D0796573

MCAD/MCSD

Developing and Implementing Windows-Based Applications with Microsoft® Visual C#™ .NET and Microsoft® Visual Studio® .NET

Exam 70-316

Amit Kalani

Training Guide

MCAD/MCSD Training Guide: Developing and Implementing Windows®-Based Applications with Microsoft® Visual C#™ .NET and Microsoft® Visual Studio® .NET, Exam (70-316)

Copyright © 2003 by Que Publishing

All rights reserved. No part of this book shall be reproduced, stored in a retrieval system, or transmitted by any means, electronic, mechanical, photocopying, recording, or otherwise, without written permission from the publisher. No patent liability is assumed with respect to the use of the information contained herein. Although every precaution has been taken in the preparation of this book, the publisher and author assume no responsibility for errors or omissions. Nor is any liability assumed for damages resulting from the use of the information contained herein.

International Standard Book Number: 0-7897-2823-0

Library of Congress Catalog Card Number: 2002108892

Printed in the United States of America

First Printing: December 2002
Reprinted with corrections: August 2003

05   04   03   4   3   2

Trademarks

All terms mentioned in this book that are known to be trademarks or service marks have been appropriately capitalized. Que cannot attest to the accuracy of this information. Use of a term in this book should not be regarded as affecting the validity of any trademark or service mark.

Microsoft is a registered trademark of Microsoft Corporation.

Windows is a registered trademark of Microsoft Corporation.

Visual C# is a registered trademark of Microsoft Corporation.

Visual Studio is a registered trademark of Microsoft Corporation.

Warning and Disclaimer

Every effort has been made to make this book as complete and as accurate as possible, but no warranty or fitness is implied. The information provided is on an "as is" basis. The author and the publisher shall have neither liability nor responsibility to any person or entity with respect to any loss or damages arising from the information contained in this book or from the use of the CD or programs accompanying it.

PUBLISHER
Paul Boger

EXECUTIVE EDITOR
Jeff Riley

DEVELOPMENT EDITOR
Steve Rowe

MANAGING EDITOR
Thomas F. Hayes

PROJECT EDITOR
Natalie Harris
Tonya Simpson

COPY EDITOR
Kitty Wilson Jarrett

INDEXER
Ginny Bess

PROOFREADER
Juli Cook

TECHNICAL EDITORS
Kourosh Ardestani
Steve Heckler

TEAM COORDINATORS
Rosemary Lewis
Kimberley Herbert

INTERIOR DESIGNER
Louisa Klucznik

COVER DESIGNER
Charis Ann Santillie

PAGE LAYOUT
Cheryl Lynch

Table of Contents

Que Certification • 201 West 103rd Street • Indianapolis, Indiana 46290

A Note from Series Editor Ed Tittel

Congratulations on your purchase of the 70-316 Training Guide, the finest exam preparation book in the marketplace!

As Series Editor of the highly regarded Training Guide series, I can assure you that you won't be disappointed. You've taken your first step toward passing the 70-316 exam, and we value this opportunity to help you on your way!

As a "Favorite Study Guide Author" finalist in a 2002 poll of CertCities readers, I know the importance of delivering good books. You'll be impressed with Que Certification's stringent review process, which ensures the books are high-quality, relevant, and technically accurate. Rest assured that at least a dozen industry experts—including the panel of certification experts at CramSession—have reviewed this material, helping us deliver an excellent solution to your exam preparation needs.

Favorite Study Guide Author

We've also added a preview edition of PrepLogic's powerful, full-featured test engine, which is trusted by certification students throughout the world.

As a 20-year-plus veteran of the computing industry and the original creator and editor of the Exam Cram series, I've brought my IT experience to bear on these books. During my tenure at Novell from 1989 to 1994, I worked with and around its excellent education and certification department. At Novell, I witnessed the growth and development of the first really big, successful IT certification program—one that was to shape the industry forever afterward. This experience helped push my writing and teaching activities heavily in the certification direction. Since then, I've worked on more than 70 certification related books, and I write about certification topics for numerous Web sites and for *Certification* magazine.

In 1997 when Exam Cram was introduced, it quickly became the best-selling computer book series since "*...For Dummies,*" and the best-selling certification book series ever. By maintaining an intense focus on the subject matter, tracking errata and updates quickly, and following the certification market closely, Exam Cram was able to establish the dominant position in cert prep books.

You will not be disappointed in your decision to purchase this book. If you are, please contact me at etittel@jump.net. All suggestions, ideas, input, or constructive criticism are welcome!

Ed Tittel

Contents at a Glance

PART IV Final Review

PART V Appendixes

PART I: Developing Window Applications

PART II: Testing, Debugging, and Deploying a Windows Application

PART III: Maintaining and Configuring a Windows Application

PART IV: Final Review

Fast Facts   1039

PART V: Appendixes

About the Author

Amit Kalani is among the first few to complete the Microsoft Certified Application Developer (MCAD) for Microsoft .NET certification.

Amit has been programming with the .NET Framework since its early beta versions. He has been a contributing author and technical reviewer for several popular books about the .NET Framework and related technologies.

In an earlier job, Amit managed a Microsoft Certified Technical Education Center (CTEC), where he designed and delivered courses on various development tools and technologies. He worked closely with students to understand their requirements, and he guided them toward passing Microsoft certification exams.

Amit lives in Michigan with his wife Priti. You can reach Amit at amit@techcontent.com.

Dedication

To my loving wife, Priti.

Acknowledgments

You see only my name on the cover, but many people have worked hard to make this book possible. It is my great pleasure to acknowledge the efforts of these people.

I'm fortunate to have worked with the talented and dedicated team of publishing professionals at Que Certification. Special thanks to Jeff Riley for giving me the opportunity and for working patiently with me at every step of the project. Thanks also to Steve Rowe for his focus on quality and for guiding me toward the goal of producing the best possible training guide. Thanks to Natalie Harris and Tonya Simpson for diligently coordinating the review process of this book.

My thanks go to Mike Gunderloy, who wrote the Visual Basic .NET version of this book. Mike generously shared his chapter drafts with me and provided me with valuable comments. It was a treat to work with him, as there was so much to learn from his vast experience and expertise.

Thanks to my technical editors, Steve Heckler and Kourosh Ardestani, for sharing their technical expertise and reviewing the contents of this book for correctness. Their constructive comments and suggestions also ensured that I did not leave out anything that is of importance to the exam.

If this book is readable, the credit must go to Kitty Wilson Jarrett. She did the copy editing for this book and did a great job in making sure that the words are right and the format is consistent.

I would also like to thank Ginny Bess, Juli Cook, and Cheryl Lynch, who were working behind the scenes to put the final manuscript between covers and on the shelf.

I would like to thank Deborah Hittel-Shoaf for starting it all. Look, Deborah, I was seeking "getting my feet wet" and I am now "neck-deep" into it.

This book has greatly benefited from the work that I did at CIStems. I have learned a lot about training from my mentor, Keshav Sharma, and the wonderful folks at CIStems.

I am grateful to my parents, Sarita and Kishan Kalani; it's their love and blessings that make it possible for me to have the opportunities that I have today.

Finally, thanks to my wife, Priti. She assisted me through the whole writing process. Her extensive knowledge of the .NET Framework and her constructive criticism were instrumental in producing the best material possible for this book.

We Want to Hear from You!

As the reader of this book, *you* are our most important critic and commentator. We value your opinion and want to know what we're doing right, what we could do better, what areas you'd like to see us publish in, and any other words of wisdom you're willing to pass our way.

As an executive editor I welcome your comments. You can email or write me directly to let me know what you did or didn't like about this book—as well as what we can do to make our books better.

Please note that I cannot help you with technical problems related to the topic of this book. We do have a User Services group, however, where I will forward specific technical questions related to the book.

When you write, please be sure to include this book's title and author as well as your name, email address, and phone number. I will carefully review your comments and share them with the author and editors who worked on the book.

Email: feedback@quepublishing.com

Mail: Jeff Riley
          Executive Editor
          Que Publishing
          800 East 96th Street
          Indianapolis, IN 46240 USA

For more information about this book or another Que title, visit our Web site at www.quepublishing.com. Type the ISBN (excluding hyphens) or the title of a book in the Search field to find the page you're looking for.

How to Use This Book

Que Certification has made an effort in its Training Guide series to make the information as accessible as possible for the purposes of learning the certification material. Here, you have an opportunity to view the many instructional features that have been incorporated into the books to achieve that goal.

CHAPTER OPENER

Each chapter begins with a set of features designed to allow you to maximize study time for that material.

List of Objectives: Each chapter begins with a list of the objectives as stated by the exam's vendor.

Objective Explanations: Immediately following each objective is an explanation of it, providing context that defines it more meaningfully in relation to the exam. Because vendors can sometimes be vague in their objectives list, the objective explanations are designed to clarify any vagueness by relying on the authors' test-taking experience.

OBJECTIVES

This chapter covers the following Microsoft-specified objective for the "Testing and Debugging" section of Exam 70-316, "Developing and Implementing Windows-Based Applications with Microsoft Visual C# .NET and Microsoft Visual Studio .NET":

Create a unit test plan.

▶ Before you release a product or component, the product needs to pass through different types of tests. This objective requires you to know the different types of tests that a product should undergo to verify its robustness, reliability, and correctness. These tests should be executed with a designed test plan that ensures that the product thoroughly meets its goals and requirements.

Implement tracing.

- **Add trace listeners and trace switches to an application.**
- **Display trace output.**

▶ Tracing helps in displaying informative messages during the application's runtime to get a fair idea of how the application is progressing. This objective requires you to know how to use Trace class properties and methods, attach trace listeners, and apply trace switches. Trace switches allow you to enable, disable, and filter tracing output that is displayed by the Trace class without recompiling programs. You can do this by just editing the configuration XML file.

CHAPTER 12

Testing and Debugging a Windows Application

OBJECTIVES

Debug, rework, and resolve defects in code.

- **Configure the debugging environment.**
- **Create and apply debugging code to components and applications.**
- **Provide multicultural test data to components and applications.**
- **Execute tests.**
- **Resolve errors and rework code.**

▶ The process of debugging helps you locate logical or runtime errors in an application. This objective requires you to know the various tools and windows that are available in Visual C# .NET to enable easy and effective debugging. These debugging tools and windows help a great deal in determining errors, executing test code, and resolving errors.

OUTLINE

Chapter Outline: Learning always gets a boost when you can see both the forest and the trees. To give you a visual image of how the topics in a chapter fit together, you will find a chapter outline at the beginning of each chapter. You will also be able to use this for easy reference when looking for a particular topic.

STUDY STRATEGIES

▶ Review the "Introduction to Instrumentation and Tracing" and "Using the Debugger" sections of the Visual Studio .NET Combined Help Collection.

▶ Try calling different methods of the Trace and Debug classes. Note the differences in the output when you run a program using the Debug and Release configurations.

▶ Experiment with attaching predefined and custom-made listeners to Trace objects. Refer to Step by Step 12.2 and Guided Practice Exercise 12.1 for examples.

▶ Know how to implement trace switches and conditional compilation in Windows applications. Refer to Step by Step 12.3 and Step by Step 12.4 for examples.

▶ Experiment with the different types of debugging windows that are available in Visual C# .NET. Understand their advantages and learn to use them effectively. They can be very helpful in resolving errors.

▶ Experiment with various techniques for debugging, such as local and remote debugging, debugging code in DLLs, and debugging SQL Server stored procedures.

Study Strategies: Each topic presents its own learning challenge. To support you through this, Que Certification has included strategies for how to best approach studying in order to retain the material in the chapter, particularly as it is addressed on the exam.

INSTRUCTIONAL FEATURES WITHIN THE CHAPTER

These books include a large amount and different kinds of information. The many different elements are designed to help you identify information by its purpose and importance to the exam and also to provide you with varied ways to learn the material. You will be able to determine how much attention to devote to certain elements, depending on what your goals are. By becoming familiar with the different presentations of information, you will know what information will be important to you as a test-taker and which information will be important to you as a practitioner.

Objective Coverage Text: In the text before an exam objective is specifically addressed, you will notice the objective is listed to help call your attention to that particular material.

Warning: In using sophisticated information technology, there is always potential for mistakes or even catastrophes that can occur through improper application of the technology. Warnings appear in the margins to alert you to such potential problems.

EXAM TIP

The Same Listeners for Debug and Trace Messages sent through the Debug and Trace objects are directed through each Listener object in the Listeners collection. Debug and Trace share the same Listeners collection, so any Listener object that is added to the Trace.Listeners collection is also added to the Debug.Listeners collection.

Exam Tip: Exam Tips appear in the margins to provide specific exam-related advice. Such tips may address what material is covered (or not covered) on the exam, how it is covered, mnemonic devices, or particular quirks of that exam.

Note: Notes appear in the margins and contain various kinds of useful information, such as tips on the technology or administrative practices, historical background on terms and technologies, or side commentary on industry issues.

INTRODUCTION

You have probably heard quite a bit of hype about *Web services* in conjunction with the .NET Framework. In fact, Microsoft has gone so far as to sometimes describe the .NET Framework as "an XML Web services platform that will enable developers to create programs that transcend device boundaries and fully harness the connectivity of the Internet" (msdn.microsoft.com/net). You may also run across a lot of complex and confusing explanations about the architecture of these Web services. But at their most basic level, Web services are simple: They are a means for interacting with objects over the Internet.

Seen in that light, Web services are part of a natural progression:

1. Object-oriented languages such as C++ and C# allow two objects within the same application interact.

2. Protocols such as the Component Object Model (COM) allow two objects on the same computer, but in different applications, interact.

3. Protocols such as the Distributed Component Object Model (DCOM) allow two objects on different computers, but in the same local network, interact.

4. Web services allow two objects on different computers—even if they're only connected by the Internet—interact.

In this chapter, I'll introduce you to Web services as they exist in the .NET Framework. You'll see how to build and use Web services in your .NET applications, and you'll learn about the major protocols that you use when you communicate with a Web service.

UNDERSTANDING WEB SERVICES

Instantiate and invoke a Web service or component.

• **Instantiate and invoke a Web service.**

Before I get into the nuts and bolts of actually working with Web services, I'll give you an overview of the way they work.

NOTE

More Web Services As you progress toward the MCAD credential, you'll find that knowledge of Web services is essential. In particular, Web services are a major component of Exam 70-320, "Developing XML Web Services and Server Components with Microsoft Visual C# .NET and the Microsoft .NET Framework."

WARNING

Working with the Internet Most of the examples in this chapter assume that you're working on a computer that is connected to the Internet. It's okay if there's a proxy server between you and the Internet, as long as you can connect to Web sites.

To create a Web service, you can build an ASP.NET project in
Visual Studio .NET.

STEP BY STEP

7.2 Creating a Web Service

1. Create a new project in Visual Studio .NET. Select the
   ASP.NET Web Service template and name the new project StringProc, as shown in Figure 7.4. You can replace
   localhost with the name of your own Web server if the
   Web server is not on your local machine.

> **NOTE** **Web Server Required** You need to
> have an IIS Web server available to
> you in order to complete Step by Step
> 7.2, Step by Step 7.3, and Guided
> Practice Exercise 7.1. IIS is a part of
> the Windows 2000 Professional,
> Windows XP Professional, and
> Windows Server operating systems.

FIGURE 7.4
The New Project dialog box allows you to create
a new Web service project in the Visual Studio
.NET IDE.

Step by Step: Step by Steps are hands-on tutorial instructions that walk you through a particular
task or function relevant to the exam objectives.

Figure: To improve readability, the figures have
been placed in the margins wherever possible so
they do not interrupt the main flow of text.

---

574   Part I DEVELOPING WINDOWS APPLICATIONS

IN THE FIELD

A CRASH COURSE IN DATABASES

Although this exam doesn't have any objectives that explicitly
demand database knowledge, you can't pass the exam without
knowing something about databases. These days, databases are
part of the pervasive understructure of computing. You're expected
to understand the basics of them, just as you understand the
basics of files and folders.

At this point you're interested in data stored in relational databases. A relational database (such as Microsoft SQL Server, which is
used in the examples in this book) stores data in tables, each of
which represents an instance of a particular entity. An *entity* is anything that you're interested in tracking in the database: a customer,
an order, an employee, or a supplier, for example. A single database can contain many tables; for example, you might have tables
named Customers, Orders, Employees, and Suppliers.

REVIEW BREAK

▶ Web services provide you with the means to create objects and
  invoke their methods even though your only connection to the
  server is via the Internet.

▶ Communication with Web services occurs via XML messages
  transported by HTTP.

▶ Because they communicate over HTTP, Web services are
  typically not blocked by firewalls.

▶ SOAP encapsulates object-oriented messages between Web
  service clients and servers.

▶ UDDI allows you to find Web services by connecting to a
  directory.

▶ WSDL lets you retrieve information on the classes and
  methods that are supported by a particular Web service.

CREATING WEB SERVICES

To better understand Web services, you should be familiar with both
sides of the conversation. In the following sections, you'll learn how
to create a Web service by using the tools built in to ASP.NET.

In the Field Sidebar: These more extensive
discussions cover material that perhaps is not as
directly relevant to the exam, but which is useful
as reference material or in everyday practice.
In the Field may also provide useful background
or contextual information necessary for understanding the larger topic under consideration.

Review Break: Crucial information is summarized at various points in the book in lists or
tables. At the end of a particularly long section,
you might come across a Review Break that is
there just to wrap up one long objective and reinforce the key points before you shift your focus to
the next section.

CHAPTER SUMMARY

KEY TERMS

- Disco
- SOAP
- UDDI
- Web method
- Web reference
- Web service
- WSDL

Web service support is one of the most significant advances in the .NET architecture. The .NET Framework supports both creating and consuming Web services through command-line tools as well as the Visual Studio .NET IDE.

Web services provide a way to invoke objects over the Internet. A Web service can expose one or more Web methods, each of which can accept parameters and return objects.

Web services use protocols and standards, including SOAP, Disco, UDDI, and WSDL, to communicate. These protocols and standards are designed to use HTTP as their transmission mechanism so that they are generally not blocked by firewalls.

Key Terms: A list of key terms appears at the end of each chapter. These are terms that you should be sure you know and are comfortable defining and understanding when you go in to take the exam.

Chapter Summary: Before the Apply Your Knowledge section, you will find a chapter summary that wraps up the chapter and reviews what you should have learned.

EXTENSIVE REVIEW AND SELF-TEST OPTIONS

At the end of each chapter, along with some summary elements, you will find a section called "Apply Your Knowledge" that gives you several different methods with which to test your understanding of the material and review what you have learned.

---

668   Part I DEVELOPING WINDOWS APPLICATIONS

APPLY YOUR KNOWLEDGE

Exercises

9.1   Embedding a Web Browser Control

One ActiveX control that you might find useful on Windows forms is the WebBrowser control, which uses the Internet Explorer rendering engine to display Web pages. In this exercise, you'll see how you can embed this control in a Windows form.

Estimated time: 15 minutes

1. Open a Visual C# .NET Windows application in the Visual Studio .NET IDE.

2. Right-click on the toolbox and select Customize Toolbox.

3. Select the COM Components tab in the Customize Toolbox dialog box.

4. Scroll down the list of components, which should include all the ActiveX controls that are registered on your computer, until you find the Microsoft Web Browser control. Click the check box for the control and click OK to add the control to the toolbox.

5. Add a new form to the application.

6. Place a TextBox control (txtURL), a Button control (btnGo), and a Web Browser control (browser1) on the form.

7. Attach the default event handlers of the form and of the Button control. Add the following code to the event handlers:

```
private void Exercise9_1_Load(
    object sender, System.EventArgs e)
{
    Object objNull=null;
    Object objStr="";
```

```
    // Initialize the browser
    // to a default URL
    browser1.Navigate(
        "http://www.quepublishing.com/",
        ref objNull, ref objStr,
        ref objStr, ref objStr);
}

private void btnGo_Click(
    object sender, System.EventArgs e)
{
    Object objNull=null;
    Object objStr="";
    // Navigate to the specified URL
    browser1.Navigate(
        txtURL.Text, ref objNull,
        ref objStr, ref objStr, ref objStr);
}
```

8. Insert the Main() method to launch the form. Set the form as the startup object for the project.

9. Run the project. Wait for the default Web page to load, or enter a URL and click the button to navigate to that URL, as shown in Figure 9.10.

Review Questions

1. What do you need to do to use an ActiveX control on a form in a Visual C# .NET Windows application?

2. What are the advantages and disadvantages of using ActiveX controls on a .NET form?

3. Name some reasons to use COM components in a .NET project.

4. What is the purpose of an RCW?

5. How do you create an RCW?

6. What should you consider when choosing how to create an RCW?

7. What extra steps do you need to take to use a COM+ component in a .NET application, as compared to using a COM component?

8. What's the difference between COM interoperability and PInvoke?

Exercises: These activities provide an opportunity for you to master specific hands-on tasks. Our goal is to increase your proficiency with the product or technology. You must be able to conduct these tasks in order to pass the exam.

Review Questions: These open-ended, short-answer questions allow you to quickly assess your comprehension of what you just read in the chapter. Instead of asking you to choose from a list of options, these questions require you to state the correct answers in your own words. Although you will not experience these kinds of questions on the exam, these questions will indeed test your level of comprehension of key concepts.

APPLY YOUR KNOWLEDGE

Review Questions

1. What do you need to do to use an ActiveX control on a form in a Visual C# .NET Windows application?

2. What are the advantages and disadvantages of using ActiveX controls on a .NET form?

3. Name some reasons to use COM components in a .NET project.

4. What is the purpose of an RCW?

5. How do you create an RCW?

6. What should you consider when choosing how to create an RCW?

7. What extra steps do you need to take to use a COM+ component in a .NET application, as compared to using a COM component?

8. What's the difference between COM interoperability and PInvoke?

9. What does the CharSet.Auto parameter in a DllImport attribute specify?

Exam Questions

1. Your application uses an instance of the Microsoft Masked Edit ActiveX control to collect data from users. You deploy the application via xcopy to the users' computers. Some of the users report that the main form of the application does not load. You've checked, and the users who are having the problem do have the .NET Framework installed. What could be the problem?

   A. The Microsoft Masked Edit control is not installed on the problem computers.

   B. The RCW for the ActiveX control needs to be registered on the problem computers.

   C. The problem computers are not connected to the Internet.

   D. Service Pack 1 for the .NET Framework is not installed on the problem computers.

2. You have imported a TriState ActiveX control to the .NET toolbox and inserted an instance of it, named Control1, on your form. This control exposes a property named State that can be set to 0, 1, or 2. Which line of code can you use to set the State property of Control1 to 2?

   A.

   `Control1.CtlState = 2;`

   B.

Answers to Exam Questions

1. **A.** RCWs are installed by xcopy, just like any other .NET assemblies. .NET does not require the Internet to run, nor do RCWs depend on Service Pack 1. When you add an ActiveX control to an application, you must make sure that that ActiveX control is installed on the target computers using a setup package. For more information, see the section "Using ActiveX Controls" in this chapter.

2. **A.** Any property named State is renamed CtlState to avoid conflicts with the AxHost.State class. For more information, see the section "Using ActiveX Controls on Windows Forms" in this chapter.

3. **B.** Moving all the code takes longer than moving part of the code, and it introduces additional risk. Because you'd like to rewrite the user interface, you should move that component to .NET before moving the server components. For more information, see the section "Using COM Components" in this chapter.

Exam Questions: These questions reflect the kinds of questions that appear on the actual vendor exam. Use them to become familiar with the exam question formats and to help you determine what you know and what you need to review or study more.

Answers and Explanations: For each of the Review and Exam questions will find thorough explanations located at the end of the section.

APPLY YOUR KNOWLEDGE

Suggested Readings and Resources

1. Visual Studio .NET Combined Help Collection, "Interoperating with Unmanaged Code"

2. Adam Nathan. *.NET and COM: The Complete Interoperability Guide.* Sams, 2002.

3. Andrew Troelsen. *COM and .NET Interoperability.* Apress, 2002.

4. Microsoft .NET/COM Migration and Interoperability. msdn.microsoft.com/library en-us/dnbda/html/cominterop.asp

5. Microsoft Support WebCast: Microsoft .NET and COM Interoperability, support.microsoft.com/servicedesks/ webcasts/wc051602/wcblurb051602.asp.

Suggested Readings and Resources: The very last element in every chapter is a list of additional resources you can use if you want to go above and beyond certification-level material or if you need to spend more time on a particular subject that you are having trouble understanding.

Introduction

MCAD/MCSD.NET Training Guide: Developing and Implementing Windows-Based Applications with Microsoft Visual C# .NET and Microsoft Visual Studio .NET is designed for developers who are pursuing the Microsoft Certified Application Developer (MCAD) or Microsoft Certified Solution Developer for Microsoft .NET (MCSD.NET) certifications from Microsoft. This book covers the "Developing and Implementing Windows-Based Applications with Microsoft Visual C# .NET and Microsoft Visual Studio .NET" exam (Exam 70-316), which is a core exam for both of those certifications. The exam is designed to measure your skill in developing Windows-based applications by using Windows forms and the other tools in the Microsoft .NET Framework, with Visual C# .NET as the programming language.

This book is designed to cover all the objectives that Microsoft has created for this exam. It doesn't offer end-to-end coverage of the Visual C# .NET language or the .NET Framework; rather, it helps you develop the specific core competencies that Microsoft says Visual C# .NET Windows-based application developers need to master. You can pass the exam by learning the material in this book, without taking a class. Of course, depending on your own personal study habits and learning style, you might benefit from studying this book *and* taking a class.

Even if you are not planning to take the exam, you might find this book useful. Understanding the wide range of topics covered by the exam objectives will certainly help you to accomplish programming tasks.

How This Book Helps You

This book gives you a self-guided tour of all the areas that are covered by the "Visual C# .NET Windows Applications" exam. The goal is to teach you the specific skills you need to achieve your MCAD or MCSD certification. You'll also find helpful hints, tips, examples, exercises, and references to additional study materials.

Organization

This book is organized around the individual objectives from Microsoft's preparation guide for the "Visual C# .NET Windows-Based Applications" exam. Every objective is covered in this book. The objectives are not covered in exactly the same order in which you'll find them in the official preparation guide (which you can download from www.microsoft.com/traincert/exams/ 70-316.asp), but they are reorganized for more logical teaching. I have also tried to make the information more accessible in several ways:

- ◆ This introduction includes the full list of exam topics and objectives.

- ◆ The Study and Exam Tips section helps you develop study strategies. It also provides you with valuable exam-day tips and information. You should read it early on.

- ◆ Each chapter starts with a list of objectives that are covered in that chapter.

◆ Each chapter also begins with an outline that provides an overview of the material for that chapter, as well as the page numbers where specific topics can be found.

◆ Each objective is repeated in the text where it is covered in detail.

Instructional Features

This book is designed to provide you with multiple ways to learn and reinforce the exam material. Here are some of the instructional features you'll find inside:

◆ **Objective explanations**—As mentioned previously, each chapter begins with a list of the objectives covered in the chapter. In addition, immediately following each objective is a detailed explanation that puts the objective in the context of the product.

◆ **Study strategies**—Each chapter offers a selected list of study strategies: exercises to try or additional material to read that will help you learn and retain the material in the chapter.

◆ **Exam tips**—Exam tips appear in the margins and provide specific exam-related advice. Exam tips address what material is likely to be covered (or not covered) on the exam, how to remember it, or particular exam quirks.

◆ **Review breaks and chapter summaries**—Crucial information is summarized at various points in the book, in lists of key points you need to remember. Each chapter ends with an overall summary of the material covered in that chapter as well.

◆ **Guided Practice Exercises**—Guided Practice Exercises offer additional opportunities to practice the material within a chapter and to learn additional facets of the topic at hand.

◆ **Key terms**—A list of key terms appears at the end of each chapter.

◆ **Notes**—Notes appear in the margins and contain various kinds of useful information, such as tips on technology, historical background, side commentary, or notes on where to go for more detailed coverage of a particular topic.

◆ **Warnings**—When you use sophisticated computing technology, there is always a possibility of mistakes or even catastrophes. Warnings appear in the margins and alert you of such potential problems, whether they're in following along with the text or in implementing Visual C# .NET in a production environment.

◆ **Step by Steps**—These are hands-on, tutorial instructions that lead you through a particular task or function related to the exam objectives.

◆ **Exercises**—Found at the end of each chapter in the "Apply Your Knowledge" section, the exercises include additional tutorial material and more chances to practice the skills that you learned in the chapter.

Extensive Practice Test Options

The book provides numerous opportunities for you to assess your knowledge and practice for the exam. The practice options include the following:

◆ **Review questions**—These open-ended questions appear in the "Apply Your Knowledge" section at the end of each chapter. They allow you to quickly assess your comprehension of what you just read in the chapter. The answers are provided later in the section.

◆ **Exam questions**—These questions appear in the "Apply Your Knowledge" section. They reflect the kinds of multiple-choice questions that appear on the Microsoft exams. You should use them to practice for the exam and to help determine what you know and what you might need to review or study further. Answers and explanations are provided later in the section.

◆ **Practice Exam**—The "Final Review" section includes a complete exam that you can use to practice for the real thing. The "Final Review" section and the Practice Exam are discussed in more detail later in this chapter.

◆ **PrepLogic**—The PrepLogic software included on the CD-ROM provides further practice questions.

> **NOTE**
> **PrepLogic Software** For a complete description of the PrepLogic test engine, please see Appendix D, "Using *PrepLogic Practice Tests, Preview Edition*, Software."

Final Review

The "Final Review" section of the book provides two valuable tools for preparing for the exam:

◆ **Fast Facts**—This condensed version of the information contained in the book is extremely useful for last-minute review.

◆ **Practice Exam**—A full practice test for the exam is included in this book. Questions are written in the style and format used on the actual exams. You should use the Practice Exam to assess your readiness for the real thing.

This book includes several valuable appendixes, including a glossary (Appendix A), an overview of the Microsoft certification program (Appendix B), and a description of what is on the CD-ROM (Appendix C). Appendix D covers the use of the PrepLogic software. Finally, Appendix E provides a list of suggested readings and resources that contain useful information on Visual C# .NET and the .NET Framework.

These and all the other book features mentioned previously will provide you with thorough preparation for the exam.

For more information about the exam or the certification process, you should contact Microsoft directly:

By email: MCPHelp@microsoft.com

By regular mail, telephone, or fax, contact the Microsoft Regional Education Service Center (RESC) nearest you. You can find lists of RESCs at www.microsoft.com/traincert/support/ northamerica.asp (for North America) and www.microsoft.com/traincert/support/ worldsites.asp (worldwide).

On the Internet: www.microsoft.com/traincert

WHAT THE "DEVELOPING AND IMPLEMENTING WINDOWS-BASED APPLICATIONS WITH MICROSOFT VISUAL C# .NET AND MICROSOFT VISUAL STUDIO .NET" EXAM (EXAM 70-316) COVERS

The "Developing and Implementing Windows-Based Applications with Microsoft Visual C# .NET and Microsoft Visual Studio .NET" exam covers seven major topic areas: "Creating User Services," "Creating and Managing Components and .NET Assemblies," "Consuming and Manipulating Data," "Testing and Debugging," "Deploying a Windows-Based Application," "Maintaining and Supporting a Windows-Based Application," and "Configuring and Securing a Windows-Based Application." The exam objectives are listed by topic area in the following sections.

Creating User Services

Create a Windows form by using the Windows Forms Designer.

- ◆ Add and set properties on a Windows Form.
- ◆ Create a Windows Form by using visual inheritance.
- ◆ Build graphical interface elements by using the System.Drawing namespace.

Add controls to a Windows Form.

- ◆ Set properties on controls.
- ◆ Load controls dynamically.
- ◆ Write code to handle control events and add the code to a control.
- ◆ Instantiate and invoke an ActiveX control.
- ◆ Configure control licensing.
- ◆ Create menus and menu items.

Implement navigation for the user interface (UI).

- ◆ Configure the order of tabs.

Validate user input.

- ◆ Validate non-Latin user input.

Implement error handling in the UI.

- ◆ Create and implement custom error messages.
- ◆ Create and implement custom error handlers.
- ◆ Raise and handle errors.

Implement online user assistance.

Display and update data.

- ◆ Transform and filter data.
- ◆ Bind data to the UI.

Instantiate and invoke a Web service or component.

- ◆ Instantiate and invoke a Web service.
- ◆ Instantiate and invoke a COM or COM+ component.
- ◆ Instantiate and invoke a .NET component.
- ◆ Call native functions by using platform invoke.

Implement globalization.

- ◆ Implement localizability for the UI.
- ◆ Convert existing encodings.
- ◆ Implement right-to-left and left-to-right mirroring.
- ◆ Prepare culture-specific formatting.

Create, implement, and handle events.

Implement print capability.

Implement accessibility features.

Creating and Managing Components and .NET Assemblies

Create and modify a .NET assembly.

- ◆ Create and implement satellite assemblies.
- ◆ Create resource-only assemblies.

Create a Windows control.

- ◆ Create a Windows control by using visual inheritance.
- ◆ Host a Windows control inside Microsoft Internet Explorer.

Consuming and Manipulating Data

Access and manipulate data from a Microsoft SQL Server database by creating and using ad hoc queries and stored procedures.

Access and manipulate data from a data store. Data stores include relational databases, XML documents, and flat files. Methods include XML techniques and ADO.NET.

Handle data errors.

Testing and Debugging

Create a unit test plan.

Implement tracing.

- ◆ Add trace listeners and trace switches to an application.
- ◆ Display trace output.

Debug, rework, and resolve defects in code.

- ◆ Configure the debugging environment.
- ◆ Create and apply debugging code to components and applications.
- ◆ Provide multicultural test data to components and applications.
- ◆ Execute tests.
- ◆ Resolve errors and rework code.

Deploying a Windows-Based Application

Plan the deployment of a Windows-based application.

- ◆ Plan a deployment that uses removable media.
- ◆ Plan a Web-based deployment.
- ◆ Plan a network-based deployment.
- ◆ Ensure that the application conforms to Windows Installer requirements and Windows Logo Program requirements.

Create a setup program that installs an application and allows for the application to be uninstalled.

◆ Register components and assemblies.

◆ Perform an install-time compilation of a Windows-based application.

Deploy a Windows-based application.

◆ Use setup and deployment projects.

Add assemblies to the Global Assembly Cache.

Verify security policies for a deployed application.

◆ Launch a remote application (URL remoting).

Maintaining and Supporting a Windows-Based Application

Optimize the performance of a Windows-based application.

Diagnose and resolve errors and issues.

Configuring and Securing a Windows-Based Application

Configure a Windows-based application.

Configure security for a Windows-based application.

◆ Select and configure authentication type. Authentication types include Windows Authentication, None, forms-based, Microsoft Passport, and custom authentication.

◆ Specify the security level for an application.

◆ Use custom attributes to configure security.

Configure authorization.

◆ Configure role-based authorization.

◆ Implement identity management.

WHAT YOU SHOULD KNOW BEFORE READING THIS BOOK

The Microsoft Visual C# .NET exams assume that you are familiar with the C# programming language and the Microsoft .NET Framework, even though there are no objectives that pertain directly to this knowledge. This book shows you tasks that are directly related to the exam objectives, but it does not include a tutorial in C# and the Microsoft .NET Framework. If you are just getting started with C# and the Microsoft .NET Framework, you should check out some of the references in Appendix E for the information that you will need to get started. For beginners, I particularly recommend these references:

◆ The samples and QuickStart Tutorials, which are installed as part of the .NET Framework SDK (which is a component of a full Visual Studio .NET installation) are an excellent starting point for information on Windows forms and common tasks.

◆ *C# How to Program,* by Harvey M. Deitel, et al. (Prentice Hall, 2002).

◆ *Special Edition Using C#,* by NIIT (Que, 2001).

◆ *C# Primer: A Practical Approach,* by Stanley B. Lippman (Addison-Wesley Professional, 2002).

◆ *Understanding .NET: A Tutorial and Analysis,* by David Chappell (Addison-Wesley Professional, 2002).

HARDWARE AND SOFTWARE YOU'LL NEED

Although you can build Visual C# .NET applications by using nothing more than the tools provided in the free .NET Framework SDK, to pass the exam you need to have access to a copy of Visual Studio .NET. Visual Studio .NET includes many tools and features that are not found in the free command-line tools. There are three editions of Visual Studio .NET:

◆ **Professional**—Visual Studio .NET Professional is the entry-level product in the product line. This edition allows you to build Windows, ASP.NET, and Web services applications. It includes visual design tools, Crystal Reports, and the Microsoft Data Engine (MSDE) version of SQL Server 2000.

◆ **Enterprise Developer**—Building on the Professional edition, the Enterprise Developer edition adds the full version of SQL Server 2000, Visual SourceSafe, Application Center Test, and Visual Studio Analyzer, as well as developer licenses for Exchange Server, Host Integration Server, and Commerce Server. It also contains additional samples and templates.

◆ **Enterprise Architect**—The high-end Enterprise Architect edition adds Visio Enterprise Architect, a development license for SQL Server, and high-end enterprise templates.

You should be able to complete all of the exercises in this book with any of the three editions of Visual Studio .NET. Your computer should meet the minimum criteria required for a Visual Studio .NET installation:

◆ A Pentium II or better CPU, running at 450MHz or faster.

◆ Windows NT 4.0 or later.

◆ The following memory, depending on the operating system you have installed: 64MB for Windows NT 4.0 Workstation, 96MB for Windows 2000 Professional, 160MB for Windows NT 4.0 Server or Windows XP Professional, or 192MB for Windows 2000 Server.

◆ 3.5GB of disk space for a full installation.

◆ A CD-ROM or DVD drive.

◆ A video card running at 800×600, with at least 256 colors.

◆ A Microsoft or compatible mouse.

Of course, those are *minimum* requirements. I recommend the following more realistic requirements:

◆ A Pentium III or better CPU running at 800MHz or faster.

◆ Windows 2000.

◆ At least 256MB of RAM, and as much more as you can afford.

◆ 5GB of disk space for a full installation.

◆ A CD-ROM or DVD drive.

◆ A video card running at 1280×1024 or higher, with at least 65,000 colors.

◆ A Microsoft or compatible mouse.

You might find it easiest to obtain access to the necessary computer hardware and software in a corporate environment. It can be difficult, however, to allocate enough time within a busy workday to complete a self-study program. Most of your study time will probably need to occur outside normal working hours, away from the everyday interruptions and pressures of your job.

ADVICE ON TAKING THE EXAM

You will find more extensive tips in the next section, "Study and Exam Prep Tips," but keep this advice in mind as you study:

◆ Read all the material in this book. Microsoft has been known to include material that is not expressly specified in the objectives for an exam. This book includes additional information that is not reflected in the objectives, in an effort to give you the best possible preparation for the examination—and for the real-world experiences to come.

◆ Complete the Step by Steps, Guided Practice Exercises, and exercises in each chapter. They will help you gain experience with Visual C# .NET. All Microsoft exams are task and experience based and require you to have experience using the Microsoft products, not just reading about them.

◆ Use the review and exam questions to assess your knowledge. Don't just read the chapter content; use the review and exam questions to find out what you know and what you don't. Study some more, review, and then assess your knowledge again.

◆ Review the exam objectives. Develop your own questions and examples for each topic listed. If you can develop and answer several questions for each topic, you should not find it difficult to pass the exam.

Remember, the primary objective is not to pass the exam: It is to understand the material. After you understand the material, passing the exam should be simple. To really work with Visual C# .NET, you need a solid foundation in practical skills. This book, and the Microsoft Certified Professional program, are designed to ensure that you have that solid foundation.

Good luck!

EXAM TIP

There's No Substitute for Experience The single best study tip that anyone can give you is to actually work with the product that you're learning! Even if you could become a "paper" MCAD or MCSD simply by reading books, you would not get the real-world skills that you need to be a Visual C# .NET success.

This section of the book provides some general guidelines for preparing for the exam "Developing and Implementing Windows-Based Applications with Microsoft Visual C# .NET and Microsoft Visual Studio .NET" (Exam 70-316). It is organized into three parts. The first part addresses your pre-exam preparation activities and covers general study tips. This is followed by an extended look at the Microsoft certification exams, including a number of specific tips that apply to the Microsoft exam formats. Finally, changes in Microsoft's testing policies and how they might affect you are discussed.

To better understand the nature of preparation for the test, it is important to understand learning as a process. You are probably aware of how you best learn new material. You might find that outlining works best for you, or you might need to see things, as a visual learner. Whatever your learning style, test preparation takes place over time. Obviously, you can't start studying for this exam the night before you take it. It is very important to understand that learning is a developmental process; understanding learning as a process helps you focus on what you know and what you have yet to learn.

Thinking about how you learn should help you recognize that learning takes place when you are able to match new information to old. You have some previous experience with computers and programming, and now you are preparing for this certification exam. Using this book, software, and supplementary materials will not just add incrementally to what you know; as you study, you actually change the organization of your knowledge and integrate this new information into your existing knowledge base. This leads you to a more comprehensive understanding of the tasks and concepts outlined in the objectives and of computing in general. Again, this happens as a repetitive process rather than as a single event. Keep this model of learning in mind as you prepare for the exam, and you will make good decisions concerning what to study and how much more studying you need to do.

Study and Exam Prep Tips

STUDY TIPS

There are many ways to approach studying, just as there are many different types of material to study. However, the tips that follow should work well for the type of material covered on this certification exam.

Study Strategies

Although individuals vary in the ways they learn information, some basic principles of learning apply to everyone. You should adopt some study strategies that take advantage of these principles. One of these principles is that learning can be broken into various depths. Recognition (of terms, for example) exemplifies a surface level of learning in which you rely on a prompt of some sort to elicit recall. Comprehension or understanding (of the concepts behind the terms, for example) represents a deeper level of learning. The ability to analyze a concept and apply your understanding of it in a new way represents a further depth of learning.

Your learning strategy should enable you to know the material at a level or two deeper than mere recognition. This will help you do well on the exams. You will know the material so thoroughly that you can easily handle the recognition-level types of questions used in multiple-choice testing. You will also be able to apply your knowledge to solve new problems.

Macro and Micro Study Strategies

One strategy that can lead to deep learning involves preparing an outline that covers all the objectives and subobjectives for the particular exam you are working on. Then you should delve a bit further into the material and include a level or two of detail beyond the stated objectives and subobjectives for the exam. Then you should expand the outline by coming up with a statement of definition or a summary for each point in the outline.

An outline provides two approaches to studying. First, you can study the outline by focusing on the organization of the material. Work your way through the points and subpoints of your outline, with the goal of learning how they relate to one another. For example, be sure you understand how each of the main objective areas is similar to and different from the others. Then do the same thing with the subobjectives; be sure you know which subobjectives pertain to each objective area and how they relate to one another.

Next, you can work through the outline, focusing on learning the details. You should memorize and understand terms and their definitions, facts, rules and strategies, advantages and disadvantages, and so on. In this pass through the outline, you should attempt to learn detail rather than the big picture (the organizational information that you worked on in the first pass through the outline).

Research has shown that attempting to assimilate both types of information at the same time seems to interfere with the overall learning process. Split your study following these two approaches, and you will perform better on the exam.

Active Study Strategies

The process of writing down and defining objectives, subobjectives, terms, facts, and definitions promotes a more active learning strategy than merely reading the material. In human information-processing terms, writing forces you to engage in more active encoding of the information. Simply reading over the information exemplifies more passive processing.

Next, you should determine whether you could apply the information you have learned by attempting to create examples and scenarios on your own. You should think about how or where you could apply the concepts you are learning. Again, you should write down this information so you can process the facts and concepts in a more active fashion.

The hands-on nature of the Step by Step tutorials, the Guided Practice Exercises, and the exercises at the end of the chapters provide further active learning opportunities that will reinforce concepts as well.

Common-Sense Strategies

Finally, you should also follow common-sense practices when studying. You should study when you are alert, reduce or eliminate distractions, take breaks when you become fatigued, and so on.

Pretesting Yourself

Pretesting enables you to assess how well you are learning. One of the most important aspects of learning is what has been called *meta-learning*. Meta-learning has to do with realizing when you know something well or when you need to study some more. In other words, you recognize how well or how poorly you have learned the material you are studying.

For most people, this can be difficult to assess objectively. Practice tests are useful in that they reveal objectively what you have learned and what you have not learned. You should use this information to guide review and further studying. Developmental learning takes place as you cycle through studying, assessing how well you have learned, reviewing, and assessing again until you feel you are ready to take the exam.

You might have noticed the practice exam included in this book. You should use it as part of the learning process. The PrepLogic software on the CD-ROM also provides a variety of ways to test yourself before you take the actual exam. By using the practice exams in the book and on the CD-ROM, you can take an entire practice test and gauge from your performance on each practice exam what areas you have mastered and what areas you still need to work on. As you complete the practice exams, one effective study method is to take notes on the items you missed as you move through the explanations of the answers.

This is active learning on your part, and with it, you are more likely to learn and remember correct answers.

You should set a goal for your pretesting. A reasonable goal would be to score consistently in the 90% range.

See Appendix D, "Using *PrepLogic Practice Tests, Preview Edition*, Software," for a more detailed explanation of the test engine.

EXAM PREP TIPS

Having mastered the subject matter, the final preparatory step is to understand how the exam will be presented. Make no mistake: A Microsoft Certified Professional (MCP) exam will challenge both your knowledge and test-taking skills. This section starts with the basics of exam design, reviews new question types, and concludes with hints targeted to each of the exam formats.

The MCP Exam

Every MCP exam is released in one of two basic formats. What is called *exam format* here is really little more than a combination of the overall exam structure and the presentation method for exam questions.

Each exam format uses the same types of questions. These types or styles of questions include multiple-rating (or scenario-based) questions, traditional multiple-choice questions, and simulation-based questions. It is important that you understand the types of questions you will be asked and the actions required to properly answer them.

Understanding the exam formats is key to good preparation because the format determines the number of questions presented, the difficulty of the questions, and the amount of time allowed to complete the exam.

Exam Forms

There are two basic formats for MCP exams: the traditional fixed-form exam and the adaptive form. As its name implies, the *fixed-form exam* presents a fixed set of questions during the exam session. The *adaptive form* uses only a subset of questions drawn from a larger pool during any given exam session.

> N O T E
>
> **Microsoft Exams and Testing Procedures**   You can find the latest information about the testing procedure for Microsoft exams at
> www.microsoft.com/traincert/mcpexams/faq/procedures.asp.

Both forms of an exam use the same set of exam objectives and exam questions; the difference is only in the way the questions are presented. Microsoft changes the exam format and questions from time to time; therefore, it does not identify the format of any given exam at the time of registration. You should know the content well and be ready to answer questions in any way the exam is presented.

Fixed-Form Exams

A fixed-form computerized exam is based on a fixed set of exam questions. The individual questions are presented in random order during a test session. If you take the same exam more than once, you won't necessarily see exactly the same questions because two or three final forms are typically assembled for every fixed-form exam Microsoft releases. These are usually labeled Forms A, B, and C. The final forms of a fixed-form exam are identical in terms of content coverage, number of questions, and allotted time, but the questions are different. Microsoft replaces exam questions regularly to minimize their exposure and to ensure that exams remain current. As the questions are replaced, any changes in the difficulty level of the exam are counterbalanced by changes in the passing score.

This ensures that consistent standards are used to certify candidates while also preventing exam piracy.

Microsoft has stopped providing numeric scores for all the exams released after December 2001. This allows Microsoft to constantly change the contents of the exam and vary the passing score according to the difficulty level of the exam. At the end of the exam, you get a result showing whether you passed or failed the exam. The typical format for a fixed-form exam is as follows:

◆ The exam contains 50 to 70 questions.

◆ Exam duration is between 60 and 300 minutes.

◆ Question review is allowed, and you have the opportunity to change your answers.

> E X A M   T I P
>
> **Confirming the Time Duration**   It is a good idea to confirm the exact time duration for an exam when you register for that exam.

The PrepLogic software on the CD-ROM that accompanies this book contains fixed-form exams. However, PrepLogic does provide numeric results of the exam to help you in your preparation.

Adaptive Exams

An adaptive-form exam has the same appearance as a fixed-form exam, but its questions differ in quantity and process of selection. Although the statistics of adaptive testing are fairly complex, the process is concerned with determining your level of skill or ability with the exam subject matter. This ability assessment begins by presenting questions of varying levels of difficulty and ascertaining at what difficulty level you can reliably answer them. Finally, the ability assessment determines whether that ability level is above or below the level required to pass the exam.

Examinees at different levels of ability see quite different sets of questions. Examinees who demonstrate little expertise with the subject matter continue to be presented with relatively easy questions. Examinees who demonstrate a high level of expertise are presented progressively more difficult questions. Individuals with both levels of expertise might answer the same number of questions correctly, but because the higher-expertise examinee can correctly answer more difficult questions, he or she receives a higher score and is more likely to pass the exam.

The typical design for an adaptive form exam is as follows:

◆ The exam contains 20 to 25 questions.

◆ You are allowed 90 minutes of testing time, although this is likely to be reduced to 45 to 60 minutes in the near future.

◆ Question review is not allowed, so you have no opportunity to change your answers.

The Adaptive-Exam Process

Your first adaptive exam will be unlike any other testing experience you have had. In fact, many examinees have difficulty accepting the adaptive testing process because they feel that they are not provided the opportunity to adequately demonstrate their full expertise.

You can take consolation in the fact that adaptive exams are painstakingly put together after months of data gathering and analysis and are just as valid as fixed-form exams. The rigor introduced through the adaptive testing methodology means that there is nothing arbitrary about what you see. It is also a more efficient means of testing, requiring less time to conduct and complete than the traditional fixed-form methodology.

As you can see in Figure 1, a number of statistical measures drives the adaptive examination process.

The measure that is most immediately relevant to you is the ability to estimate. Accompanying this test statistic are the standard error of measurement, the item characteristic curve, and the test information curve.

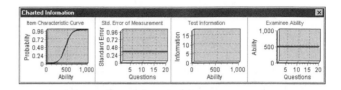

FIGURE 1
Microsoft's adaptive testing demonstration program.

The standard error, which is the key factor in determining when an adaptive exam will terminate, reflects the degree of error in the exam ability estimate. The item characteristic curve reflects the probability of a correct response relative to examinee ability. Finally, the test information statistic provides a measure of the information contained in the set of questions the examinee has answered, again relative to the ability level of the individual examinee.

When you begin an adaptive exam, the standard error has already been assigned a target value below which it must drop below in order for the exam to conclude. This target value reflects a particular level of statistical confidence in the process. The examinee's ability is initially set to the mean possible exam score (which is 500 for MCP exams).

As the adaptive exam progresses, questions of varying difficulty are presented. Based on your pattern of responses to these questions, the ability estimate is recalculated. Simultaneously, the standard error estimate is refined from its first estimated value toward the target value. When the standard error reaches the target value, the exam terminates. Thus, the more consistently you answer questions of the same degree of difficulty, the more quickly the standard error estimate drops and the fewer questions you end up seeing during the exam session. This situation is depicted in Figure 2.

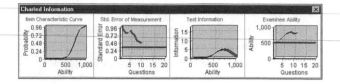

FIGURE 2
The changing statistics in an adaptive exam.

As you might suspect, one good piece of advice for taking an adaptive exam is to treat every exam question as if it is the most important. The adaptive scoring algorithm attempts to discover a pattern of responses that reflects a level of proficiency with the subject matter. Incorrect responses almost guarantee that additional questions must be answered (unless, of course, you get every question wrong). This is because the scoring algorithm must adjust to information that is not consistent with the emerging pattern.

New Question Types

A variety of question types can appear on MCP exams. Examples of multiple-choice questions and scenario-based questions appear throughout this book and the PrepLogic software. Simulation-based questions are new to the MCP exam series.

Simulation Questions

Simulation-based questions reproduce the look and feel of key Microsoft product features for the purpose of testing. The simulation software used in MCP exams has been designed to look and act, as much as possible, just like the actual product. Consequently, answering simulation questions in an MCP exam entails completing one or more tasks just as if you were using the product itself.

The format of a typical Microsoft simulation question consists of a brief scenario or problem statement, along with one or more tasks that must be completed to solve the problem.

A Typical Simulation Question

It sounds obvious, but your first step when you encounter a simulation is to carefully read the question. Do not go straight to the simulation application! You must assess the problem being presented and identify the conditions that make up the problem scenario. You should note the tasks that must be performed or outcomes that must be achieved to answer the question and review any instructions on how to proceed.

The next step is to launch the simulator by using the button provided. After clicking the button, you see a feature of the product, presented in a dialog box. The simulation application is likely to partially cover the question text. You should feel free to reposition the simulation or move between the question text screen and the simulation by using hotkeys, by using point-and-click navigation, or by clicking the simulation launch button again.

It is important to understand that your answer to the simulation question will not be recorded until you move on to the next exam question. This gives you the added capability to close and reopen the simulation application on the same question without losing any partial answer you may have made.

The third step is to use the simulator as you would the actual product, to solve the problem or perform the defined tasks. Again, the simulation software is designed to function, within reason, just as the product does. But don't expect the simulation to reproduce product behavior perfectly. Most importantly, do not allow yourself to become flustered if the simulation does not look or act exactly like the product.

Two final points will help you tackle simulation questions. First, respond only to what is being asked in the question; do not solve problems that you are not asked to solve. Second, accept what is being asked of you. You may not entirely agree with conditions in the problem statement, the quality of the desired solution, or the sufficiency of defined tasks to adequately solve the problem.

Always remember that you are being tested on your ability to solve the problem as it is presented. If you make any changes beyond those required by the question, the item will be scored as wrong on an MCP exam.

Putting It All Together

Given all these different pieces of information, I now present a set of tips that will help you successfully tackle the exam.

More Pre-Exam Preparation Tips

Generic exam-preparation advice is always useful. Tips include the following:

◆ Become familiar with the product. Hands-on experience is one of the keys to success on any MCP exam. Review the exercises, the Guided Practice Exercises, and the Step by Steps in the book.

◆ Review the current exam-preparation guide on the Microsoft MCP Web site. The documentation Microsoft makes available on the Web identifies the skills every exam is intended to test.

◆ Memorize foundational technical detail, but remember that MCP exams are generally heavy on problem solving and application of knowledge rather than just questions that require only rote memorization.

◆ Take any of the available practice tests. I recommend the one included in this book and the ones you can create by using the PrepLogic software on the CD-ROM. Although these are fixed-form exams, they provide preparation that is also valuable for taking an adaptive exam. Because of the nature of adaptive testing, these practice exams cannot be taken in the adaptive form. However, fixed-form exams use the same types of questions as adaptive exams and are the most effective way to prepare for either type.

◆ Look on the Microsoft MCP Exam Resources Web site (www.microsoft.com/traincert/mcpexams) for samples and demonstration items. These tend to be particularly valuable for one significant reason: They help you become familiar with any new testing technologies before you encounter them on an MCP exam.

Tips for the Exam Session

The following generic exam-taking advice you've heard for years applies when you're taking an MCP exam:

◆ Take a deep breath and try to relax when you first sit down for your exam session. It is very important to control the pressure you might (naturally) feel when taking exams.

◆ You will be provided with scratch paper. Take a moment to write down any factual information and technical detail that you have committed to short-term memory.

◆ Carefully read all information and instruction screens. These displays have been put together to give you information relevant to the exam you are taking.

◆ Accept the nondisclosure agreement and preliminary survey as part of the examination process. Complete them accurately and quickly move on.

◆ Read the exam questions carefully. Reread each question to identify all relevant detail.

◆ Tackle the questions in the order in which they are presented. Skipping around won't build your confidence; the clock is always counting down.

◆ Don't rush, but also don't linger on difficult questions. The questions vary in degree of difficulty. Don't let yourself be flustered by a particularly difficult or verbose question.

Tips for Fixed-Form Exams

Besides considering basic preparation and test-taking advice, you also need to consider the challenges presented by the different exam designs. Because a fixed-form exam is composed of a fixed, finite set of questions, you should add these tips to your strategy for taking a fixed-form exam:

◆ Note the time allotted and the number of questions on the exam you are taking. Make a rough calculation of how many minutes you can spend on each question and use this to pace yourself through the exam.

◆ Take advantage of the fact that you can mark a question that you want to review later before you finish your exam. When you have answered all other questions, you can easily locate marked questions and return to them. However, you should remember that if you answer a question but leave it marked, it is considered unanswered. Be sure to unmark any marked question before you end the exam.

◆ If there is session time remaining after you have completed all questions (and if you aren't too fatigued!), review your answers. Pay particular attention to questions that seem to have a lot of detail or that require graphics.

◆ As for changing your answers, the general rule of thumb here is don't! If you read a question carefully and completely and you felt like you knew the right answer, you probably did. Don't second-guess yourself. If, as you check your answers, one clearly stands out as incorrectly marked, however, of course you should change it. If you are at all unsure, go with your first instinct.

Tips for Adaptive Exams

If you are planning to take an adaptive exam, keep these additional tips in mind:

◆ Read and answer every question with great care. When reading a question, identify every relevant detail, requirement, or task that must be performed and double-check your answer to be sure you have addressed every one of them.

◆ If you cannot answer a question, use the process of elimination to reduce the set of potential answers, and then take your best guess. Careless mistakes invariably mean additional questions will be presented.

◆ You cannot review questions and change your answers. After you leave a question, whether you've answered it or not, you cannot return to it. Do not skip any questions; if you do, the item is counted as incorrect.

Tips for Simulation Questions

You might encounter simulation questions on either the fixed-form or adaptive-form exam. If you do, keep these tips in mind:

◆ Avoid changing any simulation settings that don't pertain directly to the problem solution. Solve the problem you are being asked to solve and nothing more.

◆ Assume default settings when related information has not been provided. If something has not been mentioned or defined, it is a noncritical detail that does not factor into the correct solution.

◆ Be sure your entries are syntactically correct, and pay particular attention to your spelling. Enter relevant information just as the product would require it.

◆ Close all simulation application windows after you complete the simulation tasks. The testing system software is designed to trap errors that could result when using the simulation application, but you should trust yourself over the testing software.

◆ If simulations are part of a fixed-form exam, you can return to skipped or previously answered questions and change your answers. However, if you choose to change an answer to a simulation question or even attempt to review the settings you've made in the simulation application, your previous response to that simulation question is deleted. If simulations are part of an adaptive exam, you cannot return to previous questions.

FINAL CONSIDERATIONS

Finally, a number of changes in the MCP program affect how frequently you can repeat an exam and what you see when you do:

◆ Microsoft has instituted a new exam retake policy. According to this policy, you can attempt any exam twice with no restrictions on the time between attempts. But after the second attempt, you must wait two weeks before you can attempt that exam again. After that, you are required to wait two weeks between subsequent attempts. Plan to pass the exam in two attempts or plan to increase your time horizon for receiving an MCP credential.

◆ New questions are being seeded into the MCP exams. After performance data is gathered on new questions, the examiners replace older questions on all exam forms. This means that the questions that appear on exams regularly change.

◆ Many of the current MCP exams will be republished in adaptive form in the coming months. Prepare yourself for this significant change in testing because it is entirely likely that this will become the preferred MCP exam format.

These changes mean that the brute-force strategies for passing MCP exams are much less viable than they once were. So if you don't pass an exam on the first or second attempt, it is entirely possible that the exam's form will change significantly before the next time you take it. It could be updated to adaptive form from fixed form or it could have a different set of questions or question types.

The intention of Microsoft is clearly not to make the exams more difficult by introducing unwanted change, but to create and maintain valid measures of the technical skills and knowledge associated with the different MCP credentials. Preparing for an MCP exam has always involved not only studying the subject matter but also planning for the testing experience itself. With the recent changes, this is now more true than ever.

DEVELOPING WINDOWS APPLICATIONS

This chapter covers the following Microsoft-specified objectives for the "Creating User Services" section of Exam 70-316, "Developing and Implementing Windows-Based Applications with Microsoft Visual C# .NET and Microsoft Visual Studio .NET":

Create a Windows form by using the Windows Forms Designer:

- **Add and set properties on a Windows form.**

- **Create a Windows form by using visual inheritance.**

- **Build graphical interface elements by using the System.Drawing namespace.**

▶ Windows forms are the basic user interface element of a Windows application. The exam objectives addressed in this chapter cover the basics of designing a Windows form by using the Windows Forms Designer. This exam objective addresses the following specific topics:

- How to create a Windows form and change its behavior and appearance through its built-in properties and through custom-added properties.

- How to use visual inheritance to rapidly design a Windows form by inheriting it from an existing Windows form.

- How to build various graphical interface elements by using the System.Drawing namespace.

Create, implement, and handle events.

▶ Event handling is the core part of programming a user interface. This chapter describes how to make a Windows form respond to user actions. You'll find further coverage of this exam objective in Chapter 4, "Creating and Managing .NET Components and Assemblies."

CHAPTER 1

Introducing Windows Forms

▶ Make yourself comfortable with the major properties of Windows forms. This chapter's examples and exercises introduce the most important form properties.

▶ Invest time looking at and understanding the code that is automatically generated by Visual Studio .NET for you.

▶ Make sure you fully understand event handling. This will enable you to write interactive Windows applications.

▶ Experiment with classes in the `System.Drawing` namespace. In addition to the completing the examples and exercises in this chapter, it would be a good idea for you to create a small sample program to test the behavior of a class or a property whenever you are in doubt.

▶ If you are new to object-oriented programming, consider reading all or some of the recommended material listed in the "Suggested Readings and Resources" section at the end of this chapter.

INTRODUCTION

In this chapter, the first step toward passing Exam 70-316, you will complete a lot of the groundwork required to build the foundation for the rest of this book.

This chapter starts with an overview of the .NET Framework and various development tools for developing applications for the .NET Framework. This overview will be enough to get you started; I'll continually cover advanced features as they become important for meeting exam objectives.

Next, this chapter talks about designing Windows forms, both by using a visual designer and by manually writing code. The visual designer that is built inside Visual Studio .NET helps you rapidly develop forms. As you design forms, you will also learn about many useful classes that are available in the System.Windows.Forms namespace. You will also learn how to visually inherit a Windows form from an existing form.

A user can generally interact with a Windows application. Applications can respond to users' actions thanks to event handling. In this chapter you will learn how to make programs interactive by using event handling.

Finally, this chapter talks about the various classes in the System.Drawing namespace. These classes allow you to add typography, 2-D graphics, and imaging features to applications.

KEY CONCEPTS

In this book, you will develop Windows application using Visual Studio .NET. Under the hood, you will be using the Framework Class Library (FCL) to write applications that run on the Common Language Runtime (CLR). Both FCL and CLR are part of a larger framework called the .NET Framework. In this section, I'll give you an overview of the .NET Framework, various development tools, and basic object-oriented concepts that you will need right from the beginning.

An Overview of the .NET Framework

The Microsoft .NET Framework is a new computing platform for developing distributed applications. It provides several new features that enhance application development. The following are some of these features:

◆ **Consistent development model**—The .NET Framework proves an object-oriented and consistent development model. When you learn programming in the .NET Framework, you can use your skills in developing different types of applications, such as Windows Forms applications, Web applications, and Web services.

◆ **Robust execution environment**—The .NET Framework provides an execution environment that maximizes security, robustness, and performance of applications while minimizing deployment and versioning conflicts.

◆ **Support for standards**—The .NET Framework is built around industry standards such as Extensible Markup Language (XML), Simple Object Access Protocol (SOAP), Common Language Infrastructure (CLI), and C#.

Because the .NET Framework provides new execution environments for running the applications designed for the .NET Framework, you need to install the .NET Framework on the target machine. The .NET Framework can be installed using the .NET Framework redistributable file (approximately 21MB). You can find the link to download this file from the Microsoft official Windows Forms Community site (www.windowsforms.net).

The .NET Framework has two main components:

◆ The Common Language Runtime (CLR)

◆ The Framework Class Library (FCL)

The Common Language Runtime

The CLR provides a managed and language agnostic environment for executing applications designed for the .NET Framework.

The managed runtime environment provides several services to the executing code: compilation, code safety verification, code execution, automatic memory management, and other system services. The applications designed to run under the CLR are known as managed applications because they enjoy the benefit of services offered by the managed execution environment provided by the CLR.

The CLR is based on the Common Language Infrastructure (CLI). CLI provides a rich type system that supports the types and operations found in many programming languages. If a language compiler adheres to the CLI specifications, it can generate code that can run and interoperate with other code that executes on the CLR. This allows programmers to write applications using a development language of their choice and at the same time take full advantage of the CLR, FCL, and components written by other developers.

Microsoft provides five language compilers for the .NET Framework: Visual C# .NET, Visual Basic .NET, Managed C++ .NET, Jscript .NET, and J# .NET. When you install the .NET Framework, you get only command-line compilers for C#, Visual Basic .NET, and Jscript .NET. The Managed C++ compiler is part of .NET Framework SDK and Visual Studio .NET, whereas the J# .NET compiler can be downloaded separately from the Microsoft Web site. Visual J# .NET will ship as a component of Visual Studio .NET starting with version 1.1. In addition to the compilers available from Microsoft, you can obtain CLI-compliant compilers for languages such as COBOL, Delphi, Eiffel, Perl, Python, Smalltalk, and Haskell from various independent vendors or organizations.

The CLI-compliant language compilers compile the source language to an intermediate format known as the Common Intermediate Language (CIL). At runtime, the CLR compiles the CIL code to the machine-specific native code using a technique called *just-in-time (JIT)* compilation. Microsoft's implementation of CIL is the *Microsoft Intermediate Language (MSIL)*.

The Framework Class Library

The FCL is an extensive collection of reusable types that allows you to develop a variety of applications, including

◆ Console applications

◆ Scripted or hosted applications

NOTE

C# and CLI Are ECMA Standards
The C# programming language, as well as the CLI, are ECMA standards. The standardization has motivated several vendors to support and extend the .NET Framework in various ways. Some example includes the Mono project (www.go-mono.com), which is an open-source implementation of the .NET Framework; the Delphi 7 Studio (www.borland.com/delphi), which brings Delphi language to the .NET Framework; and Covalent Enterprise Ready Servers (www.covalent.net), which supports ASP.NET on the Apache Web server.

- ◆ Desktop applications (Windows Forms)

- ◆ Web applications (ASP.NET applications)

- ◆ XML Web services

- ◆ Windows services

The FCL organizes its classes in hierarchical namespaces so that they are logically grouped and easy to identify. You will learn about several of these namespaces and the classes that relate to the Windows Forms applications in this book.

An Overview of the Development Tools

Two development tools are available from Microsoft to help you design the Windows applications that run on the .NET Framework:

- ◆ The .NET Framework SDK

- ◆ Visual Studio .NET

I discuss these tools in the following sections.

The .NET Framework SDK

The Microsoft .NET Framework Software Development Kit (SDK) is available as a free download (about 131MB). You can find the link to download it from www.windowsforms.net. When you install the .NET Framework SDK you get a rich set of resources to help you develop applications for the Microsoft .NET Framework. This includes

- ◆ **The .NET Framework**—This installs the necessary infrastructure of the .NET Framework, including the CLR and the FCL.

- ◆ **Language compilers**—The command-line–based compilers allow you to compile your applications. The language compilers installed with the SDK are Visual C# .NET, Visual Basic .NET, Jscript .NET, and a non-optimizing compiler for Managed C++ .NET.

- ◆ **Tools and debuggers**—Various tools installed with the .NET Framework SDK make it easy to create, debug, profile, deploy, configure, and manage applications and components. I discuss most of these tools as I progress through this book.

◆ **Documentation**—The .NET Framework SDK installs a rich set of documentation to quickly get you up to speed on development using the .NET Framework. These include the QuickStart tutorials, product documentation, and samples.

It's possible to develop all your programs by using just a text editor and the command-line compilers and tools provided by the .NET Framework SDK. However, Visual Studio .NET provides a much more productive development environment.

Visual Studio .NET

Visual Studio .NET provides developers with a full-service Integrated Development Environment (IDE) for building Windows Forms applications, ASP.NET Web applications, XML Web services, and mobile applications for the .NET Framework. Visual Studio .NET supports multiple languages—Visual C# .NET, Visual Basic .NET, Visual C++ .NET, and Visual J# .NET—and provides transparent development and debugging facilities across these languages in a multilanguage solution. Additional languages from other vendors can also be installed seamlessly into the Visual Studio .NET shell.

Visual Studio .NET installs the .NET Framework SDK as a part of its installation. In addition to the SDK features, some important features of Visual Studio .NET are

◆ **IDE**—Supports development, compilation, debugging, and deployment, all from within the development environment.

◆ **Editing tools**—Supports language syntaxes for multiple languages. The IntelliSense feature provides help with syntax. Visual Studio .NET also supports editing of XML, Extensible Stylesheet Language (XSL), Hypertext Markup Language (HTML), and Cascading Style Sheets (CSS) documents, among other types.

◆ **Integrated debugging**—Supports cross-language debugging, including debugging of SQL Server stored procedures. It can seamlessly debug applications that are running locally or on a remote server.

◆ **Deployment tools**—Support Windows Installer. These tools also provide graphical deployment editors that allow you to visually control various deployment settings for Visual Studio .NET projects.

◆ **Automation**—Provides tools for extending, customizing, and automating the Visual Studio .NET IDE.

You will learn about all of these features in the course of this book. As an exam requirement, this book uses Visual Studio .NET as its preferred tool for developing Windows Forms applications.

EXAM TIP

Using the IDE   Exam 70-316 requires you to know Visual Studio .NET and Visual C# .NET programming language for Windows-based application development. You might be asked questions about specific Visual Studio .NET features.

Understanding Classes, Inheritance, and Namespaces

The .NET Framework is designed to be object oriented from the ground up. I'll cover the different elements of object-oriented programming as they come up, but before I start, you should know a few terms, such as class, inheritance, and namespace that are important right from the beginning. The following sections briefly explain these terms and their meaning.

Classes

C# is an object-oriented programming language. One of the tasks of a C# developer is to create user-defined types called *classes*. A class is a reference type that encapsulates data (such as constants and fields) and defines its behaviors using programming contructs such as methods, properties, constructors, and events.

A class represents an abstract idea that you would like to include in an application. For example, the .NET Framework includes a Form class, which includes data fields for storing information such as the size of the form, the form's location, the form's background color, title bar text, and so on. The Form class also contains methods that define how a form behaves, such as a Show() method that shows the form onscreen and an Activate() method that activates the form by giving it the focus.

A class functions as the blueprint of a concept. When you want to work with a class in a program, you create instances of the class, which are called *objects*. Objects are created from the blueprint defined by the class, but they physically exist in the sense that they have memory locations allocated to them and they respond to messages. For example, to create an actual form in a program, you create an instance of the Form class. After you have that instance available, you can actually work on it—you can set its properties and call methods on it.

Each object maintains its own copy of the data that is defined by the class. This allows different instances of a class to have different data values. For example, if you have two instances of the class Human—objYou and objMe—these two objects can each have a different value for their EyeColor properties. You access the member of an object by using *ObjectName.MemberName* syntax, where *ObjectName* is name of the class instance and *MemberName* can be a field, a property, a method, or an event. When an object is created, it creates its members in a special area in memory called the *heap,* and it stores a pointer to that memory. Because classes use pointers to refer to their data, they are sometimes also called *reference types*.

In contrast with the reference types, C# also has a structure type (called a *struct*), which is defined by using the struct keyword. Structs are similar to classes, but rather than store a pointer to the memory location, a struct uses the memory location to store its members. A struct is also referred to as a *value type*.

Among the members of classes, properties warrant special attention. A property provides access to the characteristics of a class or an instance of that class (that is, an object). Examples of properties include the caption of a window, the name of an item, and the font of a string.

To the programs using a class, a property looks like a field—that is, a storage location. Properties and fields have the same usage syntax, but their implementations differ. In a class, a property is not a storage location; rather, it defines accessors that contain code to be executed when the property value is being read or written. This piece of code allows properties to preprocess the data before it is read or written, to ensure integrity of a class. Using properties is the preferred way of exposing attributes or characteristics of a class, and various classes in this chapter use properties extensively.

NOTE

Static Members of a Class A class can have static members (fields, methods, and so on). Static members belong to the class itself rather than to a particular instance. No instance of a class is required in order to access its static members. When you access a static member of a class, you do so by prefixing its name with the name of the class—for example, ClassName.*StaticMemberName*.

Inheritance

Object-oriented programming languages such as C# provide a feature called inheritance. *Inheritance* allows you to create new types that are based on types that already exist. The original type is called a *base class,* and the inherited class is called a *derived class.* When one class inherits from another class, the derived class gets all the functionality of the base class. The derived class can also choose to extend the base class by introducing new data and behavioral elements. In developing Windows forms, you will frequently inherit from the Form class to create your own custom forms; these custom forms will be at least as functional as an object of the Form class, even if you do not write any new code in the derived class. Value types such as structs cannot be used for inheritance.

It is interesting to note that every single type (other than the Object class itself) that you create or that is already defined in the framework is implicitly derived from the Object class of the System namespace. This is the case to ensure that all classes provide a common minimum functionality. Also note that a C# type can inherit from only a single parent class at a time.

Inheritance is widely used in the FCL, and you will come across classes (for example, the Form class) that get their functionality from other classes (for example, the Control class) as a result of a chain of inheritances.

Namespaces

Several hundred classes are available in the FCL. In addition, an increasingly large number of classes are available through independent component vendors. Also, you can develop classes on your own. Having a large number of classes not only makes organization impossible but can also create naming conflicts between various vendors. The .NET Framework provides a feature called a *namespace* that allows you to organize classes hierarchically in logical groups based on what they do and where they originate. Not only does a namespace organize classes, but it also helps avoid naming conflicts between vendors because each classname is required to be unique only within its namespace. A general convention is to create a namespace like this:

    CompanyName.ApplicationName

> **NOTE**
>
> **Access Modifiers** A class can define the accessibility of its member by including an access modifier in its declaration. C# has four different access modifiers:
>
> - **public**—Allows the member to be globally accessible.
> - **private**—Limits the member's access to only the containing type.
> - **protected**—Limits the member's access to the containing type and all classes derived from the containing type.
> - **internal**—Limits the member's access to within the current project.

In this case *CompanyName* is your unique company name and
ApplicationName is a unique application name within the company.
All classes related to this application then belong to this namespace.
A class is therefore identified, for example, as
`QueCertifications.Exam70316.ExamQuestions`, where
`QueCertifications` is the unique name for a company, `Exam70316` is
a unique application within that company, and `ExamQuestions` is the
name of a specific class. `QueCertifications` could have another class
with the same name, `ExamQuestions`, as long as it belongs to a different application, such as `QueCertifications.Exam70306`. The objective of namespaces is to keep the complete naming hierarchy unique
so that there are no naming conflicts.

A namespace is a string in which dots help create a hierarchy. In the
namespace `QueCertifications.Exam70316`, `Exam70316` is called a *child
namespace* of `QueCertifications`. You could organize classes at two
levels here: at the level of `QueCertifications` and also at the level of
`Exam70316`. You can create a hierarchy with as many levels as you
want.

A System namespace in the FCL acts as the root namespace for all
the fundamental and base classes defined inside the FCL. One of
the fundamental classes defined in the `System` namespace is `Object`
class (uniquely identified as `System.Object`). This class acts as the
ultimate base class for all other types in the .NET Framework.

The `System.Windows.Forms` namespace organizes classes for working
with Windows forms. The `System.Drawing` namespace organizes
classes for creating graphical elements. You will make use of many
classes from these two namespaces in this chapter.

NOTE

**Namespace Hierarchies Versus
Inheritance Hierarchy**   A namespace
hierarchy has nothing to do with inheritance hierarchy. When one class
inherits from another, the base class
and the derived class may belong to
different and unrelated namespaces.

CREATING A WINDOWS FORMS APPLICATION

In this section, you will learn how to use Visual Studio .NET to
create a Windows Forms application. In the process, you will
become familiar with the development environment and a few common classes you will use with Windows Forms applications.

Using the
`System.Windows.Forms.Form` Class

A Windows application generally consists of one or more Windows forms. A Windows form is an area on the screen (usually rectangular) over which you design the user interface of a Windows application. This area acts as a placeholder for various user interface elements, such as text boxes, buttons, lists, grids, menus, and scrollbars.

Programmatically speaking, a Windows form is an instance of the `Form` class of the `System.Windows.Forms` namespace. The `Form` class derives from the inheritance hierarchy shown in Figure 1.1.

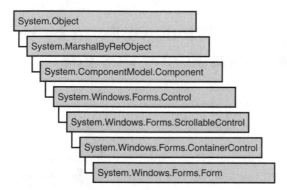

FIGURE 1.1
The `Form` class ultimately inherits from the Object class through an inheritance hierarchy.

The following points relate to the inheritance hierarchy shown in Figure 1.1 and the `Form` class:

◆ The `Form` class inherits from the `ContainerControl` class. By virtue of this inheritance, the `Form` class becomes capable of acting as a placeholder for various user interface elements or controls, such as text boxes, labels, buttons, and toolbars.

◆ A form is also a control, but it is a special type of control that is both scrollable and capable of acting as a container control. This is because the `Form` class inherits from `Control` class via the `ScrollableControl` and `ContainerControl` classes.

◆ The `Form` class is ultimately derived from the `Object` class of the `System` namespace, just like any other class. As a result of this inheritance, you can also say that a form is of type `Object`.

◆ As a result of inheritance, the Form class has access to several members (methods, properties, events, and so on) that are available to it through its parent classes. The Form class also adds a set of new members for its specific functionality. This is typical of the way that inheritance hierarchies work.

You can use the properties of a Form object (such as Size, BackColor, and Opacity) to modify the way a form appears onscreen. Methods of a Form object can be used to perform on the form actions such as Show and Hide. You can also attach to the form custom code that acts as event handlers; this enables the form to respond to different actions performed on the form.

Designing a Windows Form by Using the Windows Forms Designer

Visual Studio .NET provides the Windows Forms Designer (sometimes also called *the designer* or *the visual designer*) for designing Windows forms. To get started with the designer, you can use it to create a simple Windows form. The simple exercise shown in Step by Step 1.1 helps you become familiar with different pieces of the development environment you use to create Windows forms.

STEP BY STEP

1.1 Creating a Windows Form

1. Launch Visual Studio .NET. On the start page, click the New Project button (alternatively, you can select File, New, Project). In the New Project dialog box, select Visual C# Project as the project type and Windows Application as the template. Name the project 316C01, as shown in Figure 1.2.

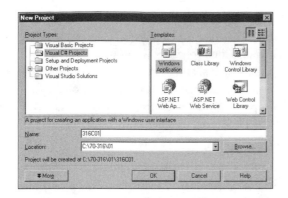

FIGURE 1.2
You can create a new Visual C# Windows application by choosing the Windows Application template for your Visual C# project.

2. The development environment is now in the design view (see Figure 1.3), and you are shown an empty form. The Solution Explorer window (see Figure 1.4) allows you to see all files that Visual Studio .NET includes in the project. If the Solution Explorer is not already visible, you can invoke it by selecting View, Solution Explorer. `Form1.cs` is the file that stores the C# code for the default Windows form that's created as part of a new project. Right-click `Form1.cs` and select Rename from the context menu. Rename the file `StepByStep1_1.cs`.

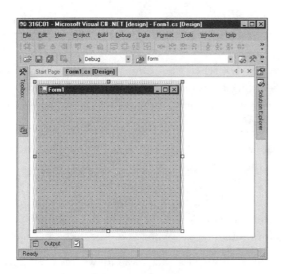

FIGURE 1.3◀
The Windows Forms Designer Environment enables you to visually develop a Windows application.

FIGURE 1.4▲
You can use the Solution Explorer to manage files within a Visual Studio .NET solution.

FIGURE 1.5
The Properties window shows the properties of an object.

FIGURE 1.6
This simple Windows form shows customized title bar text.

3. The form's title bar displays the text Form1. Title is a property of a form, and you can manipulate Title through the Properties window. Click the form so that it gets the focus, and then press F4 or select View, Properties Window. Change the Text property of the form in the Properties window to StepByStep1_1, as shown in Figure 1.5. The form's title bar now displays StepByStep1_1.

4. Select Debug, Start or click F5 to execute the project; this displays your very first Windows form. You should see something similar to Figure 1.6. Try positioning this form anywhere onscreen by dragging its title bar. You can increase or decrease the form size by dragging the form's border.

5. Click the close button of the form to end the execution of this application and return to the design view.

6. Right-click anywhere on the form and select View Code from the context menu. This opens a new window in the Visual Studio .NET environment, showing the code corresponding to the Windows form. Click the + sign next to the Windows Form Designer Generated Code region and observe all the code that the designer automatically generated for you.

In Step by Step 1.1, when you create a new Windows application, Visual Studio .NET automatically includes a Windows form inside it. The Windows form contains the code to launch itself when you run the project.

Each Windows form resides in a code file whose filename extension depends on the language you are using (for example, .cs for C#). Visual Studio .NET originally assigned the name Form1.cs to the code file, but you changed it to StepByStep1_1.cs through the Solution Explorer. This code file contains the definition of the Windows form that you saw when you executed the project.

In the Windows Forms Designer, a Windows form can be seen in two views: the design view (see Figure 1.3) and the code view (see Figure 1.7). What you see in the design view is nothing but a visual representation of the code. When you manipulate the form by using the designer, this code is automatically generated or modified based on your actions. You can also write the complete code yourself in the code view. When you switch back to the design view, the designer reads the code in order to draw the corresponding form onscreen.

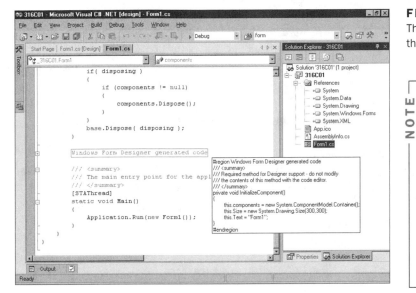

FIGURE 1.7
The code view allows you to view and modify the code associated with a Windows form.

> **NOTE**
>
> **Projects and Solutions** A *solution* is used to group one or more projects. In a typical application you first create a solution and then add projects to it. If you directly create a project, Visual Studio .NET automatically creates a solution for it. In that case, the name of the solution defaults to the name of project. For example, the project 316C01 is automatically created in solution 316C01.

Exploring the Generated Code

While exploring the code in Step by Step 1.1 you probably noticed that Visual Studio .NET groups code into blocks. This feature is called *code outlining*. You can expand and collapse code blocks by using the + and - signs near the left margin of the window in code view (see Figure 1.7). Code outlining is especially helpful when you are working with large code files. You can collapse certain areas of code that you don't want to focus on at that time and continue editing the expanded sections in which you are interested.

Step by Step 1.1 also shows a rectangular block marked Windows Form Designer Generated Code. This is a block of collapsed code that has a name. When you expand the block, you see a set of statements included between #region and #endregion directives. These directives mark the beginning and end of a named code block. You can specify a name after the #region directive to identify the code block with a name. When you collapse this region, you can easily figure out what the collapsed code block does by looking at the name associated with the region. These directives are only useful in the visual designers such as Visual Studio .NET, for effective presentation of your code. When code is compiled, these directives are not present in the executable code.

WARNING

Windows Form Designer Generated Code   The code enclosed in the code block titled Windows Form Designer Generated Code is required for Windows Forms Designer support, and you should not generally modify it.

If you collapse the Windows Form Designer Generated Code block and look at the other code that is present in the code view, you can see that almost all the code, other than a few using directives at the top, is enclosed in a namespace (I talk about using directives a bit later in this chapter). Using namespaces is a good practice because it helps you organize classes and other programming elements. Visual Studio .NET automatically organizes the classes for a new form in a namespace whose name is the same as the name of the project. (Because the project name in this case starts with a digit, Visual Studio .NET adds an underscore [_] at the beginning to make it a valid identifier.) When you create a Windows form using Visual Studio .NET, Visual Studio .NET defines a class that inherits its functionality from the standard Form class in the System.Windows.Forms namespace. In Step by Step 1.1, although you change the name of the code file containing the class from Form1.cs to StepByStep1_1.cs, the name of the class itself is not changed. Here's the class definition:

```
public class Form1 : System.Windows.Forms.Form
{
    //Form implementation goes here
}
```

Form1 is the classname that Visual Studio .NET automatically generates for you when you create a Windows application. If you want to change it, you can either change it right in the code or you can modify the Name property of the form in the design view.

The : System.Windows.Forms.Form part of the code specifies that the Form1 class inherits from the Form class that belongs to the System.Windows.Forms namespace. All the basic functionality of the Form1 class (such as moving and resizing) comes from the base Form class.

Any class can have a constructor definition. A *constructor* is a method that is used to create new instances of a class. You can easily recognize a constructor because it has the same name as the class and is defined with syntax similar to that of a method definition, but it has no return type. Here's the constructor for the Form1 class:

```
public Form1()
{
    // Required for Windows Form Designer support
    InitializeComponent();

    // TODO: Add any constructor code
    //after InitializeComponent call
}
```

NOTE

Names Can Differ   It's a good convention to keep the same names for both the form's class and the file that contains the class definition, but in the .NET Framework, it's not a law that you do so.

NOTE

Static Constructors   A class can have a *static constructor*, which is called automatically before any of the members of the class are accessed. A common use of static constructors is to initialize static fields and properties of the class.

Visual Studio .NET ignores the lines that start with // (they are comments and do not generate any code). The Windows Forms Designer puts just one line of code inside the default Form1 constructor: a call to the InitializeComponent() method of the class. The Windows Forms Designer uses the InitializeComponent() method for storing the customizations done to the form through the design view. This method is defined in the Windows Form Designer Generated Code region. When you expand this region, you see code similar to this:

```
private void InitializeComponent()
{
    //
    // Form1
    //
    this.AutoScaleBaseSize =
        new System.Drawing.Size(5, 13);
    this.ClientSize =
        new System.Drawing.Size(292, 266);
    this.Name = "Form1";
    this.Text = "StepByStep1_1";
}
```

You can see here that the Text property of Form1, which you manipulate by using the Properties window, has been inserted as a code statement. Note the use of the this keyword to qualify the property names. The this keyword refers to the current instance of the class for which the method is called.

The next piece of code after the form's constructor is the Dispose() method. In its simple form it looks like this:

```
protected override void Dispose( bool disposing )
{
    if( disposing )
    {
        if (components != null)
        {
            components.Dispose();
        }
    }
    base.Dispose( disposing );
}
```

The Dispose() method is an ideal place to put any cleanup code that you would like to be executed when you're done with the class.

NOTE

Calling Dispose() The CLR features automatic garbage collection. All memory resources that are no longer required are automatically garbage collected. Dispose() is not necessary for managed code, but it is a good place for cleanup code for any of the non-managed or non-memory resources that you create in a program.

Running a Windows Form

Finally in our code exploration comes the method that is making everything happen: the `Main()` method. Visual Studio .NET automatically generates the `Main()` method for you in the form's code. In this particular case, `Main()` is generated because you specified that the project should be created as a Windows form application. An application must have an execution starting point that is defined by the `Main()` method. When you execute the form, `Main()` is the method that receives the control first.

The `Main()` method for our simple Windows form example looks like this:

```
[STAThread]
static void Main()
{
    Application.Run(new Form1());
}
```

The first line in this code is an attribute associated with the `Main()` method. Attributes are used to specify runtime behavior of a code element. The `STAThread` attribute specifies that the default threading model for this application is Single-Threaded Apartment (STA). It's a good idea to use this attribute with the `Main()` method because it is used when your application participates in Component Object Model (COM)-interoperability or does anything that requires Object Linking and Embedding, such as drag-and-drop or Clipboard operations.

The `Main()` method has a single line of code that invokes the `Run()` method of the `Application` class. The Application class provides methods and properties for managing a Windows application. The `Run()` method starts the application by creating the specified form onscreen and sends the application into a message loop. The application stays in the loop and responds to user messages (generated by such actions as moving or resizing the form) until the message loop is terminated because the form is closed.

Using `Form1()` inside the `Application.Run` statement calls the Form1 constructor, to return an instance of the newly created form. This displays the form when the application starts.

Any form that will initiate a Windows application by launching itself should have a `Main()` method, similar to the one discussed previously, defined in it. Normally only one form in a project (the form that acts as the starting form) has a `Main()` method.

WARNING

Keeping Things Synchronized   If you modify the name of a form, either by using the code view or by using the Windows Forms Designer via the `Name` property, Visual Studio .NET does not automatically change the name of the form in the `Application.Run()` method. You have to change it manually.

If you refer to the .NET FCL documentation, you will see that the `Application` class belongs to the `System.Windows.Forms` namespace. But rather than uniquely referring to it as `System.Windows.Forms.Application`, the code refers to it as just `Application`. How is this possible? The language designers noted that typing the full namespace with a class every time it is used is a lot of typing, so they provided a shortcut for this via the `using` directive. Near the beginning of a program file, Visual Studio .NET typically includes the following `using` directives for a Windows application:

```
using System;
using System.Drawing;
using System.Collections;
using System.ComponentModel;
using System.Windows.Forms;
```

Inclusion of these `using` directives tells the C# compiler to look for each class you are using in the namespaces specified in the `using` directive. The compiler looks up each namespace one-by-one, and when it finds the given class in one of the namespaces, it internally replaces the reference of the class with `NamespaceName.ClassName` in the code.

What happens when code uses two classes that have the same name but belong to different namespaces? The usage of the `using` directive discussed so far can't handle that situation; fortunately, there is another way you can use `using` directives. You can create aliases for a namespaces with the `using` directive. These aliases save you typing and qualify classes appropriately. Here is an example:

```
//Create namespace alias here
using Q316 = QueCertifications.Exam70316;
using Q306 = QueCertifications.Exam70315;

//use aliases to distinctly refer to classes
Q316.ExamQuestions.Display();
Q306.ExamQuestions.Display();
```

When you instruct Visual Studio .NET to run the form, it first compiles the form's code, using an appropriate language compiler (C# in this case for a C# Windows application). If there are no errors at compile time, the compiler generates an executable file with the name of the project and the extension `.exe` (for example, `316C01.exe`). The default location of the file is the bin\debug directory in the project's directory. You can explore where this file is located in the project through the Solution Explorer by following the steps in Step by Step 1.2.

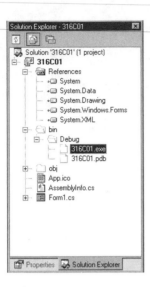

FIGURE 1.8
You can show all files in the Solution Explorer.

NOTE

Don't Confuse Library Names with Namespaces   Sometimes the name of a library may look similar to the name of a namespace. For example, earlier in this chapter I talked about a namespace System.Windows.Forms, and there is a library by the same name that exists as System.Windows. Forms.dll. Don't be mistaken: They are totally different concepts. A library exists as a file and can contain code for one or more classes. Those classes may belong to different namespaces. A namespace is a logical organization of classes and has no physical form. A library is a physical unit that stores classes as a single deployment unit. Creation of code libraries is discussed in more detail in Chapter 4.

STEP BY STEP

1.2 Using the Solution Explorer to See Hidden Files

1. Open the Solution Explorer window if it is not already open by selecting View, Solution Explorer.

2. Click on the Project name 316C01 to select it. From the toolbar in the Solution Explorer, click the Show All Files icon.

3. A dimmed folder icon named bin becomes visible in the project's file hierarchy. Expand this folder fully by clicking the + signs (see Figure 1.8). You should see a file named 316C01.exe. This is the project's executable file. The other file, named 316C01.pdb (pdb stands for *program database*), stores debugging and project information.

4. Click the project name again to select it. From the toolbar in the Solution Explorer window click Show All Files. The bin folder is now hidden.

You might be wondering whether the little code that you are seeing in the form is enough for all of its functionality. Where is the code to actually draw the form onscreen? Where is the code that responds to dragging or resizing of the form? This form is inheriting its functionality from other classes. But where is the code for those classes? Code for various classes in the FCL is packaged as libraries (that is, .dll files), and Visual Studio .NET is smart enough to automatically include references to them in your project. It selects a few common libraries, depending on the project type, and it lets you include references to other libraries. You can see what libraries are included with a project by opening the Solution Explorer and navigating to the References hierarchy within the project (refer to Figure 1.8).

Using the Application Class

The Application class is responsible for managing a Windows Application. It provides a set of properties to get information about the current application (see Table 1.1). It also provides methods to start an application, end an application, and process the Windows messages (see Table 1.2). It is important to note here that all methods and properties of the Application class are static.

Because they're static, you need not create an instance of the Application class in order to use them. You can directly call these methods by prefixing them with the name of the class. As a matter of fact, creating an instance of the Application class is not possible. The class designers assigned a private access modifier to the constructor of the Application class to prevent you from creating instances of the class. If a constructor is not accessible for a class, it cannot be instantiated.

TABLE 1.1

SOME IMPORTANT STATIC PROPERTIES OF THE Application CLASS

Property Name	Description
CompanyName	Specifies the company name associated with the application
CurrentCulture	Specifies the culture information for the current thread
CurrentInputLanguage	Specifies the current input language for the current thread
ExecutablePath	Specifies the path of the executable file that started the application
ProductName	Specifies the product name for the current application
ProductVersion	Specifies the product version for the current application

TABLE 1.2

SOME IMPORTANT STATIC METHODS OF THE Application CLASS

Method Name	Description
DoEvents()	Processes all Windows messages currently in the message queue
Exit()	Terminates the application
ExitThread()	Exits the message loop on the current thread and closes all windows on the thread
Run()	Begins a standard application message loop on the current thread

STEP BY STEP

1.3 Using Application Class Properties

1. Launch Visual Studio .NET. Select File, Open, Project. Navigate to the existing project 316C01 and open it.

2. In the Solution Explorer, right-click the project name and select Add, Add Windows Form. (Alternatively, you can do this by selecting Project, Add Windows Form). Name the new form StepByStep1_3.cs.

3. Switch to the code view, and just after the Windows Form Designer Generated Code region, insert the following Main() method:

```
[STAThread]
static void Main()
{
    Application.Run(new StepByStep1_3());
    //Display a MessageBox
    MessageBox.Show(Application.ExecutablePath,
      "Location of Executable", MessageBoxButtons.OK,
          MessageBoxIcon.Information);
}
```

4. In the Solution Explorer, right-click the project name and select Properties from the context menu. In the Property Pages window, set the startup object to _316C01.StepByStep1_3 (see Figure 1.9). Click OK to close the Property Pages window.

FIGURE 1.9
You can change the startup object by using the Property Pages window.

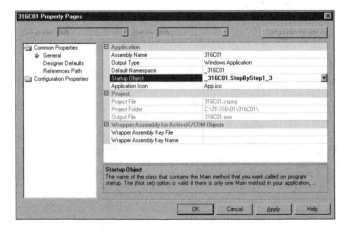

5. Select Debug, Run. The application displays the new form. When you close the form, the application displays a message box that shows the application's executable path (see Figure 1.10).

FIGURE 1.10
You can display an executable's path by using the `Application.ExecutablePath` property.

Because in Step by Step 1.3 you add another form to an existing Windows form project, the `Main()` method that starts the application is not automatically inserted in the form. The newly created form has its `Name` property properly set to `StepByStep1_3` because you explicitly specify the classname at the time of form creation. In Step by Step 1.3 you want to run the newly created form when the application starts. To accomplish this, you can manually add a `Main()` method in code and designate the newly added form as the startup object. Even though the project then contains two forms, each with a `Main()` method, only the `Main()` method of the startup object is executed when you start the project. The other form (`StepByStep1_1`) just exists there, doing nothing.

When you run the `project`, the form `StepByStep1_3` is displayed. When you close the form, it internally sends an exit message to the active application, which takes the control out of the `Application.Run()` method; the message box gets a chance to display itself.

`StepByStep1_3` uses the `Show()` method of the `MessageBox` class to display a message box to the user. The message box displays the value of the `ExecutablePath` property of the `Application` class.

Because you're calling the `Show()` method prefixed by the name of the class (`MessageBox`), `Show()` must be a static method. Note that as you type the code, Visual Studio .NET helps you with syntax, methods, and properties of various code items, by using a feature called IntelliSense (see Figure 1.11).

FIGURE 1.11

IntelliSense helps you easily complete statements.

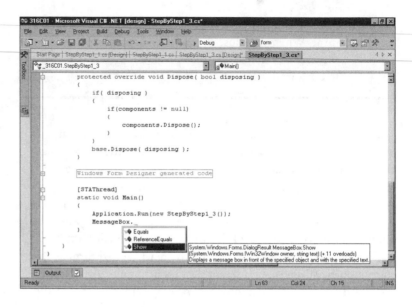

As a quick exercise, try placing the `MessageBox.Show()` method before `Application.Run()`, and note the difference in execution.

Using the `MessageBox` Class

The `MessageBox` class belongs to the `System.Windows.Forms` namespace and inherits from the `Object` class. In addition to the methods that it has as a result of its inheritance from `Object`, it provides a `Show()` method that you can use in 12 different variations (as you can see with the help of IntelliSense) to display different kinds of message boxes to the user. Some of the arguments of the `Show()` method are values of enumeration types such as `MessageBoxButtons` and `MessageBoxIcons`. *Enumeration types* (also known as *enums*) provide a set of named constants called the enumerator list. You will see an extensive usage of enumeration types in .NET FCLs. They are the preferred, type-safe, and object-oriented way of referring to a list of constant values. For example, the `MessageBoxButtons` enumeration type provides a list of enumerators. Each of these values specifies a set of buttons that can be displayed in a message box. Table 1.3 lists the values of the `MessageBoxButtons` enumeration type and their meanings.

TABLE 1.3

MessageBoxButtons ENUMERATORS

Enumerator Value	The Message Box Shows These Buttons
AbortRetryIgnore	Abort, Retry, and Ignore
OK	OK
OKCancel	OK and Cancel
RetryCancel	Retry and Cancel
YesNo	Yes and No
YesNoCancel	Yes, No, and Cancel

NOTE

Using Message Boxes Message boxes can help you quickly debug code in some instances. For example, you can use a message box to display the values of variables, fields, and properties at different stages in program execution.

The MessageBoxIcons enumeration determines the icon on a message box. Table 1.4 lists the values of the MessageBoxIcons enumerators and their meanings. (Note that some of the names have identical meanings.)

TABLE 1.4

MessageBoxIcons ENUMERATORS

Enumerator Value	The Message Box Contains This Symbol
Asterisk	A lowercase letter i in a circle
Error	A white X in a circle with a red background
Exclamation	An exclamation point in a triangle with a yellow background
Hand	A white X in a circle with a red background
Information	A lowercase letter i in a circle
None	No symbol
Question	A question mark in a circle
Stop	A white X in a circle with a red background
Warning	An exclamation point in a triangle with a yellow background

▶ Each form definition is contained in a class. Forms generally derive their functionality from the standard `System.Windows.Forms.Form` class.

▶ The Solution Explorer window allows you to manage all the files in a project.

▶ The `Main()` method acts as an entry point for a class. Execution of code inside a class begins from the `Main()` method.

▶ The `Application.Run()` method sends a form to a message loop that allows the form to listen to user interactions until the form is closed.

▶ The `MessageBox` class can be used to display various types of messages to the user.

SETTING AND ADDING PROPERTIES TO A WINDOWS FORM

Create a Windows form by using the Windows Forms Designer:

- **Add and set properties on a Windows form.**

The properties of an object provide a mechanism through which objects can expose their characteristics to the external world. In the following sections you will learn how to customize a form's appearance by using its properties. You will also learn how you can add your own properties to a form.

Using the Visual Designer to Set Windows Form Properties

A Windows form derives from several other classes, such as `Object`, `Control`, and so on, through a chain of inheritances.

As a result of this inheritance, the Windows form inherits the properties of its parent classes in addition of its own specific properties. All these properties are available for easy manipulation through the Properties window in Visual Studio .NET. Step by Step 1.4 shows you how to manipulate some of these properties to get a feel for how they affect the behavior of a form.

STEP BY STEP

1.4 Working with Windows Form Properties

1. Open the project 316C01. In the Solution Explorer right-click the project name and select Add, Add Windows Form from the context menu. Name the new form StepByStep1_4.

2. Right-click the form and select Properties from the context menu. Find the BackColor property and click the down arrow of the drop-down list. This invokes a tabbed list of colors in which three categories of colors are available: Custom, Web, and System. Click the tab titled Web and select AntiqueWhite from the list. Note that the form's surface immediately changes color to reflect this property change.

3. In the Properties window, locate the property named FormBorderStyle and change its value from Sizable to FixedSingle.

4. In the Properties window, look for the property named Size. Expand this property by clicking the + sign next to it. Change the Width subproperty to 400 and the Height subproperty to 200.

5. Go to the StartPosition property in the list of properties and change its value to CenterScreen.

6. Change the MinimizeBox property to False.

7. Right-click anywhere on the form and select View Code from the context menu. In the code view, insert the following code just after the Windows Form Designer Generated Code region:

continues

FIGURE 1.12
You can change a form's properties—such as BackColor, Size, and FormBorderStyle—to customize its appearance.

continued

```
[STAThread]
static void Main()
{
    Application.Run(new StepByStep1_4());
}
```

8. In the Solution Explorer, right-click the project name and select Properties from the context menu. In the Property Pages window, set _316C01.StepByStep1_4 as the startup object. Click OK to close the Property Pages window.

9. Select Debug, Run. The application displays the form, showing the effect of the property settings that you made. The result looks similar to that shown in Figure 1.12.

In Step by Step 1.4, you manipulate various properties of a form to change its visual appearance. When you invoke the Properties window for the form, you see a big list of properties that are available to you. These properties provide significant control over the characteristics of the form. Table 1.5 lists some of the important properties of the Form class.

TABLE 1.5

SOME IMPORTANT PROPERTIES OF THE Form CLASS

Property Name	Description
BackColor	Specifies the background color of the form
BackgroundImage	Specifies the background image displayed in the form
ClientSize	Specifies the size of the client area of the form
ControlBox	Indicates whether a control box needs to be displayed in the caption bar of the form
DesktopLocation	Specifies the location of the form on the Windows desktop
Enabled	Indicates whether a control can respond to user interaction
FormBorderStyle	Specifies the border style of the form
Handle	Gets the Window Handle (HWND) of the form
HelpButton	Indicates whether a Help button is to be displayed on the caption bar of the form

Property Name	Description
Icon	Specifies the icon for the form
MaximizeBox	Indicates whether a maximize button is to be displayed on the caption bar of the form
MaximumSize	Specifies the maximum size to which the form can be resized
MinimizeBox	Indicates whether a minimize button is to be displayed in the caption bar of the form
MinimumSize	Specifies the minimum size to which the form can be resized
Modal	Indicates whether the form is to be displayed modally
Name	Specifies the name of the form
Opacity	Specifies the opacity level of the form
ShowInTaskbar	Indicates whether the form is to be displayed in the Windows taskbar
Size	Specifies the size of the form
StartPosition	Specifies the starting position of the form at runtime
TopMost	Indicates whether the form should be displayed as the top-most form of the application

The properties in Table 1.5 have various data types. You will find that some properties, such as FormBorderStyle, are enumeration types; some properties, such as Size, are of type struct, and their values are determined by the values of their contained members (for example, X and Y); other properties, such as MinimizeBox, accept a simple Boolean value. The Properties window provides a nice user interface for working with these values.

To increase your understanding about what's going on behind the scenes, it would be a good idea to switch to the code view, expand the Windows Form Designer Generated Code region, and analyze the generated code.

Setting Windows Form Properties Programmatically

Using the Windows Forms Designer is a quick and easy way to manipulate control properties, but the designer can only set the properties at design time. What would you do if wanted to change the appearance of a form at runtime? You could write your own code in the code view.

In complex projects, as you need more functionality in an application, you will find yourself switching frequently to the code view. Sometimes you can learn a lot about the .NET Framework by using the code view because it gives you an opportunity to directly play with .NET Framework data structures.

Step by Step 1.5 lets you explore some more properties of a Windows form and programmatically code the properties that are used in Step by Step 1.4. Step by Step 1.5 also shows you how to create a form programmatically.

STEP BY STEP

1.5 Setting Windows Form Properties Programmatically

1. Open the project 316C01. In the Solution Explorer right-click the project name and select Add, Add Windows Form from the context menu. Name the new form StepByStep1_5.

2. Right-click anywhere on the form and select View Code from the context menu. In the code view, insert the following code just after the Windows Form Designer Generated Code region:

```
[STAThread]
static void Main()
{
    // Create StepByStep1_5 object
    // and set its properties
    StepByStep1_5 frm1_5 = new StepByStep1_5();
    frm1_5.BackColor = Color.AntiqueWhite;
    frm1_5.FormBorderStyle =
        FormBorderStyle.FixedSingle;
    frm1_5.Size = new Size(400,200);
    frm1_5.StartPosition =
        FormStartPosition.CenterScreen;
    frm1_5.MinimizeBox = false;
    Application.Run(frm1_5);
}
```

3. In the Solution Explorer, right-click the project name and select Properties from the context menu. In the Property Pages window, select _316C01.StepByStep1_5 as the startup object. Click OK to close the Property Pages window.

4. Select Debug, Run. The form that is displayed looks similar to the form that you created in Step by Step 1.4 (refer to Figure 1.12).

In Step by Step 1.5, when you add a new Windows form to a project, a new class representing that form is created. As you can see in the code in Step by Step 1.5, you first create an object of the class so that you can later modify the object's properties. The modified form object is then passed as a parameter to the Application.Run() method that invokes the form.

While you are typing code in the code view, you see Visual Studio .NET helping you with the properties and syntaxes via IntelliSense. You should also note that values for properties such as BackColor and FormBorderStyle are encapsulated in enumerated types. You can find out what enumerated type to use for a property by hovering your mouse pointer over a property name in the code view. This displays a ToolTip that helps you identify the type of a property.

If you compare the code that you write manually in Step by Step 1.5 with the code that is generated by the Windows Forms Designer in Step by Step 1.4, you should see that the most significant difference is that the designer includes all its code for setting form properties in the InitializeComponent() method.

You can alternatively place the code inside the form's constructor after the call to the InitializeComponent() method. Including the code in the constructor ensures that the code is executed every time an instance of the form is created. The effect in this case would be the same as the effect of placing the code in the InitializeComponent() method.

So far you have seen how to get and set properties for a Windows form. The Form class also provides a set of methods, and Step by Step 1.6 demonstrates how to use them.

> **NOTE**
>
> **Leaving the Autogenerated Code Alone** The Windows Forms Designer manages the InitializeComponent() method. Putting your own code within that method might interfere with the designer's working. It is therefore generally recommended that you avoid modifying this method.

STEP BY STEP

1.6 Invoking Methods of Windows Forms

1. Open the project 316C01. In the Solution Explorer right-click the project name and select Add, Add Windows Form from the context menu. Name the new form StepByStep1_6.

2. Right-click anywhere on the form and select View Code from the context menu. In the code view, insert the following code just after the Windows Form Designer Generated Code region:

```
[STAThread]
static void Main()
{
    // Create StepByStep1_6 object
    // and set its properties
    StepByStep1_6 frmBottom = new StepByStep1_6();
    frmBottom.BackColor = Color.AntiqueWhite;
    frmBottom.FormBorderStyle =
        FormBorderStyle.FixedSingle;
    frmBottom.Size = new Size(400,200);
    frmBottom.StartPosition =
        FormStartPosition.CenterScreen;
    frmBottom.MinimizeBox = false;

    // Create a new form and set its
    // properties to stay on top
    Form frmOnTop = new Form();
    frmOnTop.TopMost = true;
    frmOnTop.Opacity = 0.7;
    frmOnTop.Show();

    Application.Run(frmBottom);
}
```

3. In the Solution Explorer, right-click the project name and select Properties from the context menu. In the Property Pages window, select _316C01.StepByStep1_6 as the startup object. Click OK to close the Property Pages window.

4. Select Debug, Run. The application displays two forms. The top form is transparent and stays on the top, even when you click the other form (see Figure 1.13).

NOTE

The Opacity Property Transparent forms are supported only on operating systems that can display layered windows. Such operating systems include Windows 2000, Windows XP and later versions of Windows. The Opacity property has no effect when you run a program on older operating systems such as Windows 98.

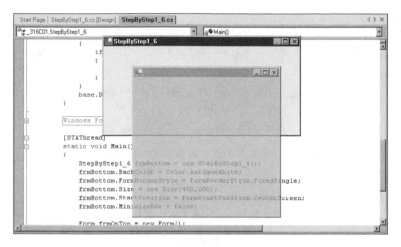

FIGURE 1.13

The Show() method sets the Visible property of a form to true.

In Step by Step 1.6 you create a new form by creating an instance of the Form class. You set the properties of the new form so that it is the topmost form in the application and then you reduce the opacity to make the form slightly transparent. Finally, you invoke the Show() method of the form to actually display the form onscreen.

There are two forms in Step by Step 1.6, but you are calling the Show() method for only one of them. When you run the program, you actually see both forms onscreen. How? It happens because frmBottom is passed as a parameter to the Application.Run() method. When the Application.Run() method starts the application by launching frmBottom onscreen, in the process it internally calls the Show() method for frmBottom. In the running program, if you close frmOnTop, you close just that form, but if you close frmBottom, you close all open forms and quit the application.

> **EXAM TIP**
>
> **Form.Close() Versus Form.Hide()**
> When you close a form by using its Close() method, all resources related to that form are released. You cannot call the Show() method to make the form visible again because the form itself does not exist anymore. If you want to temporarily hide a form and show it at a later time, you can use the form's Hide() method. Using the Hide() method is equivalent to setting the form's Visible property to false. The form still exists in memory, and you can make it visible any time by calling the Show() method of the form or by setting the form's Visible property to true.

GUIDED PRACTICE EXERCISE 1.1

You are a Windows developer for SpiderWare, Inc. In one of your applications you are required to create a form that enables users to set various options of the application. You want the form to have the following characteristics:

▶ It should have a thin title bar showing the text Options and a close button. The user should not be able to resize, minimize, or maximize this form.

continues

continued

▶ It should always appear on top of the other forms in the application.

▶ It should be always displayed in the center of the screen.

How would you create such a form?

You should try working through this problem on your own first. If you get stuck, or if you'd like to see one possible solution, follow these steps:

1. Open the project 316C01. Add a Windows form with the name GuidedPracticeExercise1_1 to the project.

2. Open the Properties window for the form. Change the value of the Text property to Options.

3. Change the FormBorderStyle property to FixedToolWindow.

4. Change the StartPosition property to CenterScreen.

5. Change the TopMost property to true.

6. Switch to the code view, and insert the following Main() method:

```
[STAThread]
static void Main()
{
    Application.Run(new GuidedPracticeExercise1_1());
}
```

7. Set the form as the startup object and execute the program.

If you have difficulty following this exercise, review the section "Designing a Windows Form by Using Windows Forms Designer," earlier in this chapter. Also spend some time looking at the various properties that are available for a form in the Properties window. Experimenting with them in addition to reading the text and examples in this chapter should help you relearn this material. After doing that review, try this exercise again.

Adding New Properties to a Windows Form

In addition to using the existing properties, you can add custom properties to a Windows form. You can use a custom property to store application-specific data.

STEP BY STEP

1.7 Adding New Properties to a Windows Form

1. Open the project 316C01. In the Solution Explorer right-click the project name and select Add, Add Windows Form from the context menu. Name the new form StepByStep1_7.

2. Right-click anywhere on the form and select View Code from the context menu. In the code view, insert the following code just after the Windows Form Designer Generated Code region:

```
//define constant values for State
public enum State{Idle, Connecting, Processing}

//use this field as storage location
//for FormState property
private State formState;

//set attributes for FormState property
[Browsable(true),
EditorBrowsable(EditorBrowsableState.Never),
Description("Sets the custom Form state"),
Category("Custom")]

//Creating FormState property
public State FormState
{
    get
    {
        return formState;
    }
    set
    {
        formState = value;
        switch (formState)
```

continues

continued

```
    {
        case State.Idle:
            this.BackColor = Color.Red;
            this.Text = "Idle";
            break;
        case State.Connecting:
            this.BackColor = Color.Orange;
            this.Text = "Connecting...";
            break;
        case State.Processing:
            this.BackColor = Color.Green;
            this.Text = "Processing";
            break;
    }
}
}
```

3. Change the form's constructor so that it looks like this:

```
public StepByStep1_7()
{
    // Default code of the Constructor
    //set the FormState property of this form
    this.FormState = State.Processing;
}
```

4. Add the following `Main()` method to the form:

```
[STAThread]
public static void Main()
{
    Application.Run(new StepByStep1_7());
}
```

5. In the Solution Explorer, right-click the project name and select Properties from the context menu. In the Property Pages window, select `_316C01.StepByStep1_7` as the startup object. Click OK to close the Property Pages window.

6. Select Debug, Run. The project shows a green-colored form onscreen.

The most important thing to note in Step by Step 1.7 is that you add a custom property named `FormState` to a form. The property that you create is even visible in the IntelliSense list when you try to access the members of this form object by typing a period (.) after the form's name in the form's constructor code.

To a program that uses the properties, the properties in Step by Step 1.7 look just like data fields, but properties by themselves do not have any storage locations, and their definitions look almost like method definitions. Properties provide two accessors (get and set) that would be called when a program would like to read from or write to the property. In Step by Step 1.7 you use a private field formState that works as a storage location for the FormState property; because formState is private, the rest of the world can access it only through the FormState public property. The data type of FormState is the enumerated type State, defined with a limited set of named constant values at the beginning of the code segment.

If you go to the design view and inspect the properties of form StepByStep1_7 through Properties window, you will not find the FormState property listed along with other properties. This is because the Properties window shows only the properties of the base class. You can think of it like this: The Properties window helps you design a new class (StepByStep1_7) in terms of a class that already exists (System.Windows.Forms.Form). So while you are designing the StepByStep1_7 class, if the Properties window would rather show the properties of the StepByStep1_7 class, then it's similar to defining a class in terms of a class that is itself under construction.

If you instead define a form by using the completely created class StepByStep1_7, it would make sense to have the FormState property available in the derived form through the Properties window. (I talk about this in a moment.)

Note that the FormState property has a big list of attributes. Such a big list isn't required to create a property, but it helps you specify the runtime behavior of the property. Table 1.6 describes how attributes can control the behavior of a property.

EXAM TIP

Read-Only and Write-Only Properties   The get and set accessors allow both read and write access to a property. If you want to make a property read-only, you should not include a set accessor in its property definition. On the other hand, if you want a write-only property, you should not include a get accessor in the property definition.

NOTE

Using the get and set Accessors   Accessors of a property can contain executable statements. The code contained in the get accessor executes when a program reads the value of a property. Similarly, when a program writes a value to a property, it executes the set accessor of the property.

TABLE 1.6

ATTRIBUTES THAT CONTROL THE BEHAVIOR OF A PROPERTY

Attribute Name	Description
Browsable	Indicates whether the property is displayed in the Properties window. Its default value is true.

continues

TABLE 1.6	*continued*

ATTRIBUTES THAT CONTROL THE BEHAVIOR OF A PROPERTY

Attribute Name	Description
EditorBrowsable	Indicates whether the property should appear in the IntelliSense list of an object in the code view. Its value is of the EditorBrowsableState enumeration type, with three possible values—Advanced, Always, and Never. Its default value is Always, which means "always list this property." If you change the value to Never, the property is hidden from the IntelliSense feature.
Description	Specifies a description string for the property. When the Description property is specified, it is displayed in the description area of the Properties window when the property is selected.
Category	Specifies the category of the property. The category is used in the Properties window to categorize the property list.

You cannot see the effect of using the attributes listed in Table 1.6 in the form you have been creating. However, you would see their effects if you inherited a form from that form. You'll learn more about this in the next section of this chapter.

REVIEW BREAK

▶ Properties let you customize the appearance and behavior of a Windows form.

▶ The Windows Forms Designer lets you define a form based on the properties that are available in its base class (which is usually the Form class).

▶ You can add custom properties to a form.

▶ Attributes let you define the runtime behavior of a property.

USING VISUAL INHERITANCE

Create a Windows form by using the Windows Forms Designer:

- **Create a Windows form by using visual inheritance**

Earlier in this chapter, in the section "Understanding Classes, Inheritance, and Namespaces," you learned that when a class inherits from its base class, it derives a basic set of functionality from the base class. No additional programming needs to be done in the derived class to enable that functionality. You are free to add extra functionality to the derived class to make it yet more useful.

Because a Windows form is a class, inheritance applies to it. In some cases you will find yourself creating new forms that are almost like ones you have previously created, but the new forms need some additional functionality. In such a case, rather than create a new form from scratch, you can inherit it from a form that has similar functionality and later customize the inherited form to add extra functionality to it.

When inheritance is applied to a Windows form, it is known as *visual inheritance* because it results in the inheritance of the visual characteristics of the form, such as its size, color, and any components placed on the form. You can also visually manipulate the properties that you inherit from the base class.

Step by Step 1.8 shows how to inherit from an existing form by using visual inheritance.

STEP BY STEP

1.8 Using Visual Inheritance

1. Open the project 316C01. In the Solution Explorer right-click the project name and select Add, Add Inherited Form from the context menu. Name the new form StepByStep1_8 and click the Open button.

2. From the Inheritance Picker dialog box (see Figure 1.14), select the component named StepByStep1_7 and click OK.

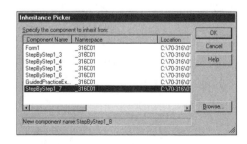

FIGURE 1.14
The Inheritance Picker dialog box allows you to choose a base class for a form.

continues

FIGURE 1.15
The FormState property is available in the Properties window in the proper category, and it has the proper description.

continued

3. Open the Properties window. Click the Categorized icon on its toolbar. In the category Custom, change the FormState property within that category to Idle (see Figure 1.15).

4. Add the following Main() method to the form:

```
[STAThread]
public static void Main()
{
    Application.Run(new StepByStep1_8());
}
```

5. In the Solution Explorer, right-click the project name and select Properties from the context menu. In the Property Pages window, select _316C01.StepByStep1_8 as the startup object. Click OK to close the Property Pages window.

6. Select Debug, Run. Because you have set the FormState property to Idle, the form displays in red.

EXAM TIP

Inheriting Private Members A derived class inherits all the members of a base class, but the private members of the base class are not accessible in the derived class because the variables with private modifiers in the base class are hidden from the derived classes.

When you run the form in Step by Step 1.8, note that the newly created form has the same behavior as the form created in Step by Step 1.7. The new form inherits its behavior from the form that already existed. In other words, the form named StepByStep1_8 is based on the form named StepByStep1_7. You have access to all browsable properties of the base form through the Properties window. When you select the FormState property of the form, you have access to its possible values in a drop-down list. Because of the run-time attribute applied to the FormState property in the base class, this property is filed in the Custom category. You are able to see the description of this property at the bottom of the Properties window when the property is selected.

After you inherit a form, you can add extra functionality to it. This functionality is available only in the newly created class and the classes you later derive from it, but it does not affect any of the base classes.

GUIDED PRACTICE EXERCISE 1.2

You are a Windows developer for SpiderWare, Inc. In one of your applications, you recently created a form that will be used to set various options of the application (refer to Guided Practice Exercise 1.1). Your application now requires another form such as the one you designed earlier. However, the color of this form should always be the same as the color of the user's desktop.

How would you create such a form?

You should try working through this problem on your own first. If you get stuck, or if you'd like to see one possible solution, follow these steps:

1. Open the project 316C01. Add an inherited form with the name GuidedPracticeExercise1_2 to this project.

2. From the Inheritance Picker dialog box select the component named GuidedPracticeExercise1_1 and click OK.

3. Open the Properties window for the form, and change the BackColor property to Desktop.

4. Switch to the code view, and insert the following Main() method:

```
[STAThread]
static void Main()
{
    Application.Run(new GuidedPracticeExercise1_2());
}
```

5. Set the form as the startup object and execute the program.

If you have difficulty following this exercise, review the sections "Designing a Windows Form by Using Windows Forms Designer" and "Using Visual Inheritance." Make sure you work through Guided Practice Exercise 1 before you attempt this one. The text and examples presented in these sections should help you relearn this material. After doing that review, try this exercise again.

NOTE

The EditorBrowsable Bug If you are inheriting a form from the same project, even though you have set the EditorBrowsable attribute for a property to be Never, you can see this property via IntelliSense help in the derived form. This feature works fine with Visual Basic .NET but is a known bug with Visual C# .NET.

The EditorBrowsable attribute works fine, however, if you are visually inheriting from a form that is present in a separate assembly. You will learn more about creating assemblies in Chapter 4.

▶ Form inheritance allows you to create a new form by inheriting it from a base form. This allows you to reuse and extend earlier coding efforts.

▶ The Windows Forms Designer lets you visually inherit a form from an existing form through the Inheritance Picker dialog box. You can also visually manipulate the inherited properties through the Properties window.

EVENT HANDLING

Create, implement, and handle events.

When you perform an action with an object, the object in turn raises events in the application. Dragging the title bar of a form and moving it around, for example, generates an event; resizing a form generates another event. A large portion of code for any typical Windows application is the code that is responsible for handling various events that the application responds to. Events are at the heart of graphical user interface (GUI)–based programming. An *event handler* is a method that is executed as a response to an event.

Not all events are triggered by user actions. Events may be triggered by changes in the environment such as the arrival of an email message, modifications to a file, changes in the time and completion of program execution, and so on.

With C#, you can define your own custom events that a class will listen to (you'll see how to do this in Chapter 4). You can also handle an event by executing custom code when the event is fired. The following sections discuss two different ways to handle events:

◆ Handling events by attaching a delegate

◆ Handling events by overriding a protected method of a base class

Handling Events by Attaching a Delegate

When you create a Windows form, it inherits from the Form class. The Form class has a set of events that are already defined and that you can access through the Properties window (see Figure 1.16). If your program needs to take actions when one of those events is fired, it must define an appropriate event handler. The event handler must be registered with the event source so that when the event occurs, the handler will be invoked (this is also referred to as *event-wiring*). It is possible to have multiple event handlers interested in responding to an event. It is also possible to have a single event handler respond to multiple events.

The visual designer uses event wiring through delegates for handling events, so for most of the book it is also the preferred approach to event handling.

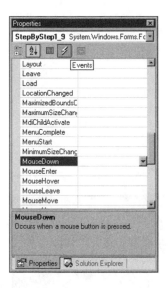

FIGURE 1.16
The Properties window lets you access events that are defined for an object.

STEP BY STEP

1.9 Handling the MouseDown Event

1. Open the project 316C01. In the Solution Explorer right-click the project name and select Add, Add Windows Form from the context menu. Name the new form StepByStep1_9 and click the Open button.

2. Open the Properties window of the form. Change the Text property to Event Handling Form.

3. In the Properties window, click the Events icon (which looks like a lightning bolt; refer to Figure 1.16) on the toolbar.

4. Look for an event named MouseDown(), and double-click the row containing the MouseDown event. This takes you to the code view, where Visual Studio .NET inserts a template for the MouseDown event handler. Add code to the event handler so that it looks like this:

continues

continued

```
private void StepByStep1_9_MouseDown(
 object sender, System.Windows.Forms.MouseEventArgs e)
{
    MessageBox.Show(
     String.Format("X ={0}, Y={1}", e.X, e.Y),
     String.Format("The {0} mouse button hit me at:",
      e.Button.ToString())));
}
```

5. Insert the following Main() method after the event handling code you just added:

```
[STAThread]
static void Main()
{
    Application.Run(new StepByStep1_9());
}
```

6. Set the form as the startup object. Run the project. Observe that whenever you click the form area, a message box appears, displaying the position of the click and whether the left or right mouse button is pressed (see Figure 1.17).

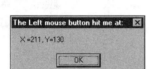

FIGURE 1.17
The event handler displays a message box showing event-related data.

Step by Step 1.9 involves responding to the MouseDown event of a form. The form inherits the MouseDown event (and many others) from its base class Form. The Properties window lets you see all the events that are available for a control or another object. You choose MouseDown from that list, and when you double-click the event name, the designer switches to the code view and inserts a template for the MouseDown event handler. You insert a line of code that generates a message box, showing the coordinates of the point at which the mouse button is pressed. This information comes from the MouseEventArgs parameter, passed to the event handling method.

The name of the event handler is StepByStep1_9_MouseDown (that is, it uses the form *ClassName_EventName*). Visual Studio .NET follows this general naming convention for naming event handlers. An event handler normally has a void return type and accepts two arguments: the object on which the event occurred and an argument of type EventArgs (or a type derived from it, such as MouseEventArgs) that contains event-related data. In the StepByStep1_9_MouseDown event handler, the second argument is of type MouseEventArgs, and it contains data that is specific to mouse events (such as the position where the button was pressed).

Table 1.7 shows the kind of information that can be retrieved from the
MouseEventArgs object. The type of the second argument depends on
the nature of event. Visual Studio .NET automatically determines it for
you, but if you write the event handler manually, you have to look in
the documentation to find its correct type. The code inside the event
handler is straightforward; it displays a message box that shows coordinates of the mouse location as well as which mouse button is pressed.

TABLE 1.7

MouseEventArgs PROPERTIES

Member	Description
Button	Returns a value of type MouseButtons that specifies which mouse button is pressed
Clicks	Returns the number of times the mouse button is pressed and released
Delta	Acts as a signed count of the number of detents (that is, notches of the mouse wheel) the mouse wheel has rotated
X	Specifies the x-coordinate of a mouse click
Y	Specifies the y-coordinate of a mouse click

How does the event handler get wired up with the actual event? The
designer does it for you, when you double-click the event name in
the Properties window. You can expand the designer-generated code
to find the following line of code:

```
this.MouseDown +=
    new System.Windows.Forms.MouseEventHandler(
        this.StepByStep1_9_MouseDown);
```

This looks like a complex statement. If you break it down to understand it properly, however, you'll see that there are three parts to it:

◆ MouseDown is the name of an event.

◆ MouseEventHandler is the delegate of the MouseDown event.

◆ StepByStep1_9_MouseDown is the name of an event handler.

And here is the role each of them is playing:

◆ The MouseDown event is raised when a mouse button is
   pressed. A set of event handlers can be attached to this event.

When the event is fired, it invokes all the attached event handlers. An event handler can be attached to this event only through its delegate object.

◆ The delegate type of the `MouseDown` event is `MouseEventHandler`. You can add event handlers to a `MouseDown` event only by adding new instances of the delegate to it. A *delegate* is a special type that is capable of storing a reference to a method with a specific signature (that is, the arguments and return type). Because it stores references of methods, a delegate can also invoke the methods dynamically when the event occurs. In the Visual Studio .NET documentation, the definition of `MouseEventHandler` delegate looks like this:

```
public delegate void MouseEventHandler(
object sender, MouseEventArgs e);
```

This means that `MouseEventHandler` is capable of storing references to any method whose return type is void and that accepts two arguments: the first one of type `System.Object` and the other one of type `MouseEventArgs`. The `StepByStep1_9_MouseDown` event handler signature matches the criteria of this delegate, and hence its reference can be stored in an instance of a delegate of type `MouseEventHandler`.

When you have an instance of the `MouseEventHandler` delegate, you can attach it to the event by using the addition syntax. `+=` is used in the example, so if any event handlers are already attached to this event by the base class, they remain in the list.

◆ `StepByStep1_9_MouseDown` is the name of the method that is responding to this event. The keyword qualifies it for the current instance of the form. When a method name is used alone, without any argument list, it works as a reference to the actual method definition. That reference is passed to the delegate. At a later stage, when the event occurs, that method is invoked through its reference that is maintained by the delegate object.

To manually write code to handle an event, you would follow these steps:

1. Look up the Visual Studio .NET documentation to find the appropriate event for a class.

2. Find out the delegate type for this event.

NOTE

Detaching an Event Handler You can detach an event handler from an event by using the `-=` syntax that is similar to the `+=` syntax. Although detaching an event handler is generally not required, you might want to detach an event if at runtime, you are no longer interested in responding to a particular event.

EXAM TIP

Adding Versus Replacing Delegates When you are attaching delegates, you should usually use the `+=` syntax rather than the `=` syntax. This is because `=` attaches the current delegate, and any other previously attached delegates are lost. Using `+=` ensures that you preserve the list of previously attached delegates.

3. Based on the delegate signature, create an event handler.

4. Create an instance of the event's delegate that contains a reference to the event handler method.

5. Add to the event the delegate instance from step 4.

From these steps, you can see that the designer takes a lot of details away from you, and what you are required to do is simply write the actual code that will be executed when the event occurs.

As mentioned earlier in this chapter, it is possible to attach multiple event handlers to an event. Step by Step 1.10 shows how to attach a second event handler to the MouseDown event from Step by Step 1.9. When you execute the code and press the mouse button on the form, both event handlers are executed.

STEP BY STEP

1.10 Attaching Multiple Event Handlers to the MouseDown Event

1. Open the project 316C01. In the Solution Explorer right-click the project name and select Add, Add Windows Form from the context menu. Name the new form StepByStep1_10 and click on the Open button.

2. Open the Properties window for the form. Change the form's Text property to Multiple Events Handling Form.

3. Search for the MouseDown event, and double-click on the row that contains the MouseDown event. Modify its event handler to look like this:

```
private void StepByStep1_10_MouseDown(object sender,
    System.Windows.Forms.MouseEventArgs e)
{
    MessageBox.Show(
      String.Format("X ={0}, Y={1}", e.X, e.Y),
      String.Format("The {0} mouse button hit me at:",
        e.Button.ToString()));
}
```

continues

continued

4. Switch to the design view, and look again for the
MouseDown event in Properties window. If you again double-click the row that contains the MouseDown event, you
see that a new event handler is not inserted. Therefore,
you need to switch to the code view and add the following
code for a second event handler:

```
private void SecondEventHandler(
  object sender, MouseEventArgs e)
{
    Form frm1_10 = (Form) sender;
    if (frm1_10.BackColor== Color.AntiqueWhite)
        frm1_10.BackColor = Color.LightCoral;
    else
        frm1_10.BackColor = Color.AntiqueWhite;
}
```

5. Insert the following Main() method after the event handling code from step 4:

```
[STAThread]
static void Main()
{
    StepByStep1_10 frm1_10= new StepByStep1_10();
    frm1_10.MouseDown += new MouseEventHandler(
      frm1_10.SecondEventHandler);
    Application.Run(frm1_10);
}
```

6. Set the form as the startup object. Run the project. Try
clicking on the form with the left and right mouse buttons, and the form changes background color in addition
to responding with a message box on every click.

In Step by Step 1.10 you add an event handler to the newly created
instance of the form StepByStep1_10. The form then has two event
handlers registered with the MouseDown event. The first event handler,
inserted through the Properties window, is attached to the event
when the InitializeComponent() event is fired as part of the
creation of a new instance of StepByStep1_10. The order in which
both event handlers are executed is the order in which they were
attached to the event.

Handling Events by Overriding a Protected Method of a Base Class

When you create a Windows form, it inherits from the Form class. By virtue of this inheritance, it has a set of public and protected methods and properties available to it from one of its base classes. The class view lets you see all the inherited members (see Figure 1.18). Some of the classes provide sets of protected methods that raise events. You can easily identify these classes because their naming convention is the word On followed by the name of the event. For example, OnMouseDown() is the protected method of the Form class that raises the MouseDown event. The Form class gets this protected method from the Control class.

The section "Handling Events by Attaching a Delegate" describes how to wire events through the use of delegate objects. An alternative way is to override the On method and write the event handling code there. Step by Step 1.11 demonstrates how to do that.

STEP BY STEP

1.11 Handling Events by Overriding the OnMouseDown Event

1. Open the project 316C01. In the Solution Explorer right-click the project name and select Add, Add Windows Form from the context menu. Name the new form StepByStep1_11 and click the Open button.

2. Open the Properties window of the form. Change the Text property of the form to Event Handling through OnMouseDown.

3. Open the class view by selecting View, Class View (or by pressing Ctrl+Shift+C). Navigate to the StepByStep1_11 node. Expand the Bases and Interfaces node. You should see a node corresponding to the base class Form. Keep expanding until you see members of the Control class (see Figure 1.18).

continues

continued

FIGURE 1.18
The class view lets you explore the complete inheritance hierarchy.

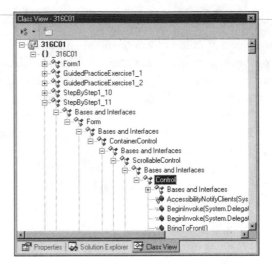

4. In the expanded tree, look for a method in the `Control` class named `OnMouseDown()`. Right-click the method name and select Add, Override from the context menu. This generates a template for the `OnMouseDown()` method in your program and switches to code view. Modify the `OnMouseDown()` method so that it looks like this:

```
protected override void OnMouseDown(
    System.Windows.Forms.MouseEventArgs e)
{
    MessageBox.Show(
      String.Format("X ={0}, Y={1}", e.X, e.Y),
      String.Format("The {0} mouse button hit me at:",
        e.Button.ToString()));
}
```

5. Enter the following code for the `Main()` method after the `OnMouseDown()` method:

```
[STAThread]
static void Main()
{
    Application.Run(new StepByStep1_11());
}
```

6. Set the form as the startup object. Run the project and click on the form surface with the left and right mouse buttons. You see the form respond to the `MouseDown` event by displaying a message box.

The result of Step by Step 1.11 is similar to the result of Step by Step 1.9, in which you handle an event by attaching a delegate to it. Only the implementation is different.

What makes the code in Step by Step 1.11 work? It works because the OnMouseDown() method (similar to other On methods) is the core method that is invoked when the mouse button is pressed. This method is responsible for notifying all registered objects about the MouseDown event. This method is not new; it was in place and working hard even when you were using the delegate-based event-handling scheme. How is that possible when you didn't code the method in your earlier programs? Recall from the section "Using Visual Inheritance" that the derived class inherits all members from its base classes in its inheritance tree. Step by Step 1.11 gets the OnMouseDown event from the Control class. In the base class Control, the OnMouseDown() method is declared as follows:

```
protected virtual void OnMouseDown(
    System.Windows.Forms.MouseEventArgs e);
```

Because the method is protected, it is available in all classes derived from Control, such as a Form and the delegate-based event-handling form StepByStep1_9. This method actually invokes the calls to delegates when the event takes place. The event-handling scheme discussed earlier keeps that fact hidden from you for the sake of simplicity.

The virtual modifier in the original declaration means that if the derived classes are not satisfied by the definition of this method in the original base class and if they need to extend it, they can do so by overriding its definition. That's what you do in Step by Step 1.11. When you override the method in a derived class, its base class version is not called. Instead, the overriding member in the most-derived class (which is StepByStep1_11 in this case) is called. That's how the version of the method that you write in Step by Step 1.11 is executed when the mouse button is pressed.

The sections "Handling Events by Attaching a Delegate" and "Handling Events by Overriding a Protected Method of a Base Class" discuss two schemes for event handling. Can these schemes exist together? To answer this question, try Step by Step 1.12.

STEP BY STEP

1.12 Mixing the Two Event Handling Schemes

1. Open the project 316C01. In the Solution Explorer right-click the project name and select Add, Add Windows Form from the context menu. Name the new form StepByStep1_12 and click the Open button.

2. Open the Properties window. Change the Text property of the form to Mixing Event Handling Techniques.

3. Search for the MouseDown event, and double-click the row that contains the MouseDown event. Modify its event handler to look like this:

```
private void StepByStep1_12_MouseDown(object sender,
    System.Windows.Forms.MouseEventArgs e)
{
    MessageBox.Show(
      String.Format("X ={0}, Y={1}", e.X, e.Y),
      String.Format("The {0} mouse button hit me at:",
        e.Button.ToString()));
}
```

4. Add the following code after the event handling code from step 3:

```
protected override void OnMouseDown(MouseEventArgs e)
{
    if (this.BackColor== Color.AntiqueWhite)
        this.BackColor = Color.LightCoral;
    else
        this.BackColor = Color.AntiqueWhite;
}
[STAThread]
static void Main()
{
    Application.Run(new StepByStep1_12());
}
```

5. Set the form as the startup object and execute it. When you click the form area, the background color changes but the message box is not displayed.

It seems that in Step by Step 1.12 you do not achieve quite what you wanted to achieve. Don't the two event handling techniques coexist?

When you click the mouse button, only the event handler code written inside the OnMouseDown() method executes, and the other handler that is wired with the help of designer does not execute. That is because Step by Step 1.12 does not code the OnMouseDown() method properly. To understand the mistake, you need to take a look at how the OnMouseDown() method works in its original form, if you hadn't overridden it. Its base class version would look something like this:

```
public event MouseEventHandler MouseDown;
protected virtual void OnMouseDown(MouseEventArgs e)
{
    if (MouseDown != null)
    {
      //Invokes the delegates.
      MouseDown(this, e);
    }
}
```

The OnMouseDown() method is invoked when the mouse button is pressed. In its code, it checks whether the associated MouseDown event has a delegate list associated with it. If the list is not empty, it raises the MouseDown event that actually fires all attached event handlers with the help of their respective delegate objects. (Recall from earlier discussions that a delegate object holds a reference to the method name and can invoke it dynamically.)

In Step by Step 1.12 , because you override the definition of the OnMousedown() method, its old base class logic that used to call other event handlers no longer executes. As a result, the events added through the delegate list are not executed. How can you fix the problem? The solution to this problem also teaches you a good programming practice: You should call the base class implementation of the protected On method whenever you override it. The modified OnMouseDown() method in Step by Step 1.12 would look like this:

```
protected override OnMouseDown(MouseEventArgs e)
{
    //fixes the problem by also calling base
    //class version of OnMouseDown method
    base.OnMouseDown(e);
    if (this.BackColor== Color.AntiqueWhite)
        this.BackColor = Color.LightCoral;
    else
        this.BackColor = Color.AntiqueWhite;}
```

This modification allows the base class implementation of the OnMouseDown() method to be executed; this is the method where the delegates are processed.

EXAM TIP

Overriding Protected Methods of a Base Class A derived class extends the functionality of its base class. It is generally a good idea to call the base class version of a method when you override a method in a derived class. That way, the derived class has at least the level of functionality offered by the base class. You can of course write more code in the overridden method to achieve extended functionality of the derived class.

On the other hand, if a derived class does not call the base class version of a method from an overridden method in derived class, you are not able to access all the functionality provided by the base class in the derived class.

REVIEW BREAK

▶ Events allow a program to respond to changes in the code's environment.

▶ Custom code can be executed when an event fires if the code is registered with the event. The pieces of code that respond to an event are called *event handlers*.

▶ Event handlers are registered with events through delegate objects.

▶ It is possible to respond to an event by overriding the On method corresponding to an event. When you use this method, you should be sure to call the corresponding On method for the base class so that you don't miss any of the event handlers registered through delegates when the event is raised.

BUILDING GRAPHICAL INTERFACE ELEMENTS BY USING THE SYSTEM.DRAWING NAMESPACE

Create a Windows form by using the Windows Forms Designer:

- **Build graphical interface elements by using the System.Drawing namespace.**

The FCLs provide an advanced implementation of the Windows Graphics Design Interface (also known as GDI+). The GDI+ classes can be used to perform a variety of graphics-related tasks such as working with text, fonts, lines, shapes, and images. One of the main benefits of using GDI+ is that it allows you to work with Graphics objects without worrying about the specific details of the underlying platform. The GDI+ classes are distributed among four namespaces:

◆ System.Drawing

◆ System.Drawing.Drawing2D

◆ `System.Drawing.Imaging`

◆ `System.Drawing.Text`

All these classes reside in a file named `System.Drawing.dll`.

Understanding the `Graphics` Objects

The `Graphics` class is one of the most important classes in the `System.Drawing` namespace. It provides methods for doing various kinds of graphics manipulations. The `Graphics` class is a sealed class and cannot be further inherited (unlike the `Form` class, for example). The only way you can work with the `Graphics` class is through its instances (that is, `Graphics` objects). A `Graphics` object is a GDI+ drawing surface that you can manipulate by using the methods of the `Graphics` class.

When you look in the documentation of the `Graphics` class, you see that there is no constructor available for this class, and hence a `Graphics` object cannot be directly created. Despite this, there are at least four ways you can get a `Graphics` object:

◆ Through the `Graphics` property of the `PaintEventArgs` argument passed to the `Paint` event handler of a control or a form. The `Graphics` object thus received represents the drawing surface of the object that was the source of the event.

◆ By calling the `CreateGraphics()` method of a control or form.

◆ By calling the `Graphics.FromHwnd()` method and passing it the handle of the current form.

◆ By calling the static `Graphics.FromImage()` method. This method takes an image object and returns a `Graphics` object that corresponds to that image. You can then use this `Graphics` object to manipulate the image.

When you have a `Graphics` object available, you have access to a drawing surface. You can use this surface to draw lines, text, curves, shapes, and so on. But before you can draw, you must understand the Windows forms coordinate system, which is discussed in the following section.

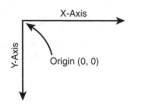

FIGURE 1.19
The Windows Forms Coordinate system is a two-dimensional coordinate system.

Understanding the Windows Forms Coordinate System

The Windows Forms library treats a Windows form as an object that has a two-dimensional coordinate system, as shown in Figure 1.19. Therefore, when you write text on the form or put controls on the form, the position is identified by a set of points. A *point* is a pair of numbers that is generally represented as (x, y) where x and y, respectively, denote horizontal and vertical distance from the origin of the form. The origin of the form is the top-left corner of the client area of the form. (The *client area* is the inner area of the form that you get after excluding the space occupied by title bar, sizing borders, and menu, if any.) The point of the origin is treated as (0, 0). The value of x increases to the right of the point of origin, and the value of y increases below the point of origin.

Two structures are available to represent points in a program—`Point` and `PointF`. These structures each represent an ordered pair of values (x and y). `Point` stores a pair of int values, whereas `PointF` stores a pair of float values. In addition to these values, these structures also provide a set of static methods and operators to perform basic operation on points.

Table 1.8 summarizes all the structures defined in the `System.Drawing` namespace.

TABLE 1.8

`System.Drawing` **Namespace** STRUCTURES

Structure	Description
`CharacterRange`	Specifies a range of character positions within a string.
`Color`	Specifies a color structure that has 140 static properties, each representing the name of a color. In addition, it also has four properties—`A`, `R`, `G`, and `B`—which specify the value for the `Alpha` (level of transparency), `Red`, `Green`, and `Blue` portions of the color. A `Color` value can be created by using any of its three static methods: `FromArgb()`, `FromKnownColor()`, and `FromName()`.
`Point`	Stores an ordered pair of integers, x and y, that defines a point in a two-dimensional plane. You can create a `Point` value by using its constructor. The `Point` structure also provides a set of methods and operators for working with points.

Structure	Description
PointF	Specifies a `float` version of the `Point` structure.
Rectangle	Stores the location and size of a rectangular region. You can create a `Rectangle` structure by using a `Point` structure and a `Size` structure. `Point` represents the top-left corner, and `Size` specifies the width and height from the given point.
RectangleF	Specifies a `float` version of the `Rectangle` structure.
Size	Represents the size of a rectangular region with an ordered pair of width and height.
SizeF	Specifies a `float` version of the `Size` structure.

Drawing Text on a Form

The `Graphics` class provides a `DrawString()` method that can be invoked on a Graphics object to render a text string on the drawing surface. There are six different forms in which the `DrawString()` method can be used. In this section, I discuss three of them; the other three forms are the same, but with one extra argument of `StringFormat` type that specifies alignment and line spacing information.

STEP BY STEP

1.13 Drawing Text on a Form

1. Open the project `316C01`. In the Solution Explorer right-click the project name and select Add Windows Form from the context menu. Name the new form `StepByStep1_13` and click the Open button.

2. Open the Properties window. Search for the `Paint` event of the form, and double-click the row that contains the `Paint` event. Modify its event handler to look like this:

```
private void StepByStep1_13_Paint(object sender,
    System.Windows.Forms.PaintEventArgs e)
{
    Graphics grfx = e.Graphics;
    String str = String.Format(
```

continues

continued

FIGURE 1.20
You can draw text on a Windows form by using the DrawString method of the Graphics class.

```
      "Form Size is: Width={0}, Height={1}",
        Width, Height);
      grfx.DrawString(str, Font, Brushes.Black, 0, 0);
}
```

3. Add the following code for the Main() method:

```
[STAThread]
static void Main()
{
    Application.Run(new StepByStep1_13());
}
```

4. Set the form as the startup object. Run the project. The form displays a string of text in black, showing the width and height of the form. Figure 1.20 shows the result.

In Step by Step 1.13, why did I choose to write the code within an event handler? There are two reasons, the foremost being that the Paint event handler provides access to the Graphics object. Second, the Paint event is fired whenever the form is redrawn, which includes when the form is first shown and when the form is restored from its minimized state, as well as when the form is shown after a window overlapping it is removed. Therefore, a Paint event handler is an appropriate place to put the code that you want to be executed whenever a form is redrawn.

The code gets the Graphics object through the Graphics property of the PaintEventArgs argument of the Paint event handler. The next step is to call the DrawString() method to draw text on the form. The DrawString() method used in Step by Step 1.13 takes five arguments and has the following signature:

```
public void DrawString(
    string, Font, Brush, float, float);
```

The first argument, string, is the string to be displayed. I use the String.Format() method to format the string.

The second argument, Font, is the font of the string. In Step by Step 1.13 I chose to display the string by using the default font of the current form through the Font property.

The third parameter, Brush, is the type of brush. The Brushes enumeration provides a variety of Brush objects, each with a distinct color. I chose the Brushes.Black value to draw text in black.

The fourth and fifth properties, `float` and `float`, specify the x and y locations for the point that marks the start of the string on the form. Both of these values are required to be of `float` type. The `0` value that the code contains is implicitly converted to a `float` value.

You might have noticed that when you resize the form in Step by Step 1.13, the `Paint` event is not triggered. An obvious idea for improving this form is to have it dynamically reflect the size of the form as you resize it. What event should you handle to do that? The `Resize` event. Step by Step 1.14 explains how to do this.

> **EXAM TIP**
>
> **Unicode Support and `DrawString`**
> GDI+ and hence the Windows Forms library have full support for Unicode. This means that you can draw text in any language supported by the operating system.

STEP BY STEP

1.14 Using the `Invalidate()` Method

1. Open the project `316C01`. In the Solution Explorer right-click the project name and select Add Windows Form from the context menu. Name the new form `StepByStep1_14` and click on the Open button.

2. Follow steps 2 and 3 from Step by Step 1.13 to include the `Paint` event handler code and `Main()` method to run the form `StepByStep1_14`.

3. Open the Properties window of the form `StepByStep1_14`. Search for the `Resize` event, and double-click on the row that contains the `Resize` event. Modify its event handler so that it looks like this:

```
private void StepByStep1_14_Resize(
    object sender, System.EventArgs e)
{
    // Call the Invalidate method
    Invalidate();
}
```

4. Set the form as the startup object. Run the project and notice that the form constantly modifies the text as it is resized.

After you complete Step by Step 1.14, the program works as desired. What's the deal with the `Invalidate()` method? The `Invalidate()` method causes the paint message to be sent to the form.

EXAM TIP

Invalidate() Method Calls When you call the `Invalidate()` method without any parameters, the `Paint` event is called for the entire area. If only a particular portion of the control needs to be refreshed, then calling `Invalidate()` for the entire area is rather taxing on application performance. In such a case you should call `Invalidate()` with a Rectangle parameter that specifies the portion of the control that you are interested in refreshing.

As a result, the `Paint` event handler is called. So this handy method can be called whenever the code in the `Paint` event handler needs to be executed. In Step by Step 1.14, the code makes a call to the `Invalidate()` method whenever the form is resized. The `Invalidate()` method is available in various forms, and you can refresh a specific portion of a form by using one of these forms.

Given the frequent requirement of calling `Paint` whenever `Resize` is fired, the Windows Forms library designers created a useful property: `ResizeRedraw`. This is a protected property that the Form class inherits from the `Control` class. When `ResizeRedraw` is set to true, it instructs a control (or a form, in this case) to redraw itself when it is resized. Its default value is `false`. Step by Step 1.15 shows how to use `ResizeRedraw`.

STEP BY STEP

1.15 Using the `ResizeRedraw` Property

1. Open the project 316C01. In the Solution Explorer right-click the project name and select Add Windows Form from the context menu. Name the new form StepByStep1_15 and click the Open button.

2. Follow steps 2 and 3 from Step by Step 1.13 to include the `Paint event` handler code and `Main()` method to run the form StepByStep1_15.

3. Switch to the code view. Modify the constructor of the form so that the modified version looks like this:

```
public StepByStep1_15()
{
    //
    // Required for Windows Form Designer support
    //
    InitializeComponent();

    // Paint when resized
    this.ResizeRedraw = true;
}
```

4. Run the project and notice that the form paints its drawing surface whenever you resize the form (just as it does in Step by Step 1.14, although the implementation is different).

The form's constructor is a good place to set the `ResizeRedraw` property. You could alternatively write it inside the `Main()` method itself.

As one more enhancement to Step by Step 1.15, you can center the text programmatically within the form. To do so, first you need to find the coordinates of the center of the form. You can find the horizontal distance by dividing the width of the client area (`ClientSize.Width`) by 2, and you can find the vertical distance by dividing the height of the client area (`ClientSize.Height`) by 2. The `ClientSize` properties give you access to a `Size` structure that represents the size of the client area of the form. But this does not really center the text onscreen because it simply causes the text to start from the center, and depending on how long it is, it might appear toward the right of the center. You need to adjust the coordinates of the center point according to the size of the string. Keep in mind that the size of the string can vary depending on what font you use for the text. A safe way to determine string size is to use the `MeasureString()` method of the `Graphics` object, as shown in the following code segment:

```
SizeF stringSize = grfx.MeasureString(str, Font);
```

You can then calculate the modified coordinates for placing the string as x = (`ClientSize.Width`−`stringSize.Width`)/2 and y = (`ClientSize.Height`−`stringSize.Height`)/2.

There is an alternative approach, however. You can use the `StringFormat` object in the following signature of the `DrawString()` method:

```
public void DrawString(
    string, Font, Brush, PointF, StringFormat);
```

The `StringFormat` argument lets you specify the text alignment and spacing options for the text. Step by Step 1.16 uses this form of `DrawString()` to center text onscreen.

STEP BY STEP

1.16 Drawing Text on a Form

1. Open the project `316C01`. In the Solution Explorer right-click the project name and select Add Windows Form from the context menu. Name the new form `StepByStep1_16` and click the Open button.

continues

continued

2. Open the Properties window of the form. Search for the Paint event, and double-click the row that contains the Paint event. Modify its event handler so that it looks like this:

```
private void StepByStep1_16_Paint(object sender,
    System.Windows.Forms.PaintEventArgs e)
{
    Graphics grfx = e.Graphics;
    String strText = String.Format(
        "Form Size is: Width={0}, Height={1}",
        Width, Height);
    PointF pt = new PointF(ClientSize.Width/2,
        ClientSize.Height/2);

    // Set the horizontal and vertical alignment
    //using StringFormat object
    StringFormat strFormat = new StringFormat();
    strFormat.Alignment = StringAlignment.Center;
    strFormat.LineAlignment = StringAlignment.Center;

    // Create Font and Brush objects
    Font fntArial = new Font("Arial", 12);
    Brush brushColor = new SolidBrush(this.ForeColor);
    // Call the DrawString method
    grfx.DrawString(
        strText, fntArial, brushColor, pt, strFormat);
}
```

3. Modify the constructor of the form so that the modified version looks like this:

```
public StepByStep1_16()
{
    // Default Code in the constructor
    // Paint when resized
    this.ResizeRedraw = true;
}
```

4. Add the following code for the Main() method:

```
[STAThread]
static void Main()
{
    Application.Run(new StepByStep1_16());
}
```

5. Set the form as the startup object. Run the project and resize the form. Notice that the text is displayed in the center of the form.

The code begins by calculating the center coordinates of the form. When you have the coordinates of the center, you want the string to be horizontally centered at that point. Calling StringAlignment.Center does this job. StringAlignment is an enumeration that is available in the System.Drawing namespace that specifies the location of the alignment of the text.

By default, when the DrawString() method draws a string, it aligns the top of the string with its x-coordinate value. This does not make much difference if the height of the text itself is not great, but as you increase the size of the font, text begins to hang down, starting from the x-axis. To center the text vertically within its own line, you can set the LineAlignment property of the StringFormat object to StringAlignment.Center.

Note the use of Font and Brush objects in Step by Step 1.16. The code creates a new Font object and specifies a font name and size. I recommend that you change its value and experiment with it. Rather than use the brush specified by the Brushes.Black value, the code in Step by Step 1.16 creates a Brush object that takes the value of its color from the current form's ForeColor property. If you change the ForeColor property of the form by using the Properties window, the change is automatically reflected here. Using a brush based on the ForeColor property of the form is a good idea as compared to using an absolute value such as Brushes.Black for a brush. For example, if the form designer has set the BackColor property of the form to black and the ForeColor property to white, text drawn using Brushes.Black would not be visible, but the brush made from the ForeColor property would be visible.

Drawing Shapes

The Graphics class allows you to draw various graphical shapes such as arcs, curves, pies, ellipses, rectangles, images, paths, and polygons. Table 1.9 lists some important drawing methods of the Graphics class.

TABLE 1.9

Some Important Drawing Methods of the Graphics Class

Method	Description
DrawArc()	Draws an arc that represents a portion of an ellipse
DrawBezier()	Draws a Bézier curve defined by four points
DrawBeziers()	Draws a series of Bézier curves
DrawClosedCurve()	Draws a closed curve defined by an array of points
DrawCurve()	Draws a curve defined by an array of points
DrawEllipse()	Draws an ellipse defined by a bounding rectangle specified by a pair of coordinates, a height, and a width
DrawIcon()	Draws the image represented by the specified Icon object at the given coordinates
DrawImage()	Draws an Image object at the specified location, preserving its original size
DrawLine()	Draws a line that connects the two points
DrawLines()	Draws a series of line segments that connect an array of points
DrawPath()	Draws a GraphicsPath object
DrawPie()	Draws a pie shape defined by an ellipse and two radial lines
DrawPolygon()	Draws a polygon defined by an array of points
DrawRectangle()	Draws a rectangle specified by a point, a width, and a height
DrawRectangles()	Draws a series of rectangles
DrawString()	Draws the given text string at the specified location, with the specified Brush and Font objects

In Step by Step 1.17 you use some of the methods shown in Table 1.9 to draw shapes on a form's surface.

STEP BY STEP

1.17 Using the Draw Methods of the Graphics Class

1. Open the project 316C01. In the Solution Explorer right-click the project name and select Add Windows Form from the context menu. Name the new form StepByStep1_17 and click the Open button.

2. Open the Properties window. Search for the Paint event, and double-click the row that contains the Paint event. You are taken to the code view.

3. On the top of the code view, along with the list of other using directives, add the following line of code:

```
using System.Drawing.Drawing2D;
```

4. Modify the code in the Paint event handler to look like this:

```
private void StepByStep1_17_Paint(object sender,
    System.Windows.Forms.PaintEventArgs e)
{
    Graphics grfx = e.Graphics;
        // Set the Smoothing mode
        // to SmoothingMode.AntiAlias
    grfx.SmoothingMode = SmoothingMode.AntiAlias;
        // Create Pen objects
    Pen penYellow = new Pen(Color.Blue, 20);
    Pen penRed = new Pen(Color.Red, 10);
    // Call Draw methods
    grfx.DrawLine(Pens.Black, 20, 130, 250, 130);
    grfx.DrawEllipse(penYellow, 20, 10, 100, 100);
    grfx.DrawRectangle(penRed, 150, 10, 100, 100);
}
```

5. Add the following code to insert the Main() method:

```
[STAThread]
static void Main()
{
    Application.Run(new StepByStep1_17());
}
```

6. Set the form as the startup object. Run the project, and you see the form as displayed in Figure 1.21.

FIGURE 1.21
You can call Draw methods of the Graphics class to draw various graphic shapes.

The Draw methods used in Step by Step 1.17 take five arguments:

◆ The first argument of each method is the Pen object that is used to draw the shape. There are several ways you can create a Pen object. The simplest way is to use a readymade Pen object from the Pens class. Or you can create a Pen object by using the Pen class constructor. Table 1.10 lists the different pen-related classes that are available in the System.Drawing namespace.

◆ The second and third arguments are the x- and y-coordinates of the upper-left corner where the desired shape is to be drawn.

◆ The fourth and fifth parameters indicate the width and height of the desired shape to be drawn. In the case of DrawLine, these indicate the x- and y-coordinates of the ending point of the line drawn.

TABLE 1.10

PEN-RELATED CLASSES IN THE System.Drawing NAMESPACE

Class	Description
Pen	Defines an object used to draw lines and curves.
Pens	Provides 140 static properties, each representing a pen of a color supported by Windows Forms.
SystemPens	Provides a set of static properties, each named after a Windows display element such as ActiveCaption, WindowText, and so on. Each of these properties returns a Pen object with a width of 1.

The reason you must include a reference to the System.Drawing.Drawing2D namespace in the program shown in Step by Step 1.17 is that you are using an enumeration named SmoothingMode. This enumeration class is defined in the namespace System.Drawing.Drawing2D, so a reference to the namespace must be present in the program if the C# compiler is to uniquely identify it.

The Graphics object has a property named SmoothingMode that can take the values of the SmoothingMode enumeration type. Table 1.11 summarizes these values. The SmoothingMode property specifies the quality of rendering. The Windows Forms library supports antialiasing, which produces text and graphics that appear to be smooth.

TABLE 1.11

SmoothingMode ENUMERATION MEMBERS

Member Name	Description
AntiAlias	Specifies an antialiased rendering.
Default	Specifies no antialiasing. Same as None.
HighQuality	Specifies a high-quality, low-performance rendering. Same as AntiAlias.
HighSpeed	Specifies a high-performance, low-quality rendering. Same as None.
Invalid	Specifies an invalid mode, raises an exception.
None	Specifies no antialiasing.

In addition to the Draw methods, the Graphics class also provides a variety of Fill methods (see Table 1.12). You can use these methods to draw a solid shape on a form.

TABLE 1.12

Fill METHODS OF THE Graphics CLASS

Method Name	Description
FillClosedCurve()	Fills the interior of a closed curve defined by an array of points
FillEllipse()	Fills the interior of an ellipse defined by a bounding rectangle
FillPath()	Fills the interior of a GraphicsPath object
FillPie()	Fills the interior of a pie section defined by an ellipse and two radial lines
FillPolygon()	Fills the interior of a polygon defined by an array of points

continues

NOTE

Antialiasing   *Antialiasing* is a technique for rendering images where partially transparent pixels are drawn close to the opaque pixels present at the edges of a drawing. This actually makes the edges kind of fuzzy, but this effect makes the edges appear smoother to human eyes than the original form. Because there are extra efforts involved in antialiasing, it makes rendering of graphics slower than not using antialiasing.

| TABLE 1.12 | *continued* |

FILL METHODS OF THE GRAPHICS CLASS

Method Name	Description
FillRectangle()	Fills the interior of a rectangle specified by a point, a width, and a height
FillRectangles()	Fills the interiors of a series of rectangles
FillRegion()	Fills the interior of a Region object

STEP BY STEP

1.18 Using the Fill Methods of the Graphics Class

1. Open the project 316C01. In the Solution Explorer right-click the project name and select Add Windows Form from the context menu. Name the new form StepByStep1_18 and click the Open button.

2. Open the Properties window of the form. Search for the Paint event, and double-click the row that contains the Paint event. You are taken to the code view.

3. Modify the code in the Paint event handler to look like this:

```
private void StepByStep1_18_Paint(object sender,
    System.Windows.Forms.PaintEventArgs e)
{
    Graphics grfx = e.Graphics;
    // Create Brush objects
    Brush brushRed = new SolidBrush(Color.Red);
    Brush brushYellow = new SolidBrush(
        Color.FromArgb(200, Color.Yellow));
    // Call Fill methods
    grfx.FillEllipse(brushRed, 20, 10, 80, 100);
    grfx.FillRectangle(brushYellow, 60, 50, 100, 100);
}
```

4. Add the following code to insert the `Main()` method:

```
[STAThread]
static void Main()
{
    Application.Run(new StepByStep1_18());
}
```

5. Set the form as the startup object. Run the project. An overlapping red ellipse and yellow rectangle appear on the form, as shown in Figure 1.22.

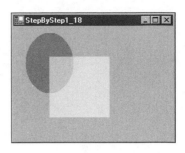

FIGURE 1.22
You can use `Fill` methods of the `Graphics` class to draw solid shapes.

The syntax of the `Fill` methods is somewhat similar to that of corresponding `Draw` methods. The only difference is that the `Fill` methods use a `Brush` object to fill a drawing object with a color.

Creating the yellow brush in Step by Step 1.18 looks interesting. While creating this color, you do an "alpha-blending" with the yellow color, to get a kind of transparent yellow color that is used to produce an overlay effect.

You use a `SolidBrush` object in Step by Step 1.18 to fill shapes. Other types of brushes can be used to create fancy filling effects; Table 1.13 lists them.

TABLE 1.13

TYPES OF BRUSHES IN THE `System.Drawing` AND `System.Drawing.Drawing2D` NAMESPACES

Class	Description
Brush	Is an abstract base class that is used to create brushes such as `SolidBrush`, `TextureBrush`, and `LinearGradientBrush`. These brushes are used to fill the interiors of graphical shapes such as rectangles, ellipses, pies, polygons, and paths.
Brushes	Provides 140 static properties, one for the name of each color supported by Windows forms.
HatchBrush	Allows you to fill the region by using one pattern from a large number of patterns available in the `HatchStyle` enumeration.
LinearGradientBrush	Is used to create two-color gradients and multicolor gradients. By default the gradient is a linear gradient that moves from one color to another color along the specified line.

continues

| TABLE 1.13 | *continued* |

TYPES OF BRUSHES IN THE System.Drawing AND System.Drawing.Drawing2D NAMESPACES

Class	Description
SolidBrush	Defines a brush of a single color. Brushes are used to fill graphics shapes, such as rectangles, ellipses, pies, polygons, and paths.
SystemBrushes	Provides a set of static properties, each named after a Windows display element, such as ActiveCaption, WindowText, and so on. Each of these properties returns a SolidBrush object that represents the color for its matching Windows display element.
TextureBrush	A class that contains properties for the Brush object that use images to fill the interior of shapes.

STEP BY STEP

1.19 Using Different Brush Types

1. Open the project 316C01. In the Solution Explorer right-click the project name and select Add Windows Form from the context menu. Name the new form StepByStep1_19 and click the Open button.

2. Open the Properties window. Search for the Paint event, and double-click the row that contains the Paint event. You are taken to the code view.

3. On the top of the code view, along with the list of other using directives, add the following lines of code:

```
using System.Drawing.Drawing2D;
```

4. Modify the code in the Paint event handler so that it looks like this:

```
private void StepByStep1_19_Paint(object sender,
    System.Windows.Forms.PaintEventArgs e)
{
    Graphics grfx = e.Graphics;
```

```
// Create a HatchBrush object
// Call FillEllipse method by passing
// the created HatchBrush object
HatchBrush hb = new HatchBrush(
    HatchStyle.HorizontalBrick,
    Color.Blue, Color.FromArgb(100, Color.Yellow));
grfx.FillEllipse(hb, 20, 10, 100, 100);

// Create a TextureBrush object
// Call FillEllipse method by passing the
// created TextureBrush object
Image img = new Bitmap("sunset.jpg");
Brush tb = new TextureBrush(img);
grfx.FillEllipse(tb, 150, 10, 100, 100);

// Create a LinearGradientBrush object
// Call FillEllipse method by passing
// the created LinearGradientBrush object
LinearGradientBrush lb = new LinearGradientBrush(
    new Rectangle(80, 150, 100, 100),
    Color.Red, Color.Yellow,
        LinearGradientMode.BackwardDiagonal);
grfx.FillEllipse(lb, 80, 150, 100, 100);
}
```

5. Add the following code to insert the `Main()` method:

```
[STAThread]
static void Main()
{
    Application.Run(new StepByStep1_19());
}
```

6. Set the form as the startup object. Run the project. Notice that ellipses filled in various styles are displayed in the form, as shown in Figure 1.23.

FIGURE 1.23
You can create fancy objects by using different brush types.

In Step by Step 1.19 you use three different `Brush` objects. The `TextureBrush` class is part of the `System.Drawing` namespace, and the other two classes (`HatchBrush` and `LinearGradientBrush`) are members of the `System.Drawing.Drawing2D` namespace.

Using `HatchBrush`, you filled the ellipse with the `HatchStyle` named `HorizontalBrick`. The `TextureBrush` class uses an image to fill the interior of a shape, and in Step by Step 1.19, the image is assumed to be in the same directory as the `.exe` file. If you have the image in some other directory, you need to change the path in the `Bitmap` constructor. The Bitmap name is a bit misleading, as it is actually capable of creating images from a variety of image formats, including BMP, GIF, JPG, and PNG.

In Step by Step 1.19 the code sets the gradient direction from the upper-right corner to the lower-left corner of the rectangle encapsulating the ellipse. Table 1.14 lists the enumeration values for `LinearGradientMode`.

TABLE 1.14

`LinearGradientMode` ENUMERATION VALUES

Member Name	Description
BackwardDiagonal	Specifies a gradient from upper-right to lower-left
ForwardDiagonal	Specifies a gradient from upper-left to lower-right
Horizontal	Specifies a gradient from left to right
Vertical	Specifies a gradient from top to bottom

Working with Images

The `System.Drawing.Image` class provides the basic functionality for working with images. However, the `Image` class is abstract, which means you can create an instance of it in your class. Instead of using the `Image` class directly, you can use the following classes that implement the `Image` class functionality:

◆ **`Bitmap`**   This class is used to work with graphic files that store information in pixel-based data such as BMP, GIF, and JPEG formats.

◆ **`Icon`**   This class creates a small bitmap that represents an Windows icon.

◆ **`MetaFile`**   This class contains embedded bitmaps and/or sequences of binary records that represent a graphical operation such as drawing a line.

Step by Step 1.20 shows how to do basic operations with the `Bitmap` class.

STEP BY STEP

1.20 Creating and Rendering Images

1. Open the project 316C01. In the Solution Explorer right-click the project name and select Add Windows Form from the context menu. Name the new form StepByStep1_20 and click the Open button.

2. Open the Properties window. Search for the Paint event, and double-click the row that contains the Paint event. You are taken to the code view.

3. On the top of the code view, along with the list of other using directives, add the following lines of code:

```
using System.Drawing.Drawing2D;
using System.Drawing.Imaging;
```

4. Modify the code in the Paint event handler to look like this:

```
private void StepByStep1_20_Paint(object sender,
    System.Windows.Forms.PaintEventArgs e)
{
    Graphics grfx = e.Graphics;
    grfx.DrawImage(new Bitmap("SampleImage.png"),
        ClientRectangle);
}
```

5. Add the following code after the event handling code from step 4:

```
[STAThread]
static void Main()
{
    // Create a Bitmap object
    Bitmap bmp = new Bitmap(
        800,600,PixelFormat.Format32bppArgb);
    // Create a Graphics object using FromImage method
    Graphics grfx = Graphics.FromImage(bmp);
    // Call the Fill Rectangle method
    // to create an outer rectangle
    grfx.FillRectangle(new SolidBrush(Color.White),
        new Rectangle(0,0,800,600));
    // Create Font and RectangleF object
    Font fntText = new Font("Verdana", 20);
    RectangleF rect = new RectangleF(
        100, 100, 250, 300);
```

continues

continued

```
// Fill the InnerRectangle
grfx.FillRectangle(
    new SolidBrush(Color.AliceBlue), rect);
// Add the text to the Inner Rectangle
grfx.DrawString("Sample Text", fntText,
  new SolidBrush(Color.Blue), rect);
// Draw a closed curve
Pen penBlack = new Pen(Color.Black, 20);
penBlack.DashStyle = DashStyle.Dash;
penBlack.StartCap = LineCap.Round;
penBlack.EndCap = LineCap.Round;
grfx.DrawClosedCurve(penBlack, new Point[] {
                     new Point(50, 50),
                     new Point(400, 50),
                     new Point(400, 400),
                     new Point(50, 400)});
// Save the newly created image file
bmp.Save("SampleImage.png", ImageFormat.Png);
Application.Run(new StepByStep1_20());
}
```

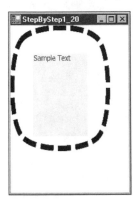

FIGURE 1.24

You can use the `Bitmap` class to work with a variety of image formats.

6. Set the form as the startup object. Run the project. The code should create an image and render it in the form, as shown in Figure 1.24.

In Step by Step 1.20 you first create an image and then render it on the form's surface. The image creation code is written in the `Main()` method, which means it is executed before the application creates the `Form` object. Three key steps are related to image manipulation:

1. You need to create a `Bitmap` object that can be used to work on images. The code for this creates the object by specifying its size in pixels and also specifying a format value from the `PixelFormat` enumeration, which belongs to the `System.Drawing.Imaging` namespace. The value `Format32bppArgb` specifies that there are 32 bits of data associated with each pixel in the image. Out of these 32 bits, 8 bits each are used for the alpha, red, green, and blue components of the pixel.

2. You need to get a `Graphics` object from the `Bitmap` object. This `Graphics` object can be used to draw on the surface of the drawing.

3. You need to call the Save() method on the Bitmap object. This method supports a variety of formats for saving graphics; these formats are available as static public properties of the ImageFormat class. The ImageFormat class is a member of the System.Drawing.Imaging namespace. Some of the possible properties are Bmp, Gif, Icon, Jpeg, Png, Tiff, and Wmf.

The rest of the code in Step by Step 1.20 draws a piece of text and a curved line on the image before saving it. Note the various properties of the Pen object that are used in this program. The code uses the customized Pen object to create a boundary around the image. Table 1.15 summarizes some important properties of the Pen class.

TABLE 1.15

SOME IMPORTANT PROPERTIES OF THE Pen CLASS

Property	Description
Alignment	Specifies the alignment for the Pen object
Brush	Specifies a Brush object that determines the attributes of the Pen object
Color	Specifies the color of the Pen object
DashCap	Specifies the cap style used at the end of the dashes that make up dashed lines
DashPattern	Specifies the array of custom dashes and spaces
DashStyle	Specifies the style used for dashed lines
EndCap	Specifies the cap style used at the end of lines
LineJoin	Specifies the join style for the ends of two consecutive lines
PenType	Specifies the style of lines
StartCap	Specifies the cap style used at the beginnings of lines
Width	Specifies the width of the Pen object

GUIDED PRACTICE EXERCISE 1.3

You are a Windows developer for SpiderWare, Inc. The Windows application you are working on should have a form that allows users to create new designs for Spider-Webs. The requirement itself is simple: The form must have a white background, where users can design using a thin black pen. Users often make mistakes while they are designing, so there should be a mechanism to erase part of the design. Users say that they will be comfortable using the left mouse button for drawing and the right mouse button for erasing. You also noted that users of the application all have high-end machines, and they want sharper-looking designs.

How would you design such a form?

You should try working through this problem on your own first. If you get stuck, or if you'd like to see one possible solution, follow these steps:

1. Open the project 316C01. Add a Windows form with the name GuidedPracticeExercise1_3 to this project.

2. Open the Properties window for the form. Change the form's BackColor property to White.

3. Look for the event named MouseMove and double-click it. This inserts a MouseMove event handler for you and switches you to the code view. In the code view, add the following statement at the top of the program:

    ```
    using System.Drawing.Drawing2D;
    ```

4. Before the MouseMove event handler code add the following line:

    ```
    Point ptPrevPosition = new Point(-1, -1);
    ```

5. Modify the MouseMove event handler to look like this:

    ```
    private void GuidedPracticeExercise1_3_MouseMove(
      object sender, System.Windows.Forms.MouseEventArgs e)
    {
        if(ptPrevPosition.X == -1)
        {
    ```

```
        // Set the previous position x-y co-ordinate
        // to the current x-y co-ordinate
        ptPrevPosition = new Point(e.X, e.Y);
    }
    Point ptCurrPosition = new Point(e.X,e.Y);
    // Get the Graphics object by calling
    // Graphics.FromHwnd() method
    Graphics g = Graphics.FromHwnd(this.Handle);
    g.SmoothingMode = SmoothingMode.AntiAlias;
    // Check if the left mouse button is pressed
    if(e.Button == MouseButtons.Left)
    {
        // Draw a line from the previous position to
        // current position using Black color
        g.DrawLine(new Pen(Color.Black),
            ptPrevPosition, ptCurrPosition);
    }
    // Check whether right mouse button is pressed
    else if(e.Button == MouseButtons.Right)
    {
        // Draw a line from the previous position to
        // current position using Form's BackColor
        g.DrawLine(new Pen(this.BackColor, 4),
            ptPrevPosition, ptCurrPosition);
    }
    // Set the Previous position to current position
    ptPrevPosition = ptCurrPosition;
}
```

6. Insert the following `Main()` method just after the event handling code:

```
[STAThread]
static void Main()
{
    Application.Run(new GuidedPracticeExercise1_3());
}
```

7. Set the form as the startup object and execute the program.

If you have difficulty following this exercise, review the sections "Event Handling" and "Drawing Shapes." The text and examples presented in those sections should help you relearn this material. After doing that review, try this exercise again.

REVIEW BREAK

▶ Windows forms follow a two-dimensional coordinate system. A point is an addressable location in this coordinate system.

▶ The Graphics object gives you access to a drawing surface. You can use it to draw lines, text, curves, and a variety of shapes.

▶ The ResizeRedraw property, when set to true, instructs the form to redraw itself when it is resized. It's a good programming practice to design forms that resize their contents based on their size. The Resize event of a form can also be used to program the resizing logic.

▶ The Graphics class provides a set of Draw methods that can be used to draw shapes such as rectangles, ellipses, and curves on a drawing surface. The Graphics class also provides a set of Fill methods that can be used to create solid shapes.

▶ An object of the Bitmap class gives you access to image manipulation. The System.Drawing namespace classes can understand a variety of image formats.

CHAPTER SUMMARY

The .NET Framework is a standards-based multilanguage platform for developing next-generation applications. Visual Studio .NET provides a productive IDE for developing .NET Framework applications.

The .NET FCLs include classes for developing Windows-based desktop and distributed applications. Visual Studio .NET provides the Windows Forms Designer, which allows you to visually drag and drop components and create applications. Various Step by Step exercises in this chapter help you familiarize yourself with the development environment and its key concepts.

A Windows form is the place where you assemble the user interface of an application. Form is a class that provides various properties through which you can get or set a form's characteristics. In this chapter you have learned how to manipulate a form's properties and how to add a custom property to a form. You have also learned how to derive from an existing form and extend the functionality of an existing form by adding your own properties and methods.

Event handling plays a key role in user interface–based programming; through event handling, you respond to various events that are fired as a result of user actions and that make programs interactive. This chapter discusses various ways to handle events. In Chapter 4 you will learn how to define your own events.

In this chapter you have also learned how to use the classes from the .NET Framework that implement graphics functionality. You have seen how to draw text, lines, and shapes, and you have learned how to work with other key graphics elements such as brushes, colors, and pens.

Chapter 2 talks more about various user interface elements that allow rapid development of powerful and interactive Windows applications.

KEY TERMS

- application
- attribute
- class
- constructor
- delegate
- enumeration
- event
- event handling
- FCL
- field
- garbage collection
- GDIT
- inheritance
- IL
- JIT compilation
- managed code
- namespace
- .NET Framework
- property
- structure
- visual inheritance
- Windows Forms Designer

APPLY YOUR KNOWLEDGE

Exercises

1.1   Responding to Keyboard Input

The Windows forms libraries provide controls such as TextBox and RichTextBox that you can use to process keyboard input from users. But sometimes you might want to program the keyboard yourself. In this exercise you will learn how to capture keyboard events and respond to them. You will design a very basic text editor named NEN (Not Even Notepad) that will let you type on a form surface and also let you edit the text by using the Backspace key.

Estimated time: 20 minutes

1. Create a new Visual C# .NET Windows application in the Visual Studio .NET IDE.

2. Add a new form to the Visual C# .NET project. Change the Text property of the form to Not Even Notepad and change the BackColor property to White.

3. In the code view, add the following using directive at the top:

   ```
   using System.Text;
   ```

4. Declare a private variable just before the form's constructor code:

   ```
   private StringBuilder text;
   ```

5. In the constructor, initialize the private variable from step 4 by including the following line of code:

   ```
   this.text = new StringBuilder();
   ```

6. Add the following code in the KeyPress event handler of the form:

```
private void Exercise1_1_KeyPress(
  object sender,
  System.Windows.Forms.KeyPressEventArgs e)
{
    // Check which key is pressed
    switch(e.KeyChar)
    {
        case '\b':
            // Backspace key is pressed
            if (sbText.Length > 0)
                sbText.Remove(
                    sbText.Length-1, 1);
            break;
        case '\r':
        case '\n':
            // Enter key is pressed
            sbText.Append('\n');
            break;
        default:
            // Other keys are pressed
            sbText.Append(e.KeyChar);
            break;
    }
    // Paint the form
    Invalidate();
}
```

7. In the form's Paint event handler, add the following code:

```
private void Exercise1_1_Paint(
  object sender,
  System.Windows.Forms.PaintEventArgs e)
{
    Graphics grfx =
      ((Form) sender).CreateGraphics();
    grfx.DrawString(text.ToString(), Font,
      Brushes.Black,ClientRectangle );
}
```

8. Insert the Main() method and set the form as the startup object of the project. Execute the application. You should see a form onscreen that shows no blinking cursor on it, but when you start typing, the form should show text. You can press the Enter key to start a new paragraph and press the Backspace key to make any changes (see Figure 1.25).

APPLY YOUR KNOWLEDGE

FIGURE 1.25
The KeyPress event allows you to capture keystrokes.

The KeyPress event is fired when you press a key on the keyboard. In its event handler, the code uses these keypresses to modify a StringBuilder object that stores the text for the small text editor. Then it calls the Invalidate() method, which in turn generates a call to the Paint event handler that is actually drawing the text onscreen. So in fact every keypress results in a total repainting of the form. Chapter 2 talks about better ways of doing this task.

1.2 Getting a List of Installed Fonts

Several Windows applications allow you to change the font of displayed text. They normally give you a list of fonts installed on your system to choose from. How do they get this list? This exercise shows you how you can work with font-related classes in the System.Drawing namespace to display a list of installed fonts.

Estimated time: 15 minutes

1. Add a new form to your Visual C# .NET project.

2. Change the Text property of the form to List of Installed Fonts and change the BackColor property to White.

3. Add a Paint event handler to the form, and add the following code to it:

```csharp
private void Exercise1_2_Paint(
    object sender,
    System.Windows.Forms.PaintEventArgs e)
{
    // Set the y coordinate to 0
    int intYCoord=0;

    // Create a Black color SolidBrush
    SolidBrush brush =
        new SolidBrush(Color.Black);

    // Iterate through the
    // FontFamily.Families
    for(int intI=0;intI <
      FontFamily.Families.Length; intI++)
    {
        FontStyle fontStyle =
            FontStyle.Regular;

        // Check whether Regular style
        // is available
        if (!FontFamily.Families[
            intI].IsStyleAvailable(
            FontStyle.Regular))
            fontStyle = FontStyle.Italic;

        // Check whether Italic style
        // is available
        if (!FontFamily.Families[
            intI].IsStyleAvailable(
            FontStyle.Italic))
            fontStyle = FontStyle.Bold;
        // Create a Font object and
        // Draw the Font Name
        Font font  = new Font(
            FontFamily.Families[intI].Name,
            12, fontStyle);
        string strFontName =
            FontFamily.Families[intI].Name;
        e.Graphics.DrawString(strFontName,
            font, brush, 0, intYCoord );
        // Increase the Y Coordinate
        // with the Font Height
        intYCoord += font.Height;
    }

}
```

4. Insert the `Main()` method and set the form as the startup object of the project. Execute the application. You should see a form that displays a list of fonts, with each font name displayed in its own font. When you increase the height of the form, you see more lines that list the fonts (see Figure 1.26).

FIGURE 1.26
You can use the `FontFamily.Families` property to get all the `FontFamily` objects associated with the current Graphics context.

The `FontFamily.Families` property stores an array of `FontFamily` objects. The code iterates over this array to display each font name in its own font style. If you remove the two `if` statements that are used in this program, you get a runtime error because not all fonts support all font styles.

In Figure 1.26 you cannot see all the fonts because the list of fonts usually contains more fonts than the number of lines that can be displayed, even on a maximized form. You'll learn how to make the contents of a form scroll in Chapter 2.

1.3   Creating Nonrectangular Forms

All the forms that you have created in this chapter so far have been rectangular forms. The Windows Forms library also allows you to create nonrectangular forms. Nonrectangular forms can be used in various applications, such as games, device simulations, and multimedia applications. In this exercise you will see how to create a nonrectangular form.

Estimated time: 10 minutes

1. Add a new form to your Visual C# .NET project.

2. In the Properties window for the form, change the `FormBorderStyle` property to `None` and change the `BackColor` property to `FireBrick`.

3. Switch to the code view and include the following `using` directive at the top of the code:

```
using System.Drawing.Drawing2D;
```

4. In the constructor of the form, include the following lines of code:

```
public Exercise1_3()
{
    //
    // Default code of the constructor
    //
    // Create a GraphicsPath object
    // AddEllipse to the GraphicsPath object
    // Set the Form's Region property for
    // the Graphics Path region
    GraphicsPath gp = new GraphicsPath();
    gp.AddEllipse(25,25,250,250);
    this.Region = new Region(gp);
}
```

APPLY YOUR KNOWLEDGE

5. Insert the `Main()` method and set the form as the startup object of the project. Run the application. You should see a circular red form.

This code first defines an elliptical region, using the `GraphicsPath` object. The `GraphicsPath` object is then used to set the `Region` property of the form. The `Region` property instructs the operating system to hide any portion of the form that lies outside the elliptical region. As a result, the form is displayed as an ellipse.

Review Questions

1. Describe the difference between a public field and a public property.

2. What is the purpose of organizing classes in namespaces?

3. What property would you use to control the shape of the mouse pointer when it enters the client area of a Windows form?

4. How can you add a custom property to a form?

5. What is visual inheritance?

6. What are the two different approaches for event handling? What is the difference between them?

7. What is the `ResizeRedraw` property? When would you want to set it to `true` for a Windows form?

8. Describe at least two ways by which you can create a `Graphics` object for a Windows form.

9. What is the difference between a `Pen` object and a `Brush` object?

Exam Questions

1. You are designing a Windows form that will work like a splash screen, giving the welcome message and product information when the application starts. What properties would you set on the form to make it look like a splash screen?

   A. Set the `FormBorderStlye` property to `FormBorderStyle.SizableToolWindow` and set `StartPosition` to `FormStartPosition.CenterScreen`.

   B. Set the `FormBorderStyle` property to `Fixed3D`, set `MinimizeBox` to `false`, set `MaximizeBox` to `false`, set `ControlBox` to `false`, and set `StartPosition` to `CenterScreen`.

   C. Set the `FormBorderStyle` property to `None`, set `StartPosition` to `CenterScreen`, and set `TopMost` to `true`.

   D. Set the `TopMost` property to `true`, set `ShowInTaskbar` to `false`, set `BackColor` to `Desktop`, and set `StartPosition` to `CenterScreen`.

2. You are designing a graphical Windows application that will allow users to design home interiors. Users are very particular about getting good-quality printing of their designs and want applications that perform quickly. What should you do while using a `Graphics` object to create lines and curves?

   A. Set the `SmoothingMode` property of the `Graphics` object to `AntiAlias`.

   B. Set the `SmoothingMode` property of the `Graphics` object to `HighSpeed`.

APPLY YOUR KNOWLEDGE

C. Set the `SmoothingMode` property of the `Graphics` object to `HighQuality`.

D. Set the `SmoothingMode` property of the `Graphics` object to `Laser`.

3. You are a Windows developer for a major component vendor. Your company is planning to launch a product that will provide a set of sophisticated Windows forms. Your customers can inherit their forms from these forms to speed up their development work. In one of the forms you have certain properties that are for advanced use only. You don't want these properties to be displayed in the Properties window, but you would like programmers to see these properties via the IntelliSense help. Which of the following attributes would you use for these properties?

A.

```
[Browsable(true), EditorBrowsable(
    EditorBrowsableState.Never)]
```

B.

```
[Browsable(false), EditorBrowsable(
    EditorBrowsableState.Always)]
```

C.

```
[Browsable(true), EditorBrowsable(
    EditorBrowsableState.Always)]
```

D.

```
[Browsable(false), EditorBrowsable(
    EditorBrowsableState.Never)]
```

4. You are a Windows developer for a company that is developing shareware software. Your task is to develop a personal information management application that will run on the Windows platform. The main form of the application has various controls placed on it. You want to resize all the controls when the form is resized. Which of the following options would you choose?

A. Write the resizing logic for each control in its own `Resize` event handler and set the `ResizeRedraw` property to `true` for each one of them.

B. Write the resizing logic in the form's `Paint` event handler.

C. Write the resizing logic in the form's `Paint` event handler and set the form's `ResizeRedraw` property to `true`.

D. Write the resizing logic for each control in its own `Paint` event handler and set the `ResizeRedraw` property to `true` for each of them.

5. You are developing a Windows application that contains a single Windows form. When the application starts, you need to do some initializations that will change the appearance of the form and assign values to some fields. Where should you put the code?

A. In the `InitializeComponent()` method

B. In the form's constructor

C. In the `Main()` method

D. Inside the Windows Form Designer Generated Code region

6. You are drawing a big line of text on a form to display the company name. You would like to fill the text with the image of the company logo. Which brush type should you use?

A. `SolidBrush`

B. `TextureBrush`

C. `HatchBrush`

D. `ImageBrush`

APPLY YOUR KNOWLEDGE

7. If you want to make a Windows form completely transparent when it is displayed, what should you do?

   A. Set the `TransparencyKey` property to `0%`.

   B. Set the `TransparencyKey` property to `100%`.

   C. Set the `Opacity` property to `0%`.

   D. Set the `Opacity` property to `100%`.

8. You can see a property in the Properties window for a Windows form, but you cannot modify it. What could be the cause?

   A. The `Browsable` attribute for the property is not set to `false`.

   B. The `Property` is a private property.

   C. The `set` accessor of the property is private.

   D. The `set` accessor of the property is not implemented.

9. Which of the following methods can be used to get a `Graphics` object for a Windows form?

   A. `Graphics.FromForm()`

   B. `Graphics.FromImage()`

   C. `Graphics.FromHwnd()`

   D. `Graphics.CreateObject()`

10. Which of the following points has coordinate (0, 0) for a Windows form?

    A. The top-left corner of the client area of the form

    B. The center of the client area of the form

    C. The top-right corner of the client area of the form

    D. The center of the user's screen

11. You want to change the property of a form so that all text placed on it will appear in bold. Which of the following statements would you use in the form's constructor?

    A.
    ```
    this.Font.Bold = true;
    ```

    B.
    ```
    this.Font = new Font(
        this.Font, FontStyle.Bold);
    ```

    C.
    ```
    this.Font.FontStyle = FontStyle.Bold;
    ```

    D.
    ```
    this.Font = new Font(
      this.Font, this.Font.Bold);
    ```

12. You are designing an interactive Windows application that will respond to several actions taken by the user. In one of the application's forms, you are required to produce a glowing effect when the mouse moves over the form. You have written an event handler and want it to attach to `MouseMove` event. What statement should you use in the form's constructor?

    A.
    ```
    this.MouseDown = new
        System.Windows.Forms.MouseEventHandler(
        this.GlowingForm_MouseDown);
    ```

    B.
    ```
    this.MouseMove = new
        System.Windows.Forms.MouseEventHandler(
        this.GlowingForm_MouseMove);
    ```

    C.
    ```
    this.MouseDown += new
        System.Windows.Forms.MouseEventHandler(
        this.GlowingForm_MouseDown);
    ```

APPLY YOUR KNOWLEDGE

D.

```
this.MouseMove += new
   System.Windows.Forms.MouseEventHandler(
   this.GlowingForm_MouseMove);
```

13. You want to create a Windows application that is capable of manipulating image files in GIF, JPG, and PNG formats. Which class you should use in the program?

    A. `Bitmap`

    B. `Image`

    C. `Icon`

    D. `Metafile`

14. You are using objects of the `HatchBrush` class in a program, but you have forgotten to include a reference to the `System.Drawing.Drawing2D` namespace through a `using` directive at the top of program. Which of the following statement holds true for this scenario?

    A. You will get a compile-time error while compiling the `using` statements.

    B. You will get an error at runtime while executing the `using` statements.

    C. The compilation should be okay as long as you refer to the `HatchBrush` class as `System.Drawing.Drawing2D.HatchBrush` in your program.

    D. The compilation should be okay as long as you refer to all objects of `HatchBrush` by prefixing them with the `System.Drawing.Drawing2D` namespace.

15. You create an object of the `GraphicsPath` class in your program. When you compile the program, you get an error saying that the type or namespace name cannot be found. What should you do?

    A. Add a reference to `System.Drawing.dll` in the program.

    B. Include using `System.Drawing` at the top of the program.

    C. Include using `System.Drawing.Drawing2D` at the top of the program.

    D. Include using `System.Drawing.Imaging` at the top of the program.

Answers to Review Questions

1. A property, unlike a field, does not have any storage location associated with it. Generally (but not necessarily) a property would use a private field to store its data and expose its value through a pair of accessors named get and set that are used for read and write operations, respectively. These accessors can encapsulate program logic that runs when the property is read or written. A property is the preferred way to expose class characteristics.

2. Namespaces serve two purposes: They help organize classes by logically grouping them and they allow you to uniquely identify classes, thereby avoiding any naming conflicts that might otherwise occur.

3. The `Cursor` property of a form can be used to specify the default mouse pointer shape for a form.

4. You can add a custom property by defining a public property in a class using the C# syntax for property declaration. The get and set accessors of the property define what happens when you attempt to read or write the property value.

APPLY YOUR KNOWLEDGE

5. Visual inheritance is a process that lets you inherit a visual element such as a form or a control based on an element that already exists. Visual inheritance helps you reuse existing code and maintain consistency between visual elements.

6. This chapter discusses two approaches to event handling. In the first one, preferred by Visual Studio .NET, you register an event handler with an event by using a delegate object. You can register or attach as many event handlers as you want. When the event fires, all the event handlers are invoked through their references that are maintained by the delegate object. The second approach is to override the On method of the base class that corresponds to the event. You must remember to call the base class version of the On method while you are overriding its definition if you want to wire the event to its base class.

7. The ResizeRedraw property indicates whether a form redraws itself if it is resized. The Form class inherits this property from the Control class. The ResizeRedraw property, when set to true for a form, causes the form's Paint event to be fired whenever the form size is changed. This property is especially useful when you want to create a form whose elements should resize proportionally with the form.

8. You can create a graphics object for a control by calling the CreateGraphics() method on the control's instance. Alternatively, you can get a Graphics object by calling the static method FromHwnd() of the Graphics class. The FromHwnd() method returns a Graphics object for the specified window handle. You can get the handle for a form through its Handle property.

9. Brush is an abstract class that is used to create classes that fill interiors of shapes such as rectangles and ellipses. SolidBrush, TextureBrush, and LinearGradientBrush are implementations of the Brush class that can be used to create Brush objects. A Pen object, on the other hand, is used to draw lines and curves. A Pen object can use a Brush object to apply various fill styles to the lines that it draws.

Answers to Exam Questions

1. **C.** When you set the FormBorderStyle property to None through the Properties window, the form has neither the title bar nor borders displayed. In addition, splash screens are generally displayed on the center of the screen and are not resizable. Given all these facts, C is the correct answer. For more information, see the section "Setting and Adding Properties to a Windows Form" in this chapter.

2. **B.** Users want high quality printing and fast speed. SmoothingMode has no effect on printing quality. Both the HighQuality and AntiAlias values of SmoothingMode use antialiasing while drawing images onscreen. This involves extra work and slows down the application. To increase speed in this case, you should select the HighSpeed option which does not use antialiasing. For more information, see the section "Drawing Shapes" in this chapter.

3. **B.** Setting the Browsable attribute of a property to false hides the property from the Properties window. The EditorBrowsable attribute specifies whether the property is available through IntelliSense help. Therefore, the correct answer is B. For more information, see the section "Using Visual Inheritance" in this chapter.

APPLY YOUR KNOWLEDGE

4. **C.** Setting the `ResizeRedraw` property to `true` for a form fires the form's `Paint` event whenever the form is resized. Programming the `Resize` event for each control does not work because when the form is resized, the control is not resized. For more information, see the section "Drawing Text on a Form" in this chapter.

5. **B.** A form's constructor is the ideal place to put all initializations because it ensures that all initializations are done at the time the form is created. Although `InitializeComponent` is also called from the form's constructor, it is not a good idea to put code there because it might interfere with the operation of the Windows Form Designer. For more information, see the section "Exploring the Forms Designer Generated Code" in this chapter.

6. **B.** Only `TextureBrush` can fill by using an image. There is no such brush as `ImageBrush`. For more information, see the section "Drawing Shapes" in this chapter.

7. **C.** `Opacity` sets the transparency level for a form, whereas `TransparencyKey` only makes transparent those form areas that match a specified color. The use of `TransparencyKey` is also wrong here. For more information, see the section "Using the Visual Designer to Set Windows Form Properties" in this chapter.

8. **D.** You can make a property read-only by not implementing the property's set accessor. The `Browsable` attribute just hides or shows the property in the Properties window; the question mentions that you are already able to see property in the Properties window. Finally, you cannot set the access modifiers, such as public and private, on accessor methods; you can only apply them to a property as a whole. For more information, see the section "Adding New Properties to a Windows Form" in this chapter.

9. **C.** `GraphicsFrom.Hwnd()` is the method that gets a graphics object for a Windows form. The `Graphics.FromImage()` method can only get the `Graphics` object for an image file. The other two methods are nonexistent. For more information, see the section "Understanding the Graphics Objects" in this chapter.

10. **A.** The top-left corner of the client area has the coordinates of (0, 0) for a Windows form. For more information, see the section "Understanding the Windows Forms Coordinate System" in this chapter.

11. **B.** You cannot directly set the `Bold` property of a `Font` object because its set accessor is not available. Therefore, the only way to set the `Font` object's `Bold` property is by calling its constructor to create a new `Font` object and then using this newly created object. For more information, see the section "Drawing Text on a Form" in this chapter.

12. **D.** Answers A and C are attaching the event handler to the `MouseDown` event and are therefore not correct. Answer B attaches the event handler to the `MouseMove` event, but it uses the = syntax. This cancels all other event handlers that are already registered with the event. Because the application is quite interactive, that is an undesirable effect. Answer D uses the correct syntax. For more information, see the section "Handling Events by Attaching a Delegate" in this chapter.

13. **A.** Image is an abstract class and does not help you much in image-related operations. `Bitmap` is the implementation of the `Image` class and can work with several types of image formats, including the GIF, JPG, and PNG. For more information, see the section "Working with Images" in this chapter.

APPLY YOUR KNOWLEDGE

14. **C.** When you are not including a `using` directive for a namespace, you need to fully qualify any class that belongs to that namespace in the program. The compiler needs to qualify only the classnames, not the object names. Therefore, Answer D is not correct. Problems with namespace qualifications can lead to compile-time errors, but not to run-time errors, so Answer B is also not correct.

Missing a `using` directive does not cause compile-time errors at the using statements, but it might cause an error later in the program if it is not able to uniquely identify a class. As a result, Answer A is incorrect. For more information, see the section "Running a Windows Form" in this chapter.

15. **C.** The `GraphicsPath` class belongs to the `System.Drawing.Drawing2D` namespace, which must be included with a `using` directive to uniquely identify the `GraphicsPath` class in a program. For more information, see the section "Drawing Shapes" in this chapter.

APPLY YOUR KNOWLEDGE

Suggested Readings and Resources

1. Visual Studio .NET Combined Help Collection:

   - ".NET Framework SDK"

   - "C# Programmer's Reference"

   - "Introduction to Windows Forms"

   - "Handling and Raising Events"

   - "Drawing and Editing Images"

2. Ben Albahari, Peter Drayton, and Brad Merrill. *C# Essentials.* O'Reilly, 2002.

3. Charles Petzold. *Programming Windows with C#.* Microsoft Press, 2001.

4. David Chappell. *Understanding .NET.* Addison-Wesley, 2001.

5. Windows forms FAQ, `www.syncfusion.com/FAQ/winforms`.

6. Windows forms community site, `www.windowsforms.net`.

7. Team Development with Visual Studio .NET and Visual SourceSafe. `msdn.microsoft.com/library/en-us/dnbda/html/tdlg_rm.asp`.

8. The .NET Show: .NET Architecture Overview. `msdn.microsoft.com/theshow/Episode006`.

9. The .NET Show: The .NET Framework. `msdn.microsoft.com/theshow/Episode007`.

10. The .NET Show: Programming in C#. `msdn.microsoft.com/theshow/Episode008`.

11. The .NET Show: What is .NET? `msdn.microsoft.com/theshow/Episode011`.

12. The .NET Show: Your First .NET Application. `msdn.microsoft.com/theshow/Episode013`.

13. The .NET Show: Understanding the Framework. `msdn.microsoft.com/theshow/Episode026`.

14. The .NET Show: The Developer Roadmap. `msdn.microsoft.com/theshow/Episode028`.

15. Microsoft Support WebCast: Working in the Microsoft Visual Studio .NET IDE, `support.microsoft.com/servicedesks/webcasts/wc042402/wcblurb042402.asp`.

This chapter covers the following Microsoft-specified objectives for the "Creating User Services" section of Exam 70-316, "Developing and Implementing Windows-Based Applications with Microsoft Visual C# .NET and Microsoft Visual Studio .NET":

Add controls to a Windows form.

- **Set properties on controls.**

- **Load controls dynamically.**

- **Write code to handle control events and add the code to a control.**

- **Create menus and menu items.**

▶ Controls are the most visible part of a Windows application. The purpose of this objective is to test your knowledge of working with the most common Windows forms controls, including working with their properties, methods, and events.

Implement navigation for the user interface (UI).

- **Configure the order of tabs**

▶ When you place controls on a form, you need to provide a logical order of keyboard-based navigation for the controls. This exam objective covers how to achieve this logical order by using Visual Studio .NET.

CHAPTER 2

Controls

▶ Experiment with the common Windows controls that are available in the Windows Forms Designer toolbox. Knowing their properties, methods, and events well will help you answer several exam questions. You will find several important members of various controls listed in tables throughout the chapter.

▶ Know how to handle events for Windows Forms controls. Make sure you read the section "Event Handling" in Chapter 1, "Introducing Windows Forms."

▶ Understand how to create controls dynamically. See Step by Step 2.2 and Step by Step 2.4 to get hands-on experience in loading controls dynamically.

▶ Know how to create menus and menu items. This includes creating both a main menu and context menus for an application.

INTRODUCTION

This chapter extends the concepts presented in Chapter 1, "Introducing Windows Forms," and discusses various aspects of user interface programming in more detail.

Windows forms controls are reusable components that encapsulate graphical user interface (GUI) functionality in Windows-based applications. The chapter starts by teaching you how to add various controls to a Windows form, how to set the properties of the controls, and how to program various events associated with the controls.

This discussion is followed by text that explains how to use common dialog boxes in applications and how to create custom dialog boxes for specific requirements.

This chapter also covers most of the commonly used controls that are available in the Visual Studio .NET toolbox. Controls are explained with examples that help you understand and appreciate how they function.

Next, the chapter teaches how to create a main menu and a context menu for Windows applications and how to associate menu items with specific actions.

ADDING CONTROLS TO A WINDOWS FORM

You can place controls on the surface of any container object. Container objects include Windows forms and panels and group box controls.

You can add controls to a form either programmatically or by using the Windows Forms Designer. Although the Windows Forms Designer provides an easy-to-use interface for adding controls to a form, you are likely to need to do some work in the code view to make programs more functional.

Adding Controls by Using the Windows Forms Designer

Add controls to a Windows form.

The Windows Forms Designer provides a toolbox that contains a variety of commonly used controls. You can drag and drop controls from the toolbox to a form and arrange them as required. You can activate the toolbox by selecting View, Toolbox or by pressing Ctrl+Alt+X. You see a rich set of controls on the Windows Forms tab of the Toolbox (see Figure 2.1). From the toolbox you can use different ways to add controls to a form or another container object, including the following:

◆ **Method 1**—You can select a control and draw it on the container surface by following these steps:

    1. Select a control by clicking on the control's icon in the toolbox (refer to Figure 2.1).

    2. Release the mouse button and move the mouse pointer to the position on the container where you want to draw the control.

    3. Hold down the mouse button and draw a rectangle on the container surface to indicate the size and position for the control instance.

◆ **Method 2**—You can drag a control onto the form at the desired location by following these steps:

    1. Select a form or another container control where you want to add a control.

    2. Drag the control's icon from the toolbox and drop it at the desired location on the container control. The control is added with its default size.

◆ **Method 3**—You can add a control to a form by double-clicking it, as in the following steps:

    1. Select a form or another container control where you want to add a control.

FIGURE 2.1

The Windows Forms Designer toolbox displays a variety of items for use in Visual Studio .NET projects.

2. Double-click the control's icon in the toolbox. This adds the control to the top-left corner of the form or other container control in its default size. You can now drag the control to its desired location on the container control.

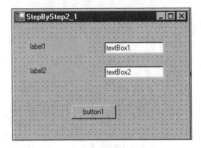

FIGURE 2.2
You can use the Windows Forms Designer to add controls to a form.

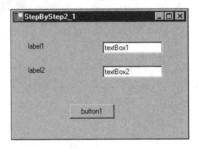

FIGURE 2.3
What you see at design time is what you get at runtime.

STEP BY STEP

2.1 Adding Controls to a Windows Form by Using the Windows Forms Designer

1. Create a new C# Windows application project in the Visual Studio .NET Integrated Development Environment (IDE). Name the project 316C02.

2. Add a new Windows form to the project. Name it StepByStep2_1.

3. Select the toolbox. On the Windows Forms tab place two controls of type Label and TextBox, and then place a control of type Button on the form's surface. Arrange the controls as shown in Figure 2.2.

4. Insert a Main() method to launch the form and set the form as the startup object for the project.

5. Run the project. You should see a Windows form that looks like the form shown in Figure 2.3. Navigate among the controls by using the Tab key.

Adding Controls Programmatically

Add controls to a Windows form.

- **Load controls dynamically.**

It is possible to add controls to a form programmatically. When you do so, you must remember to follow these three steps:

1. Create a private variable to represent each of the controls you want to place on the form.

2. In the form, place code to instantiate each control and to customize each control, using its properties, methods, or events.

3. Add each control to the form's control collection.

Step by Step 2.2 demonstrates this process.

STEP BY STEP

2.2 Adding Controls to a Windows Form Programmatically

1. Add a Windows form to existing project 316C02. Name the form StepByStep2_2.

2. Switch to the code view and add the following variables just above the form's constructor code:

```
//create variables to hold controls
private Label lblName, lblPassword;
private TextBox txtName, txtPassword;
private Button btnLogin;
```

3. Add the following code to the form's constructor:

```
//specify the form's size
this.ClientSize = new System.Drawing.Size(272, 182);

//set up the label for prompting Name
lblName = new Label();
lblName.Text = "Name: ";
//Specify the location for proper placement
//the default location will be (0, 0) otherwise
lblName.Location = new Point(16, 16);

//set up label for prompting Password
lblPassword = new Label();
lblPassword.Text = "Password: ";
lblPassword.Location = new Point(16, 80);

//setup a text box that allows user to enter Name
txtName = new TextBox();
txtName.Location = new Point(152, 16);

//setup text box for entering password
txtPassword = new TextBox();
txtPassword.Location = new Point(152, 80);
txtPassword.PasswordChar = '*';
```

continues

continued

```
//set up a command button
btnLogin = new Button();
btnLogin.Text = "Login";
btnLogin.Location = new Point(96, 128);

//Add control to the form
//Method 1: Specify the current form as
//parent container for a control
lblName.Parent = this;

//Method 2: Add a control to form's control collection
this.Controls.Add(txtName);

//Method 3: Add an array of controls to
//form's control collection
this.Controls.AddRange(
    new Control[] {lblPassword, txtPassword, btnLogin});
```

4. Insert the `Main()` method to launch the form. Set the form as the startup object for the project.

5. Run the project. The form is displayed, as shown in Figure 2.4.

FIGURE 2.4
You can programmatically add controls to a Windows form.

When you create controls programmatically, more effort is involved in finding the exact location where you would like to display the controls on the form than in plotting the controls via the Windows Forms Designer. In exchange for this small inconvenience, the code view allows you to add more functionality and power to a Windows form; typically in a project you would use a combination of the two.

This section uses examples that involve adding control to forms because the `Form` control is the container control with which you are most familiar from Chapter 1. You can easily apply these concepts to any of the container controls. A container control has a property named `Controls` that is a collection of `Control` objects. When you add or remove a control from a form, the control is added to or removed from the form's control collection.

EXAM TIP

Adding Control to a Container Control While you are creating a control programmatically, you must remember to associate it with a parent container control. If you don't do this, the control is created but not displayed.

SETTING PROPERTIES OF CONTROLS

Add controls to a Windows form.

- **Set properties on controls.**

Chapter 1 discussed how to work with properties of a `Form` object. You learned how to manipulate these properties through both the Properties window at design time and a program at runtime. The same concept carries over to Windows forms controls. Recall from the section "Using the `System.Windows.Forms.Form` Class" in Chapter 1 that a form is also a control that derives from the `Control` class.

Although this section discusses the properties of controls, some of the properties and their behaviors are similar to those of forms. Controls may also have additional properties, depending on their specific functionality.

To set a property for a control by using the Properties window, follow these steps:

1. Select the control by clicking it. This makes it the active object.

2. Activate the Properties window, and then select a property from the list and modify it.

To set a property for a control within code, follow these steps:

1. Switch to the code view. Select the method or property in which you want to write the code.

2. Use the `ControlObject.PropertyName` syntax to access the property for a control's object. `ControlObject` is an instance of the control, and `PropertyName` is any valid property name for the given control. In the code view, IntelliSense helps you access the list of properties associated with a control.

Important Common Properties of Controls

The following sections discuss several important properties that are shared by many of the standard controls.

The Anchor Property

When a form is resized, you might want its controls to move along with it, keeping a constant distance from the form's edges.

You can achieve this by anchoring the control with the edges of its container control (see Figures 2.5 and 2.6). The default value of Anchor is Top, Left; this specifies that the control is anchored to the top and left edge of the container. (Refer to Step by Step 2.4 later in this chapter for an example of how the Anchor property is used.)

FIGURE 2.5▶
You can click the down arrow in the Anchor property to display an anchoring window.

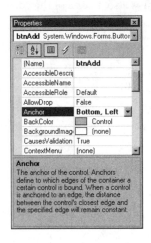

FIGURE 2.6▲
The dark bars indicate the sides to which the control is anchored.

The Dock Property

At some point you might need a control to span an entire side (left, right, top, or bottom) of its parent control. You can use the Dock property of a control to achieve this behavior (see Figures 2.7 and 2.8). The default value of the Dock property is None. This property is specially used with controls such as StatusBar and ToolBar, but it is not limited to them. (To see an example of docking with a Label control, see Step by Step 2.4 later in this chapter.)

FIGURE 2.7▶
You can click the down arrow in the Dock property to display a docking window.

FIGURE 2.8▲
You can click the edge at which you want a control to be docked.

The `Enabled` Property

The `Enabled` property of a control has a Boolean value (`true`/`false`) that can be used to determine whether a control can respond to user interactions. A disabled control (with the `Enabled` property set to `false`) does not receive the focus, does not generate any events, and appears dimmed, or "grayed out." The default value of the `Enabled` property is `true`, except for a `Timer` control, whose `Enabled` property is `false` by default.

The `Font` Property

You use the `Font` property to set the font of the text displayed by the control. The value of this property is an object of the `Font` class. When you select the `Font` property in the Properties window for a control, you see an ellipsis (…) button. Clicking this button invokes a Font dialog box (see Figure 2.9) that can be used to conveniently manipulate the `Font` property.

The `Location` Property

The `Location` property specifies the location of the top-left corner of the control with respect to the top-left corner of its container control. Its value is of type `Point`.

Four other properties depend on Location: `Left`, `Right`, `Top`, and `Bottom`. `Left` is the same as `Location.X`, `Right` is the same as `Location.X + Width`, `Top` is the same as `Location.Y`, and `Bottom` is the same as `Location.Y + Height`.

The `Name` Property

A control's `Name` property can be used to manipulate a control programmatically. When you place a control on a container object by using the Windows Forms Designer, it names the control automatically based on the type of control (for example, `label1`, `label2`). If you create a control programmatically, its name is by default an empty string. It's a good programming practice to give a meaningful name to a control. Most programmers use Hungarian notation for naming controls; in this scheme, the name of each control begins with a lowercase prefix that is an abbreviation for the name of the control. For example, an instance of a `TextBox` control storing a customer name would be named `txtCustomerName`.

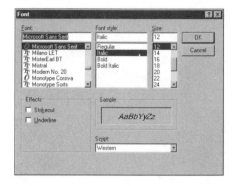

FIGURE 2.9
The Font dialog box allows you to set the `Font` property of a control.

NOTE

Programmatically Setting the `Font` Property The `Font` object is said to be *immutable* because its value cannot be modified after the control has been created. If you try to programmatically set one of its properties, you get the compilation error `Property or indexer cannot be assigned to--it is read only`.

Therefore, the only way you can change the `Font` property of a control is by assigning a newly created `Font` object to the `Font` property.

The Size Property

The Size property sets or gets the height and width of a control. The value of this property is of data type Size. Size is a struct that has properties named Height and Width that, respectively, store the height and width of the control, in pixels.

You can also individually manipulate the height and width of a control by using a control's Height and Width properties.

The Control class has a protected property named DefaultSize that specifies the default size of the control. The default size is used to draw a control if the size of the control is not explicitly specified. You can override this property in a program to specify a different default size for a control.

The TabIndex and TabStop Properties

The Tab key is used for keyboard navigation from one control to another on a Windows form. The TabIndex property of a control is an integer value that specifies the order in which controls receive focus when the user presses the Tab key.

If you do not want a control to receive focus when the user uses the Tab key, you can set the control's TabStop property to false. Its default value is true, and it allows the control to participate in keyboard navigation through the Tab key.

The TabIndex property is effective only when the TabStop property of the control is set to true.

The Text Property

The Text property is a string that indicates the text associated with the control. Different controls use the Text property in different ways: For example, a Form control displays its Text property in its title bar and a Label control displays its Text property on the face of the control. Unlike with a Form or a Label control, users can manipulate the Text property of some controls, such as TextBox and RichTextBox, at runtime by changing the contents of the controls' input boxes.

The Text property can also be used to provide a keyboard shortcut to a control. An ampersand (&) in front of a character marks it as the hotkey for that control. If you assign &Save to the Text property of a Button control, the *S* in the name is underlined. Because this is a standard Windows convention, when users see it, they know that they can press the button by pressing the Alt+S key combination.

Some controls such as Label controls cannot receive focus. If you assign a hotkey for such a control, the focus instead goes to a control with the next higher TabIndex property. You can in fact use this behavior in your favor. To identify controls such as TextBox, RichTextBox, TreeView, or ListView, you would place a Label control beside them. You can associate a hotkey with the Label control and keep the TabIndex property of Label and the corresponding control in immediate succession. This way, when you press the hotkey for the Label control, it transfers focus to the control that has the next higher TabIndex property, and the corresponding control receives focus.

The Visible Property

The Visible property is set to true by default. When you set it to false, you still see the control in the Windows Forms Designer, but users of the application cannot see the control at runtime. Be aware that setting the Visible property to false does not remove the control from its container's controls collection.

Configuring the Order of Tabs

Implement navigation for the user interface.

- **Configure the order of tabs**

Many people find it convenient to use the keyboard to navigate among the controls on a form. A Windows user expects to move from one control to another in a logical order by using the Tab key. The Windows Forms Designer provides a Tab Order Wizard that allows you to conveniently set the order in which the controls should receive focus when the Tab key is pressed. Step by Step 2.3 describes how to use this wizard.

NOTE

Visually Displaying an Ampersand in the Text Property What if you want to display an ampersand in a control's text property rather than have it function as a hotkey?

If you're working with a Label control, you can set its UseMnemonic property to false. When UseMnemonic is false, the control does not interpret the ampersand as a hotkey modifier.

But only the Label and LinkLabel controls have a UseMnemonic property. What about other controls, such as Button? With all those other controls, you can use a double ampersand (&&) in the Text property to represent a single ampersand.

NOTE

Control Transparency No property directly allows you to set transparency for a control. However, you can use the BackColor property of a control and set a color by using the Color.FromArgb() method. The Color.FromArgb() method lets you specify an alpha component that controls transparency.

FIGURE 2.10
A hotkey allows you to jump to a control by using the keyboard.

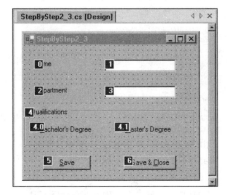

FIGURE 2.11
The Tab Order Wizard allows you to configure the order of tabs.

STEP BY STEP

2.3 Configuring the Order of Tabs

1. Add a Windows form to existing project 316C02. Name the form StepByStep2_3.

2. Place two Label controls on the form and set their Text properties to &Name and &Department.

3. Place two TextBox controls and two CheckBox controls on the form. Empty the Text property for each of the TextBox controls. Change the Text properties for the CheckBox controls as &Bachelor's degree and "&Master's degree.

4. Add two Button controls to the form and change their Text properties to &Save and Save && &Close. Resize and arrange all the controls as shown in Figure 2.10.

5. Select View, Tab Order and number the controls as shown in Figure 2.11. You can change a tab order number by clicking it.

6. Insert the Main() method to launch the form. Set the form as the startup object for the project.

7. Run the project. Use the Tab key to navigate from one control to another. Use hotkeys to directly jump to a control.

HANDLING CONTROL EVENTS

Add controls to a Windows form.

- **Set properties on controls.**
- **Load controls dynamically.**
- **Write code to handle control events and add the code to a control.**

Event handling for a control is very similar to event handling for a Windows form (refer to Chapter 1). Each control inherits a number of events from the System.Windows.Forms.Control class.

Each control type also has a set of events that is specific to its unique functionality. Every control has a default event associated with it (for example, the Click event for a Button control, Load for a Form control, and CheckedChanged for a CheckBox control). When you double-click a control in the Windows Forms Designer, the designer automatically creates an event handler for the default event and opens the code view, which allows you to add custom code inside the event handler. You can also handle an event by double-clicking the name of the event in the Properties window; doing this creates an event handler for the selected event of the control.

Step by Step 2.4 is an example of event handling as applied to controls. Step by Step 2.4 creates a Windows form that presents two buttons—Add and Remove. When you click the Add button, the code in its Click event handler dynamically adds a new Button object to the form, forming a stack of buttons. When you click the Remove button, the code in its Click event handler removes the most recently created Button object (see Figure 2.12).

Step by Step 2.4 illustrates the following points related to handling events:

◆ How to attach an event handler with a control's event

◆ How to add custom code to an event handler

◆ How to attach a single event handler to provide common behavior to several controls

◆ How to attach an event handler programmatically at runtime

Therefore, you should carefully watch the steps and the comments in the code in Step by Step 2.4.

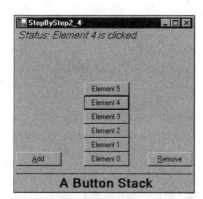

FIGURE 2.12
You can add and remove controls dynamically.

STEP BY STEP

2.4 Programming Control Events

1. Add a Windows form to existing project 316C02. Name the form StepByStep2_4.

continues

continued

N O T E

Setting a Property for Multiple Controls   To set a property for multiple controls simultaneously, click each of the controls while pressing the Ctrl key; then invoke the Properties window and set the property. The property you set is applied to all the selected controls. When you invoke the Properties window while multiple controls are selected, it shows only the properties that all the selected controls have in common. You can use the same steps to set a common event handler for multiple controls.

2. Place a Label control on the form; change the Dock property to Top, change the Name property to lblStatus, change the Font property to make it italic and size 12, change the Text property to be empty, and change the TextAlign property to MiddleCenter.

3. Place another Label control on the form; change the Dock property to Bottom, change the Name property to lblStack, change the Font property to make it bold and size 16, change the Text property to A Button Stack, and change the TextAlign property to MiddleCenter.

4. Place a Button control on the form. Change the Name property to btnAdd, change the Text property to &Add, and change the Anchor property to Bottom, Left.

5. Place another Button control on the form. Change the Name property to btnRemove, change the Text property to &Remove, and change the Anchor property to Bottom, Right.

6. Switch to the code view and add the following code before the form's constructor code:

```
//Stores the top of stack value
private int intTos;
//stores initial control count
private int intInitCtrlCount;
```

7. Add the following code in the form's constructor code after the call to the InitializeComponent() method:

```
//Initially the stack is empty
intTos = 0;
//Get the initial control count. Be sure to put this
//statement after the call to
//InitializeComponent method
intInitCtrlCount = this.Controls.Count;
//Redraw form if it is resized
this.ResizeRedraw=true;
```

8. Using the Properties window, add an event handler for the form's Paint event. Add the following code to the event handler:

```
private void StepByStep2_4_Paint(object sender,
    System.Windows.Forms.PaintEventArgs e)
{
```

```
//Gets the Graphics object for the form
Graphics grfx = e.Graphics;
//Draw a line, end-to-end on the form
grfx.DrawLine(Pens.Black, 0,
    this.lblStack.Location.Y -5, this.Width,
    this.lblStack.Location.Y - 5);
//Set the location for Add and remove buttons
// so that they get repositioned
// after the form is resized
this.btnAdd.Location    = new Point(
  0, this.lblStack.Location.Y - 40);
this.btnRemove.Location =
    new Point(this.Width-this.btnRemove.Width - 7,
    this.lblStack.Location.Y - 40);
}
```

9. Insert the following event handler in the code; you will later attach it programmatically to the dynamically created Button objects:

```
// A custom event handler that I will attach to
// Click event of all buttons added to the stack
private void Button_Click(
    object sender, System.EventArgs e)
{
    //Type cast the object to a Button
    Button btnSender = (Button)sender;
    // Change the lblStatus to show
    // that this button was clicked
    lblStatus.Text = "Status: " +
        btnSender.Text + " is clicked.";
}
```

10. In the design view, double-click the Add button. This attaches an event handler for the Click event (the default event for a button). In the event handler code, insert the following lines:

```
private void btnAdd_Click(
    object sender, System.EventArgs e)
{
    //If stack is not yet full
    if (intTos < 8)
    {
        Button btnSender = (Button) sender;
        //Create a new Button to add to the Stack
        Button btnNew = new Button();
        btnNew.Name="Element" + intTos;
        btnNew.Text = "Element " + intTos;
        btnNew.Location =
        new Point((this.Width-btnNew.Width)/2,
    btnSender.Location.Y - btnSender.Height * intTos);
```

continues

continued

```
//Attach a event handler to the Click
//event of newly created button
btnNew.Click += new System.EventHandler(
    this.Button_Click);

//Add the Button to the Container's
//Control collection
this.Controls.Add(btnNew);
lblStatus.Text = "Status: Element " +
    intTos + " added.";
intTos++;
}
else
    //Stack is full, can't add a button
    lblStatus.Text = "Status: Stack is full!";
}
```

11. In the design view, double-click the Remove button. In its `Click` event handler code, insert the following lines:

```
private void btnRemove_Click(
    object sender, System.EventArgs e)
{
    Button btnSender = (Button) sender;
    //Current control count in the
    //Form's Control collection
    int intCtrlCount = this.Controls.Count;
    //If any new buttons were created in the stack
    if (intCtrlCount > intInitCtrlCount)
    {
        //Remove the most recently added
        //control in the collection
        this.Controls.Remove(
            this.Controls[this.Controls.Count-1]);
        //Adjust the top of stack
        intTos--;
        lblStatus.Text = "Status: Element " +
            intTos + " removed.";
    }
    else
        //Stack is empty, Can't remove a button
        lblStatus.Text = "Status: Stack is empty!";
}
```

12. Insert the `Main()` method to launch the form. Set the form as the startup object for the project.

13. Run the project. Click the Add and Remove buttons. You will see that the `Button` controls are dynamically created and removed. When you click one of the dynamically created button controls, its `Click` event is fired and it displays a message on the top `Label` control (refer to Figure 2.12).

Step by Step 2.4 illustrates these important aspects of dynamic control creation:

◆ You can dynamically add or remove controls to a container by using the `Add()` and `Remove()` methods of the container object's controls collection.

◆ You can access the dynamically added control objects by iterating through the controls collection.

◆ By attaching a single event handler to a group of controls, you can provide the group with a common behavior.

Because event handling is so integrated with the nature of Windows applications, this chapter includes several examples of handling events that are associated with controls.

EXAM TIP

Control Arrays in Visual C# .NET Visual Basic 6.0 has a concept of control arrays that is often handy when you're working with a group of similar controls. Neither Visual Basic .NET nor Visual C# .NET has any built-in support for control arrays; you can instead achieve the same functionality by manipulating the Controls collection of a form or any other container control.

R E V I E W   B R E A K

▶ You can add controls to a form in two ways: by using the Windows Forms Designer or by hand-coding them in the code.

▶ The Windows Forms Designer of the Microsoft Visual Studio .NET IDE allows you to add controls to a form and design a form in a very simple manner.

▶ The Visual Studio .NET toolbox provides a varierty of controls and components to create common Windows GUI elements.

▶ When you create controls programmatically, be sure to add them to their parent containers' controls collections.

▶ You can set the properties on controls at design time by using the Properties window or at runtime by accessing them as `ControlName.PropertyName` in the code.

▶ Some of the important properties of the controls `Anchor`, `Dock`, `Enabled`, `Font`, `Location`, `Name`, `Size`, `TabIndex`, `TabStop`, and `Visible` are shared by most common Windows forms controls.

▶ The Tab Order Wizard provides a convenient way to set the tab order of controls to implement logical keyboard-based navigation of the controls in the form via Tab key.

continues

continued

▶ Controls are event driven. Events are fired when the user interacts with a control. To cause a control to take specific action when an event occurs, you need to write an event handler method and attach that to an event of a control via the control's delegate.

▶ You can attach an event handler to a control's event either by using the Properties window or programmatically by adding an event handler's delegate object to a control's event (*ControlName.EventName*) by using the += operator.

GUIDED PRACTICE EXERCISE 2.1

One of the common features of Windows-based applications is that they show or hide controls to make their user interface effective. One common example is the Find and Replace dialog box in Microsoft Word, where controls showing advance options are initially hidden but can be shown if the user wants. How would you create such an interface, where users can control visibility of controls?

In this exercise, you will create the Windows form shown in Figure 2.13. The controls on this form are grouped in two GroupBox container controls. The Console group box allows you to manipulate the controls in the Playground group box. When you choose a type of control from the combo box in the Console group box and click the Hide button, all controls of that type in the Playground container should be hidden. Similarly, when you click the Show button, the visibility of all controls of the selected type should be restored.

This exercise gives you practice on working with the controls collection of a container control. You should try working through this problem on your own first. If you get stuck, or if you'd like to see one possible solution, follow these steps:

1. Add a new form to your Visual C# .NET project. Name the form GuidedPracticeExercise2_1.cs.

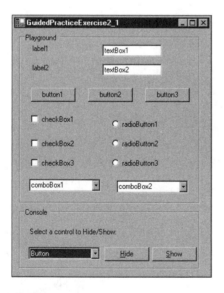

FIGURE 2.13

You can work with the Controls collection of a form to hide and show its controls dynamically at runtime.

2. Place two `GroupBox` controls on the form. Change the `Name` property of one to `grpConsole` and change the `Name` property of the other to `grpPlayground`. Add and arrange controls on these `GroupBox` controls as shown in Figure 2.13. To easily arrange and align the controls, you can use various options that are available in the Format menu (see Figure 2.14).

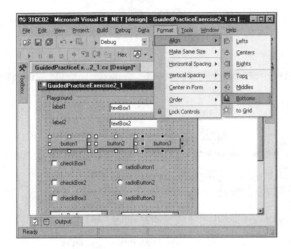

FIGURE 2.14
Format menu options allow you to arrange controls.

3. Name the combo box inside the Console group box `cboControls` and name the buttons `btnHide` and `btnShow`.

4. Invoke the Properties window for the `cboControls` control and select its `Items` property. Click the ellipsis (…) button. This invokes the String Collection Editor (see Figure 2.15). Add the following values to the editor and then close it:

```
Button
CheckBox
ComboBox
Label
TextBox
RadioButton
```

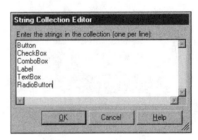

FIGURE 2.15
The String Collection Editor allows you to view and change the list of strings for a `ListControl` object such as `ComboBox`.

5. Attach `Click` event handlers with both Hide and Show buttons and enter the following code to manage the `Click` event for them:

```
private void btnShow_Click(
    object sender, System.EventArgs e)
{
```

continues

continued

```
//check each control in the grpPlayground
//container control
foreach (Control ctrl in
    this.grpPlayground.Controls)
{
    //If the type of control is what selected
    //by user in the combobox
    if (ctrl.GetType().ToString() ==
        "System.Windows.Forms." +
        this.cboControls.SelectedItem)
        //Show the control
        this.grpPlayground.Controls[
this.grpPlayground.Controls.IndexOf(ctrl)].Visible =
        true;
    }
}

private void btnHide_Click(
    object sender, System.EventArgs e)
{
    //check each control in the
    //grpPlayground container control
    foreach (Control ctrl in
        this.grpPlayground.Controls)
    {
        //If the type of control is what
        //selected by user in the combobox
        if (ctrl.GetType().ToString() ==
            "System.Windows.Forms." +
            this.cboControls.SelectedItem)
            //Hide the control
            this.grpPlayground.Controls[
this.grpPlayground.Controls.IndexOf(ctrl)].Visible =
            false;
    }
}
```

6. Insert the `Main()` method and set the form as the startup object for the project.

7. Run the project and experiment with the user interface. You'll find that when you click the Hide button after selecting a control type from the combo box, all controls of that type are hidden from the Playground group box. Similarly, clicking on the Show button displays the control of selected type again.

If you have difficulty following this exercise, review the sections "Handling Control Events" and "Important Common Properties of Controls" earlier in this chapter. Also, complete Step by Step 2.2 and Step by Step 2.4. Experimenting with those exercises and reading the specified sections should help you relearn this material. After doing that review, try this exercise again.

DIALOG BOXES

A dialog box is used to prompt the user for input. The application can then use the user input for its own processing. You can either use one of the existing dialog box components provided by the Windows Forms library or you can create a dialog box to meet your custom application requirements. The following sections cover both of these scenarios.

Common Dialog Boxes

The Windows Forms library provides the following dialog box classes that are ready to use in Windows applications:

◆ `ColorDialog`—Displays a list of colors and returns a property that contains the color selected by user.

◆ `FontDialog`—Displays a dialog box that allows the user to select a font and other text properties, such as size, style, and special effects.

◆ `OpenFileDialog`—Allows the user to browse files and folders on his or her computer and select one or more files.

◆ `PageSetupDialog`—Allows the user to select various settings related to page layout.

◆ `PrintDialog`—Allows the user to select various print-related options and sends specified documents to selected printers.

◆ `PrintPreviewDialog`—Allows the user to preview a file before printing.

◆ `SaveFileDialog`—Allows the user to browse the files and folders on his or her computer and select files that need to be saved.

These classes are also referred to as *Windows Forms dialog components*. These dialog boxes provide the same functionality found in several of the common dialog boxes that are used by the Windows operating system. Each of these dialog box classes is derived from the `CommonDialog` class, which provides the basic functionality for displaying a dialog box.

The dialog box classes provide a method named `ShowDialog` that presents a dialog box to the user. Each of the dialog box classes has a set of properties that store data that is relevant to the particular dialog box.

STEP BY STEP

2.5 Using Common Dialog Boxes

1. Add a Windows Form to existing project `316C02`. Name this form `StepByStep2_5`.

2. Place five `Button` controls on the form. Name them `btnOpen`, `btnSave`, `btnClose`, `btnColor`, and `btnFont` and change their `Text` properties to `&Open...`, `&Save...`, `Clos&e...`, `&Color...`, and `&Font...`, respectively.

3. Place a `RichTextBox` control on the form and name it `rtbText`. Arrange all the controls as shown in Figure 2.16.

4. Drag and drop the following components from the toolbox to the form: `OpenFileDialog`, `SaveFileDialog`, `ColorDialog`, and `FontDialog`. Because these are components, they are not added to the form, but they appear on the component tray in the lower area of the form (see Figure 2.16).

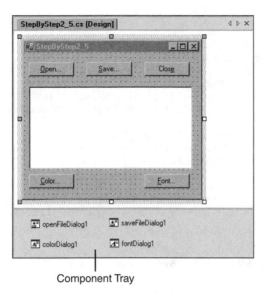

Component Tray

FIGURE 2.16
The component tray represents components that do not otherwise provide visible surfaces at runtime.

> **N O T E**
>
> **Nonvisual Controls and the Component Tray**   Controls such as common dialog box controls do not provide a runtime user interface. Instead of being displayed on the form's surface, they are displayed on a component tray at the bottom of the form. After a control has been added to the component tray, you can select the component and set its properties just as you would with any other control on the form. These nonvisual controls implement the IComponent interface and therefore are also sometimes referred to as *components*.

5. Switch to the code view and add the following using directive at the top of the program:

```
using System.IO;
```

6. Double-click the Open button to attach an event handler to the Click event. Add the following code to the event handler:

```csharp
private void btnOpen_Click(
    object sender, System.EventArgs e)
{
    //Allow to select only *.rtf files
    openFileDialog1.Filter =
        "Rich Text Files (*.rtf)|*.rtf";
    if(openFileDialog1.ShowDialog() == DialogResult.OK)
    {
        //Load the file contents in the RichTextBox
        rtbText.LoadFile(openFileDialog1.FileName,
            RichTextBoxStreamType.RichText);
    }
}
```

7. Add the following code to handle the Click event of the Save button:

```csharp
private void btnSave_Click(
    object sender, System.EventArgs e)
{
```

continues

continued

```
//Default choice to save file is *.rtf
//but user can select
//All Files to save with other extension
saveFileDialog1.Filter =
"Rich Text Files (*.rtf)|*.rtf|All Files (*.*)|*.*";
if(saveFileDialog1.ShowDialog() == DialogResult.OK)
{
    //Save the RichText content to a file
    rtbText.SaveFile(saveFileDialog1.FileName,
        RichTextBoxStreamType.RichText);
}
}
```

8. Add the following code to handle the Click event of the Close button:

```
private void btnClose_Click(
    object sender, System.EventArgs e)
{
    //close the form
    this.Close();
}
```

9. Add the following code to handle the Click event of the Color button:

```
private void btnColor_Click(
    object sender, System.EventArgs e)
{
    if(colorDialog1.ShowDialog() == DialogResult.OK)
    {
        //Change the color of selected text
        //If no text selected, change the active color
        rtbText.SelectionColor = colorDialog1.Color;
    }
}
```

10. Add the following code to handle the Click event of the Font button:

```
private void btnFont_Click(
    object sender, System.EventArgs e)
{
    if(fontDialog1.ShowDialog() == DialogResult.OK)
    {
        //Change the font of selected text
        //If no text selected, change the active font
        rtbText.SelectionFont = fontDialog1.Font;
    }
}
```

EXAM TIP

The FilterIndex Property The
FilterIndex property of the
OpenFileDialog and
SaveFileDialog components determines the index of the currently
selected filter in the list of filters
specified by the dialog box's Filter
property. Be aware that this index is
one based; that is, the first filter in
the list of filters has an index of
one instead of zero.

11. Insert the `Main()` method to launch the form. Set the form as the startup object.

12. Run the project. Click the Open button, select a Rich Text Format (RTF) file to open, experiment with changing the color and font, and save the file (see Figure 2.17).

FIGURE 2.17
The `OpenFileDialog` and `SaveFile` dialog boxes, respectively, allow you to select a file for opening and saving; the `ColorDialog` and `FontDialog` dialog boxes, respectively, allow you to select color and font.

The `Filter` property of the `OpenFileDialog` and `SaveFileDialog` components specifies the choices that appear in the Files of Type drop-down list boxes of these dialog boxes. You can use this property to filter the type of files that the user can select from the dialog box.

You will learn about the printing-related dialog box components in Chapter 11, "Printing."

Creating a Custom Dialog Box

If you need to create dialog boxes other than those already provided by the Windows Forms library, you can do so by creating a form and setting it up to behave as a dialog box. You can make the dialog box as rich as your requirements dictate by adding various controls to it.

STEP BY STEP

2.6 Creating a Custom Dialog Box

1. Add a Windows form to existing project `316C02`. Name the form `frmDialog`.

2. Set the `ControlBox` property of the form to `false`, set `FormBorderStyle` to `FixedDialog`, set `ShowIntaskBar` to `False`, set `StartPosition` to `CenterParent`, and set `Text` to `A Custom Dialog Box`.

3. Place two `Button` controls and a `TextBox` control on the form, set the `Name` property of the `Button` controls to `btnOK` and `btnCancel` and change their `Text` properties to `&OK` and `&Cancel`, respectively. Change the `TextBox` control's `Name` property to `txtDialogText` and its `Text` property to `Dialog Text`.

NOTE
Getting the File Extension The `OpenFileDialog` and `SaveFileDialog` components have a property named `FileName` that returns the name of the selected file. How can you get just the extension for this file? You can do so by using the `Extension` property of the `FileInfo` class:

```
FileInfo fiFileInfo = new
    FileInfo(openFileDialog1.
FileName);
MessageBox.Show(fiFileInfo.
Extension);
```

Similarly if you want just the name of the file, without any extensions, you can use the `Name` property of the `FileInfo` class:

```
FileInfo fiFileInfo = new
    FileInfo(openFileDialog1.
FileName);
MessageBox.Show(fiFileInfo.Name);
```

continues

continued

4. Change the form's constructor code to the following:

```
public frmDialog()
{
    //
    // Required for Windows Forms Designer support
    //
    InitializeComponent();

    //Configure OK button
    btnOK.DialogResult =
        System.Windows.Forms.DialogResult.OK;
    //Configure Cancel button
    btnCancel.DialogResult =
        System.Windows.Forms.DialogResult.Cancel;
}
```

5. Add the following code just after the constructor to create a property that holds the text entered by the user:

```
private string message;
//Stores the message entered by user
public string Message
{
    get
    {
        return message;
    }
    set
    {
        message = value;
    }
}
```

6. Add an event handler for the Click event of the OK button and add the following code in it:

```
private void btnOK_Click(
    object sender, System.EventArgs e)
{
    this.Message = this.txtDialogText.Text;
}
```

7. Add a new Windows form to the project. Name it StepByStep2_6.

8. Place a Button control and a Label control on the form. Name the Button control btnInvokeDialog, and change the Text property to Invoke Dialog. Name the Label control lblDialogResult, and change the Text property to Click the button to invoke a custom dialog box.

NOTE

Modal and Modeless Dialog Boxes
When a *modal* dialog box is open, an application can only receive input for the modal dialog box. If you want to work with other windows, you must close the modal dialog box first. An example of a modal dialog box is the one that opens when you select Help, About in Visual Studio .NET. On the other hand, a *modeless* dialog box allows an application to receive input for other windows and controls. An example of a modeless dialog box is the Find & Replace dialog box of Visual Studio .NET.

9. Attach an event handler to the Click event of
btnInvokeDialog and add the following code to it:

```
private void btnInvokeDialog_Click(
    object sender, System.EventArgs e)
{
    //Create the custom dialog box
    frmDialog dlgCustom = new frmDialog();
    //Present dialog box to the user
    dlgCustom.ShowDialog();

    if(dlgCustom.DialogResult == DialogResult.OK)
    {
        //Display the message in label
        //if user pressed OK
        this.lblDialogResult.Text = dlgCustom.Message;
    }
    else
        //Indicate that user cancelled the dialog box
        this.lblDialogResult.Text =
            "Dialog box was cancelled";
}
```

10. Insert a Main() method in StepByStep2_6 to launch the
form. Set the form as the startup object for the project.

11. Run the project. Click the Invoke Dialog button, and the
custom dialog box is displayed. Enter some text in the text
box and click the OK button. The text you enter is then
displayed on the parent form's label control (see Figure
2.18).

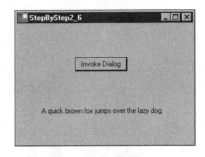

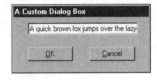

FIGURE 2.18
You can use the ShowDialog method to display
a form as a dialog box.

The ShowDialog() method displays a form as a modal dialog box. All
the buttons on the form that need to return results have their
DialogResult properties set to any of the DialogResult enumeration
values except DialogResult.None. When the user clicks one of these
buttons, the button sets the form's DialogResult property with the
DialogResult property of the button and closes the form automatically after running the Click event handler (if any).

EXAM TIP

**The Show() and ShowDialog()
Methods** When you use the
ShowDialog() method of the Form
class, the form is displayed as a
modal dialog box. If you want to display the form as a modeless dialog
box, you should use the Show()
method.

REVIEW BREAK

▶ DialogBox is used to prompt the user for input. There are a
few built-in dialog boxes available, such as ColorDialog,
FontDialog, OpenFileDialog, and SaveFileDialog, that function just like the Windows operating system's dialog boxes.

continues

continued

▶ You can build custom dialog boxes to meet custom requirements. You can create such a dialog box by creating a form and setting a few properties of the form that enable the form to behave like a dialog box.

▶ Dialog boxes can be of two types: modal and modeless. You call the ShowDialog() and Show() methods of the Form class to create modal and modeless dialog boxes, respectively.

COMMON WINDOWS FORMS CONTROLS

Add controls to a Windows form.

- **Set properties on controls.**

- **Write code to handle control events and add the code to a control.**

The Windows Forms library includes an array of commonly used GUI elements that you can assemble on a Windows form to create Windows applications. These GUI elements (or Windows forms controls) are mostly derived from the System.Windows.Forms.Control class. By virtue of this inheritance, these controls share a number of common properties, methods, and events; in addition, these controls may also have their own specific sets of properties, methods, and events that give them distinct behaviors. Figure 2.19 shows a hierarchy of important classes in the Control class.

The following sections discuss some important controls that are available in the Windows Forms Designer toolbox. The discussion and examples presented here will help you appreciate the specific nature of these controls.

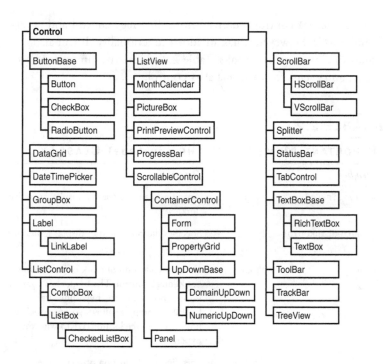

FIGURE 2.19
System.Windows.Forms.Control is the base class for all controls.

The Label and LinkLabel Controls

A Label control is used to display read-only information to the user. It is generally used to label other controls and to provide the user with any useful runtime messages or statistics. You can display both text and images on Label controls by using the Text and Image properties, respectively. Table 2.1 shows some of the properties of the Label object with which you should be familiar.

TABLE 2.1

IMPORTANT MEMBERS OF THE Label CLASS

Member	Type	Description
Image	Property	Specifies an image that is displayed on a label.
Font	Property	Specifies the font in which the text is displayed on a label.
Text	Property	Specifies the text displayed on a label.
TextAlign	Property	Specifies the alignment of the text displayed on a label. It can have one of three horizontal positions (Center, Left, or Right) and one of three vertical positions (Bottom, Middle, or Top).

The LinkLabel control is derived from the Label control and is very similar to it. However, it has an added functionality: It can also show one or more hyperlinks. Table 2.2 summarizes important properties and events for the LinkLabel control.

TABLE 2.2

IMPORTANT MEMBERS OF THE LinkLabel CLASS

Member	Type	Description
ActiveLinkColor	Property	Specifies the color used to display an active link.
DisabledLinkColor	Property	Specifies the color used to display a disabled link.
Links	Property	Gets the collection of Link objects in the LinkLabel control. The Link class contains information about the hyperlink. Its LinkData property allows you to associate a uniform resource locator (URL) with the hyperlink.
LinkArea	Property	Specifies which portion of text in the LinkLabel control is treated as part of the link.
LinkBehavior	Property	Specifies how the link appears when the mouse pointer is placed over it.
LinkClicked	Event	Occurs when a link in the LinkLabel control is clicked. Inside its event handler, the LinkLabelLinkClickedEventArgs object provides data for the event. LinkClicked is the default event for LinkLabel class.
LinkColor	Property	Specifies the color used to display a link.
VisitedLinkColor	Property	Specifies the color used to display a visited link

STEP BY STEP

2.7 Using LinkLabel Controls

1. Add a Windows form to existing project 316C02. Name the form StepByStep2_7.

2. Place two `LinkLabel` controls on the form. Change their `Name` properties to `lnkWinForms` and `lnkPrograms` and their `Text` properties to `Windows Forms Community Website` and `Launch Calculator | Open C: Drive`, respectively.

3. Switch to the code view, and add the following code in the form's constructor, after the `InitializeComponent()` method call:

```
//Add a link for Calculator in
//the first half of LinkLabel
lnkPrograms.Links.Add(
    0, "Launch Calculator".Length, "calc.exe ");
//Add a link for C: Drive in
//the second half of LinkLabel
lnkPrograms.Links.Add(lnkPrograms.Text.IndexOf(
    "Open C: Drive"), "Open C: Drive".Length, "c:\\");

//Autosize the control based on its contents
lnkPrograms.AutoSize = true;
```

4. Double-click the `lnkWinForms` link label to attach a `LinkClicked` event handler to it. Add the following code to the event handler:

```
private void lnkWinForms_LinkClicked(object sender,
System.Windows.Forms.LinkLabelLinkClickedEventArgs e)
{
    lnkWinForms.LinkVisited = true;
    //Go to Windows Forms Community Website
    System.Diagnostics.Process.Start(
        "IExplore", "http://www.windowsforms.net");
}
```

5. Double-click the `lnkPrograms` link label to attach a `LinkClicked` event handler to it. Add the following code to the event handler:

```
private void lnkPrograms_LinkClicked(object sender,
System.Windows.Forms.LinkLabelLinkClickedEventArgs e)
{
    //Launch the program stored in the hyperlink
    System.Diagnostics.Process.Start(
        e.Link.LinkData.ToString());
}
```

6. Insert the `Main()` method to launch form `StepByStep2_7`. Set this form as the startup object for the project.

7. Run the project and click the links. The form takes an appropriate action by either navigating to the Web site, launching the Calculator, or opening the folder (see Figure 2.20).

FIGURE 2.20
A `LinkLabel` control can be used to link to a Web page, an application, or a folder.

The `System.Diagnostic.Process` class lets you start and stop process-es that are running on your computer. Its `Start()` method actually starts a given process. The `Start()` method is static and therefore lets you create the process without creating an object of `System.Diagnostic.Process` class. The `LinkLabelLinkClickedEventArgs` object passed to the `LinkClicked` event handler contains a `Link` object that corresponds to the link being clicked. The `LinkData` property of this `Link` object represents the data associated with the link.

The `TextBox` and `RichTextBox` Controls

`TextBox` and `RichTextBox` both derive from the `TextBoxBase` class. The `TextBoxBase` class implements the basic functionality used by both the `TextBox` and `RichTextBox` classes.

A `TextBox` control provides an area that the user can use to input text. Depending on how you set the properties of this control, you can use it for multiline text input or you can use it like a password box that masks the characters entered by the user with a specific character (such as *). Table 2.3 summarizes the important members of the `TextBox` class.

TABLE 2.3

IMPORTANT MEMBERS OF THE TextBox CLASS

Member	Type	Description
AcceptsReturn	Property	Represents a Boolean value, where `true` indi-cates that pressing the Enter key in a multiline text box inserts a new line. This property is applicable only if the text box accepts multi-line input.
CharacterCasing	Property	Specifies whether the `TextBox` control needs to modify the case of the characters as they are entered. The value of this property can be `Lower`, `Normal`, or `Upper`. The Default value is `Normal`, which means the characters are not modified.
MultiLine	Property	Indicates whether the text box can accept multiple lines of input. The default value is `false`.

Member	Type	Description
PasswordChar	Property	Masks each character in the text box by the specified character. It is usually set when the text box inputs sensitive information such as a password, where the characters need to be masked. If no character is specified, the normal text is displayed.
ReadOnly	Property	Makes the text box appear with a gray background and text cannot be edited when set to true.
ScrollBars	Property	Specifies which scrollbars (none, horizontal, vertical, or both) should appear in a multiline textbox.
Text	Property	Specifies the text contained in the textbox.
TextChanged	Event	Occurs when the value of the Text property changes. TextChanged is the default event for the TextBox class.
WordWrap	Property	Specifies whether the control can automatically wrap words to the next line. The default value is true. Works only if the MultiLine property is set to true.

As its name suggests, the RichTextBox control is a TextBox control with rich formatting capabilities. It can upload an RTF file. It can display its contents in rich character and paragraph formatting. Any portion of the control can be displayed in various formats, depending on the settings of its properties. Table 2.4 summarizes the important members of the RichTextBox class.

TABLE 2.4

IMPORTANT MEMBERS OF THE RichTextBox CLASS

Member	Type	Description
DetectUrls	Property	Specifies whether the control automatically detects and formats URLs
Rtf	Property	Specifies the text of the RichTextBox control, including all RTF codes
SelectionColor	Property	Specifies the color of the currently selected text
SelectionFont	Property	Specifies the font of the currently selected text

continues

TABLE 2.4	*continued*

IMPORTANT MEMBERS OF THE RichTextBox CLASS

Member	Type	Description
SelectedRtf	Property	Specifies the currently selected RTF text
TextChanged	Event	Occurs when the value of the Text property changes. TextChanged is the default event for RichTextBox class.
WordWrap	Property	Specifies whether the control can automatically wrap words to the next line if required
ZoomFactor	Property	Specifies the current zoom level.

Step by Steps 2.5 and 2.18, later in this chapter, describe good usage of the RichTextBox control.

The PictureBox Control

PictureBox controls display images and graphics from metafile, icon, bitmap, JPEG, PNG, and GIF files. Table 2.5 summarizes the important members of the PictureBox class.

TABLE 2.5

IMPORTANT MEMBERS OF THE PictureBox CLASS

Member	Type	Description
Click	Event	Occurs when the control is clicked. Click is the default event for the PictureBox class.
Image	Property	Represents the image that the picture box displays.
SizeMode	Property	Indicates how the image is displayed. Holds one of the PictureBoxSizeMode enumeration values—AutoSize (picture box is autosized to the image size), CenterImage (image is displayed in the center of the picture box), Normal (image is placed in the upper-left corner of the picture box), and StretchImage (image is stretched or reduced to fit the picture box size).

Step by Steps 2.8 and 2.16, later in this chapter, show good usage of `PictureBox` control.

The GroupBox and Panel Controls

`GroupBox` is a container control that contains other controls. It is mostly used to arrange controls and group similar controls. It does not include scrollbars. Table 2.6 summarizes the important members of the `GroupBox` class.

TABLE 2.6

IMPORTANT MEMBERS OF THE GroupBox CLASS

Member	Type	Description
Controls	Property	Specifies a collection of controls contained in a group box
Text	Property	Specifies a caption for a group box

Similar to `GroupBox`, `Panel` is a container control that contains other controls. It is mostly used to arrange controls and group similar controls. It has built-in support for scrollbars. You cannot provide a caption for the `Panel` control. Table 2.7 summarizes the important members of the `Panel` class.

TABLE 2.7

IMPORTANT MEMBERS OF THE Panel CLASS

Member	Type	Description
AutoScroll	Property	Indicates whether scrollbars should be displayed when the display of all the controls exceeds the area of a panel
Controls	Property	Specifies a collection of controls contained in a panel

STEP BY STEP

2.8 Using GroupBox and Panel Controls

1. Add a Windows form to existing project 316C02. Name the form StepByStep2_8.

2. Place on the form a Label control with the Text property set to Click button to open a picture file: and a Button control with the Text property set to Browse... and the Name property set to btnBrowse. Also, add to the form an OpenFileDialog control with the Name property set to ofdPicture.

3. Place a GroupBox control on the form and add three label controls to it. Name the three label controls lblSize, lblDateModified, and lblDateAccessed. Set the GroupBox control's Name property to grpFile and Text property to File Statistics.

4. Place a Panel control in the form and add a PictureBox control to it. Set the Panel control's Name property to pnlImage and AutoScroll property to true. Set the PictureBox control's Name property to pbImage and SizeMode property to AutoSize.

5. Switch to the code view and add the following using directive at the top of the program:

```
using System.IO;
```

6. Double-click the btnBrowse button to attach a Click event handler to it. Add the following code to the event handler:

```
private void btnBrowse_Click(
    object sender, System.EventArgs e)
{
    //Set filters for graphics files
    ofdPicture.Filter=
      "Image Files (BMP, GIF, JPEG, etc.)|" +
      "*.bmp;*.gif;*.jpg;*.jpeg;*.png;*.tif;*.tiff|" +
      "BMP Files (*.bmp)|*.bmp|" +
      "GIF Files (*.gif)|*.gif|" +
      "JPEG Files (*.jpg;*.jpeg)|*.jpg;*.jpeg|" +
      "PNG Files (*.png)|*.png|" +
      "TIF Files (*.tif;*.tiff)|*.tif;*.tiff|" +
      "All Files (*.*)|*.*";
    if(ofdPicture.ShowDialog() == DialogResult.OK)
    {
```

```
//Get file information
FileInfo file = new FileInfo(
    ofdPicture.FileName);
lblSize.Text = String.Format(
    "File Size: {0} Bytes",
    file.Length.ToString());
lblDateModified.Text = String.Format(
    "Date last modified: {0}",
    file.LastWriteTime.ToLongDateString());
lblDateAccessed.Text = String.Format(
    "Date last accessed: {0}",
    file.LastAccessTime.ToLongDateString());
//Load the file contents in the PictureBox
this.pbImage.Image = new Bitmap(
    ofdPicture.FileName);
    }
}
```

7. Insert the `Main()` method to launch form `StepByStep2_8`. Set this form as the startup object for the project.

8. Run the project. Click the Browse button. The Open dialog box prompts you to open an image file. Select an appropriate image file and click OK. The `Panel` control shows the image, and the `GroupBox` control shows the file statistics (see Figure 2.21). The `Panel` control includes scrollbars if the image size exceeds the panel area.

FIGURE 2.21
The `Panel` and `GroupBox` controls show the image and file statistics.

The Button, CheckBox, and RadioButton Controls

A `Button` object is used to initiate a specific action when a user clicks it. The `Button` class derives from the `ButtonBase` class. The `ButtonBase` class provides common functionality to the `Button`, `CheckBox`, and `RadioButton` classes.

In contrast to the `Button` class, `CheckBox` and `RadioButton` are used to maintain state. They can be on or off (that is, selected or not selected, checked or unchecked). These controls are generally used in groups. A `CheckBox` control allows you to select one or more options from a group of options, and a group of `RadioButton` controls are used to select one out of several mutually exclusive options. If you want to place two groups of `RadioButton` controls on a form and have each group allow one selection, you need to place them in different container controls, such as `GroupBox` or `Panel` controls, on the form.

These container controls, as discussed earlier in the chapter, are used to group controls that have similar functionality. The GroupBox control is a popular choice for grouping RadioButton controls.

Tables 2.8, 2.9, and 2.10 summarize the important members of the Button, CheckBox, and RadioButton classes, respectively.

TABLE 2.8

IMPORTANT MEMBERS OF THE Button CLASS

Member	Type	Description
Image	Property	Specifies the image displayed on a button.
Text	Property	Specifies the text displayed on a button.
Click	Event	Occurs when the Button control is clicked. Click is the default event for the Button class.

TABLE 2.9

IMPORTANT MEMBERS OF THE CheckBox CLASS

Member	Member	Description
Checked	Property	Returns true if the check box has been checked. Otherwise, it returns false.
CheckedChanged	Event	Occurs every time a check box is checked or unchecked. CheckedChanged is the default event for the CheckBox class
CheckState	Property	Specifies the state of the check box. Its value is one of the three CheckState enumeration values: Checked, Unchecked, or Indeterminate.
ThreeState	Property	Indicates whether the check box allows three states: Checked, Unchecked, or Indeterminate. If it is set to false, CheckState can be set to Indeterminate only in code and not through the user interface.
Text	Property	Specifies the text displayed along with the check box.

EXAM TIP

A Checked Property Doesn't Always Indicate the Checked State If the ThreeState property of a CheckBox control is true, the Checked property returns true for Checked as well as for the Indeterminate check state. Therefore, the CheckState property should be used to determine the current state of the check state.

TABLE 2.10

IMPORTANT MEMBERS OF THE RadioButton CLASS

Member	Type	Description
Checked	Property	Indicates whether the radio button is selected. Returns true if the button is selected and false otherwise.
CheckedChanged	Event	Occurs every time the control is either selected or deselected. CheckedChanged is the default event of the RadioButton class.
Text	Property	Specifies the text displayed along with the radio button.

STEP BY STEP

2.9 Using CheckBox and RadioButton Controls

1. Add a Windows form to existing project 316C02. Name the form StepByStep2_9.

2. Add three GroupBox controls to the form. Change their Name properties to grpSampleText, grpEffects, and grpFontSize. To grpSampleText, add a Label control, and then add two CheckBox controls to grpEffects and three RadioButton controls to grpFontSize. Arrange the controls and change their Text properties as shown in Figure 2.22.

3. Change the Name property of the Label control to lblSampleText. Change the Name properties of the two CheckBox controls to cbStrikeout and cbUnderline. Change the Name properties of RadioButton controls to rb12Point, rb14Points, and rb16Points.

4. Double-click the CheckBox and RadioButton controls and add the following code to the default event handlers:

```
private void cbStrikeout_CheckedChanged(
    object sender, System.EventArgs e)
{
    //toggle the Strikeout FontStyle of lblSampleText
    lblSampleText.Font = new Font(
     lblSampleText.Font.Name, lblSampleText.Font.Size,
     lblSampleText.Font.Style ^ FontStyle.Strikeout);
}
```

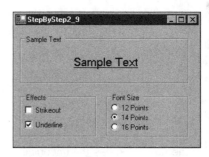

FIGURE 2.22

You use the CheckBox control to select a combination of options and the RadioButton control to select one of several mutually exclusive options.

NOTE

The AutoCheck Property When the AutoCheck property of a CheckBox or a RadioButton control is true, the Checked property (even the CheckState property, in the case of a CheckBox control) and the appearance of the control are automatically changed when the user clicks the control. You can set the AutoCheck property to false and then write code in the Click event handler to have these controls behave in a different manner.

continues

continued

<table>
<tr>
<td>

EXAM TIP

The FontStyle Enumeration and Bitwise Operations The FontStyle enumeration has a Flags attribute that allows bitwise operations on FontStyle values. For example, look at the following statement:

```
lblSampleText.Font.Style |
FontStyle.Underline
```

Here the | operator will turn on all the bits representing the Underline style, returning a FontStyle value that adds Underline to the existing font style of lblSampleText.

The following expression involves a bitwise exclusive OR (XOR) operation:

```
lblSampleText.Font.Style ^
FontStyle.Underline
```

This expression returns a FontStyle value that toggles the Underline font style of the label. If the label was already underlined, the new value has the underline removed; if the label was not under-lined already, the Underline bits are set in the new value.

The following expression involving a bitwise AND does not have any effect because using AND with 1 always returns the original value:

```
lblSampleText.Font.Style &
FontStyle.Underline
```

</td>
<td>

```csharp
private void cbUnderline_CheckedChanged(
    object sender, System.EventArgs e)
{
    //toggle the Underline FontStyle of lblSampleText
    lblSampleText.Font = new Font(
      lblSampleText.Font.Name, lblSampleText.Font.Size,
      lblSampleText.Font.Style ^ FontStyle.Underline);
}

private void rb12Points_CheckedChanged(
   object sender, System.EventArgs e)
{
    //Change the font size of lblSampleText to 12
    lblSampleText.Font = new Font(
      lblSampleText.Font.Name, 12,
      lblSampleText.Font.Style);
}

private void rb14Points_CheckedChanged(
   object sender, System.EventArgs e)
{
    //Change the font size of lblSampleText to 14
    lblSampleText.Font = new Font(
      lblSampleText.Font.Name, 14,
      lblSampleText.Font.Style);
}

private void rb16Points_CheckedChanged(
   object sender, System.EventArgs e)
{
    //Change the font size of lblSampleText to 16
    lblSampleText.Font = new Font(
      lblSampleText.Font.Name, 16,
      lblSampleText.Font.Style);
}
```

5. Insert a Main() method to launch the form StepByStep2_9. Set the form as the startup object for the project.

6. Run the project. Click the CheckBox controls, and you see that the font style of sample text changes. Then click the RadioButton controls, and you are able to select only one of three radio buttons, and when you click one, the CheckedChanged event handler immediately increases or decreases the font size (refer to Figure 2.22).

</td>
</tr>
</table>

The `ListBox`, `CheckedListBox`, and `ComboBox` Controls

A `ListBox` control allows you to select one or more values from a given list of values. It derives from the `ListControl` class, which provides common functionality for both the `ListBox` and `ComboBox` controls. Table 2.11 summarizes the important members of the `ListBox` class.

TABLE 2.11

IMPORTANT MEMBERS OF THE ListBox CLASS

Member	Type	Description
ColumnWidth	Property	Specifies the width of a column in a multi-column list box.
ItemHeight	Property	Specifies the height of an item in a list box.
Items	Property	Specifies a collection of objects representing the list of items in a list box.
FindString()	Method	Finds the first item in a list box that starts with the specified string.
FindStringExact()	Method	Finds the first item in a list box that exactly matches the specified string.
MultiColumn	Property	Indicates whether a list box supports multiple columns.
SelectedIndex	Property	Specifies an index of the currently selected item.
SelectedIndexChanged	Event	Occurs when the selected index property changes. `SelectedIndexChanged` is the default event for the `ListBox` class.
SelectedIndices	Property	Specifies a collection of indexes of the currently selected items.
SelectedItem	Property	Specifies a currently selected item.
SelectedItems	Property	Specifies a collection of currently selected items.

continues

TABLE 2.11	*continued*

IMPORTANT MEMBERS OF THE ListBox CLASS

Member	Type	Description
SelectionMode	Property	Indicates the number of items that can be selected. The values are specified by the SelectionMode enumeration and can be MultiSimple (allows multiple selections), MultiExtended (allows multiple selections, with the help of the Ctrl, Shift, and arrow keys), None (allows no selection), and One (allows a single selection).
Sorted	Property	Indicates whether the items in a list box are sorted alphabetically.

The CheckedListBox control derives from the ListBox control and inherits most of the features of the ListBox class. A CheckedListBox control displays a list of items to be selected, along with a check box for each item. The user selects an item by clicking the check box associated with the item. Because a CheckedListBox control contains check boxes, it implies that zero or more items can be selected from a CheckedListBox control. Table 2.12 summarizes important members of the CheckedListBox class.

NOTE

The SelectionMode Property of the CheckedListBox Class Unlike the ListBox class, the CheckedListBox class allows only two values of the SelectionMode enumeration for its SelectionMode property. The value None does not allow any selection, and the value One allows you to make zero or more selections. It is invalid to use the other values of the SelectionMode enumeration, such as MultiSimple and MultiExtended, with the SelectionMode property of the CheckedListBox control.

TABLE 2.12

IMPORTANT MEMBERS OF THE CheckedListBox CLASS

Member	Type	Description
CheckedIndices	Property	Specifies a collection of indexes of the currently checked items.
CheckedItems	Property	Specifies a collection of currently checked items.
ItemCheck	Event	Occurs when an item is checked or unchecked.
SelectionMode	Property	Indicates the number of items that can be checked. The values are specified by the SelectionMode enumeration and can be only None (allow no selection) or One (allow multiple selections).

STEP BY STEP

2.10 Using `ListBox` and `CheckedListBox` Controls

1. Add a Windows form to existing project 316C02. Name the form StepByStep2_10.

2. Add two `Label` controls, a `CheckedListBox` control, a `ListBox` control, and a `Button` control, and arrange them as shown in Figure 2.23. Change the `Label` control's Text properties to Select Scripts and Selected Scripts. Change the `Button` control's Name property to btnDone and change its Text property to Done.

3. Change the `ListBox` control's Text property to lbSelectedScripts and SelectionMode to MultiExtended. Name the `CheckedListBox` control clbScripts, select its Items property, and click the ellipsis (...) button. Add the following scripts in the String Collection Editor:

```
Latin
Greek
Cyrillic
Armenian
Hebrew
Arabic
Devanagari
Bengali
Gurmukhi
Gujarati
Oriya
Tamil
Telugu
Kannada
Malayalam
Thai
Lao
Georgian
Tibetan
Japanese Kana
```

4. Switch to the code view and add the following using directive:

```
using System.Text;
```

continues

continued

5. Invoke the Properties window and click the Events icon. Double-click the `ItemCheck` event to add an event handler for the event. Add the following code to the event handler:

```
private void clbScripts_ItemCheck(object sender,
    System.Windows.Forms.ItemCheckEventArgs e)
{
    //Get the item that was just checked or unchecked
    string item = clbScripts.SelectedItem.ToString();
    if (e.NewValue == CheckState.Checked)
        //Checked: Add to the ListBox
        lbSelectedScripts.Items.Add(item);
    else
        //Unchecked: Remove from the ListBox
        lbSelectedScripts.Items.Remove(item);
}
```

6. Double-click the `btnDone` control and add the following code to handle the `Click` event of the `Button` control:

```
private void btnDone_Click(
    object sender, System.EventArgs e)
{
    //Be sure to have a using directive for System.Text
    //at top of the program
    StringBuilder sbLanguages = new StringBuilder();
    if (lbSelectedScripts.SelectedItems.Count>0)
    {
        sbLanguages.Append("You Selected:\n\n");
        //If there were items selected in ListBox
        //create a string of their names
        foreach (string item in
            lbSelectedScripts.SelectedItems)
            sbLanguages.Append(item + "\n");
    }
    else
    {
        //No items selected
        sbLanguages.Append(
            "No items selected from ListBox");
    }
    MessageBox.Show(sbLanguages.ToString(),
        "Selection Status",
        MessageBoxButtons.OK,
        MessageBoxIcon.Information);
}
```

7. Insert the `Main()` method to launch the form `StepByStep2_10`. Set the form as the startup object for the project.

8. Run the project. Double-click the `CheckBox` control to select items from the `CheckedListBox` control. The selected scripts are then added to the `ListBox` control. Select some items from the `ListBox` control and then click the Done button. A message box is displayed, showing the selected scripts from the `ListBox` control (see Figure 2.23).

A `ComboBox` control is similar to a `ListBox` control, except that it has an editing field. A combo box appears with an editing text box with a down arrow at the right side of the box. When the down arrow is clicked, a drop-down list containing the predefined items to be displayed by the combo box appears. You can select only a single item from the combo box. A `ComboBox` control allows you to enter new text or select from the list of existing items in the combo box. Table 2.13 summarizes the important members of the `ComboBox` class with which you should be familiar.

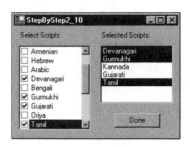

FIGURE 2.23
The `ListBox` and `CheckedListBox` controls allow the user to select a combination of values from a list of items.

TABLE 2.13

IMPORTANT MEMBERS OF THE ComboBox CLASS

Member	Type	Description
DrawMode	Property	Specifies how combo box items are drawn. It has one of the values from the `DrawMode` enumeration, `Normal`, which specifies that the list of items is drawn by the system itself. The other two values, `OwnerDrawFixed` and `OwnerDrawVariable`, specify that the elements are drawn by your own program (preferably in the `DrawItem` event handler). `OwnerDrawFixed` specifies that elements be of the same size, and `OwnerDrawVariable` specifies a variable size.

continues

TABLE 2.13	*continued*

IMPORTANT MEMBERS OF THE ComboBox CLASS

Member	Type	Description
DropDownStyle	Property	Represents the style of the combo box. Its values are specified by the DropDownStyle enumeration values DropDown (default style, click the arrow button to display the items, and the text portion is editable), DropDownList (click the arrow button to display the items, but the text portion is not editable), and Simple (no arrow button, the list portion is always visible, and the text portion is also editable).
DropDownWidth	Property	Specifies the width of the drop-down list portion of the combo box.
Items	Property	Specifies a collection of items in the combo box control.
MaxDropDownItems	Property	Represents the maximum number of items the drop-down list portion can display. If the number of items is greater than this property, a scrollbar appears.
MaxLength	Property	Indicates the maximum length of text allowed to be entered in the editable portion of the combo box.
SelectedIndex	Property	Specifies an index of the currently selected item.
SelectedIndexChanged	Event	Occurs when the SelectedIndex property changes. SelectedIndexChanged is the default event for the ComboBox class.
SelectedItem	Property	Specifies the currently selected item.
SelectedText	Property	Specifies the currently selected text in the editable portion.
Sorted	Property	Indicates whether the items are sorted alphabetically in the combo box.

EXAM TIP

The SelectedIndex Property The SelectedIndex property in the ListBox, CheckedListBox, and ComboBox controls returns –1 if no item is selected.

STEP BY STEP

2.11 Using ComboBox Controls

1. Add a Windows form to existing project 316C02. Name the form StepByStep2_11.

2. Place a Label control with the Text property Select or Enter a Color, a ComboBox control with the Name property cboColor, and a Button control with the Name property btnSet and the Text property Set Form's Back Color.

3. Change the ComboBox control's Sorted property to true and add the following scripts to the items collection via the String Collection Editor:

```
Violet
Indigo
Blue
Green
Yellow
Orange
Red
White
```

4. Double-click the btnSet control and add the following code to handle the Click event of the Button control:

```csharp
private void btnSet_Click(
    object sender, System.EventArgs e)
{
    this.BackColor = Color.FromName(cboColor.Text);
}
```

5. Insert a Main() method to launch the form StepByStep2_11. Set the form as the startup object for the project.

6. Run the project. Select a color from the list of colors in the combo box or enter a new color in the combo box. Click the button. The form's background color is changed to the color that is selected or entered in the combo box. Figure 2.24 shows the output when a desired color is entered in the combo box and the button is clicked.

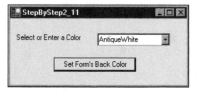

FIGURE 2.24

The ComboBox control allows you to either select from a list or enter new text.

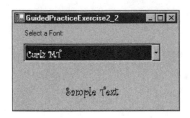

FIGURE 2.25
You can create an owner-drawn `ComboBox` control by programming the `DrawItem` event handler.

GUIDED PRACTICE
EXERCISE 2.2

Some Windows-based applications use sophisticated combo boxes that have rich user interfaces that can display things such as images and text in various fonts. Ever wonder how you would do such customization in applications?

In this exercise you will create the Windows form shown in Figure 2.25. The idea is to create a font sampler such as those used by many word processing applications. The form contains a combo box that displays a list of fonts installed on the system. But the interesting thing here is that the items in the combo box are displayed in their respective fonts. The form also contains a label control that displays a sample of the font that the user chooses from the combo box.

This exercise gives you practice on working with controls that have customized rendering. If you are looking for a starting point, try experimenting with the `DrawMode` property and the `DrawItem` event of the `ComboBox` control and then proceed with this exercise. You should try working through this problem on your own first. If you get stuck, or if you'd like to see one possible solution, follow these steps:

1. Add a new form to your Visual C# .NET project. Name the form `GuidedPracticeExercise2_2.cs`.

2. Place two `Label` controls on the form—one with the `Text` property `Select a Font` and the other with the `Name` property `lblSampleText`, the `Text` property `Sample Text`, and the `Font` property `Microsoft Sans Serif, Regular, 14`.

3. Place a `ComboBox` control on the form. Change the `Name` property to `cboFont`, change `DrawMode` to `OwnerDrawVariable`, and change `DropDownStyle` to `DropDownList`.

4. Double-click the form and add the following code to handle the `Load` event of the form:

```
private void GuidedPracticeExercise2_2_Load(
    object sender, System.EventArgs e)
{
    //Add a list of System Fonts to ComboBox
    cboFont.Items.AddRange(FontFamily.Families);
}
```

5. Add the following code in the code view:

```
private FontStyle GetFontStyle(FontFamily ff)
{
    FontStyle fontStyle = FontStyle.Regular;
    // Check whether Regular style is available
    if (!ff.IsStyleAvailable(FontStyle.Regular))
        fontStyle = FontStyle.Italic;
    // Check whether Italic style is available
    if (!ff.IsStyleAvailable(FontStyle.Italic))
        fontStyle = FontStyle.Bold;
    return fontStyle;
}
```

6. Invoke the Properties window, click the Events icon, select the
DrawItem event, and double-click to add an event handler to
DrawItem. Add the following code to the event handler:

```
// This DrawItem event handler is invoked
// to draw an item in a ComboBox if that
// ComboBox is in an OwnerDraw DrawMode.
private void cboFont_DrawItem(object sender,
    System.Windows.Forms.DrawItemEventArgs e)
{
    ComboBox cboFont = (ComboBox) sender;
    // do nothing if there is no data
    if (e.Index == -1)
        return;
    if (sender == null)
        return;

    //Make a FontFamily object from the name
    //of the font currently being drawn
    FontFamily fontFamily =
        (FontFamily) cboFont.Items[e.Index];

    // Create a Font object that will be used
    // to draw the text in ComboBox
    Font font  = new Font(fontFamily.Name, 12,
      GetFontStyle(fontFamily));

    // If the item is selected,
    // draw the correct background color
    e.DrawBackground();
    e.DrawFocusRectangle();

    // DrawItemEventArgs gives access to
    // the ComboBox Graphics object
    Graphics g = e.Graphics;

    // Draw the name of the font in the same font
    g.DrawString(fontFamily.Name, font,
      new SolidBrush(e.ForeColor),
      e.Bounds.X, e.Bounds.Y+4);
}
```

continues

continued

7. Double-click the combo box and add the following code to handle the `SelectedIndexChanged` event of the `ComboBox` control:

```
private void cboFont_SelectedIndexChanged(
    object sender, System.EventArgs e)
{
    // Get the FontFamily object for
    // current ComboBox selection
    FontFamily fontFamily =
        (FontFamily)((ComboBox) sender).SelectedItem;
    // Create a Font object and draw the Font Name
    lblSampleText.Font = new Font(fontFamily.Name,
    lblSampleText.Font.Size, GetFontStyle(fontFamily));
}
```

8. Insert the `Main()` method to launch the form and set the form as the startup object for the project.

9. Run the project. The combo box displays all the available fonts, drawn in their own fonts. The label's text is also updated to display the text in the selected font (refer to Figure 2.25).

If you have difficulty following this exercise, review the section "The `ListBox`, `CheckedListBox` and `ComboBox` Controls," earlier in this chapter. After doing that review, try this exercise again

---

REVIEW BREAK

▶ The `LinkLabel` control is derived from the `Label` control. It allows you to add links to a control. The `Links` property of the `LinkLabel` control contains a collection of all the links referenced by the control.

▶ You can display a `TextBox` control as an ordinary text box, a password text box (in which each character is masked by the character provided in the `PasswordChar` property), or a multiline text box by setting the `TextBox` control's `MultiLine` property to `true`. The `RichTextBox` control provides enriched formatting capabilities to a text box control. It can also be drawn as a single-line or multiline text box. By default, it has its `MultiLine` property set to `true`, unlike the `TextBox` control.

▶ GroupBox and Panel controls are container controls. They can be used to group similar controls. The Controls property of these controls contains a collection of the controls' child controls.

▶ The CheckBox control allows multiple check boxes to be checked from a group of check boxes, and a RadioButton control allows only one radio button to be selected from a group of mutually exclusive radio buttons.

▶ The CheckBox control can allow you to set three check states—Checked, Unchecked, and Indeterminate—if the ThreeState property is set to true.

▶ The ComboBox control allows you to select a value from a list of predefined values or to enter a value in the combo box. The ListBox control allows you to select a value from a list of values displayed.

▶ The CheckedListBox control derives from the ListBox control and inherits its functionality. However, a CheckedListBox control displays a check box along with a list of items to be checked. It allows only two selection modes: None (allows no selection) and One (allows multiple selections).

The DomainUpDown and NumericUpDown Controls

The DomainUpDown and NumericUpDown controls inherit from the System.Windows.Forms.UpDownBase class. You use them to select values from the (generally) ordered collection of values by pressing the control's up and down buttons. You can also enter values in these controls, unless the ReadOnly property is set to true.

The DomainUpDown control allows you to select from a collection of objects. When an item is selected, the object is converted to String and is displayed. If you want a control that displays numeric values, you instead use the NumericUpDown control. Table 2.14 summarizes the important members of the DomainUpDown class.

TABLE 2.14

IMPORTANT MEMBERS OF THE DomainUpDown CLASS

Member	Type	Description
Items	Property	Represents a collection of objects assigned to a control.
ReadOnly	Property	Indicates whether you can change the value in a way other than by pressing the up and down buttons.
SelectedIndex	Property	Specifies the index value of the selected item in the items collection.
SelectedItem	Property	Specifies the value of the selected item.
SelectedItemChanged	Event	Occurs when the SelectedIndex property is changed. SelectedItemChanged is the default event of the DomainUpDown class.
Sorted	Property	Indicates whether the items collection is sorted.
Wrap	Property	Indicates whether the SelectedIndex property resets to the first or the last item if the user continues past either end of the list.

The NumericUpDown control contains a single numeric value that can be increased or decreased when you click the up or down buttons of the control. You can specify the Minimum, Maximum, or Increment value to control the range of values in this control. Table 2.15 summarizes the important members of the NumericUpDown class.

TABLE 2.15

IMPORTANT MEMBERS OF THE NumericUpDown CLASS

Member	Type	Description
Increment	Property	Indicates to increase or decrease the Value property by the specified amount when the up or down button is clicked
Maximum	Property	Specifies the maximum allowed value
Minimum	Property	Specifies the minimum allowed value

Member	Type	Description
ReadOnly	Property	Indicates whether you can change the value in a way other than by pressing the up and down buttons
ThousandsSeparator	Property	Indicates whether the thousands separator should be used when appropriate
Value	Property	Specifies a value assigned to a control
ValueChanged	Event	Occurs when the Value property is changed. ValueChanged is the default event of the NumericUpDown class.

STEP BY STEP

2.12 Using DomainUpDown and NumericUpDown Controls

1. Add a Windows form to existing project 316C02. Name the form StepByStep2_12.

2. Add three Label controls, one DomainUpDown control, and one NumericUpDown control to the form and arrange them as shown in Figure 2.26.

3. Name the DomainUpDown control dudColor. Set its Text property to Black, UpDownAlign property to Left, and Wrap property to true. Select its Items property and click the ellipsis (...) button. In the String Collection Editor add the following values:

Violet
Indigo
Blue
Green
Yellow
Orange
Red
Black
White

4. Name the NumericUpDown control nudSize. Set its Maximum property to 30, Minimum to 2, Increment to 2 , Value to 12, and ReadOnly to true.

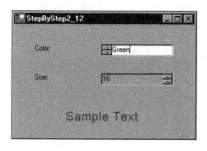

FIGURE 2.26
The DomainUpDown and NumericUpDown controls allow the user to select a value from a given list of values, by clicking up or down buttons or by directly entering a value.

continues

continued

5. Name the `Label` placed at the bottom of the form `lblSampleText`, and then change its `Text` property to `Sample Text` and its `TextAlign` property to `MiddleCenter`.

6. Attach the event handlers to the default events of the `DomainUpDown` and `NumericUpDown` controls. Add the following code to the event handlers:

```
private void dudColor_SelectedItemChanged(
    object sender, System.EventArgs e)
{
    //Typecast the object to DomainUpDown
    DomainUpDown dudColor = (DomainUpDown) sender;
    //Change color of lblsampleText to selected color
    lblSampleText.ForeColor =
        Color.FromName(dudColor.Text);
}

private void nudSize_ValueChanged(
    object sender, System.EventArgs e)
{
    //Typecast the object to NumericUpDown
    NumericUpDown nudSize = (NumericUpDown) sender;
    //Change the font of lblSampleText to selected font
    lblSampleText.Font = new Font(
        lblSampleText.Font.FontFamily,
        (float) nudSize.Value);
}
```

7. Insert the `Main()` method to launch form `StepByStep2_12`. Set the form as the startup object for the project.

8. Run the project. Click the up and down buttons of the `UpDown` controls. Their respective event handlers are fired and change the appearance of the `Text` property of the `lblSampleText` control (refer to Figure 2.26). You can enter a desired color in the `DomainUpDown` control because its `ReadOnly` property is `false`.

The `MonthCalendar` and `DateTimePicker` Controls

The `MonthCalendar` control provides a user-friendly interface to select a date or a range of dates. Table 2.16 summarizes the important members of the `MonthCalendar` class with which you should be familiar.

TABLE 2.16

IMPORTANT MEMBERS OF THE MonthCalendar CLASS

Member	Type	Description
CalendarDimensions	Property	Specifies the number of columns and rows of months to display.
DateChanged	Event	Occurs when the date that is selected in the control changes. DateChanged is the default event of the MonthCalendar class.
DateSelected	Event	Occurs when a date is selected in the control.
FirstDayOfWeek	Property	Represents the first day of the week displayed in the calendar.
MaxDate	Property	Specifies the latest allowable date that can be selected.
MaxSelectionCount	Property	Specifies the maximum number of days that can be selected.
MinDate	Property	Specifies the earliest allowable date that can be selected.
SelectionEnd	Property	Specifies the end date of the selected range of dates.
SelectionRange	Property	Specifies the selected range of dates.
SelectionStart	Property	Specifies the start date of the selected range of dates.
ShowToday	Property	Indicates whether today's date should be displayed in the bottom of the control.
ShowTodayCircle	Property	Indicates whether today's date should be circled.
ShowWeekNumbers	Property	Indicates whether the week numbers (1–52) should be displayed at the beginning of each row of days.
TodayDate	Property	Represents today's date.

The DateTimePicker control allows the user to select the date and time in different formats. The Format property determines the format in which the control displays the date and time. You can also use the DateTimePicker control to display a custom date/time format by setting the Format property to DateTimePickerFormat.Custom and the CustomFormat property to the custom format desired. Table 2.17 summarizes the important members of the DateTimePicker class.

TABLE 2.17

IMPORTANT MEMBERS OF THE DateTimePicker CLASS

Member	Type	Description
CustomFormat	Property	Represents the custom date/time format string.
Format	Property	Specifies the format of the date and time that are displayed in the control. The values are specified by the DateTimePickerFormat enumeration—Custom, Long (the default), Short, and Time. Long, Short, and Time display the date in the value formats set by the operating system. The Custom value lets you specify a custom format.
FormatChanged	Event	Occurs when the Format property changes.
MaxDate	Property	Specifies the latest allowable date and time to be selected.
MinDate	Property	Specifies the soonest allowable date and time to be selected.
ShowCheckBox	Property	Indicates whether the check box should be displayed to the left of the selected date.
ShowUpDown	Property	Indicates whether an UpDown control, rather than the default calendar control, should be displayed to allow the user to make selections.
Value	Property	Represents the value of the date and time selected.
ValueChanged	Event	Occurs when the Value property changes. ValueChanged is the default event of the DateTimePicker class.

STEP BY STEP

2.13 Using MonthCalendar and DateTimePicker Controls

1. Add a Windows form to existing project 316C02. Name the form StepByStep2_13.

2. Place three `Label` controls, one `MonthCalendar` control (`mcTravelDates`), one `DateTimePicker` control (`dtpLaunchDate`), and two `RadioButton` controls (`rbLongDate` and `rbShortDate`) on the form and arrange them as shown in Figure 2.27. Name the `Label` control that is placed adjacent to the `MonthCalendar` control `lblTravelDates`.

3. Switch to the code view and add the following `using` directive:

```
using System.Text;
```

4. Add an event handler for the `DateSelected` event for the `MonthCalendar` control. Add the following code to the event handler:

```
private void mcTravelDates_DateSelected(object sender,
    System.Windows.Forms.DateRangeEventArgs e)
{
    StringBuilder sbMessage = new StringBuilder();
    sbMessage.Append("StartDate:\n");
    sbMessage.Append(e.Start.ToShortDateString());
    sbMessage.Append("\n\nEnd Date:\n");
    sbMessage.Append(e.End.ToShortDateString());
    this.lblTravelDates.Text = sbMessage.ToString();
}
```

5. Attach the event handlers to the default events of the `RadioButton` controls. Add the following code to the event handlers:

```
private void rbLongDate_CheckedChanged(
    object sender, System.EventArgs e)
{
    if(rbLongDate.Checked)
        dtpLaunchDate.Format =
          DateTimePickerFormat.Long;
}

private void rbShortDate_CheckedChanged(
    object sender, System.EventArgs e)
{
    if(rbShortDate.Checked)
        dtpLaunchDate.Format =
          DateTimePickerFormat.Short;
}
```

6. Insert a `Main()` method to launch form `StepByStep2_13`. Set the form as the startup object for the project.

continues

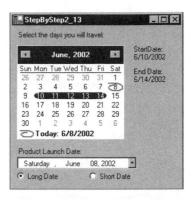

FIGURE 2.27

You can perform date selections using the `MonthCalendar` and `DateTimePicker` controls.

continued

7. Run the project. Select a range of dates from the MonthCalendar control and a date from the DateTimePicker control. The label adjacent to the MonthCalendar control displays the start date and end date from the range of the dates selected (refer to Figure 2.27). You can also change the format of the date shown by the DateTimePicker control by selecting radio buttons.

The TreeView and ListView Controls

The TreeView control is used to display a hierarchical collection of nodes. Each node represents a TreeNode object that can further have a collection of nodes, thereby forming a hierarchical structure. Table 2.18 summarizes the important members of the TreeView class.

TABLE 2.18

IMPORTANT MEMBERS OF THE TreeView CLASS

Member	Type	Description
AfterCheck	Event	Occurs after the tree node is checked.
AfterCollapse	Event	Occurs after the tree node is collapsed.
AfterExpand	Event	Occurs after the tree node is expanded.
AfterSelect	Event	Occurs after the tree node is selected. AfterSelect is the default event for the TreeView class.
CheckBoxes	Property	Indicates whether a check box should appear along with each item in the control.
ImageList	Property	Represents the ImageList control that contains node icons.
Nodes	Property	Specifies the collection of tree nodes in the control.
Scrollable	Property	Indicates whether the scrollbars need to be displayed when needed. The default value is true.
SelectedNode	Property	Represents the selected node.
Sorted	Property	Indicates whether the tree nodes are sorted.

The ListView control is used to display a list of items. Each item in the list usually has name of the item and an optional icon corresponding to it.

Table 2.19 summarizes important members of ListView class.

TABLE 2.19

IMPORTANT MEMBERS OF THE ListView CLASS

Member	Type	Description
Activation	Property	Indicates how an item can be activated—OneClick (single-click), Standard (double-click), and TwoClick (double-click and the item color changes when the mouse hovers over it). These values are defined in the ItemActivation enumeration.
CheckBoxes	Property	Indicates whether the check box should appear along with each item in the control.
CheckedIndices	Property	Specifies a collection of indexes of the currently checked items.
CheckedItems	Property	Specifies a collection of currently checked items.
ItemActivate	Event	Occurs when the item is activated.
ItemCheck	Event	Occurs when the item's check state changes.
Items	Property	Specifies a collection of items displayed by the ListView control.
LargeImageList	Property	Represents the ImageList control to be used to display large icons.
MultiSelect	Property	Indicates whether multiple items can be selected.
Scrollable	Property	Indicates whether the scrollbars need to be added when the items exceed the size of the client area. The default value is true.
SelectedIndexChanged	Event	Occurs when the selected index changes. SelectedIndexChanged is the default event of the ListView class.
SelectedIndices	Property	Specifies a collection of indexes of the currently selected items.

continues

TABLE 2.19	*continued*	

IMPORTANT MEMBERS OF THE ListView CLASS

Member	Type	Description
SelectedItems	Property	Specifies a collection of currently selected items.
SmallImageList	Property	Represents the ImageList control to be used to display small icons.
Sorting	Property	Represents the sort order of items in the control, from the SortOrder enumeration—Ascending, Descending, and None (the default).
View	Property	Represents the way items are displayed. The values are specified by the View enumeration—Details (items are displayed with multicolumn information about the item), LargeIcon (default value; item appears with a large icon, along with a label below it in multiple columns), List (single-column list in which a small icon is displayed with a label on its right), and SmallIcon (small icon with a label on the right, displayed in multiple columns).

The familiar interface of Windows Explorer uses both a tree view and a list view to present the folders and folder contents in its left and right panes, respectively. Step by Step 2.14 provides a similar functionality but on a smaller scale.

STEP BY STEP

2.14 Using TreeView and ListView Controls

1. Add a Windows form to existing project 316C02. Name the form StepByStep2_14.

2. Place a TreeView control (tvwDirectories), a ListView control (lvwFiles), and an ImageList (ilSmallIcons) control on the form. The ImageList control is added to the component tray.

3. Change the `ColorDepth` property to `Depth8Bit`. Select the `Images` property and click the ellipsis (...) button. This invokes the Image Collection Editor. Click the Add button. An Open File dialog box appears. Select a small icon image to represent items in a list view and click Open. The file is added to the Members list box in the Image Collection Editor, along with its index, as shown in Figure 2.28. Click OK to close the Image Collection Editor.

4. Change the `View` property of the `ListView` control to `List` and change the `SmallImageList` property to `ilSmallIcons`.

5. Switch to the code view and add the following line to the using directive:

```
using System.Text;
```

6. Attach the event handlers to the default events of the `TreeView` and `Form` controls. Add the following code in the code view:

```
private void StepByStep2_14_Load(
    object sender, System.EventArgs e)
{
    tvwDirectories.Nodes.Add("C:\\");
    //Load tree view with C: drive contents
    RefreshTreeView("C:\\", tvwDirectories.Nodes[0]);
}

private void tvwDirectories_AfterSelect(object sender,
    System.Windows.Forms.TreeViewEventArgs e)
{
    //Load tree view with subdirectories
    //of current selection
    RefreshTreeView(e.Node.Text, e.Node);
    //Load list view with files of current selection
    RefreshListView(e.Node.Text);
}

public void RefreshTreeView(
    string strDir, TreeNode tnRoot)
{
    //Get directory information
    string[] strDirArray =
        Directory.GetDirectories(strDir);
    if (strDirArray.Length != 0)
    {
        //Populate tree view coptrol with all
        // subdirectories in the current directory
        foreach (string dir in strDirArray)
        {
```

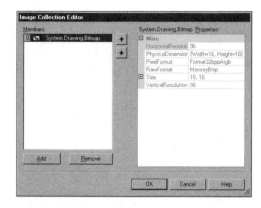

FIGURE 2.28
You can add images to an `ImageList` control by using the Image Collection Editor.

continues

continued

```
                        TreeNode tnNode = new TreeNode(dir);
                        tnRoot.Nodes.Add(tnNode);
                }
            }
        }

        public void RefreshListView(string strDir)
        {
            lvwFiles.Items.Clear();
            //Get file information
            FileInfo[] files =
              new DirectoryInfo(strDir).GetFiles();
            //Populate list view with all files
            // in the current directory
            foreach (FileInfo file in files)
            {
                ListViewItem newFile =
                    lvwFiles.Items.Add(file.Name);
                newFile.ImageIndex = 0;
            }
        }
```

7. Insert the Main() method to launch form StepByStep2_14. Set the form as the startup object for the project.

8. Run the project. The c:\ node is displayed in a tree view and the files contained in the c:\ folder are displayed in a list view. Click c:\, and notice that you are able to move through the directory structure of your c: drive in a tree view. Also notice that after you select a folder in the tree view, the list view is updated with the selected folder files (see Figure 2.29).

FIGURE 2.29

You can use the TreeView and ListView controls to partly mimic the functionality of Windows Explorer.

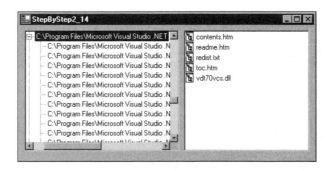

Step by Step 2.14 includes an `ImageList` component that is used to store a list of images that can be used by other Windows forms controls (for example, `ListView`). The `Images` property of the `ImageList` component is a collection that stores the list of images, and the `ImageIndex` property provides an index to those images.

The `Timer` Component and `TrackBar` and `ProgressBar` Controls

The `Timer` component is used when an event needs to be generated at user-defined intervals. Table 2.20 summarizes the important members of the `Timer` class.

TABLE 2.20

IMPORTANT MEMBERS OF THE Timer CLASS

Member	Type	Description
Enabled	Property	Indicates whether the timer is currently running.
Interval	Property	Represents the time, in milliseconds, between ticks of the timer.
Start()	Method	Starts the Timer component.
Stop()	Method	Stops the Timer component.
Tick	Event	Occurs when the timer interval elapses and the timer is enabled.

A `TrackBar` control provides an intuitive way to select a value from a given range by providing a scroll box and a scale of value. The user can slide the scroll box on the scale to point to the desired value. Table 2.21 summarizes the important members of the `TrackBar` class.

TABLE 2.21

IMPORTANT MEMBERS OF THE TrackBar CLASS

Member	Type	Description
LargeChange	Property	Indicates the number of ticks by which the Value property changes when the scroll box is moved a large distance.

continues

EXAM TIP

`System.Windows.Forms.Timer` **Versus** `System.Timers.Timer`   You should always use the `Timer` class from the `System.Windows.Forms` namespace in Windows Forms because this class is optimized to work with forms. The `System.Timers.Timer` class fires `Tick` events from another thread and may cause indeterminate results in applications.

TABLE 2.21	*continued*

IMPORTANT MEMBERS OF THE TrackBar CLASS

Member	Type	Description
Maximum	Property	Specifies the upper bound of the TrackBar control's range.
Minimum	Property	Specifies the lower bound of the TrackBar control's range.
Orientation	Property	Represents the horizontal or vertical orientation of the control.
Scroll	Event	Occurs when the scroll box is moved by a keyboard or mouse action. Scroll is the default event for the TrackBar class.
SmallChange	Property	Indicates the number of ticks by which the Value property changes when the scroll box is moved a small distance.
TickFrequency	Property	Represents the frequency within which ticks are drawn in the control.
TickStyle	Property	Represents the way the control appears. The values are specified by the TickStyle enumeration—Both, BottomRight, None, and TopLeft.
Value	Property	Represents the scroll box's current position in the control.
ValueChanged	Property	Occurs when the Value property changes via the Scroll event or programmatically.

A ProgressBar control is usually displayed to indicate the status of a lengthy operation such as installing an application, copying files, or printing documents. Table 2.22 summarizes the important members of the ProgressBar class.

TABLE 2.22

IMPORTANT MEMBERS OF THE ProgressBar CLASS

Member	Type	Description
Maximum	Property	Specifies the upper bound of the progress bar's range.
Minimum	Property	Specifies the lower bound of the progress bar's range.
Value	Property	Represents the current position of the control.

Step by Step 2.15 gives an example of using the TrackBar and ProgressBar controls. The example simulates a lengthy operation with the help of a Timer component. You can control the speed with which the process works by using a TrackBar control that changes the Interval property of the Timer component to set the time at which it will generate Tick events.

STEP BY STEP

2.15 Using the Timer Component and TrackBar and ProgressBar Controls

1. Add a Windows form to existing project 316C02. Name the form StepByStep2_15.

2. Place a Timer component on the form. This component is added to the component tray. Name the Timer component tmrTimer and set its Enabled property to true.

3. Place four Label controls, one ProgressBar control, and one TrackBar control on the form and arrange them as shown in Figure 2.30.

4. Name the ProgressBar control prgIndicator and the TrackBar control trkSpeed. For the TrackBar control, change the Maximum property to 1000, TickFrequency to 100, TickStyle to Top,Left, and Value to 100.

5. Name a Label control lblMessage. Change the label's Size - Height property to 1 and BorderStyle property to Fixed3D, to represent it as a line.

6. Double-click the Timer component and TrackBar control to attach default event handlers to their default events— Tick and Scroll, respectively. Add the following code to the event handlers:

```
private void tmrTimer_Tick(
    object sender, System.EventArgs e)
{
    if (prgIndicator.Value < prgIndicator.Maximum)
        //Increase the progress indicator
        prgIndicator.Value += 5;
    else
```

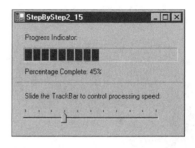

FIGURE 2.30
The Timer component updates the progress bar on every tick, and the TrackBar control controls the interval of Tick events for the Timer component.

No Line and Shape Controls Unlike in earlier versions of Visual Studio, you won't find any Line or Shape control in Visual Studio .NET. This is because all controls in the Visual Studio .NET toolbox must be windowed. The Line and Shape controls are window-less, and hence they were removed. What can you do about it? For drawing a simple line, you can use a Label control in which you can set the Height property to 1 (or more, if you want a thicker line) and set the BorderStyle property. For more advanced lines and shapes, you can use powerful GDI+ classes that are available in the Windows Forms library (refer to Chapter 1 for discussion on the System.Drawing namespace).

continues

continued

```
        //Reset the progress bar indicator
        prgIndicator.Value = prgIndicator.Minimum;
    lblMessage.Text = "Percentage Complete: " +
        prgIndicator.Value + "%";
}

private void trkSpeed_Scroll(
    object sender, System.EventArgs e)
{
    TrackBar trkSpeed = (TrackBar) sender;
    if (trkSpeed.Value >= 1)
        //Set timer value based on user's selection
        tmrTimer.Interval = trkSpeed.Value;
}
```

7. Insert the `Main()` method to launch form `StepByStep2_15`. Set the form as the startup object for the project.

8. Run the project. Slide the `TrackBar` control, and the progress bar progresses at different speeds, depending on the time interval set by the `TrackBar` control (refer to Figure 2.30).

The **HScrollBar** and **VScrollBar** Controls

The `HScrollBar` and `VScrollBar` controls display horizontal and vertical scrollbars, respectively. The `HScrollBar` and `VScrollBar` classes inherit their properties and other members from the `ScrollBar` class, which provides the basic scrolling functionality.

Usually, controls such as `Panel`, `TextBox`, and `ComboBox` include their own scrollbars. But some controls, such as `PictureBox`, do not have built-in scrollbars. You can use `HScrollBar` and `VScrollBar` to associate scrollbars with such controls. Table 2.23 summarizes the important members of `ScrollBar` class, from which the `HScrollBar` and `VScrollBar` controls inherit.

TABLE 2.23

IMPORTANT MEMBERS OF THE ScrollBar CLASS

Member	Type	Description
LargeChange	Property	Indicates the number by which the Value property changes when the scroll box is moved a large distance.
Maximum	Property	Specifies the upper bound of the scrollbar's range.
Minimum	Property	Specifies the lower bound of the scrollbar's range.
Scroll	Event	Occurs when the scroll box is moved by a keyboard or mouse action. Scroll is the default event for the ScrollBar class.
SmallChange	Property	Indicates the number by which the Value property changes when the scroll box is moved a small distance.
Value	Property	Represents the current position of the control.
ValueChanged	Event	Occurs when the Value property changes either via the Scroll event or programmatically.

STEP BY STEP

2.16 Using HScrollBar and VScrollBar Controls

1. Add a Windows form to existing project 316C02. Name the form StepByStep2_16.

2. Place a PictureBox control, an HScrollBar control, and a VScrollBar control on the form. Name the PictureBox control pbImage and set the SizeMode property to AutoSize. Select the Image property and click the ellipsis (...) button. This causes an Open File dialog box to appear. Select the image you want to have uploaded in the form.

3. Name the HScrollBar control hScroll and set its Dock property to Bottom. Change the Name property of the VScrollBar control to vScroll and set its Dock property to Right.

continues

continued

4. Double-click the HScrollBar and VScrollBar controls to attach event handlers to their default Scroll events. Add the following code to the event handlers:

```
private void vScroll_Scroll(object sender,
    System.Windows.Forms.ScrollEventArgs e)
{
    //Scroll the image vertically
    pbImage.Top = vScroll.Bottom - pbImage.Height -
        (int)getVScrollAdjustment();
}
private float getVScrollAdjustment()
{
    //Calculate vertical scroll bar changes
    float vPos =
        (float)(vScroll.Value - vScroll.Minimum);
    float vDiff =
        (float)(vScroll.Height - pbImage.Height);
    float vTicks =
        (float)(vScroll.Maximum - vScroll.Minimum);
    return (vDiff/vTicks)*vPos;
}

private void hScroll_Scroll(object sender,
    System.Windows.Forms.ScrollEventArgs e)
{
    //Scroll the image horizontally
    pbImage.Left = hScroll.Right - pbImage.Width -
        (int)getHScrollAdjustment();
}
private float getHScrollAdjustment()
{
    //Calculate horizontal scrollbar changes
    float hPos =
        (float)(hScroll.Value - hScroll.Minimum);
    float hDiff =
        (float)(hScroll.Width - pbImage.Width);
    float hTicks =
        (float)(hScroll.Maximum - hScroll.Minimum);

    return (hDiff/hTicks)*hPos;
}
```

5. Insert the Main() method to launch form StepByStep2_16. Set the form as the startup object for the project.

6. Run the project. The form displays the image, and the scrollbars that are on the right and bottom can be used to scroll through the image if the image size exceeds the allotted space, as in Figure 2.31.

FIGURE 2.31
The HScrollBar and VScrollBar classes allow you to implement scrolling functionality in an application.

The `TabControl` Control

The `TabControl` control displays a collection of tabbed pages. Each tabbed page can contain its own controls. The `TabControl` control can be useful in organizing large number of controls because when the controls are organized into various tabbed pages they occupy less space on the form. Tabbed pages appear mostly in wizards and IDEs. For example, the Visual Studio .NET IDE displays all the open files in tabbed pages. Table 2.24 summarizes the important members of the `TabControl` class.

TABLE 2.24

IMPORTANT MEMBERS OF THE TabControl CLASS

Member	Type	Description
Alignment	Property	Represents the area where the tabs will be aligned—`Bottom`, `Left`, `Right`, or `Top` (the default).
ImageList	Property	Represents the `ImageList` control from which images are displayed on tabs.
MultiLine	Property	Indicates whether tabs can be displayed in multiple rows.
SelectedIndex	Property	Represents the index of the selected tabbed page.
SelectedIndexChanged	Event	Occurs, when the selected index changes. `SelectedIndexChanged` is the default event of the `TabControl` class.
SelectedTab	Property	Specifies the selected tabbed page.
TabCount	Property	Specifies a count of the tabs in a control.
TabPages	Property	Specifies a collection of tabbed pages in a control.

Step by Step 2.17 displays a `TabControl` control to build a message box by accepting the values for the caption and the message in one tab page, the message box buttons in the second tab page, and the icon to be displayed in the third tab page.

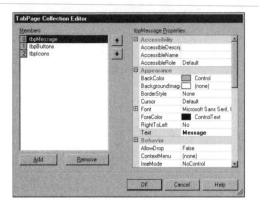

FIGURE 2.32
You can use the TabPage Collection Editor to add tab pages to a `TabControl` control.

STEP BY STEP

2.17 Using `TabControl` Controls

1. Add a Windows form to existing project 316C02. Name the form StepByStep2_17.

2. Place a `TabControl` control (tabDemo) on the form. Select the `TabPages` property and click the ellipsis (...) button. This invokes the TabPage Collection Editor. Click the Add button and a `TabPage` control is added to the collection, with its index. Name the `TabPage` control tbpMessage and change its `Text` property to `Message`. Add two more `TabPage` controls: tbpButtons with `Text` property `Buttons` and tbpIcons with `Text` property `Icons`. Figure 2.32 shows the TabPage Collection editor after you add the tab pages. Click OK to close the TabPage Collection Editor.

3. Place two `Label` controls and two `TextBox` controls (txtMessage and txtCaption) on the Message tab page, five `RadioButton` controls (rbOK, rbOKCCancel, rbRetryCancel, rbYesNo, and rbYesNoCancel) on the Buttons tab page, and five `RadioButton` controls (rbError, rbInformation, rbNone, rbQuestion, and rbWarning) on the Icons tab page. Place a `GroupBox` control on the form and four `RadioButton` controls (rbLeft, rbRight, rbTop, and rbBottom) inside it. Place a `Button` control (btnShow) on the form. Arrange all the controls and set their `Text` properties as shown in Figure 2.33.

4. Switch to the code view and add the following code before the constructor definition:

```
private MessageBoxButtons mbbButtons;
private MessageBoxIcon mbiIcon;
```

5. Add the following code in the constructor:

```
public StepByStep2_17()
{
    //
    // Required for Windows Forms Designer support
    //
    InitializeComponent();
```

```
        //Initial setting for MessageBox button
        mbbButtons = MessageBoxButtons.OK;
        //Initial setting for MessageBox icon
        mbiIcon = MessageBoxIcon.Information;
}
```

6. Add the following code in the code view:

```
//This event handler is used by the RadioButtons
//that control TabControl's alignment
private void rbAlign_CheckedChanged(
    object sender, System.EventArgs e)
{
    //Typecast sender object to a RadioButton
    RadioButton rbAlign = (RadioButton) sender;

    //Only if the radio button was checked
    if(rbAlign.Checked)
    {
        //Set the alignment of TabControl based
        //on which RadioButton was checked.
        if (rbAlign == rbLeft)
            tabDemo.Alignment = TabAlignment.Left;
        else if (rbAlign == rbRight)
            tabDemo.Alignment = TabAlignment.Right;
        else if (rbAlign == rbBottom)
            tabDemo.Alignment = TabAlignment.Bottom;
        else
            tabDemo.Alignment = TabAlignment.Top;
    }
}

private void rbButtons_CheckedChanged(
    object sender, System.EventArgs e)
{
    //find the RadioButton that was checked
    //from the Buttons tab and create a
    //MessageBoxButtons objects corresponding to it.
    if(sender == rbOKCancel)
        mbbButtons = MessageBoxButtons.OKCancel;
    else if (sender == rbRetryCancel)
        mbbButtons = MessageBoxButtons.RetryCancel;
    else if (sender == rbYesNo)
        mbbButtons = MessageBoxButtons.YesNo;
    else if (sender == rbYesNoCancel)
        mbbButtons = MessageBoxButtons.YesNoCancel;
    else
        mbbButtons = MessageBoxButtons.OK;
}

private void rbIcon_CheckedChanged(
    object sender, System.EventArgs e)
{
```

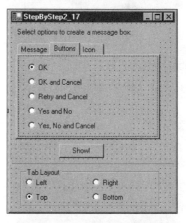
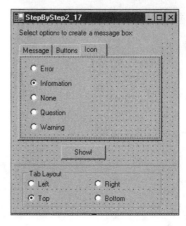

FIGURE 2.33
You can organize various controls on each tab page of a TabControl control.

continues

continued

```
//find the RadioButton that was checked
//from the Icon tab and create a
//MessageBoxIcon objects corresponding to it.
if(sender == rbError)
    mbiIcon = MessageBoxIcon.Error;
else if (sender == rbWarning)
    mbiIcon = MessageBoxIcon.Warning;
else if (sender == rbNone)
    mbiIcon = MessageBoxIcon.None;
else if (sender == rbQuestion)
    mbiIcon = MessageBoxIcon.Question;
else
    mbiIcon = MessageBoxIcon.Information;
}
```

7. Select all the RadioButton controls in the Buttons tab page. Invoke the Properties window and click the Events icon. Select the CheckedChanged event and select the rbButtons_CheckChanged event handler from the list. Repeat the same steps for the Icon tab page by selecting all the RadioButton controls in the Icon tab page, and select the rbIcon_CheckedChanged event handler. Select all the RadioButton controls in the group box and then again select the CheckedChanged event and select the rbAlign_CheckChanged event handler from the list of event handlers.

8. Double-click the Button control and add the following code to handle the Click event of the Button control:

```
private void btnShow_Click(
    object sender, System.EventArgs e)
{
    MessageBox.Show(txtMessage.Text,
        txtCaption.Text, mbbButtons, mbiIcon);
}
```

9. Insert the Main() method to launch form StepByStep2_17. Set the form as the startup object for the project.

10. Run the project. Enter the message and caption of the message in the Message tab page, select the desired button from the Buttons tab page, and select the desired icon from the Icons tab page. Click the Show! button. A message box appears, with the desired message, caption, button, and icon. You can align tabs to different directions, depending on the alignment side selected from the Tab Layout group box.

▶ DomainUpDown and NumericUpDown allow you to select from a list of defined values by pressing up and down buttons. You can also directly enter values in these controls unless their ReadOnly properties are set to true.

▶ The DateTimePicker control allows you to select a date and time, and the MonthCalendar control allows you to select a date or range of dates. The SelectionStart, SelectionEnd, and SelectionRange properties of the MonthCalendar control return the start date, end date, and range of dates selected.

▶ The TreeView control is used to display data in a hierarchical collection of nodes. Each node represents a TreeNode object. The AfterSelect event of the TreeView control occurs when a node is selected and the SelectedNode property is set with the new selection.

▶ The ListView control is used to display items in different views—such as List, Details, SmallIcon, and LargeIcon—which are similar to the view options of the Windows Explorer.

▶ ScrollBar controls can be associated with controls to provide scrolling functionality.

▶ The TabControl control provides a user interface that can be used to save space as well as organize large numbers of controls. You often see a TabControl control used in wizards.

CREATING MENUS AND MENU ITEMS

Add controls to a Windows form.

- **Create menus and menu items.**

Windows applications use menus to provide organized collections of commands that can be performed by the user. Menus can inform the user of an application's capabilities as well as its limitations. If a program has properly organized menus, users can easily find common commands as well as less familiar features. Users can also learn shortcut keys from a well-designed menu structure.

Because menus have so many benefits to the user, you should be well versed in their creation and the function they can provide. The following sections discuss the menu-related classes MainMenu, MenuItem, and ContextMenu. They also discuss two controls, the StatusBar and ToolBar controls, that are often used with menus.

All three of the menu-related classes MainMenu, MenuItem, and ContextMenu derive from the Menu class, which provides common functionality to these classes. The MainMenu class is used to create an application's top-level menu and the ContextMenu class is used to create a shortcut menu that appears when the user right-clicks a control. Both MainMenu and ContextMenu have MenuItems properties. MenuItems is a collection of MenuItem objects, each representing an individual menu item. It is interesting to note that MenuItem itself also has a menu items collection that can be used to store submenus, thereby creating a hierarchical menu structure. Table 2.25 summarizes the important members of the MenuItem class with which you should be familiar.

TABLE 2.25

IMPORTANT MEMBERS OF THE MenuItem CLASS

Member	Type	Description
Checked	Property	Indicates whether a checkmark or a radio button should appear near the menu item.
Click	Event	Occurs when the user selects the menu item.
DrawItem	Event	Occurs when a request is made to draw an owner-drawn menu item. DrawItem occurs only when the OwnerDraw property is set to true.
Enabled	Property	Indicates whether the menu item is enabled.
MenuItems	Property	Specifies the collection of MenuItem objects associated with the menu. This property can be used to create hierarchical submenus.
OwnerDraw	Property	Indicates whether you can provide your own custom code to draw a menu item instead of letting Windows handle it in a standard way.
Parent	Property	The parent with which the menu item is associated. You must specify a parent for a MenuItem object; otherwise, it is not displayed.
PerformClick	Method	Generates the Click event for the menu item as if the user had clicked it.

Member	Type	Description
Popup	Event	Occurs just before a submenu corresponding to the menu item is displayed. This event handler is generally used to add, remove, enable, disable, check, or uncheck menu items, depending on the state of an application just before these menu items are displayed.
RadioCheck	Property	Indicates whether the menu item should display a radio button instead of a checkmark when its Checked property is true.
Select	Event	Occurs when the user selects a menu item by navigating to it.
Shortcut	Property	Specifies the shortcut key combination associated with the menu item.
Text	Property	Specifies the caption of the menu item.

The MainMenu Control

The MainMenu control is a container control for a form's main menu, which is displayed just below its title bar. Visual Studio .NET provides an easy-to-use menu designer that helps you quickly design a main menu for a form.

A Windows form can have only one MainMenu object associated with it, and it is identified by the Menu property of the Form object. After you create a menu, you should be sure to set the Menu property of the form to the name of the menu you want to display on it.

The most important member of the MainMenu class is MenuItems, which is a collection of MenuItem objects.

In Step by Step 2.18 you create a simple word processing program that provides little functionality but gives a good overview of how menus are used in a Windows application. Later in this chapter you use the information from Step by Step 2.18 along with extra features such as status bars and toolbars.

You will learn the following from Step by Step 2.18:

◆ How to add menus and submenus to a form

◆ How to use Checked and RadioButton menu items, and how to select and deselect them based on user actions

◆ How to associate hotkeys and shortcuts with menu items

◆ How to write event handlers for performing actions when a user selects a menu item

STEP BY STEP

2.18 Creating a Main Menu for a Form

1. Add a Windows form to existing project `316C02`. Name the form `StepByStep2_18`.

2. Place a panel on the form and set the `Dock` property to `Fill` and `AutoScroll` to `true`.

3. Add a `RichTextBox` control to the panel. Name it `rbText` and change its `Dock` property to `Fill`.

4. From the toolbox drag a `MainMenu` control onto the form. Change the control's `Name` property to `mnuMainMenu` and change the form's `Menu` property to `mnuMainMenu`.

5. Using the menu designer (see Figure 2.34), add a top-level menu item. Set its `Text` as `&File` and name it `mnuFile`. Add the menu items listed in Table 2.26 to it.

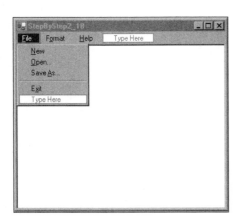

FIGURE 2.34
The Menu Designer allows you to create structured menus within the Windows Forms Designer.

TABLE 2.26

FILE MENU ITEMS

Text	Control Name	Shortcut
&New	mnuFileNew	Ctrl+N
&Open...	mnuFileOpen	Ctrl+O
Save &As...	mnuFileSaveAs	Ctrl+S
E&xit	mnuFileExit	None

6. Create the second top-level menu item, with its `Text` property as `F&ormat` and `Name` property as `mnuFormat`. Add the menu items listed in Table 2.27 to it.

TABLE 2.27

FORMAT MENU ITEMS

Text	Control Name	Shortcut
&Color	mnuFormatColor	None
&Font	mnuFormatFont	None

7. Set up the Format, Color menu according to the items listed in Table 2.28.

TABLE 2.28

FORMAT, COLOR MENU ITEMS

Text	Control Name	Shortcut	RadioCheck Setting
&All Colors...	mnuFormatAllColors	None	false
&Black	mnuFormatColorBlack	Ctrl+Shift+B	true
Bl&ue	mnuFormatColorBlue	Ctrl+Shift+U	true
&Green	mnuFormatColorGreen	Ctrl+Shift+G	true
&Red	mnuFormatColorRed	Ctrl+Shift+R	true

8. Set up the Format, Font menu according to the items listed in Table 2.29.

TABLE 2.29

FORMAT, FONT MENU ITEMS

Text	Control Name	Shortcut
&All Fonts...	mnuFormatFontAllFonts	None
&Bold	mnuFormatFontBold	Ctrl+B
&Italic	mnuFormatFontItalic	Ctrl+I
&Underline	mnuFormatFontUnderline	Ctrl+U

continues

continued

9. Name the third top-level menu mnuHelp and set its Text property to &Help. This menu has only one menu item in it: mnuHelpAbout. Set the Text property of mnuHelpAbout to &About.

10. In the menu designer, right-click the Exit menu and select Insert Separator from the context menu. Insert separators after the All Colors... and All Fonts... menu items.

11. From the toolbox drop four dialog box components: OpenFileDialog, SaveFileDialog, FontDialog, and ColorDialog. Change their Name properties to dlgOpenFile, dlgSaveFile, dlgFont, and dlgColor, respectively.

12. Select File, New. In the Properties window double-click the menu item's Click event to add an event handler to it. Add the following code to the event handler:

```
private void mnuFileNew_Click(
    object sender, System.EventArgs e)
{
    rtbText.Clear();
}
```

13. Add the following code to the Click event handler of the File, Open menu item:

```
private void mnuFileOpen_Click(
    object sender, System.EventArgs e)
{
    //Allow to select only *.rtf files
    dlgOpenFile.Filter =
        "Rich Text Files (*.rtf)|*.rtf";
    if(dlgOpenFile.ShowDialog() == DialogResult.OK)
    {
        //Load the file contents in the RichTextBox
        rtbText.LoadFile(dlgOpenFile.FileName,
            RichTextBoxStreamType.RichText);
    }
}
```

14. Double-click the File, Save As... menu item to attach a Click event handler to it. Add the following code to the event handler:

```
private void mnuFileSaveAs_Click(
    object sender, System.EventArgs e)
{
```

```
    //Default choice to save file is *.rtf
    //but user can select
    //All Files to save with other extension
    dlgSaveFile.Filter =
  "Rich Text Files (*.rtf)|*.rtf|All Files (*.*)|*.*";
    if(dlgSaveFile.ShowDialog() == DialogResult.OK)
    {
        //Save the RichText content to a file
        rtbText.SaveFile(dlgSaveFile.FileName,
            RichTextBoxStreamType.RichText);
    }
}
```

15. Double-click the File, Exit menu item to attach a `Click` event handler to it. Add the following code to the event handler:

```
private void mnuFileExit_Click(
    object sender, System.EventArgs e)
{
    //close the form
    this.Close();
}
```

16. Double-click the Format, Color, All Colors… menu item to attach a `Click` event handler to it. Add the following code to the event handler:

```
private void mnuFormatColorAllColors_Click(
    object sender, System.EventArgs e)
{
    if(dlgColor.ShowDialog() == DialogResult.OK)
    {
        //Change the color of selected text
        //If no text selected, change the active color
        rtbText.SelectionColor = dlgColor.Color;
    }
}
```

17. Insert the following event handler in the code and associate it with the `Click` event of the Format, Color, Black; Format, Color, Blue; Format, Color, Green; and Format, Color, Red menu items:

```
private void mnuFormatColorItem_Click(
    object sender, System.EventArgs e)
{
    MenuItem mnuItem = (MenuItem) sender;
    //Get color name, before that also get rid of
    //the '&' character in Control's Text
    rtbText.SelectionColor = Color.FromName(
        mnuItem.Text.Replace("&", ""));
```

continues

continued

```
//uncheck all menu items inside color menu
foreach(MenuItem m in mnuItem.Parent.MenuItems)
    m.Checked = false;
//just check the clicked menu
mnuItem.Checked = true;
}
```

18. Insert the following event handler in the code and associate it with the Popup event of Format, Color menu item:

```
private void mnuFormatColor_Popup(
    object sender, System.EventArgs e)
{
    MenuItem mnuItem = (MenuItem) sender;

    //for all menu items inside color menu
    foreach(MenuItem m in mnuItem.MenuItems)
    {
        if (m.Text.Replace("&", "") ==
            rtbText.SelectionColor.Name)
            //If it is the selected color, check it
            m.Checked = true;
        else
            //otherwise uncheck it
            m.Checked = false;
    }
}
```

19. Double-click the Format, Font, All Fonts... menu item to attach a Click event handler to it. Add the following code to the event handler:

```
private void mnuFormatFontAllFonts_Click(
    object sender, System.EventArgs e)
{
    if(dlgFont.ShowDialog() == DialogResult.OK)
    {
        //Change the font of selected text
        //If no text selected, change the active font
        rtbText.SelectionFont = dlgFont.Font;
    }
}
```

20. Insert the following event handler in the code and associate it with the Click event of the Format, Font, Bold; Format, Font, Italic; and Format, Font, Underline menu items:

```
private void mnuFormatFontItem_Click(
    object sender, System.EventArgs e)
{
```

```
    MenuItem mnuItem = (MenuItem) sender;
    mnuItem.Checked = !mnuItem.Checked;
    FontStyle fsStyle;
    //Set the FontStyle selected by user in fsStyle
    switch (mnuItem.Text.Replace("&",""))
    {
        case "Bold":
            fsStyle = FontStyle.Bold;
            break;
        case "Italic":
            fsStyle = FontStyle.Italic;
            break;
        case "Underline":
            fsStyle = FontStyle.Underline;
            break;
        default:
            fsStyle = FontStyle.Regular;
            break;
    }
    //Create a font object, toggle the FontStyle
    //and set the new font on selection
    rtbText.SelectionFont = new Font(
        rtbText.SelectionFont.FontFamily,
        rtbText.SelectionFont.Size,
        rtbText.SelectionFont.Style^fsStyle);
}
```

21. Insert the following event handler in the code and associate it with the Popup event of the Format, Font menu item:

```
private void mnuFormatFont_Popup(
    object sender, System.EventArgs e)
{
    //Set the check boxes on format menu to reflect
    //users selection of Font
    mnuFormatFontBold.Checked =
        rtbText.SelectionFont.Bold;
    mnuFormatFontItalic.Checked =
        rtbText.SelectionFont.Italic;
    mnuFormatFontUnderline.Checked =
        rtbText.SelectionFont.Underline;
}
```

22. Double-click the Help, About menu item to attach a Click event handler to it. Add the following code to the event handler:

```
private void mnuHelpAbout_Click(
    object sender, System.EventArgs e)
{
    Form frm = new frmAbout();
    //Display an About dialog box.
    frm.ShowDialog(this);
}
```

continues

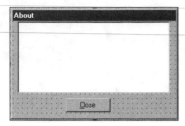

FIGURE 2.35
The About dialog box uses a RichTextBox control to display the contents of an RTF file.

EXAM TIP

The WordWrap Property and Scrollbars   When the WordWrap property of a RichTextBox control is true (the default value), the horizontal scrollbars are not displayed, regardless of the setting of the ScrollBars property.

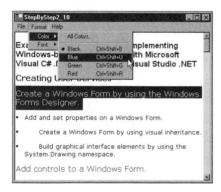

FIGURE 2.36
You can use either the mouse or hotkeys or shortcut keys to access menu commands.

---

continued

23. Add a new Windows form, named frmAbout, to the project. Change its ControlBox property to false, FormBorderStyle to FixedDialog, ShowInTaskbar to false, and Text to About.

---

24. Place a RichTextBox control and a Button control on the form and name them rtbText and btnClose, respectively. Arrange the controls as shown in Figure 2.35.

---

25. Add the following code to the form's Load event handler:

```
private void frmAbout_Load(
    object sender, System.EventArgs e)
{
    if (File.Exists("About.rtf"))
        //Load content from a file
        rtbText.LoadFile("About.rtf");
    else
        //When file not available,
        //just link to a Web site
        rtbText.Text =
        "Please visit http://www.microsoft.com/net" +
        " to learn how this product was developed";
}
```

---

26. Add the following code to the LinkClicked event handler of rtbText:

```
private void rtbText_LinkClicked(object sender,
    System.Windows.Forms.LinkClickedEventArgs e)
{
    //Start internet explorer to open the link
    System.Diagnostics.Process.Start(
        "IExplore", e.LinkText);
}
```

---

27. Add the following code to the Close event handler of btnClose:

```
private void btnClose_Click(
    object sender, System.EventArgs e)
{
    //get rid of this form.
    this.Close();
}
```

---

28. Insert the Main() method to launch the form StepByStep2_18. Set the form as the startup object for the project.

---

29. Run the project. Open or create a rich text file and use the Format menu to format the text. Also use hotkeys and shortcut keys to select menu items (see Figure 2.36).

In Step by Step 2.18, you place a panel on the form and place the RichTextBox control on the panel. Actually, this example works fine even without using the panel. However, the panel is helpful if you want to use other controls, such as StatusBar and Toolbar, in the application. By using a Panel control, it is easy to divide a form's real estate and avoid overlap problems.

The ContextMenu Control

A context menu is typically used to provide users with a small context-sensitive menu based on the application's current state and the user's current selection. A context menu is invoked when the user right-clicks a control.

You use the ContextMenu class to create a context menu. A context menu is simpler than a main menu because it has only one top-level menu that displays all the menu items. In addition, you can have submenus and other functionality, such as hide, show, enable, disable, check, and uncheck available in a context menu.

A context menu is associated with a control or a form, so you can have several ContextMenu objects in an application, each working in a different context. You must associate a ContextMenu object with a control by assigning it to the control's ContextMenu property.

The process of creating a context menu is similar to the process of creating a main menu. Step by Step 2.19 extends the application created in Step by Step 2.18 by adding a context menu for basic editing operations such as cut, copy, and paste. You will learn the following in Step by Step 2.19:

◆ How to create a context menu and its items

◆ How to associate a context menu with a control

◆ How to enable and disable menu items based on application state

◆ How to work with the Clipboard class

EXAM TIP

The RadioCheck Property Setting the RadioCheck property to true does not implicitly set mutual exclusion for menu items; you are still able to check several of them at the same time. You have to set mutual exclusion programmatically. The Popup event is an appropriate place to check a menu item and uncheck all other menu items in that group.

NOTE

Docking Controls in a Scrollable Container When docking controls within a scrollable control such as a form, you should add a child scrollable control such as the Panel control to contain any other controls, such as a RichTextBox control, that might require scrolling. You should also set the Dock property to DockStyle.Fill and the AutoScroll property to true for the child panel control. The AutoScroll property of the parent scrollable control such as a form should be set to false.

FIGURE 2.37
The Menu Designer allows you to create context menus within the Windows Forms Designer.

STEP BY STEP

2.19 Creating a Context Menu for a Form

1. Add a Windows form to existing project 316C02. Name the form StepByStep2_19.

2. Follow steps 2 to 27 from Step by Step 2.18.

3. From the toolbox, drag and drop a ContextMenu control onto the form. It is added to the component tray. Select its properties and change its name to mnuContextMenu.

4. Change the ContextMenu property of the rtbText object to mnuContextMenu.

5. Select the ContextMenu control. Notice that the context menu appears in place of the main menu. Create menu items in the context menu as shown in Figure 2.37, and define their properties as shown in Table 2.30.

TABLE 2.30

CONTEXT MENU ITEMS

Text	Control Name	Shortcut
Cu&t	mnuContextCut	Ctrl+X
&Copy	mnuContextCopy	Ctrl+C
&Paste	mnuContextpaste	Ctrl+V

6. Double-click the Cut menu item to add an event handler to it, and then add the following code to it:

```
private void mnuContextCut_Click(
    object sender, System.EventArgs e)
{
    //Set the clipboard with current selection
    Clipboard.SetDataObject(rtbText.SelectedRtf,true);
    //Delete the current selection
    rtbText.SelectedRtf = "" ;
}
```

7. Add the following event handler for the `Click` event handler of the Copy menu item:

```
private void mnuContextCopy_Click(
    object sender, System.EventArgs e)
{
    //Set the clipboard with current selection
    Clipboard.SetDataObject(rtbText.SelectedRtf,true);
}
```

8. Add the following code to the `Click` event handler of the Paste menu item:

```
private void mnuContextPaste_Click(
    object sender, System.EventArgs e)
{
    //DataObject provides format-independent data
    //transfer mechanism
    //Get data from clipboard and store
    //it in a DataObject object
    DataObject doClipboard =
        (DataObject)Clipboard.GetDataObject();
    //only if clipboard had any data
    if (doClipboard.GetDataPresent(DataFormats.Text))
    {
        //get the string data from DataObject object
        string text =
        (string)doClipboard.GetData(DataFormats.Text);
        if (!text.Equals(""))
            //If there was some text to paste
            //paste it in RTF format
            rtbText.SelectedRtf  = text;
    }
}
```

9. Double-click the `mnuContextMenu` object in the component tray. This adds an event handler for its `Popup` event, to which you should add the following code:

```
private void mnuContext_Popup(
    object sender, System.EventArgs e)
{
    //Initially disable all menu items
    mnuContextCut.Enabled = false;
    mnuContextCopy.Enabled = false;
    mnuContextPaste.Enabled = false;
    //If there was any selected text
    if (!rtbText.SelectedText.Equals(""))
    {
        //enable the cut and copy menu items
        mnuContextCut.Enabled = true;
        mnuContextCopy.Enabled = true;
    }
```

continues

continued

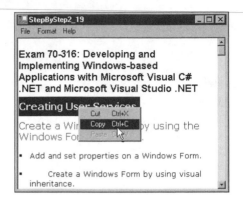

FIGURE 2.38
Menu options in the context menu are enabled or disabled based on the current context.

```
DataObject doClipboard =
    (DataObject)Clipboard.GetDataObject();
//if there is text data on clipboard,
//enable the Paste menu item
if (doClipboard.GetDataPresent(DataFormats.Text))
    mnuContextPaste.Enabled = true;
}
```

10. Insert the `Main()` method to launch form `StepByStep2_19`. Set the form as the startup object for the project.

11. Run the project. Open or create an RTF file, select some text, and right-click and copy it to the Clipboard (see Figure 2.38). Paste it at a different location. You should also see that the Cut, Copy, and Paste menu items are enabled and disabled depending on the context. For example, if there is no text selected, the Cut and Copy menu items are disabled.

Although the Clipboard operations implemented here would work fine within this application, they might fail if you are pasting different types of data from some other application. This is because you have not implemented error handling here. Error handling is covered in detail in Chapter 3, "Error Handling for the User Interface."

GUIDED PRACTICE EXERCISE 2.3

The Edit main menu is one of the most common features of all Windows-based applications. Typically, the Edit menu contains commands such as Cut, Copy, Paste, Undo, and Redo.

In this exercise, you extend the application created in Step by Step 2.19 by adding an Edit menu as a top-level menu in the form's main menu. In addition to Cut, Copy, and Paste, you also need to implement Undo and Redo menu items that allow you to undo or redo the changes made to the `RichTextBox` control. You should try working through this problem on your own first reusing as much code as you can from Step by Step 2.19. If you get stuck, or if you'd like to see one possible solution, follow these steps:

1. Add a new form to your Visual C# .NET project. Name the form GuidedPracticeExercise2_3.cs.

2. Follow steps 2 through 9 from Step by Step 2.19.

3. Select mnuContextMenu from the component tray and then in the context menu, select all menu items by pressing the Ctrl key while selecting items. Right-click and then select Copy to copy these menu items to the Clipboard. Select mnuMainMenu, right-click the top-level Format menu, and select Insert New from the shortcut menu. This creates a new menu item just before Format Menu. Change its Text property to &Edit and name the control mnuEdit. Right-click in the menu list of this newly created menu, and select Paste from the shortcut menu. All the context menu items are copied here.

4. Change the Name properties of the menu items Cut, Copy, and Paste to mnuEditCut, mnuEditCopy, and mnuEditPaste, respectively. Also change their Shortcut properties to CtrlX, CtrlC, and CtrlV, respectively.

5. Select the mnuEditCut menu item and choose mnuContextCut_Click as its Click event handler. Similarly, choose mnuContextCopy_Click and mnuContextPaste_Click as the event handlers for the mnuEditCopy and mnuEditPaste menus, respectively.

6. Insert another menu item just before the Edit, Cut menu item. Change its Text property to &Undo, change its Name property to mnuEditUndo, and change its Shortcut property to CtrlZ. Similarly, add another menu item for Redo and set Text as &Redo, Name as mnuEditRedo, and Shortcut as CtrlY. Insert a separator bar between Undo, Redo, and the other menu items in the Edit menu.

7. Create event handlers for the Click event of the mnuEditUndo and mnuEditRedo menu items. Modify the code as shown here:

```
private void mnuEditUndo_Click(
    object sender, System.EventArgs e)
{
    //Undo the last edit operation
    rtbText.Undo();
}

private void mnuEditRedo_Click(
    object sender, System.EventArgs e)
```

continues

continued

```
{
    //Redo the last operation that was undone
    rtbText.Redo();
}
```

8. Select `mnuEdit` and add the following code to its `Popup` event handler:

```csharp
private void mnuEdit_Popup(
    object sender, System.EventArgs e)
{
    //Initially disable all menu items
    mnuEditUndo.Enabled = false;
    mnuEditRedo.Enabled = false;
    mnuEditCut.Enabled = false;
    mnuEditCopy.Enabled = false;
    mnuEditPaste.Enabled = false;

    //If there was any selected text
    if (!rtbText.SelectedText.Equals(""))
    {
        //enable the cut and copy menu items
        mnuEditCut.Enabled = true;
        mnuEditCopy.Enabled = true;
    }
    DataObject doClipboard =
        (DataObject)Clipboard.GetDataObject();
    //if there is text data on clipboard,
    //enable the Paste menu item
    if (doClipboard.GetDataPresent(DataFormats.Text))
        mnuEditPaste.Enabled = true;
    //Check if Undo is possible
    if (rtbText.CanUndo)
        mnuEditUndo.Enabled = true;
    //Check if Redo is possible
    if (rtbText.CanRedo)
        mnuEditRedo.Enabled = true;
}
```

9. Insert the `Main()` method to launch form `GuidedPracticeExercise2_3.cs`. Set the form as the startup object for the project.

10. Run the project. Open or create an RTF file, select some text and select Edit, Copy to copy text to the Clipboard. Perform some cut, copy, and paste operations. Select Edit, Undo to undo the changes in the document (see Figure 2.39).

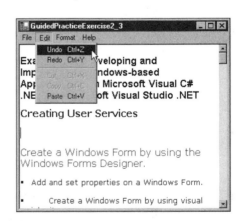

FIGURE 2.39
The Edit menu provides standard editing commands such as Undo, Redo, Cut, Copy, and Paste.

If you have difficulty following this exercise, review the sections "The MainMenu Control" and "The ContextMenu Control" earlier in this chapter. Also, spend some time looking at the various methods and properties that are available for a RichTextBox control in the Properties window. Reading the text and examples in this chapter should help you relearn this material. After doing that review, try this exercise again.

The StatusBar Control

The StatusBar control is used to display information such as help messages and status messages. A StatusBar control is normally docked at the bottom of a form. When you add a StatusBar control to a form from the toolbox, make sure to set the z-order of the control by right-clicking the status bar and selecting Send to Back from the shortcut menu. When you do this, you do not see the status bar overlapping other controls at the bottom of the form.

One of the most important properties for a StatusBar control is the Panels property. Panels is a collection of StatusBarPanel objects. Panels divide a status bar area so that you can use each area to display a different type of information, such as the status of the date and time, page number, download progress, and the Caps Lock, Num Lock, and Insert keys. Table 2.31 summarizes the important members of the StatusBarPanel class.

> **NOTE**
>
> **Layering Controls: Z-order** *Z-order* specifies the visual layering of controls on a form along the form's z-axis, which specifies its depth. Controls are stacked in descending z-order value, with the control with the greatest z-order at the top of the stack and the control with the smallest z-order on the bottom of the stack. You can set the z-order of a control relative to its container control by right-clicking the control and selecting either Send to Back or Bring to Front from the shortcut menu.

TABLE 2.31

IMPORTANT MEMBERS OF THE StatusBarPanel CLASS

Member	Type	Description
Alignment	Property	Specifies the alignment of the text and icons within the panel. Can be one of the Center, Left, or Right values of the HorizontalAlignment enumeration.

continues

NOTE

The AutoSize Property The StatusBarPanel objects that have their AutoSize properties set to StatusBarPanelAutoSize.Contents have priority placement over the StatusBarPanel objects that have their AutoSize properties set to StatusBarPanelAutoSize.Spring. That is, a StatusBarPanel object with AutoSize set to Spring is shortened if a StatusBarPanel object with AutoSize set to Contents resizes itself to take more space on the status bar.

NOTE

Icon Positioning on a Status Bar Panel An icon is always positioned on the left side of the text in a panel, regardless of the text's alignment.

TABLE 2.31 *continued*

IMPORTANT MEMBERS OF THE StatusBarPanel CLASS

Member	Type	Description
AutoSize	Property	Specifies how the panel should size itself. This property can take the values None, Contents, and Spring from the StatusBarPanelAutosize enumeration.
BorderStyle	Property	Specifies the border style. BorderStyle can have the values None, Raised, and Sunken from the StatusBarPanelBorderStyle enumeration.
Icon	Property	Specifies the icon to be displayed in the status bar.
Style	Property	Specifies whether the StatusBarPanel object is set to OwnerDraw or Text (that is, system drawn). The OwnerDraw style can be use to give custom rendering to the StatusBarPanel object.
ToolTipText	Property	Specifies the ToolTip to show for the StatusBarPanel object.

STEP BY STEP

2.20 Creating a Status Bar for a Form

1. Add a Windows form to existing project 316C02. Name the form StepByStep2_20.

2. Follow steps 2 through 8 from Guided Practice Exercise 2.3.

3. Select the form StepByStep2_20 by clicking its title bar. From the toolbox, double-click the StatusBar control to add it to the form. Name the StatusBar object sbStatus and clear its Text property. Change its ShowPanels property to true.

4. Select the status bar. Right-click it and select Send to Back from the shortcut menu.

5. Select the `Panels` property of the status bar. Click the ellipsis (…) button and create three `StatusBarPanel` objects, using the `StatusBarPanel` Collection Editor, as shown in Figure 2.40. Name the first object `sbpHelp`, change its `AutoSize` property to `Spring`, and empty its `Text` property. Name the second object `sbpDate`, change its `Alignment` property to `Right`, change `AutoSize` to `Contents`, change `ToolTipText` to `Current System Date`, and empty the `Text` property. Name the third object `sbpTime`, change its `Alignment` property to `Right`, change `AutoSize` to `Contents`, change `ToolTipText` to `Current System Time`, and empty the `Text` property.

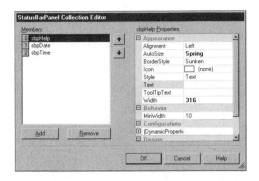

FIGURE 2.40
The `StatusBarPanel` Collection Editor allows you to create and edit panels in a status bar.

6. Add a `Timer` control to the form, name it `tmrTimer`, change its `Enabled` property to `true`, and set the `Interval` property to `1000`. Double-click the `tmrTimer` object to add an event handler for its `Tick` event, and then add the following code to it:

```
private void tmrTimer_Tick(
    object sender, System.EventArgs e)
{
    DateTime dtNow = DateTime.Now;
    //display current date in the status bar panel
    sbpDate.Text = dtNow.ToLongDateString();
    //display current time in the status bar panel
    sbpTime.Text = dtNow.ToShortTimeString();
}
```

7. Insert the following event handling code in the program:

```
private void mnuItem_Select(
    object sender, System.EventArgs e)
{
    //Get the menu item sending the event
    MenuItem mnuItem = (MenuItem) sender;
    string strHelp;
    //Check which menu it is
    //and set the appropriate help text.
    switch(mnuItem.Text.Replace("&", ""))
    {
        case "New":
            strHelp = "Create a new document";
            break;
        case "Open...":
            strHelp = "Open an existing document";
            break;
        case "Save As...":
            strHelp = "Save the active document" +
                " with a new name";
```

continues

continued

```
                break;
            case "Exit":
                strHelp = "Quit the application";
                break;
            case "Undo":
                strHelp = "Undo the last action";
                break;
            case "Redo":
                strHelp = "Redo the last undone action";
                break;
            case "Cut":
             strHelp = "Cut the selection to the clipboard";
                 break;
            case "Copy":
            strHelp = "Copy the selection to the clipboard";
                break;
            case "Paste":
                strHelp = "Insert clipboard contents";
                break;
            case "Color":
                strHelp = "Select a color";
                break;
            case "Font":
                strHelp = "Select a font";
                break;
            default:
                strHelp = "";
                break;
        }
        sbpHelp.Text = strHelp;
    }
```

8. Select `mnuItem_Select` as the event handler for the `Select` events of all the menu items, including the top-level menus.

9. Add the following event handler in the code view:

```
//Reset the help text on status bar after the
//Menu is closed
protected override void OnMenuComplete(EventArgs e)
{
    sbpHelp.Text = "";
}
```

10. Insert the `Main()` method to launch form `StepByStep2_20`. Set the form as the startup object for the project.

11. Run the project. You should see the system date and time on the status bar. As you navigate through various menu items, you should see the description of menu items in the status bar (see Figure 2.41).

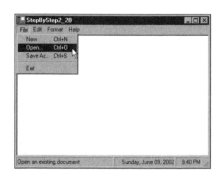

FIGURE 2.41
The `StatusBar` control is used to display various kinds of status information for an application.

The ToolBar Control

The ToolBar control can be used to create a Windows toolbar. It is normally docked on the top of the form, just below the menu bar. When you add a ToolBar control to form the toolbox, you should make sure to set the z-order of the control by right-clicking the toolbar and selecting Send to Back from the shortcut menu. When you do this, you do not see the toolbar overlapping other controls at the top of the form. Table 2.32 summarizes the important members of ToolBar class.

TABLE 2.32

IMPORTANT MEMBERS OF THE ToolBar CLASS

Member	Type	Description
Buttons	Property	Specifies a collection of ToolBarButton objects. Each ToolbarButton object represents a button on the ToolBar object.
ButtonClick	Event	Occurs when the toolbar button is clicked.
ImageList	Property	Specifies the ImageList object that stores the icons that will be displayed on the ToolBarButton objects.
SendToBack()	Method	Sends the toolbar to the back of the z-order.
ShowToolTips	Property	Specifies whether the toolbar should show ToolTips.

Normally the toolbar buttons represent shortcuts to tasks that could otherwise be done by selecting a menu option. When you respond to the ButtonClick event of a ToolBar object, you can simply invoke a corresponding menu item to accomplish a task, thereby reusing the efforts already invested in programming the menus. You can programmatically invoke a menu item by calling the PerformClick() method on a MenuItem object. So all you need to know is what menu to invoke for a particular toolbar button. The ToolBarButton control provides a useful property for this: the Tag property. You can use it to store any object that needs to be associated with a toolbar button. At program startup, you can use the Tag property of a ToolBarButton object to assign each button to a corresponding menu item. Step by Step 2.21 describes how to do this.

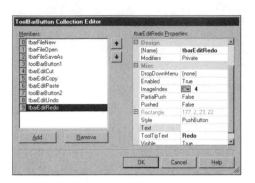

FIGURE 2.42

The ToolBarButton Collection Editor allows you to create and edit buttons in a toolbar.

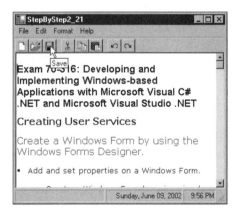

FIGURE 2.43

A toolbar contains buttons that carry out associated menu commands.

STEP BY STEP

2.21 Creating a Toolbar for a Form

1. Add a Windows form to existing project 316C02. Name the form StepByStep2_21.

2. Follow steps 2 through 9 from Step by Step 2.20.

3. Select the form StepByStep2_21 by clicking its title bar. From the toolbox, double-click the ToolBar control to add it to the form. Name the ToolBar object tbarToolBar and change both the height and width of its ButtonSize property to 16. Change the ShowToolTips property to true.

4. Drop an ImageList (imgToolBarIcons) object on the form. To its Images property, add images for New, Open, Save, Cut, Copy, Paste, Undo, and Redo operations. Change the ImageList property of the ToolBar control to imgToolBarIcons.

5. Select the ToolBar control's Buttons property. Click the ellipsis (...) button to open the ToolBarButton Collection Editor Window. Using this window, add the buttons New, Open, Save, Cut, Copy, Paste, Undo, and Redo, and name them tbarFileNew, tbarFileOpen, tbarFileSaveAs, tbarEditCut, tbarEditCopy, tbarEditPaste, tbarEditUndo, and tbarEditRedo, respectively (see Figure 2.42). Select an image for each button from the ImageIndex property and give each button an appropriate ToolTipText setting. You can also add separators between the toolbar buttons by adding a ToolBarButton control and setting its Style property to Separator. The completed toolbar should look like the one shown in Figure 2.43.

6. Add the following code to the form's constructor:

```
public StepByStep2_21()
{
    //
    // Required for Windows Forms Designer support
    //
    InitializeComponent();
```

```
// Store the references to menu items
// in the toolbar buttons
tbarFileNew.Tag = mnuFileNew;
tbarFileOpen.Tag = mnuFileOpen;
tbarFileSaveAs.Tag = mnuFileSaveAs;
tbarEditCut.Tag = mnuEditCut;
tbarEditCopy.Tag = mnuEditCopy;
tbarEditPaste.Tag = mnuEditPaste;
tbarEditUndo.Tag = mnuEditUndo;
tbarEditRedo.Tag = mnuEditRedo;
}
```

7. Double-click the toolbar to add the following event handler for its Click event:

```
private void tbarToolBar_ButtonClick(object sender,
    System.Windows.Forms.ToolBarButtonClickEventArgs e)
{
    ToolBarButton tbarButton = e.Button;
    //Get related menu item from the
    //toolbar buton's tag property
    MenuItem mnuItem = (MenuItem) tbarButton.Tag;

    //Generate the click event for related menu item
    mnuItem.PerformClick();
}
```

8. Insert the Main() method to launch form StepByStep2_21. Set this form as the startup object for the project.

9. Run the project, and you should see the toolbar. Click the various toolbar buttons to do desired tasks (refer to Figure 2.43).

Menu toolbar buttons map directly to menu items. Clicking a menu toolbar button is the same as clicking on its corresponding menu item (or pressing the hotkey for that item).

Disabling a menu item disables its toolbar button as well, but it does not change the appearance of the button. If you want the button to "look" disabled, you must do it programmatically.

CREATING MDI APPLICATIONS

So far in this chapter, you have created only single-document interface (SDI) applications. These applications allow a user to work with only one window at a time. Several large Windows applications, such as Microsoft Excel and Visual Studio .NET, allow users to work with several open windows at the same time. These applications are called *multiple-document interface* (MDI) applications. The main application window of an MDI application acts as the parent window, which can open several child windows. You need to know the following main points about an MDI application:

◆ Child windows are restricted to their parent window (that is, you cannot move a child window outside its parent window).

◆ The parent window can open several types of child windows. As an example of an MDI application, Visual Studio .NET allows you to work with several types of document windows at the same time.

◆ The child windows can be opened, closed, maximized, or minimized independently of each other, but when the parent window is closed, the child windows are automatically closed.

◆ The MDI frame should always have a menu; one of the menus that a user always expects to see in an MDI application is the Window menu (see Figure 2.44), which allows the user to manipulate various windows that are open in an MDI container form.

FIGURE 2.44
An MDI application typically has a Window menu item.

The Windows Forms in an MDI application are also created by using the standard `System.Windows.Forms.Form` class. To create an MDI parent form, you create a regular Windows form and change its `IsMdiContainer` property to `true`. To create an MDI child form, you create a regular Windows form and assign the name of the parent MDI object to the `MdiParent` property. Table 2.33 summarizes the important members of the `Form` class that are related to the MDI applications.

TABLE 2.33

IMPORTANT MEMBERS OF THE Form CLASS THAT ARE
RELATED TO MDI APPLICATIONS

Member	Type	Description
ActiveMdiChild	Property	Identifies the currently active MDI child window
IsMdiContainer	Property	Indicates whether the form is a container for MDI child forms
MdiChildActivate	Event	Occurs when anMDI child form is activated or closed within an MDI application
MdiChildren	Property	Specifies an array of forms that represent the MDI child form of the form
MdiParent	Property	Specifies the MDI parent form for the current form
LayoutMdi()	Method	Arranges the MDI child forms within an MDI parent form

Step by Step 2.22 shows how to create an MDI application. In it you can create a form that is similar to the one created in Step by Step 2.18 and you can use it as an MDI child window.

You learn the following from Step by Step 2.22:

◆ How to create an MDI parent form

◆ How to create MDI child forms

◆ How to convert an existing SDI application to an MDI application

◆ How to merge menus between MDI parent and child windows

◆ How to create Windows menus that allow users to load and rearrange MDI child forms

STEP BY STEP

2.22 Creating an MDI Application

1. Add a Windows form to existing project 316C02. Name the form MdiChild.

2. Follow steps 2 to 27 from Step by Step 2.18.

3. Select the main menu of the form and change the MergeType property of the File menu to MergeItems. Select the File, New and File, Open menus and change their MergeType properties to Remove.

4. Rename the File, Exit menu item &Close. Change the MergeOrder properties for the File, Save As; File, Close; Format; and Help menu items to 5, 3, 10, and 30, respectively. Change the MergeOrder property for the separator in the File menu to 4.

5. Switch to the code view. After the default constructor code, add another constructor with the following code:

```
public MdiChild(string fileName)
{
    //
    // Required for Windows Forms Designer support
    //
    InitializeComponent();
    rtbText.LoadFile(fileName,
        RichTextBoxStreamType.RichText);
}
```

6. Add another Windows form to existing project 316C02. Name the form StepByStep2_22 and change its IsMdiContainer property to true.

7. Add a MainMenu component to the form. Create a top-level menu item, change its Text property to &File, and name it mnuFile. Add the following menu items to it: &New (mnuFileNew), &Open... (mnuFileOpen), separator, and E&xit (mnuFileExit). Change the menu items' MergeOrder properties to 1, 2, 6, and 7, respectively.

8. Add another top-level menu. Change the Text property to &Window, and the Name property to mnuWindow, and the MdiList property to true. Add the following menu items to it: Tile &Horizontally (mnuWindowTileHorizintally), Tile &Vertically (mnuWindowTileVertically), and &Cascade (mnuWindowCascade).

9. Double-click the File, New menu item and add the following event handler to its Click event:

```
private void mnuFileNew_Click(
    object sender, System.EventArgs e)
{

    //create a new instance of child window
    MdiChild frmMdiChild = new MdiChild();
    //set its MdiParent
    frmMdiChild.MdiParent = this;
    frmMdiChild.Text = "New Document";
    //Display the child window
    frmMdiChild.Show();
}
```

10. Double-click the File, Open menu item and add the following event handler to it:

```
private void mnuFileOpen_Click(
    object sender, System.EventArgs e)
{
    //Allow to select only *.rtf files
    dlgOpenFile.Filter =
        "Rich Text Files (*.rtf)|*.rtf";
    if(dlgOpenFile.ShowDialog() == DialogResult.OK)
    {
        //create the child form by
        //loading the given file in it
        MdiChild frmMdiChild =
            new MdiChild(dlgOpenFile.FileName);
        //Set the current for as its parent
        frmMdiChild.MdiParent = this;
        //Set the file's title bar text
        frmMdiChild.Text = dlgOpenFile.FileName;
        //display the form
        frmMdiChild.Show();
    }
}
```

continues

11. Add the following event handlers to Click events of other menu items, as shown in steps 9 to 10:

```
private void mnuFileExit_Click(
    object sender, System.EventArgs e)
{
    //Close the parent window
    this.Close();
}
private void mnuWindowTileHorizontally_Click(
    object sender, System.EventArgs e)
{
    //Tile child windows horizontally
    this.LayoutMdi(MdiLayout.TileHorizontal);
}
private void mnuWindowTileVertically_Click(
    object sender, System.EventArgs e)
{
    //Tile child windows vertically
    this.LayoutMdi(MdiLayout.TileVertical);
}
private void mnuWindowCascade_Click(
    object sender, System.EventArgs e)
{
    //cascade
    this.LayoutMdi(MdiLayout.Cascade);
}
```

12. Add the following event handler to the Popup event of the mnuWindow menu item:

```
private void mnuWindow_Popup(
    object sender, System.EventArgs e)
{
    //code to enable and disable Window menu items
    //depending on if any child windows are open
    if (this.MdiChildren.Length > 0)
    {
        mnuWindowTileHorizontally.Enabled = true;
        mnuWindowTileVertically.Enabled = true;
        mnuWindowCascade.Enabled = true;
    }
    else
    {
        mnuWindowTileHorizontally.Enabled = false;
        mnuWindowTileVertically.Enabled = false;
        mnuWindowCascade.Enabled = false;
    }
}
```

13. Insert the `Main()` method to launch form `StepByStep2_22`. Set the form as the startup object for the project.

14. Run the project. From the File menu, open a new document, and then also open an existing document by selecting File, Open. Click the Window menu and select various options to arrange the child windows (see Figure 2.45).

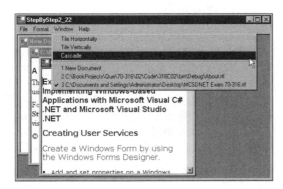

FIGURE 2.45
When you are working with an MDI application, you can use the commands from the Window menu to switch between windows or documents.

The default `MergeType` property for the `MenuItem` objects is `Add`. This means that the `MenuItem` objects in Step by Step 2.22 are added together on an MDI parent window. If you don't want to include some of the menu items, you can set their `MergeType` properties to `Remove`. The `MergeOrder` properties for the `MenuItem` objects specify the order in which they appear on the parent MDI form.

There is another interesting property of the `MenuItem` object that is used with MDI applications: the `MdiList` property. When this property is set to `true`, the `MenuItem` object is populated with a list of MDI child windows that are displayed within the associated form.

REVIEW BREAK

▶ There are two primary types of menus. The main menu is used to group all the available commands and option in a Windows application, and a context menu is used to specify a relatively smaller list of options that apply to a control, depending on the application's current context.

continues

continued

▶ You can make keyboard navigation among menu items possible by associating hotkeys in the `Text` property of the menu items. You can also associate shortcut keys, which directly invoke commands, with a menu.

▶ The `Clipboard` object consists of two public static methods, `GetDataObject()` and `SetDataObject()`, which get and set the data from the Clipboard.

▶ The `StatusBar` control creates a standard Windows status bar in an application. You can use `StatusBar` to display various messages and help text to the user.

▶ You can use toolbars to create a set of small buttons that are identified by icons. Toolbars generally provide shortcuts to operations that are available in the application's main menu. Toolbars are common in Windows applications and make an application simple to use.

▶ An MDI application allows multiple documents or windows to be open at the same time.

CHAPTER SUMMARY

Using Visual Studio .NET, you can add controls to a form in two ways: Either you can use the convenient Windows Forms Designer or you can hand code the controls and load them dynamically in application.

Visual Studio .NET comes with a whole array of Windows Forms controls, and you can set their properties at design time and run-time. Visual Studio .NET makes event handling easy by automatically creating event handlers for controls.

Visual Studio .NET comes with full-fledged menu controls that are needed by almost every real-time application. Visual Studio .NET allows you to create main menus as well as context menus. Visual Studio .NET's MDI forms support is extensive, allowing you to merge menu items with menus of child windows.

This chapter presents the rich library of Windows forms controls. It discusses most of the common Windows controls used by the applications. In fact, the .NET Framework Software Development Kit (SDK) also allows you to create your own controls. In addition, a large number of controls are available from several third-party control vendors. Chapter 4, "Creating and Managing .NET Components and Assemblies" explains how to create user controls and add them to the list of available controls.

KEY TERMS

- Clipboard
- context menu
- main menu
- MDI application
- SDI application
- tab order
- ToolTip
- z-order

APPLY YOUR KNOWLEDGE

Exercises

2.1   Adding ToolTips to Controls

In this exercise you will learn how to set ToolTips for a form. A few Windows forms controls, such as TabPage, ToolBarButton, and StatusBarPanel, have ToolTipText properties for showing ToolTips. But other commonly used controls do not have any built-in properties to which ToolTips text can be assigned. This exercise introduces the ToolTip component. When you drag the ToolTip component from the toolbox into the Windows form, this component provides a new property for all the controls on the form. This new property is named ToolTip on *tooltipComponentName* and can be edited through the Properties window. When the form executes, for each of its controls it shows the value of the ToolTip on *Tooltip ComponentName* property as the ToolTip for the control.

Estimated time: 25 minutes

1. Create a new Visual C# .NET Windows application in the Visual Studio .NET IDE.

2. Add a new form to your Visual C# .NET project. Name it Exercise2_1.cs. Change the Text property of the form to Find, change FormBorderStyle to Fixed3D, and change TopMost to true. Set the MaximizeBox, MimimizeBox, and ShowInTaskBar properties to false.

3. Place a ToolTip component on the form and name it tTip. It is added to the component tray.

4. Place one Label control (keep its default name), one TextBox control (txtTextToFind), two Button controls (btnFind and btnCancel), one CheckBox control (chkMatchCase), and a group box with two RadioButton controls (rbUp and rbDown) on the form. Arrange the controls as shown in Figure 2.46.

FIGURE 2.46
The Windows ToolTip component displays text when the user points at controls.

5. A property named ToolTip on tTip is added to all the controls placed on the form. Modify this property to enter an appropriate ToolTip message for each control on the form.

6. Insert the Main() method and set the form as the startup object of the project.

7. Run the project. The ToolTip message is displayed when you rest the mouse pointer over the control (refer to Figure 2.46).

2.2   Dynamically Creating Menu Items

While creating menus in Windows applications, you are often required to add menu items dynamically. This exercise shows you how to create menu items dynamically, and it shows a list of the recent files opened by the application.

Estimated time: 40 minutes

1. Add a new form to your Visual C# .NET project. Name it Exercise2_2.cs.

2. Place a MainMenu control (mnuMainMenu) and an OpenFileDialog control (dlgOpenFile) on the form.

3. Using the menu designer, add a top-level menu item, set its Text property to &File, and name it mnuFile. Add three menu items: &Open (mnuFileOpen), Recent &Files (mnuFileRecentFiles), and E&xit (mnuExit).

APPLY YOUR KNOWLEDGE

4. Change the Menu property of the form to mnuMainMenu.

5. Add the following code in the code view, just before the constructor:

```
//Store recently used file
//list in ArrayList
private ArrayList alRecentFiles;
private System.Windows.Forms.MainMenu
    mnuMainMenu;
//Maximum number to files to store
private const int intListSize = 4;
```

6. Add the following code in the constructor:

```
//Create ArrayList of given size
alRecentFiles = new ArrayList(intListSize);
```

7. Attach the default Click event handlers for the mnuFileExit, mnuFileOpen, and mnuFileRecentFiles menu items and add the following code to handle the Click events of the menu items:

```
private void mnuFileExit_Click(
    object sender, System.EventArgs e)
{
    this.Close();
}

private void mnuFileOpen_Click(
    object sender, System.EventArgs e)
{
    if(dlgOpenFile.ShowDialog() ==
        DialogResult.OK)
    {
        //Find if the file already
        //exists in the ArrayList
        int pos = alRecentFiles.IndexOf(
            dlgOpenFile.FileName);
        //If it exists then remove it
        if (pos >= 0)
            alRecentFiles.RemoveAt(pos);

        //If you have exceeded the size
        //of ArrayList
        //delete the oldest item from it
        if (alRecentFiles.Count >=
            intListSize)
            alRecentFiles.RemoveAt(
                intListSize-1);
```

```
        //Add the recently opened file to
        //the queue of recent files
        alRecentFiles.Insert(0,
            dlgOpenFile.FileName);

        //do some processing here...
        MessageBox.Show(
            "You selected to open: " +
            dlgOpenFile.FileName,
            "File Opened",
MessageBoxButtons.OK,
            MessageBoxIcon.Information);
    }
}
private void mnuFileRecentFilesItem_Click(
    object sender, System.EventArgs e)
{
    MenuItem mnuItem = (MenuItem) sender;
    //do some processing here
    MessageBox.Show("You selected to open: "
+
        mnuItem.Text.Substring(2),
        "File Opened", MessageBoxButtons.OK,
        MessageBoxIcon.Information);
}
```

8. Add the Popup event handler for the mnuFile menu item:

```
private void mnuFile_Popup(
    object sender, System.EventArgs e)
{
    //Check if there are any file
    //names in the list
    if (alRecentFiles.Count > 0)
    {
      //Clear old recent file list
      mnuFileRecentFiles.MenuItems.Clear();
      //Use this number to add keyboard
      //shortcut to menu items
      //Most recent file has short of 1,
      //next file has shortcut of 2..
      int intFileCount = 1;
      foreach (string fileName in
          alRecentFiles)
      {
          //Create a menu item to create
          //in File - Recent Files menu
          MenuItem mnuItem =
              new MenuItem();
```

APPLY YOUR KNOWLEDGE

```
        //Set the MenuItem text with
        //a shortcut key
        mnuItem.Text = String.Format(
          "&{0} {1}", intFileCount++,
          fileName);
        //attach an event handler
        //to this menu item
        mnuItem.Click += new
         System.EventHandler(
         mnuFileRecentFilesItem_Click);
        //Add the recently used file in
        // the File - Recent files menu
       mnuFileRecentFiles.MenuItems.Add(
           mnuItem);
    }
    //Now that I have some files in
    //the File - Recent Files menu,
    //Enable it
    mnuFileRecentFiles.Enabled = true;
  }
  else
      //If there are no recent files,
      //disable the menu item
      mnuFileRecentFiles.Enabled = false;
}
```

9. Insert the Main() method and set the form as the startup object of the project.

10. Run the project. Open a few files by selecting File, Open, and then select the Recent Files menu item. The recently opened files are added as submenu items to the Recent Files menu item. Also, the files appear in order in terms of how recently they were opened (see Figure 2.47).

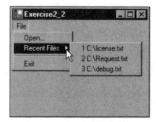

FIGURE 2.47
You can display a list of recently used files by dynamically creating menu items.

Review Questions

1. Where in a form can controls be placed? What are the two ways to add controls?

2. What is the shortcut way of creating an event handler for the default event of a control?

3. When should you choose a ComboBox control instead of a ListBox control in an application?

4. What different modes of selection are possible in a list box?

5. What are the roles of the TabIndex and TabStop properties?

6. How can you create modal and modeless dialog boxes?

7. What are the different styles for drawing combo boxes?

8. What is the function of the Tag property in a control?

9. When does the Popup event of a menu occur? What is the main reason this event is used?

10. What is the difference between the DateTimePicker and MonthCalendar controls? What do you need to do in order to display a custom format in a DateTimePicker control?

11. What is an MDI application?

12. How do you merge menu items of a child window with an MDI window?

Exam Questions

1. You are designing a data entry form that contains several Label and TextBox controls.

APPLY YOUR KNOWLEDGE

You have placed a Label control and a TextBox control beside each other. The TextBox control is used for entering the zip code, and the Label control just provides a label that identifies it. When the user presses the Alt+Z key combination, you want the focus to shift to the text box for entering the zip code. What should you do? (Select all that apply.)

A. Set the TabIndex property of the text box to one higher than the TabIndex property of the label.

B. Set the TabIndex property of the label to one higher than the TabIndex property of the text box.

C. Change the label's Text property to ^Zip Code.

D. Change the label's Text property to &Zip Code.

E. Set the UseMnemonic property of the label to true.

F. Set the UseMnemonic property of the label to false.

2. You are designing a Windows application that has a variety of controls. For some of the controls, you want to prevent the user from being able to give focus to the control under any circumstance. Which of the following would you do?

A. Set the control's TabIndex property to 0.

B. Set the control's TabStop property to 0.

C. Set the control's TabStop property to false.

D. Set the control's Enabled property to false.

3. You are using a CheckedListBox control in one of the Windows forms of an application. You want to allow the user to select multiple items from the CheckedListBox control. What value of the SelectionMode property would you choose?

A. SelectionMode.None

B. SelectionMode.One

C. SelectionMode.MultiSimple

D. SelectionMode.MultiExtended

4. You are using a TreeView control in a windows form. When the user clicks a tree node to select it, you need to access the newly selected node in your program. Which of the following would give you the correct result?

A. Use the SelectedNode property in the Click event handler of the TreeView control.

B. Use the SelectedNode property in the DoubleClick event handler of the TreeView control.

C. Use the SelectedNode property in the BeforeSelect event handler of the TreeView control.

D. Use the SelectedNode property in the AfterSelect event handler of the TreeView control.

5. You are using a CheckBox control on a Windows form; the application requires that users either check or uncheck the check box. But your program should also be capable of setting the CheckBox control to Indeterminate, depending on the application's current state. Which of the following would work for you?

A. Set the ThreeState property of CheckBox to false.

APPLY YOUR KNOWLEDGE

B. Set the `ThreeState` property of `CheckBox` to `true`.

C. Set the `CheckState` property to `CheckState.Checked`.

D. Set the `CheckState` property to `CheckState.Unchecked`.

6. You are designing a menu that has some mutually exclusive options. You have set the `RadioCheck` properties of all the menu items to `true` and their `OwnerDraw` properties to `false`. Still, you are able to check multiple items from the menu when you run the program. Which of the following events would you program to set mutual exclusion among menu items?

   A. `Click`

   B. `Select`

   C. `Popup`

   D. `DrawItem`

7. You have placed a `RichTextBox` control on a Windows form. You want both a horizontal scrollbar and a vertical scrollbar to appear with the control in all cases. Which of the following choice(s) would you make? (Select all that apply.)

   A. Set the `ScrollBars` property to `RichTextScrollBars.Both`.

   B. Set the `ScrollBars` property to `RichTextScrollBars.ForcedBoth`.

   C. Set the `WordWrap` property to `false`.

   D. Set the `WordWrap` property to `true`.

8. You are modifying an existing Windows form application, and you have placed a `TextBox` control on an existing `Panel` control. When you run the program, the `TextBox` control appears to be disabled. Which of following could be the reasons? (Select all that apply.)

   A. The `Enabled` property of `TextBox` is `false`.

   B. The `ReadOnly` property of `TextBox` is `true`.

   C. The `Enabled` property of `Panel` is `false`.

   D. The `Enabled` property of `Form` is `false`.

9. Your application represents an Extensible Markup Language (XML) document in a `TreeView` control. You are working on a module that gathers all data from the tree and stores it in an XML document. Which of the following properties gives you access to the entire collection of items in the `TreeView` control?

   A. `Controls`

   B. `Container`

   C. `Nodes`

   D. `TopNode`

10. You want to apply a bold font style to a `Label` control's text displayed on a form. This should not affect any other font style, such as italic or underline, that the control might already have. Which of the following expressions would return the correct `FontStyle` value?

    A.

    `lblSampleText.Font.Style | FontStyle.Bold`

    B.

    `lblSampleText.Font.Style ^ FontStyle.Bold`

APPLY YOUR KNOWLEDGE

C.

```
lblSampleText.Font.Style & FontStyle.Bold
```

D.

```
lblSampleText.Font.Style |
    (FontStyle.Underline & FontStyle.Italic)
```

11. You are creating a graphic application in which you will manipulate a variety of image formats. You have created an `OpenFileDialog` object in the program and have set the `Filter` property as follows:

```
ofdPicture.Filter=
    "Image Files (BMP, GIF, JPEG, etc.)|" +
    "*.bmp;*.gif;*.jpg;*.jpeg;" +
    "*.png;*.tif;*.tiff|" +
    "BMP Files (*.bmp)|*.bmp|" +
    "GIF Files (*.gif)|*.gif|" +
"JPEG Files (*.jpg;*.jpeg)|*.jpg;*.jpeg|" +
    "PNG Files (*.png)|*.png|"+
"TIF Files (*.tif;*.tiff)|*.tif;*.tiff|" +
    "All Files (*.*)|*.*";
```

You have created a button with its text property set as `Open Image...`. When you click this button, the Open File dialog box should display GIF Files as its first choice in the list of file types. Which of the following values for the `FilterIndex` property would you choose to achieve this in the event handler of the button's `Click` event?

A. 0

B. 1

C. 2

D. 3

12. You are developing a purchase order form; the form has a View menu with several menu items. One of the menu items has its `Name` property set as `mnuViewComments`, `Text` property set as `C&omments`, and `Shortcut` property set as `Ctrl0`.

You don't want to allow the user to view comments unless he or she has first created some comments. Which of the following solutions would you chose for doing this?

A. In the `Popup` event of the View menu, set the `Visible` property of `mnuViewComments` to `true` if the number of comments is greater than zero; otherwise, set the `Visible` property to `false`.

B. In the `Click` event of the View menu, set the `Visible` property of `mnuViewComments` to `true` if the number of comments is greater than zero; otherwise, set the `Visible` property to `false`.

C. In the `Popup` event of the View menu, set the `Enabled` property of `mnuViewComments` to `true` if the number of comments is greater than zero; otherwise, set the `Enabled` property to `false`.

D. In the `Popup` event of the `mnuViewComments` menu item, set the `Enabled` property to `true` if the number of comments is greater than zero; otherwise, set the `Enabled` property to `false`.

13. You are designing a form that needs to display dates in a long date format, although this format need not necessarily be the operating system format. Which format property of the `DateTimePicker Format` enumeration would you select?

A. `DateTimePickerFormat.Short`

B. `DateTimePickerFormat.Long`

C. `DateTimePickerFormat.Time`

D. `DateTimePickerFormat.Custom`

APPLY YOUR KNOWLEDGE

14. Assume that the menu designer has already been used to create a menu structure for a form. In order for menus to provide the functionality required, how would you assign program code to the menu items?

    A. Attach an event handler to the `Click` event of each menu item.

    B. Attach an event handler to the `Select` event of each menu item.

    C. Attach an event handler to the `Popup` event of each menu item.

    D. Attach an event handler to the `DrawItem` event of each menu item.

15. You are designing an MDI application where the parent container has a different menu structure from the child windows. If you need to suppress some of the menu items in the child windows that collide with parent menu items, which of the following options would you choose?

    A. Set the `MergeType` property to `MergeType.Remove` for the items that need to be suppressed.

    B. Set the `Visible` property to `false` for the items that need to be suppressed.

    C. Set the `MergeOrder` property to `0` for all the items that need to be suppressed.

    D. Set the `MdiList` property to `false` for all the items that need to be suppressed.

Answers to Review Questions

1. Controls can be placed on any container control or directly in a form. You can add controls to a container control in two ways: either using the Windows Forms Designer or by hand-coding them.

2. Double-clicking a control in the design view creates an event handler for the default event of the control.

3. A combo box can save space on a form because it does not display the full list until the user clicks the down arrow—except when the `DropDownStyle` property of the `ComboBox` control is set to `ComboBoxStyle.Simple`. Another reason for choosing a combo box might be because it contains a text box field, so the user can type in choices that are not in the list—unless the `DropDownStyle` property is set to `ComboBoxStyle.DropDownList`.

4. The different modes of selection that are possible with a `ListBox` control are multiple selections (`SelectionMode.MultiSimple`); multiple selections with the help of the Ctrl, Shift, and arrow keys (`SelectionMode.MultiExtended`); single selection (`SelectionMode.One`); and no selection (`SelectionMode.None`).

5. The `TabIndex` property of a control specifies the order in which controls receive focus when the user presses the Tab key. The `TabStop` property indicates whether the control can receive focus if the user presses the Tab key.

6. Modal and modeless dialog boxes are created in the same way, except that they are displayed by calling different methods. Modal dialog boxes are displayed by calling the `Form.ShowDialog()` method, and modeless dialog boxes are displayed by calling the `Form.Show()` method.

APPLY YOUR KNOWLEDGE

7. You can represent a combo box in different styles by setting its `DropDownStyle` property to different values of the `DropDownStyle` enumeration. First, it can appear as `DropDown`, which is the default style, where you click the arrow button to display the items and the text portion is editable. Second, it can appear as `DropDownList`, where it displays the list of items when the arrow button is clicked, but you cannot edit the text portion. Third, it can appear as `Simple`, where the list portion is always visible, without any arrow buttons, and the text portion is also editable.

8. The `Tag` property is commonly used to store data associated with a control. For example, you can store a reference to a `MenuItem` object in a `ToolBarButton` object's `Tag` property. By doing this, you have a reference available to its corresponding menu item that can be used to perform actions on the `MenuItem` object when the `ToolBarButton` object is clicked. If you are using the Properties window, you can just assign `string` data to the `Tag` property, but in your program, you are free to assign any type derived from the `Object` class to the `Tag` property.

9. The `Popup` event of a menu occurs just before the menu items are displayed. If a menu has no items in its submenu, the `Popup` event is not fired.

10. The `MonthCalendar` control allows you to select a range of dates, and the `DateTimePicker` control allows you to select a date and time. In order to display the date in a custom format, the `Format` property should be set to `DateTimePicker.Custom`, and the custom format should be assigned to `CustomFormat` property of the `DateTimePicker` control.

11. An MDI application consists of an MDI form that acts as a master form; it can open any number of child forms. A form must have its `IsMdiContainer` property set to `true` before it can work like an MDI container.

12. Menu items of child windows are automatically merged with menu items of MDI windows, depending on the setting of the `MergeType` and `MergeOrder` properties. If you want to merge two menus that are not part of an MDI application, you can use the `MergeMenu` method of the `MainMenu` or `ContextMenu` classes.

Answers to Exam Questions

1. **A, D,** and **E.** A label control cannot receive focus, Instead, it transfers focus to the control that has the next higher `TabIndex` (Answer A). The mnemonic character & (not the ^ character) specifies the keyboard shortcut key (Answer D). The `UseMnemonic` property should be `true` if the mnemonic character identifies the adjacent character as a shortcut key. If `UseMnemonic` is set to `false`, & does not have any special meaning and is displayed as an actual character (Answer E). For more information, see the section "Important Common Properties of Controls" in this chapter.

2. **D.** To prevent the user from being able to give focus to a control under any circumstance, you must set the control's `Enabled` property to `false`. All other options affect only the user's navigation with the Tab key. The user could still use the mouse, as long as the `Enabled` property was set to `true`. For more information, see the section "Configuring the Order of Tabs" in this chapter.

APPLY YOUR KNOWLEDGE

3. **B.** The CheckedListBox control supports only two values for the SelectionMode property: SelectionMode.None, which does not allow any selection, and SelectionMode.One, which allows multiple selections. If the other two selection modes are set through the Properties window, the IDE generates an error message; if the modes are set programmatically, an ArgumentException error is raised. For more information, see the section "The ListBox, CheckedListBox, and ComboBox Controls" in this chapter.

4. **D.** The Click and DoubleClick events are inherited from the Control class, and they occur before the new selection is set to the SelectedNode property. The BeforeSelect event also occurs just before a tree node is selected. Therefore, accessing the SelectedNode property in these events returns the old selection. The correct event to program is the AfterSelect event because it occurs after the newly selected node is set in the SelectedNode property. For more information, see the section "The TreeView and ListView Controls" in this chapter.

5. **A.** When the ThreeState property is set to false, CheckBox can be set to Indeterminate only through the program and not via user interaction. For more information, see the section "The Button, CheckBox, and RadioButton Controls" in this chapter.

6. **C.** The Popup event occurs just before a menu's list of items is displayed. You can use this event to check or uncheck menu items. Remember that setting the RadioCheck property to true does not implicitly set mutual exclusion for menu items; you are still able to check several of them together. So the Popup event is the right place to check the appropriate item and uncheck all others.

For more information, see the section "Creating Menus and Menu Items" in this chapter.

7. **B and C.** If the WordWrap property of RichTextBox is true (which is the default setting), the horizontal scrollbar is not displayed, regardless of the setting in the ScrollBars property. So if you need to display the horizontal scrollbar, you need to set WordWrap to false. If you want to display both the scrollbars all the time, setting the ScrollBars property to RichTextScrollBars.ForcedBoth does this only when the WordWrap property is false. For more information, see the section "The TextBox and RichTextBox Controls" in this chapter.

8. **A, C, and D.** A control's Enabled property depends on its parent container controls. So if the TextBox control is disabled, it might be because its own Enabled property is false or because any of its parent control's Enabled properties are false. For more information, see the section "The Enabled Property" in this chapter.

9. **C.** The Nodes property of a TreeView control gets the collection of TreeNode objects in the tree view. On the other hand, the TopNode control gets just the first fully visible node in the tree view. For more information, see the section "The TreeView and ListView Controls" in this chapter.

10. **A.** The FontStyle enumeration has a Flags attribute that allows bitwise operations on FontStyle values. When you use an expression like this:

    lblSampleText.Font.Style | FontStyle.Bold

    FontStyle.Bold represents the bold bit set as 1. The result of a bitwise OR operation with the value 1 is always 1, and hence the preceding expression returns a FontStyle value that adds to the existing FontStyle value of lblSampleText.

APPLY YOUR KNOWLEDGE

For more information, see the section "The Font Property" in this chapter.

11. **D.** The FilterIndex property specifies the filter that is currently selected in the File dialog box. It is a one-based index, so GIF Files has an index of 3. For more information, see the section "Common Dialog Boxes" in this chapter.

12. **C.** You should set the Enabled property of mnuViewComments to true if the number of comments is greater than zero; otherwise, set it to false. When the menu item is disabled, the user is neither able to select it from the menu nor open it by using the shortcut key associated with it. The Visible property hides the menu item from display, but the shortcut key still works because the menu item itself is actually enabled. For more information, see the section "Creating Menus and Menu Items" in this chapter.

13. **D.** You must select DateTimePickerFormat.Custom because the other three always display date and time according to the settings in the operating system. For more information, see the section "The MonthCalendar and DateTimePicker Controls" in this chapter.

14. **A.** The action associated with the menu item is performed when the menu is selected by the user by clicking on it. Therefore, you have to program the event handler for its Click event to do the associated task. For more information, see the section "Creating Menus and Menu Items" in this chapter.

15. **A.** You must set the MergeType property to MergeType.Remove in order to suppress the menu from appearing in the MDI container's main menu. If you set it to Visible, although the menu item would be hidden, it could be still invoked via its shortcut key. For more information, see the section "Creating MDI Applications" in this chapter.

APPLY YOUR KNOWLEDGE

Suggested Readings and Resources

1. Visual Studio .NET Combined Help Collection:

   - "Windows Forms Controls"

   - "Windows Forms Walkthroughs"

   - "Menus in Windows Forms"

   - "Multiple-Document Interface (MDI) Applications"

   - "What's New in Windows Forms and Controls"

2. Windows Forms QuickStart Tutorial:

   - "Getting Started"

   - "Building Applications"

   - "Control Reference"

3. Charles Petzold. *Programming Windows with C#.* Microsoft Press, 2001.

4. Richard Grimes. *Developing Applications with Visual Studio .NET.* Addison-Wesley, 2002.

5. Windows Forms FAQ, www.syncfusion.com/FAQ/winforms.

6. The .NET Show: Visual Studio .NET. msdn.microsoft.com/theshow/Episode015.

7. The .NET Show: .NET Does Windows. msdn.microsoft.com/theshow/Episode018.

This chapter covers the following Microsoft-specified objectives for the "Creating User Services" section of Exam 70-316, "Developing and Implementing Windows-Based Applications with Microsoft Visual C# .NET and Microsoft Visual Studio .NET":

Implement error handling in the UI.

- **Create and implement custom error messages**

- **Create and implement custom error handlers.**

- **Raise and handle errors.**

▶ When you run a Windows application, it may encounter problems that you thought would not occur. For example, the database server is down, a file is missing, or a user has entered improper values. A good Windows application must recover gracefully from this problem rather than abruptly shut down. This exam objective covers the use of exception handling to create robust and fault-tolerant applications. The Microsoft .NET Framework provides some predefined exception classes to help you catch these exceptional situations in your programs. It allows you to create your own exception handling classes and error messages that are specific to your application.

Validate user input.

▶ Garbage in results in garbage out. The best place to avoid incorrect data in an application is at the source—right where the data enters. The Windows Forms library provides an ErrorProvider component that can be used to display helpful error messages and error icons if data that is entered is incorrect. This exam objective covers the ErrorProvider component and various other input-validation techniques.

CHAPTER 3

Error Handling for the User Interface

STUDY STRATEGIES

▶ Review the "Exception Handling Statements" and the "Best Practices for Exception Handling" sections of the Visual Studio .NET Combined Help Collection. The Visual Studio .NET Combined Help Collection is installed as part of the Visual Studio .NET installation.

▶ Experiment with code that uses the try, catch, and finally blocks. Use these blocks with various combinations and inspect the differences in your code's output.

▶ Know how to create custom exception classes and custom error messages; learn to implement them in a program.

▶ Experiment with the ErrorProvider component, the Validating event, and other validation techniques. Use these tools in various combinations to validate data that is entered in controls.

INTRODUCTION

The .NET Framework uses the Windows structured exception handling model. Exception handling is an integral part of the .NET Framework that allows the Common Language Runtime (CLR) and your code to throw exceptions across languages and machines. Visual C# .NET helps you fire and handle these exceptions with the help of try, catch, finally, and throw statements. The Framework Class Library (FCL) provides a huge set of exception classes for dealing with various unforeseen conditions in the normal execution environment. If you feel the need to create custom exception classes to meet the specific requirements of an application, you can do so by deriving from the ApplicationException class.

In every program data must be validated before the program can proceed with further processing and storage of the input data. In this chapter I discuss the various techniques you can use to validate data and maintain the integrity of an application. This isn't just a matter of making sure that your application delivers the proper results; if you don't validate input, your application might represent a serious security hole in your systems.

UNDERSTANDING EXCEPTIONS

An *exception* occurs when a program encounters any unexpected problems such as running out of memory or attempting to read from a file that no longer exists. These problems are not necessarily caused by programming errors but mainly occur due to violations of certain assumptions that are made about the execution environment.

When a program encounters an exception, its default behavior is to throw the exception, which generally translates to abruptly terminating the program after displaying an error message. This is not a characteristic of a robust application and does not make your program popular with users. Your program should be able to handle these exceptional situations and, if possible, gracefully recover from them. This is called *exception handling*. Proper use of exception handling can make programs robust and easy to develop and maintain. However, if you do not use exception handling properly, you might end up having a program that performs poorly, is harder to maintain, and may potentially mislead its users.

Step by Step 3.1 demonstrates how an exception may occur in a program. Later in this chapter I explain how to handle these exceptions.

STEP BY STEP

3.1 Exceptions in Windows Applications

1. Create a new C# Windows application project in the Visual Studio .NET Integrated Development Environment (IDE). Name the project 316C03.

2. Add a new Windows form to the project. Name it StepByStep3_1.

3. Place three TextBox controls (txtMiles, txtGallons, and txtEfficiency) and a Button control (btnCalculate) on the form and arrange them as shown in Figure 3.1. Add Label controls as necessary.

4. Add the following code to the Click event handler of btnCalculate:

```
private void btnCalculate_Click(
    object sender, System.EventArgs e)
{
    //this code has no error checking. If something
    //goes wrong at run time,
    //it will throw an exception
    decimal decMiles =
        Convert.ToDecimal(txtMiles.Text);
    decimal decGallons =
        Convert.ToDecimal(txtGallons.Text);
    decimal decEfficiency = decMiles/decGallons;
    txtEfficiency.Text =
        String.Format("{0:n}", decEfficiency);
}
```

5. Insert the Main() method to launch the form. Set the form as the startup object for the project.

6. Run the project. Enter values for miles and gallons and click the Calculate button. The program calculates the mileage efficiency, as expected. Now enter the value 0 in the Gallons of Gas Used field and run the program. The program abruptly terminates after displaying an error message (see Figure 3.2).

FIGURE 3.1
The mileage efficiency calculator does not implement any error handling for the user interface.

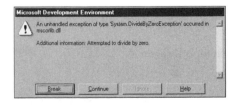

FIGURE 3.2
The development environment gives you a chance to analyze the problem when an exception occurs.

When you run the program created in Step by Step 3.1 from the IDE and the program throws an exception, the IDE gives you options to analyze the problem by debugging the program. In Step by Step 3.1, if you had instead run the program by launching the project's .exe file from Windows Explorer, the program would have terminated after displaying a message box with an error message and some debugging information (see Figure 3.3).

From the CLR's point of view, an exception is an object that encapsulates information about the problems that occur during program execution. The FCL provides two categories of exceptions:

◆ **ApplicationException**—Represents exceptions thrown by the applications

◆ **SystemException**—Represents exceptions thrown by the CLR

Both of these exception classes derive from the base class Exception, which implements the common functionality for exception handling. Neither the ApplicationException class nor the SystemException class adds any new functionality to the Exception class; they exist just to differentiate exceptions in applications from exceptions in the CLR. The classes derived from Exception share some important properties, as listed in Table 3.1

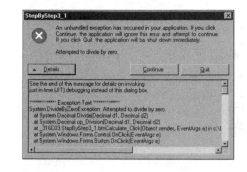

FIGURE 3.3
When a program is executed outside the Visual Studio .NET environment, debugging information is displayed when an exception is thrown.

TABLE 3.1

IMPORTANT MEMBERS OF THE Exception CLASS

Member	Type	Description
HelpLink	Property	Specifies the uniform resource locator (URL) of the help file associated with this exception.
InnerException	Property	Specifies an exception associated with this exception. This property is helpful when a series of exceptions are involved. Each new exception can preserve the information about the previous exception by storing it in the InnerException property.
Message	Property	Specifies textual information that indicates the reason for the error and provides possible resolutions.
Source	Property	Specifies the name of the application that causes the error.

continues

EXAM TIP

Floating-Point Types and Exceptions   Operations that involve floating-point types never produce exceptions. Instead, in exceptional situations, floating-point operations are evaluated by using the following rules:

- If the result of a floating-point operation is too small for the destination format, the result of the operation becomes positive zero or negative zero.

- If the result of a floating-point operation is too large for the destination format, the result of the operation becomes positive infinity or negative infinity.

- If a floating-point operation is invalid, the result of the operation becomes NaN (not a number).

TABLE 3.1   *continued*

IMPORTANT MEMBERS OF THE Exception CLASS

Member	Type	Description
StackTrace	Property	Specifies where an error has occurred. If the debugging information is available, the stack trace includes the name of the source file and the program line number.
TargetSite	Property	Represents the method that throws the current exception.

HANDLING EXCEPTIONS

Implement error handling in the user interface:

- **Create and implement custom error messages.**

- **Raise and handle errors.**

Abruptly terminating a program when an exception occurs is not a good idea. An application should be able to handle an exception and, if possible, try to recover from it. If recovery is not possible, you can have the program take other steps, such as notify the user and then gracefully terminate the application.

The .NET Framework allows exception handling to interoperate among languages and across machines. You can catch exceptions thrown by code written in one .NET language in a different .NET language. The .NET framework also allows you to handle exceptions thrown by legacy Component Object Model (COM) applications and legacy non-COM Windows applications.

Exception handling is such an integral part of the .NET framework that when you look for a method reference in the product documentation, there is always a section that specifies what exceptions a call to that method might throw.

You can handle exceptions in Visual C# .NET programs by using a combination of exception handling statements: try, catch, finally, and throw.

The `try` Block

You should place the code that might cause exceptions in a `try` block. A typical `try` block looks like this:

```
try
{
    //code that may cause exception
}
```

You can place any valid C# statements inside a `try` block, including another `try` block or a call to a method that places some of its statements inside a `try` block. The point is, at runtime you may have a hierarchy of `try` blocks placed inside each other. When an exception occurs at any point, rather than executing any further lines of code, the CLR searches for the nearest `try` block that encloses this code. The control is then passed to a matching `catch` block (if any) and then to the `finally` block associated with this `try` block.

A `try` block cannot exist on its own; it must be immediately followed by either one or more `catch` blocks or a `finally` block.

The `catch` Block

You can have several `catch` blocks immediately following a `try` block. Each `catch` block handles an exception of a particular type. When an exception occurs in a statement placed inside the `try` block, the CLR looks for a matching `catch` block that is capable of handling that type of exception. A typical `try`-`catch` block looks like this:

```
try
{
    //code that may cause exception
}
catch(ExceptionTypeA)
{
    //Statements to handle errors occurring
    //in the associated try block
}
catch(ExceptionTypeB)
{
    //Statements to handle errors occurring
    //in the associated try block
}
```

NOTE

> **Exception Handling Hierarchy** If there is no matching catch block, an unhandled exception results. The unhandled exception is propagated back to its caller code. If the exception is not handled there, it propagates further up the hierarchy of method calls. If the exception is not handled anywhere, it goes to the CLR, whose default behavior is to terminate the program immediately.

The formula the CLR uses to match the exception is simple: While matching it looks for the first catch block with either the exact same exception or any of the exception's base classes. For example, a DivideByZeroException exception would match any of these exceptions: DivideByZeroException, ArithmeticException, SystemException, and Exception. In the case of multiple catch blocks, only the first matching catch block is executed. All other catch blocks are ignored.

When you write multiple catch blocks, you need to arrange them from specific exception types to more general exception types. For example, the catch block for catching a DivideByZeroException exception should always precede the catch block for catching a ArithmeticException exception. This is because the DivideByZeroException exception derives from ArithmeticException and is therefore more specific than the latter. The compiler flags an error if you do not follow this rule.

A try block need not necessarily have a catch block associated with it, but if it does not, it must have a finally block associated with it.

STEP BY STEP

3.2 Handling Exceptions

1. Add a new Windows form to the project. Name it StepByStep3_2.

2. Create a form similar to the one created in Step by Step 3.1 (refer to Figure 3.1), with the same names for the controls.

3. Add the following code to the Click event handler of btnCalculate:

```
private void btnCalculate_Click(
    object sender, System.EventArgs e)
{
    //put all the code that may require graceful
    //error recovery in a try block
    try
    {
        decimal decMiles =
            Convert.ToDecimal(txtMiles.Text);
        decimal decGallons =
            Convert.ToDecimal(txtGallons.Text);
        decimal decEfficiency = decMiles/decGallons;
```

```
        txtEfficiency.Text =
            String.Format("{0:n}", decEfficiency);
    }
    // try block should at least have one catch or a
    // finally block. catch block should be in order
    // of specific to the generalized exceptions
    // otherwise compilation generates an error
    catch (FormatException fe)
    {
        string msg = String.Format(
            "Message: {0}\n Stack Trace:\n {1}",
            fe.Message, fe.StackTrace);
        MessageBox.Show(msg, fe.GetType().ToString());
    }
    catch (DivideByZeroException dbze)
    {
        string msg = String.Format(
            "Message: {0}\n Stack Trace:\n {1}",
            dbze.Message, dbze.StackTrace);
        MessageBox.Show(
            msg, dbze.GetType().ToString());
    }
    //catches all CLS-compliant exceptions
    catch(Exception ex)
    {
        string msg = String.Format(
            "Message: {0}\n Stack Trace:\n {1}",
            ex.Message, ex.StackTrace);
        MessageBox.Show(msg, ex.GetType().ToString());
    }
    //catches all other exceptions including
    //the NON-CLS compliant exceptions
    catch
    {
        //just rethrow the exception to the caller
        throw;
    }
}
}
```

4. Insert the `Main()` method to launch the form. Set the form as the startup object for the project.

5. Run the project. Enter values for miles and gallons and click the Calculate button. The program calculates the mileage efficiency, as expected. Now enter the value 0 in the Gallons of gas used field and run the program. Instead of abruptly terminating as in the earlier case, the program shows a message about the `DivideByZeroException` exception, as shown in Figure 3.4, and it continues running. Now enter some alphabetic characters instead of number in the fields and click the Calculate button.

continues

> **EXAM TIP**
>
> **CLS- and Non-CLS-Compliant Exceptions** All languages that follow the Common Language Specification (CLS) throw exceptions of type `System.Exception` or a type that derives from `System.Exception`. A non-CLS-compliant language may throw exceptions of other types, too. You can catch those types of exceptions by placing a general `catch` block (that does not specify any exception) with a `try` block. In fact, a general `catch` block can catch exceptions of all types, so it is the most generic of all `catch` blocks and should be the last `catch` block among the multiple `catch` blocks associated with a `try` block.

FIGURE 3.4

To get information about an exception, you can catch the `Exception` object and access its `Message` property.

continued

This time you get a FormatException exception, and the program continues to run. Now try entering very large values in both the fields. If the values are large enough, the program encounters an OverflowException exception, but because the program is catching all types of exceptions, it continues running.

The program in Step by Step 3.2 displays a message box when an exception occurs; the StackTrace property lists the methods in the reverse order of their calling sequence. This helps you understand the logical flow of the program. You can also place any appropriate error handling code in place, and you can display a message box.

When you write a catch block that catches exceptions of type Exception, the program catches all CLS-compliant exceptions. This includes all exceptions, unless you are interacting with legacy COM or Windows 32-bit Application Programming Interface (Win32 API) code. If you want to catch all kinds of exceptions, whether CLS-compliant or not, you can place a catch block with no specific type. A catch block like this must be the last catch block in the list of catch blocks because it is the most generic one.

You might be thinking that it is a good idea to catch all sorts of exceptions in your code and suppress them as soon as possible. But it is not a good idea. A good programmer catches an exception in code only if he or she can answer yes to one or more of the following questions:

◆ Will I attempt to recover from this error in the catch block?

◆ Will I log the exception information in the system event log or another log file?

◆ Will I add relevant information to the exception and rethrow it?

◆ Will I execute cleanup code that must run even if an exception occurs?

If you answer no to all these questions, then you should not catch the exception but rather just let it go. In that case, the exception propagates up to the calling code, and the calling code might have a better idea of how to handle the exception.

NOTE

checked and unchecked   Visual C# .NET provides the checked and unchecked keywords, which can be used to enclose a block of statements (for example, checked {a = c/d}) or as an operator when you supply parameters enclosed in parentheses (for example, unchecked(c/d)). The checked keyword enforces checking of any arithmetic operation for overflow exceptions. If constant values are involved, they are checked for overflow at compile time. The unchecked keyword suppresses the overflow checking and instead of raising an OverflowException exception, the unchecked keyword returns a truncated value in case of overflow.

If checked and unchecked are not used, the default behavior in C# is to raise an exception in case of overflow for a constant expression or truncate the results in case of overflow for the nonconstant expressions.

NOTE

Do Not Use Exceptions to Control the Normal Flow of Execution   Using exceptions to control the normal flow of execution can make your code difficult to read and maintain because the use of try-catch blocks to deal with exceptions forces you to fork the regular program logic between two separate locations—the try block and the catch block.

The throw Statement

A throw statement explicitly generates an exception in code. You use throw when a particular path in code results in an anomalous situation.

You should not throw exceptions for anticipated cases such as the user entering an invalid username or password; instead, you can handle this in a method that returns a value indicating whether the login is successful. If you do not have the correct permissions to read records from the user table and you try to read those records, an exception is likely to occur because a method for validating users should normally have read access to the user table.

There are two ways you can use the throw statement. In its simplest form, you can just rethrow the exception in a catch block:

```
catch(Exception e)
{
    //TODO: Add code to create an entry in event log
    throw;
}
```

This usage of the throw statement rethrows the exception that was just caught. It can be useful in situations in which you don't want to handle the exception yourself but would like to take other actions (for example, recording the error in an event log, sending an email notification about the error) when an exception occurs and then pass the exception as-is to its caller.

The second way to use the throw statement is to use it to throw explicitly created exceptions, as in this example:

```
string strMessage =
    "EndDate should be greater than the StartDate";
ArgumentOutOfRangeException newException =
    new ArgumentOutOfRangeException(strMessage);
throw newException;
```

In this example, I first create a new instance of the ArgumentOutOfRangeException object and associate a custom error message with it, and then I throw the newly created exception.

You are not required to put this usage of the throw statement inside a catch block because you are just creating and throwing a new exception rather than rethrowing an existing one. You typically use this technique in raising your own custom exceptions. I discuss how to do that later in this chapter.

WARNING

Use throw Only When Required
The throw statement is an expensive operation. Use of throw consumes significant system resources compared to just returning a value from a method. You should use the throw statement cautiously and only when necessary because it has the potential to make your programs slow.

EXAM TIP

Custom Error Messages   When you create an exception object, you should use its constructor that allows you to associate a custom error message rather than use its default constructor. The custom error message can pass specific information about the cause of the error and a possible way to resolve it.

Another way of throwing an exception is to throw it after wrapping it with additional useful information, as in this example:

```
catch(ArgumentNullException ane)
{
    //TODO: Add code to create an entry in the log file
    string strMessage = "CustomerID cannot be null";
    ArgumentNullException newException =
        new ArgumentNullException(strMessage, ane);
    throw newException;
}
```

Many times, you need to catch an exception that you cannot handle completely. In such a case you should perform any required processing and throw a more relevant and informative exception to the caller code so that it can perform the rest of the processing. In this case, you can create a new exception whose constructor wraps the previously caught exception in the new exception's `InnerException` property. The caller code then has more information available to handle the exception appropriately.

It is interesting to note that because `InnerException` is of type `Exception`, it also has an `InnerException` property that may store a reference to another exception object. Therefore, when you throw an exception that stores a reference to another exception in its `InnerException` property, you are actually propagating a chain of exceptions. This information is very valuable at the time of debugging and allows you to trace the path of a problem to its origin.

The `finally` Block

The `finally` block contains code that always executes, whether or not any exception occurs. You use the `finally` block to write cleanup code that maintains your application in a consistent state and preserves sanitation in the environment. For example, you can write code to close files, database connections, and related input/output resources in a `finally` block.

It is not necessary for a `try` block to have an associated `finally` block. However, if you do write a `finally` block, you cannot have more than one, and the `finally` block must appear after all the `catch` blocks.

Step by Step 3.3 illustrates the use of the `finally` block.

EXAM TIP

No Code in Between `try-catch-finally` Blocks When you write try, catch, and finally blocks, they should be in immediate succession of each other. You cannot write any other code between the blocks, although compilers allow you to place comments between them.

STEP BY STEP

3.3 Using the `finally` Block

1. Add a new Windows form to the project. Name it `StepByStep3_3`.

2. Place two `TextBox` controls (`txtFileName` and `txtText`), two `Label` controls (keep their default names), and a `Button` control (`btnSave`) on the form and arrange them as shown in Figure 3.5.

3. Attach the `Click` event handler to the `btnSave` control and add the following code to handle the `Click` event:

FIGURE 3.5

When you click the Save button, the code in `finally` block executes, regardless of any exception in the `try` block.

```
private void btnSave_Click(
    object sender, System.EventArgs e)
{
    // a StreamWriter writes characters to a stream
    StreamWriter sw = null;
    try
    {
        sw = new StreamWriter(txtFileName.Text);
        // Attempt to write the text box
        // contents in a file
        foreach(string line in txtText.Lines)
            sw.WriteLine(line);
        // This line only executes if there
        // were no exceptions so far
        MessageBox.Show(
          "Contents written, without any exceptions");
    }
    //catches all CLS-compliant exceptions
    catch(Exception ex)
    {
        string msg = String.Format(
            "Message: {0}\n Stack Trace:\n {1}",
            ex.Message, ex.StackTrace);
        MessageBox.Show(msg, ex.GetType().ToString());
        goto end;
    }
    // finally block is always executed to make sure
    // that the resources get closed whether or not
    // the exception occurs. Even if there is a goto
    // statement in catch or try block the final block
    // is first executed before the control goes to
    // the goto label
    finally
    {
        if (sw != null)
            sw.Close();
```

continues

continued

```
        MessageBox.Show("Finally block always " +
            "executes whether or not exception occurs");
    }
end:
    MessageBox.Show("Control is at label: end");
}
```

4. Insert a `Main()` method to launch the form. Set the form as the startup object for the project.

5. Run the project. You should see a Windows form, as shown in Figure 3.5. Enter a filename and some text. Watch the order of messages. Note that the message box being displayed in the `finally` block is always displayed prior to the message box displayed by the `end` label.

EXAM TIP

The `finally` Block Always Executes If you have a `finally` block associated with a `try` block, the code in the `finally` block always executes, whether or not an exception occurs.

Step by Step 3.3 illustrates that the `finally` block always executes. In addition, if there is a transfer-control statement such as `goto`, `break`, or `continue` in either the `try` block or the `catch` block, the control transfer happens after the code in the `finally` block is executed. What happens if there is a transfer-control statement in the `finally` block also? That is not an issue because the C# compiler does not allow you to put a transfer-control statement such as `goto` inside a `finally` block.

One of the ways the `finally` statement can be used is in the form of a `try-finally` block without any `catch` block. Here is an example:

```
try
{
    //Write code to allocate some resources
}
finally
{
    //Write code to Dispose all allocated resources
}
```

NOTE

Throwing Exceptions from the `finally` Block Although it is perfectly legitimate to throw exceptions from a `finally` block, it is not recommended. The reason for this is that when you are processing a `finally` block, you might already have an unhandled exception waiting to be caught.

This use ensures that allocated resources are properly disposed of, no matter what. In fact, C# provides a `using` statement that does the exact same job but with less code. A typical use of the `using` statement is as follows:

```
// Write code to allocate some resource. List the
// allocate resources in a comma-separated list inside
// the parentheses, with the following using block
using(...)
```

```
{
  //use the allocated resource
}
// Here, the Dispose() method is called for all the
// objects referenced in the parentheses of the
// using statement. There is no need to write
// any additional code
```

▶ An exception occurs when a program encounters any unexpected problem during normal execution.

▶ The FCL provides two main types of exceptions: SystemException and ApplicationException. SystemException represents the exceptions thrown by the CLR, and ApplicationException represents the exceptions thrown by the applications.

▶ The System.Exception class represents the base class for all CLS-compliant exceptions and provides the common functionality for exception handling.

▶ The try block consists of code that may raise an exception. A try block cannot exist on its own. It should be immediately followed by one or more catch blocks or a finally block.

▶ The catch block handles the exception raised by the code in the try block. The CLR looks for a matching catch block to handle the exception; this is the first catch block with either the exact same exception or any of the exception's base classes.

▶ If there are multiple catch blocks associated with a try block, the catch blocks should be arranged in specific-to-general order of exception types.

▶ The throw statement is used to raise an exception.

▶ The finally block is used to enclose code that needs to run, regardless of whether an exception is raised.

CREATING AND USING CUSTOM EXCEPTIONS

Implement error handling in the user interface.

- **Create and implement custom error messages.**
- **Create and implement custom error handlers.**
- **Raise and handle errors.**

EXAM TIP

Using `ApplicationException` as a Base Class for Custom Exceptions
Although you can derive custom exception classes directly from the `Exception` class, Microsoft recommends that you derive custom exception classes from the `ApplicationException` class.

The exception classes provided by the .NET Framework, combined with the custom messages created when you create a new exception object to throw or rethrow exceptions, should suffice for most of your exception handling requirements. In some cases, however, you might need exception types that are specific to the problem you are solving.

The .NET Framework allows you to define custom exception classes. To keep your custom-defined `Exception` class homogeneous with the .NET exception framework, Microsoft recommends that you consider the following when you design a custom exception class:

◆ Create an exception class only if there is no existing exception class that satisfies your requirement.

◆ Derive all programmer-defined exception classes from the `System.ApplicationException` class.

◆ End the name of your custom exception class with the word `Exception` (for example, `MyOwnCustomException`).

◆ Implement three constructors with the signatures shown in the following code:

```
public class MyOwnCustomException :
    ApplicationException
{
    // Default constructor
    public MyOwnCustomException ()
    {
    }
    // Constructor accepting a single string message
    public MyOwnCustomException (string message) :
        base(message)
    {
```

```
    }
    // Constructor accepting a string message and an
    // inner exception that will be wrapped
    // by this custom exception class
    public MyOwnCustomException(string message,
        Exception inner) : base(message, inner)
    {
    }
}
```

Step by Step 3.4 shows you how to create a custom exception.

STEP BY STEP

3.4 Creating and Using a Custom Exception

1. Add a new Windows form to the project. Name it
`StepByStep3_4`.

2. Place and arrange controls on the form as shown in Figure
3.6. Name the `TextBox` control `txtDate`, the `Button` control `btnIsLeap`, and the `Label` control inside the Results
panel `lblResult`.

3. Switch to the code view and add the following definition
for the `MyOwnInvalidDateFormatException` class to the end
of the class definition for project `StepByStep3_4`:

```
// You can create your own exception classes by
// deriving from the ApplicationException class.
// It is good coding practice to end the class name
// of the custom exception with the word "Exception"
public class MyOwnInvalidDateFormatException :
    ApplicationException
{
    // It is a good practice to implement the three
    // recommended common constructors as shown here.
    public MyOwnInvalidDateFormatException()
    {
    }
    public MyOwnInvalidDateFormatException(
        string message): base(message)
    {
        this.HelpLink =
    "file://MyOwnInvalidDateFormatExceptionHelp.htm";
    }
    public MyOwnInvalidDateFormatException(
     string message, Exception inner) :
     base(message, inner)
    {
    }
}
```

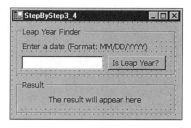

FIGURE 3.6
The leap year finder implements a custom
exception for an invalid date format.

continues

continued

4. Add the following definition for the Date class:

```
//This class does elementary date handling required
//for this program
public class Date
{
    private int day, month, year;

    public Date(string strDate)
    {
        if (strDate.Trim().Length == 10)
        {
            //Input data might be in an invalid format
            //In which case, Convert.ToDateTime()
            // method will fail
            try
            {
                DateTime dt =
                    Convert.ToDateTime(strDate);
                day = dt.Day;
                month = dt.Month;
                year = dt.Year;
            }
            //Catch the exception, attach that to the
            //custom exception and
            //throw the custom exception
            catch(Exception e)
            {
                throw new
                  MyOwnInvalidDateFormatException(
                  "Custom Exception Says: " +
                  "Invalid Date Format", e);
            }
        }
        else
            //Throw the custom exception
            throw new MyOwnInvalidDateFormatException(
                "The input does not match the " +
                "required format: MM/DD/YYYY");
    }

    //Find if the given date belongs to a leap year
    public bool IsLeapYear()
    {
        return (year%4==0) && ((year %100 !=0) ||
            (year %400 ==0));
    }
}
```

5. Add the following event handler for the Click event of btnIsLeap:

```
private void btnIsLeap_Click(
    object sender, System.EventArgs e)
{
    try
    {
        Date dt = new Date(txtDate.Text);
        if (dt.IsLeapYear())
            lblResult.Text =
                "This date is in a leap year";
        else
            lblResult.Text =
                "This date is NOT in a leap year";
    }
    //Catch the custom exception and
    //display an appropriate message
    catch (MyOwnInvalidDateFormatException dte)
    {
        string msg;
        //If some other exception was also
        //attached with this exception
        if (dte.InnerException != null)
          msg = String.Format(
          "Message:\n {0}\n\n Inner Exception:\n {1}",
          dte.Message, dte.InnerException.Message);
        else
            msg = String.Format(
                "Message:\n {0}\n\n Help Link:\n {1}",
                dte.Message, dte.HelpLink);

        MessageBox.Show(msg, dte.GetType().ToString());
    }
}
```

6. Insert a Main() method to launch the form. Set the form as the startup object for the project.

7. Run the project. Enter a date and click the button. If the date you enter is in the required format, you see a result displayed in the Results group box; otherwise, you get a message box showing the custom error message thrown by the custom exception, as in Figure 3.7.

FIGURE 3.7

You can associate a customized error message and a help link with a custom exception.

GUIDED PRACTICE
EXERCISE 3.1

You are a Windows developer for a data analysis company. For one of your applications you need to create a keyword searching form that asks for a filename and a keyword from the user (as shown in Figure 3.8). The form should search for the keyword in the file and display the number of lines that contain the keyword in the results group box. Your form assumes that the entered keyword is a single word. If it is not a single word, you need to create and throw a custom exception for that case.

How would you throw a custom exception to implement custom error messages and custom error handling in your program?

You should try working through this problem on your own first. If you get stuck, or if you'd like to see one possible solution, follow these steps:

1. Add a new form to your Visual C# .NET project. Name the form `GuidedPracticeExercise3_1.cs`.

2. Place and arrange controls on the form as shown in Figure 3.8. Name the `TextBox` control for accepting the filename `txtFileName` and the Browse control `btnBrowse`. Set the `ReadOnly` property of `txtFileName` to `true`. Name the `TextBox` control for accepting the keyword `txtKeyword` and the `Button` control `btnSearch`. Set the tab order of the form in the correct order, to ensure that the user's cursor is not placed in the read-only text box when the application starts.

3. Add an `OpenFileDialog` control to the form and change its name to `dlgOpenFile`.

4. Create a new class named `BadKeywordFormatException` that derives from `ApplicationException` and place the following code in it:

```
public class BadKeywordFormatException :
    ApplicationException
{
    public BadKeywordFormatException()
    {
    }
    public BadKeywordFormatException(string message):
        base(message)
```

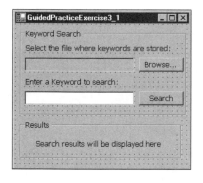

FIGURE 3.8
The keyword searching form throws a custom exception if the input is not in the required format.

```
    {
    }
    public BadKeywordFormatException(string message,
        Exception inner): base(message, inner)
    {
    }
}
```

5. Create a method named `GetKeywordFrequency()` in the `GuidedPracticeExercise3_1` class. This method should accept a string and return the number of lines that contain the string. Add the following code to the method:

```
private int GetKeywordFrequency(string path)
{
    if(this.txtKeyword.Text.Trim().IndexOf(' ') >= 0)
        throw new BadKeywordFormatException(
          "The keyword must only have a single word");

    int count = 0;
    if (File.Exists(path))
    {
        StreamReader sr =
          new StreamReader(txtFileName.Text);
        while (sr.Peek() > -1)
         if (sr.ReadLine().IndexOf(txtKeyword.Text)
           >= 0)
                count++;
    }
    return count;
}
```

6. Add the following code to the `Click` event handler of `btnBrowse`:

```
private void btnBrowse_Click(
    object sender, System.EventArgs e)
{
    if (dlgOpenFile.ShowDialog() == DialogResult.OK)
        txtFileName.Text = dlgOpenFile.FileName;
}
```

7. Add the following code to the `Click` event handler of `btnSearch`:

```
private void btnSearch_Click(
    object sender, System.EventArgs e)
{
    if (txtKeyword.Text.Trim().Length == 0)
    {
        MessageBox.Show(
            "Please enter a keyword to search for",
            "Missing Keyword");
        return;
    }
```

continues

continued

```
try
{
    lblResult.Text = String.Format(
     "The keyword: '{0}', was found in {1} lines",
      txtKeyword.Text,
      GetKeywordFrequency(txtFileName.Text));
}
catch(BadKeywordFormatException bkfe)
{
    string msg = String.Format(
        "Message:\n {0}\n\n StackTrace:\n{1}",
        bkfe.Message, bkfe.StackTrace);
    MessageBox.Show(msg, bkfe.GetType().ToString());
}
}
```

8. Insert the `Main()` method to launch the form
   `GuidedPracticeExercise3_1.cs`. Set the form as the startup
   object for the project.

9. Run the project. Click the Browse button and select an existing file. Enter the keyword to search for in the file and click
   the Search button. If the keyword entered is in the wrong format (for example, if it contains two words), the custom
   exception is raised.

If you have difficulty following this exercise, review the sections
"Handling Exceptions" and "Creating and Using Custom
Exceptions" earlier in this chapter. After reviewing, try this exercise
again.

MANAGING UNHANDLED EXCEPTIONS

The CLR-managed applications execute in an isolated environment
called an *application domain*. The `AppDomain` class of the `System`
namespace programmatically represents the application domain. The
`AppDomain` class provides a set of events that allows you to respond
when an assembly is loaded, when an application domain is
unloaded, or when an application throws an unhandled exception.

In this chapter, we are particularly interested in the UnhandledException event of the AppDomain class, which occurs when any other exception handler does not catch an exception. Table 3.2 lists the properties of the UnhandledExceptionEventArgs class.

TABLE 3.2

IMPORTANT MEMBERS OF THE UnhandledExceptionEventArgs CLASS

Member	Type	Description
ExceptionObject	Property	Specifies the unhandled exception object that corresponds to the current domain
IsTerminating	Property	Indicates whether the CLR is terminating

You can attach an event handler with the UnhandledException event to take custom actions such as logging exception-related information. A log that is maintained over a period of time may help you find and analyze patterns with useful debugging information. There are several ways you can log information that is related to an event:

◆ By using the Windows event log

◆ By using custom log files

◆ By using databases such as SQL Server 2000

◆ By sending email notifications

Among these ways, the Windows event log offers the most robust method for event logging because it requires minimal assumptions for logging events. The other cases are not as fail-safe; for example, an application could loose connectivity with the database or with the SMTP server, or you might have problems writing an entry in a custom log file.

The .NET Framework provides you access to the Windows event log through the EventLog class. Windows 2000 and later have three default logs—application, system, and security. You can use the EventLog class to create custom event logs. You can easily view the event log by using the Windows Event Viewer utility.

You should familiarize yourself with the important members of the EventLog class that are listed in Table 3.3.

NOTE

When Not to Use the Windows Event Log The Windows event log is not available on older versions of Windows, such as Windows 98. If your application needs to support computers running older versions of Windows, you might want to create a custom error log. In a distributed application, you might want to log all events centrally in a SQL Server database. To make the scheme fail-safe, you can choose to log locally if the database is not available and transfer the log to the central database when it is available again.

TABLE 3.3

IMPORTANT MEMBERS OF THE EventLog CLASS

Member	Type	Description
Clear()	Method	Removes all entries from the event log and makes it empty
CreateEventSource()	Method	Creates an event source that you can use to write to a standard or custom event log
Entries	Property	Gets the contents of the event log
Log	Property	Specifies the name of the log to read from or write to
MachineName	Property	Specifies the name of the computer on which to read or write events
Source	Property	Specifies the event source name to register and use when writing to the event log
SourceExists()	Method	Specifies whether the event source exists on a computer
WriteEntry()	Method	Writes an entry in the event log

STEP BY STEP

3.5 Logging Unhandled Exceptions in the Windows Event Log

1. Add a new Windows form to the project. Name it StepByStep3_5.

2. Place three TextBox controls (txtMiles, txtGallons, and txtEfficiency) and a Button control (btnCalculate) on the form and arrange them as shown in Figure 3.1. Add Label controls as necessary.

3. Switch to the code view and add the following using directive at the top of the program:

```
using System.Diagnostics;
```

4. Double-click the Button control and add the following code to handle the Click event handler of the Button control:

```
private void btnCalculate_Click(
    object sender, System.EventArgs e)
{
    //This code has no error checking.
    //If something goes wrong at run time,
    //it will throw an exception
    decimal decMiles =
        Convert.ToDecimal(txtMiles.Text);
    decimal decGallons =
        Convert.ToDecimal(txtGallons.Text);
    decimal decEfficiency = decMiles/decGallons;
    txtEfficiency.Text =
        String.Format("{0:n}", decEfficiency);
}
```

5. Add the following code in the class definition:

```
private static void UnhandledExceptionHandler(
    object sender, UnhandledExceptionEventArgs ue)
{
    Exception unhandledException =
        (Exception) ue.ExceptionObject;

    //If no event source exist,
    //create an event source.
    if(!EventLog.SourceExists(
           "Mileage Efficiency Calculator"))
    {
        EventLog.CreateEventSource(
            "Mileage Efficiency Calculator",
            "Mileage Efficiency Calculator Log");
    }

    // Create an EventLog instance
    // and assign its source.
    EventLog eventLog = new EventLog();
    eventLog.Source = "Mileage Efficiency Calculator";

    // Write an informational entry to the event log.
    eventLog.WriteEntry(unhandledException.Message);
    MessageBox.Show("An exception occurred: " +
        "Created an entry in the log file");
}
```

6. Insert the following `Main()` method:

```
[STAThread]
public static void Main()
{
    // Create an AppDomain object
    AppDomain adCurrent = AppDomain.CurrentDomain;
    // Attach the UnhandledExceptionEventHandler to
    // the UnhandledException of the AppDomain object
    adCurrent.UnhandledException += new
```

continues

continued

```
    UnhandledExceptionEventHandler(
      UnhandledExceptionHandler);
    Application.Run(new StepByStep3_5());
}
```

7. Set the form as the startup object for the project.

8. Run the project. Enter invalid values for miles and gallons and run the program. When an unhandled exception occurs, a message box is displayed, notifying you that the exception has been logged. You can view the logged message by selecting Event Viewer from the Administrative Tools section of the Control Panel. The Event Viewer displays the Mileage Efficiency Calculator Log and other logs in the left pane (see Figure 3.9). The right pane of the Event Viewer shows the events that are logged. You can double-click an event to view the description and other properties of the event, as shown in Figure 3.10.

FIGURE 3.9
You can view messages logged to an event log by using the Windows Event Viewer.

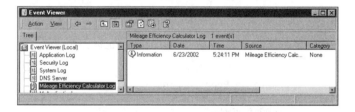

FIGURE 3.10
You can view event properties for a particular event to see the event-related details.

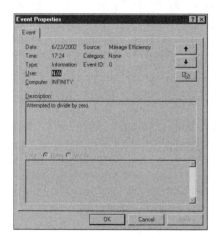

▶ If the existing exception classes do not meet your exception handling requirements, you can create new exception classes that are specific to your application by deriving them from the `ApplicationException` class.

▶ You can use the `UnhandledException` event of the `AppDomain` class to manage unhandled exceptions.

▶ You can use the `EventLog` class to log events to the Windows event log.

VALIDATING USER INPUT

Validate user input.

Garbage in results in garbage out. When designing an application that accepts data from the user, you must ensure that the entered data is acceptable for the application. The most relevant place to ensure the validity of data is at the time of data entry itself. You can use various techniques for validating data:

◆ You can restrict the values that a field can accept by using standard controls such as combo boxes, list boxes, radio buttons, and check boxes. These allow users to select from a set of given values rather than permit free keyboard entry.

◆ You can capture the user's keystrokes and analyze them for validity. Some fields may require the user to enter only alphabetic values but no numeric values or special characters; in that case, you can accept the keystrokes for alphabetic characters while rejecting others.

◆ You can restrict entry in some data fields by enabling or disabling them, depending on the state of other fields.

◆ You can analyze the contents of the data field as a whole and warn the user of any incorrect values when he or she attempts to leave the field or close the window.

The first technique is discussed relative to the use of various controls in Chapter 2, "Controls"; the following sections cover rest of these techniques.

Keystroke-Level Validation

When you press a key on a control, three events take place, in the following order:

1. KeyDown

2. KeyPress

3. KeyUp

You can program the event handlers for these events in order to perform keystroke-level validation. You choose the event to program based on the order in which the event is fired and the information that is passed in the event argument of the event handler.

The KeyPress event happens after the KeyDown event but before the KeyUp event. Its event handler receives an argument of type KeyPressEventArgs. Table 3.4 lists the properties of KeyPressEventArgs.

TABLE 3.4

IMPORTANT MEMBERS OF THE KeyPressEventArgs CLASS

Member	Type	Description
Handled	Property	Indicates whether the event has been handled
KeyChar	Property	Returns the character value that corresponds to the key

The KeyPress event fires only if the key that is pressed generates a character value. To handle keypresses for function keys, control keys, and cursor movement keys, you must use the KeyDown and KeyUp events.

The KeyDown and KeyUp events occur when the user presses and releases a key on the keyboard, respectively. Event handlers of these events receive an argument of KeyEventArgs type; it provides the properties listed in Table 3.5.

TABLE 3.5

IMPORTANT MEMBERS OF THE KeyEventArgs CLASS

Member	Type	Description
Alt	Property	Returns true if the Alt key is pressed; otherwise, returns false.
Control	Property	Returns true if the Ctrl key is pressed; otherwise, returns false.
Handled	Property	Indicates whether the event has been handled.
KeyCode	Property	Returns the keyboard code for the event. Its value is one of the values specified in the Keys enumeration.
KeyData	Property	Returns the key code for the pressed key, along with modifier flags that indicate what combination of modifier keys (Ctrl, Shift, and Alt) are pressed at the same time.
KeyValue	Property	Returns the integer representation of the KeyData property.
Modifiers	Property	Returns the modifier flags that indicate what combination of modifier keys (Ctrl, Shift, and Alt) are pressed.
Shift	Property	Returns true if the Shift key is pressed; otherwise, returns false.

The KeyPreview Property

By default, only the active control receives the keystroke events. The Form object also has the KeyPress, KeyUp, and KeyDown events, but they are fired only when all the controls on the form are either hidden or disabled.

When you set the KeyPreview property of a form to true, the form receives all three events—KeyPress, KeyUp, and KeyDown—just before the active control receives these events. This allows you to set up a two-tier validation on controls. If you want to discard certain types of characters at the form level, you can set the Handled property for the event argument to true (this does not allow the event to propagate to the active control); otherwise, the events propagate to the active control. You can then use keystroke events at the control level to perform field-specific validations, such as restricting the field to only numeric digits.

Field-Level Validation

Field-level validation ensures that the value entered in the field is in accordance with the application's requirements. If it is not, you can display an error to alert the user about the problem. These are appropriate reasons to perform field-level validations:

◆ When the user attempts to leave the field

◆ When the content of the field changes for any reason

When the user enters and leaves a field, the events occur in the following order:

1. Enter (Occurs when a control is entered.)

2. GotFocus (Occurs when a control receives focus.)

3. Leave (Occurs when focus leaves a control.)

4. Validating (Occurs when a control is validating.)

5. Validated (Occurs when a control is finished validating.)

6. LostFocus (Occurs when a control looses focus.)

The Validating event is the ideal place to store the validating logic for a field. The following sections explain the use of the Validating event and the CausesValidation property for field-level validation. They also discuss the use of the ErrorProvider component to display error messages to the user.

The Validating Event

The Validating event is the ideal place for storing the field-level validation logic for a control. The event handler for validating the event receives an argument of type CancelEventArgs. Its only property, Cancel, cancels the event when it is set to true.

Inside the Validating event, you can write code to do the following:

◆ Programmatically correct any errors or omissions made by the user.

◆ Show error messages and alerts to the user so that the user can fix the problem.

Inside the `Validating` event, you might also want to retain the focus in the current control, thus forcing the user to fix the problem before proceeding further. To do this, you can use either of the following techniques:

◆ Use the `Focus()` method of the control to transfer the focus back to the field.

◆ Set the `Cancel` property of `CancelEventArgs` to `true`. This cancels the `Validating` event, leaving the focus in the control.

A related event, `Validated`, is fired just after the `Validating` event occurs—and it enables you to take actions after the control's contents have been validated.

The `CausesValidation` Property

When you use the `Validating` event to restrict the focus in the control by canceling the event, you must also consider that you are making the control sticky.

Consider a case in which the user is currently on a control such as a `TextBox` control, with incorrect data, and you are forcing the user to fix the problem before leaving the control, by setting the `Cancel` property of `CancelEventArgs` to `true`. When the user clicks the Help button in the toolbar to check what is wrong, nothing happens unless the user makes a correct entry. This can be an annoying situation for the user, so you want to avoid it in your applications.

The `CausesValidation` property comes to your rescue in such a case. The default value of the `CausesValidation` property for a control is `true` for all controls, which means that the `Validating` event fires for any control, requiring validation before the control in question receives the focus.

When you want a control to respond, regardless of the validation status of other controls, you should set the `CausesValidation` property of that control to `false`. For example, in the previous example, the Help button in the toolbar would be set with the `CausesValidation` property set to `false`.

NOTE

The `Validating` Event and Sticky Forms The `Validating` event fires when you close a form. If inside the `Validating` event you set the `Cancel` property of the `CancelEventArgs` argument to `true`, the `Validating` event also cancels the close operation.

There is a workaround for this problem. Inside the `Validating` event, you should set the `Cancel` property of the `CancelEventArgs` argument to `true` if the mouse is in the form's client area. The close button is in the title bar that is outside the client area of the form. Therefore, when the user clicks the close button, the `Cancel` property is not set to `true`.

The ErrorProvider Component

The ErrorProvider component in the Visual Studio .NET toolbox is useful when you're showing validation-related error messages to the user. The ErrorProvider component can set a small icon next to a field when it contains an error. When the user moves the mouse pointer over the icon, an error message pops up as a ToolTip. This is a better way of displaying error messages than the old way of using message boxes because it eliminates at least two serious problems with message boxes:

◆ When you use message boxes, if you have errors on multiple controls, popping up several message boxes might annoy or scare your users.

◆ After the user dismisses a message box, the error message is no longer available for reference.

Table 3.6 lists some important members of the ErrorProvider class with which you should familiarize yourself.

TABLE 3.6

IMPORTANT MEMBERS OF THE ErrorProvider CLASS

Member	Type	Description
BlinkRate	Property	Specifies the rate at which the error icon flashes.
BlinkStyle	Property	Specifies a value that indicates when the error icon flashes.
ContainerControl	Property	Specifies the component's parent control.
GetError()	Method	Returns the error description string for the specified control.
Icon	Property	Specifies an icon to display next to a control. The icon is displayed only when an error description string has been set for the control.
SetError()	Method	Sets the error description string for the specified control.
SetIconAlignment()	Method	Sets the location at which to place an error icon with respect to the control. It has one of the ErrorIconAlignment values (BottomLeft, BottomRight, MiddleLeft, MiddleRight, TopLeft, and TopRight).
SetIconPadding()	Method	Specifies the amount of extra space to leave between the control and the error icon.

The ErrorProvider component displays an error icon next to a field, based on the error message string. The error message string is set by the SetError() method. If the error message is empty, no error icon is displayed, and the field is considered correct. Step by Step 3.5 shows how to use the ErrorProvider component.

STEP BY STEP

3.6 Using the ErrorProvider Component and Other Validation Techniques

1. Add a new Windows form to the project. Name it StepByStep3_6.

2. Place three TextBox controls (txtMiles, txtGallons, and txtEfficiency) and a Button control (btnCalculate) on the form and arrange them as shown in Figure 3.11. Add Label controls as necessary.

3. The ErrorProvider component is present in the Windows Forms tab of the Visual Studio .NET toolbox. Add an ErrorProvider component (errorProvider1) to the form. The ErrorProvider component is placed in the component tray.

4. Double-click the form and add the following code to handle the Load event handler of the Form control:

```
private void StepByStep3_6_Load(
    object sender, System.EventArgs e)
{
    // Set the ErrorProvider's Icon
    // alignment for the TextBox controls
    errorProvider1.SetIconAlignment(
        txtMiles, ErrorIconAlignment.MiddleLeft);
    errorProvider1.SetIconAlignment(
        txtGallons, ErrorIconAlignment.MiddleLeft);
}
```

5. Attach the Validating event handlers to the TextBox controls and add the following code to handle the Validating event handler of the txtMiles and txtGallons controls:

```
private void txtMiles_Validating(object sender,
    System.ComponentModel.CancelEventArgs e)
{
    try
```

continues

continued

```
    {
        decimal decMiles =
            Convert.ToDecimal(txtMiles.Text);
        errorProvider1.SetError(txtMiles, "");
    }
    catch(Exception ex)
    {
        errorProvider1.SetError(txtMiles, ex.Message);
    }
}

private void txtGallons_Validating(object sender,
    System.ComponentModel.CancelEventArgs e)
{
    try
    {
        decimal decGallons =
            Convert.ToDecimal(txtGallons.Text);
        if (decGallons > 0)
            errorProvider1.SetError(txtGallons, "");
        else
            errorProvider1.SetError(txtGallons,
              "Please enter a value > 0");
    }
    catch(Exception ex)
    {
        errorProvider1.SetError(
          txtGallons, ex.Message);
    }
}
```

6. Add the following code to the Click event handler of
btnCalculate:

```
private void btnCalculate_Click(
    object sender, System.EventArgs e)
{
    // Check whether the error description is not empty
    // for either of the TextBox controls
    if (errorProvider1.GetError(txtMiles) != "" ||
        errorProvider1.GetError(txtGallons) != "")
        return;

    try
    {
        decimal decMiles =
            Convert.ToDecimal(txtMiles.Text);
        decimal decGallons =
            Convert.ToDecimal(txtGallons.Text);
        decimal decEfficiency = decMiles/decGallons;
        txtEfficiency.Text =
            String.Format("{0:n}", decEfficiency);
    }
```

```
catch(Exception ex)
{
    string msg = String.Format(
        "Message: {0}\n Stack Trace:\n {1}",
        ex.Message, ex.StackTrace);
    MessageBox.Show(msg, ex.GetType().ToString());
}
}
```

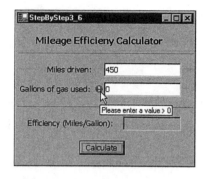

7. Insert the `Main()` method to launch the form. Set the form as the startup object for the project.

8. Run the project. Enter values for miles and gallons and click Calculate. The program calculates the mileage efficiency, as expected. When you enter an invalid value into any of the `TextBox` controls, the error icon starts blinking and displays the error message when the mouse is hovered over the error icon, as shown in Figure 3.11.

FIGURE 3.11
The `ErrorProvider` component shows the error icon and the error message in a nonintrusive way.

Enabling Controls Based on Input

One of the useful techniques for restricting user input is selectively enabling and disabling controls. These are some common cases in which you would want to do this:

◆ Your application might have a check box titled Check Here if You Want to Ship to a Different Location. Only when the user checks the check box should you allow him or her to enter values in the fields for the shipping address. Otherwise, the shipping address is the same as the billing address.

◆ In a Find dialog box, you have two buttons: Find and Cancel. You want to keep the Find button disabled initially and enable it only when the user enters search text in a text box.

The `Enabled` property for a control is `true` by default. When you set it to `false`, the control cannot receive the focus and appears grayed out.

For a control such as `TextBox`, you can also use the `ReadOnly` property to restrict user input. One advantage of using the `ReadOnly` property is that the control is still able to receive focus, so you are able to scroll through any text in the control that is not initially visible.

In addition, you can select and copy the text to the Clipboard, even if the ReadOnly property is true.

Other Properties for Validation

In addition to the techniques mentioned in the preceding sections, the properties described in the following sections allow you to enforce some restrictions on user input.

The `CharacterCasing` Property

The CharacterCasing property of the TextBox control changes the case of characters in the text box as required by the application. For example, you might want to convert all characters entered in a text box used for entering a password to lowercase so that there are no problems due to case-sensitivity.

The values of the CharacterCasing property can be set to three values: CharacterCasing.Lower, CharacterCasing.Normal (the default value), and CharacterCasing.Upper.

The `MaxLength` Property

The MaxLength property of a TextBox or ComboBox control specifies the maximum number of characters that the user can enter into the control. This property is handy when you want to restrict the size of some fields, such as fields for telephone numbers or zip codes. This property is useful in scenarios in which you are adding or updating records in a database with the values entered in the controls; in such a case you can use the MaxLength property to prevent the user from entering more characters than the corresponding database field can handle.

When the MaxLength property is zero (the default), the number of characters that can be entered is limited only by the available memory.

EXAM TIP

The Scope of the MaxLength Property The MaxLength property affects only the text that is entered into the control interactively by the user. Programmatically, you can set the value of the Text property to a value that is longer than the value specified by the MaxLength property.

GUIDED PRACTICE
EXERCISE 3.2

As a Windows developer for a data analysis company, you recently developed a keyword searching form for your Windows application (refer to Guided Practice Exercise 3.1). The form asks for a filename and a keyword from the user, and then it searches for the keyword in the file and displays the number of lines that contain the keyword in the results group box. The form assumes that the entered keyword is a single word. In the solution in Guided Practice Exercise 3.1, if the keyword is not a single word, the form creates and throws a custom exception for that case. Since you created that solution, you have studied field-level validation techniques and realized that for this scenario, the use of field-level validation provides a much more elegant solution.

You now want to modify the keyword searching form. Its basic functionality is still the same as in Guided Practice Exercise 3.1, but you need to incorporate a few changes in the user interface. Initially the keyword text box and the Search button are disabled; you should enable these controls as the user progresses through the application. If the keyword entered by the user is not a single word, instead of throwing an exception, you need to display the error icon with the keyword text box and set an error message. The keyword text box should not lose focus unless it has valid data.

How would you create such a form?

You should try working through this problem on your own first. If you get stuck, or if you'd like to see one possible solution, follow these steps:

1. Add a new form to your Visual C# .NET project. Name the form GuidedPracticeExercise3_2.cs.

2. Place and arrange the controls on the form as shown in Figure 3.8. Name the TextBox control for accepting the filename txtFileName and the Browse button btnBrowse. Set the ReadOnly property of txtFileName to true. Name the TextBox control for accepting the keyword txtKeyword and the Button control btnSearch. Set the tab order of the form in the correct order so that the user's cursor is not placed in a read-only text box when the application starts.

continues

continued

3. Add an OpenFileDialog control to the form and change its name to dlgOpenFile. Add an ErrorProvider component (errorProvider1) to the form. The ErrorProvider component is placed in the component tray.

4. Double-click the form to attach the Load event handler to the form. Add the following code to handle the Load event of the Form control:

```
private void GuidedPracticeExercise3_2_Load(
    object sender, System.EventArgs e)
{
    // Disable the keyword text box and Search button
    txtKeyword.Enabled = false;
    btnSearch.Enabled = false;
    errorProvider1.SetIconAlignment(
        txtKeyword, ErrorIconAlignment.MiddleLeft);
}
```

5. Attach TextChanged and Validating event handlers to the txtKeyword control and add the following code:

```
private void txtKeyword_TextChanged(
    object sender, System.EventArgs e)
{
    if(this.txtKeyword.Text.Length==0)
        this.btnSearch.Enabled = false;
    else
        this.btnSearch.Enabled = true;
}

private void txtKeyword_Validating(object sender,
    System.ComponentModel.CancelEventArgs e)
{
    if(this.txtKeyword.Text.Trim().IndexOf(' ') >= 0)
    {
        errorProvider1.SetError(txtKeyword,
          "You must only specify a single word");
        txtKeyword.Focus();
        txtKeyword.Select(0, txtKeyword.Text.Length);
    }
    else
        errorProvider1.SetError(txtKeyword, "");
}
```

6. Create a method named GetKeywordFrequency() that accepts a string and returns the number of lines containing it. Add the following code to the method:

```
private int GetKeywordFrequency(string path)
{
    int count = 0;
    if (File.Exists(path))
```

```
    {
        StreamReader sr =
            new StreamReader(txtFileName.Text);
        while (sr.Peek() > -1)
            if (sr.ReadLine().IndexOf(txtKeyword.Text)
                >= 0)
                count++;
    }
    return count;
}
```

7. Add the following code to the `Click` event handler of
   `btnBrowse`:

```
private void btnBrowse_Click(
    object sender, System.EventArgs e)
{
    if (dlgOpenFile.ShowDialog() == DialogResult.OK)
    {
        txtFileName.Text = dlgOpenFile.FileName;
        this.txtKeyword.Enabled = true;
        this.txtKeyword.Focus();
    }
}
```

8. Add the following code to the `Click` event handler of
   `btnSearch`:

```
private void btnSearch_Click(
    object sender, System.EventArgs e)
{
    if (errorProvider1.GetError(txtKeyword) != "")
        return;
    try
    {
        lblResult.Text = String.Format(
          "The keyword: '{0}' was found in {1} lines",
          txtKeyword.Text,
          GetKeywordFrequency(txtFileName.Text));
    }
    catch(Exception ex)
    {
        string msg = String.Format(
            "Message:\n {0}\n\n StackTrace:\n{1}",
            ex.Message, ex.StackTrace);
        MessageBox.Show(msg, ex.GetType().ToString());
    }
}
```

9. Insert the `Main()` method to launch form
   `GuidedPracticeExercise3_2.cs`. Set the form as the startup
   object for the project.

continues

continued

10. Run the project. The keyword text box and the search button are disabled. Click the Browse button and select an existing file; this enables the keyword text box. Enter the keyword to search in the file; this enables the Search button. Click the Search button. If the keyword entered is in the wrong format (for example, if it contains two words), the `ErrorProvider` component shows the error message and the icon.

If you have difficulty following this exercise, review the section "Validating User Input," earlier in this chapter, and then try this exercise again.

REVIEW   BREAK

▶ It a good practice to validate user input at the time of data entry. Thoroughly validated data results in consistent and correct data stored by the application.

▶ When a user presses a key, three events are generated, in the following order: `KeyDown`, `KeyPress`, and `KeyUp`.

▶ The `Validating` event is the ideal place for storing the field-level validation logic for a control.

▶ The `CausesValidation` property specifies whether validation should be performed. If it is set to `false`, the `Validating` and `Validated` events are suppressed.

▶ The `ErrorProvider` component in the Visual Studio .NET toolbox is used to show validation-related error messages to the user.

▶ A control cannot receive the focus and appears grayed out if its `Enabled` property is set to `false`.

Chapter Summary

The .NET Framework provides fully integrated support for exception handling. In fact, it allows you to raise exceptions in one language and catch them in a program written in another language. The `try` block is used to enclose code that might cause exceptions. The `catch` block is used to handle the exceptions raised by the code in the `try` block, and the `finally` block ensures that certain code is executed, regardless of whether an exception occurs.

The FCL provides a large number of exception classes that represent most of the exceptions that a program may encounter. If you prefer to create your own custom exception class, you can do so by deriving your exception class from the `ApplicationException` class.

This chapter describes a variety of ways to validate user input. The Windows Forms library provides an `ErrorProvider` component that is used to signal errors. You can also associate custom icons and error messages with the `ErrorProvider` component.

KEY TERMS

- exception
- exception handling
- input validation

APPLY YOUR KNOWLEDGE

Exercises

3.1   Handling Exceptions

Recall that Step by Step 2.5 in Chapter 2 demonstrates the use of common dialog boxes through the creation of a simple rich text editor. This editor allows you to open and save a rich text file. You can also edit the text and change its fonts and colors. The program works fine in all cases except when you try to open or save a file that is already open; in that case, the program throws a System.IO.IOException exception.

The objective of this exercise is to make a robust version of this program that generates a warning about the open file rather than abruptly terminating the program.

Estimated time: 15 minutes

1. Open a new Windows application in Visual C# .NET. Name it 316C03Exercises.

2. Add a Windows form to the project. Name the form Exercise3_1.

3. Place five Button controls on the form. Name them btnOpen, btnSave, btnClose, btnColor, and btnFont, and change their Text properties to &Open..., &Save..., Clos&e..., &Color..., and &Font..., respectively. Place a RichTextBox control on the form and name it rtbText. Arrange all the controls as shown in Figure 3.12.

FIGURE 3.12
This robust version of a simple rich text editor handles the exceptions of System.IO.IOException type.

4. Drag and drop the following components from the toolbox onto the form: OpenFileDialog, SaveFileDialog, ColorDialog, and FontDialog.

5. Switch to the code view and add the following using directive to the top of the program:

   using System.IO;

6. Double-click the Open button to attach an event handler to this Click event. Add the following code to the event handler:

```
private void btnOpen_Click(
    object sender, System.EventArgs e)
{
    //Allow user to select only *.rtf files
    openFileDialog1.Filter =
        "Rich Text Files (*.rtf)|*.rtf";
    if(openFileDialog1.ShowDialog()
        == DialogResult.OK)
    {
        try
        {
            //Load the file contents
            //into the RichTextBox control
            rtbText.LoadFile(
            openFileDialog1.FileName,
            RichTextBoxStreamType.RichText);
        }
        catch(System.IO.IOException ioe)
```

```
        {
            MessageBox.Show(ioe.Message,
                "Error opening file");
        }
    }
}
```

7. Add the following code to handle the `Click` event of the Save button:

```
private void btnSave_Click(
    object sender, System.EventArgs e)
{
    //Default choice for saving file
    //is *.rtf but user can select
    //All Files to save with
    //another extension
    saveFileDialog1.Filter =
     "Rich Text Files (*.rtf)|*.rtf|" +
     "All Files (*.*)|*.*";
    if(saveFileDialog1.ShowDialog()
        == DialogResult.OK)
    {
        try
        {
            //Save the RichTextBox control's
            //content to a file
            rtbText.SaveFile(
            saveFileDialog1.FileName,
            RichTextBoxStreamType.RichText);
        }
        catch(System.IO.IOException ioe)
        {
            MessageBox.Show(ioe.Message,
                "Error saving file");
        }
    }
}
```

8. Add the following code to handle the `Click` event of the Close button:

```
private void btnClose_Click(
    object sender, System.EventArgs e)
{
    //close the form
    this.Close();
}
```

9. Add the following code to handle the `Click` event of the Color button:

```
private void btnColor_Click(
    object sender, System.EventArgs e)
{
    if(colorDialog1.ShowDialog()
        == DialogResult.OK)
    {
        //Change the color of the selected
        //text. If no text is selected,
        // change the active color
        rtbText.SelectionColor =
            colorDialog1.Color;
    }
}
```

10. Add the following code to handle the `Click` event of the Font button:

```
private void btnFont_Click(
    object sender, System.EventArgs e)
{
    if(fontDialog1.ShowDialog()
        == DialogResult.OK)
    {
        //Change the font of the selected
        //text. If no text is selected,
        //change the active font
        rtbText.SelectionFont =
            fontDialog1.Font;
    }
}
```

11. Insert the `Main()` method to launch the form. Set the form as the startup object.

12. Run the project. Click on the Open button and try to open an already opened file. An error message appears, warning about the file already being open, as shown in Figure 3.13.

FIGURE 3.13
Instead of abnormal program termination, you now get an error message about the already open file.

APPLY YOUR KNOWLEDGE

3.2   Validating User Input

One technique for input validation is to force the user to fix an erroneous field before allowing him or her to move to another field. To achieve this, you can set the Cancel property of the CancelEventArgs argument of the field's Validating event to false.

In this exercise, you create a login form (see Figure 3.14) that accepts a username and password. It forces the user to enter the username. The user should also be able to close the application by clicking the Cancel button, regardless of the validation status of the fields.

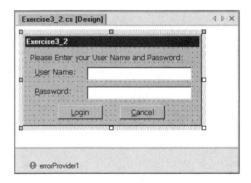

FIGURE 3.14
A nonsticky login form validates the input and allows users to close the application by clicking the Cancel button.

Estimated time: 15 minutes

1. Open a Visual C# .NET Windows application in the Visual Studio .NET IDE. Name it 316C03Exercises.

2. Add a new form to the application. Name it Exercise3_2.

3. Place three Label controls (keep their default names), two TextBox controls (txtUserName and txtPassword), two Button controls (btnLogin and btnCancel), and an ErrorProvider component (errorProvider1) on the form. The ErrorProvider component is placed in the component tray. Arrange the controls in the form as shown in Figure 3.14.

4. Change the ControlBox property of the form to false, the CharacterCasing property of the txtPassword control to Lower, and the CausesValidation property of the btnCancel control to false.

5. Double-click the Form control to attach a Load event handler; add the following code to the event handler:

```
private void Exercise3_2_Load(
    object sender, System.EventArgs e)
{
    errorProvider1.SetIconAlignment(
        txtUserName,
        ErrorIconAlignment.MiddleLeft);
    errorProvider1.SetIconAlignment(
        txtPassword,
        ErrorIconAlignment.MiddleLeft);
}
```

6. Declare the following variable outside a method block in the class:

```
//closingFlag is used to check if the
//user has clicked the Close button
private bool closingFlag = false;
```

7. Add the following code to the Click event handler of the Cancel button:

```
private void btnCancel_Click(
    object sender, System.EventArgs e)
{
    closingFlag = true;
    this.Close();
}
```

APPLY YOUR KNOWLEDGE

8. Add the following code to the `Click` event handler of the Login button:

```
private void btnLogin_Click(
    object sender, System.EventArgs e)
{
    string strMessage = String.Format(
     "The following information:" +
     "\n\nUserName: {0}\n\nPassword: {1}" +
     "\n\n can now be passed to the " +
     "middle-tier for validation",
     txtUserName.Text, txtPassword.Text);
    MessageBox.Show(strMessage,
        "User Input Validation Succeeded");
}
```

9. Attach the following event handling code to the `Validating` events of both the `txtUserName` and `txtPassword` controls:

```
private void
    txtUserNamePassword_Validating(
    object sender,
    System.ComponentModel.CancelEventArgs e)
{
    TextBox fieldToValidate =
        (TextBox) sender;

    if (!closingFlag)
    {
    if(fieldToValidate.Text.Trim().Length
        == 0)
        {
            errorProvider1.SetError(
                fieldToValidate,
     "Please enter a value for this field");
            e.Cancel = true;
        }
        else if (
    fieldToValidate.Text.Trim().IndexOf(' ')
        >=0)
        {
            errorProvider1.SetError(
                fieldToValidate,
     "You may NOT have spaces in this field");
            fieldToValidate.Select(0,
                fieldToValidate.Text.Length);
            e.Cancel = true;
        }
    }
}
```

10. Attach the following event handling code to the `Validated` event of both the `txtUserName` and `txtPassword` controls:

```
private void txtUserNamePassword_Validated(
    object sender, System.EventArgs e)
{
    TextBox fieldToValidate =
        (TextBox) sender;
    errorProvider1.SetError(
        fieldToValidate, "");
}
```

11. Insert the `Main()` method to launch the form. Set the form as the startup object.

12. Run the project. Click the Login button, and you are forced to enter the username. However, you can click the Cancel button to close the application.

Review Questions

1. What is the default behavior of the .NET Framework when an exception is raised?

2. What is the base class of all exceptions that provides basic functionality for exception handling? What are the two main types of exception classes and their purposes?

3. Explain the `Message` and `InnerException` properties of the `Exception` class.

4. What is the purpose of a `try-catch` block?

5. How many `catch` blocks can be associated with a try block? How should they be arranged?

6. What is the importance of a `finally` block?

7. Can you associate custom error messages with the exception types defined by the CLR? If yes, how do you do it?

APPLY YOUR KNOWLEDGE

8. What are some of the points you should consider before creating `Custom` exceptions?

9. What is the importance of the `Validating` event?

10. What is the purpose of the `ErrorProvider` component?

Exam Questions

1. You are creating a data import utility for a personal information system that you recently designed. When the record in the source data file is not in the required format, the application needs to throw a custom exception. You want to keep the name of this exception class as `InvalidRecordStructureException`. Which of the following classes would you choose as the base class for the custom exception class?

   A. `ApplicationException`

   B. `Exception`

   C. `SystemException`

   D. `InvalidFilterCriteriaException`

2. You are assisting a colleague in solving the compiler error that her code is throwing. This is the problematic portion of her code:

```
try
{
    bool success =
        GenerateNewtonSeries(500, 0);
    //more code here
}
catch(DivideByZeroException dbze)
{
    //exception handling code
}
catch(NotFiniteNumberException nfne)
{
```

```
    //exception handling code
}
catch(ArithmeticException ae)
{
    //exception handling code
}
catch(OverflowException e)
{
    //exception handling code
}
```

To remove the compilation error, which of the following ways would you rearrange the code?

A.

```
 try
{
    bool success =
        GenerateNewtonSeries(500, 0);
    //more code here
}
catch(DivideByZeroException dbze)
{
    //exception handling code
}
catch(ArithmeticException ae)
{
    //exception handling code
}
catch(OverflowException e)
{
    //exception handling code
}
```

 B.

```
try
{
    bool success =
        GenerateNewtonSeries(500, 0);
    //more code here
}
catch(DivideByZeroException dbze)
{
    //exception handling code
}
catch(Exception ae)
{
    //exception handling code
}
catch(OverflowException e)
```

APPLY YOUR KNOWLEDGE

```
{
    //exception handling code
}
```

C.

```
try
{
    bool success =
        GenerateNewtonSeries(500, 0);
    //more code here
}
catch(DivideByZeroException dbze)
{
    //exception handling code
}
catch(NotFiniteNumberException nfne)
{
    //exception handling code
}
catch(OverflowException e)
{
    //exception handling code
}
catch(ArithmeticException ae)
{
    //exception handling code
}
```

D.

```
try
{
    bool success =
        GenerateNewtonSeries(500, 0);
    //more code here
}
catch(DivideByZeroException dbze)
{
    //exception handling code
}
catch(NotFiniteNumberException nfne)
{
    //exception handling code
}
catch(Exception ae)
{
    //exception handling code
}
catch(ArithmeticException e)
{
    //exception handling code
}
```

3. You are required to debug a program that contains exception handling code. To understand the program better, you create a stripped-down version of it and include some `MessageBox` statements that give you clues about the flow of the program's execution. The program has the following code:

```
try
{
    int num = 100;
    int den = 0;
    MessageBox.Show("Message1");
    try
    {
        int res = num/den;
        MessageBox.Show("Message2");
    }
    catch(ArithmeticException ae)
    {
        MessageBox.Show("Message3");
    }
}
catch(DivideByZeroException dbze)
{
    MessageBox.Show("Message4");
}
finally
{
    MessageBox.Show("Message5");
}
```

Which of the following options describes the correct order of displayed messages?

A.

```
Message1
Message2
Message3
Message4
Message5
```

B.

```
Message1
Message3
Message5
```

APPLY YOUR KNOWLEDGE

C.

```
Message1
Message4
Message5
```

D.

```
Message1
Message2
Message4
Message5
```

4. In your Windows application, you want to determine the type of an exception. You have written the following code:

```
try
{
    try
    {
        throw new
            ArgumentOutOfRangeException();
    }
    catch(ArgumentException ae)
    {
        throw new ArgumentException(
            "Out of Range", ae);
    }
}
catch(Exception e)
{
    MessageBox.Show(
    e.InnerException.GetType().ToString());
}
```

When the program containing this code segment is executed, what output is displayed by the message box?

A. System.Exception

B. System.ApplicationException

C. System.ArgumentException

D. System.ArgumentOutOfRangeException

5. The Validating event of a TextBox control in your Windows application has the following code:

```
01 private void textBox1_Validating(
      object sender, CancelEventArgs e)
02 {
03    try
04    {
05        MyValidatingCode();
06    }
07    catch(Exception ex)
08    {
09
10        textBox1.Select(0,
              textBox1.Text.Length);
11        this.errorProvider1.SetError(
              textBox1, ex.Message);
12    }
13 }
```

The MyValidatingCode() method validates the contents of the text box. If the contents are invalid, the MyValidatingCode() method throws an exception and retains control in the text box. (The line numbers in the code sample are for reference purposes only.) Which of the following lines of code should be in line 9?

A.

```
e.Cancel = true;
```

B.

```
e.Cancel = false;
```

C.

```
textBox1.CausesValidation = true;
```

D.

```
textBox1.CausesValidation = false;
```

6. You have designed a windows form that works as a login screen. The form has two TextBox controls, named txtUserName and txtPassword. You want to ensure that user can enter only lowercase characters in the control. Which of the following options would you recommend?

APPLY YOUR KNOWLEDGE

A. Set the form's `KeyPreview` property to `true` and program the `KeyPress` event of the form to convert uppercase letters to lowercase letters.

B. Create a single event handler that is attached to the `KeyPress` event of both `txtUserName` and `txtPassword`. Program this event handler to convert the uppercase letters to lowercase.

C. Use the `CharacterCasing` property.

D. Use the `Char.ToLower()` method in the `TextChanged` event handler.

7. You need to create a custom exception class in a Windows application. You have written the following code for the `Exception` class:

```
public class KeywordNotFound:
    ApplicationException
{
    public KeywordNotFoundException()
    {
    }
    public KeywordNotFoundException(
        string message, Exception inner)
        : base(message, inner)
    {
    }
}
```

A peer reviewer of the code finds that you did not follow some of the best practices for creating a custom exception class. Which of the following suggestions do you need to incorporate? (Choose all that apply.)

A. Name the exception class `KeywordNotFoundException`.

B. Derive the exception class from the base class `Exception` instead of `ApplicationException`.

C. Add one more constructor to the class, with the following signature:

```
public KeywordNotFoundException(
    string message) : base(message)
{
}
```

D. Add one more constructor to the class, with the following signature:

```
public KeywordNotFoundException(
    Exception inner) : base(inner)
{
}
```

E. Derive the exception class from the base class `SystemException` instead of `ApplicationException`.

8. In your Windows application, you have created a dialog box that allows users to set options for the application. You have also created a Help button that users can press to get help on various options for the dialog box. You validate the data entered by the user in a text box titled Complex Script. If the user enters an invalid value, you set the focus back in the control by setting the `Cancel` property of the `CancelEventArgs` object to `true`. While you are testing the application, you discover that when you enter invalid data in the text box, you cannot click the Help button unless you correct the data first. What should you do to correct the problem?

A. Set the `CausesValidation` property of the `TextBox` control to `false`.

B. Set the `CausesValidation` property of the `TextBox` control to `true`.

C. Set the `CausesValidation` property of the Help button to `false`.

D. Set the `CausesValidation` property of the Help button to `true`.

APPLY YOUR KNOWLEDGE

9. You are writing exception handling code for an order entry form. When an exception occurs, you want to get information about the sequence of method calls and the line number in the method where the exception occurs. Which property of the Exception class could help you?

   A. HelpLink

   B. InnerException

   C. Message

   D. StackTrace

10. Which of the following statements is true regarding the following usage of the throw statement?

```
catch(Exception e)
{
    throw;
}
```

   A. The throw statement catches and rethrows the current exception.

   B. The throw statement catches, encapsulates, and then rethrows the current exception.

   C. The throw statement must be followed by an exception object to throw.

   D. The throw statement transfers control to the finally block that follows the catch block.

11. You are creating a Windows form that works as a login screen for an order entry system designed for the sales department of your company. Which of the following strategies would you follow?

   A. Design a ValidateUser() method. Throw a new custom exception EmployeeNotFound when the entered username is not in the database.

   B. Design a ValidateUser() method. Throw an ArgumentException exception when the user types special characters in the username field or the password field.

   C. Design a ValidateUser() method that returns true if the username and password are correct and otherwise returns false.

   D. Design a ValidateUser() method. Throw an ApplicationException exception when the entered username is not in the database.

12. You want to capture all the exceptions that escape from the exception handling code in your application and log them in the Windows event log. Which of the following techniques would you use?

   A. Write all the code of the Main() method inside a try block, attach a generic catch block to that try block, and handle the exception there.

   B. Write all the code of the Main() method inside a try block, attach a catch block that catches all exceptions of type Exception, and write code to make an entry in the event log.

   C. Program the ProcessExit event handler of the AppDomain class.

   D. Program the UnhandledException event handler of the AppDomain class.

13. Which of the following is the most robust way to record the unhandled exceptions in an application?

   A. Create an entry in the Windows event log.

   B. Create an entry in the application's custom log file.

APPLY YOUR KNOWLEDGE

C. Create an entry in a table in a Microsoft SQL Server 2000 database.

D. Send an email message using SMTP.

14. The structured exception handling mechanism of the .NET Framework allows you to handle which of the following types of exceptions? (Choose all the answers that apply.)

A. Exceptions from all CLS-compliant languages

B. Exceptions from non-CLS-compliant languages

C. Exceptions from unmanaged COM code

D. Exceptions from unmanaged non-COM code

15. Which of the following statements is true about the following code segment?

```
const int someVal1 = Int32.MaxValue;
const int someVal2 = Int32.MaxValue;
int result;
checked
{
    result = someVal1 * someVal2;
}
```

A. The code generates an `OverflowException` exception.

B. The code executes successfully without any exceptions.

C. The code causes a compile-time error.

D. The code executes successfully, but the value of the resulting variable is truncated.

Answers to Review Questions

1. The .NET Framework terminates the application after displaying an error message when an exception is raised.

2. The `Exception` class is the base class that provides common functionality for exception handling. The two main types of exceptions derived from the `Exception` class are `SystemException` and `ApplicationException`. `SystemException` represents the exceptions thrown by the CLR, and `ApplicationException` represents the exceptions thrown by the applications.

3. The `Message` property describes the current exception. The `InnerException` property represents an exception object associated with the current exception object. This property is helpful when a series of exceptions are involved because each new exception can preserve the information about the previous exception by storing it in the `InnerException` property.

4. The `try` block is used to enclose code that may raise an exception. The `catch` block handles the exception raised by the code in the `try` block.

5. Zero or more `catch` blocks can be associated with a `try` block. If there is no `catch` block associated with a `try` block, a `finally` block should follow the `try` block; otherwise, a compile-time error occurs. The `catch` blocks should be arranged from top to bottom in the order of specific to general exception types; otherwise, a compile-time error occurs.

6. The code contained by the `finally` block always executes, regardless of whether any exception occurs in the `try` block. Therefore, you can use the `finally` block to write cleanup code—such as closing data connections, closing files, and so on—that needs to happen, regardless of whether an exception occurs.

7. Yes, you can associate custom error messages with the exception classes defined by the CLR in order to provide more meaningful information to the calling code. The constructor of these classes that accepts as its parameter the exception message can be used to pass the custom error message.

8. Custom exceptions should be derived from `ApplicationException` and should be created only if any of the existing classes do not meet the requirements of your application. The custom exception classes should have names that end with the word `Exception` and should implement three constructors (a default constructor that takes no arguments, a constructor that takes a string argument, and a constructor that takes a string as well as an `Exception` object) of the base class.

9. The `Validating` event is the ideal place for storing the field-level validation logic for a control. The `Validating` event handler can be used to cancel the event if validation fails, thus forcing the focus to the control. This requires the user to enter correct data.

10. The `ErrorProvider` component in the Visual Studio .NET toolbox can be used to show validation-related error icons and error messages to the user.

Answers to Exam Questions

1. **A.** When you create a class for handling custom exceptions in your programs, the best practice is to derive it from the `ApplicationException` class. The `SystemException` class is for the system-defined exceptions. The `Exception` class is the base class for both the `ApplicationException` and `SystemException` classes and should not be subclassed. For more information, see the section "Creating and Using Custom Exceptions" in this chapter.

2. **C.** When you have multiple `catch` blocks associated with a `try` block, you must write them in the order of most specific to least specific. The `catch` block corresponding to the `ArithmeticException` exception should come at the end because it is more general than `DivideByZeroException`, `NotFiniteNumberException`, and `OverFlowException`, which are derived from it. For more information, see the section "The `catch` Block" in this chapter.

3. **B.** When an exception occurs in a `try` block, the program searches for a matching `catch` block associated with that `try` block. Because the `ArithmeticException` type is more general than the `DivideByZeroException` type, all `DivideByZeroException` exceptions are handled in the `catch` block that catches the `ArithmeticException` exception. In all cases, the `finally` block is executed. For more information, see the sections "The `catch` Block" and "The `finally` Block" in this chapter.

4. **D.** The message box displays a `System.ArgumentOutOfRangeException` exception because that is the exception that you caught and wrapped in the `InnerException` property of the exception that was caught later by the outer `catch` block. For more information, see the section "The `throw` Statement" in this chapter.

5. **A.** When you want to retain the control inside a control after the `Validating` event is processed, you must set the `Cancel` property of the `CancelEventArgs` argument in the `Validating` event to true. The correct answer is therefore `e.Cancel = true`. The `CausesValidation` property has a different purpose: It is used to decide whether a `Validating` event is fired for a control. For more information, see the section "The `Validating` Event" in this chapter.

APPLY YOUR KNOWLEDGE

6. **C.** The `CharacterCasing` property, when set to `CharacterCasing.Lower` for a `TextBox` control, converts all uppercase letters to lowercase as you type them. It is the preferred way to enforce either lowercase or uppercase input in a text box. For more information, see the section "Other Properties for Validation" in this chapter.

7. **A and C.** As a good exception handling practice, you should end the name of the exception class with the word `Exception`. In addition, an exception class must implement three standard constructors. The missing constructor is the one given in Answer C. For more information, see the section "Creating and Using Custom Exceptions" in this chapter.

8. **C.** When you want a control to respond, regardless of the validation status of other controls, you should set the `CausesValidation` property of that control to `false`. Therefore, the Help button should have its `CausesValidation` property set to `false`. For more information, see the section "The `CausesValidation` Property" in this chapter.

9. **D.** The `StackTrace` property of the `Exception` class and the classes that derive from it contain information about the sequence of method calls and the line numbers in which exceptions occur. Therefore, it is the right property to use. For more information, see the section "Understanding Exceptions" in this chapter.

10. **A.** The `throw` statement re-throws the current exception. For more information, see the section "The `throw` Statement" in this chapter.

11. **C.** It is obvious that the user might make typing mistakes while typing his or her username or password. You should not throw exceptions for these situations; you should instead design a `ValidateUser()` method that returns a result indicating whether the login is successful. For more information, see the section "Validating User Input" in this chapter.

12. **D.** To capture all unhandled exceptions for an application, you must program the `UnhandledEvent` event handler of the `AppDomain` class. For more information, see the section "Managing Unhandled Exceptions" in this chapter.

13. **A.** Logging on to the Windows event log is the most robust solution because the other solutions have more assumptions that may fail. For example, your application might loose connectivity with the database or with the SMTP server, or you might have problems writing an entry to a custom log file. For more information, see the section "Managing Unhandled Exceptions" in this chapter.

14. **A, B, C,** and **D.** The .NET Framework allows you to handle all kinds of exceptions, including cross-language exceptions, for both CLS- and non-CLS-compliant languages. It also allows you to handle exceptions from unmanaged code, both COM as well as non-COM. For more information, see the section "Understanding Exceptions" in this chapter.

APPLY YOUR KNOWLEDGE

15. **C.** When constant values appear inside the checked statement, they are checked for overflow at compile time. Because you are multiplying the two maximum possible values for integer, the result cannot be stored inside an integer.

The compiler detects this problem and generates a compile-time error. For more information, see the section "Handling Exceptions" in this chapter.

Suggested Readings and Resources

1. Visual Studio .NET Combined Help Collection:

   • "Exception Management in .NET"

   • "Exception Handling Statements"

   • "Best Practices for Exception Handling"

2. Harvey M. Dietel, et al. *C# How to Program*. Prentice Hall, 2001.

3. Jeffrey Richter. *Applied Microsoft .NET Framework Programming*. Microsoft Press, 2001.

4. Exception Management in .NET. msdn.microsoft.com/library/ en-us/dnbda/html/exceptdotnet.asp.

This chapter covers the following Microsoft-specified objectives for the "Creating and Managing Components and .NET Assemblies" and "Creating User Services" sections of Exam 70-316, "Developing and Implementing Windows-Based Applications with Microsoft Visual C# .NET and Microsoft Visual Studio .NET":

Instantiate and invoke a Web Service or component.

- **Instantiate and invoke a .NET component.**

Create a Windows control.

- **Create a Windows control by using visual inheritance.**

- **Host a Windows control inside Microsoft Internet Explorer.**

▶ The Microsoft .NET Framework allows programmers to create reusable code components. This objective requires you to know how to create components from three important classes: Component, Control, and UserControl. The Microsoft .NET Framework also supports extensibility by allowing you to create new controls that extend the functionality provided by the existing controls through a technique known as *visual inheritance*. In addition to hosting controls in a Windows form, you should know how to host them in Microsoft Internet Explorer.

CHAPTER 4

Creating and Managing .NET Components and Assemblies

Create and modify a .NET assembly.

- **Create and implement satellite assemblies.**

- **Create resource-only assemblies.**

▶ Assemblies are the basic units for reuse, versioning, security, and deployment for components and applications that are created by using the .NET Framework. This objective requires you to know about creating and modifying assemblies. This chapter helps you learn various important concepts related to assemblies: private and shared assemblies, single-file and multifile assemblies, and resource-only and satellite assemblies.

Create, implement, and handle events.

▶ The user interface programming to create a Windows-based application is mostly event driven. Events allow you to respond to changes in the environment of an application. For this exam objective you are required to know how to create and implement your own events.

▶ Review the "Component Authoring Walkthroughs" and the "Component Authoring— Decision Chart" sections of the Visual Studio .NET Combined Help Collection.

▶ Create reusable components in the different ways described in this chapter and inspect the differences between them. Host these components in a form and test the components.

▶ Experiment with creating controls by inheriting from existing user-created controls through visual inheritance. Step by Step 4.6 explains how to create controls using visual inheritance.

▶ Know how to host Windows controls in Microsoft Internet Explorer. Step by Step 4.7 shows an example.

▶ Experiment with creating your own events and implementing them. Step by Step 4.3 and Guided Practice Exercise 4.1 provide examples.

▶ Review the "Programming with Assemblies" and "Creating Satellite Assemblies" sections of the Visual Studio .NET Combined Help Collection.

▶ Understand how to create and manage different types of assemblies in the .NET Framework.

▶ Experiment with creating satellite assemblies. Refer to Step by Step 4.16 and Chapter 8, "Globalization," for examples of creating satellite assemblies. Experiment with Step by Step 4.17 to learn how to create resource-only assemblies.

INTRODUCTION

Visual C# .NET provides a rich collection of components that you can use to quickly create user interfaces and functionality for your Windows applications. For more advanced or customized functionality, you can create your own custom components or purchase them from a component vendor. Custom-created components encapsulate user interface and programming logic that you can directly plug in to your application.

The .NET Framework allows you to create components in several different ways:

◆ You can create a non-visual component by deriving from the `Component` class.

◆ You can create a control by painting its own user interface by deriving from the `Control` class, or any of its derived classes.

◆ You can create a user control (also known as a composite control) based on other existing controls by deriving from the `UserControl` class or any of its derived classes.

Visual C# .NET helps you extend the functionality of a user interface by allowing you to create new controls by inheriting from existing Windows controls. This technique is called *visual inheritance*.

The components you create cannot run by themselves; they need to be hosted in a container. The preferred place to host Windows controls is in a Windows form, although you can also host controls inside Microsoft Internet Explorer.

.NET Framework *assemblies* are the basic units for reuse, versioning, security, and deployment for components that are created by using the .NET Framework. An assembly is a collection of types and resources that together form a logical unit of functionality. There are different types of assemblies of which you should be aware: single-file and multifile assemblies, private and shared assemblies, static and dynamic assemblies, and satellite and resource-only assemblies.

In this chapter I show you how to create and manage components, events, and assemblies in .NET applications.

CREATING AND MANAGING .NET COMPONENTS

Instantiate and invoke a Web Service or component.

- **Instantiate and invoke a .NET component.**

Create a Windows control.

- **Create a Windows control by using visual inheritance.**

- **Host a Windows control inside Microsoft Internet Explorer.**

There are three main classes for creating components in the .NET Framework:

- ◆ The `Component` class

- ◆ The `Control` class

- ◆ The `UserControl` class

The most general of these three classes is the `Component` class. It is the base class for all the components in the .NET Framework. The `Component` class belongs to the `System.ComponentModel` namespace. You can derive from the `Component` class to create nonvisual components such as the `Timer` component or the `EventLog` component.

The `Control` class extends the `Component` class and enables you to create components that have a visual representation. The `Control` class belongs to the `System.Windows.Forms` namespace. Most of the Windows controls—including the `Form`, `Label`, and `Button` controls—inherit from this class. The `Control` class by itself gives you very basic functionality such as getting user input through the keyboard and mouse and participating in the message loop that allows event handling and security. The `Control` class does not implement painting of controls, so when you derive from this class, you need to implement your own rendering logic by overriding the `Paint()` method. This is desirable if you want to design a control that has a user interface that needs to be different from common Windows controls.

You might also want to design a control by assembling existing controls. For example, you might not want to have a different Paint() method but instead might want to achieve a custom functionality by having some controls work together. The .NET Framework provides the UserControl class for this purpose. The UserControl class belongs to the System.Windows.Forms namespace.

The UserControl class provides an empty control. You can create a new control by assembling existing controls on the surface of a UserControl. The UserControl class derives from the ContainerControl class and is therefore capable of acting as a container control.

Basically, when you create a class that derives directly or indirectly from the Component class, you create a .NET component. I often use the term *control* for components that are derived from the Control class or any of its child classes, including the UserControl class. I refer to components that do not render any user interface as simply *components*.

In the following section I discuss how to create a control based on the UserControl class. Later, I discuss how you can design controls that derive from the Control class and render their own user interfaces. Finally, I show you how to create a nonvisual component by deriving it from the Component class.

Creating Components by Extending the UserControl Class

To create a control by using Visual Studio .NET, you need to create a project based on the Windows Control Library template. This project allows you to package one or more controls in a dynamic link library (DLL) file. The DLL file can then be used by other applications that need to use the controls contained within the DLL file.

By default, Visual Studio .NET prefers that you create controls based on the UserControl class. When you create the Windows Control Library project, Visual Studio .NET automatically adds a class derived from UserControl to it. The design view for this class shows a borderless, captionless gray area, where you can assemble your control by selecting controls from the toolbox and placing them on the control's gray area.

NOTE

Working with Multiple Projects In this chapter, I create various types of projects, so rather than grouping all Step by Steps into a single project, I create a project for each Step by Step. Visual Studio .NET allows organization of multiple related projects in a solution.

In Step by Step 4.1 you create a ColorMixer control that allows you to select Red, Green, and Blue values to create the desired color.

STEP BY STEP

4.1 Creating Components by Extending the UserControl Class

1. Launch Visual Studio .NET. Select File, New, Blank Solution, and name the new solution 316C04.

2. In Solution Explorer, right-click the name of the solution and select Add, New Project. Select Visual C# projects from the Project Types tree and then select Windows Control Library from the list of templates on the right. Name the project StepByStep4_1. The Component Designer should show the control as a captionless, borderless form.

3. In Solution Explorer, change the name of the UserControl1.cs file to ColorMixer.cs. Right-click the control surface and select View Code from the context menu. Change the name of the class and its constructor from UserControl1 to ColorMixer.

4. Drag and drop a GroupBox control, three Label controls, and three TrackBar controls and arrange them on the form as shown in Figure 4.1. Name the TrackBar controls tbRed, tbGreen, and tbBlue, and change their Maximum properties to 255, their Orientation properties to Vertical, their TickFrequency properties to 15, and their TickStyle properties to Both.

5. Switch to the class view by selecting View, Class View. Navigate to the ColorMixer class, right-click it, and select Add, Add Property. The C# Add Property Wizard appears. Use the wizard to add three properties, one by one, and name them Red, Green, and Blue. Set the other input fields in the wizard as shown in Figure 4.2.

continues

NOTE

Visual Studio .NET Editions The templates for creating Windows Control Library and Class Library projects are not part of Visual Studio .NET Standard Edition. You need to have Visual Studio .NET Professional, Enterprise Developer or Enterprise Architect in order to use these templates.

However, you can create all components without using Visual Studio .NET by manually writing all the code that Visual Studio .NET would otherwise generate automatically for you because all the bits are in the .NET Framework Software Development Kit (SDK). It's just not nearly as easy as having Visual Studio .NET do the work for you.

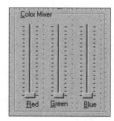

FIGURE 4.1
You can create a user control by deriving from the UserControl class.

continued

FIGURE 4.2
You can use the C# Add Property Wizard to add
a new property to a C# class.

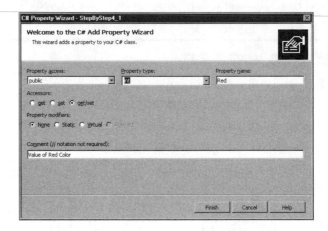

6. Switch to the code view and modify the generated code as
shown here:

```
[Category("Color"), Description("Value of Red Color")]
public int Red
{
    get
    {
        return tbRed.Value;
    }
    set
    {
        tbRed.Value = value;
    }
}
[Category("Color"),
    Description("Value of Green Color")]
public int Green
{
    get
    {
        return tbGreen.Value;
    }
    set
    {
        tbGreen.Value = value;
    }
}
[Category("Color"),
    Description("Value of Blue Color")]
public int Blue
{
    get
    {
        return tbBlue.Value;
    }
```

```
    set
    {
        tbBlue.Value = value;
    }
}
```

7. Select Build, Build StepByStep4_1. This step generates the code for your control and packages it into the file StepByStep4_1.dll, which is located in the bin\Debug or bin\Release directory of your project. You can navigate to it through Solution Explorer: Just select the project and click the Show All Files button in the Solution Explorer When you build the project, a file named StepByStep4_1.dll is created. This DLL files contains the code for the ColorMixer control.

In Step by Step 4.1, although StepByStep4_1.dll contains just the definition for one control, you can add more control definitions by adding more user controls to it. You could even make it a huge library that could be used across your organizations or commercialized.

Although the user control is created in Step by Step 4.1, you can't see it in action yet for two reasons. First, a control can't exist by itself. It needs to be placed inside a parent container control such as a Windows form. Second, the code in the DLL file can't instantiate itself because there is no Main() method in it.

In Step by Step 4.2 you create a Windows application project that hosts the ColorMixer control on a form.

STEP BY STEP

4.2 Hosting the ColorMixer Control in a Windows Application

1. Activate Solution Explorer for solution 316C04, right-click the solution name (316C04), and select Add, Add New Project. Select Windows Application as the template for the new project and name the project StepByStep4_2.

continues

continued

2. In Solution Explorer, right-click `Form1.cs` and rename it `TestColorMixer`. Open the Properties window for this form and change both its `Name` and `Text` properties to `TestColorMixer`. Switch to the code view of the form and modify the `Main()` method to launch `TestColorMixer` instead of `Form1`.

3. In Solution Explorer, right-click project `StepByStep4_2` and select Add Reference from the context menu. In the Add Reference dialog box (see Figure 4.3), select the Projects tab, select the Project named `StepByStep4_1` from the list view, and click the Select button. The selected project is then copied to the Selected Components list. Click OK. You should see a reference to `StepByStep4_1` in the reference node of your project in Solution Explorer, as shown in Figure 4.4.

FIGURE 4.3▶
The Add Reference Dialog Box allows you to add a reference to a component.

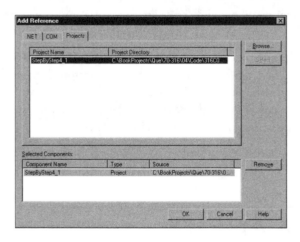

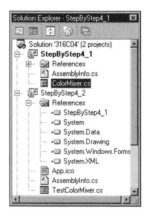

FIGURE 4.4▲
You can view the references added to a project via Solution Explorer.

4. In the toolbox, click the Windows form and scroll down the list of Windows form controls until you find a control named `ColorMixer`, as shown in Figure 4.5. Double-click the control to add it to the form. Accept the default name `colorMixer1` for the control and activate the Properties window. Arrange the properties by category by clicking the Categorized tool button (with the icon that shows tree nodes) on the Properties window. Look for the Color category and set the `Red`, `Green`, and `Blue` properties to `100` each, as shown in Figure 4.6.

5. Add a `Label` control (`lblColorSample`) and a `Button` control (`btnSetColor`) to the form and arrange the controls as shown in Figure 4.7.

6. Double-click the `Button` control to attach an event handler to the `Click` event. Add the following code to the handler:

```
private void btnSetColor_Click(object sender,
    System.EventArgs e)
{
    lblColorSample.BackColor = Color.FromArgb(
       colorMixer1.Red, colorMixer1.Green,
       colorMixer1.Blue);
}
```

7. Activate Solution Explorer, right-click the name of the solution, and select Properties. In the Solution Property Pages dialog box, select `StepByStep4_2` as the single startup project.

8. Run the project. You should see the form hosting the `ColorMixer` control. Work with the `Red`, `Green`, and `Blue` trackbars to select the color values and then click the Set Color button. The background color of the label shows the color that is created from the `Red`, `Green`, and `Blue` values you selected.

Step by Step 4.2 shows that a custom-created control can be used just like any other standard Windows form control. You can drag and drop a custom control from the Visual Studio .NET toolbox onto the form's surface and set its properties just as you would do for any standard Windows control.

FIGURE 4.5
You can customize the Visual Studio .NET toolbox to include custom created controls.

FIGURE 4.6
The Properties window allows you to view the properties of the user control; the properties can be arranged by Category.

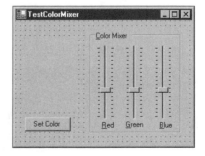

FIGURE 4.7
You can design a form that hosts a user control.

Wouldn't it be nice if the form in Step by Step 4.2 could listen to changes in the control as they happen? That way the Label control could just subscribe to changes in the ColorMixer control and have its BackColor property changed as soon as there was any change in the ColorMixer control. This would eliminate the need to press the button after making each change.

Yes, this would be really nice, but you can't really handle the events raised by TrackBar from inside the TestColorMixer form because TrackBar is a private control of the ColorMixer control and is not accessible outside it. A better idea would be to have the class ColorMixer publish a Changed event so that all interested classes could subscribe to it. I explain how to do that in the next section.

Creating and Implementing Events

Create, implement, and handle events.

Events in C# are based on the publish–subscribe model. The class that implements an event is called the *publisher* of the event, and the class that registers with a publisher to receive event notifications is called the *subscriber* of the event. A class can subscribe to an event by attaching appropriate event handlers to the event. The publisher registers all event handlers and takes the responsibility of notifying the subscribers by invoking the event handler when the event occurs.

An *event handler* is a method with a specific signature that the publisher class is capable of registering. By convention, an event handler returns void and takes two arguments. The first argument specifies the object on which the event occurs (that is, the publisher of event) and the second argument specifies information related to the event. The second argument is an object of type EventArgs or its derived classes. For example, look at the following lines of code that define a ColorMixerEventArgs class that contains information about the event occurring on the ColorMixer control:

```
//Defines the class that stores data related to event
public class ColorMixerEventArgs : EventArgs
{
    public readonly int red, green, blue;
    public ColorMixerEventArgs(
        int red, int green, int blue)
```

```
    {
        this.red = red;
        this.green = green;
        this.blue = blue;
    }
}
```

By convention, a class that is derived from EventArgs has a name that ends with EventArgs. When a Changed event occurs on the ColorMixer control, it needs to notify the Red, Green, and Blue color values to its subscribers. To do this, the ColorMixerEventArgs class derives from EventArgs and provides a mechanism for storing event-related data in its object.

Events in C# are implemented by using delegates. A *delegate* is a special class whose object is capable of storing references to methods of a particular signature. If you have a background in C/C++ programming, you can relate delegates with function pointers. In C#, the delegates are defined like this:

```
//define the prototype of the callback method
public delegate void ChangedEventHandler(
    object sender, ColorMixerEventArgs args);
```

The signature of the delegate essentially specifies the signature of the event handler methods on which it can generate a call-back.

The event itself is defined as a type of the delegate, as shown in the following code segment:

```
//define the event
public event ChangedEventHandler Changed;
```

The event internally manages a linked list of delegates. When an event occurs, the event scans this linked list and invokes the event handler that is identified by the delegate object in each node.

When the actual event occurs, the class that publishes the event takes responsibility for notifying all its subscribers that the event occurred, by executing the event handlers attached to it. The following code example shows how the publisher class does this:

```
//notify the registered objects of event
protected virtual void OnChanged(
    ColorMixerEventArgs e)
{
    //if any object registered with the event
    if (Changed != null)
```

```
        {
            //notify that object
            Changed(this, e);
        }
    }
```

When the actual event occurs, the publisher class just needs to call this `OnChanged()` method. This code checks whether there are any objects that are registered with the event. If there are any, the `OnChanged()` method invokes the event handler that is associated with the object by passing the reference to the object that publishes the event and an object that stores information about the event.

When a subscriber wants to subscribe to an event, it needs to take the following steps:

◆ Implement an event handler with the signature specified by the delegate object of the event.

◆ Create a delegate object specified for the event. This delegate should refer to the event handler method.

◆ Attach the event handler to the event. Remember to use the `+=` operator for attaching the delegate so that you don't cancel any of the previously registered delegates.

To keep the event handling simple and transparent, Visual Studio .NET hides some of the implementation details when you subscribe to an event. In Visual Studio .NET the familiar way to attach an event handler to an event is to select an appropriate event for a control in the Properties window and double-click it. This generates a template for event handler method, and you simply fill in the details.

For example, say you have a control named `colorMixer1` on your form. When you attach an event handler to its `Changed` event, this is what really happens behind the scenes:

```
//Visual Studio .NET hides this
//implementation from you by encapsulating
// this line in designer-generated code
this.colorMixer1.Changed +=
    new ColorMixer.ChangedEventHandler(
    colorMixer1_Changed);
```

Here `colorMixer1_Changed()` is the name of the event handler implemented by the class that subscribes to the `Changed` event. In this line of code, a delegate object for the `ChangedEventHandler` delegate is created. This delegate object points to the event handler method, `colorMixer1_Changed()`. Finally, the delegate object is attached to the `Changed` event itself. Notice that the line uses the `+=` syntax while attaching the event handler in order to add the delegate to a list of already existing delegates.

Step by Step 4.3 shows how to create a new version of `ColorMixer` control called `ColorMixerWithEvents`. This version implements a `Changed` event in the control, using the techniques just discussed.

STEP BY STEP

4.3 Creating a User Control That Publishes Events

1. Create a new project with the Windows Control Library template in solution `316C04`. Name the project `StepByStep4_3`.

---

2. Using Solution Explorer, drag the `ColorMixer.cs` control from `StepByStep4_1` to this project. While dragging, hold the Ctrl key so that the control is copied to the current project instead of being moved. Change the name of the control to `ColorMixerWithEvents.cs`. Switch to the code view and change all instances of `ColorMixer` to `ColorMixtureWithEvents`.

---

3. Add the following code at the end of the class `ColorMixerWithEvents`, just before its closing bracket (the end of the class definition):

```
public class ColorMixerEventArgs : EventArgs
{
    public readonly int red, green, blue;
    public ColorMixerEventArgs(
      int red, int green, int blue)
    {
        this.red = red;
        this.green = green;
        this.blue = blue;
    }
}

//define the prototype of the callback method
public delegate void ChangedEventHandler(
    object sender, ColorMixerEventArgs args);
```

continues

continued

```
//define the event
public event ChangedEventHandler Changed;

//notify the registered objects of the event
protected virtual void OnChanged(
    ColorMixerEventArgs e)
{
    //if any object registered with the event
    if (Changed != null)
    {
        //notify that object
        Changed(this, e);
    }
}
```

4. Add the following event handler in the class definition. Attach this event handler to all three TrackBar controls in the Properties window:

```
// Fire Change event when there is any
// change to the trackbar controls
private void TrackBar_ValueChanged(
    object sender, System.EventArgs e)
{
    ColorMixerEventArgs args = new ColorMixerEventArgs(
        tbRed.Value, tbGreen.Value, tbBlue.Value);
    OnChanged(args);
}
```

5. Select the project StepByStep4_3 in Solution Explorer and select Build from the context menu. This step generates the StepByStep4_3.dll file that contains the code for ColorMixtureWithEvents.

Step by Step 4.3 shows how to create a class that publishes a Changed event. Step by Step 4.4 shows how to create a Windows application that hosts this class and subscribes to its Changed event.

STEP BY STEP

4.4 Creating a Windows Application That Subscribes to Events

1. Open Solution Explorer for solution 316C04, and then right-click the solution name (316C04) and select Add, Add New Project. Select Windows Application as the template for the new project and name the project StepByStep4_4.

2. In Solution Explorer, right-click `Form1.cs` and rename it `TestColorMixerWithEvents`. Open the Properties window for this form and change both its `Name` and `Text` properties to `TestColorMixerWithEvents`. Switch to the code view of the form and modify the `Main()` method to launch `TestColorMixerWithEvents` instead of `Form1`.

3. Using Solution Explorer, add a reference for `StepByStep4_3.dll`.

4. In the toolbox, click the Windows form and scroll down the list of Window form controls until you find a control named `ColorMixerWithEvents`. Double-click the control to add it to the form. Accept the default name of the control, `colorMixerWithEvents1`. Add a `GroupBox` control and a `Label` control (`lblColorSample`) to the `GroupBox` control, set the `Label` control's `Dock` property to `Fill`, and arrange the controls as shown in Figure 4.8.

5. Access the Properties window for `colorMixerWithEvents1` and double-click its `Changed` event to add an event handler for it. Add the following code to the event handler:

```
private void colorMixerWithEvents1_Changed(
object sender,
StepByStep4_3.ColorMixerWithEvents.ColorMixerEventArgs
args)
{
    lblColorSample.BackColor = Color.FromArgb(
        args.red, args.green, args.blue);
}
```

6. Activate Solution Explorer, right-click the name of project `StepByStep4_4`, and select Set as Startup Project from the context menu.

7. Run the project. You should see the form hosting the `ColorMixerWithEvents` control. Work with the Red, Green, and Blue trackbars to select the color values. You should see that the `Label` control changes color as you change the value of any trackbar, as shown in Figure 4.8.

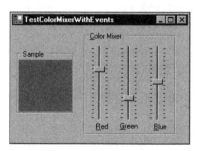

FIGURE 4.8
The `ColorMixerWithEvents` control changes the `ForeColor` property of the `Label` control as soon as the trackbars are changed.

R E V I E W   B R E A K

▶ The Microsoft .NET Framework allows programmers to create reusable code components. You can create a Windows component by deriving from the `Component`, `Control`, or `UserControl` classes or from any of their derived classes.

▶ If you want to create a control by assembling existing controls and you want to add custom-defined functionality to them, you should choose to inherit them from the `UserControl` class. You should create a Windows Control Library template to create a user control.

▶ You can drag and drop the custom-created components from the toolbox on the form and set its properties the same way you would set the properties of any standard Windows component.

▶ A delegate is a special type that can store references to methods of a specific signature. Events are objects of the delegate type.

▶ To create and implement an event, you need to take care of the following steps:

  1. Define the `EventArgs` class that will contain the event-related data. This is required only if you want to pass specific event-related information to the event handlers.

  2. Create a delegate object that can store a reference to the event handler. This is required only if you want to pass specific event-related information to the event handlers.

  3. Define the event itself as an object of delegate type.

  4. Define a method that notifies the registered objects of the event. Usually this method has a name such as `OnChanged()`, where `Changed` is a event name.

  5. Call the method defined in step 4 whenever the event occurs.

▶ You should use the += syntax while attaching an event handler to an event to add the delegate to a list of already existing delegates. Otherwise, all the previously existing delegates are cancelled and receive no notification of the event.

GUIDED PRACTICE EXERCISE 4.1

The objective of this exercise is to create a composite control by assembling two command buttons as shown in Figure 4.9.

You should be able to drag the buttons at runtime and generate two events, CrashEnter and CrashLeave. The CrashEnter event is fired when the two buttons overlap each other, and the CrashLeave event is fired when the overlap is removed. You should host this control on a Windows form, where you should display a red-colored message that says Crash! whenever the control overlaps as shown in Figure 4.10 and clear the message when the overlapping is removed.

How would you create such a control and host it on a Windows form?

This exercise helps you practice creating composite controls and implementing events. You should try working through this problem on your own first. If you get stuck, or if you'd like to see one possible solution, follow these steps:

1. Create a new project with the Windows Control Library template in solution 316C04. Name the project GuidedPracticeExercise4_1.

2. In Solution Explorer, change the name of the UserControl1.cs file to ButtonShips.cs. Right-click the control surface and select View Code from the context menu. Change the name of the class and its constructor from UserControl1 to ButtonShips.

3. Drag and drop two Button controls (btnShip1 and btnShip2) on the form, as shown in Figure 4.9.

4. Switch to the code view and define the following variables:

```
// Specifies whether mousebutton is pressed or not
private bool isMouseDown;
// Stores the position of last mouse movement
private Point ptLast;
// Are the buttons overlapping?
private bool inCrash = false;
```

continues

FIGURE 4.9
The ButtonShips composite control publishes the CrashEnter and CrashLeave events.

FIGURE 4.10
The CrashEnter event is fired when the two Button controls overlap each other.

continued

5. Double-click the control and add the following code to the
   Load event handler of the control:

```
private void ButtonShips_Load(
    object sender, System.EventArgs e)
{
    btnShip1.Location = new Point(0, 0);
    btnShip2.Location = new Point(
        this.Width - btnShip2.Width, 0);
}
```

6. Add the following code to the class to define the CrashEnter
   and CrashLeave events. Also define the methods
   OnCrashEnter(), and OnCrashLeave(), which actually raise the
   event when buttons overlap or leave the overlap state:

```
//define the event
public event EventHandler CrashEnter;

//notify the registered objects of event
protected virtual void OnCrashEnter(EventArgs e)
{
    //if any object registered with the event
    if (CrashEnter != null)
    {
        //notify that object
        CrashEnter(this, e);
    }
}

//define the event
public event EventHandler CrashLeave;

//notify the registered objects of event
protected virtual void OnCrashLeave(EventArgs e)
{
    //if any object registered with the event
    if (CrashLeave != null)
    {
        //notify that object
        CrashLeave(this, e);
    }
}
```

7. Add the following AnyButton_MouseDown(),
   AnyButton_MouseUp(), and AnyButton_MouseMove event handlers
   to the class definition and attach the event handlers to the
   MouseDown, MouseUp, and MouseMove events of both buttons:

```
private void AnyButton_MouseDown(object sender,
    System.Windows.Forms.MouseEventArgs e)
```

```
{
    isMouseDown = true;
    // Save the position of mouse down
    ptLast = new Point(e.X, e.Y);
}

private void AnyButton_MouseUp(object sender,
    System.Windows.Forms.MouseEventArgs e)
{
    isMouseDown = false;
}

private void AnyButton_MouseMove(object sender,
    System.Windows.Forms.MouseEventArgs e)
{
    if (!isMouseDown)
        return;

    //find the button causing the move operation
    Button btn = (Button) sender;

    //set the button's new positions
    btn.Top = btn.Top + (e.Y - ptLast.Y);
    btn.Left = btn.Left + (e.X - ptLast.X);

    Rectangle btn1Rect = new Rectangle(
        btnShip1.Location, btnShip1.Size);
    Rectangle btn2Rect = new Rectangle(
        btnShip2.Location, btnShip2.Size);

    if(btn1Rect.IntersectsWith(btn2Rect))
    {
        if (!inCrash)
        {
            this.OnCrashEnter(new EventArgs());
            inCrash = true;
        }
    }
    else
    {
        if(inCrash)
        {
            this.OnCrashLeave(new EventArgs());
            inCrash = false;
        }
    }
}
```

8. Select the project GuidedPracticeExercise4_1 in Solution Explorer and select Build from the context menu. This step generates the code for your control and packages it into the file GuidedPracticeExercise4_1.dll. This file is located in the bin\Debug directory of your project.

continues

continued

9. Add new projects to the solution. Select the Windows Application template and name the project `GuidedPracticeExercise4_1Test`.

10. In Solution Explorer, right-click `Form1.cs` and rename it `TestButtonShips`. Open the Properties window for this form and change both its `Name` and `Text` properties to `TestButtonShips`. Switch to the code view of the form and modify the `Main()` method to launch `TestButtonShips` instead of `Form1`.

11. Using Solution Explorer, add a reference for `GuidedPracticeExercuse4_1.dll`.

12. Add a `GroupBox` control and a `Label` control (`lblResults`) to the form. Place the `ButtonShips` control into the `GroupBox` control and set its `Dock` property to `Fill`. Arrange the controls as shown in Figure 4.10.

13. Attach event handlers for the `CrashEnter` and `CrashLeave` events of the `ButtonShips` control and add the following code to the event handlers:

```
private void buttonShips1_CrashEnter(object sender,
    System.EventArgs args)
{
    lblResult.Text = "Crash!";
}

private void buttonShips1_CrashLeave(object sender,
    System.EventArgs args)
{
    lblResult.Text = "";
}
```

14. Activate Solution Explorer, right-click the name of project `GuidedPracticeExercise4_1Test`, and select Set as Startup Project from the context menu.

15. Run the project. You should see the form hosting the `ButtonShips` control. Move the `Ship1` and `Ship2` buttons. When they overlap, the label displays Crash! (refer to Figure 4.10); the message is erased when the buttons are moved away from each other.

If you have difficulty following this exercise, review the sections "Creating Components by Extending the UserControl Class" and "Creating and Implementing Events" earlier in this chapter. After doing that review, try this exercise again.

Extending a Control by Using Visual Inheritance

Create a Windows control.

- **Create a Windows control by using visual inheritance.**

Recall from Chapter 1, "Introducing Windows Forms," that it is possible to inherit a form from another form. When you inherit, you get all the functionality of the base form, and this allows you to reuse code. The same concept of inheritance also applies to controls. The technique of inheriting one visual object from another visual object is known as *visual inheritance*.

To demonstrate how visual inheritance can help in extending the functionality of existing controls, Step by Step 4.5 shows how to create a new control that derives from ColorMixerWithEvents and add a color sampler to it.

STEP BY STEP

4.5 Extending a Control by Using Visual Inheritance

1. Create a new project based on the Windows Control Library template in solution 316C04. Name the project StepByStep4_5.

2. Right-click the UserControl1.cs file and select Delete from the context menu.

continues

continued

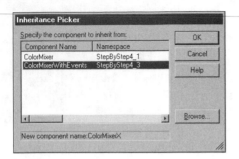

FIGURE 4.11
The Inheritance Picker dialog box allows you to choose the base component from which you want to inherit.

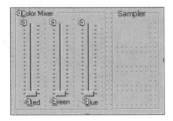

FIGURE 4.12
You can add new controls along with the inherited user control.

3. Right-click the project name and select Add, Add Inherited Control. Name the control `ColorMixerX.cs` and click the Open button. From the Inheritance Picker dialog box, select the component `ColorMixerWithEvents`, as shown in Figure 4.11. Click the OK button. You should see a control surface whose contents are from `ColorMixerWithEvents`.

4. Add a `GroupBox` control and four `Label` controls (`lblSampler`, `lblRed`, `lblGreen`, and `lblBlue`) along with the inherited control, as shown in Figure 4.12. Change the `Text` property of `groupBox1` to `Sampler` and change the `Text` property of the `Label` controls to empty string.

5. Switch to the code view of the `ColorMixerX` control and add the following lines of code in the control's constructor after the call to the `IntializeComponent()` method:

```
//set the initial display of control
lblSampler.BackColor = Color.FromArgb(
    this.Red, this.Green, this.Blue);
lblRed.Text = String.Format("R: {0}", this.Red);
lblGreen.Text = String.Format("G: {0}", this.Green);
lblBlue.Text = String.Format("B: {0}", this.Blue);
```

6. In the Properties window, double-click the `Click` event of the `ColorMixerX` control and add the following code to its event handler:

```
private void ColorMixerX_Changed(object sender,
StepByStep4_3.ColorMixerWithEvents.ColorMixerEventArgs
  args)
{
    lblSampler.BackColor = Color.FromArgb(
        args.red, args.green, args.blue);
    lblRed.Text = String.Format("R: {0}", args.red);
    lblGreen.Text = String.Format(
        "G: {0}", args.green);
    lblBlue.Text = String.Format("B: {0}", args.blue);
}
```

7. Select the project `StepByStep4_4` in Solution Explorer and select Build from the context menu. This generates a `StepByStep4_4.dll` file that contains the code for the `ColorMixtureX` control.

Step by Step 4.6 shows how to test the inherited control
ColorMixerX.

STEP BY STEP

4.6 Creating a Windows Application That Hosts an Inherited Control

1. Activate Solution Explorer for solution 316C04, right-click the solution name (316C04), and select Add, Add New Project. Select Windows Application as the template for the new project and name the project StepByStep4_6.

2. In Solution Explorer, right-click Form1.cs and rename it TestColorMixerX. Open the Properties window for this form and change both its Name and Text properties to TestColorMixerX. Switch to the code view of the form and modify the Main() method to launch TestColorMixerX instead of Form1.

3. Using Solution Explorer, add a reference for StepByStep4_5.dll.

4. Drag the ColorMixerX control from the toolbox and drop it on the form. Add a GroupBox control and add a Label control (lblDrawingBoard) to the group box. Change the label's BackColor property to System - Window and the Dock property to Fill. Arrange the controls as shown in Figure 4.13.

5. Switch to the code view. Add the following using directive at the top of the code:

```
// Required for SmoothingMode
using System.Drawing.Drawing2D;
```

6. Add the following code in the class definition that declares some new variables and modify the form's constructor as shown here:

```
// Specifies whether mousebutton is pressed or not
bool isMouseDown;
// Stores the position of last mouse movement
Point ptLast;
```

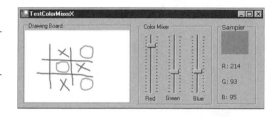

FIGURE 4.13
You can choose a color from the ColorMixerX control to draw on the drawing board with the selected color.

continues

continued

```
// Stores the currently selected color
Color clrSelected; public TestColorMixerX()
{
    // Required for Windows Form Designer support
    InitializeComponent();

    //Set the value of color when form is initialized
    clrSelected = Color.FromArgb(colorMixerX1.Red,
        colorMixerX1.Green, colorMixerX1.Blue);
}
```

7. Add the following code to the event handler for the
Changed event of the colorMixerX1 control:

```
private void colorMixerX1_Changed(object sender,
StepByStep4_3.ColorMixerWithEvents.ColorMixerEventArgs
args)
{
    clrSelected = Color.FromArgb(colorMixerX1.Red,
        colorMixerX1.Green, colorMixerX1.Blue);
}
```

8. Attach event handlers for the MouseDown, MouseUp, and
MouseMove events of the lblDrawingBoard control and add
the following event handling code to the event handlers:

```
private void lblDrawingBoard_MouseDown(object sender,
    System.Windows.Forms.MouseEventArgs e)
{
    isMouseDown = true;
    ptLast = new Point(e.X, e.Y);
}

private void lblDrawingBoard_MouseUp(object sender,
    System.Windows.Forms.MouseEventArgs e)
{
    isMouseDown = false;
}

private void lblDrawingBoard_MouseMove(object sender,
    System.Windows.Forms.MouseEventArgs e)
{
    if (!isMouseDown)
        return;
    Point ptCurr = new Point(e.X, e.Y);
    Graphics g = this.lblDrawingBoard.CreateGraphics();
    g.SmoothingMode = SmoothingMode.AntiAlias;
    g.DrawLine(new Pen(clrSelected, 2),
        ptLast, ptCurr);
    ptLast = ptCurr;
    g.Dispose();
}
```

9. Activate Solution Explorer, right-click the name of project `StepByStep4_6`, and select Set as Startup Project from the context menu.

10. Run the project. You should see the form hosting the `ColorMixerX` control. Select a color from the `ColorMixerX` control, and you should notice that you can draw on the drawing board with the selected color (see Figure 4.13).

Note that when you add a reference to the file `StepByStep4_5.dll` in Step by Step 4.6, in addition to this file, Visual Studio .NET also copies the DLL file that contains its base class (`StepByStep4_3.dll`) to the `bin\debug` or `bin\Release` folder. This is to make sure that all referenced classes are available at runtime.

> **NOTE**
>
> **Deploying Controls** In a real application, of course, you want to avoid needing to copy components to every project that needs them. Chapter 13, "Deploying a Windows Application" shows how to add assemblies to the global assembly cache (GAC) to make a component available to all projects on the computer.

Hosting a Windows Control Inside Internet Explorer

Create a Windows control.

- **Host a Windows control inside Microsoft Internet Explorer.**

In addition to hosting controls in a Windows form, you can also host a Windows controls inside Internet Explorer. Inside Internet Explorer, a control is rendered as an object, but it does not require any registration, unlike ActiveX objects. The assembly containing the Windows control should reside either in the GAC or in the same virtual directory where the Web page that renders the control resides.

You need to take the following steps in order to host a Windows control in Internet Explorer:

1. Create a virtual directory on the Web server that will deliver the control to the browser. Ensure that the directory has permission set to Scripts Only. If the permission is set as Scripts & Executables, the control might not work properly.

2. Copy the assembly (that is, the DLL file) that contains the control to the virtual directory if the assembly does not already reside in the GAC.

3. Create a Hypertext Markup Language (HTML) or ASP.NET page in the virtual directory and add to the document an object tag that references the control. The `classid` attribute of the object element should contain the path to the control library (`.dll` file) and the fully qualified name of the control, separated by a # (pound sign). Here's an example:

```
classid=
"http://localhost/StepByStep4_7/StepByStep4_5.dll#
➥StepByStep4_5.ColorMixerX"
```

STEP BY STEP

4.7 Hosting a Windows Control Inside Internet Explorer

1. Create a new project in Visual Studio .NET. Select the ASP.NET Web Application template and specify the location as `http://localhost/StepByStep4_7`, as shown in Figure 4.14. You can replace localhost with the name of your own Web server.

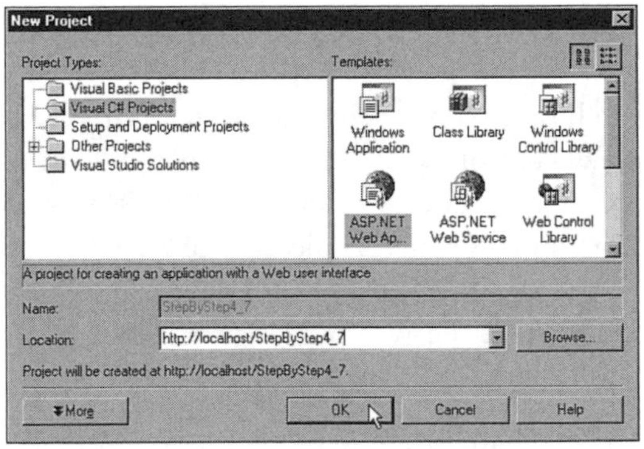

2. Right-click the `WebForm1.aspx` file in Solution Explorer and rename it `ColorMixerXIE.aspx`. Change all references to `WebForm1` to refer to `ColorMixerXIE` in the code view.

NOTE

Web Server Required   You need to have a Web server available to you in order to host Windows controls inside Microsoft Internet Explorer.

FIGURE 4.14
When you create an ASP.NET Web application project in Visual Studio .NET, a virtual directory is automatically created by the IDE.

3. Right-click the project and select Add Existing Item from the context menu. Browse to the folder where the project `StepByStep4_5` is stored and select `StepByStep4_5.dll` and `StepByStep4_3.dll` from the `bin\debug` directory under the project. These DLL files will be added to the `StepByStep4_7 project` directory where the `ColorMixerXIE.aspx` file is stored.

4. Insert the following code in the ASPX page in HTML view inside the <body> element:

```
<form id="ColorMixerXIE" method="post" runat="server">
    <object id="colorMixerX1" height="300" width="300"
    classid=
    "http://localhost/StepByStep4_7/StepByStep4_5.dll#
    ➡StepByStep4_5.ColorMixerX" >
    </object>
</form>
```

5. Right-click `ColorMixerXIE.aspx` and select Build and Browse from the context menu. You should see the `ColorMixerX` Windows forms control hosted in Internet Explorer, as shown in Figure 4.15.

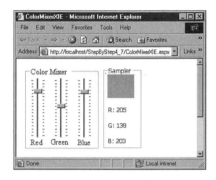

FIGURE 4.15
You can host a Windows control inside Internet Explorer.

Creating Components by Extending the `Control` Class

You can create a control by extending it directly from the `Control` class instead of from the `UserControl` class. You would especially want to do this if you wanted to design a control that has a unique user interface that you cannot create by assembling existing controls.

When you create a control by extending it from the `Control` class, the control does not have any default user interface. You need to handle the control's `Paint` event to render its user interface.

Visual Studio .NET does not provide a template for creating a control directly from the `Control` class. To deal with this, you can modify the template for the user control to extend from the `Control` class instead of from the `UserControl` class.

Step by Step 4.8 demonstrates the process of creating a custom control by designing a digital clock that renders its own user interface.

STEP BY STEP

4.8 Creating a Control That Renders Its Own User Interface

1. Create a new project based on the Windows Control Library template in solution 316C04. Name the project StepByStep4_8.

2. Rename the UserControl1.cs file DigitalClock.cs.

3. Switch to the code view and change the name of the class and its constructor from UserControl1 to DigitalClock. Change the class declaration so that its base class is now Control instead of System.Windows.Forms.UserControl. After you make these changes, the class header should look like this:

```
public class DigitalClock : Control
```

4. Switch back to the design view. You should notice that the borderless gray box for creating controls is gone. Instead, there should be a message, telling you to add components from Server Explorer or the toolbox.

5. Open the toolbox and double-click a Timer control. Note that the message in the design view is gone and the Timer control is placed there. Set the Enabled property of the Timer control to true and the Interval property to 1000. From the list of its events, double-click the Tick event to add the following event handing code to it:

```
private void timer1_Tick(
    object sender, System.EventArgs e)
{
    Invalidate();
}
```

6. Switch to the design view and click anywhere on the empty gray area so that the control DigitalClock is selected. From its Properties window, double-click the SizeChanged event to attach an event handler to it, and then add the following event handling code to the event handler:

```
private void DigitalClock_SizeChanged(
    object sender, System.EventArgs e)
{
    Invalidate();
}
```

7. Add an event handler to the Paint event of the DigitalClock control and add the following code to it:

```
private void DigitalClock_Paint(object sender,
    System.Windows.Forms.PaintEventArgs e)
{
    Graphics g = e.Graphics;
    string strTime = DateTime.Now.ToString("T");

    //Get the current string size
    SizeF sizef = g.MeasureString(strTime, Font);

    //Get the scaling factor
    float scale = Math.Min(
        ClientSize.Width/ sizef.Width,
        ClientSize.Height/ sizef.Height);

    //Scale the font as per new control size
    Font font = new Font(Font.FontFamily,
        scale*Font.SizeInPoints);

    //Get the string size for scaled font size
    sizef = g.MeasureString(strTime, font);

    //Find the position to draw the string
    PointF pos = new PointF(
        (ClientSize.Width - sizef.Width)/2,
        (ClientSize.Height - sizef.Height)/2);

    //Draw the time string
    g.DrawString(strTime, font,
        new SolidBrush(ForeColor), pos);
}
```

8. Select the project StepByStep4_8 in Solution Explorer and select Build, Build StepByStep 4_8. This generates a StepByStep4_8.dll file that contains the code for the DigitalClock control.

Note in Step by Step 4.8 when you modify the UserControl template to extend the class from Control instead of UserControl, Visual Studio .NET removes the borderless gray control area.

Another important point to note from Step by Step 4.8 is that you create an event handler for the SizeChanged event of the control.

The `SizeChanged` event is fired when you change the size of the control either at design time or at runtime. If you don't include this event handler, when you resize the control after placing it in its container, the control cannot paint itself correctly. The code in Step by Step 4.8 includes a call to the `Invalidate()` method, which ensures that the `Paint` event is generated every time the size of the control is changed.

Step by Step 4.9 shows how to host the `DigitalClock` control in a Windows form.

STEP BY STEP

4.9 Creating a Windows Application That Hosts the `DigitalClock` Control

1. Activate Solution Explorer for solution `316C04`, right-click the solution name (`316C04`), and select Add, Add New Project. Select Windows Application as the template for the new project and name the project `StepByStep4_9`.

2. In Solution Explorer, right-click `Form1.cs` and rename it `TestDigitalClock`. Open the Properties window for this form and change both its `Name` and `Text` properties to `TestDigitalClock`. Switch to the code view of the form and modify the `Main()` method to launch `TestDigitalClock` instead of `Form1`.

3. Using Solution Explorer, add a reference for `StepByStep4_8.dll`.

4. Right-click the toolbox and select Add Tab. Name the new tab My Custom Controls. Right-click the My Custom Controls tab and select Customize Toolbox from the context menu. Click the .NET Framework Components tab, and then click the Browse button to add a reference to `StepByStep4_8.dll`. Click the OK button. A `DigitalClock` control is added to the My Custom Controls tab in the toolbox.

5. Drag the `DigitalClock` control from the toolbox and drop it on the form. Resize the control. Note that the control repaints itself with text of the appropriate size.

6. Set `StepByStep4_9` as the startup project.

7. Run the project. The form that is hosting the `DigitalClock` control should show the current time, as in Figure 4.16.

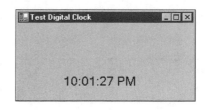

FIGURE 4.16

You can create a custom control that renders its own user interface by inheriting from the `Control` class.

Creating Components by Extending the `Component` Class

When you don't need any visual representation for components, you can extend them from the most basic of all component classes, the `Component` class. A familiar example of a nonvisual component is the `Timer` component. It does not have any user interface to show on a form, but it does provide useful properties and events that its container can use to customize and control the behavior of the control.

Visual Studio .NET does not provide a template for creating a project for a `Component` object, but Step by Step 4.10 shows how to use a Class Library project template to create a project and then add a `Component` class to it.

STEP BY STEP

4.10 Creating a `RandomNumberGenerator` Component

1. Create a new project based on the Class Library template in solution `316C04`. Name the project `StepByStep4_10`.

2. Right-click `Class1.cs` in Solution Explorer and select Delete from the context menu to delete the file from the project.

3. In Solution Explorer, right-click the project name (`StepByStep4_10`) and select Add, Add New Item. In the Add New Item dialog, select Component Class as the template of the item and name the project `RandomNumberGenerator.cs`, as shown in Figure 4.17.

continues

continued

FIGURE 4.17
You can add a `Component` class by using the Add New Item dialog box in the Visual Studio .NET IDE.

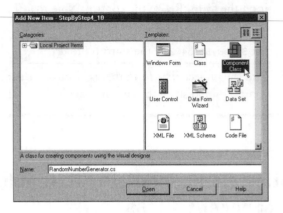

4. Add the following code just after the Component Designer generated code:

```
//stores minValue and maxValue
private int minValue=1, maxValue=100;
```

5. Use the C# Property Wizard to add two properties, `MinValue` and `MaxValue`, of type `int`. Modify the generated property code so it looks like this:

```
/// <summary>
/// Get or Set the minimum value for random number
/// </summary>
public int MinValue
{
    get
    {
        return minValue;
    }
    set
    {
        minValue = value;
    }
}

/// <summary>
/// Get or Set the maximum value for random number
/// </summary>
public int MaxValue
{
    get
    {
        return maxValue;
    }
}
```

```
    set
    {
        maxValue = value;
    }
}
```

6. Switch to the class view by selecting View, Class View. Navigate to the `RandomNumberGenerator` class, right-click it, and select Add, Add Method. The C# Method Wizard appears. Use the wizard to add a method named `GetRandomNumber()`, as shown in Figure 4.18.

NOTE

XML Documentation Visual C# .NET provides a mechanism to document code by using Extensible Markup Language (XML). Any source code line that begins with `///` and that precedes a user-defined type, a class member, or a namespace declaration can be processed as a comment and placed in a separate documentation file by the C# compiler.

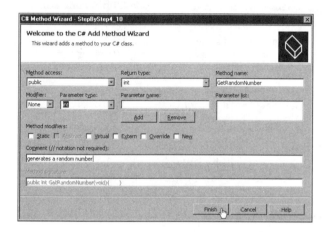

FIGURE 4.18
You can create a method via the C# Method Wizard.

7. Modify the code in the `GetRandomNumber()` method so that it looks like this:

```
/// <summary>
/// generates a random number
/// </summary>
public int GetRandomNumber()
{
    Random r = new Random();
    return r.Next(minValue, maxValue);
}
```

8. In Solution Explorer, navigate to the project `StepByStep4_10` and right-click its Reference node. Select Add Reference from the context menu. In the Add Reference dialog box, select the .NET tab and double-click the component named `System.Drawing.dll` and click OK. A reference to `System.Drawing.dll` is added to this project.

continues

continued

FIGURE 4.19
When you set the build action for a resource to Embedded Resources, the resource is embedded in to the main assembly.

> **NOTE**
>
> **Sample Graphics** Visual Studio .NET installs a small library of sample graphics files, including icon, bitmap, and some sample video files. These files are available in the Common7\Graphics subfolder of the Visual Studio .NET installation folder.

9. Insert the following line at the top of the code, along with other using directives:

```
// Required for ToolboxBitmap attribute
using System.Drawing;
```

10. Select any 16×16-pixel .bmp file (if you have a 16×16 .ico file, just rename it with a .bmp extension). Change its name to RandomNumberGenerator.bmp and add it to the project. After the .bmp file appears in Solution Explorer, right-click it and select Properties from the context menu. In the Properties window, set Build Action to Embedded Resources, as shown in Figure 4.19.

11. Add the following attribute just before the class declaration:

```
// Set the Toolbox icon
[ToolboxBitmap(typeof(RandomNumberGenerator))]
```

12. Select the project StepByStep4_10 in Solution Explorer and select Build, Build StepByStep 4_10. This generates a StepByStep4_10.dll file that contains the code for the RandomNumberGenerator component.

It is possible to change the toolbox icon for a control or a component by using the ToolboxBitMapAttribute class. This class belongs to the System.Drawing namespace. Because the component does not have any user interface, Visual Studio .NET does not automatically include a reference to System.Drawing.dll with a Component class, as it would do with a UserControl class or a Form class. In Step by Step 4.10, to have access to the ToolboxBitmapAttribute class, you add the reference to the System.Drawing.dll library manually.

Another requirement for ToolboxBitMap attribute is that the bitmap file should have the same name as the class, reside in the same folder as the class file, and have a .bmp file extension.

To see the component in action, you can create the Windows application project, as described in Step by Step 4.11.

STEP BY STEP

4.11 Creating a Windows Application That Uses the RandomNumberGenerator Component

1. Activate Solution Explorer for solution 316C04, right-click the solution name (316C04), and select Add, Add New Project. Select Windows Application as the template for the new project and name the project StepByStep4_11.

2. In Solution Explorer, right-click Form1.cs and rename it TestRandomNumberGenerator. Open the Properties window for this form and change both its Name and Text properties to TestRandomNumberGenerator. Switch to the code view of the form and modify the Main() method to launch TestRandomNumberGenerator instead of Form1.

3. Using Solution Explorer, add a reference for StepByStep4_10.dll.

4. Activate the toolbox and click the My Custom Controls tab. Right-click the toolbox. Select Customize Toolbox, click the .NET Framework Components tab, and click the Browse button to add a reference to StepByStep4_10.dll. Click the OK button. A RandomNumberGenerator component is added to the My Custom Controls tab in the toolbox, as shown in Figure 4.20.

5. Drag the RandomNumberGenerator control from the toolbox and drop it on the form. The component is added to the component tray, rather than to the form. Access the Properties window for the component and change its MinValue property to 500 and its MaxValue property to 1000 (see Figure 4.21).

6. Add a Label control (lblResults) and a Button control (btnGenerate) to the form. Empty the Label control's Text property and set the Button control's Text property to Generate a Random Number!. Double-click the Button control to add an event handler for its Click event. Add the following code to the event handler:

continues

FIGURE 4.20
You can display a custom icon in the toolbox by using the ToolboxBitmap attribute.

FIGURE 4.21
You can edit properties for the custom-created component just as you would for any other component in the Properties window of the Visual C# .NET IDE.

continued

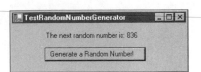

FIGURE 4.22
You can generate a random number by calling the methods of the custom-created `RandomNumberGenerator` component.

```
private void btnGenerate_Click(object sender,
    System.EventArgs e)
{
    lblResult.Text = String.Format(
        "The next random number is: {0}",
        randomNumberGenerator1.GetRandomNumber());
}
```

7. Set `StepByStep4_11` as the startup project.

8. Run the project and click the button. You should get a random number in the range 500 to 1,000 every time you press the button (see Figure 4.22).

REVIEW BREAK

▶ The technique of inheriting one visual object from another visual object is known as visual inheritance. When you inherit from a control by using visual inheritance, you get all the functionality of the base control, which allows you to reuse code.

▶ When controls are hosted inside Internet Explorer, they are rendered as object elements that do not require any registration, unlike ActiveX objects. The `classid` attribute of the object element should contain the path to the control library (`.dll` file) and the fully qualified name of the control, separated by a # (pound sign).

▶ Controls can be hosted inside Internet Explorer if the assemblies exist in the GAC of the Web server or in the same virtual directories where the Web page resides.

▶ When you create a control by extending it from the `Control` class, the control does not have a default user interface. You need to handle the control's `Paint` event in order to render its user interface.

▶ When you don't need a visual representation for your components, you can extend them from the `Component` class. This class does not have any user interface to show on a form, but it does provide useful properties, methods, and events that can be used by the component's container to customize and control the component's behavior.

GUIDED PRACTICE
EXERCISE 4.2

The objective of this exercise is to create a custom control that derives from the TextBox control. You call the derived control NumericTextBox because it allows input of only digits. If you type any characters other than digits, they are simply ignored.

How would you create the NumericTextBox control?

This exercise gives you practice extending the functionality of existing Windows forms controls. You should try working through this problem on your own first. If you get stuck, or if you'd like to see one possible solution, follow these steps:

1. Create a new project with the Windows Control Library template in solution 316C04. Name the project GuidedPracticeExercise4_2.

2. In Solution Explorer, change the name of the UserControl1.cs file to NumericTextBox.cs. Switch to the code view and change the name of the class and its constructor from UserControl1 to NumericTextBox. Change the class declaration so that its base class is now System.Winmdows.Forms.TextBox instead of System.Windows.Forms.UserControl. After making these changes, the class header should look like this:

```
public class NumericTextBox :
    System.Windows.Forms.TextBox
```

3. Switch back to the design view. The borderless gray box for creating controls should be gone. Instead, there should be a message, telling you to add components from Server Explorer or the toolbox.

4. Switch to the design view and click anywhere on the empty gray area so that the control DigitalClock is selected. From its Properties window, double-click the KeyPress event to add the following event handing code to it:

```
private void NumericTextBox_KeyPress(object sender,
    System.Windows.Forms.KeyPressEventArgs e)
{
    if(!Char.IsDigit(e.KeyChar))
        e.Handled = true;
```

continues

continued

```
        else
            e.Handled = false;
}
```

5. Select the project `GuidedPracticeExercise4_2` in Solution Explorer and select Build, Build GuidedPracticeExercise4_2. This generates a `GuidedPracticeExercise4_2.dll` file that contains the code for the `NumericTextBox` control.

6. Add a new Windows application project. Name it `GuidedPracticeExercise4_2Test`.

7. In Solution Explorer, right-click `Form1.cs` and rename it `TestNumericTextBox`. Open the Properties window for this form and change both its `Name` and `Text` properties to `TestNumericTextBox`. Switch to the code view of the form and modify the `Main()` method to launch `TestNumericTextBox` instead of `Form1`.

8. Using Solution Explorer, add a reference for `GuidedPracticeExercise4_2.dll`.

9. Right-click the toolbox and select My Custom Controls tab, created in Step by Step 4.7. Right-click the My Custom Controls tab and select Customize Toolbox. Click the .NET Framework Components tab, and then click the Browse button to add a reference to `GuidedPracticeExercise4_2.dll`. Click the OK button. The `NumericTextBox` control is added to the My Custom Controls tab in the toolbox.

10. Drag the `NumericTextBox` control from the toolbox and drop it on the form. Add a label to the form, as shown in Figure 4.23.

11. Set the project `GuidedPracticeExercise4_2Test` as the startup project.

12. Run the project. You should see the form hosting `NumericTextBox`, which allows the user to enter only numeric text (refer to Figure 4.23).

If you have difficulty following this exercise, review the section "Creating Components by Extending the `Control` Class." After doing that review, try this exercise again.

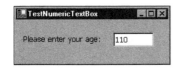

FIGURE 4.23
The `NumericTextBox` control accepts only numeric data.

CREATING AND MANAGING .NET ASSEMBLIES

Create and modify a .NET assembly.

- **Create and implement satellite assemblies.**

- **Create resource-only assemblies.**

A Windows application often consists of several different files. It typically includes the .dll and .exe files that contain the application code; the .gif, .bmp, or .ico files that contain graphics; and other data files, such as those that store strings in several languages for multilingual support. A Windows application that is created using the .NET Framework groups together a logical collection of such files into an *assembly*. (I use the term *logical* here because these files are not physically combined into a single large file. Even when these files are part of an assembly, they maintain their own physical existence. In fact, you can't even tell by looking at a file that it belongs to a particular assembly.)

One of the files in the assembly contains a special piece of information called the *assembly manifest*, which contains the metadata for the assembly. When the Common Language Runtime (CLR) loads an assembly, it first reads the manifest to get the following information:

- ◆ The name and version of the assembly

- ◆ The files that make up the assembly, including their names and hash values

- ◆ The compile-time dependency of the assembly on other assemblies

- ◆ The culture or language that the assembly supports

- ◆ The set of permissions required for the assembly to run properly

An assembly is the basic unit of deployment, scoping, versioning, and security in the .NET Framework. With the concept of assemblies, Microsoft has attempted to leverage the following key benefits in the .NET Framework:

◆ Each assembly has a version number, and all the types and resources in the assembly share the same version number. This makes it easy for applications to refer to the correct version of files and avoid versioning problems.

◆ The self-describing nature of assemblies makes it possible to deploy applications by using the XCOPY command. The XCOPY installation is sometimes also referred as zero-impact installation because it does not cause any side effects such as making Registry entries on a computer.

◆ Assemblies define a security boundary, which allows the CLR to restrict execution of a set of operations, based on the identity and origin of the assembly.

Assemblies exist in different forms, depending on how they are used. In this chapter I classify them into the following categories:

◆ Single-file and multifile assemblies

◆ Static and dynamic assemblies

◆ Private and shared assemblies

◆ Satellite and resource-only assemblies

The following sections discuss each of these categories.

Single-File and Multifile Assemblies

A *single-file assembly* has just a single EXE or DLL file. Such a file consists of code and any embedded resources, as well as the assembly manifest of the assembly. A single-file assembly is something that you are already familiar with because as you have built projects in the Step by Step exercises in this chapter, the output DLL or EXE files have been single-file assemblies. Step by Step 4.12 shows how to view the contents of an assembly file.

NOTE

The MSIL Disassembler The MSIL Disassembler can be used to view the metadata and disassembled code for .NET libraries, modules, and executables in a hierarchical tree view. Looking at MSIL can reveal a lot of information about the inner workings of a program or a component, and it can be a useful learning and debugging tool.

STEP BY STEP

4.12 Viewing Assembly Contents

1. Activate Solution Explorer. Click the Show All Files button on the toolbar. Navigate to the bin\Debug folder of project StepByStep4_11.

2. Select the StepByStep4_10.dll file, and then right-click it and select Open With from the context menu. In the Open With dialog box (see Figure 4.24), select ildasm.exe and then click Open. The Microsoft Intermediate Language (MSIL) Disassembler appears, showing the contents of StepByStep4_10.dll (see Figure 4.25).

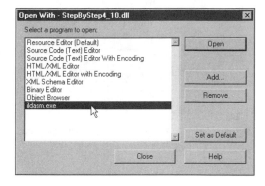

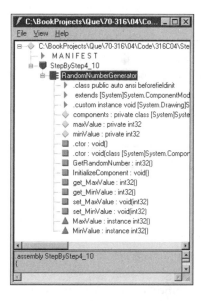

3. Expand the nodes; you should see the methods and constructors defined inside the class. Double-clicking a method node opens a window that shows disassembled code for the method.

4. At the top of the hierarchy you should find a node titled Manifest. Double-click it to open the metadata information for this assembly (see Figure 4.26). The manifest contains references to other assemblies, version information, public key token, and other information. The public key token identifies strong-named assemblies, which are discussed in Chapter 13.

FIGURE 4.24▲
The Open With dialog box allows you to select an application for opening the selected file.

FIGURE 4.25◀
The MSIL Disassembler shows the metadata and disassembled code for the .NET libraries, modules, and executables, in a hierarchical tree view.

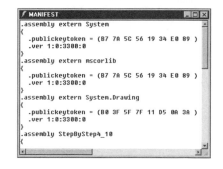

FIGURE 4.26▲
The assembly manifest contains references to other assemblies, their version information, and the public key token.

In Step by Step 4.12 when you right-click an .exe file and select Open With from the context menu, the Open With dialog box that appears does not show an option for ildasm.exe. Don't be disappointed; you can add an entry for ildasm.exe by clicking the Add button in the Open With dialog box (refer to Figure 4.24).

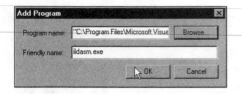

FIGURE 4.27
You can use the Add Program dialog box to add `ildasm.exe` to the list of `.exe` files.

This opens the Add Program dialog box, as shown in Figure 4.27. You have to specify the location for the `ildasm.exe` file; this file is usually located in the `FrameworkSDK\bin` folder, inside the Visual Studio .NET installation folder. Alternatively, you can launch the MSIL Disassembler from a Visual Studio .NET command prompt and open the file of your choice.

A multifile assembly is an assembly that can include multiple files. There should be at least one `.dll` or `.exe` file among these files. You can choose to attach the assembly manifest with any of these files, or you can keep it in a separate file of its own. Unfortunately, Visual Studio .NET does not support creation of multifile assemblies, so you must use command-line tools to create them. Step by Step 4.13 describes this process.

STEP BY STEP

4.13 Creating a Multifile Assembly

1. Create a new project based on the Empty Project template in solution 316C04. Name the project `StepByStep4_13`. Activate Solution Explorer and access the project's Property Pages by selecting Properties from the context menu. Set the `Output Type` property to `Class Library`.

2. Switch to the class view, right-click the project `StepByStep4_13`, and select Add, Add Class from the context menu. The C# Add Class Wizard opens, as shown in Figure 4.28. Use this wizard to create a class named `MathLib`. Using the class view, add a static method named `Add()` that returns an `int` value and accepts two `int` parameters, `first` and `second`. Modify the generated template by modifying the `Add()` method, as follows:

```
public static int Add (int first, int second)
{
    return first + second;
}
```

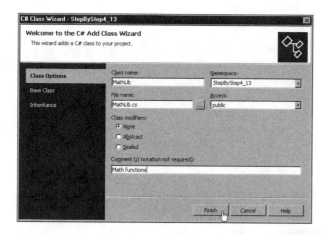

FIGURE 4.28
You can use the C# Add Class Wizard to add a class.

> **NOTE**
>
> **Two Ways to Add a Class** There are two ways to add a class to a project. The first way is to select a project in Solution Explorer and choose Add, Add Class. This adds to the project a basic template for a class file. The second and much better way to create a class is by selecting a project in the Class View and then choosing Add, Add Class. This latter method opens the C# Add Class Wizard, which allows you to customize various attributes for the class, as shown in Figure 4.28.

3. Add another class to the project and name this class StringLib. Add a static method named Concat() that returns a string and that accepts two strings, firstHalf and secondHalf. Modify the generated template by adding the following code to it, and then save all files:

```
public static string Concat(
    string firstHalf, string secondHalf)
{
    return firstHalf + secondHalf;
}
```

4. Open the Visual Studio .NET command prompt. A command window opens, ready to execute .NET Framework command-line tools.

5. Issue the following command to compile StringLib.cs as a module that is not yet part of any assembly:

```
csc /t:module StringLib.cs
```

A file named StringLib.netModule is generated.

6. Type the following command to open StringLib.netModule in the MSIL Disassembler:

```
ildasm StringLib.netModule
```

Open its manifest and be aware that this manifest is not an assembly manifest because there is no .assembly directive in it. However, there is an assembly extern directive that points to another assembly, named mscorlib, but that's different: It doesn't make this file an assembly.

continues

continued

7. Use a command similar to the one in step 5 to compile the `MathLib.cs` file into a module. When you watch the `MathLib.netModule` file through the MSIL Disassembler, you should again note that this file is just a module and not an assembly.

8. Type the following command to read both module files and create an assembly:

```
csc /t:library /out:Utils.dll
➥/addmodule:MathLib.netModule,StringLib.netModule
```

9. Open the `Utils.dll` file in the MSIL Disassembler. Note that `Utils.dll` contains just the manifest and no code. Examine the manifest and note that it has an `.assembly` `Utils` directive that identifies it as an assembly manifest for an assembly named `Utils`. The assembly directive is followed by two `.file` directives that identify other files in the assembly.

So, is `Utils.dll` from Step by Step 4.13 *the* assembly? No, it is not. It just specifies the assembly manifest. The assembly actually consists of three files: `Utils.dll`, which stores the assembly manifest, `MathLib.netModule`, and `StringLib.netModule`. So you can see that the concept of an assembly is logical and not physical. Although `Utils.dll`, `MathLib.netModule`, and `StringLib.netModule` are three distinct files physically, logically they belong to the same assembly: `Utils`.

Although you can't create multifile assemblies by using Visual Studio .NET, you can use them within a Visual Studio .NET project. Step by Step 4.14 demonstrates how to do this.

STEP BY STEP

4.14 Creating a Windows Application That Uses a Multifile Assembly

1. Activate Solution Explorer for solution `316C04`, right-click the solution name (`316C04`), and select Add, Add New Project. Select Windows Application as the template for the new project and name the project `StepByStep4_14`.

2. In Solution Explorer, right-click Form1.cs and rename it TestMultiFileAssembly. Open the Properties window for this form and change both its Name and Text properties to TestMultiFileAssembly. Switch to the code view of the form and modify the Main() method to launch TestMultiFileAssembly instead of Form1.

3. In Solution Explorer, right-click the project name and select Add Reference. In the Add Reference dialog box, browse for the file Utils.dll (it should be in the folder of project StepByStep4_13) and add a reference to it. Adding this reference copies all the files identified by the assembly manifest in Utils.dll into the bin\debug\Utils folder of the current project. You can verify this by clicking the Show All Files tool in Solution Explorer and navigating to the bin\debug\Utils folder of the current project.

4. Switch to the code view and add the following using directive at the top of the code:

```
using StepByStep4_13;
```

5. In the design view, arrange controls on the form (see Figure 4.29). In the first GroupBox control, name the TextBox controls txtFirst and txtSecond; name the Button control btnAdd; and name the Label control at the bottom lblAddResult. For the second GroupBox control, name the TextBox controls txtFirstHalf and txtSecondHalf; name the Button control btnConcat; and name the Label control at the bottom lblConcatResult.

6. Add the following event handling code to the Click event of btnAdd:

```
private void btnAdd_Click(object sender,
    System.EventArgs e)
{
    int intAddResult = MathLib.Add(
        Convert.ToInt32(txtFirst.Text),
        Convert.ToInt32(txtSecond.Text));
    lblAddResult.Text = String.Format(
        "The Result of Addition is: {0}", intAddResult);
}
```

7. Add the following event handling code to the Click event of btnConcat:

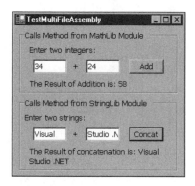

FIGURE 4.29
A Windows application can invoke methods from a multifile assembly.

continues

continued

```
private void btnConcat_Click(object sender,
    System.EventArgs e)
{
    lblConcatResult.Text =
        "The Result of concatenation is: " +
        StringLib.Concat(txtFirstHalf.Text,
        txtSecondHalf.Text);
}
```

8. Set StepByStep4_14 as the startup project.

9. Run the project. Enter two integer values in the top group box and click the Add button. This invokes the MathLib.Add() method from the MathLib.netModule file. Enter two string values in the second group box and click the Concat button. This invokes the StringLib.Concat() method from the StringLib.netModule file. You should see output similar to that shown in Figure 4.29.

Static and Dynamic Assemblies

When you compile programs by using Visual Studio .NET or the command-line compiler, they emit the files that make up an assembly. These files are physically stored on disk. Such an assembly is called a *static assembly*.

It is also possible to create and execute assemblies on-the-fly (that is, while a program is still under execution). Such assemblies are called *dynamic assemblies*. A common usage of dynamic assemblies can be seen in ASP.NET. When you execute an .aspx page, ASP.NET creates assemblies at runtime.

If needed, dynamic assemblies can be saved to disk and loaded again from there. The classes used to create dynamic assemblies are available in the System.Reflection.Emit namespace. I do not cover that namespace in this book because it is not required by the exam objectives, but if you are interested, you can explore the product documentation for the System.Reflection.Emit.AssemblyBuilder class.

Private and Shared Assemblies

Assemblies can be deployed by using two different approaches:

◆ You can deploy an assembly for use with a single application. When the assembly is deployed this way, it is called a *private assembly*.

◆ You can deploy an assembly for use with several applications. When the assembly is deployed in shared mode, it is called a *shared assembly*.

Here are some fast facts about private assemblies:

◆ Private assemblies are intended to be used only by the applications with which they are deployed.

◆ Private assemblies are deployed in the directory (or a subdirectory) where the main application is installed.

◆ Typically, a private assembly is written by the same company that writes the main application that uses the private assembly.

Because of the localized nature of private assemblies, the CLR does not impose a strict versioning policy with them. It is more or less left to application developers to decide how to version and name their assemblies.

On the other hand, a shared assembly can be used by more than one application. All the shared assemblies on a computer are stored in the GAC so that they are accessible by all applications. Because of the shared nature of the GAC, the CLR imposes special requirements of security and versioning that must be met before you can install any assembly in the GAC.

Here are some fast facts about shared assemblies and the GAC:

◆ Each assembly that is installed in the GAC must have a strong name. A strong name consists of an assembly's name, a version number, a culture, a public key, and an optional digital signature. The strong name ensures an assembly's identity.

◆ The CLR checks the assembly's integrity before installing it in the GAC. The CLR ensures that the assembly has not been tampered with by checking the assembly's strong name.

NOTE **XCOPY Deployment and the GAC** When an application needs to refer to assemblies in the GAC, you cannot deploy the application by using just the XCOPY command as you also need to install the assembly in the GAC of the target machine. In such a case, it is recommended that you deploy the application by using an installer program such as Windows Installer 2.0 that understands how to work with the GAC. Creating setup and deployment projects by using Windows Installer technology is discussed in Chapter 13.

NOTE **Private Assemblies Versus Shared Assemblies** As a general rule, you should deploy assemblies as private assemblies. You should install the assemblies in the GAC if you are explictly required to share them with other applications.

EXAM TIP

The Strong Name Tool and the File Signing Tool   Assemblies that are signed with a strong name (using `sn.exe` tool) provide a name, version, and integrity protection, but they do not provide the same high level of trust as a publisher certificate. You can use the File Signing tool (`signcode.exe`) to attach a publisher's digital signature to an assembly. The File Signing tool requires you to specify a software publisher certificate that you can obtain by verifying your identity through a Certification Authority (CA) such as Verisign or Thawte.

You can sign an assembly by using both the Strong Name tool and the File Signing tool. If you use both, you must use the Strong Name tool before you use the File Signing tool.

◆ The GAC is capable of maintaining multiple copies of an assembly with the same name but different versions.

◆ The CLR can determine what version of an assembly to load, based on the information in an application's configuration file or the machinewide configuration file (`machine.config`). This is described in more depth in Chapter 15, "Configuring a Windows Application."

To view the contents of the GAC, follow the steps outlined in Step by Step 4.15.

STEP BY STEP

4.15 Viewing the Contents of the GAC

1. Open Windows Explorer and navigate to the system folder of your computer (such as `C:\Windows` or `C:\WINNT`). Open the subfolder named `assembly`.

2. You should now be able to see the contents of the GAC (see Figure 4.30). The .NET Framework installs a Windows shell called the Assembly Cache Viewer (`Shfusion.dll`) that allows you to easily view the contents of the GAC using Windows Explorer. Select the `System.Security` assembly and right-click it, and then select Properties from the context menu. You should see information related to this assembly, as shown in Figure 4.31.

FIGURE 4.30
The Assembly Cache Viewer Shell Extension enables you to view the contents of GAC by using Windows Explorer.

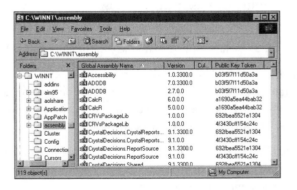

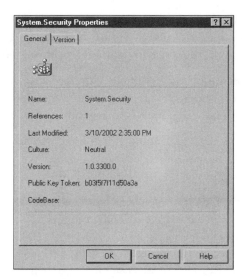

The GAC is discussed further in Chapter 13, where you learn how to deploy your own assemblies in the GAC.

Resource-Only and Satellite Assemblies

Create and modify a .NET assembly.

- **Create and implement satellite assemblies.**

- **Create resource-only assemblies.**

A Windows application typically contains resources such as images and translated strings in various cultures/languages, in addition to the code. When you add resources in a Visual Studio .NET project, their default build type is `Content`. When you compile the project, the assemblies contain just code, metadata, and links to resource files that exist externally. This means that the resource files are distributed with the application as separate files, and all these files must be available at runtime in order for the application to function correctly.

Another way of packaging resource files with an application is to embed them into the assembly itself. To achieve this, when you add resource files to a project, you need to set their build type as `Embedded Resources` instead of `Content`. You can do this through the Properties window by accessing the properties of these files.

FIGURE 4.31
You can view the properties of the selected assembly in the GAC when you double-click on the assembly.

NOTE

Native Assemblies Versus JIT-Compiled Assemblies Assemblies store code in MSIL format. When a method is invoked for the first time, the CLR compiles that method into the machine's native code in a just-in-time (JIT) fashion. The native code is stored in memory and is directly used for any subsequent calls to this method. In the JIT compilation mode, a method is slow when it is called for the first time because an additional step of compilation is involved, but any subsequent calls to that method run as fast as native code.

When you view the GAC, note that some assemblies have their type marked as Native Image. That means these assemblies were precompiled in native code before they were installed in the GAC. The advantage of using the native image format is that even the first call of any method in an assembly is as fast as its subsequent calls. You can create a native image for an assembly by using the Native Image Generator tool (`ngen.exe`) that is installed as part of the .NET Framework SDK. Creating and precomiling an assembly during deployment is discussed in Chapter 13.

When the build type is set to Embedded Resources, the contents of the resource files are included in the assembly itself at compile time. Visual Studio .NET does this in the following three steps:

1. It creates an XML resource file with the extension .resx. This file stores the resources as key/value pairs (for example, the name of a resource file and its location).

2. At the time of compilation, all resources that are referenced by the .resx file are embedded into a binary file with the extension .resources.

3. The binary resource file (.resources) is embedded into the code assembly, using the compiler options.

Of course these steps can be done manually. The .resx file is an XML file, so you can manually create it by using any text editor. You can compile it into a .resources file by using the Resource File Generator tool (resgen.exe). You can embed a .resources file in an assembly by using the C# compiler's /resource option.

These steps create an assembly that contains both code and resources. Assemblies created in such a way are not dependent on external resource files. They have all the necessary information inside themselves. Recall that in Step by Step 4.10 you embedded a resource file named RandomNumberGenerator.bmp. When Visual Studio compiled that project to create StepByStep4_10.dll, it followed the three steps described here. You can go that project's folder and search for the .resx file and .resources files. The .resx file and the .resources files should have their filenames set the same as the name of the class—but with different extensions. You can also view the .dll file in the MSIL Disassembler (ildasm.exe) to see how it is different from the other files.

Another way to attach resources in an application is by creating resource-only assemblies. These assemblies contain just resources—and no code.

With the exception of satellite assemblies, Visual Studio .NET does not allow you to create resource-only assemblies. However, you can use the command-line tools provided by the .NET Framework to create such assemblies.

The .NET Framework provides various classes, in the System.Resources namespace, that can be used to work with resource files. Some important classes of this namespace are listed in Table 4.1.

TABLE 4.1

SOME IMPORTANT CLASSES THAT DEAL WITH
RESOURCES

Class	Description
ResourceManager	Provides access to the resources at runtime. You use this class to read information from resource-only assemblies.
ResourceReader	Enables you to read resources from the binary resource (.resources) file.
ResourceWriter	Enables you to write resources to the binary resource (.resources) file.
ResXResourceReader	Enables you to read resource information from the XML-based .resx file.
ResXResourceWriter	Enables you to write resource information to the XML-based .resx file.

Step by Step 4.16 shows you how to programatically generate .resx and .resources files from given resources. The objective is to create a resource file for storing flags of different countries. You can get these graphics from the common7\graphics\icons\flag folder in your Visual Studio .NET installation. For convenient use, each file in Step by Step 4.16 is renamed with its corresponding two-letter International Standards Organization (ISO) country code.

STEP BY STEP

4.16 Creating Resource Files

1. Activate Solution Explorer for solution 316C04, right-click the solution name (316C04), and select Add, Add New Project. Select Windows Application as the template for the new project and name the project StepByStep4_16.

2. In Solution Explorer, right-click Form1.cs and rename it GenerateResourceFiles. Open the Properties window for this form and change both its Name and Text properties to GenerateResourceFiles. Switch to the code view of the form and modify the Main() method to launch GenerateResourceFiles instead of Form1.

continues

continued

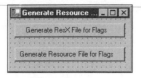

FIGURE 4.32
You can generate `.resx` and `.resources` files
by using the `ResXResourceWriter` and
`ResourceWriter` classes.

3. In Solution Explorer, right-click the project, select Add, Add Folder. Name the folder `Flags`. Right-click the `Flags` folder and select Add, Add Existing Item. Add all the icon files of country flags to this folder.

4. Place two `Button` controls (`btnGenerateResX` and `btnGenerateResources`) on the form, as shown in Figure 4.32.

5. Place the following `using` directives at the top of the code:

```
using System.Resources;
using System.IO;
```

6. Add an event handler for the `Click` event of `btnGenerateResX` and add the following code to it:

```
private void btnGenerateResX_Click(object sender,
    System.EventArgs e)
{
//Create a ResXResourceWriter object
    ResXResourceWriter rsxw =
        new ResXResourceWriter("Flags.resx");
    //the EXE will be placed in the bin\debug folder
    // so refer to the Flags folder from there
    foreach (string file in Directory.GetFiles(@
        "..\..\Flags", "*.ico"))
    {
        string countryCode = file.Substring(
          file.Length-6, 2);
        Image img = Image.FromFile(file);
        //store the Key-Value pair.
        rsxw.AddResource(countryCode,img);
    }
    rsxw.Close();
    MessageBox.Show("Flags.resx file generated");
}
```

7. Add an event handler for the `Click` event of `btnGenerateResources` and add the following code to it:

```
private void btnGenerateResources_Click(object sender,
    System.EventArgs e)
{
    //Create a ResourceWriter object
    ResourceWriter rw =
        new ResourceWriter("Flags.resources");
    //the EXE will be placed in the bin\debug folder
    // so refer to the Flags folder from there
    foreach (string file in Directory.GetFiles(@
        "..\..\Flags", "*.ico"))
```

```
        {
            string countryCode = file.Substring(
                file.Length-6, 2);
            Image img = Image.FromFile(file);
            //store the Key-Value pair
            rw.AddResource(countryCode,img);
        }
        rw.Close();
        MessageBox.Show("Flags.resources file generated");
}
```

8. Set `StepByStep4_16` as the startup project.

9. Run the project. Click each of the buttons to create both a `Flags.resx` file and a `Flags.resources` file. The location of these files is the same as the location of the project's `.exe` file.

In Step by Step 4.16 you create both a `.resx` file and a `.resources` file to demonstrate the capability of the `ResXResourceWriter` and `ResourceWriter` classes. Note that the `Flags.resources` file is not generated by compiling the `Flags.resx` file; rather, it is directly created using the `ResourceWriter` class. If you chose to create `.resources` file from a `.resx` file, you could use the following command:

```
resgen Flags.resx
```

Because you have already created a `Flags.resources` file by using Step by Step 4.16, you can ignore the `.resx` file for now. Although the `Flags.resources` file has resources embedded in it in binary format, it is not an assembly. To create an assembly for this file, you can use the Assembly Linker tool (`al.exe`), as described in Step by Step 4.17.

STEP BY STEP

4.17 Creating Resource-Only Assemblies

1. Open the Visual Studio .NET command prompt.

2. Change directory to where your project's `.exe` file is stored. Issue the following command to compile the `Flags.resources` file as a resource-only assembly:

```
al /embed:Flags.resources /out:Flags.Resources.dll
```

EXAM TIP

Linking the Modules Created in Different Programming Languages
You can use the Assembly Linker tool to create an assembly by linking together various compiled modules (that is, MSIL-translated programs without assembly manifests). This feature is especially useful if you are using multiple .NET languages in your programming environment. You can first compile the various programs, by using their corresponding language compilers, into module files and then use al.exe to link the module files together into an assembly.

FIGURE 4.33
The ResourceManager class allows you to load resources from resource-only assemblies.

Now that you know how to create a resource-only assembly, complete Step by Step 4.18 to learn how to use it from a Windows application. In Step by Step 4.18 you should especially focus on the use of the ResourceManager class to load the resources from resource-only assemblies.

STEP BY STEP

4.18 Using Resource-Only Assemblies

1. Activate Solution Explorer for solution 316C04, right-click the solution name (316C04), and select Add, Add New Project. Select Windows Application as the template for the new project and name the project StepByStep4_18.

2. In Solution Explorer, right-click Form1.cs and rename it GetCountryFlag. Open the Properties window for this form and change both its Name and Text properties to GetCountryFlag. Switch to the code view of the form and modify the Main() method to launch GetCountryFlag instead of Form1.

3. Add a TextBox control (txtCountryCode), a PictureBox control (pbFlag), a Button control (btnGetFlag), and a couple of Label controls to the form. Arrange the controls on the form (see Figure 4.33).

4. Place the following using directive at the top of the code:

```
using System.Reflection;
using System.Resources;
```

5. Add an event handler for the Click event of btnGetFlag and add the following code to it:

```
private void btnGetFlag_Click(object sender,
    System.EventArgs e)
{
    ResourceManager resource = new ResourceManager(
        "Flags",
        Assembly.LoadFrom("Flags.resources.dll"));
    pbFlag.Image = (Bitmap) resource.GetObject(
        txtCountryCode.Text.ToUpper());
}
```

6. Set `StepByStep4_18` as the startup project.

7. Run the project. Enter `US` in the text box and click the Get Flag button. The U.S. flag appears in the picture box (as shown in Figure 4.33).

A common use of resource-only assemblies is to store language- and culture-specific information. A Windows application that has been designed for international usage may package resource information for each locale in a separate assembly file. When a user downloads the application, he or she can ignore the assemblies for other cultures. Skipping the unnecessary files may significantly reduce the user's download time for the application.

The resource-only assemblies that store culture-specific information are also known as *satellite assemblies*. Step by Step 4.19 demonstrates how Visual Studio .NET can be used to generate satellite assemblies for different cultures.

STEP BY STEP

4.19 Generating Culture-Specific Satellite Assemblies

1. Activate Solution Explorer for solution `316C04`, right-click the solution name (`316C04`), and select Add, Add New Project. Select Windows Application as the template for the new project and name the project `StepByStep4_19`.

2. Drag and drop a `Label` control and a `PictureBox` control on the form. Write some text in the `Label` control, and assign an image to the `Images` property of the `PictureBox` control. The actual contents of the `Label` and `PictureBox` controls do not matter because this is just a demonstration of how to create satellite assemblies.

3. Select the `Localizable` property of the form to `true`. Set the `Language` property to `Hindi(India)`.

continues

continued

FIGURE 4.34
You can generate satellite assemblies to store culture-specific information through Visual Studio .NET.

FIGURE 4.35
You can use the MSIL Disassembler to view the assembly manifest of a satellite assembly.

4. In Solution Explorer, click the Show All Files button to see all files for the project. Click the + sign next to Form1.cs. You should see that it has attached to it a set of files with the extension .resx. These files are the XML-based resource files for storing the culture information for each language you select.

5. Go back to the form properties and set the Language property to Japanese. A .resx file is added to Solution Explorer for the Japanese language.

6. Set the project as the startup project.

7. Run the project. Navigate to the bin\debug folder. New folders that are specific to the selected language are created there. Expand the hi-IN folder to see its contents. You should see a file named StepByStep4_19.resources.dll (see Figure 4.34). This is the satellite assembly that is created by compiling the resources listed in the corresponding .resx file. Open the file in the MSIL Disassembler to view its contents and look at its assembly manifest (see Figure 4.35).

The topics of satellite assemblies and globalization of applications are covered in great detail in Chapter 8, "Globalization." For now, you can just note that Visual Studio .NET automatically creates a satellite assembly for the localized .resx file in the correct directory location, which is identified by its culture name. The .resx file is an XML-based configuration file that contains the resource information. Because it has an editable format, you can edit and modify it by using any text editor. In fact, Visual Studio .NET includes a built-in Resource Editor that allows you to edit .resx files.

R E V I E W   B R E A K

▶ Assemblies are the basic unit for reuse, versioning, security, and deployment for the components that are created by using the .NET Framework. An assembly manifest stores the assembly's metadata.

▶ Depending on the number of files that make up an assembly, it is called either a single-file or a multifile assembly.

▶ A private assembly is specific to an individual application. In contrast, a shared assembly can be referenced by more than one application and is stored in the machinewide GAC. A shared assembly must be assigned a cryptographically strong name.

▶ Resource-only assemblies are assemblies that contain just resources and no code. Resource-only assemblies that store culture-specific information are known as satellite assemblies.

CHAPTER SUMMARY

Building an efficient Visual C# .NET application requires you to create and manage .NET components and assemblies. As applications grow ever more complex, it's necessary to build them effectively by creating reusable components. The Microsoft .NET Framework allows programmers to create reusable code components. You can create a Windows component by deriving from the Component, Control, and UserControl classes, or from any of their derived classes. Your choice of base class mostly depends on what functionality you want to borrow and the type of component you want to create.

The Microsoft .NET Framework supports extensibility of components by allowing you to create new controls that can extend the functionality provided by the user controls that already exist, through a technique known as visual inheritance. In addition to hosting controls in a Windows form, you can host them in Microsoft Internet Explorer without much additional effort.

Assemblies are the basic units for reuse, versioning, security, and deployment for components created by using the .NET Framework. Assemblies are self-describing; they store their metadata inside themselves in the assembly manifest.

Assemblies can be classified in various ways: single-file and multifile assemblies, static and dynamic assemblies, private and shared assemblies, and satellite and resource-only assemblies.

Shared assemblies can be shared across applications and are stored in the machinewide GAC. Resource-only assemblies are assemblies that contain just resources and no code. The resource-only assemblies that store culture-specific information are known as satellite assemblies.

KEY TERMS

- assembly
- assembly manifest
- assembly metadata
- component
- custom control
- delegate
- GAC
- metadata
- private assembly
- resource-only assembly
- satellite assembly
- shared assembly
- strong name
- user control

APPLY YOUR KNOWLEDGE

Exercises

4.1   Creating the Odometer User Control

In this exercise, you'll learn to create a new user control from an existing user control. Your objective is to design an odometer user control that shows a three-digit odometer where each digit is displayed on a `Label` control. The odometer exposes a property named `ScrollInterval` that controls how frequently the odometer values change.

Estimated time: 20 minutes

1. Launch Visual Studio .NET. Select File, New, Blank Solution, and name the new file `316C04Exercises`.

2. Add to the solution a new project based on the Windows Control Library template. Name the project `Exercise4_1`. The Component Designer shows the control as a captionless, borderless form.

3. Drag and drop three `Label` controls (`lblHundred`, `lblTen`, and `lblUnit`) and a `Timer` component (`timer1`) on the form. Set the `Enabled` property of the `timer1` component to `true`.

4. Switch to code view and define a property in the class definition:

```
public int ScrollInterval
{
    get
    {
        return timer1.Interval;
    }
    set
    {
        timer1.Interval = value;
    }
}
```

5. Double-click the `Timer` component in the component tray to attach the default `Tick` event, and then add the following code to the event handler:

```
private void timer1_Tick(object sender,
    System.EventArgs e)
{
    int intUnit = Convert.ToInt32(
        lblUnit.Text);
    intUnit++;
    if (intUnit >= 9)
    {
        intUnit = 0;
        int intTen = Convert.ToInt32(
            lblTen.Text);
        intTen++;
        if (intTen >= 9)
        {
            intTen = 0;
            int intHundred =
                Convert.ToInt32(
                    lblHundred.Text);
            intHundred++;
            if(intHundred >= 9)
            {
                intHundred = 0;
            }
            lblHundred.Text =
                intHundred.ToString();
        }
        lblTen.Text = intTen.ToString();
    }
    lblUnit.Text = intUnit.ToString();
}
```

6. Select the project `Exercise4_1` in Solution Explorer and select Build from the context menu. This step generates the code for the control and packages it into `Exercise4_1.dll`. This file is located in the `bin\debug` or `bin\Release` directory of your project.

7. Add new projects to the solution. Select the Windows Application template and name the project `Exercise4_1Test`.

8. In Solution Explorer, right-click `Form1.cs` and rename it `TestOdometer`. Open the Properties window for this form and change both its name and `Text` properties to `TestOdometer`. Switch to the code view of the form and modify the `Main()` method to launch `TestOdometer` instead of `Form1`.

APPLY YOUR KNOWLEDGE

9. Using Solution Explorer, add a reference to Exercise4_1.dll.

10. Place the Odometer control onto the form from the toolbox.

11. Set Exercise4_1Test as the startup project.

12. Run the project. You should see the form that is hosting the Odometer control, as shown in Figure 4.36.

FIGURE 4.36
The Odometer user control inherits from the UserControl class.

4.2 Getting Types in an Assembly

The classes in the System.Reflection namespace, along with the System.Type class, allow you to obtain information about loaded assemblies at runtime. This information includes the types defined within the assemblies, such as classes, interfaces, and value types. In this exercise, you use these classes to fetch all the types in the selected assembly.

Estimated time: 20 minutes

1. Create a new project with the Windows Control Library template in solution 316C04Exercises. Name the project Exercise4_2.

2. In Solution Explorer, right-click Form1.cs and rename it GetTypes. Open the Properties window for this form and change both its Name and Text properties to GetTypes. Switch to the code view of the form and modify the Main() method to launch GetTypes instead of Form1.

3. Place a Label control, a TextBox control (txtAssemblyName), a Button control (btnLoadAssembly), and a ListBox control (lbTypes) on the form (see Figure 4.37).

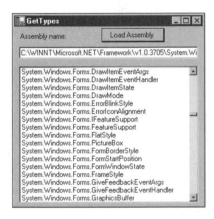

FIGURE 4.37
The System.Reflection.Assembly class helps in getting the types of an assembly through its GetTypes() method.

4. Switch to the code view and add the following using directive:

```
using System.Reflection;
```

5. Add code to handle the Load event of the form and the SelectedIndexChanged event of the ComboBox control:

```
private void btnLoadAssembly_Click(
    object sender, System.EventArgs e)
{
    if(dlgOpen.ShowDialog() ==
        DialogResult.OK)
    {
        txtAssemblyName.Text =
            dlgOpen.FileName;
        // Load the Assembly
        Assembly assem = Assembly.LoadFrom(
            txtAssemblyName.Text);
```

APPLY YOUR KNOWLEDGE

```
//Get all the types in the assembly
Type [] types = assem.GetTypes ();
lbTypes.Items.Clear();

foreach (Type type in types)
{
    // Dump the FullName of
    // the Type in the ListBox
    lbTypes.Items.Add(
        type.FullName);
}
    }
}
```

6. Set the project as the startup project.

7. Run the project. Click the Load Assembly button and select the assembly to load. You should see that all the types in the assembly appear in the list box, with their full namespaces, as shown in Figure 4.37.

Review Questions

1. What are the three different ways in which Windows components can be created?

2. What is the usual signature of an event handler?

3. What are the steps you must perform in order to create and implement an event?

4. What should be the value of classid when you are creating object elements to render Windows controls in a Web page?

5. When you create a control by inheriting from the Control class, what extra step do you need to take?

6. How can you assign a custom toolbox icon to a component?

7. What is the purpose of an assembly manifest?

8. What type of assemblies should be stored in the GAC?

9. What are resource-only assemblies and satellite assemblies?

Exam Questions

1. You want to decrease the time it takes when a component loads for the first time. Which of the following tools can help you?

   A. gacutil.exe

   B. resgen.exe

   C. sn.exe

   D. ngen.exe

2. You have converted your application's assembly files to native images by using the Native Image Generator (ngen.exe). Which of the following statements holds true for your assemblies? (Select all that apply.)

   A. Applications that use a native assembly will run faster on their initial run.

   B. Applications that use a native assembly will have consistently faster performance compared to JIT-compiled assemblies.

   C. Native assemblies are portable. You should be able to use them on any machine that has the CLR installed.

   D. Native assemblies can be used in debugging scenarios.

3. You have developed a graphics application. Before you create a setup program, you want to package some of the image files into a satellite assembly.

APPLY YOUR KNOWLEDGE

You have created an XML-based resource file for all these files and named it `App.resx`. Which of the following steps would you take to convert this file into a satellite assembly?

   A. Use `csc.exe` followed by `al.exe`.

   B. Use `resgen.exe` followed by `al.exe`.

   C. Use `resgen.exe` followed by `csc.exe`.

   D. Use `csc.exe` followed by `resgen.exe`.

4. You have developed a utility network library that will be used by several applications in your company. How should you deploy this library?

   A. Sign the library by using the Strong Name tool and place it in the GAC.

   B. Sign the library by using the File Signing tool and place it in the GAC.

   C. Sign the library by using both the Strong Name tool and the File Signing tool and place it in the `bin` directory of each application that uses it.

   D. Keep the library in a central place such as `C:\CommonComponents` and use each application's configuration files to point to it.

5. You are a programmer for a popular gaming software publishing company. The company has recently designed a series of games, using the .NET Framework. All these new game applications share some components. Some of these components are shipped in the box with the application and others are deployed over the Internet. Which of the following tools should you use for these components before packaging a game for deployment?

   A. Use `sn.exe` to sign the components.

   B. Use `signcode.exe` to sign the components.

   C. Use `sn.exe` followed by `signcode.exe` to sign the components

   D. Use `signcode.exe` followed by `sn.exe` to sign the components.

6. You want to implement a versioning policy on all components of your Windows application. Which of the following options would you use?

   A. Use `signcode.exe` to assign the version information.

   B. Use `resgen.exe` to create a resource file that contains the version information.

   C. Create an XML-based configuration file that maintains version information for each component.

   D. Use `sn.exe` to assign a strong name to each assembly.

7. You are designing a contact management system that will be used by your company's salespeople. You will often be required to create forms that are capable of accepting and validating addresses. This will involve accepting information such as name, street name, state, country, and zip code by displaying controls such as `TextBox` or `ComboBox` controls. You think it is a good idea to package your address input and validation code in a component so that you can reuse your efforts in several forms throughout the application. Which of the following classes should you use as the base class of your component?

   A. `System.Windows.Forms.Control`

   B. `System.Windows.Forms.UserControl`

   C. `System.Windows.Forms.Form`

   D. `System.ComponentModel.Component`

APPLY YOUR KNOWLEDGE

8. You are creating a time-tracking application that will be used companywide. Several forms in this application show clocks to the user. The clocks have the look and action of an analog clock, with a circular face and hands of different sizes for hour, minutes, and seconds. You decide to code the analog clock as a reusable component. Which of the following classes should you choose as the base class for creating this control?

   A. `System.Windows.Forms.Control`

   B. `System.Windows.Forms.UserControl`

   C. `System.Windows.Forms.Form`

   D. `System.ComponentModel.Component`

9. You are using the C# language compiler from the command line. You want to compile a C# program but do not want the compiler to write an assembly manifest for it. Which of the following compiler options would you choose?

   A. `/target:exe`

   B. `/target:library`

   C. `/target:module`

   D. `/target:winexe`

10. One of your colleagues is designing a `Changed` event for his control. He complains to you that his code behaves quite abnormally; it runs well some of the time and generates exceptions at other times. The following is part of his event handling code (line numbers are for reference purposes only):

```
01: public delegate void
        ChangedEventHandler(object sender,
        ColorMixerEventArgs args);

02: public event
        ChangedEventHandler Changed;
```

```
03: protected virtual void OnChanged(
        ColorMixerEventArgs e)
04: {
05:         //notify the object
06:         Changed(this, e);
07:}
```

Which of the following suggestions would solve his problem?

   A. The code in line 6 should be replaced with the following:

```
if (ChangedEventHandler != null)
{
    //notify that object
    ChangedEventHandler(this, e);
}
```

   B. The code in line 6 should be replaced with the following:

```
if (ChangedEventHandler != null)
{
    //notify that object
    Changed(this, e);
}
```

   C. The code in line 6 should be replaced with the following:

```
if (Changed != null)
{
    //notify that object
    ChangedEventHandler(this, e);
}
```

   D. The code in line 6 should be replaced with the following:

```
if (Changed != null)
{
    //notify that object
    Changed(this, e);
}
```

11. One of your colleagues is trying to host a control in Internet Explorer. He has created the control and tested it successfully on a Windows form, but he can't make it show up in Internet Explorer.

The name of the control is
`SolidControls.ColorMixer` and it lives in a file
named `SolidControlsLib.dll`. When asked, your
colleague tells you that he has placed both the
HTML page and the `.dll` file in the same virtual
directory. He shows you the HTML file that he
has designed to host the control. Here is part of
his HTML code (line numbers are for reference
purposes only):

```
01: <html>
02:     <body>
03:         <object id="colorMixerX1"
04:             classid="http://localhost/
➥WebDir/SolidControlsLib.dll"
05:             height="300" width="300">
06:         </object>
07:     </body>
08: </html>
```

What changes are necessary to make this control
work in Internet Explorer?

A. Change the code in line 4 to this:

```
classid="http://localhost/WebDir/
➥SolidControlsLib.dll#
➥SolidControls.ColorMixer"
```

B. Change the code in line 4 to this:

```
classid="http://localhost/WebDir/
➥SolidControlsLib.dll?
➥SolidControls.ColorMixer"
```

C. Change the code in line 4 to this:

```
classid="SolidControls.ColorMixer"
```

D. Change the code in line 4 to this:

```
classid="http://localhost/WebDir/
➥SolidControlsLib.dll?
➥classid=SolidControls.ColorMixer"
```

12. You have designed a composite `user` control by
assembling five `TextBox` controls and two `Button`
controls. You do not want the client application
to be able to access the contained objects within
the `user` control. Which modifier should you use
with your contained objects to achieve this goal?
(Select all that apply.)

A. `private`

B. `internal`

C. `protected`

D. `public`

13. You are designing a component that will enable
your applications to interact with the computers
in a network. The component does not have any
visual representation, but it should provide a
design-time interface that will help a client application designer set its properties and behavior.
Which of the following classes is the best choice
as the base class for creating this control?

A. `System.Windows.Forms.Control`

B. `System.Windows.Forms.UserControl`

C. `System.Windows.Forms.Form`

D. `System.ComponentModel.Component`

14. Your Windows application is using some graphics
files. You want to embed the graphics files in the
application's `.exe` file so that you don't have to
distribute additional files with your application.
What should you do?

A. Create a satellite assembly for storing
graphics.

B. Set the `BuildAction` property of the graphics
files to `Content`.

C. Set the `BuildAction` property of the graphics files to `Compile`.

D. Set the `BuildAction` property of the graphics files to `Embedded Resources`.

15. Which of the following statements is true for a multifile assembly?

   A. Each file in a multifile assembly must contain an assembly manifest.

   B. Only one of the files in the multifile assembly can contain an assembly manifest.

   C. You can find the assembly to which a file belongs by opening that file through the MSIL Disassembler (`ildasm.exe`).

   D. You can have two files with the same name but different versions in a multifile assembly without having any versioning conflicts.

Answers to Review Questions

1. These are the three different ways Windows components can be created:

   • You can create a nonvisual component by deriving from the `Component` class.

   • You can create a control by painting its own user interface by deriving from the `Control` class or any of its derived classes.

   • You can create a composite control based on existing controls by deriving from the `UserControl` class or any of its derived classes.

2. The event handler method usually contains two parameters: the object that was the target of the event and an object of type `System.EventArgs` or its derived class that contains event-related data.

3. To create and implement an event, you need to take care of the following steps:

   • Define the `EventArgs` class, which contains the event-related data. This is required only if you want to pass specific event-related information to the event handlers.

   • Create a `Delegate` object that can store a reference to the event handler. This is required only if you want to pass specific event-related information to the event handlers.

   • Define the event itself as an object of delegate type.

   • Define a method that notifies the registered objects of the event. Usually this method has a name such as `OnChanged()`, where `Changed` is an event name.

   • Call the method defined in the preceding step whenever the event occurs.

4. The `classid` attribute of the object element should contain the path to the control library (`.dll` file) and the fully qualified name of the control, separated by a # (pound sign).

5. When you create a control by inheriting from the `Control` class, the control does not have any user interface. Therefore, the `Paint` event should be handled in order to paint the desired user interface for the control.

6. You can associate a custom toolbox icon with a component by using the `ToolBoxBitmap` attribute with the class definition. You should ensure that the bitmap file is (16×16), has the same name as the component, resides in the same folder as the class file, and has a `.bmp` filename extension.

7. An assembly manifest stores the assembly's metadata. The metadata provides self-describing information such as the name of the assembly, the version of the assembly, the files that are part of the assembly and their hash values, and the assembly's dependencies on other assemblies. This subset of information in the manifest makes assemblies self-sufficient.

8. Shared assemblies (that is, assemblies that are shared by more than one application) must be stored in the machinewide GAC. Shared assemblies have strong names, and they are often digitally signed.

9. Resource-only assemblies are assemblies that contain only resources and no code. Resource-only assemblies that store culture-specific information are known as satellite assemblies.

Answers to Exam Questions

1. **D.** The Native Image Generator tool (ngen.exe) converts MSIL to processor-specific native code. A native assembly loads faster than an MSIL assembly the first time it loads because the work that the JIT compiler would normally do has already been done by ngen.exe. The other three choices are not relevant because gacutil.exe allows you to view and manipulate the contents of the GAC. resgen.exe is the Resource File Generator tool, which is used to compile XML-based resource files (that is, .resx files) into binary .resources files. sn.exe is used to assign assemblies strong names so that they can be placed in the GAC. For more information, see the section "Creating and Managing .NET Assemblies" in this chapter.

2. **A** and **D.** The native assemblies load faster the first time because the work that the JIT compiler would normally do has been already done by ngen.exe. However, on subsequent executions, they show the same performance as their JIT-compiled equivalents. The natively generated assemblies are processor specific; they can't be ported across different processor architectures. ngen.exe provides a /debug switch that can be used to generate native assemblies for debugging scenarios. For more information, see the section "Satellite and Resource-Only Assemblies" in this chapter.

3. **B.** To create a satellite assembly, you first compile the XML-based resource file into a binary resource file, using the Resource File Generator tool (resgen.exe). Then you use the Assembly Linker tool (al.exe) to create a satellite assembly. For more information, see the section "Creating and Managing .NET Assemblies" in this chapter.

4. **A.** If an assembly is used by several applications, it is a good idea to place the assembly in the GAC because the GAC provides lot of benefits, including versioning and security checks. Before you can place an assembly in the GAC, you must assign a strong name to it. You can use sn.exe to assign a strong name. signcode.exe is used to digitally sign an assembly with a third-party software publisher's certification. Its use is not required in order for an assembly to be placed in the GAC. For more information, see the section "Private and Shared Assemblies" in this chapter.

5. **C.** Because your components are being shared among several games published by your company, they are good candidates to be placed in the GAC of the target machine. Before a component can be placed in the GAC, it must be signed by using the Strong Name tool (sn.exe).

Because your company is also deploying software over the Internet, you should digitally sign your code with a software publisher's certificate, obtained from a respected certification authority. After you obtain the certificate, you can use signcode.exe to sign the component. When you are using both sn.exe and signcode.exe with an assembly, you should use sn.exe first. For more information, see the section "Private and Shared Assemblies" in this chapter.

6. **D.** Versioning is done only for assemblies that have strong names, so you must sign your components by using the Strong Name tool (sn.exe) before they can participate in versioning. For more information, see the section "Private and Shared Assemblies" in this chapter.

7. **B.** The System.Windows.Forms.UserControl class provides functionality for quickly creating a reusable component by assembling existing Windows controls. For more information, see the section "Creating and Managing .NET Components" in this chapter.

8. **A.** You should inherit from the Control class if you want to provide a custom graphical representation of a control or functionality that is not available through standard controls. For more information, see the section "Creating and Managing .NET Components" in this chapter.

9. **C.** /target:module is the only option that instructs the C# compiler not to include an assembly manifest in the compiled code. For more information, see the section "Single-File and Multifile Assemblies" in this chapter.

10. **D.** When the event occurs, the OnChange() method is called in order to notify all registered objects about the event. This is done by the event object Changed. If Changed event is null, no objects have registered themselves with this event. If it is not null, calling Changed with object and event arguments invokes the event on registered objects. ChangedEventArgs should not be used because it is a delegate that defines the type of event, rather than the event itself. For more information, see the section "Creating and Implementing Events" in this chapter.

11. **A.** You should give classid as a string that has the virtual path to the control library and the namespace-qualified name of the control class, separated by the # sign. For more information, see the section "Hosting a Windows Control Inside Internet Explorer" in this chapter.

12. **A** and **B.** When you declare the contained objects within a control as internal or private, they are not accessible to the client application for direct manipulation. For more information, see the section "Creating and Managing .NET Components" in this chapter.

13. **D.** The components that provide no visual interface should be derived directly from the System.ComponentModel.Component class. For more information, see the section "Creating and Managing .NET Components" in this chapter.

14. **D.** When you set a Build Action property of a graphics file to Embedded Resources, the file is embedded with the main project output, whether it is a .dll or an .exe. For more information, see the sections "Satellite and Resource-Only Assemblies" and "Creating Components by Extending the Component Class" in this chapter.

APPLY YOUR KNOWLEDGE

15. **B.** Only one of the files in a multifile assembly can contain the assembly manifest. You cannot find the name of an assembly to which a file belongs by viewing it in the MSIL Disassembler because only the assembly manifest contains that information. It is not possible to have two files with the same name in an assembly.

The most elementary unit of versioning is the assembly itself, so the files contained in it cannot have additional versions. For more information, see the section "Single-File and Multifile Assemblies" in this chapter.

Suggested Readings and Resources

1. Visual Studio .NET Combined Help Collection:

    - "Component Authoring Walkthroughs"

    - "Component Authoring—Decision Chart"

    - "Programming with Assemblies"

    - "Creating Satellite Assemblies"

2. Jeffrey Richter. *Applied Microsoft .NET Framework Programming.* Microsoft Press, 2001.

3. Richard Grimes. *Developing Applications with Visual Studio .NET.* Addison-Wesley, 2002.

4. Don Box. *Essential .NET Vol.1: The Common Language Runtime.* Addison-Wesley, 2002.

5. Microsoft Support Webcast: Microsoft .NET Framework and Control Licensing. support.microsoft.com/servicedesks/webcasts/wc061202/wcblurb061202.asp.

6. Microsoft Support WebCast: Developing Components and Controls with Microsoft Visual Studio .NET. support.microsoft.com/servicedesks/webcasts/wc101201/wcblurb101201.asp.

This chapter covers the following Microsoft-specified objectives for the "Creating User Services" section of Exam 70-316, "Developing and Implementing Windows-Based Applications with Microsoft Visual C# .NET and Microsoft Visual Studio .NET":

Display and update data.

- **Transform and filter data.**

- **Bind data to the UI.**

▶ Nearly every Windows application deals with data in some way. The purpose of this objective is to teach some of the skills involved in making data available on the user interface of a Windows-based application. That includes both getting the data that the user wants to see (transforming and filtering) and tying the data to the user interface (data binding). In Chapter 6, "Consuming and Manipulating Data," you'll learn more about programming with data; this objective deals with the parts of the process that you can actually see onscreen.

CHAPTER 5

Data Binding

STUDY STRATEGIES

▶ Be sure to carefully read the sections of this chapter that deal with data binding, even if you think you already know all about data binding. In the .NET world, the concept of data binding has been generalized and improved from what existed in earlier Microsoft development environments.

▶ In previous Microsoft development environments, many writers and trainers recommended avoiding data binding due to performance issues and a lack of flexibility. Microsoft has removed the bulk of these limitations in Visual Studio .NET.

▶ Make sure you understand the difference between simple and complex data binding, and know the syntax used for each.

▶ Practice working with Server Explorer. You should know how to connect an application to any data source, and you should know how to select and display the data that you want to show to the end user.

INTRODUCTION

Now that you know how to put together a user interface in Visual C# .NET, it's time to turn to the functionality behind that user interface. One of the most important parts of almost any application is to connect the data model of the application to the user interface. *Data model* is a general term: It might refer to data stored in a database, or to an array of values, or to items contained in an object from the System.Collections namespace. The data model is internal to the application. It contains information that is known to the application.

To be useful for the end users of your application, the data model must somehow be connected to the user interface. One of the easiest ways to make a connection between the data model and the user interface is to bind the data to the user interface. *Binding* refers to the process of making a link between controls on the user interface and data stored in the data model. As the user views and manipulates controls, the application takes care of translating the user's actions into reading and writing data from the data model.

Sometimes the data model contains more information than you want to show to the user. For example, you might have a list of 10,000 customers in the data model. Most likely the user wants to see the orders from a single customer or a small group of customers. Therefore, your application needs to filter (limit) the amount of information that it shows from the data model, in order to avoid overwhelming the user. You might also need to transform the data from an internal representation (for example, a customer code) to something more user friendly (such as a customer name) in the process of moving it from the data model to the user interface.

This chapter covers all these topics, using a very broad concept of data. Chapter 6 drills into the use of ADO.NET, focusing on data stored in databases.

BINDING DATA TO THE USER INTERFACE

Display and update data:

- **Bind data to the user interface.**

Data binding refers to the process of creating a link between a data model and the user interface of an application. The data model can be any source of data within the application: It might be an array of values, an Extensible Markup Language (XML) file, or data stored in a database. The user interface consists of the controls that are contained on the forms in an application.

The .NET Framework includes extremely flexible data binding capabilities. In the following sections you'll learn about many of those capabilities, including the following:

◆ Simple data binding

◆ Complex data binding

◆ One-way and two-way data binding

◆ The `BindingContext` object

◆ The Data Form Wizard

Simple Data Binding

Simple data binding means connecting a single value from the data model to a single property of a control. For example, you might bind the `Vendor` object name from a list of vendors to the `Text` property of a `TextBox` control.

STEP BY STEP

5.1 Using Simple Data Binding to Display a Vendor Name

1. Launch a new Visual C# Windows application project. Name it `315C05`.

---

2. Place a `TextBox` control on a new Windows form. Name the control `txtVendorName`.

3. Double-click the form and enter the following code in the form's `Load` event:

```
private void StepByStep5_1_Load(object sender,
    System.EventArgs e)
{
    // Create an array of vendor names
    String [] astrVendorNames =
        {"Microsoft", "Rational", "Premia"};

    // Bind the array to the text box
    txtVendorName.DataBindings.Add(
        "Text", astrVendorNames, "");
}
```

4. Insert the `Main()` method to launch the form. Set the form as the startup object for the project.

5. Run the project. The text box is now bound to the array, and it displays the first value from the array.

Looking at the code in Step by Step 5.1, you can see that the .NET Framework supplies an object model for binding. The control has a `ControlBindingsCollection` (accessed through its `DataBindings` property), which contains instances of the `Binding` class. By default there are no `Binding` objects in the collection, so when you create a control, it's not bound. To bind the control, you can add a new `Binding` object to the `ControlBindingsCollection` by using its `Add()` method.

Because the `Add()` method creates a new instance of the `Binding` class, it takes the same parameters as the constructor for that class:

◆ The name of the property to bind to

◆ The data source to bind

◆ The navigation path to the particular data; in this particular example, the navigation path is empty because there's only one thing to bind to in this array

Now that you've seen simple data binding in action, it's time to explore the topic in a bit more depth. I'll start by looking at which entities can be bound to the user interface. Then I'll talk about which properties you can bind to those entities.

Finally, I'll explain the architecture that the .NET Framework uses to manage simple data binding. You'll see that you can work directly with the objects that handle the data binding connections if you need to interact with the data binding process from code.

Bindable Entities

In Step by Step 5.1, the `Text` property of the `TextBox` control is bound to an element from an array. The `Binding` class can accept many other types of data sources, including the following:

◆ An instance of any class that implements the `IBindingList` or `ITypedList` interface, including the `DataSet`, `DataTable`, `DataView`, and `DataViewManager` classes.

◆ An instance of any class that implements the `IList` interface on an indexed collection of objects. In particular, this applies to classes that inherit from `System.Array`, including C# arrays.

◆ An instance of any class that implements the `IList` interface on an indexed collection of strongly typed objects. For example, you can bind to an array of `Vendor` objects.

Binding to a collection of strongly typed objects is a convenient way to handle data from an object-oriented data model.

STEP BY STEP

5.2 Using Simple Data Binding with a Strongly Typed `IList`

1. Add a new class named `Vendor.cs` to your project. Enter this code in the class:

```
using System;
namespace _316C05
{
    public class Vendor
    {
        private string vendorName;
        public string VendorName
        {
            get
            {
                return vendorName;
            }
```

```
            set
            {
                vendorName = value;
            }
        }
        public Vendor(string strVendorName)
        {
            this.VendorName = strVendorName;
        }
    }

}
```

2. Place a `TextBox` control on a new Windows form. Name the control `txtVendorName`.

3. Double-click the form and enter the following code in the form's `Load` event handler:

```
private void StepByStep5_2_Load(
    object sender, System.EventArgs e)
{
    // Create an array of vendor objects
    Vendor[] aVendors = new Vendor[3];
    aVendors[0] = new Vendor("Microsoft");
    aVendors[1] = new Vendor("Rational");
    aVendors[2] = new Vendor("Premia");

    // Bind the array to the text box
    txtVendorName.DataBindings.Add(
        "Text", aVendors, "VendorName");
}
```

4. Insert the `Main()` method to launch this form. Set the form as the startup object for the project.

5. Run the project. The text box is now bound to the array, and it displays the first value from the array.

> **NOTE**
>
> **Navigation Path for Objects** Step by Step 5.2 demonstrates how you can use the navigation path (the third parameter to the `DataBindings.Add` call) to specify a particular property of an object to bind to a control.

At this point, you could be forgiven for thinking that binding makes only the first element of a data source available on the user interface. In fact, bound controls are designed to let the user move through an entire collection of data. Later in this chapter you'll learn the details of the `BindingContext` object, which enables you to manipulate the data behind a bound control. But as a preview, Figure 5.1 shows a form that lets you scroll through the data in a strongly typed `IList`.

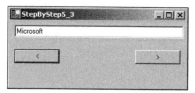

FIGURE 5.1

This form includes a bound `TextBox` control and two `Button` controls that let the user scroll through the data.

STEP BY STEP

5.3 Scrolling Through Data, Using the `BindingContext` Object

1. Place a `TextBox` control on a new Windows form. Name the control `txtVendorName`.

2. Place a `Button` control on the form. Name the control `btnPrevious` and set its `Text` property to `<`.

3. Place a second `Button` control on the form. Name the control `btnNext` and set its `Text` property to `>`.

4. Double-click the form and enter the following code:

```
// Create an array of vendor objects
Vendor aVendors = new Vendor[3];

private void StepByStep5_3_Load(object sender,
    System.EventArgs e)
{
    // Initialize the vendors array
    aVendors[0] = new Vendor("Microsoft");
    aVendors[1] = new Vendor("Rational");
    aVendors[2] = new Vendor("Premia");

    // Bind the array to the text box
    txtVendorName.DataBindings.Add(
        "Text", aVendors, "VendorName");
}
```

5. Add the following code to handle the `Click` events from the two buttons:

```
private void btnPrevious_Click(object sender,
    System.EventArgs e)
{
    // Move to the previous item in the data source
    this.BindingContext[aVendors].Position -= 1;
}

private void btnNext_Click(object sender,
    System.EventArgs e)
{
    // Move to the next item in the data source
    this.BindingContext[aVendors].Position += 1;
}
```

6. Insert the `Main()` method to launch this form. Set the form as the startup object for the project.

7. Run the project. The text box is now bound to the array, and it displays the first value from the array. You can use the two buttons to move to different values within the array.

Properties That Can Be Bound

Just as the .NET Framework allows flexibility in the source of bound data, it allows flexibility on the user interface side of the equation. You can use simple data binding with any control that has a `DataBindings` property, which includes any control that is derived from `System.Windows.Forms.Control`. In practice, that means almost any control you can drop on a Windows form.

You can bind just about any property of these bindable controls to an item of data. This gives you enormous flexibility in building a user interface that depends on data. For example, you can bind an array of `DateTime` values to the `Value` property of a `DateTimePicker` control.

STEP BY STEP

5.4 Binding Data to a DateTimePicker Control

1. Place a `DateTimePicker` control on a new Windows form. Name the control `dtBound`.

2. Place a `Button` control on the form. Name the control `btnPrevious` and set its `Text` property to `<`.

3. Place a second `Button` control on the form. Name the control `btnNext` and set its `Text` property to `>`.

4. Double-click the form and enter the following code:

```
// Create an array of dates
DateTime [] adtBound =
 {DateTime.Today , DateTime.Today.AddDays(1),
 DateTime.Today.AddDays(2), DateTime.Today.AddDays(3),
DateTime.Today.AddDays(4), DateTime.Today.AddDays(5)};

private void StepByStep5_4_Load(object sender,
    System.EventArgs e)
```

continues

continued

```
{
    // Bind the array to the date/time picker
    dtBound.DataBindings.Add("Value", adtBound, "");
}
```

5. Add the following code to handle the `Click` events from the two buttons:

```
private void btnPrevious_Click(
    object sender, System.EventArgs e)
{
    // Move to the previous item in the data source
    this.BindingContext[adtBound].Position -= 1;
}

private void btnNext_Click(
    object sender, System.EventArgs e)
{
    // Move to the next item in the data source
    this.BindingContext[adtBound].Position += 1;
}
```

6. Insert the `Main()` method to launch the form. Set the form as the startup object for the project.

7. Run the project. The `DateTimePicker` control is now bound to the array, and it displays the first value from the array. You can use the two buttons to move to different values within the array.

If you think creatively, you can find many ways to use simple data binding beyond simply displaying text in a text box. Here are some possibilities:

◆ Display a set of photos by binding them to the `Image` property of a `PictureBox` control.

◆ Show the relative magnitude of quantities with the `Value` property of a `ProgressBar` control.

◆ Color-code an area of a form by binding to the `BackColor` property of a `Panel` control.

The Architecture of Simple Data Binding

When you use simple data binding to connect a control to a data source, the .NET Framework creates a pair of objects to manage the binding: a `CurrencyManager` object and a `BindingContext` object. Depending on the number of controls on the form and the data to which they are bound, a single form might involve several of each of these objects.

The `CurrencyManager` object is responsible for keeping track of which piece of data from a data source is currently bound to the user interface. Although so far you've only seen one data bound control on each form, a single form can contain multiple bound controls. If all the controls are bound to the same data source, they can share a `CurrencyManager` object. But a single form can involve multiple `CurrencyManager` objects as well. Suppose, for example, that you built a form with an array of `Vendor` objects bound to one control and an array of `DateTime` objects bound to another control. In that case, the form would have two `CurrencyManager` objects.

Any bound form will also have at least one `BindingContext` object. The job of the `BindingContext` object is to keep track of the various `CurrencyManager` objects on the form. The indexer of the `BindingContext` object returns a `CurrencyManager` object. Consider this line of code:

```
this.BindingContext[adtBound].Position += 1;
```

That tells the `BindingContext` object for the form to return a `CurrencyManager` object for the `adtBound` data source and then to increment the `Position` property of the `CurrencyManager` object. The `CurrencyManager` object encapsulates the knowledge of how to move the pointer within the data array when the `Position` property is changed.

Like forms, container controls (such as the `GroupBox`, `Panel`, or `TabControl` controls) can have their own `BindingContext` objects. By using these separate `BindingContext` objects, you can create forms that have independently scolling views of the same data.

You'll learn about the `CurrencyManager` object in more depth later in this chapter. But first, let's look at another variety of data binding: complex data binding.

REVIEW BREAK

▶ Simple data binding refers to connecting a single entity in the data model to a single property of a control on the user interface.

▶ Any class that implements the `IBindingList`, `ITypedList`, or `IList` interface can deliver data via simple data binding.

▶ You can bind to almost any property of any control.

▶ A form control uses `CurrencyManager` and `BindingContext` objects to keep track of data binding.

Complex Data Binding

In complex data binding, you bind a user interface control to an entire collection of data, rather than to a single data item. A good example of complex data binding involves the `DataGrid` control. Figure 5.2 shows a bound `DataGrid` control displaying data from the Suppliers table in the SQL Server 2000 Northwind database.

FIGURE 5.2
By using complex data binding, you can see an entire collection of data on the user interface at one time.

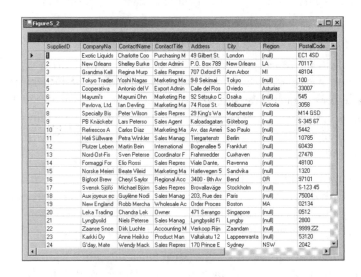

Database Terminology   In some literature you'll see the rows of a database table referred to as *records* or *tuples* and the columns referred to as *fields* or *attributes*.

EXAM TIP

You'll learn how to build this form later in the chapter, but for now, just concentrate on its features. `DataGrid` is a single control that displays many pieces of data. In this case, the data is taken from the rows and columns of the `Suppliers` table in a SQL Server 2000 database. You can click any cell in the `DataGrid` control and edit the data that the cell contains. If the form is properly programmed, these edits are reflected in the underlying data.

Obviously, complex data binding is a powerful tool for transferring large amounts of data from a data model to a user interface. The following sections dig into the mechanics of complex data binding with two examples:

◆ Binding to a `ComboBox` or `ListBox` control

◆ Binding to a `DataGrid` control

Binding to a `ComboBox` or `ListBox` Control

The `ComboBox` and `ListBox` controls both provide ways for the user to select one item from a list of data. The difference between the two is that in the `ListBox` control, the list is visible at all times, whereas in the `ComboBox` control, the list is hidden until the user clicks the drop-down arrow at the end of the box. Either of these controls can be loaded with an entire list of data via complex data binding.

> **NOTE**
>
> **The Northwind Sample Database**
> Whenever I've used data from a database in this book, I've used the Northwind sample database that comes as part of SQL Server 2000. Visual Studio .NET includes Microsoft Data Engine (MSDE), a stripped-down version of SQL Server that you can use if you don't have the full version installed. See your Visual Studio CD's `readme` file for information on installing MSDE. You can also find the Northwind sample database in any version of Microsoft Access, but the Access version does not ship with Visual Studio .NET. The code in this book assumes that you are using the SQL Server version.

STEP BY STEP

5.5 Binding Data to a List in a `ListBox` Control

1. Place a `ListBox` control on a new Windows form. Name the control `lbExams`.

2. Add a new class named `Exam.cs` to the project. Enter this code in the class:

```
using System;
namespace _316C05
{
    public class Exam
    {
        private String examNumber;
        private String examName;
```

continues

continued

```
        public String ExamNumber
        {
            get
            {
                return examNumber;
            }
        }

        public String ExamName
        {
            get
            {
                return examName;
            }
        }
        public Exam(String strExamNumber,
            String strExamName)
        {
            examNumber = strExamNumber;
            examName = strExamName;
        }
    }
}
```

3. Double-click the form and enter the following code in the form's Load event handler:

```
private void StepByStep5_5_Load(object sender,
    System.EventArgs e)
{
    // Create an array of exams
    Exam[] aExams =
    {
    new Exam("315",
        "Web Applications With Visual C# .NET"),
    new Exam("316",
        "Windows Applications With Visual C# .NET"),
    new Exam("320", "XML With Visual C# .NET"),
    new Exam("305", "Web Applications With VB.NET"),
    new Exam("306",
        "Windows Applications With VB.NET"),
    new Exam("310", "XML With VB.NET")};

    // Bind the array to the list box
    lbExams.DataSource = aExams;
    lbExams.DisplayMember = "ExamName";
}
```

4. Insert the Main() method to launch the form. Set the form as the startup object for the project.

5. Run the project. The ListBox control displays the ExamName property of every object in the array.

Step by Step 5.5 works by first creating an array of exam objects that contains all the information you'd like to display in the list portion of a `ListBox` control. It then sets the `DataSource` property of the `ListBox` control to the name of the array and the `DisplayMember` property to the name of the object property that supplies the text for the list. The result is a `ListBox` control that allows the user to choose from a list of exam names.

As it stands, Step by Step 5.5 doesn't do anything with the data after the user chooses an item from the list. But frequently you'll use a complex data-bound `ListBox` or `ComboBox` control in conjunction with a simple data-bound control such as a `TextBox` control. By selecting a row in the `ListBox` control, the user can choose a value for the `TextBox` control.

You can think of the `ListBox` control in this case as a little pump that moves data from one part of the data model to another. Step by Step 5.6 shows how you can set this up.

STEP BY STEP

5.6 Using a `ListBox` Control with Two Data Bindings

1. Start with the form from Step by Step 5.5. Add two `Label` controls, two `Button` controls, and two `TextBox` controls. Name the `TextBox` controls txtCandidateName and txtExamNumber. Name the button controls btnPrevious and btnNext. Arrange the controls as shown in Figure 5.3.

2. Add a new class named Candidate.cs to the project. Enter this code in the class:

```
using System;
namespace _316C05
{
    public class Candidate
    {
        private string examNumber;
        private string candidateName;

        public string ExamNumber
        {
            get
```

FIGURE 5.3
You can design a form with a bound `ListBox` control and other controls to see the effects of data binding.

continues

continued

```
            {
                return examNumber;
            }
            set
            {
                examNumber = value;
            }
        }

        public string CandidateName
        {
            get
            {
                return candidateName;
            }
            set
            {
                candidateName = value;
            }
        }

        public Candidate(String strCandidateName,
            String strExamNumber)
        {
            this.CandidateName = strCandidateName;
            this.ExamNumber = strExamNumber;
        }
    }
}
```

3. Attach event handlers to the form's Load event and to the btnPrevious and btnNext controls' Click events. Add the following code in the event handlers:

```
// Create an array of candidates
private Candidate[] aCandidates = {
            new Candidate("Bill Gates", "305"),
            new Candidate("Steve Ballmer", "320")};

private void StepByStep5_6_Load(object sender,
    System.EventArgs e)
{
    // Create an array of exams

    Exam[] aExams = {
    new Exam("315",
        "Web Applications With Visual C# .NET"),
    new Exam("316",
        "Windows Applications With Visual C# .NET"),
    new Exam("320", "XML With Visual C# .NET"),
    new Exam("305", "Web Applications With VB.NET"),
    new Exam("306",
        "Windows Applications With VB.NET"),
    new Exam("310", "XML With VB.NET")};
```

```
    // Bind the array to the list box
    lbExams.DataSource = aExams;
    lbExams.DisplayMember = "ExamName";
    lbExams.ValueMember = "ExamNumber";

    // Bind the candidates to the text boxes
    txtCandidateName.DataBindings.Add(
        "Text", aCandidates, "CandidateName");
    txtExamNumber.DataBindings.Add(
        "Text", aCandidates, "ExamNumber");

    // And bind the exam number to the list box value
    lbExams.DataBindings.Add(
        "SelectedValue", aCandidates, "ExamNumber");
}

private void btnPrevious_Click(object sender,
    System.EventArgs e)
{
    this.BindingContext[aCandidates].Position -= 1;
}

private void btnNext_Click(object sender,
    System.EventArgs e)
{
    this.BindingContext[aCandidates].Position += 1;
}
```

4. Insert the `Main()` method to launch the form. Set the form as the startup object for the project.

5. Run the project. As you move through the `Candidate` records, the `ListBox` control shows the exam name that matches the exam number for the candidate. If you change the value in the `ListBox` control or in the `txtExamNumber` control, the change is reflected in the other control as soon as the change is committed (that is, when you tab to another control).

Understanding Step by Step 5.6 is crucial for the effective use of `ComboBox` and `ListBox` controls in applications. Using these controls can be a little tricky because the `ListBox` control is bound to two different things. Here's a review of how it all fits together:

◆ The `ListBox` control in Step by Step 5.6 draws the list of items to display from the array of `Exam` objects. The list portion of the list box is complex-data-bound to this array. The complex binding is managed by setting the `DataSource`, `DisplayMember`, and `ValueMember` properties of the `ListBox` control.

◆ The two TextBox controls are simple-data-bound to different elements in the array of Candidate objects. As you move through that array (with the btnNext and btnPrevious controls), the data displayed in those TextBox controls changes. This is, by the way, a two-way link. If you change the data in one of the TextBox controls, it's also changed in the array; you can see this by changing an entry, scrolling to another candidate, and then scrolling back.

◆ The SelectedValue property of the ListBox control is also simple-data-bound to an element in the array of Candidate objects. This sets up the link between the two arrays. As you choose an item from the list in the ListBox control, your choice is automatically pushed to the bound value from the Candidate array.

◆ Because the SelectedValue property of the ListBox control and the Text property of the txtExamNumber control are bound to the same value, they automatically stay in sync when either one is updated.

◆ You can use the DisplayMember and ValueMember properties of the ListBox control to cause it to show one value while binding another, as in Step by Step 5.6.

Binding to a DataGrid Control

The DataGrid control provides a way to display many rows from a data model at one time. The DataGrid control is designed to let you see an entire collection of data (often called a *resultset*) at one time.

STEP BY STEP

5.7 Binding an Array of Objects to a DataGrid Control

1. Place a DataGrid control on a new Windows form. Name the control dgExams.

2. Double-click the form and enter the following code in the form's Load event handler:

```csharp
private void StepByStep5_7_Load(object sender,
    System.EventArgs e)
{
    // Create an array of exams
    Exam[] aExams ={
      new Exam("315",
          "Web Applications With Visual C# .NET"),
      new Exam("316",
          "Windows Applications With Visual C# .NET"),
      new Exam("320", "XML With Visual C# .NET"),
      new Exam("305", "Web Applications With VB.NET"),
      new Exam("306",
          "Windows Applications With VB.NET"),
      new Exam("310", "XML With VB.NET")};

    // Bind the array to the data grid
    dgExams.DataSource = aExams;
}
```

3. Insert the `Main()` method to launch the form. Set the form as the startup object for the project.

4. Run the project. The `DataGrid` control displays all the information from the aExams array.

The `DataGrid` control is a mainstay of data display for Visual C# .NET forms. As such, it is extremely configurable. Visual Studio .NET includes two interfaces for setting the display propeties of a `DataGrid` control. First, you can set individual properties to control the look of the `DataGrid` control in the Properties window. Second, you can use AutoFormats to quickly apply a whole new look to a `DataGrid` control.

STEP BY STEP

5.8 Applying an AutoFormat to a `DataGrid` Control

1. Select a `DataGrid` control on a Visual C# .NET form with the form open in the Windows Forms Designer.

2. Click the AutoFormat hyperlink, which is located directly under the properties list in the Properties window. This opens the Auto Format dialog box.

continues

FIGURE 5.4
The three DataGrid controls on this form have had three different AutoFormats applied.

continued

3. Select a format from the list and click OK to apply the new format to the DataGrid control. Figure 5.4 displays three DataGrid controls on a form, with three different AutoFormats applied. Although the controls are each bound to the same array of objects, they all look different.

When you need more precise formatting for a DataGrid control than the Auto Format dialog box allows, or when you just don't care for the look of any of the AutoFormats, you can set individual display properties for the DataGrid control. Table 5.1 lists the properties you can use to control the look of the DataGrid control.

TABLE 5.1

DataGrid CONTROL DISPLAY PROPERTIES

Property	Description
AlternatingBackColor	Specifies the background color to use for even-numbered rows in the grid.
BackColor	Specifies the background color to use for odd-numbered rows in the grid.
BackgroundColor	Specifies the color to use for any portion of the control that's not filled with data.
BorderStyle	Offers the choices None, FixedSingle, and Fixed3D for the borders of the control.
CaptionBackColor	Specifies the background color for the caption portion of the control.
CaptionFont	Specifies the font for the caption portion of the control.
CaptionText	Specifies the text to display in the caption portion of the control.
CaptionVisible	Controls whether a caption will be displayed. This is a Boolean property.
ColumnHeadersVisible	Controls whether each column will have a header. This is a Boolean property.

Property	*Description*
FlatMode	Controls whether the grid will have a 3D or a flat appearance. This is a Boolean property.
Font	Specifies the font for text in the control.
ForeColor	Specifies the foreground color for text in the control.
GridlineColor	Specifies the color for the lines of the grid.
GridlineStyle	Offers the choices None and Solid.
HeaderBackColor	Specifies the background color for column and row headers.
HeaderFont	Specifies the font for column and row headers.
HeaderForeColor	Specifies the foreground color for column and row headers.
LinkColor	Specifies the color to use for hyperlinks between sections of a control.
ParentRowBackColor	Specifies the background color to use for the parent rows area.
ParentRowsForeColor	Specifies the text color to use for the parent rows area.
ParentRowsLabelStyle	Offers the choices None, TableName, ColumnName, and Both.
ParentRowsVisible	Controls whether the parent rows area will be visible. This is a Boolean property.
PreferredColumnWidth	Specifies the default width for columns, in pixels.
PreferredRowHeight	Specifies the Default height for rows, in pixels.
RowHeadersVisible	Controls whether each row will have a header. This is a Boolean property.
RowHeaderWidth	Specifies the default width of row headers, in pixels.
SelectionBackColor	Specifies the background color for any selected cells.
SelectionForeColor	Specifies the text color for any selected cells.

Figure 5.5 shows a complex-data-bound DataGrid control that displays data from several database tables at one time, to help you understand where each of the areas mentioned in Table 5.1 is located. You'll learn how to bind database tables to the DataGrid control later in this chapter.

FIGURE 5.5

This figure displays the location of various formatting areas on a DataGrid control.

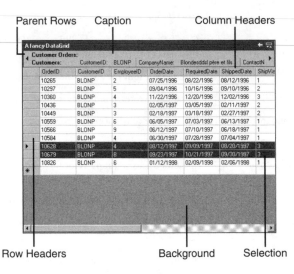

GUIDED PRACTICE EXERCISE 5.1

In this exercise, you'll be working with employee data from Skylark Spaceways. This exercise helps you review the basic syntax of both simple and complex data binding, as well as the use of the DataGrid control. Table 5.2 shows the data that you need to manage.

TABLE 5.2

SKYLARK SPACEWAYS EMPLOYEE ROSTER

Employee Number	Employee Name	Position	Home Planet
1	E.E. Smith	CEO	Earth
2	Melanie "Jets" Riggs	Chief Pilot	Mars
3	William Danforth	Pilot	Mars
4	Blaise Canton	Engineer	Luna
5	Amanda Timmel	CFO	Earth

You need to display this data in two different ways. First, you should create a form that displays information about one employee at a time, with buttons to scroll through the list. To save space, the form should show the employee names and positions in TextBox controls.

However, it should also make the home planet information available as a ToolTip on the employee names text box. There should be a button on this form to open a second form. The second form should display the entire employee roster in grid form.

How would you create such a form?

You should try working through this problem on your own first. If you get stuck, or if you'd like to see one possible solution, follow these steps:

1. Create a form that is populated with two TextBox controls (txtEmployeeName and txtPosition), two Label controls, and three Button controls (btnPrevious, btnNext, and btnRoster) arranged as shown in Figure 5.6. Also add a ToolTip control to the form.

2. Create a new class named Employee.cs in the project, using this code:

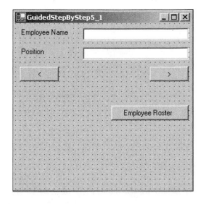

FIGURE 5.6
The design of a form that displays employee data.

```csharp
using System;
namespace _316C05
{
    public class Employee
    {
        private Int32 employeeNumber;
        private String employeeName;
        private String position;
        private String homePlanet;

        public Int32 EmployeeNumber
        {
            get
            {
                return employeeNumber;
            }
            set
            {
                employeeNumber = value;
            }
        }

        public String EmployeeName
        {
            get
            {
                return employeeName;
            }
            set
            {
                employeeName = value;
            }
        }
```

continues

continued

```csharp
public String Position
{
    get
    {
        return position;
    }
    set
    {
        position=value;
    }
}
public String HomePlanet
{
    get
    {
        return homePlanet;
    }
    set
    {
        homePlanet=value;
    }
}
public Employee(Int32 intEmployeeNumber,
    String strEmployeeName,
    String strPosition,
    String strHomePlanet)
{
    EmployeeNumber = intEmployeeNumber;
    EmployeeName = strEmployeeName;
    Position = strPosition;
    HomePlanet = strHomePlanet;
}
    }
}
```

3. Double-click the form, `btnPrevious`, `btnNext`, and `btnRoster` to attach event handlers to the default events. Add the following code to handle data creation, data binding, and navigation in the event handlers:

```csharp
// Create and stock an array of data
Employee[] aEmployees = {
    new Employee(1, "E.E. Smith", "CEO", "Earth"),
    new Employee(2, "Melanie \"Jets\" Riggs",
        "Chief Pilot", "Mars"),
    new Employee(3, "William Danforth",
        "Pilot", "Mars"),
    new Employee(4, "Blaise Canton",
        "Engineer", "Luna"),
    new Employee(5, "Amanda Timmel",
        "CFO", "Earth")};
```

```csharp
private void GuidedStepByStep5_1_Load(object sender,
    System.EventArgs e)
{
    // Bind data to the ui
    txtEmployeeName.DataBindings.Add(
        "Text", aEmployees, "EmployeeName");
    txtEmployeeName.DataBindings.Add(
        "Tag", aEmployees, "HomePlanet");
    txtPosition.DataBindings.Add(
        "Text", aEmployees, "Position");

    // Transfer the home planet info to the tooltip
    ToolTip1.SetToolTip(txtEmployeeName,
        txtEmployeeName.Tag.ToString());
}

private void btnPrevious_Click(object sender,
    System.EventArgs e)
{
    this.BindingContext[aEmployees].Position -= 1;
    ToolTip1.SetToolTip(txtEmployeeName,
        txtEmployeeName.Tag.ToString());
}

private void btnNext_Click(object sender,
    System.EventArgs e)
{
    this.BindingContext[aEmployees].Position += 1;
    ToolTip1.SetToolTip(txtEmployeeName,
        txtEmployeeName.Tag.ToString());
}

private void btnRoster_Click(object sender,
    System.EventArgs e)
{
    GuidedStepByStep5_1a f =
        new GuidedStepByStep5_1a();
    f.dgEmployees.DataSource = aEmployees;
    f.Show();
}
```

> **EXAM TIP**
>
> **Quotes in Strings** If you want to insert a quote mark (") into a string constant, you can escape the quote marks with the backslash character. For instance, in the preceding example, if you would like a string to mean exactly "Melanie "Jets" Riggs", including the quotes, you would write "Melanie \"Jets\" Riggs". Another way to ensure verbatim representation of a string is to prefix the string with the @ sign, so the name could also be written as @"Melanie "Jets" Riggs". You also can escape out other special characters, such as the single quote and backslash, using the \ and @ characters, as shown previously.

4. Create a second form and name it GuidedStepByStep5_1a (or give it any name you like and revise the code in the btnRoster_Click event handler in step 3 to match). Place a single DataGrid control on this form. Name the DataGrid control dgEmployees and set its Modifiers property to Internal.

5. Insert the Main() method to launch the first form. Set the first form as the project's startup form and test your work. You should be able to scroll through employees, view the home planet information in a ToolTip, and open a grid that contains all the employee information.

continues

continued

If you have difficulty following this exercise, review the sections "Simple Data Binding" and "Complex Data Binding," earlier in this chapter. The text and examples should help you relearn this material and help you understand what happens in this exercise. After doing that review, try this exercise again.

R E V I E W   B R E A K

▶ Complex data binding binds a user interface control to an entire collection of data.

▶ To use complex data binding with a `ListBox` or `ComboBox` control, you set the control's `DataSource` and `DisplayMember` properties.

▶ A `ListBox` or `ComboBox` control can act to pull values from one data source and place them in another.

▶ You can cause a `ListBox` or `ComboBox` control to display one value while binding to another by using the `DisplayMember` and `ValueMember` properties of the control.

▶ The `DataGrid` control displays an entire array of data in rows and columns. You specify the data to display by setting the `DataSource` property of the `DataGrid` control.

▶ The properties of the `DataGrid` control include many flexible formatting options.

One-Way and Two-Way Data Binding

Data binding in Windows forms can be one-way or two-way. In *one-way data binding*, the bound property of the control reflects changes to the data model, but changes to the control are not written back to the data model. For example, if you display a list of customers in a `ComboBox` control, the act of selecting a customer from the `ComboBox` control does not do anything to modify the list.

In *two-way data binding*, changes to the control are written back to the data model. For example, if you have a `TextBox` control that is bound to the `CustomerName` property of a `Customer` object, changing the text in the `TextBox` control changes the corresponding property of the object.

Simple data binding on Windows forms is automatically two-way. Any changes you make to the data on the form are automatically transmitted back to the data model. However, it's important to note that the data model might not be the ultimate data source. The most common exception to this occurs when you use the ADO.NET classes to access data from a database and place it in a data model. Changes to bound data on a form are written back to the data model, but they are not automatically returned to the database (though you can write code to do this).

> **N O T E** **Using the `DataAdapter` Object to Update a Data Source**   To transmit changes from a data model back to the original data source, you usually use the `Update()` method of the `DataAdapter` object. For more detailed information on the `DataAdapter` object, see Chapter 6 and the section "Using the Data Form Wizard," later in this chapter.

The `BindingContext` and `CurrencyManager` Classes

You saw the `BindingContext` and `CurrencyManager` classes earlier in the chapter, in the discussion of the overall architecture of data binding. Now that you've seen both simple and complex data binding in action, it's time to look at the `BindingContext` and `CurrencyManager` classes in somewhat more detail.

The `BindingContext` class exists primarily as a means to retrieve the `CurrencyManager` objects on a form. Table 5.3 shows the important interface members of the `BindingContext` class. In many applications, you can let Visual C# .NET manage these objects for you. But there are times when it's useful to work directly with these objects. For instance, the `CurrencyManager` class provides event hooks that let you react to modifications that the user makes to bound data.

TABLE 5.3

IMPORTANT MEMBERS OF THE BindingContext CLASS

Member	Type	Description
Contains()	Method	Indicates whether the `BindingContext` object contains a specific `BindingManagerBase` object

The BindingManagerBase class is an abstract class that is implemented in both the CurrencyManager class and the PropertyManager class. You've already seen the CurrencyManager class. The PropertyManager class is used to manipulate the current value of an individual property, rather than the property of the current object in a list; you are unlikely to have any reason to use the PropertyManager class yourself. Table 5.4 shows the important interface members of the BindingManagerBase class.

TABLE 5.4

IMPORTANT MEMBERS OF THE BindingManagerBase CLASS

Member	Type	Description
AddNew()	Method	Adds a new object to the underlying list
Bindings	Property	Gets the collection of bindings being managed by the class
CancelCurrentEdit()	Method	Cancels any edits that are in progress
Count	Property	Gets the number of rows managed by the class
Current	Property	Gets the current object
CurrentChanged	Event	Occurs when the bound value changes
EndCurrentEdit()	Method	Commits any edits that are in progress
GetItemProperties()	Method	Gets a list of item properties for the current object in the list
Position	Property	Gets or sets the position in the underlying list that is bound with this class
PositionChanged	Event	Occurs when the Position property changes
RemoveAt()	Method	Removes the object at the specified position from the underlying list
ResumeBinding()	Method	Resumes data binding
SuspendBinding()	Method	Suspends data binding

The CurrencyManager class implements most of the interfaces of the BindingManagerBase class, and it includes a few others of its own. Table 5.5 lists the important interface members of the CurrencyManager class.

TABLE 5.5

IMPORTANT MEMBERS OF THE CurrencyManager CLASS

Member	Type	Description
AddNew()	Method	Adds a new object to the underlying list
Bindings	Property	Gets the collection of bindings being managed by the class
CancelCurrentEdit()	Method	Cancels any edits that are in progress
Count	Property	Gets the number of rows managed by the class
Current	Property	Gets the current object
CurrentChanged	Event	Occurs when the bound value changes
EndCurrentEdit()	Method	Commits any edits that are in progress
GetItemProperties()	Method	Gets a list of item properties for the current object in the list
ItemChanged	Event	Occurs when the current item has been altered
List	Property	Gets the IList interface from the data source
Position	Property	Gets or sets the position in the underlying list that is bound with the class
PositionChanged	Event	Occurs when the Position property changes
Refresh()	Method	Repopulates the bound controls
RemoveAt()	Method	Removes the object at the specified position from the underlying list
ResumeBinding()	Method	Resumes data binding
SuspendBinding()	Method	Suspends data binding

> **EXAM TIP**
>
> **Understanding the Binding Objects**
> You don't need to memorize every detail of the BindingContext, BindingManagerBase, and CurrencyManager objects. Instead, concentrate on knowing the overall uses of these objects. The BindingContext class is your hook to retrieve the CurrencyManager object. The BindingManagerBase class supplies the Position property that lets you see where you are in a set of bound data. The CurrencyManager class supplies the event hooks that let you interact with user-initiated data changes.

In addition to manipulating the Position property, you'll likely find the CurrencyManager class most useful for managing events on data-bound forms. Of course, because this class doesn't have a visual, control-based representation, you need to set up these events in code. Listing 5.1 shows how you can create delegates and respond to the events of the CurrencyManager class.

LISTING 5.1

TRAPPING EVENTS FOR THE CurrencyManager CLASS

```csharp
// Create an array of vendor objects
Vendor[] aVendors = new Vendor[3];

private void Listing5_1_Load(object sender,
    System.EventArgs e)
{
    // Initialize the vendors array
    aVendors[0] = new Vendor("Microsoft");
    aVendors[1] = new Vendor("Rational");
    aVendors[2] = new Vendor("Premia");

    // Bind the array to the text box
    txtVendorName.DataBindings.Add(
        "Text", aVendors, "VendorName");

    CurrencyManager cm =
        (CurrencyManager) this.BindingContext[aVendors];

    cm.CurrentChanged += new EventHandler(
        CurrencyManager_CurrentChanged);
    cm.ItemChanged += new ItemChangedEventHandler(
        CurrencyManager_ItemChanged);
    cm.PositionChanged += new EventHandler(
        CurrencyManager_PositionChanged);
}

private void CurrencyManager_CurrentChanged(Object o,
    EventArgs e)
{
    lbEvents.Items.Add("CurrentChanged");
}

private void CurrencyManager_ItemChanged(Object o,
    System.Windows.Forms.ItemChangedEventArgs icea)
{
    lbEvents.Items.Add("ItemChanged");
}

private void CurrencyManager_PositionChanged(Object o,
    System.EventArgs ea)
{
    lbEvents.Items.Add("PositionChanged");
}

private void btnPrevious_Click(object sender,
    System.EventArgs e)
{
    // Move to the previous item in the data source
    this.BindingContext[aVendors].Position -= 1;
}
```

```
private void btnNext_Click(object sender,
    System.EventArgs e)
{
    // Move to the previous item in the data source
    this.BindingContext[aVendors].Position += 1;
}
```

EXAM TIP

An Event Mnemonic You can remember that the `CurrentChanged` event refers to the user interface changes by noting that *current* and *control* begin with the same letter.

The names of the `CurrencyManager` class events may be a bit confusing. The `ItemChanged` event is fired when the data itself is changed by an external factor. For example, if you modify the data in an array and that array is bound to the user interface, the `ItemChanged` event occurs. The `CurrentChanged` event occurs when the data is changed on the user interface. This is true whether the user changes the data by typing a control or the `CurrencyManager` changes the data by responding to a change of the `Position` property. Finally, the `PositionChanged` event occurs when the `Position` property is changed. In practice, you see a `CurrentChanged` event whenever you see a `PositionChanged` event, but you can also get `CurrentChanged` events without a change in the `Position` property.

STEP BY STEP

5.9 Using `CurrencyManager` Events

1. Create a form that is populated with two `TextBox` controls (txtEmployeeName and txtPosition), two `Label` controls, and two `Button` controls (btnPrevious and btnNext). Also add a `ToolTip` control to the form. Figure 5.7 shows the form in design mode.

2. Double-click the form and the `btnPrevious` and `btnNext` controls to attach event handlers to their default events. Enter the following code behind the form:

```
// Create and stock an array of data
Employee[] aEmployees = {
    new Employee(1, "E.E. Smith", "CEO", "Earth"),
    new Employee(2, "Melanie \"Jets\" Riggs",
        "Chief Pilot", "Mars"),
    new Employee(3, "William Danforth",
        "Pilot", "Mars"),
    new Employee(4, "Blaise Canton",
        "Engineer", "Luna"),
    new Employee(5, "Amanda Timmel", "CFO", "Earth")};
```

FIGURE 5.7
You can use `CurrencyManager` events to synchronize the ToolTip of the employee name TextBox control with its text.

continues

continued

```
private void StepByStep5_9_Load(object sender,
    System.EventArgs e)
{
    // Bind data to the ui
    txtEmployeeName.DataBindings.Add(
        "Text", aEmployees, "EmployeeName");
    txtEmployeeName.DataBindings.Add(
        "Tag", aEmployees, "HomePlanet");
    txtPosition.DataBindings.Add(
        "Text", aEmployees, "Position");

    // Transfer the home planet info to the tooltip
    ToolTip1.SetToolTip(txtEmployeeName,
        txtEmployeeName.Tag.ToString());

    // Set up an event to update the tooltip
    CurrencyManager cm =
    (CurrencyManager) this.BindingContext[aEmployees];
    cm.PositionChanged +=
    new EventHandler(CurrencyManager_PositionChanged);
}

private void btnPrevious_Click(object sender,
    System.EventArgs e)
{
    this.BindingContext[aEmployees].Position -= 1;
}

private void btnNext_Click(object sender,
    System.EventArgs e)
{
    this.BindingContext[aEmployees].Position += 1;
}

private void CurrencyManager_PositionChanged(Object o,
    System.EventArgs ea)
{
    ToolTip1.SetToolTip(txtEmployeeName,
        txtEmployeeName.Tag.ToString());
}
```

3. Insert the Main() method to launch the form. Set the form as the startup object for the project.

4. Run the project. As you scroll through the records, you see that the ToolTip for the employee name TextBox control is kept synchronized by the PositionChanged event code.

If you compare the code in Step by Step 5.9 with the code from Guided Practice Exercise 5.1, you see that using the PositionChanged event can save you from writing duplicate code in every procedure where you might change the Position property of the CurrencyManager class.

Using the Data Form Wizard

Now that you've seen the mechanics of data binding, it's time to explore one of the tools that Visual C# .NET offers for automatic data binding: the Data Form Wizard. In the following sections, you'll see how to use the wizard to build both a single-table form and a multiple-table form. This helps you ease into the broad topic of using data from databases, which occupies the rest of this chapter and all of Chapter 6.

IN THE FIELD

A CRASH COURSE IN DATABASES

Although this exam doesn't have any objectives that explicitly demand database knowledge, you can't pass the exam without knowing something about databases. These days, databases are part of the pervasive understructure of computing. You're expected to understand the basics of them, just as you understand the basics of files and folders.

At this point you're interested in data stored in relational databases. A relational database (such as Microsoft SQL Server, which is used in the examples in this book) stores data in tables, each of which represents an instance of a particular entity. An *entity* is anything that you're interested in tracking in the database: a customer, an order, an employee, or a supplier, for example. A single database can contain many tables; for example, you might have tables named Customers, Orders, Employees, and Suppliers.

Each table contains one row (or record) for each instance of an entity: If you have 50 customers, then the Customers table should have 50 rows. Each row consists of a number of columns (or fields) that describe the entity. For example, these might be the fields in a Customers table:

- Customer Number
- Customer Name

continues

continued

- City

- State

In a well-designed database, each entity can be identified by a column or combination of columns called the *primary key*. For example, the primary key for the Customers table could be the Customer Number column. Each customer would then have a unique and unchanging customer number. If you knew the customer number, you could use it to look up all the other information that the database stores about that customer.

SQL Server is called a *relational database* because it accommodates the fact that there are relationships between entities that are stored in different tables. Think about customers and orders, for example. Each order is placed by a single customer. You can indicate this by storing the customer number (the primary key of the Customers table) in the Orders table. These might be the columns of the Orders table:

- Order Number

- Customer Number

- Order Date

- Delivery Date

In this case, the Order Number column would be the primary key (the unique identifying column) of the Orders table. The Customer Number column in the Orders table serves to relate each order to a corresponding row in the Customers table. You call the Customer Number a *foreign key* in the Orders table. To specify a relationship between tables, you name the two tables and the columns that match between them. Relationships can be one-to-many (one customer can place many orders) or one-to-one (one employee has at most one pension).

Databases can contain other objects in addition to tables. These include views (which can provide a subset of information from one or more tables) and stored procedures (which are groups of SQL statements that are compiled into execution plans) and users and groups (which control the security of database objects).

If you've never worked with a database, you may find it a bit confusing at first. But if you work through the examples carefully, it should become clear to you.

NOTE   **Database Design**   For more information on relational database design and terminology, refer to Que's *SQL Server 2000 Programming* by Carlos Rojas and Fernando Guerrero.

Building a Single-Table Data Form

You'll start by building a data form that displays data from a single table: the Customers table in the Northwind sample database.

STEP BY STEP

5.10   Building a Single-Table Data Form

1. Select Project, Add New Item. In the Add New Item dialog box (shown in Figure 5.8), select the Data Form Wizard. Name the new form `StepByStep5_10.cs` and click Open.

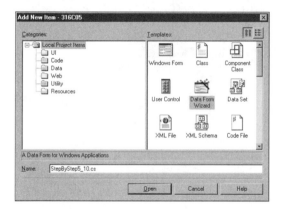

FIGURE 5.8
The Add New Item dialog box allows you to launch the Data Form Wizard.

2. Read the Welcome screen of the wizard and click Next.

3. The next screen helps you choose a `DataSet` object to use with the data form. A `DataSet` object is a .NET Framework object that you can think of as representing one or more tables from a database (it's actually more flexible than that, but that's enough for this example). On this screen, shown in Figure 5.9, choose to create a new `DataSet` object named `dsCustomers`. Click Next.

4. The next screen helps you choose or build a data connection. A data connection tells Visual C# .NET which database contains the data you want to retrieve. You haven't set up any data connections yet, so click the New Connection button. This opens the Data Link Properties dialog box.

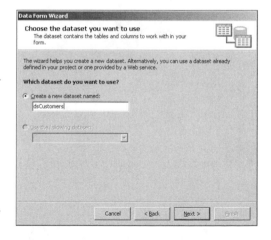

FIGURE 5.9
The Data Form Wizard allows you to create a new `DataSet` object or use an existing `DataSet` object.

continues

EXAM TIP

Specifying Connection Information
You might have to try a few things to connect to the database. For the server name, you can use the name of a computer on which SQL Server is running. If SQL Server is installed on the same computer where you're writing the code, you can use the special name (local) instead of entering a server name. For logon information, you should first try Windows NT Integrated Security, which logs on to SQL Server by using your Windows identity. If that fails, try using the specific user name sa and a blank password. If that also fails, you need to check with the person who is responsible for the SQL Server to find out what login information to use. Note the Test Connection button at the bottom of the dialog box; it is handy when you try to get your login information correct.

FIGURE 5.10
You can use the Data Form Wizard to create a data connection to the Northwind sample database.

WARNING

Blank Passwords   You might use blank passwords when developing applications. However, using blank passwords when deploying the final application is dangerous for the real data. You should always use strong passwords for production databases.

5. Click the Provider tab of the Data Link Properties dialog box and select Microsoft OLE DB Provider for SQL Server.

6. Click on the Connection tab of the Data Link Properties dialog box and enter the information that you need to use the Northwind database, as shown in Figure 5.10.

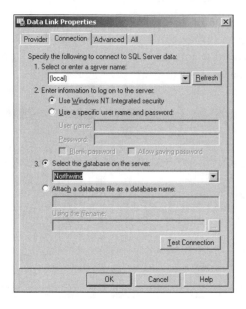

7. Click OK on the Data Link Properties dialog box to create the connection and return to the Data Form Wizard. Select the new connection in the combo box (it should have a name such as *MACHINENAME*.Northwind.dbo) and click Next.

8. On the Choose Tables or Views screen of the wizard, select the Customers table in the Available Items list and click the > button to move the table to the Selected Items list, as shown in Figure 5.11. Click Next.

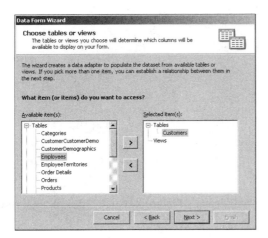

FIGURE 5.11
You can choose tables and views as data sources for data binding.

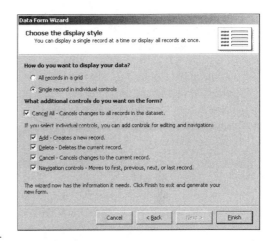

FIGURE 5.12
You can choose a display style and the additional controls on the form through the Data Form Wizard.

9. On the Choose Tables and Columns to Display on the Form screen, leave all the columns in the table selected and click Next.

10. On the Choose the Display Style screen, shown in Figure 5.12, select the single record style and check all the optional check boxes. Click Finish.

11. Insert the `Main()` method to launch the form. Set the form as the startup form for the project and run the project to experiment with the data form.

Figure 5.13 shows the finished Data Form created in Step by Step 5.10. It contains 10 buttons, which have the following functions:

- ◆ **Load**—Load all the data from the database and bind it to the form.

- ◆ **Update**—Save all changes to the database.

- ◆ **Cancel All**—Discard all changes without changing the database.

- ◆ **<<**—Move to the first row.

- ◆ **<**—Move to the previous row.

- ◆ **>**—Move to the next row.

- ◆ **>>**—Move to the last row.

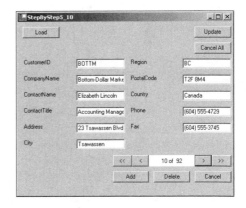

FIGURE 5.13
The finished data form displays all the data from the Customers table, providing options to delete rows, add rows, and save changes back to the original database.

NOTE

**Data Form Wizard–Generated Code
May Not Be Optimal** The Data Form
Wizard is designed to create output
for a variety of combinations of forms
(Windows forms, Web forms, and so
on), controls, and data sources.
Therefore, the code generated by the
wizard might not be the optimal code
for any one specific situation. As you
progress through this book, you will
learn techniques for optimizing the
data access code.

◆ **Add**—Add a new row.

◆ **Delete**—Delete the current row.

◆ **Cancel**—Cancel changes to the current row.

You might want to browse through the code that the wizard created
behind this form. Be warned, though, that there are more than 600
lines of code involved in implementing this functionality! Obviously,
the Data Form Wizard can save you a lot of time in building data-
bound forms.

As you continue through the book, you'll learn more about database
objects and the code that you can use to manipulate them. For now,
you'll stick to the relatively easy user interface tools as you explore
what can be done with data binding.

Building a Multiple-Table Data Form

You can use the Data Form Wizard to build a form that displays
data from more than one table. Step by Step 5.11 explains how to
do this.

STEP BY STEP

5.11 Building a Multiple-Table Data Form

1. Select Project, Add New Item. In the Add New Item dia-
    log box, select the Data Form Wizard. Name the new
    form StepByStep5_11.cs and click Open.

2. Read the Welcome screen of the wizard and click Next.

3. On the Choose a Dataset screen, choose to create a new
    DataSet object named dsCustOrders. Click Next.

4. On the Choose a Data Connection screen, select the data
    connection that you created in Step by Step 5.10, and
    click Next.

5. On the Choose Tables or Views screen, select the
    Customers table in the Available Items list and click the >
    button to move it to the Selected Items list. Also select the
    Orders table and click the > button to move it to the
    Selected Items list. Click Next.

NOTE

Relationships Creating a relationship between tables tells the wizard
which fields it should treat as primary
and foreign keys. Refer to the sidebar
"A Crash Course in Databases," earlier in this chapter if you need to review
this concept.

6. The next screen helps you specify the relationship between the two tables, Customers and Orders. Name the new relationship `relCustomerOrders`. Select Customers as the parent table and Orders as the child table. Select CustomerID as the key field in each table. Figure 5.14 shows the wizard at this point. Click the > button to create the new relationship, and then click Next.

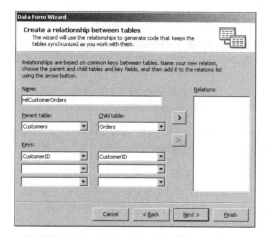

FIGURE 5.14
When you use the Data Form Wizard to create a relationship between tables, it automatically takes care of generating code to keep the tables synchronized.

7. On the Choose Tables and Columns to Display on the Form screen, leave all the columns in both tables selected and click Next.

8. On the Choose the Display Style screen, select the All Records in a Grid style and check the Cancel All check box. Click Finish.

9. Insert the `Main()` method to launch the form. Set the new form as the startup form for the project and run the project to experiment with the data form.

As you select different Customer table rows in the upper `DataGrid` control on the form created in Step by Step 5.11, the lower `DataGrid` control changes to show only the Order rows for that customer. Figure 5.15 shows an example.

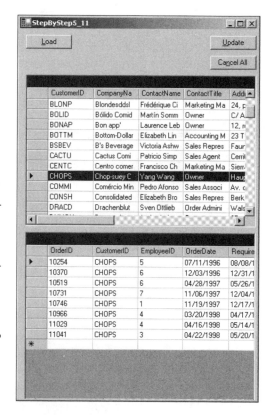

FIGURE 5.15
This two-table data form uses one `DataGrid` control for each table, and it uses code to keep the two `DataGrid` controls synchronized.

Once again, you'll find a tremendous amount of code (about 500 lines) behind this form. And once again, you'll leave it for future inspection.

REVIEW BREAK

▶ In one-way data binding, data from the data model is displayed on the form, but changes to the form do not affect the data model.

▶ In two-way data binding, data from the data model is displayed on the form, and changes to the form are also written back to the database.

▶ The .NET Framework uses `BindingContext` and `CurrencyManager` objects to manage data binding.

▶ You can use events of the `CurrencyManager` object to help react to changes in bound data.

▶ The Data Form Wizard helps you quickly create data-bound forms, both simple and complex. These forms draw their data from a relational database such as SQL Server.

TRANSFORMING AND FILTERING DATA

Display and update data:

- **Transform and filter data.**

The second test objective for this chapter involves transforming and filtering data. Especially when you're dealing with data from a database, you might find that the data is not in the exact form that you'd like to display to the user. Perhaps there are 5,000 rows in the Customer table, and you'd like to pull out the single row that interests your users. Or perhaps you'd like to show customer names with orders, but the Orders table only stores the CustomerID. The following sections look at a few of the tools that the .NET Framework offers for manipulating database data.

First, you'll dig into Server Explorer, which allows you to interact directly with SQL Server or other databases. Then you'll look at some of the ways you can filter and transform data.

Using Server Explorer

By default, the Server Explorer window in Visual Studio .NET is displayed as a small vertical tab to the left of the toolbox. When you hover the mouse over this tab, Server Explorer slides out. Figure 5.16 shows the Server Explorer window when it slides out.

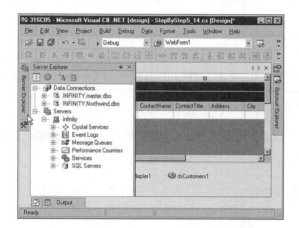

FIGURE 5.16
The Server Explorer window slides out when you move the mouse over its vertical tab.

Although you're going to use Server Explorer to work with databases, it's really a general-purpose tool for managing server resources of many types. Table 5.6 lists the resources that you can manage with Server Explorer.

TABLE 5.6

RESOURCES YOU CAN MANAGE WITH SERVER EXPLORER

Resource Type	Represents
Crystal Services	Options for Crystal Reports
Data Connection	A connection to a particular database
Event Logs	Windows event logs
Message Queues	Windows message queues
Performance Counters	Windows performance counters
Services	Windows services
SQL Servers	Microsoft SQL Servers

To work with bound data, you use the Data Connection node in Server Explorer and its children.

Adding a Data Connection

You've already seen that you can add a data connection to a project from within the Data Form Wizard. Those data connections are automatically available in Server Explorer as well. You can also add a data connection directly from Server Explorer, as described in Step by Step 5.12.

EXAM TIP

Supported Connection Types
You've probably noticed that the Data Link Properties dialog box gives you a great many choices on the Provider tab. In addition to SQL Server, connections using the Oracle or Jet providers are also fully supported by .NET. Other providers might also work, but there's no guarantee, and you should test your application carefully if you decide to use another provider.

STEP BY STEP

5.12 Adding a Data Connection from Server Explorer

1. Open Server Explorer.

2. Right-click the Data Connections node and then select Add Connection. This opens the Data Link Properties dialog box.

3. Fill in the connection information for your data source. The dialog box defaults to using the Microsoft OLE DB Provider for SQL Server, but you can change that on the Provider tab if you like.

4. Click OK to create the data connection.

Visual Studio .NET remembers your data connections across sessions and projects. Any data connection that you've created will appear in Server Explorer in all your projects, unless you right-click the data connection and choose Delete.

Object Design from Server Explorer

Even without bringing SQL Server objects into your Visual C# .NET projects, you can manipulate them from Server Explorer. Visual Studio .NET provides wide-ranging design options for SQL Server objects. Table 5.7 summarizes your options in this area.

TABLE 5.7

MANIPULATING SQL SERVER OBJECTS FROM SERVER EXPLORER

Object New?	Edit Data?	Design?	Create?
Database Diagram	N/A	Yes	Yes
Table	Yes	Yes	Yes
View	Yes	Yes	Yes
Stored Procedure	Yes	Yes	Yes
Function	Yes	Yes	Yes

EXAM TIP

Visual Studio .NET Focuses on Data, Not Management   The objects you can edit from Visual Studio .NET are those that can bring back data to an application. SQL Server contains many other objects (such as users, groups, and alerts) that are used for server management. To work with these objects, you need to use SQL Server's own design tools.

STEP BY STEP

5.13 Editing a SQL Server Table from Server Explorer

1. Open Server Explorer.

2. Expand the tree under Data Connections to show a SQL Server data connection that points to the Northwind sample database, then the Tables node of the SQL Server, and then individual tables.

3. Right-click the Products table and select Retrieve Data. The data stored in the table appears within your Visual Studio .NET workspace, as shown in Figure 5.17.

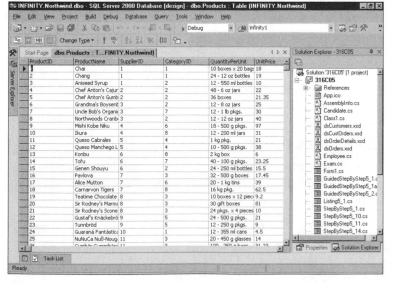

FIGURE 5.17
You can edit SQL Server data directly within Visual Studio .NET.

continues

continued

4. Edit, add, and delete values from the table.

5. Close the window that displays the Products data.

6. Reopen Server Explorer and find the Products table again. Right-click the table and select Design Table. Visual Studio .NET displays information related to the design of the table, as shown in Figure 5.18. This information includes such things as the name and data type of each column in the table.

FIGURE 5.18
You can design a SQL Server table directly within Visual Studio .NET.

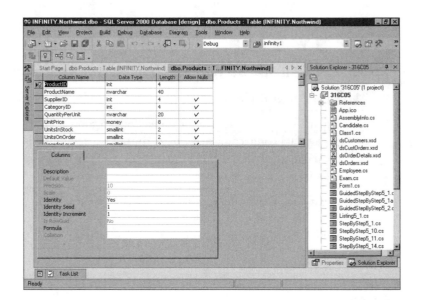

7. Close the editing window when you're done examining the design information for the table.

Drag-and-Drop from Server Explorer

Server Explorer can act as a source for drag-and-drop operations. Different visual data objects can be created, depending on what sort of object you drag from Server Explorer:

◆ Dragging and dropping a database creates a `SqlConnection` object.

◆ Dragging and dropping a table, view, table column, or view column creates a `SqlDataAdapter` object.

◆ Dragging and dropping a stored procedure or table-valued function creates a `SqlCommand` object.

These three objects are members of the `System.Data.SqlClient` namespace, which you'll learn more about in Chapter 6. This chapter concentrates more on what you can do with the objects than on the code that creates and supports them.

Figure 5.19 shows the appearance of the created objects on a Visual C# .NET form. This figure also includes a `DataSet` object; later in this chapter you'll see how to generate a `DataSet` object in the Windows Forms Designer.

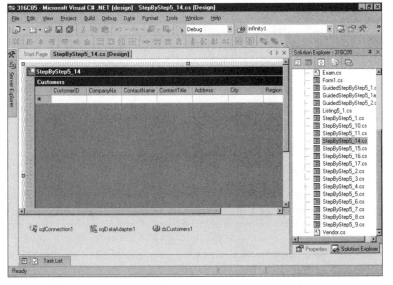

FIGURE 5.19
Visual data objects can be created in the Windows Forms Designer.

As you might guess from their placement below the form's design surface, these visual data objects are not visible at runtime. At design time, they provide access to instances of their underlying classes. For example, the `sqlConnection1` object in the designer is a visual representation of an instance of the `SqlConnection` class. If you view the code behind the form and expand the Windows Form Designer Generated Code region, you find the declaration that Visual C# .NET created when you dropped the object on the form:

```
private System.Data.SqlClient.SqlConnection
    sqlConnection1;
```

What can you use these visual data objects for? As Step by Step 5.14 shows, they can provide a fast way to design a form that has a DataGrid control that is complex-data-bound to data in a SQL Server table.

STEP BY STEP

5.14 Binding a DataGrid Control to a SQL Server Table

1. Place a DataGrid control on a new Windows form. Name the control dgCustomers. Set the CaptionText property of the control to Customers.

2. Open Server Explorer.

3. Expand the tree under Data Connections to show a SQL Server data connection that points to the Northwind sample database, then the Tables node of the SQL Server, and then individual tables.

4. Drag the Customers table from Server Explorer and drop it on the form. This creates two visual data objects, sqlConnecton1 and sqlDataAdapter1.

5. Select the sqlDataAdapter1 object. Click the Generate Dataset link below the Properties window.

6. In the Generate Dataset window (see Figure 5.20), choose to use the existing dsCustomers DataSet object. Click OK.

7. Set the DataSource property of the DataGrid control to dsCustomers1. Set the DataMember property of the DataGrid control to Customers.

8. Double-click the form and enter the following code in the form's Load event handler:

```
private void StepByStep5_14_Load(object sender,
    System.EventArgs e)
{
    // Move the data from the database
    // to the DataGrid
    sqlDataAdapter1.Fill(dsCustomers1, "Customers");
}
```

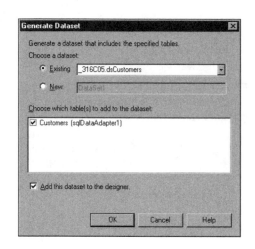

FIGURE 5.20
You can generate a DataSet object through a SqlDataAdapter object.

9. Insert the `Main()` method to launch the form. Set the form as the startup object for the project.

10. Run the project. The `DataGrid` control displays all the data from the Customers table.

NOTE

Data and XML In Visual Studio and the .NET Framework, XML is the preferred format for storing and transmitting data of all kinds. XML stores data in a standard format, which makes it easy for you to share the data between applications.

Although you only have to write one line of code for Step by Step 5.14, you actually create a number of ADO.NET objects along the way. Here's a rundown of how all the pieces fit together:

◆ The `sqlConnection1` object is an instance of the `SqlConnection` class. This object represents a connection to the SQL Server database.

◆ The `sqlDataAdapter1` object is an instance of the `SqlDataAdapter` class. This class encapsulates all the tools that are necessary to extract data via a `SqlConnection` object and to write changes back to the data source.

◆ The Generate Dataset dialog box creates an XML Schema Design (XSD) file, `dsCustomers.xsd`. This file represents the structure of the Customers table to the .NET Framework.

◆ The `dsCustomers1` object is an instance of the `DataSet` class represented by the `dsCustomers.xsd` file.

◆ The call to the `Fill()` method of the `sqlDataAdapter1` object tells it to extract all the rows from the Customers table and to place them in the `dsCustomers1` object. You can think of the `SqlDataAdapter` class as a two-way pump that can move data from the underlying database to the data model within your application and back.

◆ Setting the `DataSource` and `DataMember` properties of the `DataGrid` control uses complex data binding to show the contents of the `dsCustomers1` object on the user interface.

Filtering Data

Filtering data refers to the process of selecting only some data from a larger body of data to appear on the user interface of a form.

This can be a critical part of avoiding information overload for end users of an application. In most cases, users do not need to see every row of data in a database or even every row from a specific table. More often, they only need a small subset of the larger data body. The following sections look at two different ways to filter data in applications: by building a `DataView` object on the client or by using a server-based view to deliver only the desired data to the client.

Filtering with `DataView` Objects

To understand the `DataView` object, you need to know a little bit about the internal structure of the `DataSet` object. A `DataSet` object contains two collections. The `Tables` collection is made up of `DataTable` objects, each of which represents data from a single table in the data source. The `Relations` collection is made up of `DataRelation` objects, each of which represents the relationship between two `DataTable` objects.

The `DataView` object supplies one more piece of this puzzle: It represents a bindable, customized view of a `DataTable` object. You can sort or filter the records from a `DataTable` object to build a `DataView` object.

STEP BY STEP

5.15 Using a `DataView` Object to Filter Data

1. Place a `DataGrid` control on a new Windows form. Name the control `dgCustomers`. Set the `CaptionText` property of this control to `Customers`.

2. Open Server Explorer.

3. Expand the tree under Data Connections to show a SQL Server data connection that points to the Northwind sample database, then the Tables node of the SQL Server, and then individual tables.

4. Drag the Customers table from Server Explorer and drop it on the form. This creates two visual data objects: `sqlConnecton1` and `sqlDataAdapter1`.

5. Select the `sqlDataAdapter1` object. Click the Generate Dataset link below the Properties window.

6. In the Generate Dataset window, choose to use the existing `dsCustomers1 DataSet` object. Click OK.

7. Double-click the form and enter the following code in the form's `Load` event handler:

```
private void StepByStep5_15_Load(object sender,
    System.EventArgs e)
{
    // Move the data from the database to the data set
    sqlDataAdapter1.Fill(dsCustomers1, "Customers");

    // Create a dataview to filter the Customers table
    System.Data.DataView dvCustomers =
        new System.Data.DataView(
        dsCustomers1.Tables["Customers"]);

    // Apply a sort to the data view
    dvCustomers.Sort = "ContactName";

    // Apply a filter to the data view
    dvCustomers.RowFilter = "Country = 'France'";

    // and bind the results to the grid
    dgCustomers.DataSource = dvCustomers;
}
```

8. Insert the `Main()` method to launch the form. Set the form as the startup object for the project.

9. Run the project. The `DataGrid` control displays only the data from customers in France. Note that the customers are also sorted by the ContactName column, as shown in Figure 5.21.

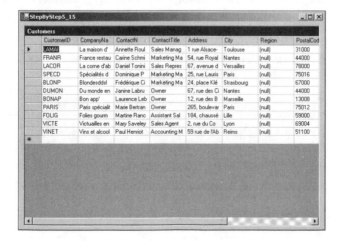

FIGURE 5.21
This `DataGrid` control is populated by binding it to a `DataView` control that filters and sorts the records from the Customers table.

Filtering at the Server

The DataView class provides a useful way to filter data, but it's inefficient if you're working with large amounts of data. That's because all the data is first retrieved from the database server and stored on the client. So if there are 10 million rows of data on the server, a DataView object retrieves all 10 million rows. After that, the DataView object can be used to quickly select a subset of the data. But what if you're never going to need all the data? In that case, you're better off filtering on the server, rather than retrieving all that data that you'll never need. One way to do this is by basing a SqlDataAdapter object on a view instead of a table, as described in Step by Step 5.16.

STEP BY STEP

5.16 Using a Server-Side View to Filter Data

1. Place a DataGrid control on a new Windows form. Name the control dgCustomers. Set the CaptionText property of this control to Customers.

2. Open Server Explorer.

3. Expand the tree under Data Connections to show a SQL Server data connection that points to the Northwind sample database, and then expand the Views node of the SQL Server.

4. Right-click the Views node and select New View.

5. In the Add Table dialog box, select the Customers table, click Add, and then click Close. This puts you in the View Designer within Visual Studio .NET.

6. Click the check boxes All Columns, ContactName, and Country in the column listing.

7. Fill in the details of the view as shown in Figure 5.22.

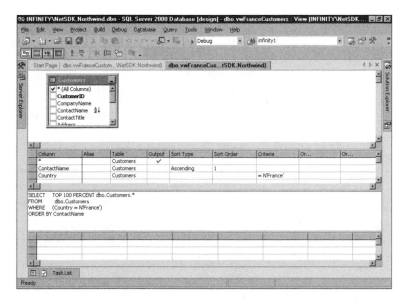

FIGURE 5.22
You can create a new SQL Server view by using the design tools in Visual Studio .NET.

8. Click the Save button and save the view as vwFranceCustomers. Close the design window for the view.

9. Drag the vwFranceCustomers view from Server Explorer and drop it on the form. You get a configuration error because the view is read-only. That's not a problem because you are not writing any data back to the database; click OK to create objects. This creates two visual data objects: sqlConnecton1 and sqlDataAdapter1.

10. Select the sqlDataAdapter1 object. Click the Generate Dataset link below the Properties window.

11. In the Generate Dataset window, choose to use the existing dsCustomers1 DataSet object. Click OK.

12. Set the DataSource property of the DataGrid control to dsCustomers1. Set the DataMember property of the DataGrid control to vwFranceCustomers.

13. Double-click the form and enter the following code in the form's Load event handler:

```
private void StepByStep5_16_Load(object sender,
    System.EventArgs e)
{
    // Move the data from the database to the DataGrid
    sqlDataAdapter1.Fill(
        dsCustomers1, "vwFranceCustomers");
}
```

continues

continued

14. Insert the Main() method to launch the form. Set the form as the startup object for the project.

15. Run the project. The DataGrid control displays only the data from customers in France. Note that the customers are also sorted by the ContactName column, as shown in Figure 5.21.

Step by Step 5.16 displays the same results as Step by Step 5.15. However, behind the scenes, things are different. Instead of retrieving all the rows of the Customers table from the server, this version retrieves only the rows that belong on the display. If you're operating over a slow network or Internet connection, this sort of server-side filtering can save you a good deal of time.

Transforming Data with Lookups

This section takes a brief look at another server-side technique: transforming data by applying lookups. A *lookup* is a technique for replacing one column of data with another column from the same table. For example, given a customer ID value, you could look up the corresponding customer name.

Figure 5.23 shows a DataGrid control bound to the Orders table.

FIGURE 5.23

This DataGrid control is bound to the Orders table; note that only the Customer ID is displayed to identify the customers.

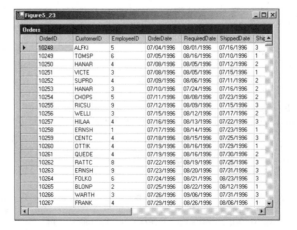

One problem with this particular form is that it displays only Customer ID values—and no other information about the customers. What if you wanted to view company names instead? You would use a new view to retrieve data from the server, as described in Step by Step 5.17.

STEP BY STEP

5.17 Using a Server-Side View to Transform Data

1. Place a DataGrid control on a new Windows form. Name the control dgOrders. Set the CaptionText property of this control to Orders.

2. Open Server Explorer.

3. Expand the tree under Data Connections to show a SQL Server data connection that points to the Northwind sample database, and then expand the Views node of the SQL Server.

4. Right-click the Views node and select New View.

5. In the Add Table dialog box, select the Customers table and click Add. Select the Orders table, click Add, and then click Close. This puts you in the View Designer within Visual Studio .NET.

6. Click the check boxes for CompanyName in the Customers table and all columns except for CustomerID in the Orders table.

7. In the grid, drag the OrderID column above the CompanyName column. Figure 5.24 shows the completed view.

8. Click the Save button and save the view as vwCustOrders. Close the design window for the view.

continues

FIGURE 5.24
You can create a new SQL Server view that
joins data from two tables.

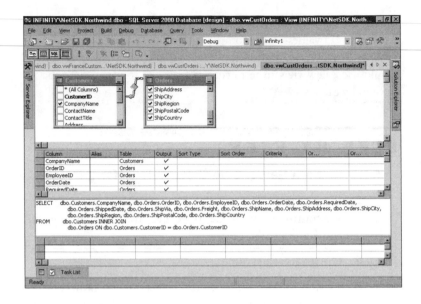

9. Drag the `vwCustOrders` view from Server Explorer and
drop it on the form. You get a configuration error because
the view is read-only. This is not a problem because you
are not writing any data back to the database; click OK to
create objects. This creates two visual data objects:
`sqlConnecton1` and `sqlDataAdapter1`.

10. Select the `sqlDataAdapter1` object. Click the Generate
Dataset link below the Properties window.

11. In the Generate Dataset window, create a new `DataSet`
object named `dsOrders`. Click OK.

12. Set the `DataSource` property of the `DataGrid` control to
`dsOrders1`. Set the `DataMember` property of the `DataGrid`
control to `vwCustOrders`.

13. Double-click the form and enter the following code in the
form's `Load` event handler:

```
private void StepByStep5_17_Load(object sender,
    System.EventArgs e)
{
    // Load the data
    sqlDataAdapter1.Fill(dsOrders1, "vwCustOrders");
}
```

14. Insert the `Main()` method to launch the form. Set the form as the startup object for the project.

15. Run the project. The `DataGrid` control displays order data with full company names, as shown in Figure 5.25.

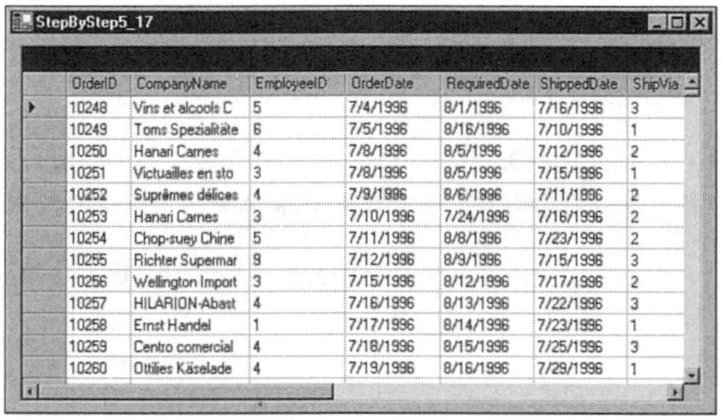

StepByStep5_17

OrderID	CompanyName	EmployeeID	OrderDate	RequiredDate	ShippedDate	ShipVia
10248	Vins et alcools C	5	7/4/1996	8/1/1996	7/16/1996	3
10249	Toms Spezialitäte	6	7/5/1996	8/16/1996	7/10/1996	1
10250	Hanari Carnes	4	7/8/1996	8/5/1996	7/12/1996	2
10251	Victuailles en sto	3	7/8/1996	8/5/1996	7/15/1996	1
10252	Suprêmes délices	4	7/9/1996	8/6/1996	7/11/1996	2
10253	Hanari Carnes	3	7/10/1996	7/24/1996	7/16/1996	2
10254	Chop-suey Chine	5	7/11/1996	8/8/1996	7/23/1996	2
10255	Richter Supermar	9	7/12/1996	8/9/1996	7/15/1996	3
10256	Wellington Import	3	7/15/1996	8/12/1996	7/17/1996	2
10257	HILARION-Abast	4	7/16/1996	8/13/1996	7/22/1996	3
10258	Ernst Handel	1	7/17/1996	8/14/1996	7/23/1996	1
10259	Centro comercial	4	7/18/1996	8/15/1996	7/25/1996	3
10260	Ottilies Käselade	4	7/19/1996	8/16/1996	7/29/1996	1

FIGURE 5.25
The `DataGrid` control displays order data with full company names instead of just a customer ID.

GUIDED PRACTICE EXERCISE 5.2

In this exercise, you'll be working with order and order detail data from the Northwind sample database. You need to design a form that lets the user select from a list of orders and then displays all the order detail data for the selected order. The list of orders should be presented in a `ComboBox` control, and the corresponding order detail data should be shown on a `DataGrid` control.

How would you create such a form?

You should try working through this problem on your own first. If you get stuck, or if you'd like to see one possible solution, follow these steps:

1. Create a form that is populated with a `ListBox` control named `lbOrders` and a `DataGrid` control named `dgOrderDetails`.

2. Open Server Explorer.

3. Expand the tree under Data Connections to show a SQL Server data connection that points to the Northwind sample database, then the Tables node of the SQL Server, and then individual tables.

continues

continued

4. Drag the Orders table from Server Explorer and drop it on the form. This creates two visual data objects: `sqlConnecton1` and `sqlDataAdapter1`. Drag the Order Details table from Server Explorer and drop it on the form. This creates one more object: `sqlDataAdapter2`.

5. Select the `sqlDataAdapter1` object. Click the Generate Dataset link below the Properties window.

6. In the Generate Dataset window, choose to use the existing `dsOrders DataSet` object. Click OK.

7. Select the `sqlDataAdapter2` object. Click the Generate Dataset link below the Properties window.

8. In the Generate Dataset window, choose to create a new `dsOrderDetails DataSet` object. Click OK.

9. Double-click the form and the list box to add event handlers to their default events and enter the following code:

```
System.Data.DataView dvOrderDetails;

private void GuidedStepByStep5_2_Load(object sender,
    System.EventArgs e)
{
    // Load the data set for the DataGrid
    sqlDataAdapter2.Fill(
        dsOrderDetails1, "Order Details");

    // and set up a dataview
    dvOrderDetails = new System.Data.DataView(
        dsOrderDetails1.Tables["Order Details"]);

    // Load the data set for the list box
    sqlDataAdapter1.Fill(dsOrders1, "Orders");

    // And bind it
    lbOrders.DataSource = dsOrders1;
    lbOrders.DisplayMember = "Orders.OrderID";
    lbOrders.ValueMember = "Orders.OrderID";
}

private void lbOrders_SelectedIndexChanged(
    object sender, System.EventArgs e)
{
```

```
        // When a new item is selected in the ListBox,
        // filter the dataview
        // Note that the SelectedItem returns
        // a System.Data.DataRowView object;
        // the OrderID is at the first indexed
        // column position in the object.
        dvOrderDetails.RowFilter = "OrderID = " +
            ((System.Data.DataRowView)
            lbOrders.SelectedItem)[0];
        dgOrderDetails.DataSource = dvOrderDetails;
    }
```

10. Insert the `Main()` method to launch the form. Set the form as the startup object for the project.

11. Run the project. The `ListBox` control displays all order numbers from the database. The `DataGrid` control displays the order details for the selected order. Figure 5.26 shows the final form.

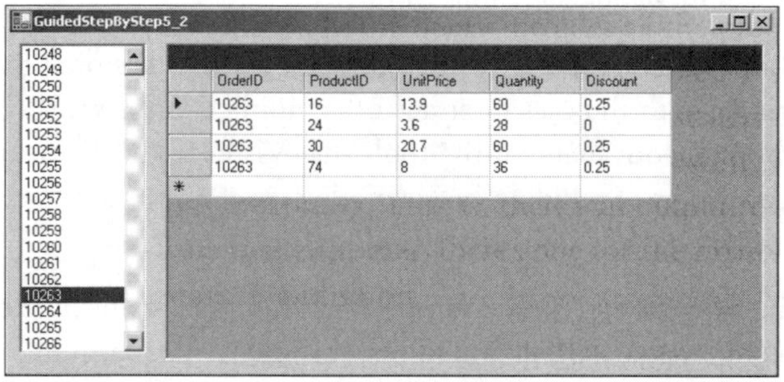

FIGURE 5.26
When you select `OrderID` from the `ComboBox` control, the order details are displayed in a `DataGrid` control.

If you have difficulty following this exercise, review the sections "Using Server Explorer," "Filtering with `DataView` Objects," and "Complex Data Binding." The text and examples should help you relearn this material and help you understand what happens in this exercise. After doing that review, try this exercise again.

REVIEW BREAK

▶ Server Explorer is a powerful tool for working with SQL Server data.

▶ You can edit and design SQL Server objects directly within Visual Studio .NET.

continues

continued

▶ The `DataView` object offers client-side sorting and filtering capabilities for data-bound objects.

▶ Using views on the server can be an efficient way to filter or transform data.

CHAPTER SUMMARY

KEY TERMS

- column
- complex data binding
- data binding
- foreign key
- one-way data binding
- primary key
- relational database
- relationship
- resultset
- row
- simple data binding
- table
- two-way data binding

Nearly every Windows application deals with data in some form. Data is often contained in a database, but it may also be in a simple array, an array of objects, or many other forms. This data is known as the data model of the application.

Data binding gives you a way to connect data that is stored in the data model with the user interface of an application. In this chapter, you learned about many of the tools that Visual C# .NET provides for data binding, including both simple and complex data binding, the Data Form Wizard, and Server Explorer.

Data binding in the .NET Framework is much more flexible than it was in any previous development environment. You can bind any class that implements `IList`, `IBindingList`, or `ITypedList` to the user interface. And any property of a user interface control can potentially be bound to data.

You also learned some programmatic approaches to data, including the use of the `BindingContext` and `CurrencyManager` classes and the creation of SQL Server views to filter or transform data. Trapping events from the `CurrencyManager` class provides additional flexibility for handling complex binding scenarios.

APPLY YOUR KNOWLEDGE

Exercises

5.1   Using Simple Data Binding to Display Information from an Array

This exercise shows you how to populate an array in code and then use simple data binding to display the information on the user interface.

Estimated time: 20 minutes

1. Create a new Visual C# .NET project to use for the exercises in this chapter.

2. Add a new class file to your project. Name the class `Computer.cs`. Enter the following code in the class file to create a class that has three properties and a constructor:

```csharp
using System;
namespace _316C05Exercises
{
    public class Computer
    {
        private String computerName;
        private String cpu;
        private Int32 ram;

        public String ComputerName
        {
            get
            {
                return computerName;
            }
            set
            {
                computerName = value;
            }
        }

        public String CPU
        {
            get
            {
                return cpu;
            }
            set
            {
```

```csharp
                cpu = value;
            }
        }

        public Int32 RAM
        {
            get
            {
                return ram;
            }
            set
            {
                ram = value;
            }
        }

        public Computer(
            String strComputerName,
            String strCPU, Int32 intRAM)
        {
            this.ComputerName =
                strComputerName;
            this.CPU = strCPU;
            this.RAM = intRAM;
        }
    }
}
```

3. Add a new form to the project. Place `Label`, `TextBox`, and `Button` controls on the form, as shown in Figure 5.27. Name the `TextBox` controls `txtComputerName`, `txtCPU`, and `txtRAM`. Name the `Button` controls `btnPrevious` and `btnNext`.

FIGURE 5.27
You can use simple data binding to display the information from an array to the user interface.

APPLY YOUR KNOWLEDGE

4. Add code to the form to create and initialize an array of `Computer` objects in the class definition, and then bind the array to the user interface, by attaching an event handler to the form's `Load` event:

```
// Create and fill an array
// of computer objects
private Computer[] aComputers = {
        new Computer("Frodo",
            "PIII-866", 512),
        new Computer("Samwise",
            "PIII-500", 256),
        new Computer("Meriadoc",
            "K6-350", 128),
        new Computer("Peregrine",
            "K6-350", 128)};

private void Exercise5_1_Load(
   object sender, System.EventArgs e)
{
    // Bind data to the user interface
    txtComputerName.DataBindings.Add(
       "Text", aComputers, "ComputerName");
    txtCPU.DataBindings.Add("Text",
       aComputers, "CPU");
    txtRAM.DataBindings.Add("Text",
       aComputers, "RAM");
}
```

5. Add the following code to the form to handle navigation by attaching event handlers to the `Click` events of the `btnPrevious` and `btnNext` controls:

```
private void btnPrevious_Click(
   object sender, System.EventArgs e)
{
   // Move to the previous item
   // in the data source
   this.BindingContext[
      aComputers].Position -= 1;
}

private void btnNext_Click(object sender,
   System.EventArgs e)
{
   // Move to the next item
   // in the data source
   this.BindingContext[
      aComputers].Position += 1;
}
```

6. Insert the `Main()` method to launch the form. Set the form as the startup form for the project and run the project. The information from the data model should appear on the user interface, and you can use the buttons to scroll through the records.

5.2   Using Simple Data Binding to Display Information from a Database

This exercise shows how you can connect to a database by using Server Explorer and then bind some of the information from the database to the user interface by using simple data binding.

Estimated time: 30 minutes

> **NOTE**
>
> **Creating the Database Connection**   This exercise assumes that you've already used Server Explorer to connect to a copy of the SQL Server 2000 Northwind sample database. If you haven't yet done that, refer to Step by Step 5.10, particularly steps 4 through 6 and the accompanying exam tip, for information on how to build a connection. After that, you can proceed with this exercise.

1. Add a new form to your Visual C# .NET project.

2. Hover your cursor over the Server Explorer tab until Server Explorer appears.

3. Expand the tree in Server Explorer to locate the Orders table in the Northwind sample database. Drag the Orders table from Server Explorer and drop it on the form.

APPLY YOUR KNOWLEDGE

4. Click the `sqlDataAdapter1` object. Click the Generate Dataset link in the Properties window. Create a new `DataSet` object named `dsOrders` and click OK.

5. Place `Label`, `TextBox`, `DateTimePicker`, and `Button` controls on the form, as shown in Figure 5.28. Name the `TextBox` controls `txtOrderID` and `txtCustomerID`. Name the `DateTimePicker` control `dtOrderDate`. Name the `Button` controls `txtPrevious` and `txtNext`.

FIGURE 5.28
You can use simple data binding to display the information from a database to the user interface.

6. Add code to the form to fill the `DataSet` object, and then bind selected items from the `DataSet` object to the user interface, by adding the following code to the form's `Load` event handler:

```
private void Exercise5_2_Load(
    object sender,System.EventArgs e)
{
    // Fill the data set
    sqlDataAdapter1.Fill(
        dsOrders1, "Orders");
    // Bind it to the user interface
    txtOrderID.DataBindings.Add(
        "Text", dsOrders1,
        "Orders.OrderID");
```

```
    txtCustomerID.DataBindings.Add(
        "Text", dsOrders1,
        "Orders.CustomerID");
    dtOrderDate.DataBindings.Add(
        "Value", dsOrders1,
        "Orders.OrderDate");
}
```

7. Add the following code to the form to handle navigation by attaching event handlers to the `Click` events of the `btnPrevious` and `btnNext` controls:

```
private void btnPrevious_Click(
    object sender, System.EventArgs e)
{
    // Move to the previous item
    // in the data source
    this.BindingContext[
        dsOrders1, "Orders"].Position -= 1;
}

private void btnNext_Click(object sender,
    System.EventArgs e)
{
    // Move to the next item in the
    // data source
    this.BindingContext[
        dsOrders1, "Orders"].Position += 1;
}
```

8. Insert the `Main()` method to launch the form. Set the form as the startup form for the project and run the project. The information from the data model appears on the user interface, and you can use the buttons to scroll through the rows of the database table.

As this exercise shows, you're not forced to use complex data binding when you use data from a database. Simple data binding works just as well. However, some syntactical complexities are introduced in this exercise because the `DataSet` object can contain more than one bindable object (remember that a `DataSet` object contains a collection of one or more `DataTable` objects).

APPLY YOUR KNOWLEDGE

The code in this exercise shows how to specify the database column to bind when adding a binding and how to specify the proper `CurrencyManager` object in your navigation code.

5.3 Using Complex and Simple Data Binding with a Combo Box

This exercise shows how to use complex data binding to fill the list in a `ComboBox` control and simple data binding to retrieve the value that the user selects from the list.

Estimated time: 10 minutes

1. Add a new form to your Visual C# .NET project. Place a `ComboBox` control named `cboComputers` and a `TextBox` control named `txtRAM` on the form.

2. Add the following code to the form to create an array and set up data bindings:

```
private void Exercise5_3_Load(
  object sender, System.EventArgs e)
{
    // Create an initialize an array
    Computer[] aComputers =
    { new Computer("Frodo",
        "PIII-866", 512),
    new Computer("Samwise",
        "PIII-500", 256),
    new Computer("Meriadoc",
        "K6-350", 128),
    new Computer("Peregrine",
        "K6-350", 128)};
    // Bind the array to the ComboBox list
    cboComputers.DataSource = aComputers;
    cboComputers.DisplayMember =
        "ComputerName";
    cboComputers.ValueMember = "RAM";
```

```
    // Bind the text box to the
    // value in the combo box
    txtRAM.DataBindings.Add("Text",
        cboComputers, "SelectedValue");
}
```

3. Insert the `Main()` method to launch the form. Set the form as the startup form for the project and run the project. The information from the data model appears on the user interface. When you select a computer name in the `ComboBox` control, you see the RAM value for that computer displayed in the `TextBox` control.

This exercise shows yet another twist on simple data binding: binding a property from one control (the `TextBox` control, in this case) to a value delivered by another control (the `ComboBox` control). This is yet another demonstration of the flexibility of data binding in the .NET Framework.

5.4 Creating a Master–Detail Data Form

This exercise lets you practice with the Visual C# .NET Data Form Wizard. You'll build a data form that shows all the employees in the Northwind sample database. When the user selects a particular employee, the form should display the orders that the employee has taken.

Estimated time: 15 minutes

1. Select Project, Add New Item. In the Add New Item dialog box, select the Data Form Wizard. Name the new form `Exercise5_4.cs` and click Open.

2. Read the Welcome screen of the wizard and click Next.

APPLY YOUR KNOWLEDGE

3. On the Choose a Dataset screen, choose to create a new `DataSet` object named `dsEmpOrders`. Click Next.

4. On the Choose a Data Connection screen, select the data connection to the Northwind sample database and click Next.

5. On the Choose Tables or Views screen, select the Employees table in the Available Items list and click the > button to move it to the Selected Items list. Also select the Orders table and click the > button to move it to the Selected Items list. Click Next.

6. On the Create a Relationship Between Tables screen, name the new relationship `relEmpOrders`. Select Employees as the parent table and Orders as the child table. Select EmployeeID as the key field in each table. Click the > button to create the new relationship, and then click Next

7. On the Choose Tables and Columns to Display on the Form screen, leave all the columns in both tables selected and click Next.

8. On the Choose the Display Style screen, select the all records in a grid style and check the Cancel All check box. Click Finish.

9. Insert the `Main()` method to launch the form. Set the new data form as the startup form for the project and run the project to experiment with it. Figure 5.29 shows the completed form.

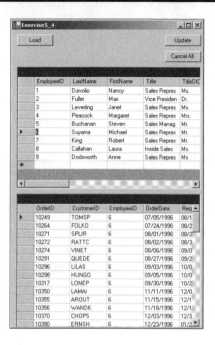

FIGURE 5.29
You can use the Data Form Wizard to create a master–detail data form.

5.5 Using a `DataView` Object to Filter Data at Runtime

This exercise guides you through the steps involved in building a form with a `DataGrid` control whose display can be filtered at runtime. The `DataGrid` control should display customers from a country that the user selects.

Estimated time: 40 minutes

1. Add a new form to your Visual C# .NET project.

2. Hover your cursor over the Server Explorer tab until Server Explorer appears.

APPLY YOUR KNOWLEDGE

3. Expand the tree in Server Explorer to locate the Customers table in the Northwind sample database. Drag the Customers table from Server Explorer and drop it on the form.

4. Click the `sqlDataAdapter1` object. Click the Generate Dataset link in the Properties window. Create a new `DataSet` object named `dsCustomers` and click OK.

5. Reopen Server Explorer.

6. Right-click the Views node and select New View.

7. In the Add Table dialog box, select the Customers table, click Add, and then click Close. This puts you in the View Designer in Visual Studio .NET.

8. Click the check box for Country in the column listing.

9. Fill in the details of the view as shown in Figure 5.30.

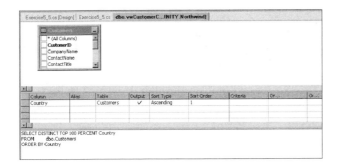

FIGURE 5.30
You can use the Visual Studio .NET View Designer to create a new SQL Server view that selects the country names from the Customers table.

EXAM TIP

SELECT DISTINCT The use of the `DISTINCT` keyword in a SQL statement tells SQL Server not to return any duplicates when running the view. You need to add the `DISTINCT` keyword by typing it in the SQL string.

10. Click on the Save button and save the view as `vwCustomerCountries`. Close the design window for the view.

11. Drag the `vwCustomerCountries` view from Server Explorer and drop it on the form. You get a configuration error because the view is read-only. That's not a problem because you are not writing any data back to the database; click OK to create objects. This creates one more visual data object: `sqlDataAdapter2`.

12. Select the `sqlDataAdapter1` object. Click the Generate Dataset link below the Properties window.

13. In the Generate Dataset window, choose to create a new `dsCountries DataSet` object. Click OK.

14. Place a `ComboBox` control named `cboCountries` on the form. Place a `DataGrid` control named `dgCustomers` on the form.

15. Add the following code to the form to fill both `DataSet` objects and to set up a `DataView` object:

```
System.Data.DataView dvCustomers;
private void Exercise5_5_Load(
    object sender, System.EventArgs e)
{
    // Fill the data set of countries
    // Bind it to the combo box
    sqlDataAdapter2.Fill(
        dsCountries1, "Countries");
```

APPLY YOUR KNOWLEDGE

```
cboCountries.DataSource =
    dsCountries1.Tables["Countries"];
cboCountries.DisplayMember = "Country";
cboCountries.ValueMember = "Country";

// Fill the data set of customers
// and set up a dataview
sqlDataAdapter1.Fill(
    dsCustomers1, "Customers");
dvCustomers = new System.Data.DataView(
    dsCustomers1.Tables["Customers"]);
}
```

16. Add the following code to the form to apply a filter to the DataView object whenever the selection in the ComboBox control changes:

```
private void
    cboCountries_SelectedIndexChanged(e
    object sender, System.EventArgs e)
{
    // Apply a filter to the dataview
    if(dvCustomers != null)
    {
        dvCustomers.RowFilter =
          "Country = '" +
          ((System.Data.DataRowView)
          cboCountries.SelectedItem)[0]
          + "'";
        // And bind the result
        // to the data grid
        dgCustomers.DataSource =
            dvCustomers;
    }
}
```

17. Insert the Main() method to launch the form. Set the form as the startup form for the project and run the project. As you select countries in the combo box, customers from the selected country are displayed on the DataGrid object.

Review Questions

1. Describe the difference between a database and a data model.

2. Describe the difference between simple and complex data binding.

3. What is the purpose of the BindingContext object?

4. What is the purpose of the CurrencyManager object?

5. Name and briefly explain two different ways to filter data.

6. Name three interfaces that support simple data binding.

7. How do the DataSource, DisplayMember, and ValueMember properties of the ComboBox control work together?

8. Name at least two SQL Server objects that you can design from within Visual Studio .NET.

9. Which is more efficient for filtering data: a server-side view or a DataView object?

Exam Questions

1. The data model for an application includes an array of Product objects named Products. Each Product object exposes public properties named ProductNumber and ProductName. You'd like to provide an interface that allows users to select the product number and see the corresponding product name. What should you do?

   A. Create two TextBox controls. Bind the ProductNumber property to one TextBox control and the ProductName property to the other TextBox control. Provide navigation buttons to allow the user to scroll through the data.

APPLY YOUR KNOWLEDGE

B. Create a DataGrid control. Bind the Products array to the DataGrid control.

C. Create a ComboBox control. Set the Products array as the data source of the control. Bind the DisplayMember property to the ProductNumber property and bind the ValueMember property to the ProductName property. Bind a TextBox control on the form to the SelectedValue property of the ComboBox control.

D. Create a TextBox control and a Label control. Bind the ProductNumber property to the TextBox control and the ProductName property to the Label control.

2. Your application's data model represents orders in a strongly typed IList of Order objects. You've used simple data binding to display the pertinent fields from the Order objects on a form. The form includes buttons to allow the user to navigate through the Order objects. What must you do in the handler for the buttons' Click events?

A. Increment or decrement the indexer of the BindingContext object for the form.

B. Call the DataBindings.Add() and DataBindings.Remove() methods to move through the objects.

C. Call the ResumeBinding() and SuspendBinding() methods of the CurrencyManager object that manages the data source.

D. Increment or decrement the Position property of the CurrencyManager object that manages the data source.

3. Your application includes a form that displays employee names in a simple-data-bound TextBox control. You'd like to add a ToolTip to the TextBox control, with the ToolTip displaying the title of the employee. The employee names and employee titles are both supplied by the same IList. How can you do this?

A. Bind the employee title to the Tag property of the TextBox control. In the event handler for the PositionChanged event of the CurrencyManager object, call the ToolTip's SetToolTip() method to copy the value from the Tag property to the ToolTip.

B. Bind the employee title to the Name property of the ToolTip control.

C. Bind the employee title to the Tag property of the TextBox control. In the event handler for the CurrentChanged event of the CurrencyManager object, call the ToolTip's SetToolTip() method to copy the value from the Tag property to the ToolTip.

D. Bind the employee title to the Tag property of the TextBox control. In the event handler for the ItemChanged event of the CurrencyManager object, call the ToolTip's SetToolTip() method to copy the value from the Tag property to the ToolTip.

4. Your application includes a database table that contains a list of course numbers and course names. You've used Server Explorer to create a SqlConnection object and a SqlDataAdapter object to access this data. You've created a DataSet object named dsCourses1 to hold this data. Your form includes code to fill the DataSet object when it's loaded.

APPLY YOUR KNOWLEDGE

Now you'd like to display the list of courses on your form in a `ListBox` control named `lbCourses`. The `ListBox` control should show the course names and return the course numbers. Which of these code snippets should you use?

A.

```
lbCourses.DataSource = dsCourses1;
lbCourses.DisplayMember = "CourseName";
lbCourses.ValueMember = "CourseNumber";
```

B.

```
lbCourses.DataSource =
    dsCourses1.Tables["Courses"];
lbCourses.DisplayMember = "CourseName";
lbCourses.ValueMember = "CourseNumber";
```

C.

```
lbCourses.DataSource =
    dsCourses1.Tables["Courses"];
lbCourses.DisplayMember = "CourseName";
lbCourses.SelectedItem = "CourseNumber";
```

D.

```
lbCourses.DataBindings.Add("DisplayMember",
    dsCourses1, "CourseName");
lbCourses.DataBindings.Add("ValueMember",
    dsCourses1, "CourseNumber");
```

5. Your application includes a `ListBox` control named `lbEmployees` that displays a list of employees. The `DisplayMember` property of the `ListBox` control is bound to the EmployeeName column of the Employees database table. The `ValueMember` property of the `ListBox` control is bound to the EmployeeNumber column of the Employees database table.

   Your form also contains a `TextBox` control named `txtEmployeeNumber`. This control uses simple data binding to display the EmployeeNumber column from the Orders table in your database.

When the user selects a new employee name in the `ListBox` control, you want to display the corresponding `EmployeeNumber` value in the `txtEmployeeNumber` control. What should you do?

A. Use the `SelectedIndexChanged` event of the `ListBox` control to copy the data from the `ListBox` control to the `TextBox` control.

B. Use simple data binding to bind the `ValueMember` property of the `ListBox` control to the `Text` property of the `TextBox` control.

C. Use simple data binding to bind the `SelectedValue` property of the `ListBox` control to the EmployeeNumber column of the Orders table.

D. Use simple data binding to bind the `SelectedValue` property of the `ListBox` control to the EmployeeNumber column of the Employees table.

6. Your application requires data from a database named College. The database includes two tables. The Departments table includes columns DepartmentID and DepartmentName. The Courses table includes columns DepartmentID, CourseName, and CourseNumber. The DepartmentID column is a primary key for the Departments table and a foreign key for the Courses table.

   A form in your application needs to display a list of CourseName values, together with the DepartmentName value for each course. This form does not need any other data. How should you retrieve only this data from the database?

APPLY YOUR KNOWLEDGE

A. Use Server Explorer to create a new SQL Server view that joins the two tables and returns only the required fields. Drag this view and drop it on a form to create a DataAdapter object that returns the required data. Build a DataSet object from the DataAdapter object and bind the DataSet object to your form.

B. Drag both the Departments table and the Courses table from Server Explorer and drop them on your form to create two separate DataAdapter objects. Use the DataAdapter objects to fill a single DataSet object. Build a DataView object from the DataSet object and use the DataView object to filter the data.

C. Drag both the Departments table and the Courses table from Server Explorer and drop them on your form to create two separate DataAdapter objects. Use the two DataAdapter objects to create two separate DataSet objects. Bind the DataSet object of Course table information to a DataGrid control. Bind the DataSet object of Department table information to a ComboBox control. Use the value in the ComboBox control to filter the information displayed on the DataGrid control.

D. Use Server Explorer to create a new SQL Server table that includes only the necessary information. Copy the data from the two separate tables to this table. Drag and drop this table from Server Explorer to your form to create a DataAdapter object. Build a DataSet object from the DataAdapter object and bind the DataSet object to your form.

7. Your application includes a SqlDataAdapter object named sqlDataAdapter1 that was created by dragging and dropping the Physicians table from a database to your form. Your application also includes a DataSet object named dsPhysicians1, based on this SqlDataAdapter object. What line of code should you use to load the data from the database into the DataSet object?

A.

```
dsPhysicians = sqlDataAdapter1.Fill(
    "Physicians");
```

B.

```
sqlDataAdapter1.Fill(
    "dsPhysicians1", "Physicians");
```

C.

```
sqlDataAdapter1.Fill(dsPhysicians1);
```

D.

```
sqlDataAdapter1.Fill(
    dsPhysicians1, "Physicians");
```

8. The application that you're designing should display employee information on a DataGrid control, by using complex data binding. Your database contains a table of departments and a table of employees. The Employees table has a foreign key that points back to the Departments table. The application should communicate with the database via a slow WAN link. The list of departments changes approximately once every two months.

The form should display all the employees from a single department. Although users will only view one department at a time, they will frequently need to view several departments during the course of a session with the application.

APPLY YOUR KNOWLEDGE

How should you design the filtering for this form?

A. Build one view on the server for each department. At runtime, have the program use the appropriate view to retrieve the requested department.

B. Each time the user requests a department, retrieve all the data into a DataSet object. Then delete all rows from the DataSet object that do not apply to this department.

C. Retrieve all the data into a DataSet object. Use a DataView object, with its RowFilter property set at runtime, to retrieve individual departments as needed.

D. Build one form for each department. Each form should be based on a view that returns only the employees for that department. At runtime, open the appropriate form. Hide the form when the user is done so that it can be opened more quickly if it's needed a second time.

9. Your application is connected to a SQL Server database that contains customer and order information. You have a form in your application that fills a DataSet object with information from the Orders table that includes the Customer ID. The DataSet object is displayed on the form by using complex data binding to a DataGrid object.

You have been asked to display the CustomerName column from the Customers table in the DataGrid object instead of the CustomerID column. How should you proceed?

A. Create a view in the SQL Server database that combines the Customers and Orders tables. Replace the DataSet object on the form with a new DataSet object based on this new view. Bind the new DataSet object to the DataGrid object.

B. Add a second DataSet object to the form. Base the second DataSet object on the Customers table from the database. Use each DataSet object to fill the appropriate columns of the DataGrid object.

C. Create a DataView object in code from the existing DataSet object. Filter the DataView object to remove the CustomerID column.

D. Add an array of Customer objects to your application and initialize it in code with customer names and IDs. Use a view to join this array to the existing DataSet object.

10. You're using simple data binding to display a DateTime value (that includes a time part) in a TextBox control. Your application uses two-way data binding so the user can edit the value in the control and have changes saved back to the data model. Unfortunately, users are not always careful, and you have a problem when invalid dates (such as February 30, 2004) are entered in the TextBox control. How should you fix this problem?

A. Write an event handler for the TextChanged event of the TextBox control. Check the text of the control in this event handler to see if it's a valid date. If it is not, revert to the original date.

B. Replace the TextBox control on the form with a DateTimePicker control. Use simple data binding to bind the data to the control's Value property.

C. Replace the `TextBox` control on the form with a `DateTimePicker` control. Use simple data binding to bind the data to the control's `Tag` property.

D. Replace the `TextBox` control on the form with a `MonthCalendar` control. Use simple data binding to bind the data to the control's `Value` property.

11. You are working with a complex form that uses `Panel` controls to organize a large amount of data. The form displays information from six different data sources. Some of the panels contain data from more than one data source.

    You have added navigation buttons to scroll through the data in one particular data source. The navigation buttons increment and decrement the `Position` property of a `CurrencyManager` object. You test the form, and the buttons do not appear to scroll the data in that data source. What could be the problem? (Choose the best two answers.)

    A. There are too many controls on the form, so your code is not getting executed.

    B. You retrieved the `CurrencyManager` object through the form's `BindingContext` object, but the `Panel` control has its own `BindingContext` object.

    C. This particular `CurrencyManager` object does not support a `Position` property.

    D. The `BindingContext` object that you're using has more than one `CurrencyManager` object, and you're working with the wrong one.

12. The data model of your application includes a task list that might have anywhere from one to eight items in it. Each item is characterized by five pieces of information. You need to display the entire task list on a single form. Your users want to be able to see all tasks at one time. What should you do?

    A. Use simple data binding to display single tasks in individual `TextBox` controls. Provide navigation buttons to scroll through the task list.

    B. Use the `System.Reflection.Emit` namespace to create the appropriate number of `TextBox` controls at runtime. Use simple data binding to bind each task to a different set of controls.

    C. Use complex data binding to display the task list in a `ComboBox` control.

    D. Use complex data binding to display the task list in a `DataGrid` control.

13. You have created an array of `Car` objects named `aCars`. Each `Car` object has a `Model` property and a `Year` property. You want to display all the `Model` property values in a `ListBox` control named `lbCars`. Which code snippet should you use for this purpose?

    A.
    ```
    lbCars.DataSource = aCars;
    lbCars.ValueMember = Model;
    ```

    B.
    ```
    lbCars.DataSource = aCars;
    lbCars.DisplayMember = Model;
    ```

    C.
    ```
    lbCars.DataSource = aCars;
    lbCars.DisplayMember = "Model";
    ```

APPLY YOUR KNOWLEDGE

D.

```
lbCars.DataSource = aCars;
lbCars.ValueMember = "Model";
```

14. You have an XML file that contains information on customers. You plan to make this information available to your users by using simple data binding to controls on the user interface. What must you do?

   A. Import the data from the XML file to a data structure that implements the IList, IBindingList, or ITypedList interfaces.

   B. Create an XML Web service to retrieve information from the file.

   C. Store the XML file in a SQL Server database.

   D. Set the Tag property of each control that you will use for data binding to XML.

15. Your data model includes an array of Date values named gadtMain. You've created a form that includes a DateTimePicker control named dtMain. Which line of code would you use to bind the control to the array?

   A.

```
dtMain.DataBindings.Add(
    "Value", gadtMain, "");
```

   B.

```
dtMain.DataBindings.Add(
    "Format", gadtMain, "");
```

   C.

```
dtMain.DataBindings.Add(
    "Value", gadtMain, "Date");
```

   D.

```
dtMain.DataBindings.Add(
    "Format", gadtMain, "Date");
```

Answers to Review Questions

1. A database is a location, such as a SQL Server database, where you can store data outside your application. A data model is the representation of data within your application.

2. Simple data binding involves connecting a single value from the data model to a single property of a control. Complex data binding involves connecting a user interface control to an entire collection of data, rather than to a single data item.

3. The BindingContext object provides access to the CurrencyManager objects on a form.

4. The CurrencyManager object is responsible for keeping track of which piece of data from a data source is currently bound to the user interface.

5. You can filter data by creating a DataView object and setting its RowFilter property or by creating a view on the database server. In the first case, all the data is returned from the server to your application and then filtered in your application. In the second case, the data is filtered on the server, and only the filtered data is returned to your application.

6. Any object that implements the IList, IBindingList, or ITypedList interfaces can be used as a data binding source.

7. The DataSource property of a ComboBox control specifies the data that will be displayed in the list portion of the combo box. The DisplayMember property specifies the exact column of data that will be shown in the list. The ValueMember property specifies the exact column of data that will be returned by the SelectedValue property of the ComboBox control.

8. You can design SQL Server database diagrams, tables, views, stored procedures, and functions from within Visual Studio .NET.

9. Which alternative is more efficient depends on what your application is doing with the data. If you only need a small portion of the data, it's more efficient to filter the data on the server with a server-side view. But if your communications link with the server is slow or you will need a variety of different subsets of the data, it can be more efficient to perform filtering on the client with a DataView object.

Answers to Exam Questions

1. **C.** Binding the ComboBox control to both the data source and a TextBox control lets the ComboBox control transfer data from the source to the TextBox control. Answer A requires searching for the data rather than choosing it. Answer B displays all the data at once. Answer D does not have any provision for choosing a product number. For more information, see the section "Complex Data Binding" in this chapter.

2. **D.** To move through the list of items, you must change the Position property of the appropriate CurrencyManager object. The indexer of the BindingContext control is used to return a CurrencyManager control. The Add() and Remove() methods make and break bindings. The ResumeBinding() and SuspendBinding() methods control whether data binding is active. For more information, see the section "Binding Data to the User Interface" in this chapter.

3. **A.** The value displayed by the ToolTip can only be set with the SetToolTip() method. It can't be bound directly. The appropriate event for renewing the ToolTip is the PositionChanged event, which occurs whenever a record becomes current. For more information, see the section "The BindingContext and CurrencyManager Classes" in this chapter.

4. **B.** The code in Answer B performs the required task. Answer A does not properly specify which data from the DataSet object to use. Answer C neglects to bind the ValueMember property, which controls the value of the ListBox control. Answer D uses simple data binding syntax, which does not display an entire list of data. For more information, see the section "Complex Data Binding" in this chapter.

5. **C.** You should use simple data binding to bind the SelectedValue property of the ListBox control to the EmployeeNumber column of the Orders table because this is the only answer that satisfies the conditions. For more information, see the section "Binding to a ComboBox or ListBox Control" and Step by Step 5.6 in this chapter.

6. **A.** Answers B and C return too much data to the client. Answer D results in storing duplicate data on the server, which is inefficient and prone to error. For more information, see the section "Filtering Data" in this chapter.

7. **D.** In a call to the Fill() method of a SqlDataAdapter object, you must specify the DataSet object to fill as an object and the table to fill as a string. For more information, see the section "Drag-and-Drop from Server Explorer" in this chapter.

8. **C.** Answers A and D require maintenance programming every time the list of departments changes. Answer B retrieves more data than necessary over the slow WAN line. For more information, see the section "Filtering with DataView Objects" in this chapter.

9. **A.** Answers B and C are unworkable. Answer D requires you to maintain the code to synchronize the array with the actual data in the database. Only Answer A lets you set up the DataGrid control so that it's automatically kept up to date. For more information, see the section "Transforming Data with Lookups" in this chapter.

10. **B.** You must use a DateTimePicker object rather than a MonthCalendar object because the latter doesn't let you specify a time. Validating the data in the TextBox control does not work because it still attempts to save the bad value to the database before validating. When you're binding a DateTimePicker object, the Value property is the one that controls the displayed date. For more information, see the section "Simple Data Binding" in this chapter.

11. **B** and **D.** All CurrencyManager objects support a Position property, and it would take a truly astronomical number of controls to cause problems with .NET's code execution. For more information, see the sections "The BindingContext and CurrencyManager classes" and "The Architecture of Simple Data Binding" in this chapter.

12. **D.** Answers A and C result in only one task being visible at a time. Answer B uses a lot of complicated programming where a single data binding call will suffice. For more information, see the section "Complex Data Binding" in this chapter.

13. **C.** You must set the DataSource and DisplayMember properties of the ListBox control to cause it to display anything. The DisplayMember property is a string, not an object. For more information, see the section "Complex Data Binding" in this chapter.

14. **A.** You should import the data from the XML file to a data structure that implements the IList, IBindingList, or ITypedList interfaces. This is the only option that produces data that can be bound. For more information, see the section "Bindable Entities" in this chapter.

15. **A.** The Value property of the DateTimePicker control is what you bind to when you want to display a particular value. You don't need a navigation path (the third parameter of DataBindings.Add) when you're binding to an array of simple types. For more information, see the section "Simple Data Binding" in this chapter.

APPLY YOUR KNOWLEDGE

Suggested Readings and Resources

1. Windows Forms QuickStart Tutorial:

   - "Databinding in Windows Forms"

   - Control topics, including "ComboBox," "DateTimePicker," and "DataGrid"

2. Visual Studio .NET Combined Help Collection "Windows Forms Data Architecture"

3. .NET Framework SDK documentation:

   - "System.Data Namespace"

   - "System.Windows.Forms Namespace"

4. Microsoft Support Webcast: An Introduction to Data Binding in Windows Forms. support.microsoft.com/servicedesks/ webcasts/wc101002/wcblurb101002.asp.

This chapter covers the following Microsoft-specified objectives for the "Consuming and Manipulating Data" section of Exam 70-316, "Developing and Implementing Windows-Based Applications with Microsoft Visual C# .NET and Microsoft Visual Studio .NET":

Consuming and manipulating data.

- **Access and manipulate data from a Microsoft SQL Server database by creating and using ad hoc queries and stored procedures.**

- **Access and manipulate data from a data store. Data stores include relational databases, XML documents, and flat files. Methods include XML techniques and ADO .NET.**

- **Handle data errors.**

▶ Visual C# .NET includes a variety of ways to manipulate data and move it from place to place. The Visual Studio .NET IDE offers tight integration with Microsoft SQL Server, making it easy to work with SQL Server data, either interactively or programmatically. The .NET Framework also offers several entire namespaces to deal with data in its various forms, including the following:

- `System.IO` for dealing with file-based storage.

- `System.Data`, `System.Data.SqlClient`, `System.Data.OleDb`, `System.Data.Common`, and `System.Data.SqlTypes` (which collectively make up ADO.NET) for using data from relational databases.

- `System.Xml` for working with XML files.

▶ In this chapter you'll learn about these many ways to manipulate data within an application.

CHAPTER 6

Consuming and Manipulating Data

OUTLINE

▶ Understand how to construct and interpret simple Transact SQL statements, including SELECT, INSERT, UPDATE, and DELETE, as well as SQL Server stored procedures. Spend some time practicing with the visual data tools in the .NET Framework or with another query front end, such as SQL Server Query Analyzer. Make sure you know how to work with the raw Transact SQL statements, not just the graphical tools.

▶ For file-based access, understand the difference between a stream and a backing store. Practice reading and writing data with FileStream, StreamReader, and StreamWriter objects.

▶ Pay attention to the uses and functions of the ADO.NET objects, and don't get confused by the similarity of the names of these objects and the names of classic ADO objects. You might encounter the claim that ADO.NET is just an evolutionary improvement on classic ADO and that your knowledge of classic ADO will help you learn ADO.NET. However, this is not true.

ADO.NET is an entirely new model for working with data.

▶ Know which objects are part of the System.Data namespace (and are therefore shared by all data providers) and which are part of specific data provider namespaces, such as System.Data.SqlClient and System.Data.OleDb.

▶ Know the objects that are contained within a DataSet object and the methods that are available to manipulate those objects. Be sure to understand when to use a strongly typed DataSet object and how this affects the syntax of data set operations.

▶ Know how to read and write XML data by using the classes from the System.Xml namespace. Understand how to synchronize an XML document with a DataSet object and some of the reasons you might want to do this.

INTRODUCTION

Now that you've learned about some of the techniques that are available for dealing with data directly from the user interface of a Visual C# .NET Windows application, it's time to take a more detailed look at the facilities that the .NET Framework offers for working with data. Data is at the core of many .NET applications, and Microsoft developers spent many hours building a flexible set of tools that you can use to work with data in your code.

I'll look at three main types of data in this chapter:

◆ Data stored in databases such as Microsoft SQL Server

◆ Data stored in disk files

◆ Data stored in Extensible Markup Language (XML)

Many classes of the .NET Framework are specially optimized to work with Microsoft SQL Server as a database, so you need to understand the language, Transact SQL (T-SQL), that's used to communicate with SQL Server. I'll start the chapter by reviewing the basic parts of the T-SQL language that you need to know to communicate effectively with SQL Server. You'll learn how you can use a small part of ADO.NET to send T-SQL statements to SQL Server and receive the results of the statements.

Next, I cover how the classes in the System.IO namespace handle the data stored in files. You'll learn how the .NET Framework handles file data as part of a more general concept of streams and backing stores.

ADO.NET is a subset of the .NET Framework that uses objects from the System.Data namespace and related namespaces. One of the key objects in ADO.NET is the DataSet object, which represents an entire relational database in a single object (with many constituent objects). In this chapter, you'll see how to create DataSet objects and fill them with data, and then you'll learn some of the many ways that you can work with that data.

XML is a key part of the .NET Framework. The classes in the System.Xml namespace give you the functionality to handle XML data. In this chapter you'll explore several classes of the System.Xml namespace that allow you to read and write XML data.

I'll close the chapter with a look at handling data errors. In particular, you'll see how the .NET error-trapping mechanisms let you deal with common database and multiuser data errors.

ACCESSING AND MANIPULATING SQL SERVER DATA

Consuming and manipulating data.

- **Access and manipulate data from a Microsoft SQL Server database by creating and using ad hoc queries and stored procedures.**

You might be a bit surprised to find a Microsoft SQL Server objective on a Visual C# .NET certification exam, but it really makes perfect sense. Many Visual C# .NET applications require a database to enable them to store data on a permanent basis, and SQL Server is one of the best databases to use with the .NET Framework. As you'll see later in this chapter, an entire namespace (`System.Data.SqlClient`) is devoted to efficient communication between .NET applications and SQL Server.

The objects in `System.Data.SqlClient`, though, won't do you any good unless you understand the language used to communicate with SQL Server: T-SQL. T-SQL is Microsoft's implementation of Structured Query Language (SQL), which is defined by a standard from the American National Standards Institute (ANSI). The core of T-SQL is based on the ANSI SQL-92 standard. SQL-92 defines a query-oriented language, in which you submit queries to the database and get back a resultset consisting of rows and columns of data. Other queries cause changes to the database (for example, adding, deleting, or updating a row of data) without returning any resultset.

There are two main ways to submit T-SQL queries to a SQL Server database for processing. First, you can write *ad hoc queries*, SQL statements that are executed directly. Second, you can write *stored procedures*, SQL statements that are stored on the server as named objects. Stored procedures can also include complex programming logic. The .NET Framework includes facilities for running both ad hoc queries and stored procedures.

EXAM TIP

SQL Statement Capitalization You usually see SQL keywords (such as SELECT, INSERT, UPDATE, and DELETE) formatted entirely in uppercase. I follow that convention in this book, but uppercase formatting isn't required by SQL Server. You might see these same keywords in mixed case or lowercase on an exam. As far as SQL Server is concerned, there's no difference between SELECT, Select, and select.

NOTE

SQL Dialects Microsoft SQL Server isn't the only product that implements the SQL-92 standard. Other products, including Microsoft Access and Oracle, also use SQL-92–based query languages. However, different databases differ in their treatment of SQL in many subtle ways. Most databases contain extensions to SQL-92 (that is, keywords that are understood only by that particular database), and most don't implement the entire SQL-92 standard. The SQL statements in this chapter are from the shared core of SQL-92 that's identical in nearly all database products, so they should work whether you're using SQL Server, Access, or Oracle (among others). But as you study the more advanced features of SQL Server, you should keep in mind that T-SQL statements do not necessarily run on other database servers without changes.

Using Ad Hoc Queries

Ad hoc T-SQL queries provide an extremely flexible way to retrieve data from a SQL Server database or to make changes to that database. In this section I'll show you several ways to send an ad hoc query to SQL Server. Then you'll learn the basics of the four main T-SQL statements that help you manipulate SQL Server data:

◆ **SELECT statements**—These statements allow you to retrieve data that is stored in the database.

◆ **INSERT statements**—These statements allow you to add new data to the database.

◆ **UPDATE statements**—These statements allow you to modify data that's already in the database.

◆ **DELETE statements**—These statements allow you to delete data from the database.

Running Queries

When you're learning T-SQL, it's useful to be able to send queries to a SQL Server database and to see the results (if any) that the server returns. You should be familiar with the many ways that are available to communicate with SQL Server. I'll show you four of them in this section:

◆ Using the Visual Studio .NET Integrated Development Environment (IDE)

◆ Using osql

◆ Using the SQL Query Analyzer

◆ Using a Visual C# .NET application

Using the Visual Studio .NET IDE

When you just need to run a query in the course of working with a project, you can run it directly from the Visual Studio .NET IDE. Step by Step 6.1 shows you how.

STEP BY STEP

6.1 Running a Query from the Visual Studio .NET IDE

1. Open a Visual C# .NET Windows application in the Visual Studio .NET IDE.

2. Open Server Explorer.

3. Expand the tree under Data Connections to show a SQL Server data connection that points to the Northwind sample database, and then expand the Views node of the selected SQL Server data connection.

4. Right-click the Views node and select New View.

5. Click Close in the Add Table dialog box.

6. In the SQL pane of the View Designer (which is the area that starts by displaying the text SELECT FROM), type this SQL statement:

```
SELECT * FROM Employees
```

7. Select Query, Run from the Visual Studio menu, or click the Run Query button on the View toolbar. The SQL statement is sent to SQL Server and the results are displayed, as shown in Figure 6.1.

NOTE

The Northwind Sample Database Whenever I've used data from a database in this book, I've used the Northwind sample database that is part of SQL Server 2000. Visual Studio .NET includes Microsoft Data Engine (MSDE), a stripped-down version of SQL Server that you can use if you don't have the full version installed. See your Visual Studio CD's readme file for information on installing MSDE.

NOTE

Creating Data Connections If you need a refresher on creating SQL Server data connections, refer to Chapter 5, "Data Binding," especially Step by Step 5.10 and Step by Step 5.12.

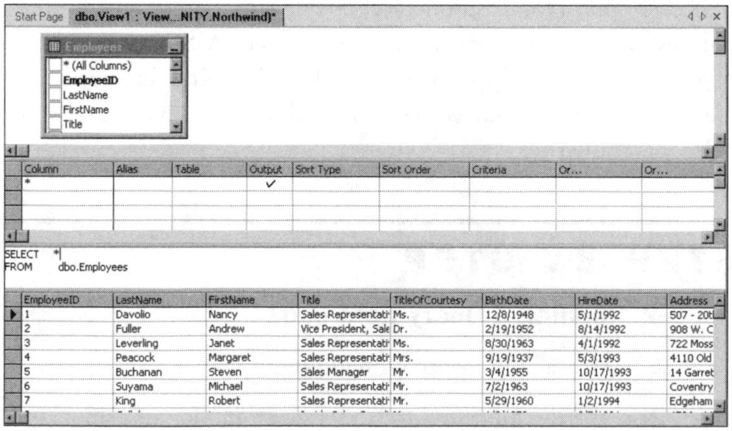

FIGURE 6.1

You can run an ad hoc query directly from the Visual Studio .NET IDE.

EXAM TIP

SQL Statement Formatting   If you look at Figure 6.1, you'll see that Visual Studio .NET made some changes to the SQL statement that you typed. This is the original statement:

```
SELECT * FROM Employees
```

This is the statement that Visual Studio .NET turns it into:

```
SELECT      *
FROM        dbo.Employees
```

Two things are going on here. First, SQL Server doesn't care about whitespace. You can insert spaces, tabs, or new lines between any SQL keywords without changing the statement. Second, every SQL Server object (such as the Employees table) has an owner. The default owner is a user named dbo (which stands for *database owner*). You can add the name of the owner of an object to the object when referring to it. In the case of SQL statements on the exam, it's likely that every object will be owned by dbo, so don't get thrown if you see the dbo prefix on a table name.

When you run the query, Visual Studio .NET sends the SQL statement to the SQL Server that is specified by the database connection that you choose in step 3. The server then processes the query (this particular query tells it to return all columns in all rows of the Employees table) and sends the results back to the client (in this case, Visual Studio .NET). The IDE then displays the results, formatted as a grid.

The View Designer in Visual Studio .NET displays up to four panes. From top to bottom, the panes are as follows:

1. **The Diagram pane**—This pane displays the tables involved in the query and the relationships between these tables, as well as all the columns that the tables contain.

2. **The Grid pane**—This pane shows the columns that have been selected as part of the query, as well as additional sorting and filtering information.

3. **The SQL pane**—This pane shows the actual SQL statement that will be executed.

4. **The Results pane**—This pane shows the results (if any) after the query has been executed.

The View toolbar includes buttons that you can use to hide or show any of these four panes. For this chapter, you need only the SQL pane and the Results pane.

Using osql

A second option for executing ad hoc queries is to use one of the utilities that ships as a part of SQL Server. The MSDE version of SQL Server that is shipped with Visual Studio .NET includes one of these utilities: osql. osql is a command-line utility that can execute SQL Server queries.

STEP BY STEP

6.2 Running a Query from osql

1. Open a Windows command prompt.

2. Type the following to launch osql and log in using Windows integrated authentication:

```
osql -E
```

3. To execute a query in `osql`, you must first tell it which database to use. To do so, type this:

```
use Northwind
```

4. Enter the query to execute:

```
SELECT FirstName, LastName FROM Employees
```

5. Tell `osql` to execute the SQL statements that you just entered:

```
GO
```

6. When you're done with `osql`, type this:

```
exit
```

Here's the entire `osql` session, including the prompts from `osql`:

```
C:\>osql -E
1> use Northwind
2> SELECT FirstName, LastName FROM Employees
3> GO
 FirstName  LastName
 ---------- --------------------
 Nancy      Davolio
 Max        Fuller
 Janet      Leverling
 Margaret   Peacock
 Steven     Buchanan
 Michael    Suyama
 Robert     King
 Laura      Callahan
 Anne       Dodsworth

(9 rows affected)
1> exit

C:\>
```

For Step by Step 6.2 you use a slightly different query for the `osql` session than you use in Step by Step 6.1. The SELECT query in Step by Step 6.2 specifies two columns from the table (FirstName and LastName), telling SQL Server to return only the contents of those two columns. If you execute SELECT * FROM Employees in `osql`, you might get a bit of a shock; the Employees table includes a bitmap image column, and when you execute SELECT * FROM Employees, the contents of that column fill a command session with junk characters.

EXAM TIP

Obtaining the SQL Query Analyzer
The SQL Query Analyzer is not included in the MSDE version of SQL Server. It's a part of all the other editions of SQL Server, so if you have another edition installed, you should have the SQL Query Analyzer available. Otherwise, you can download the 120-day trial version of SQL Server 2000 from www.microsoft.com/sql/evaluation/trial/2000/default.asp; this version contains the SQL Query Analyzer.

Using the SQL Query Analyzer

Although osql can be convenient for quick queries, it doesn't offer much in the way of tools. SQL Server offers a full-featured query environment called the SQL Query Analyzer.

STEP BY STEP

6.3 Running a Query from the SQL Query Analyzer

1. Select Start, Programs, Microsoft SQL Server, Query Analyzer. The SQL Query Analyzer is launched, and the Connect to SQL Server dialog box appears.

2. To choose a SQL Server to work with, you can type the name of a SQL Server or the special name (local) to use a SQL Server on the same computer as the SQL Query Analyzer. You can also use the Browse button to list all servers on the network. After you select a server and fill in your authentication information, click OK.

3. Select the Northwind database from the Databases combo box on the SQL Query Analyzer toolbar.

4. Type this query in the Query window:

```
SELECT * FROM Employees
```

5. Select Query, Execute, click the Execute button on the toolbar, or press F5 to run the query. The SQL statement is sent to SQL Server, and the results are displayed, as shown in Figure 6.2.

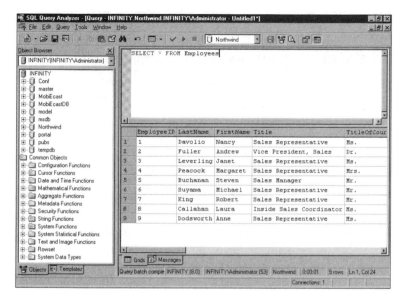

FIGURE 6.2
You can run an ad hoc query in the SQL Query Analyzer.

The SQL Query Analyzer offers an extremely flexible environment for running ad hoc queries. The features of the SQL Query Analyzer include the following:

◆ The ability to have multiple query windows open at the same time.

◆ An Object Browser in which you can see the structure of SQL Server objects

◆ Performance analysis tools

◆ Templates for common queries

For more information on using the SQL Query Analyzer, refer to *SQL Server Books Online*, the help file that is installed as part of SQL Server.

Using a Visual C# .NET Application

As a final alternative for executing ad hoc queries, you can build your own Visual C# .NET form to execute any query.

STEP BY STEP

6.4 Running a Query from a Custom Form

1. Add a new form to your Visual C# .NET project.

2. Open Server Explorer.

3. Expand the tree under Data Connections to show a SQL Server data connection that points to the Northwind sample database. Drag and drop the data connection to the form. A sqlConnection1 object is created on the form, and this object represents a connection to SQL Server.

4. Add a TextBox control (txtQuery), a Button control (btnExecute), and a DataGrid control (dgResults) to the form. Set the Multiline property of the TextBox control to true. Set the CaptionVisible property of the DataGrid control to false.

5. Switch to the code view and add the following using directives to make the ADO.NET objects available:

```
using System.Data;
using System.Data.SqlClient;
```

6. Double-click the Button control and enter this code to execute the query when the Execute Query button is clicked:

```
private void btnExecute_Click(object sender,
    System.EventArgs e)
{
    // Create a SqlCommand object to represent the query
    SqlCommand cmd = sqlConnection1.CreateCommand();
    cmd.CommandType = CommandType.Text;
    cmd.CommandText = txtQuery.Text;
    // Create a SqlDataAdapter object
     // To talk to the database
    SqlDataAdapter da = new SqlDataAdapter();
    da.SelectCommand = cmd;
    // Create a DataSet to hold the results
    DataSet ds = new DataSet();
    // Fill the data set
    da.Fill(ds, "Results");
    // And bind it to the data grid
    dgResults.DataSource = ds;
    dgResults.DataMember = "Results";
}
```

7. Insert the `Main()` method to launch the form. Set the form as the startup object for the project.

8. Run the project. Enter this query in the Query text box:

```
SELECT * FROM Employees
```

9. Click the Execute Query button. The code runs, retrieving the results to the `DataGrid` control, as shown in Figure 6.3.

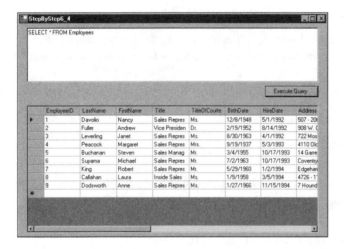

FIGURE 6.3
You can run an ad hoc query from a custom form.

> **NOTE**
>
> **Error Handling** I do not use error handling in most of the programs in this chapter, to keep the focus on specific ADO.NET features. Error handling plays an important role in designing robust programs, and you must use it in real-life programs. To learn about error handling, refer to Chapter 3, "Error Handling for the User Interface." I also discussed error handling features that are specific to ADO.NET later in this chapter, in section, "Handling Data Errors."

You'll learn about the ADO.NET objects that Step by Step 6.4 uses later in this chapter, starting in the section "The ADO.NET Object Model." So for now let's quickly review the objects used in Step by Step 6.4:

◆ The `SqlConnection` object represents a connection to a database.

◆ The `SqlCommand` object represents a single query that you can send to the server.

◆ The `DataSet` object represents the results of one or more queries.

◆ The `SqlDataAdapter` object acts as a pipeline between the `SqlConnection` and `DataSet` objects.

The code in Step by Step 6.4 uses these objects to retrieve data from SQL Server to the data set, and it uses the SQL statement that you typed in to know which data to retrieve. It then uses complex data binding (which is described in Chapter 5) to display the results on the user interface in the `DataGrid` control.

The SELECT Statement

Now that you know a variety of ways to execute ad hoc queries, it's time to dig in to the T-SQL language to see some of the possible queries, starting with the SELECT statement.

The most basic SQL statement is the SELECT statement, which is used to create a resultset. In skeleton form, a SELECT statement looks like this:

```
SELECT field_list
FROM table_list
WHERE where_clause
GROUP BY group_by_clause
HAVING having_clause
ORDER BY sort_clause
```

Each of these lines of code is called a *clause*. The SELECT and FROM clauses are required, and the rest are optional. Here's an example of a SQL statement that contains only the required clauses:

```
SELECT OrderID, CustomerID
FROM Orders
```

The resultset for this statement contains the values of the OrderID and CustomerID fields from every record in the Orders table.

There are other things you can do in the SELECT clause besides just list fields. You've already seen that there's a shortcut for all fields:

```
SELECT *
FROM Orders
```

You can also perform calculations in the SELECT clause:

```
SELECT OrderID,
CAST(ShippedDate - OrderDate AS integer) AS Delay
FROM Orders
```

The expression ShippedDate - OrderDate calculates the number of days between the two dates. The CAST function tells SQL Server to return the result as an integer. If you try this example, you'll see that the AS clause supplies a name for the calculated column.

EXAM TIP

Practicing Using SQL   You can use any of the methods described in the preceding sections to execute the statements that you're about to learn. You should execute enough of these statements to get a good idea of how the T-SQL language works. Just reading the descriptions here is no substitute for actually practicing with T-SQL. You're sure to see some SQL statements on the exam.

If you omit AS Delay, the query still works, but SQL Server returns the calculation without assigning a name to the column.

You're not limited to retrieving fields from a single table. For instance, you could try retrieving information from both the Customers and Orders tables by using this query:

```
SELECT OrderID, Customers.CustomerID
FROM Orders, Customers
```

Customers.CustomerID is known as a *fully qualified name* because it specifies both the table name and the field name. This is necessary because both the Customers and the Orders tables contain fields named CustomerID, and you need to tell SQL Server which one you want to display.

If you try this last query, though, you get more than 75,000 records back. That's many more than the number of orders in the database! This happens because although the query includes all the proper tables, it doesn't tell SQL Server how to relate those tables. This sort of query is called a *cross-product query*. SQL Server constructs the resultset by including one row in the output for each row in each combination of input table rows. That is, there's an output row for the first order and the first customer, there's one for the first order and the second customer, and so on.

A more useful query, of course, would match each order with the corresponding customer. That's the job of the INNER JOIN keyword. INNER JOIN tells SQL Server how to match two tables. Here's how the query looks for a fixed version of the original query:

```
SELECT OrderID, Customers.CustomerID
FROM Orders INNER JOIN Customers
ON Orders.CustomerID = Customers.CustomerID
```

> **NOTE**
>
> **One Keyword or Two?**   Even though it's two words, INNER JOIN is referred to as a single SQL keyword. That's because you can't have INNER in T-SQL unless you immediately follow it with JOIN.

This fixed query tells SQL Server to look at each row in the Orders table and match it with all rows in the Customers table where the CustomerID of the order equals the CustomerID of the customer. Because CustomerIDs are unique in the Customers table, using the preceding code example is the same as including only a single row for each order in the resultset.

The INNER JOIN keyword can appear more than once in a query if there are more than two tables to join. For example, the following query shows employee IDs along with order and customer IDs:

```
SELECT Orders.OrderID,
       Customers.CustomerID, Employees.EmployeeID
```

```
FROM Employees INNER JOIN
(Customers INNER JOIN Orders
ON Customers.CustomerID = Orders.CustomerID)
ON Employees.EmployeeID = Orders.EmployeeID
```

Note the use of parentheses to specify the order in which the joins should be performed.

The basic SELECT query allows you to see all the data in a table:

```
SELECT * FROM Orders
```

This query returns every bit of data in the Orders table—every column, every row. You've already seen that you can use a field list to limit the number of columns returned:

```
SELECT OrderID, CustomerID, EmployeeID FROM Orders
```

But what if you want to see only some of the rows in a table? That's where the WHERE clause comes into the picture. You can think of a WHERE clause as making a simple yes-or-no decision for each row of data in the original table, deciding whether to include that row in the resultset.

The simplest form of the WHERE clause checks for the exact contents of a field. Here's an example:

```
SELECT * FROM Orders
WHERE ShipCountry = 'Brazil'
```

This query looks at every row in the Orders table and determines whether the ShipCountry field contains the exact value 'Brazil'. If it does, the row is included in the results. If it does not, the row is discarded.

However, WHERE clauses need not be exact. The following is also a valid SQL statement:

```
SELECT * FROM Orders
WHERE Freight > 50
```

In this case, you get all the rows where the amount in the Freight field is greater than 50.

Note, by the way, that in the first of these WHERE clause examples, Brazil appears in single quotation marks but 50 does not. This is simply a matter of syntax: Text and date data need quotation marks, but numeric columns do not.

You can combine multiple tests in a single WHERE clause. Here's an example:

```
SELECT * FROM Orders
WHERE ShipCountry = 'Brazil'
 AND Freight > 50
 AND OrderDate <= '12/31/97'
```

This retrieves all orders that went to Brazil, had more than $50 of freight charges, and were shipped before the end of 1997.

The entire WHERE clause must be a single logical predicate. That is, after all the pieces are evaluated, the result must be a true or false value. Rows for which the WHERE clause evaluates to true arc included in the results; rows for which it evaluates to false are excluded.

You can also use wildcards in a WHERE clause. Consider this simple SELECT statement:

```
SELECT * FROM Customers
WHERE CustomerID = 'BLONP'
```

If you run that query, you find that it returns the record for Blondel Pere et Fils, the customer that is assigned the customer ID BLONP. So far, that's easy. But what if you remember that the customer ID starts with B, but you can't remember exactly what it is? That's when you'd use a wildcard:

```
SELECT * FROM Customers
WHERE CustomerID LIKE 'B%'
```

The % wildcard matches zero or more characters—so the result of this query is to retrieve all the customers whose customer IDs begin with *B*. Note the switch from = to LIKE when you use a wildcard; if you searched for CustomerID = 'B%', you would find only a customer with that exact ID. Now suppose you almost remember the CustomerID, but not quite: You don't know if it is BLOND or BLONP. Try this query:

```
SELECT * FROM Customers
WHERE CustomerID LIKE 'BLON_'
```

The _ wildcard matches precisely one character—so it would match BLONA, BLONB, and so on. If you're sure that it's either of these, you can use this:

```
SELECT * FROM Customers
WHERE CustomerID LIKE 'BLON[DP]'
```

[DP] acts as a character set wildcard. The square brackets tell SQL Server to match any one of the characters listed in the set. You can also use a dash in a character set to indicate a range:

```
SELECT * FROM Customers
WHERE CustomerID LIKE 'BLON[D-P]'
```

This matches BLOND, BLONE, and so on, up to BLONP. You can also invert a character set by using the ^ character. Here's an example:

```
SELECT * FROM Customers
WHERE CustomerID LIKE 'BLON[^A-O]'
```

This matches BLONP, BLONQ, and so on—but not BLONA, BLONB, or anything else that would match on the character set without the ^ character.

SQL is a set-oriented language; by default, the database engine is free to return the set of results in any order it likes. The way to guarantee a sort order is to include an ORDER BY clause in a SQL statement. For example, to see the customers from Venezuela in postal code order, you could use this statement:

```
SELECT * FROM Customers
WHERE Country = 'Venezuela'
ORDER BY PostalCode
```

This example shows the basic ORDER BY clause: a field name to sort by. You can use two keywords to modify this: ASC, for ascending sort (the default), and DESC, for descending sort. Therefore, you could just as easily write the previous SQL statement as follows:

```
SELECT * FROM Customers
WHERE Country = 'Venezuela'
ORDER BY PostalCode ASC
```

And you could get the customers sorted in reverse postal code order by using this statement:

```
SELECT * FROM Customers
WHERE Country = 'Venezuela'
ORDER BY PostalCode DESC
```

You're not limited to sorting by a single field. For example, you might want to see the entire customer list, sorted first by country and then by postal code within country:

```
SELECT * FROM Customers
ORDER BY Country, PostalCode
```

You can specify on a field-by-field basis the order of the sort:

```
SELECT * FROM Customers
ORDER BY Country ASC, PostalCode DESC
```

This would sort by country in ascending order, and then by postal code in descending order within each country.

You can also calculate a sort. For example, you can sort the customers by the length of their company names:

```
SELECT * FROM Customers
ORDER BY Len([CompanyName])
```

Here the square brackets tell the Len() function that it's being passed a column name and to retrieve that column value for each row as the input to the function.

A calculation need not have anything to do with the fields returned by the SELECT statement, as in this example:

```
SELECT * FROM Customers
ORDER BY 2+2
```

This is a perfectly valid SQL statement, although the effect is to put the records in whatever order the database engine decides it wants to use.

So far, all the SELECT statements you've seen in this chapter have returned results where each row corresponds to one row in the underlying tables. However, it's possible (and indeed common) to use SQL to return aggregate, summarized information.

For example, suppose you want to know how many customers you have in each country. Here's a query that gives you the answer:

```
SELECT Count(CustomerID) AS CustCount, Country
FROM Customers
GROUP BY Country
```

You can think of the GROUP BY clause as creating "buckets,"—in this case, one for each country. As the database engine examines each record, it tosses it in the appropriate bucket. After this process is done, the database engine counts the number of records that ended up in each bucket and outputs a row for each one. Figure 6.4 shows the start of the resultset from this query.

FIGURE 6.4

You can use a GROUP BY clause in a query to retrieve a resultset with summarized information.

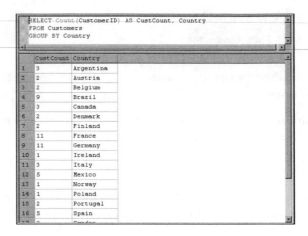

You can use ORDER BY in conjunction with GROUP BY. For example, you could sort by the number of customers in each country:

```
SELECT Count(CustomerID) AS CustCount, Country
FROM Customers
GROUP BY Country
ORDER BY Count(CustomerID) DESC
```

Or you could sort by country name:

```
SELECT Count(CustomerID) AS CustCount, Country
FROM Customers
GROUP BY Country
ORDER BY Country
```

In these SQL statements, Count() is an *aggregate function*—that is, a function that returns a result based on a number of rows. T-SQL supports a number of aggregate functions. Here are some of the most common:

◆ Count()—Returns the number of records.

◆ Sum()—Returns the total value of records.

◆ Avg()—Returns the average value of records.

◆ Min()—Returns the value of the smallest record.

◆ Max()—Returns the value of the largest record.

You can also group on more than one field. Here's an example:

```
SELECT Count(CustomerID) AS CustCount, Region, Country
FROM Customers
GROUP BY Region, Country
```

This statement sets up one bucket for each combination of region and country, and it categorizes the customers by both fields simultaneously.

So far, the GROUP BY statements you've seen have included all the records in the table. For example, consider this query:

```
SELECT ProductID,
Sum(Quantity) AS TotalSales
FROM [Order Details]
GROUP BY ProductID
ORDER BY Sum(Quantity) DESC
```

This query returns a resultset that has one row for each product found in the Order Details table, with the product ID and the total quantity of that product that was ordered. This query uses all the rows in the Order Details table to come up with its totals. There are two ways you can limit this to use only part of the table.

First, you can use a WHERE clause to limit the rows from the original query that will be included in the totals:

```
SELECT ProductID,
Sum(Quantity) AS TotalSales
FROM [Order Details]
WHERE Quantity > 10
GROUP BY ProductID
ORDER BY Sum(Quantity) DESC
```

This has the same effect as the first query, except that it just ignores any row in the Order Details table that has a quantity of 10 or under.

The other way to limit the results is by filtering on the totals with a HAVING clause:

```
SELECT ProductID, Sum(Quantity) AS TotalSales
FROM [Order Details]
GROUP BY ProductID
HAVING Sum(Quantity) > 1000
ORDER BY Sum(Quantity) DESC
```

A HAVING clause filters on the results, rather than on the input. That is, this query sums everything from the Order Details table, and then it shows you only rows where the total is greater than 1,000.

You can also combine the two types of filtering, as in this example:

```
SELECT ProductID, Sum(Quantity) AS TotalSales
FROM [Order Details]
WHERE Quantity > 10
GROUP BY ProductID
HAVING  Sum(Quantity) > 1000
ORDER BY Sum(Quantity) DESC
```

NOTE

Quoting Names This query uses square brackets to quote the name of the "Order Details" table. This is necessary because the table name has a space in it, and without the square brackets, SQL Server would try to interpret it as two names.

This query goes through the source table, sums up all the rows where the quantity is greater than 10, and then keeps only the rows where the total is greater than 1,000.

Note that WHERE and HAVING go in two different places in the SQL statement. The order of clauses is fixed, not optional.

The INSERT Statement

The purpose of the INSERT statement is to add a row or multiple rows to a table by executing a SQL statement. In its simplest form, the INSERT statement lists a target table and a set of values to insert. For example, this query (with the optional INTO keyword) adds a new row to the Order Details table:

```
INSERT INTO [Order Details]
VALUES (10248, 1, 12.00, 5, 0)
```

There are two drawbacks to this simple form of the INSERT statement. First, it's very difficult to tell which field is getting which piece of data; the values are inserted into the table fields in the order in which the fields show up in design view, but you need to remember (in this example) that the quantity is the fourth field. Second, if you use this format, you need to supply a value for every field. This is a problem when you want the default value for a field or when a field can't have data inserted into it (for example, an identity field, whose values are automatically generated by SQL Server). To get around these problems, a second format explicitly lists the fields for the target table:

```
INSERT INTO [Order Details]
  (OrderID, ProductID, UnitPrice, Quantity, Discount)
VALUES (10248, 2, 12.00, 5, 0)
```

Here, the first set of parentheses holds a column list, and the second set holds the values to insert. If a field has a default value, or can be null, or is an identity field, you can leave it out of the field list, as in this example:

```
INSERT INTO Products
  (ProductName, SupplierID, CategoryID)
VALUES ('Turnips', 25, 7)
```

This works even though no value is specified for most of the fields in the Products table. Also, you can rearrange the field list as long as you rearrange the value list to match:

```
INSERT INTO Products
  (SupplierID, ProductName, CategoryID)
VALUES (20, 'Lettuce',  7)
```

The INSERT statement isn't limited to inserting a single record. A second format inserts the results of a SELECT statement into the target table. For example, this query inserts a product from every supplier into the Products table:

```
INSERT INTO Products (SupplierID, ProductName,
CategoryID )
SELECT SupplierID, 'Trout', 8
FROM Suppliers
```

This works by building the results of the SELECT statement and then putting each row returned by the SELECT statement into the target table. Of course, the columns still need to match up properly.

The UPDATE Statement

Another very useful SQL statement is the UPDATE statement. As you can probably guess, the purpose of an UPDATE query is to update data. For example, you could update a field in a record in the Northwind database by using this query:

```
UPDATE Customers
  SET ContactName = 'Maria Anderson'
  WHERE CustomerID = 'ALFKI'
```

In this query, the UPDATE statement introduces an UPDATE query. The SET keyword tells SQL Server what to update. In this case, it's setting a field equal to a literal value. The WHERE clause tells SQL Server which row in the table to update.

You're not limited to updating a single record. If the WHERE clause selects multiple records, they are all updated, as in this example:

```
UPDATE Customers
  SET Country = 'United States'
  WHERE Country = 'USA'
```

You can even update every row in a table, by leaving out the WHERE clause:

```
UPDATE Products
  SET Discontinued = 1
```

This updates every row in the Products table—even those where the Discontinued field already has the value 1.

You can also update more than one field at a time by using an UPDATE query:

```
UPDATE Customers
  SET ContactName = 'Maria Anders', City = 'Berlin'
  WHERE CustomerID = 'ALFKI'
```

And you can update by using the result of an expression:

```
UPDATE Products
  SET UnitPrice = UnitPrice * 1.1
```

If only it were so simple to raise prices in real life!

Finally, you can update based on joined tables:

```
UPDATE Suppliers INNER JOIN Products
  ON Suppliers.SupplierID = Products.SupplierID
  SET Products.Discontinued = 1
  WHERE Suppliers.Country = 'Italy'
```

This has the effect of discontinuing all the products that are imported from Italy.

The DELETE Statement

The DELETE statement removes data from a table. The rule for constructing a DELETE query is simple: Construct a SELECT query to select the records you want to delete, and then change the SELECT keyword to DELETE. Remove any * identifier from the SELECT clause as well. That's it!

To avoid destroying existing data, let's use another query to set the stage for the DELETE statement by using the SELECT INTO statement to create a new table. For example, this statement creates a table named BadCustomers, with all the data from the existing Customers table:

```
SELECT * INTO BadCustomers
FROM Customers
```

Here's a SELECT query for selecting a single row from the new table:

```
SELECT * FROM BadCustomers WHERE CustomerID = 'GODOS'
```

Now change the SELECT * clause to DELETE:

```
DELETE FROM BadCustomers WHERE CustomerID = 'GODOS'
```

If you run this query, the specified row is deleted. There's no need for a WHERE clause if you want to get really extreme:

```
DELETE FROM BadCustomers
```

This statement deletes all the rows from the BadCustomers table.

▶ T-SQL is the Microsoft SQL Server dialect of the ANSI SQL-92 standard query language.

▶ You can execute T-SQL statements from a variety of interfaces, including the Visual Studio .NET IDE, osql, the SQL Query Analyzer, and custom applications.

▶ SELECT statements retrieve data from tables in a database.

▶ INSERT statements add new data to tables in a database.

▶ UPDATE statements modify existing data in tables in a database.

▶ DELETE statements remove data from tables in a database.

Using Stored Procedures

When you use an ad hoc query to interact with SQL Server, the SQL statements in the query are completely transient—that is, they vanish as soon as you close whatever tool you've used to execute the query. In contrast, *stored procedures* are stored permanently on the SQL Server itself. Stored procedures have two main benefits. First, you can use them to save complex SQL statements for future execution so that you don't have to re-create them from scratch. Second, SQL Server compiles stored procedures so that they run faster than ad hoc queries.

In the following sections you'll learn how to create and run stored procedures. You'll also learn about parameters, which make stored procedures flexible, and the @@IDENTITY variable, which can supply useful information any time you use a stored procedure to insert data into a table that has an identity column.

> **EXAM TIP**
>
> **When to Use Stored Procedures**
> In almost every case, stored procedures are preferable to ad hoc queries in production applications. The only time you should consider using ad hoc queries is when you're writing an application that must allow completely free-form querying by the end user. Otherwise, the additional development time required to implement stored procedures will be worth it in the end.

Creating a Stored Procedure

T-SQL includes a CREATE PROCEDURE keyword that you use to create stored procedures. You can run CREATE PROCEDURE statements from any interface that allows you to enter and execute T-SQL.

STEP BY STEP

6.5 Creating a Stored Procedure from the Visual Studio .NET IDE

1. Open Server Explorer in the Visual Studio .NET IDE.

2. Expand the tree under Data Connections to show a SQL Server data connection that points to the Northwind sample database, and then expand the Stored Procedures node of the selected SQL Server data connection.

3. Right-click the Stored Procedures node and select New Stored Procedure. This step opens the Stored Procedure Designer.

4. Replace the boilerplate code in the Stored Procedure Designer with this code:

```
CREATE PROCEDURE procFranceCustomers
AS
    SELECT * FROM Customers
    WHERE Country = 'France'
```

5. Click the Save button to save the stored procedure to the database.

6. Select Database, Run Stored Procedure to run the CREATE PROCEDURE statement. The stored procedure is created in the database.

7. Execute the new procFranceCustomers stored procedure from any tool that allows you to execute SQL Statements. For example, Figure 6.5 shows the results of executing the stored procedure in the custom form that you built in Step by Step 6.4.

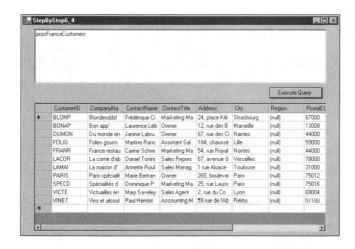

FIGURE 6.5
The results of running a stored procedure are the same as the results of running the T-SQL statements contained in the stored procedure.

You can see from Step by Step 6.5 that there are two separate executing steps in the process. Executing the CREATE PROCEDURE statement (which is itself an ad hoc query) is necessary in order to create the stored procedure. After that has been done, you can execute the stored procedure itself to return results.

Running Stored Procedures from the .NET Framework

Executing a stored procedure from the .NET Framework is very similar to executing an ad hoc query. The difference is that when you execute a stored procedure from the .NET Framework, you supply the name of the stored procedure instead of the actual SQL code as the CommandText property of a SqlCommand object and set the CommandType property to CommandType.StoredProcedure.

STEP BY STEP

6.6 Running a Stored Procedure from Visual C# .NET

1. Add a new form to your Visual C# .NET project.

2. Open Server Explorer.

continues

continued

3. Expand the tree under Data Connections to show a SQL Server data connection that points to the Northwind sample database. Drag and drop the data connection to the form. A sqlConnection1 object is created on the form.

4. Add a DataGrid control named dgResults to the form.

5. Switch to the code view and add the following using directives to make the ADO.NET objects available:

```
using System.Data;
using System.Data.SqlClient;
```

6. Double-click the form and enter this code to execute the stored procedure when you load the form:

```
private void StepByStep6_6_Load(object sender,
    System.EventArgs e)
{
    // Create a SqlCommand object to represent
    // the stored procedure
    SqlCommand cmd = sqlConnection1.CreateCommand();
    cmd.CommandType = CommandType.StoredProcedure;
    cmd.CommandText = "procFranceCustomers";
    // Create a SqlDataAdapter to talk to the database
    SqlDataAdapter da = new SqlDataAdapter();
    da.SelectCommand = cmd;
    // Create a DataSet to hold the results
    DataSet ds = new DataSet();
    // Fill the DataSet
    da.Fill(ds, "Customers");
    // And bind it to the DataGrid
    dgResults.DataSource = ds;
    dgResults.DataMember = "Customers";
}
```

7. Insert the Main() method to launch the form. Set the form as the startup object for the project.

8. Run the project. The code runs, retrieving the results to the DataGrid control, as shown in Figure 6.6.

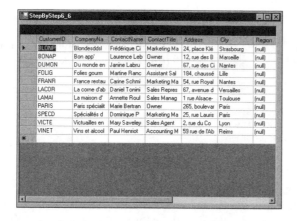

FIGURE 6.6
You set the `CommandType` property of `SqlCommand` to `CommandType.StoredProcedure` to run a stored procedure from the `SqlCommand` object.

Stored procedures are not limited to containing `SELECT` statements. You can place any SQL statement inside a stored procedure. For example, you might use this SQL statement to create a stored procedure to update the Customers table:

```
CREATE PROCEDURE procExpandCountry
AS
UPDATE Customers
 SET Country = 'United States'
 WHERE Country = 'USA'
```

When a stored procedure doesn't return a resultset, you need to use a slightly different code structure to execute it. This is described in Step by Step 6.7. Guided Practice Exercise 1.1 offers additional practice with this technique.

STEP BY STEP

6.7 Running a Stored Procedure That Does Not Return Results

1. Add a new form to your Visual C# .NET project.

2. Open Server Explorer.

3. Expand the tree under Data Connections to show a SQL Server data connection that points to the Northwind sample database. Drag and drop the data connection to the form. A `sqlConnection1` object is created on the form.

continues

continued

4. Using a tool such as the SQL Query Analyzer or the Visual Studio .NET IDE, create this stored procedure:

```
CREATE PROCEDURE procExpandCountry
AS
UPDATE Customers
 SET Country = 'United States'
 WHERE Country = 'USA'
```

5. Place a `Button` control on the form and name it `btnExecute`.

6. Switch to the code view and add the following using directives to make the ADO.NET objects available:

```
using System.Data;
using System.Data.SqlClient;
```

7. Double-click the `Button` control and enter this code to execute the stored procedure when the Execute button is clicked:

```
private void btnExecute_Click(object sender,
    System.EventArgs e)
{
    // Create a SqlCommand object to represent
    // the stored procedure
    SqlCommand cmd = sqlConnection1.CreateCommand();
    cmd.CommandType = CommandType.StoredProcedure;
    cmd.CommandText = "procExpandCountry";
    // Open the connection and
    // execute the stored procedure
    sqlConnection1.Open();
    cmd.ExecuteNonQuery();
    // Close the connection
    sqlConnection1.Close();
    MessageBox.Show("SQL statement was executed.");
}
```

8. Insert the `Main()` method to launch the form. Set the form as the startup object for the project.

9. Run the project and click the Execute Stored Procedure button. The stored procedure executes, and you are informed of that fact via a message box.

EXAM TIP

Opening and Closing Connections
When you call the methods of the `SqlDataAdapter` object, the .NET Framework automatically opens and closes the associated `SqlConnection` object as necessary. For any other operation (such as using the `SqlCommand.ExecuteNonQuery()` method) you must explicitly call the `SqlConnection.Open()` and `SqlConnection.Close()` methods in your code.

You can use the `ExecuteNonQuery()` method of the `SqlCommand` object to execute any ad hoc query or stored procedure that doesn't return any results.

Using Parameters in Stored Procedures

The examples that you've seen so far in this chapter don't begin to tap the real power of stored procedures. SQL Server supports *parameterized stored procedures*, which allow you to pass information to stored procedures at runtime; you can think of them as the T-SQL analog of Visual C# .NET methods. For example, this SQL statement defines a stored procedure that returns the total sales for a particular customer, with the customer ID specified at runtime:

```
CREATE PROC procCustomerSales
  @CustomerID char(5),
  @TotalSales money OUTPUT
AS
  SELECT @TotalSales = SUM(Quantity * UnitPrice)
  FROM ((Customers INNER JOIN Orders
  ON Customers.CustomerID = Orders.CustomerID)
  INNER JOIN [Order Details]
  ON Orders.OrderID = [Order Details].OrderID)
  WHERE Customers.CustomerID = @CustomerID
```

In this SQL statement, both @CustomerID and @TotalSales are variables (called *parameters* in T-SQL). To use the stored procedure, you must supply a value for the @CustomerID parameter. The @TotalSales parameter is marked as an OUTPUT parameter; it returns a value from the stored procedure to the calling code.

In the .NET Framework, the SqlCommand object has a collection of parameters that allow you to manage parameterized stored procedures.

STEP BY STEP

6.8 Running a Parameterized Stored Procedure

1. Add a new form to your Visual C# .NET project.

2. Open Server Explorer.

3. Expand the tree under Data Connections to show a SQL Server data connection that points to the Northwind sample database. Drag and drop the data connection to the form. A sqlConnection1 object is created on the form.

continues

continued

FIGURE 6.7
You can accept the parameters value at run-time and then execute a parameterized stored procedure.

4. Using a tool such as the SQL Query Analyzer or the Visual Studio .NET IDE, create a stored procedure with this code:

```
CREATE PROC procCustomerSales
  @CustomerID char(5),
  @TotalSales money OUTPUT
AS
  SELECT @TotalSales = SUM(Quantity * UnitPrice)
  FROM ((Customers INNER JOIN Orders
  ON Customers.CustomerID = Orders.CustomerID)
  INNER JOIN [Order Details]
  ON Orders.OrderID = [Order Details].OrderID)
  WHERE Customers.CustomerID = @CustomerID
```

5. Place two `Label` controls, two `TextBox` controls (`txtCustomerID` and `txtTotalSales`), and a `Button` control (`btnGetTotalSales`) on the form, as shown in Figure 6.7.

6. Switch to the code view and add the following using directives to make the ADO.NET objects available:

```
using System.Data;
using System.Data.SqlClient;
using System.Data.SqlTypes;
```

7. Double-click the `Button` control and enter this code to execute the stored procedure when the button is clicked:

```
private void btnGetTotalSales_Click(object sender,
    System.EventArgs e)
{
    // Create a SqlCommand to represent
    // the stored procedure
    SqlCommand cmd = sqlConnection1.CreateCommand();
    cmd.CommandType = CommandType.StoredProcedure;
    cmd.CommandText = "procCustomerSales";
    // Add the input parameter and set its value
    cmd.Parameters.Add(new SqlParameter("@CustomerID",
        SqlDbType.Text, 5));
    cmd.Parameters["@CustomerID"].Value =
        txtCustomerID.Text;
    // Add the output parameter and set its direction
    cmd.Parameters.Add(new SqlParameter("@TotalSales",
        SqlDbType.Money));
    cmd.Parameters["@TotalSales"].Direction =
        ParameterDirection.Output;
    // Execute the stored procedure
    // Display the formatted results
    sqlConnection1.Open();
    cmd.ExecuteNonQuery();
```

```
    txtTotalSales.Text = String.Format("{0:c}",
        cmd.Parameters["@TotalSales"].Value);
    sqlConnection1.Close();
}
```

8. Insert the `Main()` method to launch this form and set the form as the startup object for the project.

9. Run the project and enter a `CustomerID` from the `Customers` table in the first text box. Click the button. The form executes the stored procedure and returns the total sales for this customer in the second text box.

In ADO.NET parameters are represented by `SqlParameter` objects. The code in Step by Step 6.8 uses two different forms of the constructor for `SqlParameter` object. The first takes the parameter name, the parameter data type, and the size of the parameter; the second omits the parameter size (because the money type has a fixed size). The code works by setting the `Value` property of the `@CustomerID` parameter, executing the `SqlCommand` object, and then retrieving the `Value` property of the `@TotalSales` parameter.

Using the `@@IDENTITY` Variable

A SQL Server table can have a single identity column. An *identity column* is a column whose value is assigned by SQL Server itself whenever you add a new row to the table. The purpose of the identity column is to guarantee that each row in the table has a unique primary key.

If you're working with a table that contains an identity column, you are likely to want to add a new row to the table and then immediately retrieve the value of the identity column for the new row. SQL Server provides a variable named `@@IDENTITY` for just this purpose. The `@@IDENTITY` variable returns the most recently assigned identity column value.

Step by Step 6.9 shows how you can use a stored procedure to insert a new row in a table and return the value of the identity column so that your code can continue to work with the new row.

STEP BY STEP

6.9 Retrieving a New Identity Value

1. Add a new form to your Visual C# .NET project.

2. Open Server Explorer.

3. Expand the tree under Data Connections to show a SQL Server data connection that points to the Northwind sample database. Drag and drop the data connection to the form. A sqlConnection1 object is created on the form.

4. Using a tool such as the SQL Query Analyzer or the Visual Studio .NET IDE, create this stored procedure:

```
CREATE PROC procInsertShipper
  @CompanyName nvarchar(40),
  @ShipperID int OUTPUT
AS
  INSERT INTO Shippers (CompanyName)
    VALUES (@CompanyName)
  SELECT @ShipperID = @@IDENTITY
```

This stored procedure contains two SQL statements. The first inserts a row into the Shippers table, and the second retrieves the value of the identity column for the new row.

5. Place two Label controls, two TextBox controls (txtCompanyName and txtShipperID), and a Button control (btnAddShipper) on the form.

6. Switch to the code view and add the following using directives to make the ADO.NET objects available:

```
using System.Data;
using System.Data.SqlClient;
using System.Data.SqlTypes;
```

7. Double-click the Button control and enter this code to execute the stored procedure when the button is clicked:

```
private void btnAddShipper_Click(object sender,
    System.EventArgs e)
{
    // Create a SqlCommand to represent
    // the stored procedure
    SqlCommand cmd = sqlConnection1.CreateCommand();
    cmd.CommandType = CommandType.StoredProcedure;
    cmd.CommandText = "procInsertShipper";
```

```
    // Add the input parameter and set its value
    cmd.Parameters.Add(new SqlParameter("@CompanyName",
        SqlDbType.VarChar, 40));
    cmd.Parameters["@CompanyName"].Value =
        txtCompanyName.Text;
    // Add the output parameter and set its direction
    cmd.Parameters.Add(new SqlParameter("@ShipperID",
        SqlDbType.Int));
    cmd.Parameters["@ShipperID"].Direction =
        ParameterDirection.Output;
    // Execute the stored procedure
    // and display the result
    sqlConnection1.Open();
    cmd.ExecuteNonQuery();
    txtShipperID.Text =
        cmd.Parameters["@ShipperID"].Value.ToString();
    sqlConnection1.Close();
}
```

8. Insert the Main() method to launch the form. Set the form as the startup object for the project.

9. Run the project and enter a company name for the new shipper in the first text box. Click the button. The form executes the stored procedure and returns the identity value assigned to the new shipper in the second text box.

Step by Step 6.9 uses the same code pattern as Step by Step 6.8. The variable names and control names are different, but the two Step by Step examples show a common pattern for using stored procedures in code:

1. Create a SqlCommand object to represent the stored procedure.

2. Create SqlParameter objects to represent the parameters of the stored procedure.

3. Supply values for any input parameters.

4. Open the SqlConnection object for this stored procedure.

5. Execute the stored procedure by using the ExecuteNonQuery() method of the SqlCommand object.

6. Retrieve values of any output parameters.

7. Close the SqlConnection object.

GUIDED PRACTICE
EXERCISE 6.1

In this exercise, you design a form to enter new products into the Northwind database. Table 6.1 shows the columns that the Products table contains.

TABLE 6.1
THE NORTHWIND PRODUCTS TABLE'S COLUMNS

Column Name	Data Type	Is the Column Nullable?	Is This an Identity Column?
ProductID	int	No	Yes
ProductName	nvarchar(40)	No	No
SupplierID	int	Yes	No
CategoryID	int	Yes	No
QuantityPerUnit	nvarchar(20)	Yes	No
UnitPrice	money	Yes	No
UnitsInStock	smallint	Yes	No
UnitsOnOrder	smallint	Yes	No
ReorderLevel	smallint	Yes	No
Discontinued	bit	No	No

The task you need to perform is to allow the user to enter at least the product name and category ID, add the product to the table, and see the product ID that is assigned to the new row in the table. You may optionally allow the user to input any other data that you like.

Valid values for the CategoryID column can be determined by retrieving the CategoryID values from the Categories table, which also contains a CategoryName column. You should use a ComboBox control to display valid CategoryID field values.

How would you design such a form?

You should try working through this problem on your own first. If you get stuck, or if you'd like to see one possible solution, follow these steps:

1. Add a new form to your Visual C# .NET project.

2. Open Server Explorer.

3. Expand the tree under Data Connections to show a SQL Server data connection that points to the Northwind sample database. Drag and drop the data connection to the form. A `sqlConnection1` object is created on the form.

4. Add three `Label` controls, a `ComboBox` control (`cboCategoryID`), a `Button` control (`btnAddProduct`), and two `TextBox` controls (`txtProductName` and `txtProductID`) to the form. Figure 6.8 shows a possible design for the form.

5. Using a tool such as the SQL Query Analyzer or the Visual Studio .NET IDE, create this stored procedure:

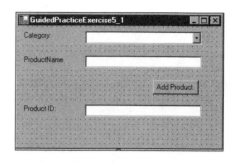

FIGURE 6.8
This form can query product information.

```
CREATE PROC procInsertProduct
  @ProductName nvarchar(40),
  @CategoryID int,
  @ProductID int OUTPUT
AS
  INSERT INTO Products (ProductName, CategoryID)
    VALUES (@ProductName, @CategoryID)
  SELECT @ProductID = @@IDENTITY
```

6. Switch to the code view and add the following `using` directives to make the ADO.NET objects available:

```
using System.Data;
using System.Data.SqlClient;
using System.Data.SqlTypes;
```

7. Double-click the form and enter the following code to fill the list in the `ComboBox` control in the form's `Load` event handler:

```
private void GuidedPracticeExercise6_1_Load(
object sender,
    System.EventArgs e)
{
    // Retrieve data for the combo box
    SqlCommand cmdCategories =
        sqlConnection1.CreateCommand();
    cmdCategories.CommandType = CommandType.Text;
    cmdCategories.CommandText =
    " SELECT CategoryID,  CategoryName" +
    " FROM Categories ORDER BY CategoryName";
```

continues

continued

```
DataSet ds = new DataSet();
SqlDataAdapter da = new SqlDataAdapter();
da.SelectCommand = cmdCategories;
da.Fill(ds, "Categories");
cboCategoryID.DataSource = ds.Tables["Categories"];
cboCategoryID.DisplayMember = "CategoryName";
cboCategoryID.ValueMember = "CategoryID";
}
```

8. Attach the `Click` event handler to the `Button` control. Enter this code to execute the stored procedure when the button is clicked:

```
private void btnAddProduct_Click(object sender,
    System.EventArgs e)
{
    // Create a SqlCommand to
    // represent the stored procedure
    SqlCommand cmd = sqlConnection1.CreateCommand();
    cmd.CommandType = CommandType.StoredProcedure;
    cmd.CommandText = "procInsertProduct";
    // Add the input parameters and set their values
    cmd.Parameters.Add(new SqlParameter(
        "@ProductName", SqlDbType.VarChar, 40));
    cmd.Parameters["@ProductName"].Value =
        txtProductName.Text;
    cmd.Parameters.Add(new SqlParameter("@CategoryID",
        SqlDbType.Int));
    cmd.Parameters["@CategoryID"].Value =
        cboCategoryID.SelectedValue;
    // Add the output parameter and set its direction
    cmd.Parameters.Add(new SqlParameter("@ProductID",
        SqlDbType.Int));
    cmd.Parameters["@ProductID"].Direction =
        ParameterDirection.Output;
    // Execute the stored procedure
    // and display the result
    sqlConnection1.Open();
    cmd.ExecuteNonQuery();
    txtProductID.Text =
        cmd.Parameters["@ProductID"].Value.ToString();
    sqlConnection1.Close();
}
```

9. Insert the `Main()` method to launch this form and set the form as the startup object for the project.

10. Run the project. Select a category for the new product from the combo box. Enter a name for the new product in the first text box. Click the button. The form executes the stored procedure and returns the identity value assigned to the new shipper in the second text box.

If you have difficulty following this exercise, review the sections "Running Queries," "The SELECT Statement," "The INSERT Statement," and "Using Stored Procedures" from this chapter as well as the section "Complex Data Binding" in Chapter 5. The text and examples should help you relearn this material and help you understand what happens in this exercise. After doing that review, try this exercise again.

REVIEW BREAK

▶ Stored procedures provide a way to keep compiled SQL statements on the database server.

▶ The ADO.NET SqlCommand object lets you execute stored procedures.

▶ Stored procedures can have both input and output parameters. Input parameters are variables that are used by the stored procedure. Output parameters let the stored procedure return results to the caller.

▶ The @@IDENTITY variable returns the most recent identity value from the connection.

ACCESSING AND MANIPULATING DATA

Consuming and manipulating data.

- **Access and manipulate data from a data store. Data stores include relational databases, XML documents, and flat files. Methods include XML techniques and ADO.NET.**

This test objective covers an immense amount of functionality within the .NET Framework. You'll need to know how to work with three types of data:

◆ File-based data

◆ Relational database data

◆ XML data

The .NET Framework includes namespaces and classes that are optimized for each of these types of data.

I cover the following major topics in this section:

◆ Working with disk files

◆ The ADO.NET object model

◆ Using DataSet objects

◆ Using XML data

Working with Disk Files

The oldest form of data that you're likely to work with in the .NET Framework is the simple disk file. This is sometimes called a *flat file*, to distinguish it from more structured forms of storage such as relational databases and XML files.

The .NET Framework includes complete support for working with flat files. In the following sections I'll introduce the concepts of streams and backing stores, and demonstrate the classes from the System.IO namespace that you can use to manipulate the data stored in disk files.

Using the File Class

The File class is used for manipulating files. The File class contains static methods that allow you to create, open, move, copy, and delete files. It also contains a set of methods that provide access to the information about the files. The File class performs security checks on all its methods.

The File class also helps in creating FileStream objects, which is discussed in the next section.

Step by Step 6.10 shows you how to create a backup copy of a file by using the methods of the File class.

STEP BY STEP

6.10 Using the `File` Class to Make a Backup Copy of a File

1. Add a new form to your Visual C# .NET project.

2. Place two `Label` controls, a `Button` control (`btnBrowse`), and two `TextBox` controls (`txtFileName` and `txtBackupName`) on the form. Arrange the controls as shown in Figure 6.9.

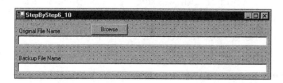

FIGURE 6.9
This form lets you create a backup copy of a file.

3. Switch to the code view and add the following `using` directive:

```
using System.IO;
```

4. Double-click the `Button` control and enter this code to handle the `Click` event of the `Button` control:

```csharp
private void btnBrowse_Click(object sender,
    System.EventArgs e)
{
    // Browse for a file to back up
    OpenFileDialog dlgOpen = new OpenFileDialog();
    dlgOpen.Title = "Select a File to back up";
    dlgOpen.Filter = "All Files(*.*)|*.*";
    if(dlgOpen.ShowDialog() == DialogResult.OK)
    {
        // Display the original and backup file names
        txtFileName.Text = dlgOpen.FileName;
        txtBackupName.Text = dlgOpen.FileName + ".bak";
        if(File.Exists(txtBackupName.Text))
        {
            // Back up file already exists
            MessageBox.Show(
              "Back up file already exists",
              "Error");
        }
        else
        {
```

continues

continued

```
// Create a backup
File.Copy(txtFileName.Text,
    txtBackupName.Text);
        }
    }
}
```

5. Insert the `Main()` method to launch the form. Set the form as the startup object for the project.

6. Run the project and click the button. The File Open dialog box opens. Select a file in the dialog box and click OK. The name of the selected file appears in the first text box, and the name of the backup file appears in the second text box. If you check your hard drive, you'll find a copy of the selected file with the extension `.bak`.

In Step by Step 6.10, when you click the Browse button, the form creates a new `OpenFileDialog` object and allows the user to select a file for which the backup needs to be created.

The `Exists()` method of the `File` class verifies whether a file with the name of the backup file exists. If the backup file already exists, an error message is displayed to the user. Otherwise, the `Copy()` method is called to create a backup copy of the file.

The .NET Framework also provides the `FileInfo` class for working with files. You can do almost everything with the `FileInfo` class that you can do with the `File` class, but unlike the `File` class, the `FileInfo` class does not contain any static methods, and therefore you need to create an instance of the `FileInfo` class before you use it.

The `File` class performs security checks whenever a static method is called, and this certainly involves additional overhead. However, in the case of the `FileInfo` class, these security checks are performed once, when the object is created, and are not repeated with each method call. For this reason, I suggest that you use the `FileInfo` class instead of the `File` class if you are going to reuse an object several times in a program.

NOTE

Directory and DirectoryInfo Along with the `File` and `FileInfo` classes, the .NET Framework provides `Directory` and `DirectoryInfo` classes that allow you to access directories. The `Directory` class provides static methods, and the `DirectoryInfo` class provides instance methods.

Using Streams and Backing Stores

File-based input and output in the .NET Framework revolve around the twin concepts of streams and backing stores. A *stream* represents a flow of raw data. A *backing* store represents some place you can put data. A backing store might be a file—but it might also be a network connection, an Internet address, or even a section of memory. The .NET Framework contains classes that let you work with data from any of these backing stores.

You find classes for working with streams and backing stores in the `System.IO` namespace. In this section, you'll learn how to use five of these classes, which apply directly to working with disk files. The `FileStream` class gives you a stream-oriented view of a disk file; it treats files as raw, typeless streams of bytes. For cases where you know more about the structure of the file, you may find the `BinaryReader` and `BinaryWriter`, or `StreamReader` and `StreamWriter` classes to be more convenient to use.

Using the `FileStream` Class

The `FileStream` class treats a file as a stream of bytes. Step by Step 6.11 shows you how to make a backup copy of a file by using the `FileStream` class.

STEP BY STEP

6.11 Using `FileStream` Objects to Make a Backup Copy of a File

1. Add a new form to your Visual C# .NET project.

2. Place two `Label` controls, a `Button` control (`btnBrowse`), and two `TextBox` controls (`txtFileName` and `txtBackupName`) on the form. Arrange the controls as shown in Figure 6.9.

3. Switch to the code view and add the following `using` directive:

```
using System.IO;
```

continues

continued

4. Double-click the `Button` control and enter this code to handle the `Click` event of the `Button` control:

```
private void btnBrowse_Click(object sender,
    System.EventArgs e)
{
    // Browse for a file to back up
    OpenFileDialog dlgOpen = new OpenFileDialog();
    dlgOpen.Title = "Select a File to back up";
    dlgOpen.Filter = "All Files(*.*)|*.*";
    if(dlgOpen.ShowDialog() == DialogResult.OK)
    {
        // Display the original and backup file names
        txtFileName.Text = dlgOpen.FileName;
        txtBackupName.Text = dlgOpen.FileName + ".bak";
        // Open the file for reading as a stream
        FileStream fsIn =
            File.OpenRead(dlgOpen.FileName);
        // Open the file for writing as a stream
        FileStream fsOut =
            File.OpenWrite(dlgOpen.FileName
         + ".bak");
        // Copy all data from in to out, byte-by-byte
        Int32 b;
        while((b = fsIn.ReadByte()) > -1)
        {
            fsOut.WriteByte((Byte) b);
        }
        // Clean up
        fsOut.Flush();
        fsOut.Close();
        fsIn.Close();
    }
}
```

5. Insert the `Main()` method to launch this form and set the form as the startup object for the project.

6. Run the project and click the button. The File Open dialog box opens. Select a file in the dialog box and click OK. The name of the selected file appears in the first text box, and the name of the backup file appears in the second text box. If you check your hard drive, you find a copy of the selected file with the extension `.bak`.

> **WARNING**
>
> **Data Loss Danger!**   Be very careful when testing the program in Step by Step 6.11. It doesn't check for the existence of the backup file, so it overwrites any existing file without warning.

The code in Step by Step 6.11 creates two `FileStream` objects, one each for the input and output files, by using static methods of the `File` object (which represents a disk file). It then reads bytes from the input file and writes those bytes to the output file.

Note the difference between the ReadByte() method, which returns an int, and the WriteByte() method, which writes a byte. The ReadByte() method uses the special value -1 (which can't be stored in a byte) to indicate that it's reached the end of the data.

When the code is done writing, it calls the Flush() method of the output stream. This is necessary to be sure that all the data has actually been written to the disk. Then the code closes both the input and output streams.

Table 6.2 shows some of the methods and properties of the FileStream object that you should be familiar with.

TABLE 6.2

IMPORTANT MEMBERS OF THE FileStream CLASS

Member	Type	Description
CanRead	Property	Indicates whether you can read from this FileStream object
CanSeek	Property	Indicates whether you can seek to a particular location in this FileStream object
CanWrite	Property	Indicates whether you can write to this FileStream object
Close()	Method	Closes the FileStream object and releases the associated resources
Flush()	Method	Writes any buffered data to the backing store
Length	Property	Specifies the length of the FileStream object, in bytes
Position	Property	Gets the position within the FileStream object
Read()	Method	Reads a sequence of bytes
ReadByte()	Method	Reads a single byte
Seek()	Method	Sets the FileStream object to a specified position
Write()	Method	Writes a sequence of bytes
WriteByte()	Method	Writes a single byte

Although the code in Step by Step 6.11 performs the desired task, it's not very efficient. Using a buffer to hold data, as shown in Step by Step 6.12, allows the operating system to optimize file activity for increased speed.

STEP BY STEP

6.12 Using `FileStream` Objects with a Buffer

1. Add a new form to your Visual C# .NET project.

2. Place two `Label` controls, a `Button` control (`btnBrowse`), and two `TextBox` controls (`txtFileName` and `txtBackupName`) on the form.

3. Switch to the code view and add the following `using` directive:

```
using System.IO;
```

4. Double-click the `Button` control and enter this code to handle the `Click` event of the `Button` control:

```csharp
private void btnBrowse_Click(object sender,
    System.EventArgs e)
{
    // Browse for a file to back up
    OpenFileDialog dlgOpen = new OpenFileDialog();
    dlgOpen.Title = "Select a File to back up";
    dlgOpen.Filter = "All Files(*.*)|*.*";
    if (dlgOpen.ShowDialog() == DialogResult.OK)
    {
        // Display the original and backup file names
        txtFileName.Text = dlgOpen.FileName;
        txtBackupName.Text = dlgOpen.FileName + ".bak";
        // Open the file for reading as a stream
        FileStream fsIn =
            File.OpenRead(dlgOpen.FileName);
        // Open the file for writing as a stream
        FileStream fsOut =
            File.OpenWrite(dlgOpen.FileName + ".bak");
        // Copy all data from in to out,
        // using a 4K buffer
        Byte[] buf = new Byte[4096];
        int intBytesRead;
        while((intBytesRead = fsIn.Read(buf, 0, 4096))
            > 0)
        {
            fsOut.Write(buf, 0, intBytesRead);
        }
        // Clean up
        fsOut.Flush();
        fsOut.Close();
        fsIn.Close();
    }
}
```

5. Insert the `Main()` method to launch the form. Set the form as the startup object for the project.

6. Run the project and click the button. The File Open dialog box opens. Select a file in the dialog box and click OK. The name of the selected file appears in the first text box, and the name of the backup file appears in the second text box. If you check your hard drive, you find a copy of the selected file with the extension `.bak`. If you experiment with large files, you should be able to see a speed difference between this version of the code and the code from Step by Step 6.11.

The `FileStream.Read()` method takes three parameters:

◆ A buffer to hold the data being read

◆ An offset in the buffer where newly read bytes should be placed

◆ The maximum number of bytes to read

The `Read()` method returns the number of bytes that were actually read. Similarly, the `Write()` method takes three parameters:

◆ A buffer to hold the data being written

◆ An offset in the buffer where the writing of bytes should begin

◆ The number of bytes to write

Using the `StreamReader` and `StreamWriter` Classes

The `FileStream` class is your best option when you don't care (or don't know) about the internal structure of the files with which you're working. But in many cases, you have additional knowledge that lets you use other objects. Text files, for example, are often organized as lines of text separated by end-of-line characters, and the `StreamReader` and `StreamWriter` classes provide you with tools for manipulating such files.

STEP BY STEP

6.13 Using StreamWriter and StreamReader Objects

1. Add a new form to your Visual C# .NET project.

2. Place a Button control (btnCreateFile) and a ListBox control (lbLines) on the form.

3. Switch to the code view and add the following using directive:

```
using System.IO;
```

4. Double-click the Button control and enter this code to handle the Click event of the Button control:

```
private void btnCreateFile_Click(object sender,
    System.EventArgs e)
{
    // Create a new file to work with
    FileStream fsOut =
        File.Create(@"c:\temp\test.txt");
    // Create a StreamWriter to handle writing
    StreamWriter sw = new StreamWriter(fsOut);
    // And write some data
    sw.WriteLine("Quotes by Gandhi");
    sw.WriteLine("Become the change you " +
        "seek in the world.");
    sw.WriteLine("To believe in something, " +
        "and not to live it is dishonest.");
    sw.WriteLine("Live simply that other may " +
        "simply live.");
    sw.WriteLine(
        "Self-respect knows no considerations.");
    sw.Flush();
    sw.Close();
    fsOut.Close();

    // Now open the file for reading
    FileStream fsIn = File.OpenRead(@"c:\temp\test.txt");
    // Create a StreamReader to handle reading
    StreamReader sr = new StreamReader(fsIn);
    // And read the data
    while (sr.Peek() > -1)
    {
        lbLines.Items.Add(sr.ReadLine());
    }
    sr.Close();
    fsIn.Close();
}
```

5. Insert the `Main()` method to launch the form. Set the form as the startup object for the project.

6. Run the project and click the button. The `c:\temp\ test.txt` file is created on your hard drive, and the list box shows the contents of the file (see Figure 6.10).

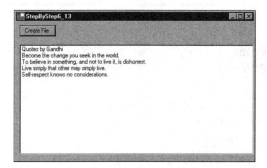

FIGURE 6.10
You can write and read lines of information from a text file by using the `StreamWriter` and `StreamReader` classes.

You can think of the `StreamWriter` and `StreamReader` classes as forming an additional layer of functionality on top of the `FileStream` class. The `FileStream` object handles opening a particular disk file, and then it serves as a parameter to the constructor of the `StreamWriter` or `StreamReader` object. The code in Step by Step 6.13 first opens a `StreamWriter` object and calls its `WriteLine()` method multiple times to write lines of text to the file. It then creates a `StreamReader` object that uses the same text file. The code makes use of the `Peek()` method of the `StreamReader` object to watch for the end of the file. This method returns the next character in the file without actually reading it, or it returns `-1` if there is no more data to be read. As long as there's data to read, the `ReadLine()` method of the `StreamReader` object can read it to place it in the list box.

In addition to the methods that you see in Step by Step 6.13, the `StreamWriter` object has a `Write()` method, which writes output without adding a newline character. The `StreamReader` class implements `Read()` and `ReadToEnd()` methods, which offer additional functionality for reading data. The `Read()` method reads a specified number of characters. The `ReadToEnd()` method reads all the remaining characters to the end of the stream.

Using the `BinaryReader` and `BinaryWriter` Classes

For files with known internal structures, the `BinaryReader` and `BinaryWriter` classes offer streaming functionality that's oriented toward particular data types.

STEP BY STEP

6.14 Using `BinaryWriter` and `BinaryReader` Objects

1. Add a new form to your Visual C# .NET project.

2. Place a `Button` control (`btnCreateFile`) and a `ListBox` control (`lbData`) on the form.

3. Switch to the code view and add the following using directive:

```
using System.IO;
```

4. Double-click the `Button` control and enter this code to handle the `Click` event of the `Button` control:

```
private void btnCreateFile_Click(object sender,
    System.EventArgs e)
{
    // Create a new file to work with
    FileStream fsOut = File.Create(@"c:\temp\test.dat");
    // Create a BinaryWriter to handle writing
    BinaryWriter bw = new BinaryWriter(fsOut);
    // And write some data
    Int32 intData1 = 7;
    Decimal dblData2 = 3.14159M;
    String strData3 = "Pi in the Sky";
    bw.Write(intData1);
    bw.Write(dblData2);
    bw.Write(strData3);
    bw.Flush();
    bw.Close();
    fsOut.Close();

    // Now open the file for reading
    FileStream fsIn = File.OpenRead(@"c:\temp\test.dat");
    // Create a BinaryReader to handle reading
    BinaryReader br = new BinaryReader(fsIn);
    // And read the data
    lbData.Items.Add("Int32: " + br.ReadInt32());
```

```
    lbData.Items.Add("Decimal: " + br.ReadDecimal());
    lbData.Items.Add("String: " + br.ReadString());
    br.Close();
    fsIn.Close();
}
```

5. Insert the `Main()` method to launch the form. Set the form as the startup object for the project.

6. Run the project and click the button. The `c:\temp\test.dat` file is created on your hard drive, and the list box shows the contents of the file (see Figure 6.11).

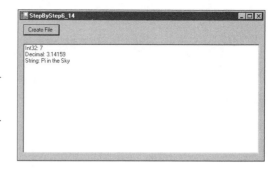

FIGURE 6.11

You can use the `BinaryWriter` and `BinaryReader` classes to write and read binary files.

Like the `StreamWriter` and the `StreamReader` classes, the `BinaryWriter` and `BinaryReader` classes provide a layer on top of the basic `FileStream` class. `BinaryWriter` and `BinaryReader` are oriented toward writing and reading particular types of data. The `BinaryWriter.Write()` method has overloads for many data types, so it can handle writing almost anything to a file. The `BinaryReader` class has methods for reading all those different data types; the code in Step by Step 6.14 shows the `ReadInt32()`, `ReadDecimal()`, and `ReadString()` methods in action.

> **WARNING**
>
> **Don't Mix Up Data Types** You must read exactly the same data types with the `BinaryReader` object that you originally wrote with the `BinaryWriter` object. Otherwise, you get garbage in your read data.

GUIDED PRACTICE EXERCISE 6.2

The goal of this exercise is to write a set of decimal numbers to two different file formats: a text file with each number on a separate line and a binary file. After you write the files, you can see which file format is more efficient for this particular data. The following are the values to write, in this order:

▶ 4.981273

▶ 45.92847

▶ 1.099

▶ 0.47162

▶ 2.44801

▶ 17.2323

continues

continued

▶ 490.00901

▶ 12.1234

▶ 23.022

▶ 1.034782

How would you create such a form?

You should try working through this problem on your own first. If you get stuck, or if you'd like to see one possible solution, follow these steps:

1. Add a new form to your Visual C# .NET project.

2. Place a Button control (btnCreateFiles) and a ListBox control (lbResults) on the form.

3. Switch to the code view and add the following using directive:

   ```
   using System.IO;
   ```

4. Double-click the Button control and enter this code to handle the Click event of the Button control:

   ```csharp
   private void btnCreateFiles_Click(object sender,
       System.EventArgs e)
   {
       // Create a new text file to work with
       FileStream fsOut =
         File.Create(@"c:\temp\TextTest.txt");
       // Create a StreamWriter to handle writing
       StreamWriter sw = new StreamWriter(fsOut);
       // And write some data
       sw.WriteLine("4.981273");
       sw.WriteLine("45.92847");
       sw.WriteLine("1.099");
       sw.WriteLine("0.47162");
       sw.WriteLine("2.44801");
       sw.WriteLine("17.2323");
       sw.WriteLine("490.00901");
       sw.WriteLine("12.1234");
       sw.WriteLine("23.022");
       sw.WriteLine("1.034782");
       sw.Flush();
       lbResults.Items.Add("Text file length = " +
           fsOut.Length);
       sw.Close();
   ```

```
      // Create a new binary file to work with
      fsOut = File.Create(@"c:\temp\BinaryTest.dat");
      // Create a BinaryWriter to handle writing
      BinaryWriter bw = new BinaryWriter(fsOut);
      // And write some data
      bw.Write(4.981273);
      bw.Write(45.92847);
      bw.Write(1.099);
      bw.Write(0.47162);
      bw.Write(2.44801);
      bw.Write(17.2323);
      bw.Write(490.00901);
      bw.Write(12.1234);
      bw.Write(23.022);
      bw.Write(1.034782);
      bw.Flush();
      lbResults.Items.Add("Binary file length = " +
         fsOut.Length);
      bw.Close();
      fsOut.Close();
   }
```

5. Insert the `Main()` method to launch the form. Set the form as the startup object for the project.

6. Run the project and click the button. The two files are created on your hard drive, and the list box control shows the lengths of the files, as shown in Figure 6.12.

If you have difficulty following this exercise, review the sections "Using the `StreamReader` and `StreamWriter` Classes" and "Using the `BinaryReader` and `BinaryWriter` Classes," earlier in this chapter. The text and examples should help you relearn this material and help you understand what happens in this exercise. After doing that review, try this exercise again.

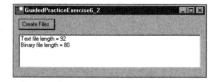

FIGURE 6.12
The relative lengths of the same data in a text file and in a binary file vary; the binary files are more compact.

R E V I E W   B R E A K

▶ The `File` class contains static methods that allow you to create, open, move, copy, and delete files.

▶ To retrieve data from disk files as raw bytes, you use the `FileStream` object.

continues

continued

▶ To retrieve data from disk files in a line-oriented fashion, you use the `StreamReader` object.

▶ To retrieve data from disk files that are formatted for binary storage, you use the `BinaryReader` object.

The ADO.NET Object Model

ADO.NET is the overall name for the set of classes (spread across a number of namespaces, including `System.Data`, `System.Data.Common`, `System.Data.SqlTypes`, `System.Data.SqlClient`, and `System.Data.OleDb`) that the .NET Framework provides for working with data in relational databases.

The ADO.NET object model is broken up into two distinct sets of objects: data provider objects and `DataSet` objects. There are two sets of objects because the .NET Framework separates the task of using data from the task of storing data. A `DataSet` object provides a memory-resident, disconnected set of objects that you can load with data. A data provider object handles the task of working directly with data sources. One of the provider objects, the `DataAdapter` object, serves as a conduit between the two sets of objects. By using a `DataAdapter` object, you can load data from a database into a `DataSet` object and later save changes back to the original data source.

Basically, the data provider objects manage the database for your application, and the `DataSet` objects manage the data model for the application.

Data Providers and Their Objects

There are five main data provider objects that you should know about:

◆ `Connection`

◆ `Command`

◆ `Parameter`

◆ `DataReader`

◆ `DataAdapter`

You've actually seen most of these objects already, but not with these names. That's because these are the generic names for the classes defined in `System.Data.Common`. Each data provider has implementations of these objects that have specific names.

A data provider is a namespace that implements these five classes (and some other classes and enumerations) for use with a particular database. For example, I've been using the SQL Server data provider, which is implemented in the `System.Data.SqlClient` namespace. In this namespace, the object names are as follows:

◆ SqlConnection

◆ SqlCommand

◆ SqlParameter

◆ SqlDataReader

◆ SqlDataAdapter

But the SQL Server data provider is not the only alternative for retrieving data in ADO.NET. The .NET Framework also ships with the OLE DB data provider, which is implemented in the `System.Data.OleDb` namespace. In this namespace, the corresponding object names are as follows:

◆ OleDbConnection

◆ OleDbCommand

◆ OleDbParameter

◆ OleDbDataReader

◆ OleDbDataAdapter

Although the .NET Framework includes only two data providers, there are other alternatives. For example, Microsoft has made an Open Database Connectivity (ODBC) data provider and an Oracle managed provider available for download. Third parties are also planning to release other providers.

I'll continue to use the SQL Server data provider objects in all the examples in this chapter. But you should keep in mind that the techniques you learn to work with objects from this namespace also work with objects from other data provider namespaces.

EXAM TIP

Not All OLE DB Are Equal
Although from the name it seems that the OLE DB data provider should work with any existing OLE DB provider, that's not the case. The OLE DB data provider is designed to work only with the SQL Server, Jet 4.0, and Oracle OLE DB providers. Other providers might work, but they are not supported.

NOTE

Managed Provider for Oracle The Oracle managed provider is an add-on in the .NET Framework. You can downloaded it from www.microsoft.com/downloads/release.asp?releaseid=40032.

The `SqlConnection` Object

The `SqlConnection` object represents a single persistent connection to a SQL Server data source. ADO.NET automatically handles connection pooling, which contributes to better application performance. When you call the `Close()` method of a `SqlConnection` object, the connection is returned to a connection pool. Connections in a pool are not immediately destroyed by ADO.NET. Instead, they're available for reuse if another part of an application requests a `SqlConnection` object that matches with the same connection details of a previously closed `SqlConnection` object.

Table 6.3 shows the most important members of the `SqlConnection` object.

TABLE 6.3

IMPORTANT MEMBERS OF THE `SqlConnection` CLASS

Member	Type	Description
`BeginTransaction()`	Method	Starts a new transaction on this `SqlConnection` object
`Close()`	Method	Returns the `SqlConnection` object to the connection pool
`ConnectionString`	Property	Specifies the server to be used by this `SqlConnection` object
`CreateCommand()`	Method	Returns a new `SqlCommand` object that executes via this `SqlConnection` object
`Open()`	Method	Opens the `SqlConnection` object

So far, all the `SqlConnection` objects you've seen in this book have been created via drag-and-drop from Server Explorer. But it's easy to create them in code yourself, as shown in Step by Step 6.15.

STEP BY STEP

6.15 Creating a `SqlConnection` Object in Code

1. Add a new form to your Visual C# .NET project.

2. Place a `Button` control (`btnConnect`) and a `TextBox` control (`txtConnectionString`) on the form.

3. Switch to the code view and add the following using directive to make the ADO.NET objects available:

```
using System.Data.SqlClient;
```

4. Double-click the Button control and enter this code to handle the Click event of the Button control:

```
private void btnConnect_Click(object sender,
    System.EventArgs e)
{
    SqlConnection cnn = new SqlConnection();
    cnn.ConnectionString = "Data Source=(local);" +
    "Initial Catalog=Northwind;" +
    "Integrated Security=SSPI";
    cnn.Open();
    txtConnectionString.Text = cnn.ConnectionString;
    cnn.Close();
}
```

5. Insert the Main() method to launch the form. Set the form as the startup object for the project.

6. Run the project and click the button. The code connects to the SQL Server database on the local computer and echoes the connection string to the TextBox control.

EXAM TIP

The Parts of a Connection String
You should know how to construct a SQL Server connection string for use with the SqlConnection object. There are three parts to the string. First is the Data Source, which is the name of the server to which you'd like to connect. You can use (local) as a shortcut name for the SQL Server instance running on the same computer as this code. Second is Initial Catalog, which is the name of the database on the server to use. Third is authentication information; it can either be Integrated Security=SSPI to use Windows authentication or User ID=*username*;Password=*password* to use SQL Server authentication. There are other optional parameters, but these three are the most important.

The SqlCommand and SqlParameter Objects

You've already seen the SqlCommand and SqlParameter objects in use in quite a few examples. The SqlCommand object represents something that can be executed, such as an ad hoc query string or a stored procedure name. The SqlParameter object represents a single parameter to a stored procedure.

Table 6.4 shows the most important members of the SqlCommand object.

TABLE 6.4

IMPORTANT MEMBERS OF THE SqlCommand CLASS

Member	Type	Description
CommandText	Property	Specifies the statement to be executed by the SqlCommand object
CommandType	Property	Indicates what type of command this SqlCommand object represents

continues

TABLE 6.4	*continued*	
IMPORTANT MEMBERS OF THE SqlCommand CLASS		
Member	*Type*	*Description*
Connection	Property	Represents the `SqlConnection` object through which this `SqlCommand` object executes
CreateParameter()	Method	Creates a new `SqlParameter` object for this `SqlCommand` object
ExecuteNonQuery()	Method	Executes a `SqlCommand` object that does not return a resultset
ExecuteReader()	Method	Executes a `SqlCommand` object and places the results in a `SqlDataReader` object
ExecuteScalar()	Method	Executes a `SqlCommand` object and returns the first column of the first row of the resultset
ExecuteXmlReader()	Method	Executes a `SqlCommand` object and places the results in an `XmlReader` object
Parameters	Property	Contains a collection of `SqlParameter` objects for this `SqlCommand` object

Step by Step 6.16 shows an example of using the `ExecuteScalar()` method, which provides you with an easy way to retrieve a single value (such as an aggregation) from a database.

FIGURE 6.13

The `ExecuteScalar()` method provides an easy way to retrieve a single value from a database.

STEP BY STEP

6.16 Using the `ExecuteScalar()` Method

1. Add a new form to your Visual C# .NET project.

2. Place a `Button` control (`btnCount`), a `TextBox` control (`txtCountry`), and a `Label` control (`lblResults`) on the form. Figure 6.13 shows the design of this form.

3. Switch to the code view and add the following `using` directives to make the ADO.NET objects available:

```
using System.Data;
using System.Data.SqlClient;
```

4. Double-click the `Button` control and enter this code to handle the `Click` event of the `Button` control:

```csharp
private void btnCount_Click(object sender,
    System.EventArgs e)
{
    // Connect to the database
    SqlConnection cnn = new SqlConnection();
    cnn.ConnectionString = "Data Source=(local);" +
    "Initial Catalog=Northwind;" +
    "Integrated Security=SSPI";
    // Create a new ad hoc query
    // To count customers in the selected country
    SqlCommand cmd = cnn.CreateCommand();
    cmd.CommandType = CommandType.Text;
    cmd.CommandText =
    "SELECT COUNT(*) FROM Customers " +
    " WHERE Country = '" + txtCountry.Text + "'";
    // Use ExecuteScalar to return results
    cnn.Open();
    lblResults.Text =
    "There are " + cmd.ExecuteScalar() +
    " customers in " + txtCountry.Text;
    cnn.Close();
}
```

5. Insert the `Main()` method to launch the form. Set the form as the startup object for the project.

6. Run the project. Enter a country name such as `France` and click the button. The code connects to the SQL Server database on the local computer and fills in the `Label` control's text with a string that includes the results of the ad hoc query.

The `SqlDataReader` Object

The `SqlDataReader` object is designed to be the fastest possible way to retrieve a resultset from a database. A `SqlDataReader` object can be constructed only by calling the `ExecuteReader()` method of a `SqlCommand` object. The resultset contained in a `SqlDataReader` object is forward-only, read-only. That is, you can only read the rows in the resultset sequentially from start to finish, and you can't modify any of the data.

STEP BY STEP

6.17 Using a `SqlDataReader` Object

1. Add a new form to your Visual C# .NET project.

2. Place a `Button` control (`btnGetCustomers`) and a `ListBox` control (`lbCustomers`) on the form.

3. Switch to the code view and add the following using directives to make the ADO.NET objects available:

```
using System.Data;
using System.Data.SqlClient;
```

4. Double-click the `Button` control and enter this code to handle the `Click` event of the `Button` control:

```
private void btnGetCustomers_Click(object sender,
    System.EventArgs e)
{
    // Connect to the database
    SqlConnection cnn = new SqlConnection();
    cnn.ConnectionString = "Data Source=(local);" +
    "Initial Catalog=Northwind;Integrated Security=SSPI";
    // Create a new ad hoc query
    // to retrieve customer names
    SqlCommand cmd = cnn.CreateCommand();
    cmd.CommandType = CommandType.Text;
    cmd.CommandText =
        "SELECT CompanyName FROM Customers "
    + " ORDER BY CompanyName";
    // Dump the data to the user interface
    cnn.Open();
    SqlDataReader dr = cmd.ExecuteReader();
    while (dr.Read())
    {
        lbCustomers.Items.Add(dr.GetString(0));
    }
    // Clean up
    dr.Close();
    cnn.Close();
}
```

5. Insert the `Main()` method to launch the form. Set the form as the startup object for the project.

6. Run the project and click the button. The code connects to the SQL Server database on the local computer and fills the `ListBox` control with a list of customers from the database.

EXAM TIP

Stored Procedures for Speed You could improve the performance of the code in Step by Step 6.17 even more by using a stored procedure instead of an ad hoc query to deliver the company names.

You can think of the SqlDataReader object as a data structure that can contain one row of data at a time. Each call to the SqlDataReader.Read() method loads the next row of data into this structure. When there are no more rows to load, the Read() method returns false, which tells you that you've reached the end of the data. To retrieve individual columns of data from the current row, the SqlDataReader object provides a series of methods (such as the GetString() method used in Step by Step 6.17) that take a column number and return the data from that column. There's also a GetValue() method that you can use with any column, but the typed methods are faster than the GetValue() method.

Table 6.5 shows the most important members of the SqlDataReader object. There's no need to memorize all the data methods (and the others that aren't shown in this table), but you should understand the pattern that they represent.

TABLE 6.5

IMPORTANT MEMBERS OF THE SqlDataReader CLASS

Member	Type	Description
Close()	Method	Closes the SqlDataReader object
GetBoolean()	Method	Gets a Boolean value from the specified column
GetByte()	Method	Gets a byte value from the specified column
GetChar()	Method	Gets a character value from the specified column
GetDateTime()	Method	Gets a date/time value from the specified column
GetDecimal()	Method	Gets a decimal value from the specified column
GetDouble()	Method	Gets a double value from the specified column
GetFloat()	Method	Gets a float value from the specified column
GetGuid()	Method	Gets a global unique identifier (GUID) value from the specified column
GetInt16()	Method	Gets a 16-bit integer value from the specified column
GetInt32()	Method	Gets a 32-bit integer value from the specified column
GetInt64()	Method	Gets a 64-bit integer value from the specified column
GetString()	Method	Gets a string value from the specified column
GetValue()	Method	Gets a value from the specified column

continues

EXAM TIP

Close Your `SqlDataReader` Objects!
The `SqlDataReader` object makes exclusive use of its `SqlConnection` object as long as it is open. You are not able to execute any other `SqlCommand` objects on that connection as long as the `SqlDataReader` object is open. Therefore, you should always call `SqlDataReader.Close()` as soon as you're done retrieving data.

TABLE 6.5   *continued*

IMPORTANT MEMBERS OF THE SqlDataReader CLASS

Member	Type	Description
GetValues()	Method	Gets an entire row of data and places it in an array of objects
IsDbNull()	Method	Indicates whether a specified column contains a null value
Read()	Method	Loads the next row of data into the `SqlDataReader` object

The `SqlDataAdapter` Object

The final data provider object that is considered in this chapter, `SqlDataAdapter`, provides a bridge between the data provider objects and the `DataSet` objects that you'll learn about in the next section. You can think of the `SqlDataAdapter` object as a two-way pipeline between the data in its native storage format and the data in a more abstract representation (the `DataSet` object) that's designed for manipulation in an application.

Table 6.6 shows the most important members of the `SqlDataAdapter` class.

TABLE 6.6

IMPORTANT MEMBERS OF THE SqlDataAdapter CLASS

Member	Type	Description
DeleteCommand	Property	Specifies the `SqlCommand` object used to delete rows from the data source
Fill()	Method	Transfers data from the data source to a `DataSet` object
InsertCommand	Property	Specifies the `SqlCommand` object used to insert rows from the data source
SelectCommand	Property	Specifies the `SqlCommand` object used to select rows from the data source
Update()	Method	Transfers data from a `DataSet` object to the data source
UpdateCommand	Property	Specifies the `SqlCommand` object used to update rows from the data source

You've seen the `SqlDataAdapter` object in use in many examples in Chapter 5 and earlier in this chapter. Later in this chapter (in the "Using `DataSet` Objects" section) you'll learn more about using the `SqlDataAdapter` object in conjunction with the `DataSet` object to manipulate data.

The `DataSet` Objects

Unlike the data provider objects, there's only one set of `DataSet` objects. The `DataSet` objects are all contained in the `System.Data` namespace. The `DataSet` objects represent data in an abstract form that is not tied to any particular database implementation. In this section, I'll introduce you to the `DataSet` object and the other objects that it contains:

- ◆ `DataSet`

- ◆ `DataTable`

- ◆ `DataRelation`

- ◆ `DataRow`

- ◆ `DataColumn`

- ◆ `DataView`

The `DataSet` object itself is a self-contained memory-resident representation of relational data. A `DataSet` object contains other objects, such as `DataTable` and `DataRelation` objects, that hold the actual data and information about the design of the data. The `DataSet` object is designed to be easy to move between components. In particular, there are methods to convert a `DataSet` object to an XML file and vice versa.

Table 6.7 shows the most important members of the `DataSet` object.

TABLE 6.7

IMPORTANT MEMBERS OF THE `DataSet` CLASS

Member	Type	Description
AcceptChanges()	Method	Marks all changes in the `DataSet` object as having been accepted
Clear()	Method	Removes all data from the `DataSet` object

continues

TABLE 6.7 | *continued*

IMPORTANT MEMBERS OF THE DataSet CLASS

Member	Type	Description
GetChanges()	Method	Gets a DataSet object that contains only the changed data in this DataSet object
GetXml()	Method	Gets an XML representation of the DataSet object
GetXmlSchema()	Method	Gets an XML Schema Definition (XSD) representation of the DataSet object's schema
Merge()	Method	Merges two DataSet objects
ReadXml()	Method	Loads the DataSet object from an XML file
ReadXmlSchema()	Method	Loads the DataSet object's schema from an XSD file
Relations	Property	Specifies a collection of DataRelation objects
Tables	Property	Specifies a collection of DataTable objects
WriteXml()	Method	Writes the DataSet object to an XML file
WriteXmlSchema()	Method	Writes the DataSet object's schema to an XSD file

As you can see, several of the DataSet object's methods deal with XML and XSD files. You'll learn more about XML files in the "Understanding XML" section, later in this chapter.

The DataTable Object

The DataTable object represents a single table within the DataSet object. A single DataSet object can contain many DataTable objects. Table 6.8 shows the most important members of the DataTable object.

TABLE 6.8

IMPORTANT MEMBERS OF THE DataTable CLASS

Member	Type	Description
ChildRelations	Property	Specifies a collection of DataRelation objects that refer to children of this DataTable object

Member	Type	Description
Clear()	Method	Removes all data from the DataTable object
ColumnChanged()	Event	Occurs when the data in any row of a specified column has been changed
ColumnChanging()	Event	Occurs when the data in any row of a specified column is about to be changed
Columns	Property	Specifies a collection of DataColumn objects
Constraints	Property	Specifies a collection of Constraint objects
NewRow()	Method	Creates a new, blank row in the DataTable object
ParentRelations	Property	Specifies a collection of DataRelation objects that refer to parents of this DataTable object
PrimaryKey	Property	Specifies an array of DataColumn objects that provide the primary key for this DataTable object
RowChanged()	Event	Fires when any data in a DataRow object has been changed
RowChanging()	Event	Fires when any data in a DataRow object is about to be changed
RowDeleted()	Event	Occurs when a row has been deleted
RowDeleting()	Event	Occurs when a row is about to be deleted
Rows	Property	Specifies a collection of DataRow objects
Select()	Method	Selects an array of DataRow objects that meet specified criteria
TableName	Property	Specifies the name of this DataTable object

As you can see, you can manipulate a DataTable object as either a collection of DataColumn objects or a collection of DataRow objects. The DataTable object also provides events that you can use to monitor data changes. For example, you might bind a DataTable object to a DataGrid control and use events to track the user's operations on the data within the DataGrid control.

The DataRelation Object

As mentioned previously, the DataSet object can represent the structure and data of an entire relational database. The DataRelation object stores information on the relationships between DataTable objects within a DataSet object. Table 6.9 shows the most important members of the DataRelation object.

TABLE 6.9

IMPORTANT MEMBERS OF THE DataRelation CLASS

Member	Type	Description
ChildColumns	Property	Specifies a collection of DataColumn objects that define the foreign key side of the relationship
ChildKeyConstraint	Property	Returns a ForeignKeyConstraint object for the relationship
ChildTable	Property	Specifies a DataTable object from the foreign key side of the relationship
ParentColumns	Property	Specifies a collection of DataColumn objects that define the primary key side of the relationship
ParentKeyConstraint	Property	Returns a PrimaryKeyConstraint object for the relationship
ParentTable	Property	Specifies a DataTable object from the primary key side of the relationship
RelationName	Property	Specifies the name of the DataRelation object

The DataRow Object

Continuing down the object hierarchy from the DataSet object past the DataTable object, we come to the DataRow object. As you can guess by now, the DataRow object represents a single row of data. When you're selecting, inserting, updating, or deleting data in a DataSet object, you normally work with DataRow objects.

Table 6.10 shows the most important members of the DataRow object.

TABLE 6.10

IMPORTANT MEMBERS OF THE DataRow CLASS

Member	Type	Description
BeginEdit()	Method	Starts editing the DataRow object
CancelEdit()	Method	Discards an edit in progress

Member	Type	Description
Delete()	Method	Deletes the DataRow object from its parent DataTable object
EndEdit()	Method	Ends an edit in progress and saves the changes
IsNull()	Method	Returns true if a specified column contains a null value
RowState	Property	Returns information on the current state of a DataRow object (for example, whether it has been changed since it was last saved to the database)

The DataColumn Object

The DataTable object also contains a collection of DataColumn objects. A DataColumn object represents a single column in a DataTable object. By manipulating the DataColumn objects, you can determine and even change the structure of the DataTable object.

Table 6.11 shows the most important members of the DataColumn object.

TABLE 6.11

IMPORTANT MEMBERS OF THE DataColumn CLASS

Member	Type	Description
AllowDbNull	Property	Indicates whether the DataColumn object can contain null values
AutoIncrement	Property	Indicates whether the DataColumn object is an identity column
ColumnName	Property	Specifies the name of the DataColumn object
DataType	Property	Specifies the data type of the DataColumn object
DefaultValue	Property	Specifies the default value of this DataColumn object for new rows of data
MaxLength	Property	Specifies the maximum length of a text DataColumn object
Unique	Property	Indicates whether values in the DataColumn object must be unique across all rows in the DataTable object

The DataView Object

The DataView object represents a view of the data contained in a DataTable object. A DataView object might contain every DataRow object from the DataTable object, or it might be filtered to contain only specific rows. That filtering can be done by SQL expressions (returning, for example, only rows for customers in France) or by row state (returning, for example, only rows that have been modified).

Table 6.12 shows the most important members of the DataView object.

TABLE 6.12

IMPORTANT MEMBERS OF THE DataView CLASS

Member	Type	Description
AddNew()	Method	Adds a new row to the DataView object
AllowDelete	Property	Indicates whether deletions can be performed through this DataView object
AllowEdit	Property	Indicates whether updates can be performed through this DataView object
AllowNew	Property	Indicates whether insertions can be performed through this DataView object
Count	Property	Specifies the number of rows in this DataView object
Delete()	Method	Deletes a row from this DataView object
Find()	Method	Searches for a row that matches the specified sort key value
FindRows()	Method	Returns an array of rows that match the specified sort key value
Sort	Property	Sorts the data in a DataView object

REVIEW BREAK

▶ The ADO.NET object model includes both database-specific data provider classes and database-independent DataSet classes.

▶ Data providers contain implementations of the `Connection`, `Command`, `Parameter`, `DataReader`, and `DataAdapter` objects optimized for a particular database product.

▶ The `SqlConnection` object represents a connection to a database.

▶ The `SqlCommand` object represents a command that can be executed.

▶ The `SqlParameter` object represents a parameter of a stored procedure.

▶ The `SqlDataReader` object provides a fast way to retrieve a resultset from a command.

▶ The `SqlDataAdapter` object implements a two-way pipeline between the database and the data model.

▶ The `DataSet` object represents the structure and data of an entire relational database in memory. It's composed of `DataTable`, `DataRelation`, `DataRow`, and `DataColumn` objects.

▶ The `DataView` object provides a filtered row of the data from a `DataTable` object.

Using `DataSet` Objects

Now that you've learned the basics about the ADO.NET objects, it's time to see what you can do with them. In particular, I concentrate on some of the basic operations, including the following:

◆ Populating a `DataSet` object from a database

◆ Moving around in `DataSet` objects and retrieving data

◆ Using strongly typed `DataSet` objects

◆ Using `DataSet` objects with multiple tables

◆ Finding and sorting data in `DataSet` objects

◆ Editing data with ADO.NET

If you're interested in exploring ADO.NET in more depth, see the list of references at the end of the chapter.

Populating a DataSet Object from a Database

Before you can do anything with data in a DataSet object, you have to get that data into the DataSet object somehow. In general, you can follow a four-step process to move data from the database to a DataSet object:

1. Create a SqlConnection object to connect to the database.

2. Create a SqlCommand object to retrieve the desired data.

3. Assign the SqlCommand object to the SelectCommand property of a SqlDataAdapter object.

4. Call the Fill() method of the SqlDataAdapter object.

STEP BY STEP

6.18 Filling a DataSet Object

1. Add a new form to your Visual C# .NET project.

2. Place a Button control (btnLoad) and a DataGrid control (dgProducts) on the form. Set the Caption property of the DataGrid control to Products.

3. Switch to the code view and add the following using directives to make the ADO.NET objects available:

```
using System.Data;
using System.Data.SqlClient;
```

4. Double-click the Button control and enter this code to handle the Click event of the Button control:

```
private void btnLoad_Click(object sender,
    System.EventArgs e)
{
    // Create a SqlConnection
    SqlConnection cnn = new SqlConnection(
    "Data Source=(local); Initial Catalog=Northwind;" +
    " Integrated Security=SSPI");
    // Create a SqlCommand
    SqlCommand cmd = cnn.CreateCommand();
    cmd.CommandType = CommandType.Text;
    cmd.CommandText = "SELECT * FROM Products " +
     " ORDER BY ProductName";
```

```
    // Set up the DataAdapter and fill the DataSet
    SqlDataAdapter da = new SqlDataAdapter();
    da.SelectCommand = cmd;
    DataSet ds = new DataSet();
    da.Fill(ds, "Products");
    // Display the data on the user interface
    dgProducts.DataSource = ds;
    dgProducts.DataMember = "Products";
}
```

5. Insert the `Main()` method to launch the form. Set the form as the startup object for the project.

6. Run the project and click the button. The code connects to the SQL Server database on the local computer and fills the `DataGrid` control with the result of executing the SQL statement, as shown in Figure 6.14.

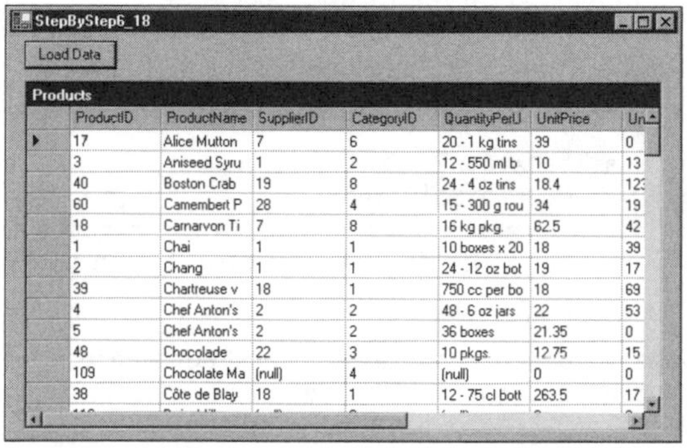

FIGURE 6.14
You can bind a `DataGrid` control to data stored in a data set.

Step by Step 6.18 demonstrates a couple shortcuts that you can use in your ADO.NET code. First, the constructor for the `SqlConnection` object has an overloaded form that lets you supply the connection string when you create the object. Second, this code doesn't explicitly call the `Open()` and `Close()` methods of the `SqlConnection` object. Instead, it lets the `SqlDataAdapter` object make those calls when it needs the data. Doing this not only cuts down the amount of code you need to write, but it also improves the scalability of your application by keeping the `SqlConnection` object open for the shortest possible period of time.

EXAM TIP

Choose a Table Name The second parameter to the `DataAdapter.Fill()` method is the name of the `DataTable` object to create from the data supplied by the `SelectCommand` property. The `DataTable` object name does not have to match the table name in the underlying database. The example in Step by Step 6.18 would work just as well if you placed data from the Products table into a `DataTable` object named Starship (although that would be a pretty poor idea from the standpoint of code maintainability).

Moving Around in DataSet Objects and Retrieving Data

If you're familiar with classic ADO, you're used to recordsets: collections of records that have a pointer to the current record. DataSet objects have no concept of a current record pointer. Instead, you move through a DataSet object by working with the collections that the DataSet contains.

STEP BY STEP

6.19 Moving Through a DataSet Object

1. Add a new form to your Visual C# .NET project.

2. Place a Button control (btnLoadData) and a ListBox control (lbData) on the form.

3. Switch to the code view and add the following using directives to make the ADO.NET objects available:

```
using System.Data;
using System.Data.SqlClient;
```

4. Double-click the Button control and enter this code to handle the Click event of the Button control:

```
private void btnLoadData_Click(object sender,
    System.EventArgs e)
{
    // Create a SqlConnection
    SqlConnection cnn = new SqlConnection(
        "Data Source=(local);
            Initial Catalog=Northwind;" +
    " Integrated Security=SSPI");
    // Create a SqlCommand
    SqlCommand cmd = cnn.CreateCommand();
    cmd.CommandType = CommandType.Text;
    cmd.CommandText = "SELECT * FROM Customers " +
        " WHERE Country = 'France'";
    // Set up the DataAdapter and fill the DataSet
    SqlDataAdapter da = new SqlDataAdapter();
    da.SelectCommand = cmd;
    DataSet ds = new DataSet();
    da.Fill(ds, "Customers");
    // Dump the contents of the DataSet
    lbData.Items.Add("DataSet: " + ds.DataSetName);
    foreach (DataTable dt in ds.Tables)
    {
```

```
        lbData.Items.Add("  DataTable: " +
            dt.TableName);
        foreach (DataRow dr in dt.Rows)
        {
            lbData.Items.Add("    DataRow");
            foreach (DataColumn dc in dt.Columns)
            {
                lbData.Items.Add("        " + dr[dc]);
            }
        }
    }
}
```

5. Insert the `Main()` method to launch the form. Set the form as the startup object for the project.

6. Run the project and click the button. The code dumps the contents of the `DataSet` object to the `ListBox` control, as shown in Figure 6.15.

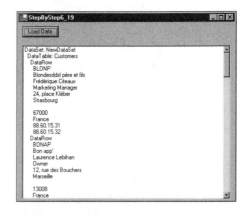

FIGURE 6.15
You can dump the contents of a `DataSet` object to a `ListBox` control.

Step by Step 6.19 shows how you can visit every piece of data in a `DataSet` object by properly selecting nested `foreach` loops. It also shows a general syntax for retrieving data: Locate the `DataRow` and `DataColumn` objects whose intersection contains the data that you're interested in, and use the `dr[dc]` indexer syntax to retrieve the actual data value. There are a variety of other syntaxes that you can use to retrieve data. Given a `DataTable` variable named `dt` that refers to the data from the Customers table, for example, either of these statements would retrieve the value in the first column of the first row of data in the `DataTable` object:

```
dt.Rows[0][0]
dt.Rows[0]["CustomerID"]
```

Using Strongly Typed `DataSet` Objects

All the syntaxes shown in the previous section for retrieving data have one thing in common: They're all late-bound. That is, the .NET Framework doesn't know until runtime that CustomerID is a valid column name. One of the innovations of ADO.NET is a provision to create strongly typed `DataSet` objects. In a strongly typed `DataSet` object, columns actually become properties of the row. This allows you to write an early-bound version of the data-retrieval expression:

```
dt.Rows[0].CustomerID
```

In addition to being faster than the late-bound syntaxes, the early-bound syntax has the added advantage of making column names show up in IntelliSense tips as you type code.

You've already seen quite a few strongly typed DataSet objects, although I didn't emphasize this while I was using them. Any time that you use the Generate DataSet link in the Properties window for a SqlDataAdapter object on a form, Visual Studio .NET builds a strongly typed DataSet object. You can also build strongly typed DataSet objects by using the XSD designer.

STEP BY STEP

6.20 Designing a Strongly Typed DataSet Object

1. Select Project, Add New Item in your Visual C# .NET project.

2. In the Add New Item dialog box, select the DataSet template. Name the new DataSet SuppliersDataSet.xsd. Click Open to create the XSD file and open it in the XSD designer.

3. Open Server Explorer.

4. Expand the tree under Data Connections to show a SQL Server data connection that points to the Northwind sample database, and then expand the Tables node of the selected SQL Server data connection. Drag the Suppliers table from Server Explorer and drop it on the design surface for the DataSet object. Figure 6.16 shows the resulting XSD design view. The E icons for each column of the table indicate that those columns have been rendered as XML elements.

5. Save the DataSet object. At this point, your project should contain a new class named SuppliersDataSet, which is a strongly typed DataSet object that you can use in code.

6. Add a new form to your Visual C# .NET project.

7. Place a Button control (btnLoadData) and a ListBox control (lbData) on the form.

FIGURE 6.16
You can create strongly typed DataSet objects in the XSD designer of Visual Studio .NET.

8. Switch to the code view and add the following using directives to make the ADO.NET objects available:

```
using System.Data;
using System.Data.SqlClient;
```

9. Double-click the Button control and enter this code to handle the Click event of the Button control:

```
private void btnLoadData_Click(object sender,
    System.EventArgs e)
{
    // Create a SqlConnection
    SqlConnection cnn = new SqlConnection(
    "Data Source=(local); Initial Catalog=Northwind;" +
    " Integrated Security=SSPI");
    // Create a SqlCommand
    SqlCommand cmd = cnn.CreateCommand();
    cmd.CommandType = CommandType.Text;
    cmd.CommandText = "SELECT * FROM Suppliers";
    // Set up the DataAdapter and fill the DataSet
    SqlDataAdapter da = new SqlDataAdapter();
    da.SelectCommand = cmd;
    SuppliersDataSet ds = new SuppliersDataSet();
    da.Fill(ds, "Suppliers");
    // Dump the contents of the DataSet
    foreach (SuppliersDataSet.SuppliersRow suppRow
      in ds.Suppliers)
    {
        lbData.Items.Add(suppRow.SupplierID +
          " " + suppRow.CompanyName);
    }
}
```

10. Insert the Main() method to launch the form. Set the form as the startup object for the project.

11. Run the project and click the button. The code displays two columns from the DataSet object in the ListBox control, as shown in Figure 6.17.

WARNING

Naming a Strongly Typed DataSet Object You should not name the DataSet object in Step by Step 6.20 as Suppliers because the corresponding code file (that is, the .cs file) created for this DataSet object contains a property Suppliers that is referred as ds.Suppliers. If you named the class with the same name, you would get the error member names cannot be the same as their enclosing type. You therefore have to choose a different name other than the name of its containing objects, such as SuppliersDataSet.

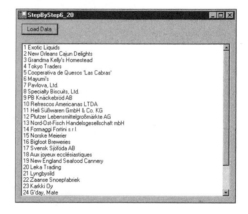

FIGURE 6.17
A strongly typed DataSet object allows you to create early-bound data retrieval expressions.

Using the SuppliersDataSet class to define the DataSet object in this case gives you several syntactical benefits. You can refer to the Suppliers DataTable object as a property of the DataSet object. You can also refer to the columns in the DataRow objects in this DataTable object as properties of the DataRow object. The strongly typed DataSet object automatically defines a class named SuppliersRow to represent one DataRow object with strong typing.

Using DataSet Objects with Multiple Tables

Every DataSet object that you've seen so far in this chapter has contained a single DataTable object. But a DataSet object is not limited to a single DataTable object; in fact, there's no practical limit on the number of DataTable objects that a DataSet object can contain. By using DataAdapter objects, you can connect a single DataSet object to more than one table in the SQL Server database. You can also define DataRelation objects to represent the relationship between the DataTable objects in the DataSet object.

STEP BY STEP

6.21 Building a DataSet Object That Contains Multiple DataTable Objects

1. Add a new form to your Visual C# .NET project.

2. Place a Button control (btnLoadData) and a DataGrid control (dgMain) on the form.

3. Switch to the code view and add the following using directives to make the ADO.NET objects available:

```
using System.Data;
using System.Data.SqlClient;
```

4. Double-click the Button control and enter this code to handle the Click event of the Button control:

```
private void btnLoadData_Click(object sender,
    System.EventArgs e)
{
    // Create a SqlConnection and a DataSet
    SqlConnection cnn = new SqlConnection(
    "Data Source=(local); Initial Catalog=Northwind;" +
    " Integrated Security=SSPI");
    DataSet ds = new DataSet();

    // Add the customers data to the DataSet
    SqlCommand cmdCustomers= cnn.CreateCommand();
    cmdCustomers.CommandType = CommandType.Text;
    cmdCustomers.CommandText = "SELECT * FROM Customers";
    SqlDataAdapter daCustomers = new SqlDataAdapter();
    daCustomers.SelectCommand = cmdCustomers;
    daCustomers.Fill(ds, "Customers");
```

```
// Add the Orders data to the DataSet
SqlCommand cmdOrders = cnn.CreateCommand();
cmdOrders.CommandType = CommandType.Text;
cmdOrders.CommandText = "SELECT * FROM Orders";
SqlDataAdapter daOrders = new SqlDataAdapter();
daOrders.SelectCommand = cmdOrders;
daOrders.Fill(ds, "Orders");

// Add the Order Details data to the DataSet
SqlCommand cmdOrderDetails = cnn.CreateCommand();
cmdOrderDetails.CommandType = CommandType.Text;
cmdOrderDetails.CommandText =
    "SELECT * FROM [Order Details]";
SqlDataAdapter daOrderDetails =
    new SqlDataAdapter();
daOrderDetails.SelectCommand = cmdOrderDetails;
daOrderDetails.Fill(ds, "OrderDetails");

// Add Relations
DataRelation relCustOrder = ds.Relations.Add(
"CustOrder",
ds.Tables["Customers"].Columns["CustomerID"],
ds.Tables["Orders"].Columns["CustomerID"]);

DataRelation relOrderOrderDetails =
    ds.Relations.Add(
      "OrderOrderDetails",
      ds.Tables["Orders"].Columns["OrderID"],
      ds.Tables["OrderDetails"].Columns["OrderID"]);

// And show the data on the user interface
dgMain.DataSource = ds;
dgMain.DataMember = "Customers";
```

}

5. Insert the Main() method to launch the form. Set the form as the startup object for the project.

6. Run the project and click the button. The code loads all three database tables into the DataSet object, and then it displays the customers' information on the data grid, as shown in Figure 6.18

FIGURE 6.18
A DataGrid control can be bound to multiple tables of a DataSet object.

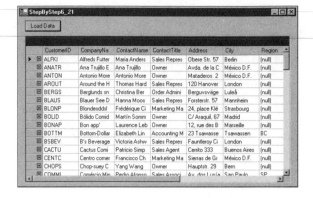

The code in Step by Step 6.21 uses three different `SqlDataAdapter` objects to move data from three different database tables into a single `DataSet` object. The data from each `SqlDataAdapter` object is stored in a separate `DataTable` object. You could also use a single `SqlDataAdapter` object for the same purpose, by changing its `SelectCommand` property each time you want to load a separate table. The code then adds `DataRelation` objects to specify the relationships between these `DataTable` objects. The `Add()` method of the `DataSet.Relations` collection takes three parameters:

◆ A name for the `DataRelation` object to be created

◆ A `DataColumn` object that represents the primary key side of the relationship

◆ A `DataColumn` object that represents the foreign key side of the relationship

Although the `DataGrid` control in Step by Step 6.21 initially displays only the customers data, all the data is available. The `DataGrid` control contains built-in logic to help navigate between related `DataTable` objects in a `DataSet` object. If you click the + sign to the left of a row of customer data, the `DataGrid` control shows a list of the relationships that involve that row, as shown in Figure 6.19.

The relationship is called a *hotlink*. Clicking the link loads all the related rows on the other side of that relationship into the `DataGrid` control, as shown in Figure 6.20. Note that the parent rows area of the `DataGrid` control contains information on the customer row where the navigation started.

FIGURE 6.19
When the DataGrid control is bound to a DataSet object that contains multiple related tables, it displays the relationship when a row node is clicked.

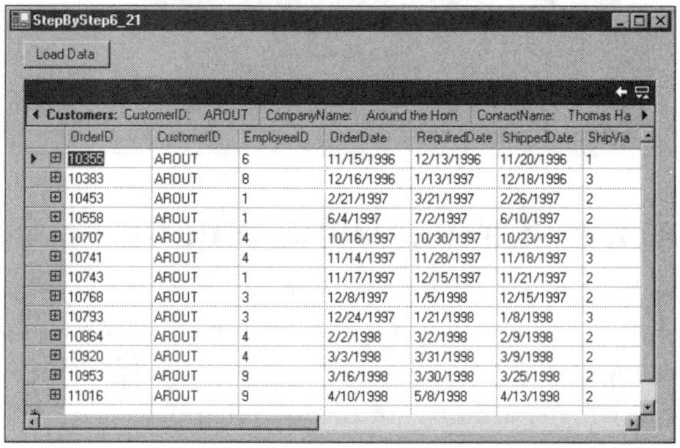

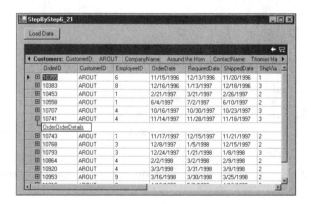

FIGURE 6.20
You can view the child table's data in a DataGrid control when the relationship link is clicked.

Because this DataSet object has another level of detail, you can repeat the process. Click the + sign next to an order to see the relationships in which that order is involved, as shown in Figure 6.21.

FIGURE 6.21
When a DataGrid control is bound to a DataSet object that contains multiple related tables, it allows you to drill into the details.

Finally, clicking the hotlink beneath an order reveals all the order detail rows for that order, as shown in Figure 6.22. The parent rows area contains details on both the customer and the order that were used to get to this point.

FIGURE 6.22
The parent rows area of the DataGrid control contains information from the Customers and the Orders tables.

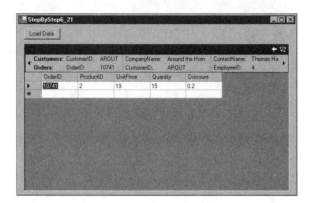

Finding and Sorting Data in DataSet Objects

The .NET Framework offers several object-oriented ways to find and sort data. In this section, I'll show you how to use two of these ways: by using the DataTable.Select() method and by using the filtering and sorting capabilities of the DataView object.

Using the Select() method of the DataTable object is a convenient way to find particular DataRow objects within the DataTable object. This method extracts an array of DataRow objects that you can work with.

STEP BY STEP

6.22 Using the DataTable.Select() Method

1. Add a new form to your Visual C# .NET project.

2. Place a Button control (btnSelect), a TextBox control (txtCountry), and a ListBox control (lbSelected) on the form.

3. Switch to the code view and add the following using directives to make the ADO.NET objects available:

```
using System.Data;
using System.Data.SqlClient;
```

4. Double-click the `Button` control and enter this code to handle the `Click` event of the `Button` control:

```
private void btnSelect_Click(object sender,
    System.EventArgs e)
{
    // Create a SqlConnection
    SqlConnection cnn = new SqlConnection(
    "Data Source=(local); Initial Catalog=Northwind;" +
    " Integrated Security=SSPI");
    // Create a SqlCommand
    SqlCommand cmd = cnn.CreateCommand();
    cmd.CommandType = CommandType.Text;
    cmd.CommandText = "SELECT * FROM Customers";
    // Set up the DataAdapter and fill the DataSet
    SqlDataAdapter da = new SqlDataAdapter();
    da.SelectCommand = cmd;
    DataSet ds = new DataSet();
    da.Fill(ds, "Customers");
    // Use the Select method
     // To get a sorted array of DataRow objects
    DataRow[] adr = ds.Tables["Customers"].Select(
    "Country = '" + txtCountry.Text + "'",
    "ContactName ASC");
    // Dump the result to the user interface
    lbSelected.Items.Clear();
    foreach(DataRow dr in adr)
    {
        lbSelected.Items.Add(dr[0] + " " + dr[1] +
        " " + dr[2]);
    }
}
```

5. Insert the `Main()` method to launch the form. Set the form as the startup object for the project.

6. Run the project. Enter a country name and click the button. You see the first three columns from the `DataRow` objects for customers in that country, as shown in Figure 6.23.

FIGURE 6.23
The `DataTable.Select()` method allows you to select a collection of rows that are sorted by a given sort expression and that match a given filter expression.

The `Select()` method of the `DataTable` object constructs an array of `DataRow` objects, based on up to three factors: a filter expression, a sort expression, and a state constant.

Filter expressions are essentially SQL WHERE clauses that are constructed according to these rules:

◆ Column names containing special characters should be enclosed in square brackets.

◆ String constants should be enclosed in single quotes.

◆ Date constants should be enclosed in pound signs.

◆ Numeric expressions can be specified in decimal or scientific notation.

◆ Expressions can be created by using AND, OR, NOT, parentheses, IN, LIKE, comparison operators, and arithmetic operators.

◆ The + operator is used to concatenate strings.

◆ Either * or % can be used as a wildcard to match any number of characters. A wildcard can be used only at the start or end of a string.

◆ Columns in a child table can be referenced with the expression *Child.Column*. If the table has more than one child table, you use the expression *Child(RelationName).Column* to choose a particular child table.

◆ The Sum, Avg, Min, Max, Count, StDev, and Var aggregates can be used with child tables.

◆ Supported functions include CONVERT, LEN, ISNULL, IIF, and SUBSTRING.

In the code in Step by Step 6.22, the filter expression is built by concatenating the text from the txtCountry control with a column comparison.

If you don't specify a sort order in the Select() method, the rows are returned in primary key order or in the order of addition, if the table doesn't have a primary key. You can also specify a sort expression that consists of one or more column names and the keywords ASC or DESC to specify ascending or descending sorts. For example, this is a valid sort expression:

```
Country ASC, CompanyName DESC
```

This expression sorts first by country, in ascending order, and then by company name within each country, in descending order.

Finally, you can also select DataRow objects according to their current state by supplying one of the DataViewRowState constants. Table 6.13 shows these constants.

TABLE 6.13

DataViewRowState CONSTANTS

Constant	Meaning
Added	Specifies new rows that have not yet been committed
CurrentRows	Specifies all current rows, whether they are unchanged, modified, or new
Deleted	Specifies deleted rows
ModifiedCurrent	Specifies modified rows
ModifiedOriginal	Specifies original data for modified rows
None	Specifies no rows
OriginalRows	Specifies original data, including rows that have been modified or deleted
Unchanged	Specifies rows that have not been changed

NOTE

From a DataTable Object to an Array
You can quickly create an array that holds all the contents of a DataTable object by calling the Select() method with no parameters:

```
DataRow[] adr = dt.Select();
```

You can also sort and filter data by using a DataView object. The DataView object has the same structure of rows and columns as a DataTable object, but it also lets you specify sorting and filtering options as properties of the DataView object. Typically you create a DataView object by starting with a DataTable object and specifying options to include a subset of the rows in the DataTable object.

STEP BY STEP

6.23 Using a DataView Object to Sort and Filter Data

1. Add a new form to your Visual C# .NET project.

2. Place a Button control (btnLoad) and a DataGrid control (dgCustomers) on the form.

3. Switch to the code view and add the following using directives to make the ADO.NET objects available:

```
using System.Data;
using System.Data.SqlClient;
```

continues

continued

4. Double-click the `Button` control and enter this code to handle the `Click` event of the `Button` control:

```
private void btnLoad_Click(object sender,
    System.EventArgs e)
{
    // Create a SqlConnection
    SqlConnection cnn = new SqlConnection(
    "Data Source=(local); Initial Catalog=Northwind;" +
    " Integrated Security=SSPI");
    // Create a SqlCommand
    SqlCommand cmd = cnn.CreateCommand();
    cmd.CommandType = CommandType.Text;
    cmd.CommandText = "SELECT * FROM Customers";
    // Set up the DataAdapter and fill the DataSet
    SqlDataAdapter da = new SqlDataAdapter();
    da.SelectCommand = cmd;
    DataSet ds = new DataSet();
    da.Fill(ds, "Customers");
    // Create a DataView based on the Customers DataTable
    DataView dv = new DataView(ds.Tables["Customers"]);
    dv.RowFilter = "Country = 'France'";
    dv.Sort = "CompanyName ASC";
    dgCustomers.DataSource = dv;
}
```

5. Insert the `Main()` method to launch the form. Set the form as the startup object for the project.

6. Run the project and click the button. The `DataGrid` control displays only the customers from France, sorted in ascending order by column `CompanyName`.

The constructor for the `DataView` object in Step by Step 6.23 specifies the `DataTable` object that includes the data from which the `DataView` object can draw. By setting the `RowFilter`, `Sort`, and `RowStateFilter` properties of the `DataView` object, you can control which rows are available in the `DataView` object, as well as the order in which they are presented. I don't use the `RowStateFilter` property in Step by Step 6.23; `RowStateFilter` allows you to select, for example, only rows that have been changed since the `DataTable` object was loaded. The `RowStateFilter` property can be set to any one of the `DataViewRowState` constants listed in Table 6.13.

GUIDED PRACTICE
EXERCISE 6.3

In this exercise, you fill a DataSet object with customer and order data. Then you allow the user to select a customer and display a DataView object that contains only that customer's orders on the user interface.

Your form should include a bound ComboBox control to allow the user to select a CustomerID value. When the user selects a new value in the combo box, you should initialize the DataView object and bind it to a DataGrid control for display.

How would you create such a form?

You should try working through this problem on your own first. If you get stuck, or if you'd like to see one possible solution, follow these steps:

1. Add a new form to your Visual C# .NET project.

2. Add a Label control, a ComboBox control (cboCustomers), and a DataGrid control (dgOrders) to the form. Figure 6.24 shows a possible design for the form.

3. Switch to the code view and add the following using directives to make the ADO.NET objects available:

```
using System.Data;
using System.Data.SqlClient;
```

4. Add the following code to the class definition:

```
// Create a SqlConnection
SqlConnection cnn = new SqlConnection(
    "Data Source=(local); Initial Catalog=Northwind;" +
    " Integrated Security=SSPI");
// DataSet to hold order information
DataSet dsOrders = new DataSet();
```

5. Double-click the form to attach an event handler to its Load event. Enter the following code to fill the list in the ComboBox control and initialize a DataSet object of orders in the event handler:

```
private void GuidedPracticeExercise6_3_Load(
 object sender,System.EventArgs e)
{
```

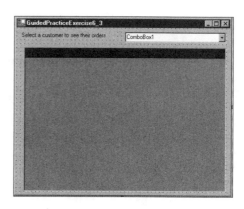

FIGURE 6.24
This form can retrieve order information by customer.

continues

continued

```
// Get all of the orders
SqlCommand cmdOrders = cnn.CreateCommand();
cmdOrders.CommandType = CommandType.Text;
cmdOrders.CommandText = "SELECT * FROM Orders";
SqlDataAdapter daOrders = new SqlDataAdapter();
daOrders.SelectCommand = cmdOrders;
daOrders.Fill(dsOrders, "Orders");
// Retrieve data for the combo box
SqlCommand cmdCustomers = cnn.CreateCommand();
cmdCustomers.CommandType = CommandType.Text;
cmdCustomers.CommandText = "SELECT CustomerID, " +
" CompanyName FROM Customers ORDER BY CompanyName";
DataSet ds = new DataSet();
SqlDataAdapter da = new SqlDataAdapter();
da.SelectCommand = cmdCustomers;
da.Fill(ds, "Customers");
cboCustomers.DisplayMember = "CompanyName";
cboCustomers.ValueMember = "CustomerID";
cboCustomers.DataSource = ds.Tables["Customers"];
}
```

6. Attach `SelectedIndexChanged` event handler to the combo box. Enter this code to load the correct orders when a value is selected from the combo box:

```
private void cboCustomers_SelectedIndexChanged(
    object sender, System.EventArgs e)
{
    // Create a DataView object
    // Containing the orders for the selected customer
    DataView dv = new DataView(
        dsOrders.Tables["Orders"]);
    dv.RowFilter = "CustomerID = '" +
        cboCustomers.SelectedValue + "'";
    dgOrders.DataSource = dv;
}
```

7. Insert the `Main()` method to launch the form. Set the form as the startup object for the project.

8. Run the project. Select a customer from the combo box. That customer's order is displayed in the data grid.

If you have difficulty following this exercise, review the sections "Running Queries," "The SELECT Statement," and "Finding and Sorting Data in DataSet Objects," as well as the material in the section "Complex Data Binding" in Chapter 5. The text and examples should help you relearn this material and help you understand what happens in this exercise. After doing that review, try this exercise again.

There are many other ways that you could meet the requirements of this particular exercise. For example, you could create stored procedures to retrieve the customer or order information (or both), or you could create a new `DataSet` object whenever you need a set of orders rather than build a `DataView` object on an existing `DataSet` object. As you practice with ADO.NET, you'll find that it's so flexible that there are almost always alternate ways to do things.

Editing Data with ADO.NET

Now that you know how to retrieve data with ADO.NET, there's one other important database-related topic to cover: editing data. ADO.NET supports all the normal database operations of updating existing data, adding new data, and deleting existing data.

As you read the following sections, you need to keep in mind the distinction between the data model and the database. As you work with data in the `DataSet` object and its subsidiary objects, you alter the data in the data model. These changes are not reflected in the underlying database until and unless you call the `Update()` method of the `SqlDataAdapter` object. So far I've only been using `SqlDataAdapter` to move data from the database to the data model; in the following sections, you'll see how to move data back from the data model to the database.

Updating Data

Updating data is easy: You simply assign a new value to the item in the `DataRow` object that you want to change. But there's more to finishing the job. In order for the `Update()` method of the `SqlDataAdapter` object to write changes back to the database, you need to set its `UpdateCommand` property to an appropriate `SqlCommand` object. Step by Step 6.24 shows you how.

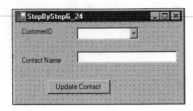

FIGURE 6.25
You can update the data in a database by using a SqlDataAdapter object.

STEP BY STEP

6.24 Using a `SqlDataAdapter` Object to Update Data in a Database

1. Add a new form to your Visual C# .NET project.

2. Place two `Label` controls, one `ComboBox` control (`cboCustomerID`), one `TextBox` control (`txtContactName`), and a `Button` control (`btnAdd`) on the form. Figure 6.25 shows the design for the form.

3. Switch to the code view and add the following `using` directives to make the ADO.NET objects available:

```
using System.Data;
using System.Data.SqlClient;
```

4. Add the following code in the class definition:

```
// Create SqlConnection, DataSet, SqlDataAdapter
// And DataRow[] ADO.NET objects
SqlConnection cnn = new SqlConnection(
    "Data Source=(local); Initial Catalog=Northwind;" +
    " Integrated Security=SSPI");
DataSet ds = new DataSet();
SqlDataAdapter da = new SqlDataAdapter();
DataRow[] adrEdit;
```

5. Double-click the form and enter this code to load data when the form is opened:

```
private void StepByStep6_24_Load(object sender,
    System.EventArgs e)
{
    // Create a SqlCommand to select data
    SqlCommand cmdSelect = cnn.CreateCommand();
    cmdSelect.CommandType = CommandType.Text;
    cmdSelect.CommandText =
      "SELECT CustomerID, ContactName FROM Customers";
    // Create a SqlCommand to update data
    SqlCommand cmdUpdate = cnn.CreateCommand();
    cmdUpdate.CommandType = CommandType.Text;
    cmdUpdate.CommandText = "UPDATE Customers SET " +
        "ContactName = @ContactName " +
        " WHERE CustomerID = @CustomerID";
    cmdUpdate.Parameters.Add("@ContactName",
      SqlDbType.NVarChar,30, "ContactName");
    cmdUpdate.Parameters.Add("@CustomerID",
      SqlDbType.NChar,5, "CustomerID");
```

```
cmdUpdate.Parameters["@CustomerID"].SourceVersion =
  DataRowVersion.Original;
// Set up the DataAdapter and fill the DataSet
da.UpdateCommand = cmdUpdate;
da.SelectCommand = cmdSelect;
da.Fill(ds, "Customers");
// Fill the data in the ComboBox
cboCustomerID.DisplayMember = "CustomerID";
cboCustomerID.ValueMember = "CustomerID";
cboCustomerID.DataSource = ds.Tables["Customers"];
}
```

6. Double-click the `ComboBox` control and enter this code to handle the `SelectedIndexChanged` event:

```
private void cboCustomerID_SelectedIndexChanged(
      object sender, System.EventArgs e)
{
    // Get just that customer's DataRow
    adrEdit = ds.Tables["Customers"].Select(
     "CustomerID = '" +
     cboCustomerID.SelectedValue + "'");
    // Make sure there's some data
    if (adrEdit != null)
    {
        txtContactName.Text =
          adrEdit[0]["ContactName"].ToString();
    }
}
```

7. Double-click the `Button` control and enter this code to handle the `Click` event of the `Button` control:

```
private void btnUpdate_Click(object sender,
    System.EventArgs e)
{
    // Make sure there's some data
    if (adrEdit != null)
    {
        // Prompt for new data and
        // put it in the DataRow object
        adrEdit[0]["ContactName"] = txtContactName.Text;
        // And save the changes
        da.Update(ds, "Customers");
        MessageBox.Show("Contact Name Updated!");
    }
}
```

8. Insert the `Main()` method to launch the form. Set the form as the startup object for the project.

9. Run the project. The code displays all the Customer ID values in the `ComboBox` control, with the corresponding

continues

continued

contact name value from the database in the text box. Select a customer ID (such as ALFKI) from the combo box and update the text box with a new contact name. Click the button. The change is written back to the database, and the update message is displayed in a message box.

The `Update()` method of the `SqlDataAdapter` object is syntactically similar to the `Fill()` method. It takes as its parameters the `DataSet` object to be reconciled with the database and the name of the `DataTable` object to be saved. You don't have to worry about which rows or columns of data are changed. The `SqlDataAdapter` object automatically locates the changed rows. It executes the `SqlCommand` object specified in its `UpdateCommand` property for each of those rows.

In Step by Step 6.24, the `UpdateCommand` property has two parameters. The `SqlParameter` objects are created by using a version of the constructor that takes four parameters rather than the three that you saw earlier in the chapter. The fourth parameter is the name of a `DataColumn` that contains the data to be used in this particular parameter. Note also that you can specify whether a parameter should be filled in from the current data in the `DataSet` object (the default) or the original version of the data, before any edits were made. In this case, the `@CustomerID` parameter is being used to locate the row to edit in the database, so the code uses the original value of the column as the value for the parameter.

Adding Data

To add data to the database, you must supply a `SqlCommand` object for the `InsertCommand` property of the `SqlDataAdapter` object.

STEP BY STEP

6.25 Using a SqlDataAdapter Object to Add Data to a Database

1. Add a new form to your Visual C# .NET project.

2. Place four Label controls, three TextBox controls (txtCustomerID, txtCompanyName, and txtContactName), and a Button control (btnAdd) on the form. Figure 6.26 shows the design for the form.

3. Switch to the code view and add the following using directives to make the ADO.NET objects available:

```
using System.Data;
using System.Data.SqlClient;
```

4. Double-click the form and enter this code to load data when the form is opened:

```
// Create some ADO.NET objects
SqlConnection cnn = new SqlConnection(
    "Data Source=(local); Initial Catalog=Northwind;" +
    " Integrated Security=SSPI");
DataSet ds = new DataSet();
SqlDataAdapter da = new SqlDataAdapter();

private void StepByStep6_25_Load(object sender,
    System.EventArgs e)
{
    // Create a SqlCommand to select data
    SqlCommand cmdSelect = cnn.CreateCommand();
    cmdSelect.CommandType = CommandType.Text;
    cmdSelect.CommandText =
        "SELECT CustomerID, CompanyName, " +
        "ContactName FROM Customers";
    // Create a SqlCommand to insert data
    SqlCommand cmdInsert = cnn.CreateCommand();
    cmdInsert.CommandType = CommandType.Text;
    cmdInsert.CommandText = "INSERT INTO Customers " +
    "(CustomerID, CompanyName, ContactName) " +
    "VALUES(@CustomerID, @CompanyName, @ContactName)";
    cmdInsert.Parameters.Add("@CustomerID",
        SqlDbType.NChar,5, "CustomerID");
    cmdInsert.Parameters.Add("@CompanyName",
        SqlDbType.NVarChar,40, "CompanyName");
    cmdInsert.Parameters.Add("@ContactName",
        SqlDbType.NVarChar,30, "ContactName");
    cmdInsert.Parameters["@CustomerID"].SourceVersion =
        DataRowVersion.Original;
```

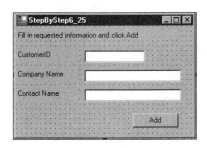

FIGURE 6.26
You can use the InsertCommand property of the SqlDataAdapter object to insert new customers into a database.

continues

```
// Set up the DataAdapter and fill the DataSet
da.SelectCommand = cmdSelect;
da.InsertCommand = cmdInsert;
da.Fill(ds, "Customers");
}
```

5. Double-click the Button control and enter this code to handle the Click event of the Button control:

```
private void btnAdd_Click(object sender,
    System.EventArgs e)
{
    // Create a new DataRow
    DataRow dr = ds.Tables["Customers"].NewRow();
    // Set values
    dr[0] = txtCustomerID.Text;
    dr[1] = txtCompanyName.Text;
    dr[2] = txtContactName.Text;
    // And append the new row to the DataTable
    ds.Tables["Customers"].Rows.Add(dr);
    // Now save back to the database
    da.Update(ds, "Customers");
    MessageBox.Show("Row added!");
}
```

6. Insert the Main() method to launch the form and set the form as the startup object for the project.

7. Run the project. Enter data in the TextBox controls and click the button. The code adds the new row to the database.

As you can see from Step by Step 6.25, the process of adding a new DataRow object to a DataTable object has several steps. First, you call the NewRow() method of the DataTable object. This returns a DataRow object that has the proper schema for that particular DataTable object. Then you can set the values of the individual items in the DataRow object. Finally, you call the Add() method of the DataTable object to actually append this DataRow object to the DataTable object.

Of course, appending the DataRow object to the DataTable object doesn't make any changes to the database. For that, you need to call the Update() method of the SqlDataAdapter object once again. If the SqlDataAdapter object finds any new rows in its scan of the database, it calls the SqlCommand object specified by its InsertCommand property once for each new row. This SqlCommand object does the actual work of permanently saving the data.

Deleting Data

The `DataRow` object supports a `Delete()` method that deletes an entire `DataRow` object from the `DataTable` object. To cause the changes to the database to persist, you need to call the `Update()` method of the `SqlDataAdapter` object.

STEP BY STEP

6.26 Using a `SqlDataAdapter` Object to Delete Data from a Database

1. Add a new form to your Visual C# .NET project.

2. Place a `Label` control, a `ComboBox` control (`cboCustomerID`) and a `Button` control (`btnDelete`) on the form.

3. Switch to the code view and add the following using directives to make the ADO.NET objects available:

```
using System.Data;
using System.Data.SqlClient;
```

4. Double-click the form and enter this code to load data when the form is opened:

```
// Create some ADO.NET objects
SqlConnection cnn = new SqlConnection(
    "Data Source=(local); Initial Catalog=Northwind;" +
    " Integrated Security=SSPI");
DataSet ds = new DataSet();
SqlDataAdapter da = new SqlDataAdapter();

private void StepByStep6_26_Load(object sender,
    System.EventArgs e)
{
    // Create a SqlCommand to select data
    SqlCommand cmdSelect = cnn.CreateCommand();
    cmdSelect.CommandType = CommandType.Text;
    cmdSelect.CommandText =
        "SELECT CustomerID, ContactName FROM Customers";
    // Create a SqlCommand to delete data
    SqlCommand cmdDelete = cnn.CreateCommand();
    cmdDelete.CommandType = CommandType.Text;
    cmdDelete.CommandText =
    "DELETE FROM Customers " +
        WHERE CustomerID = @CustomerID";
    cmdDelete.Parameters.Add("@CustomerID",
        SqlDbType.NChar,5, "CustomerID");
    cmdDelete.Parameters["@CustomerID"].SourceVersion =
```

continues

continued

```
                    DataRowVersion.Original;
    // Set up the DataAdapter and fill the DataSet
    da.SelectCommand = cmdSelect;
    da.DeleteCommand = cmdDelete;
    da.Fill(ds, "Customers");
    // Fill the data in the ComboBox
    cboCustomerID.DisplayMember = "CustomerID";
    cboCustomerID.ValueMember = "CustomerID";
    cboCustomerID.DataSource = ds.Tables["Customers"];
}
```

5. Double-click the Button control and enter this code to handle the `Click` event of the `Button` control:

```
private void btnDelete_Click(object sender,
    System.EventArgs e)
{
    // Find the specified row and delete it
    foreach( DataRow dr in ds.Tables["Customers"].Rows)
    {
        if(dr[0] == cboCustomerID.SelectedValue)
        {
            dr.Delete();
            break;
        }
    }
    // Save the changes
    da.Update(ds, "Customers");
    MessageBox.Show("Row deleted!");
}
```

6. Insert the `Main()` method to launch the form. Set the form as the startup object for the project.

7. Run the project. The form pops up with a `ComboBox` control that contains all the customer IDs and a `Button` control. Select a customer ID and click the button. The selected customer is deleted from the `DataSet` object and from the database.

Note in Step by Step 6.26 that the deletion command uses the original value of the `CustomerID` column to locate the correct row to delete from the database.

Editing with a `DataGrid` Control

The preceding examples of editing, adding, and deleting rows are functional but somewhat tedious. Fortunately, there are easier ways to set up these operations in the user interface. If you bind a `DataSet` object to a `DataGrid` control, the `DataGrid` control enables you to perform all three of the fundamental editing operations:

◆ To update the data in a row, click in the column to be updated and type a new value.

◆ To add a new row, scroll to the end of the list and type the values for the row into the last row of the `DataGrid control`.

◆ To delete a row, click on the record selector to the left of the row and click the Delete key on the keyboard.

If you use a `DataGrid` control for editing, you should supply `SqlCommand` objects to handle all the editing operations.

STEP BY STEP

6.27 Using a `DataGrid` Control to Edit Data in a Database

1. Add a new form to your Visual C# .NET project.

2. Place a `DataGrid` control (`dgCustomers`) and a Button control (`btnSaveChanges`) on the form.

3. Switch to the code view and add the following using directives to make the ADO.NET objects available:

```
using System.Data;
using System.Data.SqlClient;
```

4. Double-click the form and enter this code to load data when the form is opened:

```
// Create some ADO.NET objects
SqlConnection cnn = new SqlConnection(
    "Data Source=(local); Initial Catalog=Northwind;" +
    " Integrated Security=SSPI");
DataSet ds = new DataSet();
SqlDataAdapter da = new SqlDataAdapter();
```

continues

continued

```
private void StepByStep6_27_Load(object sender,
    System.EventArgs e)
{
    // Create a SqlCommand to select data
    SqlCommand cmdSelect = cnn.CreateCommand();
    cmdSelect.CommandType = CommandType.Text;
    cmdSelect.CommandText = "SELECT CustomerID, " +
        " CompanyName, ContactName FROM Customers";
    // Create a SqlCommand to update data
    SqlCommand cmdUpdate = cnn.CreateCommand();
    cmdUpdate.CommandType = CommandType.Text;
    cmdUpdate.CommandText = "UPDATE Customers SET " +
    "CompanyName = @CompanyName, ContactName = " +
    "@ContactName " + "WHERE CustomerID = @CustomerID";
    cmdUpdate.Parameters.Add("@ContactName",
        SqlDbType.NVarChar, 30, "ContactName");
    cmdUpdate.Parameters.Add("@CompanyName",
        SqlDbType.NVarChar, 40, "CompanyName");
    cmdUpdate.Parameters.Add("@CustomerID",
        SqlDbType.NChar, 5, "CustomerID");
    cmdUpdate.Parameters["@CustomerID"].SourceVersion
        = DataRowVersion.Original;
    // Create a SqlCommand to insert data
    SqlCommand cmdInsert= cnn.CreateCommand();
    cmdInsert.CommandType = CommandType.Text;
    cmdInsert.CommandText = "INSERT INTO Customers " +
    "(CustomerID, CompanyName, ContactName) " +
    "VALUES(@CustomerID, @CompanyName, @ContactName)";
    cmdInsert.Parameters.Add("@CustomerID",
        SqlDbType.NChar,5, "CustomerID");
    cmdInsert.Parameters.Add("@CompanyName",
        SqlDbType.NVarChar, 40, "CompanyName");
    cmdInsert.Parameters.Add("@ContactName",
        SqlDbType.NVarChar, 30, "ContactName");
    cmdInsert.Parameters["@CustomerID"].SourceVersion
        = DataRowVersion.Original;
    // Create a SqlCommand to delete data
    SqlCommand cmdDelete = cnn.CreateCommand();
    cmdDelete.CommandType = CommandType.Text;
    cmdDelete.CommandText = "DELETE FROM Customers" +
        " WHERE CustomerID = @CustomerID";
    cmdDelete.Parameters.Add("@CustomerID",
        SqlDbType.NChar, 5, "CustomerID");
    cmdDelete.Parameters["@CustomerID"].SourceVersion
        = DataRowVersion.Original;
    // Set up the DataAdapter and fill the DataSet
    da.SelectCommand = cmdSelect;
    da.UpdateCommand = cmdUpdate;
    da.InsertCommand = cmdInsert;
    da.DeleteCommand = cmdDelete;
    da.Fill(ds, "Customers");
```

```
    // And bind the data to the DataGrid
    dgCustomers.DataSource = ds;
    dgCustomers.DataMember = "Customers";
}
```

5. Double-click the `Button` control and enter this code to handle the `Click` event of the `Button` control:

```
private void btnSaveChanges_Click(object sender,
    System.EventArgs e)
{
 // Persist all changes from the
 // data model to the database
    da.Update(ds, "Customers");
}
```

6. Insert the `Main()` method to launch the form. Set the form as the startup object for the project.

7. Run the project. Make some changes in the `DataGrid` control and click the Save Changes button. If you run the project a second time, you should find that all the changes were saved to the database.

Although there's a lot of code in Step by Step 6.27, it's just a combination of the code from Step by Steps 6.24 through 6.26. To set up a `SqlDataAdapter` object to handle all possible changes, you need to supply all the necessary `SqlCommand` objects. The `Update()` method of the `SqlDataAdapter` object takes care of calling the appropriate `SqlCommand` object for each change.

REVIEW BREAK

▶ You can change data in a `DataSet` object just by treating the items in the `DataSet` object like any other variables.

▶ To cause changes from the data model to persist to the underlying database, you must call the `Update()` method of the `SqlDataAdapter` object.

▶ The `UpdateCommand` property of the `SqlDataAdapter` object specifies a `SqlCommand` object to be executed for all changed rows.

▶ The `InsertCommand` property of the `SqlDataAdapter` object specifies a `SqlCommand` object to be executed for all new rows.

continues

continued

▶ The `DeleteCommand` property of the `SqlDataAdapter` object specifies a `SqlCommand` object to be executed for all deleted rows.

▶ The `DataGrid` control can provide a convenient way to handle data changes on the user interface.

Using XML Data

The final type of data that you'll learn about in this chapter is XML data. XML is an entire family of closely related standards. For example, an XSD file is a special type of XML file for storing schema information. XSD files were used in the section "Using Strongly Typed DataSet Objects", earlier in this chapter.

The following sections introduce you to the basic terminology and format of XML files. Then you'll learn about the `XmlDocument` and `XmlNode` classes, which are part of the `System.Xml` namespace. These classes provide an internal representation of XML that your .NET applications can use. Finally, to tie things together, you'll see how you can synchronize data in a `DataSet` object with data in an `XmlDocument` object.

Understanding XML

If you're already familiar with XML, you might want to skip this section. Otherwise, you should follow along. You'll find that the basics are not that difficult, although some people seem determined to make XML harder than it has to be.

XML is just human-readable data combined with human-readable metadata. That is, XML files contain regular text, so you can read them. And they contain both data (such as customer ID values) and descriptions of that data.

Here's a concrete example to start with. This XML file represents data for two customers:

```
<?xml version="1.0" encoding="UTF-8"?>
<!-- Customer list for Bob's Tractor Parts -->
<Customers>
```

```
    <Customer CustomerNumber="1">
        <CustomerName>Lambert Tractor Works
        </CustomerName>
        <CustomerCity>Millbank</CustomerCity>
        <CustomerState>WA</CustomerState>
    </Customer>
    <Customer CustomerNumber="2">
        <CustomerName><![CDATA[Joe's Garage]]>
        </CustomerName>
        <CustomerCity>Doppel</CustomerCity>
        <CustomerState>OR</CustomerState>
    </Customer>
</Customers>
```

Even without knowing anything about XML, you can see some things just by looking at this file. In particular, XML consists of tags (which are contained within angle brackets) and data. Tags appear in pairs, with each opening tag matched by a closing tag. The closing tag has the same text as the opening tag, prefixed with a forward slash (for example, if <CustomerCity> is the opening tag, </CustomerCity> is the closing tag.

The first thing that you find in an XML file is the *XML declaration*:

```
<?xml version="1.0" encoding="UTF-8"?>
```

The declaration tells you three things about this document:

◆ It's an XML document.

◆ It conforms to the XML 1.0 specification.

◆ It uses the UTF-8 character set (a standard set of characters for the Western alphabet).

The XML tags that begin and end with a ? are called *processing instructions*. Tags in an XML document contain the names of elements. If you're familiar with Hypertext Markup Language (HTML), you know that in HTML, some elements have names dictated by the HTML specification. For example, the <H1> tag specifies a first-level heading. XML takes a different approach. You can make up any name you like for an element, subject to some simple naming rules:

◆ A name can contain any alphanumeric character.

◆ A name can contain underscores, hyphens, and periods.

◆ A name must not contain any whitespace.

◆ A name must start with a letter or an underscore.

An opening tag together with a closing tag and the content between them define an *element*. For example, here's a single element from the sample document:

```
<CustomerState>OR</CustomerState>
```

This defines an element whose name is `CustomerState` and whose value is `OR`.

Elements can be nested, but they cannot overlap. So the following is legal XML, defining an element named `Customer` that has three child elements:

```
<Customer CustomerNumber="1">
    <CustomerName>Lambert Tractor Works</CustomerName>
    <CustomerCity>Millbank</CustomerCity>
    <CustomerState>WA</CustomerState>
</Customer>
```

But the following is not legal XML because the `CustomerCity` and `CustomerState` elements overlap:

```
<Customer CustomerNumber="1">
    <CustomerName>Lambert Tractor Works</CustomerName>
    <CustomerCity>Millbank<CustomerState>
    </CustomerCity>WA</CustomerState>
</Customer>
```

Every XML document contains a single root element that contains all the other nodes of the XML document. The root element in the sample document is named `Customers`.

The effect of the rules that nesting is okay, overlapping is not okay, and there is a single root element is that any XML document can be represented as a tree of nodes.

Elements can contain attributes. An *attribute* is a piece of data that further describes an element. For example, the sample document includes this opening tag for an element:

```
<Customer CustomerNumber="1">
```

This declares an element named `Customer`. The `Customer` element includes an attribute whose name is `CustomerNumber` and whose value is `1`.

An XML document can contain one or more *namespace* declarations. The sample document does not declare a namespace. Here's an example for a namespace declaration:

```
<Customers xmlns:tr="urn:schemas-tractor-repair">
```

The namespace is declared as part of the root tag for the document. In this particular case, the namespace (introduced with the special `xmlns` characters) defines the prefix `tr` for tags within the namespace. `urn` (for the uniform resource name) is an arbitrary string whose purpose is to distinguish this namespace from other namespaces.

XML namespaces serve the same purpose as .NET namespaces: They help cut down on naming collisions. After declaring the `tr` namespace, an XML document could use a tag such as this:

```
<tr:CustomerState>OR</tr:CustomerState>
```

This indicates that this `CustomerState` tag is from the `tr` namespace and should not be confused with any other `CustomerState` tag.

XML offers two ways to deal with special characters in data. First, for individual characters you can use entity references. Five entity references are defined in the XML standard:

◆ `&lt`—Translates to < (opening angle bracket).

◆ `&gt`—Translates to > (closing angle bracket).

◆ `&amp`—Translates to & (ampersand).

◆ `&apos`—Translates to ' (apostrophe)

◆ `&quot`—Translates to " (quotation mark).

You can also use a `CDATA` section to hold any arbitrary data, whether the data contains special characters or not. The sample document uses this approach to store a customer name containing an apostrophe, as shown here:

```
<CustomerName><![CDATA[Joe's Garage]]></CustomerName>
```

Finally, an XML document can contain comments. Comments are set off by the opening string `<!--` and the closing string `-->`. Here's an example:

```
<!-- Customer list for Bob's Tractor Parts -->
```

There is a great deal more complexity available in XML than discussed in this section. But these basics are more than enough for you to understand most of the XML that you're likely to run across until you start working with XML in depth.

Using the `XmlNode`, `XmlDocument`,

XmlTextReader, and XmlTextWriter Classes

XML documents on disk are just disk files, so you could read them with the System.IO classes that you learned about earlier in the chapter. But XML is so central to the .NET Framework that the .NET Framework provides classes especially for working with XML. These classes are grouped together in the System.Xml namespace.

To understand the .NET Framework representation of an XML document, you can start with the concept of a node. A *node* is one item in an XML document: It might be an attribute, a comment, an element, or something else. In the System.Xml namespace, nodes are represented by XmlNode objects. Table 6.14 shows the most important members of the XmlNode object.

TABLE 6.14

IMPORTANT MEMBERS OF THE XmlNode CLASS

Member	*Type*	*Description*
AppendChild()	Method	Adds a new child node to the end of this node's list of children.
Attributes	Property	Specifies a collection of the attributes of this node.
ChildNodes	Property	Specifies a collection of child nodes of this node.
FirstChild	Property	Specifies the first child node of this node.
InnerText	Property	Specifies the value of this node and all its children.
InnerXml	Property	Specifies the XML code representing just the children of this node.
InsertAfter()	Method	Inserts a new node after this node.
InsertBefore()	Method	Inserts a new node before this node.
LastChild	Property	Specifies the last child node of this node.
Name	Property	Specifies the name of the node.
NextSibling	Property	Specifies the next child node of this node's parent node.
NodeType	Property	Specifies the type of this node. The XmlNodeType enumeration includes values for all possible node types.

Member	*Type*	*Description*
OuterXml	Property	Specifies the XML code representing this node and all its children.
ParentNode	Property	Specifies the parent of this node.
PrependChild()	Method	Adds a new child node to the start of this node's list of children.
PreviousSibling()	Method	Specifies the previous child node of this node's parent node.
RemoveAll()	Method	Removes all children of this node.
RemoveChild()	Method	Removes a specified child of this node.
ReplaceChild()	Method	Replaces a child node with a new node.
Value	Property	Specifies the value of the node.

> **EXAM TIP**
>
> **Get the Big Picture** You should not worry about memorizing the complete list of XmlNode members. Instead, you should concentrate on understanding the big picture: There are rich methods for navigating the tree of nodes and for altering existing nodes.

XmlNode objects are collected into an XmlDocument object. As you can probably guess, XmlDocument is the object in the System.Xml namespace that represents an entire XML document. The XmlDocument class provides an in-memory representation of an XML document. The XmlDocument class implements the W3C Document Object Model (DOM) Level 1 Core and the Core DOM Level 2 standards. The DOM provides a standard programming model for working with XML. Table 6.15 shows the most important members of the XmlDocument class.

TABLE 6.15

SOME IMPORTANT MEMBERS OF THE XmlDocument CLASS

Member	*Type*	*Description*
CreateAttribute()	Method	Creates a new attribute node
CreateElement()	Method	Creates a new element node
CreateNode()	Method	Creates a new XmlNode object
DocumentElement	Property	Returns the XmlNode object that represents the root node of this document
GetElementsByTagName()	Method	Returns a list of all elements with the specified tag name
Load()	Method	Loads an XML document into an XmlDocument object
LoadXml()	Method	Loads a string of XML data into an XmlDocument object

continues

TABLE 6.15	*continued*

SOME IMPORTANT MEMBERS OF THE XmlDocument CLASS

Member	*Type*	*Description*
Save()	Method	Saves the XmlDocument object as a file or stream
WriteTo()	Method	Saves the XmlDocument object to an XmlWriter object

STEP BY STEP

6.28 Displaying the Contents of an XML Document

1. Add a new form to your Visual C# .NET project.

2. Place a ListBox control (lbNodes) and a Button control (btnLoadXml) on the form.

3. Switch to the code view and add the following using directive:

```
using System.Xml;
```

4. Double-click the Button control and enter this code to load data when the button is clicked:

```
private void btnLoadXml_Click(object sender,
    System.EventArgs e)
{
    // Browse for an XML file
    OpenFileDialog dlgOpen = new OpenFileDialog();
    dlgOpen.Title = "Select a File";
    dlgOpen.Filter =
        "XML files (*.xml)|*.xml|All Files(*.*)|*.*";
    if(dlgOpen.ShowDialog() == DialogResult.OK)
    {
        // Create an XmlTextReader object
        // that will read in the file
        XmlTextReader xtr = new XmlTextReader(
            dlgOpen.FileName);
        xtr.WhitespaceHandling = WhitespaceHandling.None;
        // Create an XmlDocument object
        XmlDocument xd = new XmlDocument();
        // Load the file into the XmlDocument
        xd.Load(xtr);
```

```
            // Add an item representing the document
            // to the ListBox
            lbNodes.Items.Add("XML Document");
            // Find the root node, and
            // add it together with its children
            XmlNode xnod = xd.DocumentElement;
            AddWithChildren(xnod, 1);
        }
    }

    private void AddWithChildren(
    XmlNode xnod, Int32 intLevel)
    {
        // Adds a node to the ListBox, together with its
        // children. intLevel controls the
        // depth of indenting
        XmlNode xnodWorking;
        String strIndent = new String(' ', 2 * intLevel);
        // Get the value of the node (if any)
        String strValue= (String) xnod.Value;
        if(strValue != null)
        {
            strValue = " : " + strValue;
        }
        // Add the node details to the ListBox
        lbNodes.Items.Add(strIndent + xnod.Name + strValue);
        // For an element node, retrieve the attributes
        if(xnod.NodeType == XmlNodeType.Element)
        {
            XmlNamedNodeMap mapAttributes= xnod.Attributes;
            // Add the attrbutes to the ListBox
            foreach(XmlNode xnodAttribute in mapAttributes)
            {
                lbNodes.Items.Add(strIndent + "  " +
                  xnodAttribute.Name + " : " +
                  xnodAttribute.Value);
            }
            // If there are any child nodes
            // Call this procedure recursively
            if(xnod.HasChildNodes)
            {
                xnodWorking = xnod.FirstChild;
                while (xnodWorking != null)
                {
                    AddWithChildren(
                        xnodWorking, intLevel + 1);
                    xnodWorking = xnodWorking.NextSibling;
                }
            }
        }
    }
}
```

continues

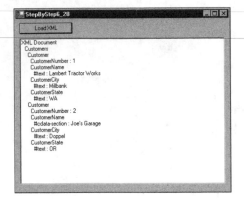

FIGURE 6.27
The XmlDocument class is an in-memory representation of an XML document.

continued

5. Insert the Main() method to launch the form. Set the form as the startup object for the project.

6. Run the project. Click the button and browse to an XML file (for example, Customers.xml). The contents of the XML code are dumped to the ListBox control, as shown in Figure 6.27.

As you can see in Figure 6.27, the object model implemented in the XmlDocument and XmlNode objects has access to the entire contents of the XML file. The code in Step by Step 6.28 uses an XmlTextReader object to read the disk file into the XmlDocument object. The XmlTextReader object has very similar functionality to the StreamReader and BinaryReader objects discussed earlier in the chapter, except that it's designed to pipe data from a disk file to an XmlDocument object. The XmlTextReader object also has other XML-specific features. For example, the WhitespaceHandling property setting in the code in Step by Step 6.28 tells it not to create nodes for extra whitespace in the XML file.

The code uses the DocumentElement property of the XmlDocument object to find the node at the root of the tree representation of the XML document. After that, it's just a matter of recursively calling a procedure that adds information about the node to the ListBox control.

One bit of added complexity in the code is necessary to deal with attributes. Attribute nodes are not included in the ChildNodes collection of a node in the XmlDocument object. Instead, you can use the Attributes property of the XmlNode object to get a collection of attribute nodes only. The code uses an XmlNamedNodeMap object to hold this collection; this object can hold an arbitrary collection of XmlNode objects of any type.

You can also modify an XML document through the XmlDocument object. To do so, you need to modify the individual XmlNode objects and then write the file back to disk.

STEP BY STEP

6.29 Modifying an XML File by Using Code

1. Add a new form to your Visual C# .NET project.

2. Place a `Button` control (`btnModify`) on the form.

3. Switch to the code view and add the following `using` directive:

```
using System.Xml;
```

4. Double-click the `Button` control and enter this code to load and modify data when the button is clicked:

```
private void btnModify_Click(object sender,
    System.EventArgs e)
{
    // Browse for an XML file
    OpenFileDialog dlgOpen = new OpenFileDialog();
    dlgOpen.Title = "Select a File";
    dlgOpen.Filter =
        "XML files (*.xml)|*.xml|All Files(*.*)|*.*";
    if(dlgOpen.ShowDialog() == DialogResult.OK)
    {
        // Create an XmlTextReader object
        // that will read in the file
        XmlTextReader xtr = new XmlTextReader(
            dlgOpen.FileName);
        xtr.WhitespaceHandling =
         WhitespaceHandling.None;
        // Create an XmlDocument object
        XmlDocument xd = new XmlDocument();
        // Load the file into the XmlDocument
        xd.Load(xtr);
        xtr.Close();
        // Find the root node, and
        // modify it together with its children
        XmlNode xnod = xd.DocumentElement;
        ModifyWithChildren(xnod);
        // Write the modified file to disk
        XmlTextWriter xtw = new XmlTextWriter(
          dlgOpen.FileName + ".new",
          System.Text.Encoding.UTF8);
        xd.WriteTo(xtw);
        xtw.Flush();
        xtw.Close();
        MessageBox.Show("Done!");
    }
}
```

continues

continued

```
private void ModifyWithChildren(XmlNode xnod)
{
    XmlNode xnodWorking;

    if (xnod.Name == "CustomerCity")
    {
        // Sets all CustomerCity nodes to uppercase
        xnod.FirstChild.Value =
            xnod.FirstChild.Value.ToUpper();
    }
    // If there are any child nodes
    // Call this procedure recursively
    if (xnod.HasChildNodes)
    {
        xnodWorking = xnod.FirstChild;
        while(xnodWorking != null)
        {
            ModifyWithChildren(xnodWorking);
            xnodWorking = xnodWorking.NextSibling;
        }
    }
}
```

> **NOTE**
>
> **XmlDocument Versus XmlTextReader and XmlTextWriter** XmlDocument loads the entire XML document in memory to form a hierarchical tree structure. This allows you to access data in any node. XmlDocument can be used to insert, update, delete, or move a node.
>
> As opposed to this, XmlTextReader and XmlTextWriter use a forward-only approach for reading and writing data respectively.

> **EXAM TIP**
>
> **When Should You Choose XmlTextReader over XmlDocument?** When you have to read data fast in forward-only manner and memory is a constraint, you should use XmlTextReader. When memory is not a constraint and you want the flexibility of inserting, deleting, and updating data in any direction, you should use XmlDocument.

5. Insert the Main() method to launch the form. Set the form as the startup object for the project.

6. Run the project. Click the button and browse to an XML file. The code makes a copy of the XML file with the added extension .new. The copy has all the CustomerCity values converted to uppercase.

Writing the XML file in Step by Step 6.29 uses one new class, XmlTextWriter. This class connects an XmlDocument object to a backing store for output, similar to the StreamWriter object discussed earlier in the chapter.

Treating XML as Relational Data

You can treat an XML document as relational data. To do this, you can use the XmlDataDocument class, which inherits from XmlDocument. The key feature of the XmlDataDocument class is that it can be synchronized with a DataSet object.

STEP BY STEP

6.30 Reading an XML Document into a DataSet Object

1. Add a new form to your Visual C# .NET project.

2. Place a Button control (btnLoadXml) and a DataGrid control (dgXml) on the form.

3. Switch to the code view and add the following using directives:

```
using System.Xml;
using System.Data;
```

4. Double-click the Button control and enter this code to load data when the button is clicked:

```
private void btnLoadXml_Click(object sender,
    System.EventArgs e)
{
    // Browse for an XML file
    OpenFileDialog dlgOpen = new OpenFileDialog();
    dlgOpen.Title = "Select a File";
    dlgOpen.Filter =
      "XML files (*.xml)|*.xml|All Files(*.*)|*.*";
    if (dlgOpen.ShowDialog() == DialogResult.OK)
    {
        // Create an XmlTextReader object
        // that will read in the file
        XmlTextReader xtr = new XmlTextReader(
            dlgOpen.FileName);
        // Create an XmlDocument object
        XmlDataDocument xdd = new XmlDataDocument();
        // Get the DataSet
        DataSet ds = xdd.DataSet;
        // Read the schema of the file to
        // initialize the DataSet
        ds.ReadXmlSchema(xtr);
        xtr.Close();
        xtr = new XmlTextReader(dlgOpen.FileName);
        xtr.WhitespaceHandling = WhitespaceHandling.None;
        // Load the file into the XmlDataDocument
        xdd.Load(xtr);
        xtr.Close();
        // And display it on the DataGrid
        dgXml.DataSource = ds;
    }
}
```

continues

continued

5. Insert the `Main()` method to launch the form. Set the form as the startup object for the project.

6. Run the project. Click the button and browse to an XML file. The code loads the XML file into the `DataSet` object and displays it on the user interface, as shown in Figure 6.28.

FIGURE 6.28
An XML File can be synchronized with a `DataSet` object, with the help of the `XmlDataDocument` class.

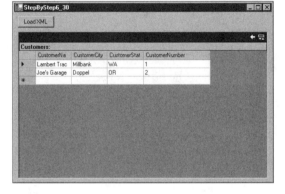

For the `DataSet` object to properly represent the XML code, it must have the same schema as the XML file. In Step by Step 6.30 I've ensured that by using the `ReadXmlSchema()` method of the `DataSet` object to load the schema from the same XML file that the `XmlDataDocument` object holds. The `XmlTextReader` object has to be closed and reopened after the schema is read because it's a forward-only object.

The synchronization between the `XmlDataDocument` object and the `DataSet` object is two way. If you derive a `DataSet` object from an `XmlDataDocument` object, modify the `DataSet` object, and then write the `XmlDataDocument` object back to disk, the changes that you made in the `DataSet` object are reflected in the XML file.

NOTE

From the `DataSet` Object to XML If you already have a `DataSet` object in your code, you can create the equivalent XML document by calling an overloaded constructor of the `XmlDataDocument` class:

```
XmlDataDocument xdd =
    new XmlDataDocument(ds);
```

GUIDED PRACTICE
EXERCISE 6.4

Northwind Traders has a new European partner that doesn't use
Microsoft SQL Server for its data storage. However, it can import an
XML file to its system. In this exercise, you need to retrieve all the
customers from France, allow the user to edit the customer informa-
tion on a form, and then save the edited version as an XML file.
The edits should *not* be saved to your own database.

How would you design such a form?

You should try working through this problem on your own first. If
you get stuck, or if you'd like to see one possible solution, follow
these steps:

1. Add a new form to your Visual C# .NET project.

2. Place a `DataGrid` control (`dgCustomers`) and a `Button` control
   (`btnSave`) on the form.

3. Switch to the code view and add the following `using` directives::

   ```
   using System.Data;
   using System.Data.SqlClient;
   using System.Xml;
   ```

4. Double-click the form and enter this code to load the data
   when the form is opened:

   ```
   private void GuidedPracticeExercise6_4_Load(
      object sender,
        System.EventArgs e)
   {
       // Create a SqlConnection
       SqlConnection cnn = new SqlConnection(
       "Data Source=(local);" +
       "Initial Catalog=Northwind;" +
       "Integrated Security=SSPI");
       // Create a SqlCommand
       SqlCommand cmd = cnn.CreateCommand();
       cmd.CommandType = CommandType.Text;
       cmd.CommandText = "SELECT * FROM Customers " +
           "WHERE Country = 'France'";
       // Set up the DataAdapter and fill the DataSet
       SqlDataAdapter da = new SqlDataAdapter();
       da.SelectCommand = cmd;
       DataSet ds = new DataSet();
       da.Fill(ds, "Customers");
   ```

continues

continued

```
// Show the data on the user interface
// so that the user can edit it
dgCustomers.DataSource = ds;
dgCustomers.DataMember = "Customers";
}
```

5. Double-click the Button control and enter this code to save the file when the user clicks the button:

```
private void btnSave_Click(object sender,
    System.EventArgs e)
{
    // Create an XmlDataDocument from the DataSet
    XmlDataDocument xdd = new XmlDataDocument(
        (DataSet) dgCustomers.DataSource);
    // And save it to a disk file
    XmlTextWriter xtw = new XmlTextWriter(
     @"c:\temp\FranceCust.xml",
     System.Text.Encoding.UTF8);
    xdd.WriteTo(xtw);
    xtw.Flush();
    xtw.Close();
    MessageBox.Show(
        @"Wrote file c:\temp\FranceCust.xml");
}
```

6. Insert the Main() method to launch the form. Set the form as the startup object for the project.

7. Run the project. The French customers appear on the user interface. Edit some of the data and then click the Save button. Open the c:\temp\FranceCust.xml file and verify that it contains the edited data.

If you have difficulty following this exercise, review the sections "Using the XmlDocument Class" and "Treating XML as Relational Data," earlier in this chapter. The text and examples should help you relearn this material and help you understand what happens in this exercise. After doing that review, try this exercise again.

There are several alternatives for meeting the requirements in Guided Practice Exercise 6.4. For example, you could choose to save the DataSet object directly, instead of working with an XmlDataDocument object, by working with the DataSet.WriteXml() method. If you'd like to let the user browse for a filename instead of hard-coding the filename, you could use the System.Windows.Forms.SaveFileDialog class.

▶ The `XmlNode` class represents a single node in an XML document (for example, an attribute, a comment, an element).

▶ The `XmlDocument` class provides an in-memory representation of an XML document.

▶ When memory is not a constraint and you want flexibility in retrieving, inserting, deleting, and updating data in any direction from XML files, you use `XmlDocument`.

▶ To read data from XML files quickly, in a forward-only manner, where memory is a constraint, you use `XmlTextReader`.

▶ The `XmlDataDocument` class can be synchronized with a `DataSet` object.

HANDLING DATA ERRORS

Consuming and manipulating data.

- **Handle data errors.**

Although error trapping has been left out of the code so far in this chapter for the sake of simplicity, in real life you can't afford to do that. You should always check for errors in any production code, so that you can take corrective action if something goes wrong. The following sections show you how to deal with two groups of data errors. First, you might attempt an operation that causes an error from the underlying database. Second, in a multiuser situation errors can be caused by two or more users editing the same row of data.

Handling Database Errors

Many things can go wrong when you're working with a database. You might try to add a duplicate value to a column that allows only unique values, or you might try to write to a table that you don't have permission to modify. In serious cases, the database server itself might run out of disk space. These are just a few of the thousands of specific conditions that can trigger SQL Server errors.

The System.Data.SqlClient namespace includes two objects to help you handle SQL Server–specific errors: the SqlException class, which inherits from System.Exception, and the SqlError class, which represents a single SQL Server error.

STEP BY STEP

6.31 Trapping SQL Server Errors

1. Add a new form to your Visual C# .NET project.

2. Place a Button control (btnNew) on the form.

3. Switch to the code view and add the following using directives to make the ADO.NET objects available:

```
using System.Data;
using System.Data.SqlClient;
```

4. Double-click the Button control and enter this code to handle the button's Click event:

```
private void btnNew_Click(object sender,
    System.EventArgs e)
{
    try
    {
        // Create a SqlConnection
        SqlConnection cnn = new SqlConnection(
          "Data Source=(local);" +
          "Initial Catalog=Northwind;"
            + "Integrated Security=SSPI");
        // Create a SqlCommand
        SqlCommand cmd = cnn.CreateCommand();
        cmd.CommandType = CommandType.Text;
        cmd.CommandText = "INSERT INTO Customers " +
            " (CompanyName) VALUES ('New Company')";
        // And execute it
        cnn.Open();
        cmd.ExecuteNonQuery();
        cnn.Close();
    }
    catch(SqlException sqlEx)
    {
        // Handle SQL Server specific errors
        foreach (SqlError err in sqlEx.Errors)
        {
            MessageBox.Show("SQL Error " +
                err.Number + ": " + err.Message);
        }
    }
```

```
        catch(Exception ex)
        {
            // Handle general errors
            MessageBox.Show("Non-SQL Exception " +
                ex.Message);
        }
}
```

5. Insert the `Main()` method to launch the form. Set the form as the startup object for the project.

6. Run the project. Click the button. You get a message box that informs you of error 515, `Cannot insert the value NULL into column 'CustomerID', table 'Northwind.dbo.Customers'; column does not allow nulls. INSERT fails.`. When you dismiss this message box, you get a second message box that informs you of error 3621, `The statement has been terminated.`.

As you can see in the code in Step by Step 6.31, the `SqlException` object exposes an `Errors` property. This property is a collection of `SqlError` objects, each of which contains a SQL Server error. A single SQL Server operation can raise multiple errors, as it does in Step by Step 6.31. You should place a similar error trap in any procedure that uses the classes from the `System.Data.SqlClient` namespace.

> **EXAM TIP**
>
> **Trapping All the Errors** The code in Step by Step 6.31 actually has two different `catch` statements. The first one catches exceptions that are packaged as a `SqlException` object. But even if you're writing data access code, it's possible for non–data-related errors to occur. That's why there's a second `catch` statement that uses the generic `Exception` object. Any time that you write code to catch exceptions of a specific type, you should remember to include a general-purpose `catch` statement, just in case.

Handling Multiuser Errors

You need to be aware of a second class of errors when you're writing database code—though actually, these are better thought of as "potentially unexpected outcomes" than as errors. Whenever you have more than one user updating the same data, concurrency issues can arise. The basic question is who wins in case of multiple updates.

Here's how the problem arises: Suppose both Alice and Bob are working with data from the Customers table in a SQL Server database. They've both downloaded to their local computers a `DataSet` object that contains the Customers table, and both are making edits in a `DataGrid` control. Alice changes the address of the first customer in the table because she's working on a stack of change-of-address requests.

Meanwhile, Bob changes the contact name for the first customer because he's updating the sales records. So now there are three versions of the row: the original one that's still on the SQL Server database, the one with a new address that's on Alice's computer, and the one with the new contact name that's on Bob's computer. Bob saves his changes by calling the Update() method of the SqlDataAdapter object so the SQL Server database contains the new contact name.

What happens when Alice saves her changes? It depends.

When you're creating the SqlCommand object that is used for the UpdateCommand property of a SqlDataAdapter object, you have to choose between two different strategies for dealing with such conflicts:

◆ **Optimistic concurrency control**—With this strategy, an update to a row succeeds only if no one else has changed that row after it is loaded into the DataSet object.

◆ **"Last one wins" concurrency control**—With this strategy, an update to a row always succeeds, whether another user has edited the row or not (as long as the row still exists).

Step by Step 6.24 shows how to implement "last one wins" concurrency control. Consider the SQL statement that the code in Step by Step 6.24 uses to update the database:

```
UPDATE Customers
SET ContactName = @ContactName
WHERE CustomerID = @CustomerID
```

The key thing to look at here is the WHERE clause. The only column that it looks at is the CustomerID column. CustomerID is the primary key of this table, a value that should never change. As long as that one column has not been changed, the UPDATE statement succeeds, no matter what may have changed about other columns in the same table.

Step by Step 6.32 shows how to implement optimistic concurrency control.

STEP BY STEP

6.32 Implementing Optimistic Concurrency Control

1. Add a new form to your Visual C# .NET project.

2. Place two Label controls, one ComboBox control (cboCustomerID), one TextBox control (txtContactName), and one Button control (btnAdd) on the form. Figure 6.25 shows the design for the form.

3. Switch to the code view and add the following using directives to make the ADO.NET objects available:

```
using System.Data;
using System.Data.SqlClient;
```

4. Double-click the form and enter this code to load data when the form is opened:

```
// Create some ADO.NET objects
SqlConnection cnn = new SqlConnection(
    "Data Source=(local); Initial Catalog=Northwind;" +
" Integrated Security=SSPI");
DataSet ds = new DataSet();
SqlDataAdapter da = new SqlDataAdapter();
DataRow[] adrEdit;

private void StepByStep6_32_Load(object sender,
    System.EventArgs e)
{
    // Create a SqlCommand to select data
    SqlCommand cmdSelect = cnn.CreateCommand();
    cmdSelect.CommandType = CommandType.Text;
    cmdSelect.CommandText =
        "SELECT CustomerID, ContactName FROM Customers";
    // Create a SqlCommand to update data
    SqlCommand cmdUpdate = cnn.CreateCommand();
    cmdUpdate.CommandType = CommandType.Text;
    cmdUpdate.CommandText =
        "UPDATE Customers" +
        " SET ContactName = @ContactName" +
        " WHERE CustomerID = @CustomerID AND " +
        " ContactName = @ContactNameOrig";
    cmdUpdate.Parameters.Add("@ContactName",
        SqlDbType.NVarChar,30, "ContactName");
    cmdUpdate.Parameters.Add("@CustomerID",
        SqlDbType.NChar,5, "CustomerID");
    cmdUpdate.Parameters["@CustomerID"].SourceVersion
        = DataRowVersion.Original;
```

continues

continued

```
cmdUpdate.Parameters.Add("@ContactNameOrig",
    SqlDbType.NVarChar,30, "ContactName");
cmdUpdate.Parameters["@ContactNameOrig"].
    SourceVersion = DataRowVersion.Original;

// Set up the DataAdapter and fill the DataSet
da.UpdateCommand = cmdUpdate;
da.SelectCommand = cmdSelect;
da.Fill(ds, "Customers");
// Fill the data in the ComboBox
cboCustomerID.DisplayMember = "CustomerID";
cboCustomerID.ValueMember = "CustomerID";
cboCustomerID.DataSource = ds.Tables["Customers"];
}
```

5. Double-click the `ComboBox` control and enter this code to handle the `SelectedIndexChanged` event:

```
private void cboCustomerID_SelectedIndexChanged(
    object sender, System.EventArgs e)
{
    // Get just that customer's DataRow
    adrEdit = ds.Tables["Customers"].Select(
     "CustomerID = '" +
     cboCustomerID.SelectedValue + "'");
    // Make sure there's some data
    if (adrEdit != null)
    {
        txtContactName.Text =
            adrEdit[0]["ContactName"].ToString();
    }
}
```

6. Double-click the `Button` control and enter this code to handle the `Click` event of the `Button` control:

```
private void btnUpdate_Click(object sender,
    System.EventArgs e)
{
    // Make sure there's some data
    if (adrEdit != null)
    {
        // Prompt for new data and put it in the DataRow
        adrEdit[0]["ContactName"] = txtContactName.Text;
        // And save the changes
        try
        {
            da.Update(ds, "Customers");
            MessageBox.Show("Contact Name Updated!");
        }
        catch(SqlException sqlEx)
        {
```

```
            // Handle SQL Server specific errors
            foreach (SqlError err in sqlEx.Errors)
            {
                MessageBox.Show(
                  "SQL Error " + err.Number +
                  ": " + err.Message);
            }
        }
        catch(Exception ex)
        {
            // Handle general errors
            MessageBox.Show("Non-SQL Exception " +
                ex.Message);
        }
    }
}
```

7. Insert the Main() method to launch the form. Set the form as the startup object for the project.

8. Run the project. The code displays all the Customer ID values in the ComboBox control, with the corresponding contact name value from the database in the text box. Select a customer ID (such as ALFKI) from the combo box and update the text box with a new contact name. Click the button. The change is written back to the database, and you can verify this by running the program a second time and changing the same customer's data.

The difference between the Step by Step 6.32 version of the update code and the version from Step by Step 6.24 is the inclusion of a try-catch block to handle exceptions and the UPDATE SQL statement, which now has a different WHERE clause:

```
UPDATE Customers
SET ContactName = @ContactName
WHERE CustomerID = @CustomerID AND
ContactName = @ContactNameOrig
```

The new WHERE clause finds a row to update only if both the CustomerID and ContactName fields are unchanged from what they were when the row was originally loaded. If you'd like to experiment with this, you can run two copies of the code at the same time. Load the data in both copies, and then change the contact name with one copy. You cannot then change the contact name with the second copy, and you get a message box with a message Non-SQL Exception Concurrency Violation: the UpdateCommand affected 0 records.

> **EXAM TIP**
>
> **Retrieving Whole Tables** Strictly speaking, you can enforce optimistic concurrency control only if you check every column of the table in the WHERE clause. If you retrieve only a few columns, it's possible to miss a change in a column that you didn't retrieve.

REVIEW BREAK

▶ Every real-world application should include error trapping. Data manipulation adds some special requirements to error trapping code.

▶ The `SqlException` and `SqlError` objects provide you with the means to retrieve SQL Server–specific error information.

▶ You can choose when you're designing update commands between optimistic concurrency and "last one wins" concurrency.

CHAPTER SUMMARY

KEY TERMS

- ad hoc query
- attribute
- backing store
- CDATA section
- data provider
- DataSet object
- DOM
- element
- identity
- "last one wins" concurrency control
- optimistic concurrency control
- osql
- parameter
- schema
- SQL Query Analyzer

The .NET Framework offers an incredible amount of flexibility for consuming and manipulating data. This chapter provides a broad survey of various techniques for dealing with data. As you continue to work with Visual C# .NET, you'll discover more advanced techniques in all these areas.

SQL Server is an important data source for .NET applications. To deal effectively with SQL Server data, you need to have an understanding of the T-SQL language. This chapter describes the basics of T-SQL, including the SELECT, INSERT, UPDATE, and DELETE statements. It also explains how to execute SQL in ad hoc queries and in stored procedures.

The .NET Framework also includes classes for manipulating disk files. These classes are part of the System.IO namespace, which treats data as streams that are supplied by backing stores. This chapter describes how to read and write files.

The major part of the chapter deals with the ADO.NET objects, which span multiple namespaces. ADO.NET includes both data provider objects, which are tied to specific data sources, and DataSet objects, which provide a purely abstract view of relational data. After describing the ADO.NET object model, this chapter shows how to apply it to a number of problems, including loading and saving data, finding and sorting data, and editing data.

CHAPTER SUMMARY

This chapter also covers the key classes that are used for dealing with XML. These classes, `XmlNode` and `XmlDocument`, are contained in the `System.Xml` namespace. XML data can also be loaded into `DataSet` objects, allowing you to treat XML files as relational databases.

Finally, this chapter describes some of the key issues involved in error handling for data-oriented applications. It talks about the classes that are available for catching SQL Server errors and the issues surrounding multiuser concurrency control.

- SQL-92
- stored procedure
- stream
- T-SQL
- XML
- XML declaration
- XML namespace

APPLY YOUR KNOWLEDGE

Exercises

6.1   Preselecting Data by Using Parameterized Stored Procedures

One of the biggest issues in working with server-side data such as SQL Server data is to minimize the amount of data that you load into an application. That's because communication with such servers is typically comparatively slow, and the servers themselves have enough processing power to quickly locate the exact data that you want. In this exercise, you'll see how you can minimize the amount of data retrieved by using a series of stored procedures with parameters.

Estimated time: 30 minutes

1. Create a new Visual C# .NET project to use for the exercises in this chapter.

2. Add a new form to the project.

3. Place a ComboBox control (cboCustomers), a Button control (btnLoad), and a DataGrid control (dgMain) on the form.

4. Switch to the code view and add the following using directives to make the ADO.NET objects available:

   ```
   using System.Data;
   using System.Data.SqlClient;
   ```

5. Using a tool such as the SQL Query Analyzer or the Visual Studio .NET IDE, create this stored procedure:

   ```
   CREATE PROC procCustomerList
   AS
   SELECT CustomerID, CompanyName
   FROM Customers
   ORDER BY CompanyName
   ```

6. Using a tool such as the SQL Query Analyzer or the Visual Studio .NET IDE, create this stored procedure:

   ```
   CREATE PROC procCustomerDetails
     @CustomerID char(5)
   AS
   SELECT * FROM Customers
   WHERE CustomerID = @CustomerID
   ```

7. Using a tool such as the SQL Query Analyzer or the Visual Studio .NET IDE, create this stored procedure:

   ```
   CREATE PROC procOrdersForCustomer
     @CustomerID char(5)
   AS
   SELECT * FROM Orders
   WHERE CustomerID = @CustomerID
   ```

8. To minimize load time, the form starts by loading only the customer list into the ComboBox control. Enter this code to load the customer list in the form's Load event handler:

   ```
   SqlConnection cnn = new SqlConnection(
       "Data Source=(local);" +
       "Initial Catalog=Northwind;" +
    "Integrated Security=SSPI");

   private void Exercise6_1_Load(
   object sender,
       System.EventArgs e)
   {
       // Load the customer list
       SqlCommand cmdCustomers =
           cnn.CreateCommand();
       cmdCustomers.CommandType =
           CommandType.StoredProcedure;
       cmdCustomers.CommandText =
           "procCustomerList";
       cnn.Open();
       DataSet ds = new DataSet();
       SqlDataAdapter da = new SqlDataAdapter();
       da.SelectCommand = cmdCustomers;
       da.Fill(ds, "Customers");
       cboCustomers.DataSource =
           ds.Tables["Customers"];
       cboCustomers.DisplayMember =
           "CompanyName";
   ```

APPLY YOUR KNOWLEDGE

```
cboCustomers.ValueMember = "CustomerID";
cnn.Close();
}
```

9. When the user clicks the Load button, the other stored procedures should load only the data of interest. Enter this code to build the `DataSet` object and bind it to the `DataGrid` control in the btnLoad `Click` event handler:

```
private void btnLoad_Click(object sender,
    System.EventArgs e)
{
    // Create a new DataSet
    DataSet ds = new DataSet();
    // Load only the customer of interest
    SqlCommand cmdCustomer =
        cnn.CreateCommand();
    cmdCustomer.CommandType =
        CommandType.StoredProcedure;
    cmdCustomer.CommandText =
        "procCustomerDetails";
    cmdCustomer.Parameters.Add(
        new SqlParameter(
            "@CustomerID", SqlDbType.Text, 5));
    cmdCustomer.Parameters["@CustomerID"].
        Value =
        cboCustomers.SelectedValue;
    SqlDataAdapter daCustomer =
        new SqlDataAdapter();
    daCustomer.SelectCommand = cmdCustomer;
    daCustomer.Fill(ds, "Customers");
    // Load the orders for this customer
    SqlCommand cmdOrders =
        cnn.CreateCommand();
    cmdOrders.CommandType =
        CommandType.StoredProcedure;
    cmdOrders.CommandText =
        "procOrdersForCustomer";
    cmdOrders.Parameters.Add(
        new SqlParameter(
            "@CustomerID", SqlDbType.Text, 5));
    cmdOrders.Parameters["@CustomerID"].
        Value =
        cboCustomers.SelectedValue;
    SqlDataAdapter daOrders =
        new SqlDataAdapter();
    daOrders.SelectCommand = cmdOrders;
    daOrders.Fill(ds, "Orders");
```

```
    // Relate the two DataTables
    DataRelation relCustOrder =
        ds.Relations.Add(
        "CustOrder",
        ds.Tables["Customers"].
        Columns["CustomerID"],
        ds.Tables["Orders"].
        Columns["CustomerID"]);
    // Bind the data to the user interface
    dgMain.DataSource = ds;
    dgMain.DataMember = "Customers";
}
```

10. Insert the `Main()` method to launch the form. Set the form as the startup form for the project.

11. Run the project. Select a customer from the list in the combo box and then press the Load button. The form displays only the information for that customer. Click on the + sign next to the customer to see the order information, as shown in Figure 6.29.

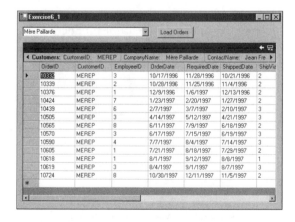

FIGURE 6.29
You can use parameterized stored procedures to minimize the amount of data that you need to load into an application.

APPLY YOUR KNOWLEDGE

6.2   Transferring Database Data to a Disk File

The `DataSet` object has facilities for saving data as XML. But sometimes file size is more important than the readability that XML brings to the table. In this exercise, you'll retrieve data from a database and then use the `BinaryWriter` class to write the data out as a compact disc file.

Estimated time: 20 minutes

1. Add a new form to your Visual C# .NET project.

2. Place a `ComboBox` control (`cboProducts`) and a `Button` control (`btnWrite`) on the form.

3. Switch to the code view and add the following using directives:

```
using System.Data;
using System.Data.SqlClient;
using System.IO;
```

4. The form initializes the list of products at load time. Enter this code to load the list of products in the form's `Load` event handler:

```
SqlConnection cnn = new SqlConnection(
    "Data Source=(local);" +
    "Initial Catalog=Northwind;" +
    "Integrated Security=SSPI");

private void Exercise6_2_Load(
    object sender, System.EventArgs e)
{
    // Load the customer list
    SqlCommand cmd = cnn.CreateCommand();
    cmd.CommandType = CommandType.Text;
    cmd.CommandText =
        "SELECT ProductName, ProductID " +
        "FROM Products ORDER BY ProductName";
    cnn.Open();
    DataSet ds = new DataSet();
    SqlDataAdapter da = new SqlDataAdapter();
    da.SelectCommand = cmd;
    da.Fill(ds, "Products");
```

```
    cboProducts.DataSource =
        ds.Tables["Products"];
    cboProducts.DisplayMember =
        "ProductName";
    cboProducts.ValueMember = "ProductID";
    cnn.Close();
}
```

5. Double-click the Button control and enter this code to handle the button's `Click` event:

```
private void btnWrite_Click(object sender,
    System.EventArgs e)
{
    // Get a file name to use
    // when saving the file
    SaveFileDialog sfd =
        new SaveFileDialog();
    sfd.Title = "Choose save file";
    if (sfd.ShowDialog() == DialogResult.OK)
    {
        // Get the full data on
        // the selected product
        SqlCommand cmdProduct =
            cnn.CreateCommand();
        cmdProduct.CommandType =
            CommandType.Text;
        cmdProduct.CommandText =
            "SELECT * FROM Products" +
            " WHERE ProductID = @ProductID";
        cmdProduct.Parameters.Add(
            new SqlParameter(
            "@ProductID", SqlDbType.Int));
        cmdProduct.Parameters["@ProductID"].Value =
            cboProducts.SelectedValue;
        // Open a BinaryWriter
        FileStream fsOut = new FileStream(
            sfd.FileName, FileMode.Create);
        BinaryWriter bw =
            new BinaryWriter(fsOut);
        // Get the data into a DataRow
        SqlDataAdapter da =
            new SqlDataAdapter();
        da.SelectCommand = cmdProduct;
        DataSet ds = new DataSet();
        da.Fill(ds, "Products");
        DataRow dr =
            ds.Tables["Products"].Rows[0];
        // And write the data
        for (int intI=0; intI <= 9; intI++)
```

APPLY YOUR KNOWLEDGE

```
{
    bw.Write(dr[intI].ToString());
}
bw.Flush();
bw.Close();
MessageBox.Show("Data written");
}
}
```

This code retrieves the `DataRow` object of interest and then uses a `BinaryWriter` object to move it, field-by-field, to a disk file. The code uses the `SaveFileDialog` class to prompt for a filename.

6. Insert the `Main()` method to launch the form. Set the form as the startup form for the project.

7. Run the project. Select a customer from the list in the combo box and click the Write button to save the corresponding `DataRow` object through a `BinaryWriter` class.

6.3 Updating Multiple Tables

You've seen how to load data from more than one table into the same `DataSet` object and how to update a database with changes that were made to a `DataSet` object. In this exercise, you'll combine the two and write code to update multiple tables that are contained in a single `DataSet` object.

Estimated time: 25 minutes

1. Add a new form to your Visual C# .NET project.

2 Place a `DataGrid` control (`dgMain`) and a `Button` control (`btnUpdate`) on the form.

3. Switch to the code view and add the following using directives to make the ADO.NET objects available:

```
using System.Data;
using System.Data.SqlClient;
```

4. Double-click the form and enter this code to load data when the form is opened:

```
private void Exercise6_3_Load(
    object sender, System.EventArgs e)
{
    // Create a SqlCommand  object
    // to select Customer data
    SqlCommand cmdSelect =
        cnn.CreateCommand();
    cmdSelect.CommandType =
        CommandType.Text;
    cmdSelect.CommandText =
        "SELECT CustomerID, CompanyName, " +
        "ContactName FROM Customers";
    // Create a SqlCommand object
    // to update Customer data
    SqlCommand cmdUpdate =
        cnn.CreateCommand();
    cmdUpdate.CommandType =
        CommandType.Text;
    cmdUpdate.CommandText =
    "UPDATE Customers SET " +
    "CompanyName = @CompanyName, " +
    "ContactName = @ContactName " +
    "WHERE CustomerID = @CustomerID";
    cmdUpdate.Parameters.Add("@ContactName",
        SqlDbType.NVarChar,30, "ContactName");
    cmdUpdate.Parameters.Add("@CompanyName",
        SqlDbType.NVarChar,40, "CompanyName");
    cmdUpdate.Parameters.Add("@CustomerID",
        SqlDbType.NChar, 5, "CustomerID");
    cmdUpdate.Parameters["@CustomerID"].
        SourceVersion =
        DataRowVersion.Original;
    // Create a SqlCommand object
    // to insert Customer data
    SqlCommand cmdInsert =
        cnn.CreateCommand();
    cmdInsert.CommandType =
        CommandType.Text;
    cmdInsert.CommandText =
        "INSERT INTO Customers (" +
        "CustomerID, CompanyName, " +
        "ContactName) VALUES(@CustomerID," +
        " @CompanyName, @ContactName)";
    cmdInsert.Parameters.Add("@CustomerID",
        SqlDbType.NChar, 5, "CustomerID");
    cmdInsert.Parameters.Add("@CompanyName",
        SqlDbType.NVarChar, 40, "CompanyName");
```

```
cmdInsert.Parameters.Add("@ContactName",
 SqlDbType.NVarChar, 30, "ContactName");
cmdInsert.Parameters["@CustomerID"].
SourceVersion = DataRowVersion.Original;
 // Create a SqlCommand object
 // to delete Customer data
SqlCommand cmdDelete =
    cnn.CreateCommand();
cmdDelete.CommandType =
    CommandType.Text;
cmdDelete.CommandText =
  "DELETE FROM Customers " +
  "WHERE CustomerID = @CustomerID";
cmdDelete.Parameters.Add("@CustomerID",
    SqlDbType.NChar, 5, "CustomerID");
cmdDelete.Parameters["@CustomerID"].
SourceVersion = DataRowVersion.Original;
 // Set up the DataAdapter object
 // and fill the DataSet
daCust.SelectCommand = cmdSelect;
daCust.UpdateCommand = cmdUpdate;
daCust.InsertCommand = cmdInsert;
daCust.DeleteCommand = cmdDelete;
daCust.Fill(ds, "Customers");
 // Now set up the commands for Orders
SqlCommand cmdSelectOrders =
    cnn.CreateCommand();
cmdSelectOrders.CommandType =
    CommandType.Text;
cmdSelectOrders.CommandText =
  "SELECT OrderID, CustomerID," +
  " OrderDate FROM Orders";
 // Create a SqlCommand object
 // to update Order data
SqlCommand cmdUpdateOrders =
    cnn.CreateCommand();
cmdUpdateOrders.CommandType =
    CommandType.Text;
cmdUpdateOrders.CommandText =
   "UPDATE Orders SET " +
   "CustomerID = @CustomerID, " +
   "OrderDate = @OrderDate " +
   "WHERE OrderID = @OrderID";
cmdUpdateOrders.Parameters.Add(
   "@CustomerID",
   SqlDbType.NChar, 5, "CustomerID");
cmdUpdateOrders.Parameters.Add(
   "@OrderDate", SqlDbType.DateTime);
cmdUpdateOrders.Parameters[
  "@OrderDate"].SourceColumn =
  "OrderDate";

cmdUpdateOrders.Parameters.Add(
 "@OrderID", SqlDbType.Int);
cmdUpdateOrders.Parameters[
  "@OrderID"].SourceColumn =
  "OrderID";
cmdUpdateOrders.Parameters[
  "@CustomerID"].SourceVersion =
  DataRowVersion.Original;
 // Create a SqlCommand object
 // to insert Order data
SqlCommand cmdInsertOrders =
    cnn.CreateCommand();
cmdInsertOrders.CommandType =
    CommandType.Text;
cmdInsertOrders.CommandText =
  "INSERT INTO Orders (" +
  "CustomerID, OrderDate) " +
  "VALUES(@CustomerID, @OrderDate)";
cmdInsertOrders.Parameters.Add(
  "@CustomerID", SqlDbType.NChar,
  5, "CustomerID");
cmdInsertOrders.Parameters.Add(
  "@OrderDate", SqlDbType.DateTime);
cmdInsertOrders.Parameters[
  "@OrderDate"].SourceColumn =
  "OrderDate";
 // Create a SqlCommand object
 // to delete Order data
SqlCommand cmdDeleteOrders =
    cnn.CreateCommand();
cmdDeleteOrders.CommandType =
    CommandType.Text;
cmdDeleteOrders.CommandText =
  "DELETE FROM Orders WHERE " +
  "OrderOD = @OrderID";
cmdDeleteOrders.Parameters.Add(
   "@OrderID", SqlDbType.Int);
cmdDeleteOrders.Parameters["@OrderID"].
  SourceColumn = "OrderID";
cmdDeleteOrders.Parameters["@OrderID"].
  SourceVersion =
  DataRowVersion.Original;
 // Add orders to the DataSet
daOrders.SelectCommand =
    cmdSelectOrders;
daOrders.UpdateCommand =
    cmdUpdateOrders;
daOrders.InsertCommand =
    cmdInsertOrders;
daOrders.DeleteCommand =
    cmdDeleteOrders;
daOrders.Fill(ds, "Orders");
```

APPLY YOUR KNOWLEDGE

```
// Relate the two tables
DataRelation relCustOrder =
    ds.Relations.Add(
    "CustOrder",
    ds.Tables["Customers"].
    Columns["CustomerID"],
    ds.Tables["Orders"].
    Columns["CustomerID"]);
// And bind the data to the DataGrid
dgMain.DataSource = ds;
dgMain.DataMember = "Customers";
}
```

5. Double-click the Button control and enter this code to handle the button's Click event. This code calls the Update property of each of the DataTable objects in the DataSet object:

```
private void btnUpdate_Click(object sender,
    System.EventArgs e)
{
    // Update both datatables
    daCust.Update(ds, "Customers");
    daOrders.Update(ds, "Orders");
}
```

6. Insert the Main() method to launch the form. Set the form as the startup form for the project.

7. Run the project. Make as many updates as you like and then click OK to make those updates a permanent part of the database.

6.4 Using Transactions with ADO.NET

Popular RDBMS software uses transactions to maintain database integrity. A *transaction* is a single unit of work. If a transaction is successful, all the data modifications made during the transaction are committed and become permanent parts of the database.

If a transaction encounters errors or is invalid, then it must be canceled or rolled back; in that case, all the data modifications in that transaction are erased.

In this exercise, I use the SqlTransaction class, which represents a T-SQL transaction on a SQL Server database. A transaction is explicitly started by using the SqlConnection.BeginTransaction() method. The newly created SqlTransaction object is then assigned to the Transaction property of the current command object. If the changes need to be committed to the database, you use SqlTransaction.Commit() method, whereas if the changes to the database need to be rolled back, you use the SqlTransaction.RollBack() method. Both the Commit() and RollBack() methods end the current transaction.

EXAM TIP

Using Transactions with ADO.NET You can create a SqlTransaction object by calling the BeginTransaction() method on the SqlConnection object. After you have the SqlTransaction object available, all subsequent operations associated with the transaction, such as Commit() and RollBack(), are performed on the SqlTransaction object instead of the SqlConnection object.

Estimated time: 25 minutes

1. Add a new form to your Visual C# .NET project.

2 Place five Label controls, four TextBox controls (txtCustomerID1, txtCompanyName1, txtCustomerID2, and txtCompanyName2), and a Button control (btnAdd) on the form.

APPLY YOUR KNOWLEDGE

3. Switch to the code view and add the following using directives to make the ADO.NET objects available:

```
using System.Data;
using System.Data.SqlClient;
```

4. Double-click the Button control and enter this code in the Click event handler:

```csharp
private void btnAdd_Click(object sender,
    System.EventArgs e)
{
    // Create a SqlConnection object
    SqlConnection cnn = new SqlConnection(
        "Data Source=(local);" +
        "Initial Catalog=Northwind;" +
        "Integrated Security=SSPI");
    // Open the connection
    cnn.Open();
    // Create a SqlTransaction object
    SqlTransaction trans =
        cnn.BeginTransaction();
    // Create a SqlCommand object for
    // the SqlConnection object
    SqlCommand cmd = cnn.CreateCommand();
    // Assign the transaction object to the
    // SqlCommand object's
    // Transaction property
    cmd.Transaction = trans;
    try
    {
        // Set the CommandType and
        // CommandText property
        // of the SqlCommand object
        // Execute the Query
        cmd.CommandType = CommandType.Text;
        cmd.CommandText =
            "INSERT INTO Customers " +
            "(CustomerID, CompanyName)" +
            " VALUES ('" +
            txtCustomerID1.Text + "', " +
            "'" + txtCompanyName1.Text +
            "')";
        cmd.ExecuteNonQuery();

        // Set the Command Type and
        // CommandText property
        // of the SqlCommand object
```

```csharp
        // Execute the Query
        cmd.CommandType = CommandType.Text;
        cmd.CommandText =
            "INSERT INTO Customers " +
            "(CustomerID, CompanyName)" +
            " VALUES ('" +
            txtCustomerID2.Text + "', " +
            "'" + txtCompanyName2.Text +
            "')";
        cmd.ExecuteNonQuery();

        // Commit the transaction
        trans.Commit();
        MessageBox.Show(
            "Customers added successfully",
            "Commit");
    }
    catch(Exception ex)
    {
        MessageBox.Show(ex.Message,
            "Rollback");
        // Rollback the transaction
        trans.Rollback();
    }
    finally
    {
        // Close the SqlConnection object
        cnn.Close();
    }
}
```

5. Insert the Main() method to launch the form. Set the form as the startup form for the project.

6. Run the project. Add information about two customers in the text boxes and then click the Add the Customers button. If no error occurs while the database is being updated, the transaction is committed. In case of any error, the transaction is rolled back and the database remains unaffected.

Review Questions

1. Describe the difference between an ad hoc query and a stored procedure.

APPLY YOUR KNOWLEDGE

2. List and describe the four basic T-SQL statements.

3. Name four ways that you can execute SQL statements.

4. In a T-SQL SELECT statement, what is the difference between the WHERE clause and the HAVING clause?

5. What is the purpose of the @@IDENTITY variable?

6. What is a stream? What is a backing store?

7. How should you decide between using a StreamReader object and using a BinaryReader object?

8. Describe the difference between the data provider objects and the DataSet objects.

9. Which ADO.NET object do you use to execute a stored procedure?

10. Which ADO.NET object transfers data between the database and the data model?

11. What are the advantages of strongly typed DataSet objects?

12. Which XML object can you synchronize with a DataSet object?

13. Name and describe the two main types of concurrency control that you can implement in .NET.

Exam Questions

1. Your SQL Server database contains a table, Sales, with these columns:

SalesID (int, identity)

StoreNumber (int)

Sales (int)

You want to see a list of the stores, together with their total sales. The list should be filtered to include only stores whose total sales are more than 10. Which SQL statement should you use?

A.
```
SELECT StoreNumber, Sales
FROM Sales
WHERE Sales > 10
```

B.
```
SELECT StoreNumber, SUM(Sales)
FROM Sales
WHERE Sales > 10
GROUP BY StoreNumber
```

C.
```
SELECT StoreNumber, SUM(Sales)
FROM Sales
GROUP BY StoreNumber
HAVING SUM(Sales) > 10
```

D.
```
SELECT StoreNumber, SUM(Sales)
FROM Sales
WHERE Sales > 10
GROUP BY StoreNumber
HAVING SUM(Sales) > 10
```

2. Your SQL Server database contains a table, Sales, with these columns:

SalesID (int, identity)

StoreNumber (int)

Sales (int)

APPLY YOUR KNOWLEDGE

You want to see a list of the stores, together with their total sales. The list should be filtered to include only rows from the table where the sales are more than 10. Which SQL statement should you use?

A.

```
SELECT StoreNumber, Sales
FROM Sales
WHERE Sales > 10
```

B.

```
SELECT StoreNumber, SUM(Sales)
FROM Sales
WHERE Sales > 10
GROUP BY StoreNumber
```

C.

```
SELECT StoreNumber, SUM(Sales)
FROM Sales
GROUP BY StoreNumber
HAVING SUM(Sales) > 10
```

D.

```
SELECT StoreNumber, SUM(Sales)
FROM Sales
WHERE Sales > 10
GROUP BY StoreNumber
HAVING SUM(Sales) > 10
```

3. Your SQL Server database contains a table, Experiments, with the following columns:

ExperimentID (int, identity)

ExperimentType (char(1))

ExperimentDate (datetime)

You want to delete all rows from the table where the ExperimentType value is either A or C. You do not want to delete any other rows. Which SQL statement should you use?

A.

```
DELETE FROM Experiments
WHERE ExperimentType LIKE '[AC]'
```

B.

```
DELETE FROM Experiments
WHERE ExperimentType LIKE '[A-C]'
```

C.

```
DELETE FROM Experiments
WHERE ExperimentType LIKE 'A' OR 'C'
```

D.

```
DELETE * FROM Experiments
WHERE ExperimentType IN ('A', 'C')
```

4. Your SQL Server database contains a table, Sales, with these columns:

SalesID (int, identity)

StoreNumber (int)

Sales (int)

You want to create a stored procedure that accepts as inputs the store number and sales, inserts a new row in the table with this information, and returns the new identity value. Which SQL statement should you use?

A.

```
CREATE PROCEDURE procInsertSales
  @StoreNumber int,
  @Sales int,
  @SalesID int
AS
  INSERT INTO Sales (StoreNumber, Sales)
  VALUES (@StoreNumber, @Sales)
  SELECT @SalesID = @@IDENTITY
```

APPLY YOUR KNOWLEDGE

B.

```
CREATE PROCEDURE procInsertSales
  @StoreNumber int,
  @Sales int,
  @SalesID int OUTPUT
AS
  INSERT INTO Sales (
    SalesID, StoreNumber, Sales)
  VALUES (@SalesID, @StoreNumber, @Sales)
```

C.

```
CREATE PROCEDURE procInsertSales
  @StoreNumber int,
  @Sales int,
  @SalesID int OUTPUT
AS
  INSERT INTO Sales (
    SalesID, StoreNumber, Sales)
  VALUES (0, @StoreNumber, @Sales)
  SELECT @SalesID = @@IDENTITY
```

D.

```
CREATE PROCEDURE procInsertSales
  @StoreNumber int,
  @Sales int,
  @SalesID int OUTPUT
AS
  INSERT INTO Sales (StoreNumber, Sales)
  VALUES (@StoreNumber, @Sales)
  SELECT @SalesID = @@IDENTITY
```

5. Your application has two `FileStream` objects. The `fsIn` object is open for reading, and the `fsOut` object is open for writing. Which code snippet would copy the contents of `fsIn` to `fsOut` using a 2KB buffer?

A.

```
Int32[] buf = new  Int32[2048];
Int32 intBytesRead;
while((intBytesRead =
   fsIn.Read(buf, 0, 2048)) > 0)
{
    fsOut.Write(buf, 0, intBytesRead);
}
//Clean up
fsOut.Flush();
fsOut.Close();
fsIn.Close();
```

B.

```
Int32[] buf = new  Int32[2048];
Int32 intBytesRead;
while((intBytesRead =
    fsIn.Read(buf, 0, 2048)) > 1)
{
    fsOut.Write(buf, 0, intBytesRead);
}
//Clean up
fsOut.Flush();
fsOut.Close();
fsIn.Close();
```

C.

```
Byte[] buf = new  Byte[2048];
Int32 intBytesRead;
while((intBytesRead =
   fsIn.Read(buf, 0, 2048)) > 0)
{
    fsOut.Write(buf, 0, intBytesRead);
}
//Clean up
fsOut.Flush();
fsOut.Close();
fsIn.Close();
```

D.

```
Byte[] buf = new  Byte[2048];
Int32 intBytesRead;
while((intBytesRead =
    fsIn.Read(buf, 0, 2048)) > 1)
{
    fsOut.Write(buf, 0, intBytesRead);
}
//Clean up
fsOut.Flush();
fsOut.Close();
fsIn.Close();
```

6. Your application includes 15 double-precision floating-point numbers that you want to write out to a disk file. You'd like to minimize the size of the disk file. Which object should you use to write the file?

A. `FileStream`

B. `StreamWriter`

C. BinaryWriter

D. XmlTextWriter

7. Your application needs to return the total number of customers in a database. What is the fastest way to do this?

A. Write ad hoc SQL queries to return the total number of customers. Use the SqlCommand.ExecuteScalar() method to execute the SQL statement.

B. Write ad hoc SQL queries to return the total number of customers. Use the SqlDataAdapter.Fill() method to execute the SQL statement.

C. Create a stored procedure to return the total number of customers. Use the SqlCommand.ExecuteScalar() method to execute the stored procedure.

D. Create a stored procedure to return the total number of customers. Use the SqlDataAdapter.Fill() method to execute the stored procedure.

8. Your application needs to retrieve a list of customer balances from a SQL Server database. The application should move through the list once, processing each balance in turn. The application does not need to write to the database. Which object should you use to hold the list in the data model?

A. DataSet

B. SqlDataReader

C. DataTable

D. DataView

9. Your SQL Server database contains customer and order information. The Orders table includes a foreign key that refers to the Customers table. You have loaded the Customers and Orders tables into a single DataSet object through two separate SqlDataAdapter objects. The DataSet object is bound to a DataGrid control on the application's user interface. When you run the application, only customer information appears in the DataGrid control. You have verified that there are orders in the database. What is the most likely cause of this problem?

A. You must use a single SqlDataAdapter object to load both tables.

B. You have neglected to create a DataRelation object in the DataSet object.

C. There are no orders for the first customer displayed on the DataGrid control.

D. The DataGrid control can display information from only a single table.

10. Your application uses a SqlDataReader object to retrieve information about customer balances. When you find a past-due balance, you want to write a new entry to a billing table by executing a stored procedure in the same database. You have used a SqlCommand object to represent the stored procedure. Calling the ExecuteNonQuery() method of the SqlCommand object is causing an error. What is the most likely cause of this error?

A. You must use a SqlDataAdapter object to execute the stored procedure.

B. You must use an ad hoc SQL statement rather than a stored procedure to insert new rows in a database.

C. You are using the `ExecuteNonQuery` method of the `SqlCommand` object, and you should be using the `ExecuteScalar` method instead.

D. You are using the same `SqlConnection` object for both the `SqlDataReader` object and the `SqlCommand` object, and the `SqlDataReader` object is still open when you try to execute the `SqlCommand` object.

11. Your application allows the user to edit product data on a `DataGrid` control. The `DataGrid` control is bound to a `DataSet` object. The `DataSet` object is filled through a `SqlDataAdapter` object. The `InsertCommand`, `UpdateCommand`, and `DeleteCommand` properties of the `SqlDataAdapter` object are set to `SqlCommand` objects, and you have tested the SQL in those `SqlCommand` objects.

When users exit the application, none of their changes are saved to the database, and they do not receive any errors. What could be the problem?

A. You have neglected to call the `SqlDataAdapter.Update()` method in your code.

B. The users do not have permission to write to the database.

C. You have neglected to fill the `DataSet` object from the `DataGrid` control after the users finish editing the data.

D. The `DataSet` object is a read-only object.

12. Your application includes a `DataSet` object that contains a `DataTable` object named `Suppliers`. This `DataTable` object contains all rows from the Suppliers table in your database. You want to bind an object to a `DataGrid` control on a form such that the `DataGrid` control displays only the suppliers from Pennsylvania. What should you do?

A. Create a filtered array by calling the `DataTable.Select()` method on the `Suppliers` data table and bind the array to the `DataGrid` control.

B. Create a new `SqlCommand` object to retrieve only suppliers from Pennsylvania. Use a new `SqlDataAdapter` object to fill a new `DataSet` object with these suppliers. Bind the new `DataSet` object to the `DataGrid` control.

C. Use a `foreach` loop to move through the entire `Suppliers` data table. Each time you find a `DataRow` object that represents a supplier from Pennsylvania, bind that `DataRow` object to the `DataGrid` control.

D. Create a filtered `DataView` object from the `Suppliers` data table and bind the `DataView` object to the `DataGrid` control.

13. You allow users to edit product information on a `DataGrid` control that is bound to a `DataSet` object. When the user clicks the Update button on the form, you call the `SqlDataAdapter.Update()` method to cause the changes from the `DataSet` object to persist to the underlying database.

Users report that new records and updated rows are saved properly but that deleted rows are reappearing the next time they run the application. What could be the problem?

A. The users do not have permission to update the underlying table.

B. The `Update()` method does not delete rows.

C. Someone is restoring an old version of the database between the two executions of the program.

D. The `DeleteCommand` property of the `SqlDataAdapter` object points to a `SqlCommand` object that does not properly delete rows.

APPLY YOUR KNOWLEDGE

14. Your application recursively calls the `FirstChild()` and `NextChild()` methods of `XmlNode` objects to visit every node in an XML file. When you find a node that includes customer name information, you store the information. The application is not returning all the customer names from the file. What could be the problem?

    A. The XML file is not well formed.

    B. The XML file has more than one root node.

    C. The customer name information is stored in XML attributes.

    D. The `HasChildNodes` property is not properly set on all nodes.

15. Your application reads an XML file from disk into an `XmlDocument` object, and then it modifies some of the nodes in the document. Which object should you use to write the modified `XmlDocument` object back to disk?

    A. `XmlTextWriter`

    B. `FileStream`

    C. `StreamWriter`

    D. `BinaryWriter`

    E. `TextWriter`

16. You have designed an application to use optimistic concurrency control. Alice and Bob each retrieve the Products table to the application at 8:00 a.m. The initial price of a widget is $3. At 8:05 a.m., Alice changes the price of a widget to $4 and saves her changes to the database. At 8:10 a.m., Bob changes the price of a widget to $5 and saves his changes to the database.

What would be the price of a widget in the database at 8:11 a.m. if no one made any other changes?

    A. $3

    B. $4

    C. $5

    D. $9

Answers to Review Questions

1. An ad hoc query consists of SQL statements that are sent to the server. A stored procedure consists of SQL statements that are permanently stored on the server.

2. The `SELECT` statement retrieves data, the `UPDATE` statement updates existing data, the `INSERT` statement adds new data, and the `DELETE` statement deletes data.

3. Using the Visual Studio .NET IDE, through `osql`, through the SQL Query Analyzer, or with your own home-grown solutions.

4. The `WHERE` clause restricts the rows that are used as input to an aggregate. The `HAVING` clause restricts the rows that are output from an aggregate.

5. The `@@IDENTITY` variable returns the last identity value to have been assigned to a table.

6. A stream is a file viewed as a list of bytes. A backing store is a place where data can be stored.

7. The `StreamReader` object is most useful when you're dealing with a line-oriented text file. The `BinaryWriter` object is most useful when you're working with a file in a particular format.

8. There are multiple sets of platform- and product-specific data provider objects. A single set of `DataSet` objects holds abstract data that's not directly associated with any database.

9. The `SqlCommand` object can be used to execute a stored procedure.

10. The `SqlDataAdapter` object is the pipeline between the data model and the `DataSet` object.

11. Strongly typed `DataSet` objects give you the benefit of IntelliSense at design time. They also provide earlier data binding than late data binding by ordinary `DataSet` objects.

12. The `XmlDataDocument` object can be synchronized with a `DataSet` object.

13. With optimistic concurrency control, an update to a row succeeds only if no one else has changed that row after it is loaded into the `DataSet` object. With "last one wins" concurrency control, an update to a row always succeeds, whether another user has edited the row or not (as long as the row still exists).

Answers to Exam Questions

1. **C.** The GROUP BY clause is required to obtain aggregate numbers. The HAVING clause filters the results after the aggregation has been performed. The answers that contain the WHERE clause are incorrect because WHERE filters the input to the aggregations. For more information, see the section "The SELECT Statement" in this chapter.

2. **B.** The GROUP BY clause is required to obtain aggregate numbers. The WHERE clause filters rows before aggregating them. The answers that contain the HAVING clause are incorrect because HAVING filters the results after aggregation.

For more information, see the section "The SELECT Statement" in this chapter.

3. **A.** Answer B would also delete rows with an ExperimentType value of B. Answer C would take the OR of A and C before evaluating the LIKE clause. DELETE * is not valid T-SQL syntax. For more information, see the section "The DELETE Statement" in this chapter.

4. **D.** Answer A does not indicate that @SalesID is an output parameter. Answers B and C attempt to insert values into the identity column, rather than let SQL Server assign the new value. For more information, see the section "Using Stored Procedures" in this chapter.

5. **C.** The Read() method returns the number of bytes read, so Answers B and D fail when there is 1 byte in the file. The Read() method reads to a byte array, so Answers A and B fail because the buffer has the wrong data type. For more information, see the section "Using the FileStream Class" in this chapter.

6. **C.** The BinaryWriter object provides a compact format for data storage on disk, as long as you don't need the data to be human-readable. All the other objects store the data as ASCII text, which takes more space. For more information, see the section "Using the BinaryReader and BinaryWriter Classes" in this chapter.

7. **C.** Stored procedures execute faster than the corresponding ad hoc SQL statements because stored procedures are stored in the database in compiled form. Using the ExecuteScalar() method is faster than filling a DataSet object for returning a single value. For more information, see the section "The SqlCommand and SqlParameter Objects" in this chapter.

APPLY YOUR KNOWLEDGE

8. **B.** The `SqlDataReader` object gives you a fast, forward-only, read-only view of the data. It is ideal for processing all rows once, without extra overhead. For more information, see the section "The `SqlDataReader` Object" in this chapter.

9. **B.** Even though the two tables are related in the database, you must still tell the `DataSet` object what the relationship is by creating a `DataRelation` object. For more information, see the section "Using `DataSet` Objects" in this chapter.

10. **D.** While a `SqlDataReader` object is open, you cannot execute other commands on the `SqlConnection` object that the `SqlDataReader` object is using. For more information, see the section "The `DataProviders` Objects" in this chapter.

11. **A.** If you do not call the `SqlDataAdapter.Update()` method, all changes to the data model are lost. Answer B would return an error to the users. Answer C is incorrect because a bound `DataSet` object automatically reflects changes to the `DataGrid` control. Answer D is incorrect because `DataSet` objects are designed to be edited. For more information, see the section "Using `DataSet` Objects" in this chapter.

12. **D.** Answers A and C do not give you objects that

can be bound to the `DataGrid` control. Answer B works, but retrieving the data from the database a second time is slower than filtering it from the existing `DataTable` object. For more information, see the section "Finding and Sorting Data in `DataSet` Objects" in this chapter.

13. **D.** If Answers A or C were the case, none of the changes would be saved. Answer B is simply incorrect. For more information, see the section "Editing Data with ADO.NET" in this chapter.

14. **C.** By default, XML attributes do not appear as part of the `XmlNodes` that is traversed by the `FirstChild` and `NextSibling` properties. If Answers A or B were the case, you would not be able to load the file into an `XmlDocument` object. Answer D is incorrect because `HasChildNodes` is automatically set by the .NET Framework. For more information, see the section "Using XML Data" in this chapter.

15. **A.** The `XmlTextWriter` object is designed to write XML files, preserving the proper XML structure. For more information, see the section "Using XML Data" in this chapter.

16. **B.** With optimistic concurrency control, Bob's change is not written to the database. For more information, see the section "Handling Multiuser Errors" in this chapter.

APPLY YOUR KNOWLEDGE

Suggested Readings and Resources

1. SQL Server Books Online, "Transact-SQL Reference"

2. Visual Studio .NET Combined Help Collection:

   - "Overview of ADO.NET"

   - "XML in Visual Studio"

3. .NET Framework SDK documentation:

   - "Accessing Data with ADO.NET"

   - "Basic File I/O"

4. Bob Beauchemin. *Essential ADO.NET*. Addison-Wesley, 2002.

5. David Sceppa. *Microsoft ADO.NET (Core Reference)*. Microsoft Press, 2002.

6. Kalen Delaney. *Inside SQL Server 2000*. Microsoft Press, 2000.

7. .NET Data Access Architecture Guide. `msdn.microsoft.com/library/en-us/dnbda/html/daag.asp`.

8. Designing Data Tier Components and Passing Data Through Tiers. `www.microsoft.com/downloads/release.asp?ReleaseID=44269`.

9. Microsoft Support Webcast: XML Integration in ADO.NET. `support.microsoft.com/servicedesks/webcasts/wc022202/wcblurb022202.asp`.

10. Microsoft Support Webcast: Microsoft ADO.NET: Programming ADO.NET Datasets. `support.microsoft.com/servicedesks/webcasts/wc041202/wcblurb041202.asp`.

11. Microsoft Support Webcast: Programming XML in the Microsoft .NET Framework Part I. `support.microsoft.com/servicedesks/webcasts/wc121801/wcblurb121801.asp`.

12. Microsoft Support Webcast: Programming XML in the Microsoft .NET Framework Part II. `support.microsoft.com/servicedesks/webcasts/wc010302/wcblurb010302.asp`.

13. Microsoft Support WebCast: Accessing Data with Microsoft Visual C# Applications. `support.microsoft.com/servicedesks/webcasts/wc092101/wcblurb092101.asp`.

14. Microsoft Support WebCast: ADO.NET. `support.microsoft.com/servicedesks/webcasts/wc081401/wcblurb081401.asp`.

15. The .NET Show: ADO.NET. `msdn.microsoft.com/theshow/Episode017`.

This chapter covers the following Microsoft-specified objectives for the "Creating User Services" section of Exam 70-316, "Developing and Implementing Windows-Based Applications with Microsoft Visual C# .NET and Microsoft Visual Studio .NET":

Instantiate and invoke a Web service or component.

- **Instantiate and invoke a Web service.**

▶ Although the exam has only a single objective related to Web services, this is a major area of the .NET Framework. With the release of the .NET Framework, it's become easier than ever to build, deploy, and use Web services. In this chapter you'll first learn what Web services are and how they fit into the overall .NET architecture. Then you'll see how to perform basic Web service tasks such as the following:

- Create a Web service

- Discover a Web service

- Instantiate and invoke a Web service

CHAPTER 7

Web Services

STUDY STRATEGIES

▶ Use ASP.NET to create a simple Web service. Then use the `wsdl.exe` tool to create a proxy class for that Web service and instantiate the Web service within your application. Make sure you understand how to make all the pieces of the process work together.

▶ Use the registry at `www.uddi.org` to explore some available Web services.

▶ Use the Web Reference feature of Visual Studio .NET to locate Web services and automatically generate proxy classes for them.

▶ If you're reviewing references on Web services to study for the exam, make sure they're specifically about Microsoft's approach to Web services. Although Web services are broadly interoperable between manufacturers, there are implementation differences.

▶ Use a tool such as .NET WebService Studio to inspect SOAP message and WSDL files to see what's happening as you interact with a Web service.

INTRODUCTION

You have probably heard quite a bit of hype about *Web services* in conjunction with the .NET Framework. In fact, Microsoft has gone so far as to sometimes describe the .NET Framework as "an XML Web services platform that will enable developers to create programs that transcend device boundaries and fully harness the connectivity of the Internet" (msdn.microsoft.com/net). You may also run across a lot of complex and confusing explanations about the architecture of these Web services. But at their most basic level, Web services are simple: They are a means for interacting with objects over the Internet.

Seen in that light, Web services are part of a natural progression:

1. Object-oriented languages such as C++ and C# allow two objects within the same application interact.

2. Protocols such as the Component Object Model (COM) allow two objects on the same computer, but in different applications, interact.

3. Protocols such as the Distributed Component Object Model (DCOM) allow two objects on different computers, but in the same local network, interact.

4. Web services allow two objects on different computers—even if they're only connected by the Internet—interact.

In this chapter, I'll introduce you to Web services as they exist in the .NET Framework. You'll see how to build and use Web services in your .NET applications, and you'll learn about the major protocols that you use when you communicate with a Web service.

> **NOTE**
>
> **More Web Services** As you progress toward the MCAD credential, you'll find that knowledge of Web services is essential. In particular, Web services are a major component of Exam 70-320, "Developing XML Web Services and Server Components with Microsoft Visual C# .NET and the Microsoft .NET Framework."

UNDERSTANDING WEB SERVICES

Instantiate and invoke a Web service or component.

- **Instantiate and invoke a Web service.**

Before I get into the nuts and bolts of actually working with Web services, I'll give you an overview of the way they work.

The key to understanding Web services is to know something about the protocols that make them possible:

◆ Simple Object Access Protocol (SOAP)

◆ Disco and Universal Description, Discovery, and Integration (UDDI)

◆ Web Services Description Language (WSDL)

One important thing to realize is that, by default, all communication between Web services servers and their clients is through Extensible Markup Language (XML) messages transmitted over Hypertext Transfer Protocol (HTTP). This has several benefits. First, because Web services messages are formatted as XML, they're reasonably easy for human beings to read and understand. Second, because those messages are transmitted over the pervasive HTTP, they can normally reach any machine on the Internet without being blocked by firewalls.

SOAP

EXAM TIP

SOAP over Other Protocols You often read that SOAP messages travel over HTTP. Although this is the default for SOAP as implemented by Visual Studio .NET, it's not a part of the SOAP specification. SOAP messages could be sent by email or File Transfer Protocol (FTP) without losing their content. As a practical matter, SOAP today uses HTTP in almost all cases.

For Web services to manipulate objects through XML messages, there has to be a way to translate objects (as well as their methods and properties) into XML. SOAP is a way to encapsulate object calls as XML sent via HTTP.

There are two major advantages to using SOAP to communicate with Web services. First, because HTTP is so pervasive, it can travel to any point on the Internet, regardless of intervening hardware or firewalls. Second, because SOAP is XML based, it can be interpreted by a wide variety of software on many operating systems. Although you'll only work with the Microsoft implementation of Web services in this chapter, numerous Web services tools from other vendors can interoperate with Microsoft-based Web services.

Here's a typical SOAP message sent from a Web services client to a Web services server:

```
<?xml version="1.0" encoding="utf-8"?>
<soap:Envelope
  xmlns:soap=
      "http://schemas.xmlsoap.org/soap/envelope/"
  xmlns:soapenc=
      "http://schemas.xmlsoap.org/soap/encoding/"
```

```
xmlns:tns=
    "http://www.capeclear.com/AirportWeather.wsdl"
xmlns:types="http://www.capeclear.com/
  AirportWeather.wsdl/encodedTypes"
xmlns:xsi=
    "http://www.w3.org/2001/XMLSchema-instance"
xmlns:xsd="http://www.w3.org/2001/XMLSchema">
<soap:Body soap:encodingStyle=
  "http://schemas.xmlsoap.org/soap/encoding/">
  <q1:getLocation
    xmlns:q1="capeconnect:AirportWeather:Station">
    <arg0 xsi:type="xsd:string">KSEA</arg0>
  </q1:getLocation>
</soap:Body>
</soap:Envelope>
```

Even without digging into this file in detail, you can see some obvious points:

◆ The SOAP message consists of an envelope that contains a body, each marked with a specific XML tag.

◆ This particular message invokes a method named `getLocation` from a specified uniform resource locator (URL).

◆ The method takes a single parameter, `arg0`, which is transmitted as an XML element.

> **NOTE**
>
> **XML Files** If you need a refresher on the parts of an XML file, see Chapter 6, "Consuming and Manipulating Data."

Here's a portion of the SOAP message that comes back from the server:

```
<?xml version="1.0" encoding="utf-8"?>
<SOAP-ENV:Envelope
  xmlns:SOAP-ENV=
      "http://schemas.xmlsoap.org/soap/envelope/"
  xmlns:xsd="http://www.w3.org/2001/XMLSchema"
  xmlns:cc1=
      "http://www.capeclear.com/AirportWeather.xsd"
  xmlns:xsi=
      "http://www.w3.org/2001/XMLSchema-instance"
  xmlns:SOAP-ENC=
      "http://schemas.xmlsoap.org/soap/encoding/">
<SOAP-ENV:Body SOAP-ENV:encodingStyle=
  "http://schemas.xmlsoap.org/soap/encoding/">
  <cc2:getLocationResponse
    xmlns:cc2="capeconnect:AirportWeather:Station"
    SOAP-ENC:root="1">
    <return xsi:type="xsd:string">
      Seattle, Seattle-Tacoma International Airport,
      WA, United States</return>
  </cc2:getLocationResponse>
</SOAP-ENV:Body>
</SOAP-ENV:Envelope>
```

In the response message, the getLocationResponse element is the
result of the call to the object on the server. It includes a string
wrapped up as an XML element.

Disco and UDDI

Before you can use a Web service, you need to know where to find
the service. Handling such requests is the job of several protocols,
including Disco and UDDI. These protocols allow you to communicate with a Web server to discover the details of the Web services
that are available at that server. You'll learn more about these protocols later in the chapter.

WSDL

Another prerequisite for using a Web service is knowledge of the
SOAP message types that it can receive and send. You can obtain
this knowledge by parsing WSDL files. WSDL is a standard by
which a Web service can tell clients what messages it accepts and
which results it will return.

Here's a portion of a WSDL file:

```
<?xml version="1.0" encoding="utf-16"?>
<definitions
  xmlns:http="http://schemas.xmlsoap.org/wsdl/http/"
  xmlns:soap="http://schemas.xmlsoap.org/wsdl/soap/"
  xmlns:s="http://www.w3.org/2001/XMLSchema"
  xmlns:s0=
    "http://www.capeclear.com/AirportWeather.xsd"
  xmlns:soapenc=
    "http://schemas.xmlsoap.org/soap/encoding/"
  xmlns:tns=
    "http://www.capeclear.com/AirportWeather.wsdl"
  xmlns:tm=
    "http://microsoft.com/wsdl/mime/textMatching/"
  xmlns:mime="http://schemas.xmlsoap.org/wsdl/mime/"
  targetNamespace=
    "http://www.capeclear.com/AirportWeather.wsdl"
  name="AirportWeather"
  xmlns="http://schemas.xmlsoap.org/wsdl/">
<types>
  <s:schema targetNamespace=
    "http://www.capeclear.com/AirportWeather.xsd">
    <s:complexType name="WeatherSummary">
      <s:sequence>
```

```
            <s:element minOccurs="1" maxOccurs="1"
              name="location" nillable="true"
              type="s:string" />
            <s:element minOccurs="1" maxOccurs="1"
              name="wind" nillable="true"
              type="s:string" />
            <s:element minOccurs="1" maxOccurs="1"
              name="sky" nillable="true"
              type="s:string" />
            <s:element minOccurs="1" maxOccurs="1"
              name="temp" nillable="true"
              type="s:string" />
            <s:element minOccurs="1" maxOccurs="1"
              name="humidity" nillable="true"
              type="s:string" />
            <s:element minOccurs="1" maxOccurs="1"
              name="pressure" nillable="true"
              type="s:string" />
            <s:element minOccurs="1" maxOccurs="1"
              name="visibility" nillable="true"
              type="s:string" />
          </s:sequence>
        </s:complexType>
      </s:schema>
    </types>
    <message name="getHumidity">
      <part name="arg0" type="s:string" />
    </message>
    <message name="getHumidityResponse">
      <part name="return" type="s:string" />
    </message>
    <message name="getLocation">
      <part name="arg0" type="s:string" />
    </message>
    <message name="getLocationResponse">
      <part name="return" type="s:string" />
    </message>
    <message name="getOb">
      <part name="arg0" type="s:string" />
    </message>
    ...
```

WSDL files define everything about the public interface of a Web service, including the following:

◆ The data types that it can process

◆ The methods that it exposes

◆ The URLs through which those methods can be accessed

EXAM TIP

Exposure Is Optional Although UDDI and WSDL files make it possible to interact with Web services without any prior knowledge, these files are not required in order for a Web service to function. You can make a Web service available on the Internet without any UDDI or WSDL file. In that case, only clients who already know the expected message formats and the location of the Web service are able to use it.

> **WARNING**
>
> **Working with the Internet** Most of the examples in this chapter assume that you're working on a computer that is connected to the Internet. It's okay if there's a proxy server between you and the Internet, as long as you can connect to Web sites.

> **NOTE**
>
> **Airport Codes** You can find a list of four-letter ICAO airport codes to use with this Web service at www.house747. freeserve.co.uk/aptcodes.htm. Codes for airports in the United States all start with K; codes for Canadian airports all start with C.

> **WARNING**
>
> **Web Service Stability** Web services come and go, and there's no guarantee that the one I use in this chapter will still be available when you try to test it. If the Airport Weather Web service doesn't seem to be available, one good way to find others is to use your favorite search engine to look for the phrase "Web service examples."

Invoking Your First Web Service

At this point, I'd like to show you a Web service in action. Step by Step 7.1 shows how you can use a Web service—in this case, one that supplies the weather at any airport worldwide.

STEP BY STEP

7.1 Invoking a Web Service

1. Open a Visual C# .NET Windows application in the Visual Studio .NET Integrated Development Environment (IDE).

2. Right-click the References folder in Solution Explorer and select Add Web Reference. The Add Web Reference dialog box appears.

3. Type http://live.capescience.com/wsdl/ AirportWeather.wsdl in the Address bar of the Add Web Reference dialog box and press Enter. This connects to the Airport Weather Web service and downloads the information shown in Figure 7.1.

FIGURE 7.1
The Add Web Reference dialog box allows you to connect to a Web service over the Internet.

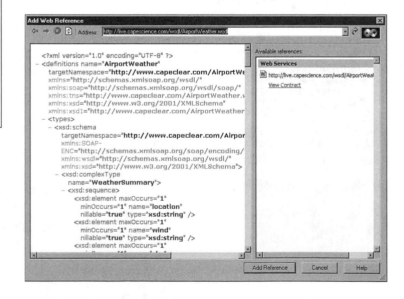

4. Click the Add Reference button.

5. Add a new form to your Visual C# .NET project.

6. Place a `Label` control, a `TextBox` control (`txtCode`), a `Button` control (`btnGetWeather`), and a `ListBox` control (`lbResults`) on the form. Figure 7.2 shows this form in the design view.

7. Double-click the `Button` control and enter the following code to invoke the Web service when the user clicks the Get Weather button:

```
private void btnGetWeather_Click(object sender,
    System.EventArgs e)
{
    // Declare the Web service main object
    com.capescience.live.AirportWeather aw =
        new com.capescience.live.AirportWeather();

    // Invoke the service to get a summary object
    com.capescience.live.WeatherSummary ws =
        aw.getSummary(txtCode.Text);

    // And display the results
    lbResults.Items.Clear();
    lbResults.Items.Add(ws.location);
    lbResults.Items.Add("Wind " + ws.wind);
    lbResults.Items.Add("Sky " + ws.sky);
    lbResults.Items.Add("Temperature " + ws.temp);
    lbResults.Items.Add("Humidity " + ws.humidity);
    lbResults.Items.Add("Barometer " + ws.pressure);
    lbResults.Items.Add("Visibility " +
        ws.visibility);
}
```

8. Insert the `Main()` method and set the form as the startup object for the project.

9. Run the project and enter a four-digit ICAO airport code. Click the Get Weather button. After a brief pause while the Web service is invoked, you see the current weather at that airport in the list box, as shown in Figure 7.3.

You'll learn more about the techniques used in Step by Step 7.1 later in this chapter, but you should be able to see the broad outlines of Web services already. In one sense, there's not much new here, compared to invoking any other object. After you've set a reference to the server, you can create objects from that server, invoke their methods, and examine the results. You could do the same with objects from a .NET library on your own computer.

FIGURE 7.2
The form invokes the Airport Weather Web service.

NOTE

IntelliSense with Web Services You'll see as you type this code that IntelliSense operates even though the objects you're working with are on the remote server.

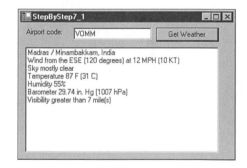

FIGURE 7.3
You can invoke a remote Web service and access the objects returned by the Web service.

But in another sense, there's a lot of revolutionary work going on here, even though you don't see most of it happening. When you create the Web reference, for example, Visual Studio .NET reads the appropriate WSDL file to determine which classes and methods are available from the remote server. When you call a method on an object from that server, the .NET infrastructure translates your call and the results into SOAP messages and transmits them without any intervention on your part.

Depending on the speed of your Internet connection, you might notice that the Web service client that you created in Step by Step 7.1 "freezes" when you invoke the Web service. That is because this program uses synchronous method to communicate with the Web service, waiting for the SOAP response before allowing any other code to execute. You will learn later in this chapter. in Exercise 7.1, how to call a Web service asynchronously to increase the responsiveness of the client program.

REVIEW BREAK

- ▶ Web services provide you with the means to create objects and invoke their methods even though your only connection to the server is via the Internet.

- ▶ Communication with Web services occurs via XML messages transported by HTTP.

- ▶ Because they communicate over HTTP, Web services are typically not blocked by firewalls.

- ▶ SOAP encapsulates object-oriented messages between Web service clients and servers.

- ▶ UDDI allows you to find Web services by connecting to a directory.

- ▶ WSDL lets you retrieve information on the classes and methods that are supported by a particular Web service.

CREATING WEB SERVICES

To better understand Web services, you should be familiar with both sides of the conversation. In the following sections, you'll learn how to create a Web service by using the tools built in to ASP.NET.

Although this material does not appear directly on the exam, it helps enhance your understanding of the skills that the exam measures.

Creating a Web Service Project

To create a Web service, you can build an ASP.NET project in Visual Studio .NET.

STEP BY STEP

7.2 Creating a Web Service

1. Create a new project in Visual Studio .NET. Select the ASP.NET Web Service template and name the new project `StringProc`, as shown in Figure 7.4. You can replace `localhost` with the name of your own Web server if the Web server is not on your local machine.

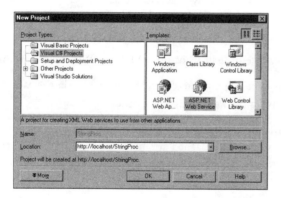

NOTE

Web Server Required You need to have an IIS Web server available to you in order to complete Step by Step 7.2, Step by Step 7.3, and Guided Practice Exercise 7.1. IIS is a part of the Windows 2000 Professional, Windows XP Professional, and Windows Server operating systems.

FIGURE 7.4
TheNew Project dialog box allows you to create a new Web service project in the Visual Studio .NET IDE.

2. Right-click the `Service1.asmx` file in Solution Explorer and rename it `Strings.asmx`.

3. Click the hyperlink on the `Strings.asmx` design surface to switch to the code view. Add the `following` attribute before the `Strings` class definition:

```
[WebService(Namespace=
    "http://NetExam.org/StringProc")]
public class Strings : System.Web.Services.WebService
```

continues

---

continued

4. Enter the following methods in the class definition:

```
[WebMethod()]
public String ToUpper(String inputString)
{
    return inputString.ToUpper();
}
[WebMethod()]
public String ToLower(String inputString)
{
    return inputString.ToLower();
}
```

5. Save the project.

6. Select Build, Build Solution to create the Web service on the server.

EXAM TIP

The Web Service Namespace If you use the `WebService` attribute, you must supply a value for the `Namespace` property. This value (`http://NetExam.org/StringProc`, in Step by Step 7.2) is purely arbitrary. It doesn't have to resolve to an actual Web site. This string is just a unique identifier for your Web service. If you leave the default value instead of changing it, you get a warning from Visual Studio .NET.

You now have a functioning Web service on your Web server. Congratulations! Although there is lots of plumbing involved in properly hooking up a Web service, Visual Studio .NET protects you from having to set up any of it. Instead, you only have to do three things:

1. Build the project from the ASP.NET Web Service template.

2. Mark the classes that should be available via the Web service by using the `WebService` attribute.

3. Mark the methods that should be available via the Web service by using the `WebMethod` attribute. The methods marked with the `WebMethod` attribute are also known as Web methods.

Testing the Web Service Project

Visual Studio .NET includes built-in tools for testing a Web service project from your browser without building any client applications for the Web service. Step by Step 7.3 shows how to use these tools, which can save you time when you're debugging a Web service.

STEP BY STEP

7.3 Testing a Web Service

1. Run the Web Service project from Step by Step 7.2. A browser is launched, showing the test page in Figure 7.5.

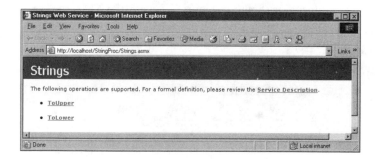

FIGURE 7.5
When you view a Web service in a browser, a Web service test page with hyperlinks to Web methods is displayed.

2. Click the Service Description link on the test page. You are able to view the WSDL file for this Web service. Click the Back button in the browser to return to the test page.

3. Click the ToUpper link on the test page. A page for testing the ToUpper() method appears, as shown in Figure 7.6.

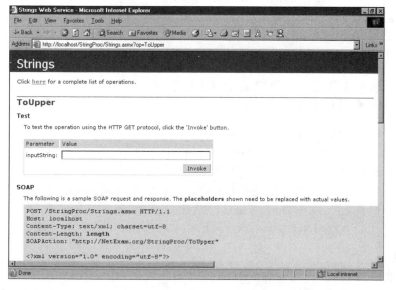

FIGURE 7.6
The Web method test page allows you to test the Web method by using the HTTP GET protocol.

4. The Web method test page shows the SOAP messages and other messages that the Web service understands. It also contains a form that allows you to test the Web method.

5. Enter a string with mixed upper- and lowercase characters at the inputString prompt.

6. Click the Invoke button. A second browser window opens, as shown in Figure 7.7, with the XML message that the Web service sends back when you call the ToUpper() method on the test string.

FIGURE 7.7
The Web service returns results in the XML format.

7. Experiment with the ToLower() method in the same way you experimented with the ToUpper() method. When you click the Invoke button, the test page constructs the appropriate XML message and passes it to the Web service, which returns the results.

GUIDED PRACTICE EXERCISE 7.1

In this exercise, you must create a Web service to allow the client applications to perform database lookup for a SQL Server database. Specifically, you need to perform these tasks:

1. Build a Web service that exposes a single class named Customer. The Customer class should expose a Web method named GetCustomers(). The GetCustomers() Web method should accept a country name and return a DataSet object that contains all the customers from that country. You should use the data from the Customers table of the Northwind sample database.

2. Build a client application that uses the Web service from step 1. The user should be able to enter a country name and see all the customers from that country.

How would you accomplish these tasks?

You should try working through this problem on your own first. If you get stuck, or if you'd like to see one possible solution, follow these steps:

1. Create a new project in Visual Studio .NET. Select the ASP.NET Web Service template and name the new project Northwind.

2. Right-click the Service1.asmx file in Solution Explorer and rename it Customer.asmx.

3. Click the hyperlink on the Customer.asmx design surface to switch to the code view. Change the name of the class to Customer and enter this code at the top of the file:

```
using System.Data.SqlClient;
```

4. Enter this code to create the GetCustomers() Web method:

```
[WebMethod()]
public DataSet GetCustomers(String Country)
{
    // Create a SqlConnection
    SqlConnection cnn = new SqlConnection(
    "Data Source=(local);" +
    "Initial Catalog=Northwind;" +
    "Integrated Security=SSPI");
    // Create a SqlCommand
    SqlCommand cmd = cnn.CreateCommand();
    cmd.CommandType = CommandType.Text;
    cmd.CommandText =
        "SELECT * FROM Customers " +
        " WHERE Country = '" + Country + "'";
    // Set up the DataAdapter and
    // fill the Dataset object
    SqlDataAdapter da = new SqlDataAdapter();
    da.SelectCommand = cmd;
    DataSet ds = new DataSet();
    da.Fill(ds, "Customers");
    // And return it to the client
    return ds;
}
```

5. Select Build, Build Solution to create the Web service on the server.

continues

FIGURE 7.8
You can test the Web methods that return complex objects through a Windows form.

continued

6. Build the client application. Open your Windows application for this chapter and add a new form to the project.

7. Place a `Label` control, a `TextBox` control named `txtCustomers`, a `Button` control named `btnGetCustomers`, and a `DataGrid` control named `dgCustomers` on the form. Figure 7.8 shows a possible design of the form.

8. Right-click the References folder in Solution Explorer and select Add Web Reference. The Add Web Reference dialog box appears.

9. Type `http://localhost/Northwind/Customer.asmx` (substituting your own Web server name for `localhost`, if the Web server is not on your local machine) in the Address bar of the Add Web Reference dialog box and press Enter. You are then connected to the server, where you can download the information about the Northwind Web service.

10. Click the Add Reference button.

11. Switch to the code view of the form. Add the following using directives:

```
using System.Data;
using System.Data.SqlClient;
```

12. Double-click the `Button` control on the form. Enter the following code to handle the button's `click` event (replace `localhost` with the name of your own Web server):

```
private void btnGetCustomers_Click
    (object sender, System.EventArgs e)
{
    // Create a DataSet object
    // to hold the customers of interest
    DataSet dsCustomers;
    // Connect to the Web service
    // and retrieve customers
    localhost.Customer cust =
        new localhost.Customer();
    dsCustomers = cust.GetCustomers(
        txtCountry.Text);
    // Bind the results to the user interface
    dgCustomers.DataSource = dsCustomers;
    dgCustomers.DataMember = "Customers";
}
```

13. Insert the `Main()` method to launch the form. Set the form as the startup object for the project.

14. Run the project and enter a country name (such as France). Click the GetCustomers button. After a brief delay while the project contacts the Web service, the data grid fills with data, as shown in Figure 7.9.

FIGURE 7.9
This Windows form displays the data supplied by the `GetCustomers()` Web method.

As this exercise shows, you can return complex objects from a Web service as easily as you can return simple types. The Web service takes care of all the details of converting the `DataSet` object to an XML representation, wrapping it in a SOAP message, sending it to the client, and reconstituting the `DataSet` object there.

If you have difficulty following this exercise, review the sections "Invoking Your First Web Service" and "Creating a Web Service Project," earlier in this chapter. Also review the section "Running Queries" in Chapter 6. After doing that review, try this exercise again.

R E V I E W   B R E A K

▶ Visual Studio .NET includes an ASP.NET Web Service template that you can use to build your own Web services.

▶ To make a class available via a Web service, you mark the class with the `WebService` attribute.

▶ To make a method available via a Web service, you mark the method with the `WebMethod` attribute.

▶ To test a Web service, run the project in the Visual Studio .NET IDE.

DISCOVERING WEB SERVICES

One of the problems with Web services is simply finding them. Because Web services aren't installed on your computer, you need some way to determine what messages they accept and what services they provide.

The usual term for this process is *discovery*, which encompasses both finding Web services and determining their interfaces. You should know about three protocols in this area:

- ◆ Disco
- ◆ UDDI
- ◆ WSDL

Disco and UDDI

Disco is a Microsoft standard for the creation of discovery documents. A Disco document is kept at a standard location on a Web services server, and it contains paths and other information for retrieving useful information, such as the WSDL file that describes a service. Disco is generally not used outside the .NET world.

UDDI is a protocol for finding services by referring to a central directory. These can be Web services, URLs for information, or any other online resources. UDDI registries are sites that contain information that is available via UDDI; you can search such a registry to find information about Web services.

UDDI registries come in two forms, *public* and *private*. A public UDDI registry is available to all comers via the Internet and serves as a central repository of information about Web and other services for businesses. A private UDDI registry follows the same specifications as a public UDDI registry but is located on an intranet for the use of workers at one particular enterprise.

NOTE

The UDDI Project The UDDI specification is being developed jointly by several industry partners, including Microsoft and IBM. For more information and a public directory, visit `www.uddi.org`.

Using the Web Services Discovery Tool (`disco.exe`)

When you set a Web reference inside Visual Studio .NET, the software automatically handles the details of discovery for you. But you can also get into the details of the process yourself. One of the tools included in the .NET Framework Software Development Kit (SDK)—and also in Visual Studio .NET—is the Web Services Discovery tool, `disco.exe`. This command-line tool assists you in the discovery process.

STEP BY STEP

7.4 Using the Web Services Discovery Tool

1. Select Start, Programs, Microsoft Visual Studio .NET, Visual Studio .NET Tools, Visual Studio .NET Command Prompt. A command prompt window opens, and the environment is set up so that you can use any of the command-line tools from the .NET Framework SDK.

2. Enter the following command to discover the details of the CapeScience Airport Weather Web service:

```
disco
➥http://live.capescience.com/wsdl/AirportWeather.wsdl
```

   As you can see, you need to know the base address of the Web service in order to use this tool.

3. The tool contacts the Web service and (in this case) creates two files of results: `AirportWeather.wsdl` and `results.discomap`. If the Web service includes a static discovery document (`.disco` file), the tool also retrieves that document.

4. Open these files in Visual Studio .NET to see the results of the discovery process. The `results.discomap` file is an XML file that shows you the name of the other file (`AirportWeather.wsdl`) and the URL from which its contents were retrieved. The `AirportWeather.wsdl` file is an XML file that contains information about the interface of the Web service, including details about the messages, parameters, and objects with which you can interact. This file gives Visual Studio .NET the details it needs in order to let you use a Web service.

> **NOTE**
>
> **The .disco File**—The `disco.exe` file also retrieves the discovery document if the Web service includes a static discovery document (`.disco` file). The `.disco` file is an XML file that contains useful URLs, including the URL for the WSDL file describing the service, the URL for the documentation of the service, and the URL to which SOAP messages should be sent.

REVIEW BREAK

▶ Disco is Microsoft's standard format for discovery documents, which contain information about Web services.

▶ UDDI is a multivendor standard for discovering online resources, including Web services.

continues

continued

▶ The Web Services Discovery tool, `disco.exe`, can retrieve discovery information from a server that exposes a Web service.

INSTANTIATING AND INVOKING WEB SERVICES

After you have discovered a Web service and retrieved information about its interface, you can instantiate an object that represents that Web service and then invoke its methods. In this section you'll learn about two methods for integrating Web services into your applications, and you'll learn about testing a Web service, as a consumer.

Creating Proxy Classes with the Web Services Description Language Tool (`wsdl.exe`)

The .NET Framework SDK includes the Web Services Description Language tool, `wsdl.exe`. This tool can take a WSDL file and generate a corresponding proxy class that you can use to invoke the Web service. Step by Step 7.5 shows you how.

STEP BY STEP

7.5 Using the Web Services Description Language Tool

1. Select Start, Programs, Microsoft Visual Studio .NET, Visual Studio .NET Tools, Visual Studio .NET Command Prompt. A command prompt window opens, and the environment is set up so that you can use any of the command-line tools from the .NET Framework SDK.

2. Navigate to the folder that contains the WSDL file that you created in Step by Step 7.4.

3. Enter the following command to create a proxy class to call the Airport Weather Web service:

```
wsdl /language:CS
➥/out:AirportWeatherProxy.cs AirportWeather.wsdl
```

The tool reads the WSDL file and creates a new file, named `AirportWeatherProxy.cs`.

4. Add the `AirportWeatherProxy.cs` file to your Visual Studio .NET Windows application project by selecting File, Add Existing Item.

5. Add a new form to your Visual C# .NET project.

6. Place a `Label` control, a `TextBox` control (`txtCode`), a `Button` control (`btnGetWeather`), and a `ListBox` control (`lbResults`) on the form. Refer to Figure 7.2 for the design of this form.

7. Double-click the `Button` control and enter the following code to invoke the Web service when the user clicks the Get Weather button:

```
private void btnGetWeather_Click(object sender,
    System.EventArgs e)
{
    // Connect to the Web service by declaring
    // a variable of the appropriate type
    // available in the proxy
    AirportWeather aw = new AirportWeather();

    // Invoke the service to get a summary object
    WeatherSummary ws = aw.getSummary(txtCode.Text);

    // And display the results
    lbResults.Items.Clear();
    lbResults.Items.Add(ws.location);
    lbResults.Items.Add("Wind " + ws.wind);
    lbResults.Items.Add("Sky " + ws.sky);
    lbResults.Items.Add("Temperature " + ws.temp);
    lbResults.Items.Add("Humidity " + ws.humidity);
    lbResults.Items.Add("Barometer " + ws.pressure);
    lbResults.Items.Add("Visibility " +
        ws.visibility);
}
```

8. Insert the `Main()` method to launch the form. Set the form as the startup object for the project.

continues

continued

9. Run the project and fill in a value for the airport code. Click the Get Weather button. After a brief pause while the Web service is invoked, you see some information in the `ListBox` control, as shown in Figure 7.3. This information is delivered from the server where the Web service resides, as properties of the `WeatherSummary` object. The difference between this and the version in Step by Step 7.1 is that this code explicitly defines the objects that it uses rather than discovering them at runtime. The `AirportWeather` and `WeatherSummary` objects are proxy objects that pass calls to the Web service and return results from the Web service.

Table 7.1 shows some of the command-line options that you can use with `wsdl.exe`. You don't need to memorize this material, but you should be familiar with the overall capabilities of the tool. You can use either the path to a local WSDL or Disco file or the URL of a remote WSDL or Disco file with this tool.

TABLE 7.1

COMMAND-LINE OPTIONS FOR `wsdl.exe`

Option	*Description*
`/domain:DomainName` `/d:DomainName`	Specifies the domain name to use when connecting to a server that requires authentication.
`/language:LanguageCode` `/l:LanguageCode`	Specifies the language for the generated class. The *LanguageCode* parameter can be `CS` (for C#), `VB` (for Visual Basic .NET) or `JS` (for JScript).
`/namespace:Namespace` `/n:Namespace`	Specifies a namespace for the generated class.
`/out:Filename/o:FileName`	Specifies the filename for the generated output. If this option is not used, the filename is derived from the Web service name.
`/password:Password` `/p:Password`	Specifies the password to use when connecting to a server that requires authentication.
`/server`	Generates a class to create a server based on the input file. By default, the tool generates a client proxy object.

Option	Description
/username:*Username* /u:*Username*	Specifies the username to use when connecting to a server that requires authentication.
/?	Displays full help for the tool.

Using Web References

As an alternative to using the Web Services Discovery tool and the Web Services Description Language tool to create explicit proxy classes, you can simply add a Web reference to a project to enable the project to use the Web service. You've seen Web references several times in this chapter, starting in Step by Step 7.1.

In fact, there's no difference in the end result between using the tools to create a proxy class and adding a Web reference. That's because, behind the scenes, a Web reference creates its own proxy class. To see this, click the Show All Files toolbar button in Solution Explorer, and then expand the Solution Explorer node for a Web reference. You see a set of files similar to that shown in Figure 7.10.

The .wsdl file is the same file that would be generated by running the Web Services Discovery tool on the URL of the Web reference. The .map file is same as the .discomap file generated by the Web Services Discovery tool. The .cs file defines the proxy objects to be used with the Web service represented by this Web reference, as you can see by opening this file. The major difference between this file and the proxy that you generate with the Web Services Description Language tool is that the autogenerated file uses a namespace that is based on the name of the Web reference.

Testing a Web Service

If you'd like to test a Web service without building an entire client application, you can use a testing tool. Several of these tools are easily available:

◆ NetTool is a free Web services proxy tool from CapeClear. You can get a copy from capescience.capeclear.com/articles/ using_nettool.

FIGURE 7.10
When you add a Web reference, the proxy class is automatically generated.

EXAM TIP

Why Use a Web Reference? The major benefit of using a Web reference (as compared to constructing proxy classes with the command-line tools) is that it's easier to update the proxy classes if the Web service changes. All you need to do in that case is right-click the Web reference node in Solution Explorer and select Update Web Reference.

◆ The .NET WebService Studio tool comes from Microsoft. You can download a free copy from `www.gotdotnet.com/team/tools/web_svc/default.aspx`.

◆ XML Spy includes a SOAP debugger that can be used to test Web services. You can download a trial copy of this XML editor and toolkit from `www.xmlspy.com`.

All three of these tools work in the same basic way: They intercept SOAP messages between Web service clients and servers so that you can inspect and, if you like, alter the results. In Step by Step 7.6 you use one of these tools to see a Web service in action.

STEP BY STEP

7.6 Testing a Web Service Without a Client Project

1. Download the .NET WebService Studio tool from `www.gotdotnet.com/team/tools/web_svc/default.aspx` and install it on your computer.

2. Launch the `WebServiceStudio.exe` application.

3. Enter `http://live.capescience.com/wsdl/AirportWeather.wsdl` as the WSDL endpoint and click the Get button.

4. The tool reads the WSDL file from the Web service and constructs the necessary proxy classes to invoke it. Click the getSummary entry on the Invoke tab to use the `getSummary` Web method.

5. In the Input section, select the `arg0` item. You can now enter a value for this item in the Value section. Enter an airport code such as KSEA for the value.

6. Click the Invoke button. The tool sends a SOAP message to the Web service, using your chosen parameters, and then displays the results, as shown in Figure 7.11.

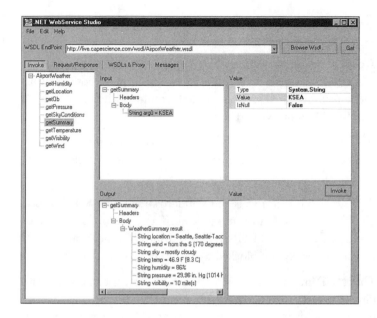

FIGURE 7.11
The .NET WebService Studio tool allows you to test a Web service without creating any client application.

7. Click the Request/Response tab to view the outgoing and incoming SOAP messages.

8. Click the WSDLs & Proxy tab to see the WSDL file and the generated proxy class for this Web service.

REVIEW BREAK

▶ You can manually generate proxy classes for a Web service by using the Web Services Description Language tool.

▶ You can automatically generate proxy classes for a Web service by setting a Web reference to point to the Web service.

▶ You can test and debug a Web service without a client application by using one of several SOAP proxy tools.

CHAPTER SUMMARY

KEY TERMS

- Disco
- SOAP
- UDDI
- Web method
- Web reference
- Web service
- WSDL

Web service support is one of the most significant advances in the .NET architecture. The .NET Framework supports both creating and consuming Web services through command-line tools as well as the Visual Studio .NET IDE.

Web services provide a way to invoke objects over the Internet. A Web service can expose one or more Web methods, each of which can accept parameters and return objects.

Web services use protocols and standards, including SOAP, Disco, UDDI, and WSDL, to communicate. These protocols and standards are designed to use HTTP as their transmission mechanism so that they are generally not blocked by firewalls.

The .NET Framework includes command-line tools to aid in the discovery and use of Web services. Visual Studio .NET enables you to easily use these tools by simply setting a Web reference. Either of these methods produces local proxy classes that you can use to send messages to a Web service and that return the results from the Web service to the rest of the application.

Exercises

7.1 Calling a Web Service Asynchronously

Depending on the speed of your Internet connection, you may have noticed that the Web service client applications you constructed earlier in Step by Step 7.1, "freeze" when you invoke the Web service. That's because by default these applications use synchronous methods to communicate with the Web service, waiting for the SOAP response before allowing any other code to execute. But the proxy classes constructed by .NET include asynchronous methods as well. In this exercise, you'll learn how to call a Web service asynchronously.

Estimated time: 30 minutes

1. Create a new Visual C# .NET Windows application in the Visual Studio .NET IDE.

2. Right-click the References folder in Solution Explorer and select Add Web Reference. The Add Web Reference dialog box appears.

3. Type `http://live.capescience.com/wsdl/AirportWeather.wsdl` in the Address bar of the Add Web Reference dialog box and press Enter. This connects to the Airport Weather Web service and downloads the information shown in Figure 7.1.

4. Click the Add Reference button.

5. Add a new form to your Visual C# .NET project.

6. Place a `Label` control, a `TextBox` control (txtCode), a `Button` control (btnGetWeather), and a `ListBox` control (lbResults) on the form. Refer to Figure 7.2 for the design of this form.

7. Double-click the `Button` control and enter the following code to invoke the Web service when the user clicks the Get Weather button:

```
private void btnGetWeather_Click(
    object sender, System.EventArgs e)
{
  // Declare the Web service main object
  com.capescience.live.AirportWeather aw =
  new com.capescience.live.AirportWeather();

    // Invoke the Web service.
    // This may take some time, so
    // call it asynchronously.
    // First, create a callback method
    AsyncCallback wcb = new AsyncCallback(
        WebServiceCallback);
    // And then initiate the
    // asynchronous call
    aw.BegingetSummary(
        txtCode.Text, wcb, aw);

}
// This method will get called
// when the Web service call is done
public void WebServiceCallback(
    IAsyncResult ar)
{
  // Retrieve the state of the proxy object
  com.capescience.live.AirportWeather aw =
    (com.capescience.live.AirportWeather)
    ar.AsyncState;

    // Call the End method to
    // finish processing
    com.capescience.live.WeatherSummary ws =
        aw.EndgetSummary(ar);

    // And display the results
    lbResults.Items.Clear();
    lbResults.Items.Add(ws.location);
    lbResults.Items.Add("Wind " + ws.wind);
    lbResults.Items.Add("Sky " + ws.sky);
    lbResults.Items.Add("Temperature " +
        ws.temp);
    lbResults.Items.Add("Humidity " +
        ws.humidity);
    lbResults.Items.Add("Barometer " +
        ws.pressure);
    lbResults.Items.Add("Visibility " +
        ws.visibility);
}
```

APPLY YOUR KNOWLEDGE

8. Insert the `Main()` method to launch the form. Set the form as the startup object for the project.

9. Run the project and enter a four-digit ICAO airport code. Click the Get Weather button. Wait a few moments; you'll see the current weather at that airport in the list box. Note that while you're waiting, you can still drag the form around the screen, which shows that it is not blocked by the Web service call.

If you compare the code for this exercise with the code from Step by Step 7.1, you should find some significant changes. In the .NET Framework, asynchronous Web service calls are managed by callback methods. When you add a Web reference, the proxy class includes `Begin` and `End` methods for each Web method. In this case, those are the `BegingetSummary()` and `EndgetSummary()` methods.

The `Begin` method takes all the same parameters as the underlying Web method, as well as two others: The first is the address of a callback method, and the second is an object whose properties should be available in the callback method. When you call the `Begin` method, the .NET Framework launches the call to the Web service in the background. When the Web method call completes, the callback method is invoked. The code in this exercise shows how you can then retrieve the original object and use its `End` method to finish the work of using the Web service.

Review Questions

1. What is the purpose of a Web service proxy class?

2. Describe the general purpose of SOAP.

3. Describe the general purpose of Disco and UDDI.

4. Describe the general purpose of WSDL.

5. Can a Web service exist without a WSDL file?

6. Explain two ways in which you can create proxy classes for a Web service.

7. List three steps involved in building a Web service by using Visual Studio .NET.

8. What tools can you use to make local copies of the configuration files for a Web service?

9. How can you test a Web service without building a client application?

10. What is the advantage of sending SOAP messages over HTTP?

Exam Questions

1. You want to use a Web service that supplies inventory level information in your application. You know the URL of the `.asmx` file published by the Web service. What step should you take first?

   A. Open the `.asmx` file in a Web browser.

   B. Run the XML Schema Definition tool

   C. Run the Web Services Discovery tool.

   D. Copy the `.asmx` file to your client project.

2. Your application includes a Web reference to a Web service that delivers customer information as an object with multiple properties. The developer of the Web service has added a new property named `CreditRating` to the object. What should you do to be able to use the `CreditRating` property in your code?

   A. Create an entirely new client application, and add to the new application a Web reference for the Web service.

B. Delete and re-create the Web reference in the existing application.

C. Update the Web reference in the existing application.

D. Use a generic `Object` variable to hold customer information, so you can call any property you like.

3. You have created a Web service to return financial information using ASP.NET. One of the methods in your Web service is defined with this code:

```
public Double Cash()
{
    // Calculations omitted
}
```

Potential consumers of your Web service report that although they can set a reference to the Web service, the `Cash()` method is not available. What could be the problem?

A. The `.asmx` file for the Web service is not available on your Web server.

B. The `WebService` class is not marked with the `[WebService]` attribute.

C. The `Cash()` method is not marked with the `[WebMethod]` attribute.

D. Web services can return only string values.

4. You have created a new Web service to perform financial calculations. You're working in an ASP.NET project within Visual Studio .NET. What's the easiest way to test your new Web service to make sure it's returning the proper results?

A. Cut and paste the code into a Windows application project and test it in the new project.

B. Run the Web service project and use the test page that it opens in the browser.

C. Use a tool such as WebService Studio to send SOAP requests directly to the server.

D. Have a large number of beta testers use the application and monitor the server for odd behavior.

5. Your application uses a Web service named Northwind. The Northwind Web service includes a Web method named `Suppliers()` that returns a `DataSet` object containing all the company's suppliers. What data type should you use to declare an object to hold the result of the `Suppliers()` method?

A. `Suppliers.DataSet`

B. `DataSet`

C. `Northwind.DataSet`

D. `DataRow[]`

6. You're using the Web Services Discovery tool to determine information about a Web service on a particular server. You receive the error message `The HTML document does not contain Web service discovery information`. What could be the problem?

A. The server address that you typed does not exist.

B. The server requires authentication, and you have entered improper credentials.

C. The Web Services Discovery tool works only on your local computer.

D. There is no WSDL or Disco file available at the address you typed.

7. You are using the Web Services Description Language tool to create a proxy class for a Web service. The Web service exposes a class named `Customer`. You already have a `Customer` class in your application. What should you do to allow both classes to coexist in the same application?

   A. Use the `/namespace` option of the Web Services Description Language tool to specify a unique namespace for the new class.

   B. Rename the existing class.

   C. Use the `/out` option of the Web Services Description Language tool to specify a unique output filename for the new class.

   D. Manually edit the generated proxy class to change the classname that it contains.

8. You have used a UDDI registry to locate a Web service that might be able to supply information for your business. You want to test the interface of the Web service to make sure it meets your requirements before you invest the effort to build a client application. How should you proceed?

   A. Use the Web Services Discovery tool to download the WSDL file for the Web service and inspect it in an XML editor.

   B. Use the Web Services Description Language tool to create a proxy class for the Web service and inspect the class using a text editor.

   C. Craft SOAP messages in an XML editor and use them to test the Web service.

   D. Use a tool such as WebService Studio to test the interface of the Web service.

9. Your application calls a Web service that performs complex, time-consuming calculations.

Users complain that the user interface of the application freezes while it's recalculating. Which of the following approaches is guaranteed to solve this problem?

   A. Move the application to a faster computer.

   B. Install a faster link to the Internet.

   C. Install more memory in the computer.

   D. Use asynchronous calls to invoke the Web service.

10. One of your business partners has informed you that it is making its inventory information available via a Web service. You do not know the URL of the Web service. How can you discover the URL?

   A. Use the Web Services Discovery tool to download the information.

   B. Use the Web Services Description Language tool to create a proxy class.

   C. Use a UDDI registry to locate the Web service.

   D. Use a search engine to explore your partner's Web site.

11. What must a developer do to make a Web service available asynchronously?

   A. Nothing. The client can always call a Web service asynchronously.

   B. Use a separate `Thread` object for each invocation of the Web service.

   C. Provide callback methods to invoke the Web service.

   D. Host the Web service on an Internet Information Server 6.0 server.

APPLY YOUR KNOWLEDGE

12. You are invoking a Web service that returns a `DataSet` object. Which project in this scenario requires a reference to the `System.Data` namespace?

    A. The client project.

    B. The Web service project.

    C. Both the client project and the Web service project.

    D. Neither project.

13. Your application invokes a Web service named Northwind that includes a Web method named `GetOrders()`. `GetOrders()` returns a `DataSet` object containing order information. What must you do to use this `DataSet` object in your client application?

    A. Create a new `DataSet` object and use the `ReadXml()` method of the `DataSet` object to initialize it from the returning SOAP message.

    B. Obtain an XSD file that specifies the schema of the `DataSet` object. Use this XSD file to instantiate a `DataSet` object from the returned data from the `GetOrders()` method.

    C. Assign the return value from the `GetOrders()` method to an array of `DataRow` variables. Loop through the array to build the `DataSet` object.

    D. Assign the return value from the `GetOrders()` method to a `DataSet` variable.

14. You have used the Web Services Discovery tool to retrieve information about a Web service named ZipcodeService. Which file would contain the URL for any documentation of the ZipcodeService Web service?

    A. `disco.exe`

    B. `results.discomap`

    C. `ZipcodeService.wsdl`

    D. `ZipcodeService.disco`

15. You have used the Web Services Description Language tool to create a proxy class for a Web service. When you add the proxy class to your project, you discover that it is coded in Visual Basic .NET. What must you do to get the proxy class in C# instead of Visual Basic .NET?

    A. Manually convert the Visual Basic .NET code to C# code.

    B. Rerun the tool, using the `/language:CS` option.

    C. Rerun the tool, using the `/namespace:CS` option.

    D. Select File, Save As and save the file with the `.cs` extension.

Answers to Review Questions

1. A Web service proxy class is an object that you can create on the client to communicate with a Web service. The proxy accepts messages and forwards them to the Web service, and it returns the results of those messages.

2. SOAP is designed to encapsulate objects as XML messages. Those objects can then be sent via HTTP or other standard communications channels.

3. Disco and UDDI are designed to help discover the interface details of a Web service.

APPLY YOUR KNOWLEDGE

4. WSDL exists to supply information on the interface of a Web service.

5. A Web service can exist without a WSDL file, but you must then know the exact incoming SOAP message that the Web service expects before you can use it.

6. You can create proxy classes for a Web service by using the `disco.exe` and `wsdl.exe` tools or by creating a Web reference within Visual Studio .NET.

7. To build a Web service you must create a new Web service application, mark the classes to be exposed with the `[WebService]` attribute, and mark the methods to be exposed with the `[WebMethod]` attribute.

8. The `disco.exe` tool makes local copies of the configuration files for a Web service. Creating a new Web reference also creates these files.

9. You can use a tool such as .NET WebService Studio to test a Web service without building a client application.

10. Using HTTP as the transport protocol for SOAP messages means that the messages can take advantage of pervasive Internet connectivity to reach their destination; they are not blocked by firewalls.

Answers to Exam Questions

1. **C.** The Web Services Discovery tool retrieves copies of the files that you need to proceed with this project. For more information, see the section "Discovering Web Services" in this chapter.

2. **C.** The Update Web Reference menu item for a Web reference refreshes local configuration information from the server that hosts the Web service. For more information, see the section "Using Web References" in this chapter.

3. **C.** All exposed methods of a Web service must be marked with the `[WebMethod]` attribute. For more information, see the section "Creating Web Services" in this chapter.

4. **B.** When you're creating a Web service in ASP.NET, running the project opens a testing form in a browser window. For more information, see the section "Testing a Web Service" in this chapter.

5. **B.** The client needs to declare the same data type that the server is returning—in this case the DataSet object. For more information, see the section "Testing the Web Service Project" and Guided Practice Exercise 7.1 in this chapter.

6. **D.** The Web Services Discovery tool requires the URL to a Disco or WSDL file in order to function. For more information, see the section "Using the Web Services Discovery Tool (`disco.exe`)" in this chapter.

7. **A.** Specifying a unique namespace for the new object eliminates the possibility that it could clash with a preexisting object name. For more information, see the section "Creating Proxy Classes with the Web Services Description Language Tool (`wsdl.exe`)" in this chapter.

8. **D.** By using an automated tool, you can avoid tedious and error-prone inspection of XML files. For more information, see the section "Testing a Web Service" in this chapter.

APPLY YOUR KNOWLEDGE

9. **D.** Speeding up the client computer does nothing to speed up the Web service, which runs on the server computer. For more information, see the section "Invoking Your First Web Service" in this chapter.

10. **C.** UDDI registries exist so that you can find business services by browsing or searching. For more information, see the section "Disco and UDDI" in this chapter.

11. **A.** Building the proxy class, either with `wsdl.exe` or by setting a Web reference, automatically creates methods for invoking the Web service asynchronously. For more information, see the section "Instantiating and Invoking Web Services" in this chapter.

12. **C.** Web services client and server applications must agree on the definition of the data to be exchanged.

For more information, see the section "Instantiating and Invoking Web Services" in this chapter.

13. **D.** The only thing you need to do to use a complex variable returned by the Web service is to declare an instance of the same data type in the client application. For more information, see the section "Instantiating and Invoking Web Services" in this chapter.

14. **D.** The `.disco` file is the only one that contains pointers to non-XML resources. For more information, see the section "Discovering Web Services" in this chapter.

15. **B.** The `/language` option controls the output language of the `wsdl.exe` tool. For more information, see the section "Creating Proxy Classes with the Web Services Description Language Tool (`wsdl.exe`)" in this chapter.

Suggested Readings and Resources

1. Visual Studio .NET Combined Help Collection.

2. .NET Framework SDK Documentation, including "XML Web Services Created Using ASP.NET and XML Web Service Clients."

3. Kenn Scribner & Mark C. Stiver. *Applied SOAP: Implementing .NET XML Web Services.* Sams, 2001.

4. Scott Short. *Building XML Web Services for the Microsoft .NET Platform.* Microsoft Press, 2002.

5. Eric Newcomer. *Understanding Web Services: XML, WSDL, SOAP, and UDDI.* Addison-Wesley, 2002.

6. Microsoft Support WebCast: "Microsoft .NET: Introduction to Web Services," `support.microsoft.com/servicedesks/webcasts/wc012902/wcblurb012902.asp`.

This chapter covers the following Microsoft-specified objectives for the "Creating User Services" section of Exam 70-316, "Developing and Implementing Windows-Based Applications with Microsoft Visual C# .NET and Microsoft Visual Studio .NET":

Implement globalization.

- **Implement localizability for the UI.**

- **Convert existing encodings.**

- **Implement right-to-left and left-to-right mirroring.**

- **Prepare culture-specific formatting.**

Validate user input.

- **Validate non-Latin user input.**

▶ The goal of this exam objective is to test your ability to produce what Microsoft calls "world-ready" applications. A *world-ready* application is one that can be translated for a new culture with a minimum of recoding (ideally, with no recoding at all). This means that you need some way to deal with issues such as these:

- Different currency symbols for different countries.

- Changes of language on the user interface.

- Cultures that read right-to-left instead of left-to-right.

The .NET Framework offers good support for the process of producing world-ready applications.

CHAPTER 8

Globalization

▶ Review the "Globalization" section of the *Common Tasks QuickStart* tutorial. The QuickStart tutorials are installed as part of the .NET Framework installation.

▶ Experiment with code that uses the `CurrentCulture` and `CurrentUICulture` properties.

Set these properties to several different values and inspect the differences in your code's output.

▶ Change the mirroring of a complex form from one of your own applications and watch how its properties change at runtime.

INTRODUCTION

In the pre-Internet days, it wasn't unusual to design an application to be used in only a single country. Large companies such as Microsoft sometimes produced their applications in a dozen or more languages, but that was unusual. The majority of applications were written in a single human language, and all the users and developers spoke the same language.

These days, though, that approach can seriously limit the market for your software. Most developers need to think from the beginning of a project about translating a user interface into multiple languages—a process known as *localization*. With the Internet as a marketing tool, there's no telling where your next customer will come from.

In support of this new way of working, the .NET Framework provides excellent capabilities for localizing applications. Localization goes far beyond simply translating the text on a user interface. These are some of the topics you need to consider:

- ◆ Translating user interface text, message boxes, and so on.
- ◆ Using encodings to translate characters from one representation to another.
- ◆ Using mirroring to change the direction of text in controls on the user interface.
- ◆ Formatting things such as currency and dates that are presented in different ways in different locales.
- ◆ Managing data sorts to take into account different alphabets.

In this chapter you'll learn about the concepts and techniques that the .NET Framework makes available for localization. You need a basic understanding of the entire process to pass the "Implement globalization" section of the certification exam.

UNDERSTANDING LOCALIZATION AND GLOBALIZATION

Implement globalization.

- **Prepare localizability for the UI.**

If you consider the process of developing an application for multiple locations around the world (say, the United States, Singapore, and Peru), you can see two basic ways to undertake the job:

◆ Write three completely different sets of source code, one for each location where the application will be used.

◆ Write one set of source code and build in the ability to customize the application for different locations.

The first of these alternatives is likely to be prohibitively expensive. Using three different sets of source code would require three times as many developers, testers, and managers as building a single version of the application. Perhaps worse, a bug that's found and fixed in one version might slip through the cracks and ship in another version. If you later needed to ship a version for a fourth location, you'd have to repeat the entire process again.

Not surprisingly, Visual C# .NET encourages you to take the second approach. An application built from a single code base can be easily customized for multiple locations through techniques such as locale-aware formatting methods and resource files. You don't have to worry about different versions getting out of sync—because they're all built from the same source code—and building a new version requires no work beyond translating strings into a new language.

The Localization Process

The technical term for the process of preparing an application for shipment in a new location-specific version is *localization*. Microsoft divides this process of preparing a world-ready application into three phases:

◆ **Globalization**—In the globalization stage, you identify all the localizable resources in the application and separate them from the executable code so that they can be modified easily. Ideally, you perform the globalization step during the design phase so that the resources always remain separate from the code.

◆ **Localizability**—In the localizability stage, you check to make sure that translating the application for a new location won't require design changes. If you've planned for localization from the beginning, localizability will typically be part of your quality assurance (QA) process.

WARNING

> **Flexible Terms** Although in theory the terms *globalization*, *localizability*, and *localization* are precise and distinct, in practice they tend to be used interchangeably. Indeed, even the objectives for the certification exam are not careful in the way that they use these terms. In this chapter I often use the terms *globalization* and *localization* to mean the same thing—developing world-ready applications.

◆ **Localization**—In the localization phase, you customize the application for new locales. This consists primarily of translating resources that you identified during the globalization phase.

What Should Be Localized?

Obviously, you must modify text that shows on the user interface when you're localizing an application. This includes text on forms, in error messages, and in message boxes, and any other text that is shown to the user. But there are many other things that you might need to localize in any given application. Here's a list of resources that are commonly localized, depending on the target locale:

◆ Menu item text.

◆ Form layouts. Text in German, for example, is generally nearly twice as long as the same text in English. You might need to move and resize controls to accommodate this.

◆ The display format for dates and times.

◆ The display format for currency.

◆ The display format for numbers (for example, some countries use commas as the thousands separator in long numbers).

◆ Data input fields (what if you're asking for a postal code in a country other than the United States?).

◆ Maps, road signs, photos, or other graphics with local content.

◆ Shortcut keys. Not every character you know appears on every keyboard.

◆ Calendars. Countries such as Korea and Saudi Arabia use completely different calendars from each other.

◆ Alphabetical order.

You need to use some judgment in deciding which of these things really need to be localized in an application. You might decide, for example, that a set of general-purpose data entry fields can serve your needs for collecting addresses, rather than try to research address formats worldwide.

IMPLEMENTING LOCALIZATION FOR THE USER INTERFACE

Implement globalization.

- **Prepare culture-specific formatting.**

The `System.Globalization` namespace in the .NET Framework provides most of the support in the .NET Framework for localization in Visual C# .NET applications. I'll start looking at localization code by exploring some of the concepts and classes you'll need to understand to build your own world-ready applications.

The two key pieces to keep in mind are cultures and resource files. A *culture*, as you'll see, is an identifier for a particular locale. A *resource file* is a place where you can store some culture-dependent resources such as strings and bitmaps. (The .NET Framework handles translating other resources, such as date formats, automatically.)

Understanding Cultures

Before you can start localizing applications, you need to understand the concept of a culture. A culture, in .NET terms, is a more precise identifier than a location or a language. A culture identifies all the things that might need to be localized in an application, which requires you to know more than just the language. For example, just knowing that an application uses English as its user interface language doesn't give you enough information to completely localize it; should you format dates and currency amounts in that application in a way that is appropriate the the United States, the United Kingdom, Canada, Australia, or New Zealand (among other possibilities)? Similarly, just knowing the location isn't enough; if an application will be used in Switzerland, there are four possibilities for the user interface language. Each combination of location and language identifies a culture.

About Culture Codes

The .NET Framework follows the IETF Standard RFC 1766 to identify cultures, using abbreviations called *culture codes*. A full culture code consists of a neutral culture code (written in lowercase), followed by one or more subculture codes (written in mixed case or uppercase). Here are a few culture codes as samples:

◆ `de` identifies the German culture. This is a neutral culture—a culture that does not specify a subculture code. Neutral cultures generally do not provide sufficient information to localize an application.

◆ `en-GB` identifies the English (United Kingdom) culture. This is a specific culture—a culture that provides enough information to localize an application (in this case, for English speakers in Great Britain).

◆ `az-AZ-Cyrl` is an example of a specific culture with two subculture codes. This particular culture refers to the Azeri language in Azerbaijan, written with Cyrillic characters.

The `CultureInfo` Class

The .NET Framework represents cultures with the `System.Globalization.CultureInfo` class. This class lets you retrieve a wide variety of information about any particular culture.

STEP BY STEP

8.1 Retrieving Culture Information

1. Open a Visual C# .NET Windows Application in the Visual Studio .NET Integrated Development Environment (IDE).

2. Add a new form to your Visual C# .NET project.

3. Place a `Button` control named `btnGetInfo`, a `TextBox` control named `Culture`, and a `ListBox` control named `lbInfo` on the form.

4. Switch to the code view and add the following `using` directive:

```
using System.Globalization;
```

5. Double-click the `Button` control and enter the following code to handle the button's `Click` event:

```
private void btnGetInfo_Click(object sender,
    System.EventArgs e)
{
```

```
// Create a CultureInfo object
// for the specified culture
CultureInfo ci = new CultureInfo(txtCulture.Text);
// Dump information about the culture
lbInfo.Items.Clear();
lbInfo.Items.Add("Display Name: " +
    ci.DisplayName);
lbInfo.Items.Add("English Name: " +
    ci.EnglishName);
lbInfo.Items.Add("Native Name: " + ci.NativeName);
// Get day names
lbInfo.Items.Add("Day Names:");
String[] strDayNames = ci.DateTimeFormat.DayNames;
foreach(String strDay in strDayNames)
{
    lbInfo.Items.Add("    " + strDay);
}
// Get the current year
lbInfo.Items.Add("Current year: " +
  ci.Calendar.GetYear(DateTime.Today));
// And the currency symbol
lbInfo.Items.Add("Currency symbol: " +
  ci.NumberFormat.CurrencySymbol);
}
```

6. Insert the Main() method to launch the form. Set the form as the startup object for the project.

7. Run the project and enter the name of a culture in the text box. Click the Get Information button. The form retrieves and displays some of the information that the CultureInfo object can return, as shown in Figure 8.1.

FIGURE 8.1
You can retrieve information about a culture by using the CultureInfo class.

Step by Step 8.1 works by creating a CultureInfo object to represent the specified culture. It then uses properties of the CultureInfo object (and of the objects that the CultureInfo contains, such as the DateTimeFormat, NumberFormat, and Calendar objects) to retrieve information about that culture. This information is useful in localizing applications, and it's all built right in to the .NET Framework.

The CultureInfo class is the key to localizing applications. After you've retrieved the proper CultureInfo object, you can derive a wide variety of information from it.

EXAM TIP

Enumerating Cultures You might have occasion to want a list of all supported cultures. The static CultureInfo.GetCultures() method returns an array of CultureInfo objects that you can enumerate to get that list.

NOTE

The `Thread` Object The `Thread` object is a member of the `System.Threading` namespace, which allows you to write multithreaded applications. Multithreading is an advanced topic that is not covered in this book. For a normal Windows application, there is a single thread of execution, represented by the `Thread.CurrentThread` object.

The `CurrentCulture` and `CurrentUICulture` Properties

The .NET Framework handles localization on a thread-by-thread basis. Each thread has two properties that are used for determining the culture to use: `CurrentCulture` and `CurrentUICulture`. You can set or view these properties for the `Thread.CurrentThread` object.

The `CurrentUICulture` property tells the Common Language Runtime (CLR) which culture to use when choosing resources for the user interface. You'll see later in this chapter how to provide multiple sets of resources for the CLR to use.

The `CurrentCulture` property is also used by the CLR to manage localization, but it's used in a different way. The `CurrentCulture` property dictates the format for dates, times, currency, and numbers, as well as other culture-specific functionality, such as string comparison rules and casing rules.

The Invariant Culture

There's one more culture that you should know about: the invariant culture. This is a special culture that doesn't have an abbreviation. The invariant culture has two purposes:

◆ To interact with other software, such as system services, where no user is directly involved.

◆ To store data in a culture-independent format that is not displayed directly to end users.

There are two ways to create a `CultureInfo` object that represents the invariant culture:

```
CultureInfo ciInv = new CultureInfo("");
CultureInfo ciInv = CultureInfo.InvariantCulture;
```

R E V I E W   B R E A K

▶ Localization is a three-step process that consists of globalization (identifying resources), localizability (verifying separation of resources from code), and localization (translating resources).

▶ Many resources might need to be localized, including user interface text, dates, times, currency amounts, and calendars.

▶ Cultures are identified by culture codes. A neutral culture code specifies only a location, and cannot be used for localization. A specific culture code specifies both a location and a language, and it provides enough information for localization.

▶ The `CultureInfo` object represents a culture in the .NET Framework.

Displaying Localized Information

Now that you know how culture information is stored in the .NET Framework, you're ready to see its use in code.

STEP BY STEP

8.2 Displaying Localized Information

1. Add a new form to your Visual C# .NET project.

2. Place a `Label` control, a `ComboBox` control (`cboSelectCulture`), and four `TextBox` controls (`txtCulture`, `txtDate`, `txtCurrency`, and `txtNumber`) on the form.

3. Switch to the code view and enter the following using directives:

```
using System.Globalization;
using System.Threading;
```

4. Attach event handlers to the form's `Load` event and the combo box's `SelectedIndexChanged` event. Enter the following code in the event handlers:

```
private void StepByStep8_2_Load(object sender,
    System.EventArgs e)
{
    // Stock the combo box
    foreach (CultureInfo ci in
    CultureInfo.GetCultures(
        CultureTypes.SpecificCultures))
```

continues

continued

```
        {
            cboSelectCulture.Items.Add(ci.Name);
        }
        // Display the name of the default culture
        txtCulture.Text =
          Thread.CurrentThread.CurrentCulture.EnglishName;
        // Display some data
        DisplayData();
    }

    private void cboSelectCulture_SelectedIndexChanged(
        object sender, System.EventArgs e)
    {
        // Create an appropriate CultureInfo
        // object for the thread
        Thread.CurrentThread.CurrentCulture =
            new CultureInfo(cboSelectCulture.Text);
        // Display the name of the culture
        txtCulture.Text =
          Thread.CurrentThread.CurrentCulture.EnglishName;
        // Refresh the display of the data
        DisplayData();
    }

    private void DisplayData()
    {
        DateTime dtNow = DateTime.Now;
        Double dblcurrency = 13472.85;
        Double dblnumber = 1409872.3502;

        txtDate.Text = dtNow.ToLongDateString();
        txtCurrency.Text = dblcurrency.ToString("c");
        txtNumber.Text = dblnumber.ToString("n");
    }
```

5. Insert the Main() method to launch the form. Set the form as the startup object for the project.

6. Run the project. Select a culture from the combo box. The form refreshes to display localized information, as shown in Figure 8.2.

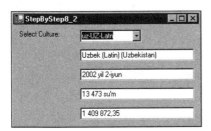

FIGURE 8.2
You can set the culture for the currently running thread by using its CurrentCulture property.

When you select a culture from the combo box in Step by Step 8.2, the code uses that information to create a CultureInfo object assigned to the CurrentCulture property of the current thread.

It then calls a method to display some data on the form. Note that the display method simply uses the `ToLongDateString()` and `ToString()` methods to format the data it displays. You don't have to do anything special to tell these methods which culture to use. They automatically use the culture specified by the `CurrentCulture` property.

Setting Culture Properties

When you set the `CurrentCulture` and `CurrentUICulture` properties, you have two choices: You can set them based on information stored in the user's operating system or you can provide a user interface to let the user choose a culture for formatting.

To use the culture of the operating system, you don't have to do anything. If the application is being executed on the Multiple User Interface (MUI) version of Windows 2000 or Windows XP, the .NET Framework automatically defaults to the culture that's currently selected by the user. If the application is being executed on another version of Windows, the .NET Framework automatically defaults the culture to the language used by the operating system.

Although letting the .NET Framework choose the appropriate culture is the easy way to handle things, it's not always workable. That's because the user might be using a version of Windows that doesn't match his own preferred language. For example, in a public kiosk setting, your application might execute on the English version of Windows XP but need to cater to users with a wide variety of language preferences.

If you want to let the user choose the culture to use, you can follow a strategy similar to the one you just saw: You can provide a control to select a culture and update the `CurrentCulture` property when the user makes a selection from this control.

Working with Resource Files

So far you've seen how to use the `CurrentCulture` property to handle localized formatting of things such as currency, dates, and numbers.

NOTE

No Localized Business Rules Although the sample code in Step by Step 8.2 changes the currency symbol when you select a new culture, it makes no attempt to convert the currency value into local units. The built-in localization support in the .NET Framework deals strictly with the user interface, not with business rules.

But localizing the text displayed on the user interface is perhaps even more important. The .NET Framework offers support for user interface localization through its ability to select a set of user interface resources at runtime. You can choose three different places to store localized user interface resources:

- ◆ **External resource**—You use the `resgen.exe` tool to create external resource files from plain-text files that contain key–value pairs. External resource files are useful when you're depending on an outside contractor to provide localized text because their source files are simple text files.

- ◆ **Satellite assemblies**—You create satellite assemblies by compiling external resource files into DLLs. Satellite assemblies are most useful when you want to be able to supply additional languages after shipping a product.

- ◆ **Assembly resource files**—Assembly resource files are specially formatted Extensible Markup Language (XML) files that contain localized text. Visual Studio .NET allows you to work directly with assembly resource files.

For most applications, assembly resource files are the easiest of these alternatives to work with. The following sections demonstrate how to use Visual Studio .NET to localize the user interface of a simple application.

Localizing Forms in the Designer

The easiest way to localize user interface resources is to use the Windows Forms Designer. Step by Step 8.3 shows you how.

STEP BY STEP

8.3 Localizing a Form in the IDE

1. Add a new form to your Visual C# .NET project. Name it `StepByStep8_3.cs`.

2. Place a `Label` control, three `RadioButton` controls, and a `Button` control on the form. It doesn't matter what you name these controls because they are only going to be used to demonstrate localization. Set the text of the controls as shown in Figure 8.3.

FIGURE 8.3
You can use the Visual Studio .NET IDE to create a form in English.

3. Set the Localizable property of the form to true. Set the Language property of the form to French (France).

4. Change the text of the controls to the French translations, as shown in Figure 8.4. Note that you can resize the Button control so that the French text fits.

5. Add another new form to your Visual C# .NET project. Name this form StepByStep8_3a.cs.

6. Place a ComboBox control named cboCulture and a Button control named btnOpenForm on the form.

7. Switch to the code view and enter the following using directives:

```
using System.Globalization;
using System.Threading;
```

8. Attach event handlers to the form's Load event, the buttons' Click events, and the combo box's SelectedIndexChanged event. Enter the following code in the event handlers:

```
private void StepByStep8_3a_Load(object sender,
    System.EventArgs e)
{
    // Put language choices in the combo box
    cboCulture.Items.Add("English");
    cboCulture.Items.Add("French");
}

private void btnOpenForm_Click(object sender,
    System.EventArgs e)
{
    StepByStep8_3 f = new StepByStep8_3();
    f.Show();
}

private void cboCulture_SelectedIndexChanged(
    object sender, System.EventArgs e)
{
    // When the user selects a language
    // Change the UI culture
    switch (cboCulture.Text)
    {
        case "English":
            Thread.CurrentThread.CurrentUICulture =
                new CultureInfo("en-US");
            break;
```

continues

FIGURE 8.4

You can create a French version of a form by setting the Localizable property to true and the Language property to French (France).

continued

```
                         case "French":
                             Thread.CurrentThread.CurrentUICulture =
                                 new CultureInfo("fr-FR");
                             break;
                 }
         }
```

9. Insert the `Main()` method in the `StepByStep8_3a.cs` form so that it will launch itself. Set the form as the startup object for the project.

10. Run the project. Click the Open Form button. Select French in the combo box and click the button again. Figure 8.5 shows the results of this procedure.

FIGURE 8.5

You can select a value from the combo box to set the `CurrentUICulture` property for the currently running thread.

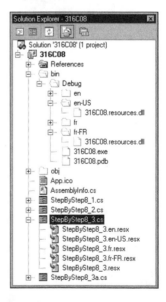

FIGURE 8.6

Visual Studio .NET automatically creates the `.resx` files to store culture-specific information and compile it into satellite assemblies.

When you select a value from the combo box on the first form in Step by Step 8.3, the code behind that form sets `CurrentUICulture` to a new `CultureInfo` object that represents the selected culture. Then, the .NET Framework automatically uses that culture when creating new forms and the controls on those forms. It does this by using resources that were automatically compiled into satellite assemblies when you localized the form in the designer.

If you click the Show All Files button in Solution Explorer and expand the tree, you find the files shown in Figure 8.6. As you can see, the designer creates a `.resx` file (which contains the localized resources) and a `.dll` file (which contains the satellite assembly) for each culture selected in the designer.

Creating Resource Files

As an alternative to creating satellite assemblies with the Windows Forms Designer, you can create your own assembly resource files to hold localizable strings. Step by Step 8.4 demonstrates this approach.

STEP BY STEP

8.4 Localizing a Form with Resource Files

1. Add a new form to your Visual C# .NET project.

2. Place a Label control (lblFolder), three RadioButton controls (rbMyDocuments, rbDesktop, and rbNewFolder), a ComboBox control (cboCulture), and a Button control (btnSave) on the form. Figure 8.7 shows the form in the design view.

3. Select Project, Add New Item. Select the Assembly Resource File template. Name the new item AppStrings.resx and click Open to create the file. The new file opens in the Visual Studio .NET IDE with a grid-based editing interface.

4. Enter names and values to identify all the text strings on the user interface, as shown in Figure 8.8. You can optionally enter a comment for each string. The Type and Mimetype columns are not used for localizing strings.

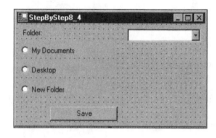

FIGURE 8.7
You can use resource files to localize a form at runtime.

Data for data

name	value	comment	type	mimetype
Folder	Folder	(null)	(null)	(null)
My_Documents	My Documents	(null)	(null)	(null)
Desktop	Desktop	(null)	(null)	(null)
New_Folder	New Folder	(null)	(null)	(null)
Save	Save	(null)	(null)	(null)

FIGURE 8.8
You can enter invariant resources with the help of the grid-based editing interface provided by the Assembly Resource File template.

5. Add two more assembly resource files to the project. The first, named AppStrings.en-US.resx, should contain another copy of the strings in English. The second, named AppStrings.fr-FR.resx, should contain the strings in French, as shown in Figure 8.9. Note that the Name column is the same in the English and French version; only the Value column changes.

continues

continued

FIGURE 8.9
You can enter culture-specific resources with
the help of grid-based editing interface provided
by the Visual Studio .NET IDE.

name	value	comment	type	mimetype
Folder	Dossier	(null)	(null)	(null)
My_Documents	Mes documents	(null)	(null)	(null)
Desktop	Bureau	(null)	(null)	(null)
New_Folder	Nouveau dossier	(null)	(null)	(null)
Save	Enregistrer	(null)	(null)	(null)

6. Switch to code view and enter the following using directives:

```
using System.Globalization;
using System.Resources;
using System.Threading;
```

7. Attach event handlers to the form's Load event and the combo box's SelectedIndexChanged event. Enter the following code in the event handlers:

```
private void StepByStep8_4_Load(object sender,
    System.EventArgs e)
{
    // Put language choices in the combo box
    cboCulture.Items.Add("English");
    cboCulture.Items.Add("French");
    // Initialize the UI text
    SetUIText();
}

private void cboCulture_SelectedIndexChanged(
    object sender, System.EventArgs e)
{
    // When the user selects a language
    // Change the UI culture
    switch (cboCulture.Text)
    {
        case "English":
            Thread.CurrentThread.CurrentUICulture =
                new CultureInfo("en-US");
            break;
        case "French":
            Thread.CurrentThread.CurrentUICulture =
                new CultureInfo("fr-FR");
            break;
    }
    // Initialize the UI text
    SetUIText();
}
private void SetUIText()
{
```

```
ResourceManager rm = new ResourceManager(
  "_316C08.AppStrings",
    Type.GetType("_316C08.StepByStep8_4").Assembly);
lblFolder.Text = rm.GetString("Folder");
rbMyDocuments.Text = rm.GetString("My_Documents");
rbDesktop.Text = rm.GetString("Desktop");
rbNewFolder.Text = rm.GetString("New_Folder");
btnSave.Text = rm.GetString("Save");
}
```

8. Insert the `Main()` method to launch the form. Set the form as the startup object for the project.

9. Run the project. As you select languages in the combo box, the user interface is refreshed with the appropriate resources.

N O T E

Finding the Project Namespace
This code assumes that your C# .NET project is named 316C08. If it has some other name, you need to alter the first and second parameters to the constructor for the `ResourceManager` object. You can find the name of the namespace by right-clicking the project node in Solution Explorer. Select Properties, and find the default namespace in the General section.

The naming of the resource files in Step by Step 8.4 follows a required pattern. The .NET Framework looks for several specific files when it's loading resources, depending on the base name of the resources and the selected culture. The base name is the second part of the first parameter to the `ResourceManager` constructor—in this case, `AppStrings`. When `CurrentUICulture` is set to a `CultureInfo` object representing the `fr-FR` (French in France) culture, the .NET Framework checks for resources in three possible files, in this order:

1. A specific culture file—in this case, `AppStrings.fr-FR.resx`.

2. A neutral culture file—in this case, `AppStrings.fr.resx`.

3. An invariant culture file—in this case, `AppStrings.resx`.

In other words, the .NET Framework falls back on increasingly more general resources when trying to load resources for a form.

Localizing Resources at Runtime

Runtime user interface resources are actually loaded by an instance of the `System.Resources.ResourceManager` class. After you have initialized a `ResourceManager` object by calling one of the class's constructors, there are two methods you can use to retrieve localized resources:

◆ `GetObject()` returns an object from the appropriate resource file.

◆ `GetString()` returns a string from the appropriate resource file.

If you're just dealing with text displayed directly on a form, the satellite assembly approach (which is shown in Step by Step 8.3) and the assembly resource file approach (which is shown in Step by Step 8.4) are equivalent. But there are times when one approach is preferred over the other.

If you need to move and resize controls, the satellite assembly approach is most convenient. That's because you can move and resize the controls directly in the Windows Forms Designer. If you need to move and resize controls when using assembly resource files, you need to store position and size information somewhere and apply them to the controls' properties in code yourself.

On the other hand, assembly resource files offer a substantial benefit in that they allow you to easily localize text that doesn't appear directly on the user interface. Message box and other informative text, for example, is most easily localized by using an assembly resource file.

Assembly resource files also let you change text on-the-fly, whereas satellite assemblies are used only when a form is first created.

You can also consider hybrid solutions for complex applications, using satellite assemblies to localize controls, and also embedding assembly resource files to localize other resources in the same project.

GUIDED PRACTICE EXERCISE 8.1

The goal of this exercise is to build a form that displays the current date. The form should offer two choices:

◆ A choice between two different cultures on the user interface.

◆ A choice between long date and short date display formats.

How would you design such a form?

This exercise gives you an opportunity to combine the two types of localization that you have seen in this chapter, by using both the CurrentCulture and the CurrentUICulture properties in a single project.

You should try working through this problem on your own first. If you get stuck, or if you'd like to see one possible solution, follow these steps:

1. Add a new form to your Visual C# .NET project. Name the form `GuidedPracticeExercise8_1.cs`.

2. Place a `ComboBox` control (`cboCulture`), two `RadioButton` controls (`rbLongDate` and `rbShortDate`), and a `TextBox` control (`txtDate`) on the form. Set the `Checked` property of `rbLongDate` to `true`. Figure 8.10 shows the design for this form.

3. Add a new assembly resource file to your project. Name the file `GPE1.resx`. Enter two strings in the file. The first one should be named `strLongDate` and have the value `Long Date`. The second should be named `strShortDate` and have the value `Short Date`.

4. Add a second assembly resource file to your project. Name the file `GPE1.en-US.resx`. This file should have the same contents as the `GPE1.resx` file.

5. Add a third assembly resource file to your project. Name the file `GPE1.de-DE.resx`. In this file, use the value `Langes Datum` for the `strLongDate` resource and the value `Kurzes Datum` for the `strShortDate` resource.

6. Switch to the code view and enter these `using` directives:

```
using System.Globalization;
using System.Resources;
using System.Threading;
```

7. Attach event handlers to the form's `Load` event, the combo box's `SelectedIndexChanged` event, and the radio button's `CheckedChanged` event. Enter the following code in the event handlers:

```
private void cboCulture_SelectedIndexChanged(
    object sender, System.EventArgs e)
{
    // Set the current cultures
    // to the selected culture
    Thread.CurrentThread.CurrentCulture =
        new CultureInfo(cboCulture.Text);
    Thread.CurrentThread.CurrentUICulture =
        new CultureInfo(cboCulture.Text);
```

FIGURE 8.10

You can set both the `CurrentCulture` and `CurrentUICulture` properties to implement localizability.

continues

continued

```
        // Refresh the display
        DisplayData();
    }

    private void GuidedPracticeExercise8_1_Load(
        object sender, System.EventArgs e)
    {
        // Put some choices in the combo box
        cboCulture.Items.Add("en-US");
        cboCulture.Items.Add("de-DE");
        // Refresh the display
        DisplayData();
    }

    private void rbLongDate_CheckedChanged(object sender,
        System.EventArgs e)
    {
        // Refresh the display
        DisplayData();
    }

    private void rbShortDate_CheckedChanged(object sender,
        System.EventArgs e)
    {
        // Refresh the display
        DisplayData();
    }

    private void DisplayData()
    {
        // Reformat the date according
        // to the user's choices
        if(rbLongDate.Checked)
        {
            txtDate.Text =
                DateTime.Today.ToLongDateString();
        }
        else
        {
            txtDate.Text =
                DateTime.Today.ToShortDateString();
        }
        // Update the user interface text
        ResourceManager rm = new ResourceManager(
          "_316C08.GPE1",
          Type.GetType(
          "_316C08.GuidedPracticeExercise8_1").Assembly);
        rbLongDate.Text = rm.GetString("strLongDate");
        rbShortDate.Text = rm.GetString("strShortDate");
    }
```

8. Insert the `Main()` method to launch the form. Set the form as the startup object for the project.

9. Run the project and experiment with the user interface. You can select either English or German, and both the user interface text and the date formats change accordingly.

If you have difficulty following this exercise, review the section "Implementing Localization for the User Interface," earlier in this chapter. After doing that review, try this exercise again.

▶ The `CurrentUICulture` property specifies to the CLR which culture to use when choosing resources for the user interface.

▶ The `CurrentCulture` property dictates the format for dates, times, currency, and numbers, as well as other culture-specific functionality, such as string comparison rules and casing rules.

▶ You must set the `Localizable` property and the `Language` property to directly localize a form.

▶ You can extract resources from an assembly resource file via a `ResourceManager` object at any time.

CONVERTING EXISTING ENCODINGS

Implement globalization.

• **Convert existing encodings.**

Many different schemes have been developed for representing the characters in a language as numeric codes within a computer. These schemes are referred to as *encodings*. For example, the venerable ASCII encoding represents common Latin characters as numeric codes ranging from 0 to 127. The .NET Framework provides support for encodings through the `System.Text.Encoding` class.

Understanding Unicode and Encodings

Internally, the .NET Framework's preferred encoding for characters is 16-bit Unicode, commonly known as UTF-16. This encoding represents characters as 16-bit numbers, giving it the ability to represent approximately 65,000 distinct characters. That's enough to represent every character commonly in use. Additional features of the full Unicode specification allow for the representation of another million characters.

Over time, Windows has been moving toward Unicode as the basis for encoding characters, but that wasn't always the case. Earlier versions of Windows used code pages to represent character sets. A code page could hold 256 characters, and the system supplied different code pages for different character sets, such as Greek characters or Latin characters.

Although Unicode is the native character encoding for .NET, the .NET Framework supports conversion to and from older encodings, such as ASCII or code pages, for compatability with older applications.

> **NOTE**
>
> **Unicode Details** You can find everything you need to know about Unicode at the Unicode home page, www.unicode.org.

Converting Encodings

The `System.Text` namespace contains classes that are designed to let you convert characters from the UTF-16 encoding to other encodings and vice versa.

STEP BY STEP

8.5 Converting Character Encodings

1. Add a new form to your Visual C# .NET project.

2. Place two `Label` controls, a `TextBox` control (`txtUnicode`), a `Button` control (`btnConvert`), and a `ListBox` control (`lbAscii`) on the form.

3. Switch to code view and enter this `using` directive:

```
using System.Text;
```

4. Double-click the `Button` control and enter the following code to handle the `Button` control's `Clickevent`:

```
private void btnConvert_Click(object sender,
    System.EventArgs e)
{
    // Get an encoding object for ascii
    ASCIIEncoding encASCII = new ASCIIEncoding();
    // Convert the string to an array of ASCII bytes
    Byte[] bytEncodedCharacters = encASCII.GetBytes(
        txtUnicode.Text);
    for (Int32 intI=0; intI
      <bytEncodedCharacters.Length ;
      intI++)
    {
        lbASCII.Items.Add(bytEncodedCharacters[intI]);
    }
}
```

5. Insert the `Main()` method to launch the form. Set the form as the startup object for the project.

6. Run the project. Enter some text in the text box control and click the Convert button. The Unicode text from the text box is converted into a series of ASCII byte codes and displayed in the list box, as shown in Figure 8.11.

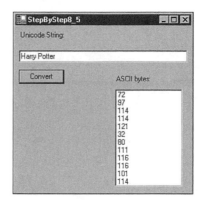

FIGURE 8.11
You can use the `ASCIIEncoding` class to convert Unicode characters to ASCII bytes.

The code sample in Step by Step 8.5 uses the `GetBytes()` method of the `ASCIIEncoding` object to convert a Unicode string into an array of ASCII bytes. Although not used in Step by Step 8.5, there's a matching `GetChars()` method that converts ASCII bytes into Unicode text.

The `ASCIIEncoding` class is a subclass of `System.Text.Encoding`. Table 8.1 lists the other available subclasses that help you convert to and from other encodings.

TABLE 8.1

ENCODING CLASSES IN THE System.Text NAMESPACE

Class	Use
ASCIIEncoding	Converts characters between Unicode and ASCII.
Encoding	Functions as a general-purpose class. The `Encoding.GetEncoding()` static method returns encodings that can be used for legacy code page compatibility.

continues

| TABLE 8.1 | *continued* |

ENCODING CLASSES IN THE System.Text NAMESPACE

Class	Use
UnicodeEncoding	Converts characters to and from Unicode, encoded as consecutive bytes in either big-endian or little-endian order.
UTF7Encoding	Converts characters to and from 7-bit Unicode encoding.
UTF8Encoding	Converts characters to and from 8-bit Unicode encoding.

IMPLEMENTING MIRRORING

Implement globalization.

- **Implement right-to-left and left-to-right mirroring.**

There are many differences between human languages. Of course different languages use different character sets, but there are differences beyond that. One of the most important differences is whether the language reads from left-to-right (like English) or from right-to-left (like Arabic). The .NET Framework supports both reading directions.

Understanding Mirroring

The process of switching a user interface between a left-to-right language such as German or English and a right-to-left language such as Hebrew or Arabic is called *mirroring*. Mirroring in the Windows environment involves changes beyond simply reversing the order of text strings. Figure 8.12, for example, shows part of the user interface from Arabic Windows.

As you can see, the entire format of the Windows user interface is reversed when you use mirroring. The close, minimize, and other buttons appear at the upper left of the window. Menus appear to the right of the menu bar. Combo box arrows are located to the left of the combo boxes, and check box text appears on the left of the check box.

FIGURE 8.12

Mirroring allows you to display the Windows user interface for right-to-left languages such as Arabic.

Mirroring in .NET

The .NET Framework offers partial support for mirroring through the RightToLeft property of forms.

STEP BY STEP

8.6 Mirroring a Form

1. Add a new form to your Visual C# .NET project.

2. Place a TextBox control, a ComboBox control, a CheckBox control, a RadioButton control, and a MainMenu control on the form. Add some items to the MainMenu control. Figure 8.13 shows what the form might look like in the design mode.

3. Set the RightToLeft property of the form to Yes.

4. Insert the Main() method to launch the form. Set the form as the startup object for the project.

5. Run the project. The form is partially mirrored, as shown in Figure 8.14.

FIGURE 8.13
You can use this form to test mirroring.

FIGURE 8.14
You can use the RightToLeft property of a Windows form to enable mirroring.

Mirroring in the .NET Framework manages most of the essentials. The form's text moves to the right end of the title bar. Controls fill from right-to-left as you enter text. ComboBox, RadioButton, and CheckBox controls reverse their appearance as well. Menus show up at the right end of the menu bar.

But the mirroring support in the .NET Framework is imperfect. The system menu and the other window buttons (such as the close and minimize buttons) don't switch positions. Controls are not mirrored to the opposite position on the form from their initial design (although, of course, you can manage that by using satellite assemblies to hold alternate form resources, as discussed earlier in the chapter).

> **EXAM TIP**
>
> **Mirroring Part of a Form**   If you want to mirror only part of a form, you can set the RightToLeft property to Yes on individual controls instead of on the entire form.

> **NOTE**
>
> **True Mirroring**   To completely mirror a form, you can call the SetProcessDefaultLayout Windows API call. You will learn how to call Windows API functions in Chapter 9, "Working with Legacy Code."

VALIDATING NON-LATIN USER INPUT

Validate user input.

- **Validate non-Latin user input.**

Another area where world-ready applications may require code changes is in handling character strings. The following sections look at two areas where different alphabets may require you to implement code changes: string indexing and data sorting. These areas require the most coding attention for non-Latin characters (such as Arabic, Hebrew, or Cyrillic characters), but they can be important when you're dealing with Latin characters as well.

String Indexing

String indexing refers to the process of extracting single characters from a text string. You might think that you could simply iterate through the data that makes up the string 16 bits at a time, treating each 16 bits as a separate character. But things aren't that simple in the Unicode world.

Unicode supports surrogate pairs and combining character sequences. A *surrogate pair* is a set of two 16-bit codes that represent a single character from the extended 32-bit Unicode character space. A *combining character sequence* is a set of 16-bit codes that represents a single character. Combining character sequences are often used to combine diacritical marks such as accents with base characters.

This presents a problem: If characters in a string aren't all the same length, how can you move smoothly from one character to the next? The answer, of course, is to use a class from the .NET Framework that knows how to perform this task. The `System.Globalization.` `StringInfo` class is designed to be able to iterate through the elements in a string.

STEP BY STEP

8.7 Iterating with the StringInfo Class

1. Add a new form to your Visual C# .NET project.

2. Place a TextBox control (txtText), a Button control (btnIterate), and a ListBox control (lbIterate) on the form.

3. Switch to the code view and enter the following using directive:

```
using System.Globalization;
```

4. Double-click the btnIterate control and add the following code to handle the Click event of the button:

```
private void btnIterate_Click(object sender,
    System.EventArgs e)
{
    lbIterate.Items.Clear();
    // Get an iterator for the entered text
    TextElementEnumerator iter =
        StringInfo.GetTextElementEnumerator(
          txtTest.Text);
    // The iterator starts before the string, have to
    // move it forward once to reach the first element
    iter.MoveNext();
    do
        lbIterate.Items.Add("Element " +
          iter.ElementIndex
          + ": " + iter.Current);
    while(iter.MoveNext());
}
```

5. Insert the Main() method to launch the form. Set the form as the startup object for the project.

6. Run the project. Paste or enter any text you like in the text box and then click the Iterate button. The code splits the string into its constituent characters, as shown in Figure 8.15.

FIGURE 8.15
You can use the StringInfo class to split a string into its constituent characters.

This code uses the static GetTextElementEnumerator() method of the StringInfo class. Given any Unicode string, this method returns an iterator that you can use to move through the string one character at a time, properly handling surrogate pairs and combining characters.

The iterator has a MoveNext() method that returns false when it has exhausted the characters in the string. The Current property of the iterator returns a single character from the current position of the iterator.

Comparing and Sorting Data

Another area where you might need to alter code to produce a world-ready application is in working with strings. Different cultures use different alphabetical orders to sort strings, and different cultures compare strings differently. For example, the single-character ligature Æ is considered to match the two characters *AE* in some cultures but not in others.

For the most part, you don't have to do any special programming to account for these factors in the .NET Framework. To make your application world-ready, you're more likely to need to remove old code—for example, code which assumes that characters are properly sorted if you sort their ASCII character numbers. Specifically, the .NET Framework provides the following culture-aware features:

◆ The String.Compare method compares strings according to the rules of the CultureInfo class referenced by the CurrentCulture property.

◆ The CultureInfo.CompareInfo object can search for substrings according to the comparison rules of the current culture.

◆ The Array.Sort() method sorts the members of an array by the alphabetic order rules of the current culture.

◆ The SortKey.Compare() method compares strings according to the rules of the current culture.

R E V I E W   B R E A K

▶ Internally, .NET applications use 16-bit Unicode as their preferred character encoding.

▶ The System.Text.Encoding class and its subclasses allow you to convert text from one encoding to another.

▶ In some languages, the user interface is read from right-to-left instead of from left-to-right. Converting a form for one of these languages is referred to as mirroring.

▶ The .NET Framework provides partial support for mirroring through the `RightToLeft` property on forms and controls.

▶ To iterate through the elements of a string in a world-ready application, you should use the `GetTextElementEnumerator()` method of the `StringInfo` class.

▶ Searching, sorting, and comparing strings in a world-ready application requires using standard objects and methods rather than clever programming tricks.

CHAPTER SUMMARY

The .NET Framework is designed to help you develop world-ready applications quickly and consistently. The localization process includes globalization (planning for localized versions), localizability (testing to make sure resources can be localized), and localization (actually translating the resources).

The .NET Framework contains a number of useful localization classes in the `System.Globalization` namespace. Key among these classes is the `CultureInfo` class, which provides the ability for .NET applications to properly display dates, times, currencies, and other culture-specific data properly.

Visual Studio .NET provides several ways to localize the user interface of an application, including satellite assemblies and assembly resource files. You can create satellite assemblies by manipulating user interface elements directly in the Visual Studio IDE. To create assembly resource files, you list resources in special files that can be loaded at runtime.

Other important globalization topics include encoding (translating from one representation of text characters to another), mirroring (handling right-to-left language input and output), and working with character sorts, comparisons, and iteration.

KEY TERMS

- culture
- culture code
- encoding
- globalization
- localizability
- localization
- resource file
- Unicode

APPLY YOUR KNOWLEDGE

Exercises

8.1 Using Localized Calendars

In addition to the features described earlier in the chapter, the CultureInfo class can supply localized calendars for different cultures. In this exercise, you'll see how you can retrieve culture-specific calendar information.

Estimated time: 20 minutes

1. Open a Visual C# .NET Windows application in the Visual Studio .NET IDE.

2. Add a new form to the application.

3. Place a Label control, a ComboBox control (cboCultures), and a ListBox control (lbInfo) on the form.

4. Switch to the code view and add the following using directive:

```
using System.Globalization;
```

5. Add code to handle the Load event of the form and the SelectedIndexChanged event of the ComboBox control:

```
private void Exercise8_1_Load(
    object sender, System.EventArgs e)
{
    // Fill the combo box with cultures
    foreach (CultureInfo ci in
        CultureInfo.GetCultures(
        CultureTypes.SpecificCultures))
    {
        cboCultures.Items.Add(ci.Name);
    }
}

private void
    cboCultures_SelectedIndexChanged(
    object sender, System.EventArgs e)
{
```

```
    // Get the selected CultureInfo
    // and some other objects
    CultureInfo ci = new CultureInfo(
        cboCultures.Text);
    Calendar cal = ci.Calendar;
    DateTimeFormatInfo dtfi =
        ci.DateTimeFormat;
    lbInfo.Items.Clear();
    DateTime dt = DateTime.Today;
    // List the culture and the calendar
    lbInfo.Items.Add("The culture is " +
        ci.EnglishName);
    lbInfo.Items.Add("The calendar is " +
        cal.GetType().ToString());
    // Get the current day, month, and year
    lbInfo.Items.Add("Today is day " +
        cal.GetDayOfMonth(dt));
    lbInfo.Items.Add(" of month " +
        cal.GetMonth(dt));
    lbInfo.Items.Add(" of year " +
        cal.GetYear(dt));
    lbInfo.Items.Add("This is day " +
        cal.GetDayOfWeek(dt) +
        " of the week");
    lbInfo.Items.Add("The day name is " +
        dtfi.DayNames[(Int32)
        cal.GetDayOfWeek(dt)]);
    lbInfo.Items.Add("The month name is " +
dtfi.MonthNames[cal.GetMonth(dt) - 1]);
    lbInfo.Items.Add("There are " +
    cal.GetMonthsInYear(cal.GetYear(dt)) +
    " months in this year");
}
```

6. Insert the Main() method to launch the form. Set the form as the startup object for the project.

7. Run the project. Select cultures from the combo box to see some of their calendar information in the list box, as shown in Figure 8.16. You might try ar-SA, he-IL, and th-TH to get some sense of the calendars that the .NET Framework supports.

APPLY YOUR KNOWLEDGE

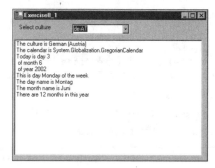

FIGURE 8.16
The CultureInfo class can supply localized calendars for different cultures.

This exercise shows you some of the methods that are available from the Calendar class (and its subclasses, such as GregorianCalendar). Here's a more extensive list of the available methods of the Calendar class; their uses are self-evident from their names:

- ◆ AddDays()

- ◆ AddHours()

- ◆ AddMilliseconds()

- ◆ AddMinutes()

- ◆ AddMonths()

- ◆ AddSeconds()

- ◆ AddWeeks()

- ◆ AddYears()

- ◆ GetDayOfMonth()

- ◆ GetDayOfWeek()

- ◆ GetDayOfYear()

- ◆ GetDaysInMonth()

- ◆ GetDaysInYear()

- ◆ GetEra()

- ◆ GetHour()

- ◆ GetMilliseconds()

- ◆ GetMinute()

- ◆ GetMonth()

- ◆ GetMonthsInYear()

- ◆ GetSecond()

- ◆ GetWeekOfYear()

- ◆ GetYear()

- ◆ IsLeapDay()

- ◆ IsLeapMonth()

- ◆ IsLeapYear()

- ◆ ToDateTime()

- ◆ ToFourDigitYear()

8.2   Retrieving Region Information

The RegionInfo object is an important part of the System.Globalization namespace. This object provides some additional information on a particular geographic region. In this exercise, you'll see how to retrieve the information that's available from the RegionInfo object.

Estimated time: 15 minutes

1. Open a Visual C# .NET Windows application in the Visual Studio .NET IDE.

2. Add a new form to the application.

3. Place a Label control, a ComboBox control (cboCultures), and a ListBox control (lbInfo) on the form.

APPLY YOUR KNOWLEDGE

4. Switch to the code view and add the following using directive:

```
using System.Globalization;
```

5. Add the following code to handle the Load event of the form and the SelectedIndexChanged event of the ComboBox control:

```
private void Exercise8_2_Load(
    object sender, System.EventArgs e)
{
    // Fill the combo box with cultures
    foreach (CultureInfo ci in
    CultureInfo.GetCultures(
        CultureTypes.SpecificCultures))
    {
        cboCultures.Items.Add(ci.Name);
    }
}

private void
    cboCultures_SelectedIndexChanged(
    object sender, System.EventArgs e)
{
    // Attempt to get the
    // correct RegionInfo object
    RegionInfo rgi = new RegionInfo(
    cboCultures.Text.Substring(
        cboCultures.Text.Length - 2));
    lbInfo.Items.Clear();
    // List the region info
    lbInfo.Items.Add("The region is "
        +rgi.Name);
    lbInfo.Items.Add("Display Name: "
        +rgi.DisplayName);
    lbInfo.Items.Add("English Name: "
        +rgi.EnglishName);
    lbInfo.Items.Add("Currency symbol: "
        +rgi.CurrencySymbol);
    if (rgi.IsMetric)
    {
        lbInfo.Items.Add(
        "Region uses metric measurements.");
    }
    else
    {
        lbInfo.Items.Add("Region does" +
            " not use metric measurements.");
    }
```

```
    lbInfo.Items.Add(
        "ISO Currency symbol: " +
        rgi.ISOCurrencySymbol);
    lbInfo.Items.Add(
        "ISO three-letter code: " +
        rgi.ThreeLetterISORegionName);
}
```

6. Insert the Main() method to launch the form. Set the form as the startup object for the project.

7. Run the project. Select cultures from the combo box to see some of their region information in the list box, as shown in Figure 8.17.

FIGURE 8.17
Region information can be obtained with the help of the RegionInfo class.

Regions are identified by two-letter codes assigned by the International Standards Organization (ISO). These codes usually match the subculture codes, so this example cheats and uses the rightmost two characters of culture codes to locate regions.

APPLY YOUR KNOWLEDGE

E X A M   T I P

The CurrentRegion Property To retrieve the region being used by the operating system, you can read the static Thread.CurrentThread. CurrentRegion property.

Review Questions

1. List some things that might need to be localized in a world-ready application.

2. Name and briefly describe the three steps of the localization process.

3. Describe the differences between neutral, specific, and invariant cultures.

4. What is the difference between the CurrentCulture property and the CurrentUICulture property of the currently executing thread?

5. Explain the naming convention for .resx files.

6. What properties must you set to directly localize a form within the Visual Studio .NET IDE?

7. What advantages do assembly resource files have over satellite assemblies?

8. How many bits does a single UTF-16 character consist of?

9. Name some things that should change when a form is mirrored.

10. What class can you use to iterate through a string character-by-character in all cases?

Exam Questions

1. Your application displays order information, including the total cost of each order. You are beginning to sell this application in multiple countries. How should you ensure that the correct currency symbol is used in all cases?

   A. Allow the user to select a culture from a list. Create a CultureInfo object based on the user's selection and assign it to the Thread.CurrentThread.CurrentCulture property. Use the ToString() method to format currency amounts.

   B. Accept the Thread.CurrentThread. CurrentCulture property as it is set when you run the application. Use the ToString() method to format currency amounts.

   C. Prompt the user for a currency symbol and store it in the Registry.

   D. Allow the user to select a currency symbol from a list of supported symbols.

2. Your application allows users to select a culture, such as English, French, or Spanish, from an options dialog box. Users complain that some information is not displayed correctly, even after they select the proper culture. What could be the problem?

   A. The users are running your application on an English-only version of Windows.

   B. You're using a neutral CultureInfo object to retrieve information instead of a specific CultureInfo object.

   C. The users have not yet installed .NET Framework Service Pack 1.

   D. Your application is constructed as an executable file rather than a satellite library.

APPLY YOUR KNOWLEDGE

3. Users would like to include the day of the week when your application displays dates. They want this to be in the language of their Windows installation. What can you do to address this need? (Select the two best answers.)

   A. Use the `DateTime.ToLongDateString()` method to format dates.

   B. Use the `CultureInfo.DateTimeFormat` property to retrieve the names of the weekdays, and select the proper name from that array.

   C. Force the user to enter the day of the week whenever he or she enters a date in the system.

   D. Use the `RegionInfo` object to retrieve the names of the weekdays, and select the proper name from that array.

4. A user would like to see French dates and currencies displayed in an application but wants the user interface to remain in English. How can you accomplish this?

   A. Set the `Thread.CurrentThread.CurrentCulture` property to a `CultureInfo` object that represents the `fr-FR` culture, and set the `Thread.CurrentThread.CurrentUICulture` property to a `CultureInfo` object that represents the `en-US` culture.

   B. Set the `Thread.CurrentThread.CurrentCulture` property to a `CultureInfo` object that represents the `en-US` culture, and set the `Thread.CurrentThread.CurrentUICulture` property to a `CultureInfo` object that represents the `fr-FR` culture.

   C. Set the `Thread.CurrentThread.CurrentCulture` property to a `CultureInfo` object that represents the `fr-FR` culture, and set the `Thread.CurrentThread.CurrentUICulture` property to a `CultureInfo` object that represents the `fr-FR` culture.

   D. Set the `Thread.CurrentThread.CurrentCulture` property to a `CultureInfo` object that represents the `en-US` culture, and set the `Thread.CurrentThread.CurrentUICulture` property to a `CultureInfo` object that represents the `en-US` culture.

5. Your application is named `1st_Class_Tracer`. You are using embedded assembly resource files to localize the application. When you try to compile the localized application, you receive an error message. What could be the problem?

   A. This application must use satellite assemblies rather than assembly resource files.

   B. You did not include resources for every possible culture in your application.

   C. You did not include a way for the user to switch cultures in your application.

   D. You used `1st_Class_Tracer` rather than `_1st_Class_Tracer` as the namespace for your resources.

6. You are using satellite assemblies to hold localization resource for the user interface of your application. The application's main form includes a menu that lets users select English, French, Spanish, or German as the user interface language. When the user makes a selection, your code creates an appropriate `CultureInfo` object and assigns it to the `Thread.CurrentThread.CurrentUICulture` property.

APPLY YOUR KNOWLEDGE

Users report that the user interface does not change languages when they make a selection from the menu. What can you do to fix this bug?

A. Instruct the users to close and reopen the application after making a selection.

B. Switch to assembly resource files to hold the resources. Use a `ResourceManager` object to extract the resources whenever they're needed.

C. Verify that your code contains the correct namespace name for your application in the class that selects the resources to use.

D. Spawn a second copy of the main form, this one with the correct user interface language.

7. Your application includes three assembly resource files: `Strings.resx` contains the default (English) resources; `Strings.en-US.resx` contains the English resources; and `Strings.France.resx` contains the French resources. Users report that they are getting the default English user interface when they've selected the option for a French user interface. What should you do?

A. Instruct users to close and reopen the application after selecting a new user interface language.

B. Add French resources to the `Strings.resx` file.

C. Rename the French resource file `Strings.fr-FR.resx`.

D. Delete the `Strings.en-US.resx` file from the project.

8. Your application contains Unicode strings encoded in UTF-16 format. You would like to save a copy of those strings to disk in UTF-8 format.

Your application needs to take the smallest amount of disk space possible. What should you do?

A. Use the `Unicode.GetBytes()` method to perform the conversion.

B. Use the `Unicode.GetChars()` method to perform the conversion.

C. Use the `UTF8Encoding.GetBytes()` method to perform the conversion.

D. Use the `UTF8Encoding.GetChars()` method to perform the conversion.

9. You are localizing a Windows form for use in Saudi Arabia (the `ar-SA` culture). Which of these steps should you perform as part of the process? (Select the two best answers.)

A. Set the `Tag` property to `ar-SA`.

B. Set the `Language` property to `Arabic (Saudi Arabia)`.

C. Set the `Localizable` property to `false`.

D. Set the `RightToLeft` property to `Yes`.

10. A dialog box in your application reports the number of characters in a particular data entry form. You're dividing the number of bits taken up by the data by 16 to arrive at this figure. Users of the localized version in Saudi Arabia complain that the number of characters is consistently overestimated. What should you do?

A. Divide the number of bits by 32 to arrive at a more accurate figure.

B. Use the `String.Length` property to retrieve the actual length of the string.

C. Divide the number of bits by 8 to arrive at a more accurate figure.

D. Use a `TextElementEnumerator` object to enumerate the characters.

11. Arabic-speaking users of your application would like to see dates displayed using the Arabic calendar. How can you accomplish this?

   A. Retrieve a `Calendar` object from `Thread.CurrentThread.CurrentCulture` and use its methods to format the dates.

   B. Retrieve a `Calendar` object from `Thread.CurrentThread.CurrentUICulture` and use its methods to format the dates.

   C. Retrieve a `DateTime` object from `Thread.CurrentThread.CurrentCulture` and use its methods to format the dates.

   D. Retrieve a `DateTime` object from `Thread.CurrentThread.CurrentCulture` and use its methods to format the dates.

12. You are shipping an application to France and Russia, and you are using satellite assemblies to hold form localization resources. Now you need to start shipping to Spain. If the application is run on the Spanish version of Windows, you want to show the user interface in Spanish. What should you do?

   A. Create an assembly resource file to hold the user interface text translated into Spanish.

   B. Build a new project that contains only the Spanish version of the form, and then build this new project to sell in Spain.

   C. Set the form's language to `Spanish (Spain)` in the IDE and translate the controls.

D. Create a new `CultureInfo` object for the `Spanish (Spain)` culture. Assign this object to the `Thread.CurrentThread.CurrentUICulture` property.

13. Your application contains an options dialog box that allows the users to select a culture for localizing dates, times, and currency. What should you do to make sure that all possible valid choices are available in this dialog box?

   A. Retrieve the list of supported cultures by using the static `CultureInfo.GetCultures()` method.

   B. Look up the list of available cultures in the .NET Framework help and hard-code that list into your application.

   C. Retrieve the list of supported cultures from the Windows Registry.

   D. Allow users to enter cultures as they need them and store a list of entered cultures for future use.

14. You are writing an application on a system that uses U.S. English Windows (culture `en-US`). The application will run on a system that uses Japanese Windows (culture `jp-JP`). The application will send information to Windows services on the target computer. Which culture should you use to format your application's output?

   A. `en-US`

   B. `jp-JP`

   C. `jp`

   D. The invariant culture

APPLY YOUR KNOWLEDGE

15. Your application needs to search for substrings in longer strings. This searching should be culture aware. What should you use to perform these searches?

    A. `CultureInfo.CompareInfo`

    B. `Array.Sort()`

    C. `String.IndexOf()`

    D. `String.IndexOfAny()`

Answers to Review Questions

1. Items that might need to be localized include text on the user interface; form layouts; date, time, and currency formats; data input fields; graphics with local content; shortcut keys; calendars; and alphabetical order.

2. The three steps are globalization (identification of resources to be localized), localizability (verification that localizable resources have been separated from code), and localization (translation of localized resources).

3. A neutral culture specifies a culture but not a subculture. A specific culture specifies a culture and one or more subcultures. The invariant culture does not specify either a culture or a subculture.

4. The `CurrentCulture` property is used by culture-aware methods such as `ToString()`. The `CurrentUICulture` is used to locate appropriate resources to display on the user interface.

5. A default resource file has a name such as `MyResources.resx`. A neutral resource file has a name such as `MyResources.fr.resx`.

A specific resource file has a name such as `MyResources.fr-FR.resx`. When searching for resources to load, the .NET CLR first tries to find a specific resource file, then a neutral resource file, and then a default resource file.

6. You must set the `Localizable` property and the `Language` property to directly localize a form.

7. You can extract resources from an assembly resource file via a `ResourceManager` object at any time. Satellite assemblies are used only when a form is loaded.

8. Usually, a single UTF-16 character consists of 16 bits. However, surrogate characters and composed characters mean that a single UTF-16 character may consist of 32 bits or more.

9. When a form is mirrored, the location of controls should be flipped from one side of the form to the other, menus and the caption bar text should move to the right, and controls should fill with data starting at the right.

10. The `StringInfo` class supports iterating through any string, regardless of culture.

Answers to Exam Questions

1. **A.** Allowing the user to choose a culture is better than accepting the existing culture of the application because the user might be running on a version of Windows that's not appropriate for his or her culture. There's no need to prompt or store a currency symbol when all necessary currency symbols are stored in the .NET Framework. For more information, see the section "Setting Culture Properties" in this chapter.

APPLY YOUR KNOWLEDGE

2. **B.** Neutral cultures do not contain enough information to properly localize an application. You should be using the appropriate specific culture instead. For more information, see the section "Understanding Cultures" in this chapter.

3. **A** and **B.** The `RegionInfo` object does not expose weekday names, and there's no point in forcing the user to enter days when you've already got them available. Both the `DateTime` class and the `CultureInfo` class can supply the information that you need here. For more information, see the section "Understanding Cultures" in this chapter.

4. **A.** The `CurrentCulture` property controls formatting, and the `CurrentUICulture` property controls user interface resource loading. For more information, see the section "The `CurrentCulture` and `CurrentUICulture` Properties" in this chapter.

5. **D.** The namespace for resources must exactly match the namespace that .NET assigns to the project. In the case of a project whose name begins with a digit, .NET prepends an underscore to create the namespace. For more information, see the section "Working with Resource Files" in this chapter.

6. **B.** Satellite assemblies are used only when a form is first opened. For more responsive resource switching, you should switch to using assembly resource files. For more information, see the section "Working with Resource Files" in this chapter.

7. **C.** Naming for assembly resource files must follow the scheme that the .NET Framework expects. Otherwise, the .NET Framework is not able to find the resource file. For more information, see the section "Creating Resource Files" in this chapter.

8. **C.** The `UTF8Encoding.GetBytes()` method translates from Unicode characters to bytes that are appropriate for the `Encoding` object that's in use. Using the `UTF8Encoding.GetBytes()` method takes less disk space than using the `UTF8Encoding.GetChars()` method. For more information, see the section "Converting Existing Encodings" in this chapter.

9. **B** and **D.** The `Tag` property has no effect on the localization process (or on anything else), and the `Localizable` property must remain set to `true` in order for you to localize a form. For more information, see the section "Working with Resource Files" in this chapter.

10. **D.** The problem is that the algorithm for simple division by 16 does not take into account composed characters. For more information, see the section "Validating Non-Latin User Input" in this chapter.

11. **A.** The `Calendar` object contains localized date and time formatting resources. The `CurrentCulture` property, not the `CurrentUICulture` property, controls which `CultureInfo` object is used to supply formatting information. For more information, see the section "The `CurrentCulture` and `CurrentUICulture` Properties" in this chapter.

12. **C.** If you set the language property and translate the controls, the .NET Framework automatically builds the necessary resources for you. For more information, see the section "Localizing Forms in the Designer" in this chapter.

13. **A.** To get a list of cultures that the .NET Framework can work with, you should retrieve the .NET Framework's own list by iterating over the `CultureInfo.GetCultures` property.

APPLY YOUR KNOWLEDGE

For more information, see the section "The `CultureInfo` Class" in this chapter.

14. **D.** You should always use the invariant culture for communication with Windows services, no matter what language Windows is using. For more information, see the section "Understanding Cultures" in this chapter.

15. **A.** `Array.Sort()` does not locate substrings. `String.IndexOf()` and `String.IndexOfAny()` can find substrings but are not culture aware. For more information, see the section "Comparing and Sorting Data" in this chapter.

Suggested Readings and Resources

1. Visual Studio .NET Combined Help Collection, "Developing World Ready Applications."

2. Nick Symmonds. *Internationalization and Localization Using Microsoft .NET*. Apress, 2001.

3. Microsoft Global Software Development Archives, `www.microsoft.com/globaldev/articles/articles.asp`.

This chapter covers the following Microsoft-specified objectives for the "Creating User Services" section of Exam 70-316, "Developing and Implementing Windows-Based Applications with Microsoft Visual C# .NET and Microsoft Visual Studio .NET":

Add controls to a Windows form.

- **Instantiate and invoke an ActiveX control.**

Instantiate and invoke a Web service or component.

- **Instantiate and invoke a COM or COM+ component.**

- **Call native functions by using platform invoke.**

▶ Although the .NET Framework can handle nearly all your application development needs, most organizations have already accumulated a large amount of useful code before they begin using the .NET Framework. It doesn't make sense to simply throw away this legacy code and rewrite everything from scratch. Fortunately, if you've followed recommendations to encapsulate your code into components over the years, you don't need to abandon old code to start getting the benefits of the .NET Framework. Instead, you can make use of the .NET Framework's interoperability features to use several types of legacy code:

- ActiveX controls can be placed on Windows forms.

- Component Object Model (COM) and COM+ components can be instantiated and invoked by .NET code.

- The .NET platform invoke capability (usually referred to as PInvoke) can be used to call the Windows application programming interface (API).

By using these interoperability features, you can ease your migration to .NET development. Making use of legacy components from .NET code means that you can migrate an application piece-by-piece rather than trying to do it all at once.

CHAPTER 9

Working with Legacy Code

STUDY STRATEGIES

▶ Convert several ActiveX controls for use in the
.NET Framework. Try using both the ActiveX
Control Importer and the Visual Studio .NET
tools for converting the ActiveX controls.

▶ If you have an existing COM or COM+ object to
work with, create a runtime callable wrapper for
the object to investigate the conversion
process. If you don't have any existing objects,
you can build one with an older version of
Visual Basic or Visual C++.

▶ Experiment with PInvoke to invoke some common Windows API calls.

INTRODUCTION

Migrating to a new development platform can be a painful process. In extreme cases, you might have to throw away the results of years of work when you decide it's time for a new set of tools. This can make switching to a new platform a very difficult decision.

Fortunately, Microsoft recognized the need to provide easy migration paths from previous versions of its tools to the .NET world. In particular, if you heeded the advice to use COM for intercomponent communications and to design your applications as sets of COM servers and clients, you'll find the upgrade path to .NET smooth. That's because the .NET Framework includes good support for interoperating with existing COM-based code.

From .NET components, you can easily instantiate and call COM components such as ActiveX controls or COM libraries. (In fact, interoperability works in the other direction, too, with COM components able to call .NET code, although I don't cover those techniques here). Combine this with an existing modular architecture, and you get an easy migration path: Move one module at a time from COM to .NET, and use the .NET interoperability features so that the components can continue to talk to one another.

In this chapter you'll learn about the facilities that the .NET Framework provides for using COM components and other legacy code. In particular, you'll learn about the tools and techniques that are necessary to call ActiveX controls, COM components, and Windows API code from the .NET Framework.

USING ACTIVEX CONTROLS

Add controls to a Windows form.

- **Instantiate and invoke an ActiveX control.**

With their roots in the Visual Basic custom control standard, ActiveX controls have become a major means of delivering encapsulated functionality to Windows applications. The key advance underlying ActiveX controls is that they have a standard set of interfaces through which they communicate with the hosting form.

By supporting these interfaces, any application can make use of any ActiveX control, without any knowledge of the internal workings of that control.

This concept has turned out to be so popular that thousands of ActiveX controls are now available commercially. You can find controls to display unusual graphs, controls that implement common Internet protocols, controls that emulate spreadsheets, and many more.

But in the .NET world, an ActiveX control is useless. .NET Framework Windows forms can only contain instances of classes that are derived from the `System.Windows.Forms.Control` class. ActiveX controls, which are built using previous technologies, do not derive from this class. So how can you possibly use an ActiveX control on a Windows form?

The answer lies in the creation of a wrapper. In programming terms, a *wrapper* is a layer of software whose job is to translate one set of interfaces into another. The `System.Windows.Forms` namespace contains a wrapper class, `AxHost`, whose job is to make ActiveX controls available to Windows forms. To a Windows form, this class appears to be a regular Windows forms control. To an ActiveX control, this class appears to be an ActiveX control container. When the form sends a message to the control, or vice versa, the wrapper class translates the message so that the recipient component can understand it.

The `AxHost` class needs to be customized to work with a particular ActiveX control. That customization is the job of the Windows Forms ActiveX Control Importer, a utility that ships with the .NET Framework.

The Windows Forms ActiveX Control Importer Tool (`aximp.exe`)

To illustrate the Windows Forms ActiveX Control Importer (`aximp.exe`), Step by Step 9.1 shows you how to use the SysInfo control, which ships as a part of Visual Basic 6, on a Windows form.

STEP BY STEP

9.1 Using the Windows Forms ActiveX Control Importer Tool

1. Create a new folder on your hard drive to house the imported control.

2. Launch a .NET command prompt by selecting Start, Programs, Microsoft Visual Studio .NET, Visual Studio .NET Tools, Visual Studio .NET Command Prompt.

3. Inside the command prompt window, navigate to the folder that you created in step 1.

4. Enter this command line to run the importer:

```
aximp c:\winnt\system32\sysinfo.ocx
```

The importer lists the names of the files that it creates as part of the import process:

```
SysInfoLib.dll
AxSysInfoLib.dll
```

5. Open a Visual C# .NET Windows application and add a new form to the project. Name the new form `StepByStep9_1.cs`.

6. Right-click the References node in Solution Explorer and select Add Reference. Select the COM tab in the Add Reference dialog box. Browse to the folder you created in step 1. Add references to both `SysInfoLib.dll` and `AxSysInfoLib.dll`.

7. Right-click the form and select View Code from the context menu. Expand the Windows Form Designer Generated Code region. Modify the code for the form as follows:

```
public class StepByStep9_1 : System.Windows.Forms.Form
{
    /// <summary>
    /// Required designer variable.
    /// </summary>
    private System.ComponentModel.Container components
        = null;
    private AxSysInfoLib.AxSysInfo sysInfo1;
    public StepByStep9_1()
```

continues

> **WARNING**
>
> **Check the Path** You might need to modify the command line for the importer if you're running an operating system other than Windows NT or Windows 2000.

continued

```
{
    //
    // Required for Windows Form Designer support
    //
    InitializeComponent();
    //
    // TODO: Add any constructor code after
    // InitializeComponent call
    //
}

/// <summary>
/// Clean up any resources being used.
/// </summary>
protected override void Dispose( bool disposing )
{
    if( disposing )
    {
        if(components != null)
        {
            components.Dispose();
        }
    }
    base.Dispose( disposing );
}

#region Windows Form Designer generated code
/// <summary>
/// Required method for Designer support-
/// do not modify the contents of
/// this method with the code editor.
/// </summary>
private void InitializeComponent()
{
    System.Resources.ResourceManager resources =
        new System.Resources.ResourceManager(
        Type.GetType("_316C09.StepByStep9_1"));
    this.sysInfo1 = new AxSysInfoLib.AxSysInfo();
    ((System.ComponentModel.ISupportInitialize)
        this.sysInfo1).BeginInit();
    this.SuspendLayout();
    //
    //SysInfo1
    //
    this.sysInfo1.Enabled = true;
    this.sysInfo1.Name = "sysInfo1";
    this.sysInfo1.OcxState =
    (System.Windows.Forms.AxHost.State)
     resources.GetObject("SysInfo1.OcxState");
    this.sysInfo1.Size = new System.Drawing.Size(
        38, 38);
    this.sysInfo1.TabIndex = 0;
```

```
//
// StepByStep9_1
//
this.AutoScaleBaseSize =
 new System.Drawing.Size(5, 13);
this.ClientSize =
 new System.Drawing.Size(292, 273);
this.Controls.AddRange(
new System.Windows.Forms.Control[]
{this.sysInfo1});
this.Name = "StepByStep9_1";
this.Text = "StepByStep9_1";
this.Load +=
    new System.EventHandler(
    this.StepByStep9_1_Load);
((System.ComponentModel.ISupportInitialize)
    this.sysInfo1).EndInit();
this.ResumeLayout(false);

}
#endregion
[STAThread]
static void Main()
{
    Application.Run(new StepByStep9_1());
}

private void StepByStep9_1_Load(object sender,
    System.EventArgs e)
{
    MessageBox.Show(sysInfo1.OSVersion.ToString());
}
}
```

FIGURE 9.1

You can use an ActiveX control on a Windows
form by creating a wrapper class using
Windows Forms ActiveX Control Importer tool.

8. Switch back to the design view of the form. You should see
an instance of the SysInfo control, as shown in Figure 9.1.

9. Set the form as the startup object for the project.

10. Run the project. You get a message box that displays the
major version number of the operating system.

Although the Windows Forms ActiveX Control Importer does the
work of building the necessary wrapper classes for you, you still have
to do a lot of work to use those classes. Because the importer does
not add the control to the toolbox in Visual Studio .NET, you need
to write all the code to initialize the code yourself. Getting this code
right can be tricky. Fortunately, there's an easier way to bring an
ActiveX control into your .NET Windows application project. You'll
learn about that technique in the next section.

Importing Controls with the Toolbox

If you're using Visual Studio .NET to build Visual C# .NET applications (and I assume that you are), you don't have to bother with the Windows Forms ActiveX Control Importer. Instead, you can use the toolbox to add any ActiveX control from your system to the .NET environment. As you'll see, this method takes care of most of the work for you.

STEP BY STEP

9.2 Using the Toolbox to Add an ActiveX Control to a Windows Form

1. Create a new form in your Visual C# .NET application.

2. Right-click the toolbox and select Customize Toolbox.

3. Select the COM Components tab in the Customize Toolbox dialog box.

4. Scroll down the list of components, which should include all the ActiveX controls that are registered on your computer, until you find the control you want to add to your project. Click the check box for the control. Figure 9.2 shows the Microsoft Masked Edit control being selected.

FIGURE 9.2
You can add an ActiveX control to a Windows form by adding the control to the Visual Studio .NET toolbox.

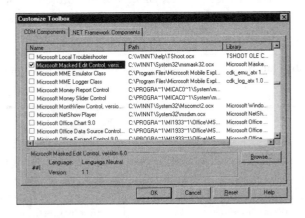

NOTE

ActiveX Control Properties ActiveX control properties are directly integrated into the Properties window. You can also click the ActiveX-Properties hyperlink at the bottom of the Properties window to open a property sheet for the control.

5. Click OK to add the control to the toolbox.

6. The new control shows up at the bottom of the toolbox, as shown in Figure 9.3. You can click and drag the control to a form just like any native .NET control. Place an instance of the Masked Edit control on your form. Set the `Mask` property of the Masked Edit control to `##/##/##`.

7. Insert the `Main()` method to launch the form. Set the form as the startup object for the project.

8. Run the project. The form accepts only the numeric characters allowed by the Masked Edit control.

FIGURE 9.3
An ActiveX control can appear in the Visual Studio .NET toolbox just like any other .NET control.

Using ActiveX Controls on Windows Forms

As you've probably guessed by now, using ActiveX controls on Windows forms is easy. Just import the ActiveX control to the .NET Framework (either by running the Windows Forms ActiveX Control Importer or by adding the control to the toolbox), and you can treat it as if it were a native .NET control. But there are a few things you should consider before you use ActiveX controls in your .NET applications.

First and foremost, you should recognize that there's an inevitable performance decrease when you use ActiveX controls on a .NET form. Although the wrapper architecture allows you to seamlessly use an ActiveX control, it imposes a performance penalty. That's because every call to the control is actually a call to the wrapper class, which then must call the control itself after suitably transforming the parameters of the call. Thus your code has to do twice as much work to interact with an ActiveX control as with a native .NET control. If you're using only a few ActiveX controls in a limited number of forms, this performance decrease might not be noticeable, but if you overuse ActiveX controls, it adds up.

When you import some ActiveX controls to the .NET Framework, their names may change to avoid conflicts with existing objects. You're most likely to see this happen if a control has a property named `State`; such a property is named `CtlState` after the import.

The code that runs under the services provided by the Common Language Runtime (CLR) is called *managed code*. Because ActiveX controls are not managed code, they don't get any of the protection that the CLR brings to .NET applications. An ActiveX control is free to access memory that doesn't belong to it or indulge in other buggy behavior that could crash your entire application.

Finally, using ActiveX controls makes it more difficult to deploy .NET applications. In addition to installing the .NET Framework and your own application, you need to make sure that the target machine has a copy of the ActiveX control properly installed and registered.

Because of these drawbacks, you should use ActiveX controls sparingly (if at all). Before importing an ActiveX control into a project, you should consider whether a native .NET control can fill your requirements.

R E V I E W   B R E A K

▶ You can use the Windows Forms ActiveX Control Importer to create wrapper classes. These wrapper classes let you host the ActiveX control on a .NET Windows form.

▶ You can import an ActiveX control to a Visual Studio .NET project by adding it to the toolbox.

▶ After you import ActiveX controls, you can use them just like native .NET controls.

▶ ActiveX controls impose a performance penalty and have other drawbacks.

Using COM Components

Instantiate and invoke a Web service or component.

• **Instantiate and invoke a COM or COM+ component.**

Using ActiveX controls on a Windows form is a special case of a more general problem: using legacy COM code from a .NET application.

You might already have a lot of development done in your organization that you would like to reuse with .NET development as you slowly migrate toward it. Fortunately, if your old programs use COM architecture, you don't have to do a "big bang" migration all at once. .NET components can call COM components, and COM components can call .NET components. This means that you can migrate one component (a control, a class library, and so on) at a time, and still keep all your code working together.

Why might you want to undertake such a gradual migration? There are four basic reasons for maintaining part of a system in COM components while moving other parts to .NET components:

◆ It takes time to learn enough about Visual C# .NET and the .NET Framework to be productive. While you're making your way up the learning curve, you may have to continue development of existing COM components.

◆ You may have components that can't be easily moved to .NET because they use language features that are no longer supported or because of other implementation quirks.

◆ It takes time to move code from one system to the other. Unless you can afford extended downtime, a gradual move lets you write the converted code at a slower pace.

◆ Your application may depend on third-party controls or libraries for which you do not have the source code.

In the following sections you'll learn how to encapsulate COM components for use with .NET applications. As with ActiveX controls, there are both command-line and GUI tools for working with COM components. Before I talk about those tools, though, you should know a bit more about wrapper classes.

Understanding Runtime Callable Wrappers

As you probably already know, Visual C# .NET creates code that operates within the .NET CLR. Code that operates within the CLR is called *managed code*. Managed code benefits from the services that the CLR offers, including garbage collection, memory management, and support for versioning and security.

Code that does not operate within the CLR is called *unmanaged code*. Code that was created by tools that are older than the .NET Framework is by definition unmanaged code. COM components are unmanaged code because COM was designed before the CLR existed, and COM components don't make use of any of the services of the CLR.

Managed code expects that all the code with which it interacts will use the CLR. This is an obvious problem for COM components. How can you take a component that was developed before the advent of .NET and make it look like a .NET component to other .NET components? The answer is to use a proxy. In general terms, a *proxy* accepts commands and messages from one component, modifies them, and passes them to another component. The particular type of proxy that allows you to use COM components within a .NET application is called a *runtime callable wrapper (RCW)*. That is, it's a proxy that can be called by the CLR.

Figure 9.4 shows schematically how the pieces fit together.

To see how COM interoperability works, you need a COM library. Step by Step 9.3 shows how to build a simple one.

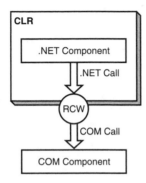

FIGURE 9.4
An RCW allows you to use COM components within the .NET framework.

STEP BY STEP

9.3 Building a COM Dynamic Link Library (DLL)

1. Launch Visual Basic 6. Create a new ActiveX DLL project.

2. Select the Project1 node in the Project Explorer window and rename it `MyCustomer`.

3. Select the Class1 node in the Project Explorer window and rename it `Balances`.

4. Add this code to the `Balances` class:

```
Option Explicit

Private mintCustomerCount As Integer
Private macurBalances(1 To 10) As Currency
```

```
' Create a read-only CustomerCount property
Public Property Get CustomerCount() As Integer
    CustomerCount = mintCustomerCount
End Property

' Create a GetBalance method
Public Function GetBalance( _
    CustomerNumber As Integer) As Currency
    GetBalance = macurBalances(CustomerNumber)
End Function

' Initialize the data
Private Sub Class_Initialize()
    Dim intI As Integer
    mintCustomerCount = 10

    For intI = 1 To 10
        macurBalances(intI) = _
            Int(Rnd(1) * 100000) / 100
    Next intI
End Sub
```

5. Save the Visual Basic project.

6. Select File, Make MyCustomer.dll to create the COM component.

> **NOTE**
>
> **If You Don't Have Visual Basic** Even if you don't have Visual Basic, you can still test COM interoperability by working with a COM library that's already installed on your computer. A variety of Microsoft components, including Office, SQL Server, and ADO, install COM libraries.

Using the Type Library Importer Tool (`tlbimp.exe`)

The task of using COM components from the .NET Framework is substantially facilitated by the fact that COM components, like .NET components, have metadata that describes their interfaces. For .NET components, the metadata is embedded in the assembly manifest. For COM components, the metadata is stored in a type library. A type library can be a separate file, or (as with Visual Basic 6 class libraries) it can be embedded within another file.

The .NET Framework includes a tool, the Type Library Importer tool (`tlbimp.exe`), that can create an RCW from COM metadata contained in a type library.

STEP BY STEP

9.4 Using the Type Library Importer Tool

1. Launch a .NET command prompt by selecting Start, Programs, Microsoft Visual Studio .NET, Visual Studio .NET Tools, Visual Studio .NET Command Prompt.

2. Inside the command prompt window, navigate to the folder that contains the `MyCustomer.dll` COM library.

3. Enter this command line to run the Type Library Importer:

```
tlbimp MyCustomer.dll /out:NETMyCustomer.dll
```

4. Add a new form to your Visual C# .NET application.

5. Place three `Label` controls, three `TextBox` controls (`txtCustomerCount`, `txtCustomerNumber`, and `txtBalance`), and a `Button` control (`btnGetBalance`), on the form. Figure 9.5 shows the design of this form.

6. Right-click the References node in Solution Explorer and select Add Reference.

7. Click the Browse button in the Add Reference dialog box. Browse to the `NETMyCustomer.dll` file that you created in step 3. Click OK to add the reference to the project.

8. Switch to the form's code view and add the following `using` directive:

```
using NETMyCustomer;
```

9. Double-click the form and the `Button` control and enter the following code in the event handlers:

```
Balances b;

private void StepByStep9_4_Load(object sender,
   System.EventArgs e)
{
    b = new Balances();
    txtCustomerCount.Text =
        b.CustomerCount.ToString();
}
```

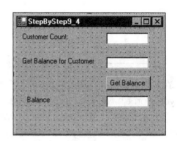

FIGURE 9.5
You can use the Type Library Importer tool to create an RCW for a COM component.

```
private void btnGetBalance_Click(object sender,
    System.EventArgs e)
{
    Int16 custNumber =
        Int16.Parse(txtCustomerNumber.Text);
    txtBalance.Text =
        b.GetBalance(ref custNumber).ToString();
}
```

10. Insert the `Main()` method to launch the form. Set the form as the startup object for the project.

11. Run the project. The form displays the customer count in the Customer Count `TextBox` control. Enter a number between 1 and 10 in the Customer Number `TextBox` control and click the Get Balance button to see that customer's balance.

In Step by Step 9.4, you use the Type Library Importer to create an RCW for the COM type library. This RCW is a library that you can add to your .NET project as a reference. After you do that, the classes in the COM component can be used just like native .NET classes. When you use a class from the COM component, .NET makes the call to the RCW, which in turn forwards the call to the original COM component and returns the results to your .NET managed code.

The Type Library Importer supports the command-line options listed in Table 9.1.

TABLE 9.1

COMMAND-LINE OPTIONS FOR THE TYPE LIBRARY IMPORTER

Option	Meaning
/asmversion:*versionNumber*	Specifies the version number for the created assembly
/delaysign	Prepares the assembly for delay signing
/help	Displays help for command-line options
/keycontainer:*containerName*	Signs the assembly with the strong name from the specified key container

continues

TABLE 9.1	*continued*

COMMAND-LINE OPTIONS FOR THE TYPE LIBRARY IMPORTER

Option	*Meaning*
`/keyfile:`*`filename`*	Signs the assembly with the strong name from the specified key file
`/namespace:`*`namespace`*	Specifies the namespace for the created assembly
`/out:filename`	Specifies the name of the created assembly
`/primary`	Produces a primary interop assembly
`/publickey:`*`filename`*	Specifies the file containing a public key that is used to sign the resulting file
`/reference:`*`filename`*	Specifies a file to be used to resolve references from the file being imported
`/silent`	Suppresses information that would otherwise be displayed on the command line during conversion
`/strictref`	Refuses to create the assembly if one or more references cannot be resolved
`/sysarray`	Imports COM SAFEARRAYs as instances of the `System.Array` type
`/unsafe`	Creates interfaces without the .NET Framework security checks
`/verbose`	Displays additional information on the command line during conversion
`/?`	Displays help about command-line options

EXAM TIP

Options Overview You don't need to memorize all the options for the Type Library Importer. You should know that most of the options deal with the security of the resulting RCW and the code that it contains.

Using COM Components Directly

As with ActiveX controls, the Visual Studio .NET interface provides a streamlined way to use a COM component from your .NET code.

STEP BY STEP

9.5 Using Direct Reference with a COM Library

1. Add a new form to your Visual C# .NET application.

2. Place three Label controls, three TextBox controls (txtCustomerCount, txtCustomerNumber, and txtBalance), and a Button control (btnGetBalance), on the form. Figure 9.5 shows the design of this form.

3. Right-click the References node in Solution Explorer and select Add Reference.

4. Select the COM tab in the Add Reference dialog box. Scroll down the list of COM components until you come to the MyCustomer library. Select the MyCustomer library, click Select, and then click OK.

5. Double-click the form and the Button control and enter the following code in the event handlers in code view:

```
MyCustomer.Balances b;

private void StepByStep9_5_Load(object sender,
    System.EventArgs e)
{
    b = new MyCustomer.Balances();
    txtCustomerCount.Text =
        b.CustomerCount.ToString();
}

private void btnGetBalance_Click(object sender,
    System.EventArgs e)
{
    Int16 custNumber =
        Int16.Parse(txtCustomerNumber.Text);
    txtBalance.Text =
      b.GetBalance(ref custNumber).ToString();
}
```

6. Insert the Main() method to launch the form. Set the form as the startup object for the project.

7. Run the project. The form displays the customer count in the Customer Count TextBox control. Enter a number between 1 and 10 in the Customer Number TextBox control and click the Get Balance button to see that customer's balance.

> **NOTE**
>
> **COM DLL Must Be Registered Before It Is Used** MyCustomer.dll will not be in the COM tab of the Add Reference dialog box if it was not built in Step by Step 9.3. When you build the DLL using Visual Basic 6.0, it automatically registers the DLL in Windows Registry. If you are using the code files from the CD, you will need to register MyCustomer.dll using regsvr32.exe, as shown here, before selecting it in the COM tab:
>
> regsvr32 MyCustomer.dll
>
> This also applies to the Numeric.dll that is used in Guided Practice Exercise 9.1, later in the chapter.

When you directly reference a COM library from the Visual Studio .NET Integrated Development Environment (IDE), the effect is almost the same as if you used the Type Library Importer to import the same library. Visual Studio .NET creates a new namespace with the name of the original library and then exposes the classes from the library within that namespace.

Although you can use either of the two methods described in this chapter to call a COM component from a .NET component, there are reasons to prefer one method over the other:

◆ For a COM component that will only be used in a single Visual C# .NET project and that you wrote yourself, use the easiest method: direct reference from the .NET project. This method is suitable only for a truly private component that does not need to be shared by the other projects.

◆ If a COM component is shared among multiple projects, use the Type Library Importer so that you can sign the resulting assembly and place it in the global assembly cache (GAC). Shared code must be signed.

◆ If you need to control details of the created assembly—such as its name, namespace, or version number—you must use the Type Library Importer. The direct reference method gives you no control over the details of the created assembly.

> **WARNING**
>
> **Import Only Your Own Code**   You should not use either of the import methods on code that is written by another developer. That's because you are not allowed to sign code that is written by someone else. If you need to use a COM component from another developer, you should obtain a primary interop assembly (PIA) from the original developer of the component. Microsoft supplies PIAs for all its own common libraries.

USING COM+ COMPONENTS

COM+ is the component services layer of Windows 2000 and later operating systems. COM+ supplies a number of services to components running under Windows, including the following:

◆ Role-based security

◆ Object pooling and reusability

◆ Queued components for asynchronous calls

◆ Transactional processing

◆ A publish-and-subscribe events model

Despite the significant differences between COM+ and straight COM, you don't have to do anything different to use a COM+ component than to use a COM component. To the consumer, a COM+ component looks much like a COM component. The Type Library Importer tool and Visual Studio .NET can both create wrappers for COM+ components, using the same procedures that they use for COM components.

GUIDED PRACTICE EXERCISE 9.1

The goal of this exercise is to compare the performance of two implementations of the same code, using a COM library for one implementation and a native .NET class for the other implementation. You should choose some code that takes a reasonably long time to run so that you can detect any differences between the two implementations.

How would you create such a form?

You should try working through this problem on your own first. If you get stuck, or if you'd like to see one possible solution, follow these steps:

1. Launch Visual Basic 6. Create a new ActiveX DLL project.

2. Select the Project1 node in the Project Explorer window and rename it Numeric.

3. Select the Class1 node in the Project Explorer window and rename it Primes.

4. Add this code to the Primes class:

```
Option Explicit

Public Function HighPrime(Max As Long) As Long
        Dim a() As Byte
        Dim lngI As Long
        Dim lngJ As Long

        ReDim a(Max)
```

continues

NOTE

Serviced Components A .NET component that uses COM+ services is also called a *serviced component* to distinguish it from the standard managed components. For an in-depth discussion of serviced components, see *MCAD/MCSD Training Guide (Exam 70-320): Developing XML Web Services and Server Components with Visual C# and the .NET Framework* (Que Publishing).

EXAM TIP

Timing Code To tell how long a piece of code takes to run, you can use arithmetic with two instances of the DateTime class to produce a TimeSpan object.

continued

```
' In the array, 1 indicates a prime,
' 0 indicates nonprime.
' Start by marking multiples
' of 2 as nonprime
For lngI = 0 To Max
    If lngI Mod 2 = 0 And lngI <> 2 Then
        a(lngI) = 0
    Else
        a(lngI) = 1
    End If
Next lngI
' Now execute the usual sieve
' of erasthones algorithm
For lngI = 3 To Sqr(Max) Step 2
    If a(lngI) = 1 Then
      ' This is a prime,
      ' so eliminate its multiples
        For lngJ = lngI + lngI To Max _
            Step lngI
            a(lngJ) = 0
        Next lngJ
    End If
Next lngI
' Find the largest prime by working backwards
For lngI = Max To 1 Step -1
    If a(lngI) = 1 Then
        HighPrime = lngI
        Exit For
    End If
Next lngI
```

```
End Function
```

5. Save the Visual Basic project.

6. Select File, Make Numeric.dll to create the COM component.

7. In your Visual C# .NET project, right-click the References node of Solution Explorer and select Add Reference.

8. Select the COM tab in the Add Reference dialog box. Scroll down the list of COM components until you come to the Numeric library. Select the Numeric library, click Select, and then click OK.

9. Add a new class to your Visual C# .NET project. Name the class Primes.cs.

10. Add this code to the `Primes.cs` class:

```
public class Primes
{
public int HighPrime(int max)
{
    Byte[] a = new Byte[max];
    Int32 intI;
    Int32 intJ;

    // In the array, 1 indicates a prime,
    // 0 indicates nonprime.
    // Start by marking multiples
    // of 2 as nonprime
    for(intI = 0;intI < max; intI++)
    {
        if((intI % 2 == 0) && (intI != 2))
            a[intI] = 0;
        else
            a[intI] = 1;
    }

    // Now execute the usual sieve
    // of erasthones algorithm
    for(intI = 3; intI <= System.Math.Sqrt(max);
        intI=intI+2)
    {
        if (a[intI] == 1)
        {
            // This is a prime,
            // so eliminate its multiples
            for(intJ = intI + intI; intJ < max;
                intJ=intJ+intI)
                a[intJ] = 0;
        }
    }
    // Find the largest prime by working backwards
    for(intI = max-1; intI > 0; intI--)
    {
        if (a[intI] == 1)
        {
            break;
        }
    }
    return intI;
}
}
```

11. Add a new form to your Visual C# .NET project. Name the form `GuidedPracticeExercise9_1.cs`.

12. Place five `Label` controls (`lblCOMresults` and `lblNETresults`), a `Button` control (`btnGo`), and a `TextBox` control (`txtMaximum`) on the form. Figure 9.6 shows the design for this form.

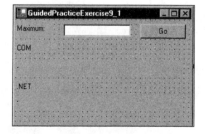

FIGURE 9.6

A form that compares execution speed between COM and .NET components.

WARNING

The Pitfalls of Performance   In Guided Practice Exercise 9.1, the .NET class was much faster than the COM class. But timing performance on Windows is notoriously difficult— for several reasons. First, although you can measure things down to the timer tick, the hardware does not provide precise-to-the-tick numbers. Second, because of caching and because other programs are in memory, timings tend not to be repeatable. Finally, it's hard to write exactly equivalent COM and .NET code. Nevertheless, repeated runs of a program such as this example can give you general information on which of two alternatives is faster.

13. Double-click the `Button` control and add the following code to handle the `Click` event of the `Button` control:

```
private void btnGo_Click(object sender,
    System.EventArgs e)
{
    Int32 maxNumber = Int32.Parse(txtMaximum.Text);
    Int32 intHighPrime;
    Numeric.Primes COM_Primes = new Numeric.Primes();
    DateTime dt1 = DateTime.Now;
    intHighPrime =
        COM_Primes.HighPrime(ref maxNumber);
    TimeSpan ts1 = DateTime.Now.Subtract(dt1);
    lblCOMresults.Text = "High prime = " +
        intHighPrime.ToString() + " took " +
        ts1.Ticks.ToString() + " ticks";

    Primes NET_Primes = new Primes();
    DateTime dt2 = DateTime.Now;
    intHighPrime = NET_Primes.HighPrime(maxNumber);
    TimeSpan ts2 = DateTime.Now.Subtract(dt2);
    lblNETresults.Text = "High prime = " +
        intHighPrime.ToString() + " took " +
        ts2.Ticks.ToString() + " ticks";
}
```

14. Insert the `Main()` method to launch the form. Set the form as the startup object for the project.

15. Run the project. Enter a fairly large number in the `TextBox` control and click the Go button. The code finds the largest prime number that is smaller than the number you entered, first with the COM library and then with the native .NET class. It displays the relative execution times for the two versions, as shown in Figure 9.7.

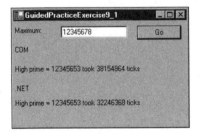

FIGURE 9.7
Running .NET code is much faster than running COM code in the .NET Framework.

If you have difficulty following this exercise, review the section "Using COM Components," earlier in this chapter. After doing that review, try this exercise again.

USING PINVOKE

Instantiate and invoke a Web service or component.

- **Call native functions by using platform invoke.**

So far in this chapter, you've seen interoperability between managed code and unmanaged code by way of method calls to classes in COM libraries. There's a second way that the .NET Framework can interoperate with unmanaged code, though: through functional calls to unmanaged libraries. The PInvoke feature of .NET allows .NET code to call functions from unmanaged libraries such as the Windows API.

STEP BY STEP

9.6 Using PInvoke with the Windows API

1. Add a new form to your Visual C# .NET application.

2. Place a `Label` control named `lblComputerName` on the form.

3. Switch to the code view. Enter the following using directives:

```
using System.Text;
using System.Runtime.InteropServices;
```

4. Add the following lines of code in the class definition, which indicates that the `GetComputerName()` method is implemented in `kernel32.dll`:

```
[DllImport("kernel32.dll", CharSet=CharSet.Auto)]
public static extern int GetComputerName(
    StringBuilder buffer, ref uint size);
```

> **NOTE**
> **Reference Parameters** In Visual C# .NET, the `ref` and `out` keywords are used to pass reference parameters.

5. Double-click the form to add the following code to handle the `Load` event handler of the form:

```
private void StepByStep9_6_Load(object sender,
    System.EventArgs e)
{
        StringBuilder sbBuf = new StringBuilder(128);
        UInt32 intLen = (uint) sbBuf.Capacity;
        Int32 intRet=0;

        // Call the Win API method
        intRet = GetComputerName(sbBuf, ref intLen);

        lblComputerName.Text =
            "This computer is named " +
            sbBuf.ToString();
}
```

continues

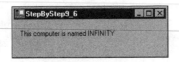

FIGURE 9.8
The PInvoke feature of .NET allows .NET code to call functions from the the Windows API.

continued

6. Insert the `Main()` method to launch the form. Set the form as the startup object for the project.

7. Run the project. The form displays the name of the computer where the code is run, as shown in Figure 9.8.

In Step by Step 9.6 the `DllImport` attribute tells the CLR where to find the implementation of the `extern` method (in this case, `GetComputerName()`) by specifying the name of the library (in this case, `kernel32.dll`). After the method is declared, you can use it in Visual C# .NET just like you use any other method. The `DllImport` attribute can also have additional fields other than the name of the library (see Table 9.2).

TABLE 9.2

IMPORTANT FIELDS OF THE `DllImportAttribute` CLASS

Field	Description
CallingConvention	Defines the calling convention to use. The values are specified by the `CallingConvention` enumeration— `Cdecl`, `FastCall`, `StdCall` (default value), `ThisCall`, and `Winapi`.
CharSet	Specifies the character set to use. By default it uses `CharSet.Ansi`. The other possible values are `CharSet.Auto`, `CharSet.Unicode`, and `CharSet.None` (which is obsolete and behaves as `CharSet.Ansi`).
EntryPoint	Represents the name of the entry point in the DLL. If the `EntryPoint` field is not passed, the name of the method is used as the entry point.
ExactSpelling	Specifies whether the name of the entry point should exactly match the name of the function in the unmanaged DLL. By default the value is `false`.
PreserveSig	Indicates whether the method signature should be preserved or can be changed. By default the value is `true`.
SetLastError	Specifies whether the last error of `Win32` should be preserved. By default the value is `false`.

In Step by Step 9.6, note the use of the `CharSet.Auto` parameter in the `DllImport` attribute of the `GetComputerName()` method declaration. You might know that many Windows API calls come in two versions, depending on the character set that you're using. For example, `GetComputerName` really exists as `GetComputerNameA` (for ANSI characters) and `GetComputerNameW` (for Unicode characters). The `Auto` modifier instructs the .NET Framework to use the appropriate version of the API call for the platform where the code is running.

PInvoke can also handle API calls that require structures as parameters. For example, the `GetWindowRect` API call fills in a structure that consists of four members that indicate the position of a window onscreen.

> **EXAM TIP**
>
> **StringBuilder Necessary** In Viusal C# .NET, you should use a `StringBuilder` object for a Windows API call that expects a string buffer to be modified by the function.

STEP BY STEP

9.7 Using PInvoke with a struct Parameter

1. Add a new form to your Visual C# .NET application.

2. Place a `Button` control (`btnGetCoordinates`), four Label controls, and four `TextBox` controls (`txtTop`, `txtBottom`, `txtLeft`, and `txtRight`) on the form.

3. Switch to the code view and add the following `using` directive:

```
using System.Runtime.InteropServices;
```

4. Add the following lines of code in the class definition:

```
[StructLayout(LayoutKind.Explicit)]
public struct Rect
{
    [FieldOffset(0)] public Int32 left;
    [FieldOffset(4)] public Int32 top;
    [FieldOffset(8)] public Int32 right;
    [FieldOffset(12)] public Int32 bottom;
}

[DllImport("user32.dll", CharSet=CharSet.Auto)]
private static extern int GetWindowRect(
    IntPtr hwnd, out Rect aRect );
```

continues

continued

5. Double-click the `Button` control and add the following code to handle the `Click` event of the `Button` control:

```
private void btnGetCoordinates_Click(object sender,
    System.EventArgs e)
{
    Rect r;
    Int32 ret;
    // Get the form's handle
    IntPtr hwnd = this.Handle;

    // call the Win32 API method
    ret = GetWindowRect(hwnd, out r);

    // if successful display the struct fields
    if(ret != 0)
    {
        txtTop.Text = r.top.ToString();
        txtBottom.Text = r.bottom.ToString();
        txtLeft.Text = r.left.ToString();
        txtRight.Text = r.right.ToString();
    }
}
```

FIGURE 9.9
PInvoke can handle API calls that require structures as parameters.

6. Insert the `Main()` method to launch the form. Set the form as the startup object for the project.

7. Run the project. Move and resize the form, and then click the Get Coordinates button. The form reports its own coordinates, as shown in Figure 9.9.

The tricky part of the code in Step by Step 9.7 lies in the declaration of the structure. The `StructLayout` attribute tells the Visual C# .NET compiler that you'll explicitly specify the location of the individual fields within the structure. The `FieldOffset` attribute specifies the starting byte of each field within the structure. By using these attributes, you can ensure that the .NET Framework constructs the same structure that the API function is expecting to receive.

R E V I E W   B R E A K

▶ Using COM or COM+ components from .NET managed code requires the creation of an RCW.

▶ You can create an RCW for a COM component by using the Type Library Importer tool or by directly referencing the COM component from your .NET code.

▶ To use COM components that you did not create, you should obtain a PIA from the creator of the component.

▶ RCWs impose a performance penalty on COM code.

▶ You can use the .NET Framework PInvoke facility to call functions from Windows libraries, including the Windows API.

CHAPTER SUMMARY

Although the .NET Framework is extensive, it is not all-encompassing. Many projects need to use a mixture of old (COM or Windows) components and new (.NET) components. Even if all the necessary facilities are available within the .NET Framework, it might not be feasible to migrate an entire existing application to .NET all at once.

The .NET Framework and Visual Studio .NET include a variety of features that are designed to make it easy to use legacy components. In this chapter, you learned about three of those features:

◆ The ability to use ActiveX controls on a Windows form

◆ The ability to instantiate and invoke objects from a COM component

◆ The ability to call functions from a Windows API or another DLL

You can create a wrapper for an ActiveX control by using the Windows Forms ActiveX Control Importer tool or by adding the control directly to the Visual Studio .NET toolbox. Either method creates wrapper classes to help host the control. The wrapper classes present the interfaces of the `Control` class to the Windows form, and they also present the interfaces of an ActiveX control container to the control.

COM components also depend on wrappers called RCWs to work with the .NET Framework. An RCW is a proxy that sends data back and forth between the COM component and .NET components. You can create RCWs with the Type Library Importer command-line tool or by adding the COM component to the references collection of a .NET project.

You might need to call functions from the Windows API or other DLLs. The .NET PInvoke functionality lets you do this. By using the `DllImport` attribute, you can tell the .NET Framework where to find the implementation of a method call.

KEY TERMS

- managed code
- PInvoke
- RCW
- unmanaged code

APPLY YOUR KNOWLEDGE

Exercises

9.1   Embedding a Web Browser Control

One ActiveX control that you might find useful on Windows forms is the `WebBrowser` control, which uses the Internet Explorer rendering engine to display Web pages. In this exercise, you'll see how you can embed this control in a Windows form.

Estimated time: 15 minutes

1. Open a Visual C# .NET Windows application in the Visual Studio .NET IDE.

2. Right-click on the toolbox and select Customize Toolbox.

3. Select the COM Components tab in the Customize Toolbox dialog box.

4. Scroll down the list of components, which should include all the ActiveX controls that are registered on your computer, until you find the Microsoft Web Browser control. Click the check box for the control and click OK to add the control to the toolbox.

5. Add a new form to the application.

6. Place a `TextBox` control (`txtURL`), a `Button` control (`btnGo`), and a Web Browser control (`browser1`) on the form.

7. Attach the default event handlers of the form and of the `Button` control. Add the following code to the event handlers:

```csharp
private void Exercise9_1_Load(
    object sender, System.EventArgs e)
{
    Object objNull=null;
    Object objStr="";
```

```csharp
    // Initialize the browser
    // to a default URL
    browser1.Navigate(
        "http://www.quepublishing.com/",
        ref objNull, ref objStr,
        ref objStr, ref objStr);
}

private void btnGo_Click(
    object sender, System.EventArgs e)
{
    Object objNull=null;
    Object objStr="";
    // Navigate to the specified URL
    browser1.Navigate(
        txtURL.Text, ref objNull,
        ref objStr, ref objStr, ref objStr);
}
```

8. Insert the `Main()` method to launch the form. Set the form as the startup object for the project.

9. Run the project. Wait for the default Web page to load, or enter a URL and click the button to navigate to that URL, as shown in Figure 9.10.

FIGURE 9.10
The `WebBrowser` ActiveX control uses the Internet Explorer rendering engine to display Web pages.

APPLY YOUR KNOWLEDGE

Review Questions

1. What do you need to do to use an ActiveX control on a form in a Visual C# .NET Windows application?

2. What are the advantages and disadvantages of using ActiveX controls on a .NET form?

3. Name some reasons to use COM components in a .NET project.

4. What is the purpose of an RCW?

5. How do you create an RCW?

6. What should you consider when choosing how to create an RCW?

7. What extra steps do you need to take to use a COM+ component in a .NET application, as compared to using a COM component?

8. What's the difference between COM interoperability and PInvoke?

9. What does the `CharSet.Auto` parameter in a `DllImport` attribute specify?

Exam Questions

1. Your application uses an instance of the Microsoft Masked Edit ActiveX control to collect data from users. You deploy the application via xcopy to the users' computers. Some of the users report that the main form of the application does not load. You've checked, and the users who are having the problem do have the .NET Framework installed. What could be the problem?

   A. The Microsoft Masked Edit control is not installed on the problem computers.

   B. The RCW for the ActiveX control needs to be registered on the problem computers.

   C. The problem computers are not connected to the Internet.

   D. Service Pack 1 for the .NET Framework is not installed on the problem computers.

2. You have imported a TriState ActiveX control to the .NET toolbox and inserted an instance of it, named `Control1`, on your form. This control exposes a property named `State` that can be set to `0`, `1`, or `2`. Which line of code can you use to set the `State` property of `Control1` to `2`?

   A.
   ```
   Control1.CtlState = 2;
   ```

   B.
   ```
   Control1.ActiveXState = 2;
   ```

   C.
   ```
   Control1.AxState = 2;
   ```

   D.
   ```
   Control1.State = 2;
   ```

3. You are responsible for migrating an existing COM application to Visual C# .NET. The existing application consists of eight COM server components and a single client user interface component that instantiates and invokes objects from the server components. You want to give the user interface of the application an overhaul and migrate to Visual C# .NET with low risk and minimal downtime. How should you proceed?

   A. Completely rewrite the entire application, using Visual C# .NET.

   B. Bring only the user interface code into Visual C# .NET. Use COM interoperability to call the existing COM servers from the .NET user interface code. Migrate the servers one by one.

APPLY YOUR KNOWLEDGE

C. Bring all the servers into Visual C# .NET. Use COM interoperability to call the migrated servers from the existing user interface code.

D. Cut and paste all the existing code into Visual C# .NET.

4. Your company supplies a COM component to provide advanced data analysis for your clients. Some of your clients are moving to the .NET Framework and require an RCW for your component. How should you proceed?

A. Use the ActiveX Library Importer to create and sign a PIA for your component.

B. Use the Type Library Importer to create and sign a PIA for your component.

C. Set a reference to your component from any Visual C# .NET project to create an RCW for your component.

D. Create a class that uses PInvoke to call functions from your component.

5. You wrote a COM component to supply random numbers in a specific distribution to a simple statistical client program. Now you're moving that client program to the .NET Framework. The COM component is used nowhere else, and you have not shipped copies to anyone else. You want to call the objects in the COM server from your new .NET client. How should you proceed?

A. Set a direct reference from your .NET client to the COM server.

B. Use the Type Library Importer to create an unsigned RCW for the COM component.

C. Use the Type Library Importer to create a signed RCW for the COM component.

D. Use PInvoke to instantiate classes from the COM component.

6. You have written several applications for your own use, all of which share classes from a COM component that you also wrote. You are moving the applications to .NET, but you intend to leave the COM component untouched. How should you proceed?

A. Set a direct reference from each application to the existing COM component.

B. Use the Type Library Importer to create an unsigned RCW for the COM component. Place a copy of this RCW in each application's directory.

C. Use PInvoke to call functions from the existing COM component in each application.

D. Use the Type Library Importer to create a signed RCW for the COM component. Place this RCW in the GAC.

7. Your application uses a communications library from a third-party developer. This library is implemented as a COM component. You are migrating your application to .NET. What should you do to continue to use the classes and methods in the communications library?

A. Obtain a PIA from the developer of the library. Install the PIA in the GAC.

B. Use the Type Library Importer to create a signed RCW for the library. Install the RCW in the GAC.

C. Use the Type Library Importer to create an unsigned RCW for the library. Install the RCW in the GAC.

D. Create wrapper code that uses PInvoke to call functions from the library. Import this wrapper code into your application.

8. Your Visual C# .NET application uses functions from a Visual Basic 6 COM library implemented as a DLL via an RCW. You built the RCW by directly referencing the COM DLL. Users are complaining of poor performance. Which of these changes is most likely to improve the performance of your application?

   A. Recompile the Visual Basic 6 library as an .exe file.

   B. Switch your .NET application from Visual C# .NET to Visual Basic .NET.

   C. Use the Type Library Importer to create a new RCW.

   D. Rewrite the Visual Basic 6 library as a native .NET library.

9. Your project contains the following API declaration:

```
[DllImport("kernel32.dll",
CharSet=CharSet.Auto)]
public static extern int GetComputerName(
    String buffer, ref uint size);
```

The project also contains code to use this API to display the computer name:

```
public static void ShowName()
{
        String buf = "";
        UInt32 intLen=128;
        Int32 intRet;

        // Call the Win API function
        intRet = GetComputerName(
            buf, ref intLen);

        Console.WriteLine(
            "This computer is named " +
            buf.ToString());
}
```

Users report that no computer name is displayed. What should you do?

A. Use ref with the variable buf in the call to the GetComputerName() function.

B. Tell the users that their computers have no names set in their network properties.

C. Replace the use of String with StringBuilder in the code.

D. Use out with the variable buf in the call to the GetComputerName() function.

10. You want to use the SysInfo ActiveX control in your Visual C# .NET application. How can you make this control available for your Windows forms? (Select the two best answers.)

   A. Use the Type Library Importer tool.

   B. Use the Windows Forms ActiveX Control Importer tool.

   C. Add the control directly to the Visual C# .NET toolbox.

   D. Add a reference to the control's library.

11. You are using three classes from a COM component in your Visual C# .NET application. You'd like to give the RCW for the COM component the same version number as the rest of your components when you ship the application. What should you do?

   A. Use PInvoke to call functions from the COM component, thus eliminating the RCW.

   B. Directly import the COM component into the References list. Right-click the reference and select Properties to set the version number.

   C. Recompile the existing COM library with the desired version number before creating the RCW.

   D. Use the Type Library Importer with the /asmversion option to explicitly set the version of the RCW.

APPLY YOUR KNOWLEDGE

12. You are planning to use two classes from a COM component in your .NET application. You'd like to place these two classes into a namespace named ComComponents. What must you do?

A. Set a direct reference to the COM component. Create an empty class file in your .NET project. Specify the ComComponents namespace in that file and import the wrapper class.

B. Use the Type Library Importer with the /namespace option to set the namespace within the RCW.

C. Use the Type Library Importer with the /out option to create a file with the desired name.

D. Use PInvoke within a namespace declaration to import the classes.

13. Your application will use functions from a COM+ component that makes use of COM+ for publish-and-subscribe events and object pooling. Which of these methods can you use to access the classes in the COM+ component? (Select the two best answers.)

A. Use PInvoke to declare the functions within the COM+ component.

B. Add the COM+ component directly to the Visual C# .NET toolbox.

C. Set a direct reference to the COM+ component.

D. Use the Type Library Importer to create an RCW for the COM+ component.

14. You have an existing COM component that contains shared classes. These classes encapsulate functionality that you want to use in your .NET application. How can you use these classes while maintaining the benefits of managed code, such as type safety and automatic garbage collection?

A. Use the Type Library Importer with the /strictref option to create an RCW for the COM component.

B. Call the methods from the COM component directly via PInvoke.

C. Add a direct reference to the COM component.

D. Rewrite the COM component as a .NET component.

15. Your application uses the GetComputerName API function. This function exists in kernel32.dll in both ANSI and Unicode versions. Your declaration is as follows:

```
[DllImport("kernel32.dll")]
public static extern int GetComputerName(
    StringBuilder buffer, ref uint size);
```

Your code is failing, with a System.EntryPointNotFoundException exception when you call this function. What should you do to fix this failure?

A. Supply the full path for kernel32.dll.

B. Add the CharSet.Auto parameter to the DllImport attribute.

C. Declare the function as GetComputerNameA instead of GetComputerName.

D. Declare the function as GetComputerNameW instead of GetComputerName.

APPLY YOUR KNOWLEDGE

Answers to Review Questions

1. You can use the Windows Forms ActiveX Control Importer to create a set of wrapper classes for the control, or you can add the control directly to the Visual Studio .NET toolbox.

2. The advantage of using an ActiveX control is that it might provide functionality that is not otherwise available to .NET applications. The disadvantages are that ActiveX controls impose a performance penalty, they are unmanaged code, and they make the distribution of your application more complex.

3. You might use COM components in a .NET project because you need to migrate an existing application in small pieces or because the COM components contain unique functionality for which you do not have source code.

4. RCWs provide a proxy between .NET applications and COM components. The RCW translates .NET calls into COM calls and returns the COM results as .NET results.

5. You can create an RCW by using the Type Library Importer or by adding a direct reference to the COM component.

6. When deciding how to create an RCW, you should consider whether you own the source code for the COM component, whether the RCW needs to go into the GAC, and how many .NET applications will make use of the COM component.

7. You don't need to take any extra steps. For purposes of calling from a .NET application, COM components and COM+ components are identical.

8. COM interoperability allows you to instantiate COM classes within a .NET application and to invoke their members. PInvoke allows you to call functions from a DLL.

9. The `CharSet.Auto` parameter of the `DllImport` attribute tells the CLR to choose the correct version—ANSI or Unicode—of an API for the particular platform on which you are running the code.

Answers to Exam Questions

1. **A.** RCWs are installed by xcopy, just like any other .NET assemblies. .NET does not require the Internet to run, nor do RCWs depend on Service Pack 1. When you add an ActiveX control to an application, you must make sure that that ActiveX control is installed on the target computers using a setup package. For more information, see the section "Using ActiveX Controls" in this chapter.

2. **A.** Any property named `State` is renamed `CtlState` to avoid conflicts with the `AxHost.State` class. For more information, see the section "Using ActiveX Controls on Windows Forms" in this chapter.

3. **B.** Moving all the code takes longer than moving part of the code, and it introduces additional risk. Because you'd like to rewrite the user interface, you should move that component to .NET before moving the server components. For more information, see the section "Using COM Components" in this chapter.

APPLY YOUR KNOWLEDGE

4. **B.** As the vendor of the component, it's your responsibility to supply the PIA. For more information, see the section "Using COM Components" in this chapter.

5. **A.** For components that are used in a single project, and that you wrote, the simplest method of creating the RCW is best. For more information, see the section "Using COM Components Directly" in this chapter.

6. **D.** Shared libraries should be placed in the GAC. Code must be signed before it can be placed in the GAC, and only the Type Library Importer can sign an RCW. For more information, see the section "Using COM Components" in this chapter.

7. **A.** Because you did not write the code for the communications library, the proper way to proceed is to obtain a PIA from the original author. For more information, see the section "Using COM Components" in this chapter.

8. **D.** Changing from a DLL to an `.exe` file or from C# to Visual Basic .NET has no significant effect on performance. RCWs are the same no matter how they're created. But rewriting the library into .NET is likely to speed it up because it eliminates the extra calls in the proxy layer. For more information, see the section "Using COM Components" in this chapter.

9. **C.** In the PInvoke calls, you should use `StringBuilder` instead of `String` to hold the return value. For more information, see the section "Using PInvoke" in this chapter.

10. **B** and **C.** These are the two methods for using an ActiveX control within a .NET project. For more information, see the section "Using ActiveX Controls" in this chapter.

11. **D.** Only the Type Library Importer can explicitly set the version number for an RCW. For more information, see the section "Using the Type Library Importer Tool (`tlbimp.exe`)" in this chapter.

12. **B.** Only the Type Library Importer can set the namespace for an RCW. For more information, see the section "Using the Type Library Importer Tool (`tlbimp.exe`)" in this chapter.

13. **C** and **D.** You can use COM+ components by using the same techniques you use with COM components. For more information, see the sections "Using COM Components" and "Using COM+ Components" in this chapter.

14. **D.** Only managed code benefits from the features of the CLR. The only way to turn the component into managed code is to rewrite it in .NET. For more information, see the section "Using COM Components" in this chapter.

15. **B.** The `CharSet.Auto` parameter is necessary to tell the CLR to use the ANSI or Unicode versions of the function, as appropriate to the operating system. For more information, see the section "Using PInvoke" in this chapter.

APPLY YOUR KNOWLEDGE

Suggested Readings and Resources

1. Visual Studio .NET Combined Help Collection, "Interoperating with Unmanaged Code."

2. Adam Nathan. *.NET and COM: The Complete Interoperability Guide*. Sams, 2002.

3. Andrew Troelsen. *COM and .NET Interoperability*. Apress, 2002.

4. Microsoft .NET/COM Migration and Interoperability. `msdn.microsoft.com/library/ en-us/dnbda/html/cominterop.asp`.

5. Microsoft Support WebCast: Microsoft .NET and COM Interoperability, `support.microsoft.com/servicedesks/ webcasts/wc051602/wcblurb051602.asp`.

This chapter covers the following Microsoft-specified objectives for the "Creating User Services" section of Exam 70-316, "Developing and Implementing Windows-Based Applications with Microsoft Visual C# .NET and Microsoft Visual Studio .NET":

Implement online user assistance.

Implement accessibility features.

▶ Perhaps at one time an application was finished when the code functioned properly, but that is certainly no longer the case. Users and managers alike expect more than properly functioning code in a useful and usable application. From the process of defining requirements right through the necessity to supply postinstallation support, applications exist as part of a wide range of features and activities. This chapter looks at two of the necessary parts of shipping any complex Windows application:

- *User assistance* refers to the process of providing help within an application through a variety of means.

- *Accessibility* refers to the coding you must do to make your application usable by people who have disabilities.

Developers sometimes think of user assistance and accessibility features as being the "icing on the cake" that can be left out if they're in a hurry. That's a fundamental misunderstanding of the importance of these features. User assistance and accessibility should be designed into applications right from the start and implemented as a matter of course with each new feature you add.

CHAPTER 10

User Assistance and Accessibility

▶ Use the standalone Hypertext Markup Language (HTML) Help Workshop or the integrated Help Workshop to create an HTML help file for one of your own applications. Make sure you understand how to create help topics and how to hook them up to the user interface.

▶ Use the `ToolTip` component to add ToolTips to one of your own applications.

▶ Review the documentation from the HTML Help Software Development Kit (SDK) to get an idea of the advanced capabilities of HTML Help.

▶ Refer to the topic "Walkthrough: Creating an Accessible Windows Application" in the Visual Studio .NET Combined Help Collection for another example of setting accessibility properties.

▶ Use the testing strategies described in this chapter to evaluate some existing Windows applications for accessibility.

INTRODUCTION

Building the best program in the world is useless if no one but the original developer can use it. As applications grow ever more complex, it's incumbent upon their developers to provide help for end users of these applications. Visual Studio .NET provides strong support for two specific types of help: user assistance and accessibility.

User assistance refers to the type of help that you get from the traditional help file: a set of short topics designed to teach you what you need to know to effectively use the capabilities of an application. Windows forms are designed to integrate with HTML Help, Microsoft's current standard for building application help. They also support more immediate help through the use of ToolTips, which are short messages that pop up when the user hovers the cursor over a control.

Accessibility refers to making sure that users who have disabilities can work with an application. In the United States alone, more than 30 million people have some disability that can affect their ability to use software, according to U.S. government figures. Windows and the .NET Framework include a variety of tools and techniques to help you make applications accessible to these users.

In this chapter you'll learn how to create HTML Help files and how to integrate those files with your applications. You'll also learn how to design an application for accessibility, as well as methods for implementing and testing accessibility.

SELECTING A HELP COMPILER

When you create an HTML Help file by using Microsoft tools, you have two choices: HTML Help 1.3 and HTML Help 2.

As I write this, in mid-2002, the latest released version of HTML Help is HTML Help 1.3. This is the version that's installed with Visual Studio .NET, and it's the version that has been in use for some time now.

But there's another alternative that provides more modern-looking help. HTML Help 2 is in beta right now, and it should ship some time in 2003. This new version is readily available, and you might choose to work with it.

If company policy or personal preference dictates that you use only released software, then HTML Help 1.3 is probably your best bet. If you like being on the cutting edge, you can download HTML Help 2. Of course, after HTML Help 2 is released, it will be the current version, suitable for everyone. Fortunately, HTML Help 2 includes tools to convert HTML Help 1.3 projects, so if you decide to wait to start using HTML Help 2, you won't lose any effort that you put into writing HTML Help 1.3 files.

I discuss both versions of HTML Help in this chapter, starting with HTML Help 1.3.

> **WARNING**
>
> **Context-Sensitive Help**   As of this writing, Microsoft has documented how to create HTML Help 2 files, but it has not yet released the Application Programming Interface (API) that is necessary to call them from a Visual C# .NET form. If you want context-sensitive help in your applications, you should stick with HTML Help 1.3 until HTML Help 2 is released.

CREATING HELP PROJECTS USING HTML HELP 1.3

Implement online user assistance.

Various versions of Windows have included several standards for help files. The standard help system for .NET applications is HTML Help, Microsoft's familiar multiple-pane help system whose contents are created in HTML. If you install Visual Studio .NET, the HTML Help SDK version 1.3 is also installed by default. This SDK contains the tools and documentation that you need to create your own help files. Figure 10.1 shows a typical HTML Help file (in this case, the help file for the HTML Help SDK itself).

> **NOTE**
>
> **Latest Version**   If you didn't install the HTML Help SDK, or if you'd like to check for a later version, visit the HTML Help download page on the Microsoft Developer Network (MSDN) Web site at msdn.microsoft.com/ library/default.asp?url=/library/ en-us/htmlhelp/html/ hwMicrosoftHTMLHelpDownloads.asp.

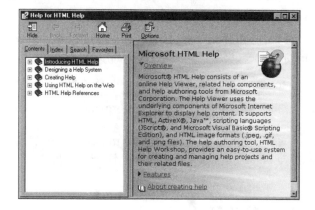

FIGURE 10.1
This HTML Help file shows help for the HTML Help.

The HTML Help SDK includes a number of components:

◆ HTML Help Workshop, an Integrated Development Environment (IDE) for developing HTML Help files

◆ The HTML Help ActiveX control and HTML Help Java Applet, components that can be used for advanced navigation in HTML Help files

◆ The HTML Help Viewer, a host application that can display HTML Help files

◆ The HTML Help Image Editor, which can capture screenshots and perform graphics editing tasks

◆ The HTML Help executable program, which executes HTML Help files outside the browser

◆ The HTML Help compiler, which converts files from HTML Help Workshop into actual HTML Help files

◆ The HTML Help Authoring Guide, which contains help for developers of HTML Help files

A number of files are included in a full HTML Help 1.3 system. These files can all be created and manipulated within HTML Help Workshop. The HTML Help system includes the following parts:

◆ A help project file, which determines the overall structure of the HTML help file

◆ Topic files, which are individual pieces of help written as HTML files

◆ Graphics, sound, animation, and other multimedia files that can be embedded within HTML Help files

◆ Contents files, which contain table of contents information

◆ Index files, which contain index information

In the following sections you'll learn how to use HTML Help Workshop to build and test a simple HTML Help file.

Creating HTML Help 1.3 Project

The first step in creating an HTML Help 1.3 file is to create a new help project. Step by Step 10.1 guides you through this process.

STEP BY STEP

10.1 Creating an HTML Help 1.3 Project File

1. Launch HTML Help Workshop by selecting Start, Programs, HTML Help Workshop, HTML Help Workshop.

2. Select File, New. In the New dialog box, select Project as the type of file to create and click OK. The New Project Wizard opens.

3. Read the introductory screen of the wizard and click Next.

4. On the Destination screen of the New Project Wizard, name the new project file Random.hhp. Browse to choose an appropriate location for this file. Click Next.

5. Leave the check boxes on the Existing Files screen of the New Project Wizard unchecked and click Next.

6. Click Finish to create the new help project file.

7. Click the Change Project Options button on the Project tab in the HTML Help Workshop IDE.

8. Set the Title property for the help file to Help for Random and click OK.

9. Click the Save button to save the help project file. Figure 10.2 shows the new file open in HTML Help Workshop.

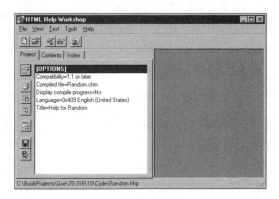

FIGURE 10.2
You can create an HTML help project by using HTML Help Workshop.

Creating Topic Files in HTML Help 1.3

After you have created a help project, the next step is to populate the project with topic files. *Topic files* are HTML pages, each of which is designed to give help to the user in a specific situation. Of course, writing help topics requires that you actually know what the application will do. So let's take a detour now and build a simple application to deliver random numbers to the user interface. Over the course of this chapter you will use this application as a testbed for help and accessiblity features.

STEP BY STEP

10.2 Building an Application That Requires User Assistance

1. Launch Visual Studio .NET and create a new Visual C# .NET Windows application.

2. Add a new form to the application. Name the form `RandomForm.cs` and set its `Text` property to `Random Number Server`.

3. Add to the form a `MainMenu` control (accept the default name), a `Label` control (`lblRange`), a `TextBox` control (`txtRandom`, with the `Text` property cleared), and a `Button` control (`btnGetRandom`, with `Text` set to `&Get Random`).

4. Add a top-level menu named `mnuTools` with the text of `&Tools`. Add to this menu a menu item named `mnuToolsOptions` with the text `&Options`. Add a top-level menu named `mnuHelp` with the text `&Help`. Add to this menu a menu item named `mnuHelpContents` with the text `&Contents`.

5. Add a second form to the project. Name this form `frmOptions`. Set its `Text` property to `Options`, its `MaximizeButton` and `MinimizeButton` properties to `false`, its `HelpButton` property to `true`, and its `FormBorderStyle` property to `FixedDialog`.

6. Place two `Label` controls, two `TextBox` controls (`txtMin`, with `Text` set to 1, and `txtMax`, with `Text` set to 1000), and two `Button` controls (`btnOK` and `btnCancel`) on the `frmOptions` form. Set the `DialogResult` property of `btnOK` to `OK`, and set the `DialogResult` property of `btnCancel` to `Cancel`. Figure 10.3 shows the design for this form.

7. Double-click the `frmOptions` form to switch to the code view. Add the following property definition in the class definition:

```
public Int32 Min
{
    get
    {
        return Int32.Parse(txtMin.Text);
    }
    set
    {
        txtMin.Text = Min.ToString();
    }
}
public Int32 Max
{
    get
    {
        return Int32.Parse(txtMax.Text);
    }
    set
    {
        txtMax.Text = Max.ToString();
    }
}
```

8. Double-click the `RandomForm` form to switch to the code view. Add the following code to declare two integer variables:

```
private int intMin;
private int intMax;
```

9. Double-click the form and attach the following code to the `Load` event handler:

```
private void RandomForm_Load(object sender,
   System.EventArgs e)
{
    intMin = 1;
    intMax = 1000;
}
```

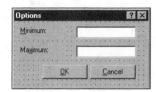

FIGURE 10.3
The Options form accepts the maximum and minimum value range to generate random numbers for the sample project.

continues

continued

10. Attach the following code to the `Click` event handler of the `mnuToolsOptions` menu item:

```
private void mnuToolsOptions_Click(object sender,
    System.EventArgs e)
{
    frmOptions f = new frmOptions();
    f.Min = intMin;
    f.Max = intMax;
    f.ShowDialog();
    if(f.DialogResult == DialogResult.OK)
    {
        intMin = f.Min;
        intMax = f.Max;
        lblRange.Text =
            "Generate a random number between "
            + intMin.ToString() + " and " +
            intMax.ToString();
    }
}
```

11. Attach the following code to the `Click` event handler of the `btnGetRandom` control:

```
private void btnGetRandom_Click(object sender,
    System.EventArgs e)
{
    Random r = new Random();
    txtRandom.Text = r.Next(
        intMin, intMax).ToString();
}
```

12. Insert the `Main()` method to launch the `RandomForm` form. Set the `RandomForm` form as the startup object for the project.

13. Run the project. Click the `Button` control to get a random number. Select Tools, Options to open the Options form. Adjust the minimum and maximum and click OK. Verify that random numbers appear in the new range.

For the simple application created in Step by Step 10.2, you need to create three help topics:

◆ An introductory topic that explains the purpose and use of the application

◆ A topic that can be invoked from the main `RandomForm` form that explains how to generate random numbers

◆ A topic that can be invoked from the `frmOptions` form that explains how to set the program options

Step by Step 10.3 shows how to use HTML Help Workshop to create these topics.

STEP BY STEP

10.3 Creating Help Topics in HTML Help 1.3

1. In HTML Help Workshop, select File, New or click the New button on the toolbar. Select HTML File in the New dialog box and click OK.

2. Set the title of the new file to `Welcome to Random` and click OK. The new file opens in the HTML Help Workshop workspace, as shown in Figure 10.4.

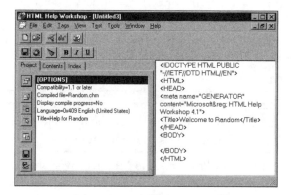

FIGURE 10.4
You can create an HTML Help topic with the aid of HTML Help Workshop.

3. Modify the HTML file so it looks like this:

```
<!DOCTYPE HTML PUBLIC "-//IETF//DTD HTML//EN">
<HTML>
<HEAD>
<meta name="GENERATOR" content="Microsoft&reg;
   HTML Help Workshop 4.1">
<Title>Welcome to Random</Title>
</HEAD>
```

continues

continued

> **EXAM TIP**
>
> **Creating HTML Help Topics**   HTML Help topics are simply standard HTML files. If you don't feel comfortable writing raw HTML, you can create these files with any HTML authoring tool you like, such as Microsoft FrontPage. Then, just cut and paste the HTML into HTML Help Workshop.

```
<BODY>
<h1>Welcome to the Random Server</h1>
<p>The Random Server application is designed to serve
all of your integer randomnumber needs. Just run the
program and click to get as many random numbers as you
would like. The numbers can be in any range you like.
Randomness guaranteed or your money back
(this application is 100% free)!</p></BODY>
</HTML>
```

4. Select File, Save File and save the file as `Welcome.htm`.

5. Add a second new HTML file. Give this file the title `Generating Random Numbers`. Modify its text as follows:

```
<!DOCTYPE HTML PUBLIC "-//IETF//DTD HTML//EN">
<HTML>
<HEAD>
<meta name="GENERATOR" content="Microsoft&reg;
    HTML Help Workshop 4.1">
<Title>Generating Random Numbers</Title>
</HEAD>
<BODY>
<h1>Generating Random Numbers</h1>
<p><img src="Main.jpg"></p>
<p>This is the main form of the Random Number Server.
Click the button to generate a random number in the
specified range. If you'd like to change the range,
select Tools, Options to open the Options dialog box.
</p>
</BODY>
</HTML>
```

6. Run the `RandomServer` project so that you can capture an image of the main form. Click the button on the form so that the form displays a random number.

7. Select Start, Programs, HTML Help Workshop, HTML Image Editor to launch the HTML Image Editor.

8. Select Capture, Using the Mouse in the HTML Image Editor window. HTML Image Editor is minimized. Move the mouse pointer over the main `RandomForm` form and click the primary mouse button.

9. Select File, Save As. Save the captured image as `Main.jpg`. Accept the defaults in the JPG Image Options dialog box.

10. Save the HTML file as `Main.htm`.

11. Add a third new HTML file. Give this file the title `Setting Options`. Modify its text as follows:

```
<!DOCTYPE HTML PUBLIC "-//IETF//DTD HTML//EN">
<HTML>
<HEAD>
<meta name="GENERATOR" content="Microsoft&reg;
    HTML Help Workshop 4.1">
<Title>Setting Options</Title>
</HEAD>
<BODY>
<h1>Setting Options</h1>
<p><img src="Options.jpg"></p>
<p>This is the options form of the Random Number
server. Enter the minimum and maximum values you would
like to set for random numbers and click OK. You can
also click Cancel to keep the settings unchanged.
</p></BODY>
</HTML>
```

12. Display the options dialog box and capture it as `Options.jpg`.

13. Save the third HTML page as `Options.htm`.

At this point, you have created all the content you need for the help file for the help application. But there are still tasks to perform before the help file is ready for use. The next step is to add links between topics.

Working with Links in HTML Help 1.3

One of the most important features of HTML is its support for hyperlinks. This is as true in an HTML Help file as it is on the World Wide Web. When the user presses F1 to display help, your job is to display the help topic that is most likely to apply to the user's current situation. But you need to also provide ways to quickly navigate to other topics, just in case your best guess was wrong. Step by Step 10.4 describes how to create links between topics in an HTML Help file, as well as how to insert a link to an external Web site.

STEP BY STEP

10.4 Inserting Links in HTML Help 1.3

1. In HTML Help Workshop, select the `Welcome.htm` file. Add two links to the bottom of this file by inserting the following text just before the `</BODY>` tag:

```
<p><a href="main.htm">
   Generating Random Numbers</a></p>
<p><a href="options.htm">Setting Options</a></p>
```

2. Add two links to the bottom of the `Main.htm` file by inserting this text just before the `</BODY>` tag:

```
<p><a href="http://random.mat.sbg.ac.at/">
About random numbers</a></p>
<p><a href="options.htm">Setting Options</a></p>
```

> **NOTE**
>
> **Special Link Types** HTML Help supports several special link types, including a keyword link for finding topics on a particular keyword and an associative link for grouping related topics. Refer to the HTML Help SDK documentation for more information on these links.

As you can see from Step by Step 10.4, there isn't a lot to know about inserting links. Links in an HTML Help file use the same tags as links in any other HTML file. You can link to local files by using their names as the link targets or to external Web sites by including their complete uniform resource locators (URLs).

Creating a Table of Contents and an Index in HTML Help 1.3

Two features that most professional help files should have are a table of contents and an index.

STEP BY STEP

10.5 Creating a Table of Contents and an Index in HTML Help 1.3

1. In HTML Help Workshop, select File, New. In the New dialog box, select Table of Contents and click OK. The Table of Contents editor window opens in the HTML Help Workshop workspace.

2. Save the Table of Contents file as `Table of Contents.hhc`.

3. Click the Options button on the Project tab of HTML Help Workshop. On the General tab, set the default file to `Welcome.htm`. On the Files tab, set the contents file to the `Table of Contents.hhc` file you just created. Click OK.

4. Select Edit, Insert Topic. On the Entry tab of the Table of Contents Entry dialog box, set the entry title to `Welcome`. Click the Add button. In the Path or URL dialog box, select the `Random.hhp` project file. Click the Browse button and browse to the `Welcome.htm` file. Click OK to add this file to the Welcome table of contents entry. Figure 10.5 shows the Table of Contents Entry dialog box at this point. Click OK to create the entry.

5. With the `Welcome.htm` file selected in the Table of Contents editor window, select Edit, Insert Heading. Click No in answer to the prompt asking if you would like to insert the new topic at the beginning of the table of contents. Set the entry title to Help Topics and click OK.

6. With the Help Topics folder selected in the Table of Contents editor window, select Edit, Insert Topic. On the Entry tab of the Table of Contents Entry dialog box, set the entry title to `Generating Random Numbers`. Click the Add button. In the Path or URL dialog box, select the `Random.hhp` project file. Click the Browse button and browse to the `Main.htm` file. Click OK to add this file to the Welcome table of contents entry. Click OK to create the entry.

7. With the Generating Random Numbers entry selected in the Table of Contents editor window, select Edit, Insert Topic. On the Entry tab of the Table of Contents Entry dialog box, set the entry title to `Setting Options`. Click the Add button. In the Path or URL dialog box, select the `Random.hhp` project file. Click the Browse button and browse to the `Options.htm` file. Click OK to add this file to the Welcome table of contents entry. Click OK to create the entry. Figure 10.6 shows the completed table of contents in the Table of Contents editor. Click the Save button to save the table of contents.

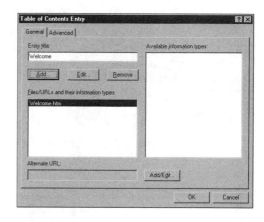

FIGURE 10.5

The Table of Contents Entry dialog box provides a convenient way to create a new table of contents entry in HTML Help 1.3.

continues

continued

FIGURE 10.6
The Table of Contents editor helps you organize table of contents entries in HTML Help 1.3.

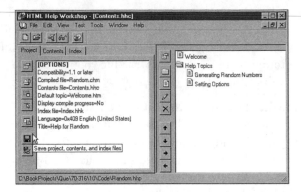

8. In HTML Help Workshop, select File, New. In the New dialog box, select Index and click OK. The Index editor window opens in the HTML Help Workshop workspace.

9. Save the Index file as Index.hhk.

10. Select Edit, Insert Keyword. Enter the keyword Random and click the Add button. In the Path or URL dialog box, select the Random.hhp project file. Click the Browse button and browse to the Main.htm file. Set the title to Generating Random Numbers. Click OK to add this file to the Random index entry. Click the Add button again and add the Options.htm file to this keyword as well. Click OK to create the entry.

11. Select Edit, Insert Keyword. Enter the keyword Options and click the Add button. In the Path or URL dialog box, select the Random.hhp project file. Click the Browse button and browse to the Options.htm file. Set the title to Setting Options. Click OK to add this file to the Options index entry. Click OK to create the entry.

12. Click the Options button on the Project tab of HTML Help Workshop. On the Files tab, set the index file to the Index.hhk file you just created. Click OK.

A help file for a large application might contain hundreds of table of contents and index entries, and they are all created by using the process outlined in Step by Step 10.5. The table of contents provides a structured way for the user to view the contents of the help file. The index provides a quick way for the user to search for specific information.

Compiling and Testing a Help File in HTML Help 1.3

Now you are ready to build a help file and try it out. The help file is compiled into a single .chm file. That's the subject of Step by Step 10.6.

STEP BY STEP

10.6 Compiling and Testing a Help File in HTML Help 1.3

1. In HTML Help Workshop, save and close all the source files for the HTML Help file.

2. Select File, Compile. In the Create a Compiled File dialog box, select the appropriate check boxes to save files or to display the finished help file when the compilation step is completed. Assign a name to the completed file and click Compile.

3. HTML Help Workshop displays a log of compile actions, as shown in Figure 10.7.

4. Click the View Compiled File button on the toolbar. Browse to the HTML Help file that you just created and click View. The newly created help file opens in the HTML Help viewer, as shown in Figure 10.8. You should be able to manipulate it just like any other help file.

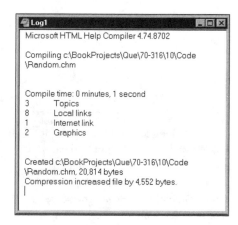

FIGURE 10.7

When you compile an HTML help file, it creates a single .chm file that contains all the contents of the Help file.

FIGURE 10.8
The compiled Help file shows the table of contents, index, and the topic files.

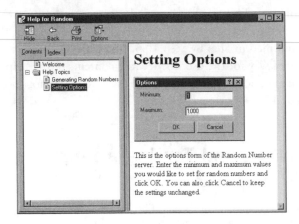

In a typical organization, three different groups work with help files while an application is being built:

◆ User assistance specialists create the help file.

◆ Developers hook up the help file with the user interface (see the section "Implementing User Assistance," later in this chapter).

◆ Testers check the work of the other two groups.

The goal of testing a help file is to make sure it will effectively deliver assistance to users. Here are some things the testers should check:

◆ Does the HTML Help file compile with no error messages?

◆ Does the Help menu item in the application open the correct help file to the correct topic?

◆ Does pressing F1 within the application bring up the correct context-sensitive help?

◆ Do all links go to the proper location?

◆ Do all entries in the table of contents load the proper topics?

◆ Do all index entries open the proper topics?

◆ Is the formatting consistent throughout the help file?

◆ Are the spelling and grammar of information in the help file correct?

◆ Is the information in the help file clear, complete, and accurate?

NOTE

Other Choices for Creating Help I use HTML Help Workshop to build a help file in this section because it is the help file solution that ships with Visual Studio .NET. However, you can use a wide variety of other programs to create help files. These range from shareware programs such as FAR (www.mvps.org/htmlhelpcenter/far.htm) to full-featured commercial programs such as RoboHelp (www.ehelp.com). If you're involved in creating help files as an ongoing activity, you should evaluate these and other alternatives.

▶ Visual Studio .NET includes the HTML Help 1.3 SDK for the creation of HTML Help files.

▶ HTML Help files are composed of multiple HTML source files, compiled into a single .chm file.

▶ You can create HTML Help topics with any HTML authoring tool. HTML Help Workshop provides a convenient way to organize help projects.

▶ HTML Help files can include navigation aids such as a table of contents and an index.

CREATING HELP PROJECT USING HTML HELP 2

The latest standard for HTML Help is HTML Help 2. Currently, you can obtain HTML Help 2 tools as part of the Visual Studio .NET Help Integration Kit (VSHIK). The VSHIK is designed to build help files that are integrated into the Visual Studio .NET shell, but you can also use it to build standalone HTML Help 2 files for your own components. Figure 10.9 shows a typical HTML Help 2 file (in this case, a part of the help for the VSHIK itself).

NOTE

Obtaining the VSHIK   You can download the VSHIK from the MSDN Web site. The VSHIK home page is located at msdn.microsoft.com/library/default.asp?url=/library/en-us/htmlhelp/html/hwmscExtendingNETHelp.asp.

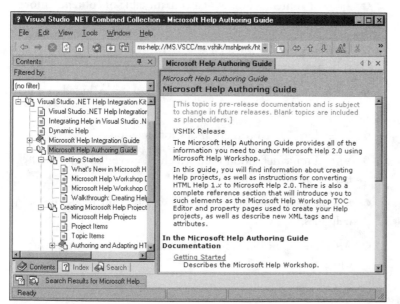

FIGURE 10.9
The help file for VSHIK is an HTML Help 2 file.

The VSHIK includes a number of components:

◆ Microsoft Help Workshop, which is a set of tools for developing HTML Help 2 files. As you'll see in the next few sections of this chapter, these tools are integrated directly into the Visual Studio .NET IDE.

◆ The Microsoft Help Authoring Guide, which contains help for developers of HTML Help 2 files.

◆ The Visual Studio Help Integration Guide, which contains help for integrating help files with Visual Studio .NET's own help. This guide is mainly of interest to people writing tools and add-ins for Visual Studio .NET.

◆ White papers that detail the process of integrating your own help to the Visual Studio .NET shell.

A number of files are included in a full HTML Help 2 system. These files can all be created and manipulated within Microsoft Help Workshop. The HTML Help system includes the following parts:

◆ Topic files, which are individual pieces of help written as HTML files. You can also use text files and Extensible Markup Language (XML) files as topic files.

◆ Graphics, sound, animation, and other multimedia files that can be embedded within HTML Help files.

◆ Table of contents files, which contain table of contents information.

◆ Collection definition files, which define the basic structure of your help file.

◆ Include files, which identify the topics to be included in a help file.

◆ Index files, which contain index information.

◆ Virtual topic definition files, which allow you to associate help keywords with Internet URLs.

◆ Sample definition files, which allow you to include samples in help files.

◆ Attribute definition files, which help you classify topics into categories.

Most of these files are specialized XML files. If you work with the Microsoft Help Workshop, though, you don't have to worry about the XML structure of these files. In the following sections you'll learn how to use Microsoft Help Workshop to build and test a simple HTML Help 2 file.

Creating an HTML Help 2 Project

The first step in creating an HTML Help 2 file is to create a new help project. Step by Step 10.7 guides you through this process.

STEP BY STEP

10.7 Creating an HTML Help 2 Project File

1. Install the VSHIK on a computer that already has Visual Studio .NET installed.

2. Launch Visual Studio .NET. On the Start page, click the New Project button.

3. Expand the Other Projects section of the Project Types tree view and select Help Project. Select the New Help Project template. Name the new help project Random and select a suitable location (see Figure 10.10). Click OK.

NOTE

Other Choices for Starting a New Project   You can choose to start a new HTML Help 2 project by converting an HTML Help 1.x project, decompiling an HTML Help 1.x help file, or decompiling an existing HTML Help 2 file.

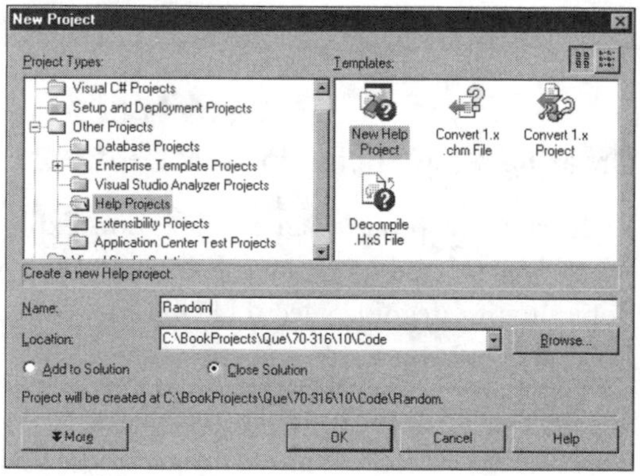

FIGURE 10.10
The New Project dialog box in Visual Studio .NET allows you to create a new HTML Help 2 project.

continues

continued

4. Microsoft Help Workshop creates a new project that includes a collection file with the extension .hxc and an index file with the extension .hxf. Right-click the project file in Solution Explorer and select Properties.

5. On the General tab of the Random Property Pages dialog box, set the title to Random Help and the version to 1.0.0.0. Click OK to save the properties.

Creating Topic Files in HTML Help 2

After you have created a help project, the next step is to populate the project with topic files. As mentioned earlier in the chapter, *topic files* are HTML pages, each of which is designed to give help to the user in a specific situation. Microsoft Help Workshop allows you to use plain-text files as topic files when you don't need the rich formatting that HTML makes possible. Topic files can also include XML data islands to define index entries and other special formatting. You'll see an example of an XML data island later in this chapter, when you create an index for your help file.

In Step by Step 10.8 you use Microsoft Help Workshop to create an HTML Help 2 version of the help topics for the Random application.

STEP BY STEP

10.8 Creating Help Topics in HTML Help 2

1. Right-click the project name in Solution Explorer and select Project, Add New Item. Select the Help Workshop Topic Items category. Select HTML File. Name the new HTML file Welcome.htm and click Open.

2. The new HTML file opens in the Visual Studio .NET workspace. You can use all of Visual Studio's editing tools to compose the HTML file visually, if you like. Alternatively, you can use the HTML tab at the bottom of the design view to switch to HTML mode and edit the source for the page directly.

3. Switch to the HTML view and modify the HTML file so it looks like this:

```
<HTML xmlns:MSHelp="http://msdn.microsoft.com/mshelp">
    <HEAD>
        <meta name="vs_targetSchema" content="HTML 4.0">
            <TITLE>Welcome to Random Server</TITLE>
    </HEAD>
    <BODY>
    <h1>Welcome to the Random Server</h1>
            <p>The Random Server application is designed
                to serve all  of your integer random number
                needs. Just run the program and click to
                get as many random numbers as you would
                like. The numbers can be in any range you
                like. Randomness guaranteed or your money
                back (this application is 100% free)!</p>
    </BODY>
</HTML>
```

4. Copy the `Main.jpg` and `Options.jpg` files that you created in Step by Step 10.3 to the folder that contains your HTML Help 2 project. Select Project, Add Existing Item and add these two graphics files to your project.

5. Add a second new HTML file. Name this file `Main.htm`. Use the Properties window to change the title of this document to `Generating Random Numbers`.

6. Click in the design window and type `Generating Random Numbers`. Select this text and use the font size drop-down list on the toolbar to change it to font size 6.

7. Drag and drop an image control from the HTML toolbox onto the page. Use the Properties window to change the source of the image to `Main.jpg`.

8. Type this help text for the topic:

```
This is the main form of the Random Number Server.
Click the button to generate a random number in the
specified range. If you'd like to change the range,
select Tools, Options to open the Options dialog box.
```

9. Add a third new HTML file. Name this file `Options.htm`. Switch to the HTML view and modify the HTML file so it looks like this:

```
<HTML xmlns:MSHelp="http://msdn.microsoft.com/mshelp">
    <HEAD>
        <meta name="vs_targetSchema" content="HTML 4.0">
            <TITLE>Setting Options</TITLE>
    </HEAD>
```

NOTE

Existing Files If you would like to add existing HTML files as topics to a help file, you can drag and drop them from Windows Explorer to Solution Explorer within Visual Studio .NET.

NOTE

Image Capture Unlike HTML Help Workshop, Microsoft Help Workshop does not include an integrated image capture application. A number of excellent programs are available for this purpose.

continues

continued

```
<BODY>
    <h1>Setting Options</h1>
    <p><img src="Options.jpg"></p>
    <p>This is the options form of the Random
        Number server. Enter the minimum and
        maximum values you would like to set for
        random numbers and click OK. You can also
        click Cancel to keep the settings
        unchanged.</p>
</BODY>
</HTML>
```

At this point, you have created all the content that you need for the help file for this application. As you can see, Microsoft Help Workshop offers great flexibility in creating help content. But there are still tasks to perform before the help file is ready to be used. The next step is to add links between topics.

Working with Links in HTML Help 2

As in HTML Help 1.3, you can have links between topics in HTML Help 2. Links help users make the most of your help file. Step by Step 10.9 describes how to create links between topics in an HTML Help file, as well as how to insert a link to an external Web site.

STEP BY STEP

10.9 Inserting Links in HTML Help 2

1. In Solution Explorer, select the `Welcome.htm` file. Switch to the HTML view. Add two links to the bottom of this file by inserting the following text just before the `</BODY>` tag:

```
<p><a href="main.htm">
    Generating Random Numbers</a></p>
<p><a href="options.htm">Setting Options</a></p>
```

2. Open the `Main.htm` file. Type the text `About Random Numbers` at the bottom of this file. Highlight this text and select Insert, Hyperlink. In the Hyperlink dialog box, shown in Figure 10.11, fill in the URL `http://random.mat.sbg.ac.at`. Click OK to create the hyperlink.

3. Type the text `Setting Options` after the `About Random Numbers` hyperlink. Use the Hyperlink dialog box to link it to the `options.htm` file, using the URL `/options.htm`. (The leading slash specifies the root directory of the project.)

As you can see, there isn't a lot to know about inserting links. Links in an HTML Help file use the same tags as links in any other HTML file. You can link to local files by using their names as the link target or to external Web sites by including their complete URLs.

FIGURE 10.11
The Hyperlink dialog box provides an easy way to insert hyperlinks.

> **NOTE**
> **Special Link Types** HTML Help supports several special types of links, including a keyword link to find topics on a particular keyword and keyword links that display an entire list of related topics. Refer to the VSHIK documentation for more information on these links.

Creating a Table of Contents and an Index in HTML Help 2

Two more features that most professional help files should have are a table of contents and an index. Step by Step 10.10 helps you create these items.

STEP BY STEP

10.10 Creating a Table of Contents and an Index in HTML Help 2

1. In Microsoft Help Workshop, select Project, Add New Item. Select the Help Workshop Project Items category. Select the Table of Contents template. Name the file `Random.hxt` and click Open. The new table of contents opens in the Visual Studio design window.

2. Drag the `Welcome.htm` file from Solution Explorer and drop it on top of the Global TOC node in the table of contents.

continues

continued

> **EXAM TIP**
>
> **Table of Contents Nodes**   An HTML Help 2 table of contents must always have a Global TOC node and at least one topic node. You can't delete the default New Topic node until you have added at least one other node.

FIGURE 10.12

An HTML Help 2 table of contents must always have a Global TOC node and at least one topic node.

3. Right-click the default New Topic node and select Delete Node.

4. Use the Properties window to change the title of the new node to Welcome.

5. Right-click the Welcome node and select Add Blank Node. Name the new node Help Topics.

6. Right-click the Help Topics node and select Add Node from File. In the Select File for TOC dialog box, select the `Main.htm` file and click Open. Accept the default node title, Generating Random Numbers, which is derived from the page's `<title>` tag.

7. Right-click the Generating Random Numbers node and select Move Node Right. Note that the Help Topics node changes from a document icon to an open book icon.

8. Drag the `Options.htm` file from Solution Explorer and drop it on the Generating Random Numbers node. Accept the default title. Figure 10.12 shows the completed table of contents.

9. Select Project, Add New Item. Select the Help Workshop Project Items category. Select the Keyword Index template. Name the file `Random.hxk` and click Open. The new index opens in the Visual Studio design window. Index files are edited as raw XML.

10. Modify the `Random.hxk` so it looks like this:

```
<?xml version="1.0"?>
<!DOCTYPE HelpIndex SYSTEM
"ms-help://hx/resources/HelpIndex.DTD">

<HelpIndex DTDVersion="1.0" Name="K">
  <Keyword Term="Random">
    <Jump Url="/Main.htm" />
  </Keyword>
</HelpIndex>
```

11. Open the `Options.htm` file in the HTML view. Add the following XML data island to the page, just before the `</HEAD>` tag:

```
<xml>
  <MSHelp:Keyword Index="K" Term="Random" />
  <MSHelp:Keyword Index="K" Term="Options" />
</xml>
```

12. To set a default home page for the help file, you need to add a second index, called a named URL index. Select Project, Add New Item. Select the Help Workshop Project Items category. Select the Keyword Index template. Name the file `NamedUrlIndex.hxk` and click Open.

13. Edit the `NamedUrlIndex.hxk` file so it looks like this (the only change is in the index name):

```
<?xml version="1.0"?>
<!DOCTYPE HelpIndex SYSTEM
"ms-help://hx/resources/HelpIndex.DTD">

<HelpIndex DTDVersion="1.0" Name="NamedUrlIndex">
  <!-- Insert keywords here -->
</HelpIndex>
```

14. Open the `Welcome.htm` file in the HTML view and add this XML data island directly before the `</HEAD>` tag to specify this as the home page for the help file:

```
<xml>
  <MSHelp:Keyword Index="NamedURLIndex"
     Term="HomePage"/>
</xml>
```

NOTE

Index Types The letter K within the name of the `Random.hxk` file indicates that this particular index is a keyword index. You can also create an associative index that provides links between help topics (even across help files), or a context-sensitive help index. For details on these other index types, refer to the VSHIK documentation.

Note that there are two different ways to define the entries that appear in a keyword index. If you prefer to have all this information in one place, you can define all the keywords and the topics to which they jump directly within the XML index file. Alternatively, you can insert XML data islands within the help topics themselves. The latter method is often more convenient if you have multiple authors working on a single help file. All this information is combined into a single index by the help compiler.

A help file for a large application might contain hundreds of table of contents and index entries, and they are created by using the process outlined in Step by Step 10.10. The table of contents provides a structured way for the user to view the contents of the help file. The index provides a quick way for the user to search for specific information.

Compiling and Testing a Help File in HTML Help 2

Now you are ready to build the help file and try it out. That's the subject of Step by Step 10.11.

STEP BY STEP

10.11 Compiling and Testing a Help File in HTML Help 2

1. In Microsoft Help Workshop, save the entire source files for the HTML Help 2 file.

2. Select Build, Build Solution. The Visual Studio .NET output window displays the results of the build.

3. If there are no build errors, select Debug, Start to view the completed help file. Figure 10.13 shows the sample help file, opened in the HTML Help 2 viewer.

FIGURE 10.13
This is the user interface of a finished HTML Help 2 file.

Although the process of building the help file with the new Microsoft Help Workshop differs from that of the older HTML Help Workshop, the end result is the same: a file that is designed to provide help to the end user. Therefore, you can apply the same testing rules to HTML Help 2 files that are shown earlier in the chapter for HTML Help 1.3 files.

▶ HTML Help 2 is Microsoft's latest standard for help files.

▶ The VSHIK includes the tools that are necessary to build HTML Help 2 files, including Microsoft Help Workshop.

IMPLEMENTING USER ASSISTANCE

Building a help file is only part of providing user assistance. You also need to make the information in the help file available to users and implement the other ways in which users expect to be able to get help with an application. This section demonstrates the three main ways in which the .NET Framework enables you to provide user assistance:

◆ By using the `HelpProvider` component to show a traditional help file

◆ By using the `HelpProvider` component to provide pop-up help for a dialog box

◆ By using the `ToolTip` component to provide quick help for individual controls

Although I'm focusing on the mechanics of providing user assistance in code, you should consider this as just one facet of an overall user assistance strategy. Depending on your organization and the applications involved, user assistance may include any or all of the following:

◆ A `readme` file or other introductory material for the user to refer to even before installing the application

◆ Printed, online, or electronic documentation

◆ Email, telephone, or on-site support from a product specialist

NOTE

User Assistance with HTML Help 1.3
Because Microsoft has not yet provided a documented way to tie HTML Help 2 to Windows forms, I use the HTML Help 1.3 format help file for the remainder of this chapter.

◆ Wizards, builders, and other user interface components that are designed to guide the user through a process

Training and tutorials are also valuable complements to a well-designed help system.

Using the `HelpProvider` Component

The `HelpProvider` component is designed to provide the link between an application and a help file. Like other components that do not have runtime user interfaces, it is displayed in the component tray at design time.

STEP BY STEP

10.12 Using the `HelpProvider` Component

1. Open the `RandomServer` Visual C# .NET application.

2. Copy the `Random.chm` HTML Help file that you created in Step by Step 10.6 to the `bin\Debug` or `bin\Release` folder of the `RandomServer` project.

3. Open the `RandomForm.cs` form in the design view. Drag and drop a `HelpProvider` control onto the form. Accept the default name, `helpProvider1`.

4. Set the `HelpNamespace` property of the `HelpProvider` component to `Random.chm`.

5. Open the Properties window for the `RandomForm.cs` form. Set `HelpKeyword` on `helpProvider1` property of the form to `Main.htm`, the `HelpNavigator` on `helpProvider1` property of the form to `Topic`, and the `ShowHelp` on `helpProvider1` property of the form to `true`.

6. Double-click the Help, Contents menu item. Enter this code to handle the menu item's `Click` event:

```
private void mnuHelpContents_Click(object sender,
  System.EventArgs e)
{
    Help.ShowHelp(this, "Random.chm");
}
```

7. Open the `frmOptions.cs` form in the design view. Drag and drop a `HelpProvider` control onto the form. Accept the default name, `helpProvider1`.

8. Set the `HelpNamespace` property of the `HelpProvider` component to `Random.chm`.

9. Open the Properties window for the `frmOptions.cs` form. Set the `HelpKeyword onhelpProvider1` property of the form to `Options.htm`, the `HelpNavigator on helpProvider1` property of the form to `Topic`, and the `ShowHelp on helpProvider1` property of the form to `true`.

10. Run the project. Press F1 with the focus on the main form of the project, and then press F1 with the focus on the options form. Also try using the Help, Contents menu item from the main form.

Step by Step 10.12 uses two different objects to provide user assistance. The first, the `HelpProvider` component, works by extending other objects on a form to include help-related properties. The `HelpNamespace` property of the `HelpProvider` control itself specifies the name of the help file to use. The `HelpNavigator` and `HelpKeyword` properties then specify the exact information to show from the help file. Table 10.1 shows the possible values for the `HelpNavigator` property.

TABLE 10.1

VALUES OF THE `HelpProvider.HelpNavigator` PROPERTY

Value	*Meaning*
`AssociateIndex`	Displays the first topic listed in the index for the specified `HelpKeyword` property
`Find`	Displays the search page of the specified help file
`Index`	Displays the index for the specified help file
`KeywordIndex`	Displays the index for the specified `HelpKeyword` property
`TableOfContents`	Displays the table of contents for the specified help file
`Topic`	Displays the topic identified by the specified `HelpKeyword` property

EXAM TIP

Getting Help from a Web Page You can supply the URL for a Web page as the `HelpNamespace` property of the `HelpProvider` component. When you do, requests for help load the specified Web page into the browser, and the `HelpKeyword` property provides an anchor name to jump to on the page.

The other object used in Step by Step 10.12 is the static Help object. This object has a ShowHelp() method, which displays the contents of a specified help file, and a ShowHelpIndex() method, which displays the index of a specified help file. This object and its methods are useful when you want to open a help file to its default topic rather than to a specific topic.

Creating Pop-up Help for Dialog Boxes

For dialog boxes, pop-up help (sometimes called *what's-this help*) offers an alternative to using an external help file. Dialog boxes are meant to keep the user focused on a particular task until that task is complete. Thus, a dialog box does not allow you to move to a different form or to the help within the application. Using pop-up help allows you to show help for a dialog box without making the user switch focus to another window.

STEP BY STEP

10.13 Displaying Pop-up Help

1. Open the RandomServer Visual C# .NET application.

2. If you have not already done so, open the frmOptions.cs form in the design view. Drag and drop a HelpProvider control onto the form. Accept the default name, helpProvider1.

3. Set the HelpNamespace property of the HelpProvider component to Random.chm.

4. Set the HelpString on helpProvider1 property of txtMin to Enter the miminum random value to be generated.

5. Set the HelpString on helpProvider1 property of txtMax to Enter the maximum random value to be generated.

6. Set the HelpString on helpProvider1 property of btnOK to Set the specified values, close this form, and return to the main form.

> **EXAM TIP**
>
> **Displaying the Help Button** To display a help button on a form, you must set the form's HelpButton property to true, its MinButton property to false, and its MaxButton property to false.

7. Set the `HelpString on helpProvider1` property of `btnCancel` to `Return to the main form without making any changes.`

8. Run the project. Select Tools, Options to open the Options dialog box. Click the Help button in the form's caption bar, and then click any control. The specified help string is displayed, as shown in Figure 10.14.

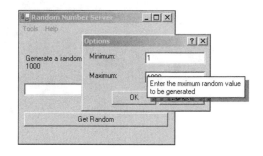

FIGURE 10.14
You can display pop-up help to provide help without switching the focus to any other window.

Using the `ToolTip` Component

The third method to display user assistance on forms is to use ToolTips. *ToolTips* are short help strings that are displayed in a pop-up window when the user hovers the mouse over a particular control. An example of using ToolTips is provided in Exercise 2.1 in Chapter 2, "Controls." In Step by Step 10.14 you use the `ToolTip` component to add ToolTips to the `RandomServer` main form.

STEP BY STEP

10.14 Displaying ToolTips

1. Open the `RandomServer` Visual C# .NET application.

2. Drag a `ToolTip` component from the toolbox and drop it onto the `RandomForm.cs` form. Accept the default name, `toolTip1`.

3. Set the `ToolTip on toolTip1` property of the `btnGetRandom` button to `Click here for a random number.`

4. Set the `ToolTip on toolTip1` property of the `txtRandom` text box to `Your a random number.`

5. Run the project. Hover your mouse over the `btnGetRandom` and `txtRandom` controls to see the ToolTips. Note that there is a longer delay to display the first ToolTip than there is to switch to a second ToolTip.

> **EXAM TIP**
>
> **Avoiding Conflicts** Generally, you should not use ToolTips and pop-up help on the same control. Having two different pieces of assistance in the same interface tends to confuse users.

You can set four properties on the `ToolTip` component to control the timing of ToolTips displays:

◆ **`InitialDisplay`**—Specifies the time (in milliseconds) before the initial ToolTip is displayed.

◆ **`AutoPopDelay`**—Specifies the time (in milliseconds) that a ToolTip remains visible.

◆ **`ReshowDelay`**—Specifies the time (in milliseconds) before subsequent ToolTips are displayed as the mouse pointer moves between controls.

◆ **`AutomaticDelay`**—Specifies a single value that is used to set the `InitialDisplay`, `AutoPopDelay`, and `ReshowDelay` properties. If you set `AutomaticDelay`, then `InitialDelay` is set equal to `AutomaticDelay`, `AutoPopDelay` is set to 10 times `AutomaticDelay`, and `ReshowDelay` is set to one-fifth of `AutoDelay`.

R E V I E W   B R E A K

▶ The `HelpProvider` component is the bridge between a .NET Framework application and an HTML Help file.

▶ You can use the `HelpProvider` component to display topics from a help file, Web pages, or pop-up help strings.

▶ Pop-up help is appropriate for dialog boxes, where you don't want the users to switch focus to another task.

▶ ToolTips let you provide quick help for individual controls.

IMPLEMENTING ACCESSIBILITY FEATURES

Implement accessibility features.

According to Microsoft, more than 30 million people in the United States alone have disabilities that can affect their ability to use computer hardware and software. Although software developers have long ignored this issue, modern software design takes accessibility strongly into account. From both ethical and economic standpoints, as well as to comply with the law, designing software for accessibility simply makes sense.

In fact, Microsoft has made accessibility a key feature of the Windows logo certification program, which allows applications to display the "designed for Windows" logo.

Five basic principles are related to accessible design:

◆ **Flexibility**   The user interface should be flexibile and customizable, so that users can adjust it to their own individual needs and preferences.

◆ **Choice of input methods**   Different users have different abilities and preferences when it comes to using a mouse or keyboard to perform tasks. All operations in an application should be accessible to the keyboard, and basic operations should be available via the mouse as well. In the future, voice and other types of input may also be considered.

◆ **Choice of output methods**   You should not depend on a single method of output (such as sound, color, or text) for important information.

◆ **Consistency**   Your application should be consistent with the Windows operating system and other applications to minimize difficulties in learning and using new interfaces.

◆ **Compatibility with accessibility aids**   Windows includes a number of accessibility aids such as the Magnifier (which can blow up text or graphics to larger sizes) and the On-Screen Keyboard (which enables keyboard input via the mouse). An application should not circumvent these accessibility aids.

As an example of implementing these principles, the Windows logo certification requirements include these items:

◆ An application must support the standard system size, color, font, and input settings.

◆ An application must ensure compatibility with the high-contrast display setting. With this setting, the application can use only colors from the Control Panel or colors explicitly chosen by the user.

◆ An application must provide documented keyboard access to all features.

EXAM TIP

Accessibility on the Web   You can find information on accessibility on the Microsoft Accessibility Web site. A good starting point for developers is www.microsoft.com/enable/dev.

◆ It must always be obvious to both the user and programmatically where the keyboard focus is located. This is necessary in order for the Magnifier and Narrator accessibility aids to function properly.

◆ An application must not convey information by sound alone.

In the following sections you'll learn more about accessible design guidelines and see how to implement those guidelines for a Visual C# .NET Windows application.

Understanding Accessible Design Guidelines

Table 10.2 lays out some of the important accessibility guidelines that you should consider for any application.

TABLE 10.2

ACCESSIBILITY GUIDELINES FOR APPLICATION DESIGN

Area	Guidelines
Color	Use color to enhance or highlight information, but do not use color as the sole means to convey important information. Remember that not all users can distinguish all colors.
Disks	Do not make the user insert or swap removable media such as disks or CD-ROMs during the normal operation of an application.
General user interface	The fundamental rule of accessibility is to provide a user interface that is flexible enough to accommodate the varying needs and preferences of different users.
Keyboard focus	Many accessibility aids need to identify the location of the keyboard focus in order to function properly. The .NET Framework normally takes care of this guideline for you.
Keyboard input	All applications should be accessible via keyboard input. Alternative input devices often emulate the keyboard, so if an application is available via the keyboard, it is available to these devices as well.
Layout	Every item onscreen should be identified by a label or other text. This helps users who cannot see the entire screen at one time.

Area	*Guidelines*
Mouse input	Some people can use a mouse (or a device whose interface emulates a mouse) more easily than a keyboard. An application should be available via the mouse.
Multitasking	Applications should not "hog the CPU." Excessive consumption of processor power can interfere with accessibility aids.
Size	You should follow the system metrics and allow users to resize items onscreen to accommodate their preferences.
Sound	You should use sound to enhance or highlight information, but you should not use sound as the sole means to convey important information. Hearing-impaired users or those in noisy environments may be unable to distinguish sound cues.
Timing	Timed events should be adjustable by the user, so that those with difficulty reading or reacting to information quickly can use your application.

Setting Control Properties for Accessibility

Some control properties listed in Table 10.3 are critical to implement accessibility in an application:

TABLE 10.3

CONTROL PROPERTIES FOR ACCESSIBILITY

Property	*Description*
AccessibleDescripton	Describes the control that will be reported to accessibility aids.
AccessibleName	Specifies the name of the control that will be reported to accessibility aids.
AccessibleRole	Specifies the role of the control that will be reported to accessibility aids.
BackColor, ForeColor	Specify screen colors. You should leave these properties at their default values to use the user's selected screen colors.

continues

TABLE 10.3	*continued*

CONTROL PROPERTIES FOR ACCESSIBILITY

Property	Description
BackgroundImage	Specifies background images. You should leave this property empty to help users read text on your forms.
Font.Size	Specifies the font size on the form. If the font size on a form is fixed, it should be set to at least 10 point.
TabIndex	Ensures a sensible navigation path and makes sure shortcut keys work for accessing controls such as TextBox controls.
Text	Creates shortcut keys using the ampersand character and ensures keyboard access to controls.

In Step by Step 10.15 you begin modifying the RandomServer application for accessibility.

STEP BY STEP

10.15 Setting Control Properties for Accessibility

1. Open the RandomServer Visual C# .NET application.

2. Open the RandomForm.cs form in the design view.

3. Open the Properties window for the form. Set the form's AccessibleDescription property to Random number generation form and its AccessibleName property to Random Form.

4. Select the Label control lblRange. Set its AccessibleDescription property to Range of random numbers and its AccessibleName property to Range Label.

5. Select the TextBox control txtRandom. Set its AccessibleDescription property to Returned random number and its AccessibleName property to Random Number.

6. Select the Button control btnGetRandom. Set its Text property to &Get Random, set its AccessibleDescription property to Get random number, and set its AccessibleName property to Get Random Button.

7. Open the `frmOptions` form in the design view.

8. Select the `Label` control `lblMinimum`. Set its `Text` property to `&Minimum`, set its `AccessibleDescription` property to `Minimum label`, and set its `AccessibleName` property to `Minimum label`.

9. Select the `TextBox` control `txtMinimum`. Set its `AccessibleDescription` property to `Minimum value for random numbers` and set its `AccessibleName` property to `Minimum value`.

10. Select the `Label` control `lblMaximum`. Set its `Text` property to `Ma&ximum:`, set its `AccessibleDescription` property to `Maximum label`, and set its `AccessibleName` property to `Maximum label`.

11. Select the `TextBox` control `txtMaximum`. Set its `AccessibleDescription` property to `Maximum value for random numbers` and set its `AccessibleName` property to `Maximum value`.

12. Select the `Button` control `btnOK`. Set its `Text` property to `&OK`, its `AccessibleDescription` property to `OK button`, and its `AccessibleName` property to `OK button`.

13. Select the `Button` control `btnCancel`. Set its `Text` property to `&Cancel`, its `AccessibleDescription` property to `Cancel button`, and its `AccessibleName` property to `Cancel button`.

14. Select View, Tab Order and verify that the `Label` controls directly precede the associated `TextBox` controls in the tab order.

Supporting High-Contrast Mode

The `RandomServer` application uses Windows defaults for color and font everywhere, so it's already compatible with high-contrast mode. But in some cases you might need to make changes to properties at runtime, in case the user has his or her computer set to high-contrast mode or if the user switches to that mode at runtime.

In high-contrast mode, you should do the following:

◆ Use only system colors to display controls.

◆ Add visual cues (such as boldface or special icons) to any information that is ordinarily conveyed by color.

◆ Remove any background images or patterns.

You can determine programatically whether the user is in high-contrast mode by checking the value of the Boolean `SystemInformation.HighContrast` property. Typically, you should check this property in your form's constructor and adjust control properties as necessary if the property returns `true`. You should also add an event handler for the `SystemEvents.UserPreferenceChanged` event, which is raised whenever the `HighContrast` property changes.

Testing Application Accessibility

Before you ship an application, you should test the accessibility features. These are some tests you should perform:

◆ Navigate your user interface by using only the keyboard. Make sure all functionality is accessible by using the keyboard alone.

◆ Select the Accessibility icon in the Control Panel. On the Display tab, check the High Contrast box. Ensure that all of your application's user interface is displayed properly in this mode and that any background images are removed.

◆ Launch the Magnifier by choosing Start, Programs, Accessories, Accessibility, Magnifier. Verify that the Magnifier window follows the keyboard focus as you use the keyboard and mouse to navigate through the application.

EXAM TIP

Accessibility Tools You can download other tools for testing accessibility as part of the Active Accessibility SDK, which is available at www.msdn.microsoft.com/ library/default.asp?url=/nhp/ Default.asp?contentid=28000544.

GUIDED PRACTICE
EXERCISE 10.1

The goal of this exercise is to add code to the `RandomServer` application's `RandomForm` form to properly implement high-contrast mode.

How would you create such a form?

You should try working through this problem on your own first. If you get stuck, or if you'd like to see one possible solution, follow these steps:

1. Open the RandomServer Visual C# .NET application.

2. Select the RandomForm.cs form, Switch to the code view and add this procedure:

```
private void AdjustBackground()
{
    if(SystemInformation.HighContrast)
        this.BackColor = SystemColors.Window;
    else
        this.BackColor = Color.Red;
}
```

3. Add an event handler for the
Microsoft.Win32.SystemEvents.UserPreferenceChanged event:

```
public void SystemEvents_UserPreferenceChanged(
    object sender,
    Microsoft.Win32.UserPreferenceChangedEventArgs e)
{
    AdjustBackground();
}
```

4. Modify the form's constructor to call the AdjustBackground procedure and the attach the
SystemEvents_UserPreferenceChanged event handler to the
UserPreferenceChanged event:

```
public RandomForm()
{
    //
    // Required for Windows Form Designer support
    //
    InitializeComponent();
    //
    // TODO: Add any constructor code after
    // InitializeComponent call
    //
    AdjustBackground();
    Microsoft.Win32.SystemEvents.UserPreferenceChanged
        += new
    Microsoft.Win32.UserPreferenceChangedEventHandler(
      SystemEvents_UserPreferenceChanged);
}
```

continues

continued

5. Modify the form's `Dispose()` method to detach the
   `SystemEvents_UserPreferenceChanged` event handler from the
   `UserPreferenceChanged` event:

```
protected override void Dispose( bool disposing )
{
    if( disposing )
    {
        if(components != null)
        {
            components.Dispose();
        }
    }
    Microsoft.Win32.SystemEvents.UserPreferenceChanged
        -=  new
    Microsoft.Win32.UserPreferenceChangedEventHandler(
        SystemEvents_UserPreferenceChanged);

    base.Dispose( disposing );
}
```

6. Run the project. The form should show up with a red background. Select the Accessibility icon in the Control Panel. On
   the Display tab, check the High Contrast box. The form
   should change, using the system background color.

If you have difficulty following this exercise, review the section
"Supporting High-Contrast Mode," earlier in this chapter. After
doing that review, try this exercise again.

CHAPTER SUMMARY

User assistance and accessibility are important parts of an application. Just having code that performs properly isn't enough. You must also help the user understand how to use your application effectively and accommodate users who have disabilities that affect their use of software and hardware.

One of the components of Visual Studio .NET is the HTML Help SDK. This SDK, which includes HTML Help Workshop and other tools, helps you build HTML Help files for your applications. HTML Help is Microsoft's standard for constructing help files, and it should be familiar to any Windows user.

HTML Help files are created from individual HTML files that represent help topics, as well as other files that represent such items as the table of contents or the index of the HTML Help file. HTML Help Workshop includes editors for these items as well as a compiler to build the HTML Help file from its component parts.

Windows forms offer several ways to display user assistance text. You can use the `HelpProvider` component to display a particular topic from an HTML Help file or the `Help` object to display the default page from a help file. The `HelpProvider` component also supports the creation of pop-up help for dialog box controls. Finally, the `ToolTip` component can display a short piece of help text related to a particular control.

Accessibility guidelines dictate the design of an application in certain areas. You must be prepared to handle either keyboard or mouse input, accessibility aids, different color schemes, and users who may not be able to process information provided in various ways. Visual Studio .NET offers excellent support for accessibility programming.

KEY TERMS

- accessibility
- HTML Help
- pop-up help
- user assistance

APPLY YOUR KNOWLEDGE

Exercises

10.1 Using a Web Page for User Assistance

Sometimes an application is so small or simple that it doesn't make sense to build an entire HTML Help file to provide user assistance. In such a case, you can use a simple Web page instead.

In this exercise, you'll learn how to use Web pages to provide user assistance.

Estimated time: 15 minutes

1. Open a Visual C# .NET Windows application in the Visual Studio .NET IDE. Add a new form to the application.

2. Add a GroupBox control, two RadioButton controls (rbLongDate and rbShortDate), a Label control (lblDate), and a Button control (btnUpdate) to the form. Figure 10.15 shows the design for this form.

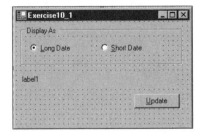

FIGURE 10.15
You can display a Web page as help for a Windows form.

3. Double-click the form, the RadioButton controls, and the Button control to add default event handlers. Add the following code to handle the events:

```csharp
private void UpdateDate()
{
    if (rbLongDate.Checked)
        lblDate.Text =
            DateTime.Now.ToLongDateString();
    else
        lblDate.Text =
            DateTime.Now.ToShortDateString();
}

private void Exercise10_1_Load(
    object sender, System.EventArgs e)
{
    UpdateDate();
}

private void rbLongDate_CheckedChanged(
    object sender, System.EventArgs e)
{
    UpdateDate();
}

private void rbShortDate_CheckedChanged(
    object sender, System.EventArgs e)
{
    UpdateDate();
}

private void btnUpdate_Click(
    object sender, System.EventArgs e)
{
    UpdateData();
}
```

4. Add a new HTML file to your project. Name the new file Exercise10_1.htm.

5. Switch to the HTML view and enter the following HTML for this page:

```html
<!DOCTYPE HTML PUBLIC
    "-//W3C//DTD HTML 4.0 Transitional//EN">
<html>
    <head>
        <title>Exercise10_1</title>
        <meta name="vs_defaultClientScript"
         content="JavaScript">
        <meta name="vs_targetSchema"
         content=
         "http://schemas.microsoft.com
        ➡/intellisense/ie5">
```

APPLY YOUR KNOWLEDGE

```html
<meta name="GENERATOR"
 content=
 "Microsoft Visual Studio.NET 7.0">
<meta name="ProgId"
    content="VisualStudio.HTML">
<meta name="Originator"
content=
 "Microsoft Visual Studio.NET 7.0">
</head>
<body>
    <h1>Welcome to the date
      display application</h1>
    <p>To use this application, just
      open the form. It will display
      the date in long date format
      by default.</p>
    <p>You can switch between long date
      and short date format by
      selecting the appropriate radio
      button.</p>
    <h2>Updating</h2>
    <p>If you leave the application
      running past midnight, you can
      click the Update button to
      update the display to the
      current date.</p>
</body>
</html>
```

6. Place a `HelpProvider` component on the form. Set the `HelpNamespace` property of the `HelpProvider` component to `..\..\Exercise10-1.htm`.

7. Set the `ShowHelp on helpProvider1` property of the form to `true`.

8. Insert the `Main()` method to launch the form. Set the form as the startup object for the project.

9. Run the project. Press the F1 key. The HTML file appears in a new browser window.

In addition to being useful for very short help files, this technique is also useful when the user assistance content changes rapidly. For example, you might have an application that periodically downloads updates from the Internet.

Rather than download a new help file every time, you might choose to keep the user assistance on the Internet as a Web site and have a `HelpProvider` component open pages from that Web site.

10.2 Augmenting Sound with the FlashWindowEx API Call

As mentioned earlier in this chapter, when you are providing accessibility in an application, you should not depend solely on sound to convey information. This exercise shows you how you can use the `FlashWindowEx` API call to notify the user visually.

Estimated time: 15 minutes

1. Add a new form to your Visual C# .NET application.

2. Add two `Label` controls, a `TextBox` control (`txtNumber`), and a `Button` control (`btnTest`) to the form. Name the blank `Label` control `lblResults`. Figure 10.16 shows the design for this form.

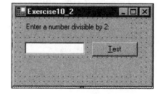

FIGURE 10.16
You can use the FlashWindowEx Windows API call to provide accessibility features on a Windows form.

3. Add the following using directive in the code view:

```csharp
using System.Runtime.InteropServices;
```

APPLY YOUR KNOWLEDGE

4. Double-click the `Button` control and add the following code in the code view:

```
[DllImport("kernel32.dll")]
public static extern bool Beep(
    int Frequency, int Duration);
private void btnTest_Click(object sender,
    System.EventArgs e)
{
    if (Int32.Parse(txtNumber.Text) % 2
      == 0)
    {
        lblResults.Text = "OK!";
    }
    else
    {
        lblResults.Text = "";
        Beep();
    }
}
```

5. Insert the `Main()` method to launch the form. Set the form as the startup object for the project.

6. Run the project. Enter some numbers and click the Test button. Note that for even numbers you get a message on the form, but for odd numbers the only feedback is the computer's beep.

7. Stop the project. Add the following code in the class definition:

```
// Structure used by FlashWindowEx
public struct FLASHWINFO
{
    // Size of the structure
    public Int32 cbSize;
    // Handle of the window to flash
    public IntPtr hwnd;
    // One of the FLASHW flags
    public Int32 dwFlags;
    // Number of times to flash
    public Int32 uCount;
    public Int32 dwTimeout;
    // Time of each flash, zero for default
}

// FlashWindowEx constants
// Stop flashing
public readonly int FLASHW_STOP = 0;
```

```
// Flash the window caption
public readonly int FLASHW_CAPTION = 1;
// Flash the taskbar button
public readonly int FLASHW_TRAY = 2;
// Flash the caption and the taskbar button
public readonly int FLASHW_ALL = 3;
// Flash continuously until
// called again with FLASHW_STOP
public readonly int FLASHW_TIMER = 4;
// Flash continuously until window is
// called to the foreground
public readonly int FLASHW_TIMERNOFG = 12;

[DllImport("user32.dll")]
public static extern int FlashWindowEx(
ref FLASHWINFO pwfi);
```

8. Modify the code of the button event handler to call the `FlashWindowEx` API:

```
private void btnTest_Click(object sender,
    System.EventArgs e)
{
    if (Int32.Parse(txtNumber.Text) % 2
      == 0)
    {
        lblResults.Text = "OK!";
    }
    else
    {
        lblResults.Text = "";
        Beep(200, 250);

        FLASHWINFO pwfi = new FLASHWINFO();
        pwfi.cbSize = Marshal.SizeOf(pwfi);
        pwfi.hwnd = this.Handle;
        pwfi.dwFlags = FLASHW_ALL;
        pwfi.uCount = 3;
        pwfi.dwTimeout = 0;
        Int32 intRet =
            FlashWindowEx(ref pwfi);
    }
}
```

9. Run the project. Enter some numbers and click the Test button. Note that for even numbers you get a message on the form and for odd numbers you get a beep and a flashing caption and taskbar button.

APPLY YOUR KNOWLEDGE

Review Questions

1. What methods can you use to provide user assistance within a .NET Windows application?

2. What help file formats can the `HelpProvider` component use?

3. What is the standard help file format for .NET applications?

4. Name some of the parts of an HTML Help system.

5. Name some areas you should test in a help file.

6. What tools can you use to create HTML Help topics?

7. Name two uses for the `HelpProvider` component.

8. What is the purpose of pop-up help?

9. Name the five basic principles of accessible design.

10. Name some of the Windows logo certification program accessibility requirements.

Exam Questions

1. You have created an HTML Help file for an application and placed it in the same folder as the application's executable file. You have placed a `HelpProvider` component on the application's main form and set the `HelpNamespace` property of the `HelpProvider` component to refer to the HTML Help file. When you run the application and press F1, the HTML Help file displays its default topic. What must you do to display a specific topic related to the main form?

   A. Set the `Name` property of the main form to the name of the help topic (`.htm`) file.

   B. Set the `Text` property of the main form to the name of the help topic (`.htm`) file.

   C. Set the `HelpKeyword` property of the main form to the name of the help topic (`.htm`) file.

   D. Set the `HelpString` property of the main form to the name of the help topic (`.htm`) file.

2. You want to display pop-up help for controls on a dialog box form. How should you set the properties of the form?

   A. Set `FormBorderStyle` to `FixedDialog` and `HelpButton` to `true`.

   B. Set `MaximizeBox` to `false`, `MinimizeBox` to `false`, and `HelpButton` to `true`.

   C. Set `MaximizeBox` to `true`, `MinimizeBox` to `true`, and `HelpButton` to `true`.

   D. Set `ControlBox` to `true` and `HelpButton` to `true`.

3. Your form contains a menu item named `mnuHelpContents`. You want to use this menu item to display the contents page of a help file named `MyApp.chm`. Which code snippet should you use for this purpose?

   A.
```
private void mnuHelpContents_Click(
  object sender, System.EventArgs e)
{
    helpProvider1.HelpNamespace =
        "MyApp.chm";
}
```

APPLY YOUR KNOWLEDGE

B.

```csharp
private void mnuHelpContents_Click(
    object sender, System.EventArgs e)
{
    helpProvider1.SetHelpNavigator(
        "MyApp.chm");
}
```

C.

```csharp
private void mnuHelpContents_Click(
    object sender, System.EventArgs e)
{
    Help.ShowHelp(this, "MyApp.chm");
}
```

D.

```csharp
private void mnuHelpContents_Click(
    object sender, System.EventArgs e)
{
    Help.ShowHelpIndex(this, "MyApp.chm");
}
```

4. You have created a dialog box for which you wish to display pop-up help. You have set the form properties so that the Help button appears and placed a `HelpProvider` component on the form. For the OK button on the form, you have set the `HelpKeyword` property to `Click here to save settings and return to the main form`.

When you click the Help button and then click the OK button, no help is displayed. What must you do to display the pop-up help?

A. Add pop-up help to every control on the form.

B. Set the `HelpNamespace` property of the `HelpProvider` control to the name of a help file.

C. Set the `ControlBox` property of the form to `false`.

D. Place the help string in the `HelpString` property instead of in the `HelpKeyword` property.

5. Your application provides users with quick help via ToolTips. Users complain that the ToolTips take too long to display. How can you fix this problem?

A. Decrease the value of the `AutoPopDelay` property.

B. Move the application to a faster computer.

C. Decrease the value of the `InitialDisplay` property.

D. Increase the value of the `AutomaticDelay` property.

6. Your application displays sales information on a form. Users complain that the application does not properly respond to the high-contrast setting on their computers. What two things must you do to accommodate this setting? (Choose the best two answers.)

A. Use only system colors on the form and its controls.

B. Remove any background images or patterns from the form.

C. Use only black and white on the form and its controls.

D. Increase the font size on the form.

7. Your application allows data entry through a form. The form uses the system default colors and fonts throughout. When the user makes a data entry mistake, the computer beeps, and the cursor remains in place. When the user saves a record, the entry colors are cleared and the cursor is returned to the first control on the form.

What should you do to make this form more accessible?

A. Prompt the user before clearing the form.

B. Set the form's `BackColor` property to `White` instead of depending on the system properties.

C. Provide audio notification of saves.

D. Provide an additional, nonaudio, means of notification for data entry errors.

8. Your application will be used by people who depend on accessibility aids such as screen readers. Which properties should you explicitly set for every control? (Choose the best two answers.)

A. `ForeColor`

B. `AccessibleName`

C. `AccessibleDescription`

D. `AccessibleRole`

9. You want your application to monitor changes to the high-contrast setting at runtime, so that it can remove a background image from a form if necessary. Which event must you trap?

A. `this.Paint`

B. `SystemEvents.PaletteChanged`

C. `this.StyleChanged`

D. `SystemEvents.UserPreferenceChanged`

10. You have created an application that displays financial information. The information displayed is retrieved from a Web service and changes frequently. How should you provide user assistance in interpreting this information?

A. Place an explanation of the information on a Web page on an Internet server and use a `HelpProvider` component to display the information.

B. Place an explanation of the information on a Web page on an Internet server and use a `ToolTip` component to display the information.

C. Place an explanation of the information in an HTML Help file and use a `HelpProvider` component to display the information.

D. Place an explanation of the information in an HTML Help file and use a `ToolTip` component to display the information.

11. You are developing a checkbook application. Currently, the application plays a music file when the checkbook is in balance. Which of these modifications would make the application more accessible? (Choose the best two answers.)

A. Add a message box that is displayed when the checkbook is in balance.

B. Allow the user to select a custom music file to play when the checkbook is in balance.

C. Allow the user to set the volume of the music played when the checkbook is in balance.

D. Use the `FlashWindowEx` API to flash the caption of the application when the checkbook is in balance.

12. You have developed a complex form that performs mathematical calculations. The instructions for using the form are quite complex, and users will need to refer to the instructions while entering information. Which type of user assistance should you supply?

A. Pop-up help

B. An HTML Help file

C. ToolTips

D. The `AccessibleDescription` property

APPLY YOUR KNOWLEDGE

13. You have created an HTML Help file for your application and compiled it with help topics. You are now ready to set the properties of controls on your form so that the proper help topics are displayed, but you can't find the `HelpKeyword` and `HelpNavigator` properties for the controls. What must you do?

    A. Place a `HelpProvider` component on the form.

    B. Place the help file in the same folder as the executable file.

    C. Place a `ToolTip` component on the form.

    D. Declare an instance of the `Help` object in the form's constructor.

14. You have created an HTML Help file for your application and connected it with a form that has a `HelpProvider` component. The `HelpString` property of the `txtFirstName` text box is set to `FirstName.htm`. When you place the cursor in that text box and press F1, the default help for the form is displayed. What is the most likely cause of the problem?

    A. The `HelpKeyword` property of the control is not set to `FirstName.htm`.

    B. The HTML Help file does not contain a topic named `FirstName.htm`.

    C. The HTML Help file is not located in the proper folder.

    D. The `HelpProvider` component has an empty `HelpNamespace` property.

15. You have developed a complex dialog box that has its own F1 help already implemented. Now you want to add pop-up help as a way for users to get quick reminders of the form's functionality.

What should you do?

    A. Set the form's properties to show the Help button and add `HelpString` properties to the controls on the form.

    B. Add a second `HelpProvider` component to the form, set the form's properties to show the Help button, and add `HelpString` properties to the controls on the form.

    C. Add a `ToolTip` component to the form, set the form's properties to show the Help button, and add `HelpString` properties to the controls on the form.

    D. You cannot have both F1 help and pop-up help on the same form.

Answers to Review Questions

1. You can use a help file, pop-up help, or ToolTips to provide user assistance within a .NET Framework application.

2. The `HelpProvider` component can use HTML Help (`.chm`) and HTML (`.htm`) files.

3. .NET applications use HTML Help as their standard help file format.

4. The parts of an HTML Help system include a help project file, topic files, multimedia files, contents files, and index files.

5. The areas to test in a help file include proper compilation, context sensitivity, validity of links in topics, the table of contents and the index, consistent formatting, spelling and grammar, and the accuracy and completeness of information.

6. You can use any tool that is capable of saving HTML to create HTML Help topics.

7. The `HelpProvider` component can be used to display F1 help or to display pop-up help.

8. Pop-up help is designed to provide help for modal dialog boxes, without requiring the user to refocus his or her attention.

9. The basic principles of accessible design are flexibility, choice of input methods, choice of output methods, consistency, and compatibility with accessibility aids.

10. The Windows logo certification program accessibility requirements include support for system size, color, font, and input settings; compatibility with the high-contrast display setting; keyboard access to all features; obvious keyboard focus; and alternatives to sound for conveying information.

Answers to Exam Questions

1. **C.** The correct property to use to connect a form or control to a particular help topic is the `HelpKeyword` property. The `HelpString` property is used only for text to be displayed as pop-up help. For more information, see the section "Implementing User Assistance" in this chapter.

2. **B.** Although the `ControlBox` property is normally set to `true` and the `FormBorderStyle` property to `FixedDialog`, for dialog box forms, these properties can be set either way without affecting the Help button. For more information, see the section "Creating Pop-up Help for Dialog Boxes" in this chapter.

3. **C.** The static `Help.ShowHelp()` method displays the contents of a help file. For more information, see the section "Implementing User Assistance" in this chapter.

4. **D.** The `HelpKeyword` property holds the topic name for a regular help topic. The `HelpString` property holds the string to display as pop-up help. For more information, see the section "Implementing User Assistance" in this chapter.

5. **C.** The time to display a ToolTip is controlled by the `InitialDelay` property, and it is independent of the speed of the computer. The `AutoPopDelay` property controls how long the ToolTip remains onscreen. Increasing the `AutomaticDelay` property makes ToolTips display more slowly rather than more quickly. For more information, see the section "Using the ToolTip Component" in this chapter.

6. **A** and **B.** The high-contrast setting is designed to aid those who need additional contrast for visibility. For more information, see the section "Supporting High-Contrast Mode" in this chapter.

7. **D.** Accessible applications should not depend on sound as the sole means of feedback. For more information, see the section "Understanding Accessible Design Guidelines" in this chapter.

8. **B** and **C.** The `AccessibleDescription` and `AccessibleName` properties provide important information for screen readers. The `AccessibleRole` property needs to be set only in special situations. The `ForeColor` property need not be set; if it's left at its default value, the user can adjust colors through the Control Panel. For more information, see the section "Setting Control Properties for Accessibility" in this chapter.

APPLY YOUR KNOWLEDGE

9. **D.** The `SystemEvents.`
   `UserPreferenceChangedevent` is triggered by
   changing the high-contrast setting. For more
   information, see the section "Supporting High-
   Contrast Mode" in this chapter.

10. **A.** Using a Web page to hold the user assistance
    for the application allows you to update the
    information frequently without installing new
    files on the client. A `HelpProvider` component is
    more suited for extensive help information than a
    `ToolTip` component. For more information, see
    the section "Implementing User Assistance" in
    this chapter.

11. **A** and **D.** To make an application that depends on
    sounds for notification more accessible, you must
    add a nonaudio means of notification. For more
    information, see the section "Understanding
    Accessible Design Guidelines" in this chapter.

12. **B.** For extensive help, an HTML Help file
    is most appropriate. The other types of user
    assistance do not remain onscreen while
    the user works with the application.

For more information, see the section
"Implementing User Assistance" in this chapter.

13. **A.** The `HelpKeyword` and `HelpNavigator` properties
    are provided to controls by the `HelpProvider`
    component. For more information, see the sec-
    tion "Using the HelpProvider Component" in
    this chapter.

14. **A.** The help file is in the right place and correctly
    connected to the `HelpProvider`; otherwise, the
    help file would not be displayed at all. For regular
    help, you must set the `HelpKeyword` property. The
    `HelpString` property is reserved for pop-up help.
    For more information, see the section
    "Implementing User Assistance" in this chapter.

15. **A.** The same `HelpProvider` control can provide
    both F1 help and pop-up help. All you need to
    do in this case is make the changes necessary to
    implement the pop-up help. For more informa-
    tion, see the section "Using the HelpProvider
    Component" in this chapter.

Suggested Readings and Resources

1. Visual Studio .NET Combined Help
   Collection:

   - "Application Assistance"

   - "HelpProvider Component"

   - "Designing Accessible Applications"

2. The Microsoft HTML Help SDK

3. The Visual Studio .NET Help Integration Kit

This chapter covers the following Microsoft-specified objectives for the "Creating User Services" section of Exam 70-316, "Developing and Implementing Windows-Based Applications with Microsoft Visual C# .NET and Microsoft Visual Studio .NET":

Implement print capability.

▶ Many applications require some sort of portable, permanent record of their activities. In some cases, this requirement can be satisfied by storing a file on disk or CD-ROM. But other applications require the use of a printer to produce a paper record. The .NET Framework handles printing support by defining the printer as a location where a Graphics object can be located and allowing you to use the methods of the Graphics object to construct the image to be printed. Printing itself is managed by an instance of the PrintDocument class.

The Visual Studio .NET IDE adds to this basic object-oriented printing scheme by defining a number of controls that you can use on a Windows form. With these controls and a minimal amount of code, you can print anything you can draw.

CHAPTER **11**

Printing

STUDY STRATEGIES

▶ Use the Object Browser tool in Visual C# .NET to drill into the System.Drawing.Printing namespace. This is the best way to learn which printer settings are under direct control via the class hierarchy.

▶ Add printing capability to one of your own applications by using the PrintDocument component.

▶ Implement PrintPreviewDialog and PageSetupDialog components in an application. Experiment with the page setup settings to understand their effect on print preview and printing.

INTRODUCTION

The Visual C# .NET method of printing is anchored by the `PrintDocument` class. This class represents a connection between an application and a printer, and it abstracts all the specific printer functions into a single set of methods and properties. All the complexities and details of printing are hidden within this class. After you learn how to manage the `PrintDocument` class, you don't need to worry at all about the details of programming any particular printer.

The `PrintDocument` class raises an event for each page to be printed. You need to write code to handle this event, which supplies the actual text or graphics to be printed. If you recall the details of drawing graphics from Chapter 1, "Introducing Windows Forms," you'll see that printing is very similar to drawing. Indeed, the classes that handle printing are contained within the `System.Drawing.Printing` namespace.

In this chapter you'll learn about printing directly from Visual C# .NET. You'll see how to use the `PrintDocument` component to print both text and graphics, and you'll learn about the additional controls that give you access to the printing-related common dialog boxes that are part of Windows.

> **NOTE**
>
> **Crystal Reports**   One thing that the exam doesn't cover is the use of Crystal Reports, the high-end reporting component that ships as a part of Visual Studio .NET. Crystal Reports is designed to allow you to put together flexible data-based reports. However, it can't handle the sort of general, low-level printing chores that I cover in this chapter.

USING THE `PrintDocument` COMPONENT

Implement print capability.

Printing in the .NET Framework is managed by the `PrintDocument` class. Typically, you create a new instance of the `PrintDocument` class, set its properties, and call its `Print()` method. Calling the method causes the `PrintDocument.PrintPage` event to occur. You determine what will be printed by adding a handler for this event. In the `PrintPage` event, you can retrieve and manipulate a `Graphics` object that lets you treat the next page to be printed as a canvas to draw on. By using the methods of the `Graphics` class, as well as associated objects (such as the `Font` or `Brush` objects), you can determine what to print.

The following sections explain how you can use this printing scheme to print both text and graphics. They also discuss the other events that are fired by the PrintDocument object that allow you to perform initialization and cleanup tasks.

Printing Text

To the .NET Framework printing mechanism, text is just a special case of graphics. You can handle text printing by calling the DrawString() method of the Graphics class.

STEP BY STEP

11.1 Printing Text

1. Create a new Visual C# .NET Windows application. Add a form to the application.

2. Place a TextBox control and a Button control on the form. Name the TextBox control txtText and set its MultiLine property to true. Name the Button control btnPrint and set its Text property to &Print.

3. Drag a PrintDocument component from the toolbox to the form. This component has no runtime image, so it is displayed in the component tray. Set its DocumentName property to NetDocument11-1.

4. Switch to the code view and add the following using directive:

```
using System.Drawing.Printing;
```

5. Add the following code to the Button control's Click event handler to print the document:

```
private void btnPrint_Click(object sender,
    System.EventArgs e)
{
    printDocument1.Print();
}
```

6. Add an event handler for the `PrintDocument` object's `PrintPage` event and add the following code to it:

```
private void printDocument1_PrintPage(object sender,
    System.Drawing.Printing.PrintPageEventArgs e)
{
    // Create a font to print with
    Font fnt = new Font("Arial", 10,
        FontStyle.Regular, GraphicsUnit.Point);
    // Print the text
    e.Graphics.DrawString(txtText.Text, fnt,
            Brushes.Black, 0, 0);
    // And indicate that there are no more pages
    e.HasMorePages = false;
}
```

7. Insert the `Main()` method to launch the form. Set the form as the startup object for the project.

8. Run the project. Enter some text in the text box and click the Print button.

NOTE

Printer Required In order for this example (and most of the others in this chapter) to function, you need to have a default printer installed.

Step by Step 11.1 demonstrates the basic steps involved in printing in the .NET Framework:

1. Declare an instance of the `PrintDocument` class (this is what the `PrintDocument` component does when you drop it on a form, and you can confirm this by expanding the Windows Form Designer Generated Code area).

2. When you're ready to print, call the `Print()` method of the `PrintDocument` object.

3. Write code in the `PrintDocument` object's `PrintPage` event handler to perform the actual printing. Within this event, you can retrieve a `Graphics` object that represents the page that is about to be printed. Manipulating this object lets you dictate what will be printed.

4. At the end of the `PrintPage` event handler, set the `HasMorePages` property of the event arguments to indicate whether there is at least one more page to print.

Step by Step 11.1 takes the text from the `TextBox` control, including any newline characters, and draws it on the `Graphics` object by using the `DrawString()` method. It draws the string at coordinates 0,0—the upper-left corner of the drawing space.

If you have more than one string of text to print, you need to think about the location of each string. If you just use the code from Step by Step 11.1, the DrawString() method places each line at 0,0—which means that the lines will all overlap. You need to keep track of the printing position and change the coordinates in code. Step by Step 11.2 shows you how to do this.

FIGURE 11.1
You can print multiple lines of text by using the font height to calculate the vertical position where the text should be printed.

STEP BY STEP

11.2 Printing Multiple Lines of Text

1. Add a new form to your Visual C# .NET application.

2. Place a TextBox control (txtText), a Label control, a NumericUpDown control (nudCopies), a FontDialog component (fontDialog1), and two Button controls (btnSetFont and btnPrint) on the form. Figure 11.1 shows the design for this form.

3. Drag a PrintDocument component (printDocument1) from the toolbox to the form. Set its DocumentName property to NetDocument11-2.

4. Switch to the code view and add the following using directive:

```
using System.Drawing.Printing;
```

5. Add the following code to the class definition:

```
// Create a default font to print with
Font fnt = new Font("Arial", 10, FontStyle.Regular,
    GraphicsUnit.Point);
```

6. Double-click the Print and Font buttons and add the following code to their Click event handlers:

```
private void btnPrint_Click(object sender,
    System.EventArgs e)
{
    printDocument1.Print();
}
private void btnSetFont_Click(object sender,
    System.EventArgs e)
{
    // Start with the current font
    fontDialog1.Font = fnt;
```

```
    // If the user clicks OK, set a new font
    if(fontDialog1.ShowDialog() == DialogResult.OK)
    {
        fnt = fontDialog1.Font;
    }
}
```

7. Add an event handler for the `PrintDocument` object's `PrintPage` event:

```
private void printDocument1_PrintPage(object sender,
    System.Drawing.Printing.PrintPageEventArgs e)
{
    // Determine the height of the font
    float fltFontHeight = fnt.GetHeight(e.Graphics);
    // Vertical position for the next line of text
    float fltCurrentY = 0;

    for(int intI=0; intI < nudCopies.Value ; intI++)
    {
        // Print the text, using the selected font
        e.Graphics.DrawString(txtText.Text, fnt,
            Brushes.Black, 0, fltCurrentY);
        fltCurrentY += fltFontHeight;
    }
    // And indicate that there are no more pages
    e.HasMorePages = false;
}
```

8. Insert the `Main()` method to launch the form. Set the form as the startup object for the project.

9. Run the project. Enter some text in the text box and use the `NumericUpDown` control to set the number of times to print the text. Click the Set Font button to set the font of the text. Click the Print button to print the results.

Step by Step 11.2 shows how you can calculate the printed height of a font by using the `GetHeight()` method of the font. Note that this method takes a `Graphics` object as a parameter. That's because it calculates the height for the font on that particular `Graphics` object, which of course represents a particular device to which you can print.

Step by Step 11.2 works as long as all the lines fit on a single page. But what if there are more lines than will fit? In that case, you need to determine the page height and maintain the `HasMorePages` property correctly.

STEP BY STEP

11.3 Printing Multiple Pages of Text

1. Add a new form to your Visual C# .NET application.

2. Place a TextBox control (txtText), a Label control, a NumericUpDown control (nudCopies), a FontDialog control (fontDialog1), and two Button controls (btnSetFont and btnPrint) on the form. You can reuse the form design shown in Figure 11.1.

3. Drag a PrintDocument component (printDocument1) from the toolbox to the form. Set its DocumentName property to NetDocument11-3.

4. Switch to the code view and add the following using directive at the top:

```
using System.Drawing.Printing;
```

5. Add the following code to the class definition:

```
// Create a default font to print with
Font fnt = new Font("Arial", 10, FontStyle.Regular,
    GraphicsUnit.Point);
// Number of lines printed so far
Int32 intLines = 0;
```

6. Double-click the Print and Font buttons and add the following code to their Click event handlers:

```
private void btnPrint_Click(object sender,
    System.EventArgs e)
{
    intLines=0;
    printDocument1.Print();
}
private void btnSetFont_Click(object sender,
    System.EventArgs e)
{
    // Start with the current font
    fontDialog1.Font = fnt;
    // If the user clicks OK, set a new font
        if(fontDialog1.ShowDialog() == DialogResult.OK)
        {
            fnt = fontDialog1.Font;
        }
}
```

7. Add an event handler for the `PrintDocument` object's `PrintPage` event:

```csharp
private void printDocument1_PrintPage(object sender,
    System.Drawing.Printing.PrintPageEventArgs e)
{

    // Determine the height of the font
    float fltFontHeight = fnt.GetHeight(e.Graphics);
    // Vertical position for the next line of text
    float fltCurrentY = 0;
    bool pageDone = false;
    while (!pageDone)
    {
     // Check to see whether there's more
     // space on the page
        if(fltCurrentY <= e.MarginBounds.Height)
        {
            // Increment the line number
            intLines += 1;
            if(intLines <= nudCopies.Value)
            {
                // Print the text,
                // using the selected font
                e.Graphics.DrawString(txtText.Text,
                  fnt, Brushes.Black, 0, fltCurrentY);
                // Increment the vertical
                // location on the page
                fltCurrentY += fltFontHeight;
            }
            else
            {
                // We've printed all the copies
                // We need to print.
                // In this case, set the flags to
                // indicate that this page is done.
                // But there are no more pages
                pageDone = true;
                e.HasMorePages = false;
            }
        }
        else
        {
            // We want to print another line,
            // But there's no space
            pageDone = true;
            e.HasMorePages = true;
        }
    }
}
```

8. Insert the `Main()` method to launch the form. Set the form as the startup object for the project.

continues

continued

9. Run the project. Enter some text in the text box and use the NumericUpDown control to set the number of times to print the text. Click the Set Font button to set the font of the text. Click the Print button to print the results. If necessary, the code prints on multiple pages.

None of the additional complexity in the code in Step by Step 11.3 comes from the act of printing itself; it's all just the math required to manage what gets printed on each page. Table 11.1 shows all the properties of the PrintPageEventArgs object that is passed to the PrintPage event. One of these, MarginBounds provides a Rectangle structure that represents the printable area of the page, taking into account the current margins. The code checks whether each line of text would go past the bottom of this rectangle. If it would, the code stops the current PrintPage event but sets the HasMorePages property to true in order to tell the .NET Framework that there is more to print and to trigger the PrintPage event another time.

TABLE 11.1

PROPERTIES OF THE PrintPageEventArgs CLASS

Property	*Description*
Cancel	Gets or sets a value that indicates whether the print job should be canceled
Graphics	Specifies a Graphics object that represents the page to be printed
HasMorePages	Specifies a Boolean value that indicates whether there are more pages to print
MarginBounds	Specifies a Rectangle structure that represents the printable area of the page
PageBounds	Specifies a Rectangle structure that represents the entire page
PageSettings	Specifies an PageSettings object that gets or sets page settings (such as portrait or landscape orientation)

Printing Graphics

Printing graphics is very similar to printing text. The only major difference is that you use different methods of the Graphics object to print graphics.

STEP BY STEP

11.4 Printing Graphics

1. Add a new form to your Visual C# .NET application.

2. Place a Button control (btnPrintGraphics) and a PrintDocument component (printDocument1) on the form. Set the DocumentName property of the PrintDocument object to NetDocument11-4.

3. Add the following using directives in the code view:

```
using System.Drawing.Printing;
using System.Drawing.Drawing2D;
```

4. Double-click the Button control and add the following code to handle the Click event of the Button control:

```
private void btnPrintGraphics_Click(object sender,
    System.EventArgs e)
{
    printDocument1.Print();
}
```

5. Double-click the PrintComponent component and add the following code to handle the PrintPage event:

```
private void printDocument1_PrintPage(object sender,
    System.Drawing.Printing.PrintPageEventArgs e)
{
    Graphics grfx = e.Graphics;
    // Set the Smoothing mode
    // to SmoothingMode.AntiAlias
    grfx.SmoothingMode = SmoothingMode.AntiAlias;
    // Create Pen objects
    Pen penYellow = new Pen(Color.Blue, 20);
    Pen penRed = new Pen(Color.Red, 10);
    // Call Draw methods
    grfx.DrawLine(Pens.Black, 20, 130, 250, 130);
    grfx.DrawEllipse(penYellow, 20, 10, 100, 100);
    grfx.DrawRectangle(penRed, 150, 10, 100, 100);
    // No more pages to print
    e.HasMorePages = false;
}
```

continues

continued

NOTE

Device Independence The code in Step by Step 11.4 demonstrates the way GDI+ enables you to create output without worrying about the differences between various devices. If you refer to Chapter 1, you'll find that the code in Step by Step 1.17 is nearly identical to the code in Step by Step 11.4; the only difference is the addition of the setting for the HasMorePages property. Of course, if you don't have a color printer, the output is in black and white—but you don't need to handle that problem explicitly in code.

6. Insert the Main() method to launch the form. Set the form as the startup object for the project.

7. Run the project. Click the button. The form prints a rectangle, an ellipse, and a line on the page.

All the methods of the Graphics object and associated objects such as brushes and pens work just as well on the printed page as they do onscreen.

STEP BY STEP

11.5 Printing Graphics Using Different Brush Types

1. Add a new form to your Visual C# .NET application.

2. Place a Button control (btnPrintGraphics) and a PrintDocument component on the form. Set the DocumentName property of the PrintDocument object to NetDocument11-5.

3. Add the following using directives in the code view:

```
using System.Drawing.Printing;
using System.Drawing.Drawing2D;
```

4. Double-click the Button control and add the following code to handle the Click event of the Button control:

```
private void btnPrintGraphics_Click(object sender,
    System.EventArgs e)
{
    printDocument1.Print();
}
```

5. Double-click the PrintComponent component and add the following code to handle the PrintPage event:

```
private void printDocument1_PrintPage(object sender,
    System.Drawing.Printing.PrintPageEventArgs e)
{
    Graphics grfx = e.Graphics;
```

```
// Create a TextureBrush object
// Call the FillEllipse method by passing the
// created TextureBrush object
Image img = new Bitmap("sunset.jpg");
Brush tb = new TextureBrush(img);
grfx.FillEllipse(tb, 100, 20, 200, 200);

// Create a LinearGradientBrush object
// Call the FillEllipse method by passing the
// created LinearGradientBrush object
LinearGradientBrush lb = new LinearGradientBrush(
    new Rectangle(160, 300, 200, 200), Color.Red,
    Color.Yellow,
    LinearGradientMode.BackwardDiagonal);
grfx.FillEllipse(lb, 100, 300, 200, 200);

e.HasMorePages = false;
}
```

6. Insert the `Main()` method to launch the form. Set the form as the startup object for the project.

7. Run the project. Click the button. The form prints the sunset image with the `TextureBrush` object and an `Ellipse` object filled with the `LinearGradientBrush` object.

> **NOTE**
>
> **The `Graphics` Object** For more details on the `Graphics` object and the other drawing classes in the .NET Framework, refer to Chapter 1.

Printing Initialization and Cleanup

In addition to the `PrintPage` event, the `PrintDocument` class supplies three other events:

◆ The `BeginPrint` event occurs once, before the first page of the job prints.

◆ The `EndPrint` event occurs once, after the last page of the job prints.

◆ The `QueryPageSettings` event occurs immediately before each `PrintPage` event. During this event you can modify the `QueryPageSettingsEventArgs.PageSettings` property to control the page settings (for example, portrait or landscape mode) of the next page to be printed.

STEP BY STEP

11.6 Using PrintDocument Events

1. Add a new form to your Visual C# .NET application.

2. Place a TextBox control (txtText), a Label control, a NumericUpDown control (nudCopies), a FontDialog component (fontDialog1), and two Button controls (btnSetFont and btnPrint) on the form. You can reuse the form design shown in Figure 11.1.

3. Drag a PrintDocument component (printDocument1) from the toolbox to the form. Set its DocumentName property to NetDocument11-6. Drag a second PrintDocument component (printDocument2) from the toolbox to the form. Set its DocumentName property to CoverSheet.

4. Switch to the code view and add the following using directive:

```
using System.Drawing.Printing;
```

5. Add the following code to the class definition:

```
// Create a default font to print with
Font fnt = new Font("Arial", 10, FontStyle.Regular,
    GraphicsUnit.Point);
// Number of lines printed so far
Int32 intLines = 0;
// Number of pages printed so far
Int32 intPages = 0;
```

6. Double-click the Print and Font buttons and add the following code to their Click event handlers:

```
private void btnPrint_Click(object sender,
    System.EventArgs e)
{
    printDocument1.Print();
}
private void btnSetFont_Click(object sender,
    System.EventArgs e)
{
    // Start with the current font
    fontDialog1.Font = fnt;
    // If the user clicks OK, set a new font
        if(fontDialog1.ShowDialog() == DialogResult.OK)
        {
            fnt = fontDialog1.Font;
        }
}
```

7. Attach default event handlers to both of the
PrintDocument objects and add the following code to handle the PrintPage event:

```csharp
private void printDocument1_PrintPage(object sender,
    System.Drawing.Printing.PrintPageEventArgs e)
{
    // Determine the height of the font
    float fltFontHeight = fnt.GetHeight(e.Graphics);
    // Vertical position for the next line of text
    float fltCurrentY = 0;
    bool pageDone = false;
    while (!pageDone)
    {
        // Check to see whether there's more
        // space on the page
        if(fltCurrentY <= e.MarginBounds.Height)
        {
            // Increment the line number
            intLines += 1;
            if(intLines <= nudCopies.Value)
            {
                // Print the text,
                // using the selected font
                e.Graphics.DrawString(txtText.Text,
                    fnt, Brushes.Black, 0, fltCurrentY);
                // And increment the vertical location
                // on the page
                fltCurrentY += fltFontHeight;
            }
            else
            {
                // We've printed all the copies we
                // need to print. In this case, set
                // the flags to indicate that this
                // page is done, but
                // there are no more pages
                pageDone = true;
                e.HasMorePages = false;
                intPages ++;
            }
        }
        else
        {
            // We want to print another line,
            // but there's no space
            pageDone = true;
            e.HasMorePages = true;
            intPages ++;
        }
    }
}
```

continues

continued

```csharp
private void printDocument2_PrintPage(object sender,
    System.Drawing.Printing.PrintPageEventArgs e)
{
    // Print a cover sheet for the job
    // Height of a line of text
    float fltFontHeight = fnt.GetHeight(e.Graphics);
    // Print the text
    e.Graphics.DrawString("Printed at " +
        DateTime.Now.ToShortTimeString(),
        fnt, Brushes.Black, 0, 0);
    // Print some printer information
    e.Graphics.DrawString("Color: " +
        e.PageSettings.Color.ToString(),
        fnt, Brushes.Black, 0, fltFontHeight);
    e.Graphics.DrawString("Printer Name: " +
        e.PageSettings.PrinterSettings.PrinterName,
        fnt, Brushes.Black, 0, fltFontHeight * 2);
    // And indicate that there are no more pages
    e.HasMorePages = false;
    intPages++;
}
```

8. Attach `BeginPrint` and `EndPrint` event handlers to the `printDocument1` object and add the following code:

```csharp
private void printDocument1_BeginPrint(object sender,
    System.Drawing.Printing.PrintEventArgs e)
{
    intPages=0;
    intLines=0;
    // Prompt for cover sheet
    if(MessageBox.Show("Print Cover Sheet?",
      "Print Job", MessageBoxButtons.YesNo,
      MessageBoxIcon.Question) == DialogResult.Yes)
    {
        printDocument2.Print();
    }
}

private void printDocument1_EndPrint(object sender,
    System.Drawing.Printing.PrintEventArgs e)
{
    // Tell the user printing is done
    MessageBox.Show("Print job finished. Printed " +
        intPages + " page(s)");
}
```

9. Insert the `Main()` method to launch the form. Set the form as the startup object for the project.

10. Run the project. Enter some text in the text box and use the `NumericUpDown` control to set the number of times to print the text. You can click the Set Font button to set the font of the text. Click the Print button to print the results. The code prompts you about whether it should print a cover page; answer yes to get a cover page. If necessary, the code prints multiple pages. When printing is done, a message box displays the total number of pages printed.

Step by Step 11.6 builds on the code in Step by Step 11.3. The additional code in Step by Step 11.6 does two things. First, to print a cover page, it calls the `Print()` method of the second `PrintDocument` object. This code uses some of the properties of the `PageSettings` and `PrinterSettings` objects; you can find complete lists of those properties in Tables 11.2 and 11.3, respectively. Second, the code uses a class-level variable to track the number of pages that have been printed, and it displays this number after the print job is finished.

> **EXAM TIP**
>
> **Printer Capabilities** You don't need to memorize all the properties in Tables 11.2 and 11.3 for the exam, but you should have a sense of which printer settings are under the control of the .NET Framework objects.

TABLE 11.2

PROPERTIES OF THE `PageSettings` CLASS

Property	Description
Bounds	Specifies the size of the page, taking into account the page orientation
Color	Gets or sets a value that indicates whether to print in color
Landscape	Is set to `true` if the page is in landscape orientation
Margins	Gets or sets the margins for the page
PaperSize	Gets or sets the paper size for the page
PaperSource	Gets or sets the paper source for the page
PrinterResolution	Gets or sets the resolution for the page
PrinterSettings	Returns the current `PrinterSettings` object

TABLE 11.3

PROPERTIES OF THE PrinterSettings CLASS

Property	Description
CanDuplex	Is set to true if the printer supports duplex printing
Collate	Is set to true if the printer output is collated
Copies	Gets or sets the number of copies to print
DefaultPageSettings	Returns a PageSettings object for the printer
Duplex	Gets or sets the duplex setting
FromPage	Gets or sets the first page number to print
InstalledPrinters	Gets the names of all the printers on the system
IsDefaultPrinter	Indicates whether this is the default printer
IsPlotter	Indicates whether this is a plotter
IsValid	Indicates whether the PrinterName property designates a valid printer
LandscapeAngle	Specifies the number of degrees of rotation from portrait to landscape output
MaximumCopies	Specifies the maximum number of copies that you can print at once
MaximumPage	Specifies the largest page number that can be selected in a print dialog box
MinimumPage	Specifies the smallest page number that can be selected in a print dialog box
PaperSizes	Specifies the paper sizes that are supported by this printer
PaperSources	Specifies the paper sources that are supported by this printer
PrinterName	Gets or sets the name of the printer to use; you change this property to change printers
PrinterResolutions	Specifies the resolutions supported by the printer
PrintRange	Specifies the page numbers specified for printing
PrintToFile	Is set to true if output is redirected to a file
SupportsColor	Is set to true if the printer supports color
ToPage	Gets or sets the last page number to print

EXAM TIP

Read-Only Settings You can retrieve the PrinterSettings and PageSettings values for any printer, but not all printers let you set all these values. Always use a try-catch block to catch any errors when making printer settings.

GUIDED PRACTICE EXERCISE 11.1

You are required to develop a Windows form that prompts the user to enter an arbitrary SQL query. The form allows the user to print the results of the input query.

How would you design such a form?

You should try working through this problem on your own first. If you get stuck, or if you'd like to see one possible solution, follow these steps:

1. Add a new form to your Visual C# .NET application.

2. Place a `Label` control, a `TextBox` control named `txtSQL` with its `MultiLine` property set to `true`, a `Button` control named `btnPrint`, and a `PrintDocument` component (`printDocument1`) on the form. Set the `DocumentName` property of the `PrintDocument` component to `SQL Query Results`. Figure 11.2 shows a possible design for this form.

3. Switch to the code view and add the following using directives:

   ```
   using System.Data;
   using System.Data.SqlClient;
   using System.Drawing.Printing;
   ```

4. Add the following code to the class definition:

   ```
   // Create Connection and DataSet objects
   SqlConnection cnn = new SqlConnection(
       "data source=(local);initial catalog=Northwind;" +
       "integrated security=SSPI");
   DataSet ds = new DataSet();
   // Create a default font to print with
   Font fnt = new Font("Arial", 10, FontStyle.Regular,
       GraphicsUnit.Point);
   // Number of rows of data to print
   Int32 intRows=0;
   // Number of rows printed
   Int32 intRowsPrinted=0;
   ```

5. Double-click the Print button and add the following code to its `Click` event handler:

   ```
   private void btnPrint_Click(object sender,
       System.EventArgs e)
   {
       printDocument1.Print();
   }
   ```

FIGURE 11.2

This is a possible design of the form that prompts the user to enter a SQL query.

continues

continued

6. Add an event handler for the PrintDocument object's PrintPage event:

```
private void printDocument1_PrintPage(object sender,
    System.Drawing.Printing.PrintPageEventArgs e)
{
    // Determine the height of the font
    float fltFontHeight = fnt.GetHeight(e.Graphics);
    // Vertical position for the next line of text
    float fltCurrentY = 0;
    bool pageDone = false;
    while (!pageDone)
    {
        // Check to see whether there's
        // more space on the page
        if(fltCurrentY <= e.MarginBounds.Height)
        {
            // Increment the line number
            intRowsPrinted += 1;
            if(intRowsPrinted <= intRows)
            {
                // Retrieve the DataRow
                DataRow dr = ds.Tables[
                  "Results"].Rows[intRowsPrinted - 1];
                // Print a row header
                e.Graphics.DrawString("Row Number " +
                    intRowsPrinted, fnt,
                    Brushes.Black, 0, fltCurrentY);
                // Build and print a string of data
                String strPrint = "  ";
                for(int intI = 0; intI <
                    ds.Tables["Results"].Columns.Count;
                    intI++)
                {
                    DataColumn dc =
                    ds.Tables["Results"].Columns[intI];
                    strPrint = strPrint +
                        dc.ColumnName + ": " +
                        dr[intI].ToString() + " ";
                    e.Graphics.DrawString(strPrint,
                        fnt, Brushes.Black, 0,
                        fltCurrentY + fltFontHeight);
                }
                // And increment the vertical location
                // on the page
                fltCurrentY += (2 * fltFontHeight);
            }
            else
            {
```

```
                    // We've printed all the copies we
                    // need to print. In this case, set
                    // the flags to indicate that this page
                    // is done, but there are no more pages
                     pageDone = true;
                     e.HasMorePages = false;
                }
            }
            else
            {
                // We want to print another line,
                // but there's no space
                pageDone = true;
                e.HasMorePages = true;
            }
        }
    }
```

7. Attach `BeginPrint` and `EndPrint` event handlers to the `printDocument1` object and add the following code:

```
private void printDocument1_BeginPrint(object sender,
    System.Drawing.Printing.PrintEventArgs e)
{
    // Get the data to print
    SqlCommand cmd = cnn.CreateCommand();
    cmd.CommandType = CommandType.Text;
    cmd.CommandText = txtSQL.Text;
    SqlDataAdapter da = new SqlDataAdapter();
    da.SelectCommand = cmd;
    cnn.Open();
    da.Fill(ds, "Results");
    intRows = ds.Tables["Results"].Rows.Count;
    intRowsPrinted=0;
}

private void printDocument1_EndPrint(object sender,
    System.Drawing.Printing.PrintEventArgs e)
{
    // Clear the dataset
    // Close the database connection
    ds.Clear();
    cnn.Close();
}
```

8. Insert the `Main()` method to launch the form. Set the form as the startup object for the project.

9. Run the project. Enter a query such as the following for the Northwind database:

```
SELECT CustomerID, CompanyName
FROM Customers
WHERE Country = 'France'
```

continues

continued

10. Click the Print button. The results of the query are printed.

This exercise demonstrates another good use for the `BeginPrint` and `EndPrint` events: They can be used to set up and destroy database objects that retrieve the data to be printed.

If you have difficulty following this exercise, review the section "Printing Text," earlier in this chapter, and the section "Running Queries" in Chapter 6, "Consuming and Manipulating Data." After doing that review, try this exercise again.

REVIEW BREAK

▶ Printing in the .NET Framework is managed by the `PrintDocument` class. The `Print()` method of the `PrintDocument` class is used to print from a .NET Windows form.

▶ The `PrintDocument` class supports the `BeginPrint` (occurs once, before printing starts), `QueryPageSettings` (occurs before each page is printed), `PrintPage` (occurs when each page is printed), and `EndPrint` (occurs once, when printing finishes) events.

▶ The only difference between drawing on a form and drawing on a printed page is in the `Graphics` object that you use. You should retrieve a `Graphics` object from the `PrintPageEventArgs` object in the `PrintPage` event to draw on a printed page.

▶ The `PrintDocument` class raises an event for each page to be printed. You should set the `PrintPageEventArgs.HasMorePages` property to `true` within the `PrintPage` event to have the event fire again to print another page.

USING THE PRINTING CONTROLS

You could use the PageSettings and PrinterSettings classes directly
to allow the user to set such things as the orientation of the printer
or the paper tray to use. But that would require you to develop a
user interface for changing such settings. Windows includes a standard Page Setup dialog box, as well as other standard printer-related
dialog boxes. Fortunately, these dialog boxes are available directly to
Windows forms. In fact, four components can be handy when you're
dealing with printing issues:

◆ The PageSetupDialog component

◆ The PrintDialog component

◆ The PrintPreviewDialog component

◆ The PrintPreviewControl control

The remainder of this chapter describes how you can use these components to add standard Windows printing features to applications.

The PageSetupDialog, PrintDialog, and PrintPreviewDialog Components

The PageSetupDialog component displays the Windows common
Page Setup dialog box, which allows the user to set margins, paper
orientation, and other characteristics of the printer that control the
output.

The PrintDialog component allows you to give the user control over
the printer and its properties.

In the examples you've seen so far in this chapter, output has gone
directly to the printer. But of course in a real application, you often
want to provide print preview capabilities. Print preview allows users
to see the results of a print job onscreen, before using time and
paper to actually print it. This makes it much easier to adjust the job
until it's perfect, and it is a convenience that Windows users have
grown to expect.

The .NET Framework offers both a component and a control for print preview. The PrintPreviewDialog component is described first, in Step by Step 11.7.

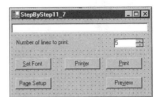

FIGURE 11.3
You can allow the user to control settings related to printing a job by displaying common print dialog boxes, using the PageSetupDialog, PrintDialog, and PrintPreviewDialog components.

STEP BY STEP

11.7 Using the PageSetupDialog, PrintDialog, and PrintPreviewDialog Components

1. Add a new form to your Visual C# .NET application.

2. Place a TextBox control (txtText), a Label control, a NumericUpDown control (nudCopies), and five Button controls (btnSetFont, btnPageSetup, btnPrinter, btnPreview, and btnPrint) on the form. Figure 11.3 shows the design for this form.

3. Drag a FontDialog component (fontDialog1), a PageSetupDialog component (pageSetupDialog1), a PrintDialog component (printDialog1), a PrintPreviewDialog component (printPreviewDialog1), and a PrintDocument component from the toolbox to the form. Set the PrintDocument object's DocumentName property to NetDocument11-7. Set the Document property of the PrintPreviewDialog component to printDocument1.

4. Switch to the code view and add the following using directive:

```
using System.Drawing.Printing;
```

5. Add the following code to the class definition:

```
// Create a default font to print with
Font fnt = new Font("Arial", 10, FontStyle.Regular,
    GraphicsUnit.Point);
// Number of lines printed so far
Int32 intLines = 0;
```

6. Double-click the Print, Font, Page Setup, Printer, and Preview buttons and add the following code to their Click event handlers:

```
private void btnPrint_Click(object sender,
    System.EventArgs e)
{
```

```
    intLines=0;
    printDocument1.Print();
}
private void btnSetFont_Click(object sender,
    System.EventArgs e)
{
    // Start with the current font
    fontDialog1.Font = fnt;
    // If the user clicks OK, set a new font
        if(fontDialog1.ShowDialog() ==
            DialogResult.OK)
        {
            fnt = fontDialog1.Font;
        }
}
private void btnPageSetup_Click(object sender,
    System.EventArgs e)
{
    // Create a PageSettings object
    // Send it to the dialog
    pageSetupDialog1.PageSettings =
            new PageSettings();
    if(pageSetupDialog1.ShowDialog() ==
            DialogResult.OK)
    {
        printDocument1.DefaultPageSettings =
            pageSetupDialog1.PageSettings;
    }
}
private void btnPrinter_Click(object sender,
    System.EventArgs e)
{
    // Create a PrinterSettings object
    // Send it to the dialog
    printDialog1.PrinterSettings =
            new PrinterSettings();
    if(printDialog1.ShowDialog() == DialogResult.OK)
    {
        printDocument1.PrinterSettings =
            printDialog1.PrinterSettings;
    }
}

private void btnPreview_Click(object sender,
    System.EventArgs e)
{
    printPreviewDialog1.ShowDialog();
}
```

---

7. Add an event handler for the PrintDocument object's PrintPage event:

```
private void printDocument1_PrintPage(object sender,
    System.Drawing.Printing.PrintPageEventArgs e)
{
```

continues

continued

```
// Determine the height of the font
float fltFontHeight = fnt.GetHeight(e.Graphics);
// Vertical position for the next line of text
float fltCurrentY = 0;
bool pageDone = false;
while (!pageDone)
{
    // Check to see whether there's
    // more space on the page
    if(fltCurrentY <= e.MarginBounds.Height)
    {
        // Increment the line number
        intLines += 1;
        if(intLines <= nudCopies.Value)
        {
            // Print the text,
            // using the selected font
            e.Graphics.DrawString(txtText.Text,
              fnt, Brushes.Black, 0, fltCurrentY);
            // And increment the vertical location
            // on the page
            fltCurrentY += fltFontHeight;
        }
        else
        {
            // We've printed all the copies we
            // need to print. In this case, set
            // the flags to indicate that this
            // page is done, but there
            // are no more pages
            pageDone = true;
            e.HasMorePages = false;
        }
    }
    else
    {
        // We want to print another line,
        // but there's no space
        pageDone = true;
        e.HasMorePages = true;
    }
}
```

> **NOTE**
>
> **Reused Code** With the exception of the `btnPageSetup_Click()`, `btnPrinter_Click()`, and `btnPreview_Click` event handlers, this is exactly the same code as in Step by Step 11.3.

8. Insert the `Main()` method to launch the form. Set the form as the startup object for the project.

9. Run the project. Enter some text in the text box and use the NumericUpDown control to set the number of times to print the text. Click the Set Font button to set the font of the text. Click the Page Setup button to see the Page Setup dialog box, shown in Figure 11.4. Click the Printer button to open the Print dialog box, as shown in Figure 11.5; click the Preview button to see the document in print preview mode, as shown in Figure 11.6; and click the Print button to print the results.

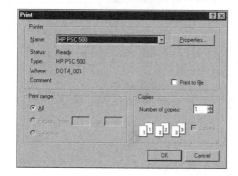

FIGURE 11.4▲
The PageSetupDialog component allows you to give the user control over setting margins, paper orientation, and other characteristics.

FIGURE 11.5◀
The PrintDialog component allows you to give the user control over the printer and its properties.

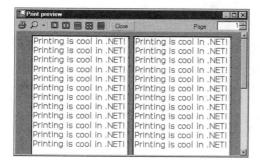

FIGURE 11.6◀
The PrintPreviewDialog component allows users to see the results of a print job onscreen.

If you inspect the code in Step by Step 11.7, you'll see that the PageSetupDialog class and the PrintDialog class are used in a similar fashion. You supply a PageSettings variable to the PageSetupDialog object and a PrinterSettings variable to the PrintDialog object, call their ShowDialog() methods, and then set the returned object's PageSettings variable and PrinterSettings variable into the DefaultPageSettings and PrinterSettings properties of the PrintDocument object, respectively.

The PageSetupDialog component has four properties that you can use to enable or disable different sections of the dialog box:

◆ **AllowMargins**—Set this to false to disable the margin settings.

◆ **AllowOrientation**—Set this to false to disable the Orientation group box of the dialog box.

◆ **AllowPaper**—Set this to false to disable the Paper group box of the dialog box.

◆ **AllowPrinter**—Set this to false to disable the Printer button in the dialog box.

Adding print preview to the code in Step by Step 11.7 takes only two lines of code: one to set the Document property of the PrintPreviewDialog object (so that it knows what it should display) and one to call the ShowDialog() method of the component. Everything else is built in to the .NET Framework and Windows itself.

The Print Preview dialog offers these features:

◆ Printing from the preview

◆ Adjustable zoom

◆ One-, two-, three-, four-, and six-page display modes

◆ The ability to scroll through all pages of the document that is being printed

If you set a breakpoint in the form's code, the code in the PrintDocument object's events is executed in preview mode as well as in print mode.

The **PrintPreviewControl** Control

If you want more control over the presentation of print previews than you get with the PrintPreviewDialog component, you can use the PrintPreviewControl control. This control can be embedded in a form to provide the core graphical functionality of the PrintPreviewDialog component. In fact, the area of the PrintPreviewDialog component that presents the preview is itself a PrintPreviewControl control.

STEP BY STEP

11.8 Using the `PrintPreviewControl` Control

1. Add a new form to your Visual C# .NET application.

2. Place a `TextBox` control (`txtText`), a `Label` control, a `NumericUpDown` control (`nudCopies`), a `FontDialog` component (`fontDialog1`), a `PrintPreviewControl` control (`printPreviewControl1`), and three `Button` controls (`btnSetFont`, `btnPreview`, and `btnPrint`) on the form.

3. Drag a `PrintDocument` component from the toolbox to the form. Set its `DocumentName` property to `NetDocument11-8`.

4. Switch to the code view and add the following `using` directive:

```
using System.Drawing.Printing;
```

5. Add the following code to the class definition:

```
// Create a default font to print with
Font fnt = new Font("Arial", 10, FontStyle.Regular,
    GraphicsUnit.Point);
// Number of lines printed so far
Int32 intLines = 0;
```

6. Double-click the Preview, Print, and Font buttons and add the following code to their `Click` event handlers:

```
private void btnPreview_Click(object sender,
    System.EventArgs e)
{
    intLines=0;
    // Set the Document property of the control
    // to printDocument1
    printPreviewControl1.Document=printDocument1;
}
private void btnPrint_Click(object sender,
    System.EventArgs e)
{
    intLines=0;
    printDocument1.Print();
}
private void btnSetFont_Click(object sender,
    System.EventArgs e)
{
    // Start with the current font
    fontDialog1.Font = fnt;
```

continues

continued

```
// If the user clicks OK, set a new font
if(fontDialog1.ShowDialog() ==
    DialogResult.OK)
{
    fnt = fontDialog1.Font;
}
}
```

7. Add an event handler for the PrintDocument object's PrintPage event:

```
private void printDocument1_PrintPage(object sender,
    System.Drawing.Printing.PrintPageEventArgs e)
{

    // Determine the height of the font
    float fltFontHeight = fnt.GetHeight(e.Graphics);
    // Vertical position for the next line of text
    float fltCurrentY = 0;
    bool pageDone = false;
    while (!pageDone)
    {
        // Check to see whether there's more space
        // on the page
        if(fltCurrentY <= e.MarginBounds.Height)
        {
            // Increment the line number
            intLines += 1;
            if(intLines <= nudCopies.Value)
            {
                // Print the text,
                // using the selected font
                e.Graphics.DrawString(txtText.Text,
                    fnt, Brushes.Black, 0, fltCurrentY);
                // And increment the vertical location
                // on the page
                fltCurrentY += fltFontHeight;
            }
            else
            {
                // We've printed all the copies we
                // need to print. In this case, set the
                // flags to indicate that this page is
                // done, but there are no more pages
                pageDone = true;
                e.HasMorePages = false;
            }
        }
        else
        {
```

```
            // We want to print another line,
            // but there's no space
            pageDone = true;
            e.HasMorePages = true;
        }
    }
}
```

8. Insert the `Main()` method to launch the form. Set the form as the startup object for the project.

9. Run the project. Enter some text in the text box and use the `NumericUpDown` control to set the number of times to print the text. Click the Set Font button to set the font of the text. Click the Preview button to see the document in print preview mode, as shown in Figure 11.7, or click the Print button to print the results.

FIGURE 11.7
You can embed print preview in a form with the help of the `PrintPreviewControl` control.

The `PrintPreviewControl` control doesn't have any of the user interfaces of the `PrintPreviewDialog` component beyond the print area itself. But you can manipulate the properties listed in Table 11.4 to get the same effects by using the `PrintPreviewControl` control, with whatever user interface you like.

TABLE 11.4

IMPORTANT PROPERTIES OF THE `PrintPreviewControl` CONTROL

Property	Description
AutoZoom	Is set to `true` to automatically change the zoom factor when the control is resized
Columns	Specifies the number of columns of pages to display in print preview
Rows	Specifies the number of rows of pages to display in print preview
StartPage	Specifies the page number of the first page to display
UseAntiAlias	Is set to `true` to use antialiasing—which shows higher-quality text but takes longer to render—when displaying the print preview
Zoom	Specifies the zoom factor to use when displaying the print preview

> **EXAM TIP**
>
> **`PrintPreviewControl` Property** To programatically make changes to a `PrintPreviewDialog` component at runtime, you can retrieve its `PrintPreviewControl` property and use the properties listed in Table 11.4.

REVIEW BREAK

▶ The `PageSetupDialog` component displays a dialog box that allows the user to set page-related printing properties.

▶ The `PrintDialog` component allows the user to set printer-related printing properties.

▶ The `PrintPreviewDialog` component displays a preview of the document before it is printed.

▶ The `PrintPreviewControl` control lets you embed a print preview in a Windows form.

CHAPTER SUMMARY

KEY TERM
• PrintDocument

The .NET Framework helps you give your applications complete printer control through a set of custom classes. The key object involved is an instance of the `PrintDocument` class, which represents a document to be printed. When you call the `PrintDocument.Print()` method, it triggers the `PrintPage` event of the class. In the `PrintPage` event, you can retrieve a `Graphics` object that represents the page to be printed and draw on it by using the familiar methods of the `Graphics` object.

Other events of the `PrintDocument` object let you manage initialization and cleanup for printing and manipulate page settings on a page-by-page basis.

The .NET Framework also provides components that give you access to the built-in common dialogs for printing. You can manipulate page settings and printer settings through these dialog boxes. You can also preview a document before it is printed, either in a separate dialog box or directly on a form.

APPLY YOUR KNOWLEDGE

Exercises

11.1 Printing Multiple Columns

The methods of the `Graphics` object give you complete flexibility to place text or objects at any point in any drawing area. In this exercise, you use these positioning capabilities to print a database table in multiple columns. This exercise also shows how you can use the `QueryPageSettings` event to force the printed output to be in landscape mode.

Estimated time: 25 minutes

1. Open a Visual C# .NET Windows application in the Visual Studio .NET Integrated Development Environment (IDE). Add a new form to the application.

2. Add a `Label` control, a `TextBox` control (txtSQL), and two `Button` controls (btnPreview and btnPrint) to the form. Set the `MultiLine` property of the `TextBox` control to `true`. Figure 11.8 shows the design for this form.

FIGURE 11.8
You can print text in multiple columns by using positioning capabilities of the `Graphics` object.

3. Add a `PrintDocument` component (printDocument1) and a `PrintPreviewDialog` component (printPreviewDialog1) to the form.

Set the `DocumentName` property of the `PrintDocument` component to `SQL Query Results`. Set the `Document` property of the `PrintPreviewDialog` component to `printDocument1`.

4. Switch to the code view and add the following using directives:

```
using System.Data;
using System.Data.SqlClient;
using System.Drawing.Printing;
```

5. Add the following code to the class definition:

```
// Create a Connection and DataSet object
SqlConnection cnn = new SqlConnection(
    "data source=(local);" +
    "initial catalog=Northwind; " +
    "integrated security=SSPI");
DataSet ds = new DataSet();
// Number of rows of data to print
Int32 intRows=0;
// Number of rows printed
Int32 intRowsPrinted=0;
```

6. Double-click the Preview and Print buttons and add the following code to their `Click` event handlers:

```
private void btnPreview_Click(
    object sender, System.EventArgs e)
{
    printPreviewDialog1.ShowDialog();
}
private void btnPrint_Click(object sender,
    System.EventArgs e)
{
    printDocument1.Print();
}
```

7. Attach event handlers for the `PrintPage`, `BeginPrint`, `EndPrint`, and `QueryPageSettings` events to the `PrintDocument` component and add the following code to handle these events:

APPLY YOUR KNOWLEDGE

```csharp
private void printDocument1_PrintPage(
object sender,
System.Drawing.Printing.PrintPageEventArgs
 e)
{
    // Create some fonts to print with
    Font fnt = new Font("Arial", 10,
      FontStyle.Regular,
      GraphicsUnit.Point);
    Font fntHeader = new Font("Arial", 10,
        FontStyle.Bold,
        GraphicsUnit.Point);
    // Determine the height of the font
    float fltFontHeight = fnt.GetHeight(
        e.Graphics);
    // Vertical position for
    // the next line of text
    float fltCurrentY = 0;
    bool pageDone = false;

    // Print a header row first
    for(int intI = 0; intI <
        ds.Tables["Results"].Columns.Count;
        intI++)
    {
        DataColumn dc =
        ds.Tables["Results"].Columns[intI];
        e.Graphics.DrawString(
            dc.ColumnName, fntHeader,
            Brushes.Black, intI * 200, 0);
    }
    // And increment the vertical
    // location on the page
    fltCurrentY += fntHeader.GetHeight(
        e.Graphics);

    while (!pageDone)
    {
        // Check to see whether there's
        // more space on the page
        if(fltCurrentY <=
            e.MarginBounds.Height)
        {
            // Increment the line number
            intRowsPrinted += 1;
            if(intRowsPrinted <= intRows)
            {
                // Retrieve the DataRow
                DataRow dr =
                 ds.Tables["Results"].Rows[
                 intRowsPrinted - 1];
                // Build and print a
                // string of data
                String strPrint = "  ";
                for(int intI = 0; intI <
              ds.Tables["Results"].Columns.Count;
                    intI++)
                {
                    DataColumn dc =
                      ds.Tables[
                    "Results"].Columns[intI];
                    strPrint = strPrint +
                        dc.ColumnName + ": " +
                        dr[intI].ToString() +
                        " ";
                    e.Graphics.DrawString(
                        dr[intI].ToString(),
                        fnt, Brushes.Black,
                        intI*200,
                        fltCurrentY );
                }
                // And increment the
                // vertical location
                // on the page
                fltCurrentY +=
                    fltFontHeight;
            }
            else
            {
                // We've printed all the
                // copies we need to print.
                // In this case, set the
                // flags to indicate that
                // this page is done, but
                // there are no more pages
                pageDone = true;
                e.HasMorePages = false;
            }
        }
        else
        {
            // We want to print another
            // line, but there's no space
            pageDone = true;
            e.HasMorePages = true;
        }
    }
}
```

APPLY YOUR KNOWLEDGE

```csharp
private void printDocument1_BeginPrint(
  object sender,
  System.Drawing.Printing.PrintEventArgs e)
{
    // Get the data to print
    SqlCommand cmd = cnn.CreateCommand();
    cmd.CommandType = CommandType.Text;
    cmd.CommandText = txtSQL.Text;
    SqlDataAdapter da =
        new SqlDataAdapter();
    da.SelectCommand = cmd;
    cnn.Open();
    da.Fill(ds, "Results");
    intRows = ds.Tables[
        "Results"].Rows.Count;
    intRowsPrinted=0;
}

private void printDocument1_EndPrint(
  object sender,
  System.Drawing.Printing.PrintEventArgs e)
{
    // Clear the dataset and
    // Close the database connection
    ds.Clear();
    cnn.Close();
}

private void
printDocument1_QueryPageSettings(
object sender,
System.Drawing.Printing.
QueryPageSettingsEventArgs e)
{
    // Assign the page into landscape mode
    e.PageSettings.Landscape = true;
}
```

8. Insert the `Main()` method to launch the form. Set the form as the startup object for the project.

9. Run the project. Enter a SQL query such as this:

```sql
SELECT CustomerID, CompanyName
FROM Customers
WHERE Country = 'France'
```

Click the Preview button or the Print button to see how the results are formatted.

This code works by placing columns every 2 inches (200 graphics units) across the page. You force the page to landscape mode by setting the `PageSettings.Landscape` property to `true` to make room for the maximum possible number of columns. From there, it's just simple math to calculate the x- and y-coordinates for printing each string to the `Graphics` object.

Of course, this example has limitations. The most notable is that it doesn't have any way to check whether the columns will all fit on the page or whether the text will fit into the columns. If you need to print arbitrary data on a page, you should investigate the `Graphics.MeasureString()` method, which can return the size of the rectangle needed to print a given string of text to a particular `Graphics` object with a given font and brush.

11.2 Setting Preview Properties

This exercise shows you how to use the properties of the `PrintPreviewControl` class to customize the initial view of a document in print preview mode.

Estimated time: 15 minutes

1. Add a new form to your Visual C# .NET application.

2. Add a `TextBox` control (txtText), three `Label` controls, three `NumericUpDown` controls (nudCopies, nudRows, and nudColumns), and three `Button` controls (btnSetFont, btnPreview, and btnPrint) to the form. Figure 11.9 shows the design for this form.

APPLY YOUR KNOWLEDGE

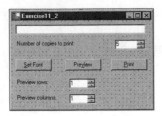

FIGURE 11.9
You can create a custom print preview dialog box by setting the properties of the `PrintPreviewDialog` component's `PrintPreviewControl` property.

3. Drag a FontDialog component (fontDialog1), a PrintPreviewDialog component (printPreviewDialog1), and a PrintDocument (printDocument1) component from the toolbox to the form. Set the DocumentName property of the PrintDocument component to Preview Properties. Set the Document property of the PrintPreviewDialog component to printDocument1.

4. Switch to the code view and add the following using directive:

```
using System.Drawing.Printing;
```

5. Add the following code to the class definition:

```
// Create a default font to print with
Font fnt = new Font("Arial", 10,
    FontStyle.Regular,
    GraphicsUnit.Point);
// Number of lines printed so far
Int32 intLines = 0;
```

6. Double-click the Preview, Print, and Font buttons and add the following code to their Click event handlers:

```
private void btnPreview_Click(
    object sender, System.EventArgs e)
{
    intLines=0;
```

```
    // Set up the specified rows and columns
    printPreviewDialog1.
        PrintPreviewControl.Rows =
            (int) nudRows.Value;
    printPreviewDialog1.
        PrintPreviewControl.Columns =
            (int) nudColumns.Value;
    // And show the preview
    printPreviewDialog1.ShowDialog();
}
private void btnPrint_Click(object sender,
    System.EventArgs e)
{
    intLines=0;
    printDocument1.Print();
}
private void btnSetFont_Click(
    object sender, System.EventArgs e)
{
    // Start with the current font
    fontDialog1.Font = fnt;
    // If the user clicks OK, set a new font
        if(fontDialog1.ShowDialog() ==
            DialogResult.OK)
        {
            fnt = fontDialog1.Font;
        }
}
```

7. Add an event handler for the PrintDocument object's PrintPage event:

```
private void printDocument1_PrintPage(
 object sender,
 System.Drawing.Printing.PrintPageEventArgs
 e)
{
    // Determine the height of the font
    float fltFontHeight =
        fnt.GetHeight(e.Graphics);
    // Vertical position for the
    // next line of text
    float fltCurrentY = 0;
    bool pageDone = false;
    while (!pageDone)
    {
        // Check to see whether there's
        // more space on the page
        if(fltCurrentY <=
            e.MarginBounds.Height)
        {
```

APPLY YOUR KNOWLEDGE

```
// Increment the line number
intLines += 1;
if(intLines <= nudCopies.Value)
{
    // Print the text,
    // using the selected font
    e.Graphics.DrawString(
        txtText.Text, fnt,
        Brushes.Black, 0,
        fltCurrentY);
    // And increment the
    // vertical location
    // on the page
    fltCurrentY +=
        fltFontHeight;
}
else
{
    // We've printed all the
    // copies we need to print.
    // In this case, set the
    // flags to indicate that
    // this page is done, but
    // there are no more pages
    pageDone = true;
    e.HasMorePages = false;
}
}
else
{
    // We want to print another
    // line, but there's no space
    pageDone = true;
    e.HasMorePages = true;
}
}
}
}
```

8. Insert the `Main()` method to launch the form. Set the form as the startup object for the project.

9. Run the project. Enter text and a repeat count for the document. Enter a number of rows and columns and then click Preview to see the preview. Figure 11.10 shows a sample preview at two rows by three columns.

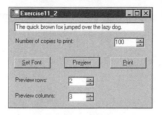

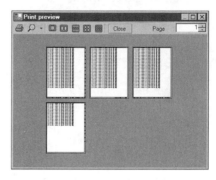

FIGURE 11.10
The `PrintPreviewControl` object's `Columns` and `Rows` properties are set to 3 and 2, resulting in output being displayed in three columns and two rows.

Review Questions

1. What method do you call to print a document from a .NET Framework Windows form?

2. What events does the `PrintDocument` object support?

3. How can you print multiple pages from a `PrintDocument` object?

4. How can you determine the height of a string of text on the printed page?

5. What is the difference between drawing on a Windows form and printing graphics via the `PrintDocument` class?

APPLY YOUR KNOWLEDGE

6. What happens when you try to print colored graphics to a black-and-white printer?

7. What common dialog boxes does the .NET Framework supply to aid in printing?

8. How can you allow users to set paper orientation without allowing them to change printers?

Exam Questions

1. Your application is printing a number of copies of a text string, using this code:

```
// Create a default font to print with
Font fnt = new Font("Arial", 10,
    FontStyle.Regular,
    GraphicsUnit.Point);
// Number of lines printed so far
Int32 intLines=0;
private void printDocument1_PrintPage(
 object sender,
 System.Drawing.Printing.PrintPageEventArgs
 e)
{
    // Determine the height of the font
    float fltFontHeight =
        fnt.GetHeight(e.Graphics);
    // Vertical position for the
    // next line of text
    float fltCurrentY = 0;
    bool pageDone = false;
    while (!pageDone)
    {
        // Check to see whether there's
        // more space on the page
        if(fltCurrentY <=
            e.MarginBounds.Height)
        {
            // Increment the line number
            intLines += 1;
            if(intLines <= nudCopies.Value)
            {
                // Print the text,
                // using the selected font
                e.Graphics.DrawString(
                    txtText.Text, fnt,
                    Brushes.Black, 0,
                    fltCurrentY);
```

```
                // And increment the
                // vertical location
                // on the page
                fltCurrentY +=
                    fltFontHeight;
            }
            else
            {
                pageDone = true;
            }
        }
        else
        {
            // We want to print another
            // line, but there's no space
            pageDone = true;
        }
    }
}
```

The application prints one page and then stops, regardless of the number of lines you've told it to print. What should you do to fix this code?

A. Set `PrintPageEventArgs.HasMorePages` to true when there is more to print but no space.

B. Set `PrintPageEventArgs.HasMorePages` to false when there is more to print but no space.

C. Set `PrintPageEventArgs.MarginBounds.Height` to a value that is greater than the length of the page to force another page.

D. Set `PrintPageEventArgs.PageBounds.Height` to a value that is greater than the length of the page to force another page.

2. Your application contains the following code:

```
private void printDocument1_PrintPage(
 object sender,
 System.Drawing.Printing.PrintPageEventArgs
 e)
{
    // Create a font to print with
    Font fnt = new Font("Arial", 10,
        FontStyle.Regular,
        GraphicsUnit.Point);
```

```
// Print the text
for(int intI=0; intI<5; int++)
{
        e.Graphics.DrawString(
            txtText.Text, fnt,
            Brushes.Black, 0, 0);
}
// And indicate that
// there are no more pages
e.HasMorePages = false;
}
```

When you call the `Print()` method of the `printDocument1` object, only a single line of text is printed on the form. What could be the reason you don't see five lines of output?

A. The printer is incompatible with Windows.

B. The code prints the line of text five times in the same place.

C. You need to create a new `Font` object for each line of text.

D. You need to set the `PrintPageEventArgs.HasMorePages` property to `true`.

3. You have designed a form that includes this code to print 10 lines of text:

```
private void printDocument1_PrintPage(
 object sender,
 System.Drawing.Printing.PrintPageEventArgs
 e)
{
    // Create a default font to print with
    Font fnt = new Font("Arial", 10,
        FontStyle.Regular,
        GraphicsUnit.Point);
    // Determine the height of the font
    float fltFontHeight = fnt.GetHeight(
        this.CreateGraphics());
    // Vertical position for
    // the next line of text
    float fltCurrentY = 0;

    for(int intI=0; intI < 10 ; intI++)
    {
```

```
    // Print the text,
    // using the selected font
    e.Graphics.DrawString(
        txtText.Text, fnt,
        Brushes.Black, 0, fltCurrentY);
    fltCurrentY += fltFontHeight;
    }
    // And indicate that there
    // are no more pages
    e.HasMorePages = false;
}
```

When you execute the code, it prints 10 copies of the text string, but the line spacing is wrong. What could be the problem?

A. The printer is incompatible with the .NET Framework.

B. A font height retrieved using the form's `Graphics` object does not necessarily match a font height for the printer's `Graphics` object.

C. You need to append a `newLine` character to the end of each text string to reset the print position.

D. You need to set `PrintPageEventArgs.HasMorePages` to `true` before printing.

4. You want to make sure that all pages of a document are printed in portrait mode, no matter what settings the user has chosen. How should you do this?

A. Set the `DefaultPageSettings.Landscape` property to `false` in the `PrintPage` event.

B. Display the Page Setup dialog box to the user, with instructions to choose portrait mode.

C. Set the `PageBounds` property to reflect a portrait page in the `BeginPrint` event.

D. Set the `PageSettings.Landscape` property to `false` in each `QueryPageSettings` event.

5. You are using this code to print numbers on a page, using a font that is defined at the class level:

```
// Create a default font to print with
Font fnt = new Font("Arial", 10,
    FontStyle.Regular,
    GraphicsUnit.Point);

private void printDocument1_PrintPage(
 object sender,
 System.Drawing.Printing.PrintPageEventArgs
 e)
{
    // Determine the height of the font
    float fltFontHeight =
        fnt.GetHeight(e.Graphics);
    // Vertical position for
    // the next line of text
    float fltCurrentY = 0;
    int intI=0;
    while(fltCurrentY <
        e.PageBounds.Height)
    {
        intI+=1;
        // Print the text,
        // using the selected font
        e.Graphics.DrawString(
            intI.ToString(), fnt,
            Brushes.Black, 0,
            fltCurrentY);
        fltCurrentY += fltFontHeight;
    }
    MessageBox.Show("Printed " +
        intI.ToString() + " lines");
    // And indicate that there
    // are no more pages
    e.HasMorePages = false;
}
```

When you run this code, it claims to print 26 lines, but on inspecting the printed page, you find that only 24 lines are on the page. How should you fix this problem?

A. Fix the off-by-one error in the loop.

B. Declare the Font object within the event procedure.

C. Check the `PrintPageEventArgs.MarginBounds.Height` property instead of the `PrintPageEventArgs.PageBounds.Height` property.

D. Initialize `fltCurrentY` to `fltFontHeight` instead of to zero.

6. Your application needs to print information retrieved from a Web service on the Internet. The information is delivered in a single method call from the Web service, but you need to break it up into multiple pages during printing. In which event of the `PrintDocument` object should you retrieve the information?

A. `PrintPage`

B. `QueryPrintSettings`

C. `EndPrint`

D. `BeginPrint`

7. You have developed complex logic within the `PrintPage` event of a `PrintDocument` object to print your company logo using graphics object. You'd like to reuse this logic on multiple forms. What should you do?

A. Cut and paste your custom logic to individual `PrintDocument` instances on each form.

B. Move your logic to a public method in a class and call that method from each `PrintDocument` instance.

C. Keep one form open with a `PrintDocument` object and use that `PrintDocument` object for every print job.

D. Derive a class from the `PrintDocument` object, override the `PrintPage` event, and put your logic in that event. Use an instance of the derived class whenever you need to print.

APPLY YOUR KNOWLEDGE

8. Users of your application want to be able to select the margins and paper orientation of their print jobs. Which component should you add to your form to enable this easily?

   A. `PrintDocument`

   B. `PrintDialog`

   C. `PrintPreviewDialog`

   D. `PageSetupDialog`

9. You are using a `PrintPreviewDialog` component in your application to display print jobs before they are printed. Users would like to be able to view eight pages at a time in the print preview, but that isn't one of the choices on the toolbar of the Print Preview dialog box. How can you display eight pages in print preview? (Select the two best answers.)

   A. Set the `PrintPreviewDialog.` `PrintPreviewControl.Rows` and `PrintPreviewDialog.PrintPreviewControl.Co` `lumns` settings to 2 and 4, respectively, before showing the dialog.

   B. Use the `PageSetupDialog` class to reduce the size of the pages so that more will fit in the display.

   C. Use a `PrintPreviewControl` control to create your own custom Print Preview dialog box.

   D. Use two `PrintPreviewDialog` components and display four pages in each one.

10. Your application uses an instance of the `PageSetupDialog` component to allow users to set the margins of their print jobs. All print jobs are sent to a departmental printer with multiple paper trays. The accounting department complains that your users are using the check stock from one of the reserved paper trays.

What can you do to prevent users from printing from that tray?

   A. Set the `AllowPaper` property of the `PageSetupDialog` component to `false` before showing the Page Setup dialog box.

   B. Set the `AllowPrinter` property of the `PageSetupDialog` component to `false` before showing the Page Setup dialog box.

   C. Set the `AllowMargins` property of the `PageSetupDialog` component to `false` before showing the Page Setup dialog box.

   D. Set the `AllowPaper` property of the `PageSetupDialog` component to `true` before showing the Page Setup dialog box.

11. Your application creates and displays a `PrintPreviewControl` control at runtime. Users would like to have the display in this control automatically sized to fit when the control is resized. What should you do?

   A. Set the `UseAntiAlias` property to `true`.

   B. Set the `UseAntiAlias` property to `false`.

   C. Set the `AutoZoom` property to `true`.

   D. Set the `AutoZoom` property to `false`.

12. Your application needs to print the contents of a database table. The print job may span multiple pages, depending on the number of rows in the table. In which event of the `PrintDocument` control should you connect to the database?

   A. `PrintPage`

   B. `QueryPrintSettings`

   C. `EndPrint`

   D. `BeginPrint`

APPLY YOUR KNOWLEDGE

13. You need to print the contents of a `TextBox` control from your form. You have added a `PrintDocument` component to the form and created a `Button` control that calls the `Print()` method of the `PrintDocument` component. When you click the button, nothing prints. What should you do?

    A. Add code to the `PrintPage` event of the `PrintDocument` component to tell it what to print.

    B. Add a `PrintDialog` component to your form.

    C. Add code to the `BeginPrint` event of the `PrintDocument` component to tell it what to print.

    D. Add a `PrintPreviewDialog` component to your form.

14. Your application allows the user to print documents, and then it places an entry in the Windows event log with the total number of pages for each document. In which event of the `PrintDocument` object should you place the event log code?

    A. `BeginPrint`

    B. `EndPrint`

    C. `QueryPageSettings`

    D. `PrintPage`

15. Your application lets the user choose a font for printing. Users complain that when they choose a large font, the lines on the printed page overlap. What should you do to fix this problem?

    A. Call the `Graphics.MeasureString()` method to get the width of the text before it is printed.

    B. Set the `AutoZoom` property of the associated `PrintPreviewDialog` component to `true`.

    C. Check the size of the font that the user selects and reduce it if it is too large.

    D. Call the `Font.GetHeight()` method to determine the vertical size of the font.

Answers to Review Questions

1. The `Print()` method of the `PrintDocument` class is used to print from a .NET Windows form.

2. The `PrintDocument` class supports the `BeginPrint` (occurs once, before printing starts), `QueryPageSettings` (occurs before each page is printed), `PrintPage` (occurs when each page is printed), and `EndPrint` (occurs once, when printing finishes) events.

3. Set the `PrintPageEventArgs.HasMorePages` property to `true` within the `PrintPage` event to have the event fired again to print another page.

4. Use the `GetHeight()` method of the `Font` object to determine the height of a font.

5. The only difference between drawing on a form and drawing on the printed page is in the `Graphics` object that you use. When you have the appropriate `Graphics` object, the code is exactly the same.

6. Windows takes care of the details of reducing the color to something that the printer can handle.

7. The .NET Framework gives you common dialog boxes to handle page setup, printer setup, and print preview.

APPLY YOUR KNOWLEDGE

8. Call the `PageSetupDialog` component with the `AllowPrinters` property set to `false` to allow the users to set paper orientation without allowing them to switch printers.

Answers to Exam Questions

1. **A.** To indicate to the `PrintDocument` class that it should print another page, set the `PrintPageEventArgs.HasMorePages` property to `true` in the `PrintPage` event. For more information, see the section "Printing Text" in this chapter.

2. **B.** The `DrawString()` method takes an X and a Y argument as its last two parameters. If you don't vary these parameters, the method continues printing in the same place. For more information, see the section "Printing Text" in this chapter.

3. **B.** All print operations need to be carried out with the printer's `Graphics` object, which can be retrieved from the arguments to the `PrintPage` event. For more information, see the section "Printing Text" in this chapter.

4. **D.** The `QueryPageSettings` event is the appropriate place to change page settings. When the `PrintPage` event occurs, it's too late to change any settings for that page. For more information, see the section "Printing Initialization and Cleanup" in this chapter.

5. **C.** The `PageBounds` property returns a `Rectangle` structure that represents the entire page. The `MarginBounds` property returns a `Rectangle` structure that represents the printable area of the page. For more information, see the section "Printing Text" in this chapter.

6. **D.** The `BeginPrint` event is appropriate for one-time actions that need to be performed before a print job starts delivering output. For more information, see the section "Printing Initialization and Cleanup" in this chapter.

7. **D.** Using a derived class allows you to encapsulate and reuse custom logic without duplicating code or losing any of the object-oriented benefits of the `PrintDocument` class. For more information, see the section "Using the `PrintDocument` Component" in this chapter.

8. **D.** The `PageSetupDialog` includes sections for setting margins and orientation. For more information, see the section "The `PageSetupDialog`, `PrintDialog`, and `PrintPreviewDialog` Components" in this chapter.

9. **A and C.** The `Rows` and `Columns` properties of the `PrintPreviewControl` control let you customize the display of thumbnails. You can either create your own instance of this control or retrieve the control from the built-in `PrintPreviewDialog` component. For more information, see the section "The `PrintPreviewControl` Control" and Exercise 11.2 in this chapter.

10. **A.** To disable a section of the Page Setup dialog box, you set the corresponding variable to `false` before showing the dialog box. For more information, see the section "The `PageSetupDialog`, `PrintDialog`, and `PrintPreviewDialog` Components" in this chapter.

11. **C.** Setting the `AutoZoom` property to `true` tells the control to display the document as large as it can, based on the current size of the control. For more information, see the section "The `PrintPreviewControl` Control" in this chapter.

APPLY YOUR KNOWLEDGE

12. **D.** By connecting to the database in the `BeginPrint` event, you can ensure that the data is available for the duration of the print job. For more information, see the section "Printing Initialization and Cleanup" in this chapter.

13. **A.** The `Print()` method triggers the `PrintPage` event, which is where the actual work of printing takes place. For more information, see the section "Using the `PrintDocument` Component" in this chapter.

14. **B.** The `EndPrint` event is appropriate for actions that need to be performed once when a print job is finished. For more information, see the section "Printing Initialization and Cleanup" in this chapter.

15. **D.** If you use the `Font.GetHeight()` method to get the height of the font, you can calculate the proper spacing of printed lines for that font. For more information, see the section "Printing Text" in this chapter.

Suggested Readings and Resources

1. Visual Studio .NET Combined Help Collection, "Windows Forms Print Support."

2. Windows Forms Quickstarts, "Working with Printing."

3. Charles Petzold. *Programming Microsoft Windows with C#.* Microsoft Press, 2001.

TESTING, DEBUGGING, AND DEPLOYING A WINDOWS APPLICATION

This chapter covers the following Microsoft-specified objective for the "Testing and Debugging" section of Exam 70-316, "Developing and Implementing Windows-Based Applications with Microsoft Visual C# .NET and Microsoft Visual Studio .NET":

Create a unit test plan.

▶ Before you release a product or component, the product needs to pass through different types of tests. This objective requires you to know the different types of tests that a product should undergo to verify its robustness, reliability, and correctness. These tests should be executed with a designed test plan that ensures that the product thoroughly meets its goals and requirements.

Implement tracing.

- **Add trace listeners and trace switches to an application.**

- **Display trace output.**

▶ Tracing helps in displaying informative messages during the application's runtime to get a fair idea of how the application is progressing. This objective requires you to know how to use Trace class properties and methods, attach trace listeners, and apply trace switches. Trace switches allow you to enable, disable, and filter tracing output that is displayed by the Trace class without recompiling programs. You can do this by just editing the configuration XML file.

CHAPTER 12

Testing and Debugging a Windows Application

Debug, rework, and resolve defects in code.

- **Configure the debugging environment.**

- **Create and apply debugging code to components and applications.**

- **Provide multicultural test data to components and applications.**

- **Execute tests.**

- **Resolve errors and rework code.**

▶ The process of debugging helps you locate logical or runtime errors in an application. This objective requires you to know the various tools and windows that are available in Visual C# .NET to enable easy and effective debugging. These debugging tools and windows help a great deal in determining errors, executing test code, and resolving errors.

▶ Review the "Introduction to Instrumentation and Tracing" and "Using the Debugger" sections of the Visual Studio .NET Combined Help Collection.

▶ Try calling different methods of the Trace and Debug classes. Note the differences in the output when you run a program using the Debug and Release configurations.

▶ Experiment with attaching predefined and custom-made listeners to Trace objects. Refer to Step by Step 12.2 and Guided Practice Exercise 12.1 for examples.

▶ Know how to implement trace switches and conditional compilation in Windows applications. Refer to Step by Step 12.3 and Step by Step 12.4 for examples.

▶ Experiment with the different types of debugging windows that are available in Visual C# .NET. Understand their advantages and learn to use them effectively. They can be very helpful in resolving errors.

▶ Experiment with various techniques for debugging, such as local and remote debugging, debugging code in DLLs, and debugging SQL Server stored procedures.

INTRODUCTION

Building a quality Windows application requires thorough testing to ensure that the application has the fewest possible defects. Therefore, you need to chart an effective test plan. Complex applications require multiple levels of testing, including unit testing, integration testing, and regression testing.

Tracing is the process of monitoring an executing program. You trace a program by placing tracing code in the program with the help of the `Trace` and `Debug` classes. The tracing messages can be sent to a variety of destinations, including the Output window, a text file, an event log, or any other custom-defined trace listener, where they can be recorded to analyze the behavior of the program. Trace switches can be used to change the types of messages being generated without recompiling the application.

The process of testing may reveal various logical errors, or bugs, in a program. The process of finding the exact locations of these errors may be time-consuming. Visual C# .NET provides a rich set of debugging tools that makes this process very convenient.

In this chapter I first discuss the test plan and various common testing techniques. I then discuss how to put tracing code in a program to monitor its execution. Finally, I talk about the debugging capabilities of Visual Studio .NET.

TESTING

NOTE

Correctness, Robustness, and Reliability *Correctness* refers to the ability of a program to produce expected results when the program is given a set of valid input data. *Robustness* is the ability of a program to cope up with invalid data or operations. *Reliability* is the ability of a program to produce consistent results on every use.

Testing is the process of executing a program with the intention of finding errors (bugs). By *error* I mean any case in which a program's actual results fail to match the expected results. The criteria of the expected results may not include just the correctness of the program; they may also include other attributes, such as usability, reliability, and robustness. The process of testing may be manual, automated, or a mixture of both techniques.

In this increasingly competitive world, testing is more important than ever. A software company cannot afford to ignore the importance of testing. If a company releases buggy code, not only will it end up spending more time and money fixing and redistributing the corrected code, but it will also lose goodwill. In the Internet world, the competition is not even next door: It is just a click away!

Creating a Test Plan

Create a unit test plan.

A *test plan* is a document that guides the process of testing. A good test plan should typically include the following information:

◆ Which software components needs to be tested

◆ What parts of a component's specification are to be tested

◆ What parts of a component's specification are not to be tested

◆ What approach needs to be followed for testing

◆ Who will be responsible for each task in the testing process

◆ What the schedule is for testing

◆ What the criteria are for a test to fail or pass

◆ How the test results will be documented and used

Executing Tests

Debug, rework, and resolve defects in code.

• **Execute tests.**

Incremental testing (sometime also called *evolutionary testing*) is a modern approach to testing that has proven very useful for rapid application development (RAD). The idea of incremental testing is to test the system as you build it. Three levels of testing are involved in incremental testing:

◆ **Unit testing**—Unit testing involves testing elementary units of the application (usually classes).

◆ **Integration testing**—Integration testing tests the integration of two or more units or the integration between subsystems of those units.

◆ **Regression testing**—Regression testing usually involves the process of repeating the unit and integration tests whenever a bug is fixed, to ensure that the old bugs do not exist and that no new ones have been introduced.

Unit Testing

Units are the smallest building blocks of an application. In Visual C# .NET, these building blocks often refer to components or class definitions. Unit testing involves performing basic tests at the component level to ensure that each unique path in the component behaves exactly as documented in its specifications.

Usually, the same person who writes the component also does unit testing for it. Unit testing typically requires that you write special programs that use the component or class being tested. These programs are called *test drivers*; they are used throughout the testing process, but they are not part of the final product.

The following are some of the major benefits of unit testing:

◆ It allows you to test parts of an application without waiting for the other parts to be available.

◆ It allows you to test exceptional conditions that are not easily reached by external inputs in a large, integrated system.

◆ It simplifies the debugging process by limiting the search for bugs to a small unit rather than to the complete application.

◆ It helps you avoid lengthy compile-build-debug cycles when debugging difficult problems.

◆ It enables you to detect and remove defects at a much lower cost than with other, later, stages of testing.

NOTE

NUnit NUnit is a simple framework for writing repeatable tests in any .NET language. For more information, visit http://nunit.sourceforge.net.

Integration Testing

Integration testing verifies that the major subsystems of an application work well with each other. The objective of integration testing is to uncover the errors that might result because of the way units integrate or interface with each other.

Visualize the whole application as a hierarchy of components; integration testing can be performed in any of the following ways:

◆ **Bottom-up approach**—With this approach, the testing progresses from the smallest subsystem and then gradually progresses up in the hierarchy to cover the whole system. This approach may require you to write a number of test-driver programs that test the integration between subsystems.

◆ **Top-down approach**—This approach starts with the top-level system, to test the top-level interfaces, and gradually comes down and tests smaller subsystems. You might be required to write *stubs* (that is, dummy modules that mimic the interface of a module but have no functionality) for the modules that are not yet ready for testing.

◆ **Umbrella approach**—This approach focuses on testing the modules that have a high degree of user interaction. Normally, stubs are used in place of process-intensive modules. This approach enables you to release graphical user interface (GUI)-based applications early and allows you to gradually increase functionality. It is called the *umbrella approach* because when you look at the application hierarchy (as shown in Figure 12.1), the input/output modules are generally present on the edges, forming an umbrella shape.

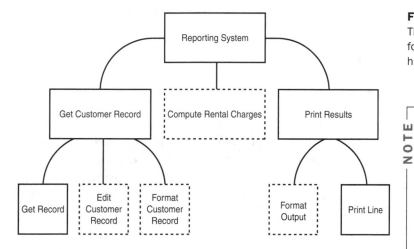

FIGURE 12.1
The umbrella approach of integration testing focuses on testing the modules that have a high degree of user interaction.

Regression Testing

Regression testing should be performed any time a program is modified, either to fix a bug or to add a feature. The process of regression testing involves running all the tests mentioned in the preceding sections as well as any newly added test cases to test the added functionality. Regression testing has two main goals:

◆ Verify that all known bugs are corrected.

◆ Verify that the program has no new bugs.

NOTE

Limitations of Testing   Testing can show the presence of errors, but it can never confirm the absence of errors. Various factors such as the complexity of the software, requirements such as interoperability with various software and hardware, and globalization issues such as support for various languages and cultures, can create excessive input data and too many execution paths to be tested. Many companies do their best to capture most of the test cases by using automation (that is, using computer programs to find errors) and beta-testing (that is, involving product enthusiasts to find errors), but errors in final products are still a well-known and acknowledged fact.

Testing International Applications

Debug, rework, and resolve defects in code.

- **Provide multicultural test data to components and applications.**

Testing an application designed for international usage involves checking the country and language dependencies of each locale for which the application has been designed. When testing international applications, you need to consider the following:

- ◆ You should test the application's data and user interface to make sure that they conform to the locale's standards for date and time, numeric values, currency, list separators, and measurements for the countries in which you plan to sell your product.

- ◆ You should test your application on as many language and culture variants as necessary to cover your entire market for the application. Operating systems such as Windows 2000 and Windows XP support the languages used in more than 120 cultures/locales.

- ◆ You should use Unicode for your applications. Applications that use Unicode run without requiring any changes on Windows 2000 and XP. If an application instead uses Windows code pages, you need to set the culture/locale of the operating system according to the localized version of the application that you are testing. Each such change requires you to reboot the computer.

- ◆ While testing a localized version of an application, you should make sure to use the input data in the language that is supported by the localized version. This makes the testing scenario similar to the scenario in which the application will be actually used.

For more discussion about support for globalization in a Windows application, refer to Chapter 8, "Globalization."

▶ Testing is the process of executing a program with the intention of finding errors. You should design an effective test plan to ensure that your application is free from all likely defects and errors.

▶ Unit testing ensures that each unit of an application functions precisely as desired. It is the lowest level of testing.

▶ Integration testing ensures that different units of an application function as expected by the test plan after they are integrated.

▶ Whenever code is modified or a new feature is added in an application, you should run all the existing test cases, along with a new set of test cases, to check the new feature. This helps you develop robust applications.

TRACING

Debug, rework, and resolve defects in code.

- **Create and apply debugging code to components and applications.**

The process of testing can reveal the presence of errors in a program, but to find the actual cause of a problem, you sometimes need the program to generate information about its own execution. Analysis of this information may help you understand why the program is behaving in a particular way and may lead to possible resolution of the error.

This process of collecting information about program execution is called *tracing*. You trace a program's execution in Visual C# .NET by generating messages about the program's execution with the use of the Debug and Trace classes.

The Trace and Debug classes have several things in common:

◆ They both belong to the System.Diagnostics namespace.

◆ They have members with the same names.

◆ All their members are static.

◆ They are conditionally compiled (that is, their statements are included in the object code only if a certain symbol is defined).

The only difference between the Debug and Trace classes is that the members of the Debug class are conditionally compiled, but only when the DEBUG symbol is defined. On the other hand, members of the Trace class are conditionally compiled, but only when the TRACE symbol is defined.

Visual C# .NET provides two basic configurations for a project: Debug and Release. Debug is the default configuration. When you compile a program by using the Debug configuration, both TRACE and DEBUG symbols are defined, as shown in Figure 12.2. When you compile a program in the Release configuration, only the TRACE symbol is defined. You can switch between the Debug and Release configurations using the Solution Configurations combo box on the standard toolbar (as shown in Figure 12.3) or by using the Configuration Manager dialog box (as shown in Figure 12.4) from the project's Property Pages dialog box.

FIGURE 12.2

Both the TRACE and DEBUG symbols are defined in the Debug configuration.

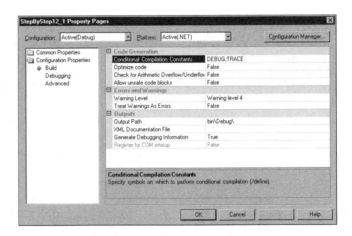

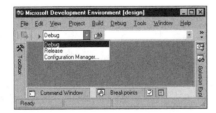

FIGURE 12.3

The standard toolbar of Visual Studio .NET contains a solutions configuration combo box to allow users to easily change solution configuration.

Later in this chapter, you will learn how to make these changes from within the program and through the command-line compilation options.

When you compile a program by using the Debug configuration, the code that uses the Debug and the Trace classes is included in the compiled code. When you run such a program, messages are generated by both the Debug and Trace classes. On the other hand, when a program is compiled by using the Trace configuration, it does not include any calls to the Debug class. Thus, when such a program is executed, you get only the messages generated by using the Trace class.

Table 12.1 summarizes the members of both the Trace and Debug classes.

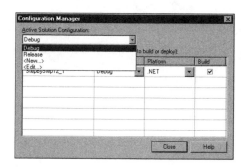

FIGURE 12.4
The Configuration Manager dialog box allows you to set configuration for projects in a solution.

NOTE

Tracing Helps in Resolving Hard-to-Reproduce Errors When programs run in a production environment, they sometimes report errors (mostly related to performance or threading problems) that are difficult to reproduce in a simulated testing environment. Tracing a production application can help you get runtime statistics for the program; this might help you in trapping these hard-to-reproduce errors.

TABLE 12.1

MEMBERS OF Debug AND Trace CLASSES

Member	Type	Description
Assert()	Method	Checks for a condition and displays a message if the condition is false.
AutoFlush	Property	Specifies whether the Flush() method should be called on the listeners after every write.
Close()	Method	Flushes the output buffer and then closes the listeners.
Fail()	Method	Displays an error message.
Flush()	Method	Flushes the output buffer and causes the buffered data to be written to the listeners.
Indent()	Method	Increases the current IndentLevel property by one.
IndentLevel	Property	Specifies the indent level.
IndentSize	Property	Specifies the number of spaces in an indent.
Listeners	Property	Specifies the collection of listeners that is monitoring the trace output.
Unindent()	Method	Decreases the current IndentLevel property by one.
Write()	Method	Writes the given information to the trace listeners in the Listeners collection.
WriteIf()	Method	Writes the given information to the trace listeners in the Listeners collection only if a condition is true.

continues

| TABLE 12.1 | *continued* |

MEMBERS OF Debug AND Trace CLASSES

Member	*Type*	*Description*
WriteLine()	Method	Acts the same as Write(), but appends the information with a newline character.
WriteLineIf()	Method	Acts the same as WriteIf(), but appends the information with a newline character.

Using Trace and Debug to Display Information

Implement tracing.

- **Display trace output**

Step by Step 12.1 demonstrates how to use some of the methods of the Trace and Debug classes.

STEP BY STEP

12.1 Using the Trace and Debug Classes to Display Debugging Information

1. Launch Visual Studio .NET. Select File, New, Blank Solution and name the new solution 316C12.

2. In Solution Explorer, right-click the name of solution and select Add, New Project. Select Visual C# Projects from the Project Types tree and then select Windows Application from the list of templates on the right. Name the project StepByStep12_1.

3. In Solution Explorer, right-click Form1.cs and rename it FactorialCalculator. Open the Properties window for this form and change its Name property to FactorialCalculator and Text property to Factorial Calculator 12_1. Switch to the code view of the form and modify the Main() method to launch FactorialCalculator instead of Form1.

4. Add two TextBox controls (txtNumber and txtFactorial) and a Button control (btnCalculate) to the form and arrange the controls as shown in Figure 12.5.

5. Add the following using directive in the code view:

```
using System.Diagnostics;
```

6. Add the following code to the Click event handler of btnCalculate:

```
private void btnCalculate_Click(object sender,
    System.EventArgs e)
{
    // write a debug message
    Debug.WriteLine(
        "Inside Button Click event handler");
    // start indenting messages now
    Debug.Indent();
    int intNumber = Convert.ToInt32(txtNumber.Text);
    // make a debug assertion
    Debug.Assert(intNumber >= 0, "Invalid value",
        "negative value in debug mode");
    // write a trace assertion
    Trace.Assert(intNumber >= 0, "Invalid value",
        "negative value in trace mode");

    int intFac = 1;
    for (int i = 2; i <= intNumber; i++)
    {
        intFac = intFac * i;
        // write a debug message
        Debug.WriteLine(i,
            "Factorial Program Debug, Value of i");
    }
    // write a trace message if the condition is true
    Trace.WriteLineIf(intFac < 1,
        "There was an overflow",
        "Factorial Program Trace");
    // write a debug message if the condition is true
    Debug.WriteLineIf(intFac < 1,
        "There was an overflow",
        "Factorial Program Debug");

    txtFactorial.Text = intFac.ToString();
    // decrease the indent level
    Debug.Unindent();

    // write a debug message
    Debug.WriteLine(
        "Done with computations, returning...");
}
```

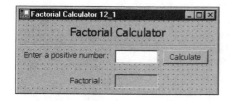

FIGURE 12.5

You can design a form that calculates the factorial of a given number.

continues

continued

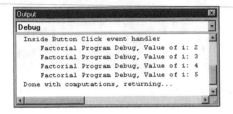

FIGURE 12.6
`Debug` and `Trace` messages are by default
always displayed in the Output window.

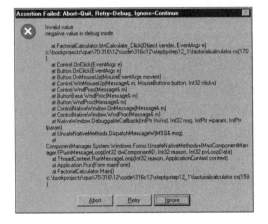

FIGURE 12.7
The Assertion Failed dialog box is displayed
when an assertion that is made in the
`Assert()` method fails.

7. Run the project. Keep the program running and switch to the Visual Studio .NET Integrated Development Environment (IDE). Select View, Other Windows, Output. Push the pin on the title bar of the output window so that it does not hide automatically. Now switch to the running program; enter 5 in the text box and click the Calculate button. You should see `Debug` messages that are generated by the program (see Figure 12.6).

8. Now switch to the running program and enter the value 100 and click the Calculate button. Messages from both the `Debug` class and the `Trace` class overflow are displayed in the Output window. Note that the default configuration is the `Debug` configuration, where both the `TRACE` and `DEBUG` symbols are defined.

9. Enter a negative value, such as -1, and click the Calculate button. This causes the assertion to fail, and you see a dialog box that shows an assertion failed message, as shown in Figure 12.7. This message box is generated by the `Debug.Assert()` method in the code. The dialog box gives you three choices: Abort, to terminate the program; Retry, to break the program execution so that you can debug the program; and Ignore, to continue the execution as if nothing has happened. Click Ignore, and you see another Assertion Failed dialog box. This one was generated by the `Trace.Assert()` method in the code. Click the Abort button to terminate the program execution.

10. From the Solution Configurations combo box on the standard toolbar, select the `Release` configuration. (The `Release` configuration defines only the `TRACE` symbol.) Run the program again. Enter the value 5 and click the Calculate button. The factorial is calculated, but no messages appear in the Output window. Enter the value 100 and click the Calculate button. You should now see the trace overflow message in the Output window. Finally, try calculating the factorial of -1. You should see just one dialog box, showing an assertion failed message. Click the Abort button to terminate the program.

Note from Step by Step 12.1 that you can use the methods of the Debug and Trace classes (for example, the WriteIf() and WriteLineIf() methods) to display messages based on conditions. This can be a very useful technique if you are trying to understand the flow of logic of a program. Step by Step 12.1 also demonstrates the use of the Assert() method. The Assert() method tests your assumption about a condition at a specific place in the program. When an assertion fails, the Assert() method pinpoints the code that is not behaving according to your assumptions. A related method is Fail(). The Fail() method displays a dialog box similar to the one that Assert() shows, but it does not work conditionally. Fail() signals unconditional failure in a branch of code execution.

Trace Listeners

Implement tracing.

- **Add trace listeners and trace switches to an application.**

Listeners are the classes that are responsible for forwarding, recording, and displaying the messages generated by the Trace and Debug classes. You can have multiple listeners associated with the Trace and Debug classes, by adding Listener objects to their Listeners property. The Listeners property is a collection that is capable of holding any objects derived from the TraceListener class. The Debug and Trace classes share a Listeners collection, so an object that is added to the Listeners collection of the Debug class is automatically available in the Trace class and vice versa.

The TraceListener class is an abstract class that belongs to the System.Diagnostics namespace and has three implementations:

◆ **DefaultTraceListener**—An object of this class is automatically added to the Listeners collection. Its behavior is to write messages on the Output window.

◆ **TextWriterTraceListener**—An object of this class writes messages to any class that derives from the Stream class and that includes the console or a file.

◆ **EventLogTraceListener**—An object of this class writes messages to the Windows event log.

EXAM TIP

The Same Listeners for Debug and Trace   Messages sent through the Debug and Trace objects are directed through each Listener object in the Listeners collection. Debug and Trace share the same Listeners collection, so any Listener object that is added to the Trace.Listeners collection is also added to the Debug.Listeners collection.

If you want a listener object to perform differently from these three listener classes, you can create your own class that inherits from the TraceListener class. When doing so, you must at least implement the Write() and WriteLine() methods.

Step by Step 12.2 shows how to create a custom listener class that implements the TraceListener class to send debug and trace messages through email.

STEP BY STEP

12.2 Creating a Custom TraceListener Object

1. Create a new Windows application project in solution 316C12. Name the project StepByStep12_2.

2. In Solution Explorer, copy the FactorialCalculator.cs form from the StepByStep12_1 project to the current project. Change the Text property of the form to Factorial Calculator 12_2. Switch to the code view and change the namespace of the form to StepByStep12_2.

3. In Solution Explorer, right-click Form1.cs and select Delete from the context menu.

4. Add to the project a reference to System.Web.dll.

5. Using the Add Class Wizard, add a new class to the project. Name the class EmailTraceListener and add the following code to it (changing the From address to a valid email address):

```
using System;
using System.Diagnostics;
using System.Text;
using System.Web.Mail;

namespace StepByStep12_2
{
    public class EmailTraceListener : TraceListener
    {
        // Message log will be sent to this address
        private string mailto;
        // Store the message log
        private StringBuilder message;

        public EmailTraceListener(string mailto)
        {
            this.mailto = mailto;
        }
```

```
// A custom listener must
// override Write() method
public override void Write(string message)
{
    if (this.message == null)
        this.message = new StringBuilder();
    this.message.Append(message);
}

// A custom listener must
// override WriteLine() method
public override void WriteLine(string message)
{
    if (this.message == null)
        this.message = new StringBuilder();
    this.message.Append(message);
    this.message.Append('\n');
}

// use the close method to send mail.
public override void Close()
{
    // ensure that the listener is flushed
    Flush();
    // MailMessage belongs to the
    // System.Web.Mail namespace
    // but can be used from
    // any managed application
    if (this.message != null)
    {
        // Create a MailMessage object
        MailMessage mailMessage =
            new MailMessage();
        mailMessage.From =
            "tracelistener@youraddress.com";
        mailMessage.To = this.mailto;
        mailMessage.Subject =
        "Factorial Program Debug/Trace output";
        mailMessage.Body =
            this.message.ToString();
        //send the mail
        SmtpMail.Send(mailMessage);
    }
}

public override void Flush()
{
    // nothing much to do here
    // so call the base class's implementation
    base.Flush();
}
    }
}
```

> **NOTE**
>
> **Sending Email Messages** The types in the System.Web.Mail namespace can be used from any managed application, including both Web and Windows applications. This functionality is supported only in the Windows 2000, Windows XP Professional, and Windows .NET Server operating systems. For other operating systems, you can send email messages by manually establishing Simple Mail Transfer Protocol (SMTP) connections through the System.Net.TcpClient class or by using an SMTP component, which you might be able to get from a component vendor for free.

continues

continued

6. Add the following code to the Load event of the FactorialCalculator form, changing the email address *Insert@youraddress.here* to a real address that can receive emails:

```
private void FactorialCalculator_Load(object sender,
    System.EventArgs e)
{
    // Add a custom listener to
    // the Listeners collection
    Trace.Listeners.Add(new EmailTraceListener(
        "Insert@youraddress.here"));
}
```

7. Add the following code to the Closing event of the FactorialCalculator form:

```
private void FactorialCalculator_Closing(
    object sender,
    System.ComponentModel.CancelEventArgs e)
{
    // call the Close() method for all listeners
    Trace.Close();
}
```

8. Set project StepByStep12_2 as the startup project.

9. Run the project, using the default Debug configuration. Enter a value and click the Calculate button. Close the form. Note that both Debug and Trace messages appear on the Output window, and they are emailed to the specified address by using the local SMTP server. Run the project again in the Release mode. Enter a large value, such as 100, and click the Calculate button. The overflow message appears in the Output window. Close the form. While you are closing the form, an email message containing the Trace messages are sent to the specified email address.

Trace Switches

Implement tracing.

- **Add trace listeners and trace switches to an application.**

So far in this chapter, you have learned that the `Trace` and `Debug` classes can be used to display valuable information related to program execution. You have also learned that it is possible to capture messages in a variety of formats. In this section, you will learn how to control the nature of messages that you want to get from a program.

You can use trace switches to set the parameters that control the level of tracing that needs to be done on a program. You set these switches via an Extensible Markup Language (XML) based external configuration file. This is especially useful when the application you are working with is in production mode. You might initially want the application not to generate any trace messages. However, if the application later has problems or you just want to check on the health of the application, you might want to instruct the application to emit a particular type of trace information by just changing the configuration file. You are not required to recompile the application; the application automatically picks up the changes from the configuration file when it restarts.

There are two predefined classes for creating trace switches: the `BooleanSwitch` class and the `TraceSwitch` class. Both of these classes derive from the abstract `Switch` class. You can also define your own trace switch classes by deriving classes from the `Switch` class.

You use the `BooleanSwitch` class to differentiate between two modes of tracing: trace-on and trace-off. Its default value is zero, which corresponds to the trace-off state. If it is set to any nonzero value, it corresponds to the trace-on state.

Unlike `BooleanSwitch`, the `TraceSwitch` class provides five different levels of tracing switches. These levels are defined by the `TraceLevel` enumeration and are listed in Table 12.2. The default value of `TraceLevel` for a `TraceSwitch` object is `0` `(Off)`.

EXAM TIP

Out-of-Range Values for BooleanSwitch and TraceSwitch For a BooleanSwitch object, if any nonzero (negative or positive) value is specified in the configuration file, the BooleanSwitch object's Enabled property is set to true. For a TraceSwitch object, if a value greater than 4 is specified, the Level property of the object is set to TraceLevel.Verbose (4). If a negative value is specified, a StackOverflow exception occurs at runtime.

TABLE 12.2

THE TraceLevel ENUMERATION

Enumerated Value	Integer Value	Type of Tracing
Off	0	None
Error	1	Only error messages
Warning	2	Warning messages and error messages
Info	3	Informational messages, warning messages, and error messages
Verbose	4	Verbose messages, informational messages, warning messages, and error messages

Table 12.3 displays the important properties of the TraceSwitch class.

TABLE 12.3

IMPORTANT PROPERTIES OF THE TraceSwitch CLASS

Property	Description
Description	Describes the switch (inherited from Switch).
DisplayName	Specifies a name used to identify the switch (inherited from Switch).
Level	Specifies the trace level that helps select which trace and debug messages will be processed. Its value is one of the TraceLevel enumeration values (refer to Table 12.2).
TraceError	Returns true if Level is set to Error, Warning, Info, or Verbose; otherwise, it returns false.
TraceInfo	Returns true if Level is set to Info or Verbose; otherwise, it returns false.
TraceVerbose	Returns true if Level is set to Verbose; otherwise, it returns false.
TraceWarning	Returns true if Level is set to Warning, Info, or Verbose; otherwise, it returns false.

Step by Step 12.3 demonstrates how to use trace switches in a Windows application.

STEP BY STEP

12.3 Using the TraceSwitch Class

1. Create a new Windows application project in solution 316C12. Name the project StepByStep12_3.

2. In Solution Explorer, copy the FactorialCalculator.cs form from the StepByStep12_1 project to the current project. Change the Text property of the form to Factorial Calculator 12_3. Switch to the code view and change the namespace of the form to StepByStep12_3.

3. Delete the default Form1.cs.

4. Declare the following static variable at the class level, just after the Main() method:

```
static TraceSwitch traceSwitch =
        new TraceSwitch("FactorialTrace",
        "Trace the factorial application");
```

5. Change the Click event handler of the Calculate button so that it has the following code:

```
private void btnCalculate_Click(object sender,
    System.EventArgs e)
{
    if (traceSwitch.TraceVerbose)
        // write a debug message
        Debug.WriteLine(
            "Inside the Button Click event handler");

    // start indenting messages now
    Debug.Indent();
    int intNumber = Convert.ToInt32(txtNumber.Text);

    if (traceSwitch.TraceError)
    {
        // make a debug assertion
        Debug.Assert(intNumber >= 0, "Invalid value",
            "negative value in debug mode");
    }

    int intFac = 1;
    for (int i = 2; i <= intNumber; i++)
    {
        intFac = intFac * i;
        // write a debug message
        if (traceSwitch.TraceInfo)
            Debug.WriteLine(i,
                "Factorial Program Debug, Value of i");
    }
```

continues

continued

```
if (traceSwitch.TraceWarning)
    // write a debug message
    // if the condition is true
    Debug.WriteLineIf(intFac < 1,
        "There was an overflow",
        "Factorial Program Debug");

txtFactorial.Text = intFac.ToString();
// decrease the indent level
Debug.Unindent();

if (traceSwitch.TraceVerbose)
    // write a debug message
    Debug.WriteLine(
        "Done with computations, returning...");
}
```

6. In Solution Explorer, select View All Files from the tool-bar. Navigate to the `bin\debug` folder. Right-click the `debug` folder and then select Add, Add New Item. Choose to create an XML file and name the XML file `StepByStep12_3.exe.config`.

7. In the XML editor, type the following configuration data in the XML file:

```xml
<?xml version="1.0" encoding="utf-8" ?>
<configuration>
    <system.diagnostics>
        <switches>
            <add name="FactorialTrace" value="4" />
        </switches>
    </system.diagnostics>
</configuration>
```

8. Set project `StepByStep12_3` as the startup project.

9. Run the project, using the default `Debug` configuration. Enter the value `5`; note that all messages appear in the out-put window. Enter a negative value and then a large value, and you see all the errors and warning messages. Close the form. Modify the XML file to change the value of `FactorialTrace` to `3`. Run the project again, you should now see all messages except the one set with `TraceLevel` as `Verbose`. Repeat the process, with values of `FactorialTrace` in the configuration file changed to `2`, `1`, and `0`.

10. Modify the program to change all Debug statements to Trace statements. Copy the XML configuration file to the bin\Release folder in the project and then repeat step 9, using the Release configuration.

Conditional Compilation

The C# programming language provides a set of preprocessing directives. You can use these directives to skip sections of source files for compilation, to report errors and warnings, or to mark distinct regions of source code.

Table 12.4 summarizes the preprocessing directives that are available in C#.

C# and the Preprocessor There is no separate preprocessor in the Visual C# .NET compiler. The lexical analysis phase of the compiler processes all the preprocessing directives. C# uses the term *preprocessor* from a conventional point of view, in contrast to languages such as C and C++ that have separate preprocessors for taking care of conditional compilation.

TABLE 12.4

C# PREPROCESSING DIRECTIVES

Directives	*Description*
#if, #else, #elif, and #endif	These directives conditionally skip the sections of code. The skipped sections are not part of the compiled code.
#define and #undef	These directives define or undefine symbols in the code.
#warning and #error	These directives explicitly generate error or warning messages. The compiler reports errors and warnings in the same way it reports other compile-time errors and warnings.
#line	This directive alters the line numbers and source file filenames reported by the compiler in warning and error messages.
#region and #endregion	These directives mark sections of code. A common example of these directives is the code generated by Windows Forms Designer. Visual designers such as Visual Studio .NET can use these directives to show, hide, and format code.

In addition to providing preprocessing directives, the C# programming language also provides a ConditionalAttribute class.

You can mark a method as conditional by applying the `Conditional` attribute to it. The `Conditional` attribute takes one argument that specifies a symbol. The conditional method is either included or omitted from the compiled code, depending on the definition of the specified symbol at that point. If the symbol definition is available, the code of the method is included; otherwise, the code of the method is excluded from the compiled code.

The conditional compilation directives and methods with the `Conditional` attribute allow you to keep debugging-related code in the source code but exclude it from the compiled version. This removes the extraneous messages and the production programs do not encounter performance hits due to processing of additional code. In this case, if you want to resolve some errors, you can easily activate the debugging code by defining a symbol and recompiling the program.

Step by Step 12.4 demonstrate the use of `ConditionalAttribute` and the conditional compilation directives.

> **EXAM TIP**
>
> **Conditional Methods**   A method must have its return type set to `void` in order to have the `Conditional` attribute applied to it.

STEP BY STEP

12.4 Using Conditional Compilation

1. Create a new Windows application project in solution `316C12`. Name the project `StepByStep12_4`.

2. In Solution Explorer, copy the `FactorialCalculator.cs` form from the `StepByStep12_1` project to the current project. Set the `Text` property of the form to `Factorial Calculator 12_4`. Switch to the code view and change the namespace of the form to `StepByStep12_4`.

3. Delete the default `Form1.cs`.

4. Add the following two conditional methods to the class definition:

```
[Conditional("DEBUG")]
public void InitializeDebugMode()
{
    label1.Text = "Factorial Calculator: Debug Mode";
}
```

```
[Conditional("TRACE")]
public void InitializeReleaseMode()
{
    label1.Text = "Factorial Calculator Version 1.0";
}
```

5. Attach an event handler to the form's Load event and add the following code:

```
private void StepByStep12_4_Load(
    object sender, System.EventArgs e)
{
    #if !DEBUG && !TRACE
        #error you should have either
➥DEBUG or TRACE defined
    #endif

    #if DEBUG
        Debug.WriteLine(
            "Program started in debug mode");
        InitializeDebugMode();
    #else
        Trace.WriteLine(
            "Program started in release mode");
        InitializeReleaseMode();
    #endif
}
```

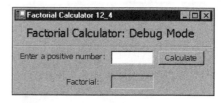

FIGURE 12.8
The factorial calculator can be conditionally compiled by using the Debug configuration.

6. Set project StepByStep12_4 as the startup project.

7. Run the project, using the default Debug configuration. The heading of the form displays "Factorial Program: Debug Mode" (see Figure 12.8). The Output window also displays a string: "Program started in debug mode." Close the program and start it again in the Release mode. A different heading appears in the form (see Figure 12.9) and a different message appears in the Output window.

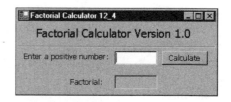

FIGURE 12.9
The factorial calculator can be conditionally compiled by using the Release configuration.

8. Add the following line as the very first line of the code:

```
#undef DEBUG
```

Run the program, using the Debug configuration. Note that the program is executed as if it were executed in the Trace configuration. This is because the Debug configuration defines both the DEBUG and TRACE symbols. Because DEBUG is undefined using the #undef preprocessing directive in the code you added, the compiled code includes the #else part of the preprocessing directive.

continues

continued

9. Add the following line just after the directive placed in step 8:

```
#undef TRACE
```

Try running the program. Rather than run the program, the compiler throws an error message, complaining that both DEBUG and TRACE are undefined. This message is caused by the conditional logic in the Load event handler of the form.

You can define the DEBUG and TRACE symbols for the compiler in the following ways:

◆ By defining the constants in the project's property pages dialog box

◆ By using the #define directive at the beginning of the code file

◆ By using the /define (/d for short) option with the command-line C# compiler

Step by Step 12.4 demonstrates conditional compilation with the DEBUG and TRACE symbols. You can also use conditional compilation with any other custom-defined symbols to perform conditional compilation.

GUIDED PRACTICE EXERCISE 12.1

The goal of this exercise is to add an EventLogTraceListener object to the Factorial Calculator program so that it will write all Trace and Debug messages to the Windows event log.

This exercise will give you good practice using trace listeners. How would you create such a form?

You should try working through this problem on your own first. If you get stuck, or if you'd like to see one possible solution, follow these steps:

1. Create a new Visual C# Windows application in solution 316C12. Name the project GuidedPracticeExercise12_1.

2. In Solution Explorer, copy the FactorialCalculator.cs form from the StepByStep12_1 project to the current project. Set the Text property of the form to Factorial Calculator GuidedPracticeExercise12_1. Switch to the code view and change the namespace of the form to GuidedPracticeExercise12_1.

3. Delete the default Form1.cs.

4. Double-click the form to add an event handler for the Load event. Add the following code to the event handler:

```
private void FactorialCalculator_Load(object sender,
    System.EventArgs e)
{
    //Add a event log listener to
    //the Listeners collection
    Trace.Listeners.Add(new EventLogTraceListener(
        "FactorialCalculator"));
}
```

5. Set project GuidedPracticeExercise12_1 as the startup project.

6. Run the project. Enter a value for finding a factorial. Click the Calculate button. Close the program. Select View, Server Explorer. Navigate to your computer, and expand the Event Logs node, the Application node, and the FactorialCalculator node. The messages generated by the Trace and Debug classes are added to the Application event log, as shown in Figure 12.10.

If you have difficulty following this exercise, review the sections "Trace Listeners" and "Using Trace and Debug to Display Information," earlier in this chapter. After doing that review, try this exercise again.

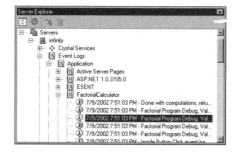

FIGURE 12.10
You can view the Windows Event Log from Server Explorer.

REVIEW BREAK

▶ The Trace and Debug classes can be used to display informative messages in an application when the DEBUG and TRACE symbols are defined, respectively, at the time of compilation.

▶ By default, both TRACE and DEBUG symbols are defined in the Debug configuration for compilation, and only the TRACE symbol is defined for the Release configuration for compilation.

▶ Listeners are objects that receive trace and debug output. By default, both Trace and Debug classes have the DefaultTraceListener object in their Listeners collections. The DefaultTraceListener object displays messages in the Output window.

▶ Debug and Trace objects share the same Listeners collection. Therefore, any listener object added to the Trace.Listeners collection is also added to the Debug.Listeners collection.

▶ Trace switches allow you to change the type of messages traced by a program, depending on the value stored in the XML configuration file. You need not recompile the application for this change to take effect; you just restart it. You need to implement code to display the messages, depending on the value of the switch.

▶ C# preprocessing directives allow you to define and undefine symbols in an application, report errors or warnings, mark regions of code, and conditionally skip code for compilation.

▶ The Conditional attribute allows you to conditionally add or skip a method for compilation, depending on the value of the symbol that is passed as a parameter to the attribute.

DEBUGGING

Debug, rework, and resolve defects in code.

- **Configure the debugging environment.**

Debugging is the process of finding the causes of errors in a program, locating the lines of code that are causing those errors, and fixing those errors.

Without tools, the process of debugging can be very time-consuming and tedious. Thankfully, Visual Studio .NET comes loaded with a large set of tools to help you with various debugging tasks.

Stepping Through Program Execution

A common technique for debugging is to execute a program step-by-step. This systematic execution allows you to track the flow of logic, to ensure that the program is following the same paths of execution that you expect it to follow. If it does not, you can immediately identify the location of the problem.

Using step-by-step execution of a program also gives you an opportunity to monitor the program's state before and after a statement is executed. For example, you can check the values of variables, the records in a database, and other changes in the environment. Visual Studio .NET provides tools to make these tasks convenient.

The Debug menu provides three options for step-by-step execution of a program (see Table 12.5). The keyboard shortcuts listed in Table 12.5 correspond to the default keyboard scheme of the Visual Studio .NET IDE. If you have personalized the keyboard scheme either through the Tools, Options, Environment, Keyboard menu or through the Visual Studio . NET Start Page, you might have a different keyboard mapping. You can check out the keyboard mappings available for your customization through Visual Studio .NET's context-sensitive help.

NOTE

Runtime Errors and Compile-Time Errors *Compile-time errors* are produced when a program does not comply with the syntax of the programming language. These errors are trivial and are generally pointed out by compilers themselves. *Runtime errors* occur in programs that are compiled successfully but do not behave as expected. The process of testing and debugging applies to runtime errors only. Testing reveals these errors, and debugging repairs them.

TABLE 12.5

DEBUG OPTIONS FOR STEP-BY-STEP EXECUTION

Debug Menu Item	Keyboard Shortcut	Purpose
Step Into	F11	You use this option to execute code in step mode. If a method call is encountered, the program execution steps into the code of the method and executes the method in step mode.

continues

| TABLE 12.5 | *continued* |

DEBUG OPTIONS FOR STEP-BY-STEP EXECUTION

Debug Menu Item	Keyboard Shortcut	Purpose
Step Over	F10	You use this option when a method call is encountered and you do not want to step into the method code. When this option is selected, the debugger executes the entire method without any step-by-step execution (interruption), and then it steps to the next statement after the method call.
Step Out	Shift+F11	You use this option inside a method call to execute the rest of the method without stepping, and you resume step execution mode when control returns to the calling method.

STEP BY STEP

12.5 Trying Step-by-Step Execution of a Windows Application

1. Set project StepByStep12_4 as the startup project.

2. Select Debug, Step Into. The program pauses its execution at the first executable statement and shows the statement highlighted, as shown in Figure 12.11. An arrow appears in the left margin of the code, and it points at the next statement to be executed.

3. Press F11 to proceed to the next step. The debugger steps into the Windows Form Designer Generated Code section, where it executes the constructor code of the FactorialCalculator form to create its new instance, as requested by the Application.Run() method. Press F11 a couple times.

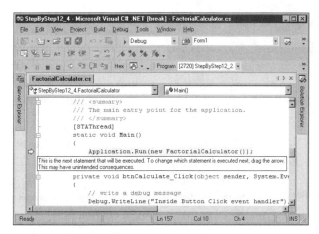

FIGURE 12.11
You can step through a program's execution by selecting Debug, StepInto from the Visual Studio .NET menu.

4. Drag the yellow arrow back one line. In this way you can instruct the debugger to change what statement will be executed next. Press F11 two times to see the effect of dragging the debugger back. Now press Shift+F11. This automates the execution for the rest of the current method, and the execution breaks again at the next statement to be executed in the calling code.

5. Control comes back to the Application.Run() method call. The form is now created and is ready to be launched, as soon as you initiate the next step by pressing F11. Press the F11 key, and you see the form execute.

6. Enter a positive number in the form and press the Calculate button. The form calculates the factorial and displays it almost instantly. Note that the application is no longer running in step mode. Pressing F11 either on the form or in the code view has no effect.

The lesson from Step by Step 12.5 is that when you start an application in step mode, after the Application.Run() method is executed and the form is launched, you cannot really go back to step-by-step execution of the code. To step into the code of various event handlers of a form, you need to mark breakpoints in the code, as described in the following section.

Setting Breakpoints

Breakpoints are markers in code that signal the debugger to pause execution. When the debugger pauses at a breakpoint, you can take your time to analyze variables, data records, and other settings in the environment to determine the state of the program. You can also choose to execute the program in step mode from this point onward.

If you have placed a breakpoint in the `Click` event handler of a button, the program pauses when you click the button and the execution reaches the breakpoint. You can then step through the execution for the rest of the event handler. When the execution of the event handler code finishes, the control is transferred back to the form. If you have another button on the form for which a breakpoint is not set in the event handler, then the program is no longer under step execution. You should mark breakpoints at all the places you would like execution to pause.

STEP BY STEP

12.6 Working with Breakpoints

1. Create a new Windows application project in solution `316C12`. Name the project `StepByStep12_6`.

2. In Solution Explorer, copy the `FactorialCalculator.cs` form from the `StepByStep12_1` project to the current project. Change the `Text` property of the form to `Factorial Calculator 12_6`. Switch to the code view and change the namespace of the form to `StepByStep12_6`.

3. Delete the default `Form1.cs`.

4. Set project `StepByStep12_6` as the startup project.

5. Add the following method to the class:

```
private int Factorial(int intNumber)
{
    int intFac = 1;
    for (int i = 2; i <= intNumber; i++)
    {
        intFac = intFac * i;
    }
    return intFac;
}
```

6. Modify the `Click` event handler of `btnCalculate` so that it looks like this:

```
private void btnCalculate_Click(object sender,
    System.EventArgs e)
{
    int intNumber, intFactorial;
    try
    {
        intNumber = Convert.ToInt32(txtNumber.Text);
        intFactorial = Factorial(intNumber);
        txtFactorial.Text = intFactorial.ToString();
    }
    catch(Exception ex)
    {
        Debug.WriteLine(ex.Message);
    }
}
```

7. In the event handler added in step 6, right-click the beginning of the line that makes a call to the `Factorial()` method and select Insert Breakpoint from the context menu. Note that the line of code is highlighted with red and that a red dot appears in the left margin, as in Figure 12.12. Alternatively, you could create a breakpoint by clicking the left margin adjacent to a line.

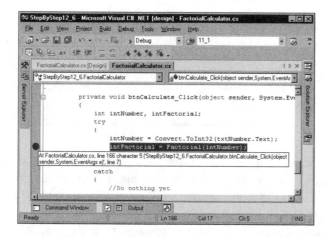

FIGURE 12.12
You can enter step-by-step execution mode by setting a breakpoint in a program.

8. Execute the project. The Factorial form appears. Enter a value and click the Calculate button. Note that execution pauses at the location where you have marked the breakpoint.

NOTE

The Disassembly Window Shows Native Code Instead of MSIL
Although C# programs are compiled to Microsoft Intermediate Language (MSIL), they are just-in-time compiled to native code only at the time of their first execution. This means the executing code is never in IL; it is always in native code. Thus, you will always see native code instead of IL in the Disassembly window.

continues

9. Press F11 to step into the code of the Factorial() method. Move the mouse pointer over various variables in the Factorial() method, and you see the current values of these variables.

10. Select Debug, Windows, Breakpoints. The Breakpoints window appears, as shown in Figure 12.13. Right-click the breakpoint listed in the window and select Goto Disassembly. The Disassembly window appears, showing the object code of the program along with the disassembled source code.

FIGURE 12.13
The Breakpoints window gives you convenient access to all breakpoint-related tasks in one place.

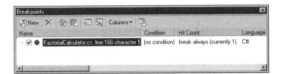

11. Close the Disassembly window. Select Debug, Step Out to automatically execute the rest of the Factorial() method and again start the step mode in the event handler at the next statement. Step through the execution until you see the form again.

12. Select Debug, Stop Debugging. The debugging session ends and the application is terminated.

13. In the code view, right-click the statement where you have set the breakpoint and select Disable Breakpoint from the context menu.

> **NOTE**
>
> **The Debug Configuration**
> Breakpoints and other debugging features are available only when you compile a program by using the Debug configuration.

> **NOTE**
>
> **Disabling Versus Removing a Breakpoint** When you remove a breakpoint, you loose all the information related to it. Instead of removing a breakpoint, you can choose to disable it. Disabling a breakpoint does not pause the program at the point of the breakpoint, but Visual C# .NET will remember the breakpoint settings. At any time, you can select Enable Breakpoint to reactivate the breakpoint.

To set advanced options in a breakpoint, you can choose to create a new breakpoint by selecting New from the context menu of the code or from the toolbar in the Breakpoints window. The New Breakpoint dialog box (see Figure 12.14) has four tabs. You can use these tabs to set a breakpoint in a function, in a file, at an address in the object code, and when a data value (that is, the value of a variable) changes.

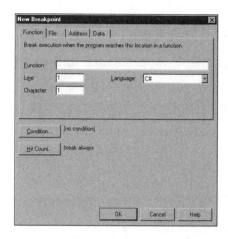

The New Breakpoint dialog box allows you to create a new breakpoint.

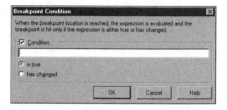

FIGURE 12.15▲
The Breakpoint Condition dialog box allows you to set a breakpoint that is based on the value of an expression at runtime.

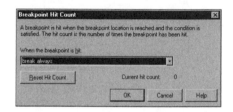

FIGURE 12.16▲
The Breakpoint Hit Count dialog box enables you to break program execution only if the specified breakpoint has been hit a given number of times.

Clicking the Condition button opens the Breakpoint Condition dialog box, as shown in Figure 12.15. The Breakpoint Condition dialog box allows you to set a breakpoint based on the runtime value of an expression.

Clicking the Hit Count button opens the Breakpoint Hit Count dialog box, as shown in Figure 12.16. This dialog box enables you to break the program execution only if the specified breakpoint has been hit a given number of times. This can be especially helpful if you have a breakpoint inside a lengthy loop and you want to step-execute the program only near the end of the loop.

Analyzing Program State to Resolve Errors

Debug, rework, and resolve defects in code.

- **Resolve errors and rework code.**

When you break the execution of a program, the program is at a particular state in its execution cycle. You can use various debugging tools to analyze the values of variables, the results of expressions, the path of execution, and so on, to help identify the cause of the error that you are debugging.

Step by Step 12.7 demonstrates various Visual C# .NET debugging tools, such as the Watch, Autos, Locals, This, Immediate, Output and the Call Stack windows.

STEP BY STEP

12.7 Analyzing Program State to Resolve Errors

1. Create a new Windows application project in solution 316C12. Name the project StepByStep12_7.

2. In Solution Explorer, copy the FactorialCalculator.cs form from the StepByStep12_6 project to the current project. Change the Text property of the form to Factorial Calculator 12_7. Switch to the code view and change the namespace of the form to StepByStep12_7.

3. Delete the default Form1.cs.

4. Set project StepByStep12_7 as the startup project.

5. Change the code in the Factorial() method to the following:

```
private int Factorial(int intNumber)
{
    int intFac = 1;
    for (int i = 2; i < intNumber; i++)
    {
        intFac = intFac * i;
    }
    return intFac;
}
```

   Note in this code that I have introduced a logical error that I will later "discover" through debugging.

6. Run the program. Enter the value 5 in the text box and click the Calculate button. You should see that the result is not correct; this program needs to be debugged.

7. Set a breakpoint in the Click event handler of btnCalculate at the line where a call to the Factorial() method is being made. Execute the program. Enter the value 5 again, and click the Calculate button.

8. Press the F11 key to step into the Factorial() method. Select Debug, Windows, Watch, Watch1 to add a Watch window. Similarly, select the Debug, Windows menu and add the Locals, Autos, This, Immediate, Output and Call Stack windows. Pin down the windows so that they always remain in view and are easy to watch as you step through the program.

9. Look at the Call Stack window shown in Figure 12.17. It shows the method call stack, giving you information about the path taken by the code to reach its current point of execution. The currently executing method is at the top of the stack, as indicated by a yellow arrow. When this method is finished executing, the next entry in the stack will be the method receiving the control of execution.

10. Look at the This window, shown in Figure 12.18. In the This window you can examine the members associated with the current object (the Factorial form). You can scroll down to find the txtNumber object. You can change the values of these objects here. At this point, you don't need to change any values.

11. Activate the Autos window, which is shown in Figure 12.19. The Autos window displays the variables used in the current statement and the previous statement. The debugger determines this information for you automatically; that is why the name of this window is Autos.

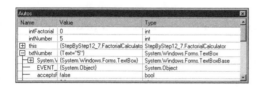

12. Invoke the Locals window, which is shown in Figure 12.20. The Locals window displays the variables that are local to the current context (that is, the current method under execution) with their current values. Figure 12.20 shows the local variables in the Factorial() method.

13. Invoke the Immediate window. Type intNumber in the Immediate window and press Enter. The Immediate window immediately evaluates and displays the current value of this variable in the next line. Now type the expression Factorial(intNumber). The Immediate window calls the Factorial() method for a given value and prints the result.

continues

FIGURE 12.17▲
The Call Stack window enables you to view the names of methods on the call stack, parameter types, and their values.

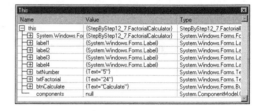

FIGURE 12.18▲
The This window enables you to examine the members associated with the current object.

FIGURE 12.19◄
The Autos window displays the variables that are used in the current statement and the previous statement.

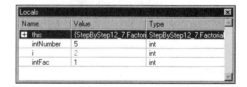

FIGURE 12.20▲
The Locals window displays the variables that are local to the method currently under execution.

continued

NOTE

Two Modes of the Command Window
The command window has two modes: the command mode and the immediate mode. When you select View, Other Windows, Command Window, the command window is invoked in the command mode. You can distinctly identify the command mode as in this mode the command window shows the > prompt (see Figure 12.21). You can use the command mode to evaluate expressions or to issue commands such as Edit to edit text in a file. You can also use regular expressions with the Edit command to make editing operations quick and effective.

On the other hand, when you invoke the command window by selecting Debug, Window, Immediate, it opens in the immediate mode. You can use the immediate mode to evaluate expressions in the currently debugged program. The immediate mode does not show any prompt (see Figure 12.21). You can switch from immediate mode to command mode by typing >cmd, and you can switch from command mode to immediate mode by typing immed in the Command window.

FIGURE 12.21
The Command window can appear in two modes: the command mode and the immediate mode.

The Immediate window can therefore be used to print values of variables and expressions while you are debugging a program.

14. Invoke the Watch1 window. The Watch window enables you to evaluate variables and expressions. Select the variable intFac from the code and drag and drop it in the Watch1 window. You can also double-click the next available row and add a variable to it. Add the variables i and intNumber to the Watch1 window, as shown in Figure 12.22.

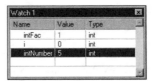

FIGURE 12.22
The Watch window enables you to evaluate variables and expressions.

15. Step through the execution of the program by pressing the F11 key. Keep observing the way values change in the Watch1 (or Autos or Locals) window. After a few steps, the method terminates. Note that the program executed only until the value of i was 4 and that the loop was not iterated back when the value of i was 5. This causes the incorrect output in the program.

16. Change the condition in the for loop to use the <= operator instead of < and press F11 to step through. The Unable to Apply Code Changes dialog box appears, as shown in Figure 12.23. This dialog box appears because after you have identified the problem and corrected the code, the source code is different from the compiled version of the program. If you choose to continue at this stage, your source code and program in execution are different, and that might mislead you. I recommend that you always restart execution in this case by clicking the Restart button. The code is then recompiled, and the program is started again.

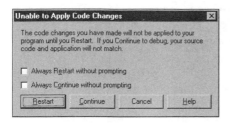

FIGURE 12.23
The Unable to Apply Code Changes dialog box appears if you edit code and then try to continue execution.

17. Enter the value 5 and click the Continue button. The program breaks into the debugger again because the breakpoint is still active. Step through the program and watch the values of the variables. The loop is executed the correct number of times, and you get the correct factorial value.

> N O T E
>
> **Support for Cross-Language Debugging** Visual Studio .NET supports debugging of projects that contain code written in several managed languages. The debugger can transparently step into and out of languages, making the debugging process smooth for you as a developer. Visual Studio .NET also extends this support to nonmanaged languages, but with minor limitations.

Debugging on Exceptions

You can control the way the debugger behaves when it encounters a line of code that throws an exception. You can control this behavior through the Exceptions dialog box, which is shown in Figure 12.24 and is invoked by selecting Debug, Exceptions. The Exceptions dialog box allows you to control the debugger's behavior for each type of exception defined on the system. In fact, if you have defined your own exceptions, you can also add them to this dialog box.

FIGURE 12.24
The Exceptions dialog box allows you to control the debugger's behavior for system and custom-defined exceptions.

There are two levels at which you can control the behavior of the debugger when it encounters exceptions:

◆ **When the exception is thrown**—You can instruct the debugger to either continue or break the execution of the program when an exception is thrown. The default setting for Common Language Runtime (CLR) exceptions is to continue the execution, possibly in anticipation that there will be an exception handler.

◆ **If the exception is not handled**—If the program you are debugging fails to handle an exception, you can instruct the debugger to either ignore it and continue or to break the execution of the program. The default setting for CLR exceptions is to break the execution, warning the programmer of the possibly problematic situation.

GUIDED PRACTICE EXERCISE 12.2

The Factorial Calculator program created in Step by Step 12.4 throws exceptions of type System.FormatException and System.OverflowException when users are not careful about the numbers they enter.

The later versions of this program (created in Step by Step 12.6 and 12.7) catch the exception to prevent users from complaining about the annoying exception messages.

The goal of this exercise is to configure the debugger in Step by Step 12.7 so that when the reported exception occurs, you get an opportunity to analyze the program.

How would you configure the debugger?

In this exercise you will practice configuring the exception handling for the Visual Studio .NET debugger environment. You should try working through this problem on your own first. If you get stuck, or if you'd like to see one possible solution, follow these steps:

1. Open the Windows application project StepByStep12_7.

2. Activate the Exceptions dialog box by selecting Debug – Exceptions.

3. In the Exceptions dialog box, click the Find button. Enter System.FormatException and click the OK button. You are quickly taken to the desired exception in the exception tree view.

4. Select Break into the Debugger from the When the Exception Is Thrown group box.

5. Repeat the steps 3 and 4 for System.OverFlowException.

6. Run the project. Enter a nonnumeric value for which to find the factorial. This causes a System.FormatException error, and the debugger prompts you to either break or continue the execution. Select to break. You can see the values of various variables at this stage either by moving the mouse pointer over them or by adding the variables to the Watch window. On the next execution of the program, enter a very large value. This causes a System.OverFlowException error. Select to break when prompted by the debugger, and then analyze the values of the various variables.

If you have difficulty following this exercise, review the section "Debugging on Exceptions," earlier in this chapter. After doing that review, try this exercise again.

Debugging a Running Process

Until this point in the chapter, you have only seen how to debug programs by starting them from the Visual Studio .NET environment. However, Visual Studio .NET also allows you to debug processes that are running outside the Visual Studio .NET debugging environment.

To access external processes from Visual Studio .NET, you need to invoke the Processes dialog box, shown in Figure 12.25. You can do this in two ways:

◆ When you have a solution open in Visual Studio .NET, you can invoke the Processes dialog box by selecting Debug, Processes.

◆ When there is no solution open in Visual Studio .NET, you don't see any Debug menu, but you can still invoke the Processes dialog box by selecting Tools, Debug Processes.

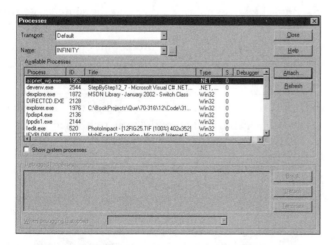

FIGURE 12.25
The Processes dialog box allows you to attach a debugger to a process that is under execution.

Step by Step 12.8 demonstrates how to attach the debugger to a process that is being executed.

STEP BY STEP

12.8 Attaching the Debugger to a Process That Is Being Executed

1. Using Windows Explorer, navigate to the bin\Debug folder inside the project folder for StepByStep12_7. Double-click the .exe file to launch the program.

2. Start a new instance of Visual Studio .NET and select Tools, Debug Processes. The Processes dialog box appears, as shown in Figure 12.25. You may have a different process list from what is shown in the figure.

3. Select the process named StepByStep12_7.exe and click the Attach button. This invokes an Attach to Process dialog box, as shown in Figure 12.26. Select the Common Language Runtime as the program type and keep all other options unchecked. Click the OK button. You should now see the selected process in the Debugged Processes section of the Processes dialog box.

4. Click the Break button to break into the running process. Click the Close button to close the Processes dialog box for now.

5. Both the Disassembly window and the source code window open in the debugging environment. Switch to the source code window. Set a breakpoint on the line of code that makes a call to the Factorial() method. Press F11 to step into the program.

6. Enter the value 5 in the form and click the Calculate button. The debugger breaks the execution when the breakpoint is reached.

7. Select Watch, Locals, Autos to analyze variables and step through the program execution.

8. When the factorial result is displayed, invoke the Processes window again by selecting Debug, Processes. From the list of debugged processes, select StepByStep12_7 and click the Detach button.

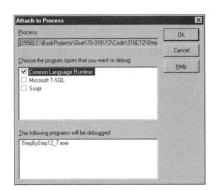

FIGURE 12.26
The Attach to Process dialog box allows you to attach to a program that is running in a process outside Visual Studio .NET.

9. Click the Close button to close the Processes dialog box. `StepByStep12_7.exe` is still executing, as it was when you initiated the debugging process.

Debugging a Remote Process

The process of debugging a remote process is almost the same as the process of debugging an already running process. The only difference is that prior to selecting a running process from the Processes dialog box, you need to select the remote machine name from the Processes dialog box (refer to Figure 12.25).

Before you can remotely debug processes, you need to do a one-time configuration on the remote machine (where the processes are running). To do so, you take one of the following steps:

◆ Install Visual Studio .NET on the remote machine.

◆ Install Remote Components Setup on the remote machine (you can start this from the Visual Studio .NET Setup Disc 1).

Using either of these methods, you can set up Machine Debug Manager (`mdm.exe`) on the remote computer. `mdm.exe` runs as a background service on the computer, providing remote debugging support. In addition, when you use either of these methods, you can add the logged-on user to the Debugger Users group. A user needs to be a member of this group in order to remotely access this computer. You can later add other usernames to this group by using the Computer Management MMC Snap-in on the remote computer.

If SQL Server is installed on the remote machine, the setup process just described also configures the machine for SQL Server stored procedures debugging, which is demonstrated at the end of this chapter, in Exercise 12.2.

For a different configuration or requirement, you might want to refer to the "Setting Up Remote Debugging" topic in the Visual Studio .NET Combined Help Collection.

> **EXAM TIP**
>
> **Debugging a Remote Process**
> The local computer and the remote computer must be members of a trusted domain in order for remote debugging to be possible.

Debugging the Code in DLL Files

The process of debugging a DLL file is similar to the process of debugging an EXE file. There is one difference though: The code in the DLL file cannot be directly invoked, so you need to have a calling program that calls various methods/components of the DLL files.

You typically need to take the following steps in order to debug code in a DLL file:

1. Launch the EXE file that uses the components or methods in the DLL file.

2. Launch Visual Studio .NET and attach the debugger to the EXE file. Set a breakpoint where the method in the DLL file is called. Continue with the execution.

3. The execution breaks when the breakpoint is reached. At this point, select Debug, Step Into to step into the code of the DLL file. Execute the code in the DLL file in step mode while you watch the value of its variables.

In addition, if the code files are executing on a remote machine, you need to make sure that the remote machine is set up with remote debugging support, as explained in the previous section.

REVIEW BREAK

▶ Debugging is the process of finding the causes of errors in a program, locating the lines of code that are causing the error, and fixing the errors.

▶ The three options available while performing step-by-step execution are Step Into, Step Over, and Step Out.

▶ Breakpoints allow you to mark code that signals the debugger to pause execution. After you encounter a breakpoint, you can choose to continue step-by-step execution or resume the normal execution by pressing F5 or by clicking the Resume button, or the Continue button.

▶ The various tool windows, such as This, Locals, Immediate, Autos, Watch, and Call Stack, can be of great help in tracking the execution path and the status of variables in the process of debugging an application in Visual Studio .NET.

▶ When an exception is thrown by an application, you can either choose to continue execution or break into the debugger (in order to start debugging operations such as step-by-step execution). You can customize this behavior for each exception object by using the Exceptions dialog box.

▶ You can attach the debugger to a running process (either local or remote) with the help of the Processes dialog box.

CHAPTER SUMMARY

This chapter starts with a discussion of the various types of tests and how important testing is for an application. You have learned that designing and executing a comprehensive test plan is desirable to ensure that an application is robust, accurate, and reliable.

The .NET Framework provides various classes and techniques that implement tracing in applications. You use tracing to display informative messages during execution of a program. The Trace and Debug classes provide different methods to generate messages at specific locations in the code. You have learned how trace switches can be applied to an application to give you control over the type of tracing information generated by an application without even needing to recompile the application.

You have also learned about the various C# preprocessing directives that are available in Visual C# .NET. You have seen how you can use the Conditional attribute to conditionally compile methods.

The compiler flags syntactical errors at compile time. The tough job is to find logical and runtime errors in an application. Visual C# .NET offers lots of tools for debugging. In this chapter you have learned about various tools available for debugging. You have also learned how to debug an already running process, debug a process running on a remote machine and debug DLL files. As you continue to work with Visual C# .NET, you'll discover more benefits of these debugging tools.

KEY TERMS

- debugging
- testing
- tracing

APPLY YOUR KNOWLEDGE

Exercises

12.1 Creating a Custom Trace Switch

The TraceSwitch and BooleanSwitch classes are two classes that provide trace switch functionality. If you need different trace levels or different implementations of the Switch class, you can inherit from the Switch class to implement your own custom trace switches.

In this exercise, you will learn how to create a custom switch. You will create a FactorialSwitch class that can be set with four values (Negative (-1), Off (0), Overflow (1), and Both (2)) for the Factorial Calculator form. The class will have two properties: Negative and Overflow.

Estimated time: 25 minutes

1. Launch Visual Studio .NET. Select File, New, Blank Solution, and name the new project 316C12Exercises.

2. Add a new Windows application project to the solution. Name the project Exercise12_1.

3. Using the Add Class Wizard, add a new class to the project. Name the class FactorialSwitch and modify the class definition so that it has the following code:

```
using System;
using System.Diagnostics;

namespace Exercise12_1
{
    // The possible values for new switch
    public enum FactorialSwitchLevel
    {
        Negative    = -1,
        Off         = 0,
        Overflow    = 1,
        Both        = 2
    }
```

```
public class FactorialSwitch : Switch
{
    public FactorialSwitch(
        string displayName,
        string description)
        : base(displayName, description)
    {
    }
    public bool Negative
    {
        get
        {
            // return true if the
            // SwitchSetting is
            // Negative or Both
            if( (SwitchSetting == -1) ||
                (SwitchSetting == 2))
                return true;
            else
                return false;
        }
    }
    public bool Overflow
    {
        get
        {
            // return true if the
            // SwitchSetting is
            // Overflow or Both
            if ((SwitchSetting == 1) ||
                (SwitchSetting == 2))
                return true;
            else
                return false;
        }
    }
}
}
```

4. In Solution Explorer, right-click Form1.cs and rename it FactorialCalculator. Open the Properties window for the form and change its Name property to FactorialCalculator and Text property to Factorial Calculator Exercise 12_1. Switch to the code view of the form and modify the Main() method to launch FactorialCalculator instead of Form1.

APPLY YOUR KNOWLEDGE

5. Place two `TextBox` controls (`txtNumber` and `txtFactorial`), three `Label` controls, and a `Button` control (`btnCalculate`) on the form and arrange the controls as shown in Figure 12.5.

6. Open `FactorialCalculator.cs` in the code view. Add the following code in the class definition:

```
static FactorialSwitch facSwitch =
    new FactorialSwitch("FactorialTrace",
    "Trace the factorial application " +
    "using Factorial Switch");
```

7. Attach a `Click` event handler to the `btnCalculate` control with the following code:

```
private void btnCalculate_Click(
    object sender, System.EventArgs e)
{
    int intNumber = Convert.ToInt32(
        txtNumber.Text);

    if (facSwitch.Negative)
    {
        // make a debug assertion
        Debug.Assert(
            intNumber >= 0, "Invalid value",
            "negative value in debug mode");
    }

    int intFac = 1;
    for (int i = 2; i <= intNumber; i++)
    {
        intFac = intFac * i;
    }

    if (facSwitch.Overflow)
        // write a debug message if
        // the condition is true
        Debug.WriteLineIf(intFac < 1,
            "There was an overflow",
            "Factorial Program Debug");
    txtFactorial.Text = intFac.ToString();
}
```

8. In Solution Explorer, select View All Files from the toolbar. Navigate to the `bin\debug` folder. Right-click the `debug` folder and select Add, Add New Item. Choose to create an XML file and name it `Exercise12_1.exe.config`.

9. In the XML editor, type the following configuration data in the XML file:

```
<?xml version="1.0" encoding="utf-8" ?>
<configuration>
    <system.diagnostics>
        <switches>
            <add name="FactorialTrace"
                value="2" />
        </switches>
    </system.diagnostics>
</configuration>
```

10. Set `Exercise12_1` as the startup project.

11. Run the project, using the default `Debug` configuration. Notice that the Assertion Failed dialog box is displayed only if the switch is set with the value -1 or 2. Similarly, the overflow message is displayed in the Output window only if the switch value is set to 1 or 2.

12. Modify the program to change all `Debug` statements to `Trace` statements. Copy the XML configuration file to the `bin\Release` folder in the project and then repeat step 11, using the `Release` configuration.

The value set in the configuration file can be accessed through the `SwitchSetting` property of the `Switch` class. The `Negative` and `Overflow` properties of the `FactorialSwitch` class return `true` or `false`, depending on the value of the `SwitchSetting` property.

12.2 Debugging SQL Server Stored Procedures Using Visual C# .NET

You can perform step-by-step execution of SQL Server stored procedures in Visual C# .NET. This exercise shows you how.

Estimated time: 30 minutes

1. Add a new Windows application project to the solution. Name the project `Exercise12_2`.

2. Rename the `Form1.cs` form `MostExpensiveProdcuts.cs`. Change all occurrences of `Form1.cs` to `MostExpensiveProducts.cs`.

3. Select Project, Properties from the main menu. Select `Debugging` under the `Configuration Properties` node in the left pane of the project's Property Pages dialog box. In the right pane, under the `Debuggers` node, choose `true` for `Enable SQL Debugging`, as shown in Figure 12.27.

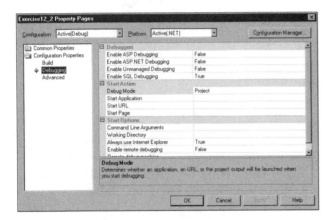

FIGURE 12.27
You can enable SQL debugging in the project's Property Pages dialog box to allow debugging of SQL Server stored procedures.

4. Drag a `SqlDataAdapter` component to the form. This activates the Data Adapter Configuration Wizard. Click Next. Select the Northwind database connection that you have created in the earlier chapters (Chapters 5, "Data Binding," and 6, "Consuming and Manipulating Data,") or click the New Connection button to create a Northwind database connection. Click Next.

5. Choose the Use Existing Stored Procedures option in the Choose a Query Type page. Click Next. Select Ten Most Expensive Products from the Select combo box, as shown in Figure 12.28. Click Next and then click Finish. A `SqlConnection` component is created in the component tray.

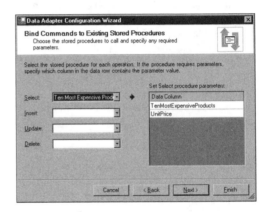

FIGURE 12.28
The Bind Commands to Existing Stored Procedures dialog box allows you to choose the SQL stored procedures to bind to the `SqlCommand` object.

6. Select the `sqlDataAdapter1` component, and then right-click and select Generate DataSet from the context menu. Select the New radio button and choose Ten Most Expensive Products from the checked list box. Click OK to create a `dataSet11` component in the component tray.

7. Place a `Button` control (`btnGetProducts`) and a `DataGrid` control (`dataGrid1`) on the form. Change the `DataGrid` control's `DataSource` property to `dataSet1` and `DataMember` property to `Ten Most Expensive Products`.

APPLY YOUR KNOWLEDGE

8. Add the following code in the `Click` event of the `Button` control:

```
private void btnGetProducts_Click(
    object sender, System.EventArgs e)
{
    sqlDataAdapter1.Fill(this.dataSet11);
}
```

9. Insert a breakpoint in the `Click` event handler, at the point of a call to the `Fill()` method of the `sqlDataAdapter1` object.

10. Open Server Explorer. Open the `Data Connections` node and select the stored procedure Ten Most Expensive Products. Right-click the stored procedure and select Edit Stored Procedure. Insert a breakpoint in the starting code line of the stored procedure, as shown in Figure 12.29.

FIGURE 12.29
You can insert breakpoints in SQL Server stored procedures.

11. Run the project. Click the button. The program starts step-by-step execution as soon as it encounters the breakpoint in the `Fill()` method call line. Press F11. You are taken to the stored procedure code, where you can perform step-by-step execution.

This exercise teaches you how to debug SQL Server stored procedures by using step-by-step execution.

In Figure 12.29, notice the `SELECT` statement enclosed in a blue outline, which represents each step in the stored procedure (if the step occupies more than a line).

> **EXAM TIP**
>
> **Watching SQL Server Variables**
> You can use various tools, such as the Watch and Locals windows, to keep track of the values of the variables that are defined in the stored procedures during step-by-step execution. These tools are very helpful when you are debugging complex stored procedures.

12.3 Setting Conditional Breakpoints by Using Visual C# .NET

This exercise shows you how to set conditional breakpoints. You set a breakpoint in the factorial calculation to break when the factorial value overflows (that is, when it becomes negative).

Estimated time: 30 minutes

1. Add a new Windows application project to the solution. Name the project `Exercise12_3`.

2. In Solution Explorer, right-click `Form1.cs` and rename it `FactorialCalculator`. Open the Properties window for this form and change its `Name` property to `FactorialCalculator` and Text property to `Factorial Calculator Exercise 12_3`. Switch to the code view of the form and modify the `Main()` method to launch `FactorialCalculator` instead of `Form1`.

3. Place two `TextBox` controls (`txtNumber` and `txtFactorial`), three `Label` controls, and a `Button` control (`btnCalculate`) on the form and arrange the controls as shown in Figure 12.5.

APPLY YOUR KNOWLEDGE

4. Attach a `Click` event handler to the `btnCalculate` control and add the following code in the event handler:

```
private void btnCalculate_Click(
    object sender, System.EventArgs e)
{
    int intNumber =
        Convert.ToInt32(txtNumber.Text);

    int intFac = 1;
    for (int i = 2; i <= intNumber; i++)
    {
        intFac = intFac * i;
    }
    txtFactorial.Text = intFac.ToString();
}
```

5. Right-click the following line in the button `Click` event handler and select New Breakpoint from the context menu:

```
intFac=intFac*i;
```

The New Breakpoint dialog box appears. Select the File tab. Note that File, Line, and Character position are already marked correctly. Click the Condition button. This opens the Breakpoint Condition dialog box. Set the values in the dialog box as shown in Figure 12.30. Select the Condition checkbox. Enter `intFac < 1` in the Condition text box and select the Is True option. Click OK twice to dismiss the New Breakpoint dialog box.

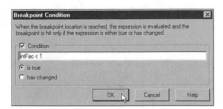

FIGURE 12.30
You can set conditional breakpoints with the Breakpoint Condition dialog box.

6. Run the project using the default `Debug` configuration. Enter `100` and click the Calculate button. Notice that the running page breaks into the debugger when `intFac` has a negative value and the breakpoint is reached.

Review Questions

1. For what do you use a test plan?

2. What is the purpose of the `Assert()` method in the `Debug` and `Trace` classes?

3. What is the main purpose of `TraceListener` class? What classes implement `TraceListener` in the Framework Class Library?

4. What are the two built-in trace switches in the .NET Framework Class Library?

5. What is the main advantage of trace switches?

6. What types of methods can be marked with the `Conditional` attribute?

7. What are the purposes of the `#error` and `#warning` preprocessing directives?

8. What are the three commands can you use to step through code while debugging?

9. What happens when you put a breakpoint in code?

10. What are some of the different windows that are available for debugging?

11. How can you attach the debugger to a running process in Visual C# .NET?

12. In order to verify that remote debugging is enabled on a system, what should you check?

APPLY YOUR KNOWLEDGE

Exam Questions

1. Which of the following activities correctly defines a typical unit test?

    A. Locate and fix errors.

    B. Run the application with carefully planned test data and determine whether it works according to its specification.

    C. Run a module with carefully planned test data and determine whether it works according to its specification.

    D. Verify that a program module integrates well with other modules in an application.

2. Which of the following actions would enable tracing for a Visual C# .NET Windows application? (Select all that apply.)

    A. Compile the Windows application with the `/define:TRACE` option.

    B. Add the following statement at the top of the source code:

    ```
    #define TRACE
    ```

    C. Start the application with the `/define:TRACE` option.

    D. Add the following code to the application's configuration file and then execute the Windows application:

    ```
    <system.diagnostics>
        <switches>
            <add name="TraceLevelSwitch"
                value="1" />
        </switches>
    </system.diagnostics>
    ```

3. You are developing a Windows application, using Microsoft Visual Studio .NET. You have included the following line at the top of the source code:

    ```
    #undef DEBUG
    ```

    Which of the following statements are true with respect to program execution? (Select all that apply.)

    A. You will see the trace messages while running the program in the `Debug` configuration.

    B. You will see the trace messages while running the program in the `Release` configuration.

    C. You will see only the trace messages generated by the methods of Debug class.

    D. You will not see any trace messages.

4. You have added the following statement to the Load event handler of a single-form Windows application:

    ```
    Trace.Listeners.Add(
        new TextWriterTraceListener(
        "TraceLog.txt"))
    ```

    Which of the following statements are true with respect to program execution? (Select all that apply.)

    A. `TextWriterTraceListner` will listen to all messages generated by the methods of the `Debug` and `Trace` classes.

    B. `TextWriterTraceListner` will listen only to the messages generated by the methods of the `Trace` class.

    C. All the trace messages will be stored in a file named `TraceLog.txt`.

    D. The trace messages will be displayed in the output window while the program is run in either the `Debug` or the `Release` configurations.

5. In your C# program, you have the following lines of code:

```
TraceSwitch myTraceSwitch =
    new TraceSwitch(
    "SwitchOne", "The first switch");
myTraceSwitch.Level = TraceLevel.Info;
```

Which of the following expressions in your program would evaluate to false?

A. myTraceSwitch.TraceInfo

B. myTraceSwitch.TraceWarning

C. myTraceSwitch.TraceError

D. myTraceSwitch.TraceVerbose

6. You want to control the tracing and debug output of a Windows application without recompiling your code. Which of the following classes would enable you to do this?

A. TraceListener

B. TraceSwitch

C. Trace

D. Debug

7. You are asked to implement tracing in a Windows application such that the application should display both warning and error messages when the application is run by using the Debug configuration and should display only error messages when it is run by using the Release configuration of Visual C# .NET. Which of the following code segments best meets this requirement?

A.

```
TraceSwitch traceSwitch =
    new TraceSwitch("MySwitch",
    "Error and Warning Switch");

#if DEBUG
    traceSwitch.Level = TraceLevel.Warning;
```

```
#else
    traceSwitch.Level = TraceLevel.Error;
#endif

Trace.WriteLineIf(traceSwitch.TraceWarning,
    "Warning Message");
Trace.WriteLineIf(traceSwitch.TraceError,
    "Error Message");
```

B.

```
TraceSwitch traceSwitch = new TraceSwitch(
    "MySwitch",
    "Error and Warning Switch");
#if DEBUG
    traceSwitch.Level = TraceLevel.Warning;
#else
    traceSwitch.Level = TraceLevel.Error;
#endif

Debug.WriteLineIf(traceSwitch.TraceWarning,
    "Warning Message");
Debug.WriteLineIf(traceSwitch.TraceError,
    "Error Message");
```

C.

```
TraceSwitch traceSwitch = new TraceSwitch(
    "MySwitch",
    "Error and Warning Switch");

#if TRACE
    traceSwitch.Level = TraceLevel.Warning;
#else
    traceSwitch.Level = TraceLevel.Error;
#endif

Trace.WriteLineIf(traceSwitch.TraceWarning,
    "Warning Message");
Trace.WriteLineIf(traceSwitch.TraceError,
    "Error Message");
```

D.

```
TraceSwitch traceSwitch = new TraceSwitch(
    "MySwitch",
    "Error and Warning Switch");

#if TRACE
    traceSwitch.Level = TraceLevel.Error;
#else
    traceSwitch.Level = TraceLevel.Warning;
#endif
```

```
Trace.WriteLineIf(traceSwitch.TraceWarning,
    "Warning Message");
Trace.WriteLineIf(traceSwitch.TraceError,
    "Error Message");
```

8. The configuration file of a Windows application has the following contents:

```
<system.diagnostics>
   <switches>
      <add name="BooleanSwitch"
            value="-1" />
      <add name="TraceLevelSwitch"
            value="33" />
   </switches>
</system.diagnostics>
```

You are using the following statements to create switch objects in your code:

```
BooleanSwitch booleanSwitch =
    new BooleanSwitch(
    "BooleanSwitch", "Boolean Switch");
TraceSwitch traceSwitch =
    new TraceSwitch(
    "TraceLevelSwitch", "Trace Switch");
```

Which of the following options is correct regarding the values of these switch objects?

A. The booleanSwitch.Enabled property is set to false and traceSwitch.Level is set to TraceLevel.Verbose.

B. The booleanSwitch.Enabled property is set to true and traceSwitch.Level is set to TraceLevel.Verbose.

C. The booleanSwitch.Enabled property is set to false and traceSwitch.Level is set to TraceLevel.Error.

D. The booleanSwitch.Enabled property is set to false and traceSwitch.Level is set to TraceLevel.Info.

9. You are developing a Windows application. Your application's configuration files have the following code:

```
<system.diagnostics>
   <switches>
      <add name="TraceLevelSwitch"
            value="3" />
   </switches>
</system.diagnostics>
```

You have written the following tracing code in your program:

```
static TraceSwitch traceSwitch =
   new TraceSwitch(
   "TraceLevelSwitch",
   "Trace the application");

[Conditional("DEBUG")]
private void Method1()
{
    Trace.WriteLineIf(
        traceSwitch.TraceError,
        "Message 1", "Message 2");
}

[Conditional("TRACE")]
private void Method2()
{
    Trace.WriteLine("Message 3");
}

private void btnCalculate_Click(
    object sender, System.EventArgs e)
{
    if(traceSwitch.TraceWarning){
        Trace.WriteLine("Message 10");
        Method1();
    }
    else{
        Trace.WriteLineIf(
            traceSwitch.TraceInfo,
            "Message 20");
        Method2();
    }

    if (traceSwitch.TraceError)
        Trace.WriteLineIf(
            traceSwitch.TraceInfo,
            "Message 30");
    Trace.WriteLineIf(
        traceSwitch.TraceVerbose,
            "Message 40");
}
```

What tracing output would be generated if you ran your program in Debug mode and clicked the btnCalculate button?

A.

```
Message 10
Message 1
Message 2
Message 30
```

B.

```
Message 10
Message 2: Message 1
Message 30
```

C.

```
Message 10
Message 2
Message 30
Message 40
```

D.

```
Message 20
Message 3
Message 30
Message 40
```

10. You have following segment of code in your program:

```
EventLogTraceListener traceListener =
    new EventLogTraceListener("TraceLog");

Trace.Listeners.Add(traceListener);
Debug.Listeners.Add(traceListener);

Trace.WriteLine("Sample Message");
Debug.WriteLine("Sample Message");
```

When you debug the program through Visual Studio .NET, how many times would the message "Sample Message" be written to the trace log?

A. 1

B. 2

C. 3

D. 4

11. Which of the following statements are true for remote debugging of processes? (Select the two best answers.)

A. Both the local and the remote machine should have Visual Studio .NET installed.

B. Only the local machine needs Visual Studio .NET.

C. Remote Components Setup is required on local machine.

D. Remote Components Setup is required on the remote machine.

12. While you are debugging in Visual Studio .NET, you want to watch the value of only those variables that are in use in the current statement and the previous statement. Which of the following debugger windows is the easiest window to use to watch these variables?

A. Autos

B. Locals

C. This

D. Watch

13. You are debugging a Windows form. The form involves long calculation and iterations. You want to break into the code to watch the value of variables whenever the value of intValue changes in the following statement:

```
intValue = ProcessValue(intValue);
```

Which of the following options would allow you to quickly achieve this?

A. Run the application by using step execution mode. Use the Step Out key to step out of execution from the ProcessValue() method. Use the Immediate window to display the value of intValue before and after this line of code executes.

B. Set a breakpoint at the given statement. Set the Hit Count option Break When Hitcount Is Equal To to 1.

C. Set the breakpoint at the given statement. In the Breakpoint Condition dialog box, enter intValue != intValue and check the Is True option.

D. Set the breakpoint at the given statement. In the Breakpoint Condition dialog box, enter intValue and check the Has Changed option.

14. You want to debug a remote process. The remote machine does not have Visual Studio .NET installed on it. Which of the following options should you choose?

A. Start the process on the remote machine first and then launch Visual Studio .NET on the local machine. Attach the debugger to the running process. Break into the execution of the remote process.

B. Open the project of the remote process in Visual Studio .NET, set a breakpoint, and execute the process.

C. Copy the remote application project to the local machine and debug it by using Visual Studio .NET debugger.

D. Open the project of the remote process in Visual Studio .NET on the remote machine and then set a breakpoint. Run Visual Studio .NET on the local machine and attach the debugger to the project.

15. You have created a DLL file project in Visual Studio .NET. How would you debug the code for this file?

A. Open the DLL file project, set the breakpoint at the desired location, and start the debugger.

B. Create an EXE project that uses the DLL file and start the debugger.

C. Create an EXE project that uses the DLL file, set the breakpoint in the EXE project, and start the debugger.

D. Select the DLL file through the Processes dialog box and attach the debugger to it. Click the Break button to break the execution into the DLL code.

16. You want to debug a remote process that is running on a Windows 2000 Server computer that is not in the domain of your local computer. The remote server has a full installation of Visual Studio .NET. The two domains do not have two-way trust established, but you do have a username and password on the remote Windows 2000 server. Which of the following would allow you to debug a process on that machine?

A. Ask the administrator of the remote machine to start the Machine Debug Manager, and then launch Visual Studio .NET on your local machine and attach the debugger to the remote process.

B. Ask the administrator of the remote machine to include your username and password in the Debugger Users group, and then launch Visual Studio .NET on your local machine and attach the debugger to the remote process.

C. Use Terminal Server to log in to the remote machine. Launch Visual Studio on the remote machine and debug the process by attaching the debugger to it.

D. Use Terminal Server to log in to the remote machine. Launch Visual Studio .NET on the local machine and debug the process by attaching the debugger to it.

17. You are trying to debug a Windows application by using Visual Studio .NET installed on your local machine. The Windows application is deployed on a remote server. When you attempt to debug the application, you get a DCOM configuration error. Which of the following steps should you take to resolve this problem?

   A. Add your account to the Power Users group on the local computer.

   B. Add your account to the Power Users group on the remote computer.

   C. Add your account to the Debugger Users group on the local computer.

   D. Add your account to the Debugger Users group on the remote computer.

18. You are developing a Windows application that heavily uses SQL Server stored procedures. You are debugging a Windows form that calls the YTDSales stored procedure. The stored procedure uses a variable named @Sales. You want to see how the value of this variable changes as the code in the stored procedure executes. Which of the following options would allow you to do this?

   A. Use the SQL Server PRINT command to display the value of the @Sales variable at different places.

B. Use the Debug.Write statement to print the value of the @Sales variable.

C. Use the Trace.Write statement to print the value of the @Sales variable.

D. Use the Locals window to monitor the value of @Sales as you step through the stored procedure.

Answers to Review Questions

1. A test plan is a document that guides the process of testing. This document should clearly specify the different approaches to testing, the test cases, the validation criteria of the tests, and so on.

2. The Assert() method takes a condition as its first parameter and then displays an Assertion Failed dialog box if the condition evaluates to false.

3. TraceListener is an abstract class that provides functionality for receiving trace and debug messages. DefaultTraceListener, TextWriterTraceListener, and EventLogTraceListener are the three built-in classes that implement TraceListener.

4. The two built-in trace switches in the .NET Framework Class Library are BooleanSwitch and TraceSwitch.

5. You can easily change the value of trace switches by editing the application configuration (XML) file, using any text editor. To make these changes take effect, you need not recompile the application; you just need to restart it.

6. Before you can apply the Conditional attribute to a method, the method should have its return type set to void.

7. The `#error` and `#warning` preprocessing directives let you explicitly generate errors and warnings from code. The compiler reports errors and warnings in the same way it reports other compile-time errors and warnings.

8. The three commands that allow you to step through code are Step Into (steps into each statement of the method called), Step Over (performs the entire method call in one step), and Step Out (steps out of the method call).

9. When the debugger encounters a breakpoint in code, it pauses the execution of the application. The execution can be resumed via the stepping commands.

10. Visual Studio .NET provides a variety of windows to ease the debugging process. Some of these windows are This, Locals, Autos, Watch, Call Stack, and Breakpoints.

11. To attach the debugger to a running process, open Visual C# .NET, invoke the Processes dialog, select the process from the list of processes, and click the Attach button.

12. You should verify that the remote machine has Machine Debug Manager (`mdm.exe`) running as a background process to enable debugging support. You should also verify that you are a member of the Debugger Users group in order to remotely access the machine for debugging.

Answers to Exam Questions

1. **C.** A unit test involves running a module against carefully planned test data and checking whether it works according to its specification. Debugging is the process of locating and fixing errors.

When you run a complete application against test data, you are performing system testing. Checking whether the modules integrate well is part of integration testing. For more information, see the section "Executing Tests" in this chapter.

2. **A** and **B.** To enable tracing in a Windows application, you must have either TRACE or DEBUG symbols defined in an application. You can do this in either of the two ways mentioned in Answers A and B. The first is to compile the program with a `/define:TRACE` switch, and the second is to define the symbol at the top of the source code by using the `#define` compilation directive. For more information, see the section "Conditional Compilation" in this chapter.

3. **A** and **B.** When you develop a Windows application by using Visual Studio .NET, two project configurations are set for you: the default Debug configuration, which has both TRACE and DEBUG symbols defined, and the Release configuration, which has just one symbol, TRACE, defined. So even if you undefine the DEBUG symbol by using a compiler directive, you still have the TRACE symbol defined for both the Debug and Release configurations. After you undefine the DEBUG symbol, you do not see any tracing messages generated by the Debug class. Because the TRACE symbol is still defined, you can see messages generated by the methods of the Trace class. For more information, see the section "Tracing" in this chapter.

4. **A, C,** and **D.** When you add a listener to the Trace.Listeners collection, it listens to the messages generated by both the Trace and Debug classes. When the new listener is added, it is added to the Listeners collection. The Listeners collection already has a DefaultTraceListener object that sends messages to the Output window.

Therefore, you have messages in TraceLog.txt as well as in the Output window. For more information, see the section "Trace Listeners" in this chapter.

5. **D.** Setting the Level property of TraceSwitch to TraceLevel.Info allows it to capture all informational, warning, and error messages, but not the verbose messages. Thus the TraceInfo, TraceWarning, and TraceError properties of the switch evaluate to true but the TraceVerbose property evaluates to false. For more information, see the section "Trace Switches" in this chapter.

6. **B.** The TraceSwitch class provides a multilevel switch that allows you to control tracing output of a Windows application without needing to recompile the code. You can implement the changes in behavior by just changing the application's configuration file. For more information, see the section "Trace Switches" in this chapter.

7. **A.** In Answer A, for the Debug configuration where the DEBUG symbol is defined, the Level property of traceSwitch is set to TraceLevel.Warning. This causes both the TraceWarning and TraceError properties of this object to evaluate to true in the Debug configuration, causing both of the messages to be displayed. In the Release configuration, where only the TRACE symbol is defined, the Level property of traceSwitch is set to TraceLevel.Error. This causes the TraceWarning property to result in a false value and the TraceError property to return a true value, causing only the error messages to be displayed. For more information, see the section "Trace Switches" in this chapter.

8. **B.** For BooleanSwitch, a value of 0 corresponds to Off, and any nonzero value corresponds to On. For TraceSwitch any number greater than 4 is treated as Verbose. From the given values in the configuration file, the booleanSwitch object should have its Enabled property set as true and the traceSwitch object should have its Level property set to TraceLevel.Verbose. For more information, see the section "Trace Switches" in this chapter.

9. **B.** The XML file has 3 as the value for TraceLevelSwitch, which causes the Level property to be set to TraceLevel.Info. This causes the TraceError, TraceWarning, and TraceInfo properties of the traceSwitch to be true; only the TraceVerbose property evaluates to false. Also, the third parameter of the WriteLineIf() method is used to categorize the output by specifying its value, followed by a colon (:) and then the trace message. For more information, see the section "Trace Switches" in this chapter.

10. **D.** The message SampleMessage will be written four times. This is because two instances of EventLogTraceListeners are added to the Listeners collection. Any message generated by the Trace and Debug classes will be listed twice. Because the program is running in the Debug mode, both the Trace and Debug statements will be executed. The net effect is that both the Trace.WriteLine and Debug.WriteLine messages will be written twice, making four entries in the trace log. For more information, see the section "Trace Listeners" in this chapter.

11. **B** and **D.** For remote debugging, Visual Studio .NET is not required on the remote machine.

APPLY YOUR KNOWLEDGE

In this case, you need to run Remote Components Setup on the remote machine. You need to have Visual Studio .NET on the local machine in order to debug the remote processes. For more information, see the section "Debugging a Remote Process" in this chapter.

12. **A.** The Autos window gives you the most convenient access because it automatically displays names and values of all variables in the current statement and the previous statement at every step. For more information, see the section "Analyzing Program State to Resolve Errors" in this chapter.

13. **D.** When you want to break into the code when the value of a variable changes, the quickest way is to set a conditional breakpoint where you specify the variable name and check the Has Changed option. For more information, see the section "Setting Breakpoints" and Exercise 12.3 in this chapter.

14. **A.** To debug a remote process, the process first needs to be started on the remote machine. You can then open Visual Studio .NET on the local machine and attach the debugger to the running process. After the debugger is attached, you can break into the code of the remote process and do step-by-step execution or set a breakpoint. For more information, see the section "Debugging a Remote Process" in this chapter.

15. **C.** A DLL project cannot be instantiated by itself, so you need to first create an EXE project that calls the classes and methods from the DLL file.

You then need to set the breakpoint on the EXE project and start the debugger. When the code steps to a method inside the DLL file, you step into the code to debug the code in the DLL file. For more information, see the section "Debugging the Code in DLL Files" in this chapter.

16. **C.** If your local machine's domain does not have a two-way trust relationship with the remote computer's domain then you cannot debug a remote process. The only option you have is to log on to the remote machine by using Terminal Server, start Visual Studio .NET on the remote machine, and use Visual Studio .NET to attach the debugger to the process that is running on the same machine. You then debug as if you were debugging a process running on your local machine. For more information, see the section "Debugging a Remote Process" in this chapter.

17. **D.** If you get a DCOM configuration error while debugging, possibly you are not the member of the Debugger Users group on the remote machine. To resolve this, you add your account on the remote machine to the Debugger Users group. For more information, see the section "Debugging a Remote Process" in this chapter.

18. **D.** You can use the Locals window to keep track of the values of the variables defined in the stored procedures during step-by-step execution. For more information, see the section "Analyzing Program State to Resolve Errors" and Exercise 12.2 in this chapter.

APPLY YOUR KNOWLEDGE

Suggested Readings and Resources

1. Windows Forms QuickStart Tutorial:

   - "Tracing Topics" under "Diagnostics in How Do I"

2. Visual Studio .NET Combined Help Collection:

   - "Introduction to Instrumentation and Tracing"

   - "Using the Debugger"

3. Kevin Burton. *.NET Common Language Runtime Unleashed*. Sams, 2002.

4. Richard Grimes. *Developing Applications with Visual Studio .NET*. Addison-Wesley, 2002.

5. The .NET Show: Debugging with Visual Studio .NET. `msdn.microsoft.com/theshow/Episode022`.

This chapter covers the following Microsoft-specified objectives for the "Deploying a Windows-Based Application" section of Exam 70-316, "Developing and Implementing Windows-Based Applications with Microsoft Visual C# .NET and Microsoft Visual Studio .NET":

Deploy a Windows-based application.

- **Use setup and deployment projects.**

▶ Microsoft Visual C# .NET ships with a new project category, Setup and Deployment projects. These projects contain templates that help in building user-friendly installation packages for different types of applications. This objective requires you to know how to create various setup projects that help in deploying Windows applications.

Create a setup program that installs an application and allows for the application to be uninstalled.

- **Register components and assemblies.**

- **Perform an install-time compilation of a Windows-based application.**

▶ Visual Studio .NET creates installation packages based on the Microsoft Windows Installer technology. Microsoft Windows Installer 2.0 handles the execution of tasks involved in installing, uninstalling, and repairing Windows applications. You only have to focus on what files need to be installed, where they should be located, what Registry entries need to be made, what type of user interface needs to be displayed to the end user, and whether any condition is to be checked or custom action to be performed during the installation process. This objective requires you to know how to deploy components and assemblies and also how to perform native compilation (that is, compiling .NET assemblies to processor-specific native code) of the assemblies at the time of installation.

CHAPTER 13

Deploying a Windows Application

Add assemblies to the global assembly cache.

▶ The .NET Framework allows you to place shared assemblies (assemblies intended to be used by more than one application) in a central location called the global assembly cache (GAC). The assemblies that are placed in the GAC must have strong names. This objective requires you to know how to assign a strong name to an assembly and install files in the GAC on the target machine during deployment.

Plan the deployment of a Windows-based application.

- **Plan a deployment that uses removable media.**

- **Plan a Web-based deployment.**

- **Plan a network-based deployment.**

- **Ensure that the application conforms to Windows Installer requirements and Windows Logo Program requirements.**

▶ This objective requires you to know the various techniques by which you can deploy applications. You can choose to deploy them through removable media such as floppy disks, CDs, or DVDs; you can use a network-based deployment; or you can make your installation package available over the Web, so that the end user can download the package.

This objective also requires you to know what is involved in creating applications that conform to the Windows Installer and Windows Logo Program requirements.

Verify security policies for a deployed application.

- **Launch a remote application (URL remoting).**

▶ You can deploy a Windows application on a network server or a Web server. This deployment method does not require you to install the application on each desktop that will use it. At runtime users can launch the application by typing the uniform resource locator (URL) in Internet Explorer. All necessary files are then downloaded to the user's computer and can be executed from there. This deployment method is called *zero deployment* because no installation is required on client machines. However, security is a concern with code downloaded from the Internet. This objective also requires you to know how to configure a security policy for the target machine in order to allow good code while restricting bad code from executing on the user's computer.

STUDY STRATEGIES

▶ Review the "Deployment Concepts" and "Deploying Applications" sections of the Visual Studio .NET Combined Help Collection.

▶ Experiment with using setup projects and merge module projects to deploy Windows applications. Understand when you should choose to create a setup project versus a merge module project.

▶ Work with the different editors that are available in setup and merge module projects and thoroughly understand the purpose of each of these editors.

▶ Experiment with the Strong Name tool (sn.exe) to create a public/private key pair and then use the key pair to assign a strong name to an assembly. Work with the delay-signing feature and understand the scenarios in which it can be helpful.

▶ Experiment with placing assemblies in the GAC. Understand the steps performed by the runtime to locate assemblies.

▶ Experiment with creating custom actions to compile assemblies into machine-specific code at install time.

▶ Understand the runtime security policy and how you can use it to your advantage to allow useful applications to run while blocking malicious code.

▶ Understand the various ways to deploy a Windows application and their benefits and shortcomings. Understand when to use XCOPY deployment versus Windows Installer deployment.

▶ Understand the requirements of the Windows Logo Program.

INTRODUCTION

After you have developed and tested a Windows application, the next step is to deploy the application so that the end user can use it. You should keep in mind the complexity and requirements of the application so that you can choose the right deployment tool. The .NET Framework simplifies deployment by making it possible to deploy simple applications by using just the XCOPY command. However, for applications that are packaged and shipped to the user, Microsoft recommends using Microsoft Windows Installer.

This chapter discusses how to use Visual Studio .NET to create Windows Installer–based setup and deployment projects. I discuss the setup project that is used to package Windows applications and the merge module project that is used to package shared components.

Chapter 4, "Creating and Managing .NET Components and Assemblies," introduced the concept of shared assemblies. *Shared assemblies* are components that are shared between several applications. In this chapter I delve into the details of creating and installing shared assemblies.

The .NET Framework provides a new model for deploying Windows applications: the no-touch (or zero deployment) model. This chapter explores how to use this installation model to execute a Windows application by just pointing to a URL. It also discusses how to configure security on the client machine to deal with the hazards of malicious mobile code while executing the code that you really want to execute.

This chapter also talks about various ways in which an application can be deployed. Finally, it discusses the Windows Logo Program and requirements that must be met in order for a Windows-based application to be qualified for using the various Windows logos.

DEPLOYMENT TOOLS

A *deployment tool* helps you set up an application on the user's computer. Choosing the right deployment tool is important because the correct tool not only eases the process of deployment but also minimizes the total cost of ownership for the application's users.

The choice of tool depends on the nature of the application. For installing simple applications, sometimes a tool as simple as the XCOPY command can be used. For sophisticated requirements, you might want to use a tool that creates a Windows Installer–based setup package for the application.

XCOPY Deployment

The .NET Framework simplifies application deployment by making zero-impact installation and XCOPY deployment feasible. You can install a .NET application that uses only managed code and private assemblies by just copying all the necessary files to the desired destination. No Registry entries need to be created, and no files need to be copied to the Windows system directory (thereby causing zero impact on the configuration of user's computer).

However, in some scenarios XCOPY is not a sufficient deployment tool. The following are some common installation tasks that are difficult or impossible to perform by using the XCOPY command:

◆ Creating shortcuts

◆ Allowing users to select features during installation

◆ Copying files to relative paths on the target machine that differ from the paths on the source machine

◆ Adding assemblies to the GAC

◆ Creating or configuring databases during the installation

◆ Adding custom event logs and performance counters to the target machine

◆ Checking whether the .NET Framework is installed on the target machine

◆ Presenting a user-friendly and branded user interface

◆ Allowing license key management and user registration

For these scenarios, the preferred alternative is to use a Microsoft Windows Installer–based installation program instead of using XCOPY to deploy an application.

Microsoft Windows Installer

Microsoft Windows Installer is an installation and configuration service that is built into the Windows operating system. It gives you complete control over the installation of an application, a component, or an update.

Windows Installer includes many built-in actions for performing the installation process. In addition to performing the standard actions, such as installing files, creating shortcuts to files, making Start menu entries, and writing Registry entries, Windows Installer also offers several advanced features, some of which are listed here:

- It provides the ability to take custom actions during application installation. For example, you might want to run a SQL script to install an application database during application installation.

- It provides on-demand installation of features. This capability allows the user to install, at a later stage, a feature that was not installed during the application's initial installation. On-demand installation does not force the user to reinstall the entire installation package; the user can just add a single feature.

- It provides the ability to roll back an installation. Windows Installer maintains an undo operation for every operation that is performed during an application installation. If Windows Installer encounters any error while installing an application, it can uninstall everything that was installed during the installation.

- It allows you to uninstall an application without breaking any other application that depends on it.

- It allows you to fix an application or one of its components if it becomes corrupted. This way, users spend less time uninstalling and reinstalling applications.

Windows Installer manages all installed components on a system by keeping a database of information about every application that it installs, including files, Registry keys, and components.

NOTE

Updating Microsoft Windows Installer Although Windows Installer is built in, you might need to install a redistributable file in order to get the latest version. Later in this chapter you will see how to create a Windows Installer bootstrapper to ensure that Windows Installer is updated (if necessary) on target machines.

NOTE

Windows Installer Requirements Windows Installer version 2.0 (the version used to install .NET applications) requires Windows NT 4.0 with Service Pack 6 or later, Windows XP, Windows .NET Server, Windows 2000, or Windows Me. Earlier Windows Installer versions require Windows NT 4.0 with Service Pack 3 or later, Windows XP, Windows 2000, or Windows Me. Windows Installer is also available as a redistributable file for Windows NT 4.0, Windows 95, and Windows 98, and it can be downloaded from www.microsoft.com/ msdownload/platformsdk/ sdkupdate/psdkredist.htm.

NOTE

Using Windows Installer Microsoft recommends the use of Windows Installer to install and configure .NET applications on an end user's system.

When you create an installation program for Windows Installer, you need to create a Windows Installer (`.msi`) package. This package includes a number of database tables that describe the application to Windows Installer. When this package is executed on the target machine, Windows Installer installs the program by reading the installation information stored in the Windows Installer package.

There are several ways to create a Windows Installer package. The most basic option is to manually create it by using the Windows Installer Software Development Kit (SDK), but for most practical requirements you would instead use a visual tool that can help with the process. In this chapter, I use the setup and deployment projects of Visual Studio .NET to create setup packages by using Windows Installer. A lot of people also use installation tools from independent vendors, such as InstallShield and Wise Solutions. Specialized tools from these and other vendors provide a much higher level of customization and ease for creating Windows Installer–based setup programs.

DEPLOYING A WINDOWS APPLICATION

Deploy a Windows-based application.

- **Use setup and deployment projects**

Microsoft Visual Studio .NET allows you to create Windows Installer–based installation packages. It offers four types of deployment project templates:

◆ **Setup Project**—You use this template to create installation packages for deploying Windows-based applications.

◆ **Web Setup Project**—You use this template to create installation packages for deploying Web-based applications.

◆ **Merge Module Project**—You use this template to create installation packages for components that may be shared by multiple applications.

◆ **Cab Project**—You use this template to package ActiveX components so that they can be downloaded over the Internet.

Visual Studio .NET also has a Setup Wizard that helps you interactively create these deployment templates. This chapter mainly discusses the Setup Project and the Merge Module Project templates. For more details on the Web Setup Project template, refer to *MCAD/MCSD Training Guide (70-315): Designing and Implementing Web Applications with Visual C# .NET and Visual Studio .NET.*

Before you delve in the details of creating deployment projects with the help of Visual Studio .NET, you need to create an application that can be deployed. In Step by Step 13.1, you create a simple Windows application named NetSql that returns the result of any SELECT query from the SQL Server Northwind database. This application will serve as a testbed for exploring various deployment features throughout this chapter.

N O T E

Setup Projects Versus Web Setup Projects The main distinction between a setup project and a Web setup project is where the files are deployed. A setup project (usually) installs files to the Program Files directory on the target computer, whereas a Web setup project installs files to a virtual directory of a Web server.

STEP BY STEP

13.1 Building an Application That Needs to Be Deployed

1. Launch Visual Studio .NET. Select File, New, Blank Solution, and name the new solution 316C13.

2. In Solution Explorer, add a Visual C# Windows application project to the solution. Name the project NetSql.

3. Rename the Form1.cs file NetSql.cs in the project. Switch to the code view of the form and modify all references to Form1 so that they refer to NetSql instead.

4. Open Server Explorer. Expand the tree under Data Connections to show a SQL Server data connection that points to the Northwind sample database. Drag and drop the data connection to the form. A sqlConnection1 object is created on the form. This object represents a connection to SQL Server.

5. Place a TextBox control (txtQuery), a Button control (btnExecute), and a DataGrid control (dgResults) on the form. Set the Multiline property of the TextBox control to true. Set the CaptionVisible property of the DataGrid control to false.

continues

continued

6. Switch to the code view. Add the following lines to the using directives:

```
using System.Data.SqlClient;
using System.IO;
```

7. Add the following member declaration in the class definition:

```
static private String query="";
```

8. Add the following code to the Load event handler of the form:

```
private void NetSql_Load(
    object sender, System.EventArgs e)
{
    this.txtQuery.Text = query;
}
```

9. Modify the Main() method so that it has the following code:

```
[STAThread]
static void Main(string[] args)
{
    // Check if any arguments
    if(args.Length !=0)
    {
        // Assume the first argument to be a file
        // Display the contents of the file
        // in the query textbox.
        StreamReader sr = new StreamReader(args[0]);
        query = sr.ReadToEnd();
        sr.Close();
    }
    Application.Run(new NetSql());
}
```

10. Enter this code to execute the query when the Button control is clicked:

```
private void btnExecute_Click(object sender,
    System.EventArgs e)
{
    // Create a SqlCommand to represent the query
    SqlCommand cmd = sqlConnection1.CreateCommand();
    cmd.CommandType = CommandType.Text;
    cmd.CommandText = txtQuery.Text;
    // Create a SqlDataAdapter to talk to the database
    SqlDataAdapter da = new SqlDataAdapter();
    da.SelectCommand = cmd;
```

```
    // Create a DataSet to hold the results
    DataSet ds = new DataSet();
    try
    {
        // Fill the DataSet
        da.Fill(ds, "Results");
        // And bind it to the DataGrid
        dgResults.DataSource = ds;
        dgResults.DataMember = "Results";
    }
    catch (Exception ex)
    {
        MessageBox.Show(
          ex.Message, "Error executing query",
          MessageBoxButtons.OK, MessageBoxIcon.Error);
    }
}
```

11. Change the solution configuration to `Release` mode. Run the application. Enter in the text box a `SELECT` query for the Northwind database.

12. Click the button. The code runs, retrieving the results in the `DataGrid` control, as shown in Figure 13.1.

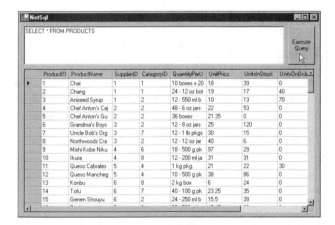

FIGURE 13.1

The `NetSql` application returns select query results from the Northwind database.

13. Add a few files that will be required when you deploy this application. Launch WordPad and create a `ReadMe.rtf` file that contains the following text:

```
NetSql Version 1.0
This application allows you to SELECT data from the
Northwind database. Just type any valid SELECT
statement and you will see the results of the
query instantly!
```

continues

continued

14. Create another file, named `License.rtf`, that contains the following text:

```
NetSql End User License Agreement
You should carefully read the following terms and
conditions before using this software.
If you do not agree to any of the terms of this
License, then do not install, distribute or use
this copy of NetSql. This software, and all
accompanying files, data and materials, are
distributed "AS IS" and with no warranties
of any kind, whether express or implied. Good data
processing procedure dictates that any program be
thoroughly tested with non-critical data before
relying on it.  The user must assume the entire
risk of using the program.
(c) All rights reserved.
```

Now that you have created an application, the following section demonstrates how to create a setup project to install this application.

Creating a Setup Project

Visual Studio .NET provides the Setup Project template so that you can create installers for Windows applications. It also provides the Setup Wizard, which helps you create different types of setup and deployment projects, using an interactive interface. Step by Step 13.2 guides through the process of creating a simple installer for the NetSql application created in Step by Step 13.1 by using the Setup Wizard.

STEP BY STEP

13.2 Creating a Setup Project for the NetSql Project by Using the Setup Wizard

1. In Solution Explorer, right-click Solution and select Add, New Project. Select Setup and Deployment projects from the Project Types tree and then select Setup Wizard from the list of templates on the right, as shown in Figure 13.2.

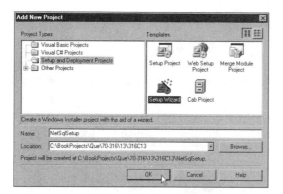

FIGURE 13.2◀
You can add a new setup project via the Setup Wizard.

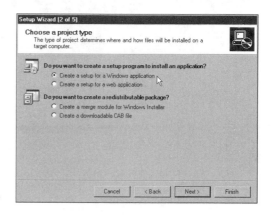

2. Name the project `NetSqlSetup`. Click OK. The Setup Wizard appears. The first screen of the wizard is the Welcome screen. Click Next.

3. The second screen of the wizard is the Choose a Project Type screen. Choose Create a setup for a Windows application from the first group of options, as shown in Figure 13.3. Click Next.

4. The third screen of the wizard is the Choose Project Outputs to Include screen. Select Primary Output from NetSql, as shown in Figure 13.4. Click Next.

5. The fourth screen of the wizard is the Choose Files to Include screen. Click the Add button and include the `ReadMe.rtf` and `License.rtf` files from the `NetSql` project folder. After including the files, the screen looks like the screen shown in Figure 13.5. Click Next.

FIGURE 13.3▲
The Choose a Project Type screen in the Setup Wizard prompts the user to select the project type.

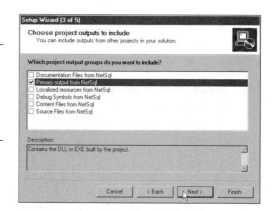

FIGURE 13.4▲
The Choose Project Outputs to Include screen in the Setup Wizard prompts the user to select the project output that will be deployed by the installer.

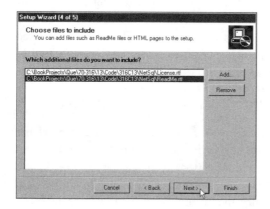

FIGURE 13.5◀
The Choose Files to Include screen in the Setup Wizard allows you to add any additional files to the setup projects.

continues

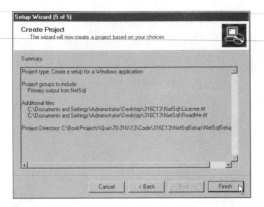

FIGURE 13.6▲
The Project Summary screen in the Setup Wizard shows the summary of the files to be included in the setup project.

FIGURE 13.7▶
The Properties window allows you to set properties of the setup project.

FIGURE 13.8▲
The Select Installation Folder screen allows the user to specify a custom installation folder during the installation process.

6. The final screen of the wizard is the Project Summary screen, as shown in Figure 13.6. Click Finish to create the project.

7. Select the new project `NetSqlSetup` in Solution Explorer. Activate the Properties window. Set `Manufacturer` to `NetSql Software`, `ProductName` to `NetSql`, and `Title` to `NetSql Installer`, as shown in Figure 13.7.

8. Build the `NetSqlSetup` project. Open Windows Explorer and navigate to the `Release` folder inside the project folder. Run `setup.exe`. Alternatively, on the development machine, you can install by right-clicking the project in Solution Explorer and choosing the Install option from the context menu. This opens the `NetSql` Setup Wizard with a welcome screen. Click Next. The Select Installation Folder screen appears, as shown in Figure 13.8. Select the default settings and click Next. Click Next again to start the installation. Click Close.

9. Open Windows Explorer and navigate to the installation folder path. If you did not change the default settings during installation, the path is `C:\Program Files\NetSql Software\NetSql`. Run the `NetSql.exe` file from the folder. The `NetSql` application is launched. Enter a query and click the button to get the results of the query.

10. Select Start, Settings, Control Panel, Add/Remove Programs to open the Add/Remove Programs dialog box. Select the Change or Remove Programs icon from the left pane and select `NetSql` from the right pane. Click the Remove button to uninstall the `NetSql` application and then click Yes. The `NetSql` application is uninstalled from your system. Alternatively, on the development machine, you can uninstall by right-clicking the project in Solution Explorer and choosing the Uninstall option from the context menu.

Step by Step 13.2 illustrates the process of creating a setup project. When the project is compiled, the output files are placed in the `Release` folder (that is, the active configuration folder). The contents of the folder are an installer package (an `.msi` file), executables (`.exe` files), and initialization file (`.ini` file). The `.msi` file is the installation package, in Microsoft Windows Installer format. If Windows Installer is installed on your computer, you can directly start the installation by running this file. The executable files consist of `setup.exe`, `InstMsiA.exe`, and `InstMsiW.exe`. The `setup.exe` file (also called the Windows Installer bootstrapper) bootstraps the installation process by first testing for the presence of Windows Installer on the target machine. If Windows Installer is not installed, `setup.exe` first installs it by using either `InstMsiA.exe` (for Windows 9x and Me) or `InstMsiW.exe` (for Windows NT/2000/XP) and then instructs Windows Installer to execute the installation based on the information stored in the installation package (`.msi` file). The `setup.ini` file stores the initialization settings, such as the name of the installation database, for the `setup.exe`.

There is one catch here. This setup project works only on the computers where the .NET Framework Common Language Runtime (CLR) has already been installed. In fact, when you build the setup project, you see the following message in the output window of Visual Studio .NET:

"WARNING: This setup does not contain the .NET Framework which must be installed on the target machine by running dotnetfx.exe before this setup will install. You can find dotnetfx.exe on the Visual Studio .NET 'Windows Components Update' media. Dotnetfx.exe can be redistributed with your setup."

On the other hand, when you look at the setup project folder in Solution Explorer, you see that the setup project has created a `Detected Dependencies` folder and included a file named `dotnetfxredist_x86_enu.msm` in it. But the `Exclude` property of this file is set to `true`. `dotnetfxredist_x86_enu.msm` is basically just a placeholder module that stops Visual Studio .NET from automatically including in the project the .NET Framework files from your installation of the .NET Framework. If you try changing the `Exclude` property of the `dotnetfxredist_x86_enu.msm` file to `false`, Visual Studio .NET does not allow you to do it, and you get an error when you build the project:

> "ERROR: dotNETFXRedist_x86_enu.msm must not be used to redistribute the .NET Framework. Please exclude this merge module."

Ideally, you should leave the `Exclude` property at its default value, `true`, for the `dotNETFXRedist_x86_enu.msm` dependency.

The .NET Framework cannot be included in a Windows Installer setup package that is created by using Visual Studio .NET deployment tools. It must be installed separately. There are several ways you can do this, including the following:

◆ Ask the user to run setup for the .NET Framework from the Windows Component Upgrade CD-ROM that comes with Visual Studio .NET.

◆ Ask the user to download the .NET Framework from the Microsoft Developer Network (MSDN) Download Center or from the Microsoft Windows Update Web site, `http://windowsupdate.microsoft.com`.

◆ Use the .NET Framework bootstrapper, `setup.exe`, which checks for the availability of the .NET Framework and installs it by using the specified location of `dotnetfx.exe` if it is not already installed.

Of course, for a professional installation, you would not want to leave it to the users to perform manual installation of the .NET Framework. So using the bootstrapper `setup.exe` is a good idea. Microsoft provides a sample bootstrapper `setup.exe` that you can readily use in projects. I tell you where to get and how to use this bootstrapper `setup.exe` later in this chapter, in Exercise 13.1.

For now let's assume that the .NET Framework is available on the machine where you will deploy applications.

You can modify the configuration settings for a setup project by selecting the project in Solution Explorer and choosing Project, Properties from the main menu. The project's Property Pages dialog box appears, as shown in Figure 13.9.

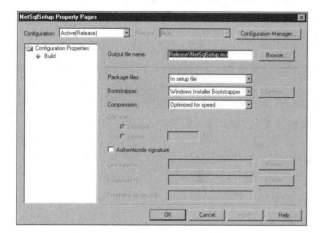

FIGURE 13.9
The Property Pages dialog box displays the configuration properties of the setup project.

In this dialog box there are five main configuration properties:

◆ **Output file name**—Specifies the output filename of the installation package (.msi file).

◆ **Package files**—Specifies how to package the files. The options are As loose uncompressed files, In setup file, and In cabinet file(s). If the In cabinet file(s) option is selected, you can also specify the size of the CAB files.

◆ **Bootstrapper**—Specifies whether any bootstrap file needs to be created for launching the installation program. A bootstrap is required when the target machine does not have Windows Installer already installed. The None option generates only the installation package (.msi file), whereas the Windows Installer Bootstrapper option creates a setup.exe file that is capable of installing Windows Installer if it is not already installed.

◆ **Compression**—Specifies whether to optimize the installation files for size or speed or whether no optimization is required. The value Optimized for speed uses a faster compression algorithm that quickly unpacks the files at install time.

A faster compression algorithm usually results in larger installation files. The value Optimized for size uses a compression algorithm that runs more slowly but that tightly packs the files. If the value None is selected, no optimization is performed.

◆ **Authenticode signature**—Allows you to specify what file contains the Authenticode certificate, the private key file, and the timestamp server URL (which is provided by the certification authority).

The output files that are generated can be deployed (that is, copied) to any target machine and can then be installed and later uninstalled. When an application is uninstalled, all the actions done by the installer application during the installation on the target machine are undone, leaving the target machine in its original state. You can choose to repair or reinstall an application by clicking the Change button in the Add/Remove Programs dialog box.

REVIEW BREAK

▶ Although the .NET Framework supports XCOPY deployment, XCOPY is not sufficient for advanced deployment requirements. For advanced requirements, you should instead use a Microsoft Windows Installer–based installation package to deploy applications.

▶ Microsoft Windows Installer is the built-in installation and configuration service of the Windows operating system. In addition to providing several advanced installation features, it provides features such as the ability to roll back an installation process, uninstall an application, and repair a component or an application.

▶ Visual Studio .NET provides four types of deployment templates: Setup Project (for Windows-based applications), Web Setup Project (for Web-based applications), Merge Module Project (for shared components and assemblies), and Cab Project (for ActiveX components to be downloaded over the Internet). It also provides the Setup Wizard, which helps in creating installation packages for any of these deployment projects.

CUSTOMIZING A SETUP PROJECT

Deploy a Windows-based application.

- **Use setup and deployment projects.**

When you are creating a professional application, you don't want the user to have to navigate to the installation folder to run the application. You instead want to create menu options and shortcuts in the target machine so that the end user can easily run the application. You might also like the installation program to provide different custom features and actions while performing installation.

Visual Studio .NET provides different types of editors to customize various aspects of the installation process:

- ◆ File System Editor
- ◆ Registry Editor
- ◆ File Types Editor
- ◆ User Interface Editor
- ◆ Custom Actions Editor
- ◆ Launch Conditions Editor

You can view an editor by either choosing its icon from Solution Explorer or by right-clicking the project in Solution Explorer and choosing View and the respective editor option from the shortcut menu, as shown in Figure 13.10.

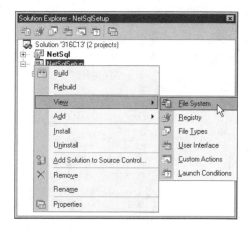

FIGURE 13.10
You can launch various editors for a setup project via Solution Explorer.

Using the File System Editor

The File System Editor provides mapping of the file system on the target machine. Each folder is referred to with a special name that is converted to represent the folder on the target machine during the installation process. For example, at the time of installation, the special folder User's Desktop is converted to the actual desktop path on the target machine.

You can add special folders by selecting the File System on Target Machine node in the left pane of the File System Editor and choosing the Add Special Folder option from the context menu.

There are many types of special folders, such as the `Application Folder`, `Common Files Folder`, `Program Files Folder`, `User's Desktop`, `System Folder`, `User's Startup Folder`, and many others, each of which represents a particular folder on the target machine.

In Step by Step 13.3, you add menu options to the Windows Program menu to launch the application and display the contents of the `ReadMe.rtf` file. You also create a shortcut to the application on the user's desktop and associate icons with the shortcut.

STEP BY STEP

13.3 Using the File System Editor

1. Select the `NetSqlSetup` project in Solution Explorer. Right-click the project node and select Add, File from the context menu. The Add Files dialog box appears. Add two icon files to represent the `NetSql` application and the `ReadMe` file.

2. Right-click the `NetSqlSetup` project in Solution Explorer and select View, File System Editor. In the editor, select Application Folder under the File System on Target Machine node in the left pane of the editor.

3. Right-click Primary Output from NetSql (Active) and select Create Shortcut to Primary Output from NetSql (Active), as shown in Figure 13.11. Alternatively, you could select the `Primary Output from NetSql (Active)` file and select Action, Create Shortcut to Primary Output from NetSql (Active). Rename the shortcut `Run NetSql`.

FIGURE 13.11
You can create shortcuts via the File System Editor.

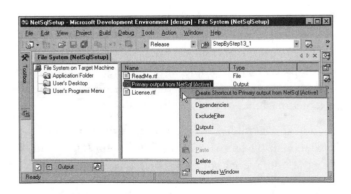

4. Move the shortcut you just created to the `User's Desktop` folder, either by dragging and dropping or by using Cut and Paste from the context menu.

5. Open the Properties window for the shortcut and select the `Icon` property. Click the ellipsis (…) button. The Icon dialog box appears.

6. Click the Browse button in the Icon dialog box. The Select Item in Project dialog box appears. Select `NetSql.ico` from the Application Folder node, as shown in Figure 13.12. Click OK. Select the icon from the Icon dialog box, as shown in Figure 13.13, and click OK.

7. Right-click the `User's Programs Menu` folder in the left pane of the editor and select Add, Create Folder. Rename the new folder `NetSql`.

8. Create shortcuts for `ReadMe.rtf` and Primary Output from NetSql (Active) and move them to the newly created folder `NetSql` under the `User's Programs Menu` folder. Name the newly created shortcuts Read Me and Run NetSql, respectively.

9. Set the `Icon` properties of the new shortcuts to `ReadMe.ico` and `NetSql.ico`, following the steps in steps 5 and 6.

10. Build the `NetSqlSetup` project. Right-click the project in Solution Explorer and select the Install option. Install the project.

11. The desktop now contains a shortcut to run the `NetSql` application, with the icon attached to the shortcut. Double-click the shortcut to verify that it works as expected.

12. Select Start, Programs, NetSql. The shortcuts named `Read Me` and `NetSql` appear as options in the menu. Click them to verify that they work as desired.

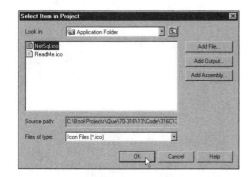

FIGURE 13.12
The Select Item in Project dialog box allows you to pick files or folders from within a deployment project.

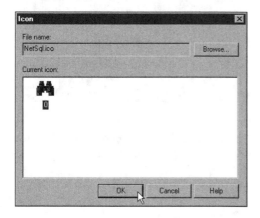

FIGURE 13.13
The Icon dialog box allows you to select icons and associate them with a file.

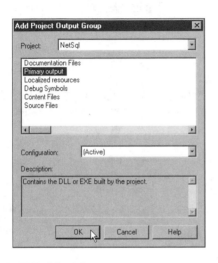

FIGURE 13.14
The Add Project Output Group dialog box allows you to add different project resources to the setup project.

GUIDED PRACTICE
EXERCISE 13.1

The goal of this exercise is to create a setup project by using the Setup Project template rather than the Setup Wizard. The project should install the NetSql application and create shortcuts on the user's desktop for the NetSql executable file and the ReadMe.rtf file.

How would you create such an installation package?

In this exercise, you will practice creating setup projects by using the setup project template. You should try working through this problem on your own first. If you get stuck, or if you'd like to see one possible solution, follow these steps:

1. In Solution Explorer, right-click Solution and select Add, New Project. Select Setup and Deployment projects from the Project Types tree and then select Setup Project from the list of templates on the right. Name the project GuidedPracticeExercise13_1.

2. In Solution Explorer, right-click the project and select Add, Project Output from the context menu. The Add Project Output Group dialog box appears, as shown in Figure 13.14. Select NetSql as the project and select Primary Output from the list box. Click OK.

3. Select Add, File from the context menu. The AddFiles dialog box appears. Navigate to the NetSql project folder and add the ReadMe.rtf file to it.

4. Open the File System Editor by clicking the File System Editor icon in Solution Explorer. Select Application Folder under the File System on Target Machine node in the left pane of the editor.

5. Right-click ReadMe.rtf and select Create Shortcut to ReadMe.rtf. Rename the shortcut Read Me. Move this shortcut to the User's Desktop folder.

6. Add another shortcut to the Primary output from NetSql (Active) file and move it to the User's Desktop folder.

7. Select the new project in Solution Explorer. Activate the Properties window. Set Manufacturer to NetSql SoftwareGPE and set ProductName to NetSqlGPE.

8. Build the GuidedPracticeExercise13_1 project. Right-click the project in Solution Explorer and select the Install option. Install the project.

9. The desktop now contains two shortcuts, one to the NetSql.exe application and the other to the ReadMe.rtf file. Double-click the shortcuts to verify that they work as expected.

If you have difficulty following this exercise, review the sections "Creating a Setup Project" and "Using the File System Editor," earlier in this chapter. After doing that review, try this exercise again.

Using the Registry Editor

The Registry Editor allows you to specify Registry keys, subkeys, and values that are added to the Registry in the target machine during installation. You can also import Registry files into the Registry Editor.

STEP BY STEP

13.4 Using the Registry Editor

1. Select the NetSqlSetup project in Solution Explorer. Open the Registry Editor by clicking the Registry Editor icon in Solution Explorer.

2. In the left pane, select HKEY_LOCAL_MACHINE, Software, [Manufacturer]. Right-click the selected node and select the New, DWORD Value from the context menu, as shown in Figure 13.15. Name the key value FreeWare. Change the Value property of the FreeWare key to 1 in the Properties window.

continues

continued

FIGURE 13.15
You can add Registry keys and values on the target machine via the Registry Editor.

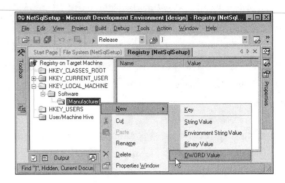

3. Build the NetSqlSetup project. Right-click on the project in Solution Explorer and select the Install option. Install the project.

4. Select Start, Run and type regedit in the Open combo box. Click OK to launch the Windows Registry Editor. In the left pane of the editor, select MyComputer, HKEY_LOCAL_MACHINE, Software, NetSql Software to view the FreeWare value you added, as shown in Figure 13.16.

FIGURE 13.16
The Registry keys and values can be added via setup projects to the target machine's Registry.

> **WARNING**
>
> **Working with the Registry**   Be extra careful when working with the Windows Registry. Take special care with the DeleteAtUninstall property of the Registry Settings Properties. Setting DeleteAtUninstall to true for a wrong key (such as HKEY_LOCAL_MACHINE\SOFTWARE) might have a very bad impact on the target computer.

Using the File Types Editor

The File Types Editor enables you to associate file extensions and actions with applications. For example, files with the extension .qry and the Open action can be associated with the NetSql application so that the NetSql application is launched whenever the user opens a .qry file.

STEP BY STEP

13.5 Using the File Types Editor

1. Select the NetSqlSetup project in Solution Explorer. Open the File Types Editor by clicking the File Types Editor icon in Solution Explorer.

2. Select the File Types on Target Machine node and choose Action, Add File Type. Open the Properties window, select the Command property, and click the ellipsis (…) button. The Select Item in Project dialog box appears. Select Primary Output from NetSql (Active) from the Application Folder node and click OK.

3. Change the Name property to QueryFiles, the Description property to Query Files, and the Extensions property to qry;sql in the Properties window for the newly added file type, as shown in Figure 13.17.

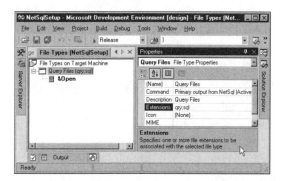

FIGURE 13.17
You can associate file types with the deployed applications via the File Types Editor.

4. Build the NetSqlSetup project. Right-click the project in Solution Explorer and select the Install option. Install the project.

5. Create a new file with the following SQL select statement:

```
SELECT * FROM EMPLOYEES
```

6. Save the file to the desktop with a .qry or .sql extension. Open the file by double-clicking it on the desktop. The file launches the NetSql application. Interestingly, the text box in the application contains the query, stored in the file. This happens because of the query member declaration and the code you added in the Main() method and the form's Load event handler of the NetSql.cs class in Step by Step 13.1.

The Command property specifies the executable file to be invoked when an action occurs on a file that has a specified extension. By default, an Open action with the verb open is added to the file type. You can also add custom actions with different verbs such as print and edit.

Using the User Interface Editor

The User Interface Editor allows you to customize the user interface that is provided to the user during the installation process. The *user interface* is the various dialog boxes that appear during the installation process. The user interface provided to the user is divided into three stages: start, progress, and end. You can add different types of dialog boxes for each stage. Each stage allows only certain types of dialog boxes to be added.

The User Interface Editor displays the user interface that is applicable during both end user installation and administrative installation. You can customize the user interface for both of these types of installations. The administrative installation occurs when you run the msiexec command-line tool with the /a option. You will find more details about administrative installation later in the chapter.

STEP BY STEP

13.6 Using the User Interface Editor

1. Select the NetSqlSetup project in Solution Explorer. Open the User Interface Editor by clicking the User Interface Editor icon in Solution Explorer.

2. Right-click the Start node under the Install tree and select Add Dialog from the context menu. The Add Dialog dialog box appears. Select License Agreement, as shown in Figure 13.18. Click OK. Right-click License Agreement and choose Move Up twice to move the License Agreement dialog box to appear after the Welcome dialog box. Select the LicenseFile property in the Properties window and select (Browse...) from the drop-down list. The Select Item in Project dialog box appears. Navigate to the Application folder and select License.rtf.

NOTE

The LicenseFile and ReadmeFile Properties The LicenseFile and ReadmeFile properties of the User Interface dialog box only work with Rich Text Format (RTF) files. If you specify a file of any other format, you don't get an error, but the contents of the file are not displayed.

3. Add a Read Me dialog box to the End node under the Install tree. Move the Read Me dialog box before the Finished dialog box. The dialog boxes should appear in the User Interface Editor as shown in Figure 13.19. Set the `ReadmeFile` property to the `ReadMe.rtf` file.

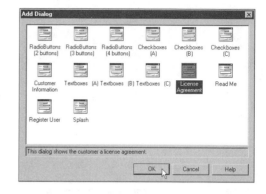

FIGURE 13.18▲
You can use the Add Dialog dialog box to add dialog boxes in the User Interface Editor.

FIGURE 13.19◄
You can customize the user interface of the installation program via the User Interface Editor.

4. Build the `NetSqlSetup` project. Right-click the project in Solution Explorer and select the Install option. Install the project. A License Agreement screen appears. Only when you select the I Agree option is the Next button enabled, as shown in Figure 13.20. The Read Me screen appears before the Close screen is shown.

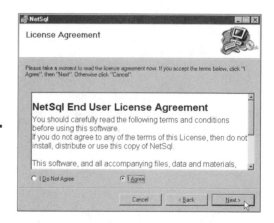

FIGURE 13.20▲
The customized License Agreement dialog box is added to the user interface to display the license agreement during the installation process.

Using the Custom Actions Editor

The Custom Actions Editor allows you to run compiled `.dll` files, `.exe` files, scripts, assembly files, or assemblies at the end of an installation. These files can be used to perform custom actions that are vital but were not carried out during the installation. If the custom action fails, the entire installation process is rolled back. For example, you might have to install the database that is required by your application during the installation process.

There are four phases in which a custom action can be performed: install, commit, rollback, and uninstall. In Step by Step 13.7 you create a simple custom action to launch the NetSql application toward the end of installation.

STEP BY STEP

13.7 Using the Custom Actions Editor

1. In Solution Explorer, right-click Solution and select Add, New Project. Select Visual C# Projects from the Project Types tree and then select Empty Project from the list of templates on the right. Name the project LaunchNetSql.

2. Right-click the project in Solution Explorer and select Add, Add Class from the context menu. Name the class LaunchNetSql.cs.

3. Modify the class definition so that it looks like this:

```
using System;
using System.Diagnostics;
namespace LaunchNetSql
{
    public class LaunchNetSql
    {
        public static void Main(string[] args)
        {
            // Create a ProcessStartInfo object
            ProcessStartInfo psi =
              new ProcessStartInfo();
            psi.FileName = "NetSql.exe ";
            // The arguments to the file specify the
            // working directory. Since the directory
            // can contain spaces,
            // join all the arguments
            psi.WorkingDirectory =
                String.Join(" ",args);
            // Start the process
            Process.Start(psi);
        }
    }
}
```

4. Right-click the project in Solution Explorer and select Properties. The Project Property Pages dialog box appears. In the left pane, select the General node under the Common Properties tree. Set the Output Type property to Windows Application under the Application node in the right pane. Click OK to build the LaunchNetSql project.

> **NOTE**
> **The Process and ProcessInfo Classes** I discuss the Process and ProcessInfo classes in great detail in Chapter 14, "Maintaining and Supporting a Windows Application."

5. In Solution Explorer, right-click the NetSqlSetup project and select Add, Project Output from the context menu. The Add Project Output Group dialog box appears. Select LaunchNetSql as the project and select Primary Output from the list box. Click OK.

6. Select the NetSqlSetup project in Solution Explorer. Open the Custom Actions Editor by clicking the Custom Actions Editor icon in Solution Explorer.

7. Select the Install node under the Custom Actions tree. Select Action, Add Custom Action. The Select Item in Project dialog box appears. Navigate to the Application folder and select Primary Output from LaunchNetSql (Active). Rename the action LaunchNetSql.

8. Select the custom action LaunchNetSql and open the Properties window. Set the Arguments property to [TARGETDIR] and the InstallerClass property to false, as shown in Figure 13.21.

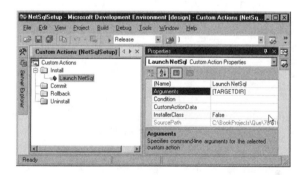

FIGURE 13.21
You can add the custom actions to be performed during the installation process via the Custom Actions Editor.

9. Build the NetSqlSetup project. Right-click the project in Solution Explorer and select the Install option. Install the project. The NetSql application is launched during the installation process.

In Step by Step 13.7 the Arguments property is used to pass any command-line arguments to the custom action that is launched. This property is set to the Windows Installer property [TARGETDIR], which maps to the directory where the application is installed on the target machine.

This argument is passed to the LaunchNetSql application to specify the path of the NetSql application. The InstallerClass property is set to false because the LaunchNetSql class does not inherit from the Installer class. The .NET Framework includes the Installer class to provide a base for custom installations. I discuss the Installer class in more detail later in the chapter.

Using the Launch Conditions Editor

The Launch Conditions Editor allows you to set conditions that are to be evaluated when an installation begins on a target machine. If the conditions are not met, the installation stops. For example, let's say you would like to install a Visual C# .NET application only if the .NET Framework CLR exists on the target machine. This condition is by default added by Visual Studio .NET. You might also need to perform other checks, such as whether a particular file exists on the target machine, or verify a particular Registry key value on the target machine.

The Launch Conditions Editor allows you to perform searches on the target machine for a file, a Registry entry, or Windows Installer components. For example, you can search whether Microsoft Data Access Components (MDAC) is installed on the target machine by searching in the Registry for that particular Registry key value (see Figure 13.22).

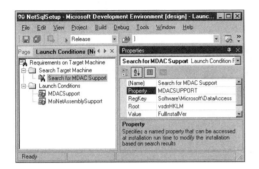

FIGURE 13.22
You can perform a search on the Registry of the target machine during the installation process via the Launch Conditions Editor.

You can then add conditions to be evaluated for the search performed on the target machine. If the conditions fail, the installation ends. For example, you could add a condition that the MDAC that is installed should be version 2.7 or higher in order for the installation to continue, by checking against the Registry key value retrieved by the Registry search (see Figure 13.23).

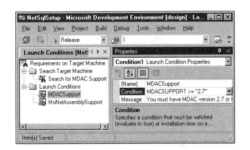

FIGURE 13.23
You can add launch conditions on the target machine during the installation process via the Launch Conditions Editor.

STEP BY STEP

13.8 Using the Launch Conditions Editor

1. Select the NetSqlSetup project in Solution Explorer. Open the Launch Conditions Editor by clicking the Launch Conditions Editor icon in Solution Explorer.

2. Select the Requirements on Target Machine node and select Action, Add Registry Launch Condition. This adds two nodes—one under the Search Target Machine node and one under the Launch Conditions node.

3. Select the newly created node under the Search Target Machine node and open the Properties window. Set the Name property to Search for MDAC Support, Property to MDACSUPPORT, Root to vsdrrHKLM, RegKey to Software\Microsoft\DataAccess, and Value to FullInstallVer, as shown in Figure 13.22.

4. Select the newly created node under the Search Target Machine node and open the Properties window. Set the Name property to MDACSupport, Condition to MDACSUPPORT >= "2.7", and set Message to You must have MDAC version 2.7 or higher installed on this computer. Please contact the administrator for installation information., as shown in Figure 13.23.

5. Build the NetSqlSetup project. Right-click the project in Solution Explorer and select the Install option. Install the project. If the target computer does not have MDAC 2.7 or higher installed, the installation process of the NetSql project is interrupted, and the user sees the error message set in the Message property of the launch condition.

NOTE

The Condition Property The different editor elements in the setup and deployment projects—such as folders, files, Registry keys, custom actions, and launch conditions—have the Condition property. The Condition property consists of a valid conditional statement in the form of a string that evaluates to either true or false.

The conditional statement is executed during installation, and if it returns true, the action associated with that particular element is performed on the target machine. For example, say a condition is applied to a Registry key value; if the statement defined in the Condition property evaluates to false during installation, the particular key value will not be entered in the Registry on the target machine.

GUIDED PRACTICE EXERCISE 13.2

The goal of this exercise is to add a few sample files to the NetSqlSetup project and then provide an option to include or omit installation of sample files on the target machine. You should use the User Interface Editor to provide the user interface to select or deselect the Samples installation option. You should use the Condition property of the files to check whether the Samples option is selected by the end user.

How would you provide such an option during the installation process?

continues

continued

In this exercise you practice on performing conditional deployment. You should try working through this problem on your own first. If you get stuck, or if you'd like to see one possible solution, follow these steps:

1. Open the `NetSql` project in Solution Explorer.

2. Add to the `NetSql` project the sample query file `CustomersFromBrazil.sql`, with the following text:

   ```
   SELECT *
   FROM CUSTOMERS
   WHERE COUNTRY = 'Brazil'
   ORDER BY COMPANYNAME
   ```

3. Add to the `NetSql` project another sample query file, `TenMostExpensiveProducts.qry`, with the following text:

   ```
   SELECT TOP 10
   Products.ProductName AS TenMostExpensiveProducts,
   Products.UnitPrice
   FROM Products
   ORDER BY Products.UnitPrice DESC
   ```

4. Open the File System Editor of the `NetSqlSetup` project. Select Application Folder and choose Add, Folder from the context menu. Rename the newly added folder `Samples`.

5. Select the `Samples` folder and choose Add, File from the context menu. The Add Files dialog box appears. Navigate to the sample query files created in the previous steps and add them to the Application Folder node.

6. Open the User Interface Editor of the `NetSqlSetup` project. Right-click the Start node under the Install tree and select Add Dialog from the context menu. The Add Dialog dialog box appears. Select Radio Buttons (2 Buttons) dialog. Click OK. Place the newly added dialog in between License Agreement and Installation Folder.

7. Set `BannerText` to `NetSql Samples`, `BodyText` to `Do you want to install Samples?`, `Button1Label` to `Yes`, `Button1Value` to `1`, `Button2Label` to `No`, `Button2Value` to `2`, `ButtonProperty` to `NETSQLSAMPLES`, and `DefaultValue` to `1`, as shown in Figure 13.24.

8. Open the File System Editor and select the `Samples` folder. Change the `Condition` properties of both the sample files to `NETSQLSAMPLES=1`.

FIGURE 13.24
The Radio Buttons dialog box can provide a customized user interface to allow the user to perform conditional deployment.

9. Build the `NetSqlSetup` project. Right-click the project in Solution Explorer and select the Install option. Install the project. During the installation process, the Samples dialog box appears, with the `Yes` option selected, as shown in Figure 13.25.

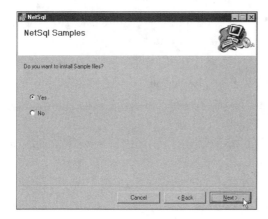

FIGURE 13.25
The customized Samples dialog box gives an option for installing the sample files during the installation process.

10. If you choose the option Yes, sample files appear in the `Samples` folder under the installation folder (which is `C:\Program Files\NetSql Software\NetSql\Samples` if you do not change the folder during installation). On the other hand, if the No option is selected in the Samples dialog box, the `Samples` folder and the sample files are not installed.

If you have difficulty following this exercise, review the sections "Using the File System Editor" and "Using the User Interface Editor," earlier in this chapter. After doing that review, try this exercise again.

R E V I E W   B R E A K

▶ The File System Editor provides a mapping of the file system on the target machine. The folders are referred to by special names that during the installation process are converted to represent the folders as per the file system on the target machine.

continues

continued

▶ The Registry Editor allows you to specify Registry keys, sub-keys, and values that are added to the Registry in the target machine during installation.

▶ The File Types Editor allows you to associate a file extension with a Windows application.

▶ The User Interface Editor allows you to customize the user interface of the installation process. You can provide different types of user interface for end user installation and administrative installation.

▶ The User Interface Editor and Launch Conditions Editor provide special properties (such as `Property` and `ButtonProperty`) whose values can be evaluated to perform the installation as per the end user's choice.

▶ The Custom Actions Editor allows you to add custom actions to be performed during the installation process. It allows you to run `.dll`, `.exe`, scripts or assembly files. Custom actions can be performed during four phases: install, commit, rollback, and uninstall.

▶ The Launch Conditions Editor allows you to set conditions to be evaluated when the installation begins on the target machine. If the conditions are not met, the installation stops.

SHARED ASSEMBLIES

Add assemblies to the global assembly cache.

Chapter 4 briefly discusses shared assemblies. This section further explores shared assemblies and how to deploy them.

A shared assembly is shared among multiple applications on a machine. It is therefore stored in a central location, the GAC and it enjoys special services such as file security, shared location, and side-by-side versioning.

Because shared assemblies are all installed in a central location, distingushing them with just a filename is not enough. You would not want an application to break when some other vendor installed an assembly with the same name in the GAC. To avoid this possibility, Microsoft requires you to assign each assembly a strong name before placing it in the GAC.

Assigning a Strong Name to an Assembly

An assembly is identified by its text name (usually the name of the file, without the file extension), version number, and culture information. However, these pieces of information do not guarantee that an assembly will be unique. There might be a case when two software publishers might use the same identity for an assembly, thereby causing applications using those assemblies to behave abnormally. You can greatly reduce the possibility of this problem occurring by assigning a strong name to an assembly. A strong name strengthens an assembly's identity by qualifying it with the software publisher's identity. The .NET Framework uses a standard cryptography technique known as *digital signing* to ensure the uniqueness of an assembly.

The process of digital signing involves two related pieces of binary data: a public key and a private key. The *public key* represents the software publisher's identity and is freely distributed. While you are creating a strongly named assembly, the public key is stored in the assembly manifest, along with other identification information, such as name, version number, and culture. This scheme does not look foolproof because the public key is available freely and nobody can stop a software publisher from forging an assembly identity with some other company's public key. To verify that only the legitimate owner of the public key has created the assembly, an assembly is signed, using publisher's private key. The private key is assumed to be known only to the publisher of the assembly. The processes of signing an assembly and verifying its signature work like this:

◆ **Signing an assembly**—You create a signature computing a cryptographic hash from the contents of the assembly. The hash is encoded with the private key. This signature is then stored within the assembly.

> **NOTE**
>
> **Signing a Multifile Assembly**   If an assembly consists of multiple files, just the file that contains the assembly manifest needs to be signed. This is because the assembly manifest already contains file hashes for all the files that constitute the assembly implementation. The CLR can easily determine whether a file has been tampered with by matching its actual hash with what is stored in the assembly manifest.

♦ **Verifying the signature**—When the common language runtime verifies an assembly's identity, it reads the public key from the assembly manifest and uses it to decrypt the cryptographic hash that is stored in the assembly. It then recalculates the hash for the current contents of the assembly. If the two hashes match, this ensures two things: the contents of the assembly were not tampered with after the assembly was signed and only the party that has a private key associated with the public key stored in the assembly has signed the assembly.

You can easily generate public/private key pairs by using the Strong Name tool (`sn.exe`), which is available in the .NET Framework SDK.

STEP BY STEP

13.9 Creating a Public/Private Key Pair by Using the Strong Name Tool (`sn.exe`)

1. From the Visual Studio .NET program group in the Windows Start menu, launch the Visual Studio .NET command prompt.

2. Issue the following command to create a pair of public/private keys:

```
sn -k RandNumCorpKeys.snk
```

3. Both the public and private keys are created and stored in a file named `RandNumCorpKeys.snk`, as shown in Figure 13.26. Note the directory where this file is created; you will be using it in Step by Step 13.10.

FIGURE 13.26
You can create a public/private key pair by using the Strong Name tool.

Step by Step 13.10 shows how to create a strongly named assembly. You use the key file generated in Step by Step 13.9 to digitally sign an assembly.

STEP BY STEP

13.10 Creating a Component with a Strong Name

1. Create a new Visual C# Class Library project in the solution 316C13. Name the project RandomNumberGenerator.

2. Add a Component class to the project and name it RandomNumberGenerator.cs. Delete Class1.cs.

3. Add a reference to System.Drawing.dll and insert the following code along with the other using directives:

```
//Required for ToolboxBitmap attribute
using System.Drawing;
```

4. Add an icon for the component and name it RandomNumberGenerator.bmp. Set its Build Action property to Embedded Resources.

5. Add the following attribute just before the class declaration:

```
//Set the Toolbox icon
[ToolboxBitmap(typeof(RandomNumberGenerator))]
```

6. Add the following line of code just after the Component Designer generated code section:

```
//stores minValue and maxValue
private int minValue=1, maxValue=100;

public int MinValue
{
    get
    {
        return minValue;
    }
    set
    {
        minValue = value;
    }
}

public int MaxValue
{
    get
    {
        return maxValue;
    }
```

continues

continued

```
        set
        {
            maxValue = value;
        }
    }
    public int GetRandomNumber()
    {
        Random r = new Random();
        return r.Next(minValue, maxValue);
    }
```

7. Add to this project the `RandNumCorpKeys.snk` file generated in Step by Step 13.9.

8. Open the `AssemblyInfo.cs` file. Scroll down in the file and change the `AssemblyVersion` and `AssemblyKeyFile` attributes as follows:

```
[assembly: AssemblyVersion("1.0")]
[assembly: AssemblyKeyFile(
    @"..\..\RandomNumCorpKeys.snk")]
```

9. Build the project. A `RandomNumberGenerator.dll` is generated, and a strong name is assigned to the file based on the specified key file.

In Step by Step 13.10 you change the `AssemblyVersion` attribute of the assembly from `1.0.*` to `1.0`. The assembly's version consists of up to four parts:

```
<major>.<minor>.<build>.<revision>
```

If you want to use a fixed value, you can hard-code it. The default value of the version uses an asterisk in place of build and revision numbers; this changes the build and revision each time you compile the project. The build is calculated as the number of days since January 1, 2000, and the revision is calculated as the number of seconds since midnight divided by 2.

At runtime the CLR uses this information to load the assembly. In the next few examples, you may compile your projects several times and thereby change the version of the assembly if you use the default version property. The GAC allows you to install multiple versions of the same assembly. Therefore, in this chapter you can hard-code the version of the application's assembly to keep matters simple.

In Step by Step 13.10 you use Visual Studio .NET to attach a strong name to an assembly. If you want to do this manually, you can use the Assembly Linker tool (al.exe) with the -keyfile option.

Adding an Assembly to the GAC

After you have associated a strong name with an assembly, you can place it in the GAC. There are several ways you can add an assembly to the GAC. Using the Windows Installer is the recommended approach, but there are some quick alternatives, too. However, you should use these quick approaches only for development purposes; they are not recommended for installing assemblies on the end user's computer.

> **NOTE**
> **Working with the GAC** You need to have administrative privilages on a computer in order to manage its GAC.

Using Windows Installer to Add an Assembly to the GAC

Using Microsoft Windows Installer is the preferred way of adding assemblies to the GAC. Windows Installer maintains a reference count for assemblies in the GAC and provides uninstallation support. You will learn how to add assemblies using Windows Installer technology through the setup and deployment projects of Visual Studio .NET a little later in this chapter.

Using Windows Explorer to Add an Assembly to the GAC

When the .NET Framework is installed, the Assembly Cache Viewer Shell Extension (shfusion.dll) is also installed. This extension allows you to view the complex structure of the GAC folder in a navigable and understandable manner using Windows Explorer. Because the GAC is integrated with the Windows shell, you can view and manage GAC's contents with the help of Windows Explorer.

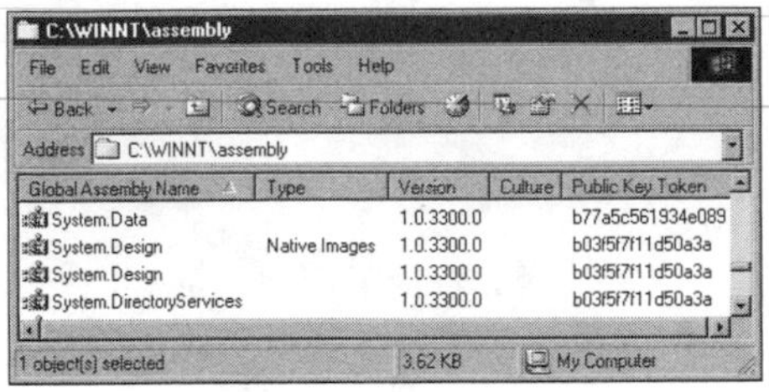

FIGURE 13.27

The Assembly Cache Viewer Shell Extension enables you to view and manage the contents of the assembly cache by using Windows Explorer.

STEP BY STEP

13.11 Adding an Assembly to the GAC by Using Windows Explorer

1. Open Windows Explorer. Navigate to the assembly cache folder. It is usually `c:\WINNT\assembly` or `C:\Windows\assembly` (see Figure 13.27).

2. Using Windows Explorer, drag the `RandomNumberGenerator.dll` file created in Step by Step 13.10 and drop it in the assembly cache folder.

3. In the assembly cache folder, right-click `RandomNumberGenerator.dll` and select Properties from the shortcut menu. The Properties dialog box appears, as shown in Figure 13.28.

FIGURE 13.28

You can view the properties of the `RandomNumberGenerator` assembly that is installed in the GAC.

> **N O T E**
>
> **The Assembly Cache Folder** The assembly cache folder actually contains two caches: the GAC and the native image cache. When you view the assembly cache folder by using Windows Explorer, the Assembly Cache Viewer Shell Extension shows you a combined list of both caches. You can determine whether an assembly is from the GAC or from the native image cache by looking at the Type field in the list. When you add an assembly to the assembly cache folder by using Windows Explorer, it is added to the GAC. You will learn about the native image cache and how to add assemblies to it later in this chapter.

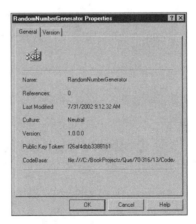

If you want to remove a file from the GAC, you just delete it from Windows Explorer by selecting File, Delete or by selecting Delete from the assembly's shortcut menu.

Using the .NET Framework Configuration Tool to Add an Assembly to the GAC

You can also use the .NET Framework Configuration tool (`mscorcfg.msc`) to manage an assembly in the GAC. Step by Step 13.12 guides you through the process of adding an assembly to the GAC by using the .NET Framework Configuration tool.

STEP BY STEP

13.12 Adding an Assembly to the GAC by Using the .NET Framework Configuration Tool

1. Open the Administrative Tools section of Windows Control Panel. Open the tool named .NET Framework Configuration. Select the assembly cache folder on the left pane under the My Computer node (see Figure 13.29).

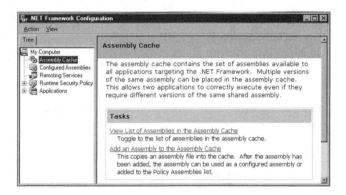

FIGURE 13.29
The .NET Framework Configuration tool allows you to manage the assembly cache.

2. In the right pane, click the hyperlink Add an Assembly to the Assembly Cache. The Add an Assembly dialog box appears. Navigate to the `RandomNumberGenerator.dll` file in the `RandomNumberGenerator` project and click the OK button.

3. Click the other hyperlink, View List of Assemblies in the Assembly Cache. A list of installed assemblies appears. Ensure that `RandomNumberGenerator` is in this list, as shown in Figure 13.30.

FIGURE 13.30
You can add assemblies in the GAC by using the .NET Framework Configuration tool.

To uninstall an assembly by using the .NET Framework Configuration tool, you just select Action, Delete or select Delete from the assembly's shortcut menu.

In addition to helping you add or remove assemblies, the .NET Framework Configuration tool helps you configure assemblies and manage their runtime security policies.

Using the Global Assembly Cache Tool (gacutil.exe) to Add an Assembly to the GAC

GacUtil.exe is a command-line tool that is especially useful for adding and removing assemblies from the GAC via a program script or a batch file.

STEP BY STEP

13.13 Adding an Assembly to the GAC by Using the Global Assembly Cache Tool

1. From the Visual Studio .NET program group in the Windows Start menu, launch the Visual Studio .NET command prompt.

2. Change the directory to the folder where the RandomNumberGenerator.dll file resides in the RandomNumberGenerator project—in this case, the project's bin\Release directory.

3. Issue the following command to install the assembly to the GAC, as shown in Figure 13.31:

```
gacutil /i RandomNumberGenerator.dll
```

FIGURE 13.31
You can add an assembly to the GAC by using the Global Assembly Cache tool.

You can list all the assemblies in the GAC by using the `gacutil.exe` tool with the `/l` option. You can use the `/u` option with the name of the assembly (without the file extension) to uninstall the assembly from the GAC:

```
gacutil /u RandomNumberGenerator
```

You can also choose to uninstall from the GAC an assembly of a specific version and specific culture by specifying its version, culture, and public key, along with the name of the assembly:

```
gacutil /u RandomNumberGenerator,Version=1.0.0.0,
➥Culture=neutral,PublicKeyToken=f26af4dbb33881b1
```

Referencing an Assembly from the GAC

Normally when you refer an assembly in a Windows application project, you can invoke the Add Reference dialog box and browse to the desired assembly. But after you have added an assembly to the GAC, this approach does not work because the GAC has a complex structure that cannot be directly enumerated by the Add Reference dialog box.

When you view the GAC by using the tools mentioned in the preceding section, you see an abstraction of its structure. If you instead switch to the command prompt and change directory to the GAC folder, you see that the GAC is actually made up of various subdirectories, one for each assembly. Each of these directories has subdirectories, whose names depend on the assemblies' versions and public keys. Each subdirectory stores the actual assembly file, along with some additional assembly information. Figure 13.32 shows how the GAC entry is made for the `RandomNumberGenerator` component on my computer.

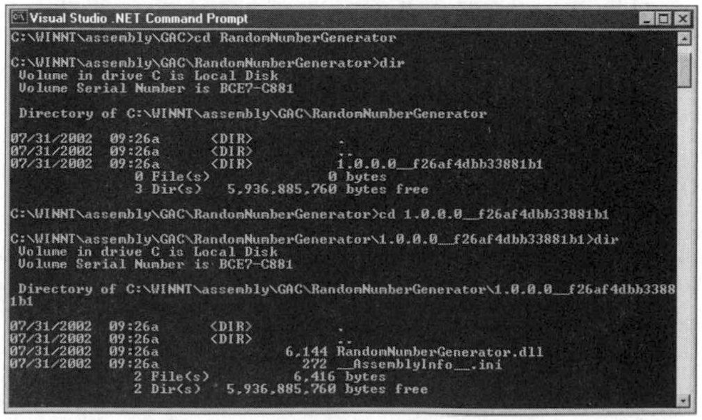

FIGURE 13.32
You can see how the assemblies are maintained in the GAC by exploring the GAC through the command window.

A good practice is to keep a copy of the assemblies installed in the GAC somewhere outside the GAC, where they are easily accessible via a pathname. You can then easily reference these assemblies through the Add Reference dialog box, by browsing to the correct path. In fact, the .NET Framework uses the same techniques for all of its own assemblies stored in the GAC. The .NET Framework also stores copies of those assemblies in the folder where the .NET Framework is installed.

Although you can add a reference to an assembly by browsing to the folder where it is stored, the convenient way is to have its name directly displayed in the Add Reference dialog box so that you can just check it to select it.

Step by Step 13.14 shows how to instruct Visual Studio .NET to add assemblies that are stored in a custom folder to the Add Reference dialog box.

STEP BY STEP

13.14 Displaying an Assembly in the Add Reference Dialog Box

1. Open the Registry Editor by launching `regedit.exe` from the Run dialog box, which you access by selecting Start, Run.

2. In the Registry Editor, browse to the key named `HKEY_LOCAL_MACHINE\SOFTWARE\Microsoft\.NETFramework\ AssemblyFolders`.

3. At this level create a new key and name it `MyAssemblies`.

4. Double-click the (Default) value in the new key and change its value to the location of `RandomNumberGenerator.dll` in the `bin\Release` folder of the `RandomNumberGenerator` project, as shown in Figure 13.33.

5. Close the Registry Editor. Close all instances of Visual Studio .NET.

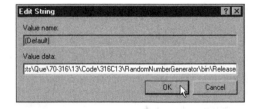

FIGURE 13.33
You can set value of a Registry key via the Edit String dialog box.

In Step by Step 13.15 you create a small Windows application that, when executed, loads the components that are installed in the GAC. Before you begin this Step by Step, make sure you have already installed the file RandomNumberGenerator.dll in the GAC.

STEP BY STEP

13.15 Creating a Windows Application That Uses the RandomNumberGenerator Component

1. Add a new Windows application project to the solution 316C13 and name it RandomNumberApplication.

2. In Solution Explorer, rename the Form1.cs file RandomNumberApplication.cs in the project. Switch to the code view of the form and modify all references to Form1 so that they refer to RandomNumberApplication instead.

3. Using the Add Reference dialog box, add a reference for RandomNumberGenerator.dll. Set the Copy Local property of the RandomNumberGenerator.dll file to false.

4. Activate the toolbox and click the My Custom Control tab. Right-click the toolbox and select Customize Toolbox. Click the .NET Framework Components tab and select RandomNumberGenerator.dll.

5. Drag the Random Number Generator control from the toolbox and drop it on the form. Change its MinValue property to 500 and change MaxValue to 1000.

6. Add a Label control (lblResults) and a Button control (btnGenerate) to the form. Empty the Label control's Text property and set the Button control's Text property to Generate a Random Number!. Double-click the Button control to add an event handler for its Click event. Add the following code to the event handler:

```
private void btnGenerate_Click(object sender,
    System.EventArgs e)
{
    lblResults.Text = String.Format(
        "The next random number is: {0}",
        randomNumberGenerator1.GetRandomNumber());
}
```

continues

continued

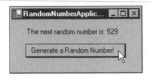

FIGURE 13.34
The form generates a random number by using
the RandomNumberGenerator component
installed in the GAC.

7. Set the project RandomNumberApplication as the startup project.

8. Run the solution. Click the button. A random number between 500 and 1,000 appears every time you press the button, as shown in Figure 13.34.

In Step by Step 13.15 you add a reference to the assembly stored in the bin\Release folder of the RandomNumberGenerator project. However, the application loads the assembly from the GAC instead of its copy in the bin\Release folder. To understand this, you need to understand how the CLR locates assemblies; this is discussed in the following section.

How the CLR Locates Assemblies

The CLR uses the following steps to locate an assembly:

1. It tries to determine the version of the assembly to be located. (This information may be available in the application's configuration files.)

2. It checks whether the assembly is already loaded. If the requested assembly has been loaded in one of the previous calls, it uses the previously loaded assembly.

3. It checks the GAC. If the assembly is in the GAC, it loads the assembly from there.

4. If there is a <codebase> element specified in the application's configuration file, the CLR locates the assembly by using the path specified by the <codebase> element.

5. If there is no <codebase> element specified in the configuration files and if there is no culture information available for the assembly, the CLR checks the following locations (in the order listed here) for the assembly:

```
[ApplicationBase]\[AssemblyName].dll
[ApplicationBase]\[AssemblyName]\[AssemblyName].dll
[ApplicationBase]\[PrivatePath1]\[AssemblyName].dll
[ApplicationBase]\[PrivatePath1]\[AssemblyName]\
➥[AssemblyName].dll
[ApplicationBase]\[PrivatePath2]\[AssemblyName].dll
[ApplicationBase]\[PrivatePath2]\[AssemblyName]\
➥[AssemblyName].dll
    .
    .
    .
```

In this case ApplicationBase is the root directory where the application is installed. AssemblyName is the text name of the assembly. PrivatePath1, PrivatePath2, and so on are the user-defined subdirectories specified either in the application's configuration file, using the <probing> element, or via the AppendPrivatePath property for an application domain.

6. If there is no <codebase> element specified in the configuration files and if the culture information is available, the CLR checks the following locations (in the order listed here) for the assembly:

```
[ApplicationBase]\[culture]\[AssemblyName].dll
[ApplicationBase]\[culture]\[AssemblyName]\
➥[AssemblyName].dll
[ApplicationBase]\[culture]\[PrivatePath1]\
➥[AssemblyName].dll
[ApplicationBase]\[culture]\[PrivatePath1]\
➥[AssemblyName]\[AssemblyName].dll
[ApplicationBase]\[culture]\[PrivatePath2]\
➥[AssemblyName].dll
[ApplicationBase]\[culture]\[PrivatePath2]\
➥[AssemblyName]\[AssemblyName].dll
    .
    .
    .
```

In this case ApplicationBase is the root directory where the application is installed. AssemblyName is the text name of the assembly. PrivatePath1, PrivatePath2, and so on are the user-defined subdirectories specified either in the application's configuration file, using the <probing> element, or via the AppendPrivatePath property for an application domain.

In the case of an assembly that is stored in the GAC, these rules ensure that the GAC copy is always the one that is used.

Delay Signing an Assembly

In Step by Step 13.10, when you sign an assembly, you use a key file that contains both the public key and a private key for a company. But as discussed earlier in the chapter, the private key ensures that the assembly is signed only by its advertised publisher. Thus, in most companies, the private key is stored securely, and only a few people have access to it.

If the keys are highly protected, it might be difficult to frequently access assemblies when multiple developers of a company are building assemblies several times a day. To solve this problem, the .NET Framework uses the delay signing technique for assemblies.

When you use delay signing, you use only the public key to build an assembly. Associating public keys with an assembly allows you to place the assembly in the GAC and complete most of the development and testing tasks with the assembly. Later, when you are ready to package the assembly, someone who is authorized signs the assembly with the private key. Signing with the private key ensures that the CLR will provide tamper protection for the assembly. The following list summarizes the various steps involved with delay signing:

1. **Extract a public key from the public/private key pair**—To extract the public key from a file that is storing the public/private key pair, you use the Strong Name tool as follows:

   ```
   sn.exe -p RandNumCorpKeys.snk RandNumCorpPublicKey.snk
   ```

   At this stage, the `RandNumCorpPublicKey.snk` file can be freely distributed to the development team, and the `RandNumCorpKeys.snk` file that contains both the private and public keys can be stored securely, possibly on a hardware device such as smart card.

2. **Delay signing an assembly using Visual Studio .NET**—To use delay signing in a Visual Studio .NET project, you need to modify the following two attributes of the project's `AssemblyInfo.cs` file and build the assembly:

   ```
   [assembly: AssemblyDelaySign(true)]
   [assembly: AssemblyKeyFile(
       "RandNumCorpPublicKey.snk")]
   ```

3. **Turn off verification for an assembly in the GAC**—By default, the GAC verifies the strong name of each assembly. If the assembly is not signed by using the private key, this verification fails. So for development and testing purposes, you can relax this verification for an assembly by issuing the following command:

```
sn.exe -Vr RandomNumberGenerator.dll
```

If you execute this command, the GAC always skips the verification for this assembly in the future.

4. **Sign a delay-signed assembly with the private key**—When you are ready to deploy a delay-signed assembly, you need to sign it with the company's private key:

```
sn.exe -R RandomNumberGenerator.dll
➥RandNumCorpKeys.snk
```

5. **Turn on verification for an assembly in the GAC**—Finally, you can instruct the GAC to turn on verification for an assembly by issuing the following command:

```
sn.exe -Vu RandomNumberGenerator.dll
```

Delay Signing Using the Assembly Linker Tool

The Assembly Linker tool (`al.exe`) generates an assembly with an assembly manifest from the given modules or resource files. Remember that a module is a Microsoft Intermediate Language (MSIL) file without an assembly manifest.

While generating an assembly, you can also instruct the Assembly Linker tool to sign or delay sign an assembly with the given public/private key file. When you use `al.exe` for delay signing, you also use the arguments listed in Table 13.1.

TABLE 13.1

ARGUMENTS PASSED TO al.exe FOR DELAY SIGNING

Argument	Description
<sourcefiles>	You replace *<sourcefiles>* with the names of one or more complied modules that will be the parts of the resulting assembly.

continues

TABLE 13.1   *continued*

ARGUMENTS PASSED TO al.exe FOR DELAY SIGNING

Argument	Description
/delay[sign][+|-]	You can use either the delay argument or the delay[sign] argument for delay signing. The option + is used to delay sign the assembly by storing just the public key manifest in the assembly manifest.
	The – option is used to fully sign an assembly by using both public and private keys.
	If you do not use either + or -, the default value of – is assumed.
/keyf[ile]:<filename>	You can use either keyf or keyfile to specify the key file. You replace <filename> with the name of the file that stores the key(s).
/out:<filename>	You replace <filename> with the desired name of the output assembly file.

Assume that you want to create an assembly by linking two modules, Sample1.netmodule and Sample2.netmodule. The public key file is SamplePublicKey.snk, and the desired output assembly is SignedSample.exe. You would use the al.exe command as follows:

```
al.exe Sample1.netmodule,Sample2.netmodule
➥/delaysign+/keyfile:SamplePublicKey.snk
➥/out:SignedSample.exe
```

Creating a Merge Module Project

Create a setup program that installs an application and allows for the application to be uninstalled.

- **Register components and assemblies.**

This section describes how to create a setup project for distributing a component such as the RandomNumberGenerator. The process of packaging a component is different from the process of packaging Windows applications. When you have a component that will be shared among multiple applications, you should package it as a merge module (.msm file). A merge module includes the actual component, such as a .dll file, along with any related setup logic, such as resources, Registry entries, custom actions, and launch conditions.

EXAM TIP

The Strong Name and the Authenticode Signature   An assembly signed with a strong name does not automatically assert a company's identity, such as its name. For that purpose you can use an Authenticode signature, in which case the company's identity is asserted by a third-party certification authority (such as Verisign or Thawte). You can use the File Signing tool (signcode.exe) to attach an authenticode signature to the assembly.

An important thing to know is the order of commands when signing an assembly using both sn.exe and signcode.exe. You must sign your assembly with the Strong Name tool (sn.exe) before you sign it with the File Signing tool (signcode.exe).

Merge modules cannot be directly installed. They need to be merged with the installation program of an application that uses the shared component, packaged into a merge module.

When you modify a component to release new versions, you create a new merge module for each of the new versions. A new merge module should be created for each successive version of a component in order to avoid version conflicts.

STEP BY STEP

13.16 Creating a Merge Module Project by Using the Setup Wizard to Package a Shared Component for Deployment

1. In Solution Explorer, right-click Solution and select Add, New Project. Select Setup and Deployment projects from the Project Types tree and then select Setup Wizard from the list of templates on the right. Name the project `RandomNumberMergeModule`.

2. The first screen of the wizard that appears is the Welcome screen. Click Next. The second screen is the Choose a Project Type screen. Choose Create a merge module for Windows Installer in the second group (Do You Want to Create a Redistributable Package?). Click Next.

3. The third screen of the wizard is the Choose Project Outputs to Include screen. Select Primary Output from RandomNumberGenerator. Click Next. Click Next on the fourth screen of the wizard as well, and then click Finish.

4. Open the File System Editor for the merge module project. Add a new folder `RandNumCorp` to the `Common Files` folder. Move the `Primary output from RandomNumberGenerator (Active)` file in the `Common Files` Folder to the `RandNumCorp` folder.

5. Select the File System on Target Machine node and choose Add Special Folder, Global Assembly Cache Folder from the context menu. Select the Global Assembly Cache Folder and select Add, Project Output from the context menu.

continues

continued

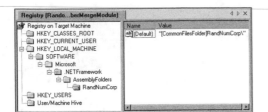

FIGURE 13.35
You can set the keys and values in the Registry Editor to add an assembly to the Add Reference dialog box.

6. The Add Project Output Group dialog box appears. Select the RandomNumberGenerator project and select Primary Output from the list of items to be added. Click OK.

7. Open the Registry Editor for the merge module project. Select the HKEY_LOCAL_MACHINE node and hierarchically add new keys to the node in the order HKEY_LOCAL_MACHINE, SOFTWARE, .NETFramework, AssemblyFolders, RandNumCorp, as shown in Figure 13.35.

8. Add a new string value to the newly added RandNumCorp key. Select the value and invoke the Properties window. Empty the Name property. When you do this, the (Default) name of the value is set (see Figure 13.35). Set the Value property to [CommonFilesFolder]RandNumCorp\. This is folder where the assembly file copy is stored.

9. Build the RandomNumberMergeModule project. Open Windows Explorer and navigate to the Release folder inside the project folder. Notice that the merge module RandomNumberMergeModule.msm has been created.

If you later want to distribute the RandomNumberGenerator component with a Windows application, you can just add the merge module created in Step by Step 13.16 to your application's setup project.

GUIDED PRACTICE EXERCISE 13.3

The goal of this exercise is to create a setup project that installs the Windows application RandomNumberApplication and includes the merge module RandomNumberMergeModule for installing the component RandomNumberGenerator.dll.

How would you create such an installer package?

In this exercise you practice creating installers for applications that have components that are packaged into merge modules. You should try working through this problem on your own first. If you get stuck, or if you'd like to see one possible solution, follow these steps:

1. In Solution Explorer, right-click Solution and select Add, New Project. Select Setup and Deployment projects from the Project Types tree and then select Setup Wizard from the list of templates on the right. Name the project `RandomNumberAppSetup`. Click OK. The Setup Wizard appears, and the first screen is the Welcome screen. Click Next.

2. The second screen of the wizard is the Choose a Project Type screen. Choose create a setup for Windows application in the first group of options.

3. The third screen of the wizard is the Choose Project Outputs to Include screen. Select Primary Output from RandomNumberApplication and select Merge Module from RandomNumberMergeModule, as shown in Figure 13.36. Click Next, click Next again, and then click Finish to create the project.

4. Notice that the `Application Folder` in the File System Editor has two files: `Primary Output from RandomNumberApplication (Active)` and `RandomNumberGenerator.dll`. The `RandomNumberGenerator.dll` file is included because by default the dependencies of the `RandomNumberApplication` project are included as well. Set the `Exclude` property of the `RandomNumberGenerator.dll` file to `true` because the `RandomNumberMergeModule` already places the assembly copy into the GAC.

5. Select the setup project `RandomNumberAppSetup` in Solution Explorer. Activate the Properties window. Set `Manufacturer` to `Random Number Corporation`, `ProductName` to `Random Number Application`, and `Title` to `Random Number Application`.

6. Build the `RandomNumberAppSetup` project. Open Windows Explorer and navigate to the `Release` folder inside the project folder. Run `setup.exe` and install the project.

7. Open Windows Explorer and navigate to the assembly cache folder (which is typically `C:\Winnt\assembly` or `C:\Windows\assembly`). Scroll down the assemblies and notice that the `RandomNumberGenerator` assembly is added to the GAC. Navigate to `C:\Program Files\Common Files\RandNumCorp` (`[CommonFilesFolder]RandNumCorp`). You should find a copy of the `RandomNumberGenerator.dll` file in this folder.

continues

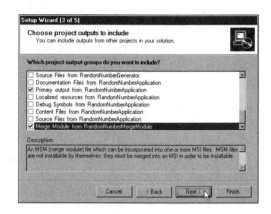

FIGURE 13.36
You can create a merge module project to package a reusable component.

continued

8. Open the Registry Editor by launching `regedit.exe` from the Run dialog box (which you access by selecting Start, Run). In the Registry Editor, browse to the key named `HKEY_LOCAL_MACHINE\SOFTWARE\Microsoft\.NETFramework\ AssemblyFolders`. Notice that a key with `RandNumCorp` is created, with its default value being `C:\Program Files\Common Files\RandNumCorp` (`[CommonFilesFolder]RandNumCorp\`). This happens because of the actions performed in Step by Step 13.16 by the merge module project.

9. Close all instances of Visual Studio .NET (if any are open). Restart Visual Studio .NET. Open the Add Reference dialog box by loading any Windows application. Select the .NET tab, and browse through to find the `RandomNumberGenerator` component. Notice that a reference to the `C:\Program Files\ Common Files\RandNumCorp\RandomNumberGenerator.dll` is added, as shown in Figure 13.37.

FIGURE 13.37

To show the references of a custom-created .NET component in the Add Reference dialog box, you need to make an entry in the Registry.

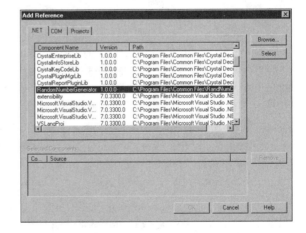

10. Navigate to the installation folder path. If you have not changed the default settings, the path is `C:\Program Files\ Random Number Corporation\Random Number Application`. Notice that only the `RandomNumberApplication.exe` file exists in the folder. Run the file from the folder. Notice that the Random Number application is launched. Click the button, and a random number is displayed in the label. The application loads the `RandomNumberGenerator` assembly from the GAC.

If you have difficulty following this exercise, review the sections "Creating a Setup Project" and "Creating a Merge Module Project," earlier in this chapter. After doing that review, try this exercise again.

▶ Shared assemblies are used by multiple applications on a machine. They are placed in the GAC and enjoy special priviliges such as file security (because they are placed in the System folder), shared location, and side-by-side versioning.

▶ You generate public/private key pairs by using the Strong Name tool (sn.exe). These pairs can be used to digitally sign assemblies.

▶ You can add a shared assembly to the GAC by using Windows Explorer, the .NET Framework Configuration tool, the Global Assembly Cache tool, and the Windows Installer.

▶ The best way to add an assembly in the GAC during deployment is to use Microsoft Windows Installer. The Windows Installer provides assembly reference-counting features and manages removal of assemblies at the time of uninstallation.

▶ When viewed in Windows Explorer, the assembly cache folder in the System folder displays assemblies from the GAC and native image cache.

▶ The CLR first searches the GAC to locate assemblies, and then it looks into the files and folders where the assembly is installed. Thus, loading shared assemblies from the GAC is efficient because the CLR does not engage itself in looking into the <codebase> and <probing> elements of the applicable configuration files.

▶ Delay signing allows you to place a shared assembly in the GAC by signing the assembly with just the public key. This allows the assembly to be signed with the private key at a later stage, when the development process is complete and the component or assembly is ready to be deployed.

continues

continued

This process allows developers to work with shared assemblies as if they were strongly named, and it also secures the private key of the signature from being accessed at different stages of development.

▶ Merge module project allows you to create reusable setup components that help in deploying shared assemblies. Merge modules cannot be directly installed. They need to be merged with the installation program of an application that uses the shared component, packaged into a merge module.

CREATING INSTALLATION COMPONENTS

Create a setup program that installs an application and allows for the application to be uninstalled.

- **Perform an install-time compilation of a Windows-based application.**

When you develop an application by using Visual Studio .NET, you use several resources, such as databases, event logs, performance counters, and message queues. However, when you install a program on a user's machine, these resource might not be present on the target machine. A good installation program ensures that all necessary resources that are required by an application exist on the target machine.

The .NET Framework provides you with the Installer class, which is defined in the System.Configuration.Install namespace. This class is specifically designed to help you perform customized installation actions such as those just mentioned. This section explores various ways in which you can use the Installer class to create powerful installation programs.

It shows you how to use the predefined installation classes that are available with several components of Visual Studio .NET. It also shows you how to create your own classes that extend the Installer class, to perform specialized tasks at the time of installation.

Understanding the `Installer` Class

The `System.Configuration.Install.Installer` class works as a base class for all the custom installers in the .NET Framework. Some of the important members of the `Installer` class are listed in Table 13.2.

TABLE 13.2

SOME IMPORTANT MEMBERS OF THE `Installer` CLASS

Member Name	Type	Description
`Commit()`	Method	Executes if the `Install()` method executes successfully.
`Install()`	Method	Performs the specified actions during an application's installation.
`Installers`	Property	Specifies a collection of `Installer` objects that are needed in order for this `Installer` instance to successfully install a component.
`Rollback()`	Method	Is called if the `Install()` method fails for some reason, to undo any custom actions performed during the `Install()` method.
`Uninstall()`	Method	Performs the specified actions when a previously installed application is uninstalled.

You can derive a class from the `Installer` class and override the methods listed in Table 13.2 to perform any custom actions.

If you want the derived `Installer` class to execute when an assembly is installed by using a setup project or by using the Installer tool (`installutil.exe`), you need to apply the `RunInstaller` attribute on the class and set its value to `true`:

```
[RunInstaller(true)]
```

The `Installer` classes facilitate the infrastructure for making installation a transactional process. If an error is encountered during the `Install()` method, The `Rollback()` method tracks back all the changes and undoes them, to leave the machine in the clean state it was in before the installation process started. The `Rollback()` method must know the order in which the installation steps were performed and exactly what changes were made so that it can undo those changes in the right order.

Similarly, when an application is uninstalled, the Uninstall() method of the Installer class is called. The responsibility of the Uninstall() method is to revert the changes done by the installation process so that the machine is left as clean as if the program had never been installed on it.

How does the Install() method communicate its installation information with the Rollback() and Uninstall() methods? This question is especially interesting when you see that the Install() and Uninstall() methods are not called in the same process. Install() is called when the application is installed, and Uninstall() is called when the application is uninstalled. These two events might be separated by several days and numerous computer restarts.

The Install() method communicates the installation state by persisting it in a file that has the extension .InstallState, called an *InstallState* file. This file is placed in the installation directory of the application. The Installer class makes this file available to each of the Install(), Commit(), Rollback(), and Uninstall() methods by passing an IDictionary object with the contents of this file. The Rollback() and Uninstall() methods use the contents of the InstallState file to perform the required cleanup operation.

Working with Predefined Installation Components

Most of the components that are available through Server Explorer have predefined installation components associated with them. For example, when you create an instance of the EventLog component in a project, it allows you to add to your project an installer that corresponds to it. When you set the properties of an EventLog object in the program, the Installer component remembers those properties and reproduces them on the target machine when the application is deployed.

Step by Step 13.17 shows how to create the required event log resources on a target machine at the time of installation, with the help of predefined installation components.

STEP BY STEP

13.17 Using a Predefined Component to Install an Event Source on a Target Computer

1. Add a new Visual C# Windows application project to the solution 316C13. Name the project `EventLogApplication`.

2. Rename the `Form1.cs` file `EventLogApplication.cs` in the project. Switch to the code view of the form and modify all references to `Form1` so that they refer to `EventLogApplication` instead.

3. Open Server Explorer. Expand the tree under Event Logs. Drag and drop the Application event log to the form. This creates an `eventLog1` object that you can see in the component tray.

4. Access the properties of the `eventLog1` object and change its `Source` property to `EventLogApplication`. Click the Add Installer link just above the description area in the Properties window, as shown in Figure 13.38. A new class named `ProjectInstaller.cs` is added to the project. In design mode you can see that `ProjectInstaller.cs` contains an object named `eventLogInstaller1`. This is an installation component for the `EventLog` object that is created in the `EventLogApplication.cs` form.

5. Switch to the code view of `ProjectInstaller.cs`. Note the use of the following attribute with the `ProjectInstaller` class:

```
[RunInstaller(true)]
```

This attribute specifies whether the `ProjectInstaller` class should be invoked during the execution of an assembly. View the Component Designer generated code section for this class, and you should see all the necessary coding for installing an event log or event source on the target machine.

FIGURE 13.38
You can add an `Installer` class for the `EventLog` component through the Add Installer hyperlink in the Properties window.

continues

continued

6. Switch to the design view of `EventLogApplication` and add a `TextBox` control (`txtMessage`) and a `Button` control (`btnWrite`) to the form. Double-click the `Button` control to attach an event handler to its `Click` event. Add the following code to the event handler:

```
private void btnWrite_Click(object sender,
    System.EventArgs e)
{
    eventLog1.WriteEntry(txtMessage.Text);
}
```

7. Build the project by using the `Release` mode. Run the project. Enter a value in the text box and click the button. Open Server Explorer. Drill down to the Event Logs node and select the Application node under it. You should see a new source added to the Application event log, with a message that appears in the text box when you click the button. The project is now ready for deployment.

As shown in Step by Step 13.17, when you click the Add Installer link for an `EventLog` component, a `ProjectInstaller` class is created in the project, and the installation component for the `EventLog` component is added to that class. If you add to this project additional installation components (for example, a `PerformanceCounter` installation component), they are all added to this `ProjectInstaller` class. They are actually added to the `Installers` collection of this class. After you compile the project to build an `.exe` or a `.dll` file, the `ProjectInstaller` class is part of the output assembly.

Deploying an Assembly That Contains the Installation Components

There are two ways you can deploy an assembly that contains installation components:

◆ By using the setup and deployment projects

◆ By using the Installer tool (`installutil.exe`)

The following sections show you how to deploy an application that contains installation components by using both of these techniques.

Deploying an Installation Component by Using the Setup Project

To deploy an application that consists of installation components, you need to create a setup project as you would do normally. But in this case, you use the Custom Actions Editor to deploy the additional resources needed for the application. At the time of deployment, the deployment project will execute the `ProjectInstaller` class as a part of its custom installation action to create component resources. Step by Step 13.18 shows you how.

STEP BY STEP

13.18 Using a Setup Project to Install Component Resources

1. Add a new setup project to the solution. Name the project `EventLogApplicationSetup`.

2. Right-click the `EventLogApplicationSetup` project in Solution Explorer, and select Add, Project Output from the shortcut menu. In the Add Project Output Group dialog box, select Primary Output of EventLogApplication Project.

3. Open the Custom Actions Editor for the `EventLogApplicationSetup` project. Right-click the Custom Actions node and then select Add Custom Action from the shortcut menu. The Select Item in Project dialog box appears. Look in the `Application` folder and select Primary Output from `EventLogApplication(Active)`. Click OK. The primary output is added to these four nodes under Custom Actions: Install, Commit, Rollback, and Uninstall.

4. Select the new project in Solution Explorer. Activate the Properties window. Set the `Manufacturer` to `EventLog Application` and set `ProductName` to `EventLogApplication`.

continues

continued

5. Build the `EventLogApplicationSetup` project. Take the project's output to a computer that does not already have an event source for the `EventLogApplication`. Run the installation. You will note that the setup program will install the `EventLogApplication` along with the required event source.

6. Run the application's executable file from the installation folder. Enter some text and click the button. Launch the Event Viewer from the Administrative Tools section of Windows Control Panel. Select the Application log under the Event Viewer node. Notice your event log entries in the right pane of the Event Viewer.

Deploying an Installation Component by Using the Installer Tool (`installutil.exe`)

You can use the command-line Installer tool (`installutil.exe`) to install assemblies that contain additional component resources.

To install the resources contained in an assembly named `Assembly1.dll`, you use the following form of the `installutil.exe` command:

```
installutil.exe Assembly1.dll
```

You can also install resources that are contained in multiple assemblies together, like this:

```
installutil.exe Assembly1.dll Assembly2.dll
➥Assembly3.dll
```

If you want to launch the uninstaller for installation classes stored in an assembly, you will use the `/u` or `/uninstall` option with the command, as follows:

```
installutil.exe /u Assembly1.dll
```

EXAM TIP

`installutil.exe` **Performs Installations in a Transactional Manner** If you are installing components from multiple assemblies by using the `installutil.exe` command, if any assembly fails to install, `installutil.exe` rolls back the installations of all other assemblies. However, the process of uninstallation is not transactional.

Working with Installer Classes

You can add your own `Installer` classes to a project to perform custom actions during installation, such as compiling the code to native image format or creating a database on a target computer.

These compiled `Installer` classes from the project are then added to the deployment project as custom actions that are run at the end of the installation. The following are typical actions that you would perform while creating a Custom Installer class:

1. Inherit a class from the `Installer` class.

2. Make sure that the `RunInstaller` attribute is set to `true` in the derived class.

3. Override the `Install()`, `Commit()`, `Rollback()`, and `Uninstall()` methods to perform any custom actions.

4. In a setup project, use the Custom Actions Editor to invoke this derived class to do the required processing.

5. If needed, pass arguments from the Custom Actions Editor to the custom `Installer` class by using the `CustomActionData` property.

In the following section, I'll show you how to use these steps to create a custom installation program that translates the MSIL assemblies to native images by using the Native Code Generation tool (`ngen.exe`) tool.

Performing Install-Time Compilation

Create a setup program that installs an application and allows for the application to be uninstalled.

- **Perform an install-time compilation of a Windows-based application.**

When assemblies are loaded at runtime, the CLR compiles the requested MSIL code into native code by using a technique known as just-in-time (JIT) compilation. The advantage of JIT compilation is that the next time a piece of code is called, it need not be converted again to the native code, and it therefore executes faster.

Because of JIT compilation, an application that executes a lot of startup code is rather slow when it starts. You can solve this problem by precompiling the MSIL code to native code. The best time to do this conversion is at installation time because at that time the compilation can be done according to the exact architecture of the machine that will execute the code.

You can compile from MSIL to native code by using the Native Code Generation tool (ngen.exe) on the target machine. If you are using this tool at the install time, you typically have to take the following steps:

◆ Find the location where the .NET Framework CLR is installed on the target computer. This is the path where ngen.exe is located.

◆ Execute ngen.exe for each assembly that you want to compile into native code. Assemblies may be present either in a common location such as the Common Files Folder or a location specified by the user at the time of compilation. You need to determine this path so that you can create the correct command line for calling ngen.exe.

Step by Step 13.19 shows how to create a custom Installer class that runs ngen.exe and how to call the class from a setup project.

STEP BY STEP

13.19 Adding a Custom Action to Perform Install-Time Compilation

1. In Solution Explorer, add a Visual C# Class Library project to the solution. Name the project GenerateNativeImage.

2. Right-click the project GenerateNativeImage and choose Add, Add New Item from the context menu. The Add New Item dialog box appears. Select Installer Class from the right pane, as shown in Figure 13.39. Name the new class GenerateNativeImage.cs.

FIGURE 13.39
You can add an Installer class via the Add New Item dialog box.

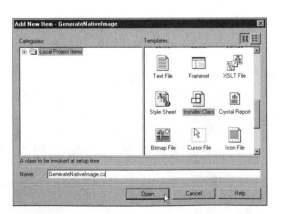

3. Open the `GenerateNativeImage.cs` file in the code view. Add the following using directives:

```
using System.Diagnostics;
using System.Runtime.InteropServices;
using System.Text;
```

4. Add the following code after the Component Designer generated code section in the class definition:

```
// Gets the install directory for the version of the
// runtime that is loaded in the current process
[DllImport("mscoree.dll")]
private static extern int GetCORSystemDirectory(
    [MarshalAs(UnmanagedType.LPWStr)]
    StringBuilder buffer, int bufferLength,
    out int length);


public override void Install(
    System.Collections.IDictionary savedState)
{
    // Call the Install() method of the base class
    base.Install(savedState);
    // Get the arguments pass to the class
    string strArgs = this.Context.Parameters["Args"];
    if (strArgs == "")
        throw new InstallException(
            "No arguments specified");

    // Declare a StringBuilder to hold the path of
    // the ngen.exe on the target machine
    StringBuilder strPath = new StringBuilder(1024);
    // holds the size of the returned string
    int intSize;

    // Call the mscoree.dll's
    // GetCORSystemDirectory method
    GetCORSystemDirectory(strPath,
        strPath.Capacity, out intSize);

    // Run the ngen process with the
    // arguments passed to the class
    ProcessStartInfo si = new ProcessStartInfo(
        strPath.ToString() +
        "ngen.exe ", "\"" + strArgs + "\"");
    si.WindowStyle = ProcessWindowStyle.Hidden;
    try
    {
        Process p = Process.Start(si);
        p.WaitForExit();
    }
```

continues

continued

```
        catch(Exception e)
        {
            throw new InstallException(e.Message);
        }
    }

    public override void Commit(
        System.Collections.IDictionary savedState)
    {
        // Call the Commit() method of the base class
        base.Commit(savedState);
    }
    public override void Rollback(
        System.Collections.IDictionary savedState)
    {
        // Call the Rollback() method of the base class
        base.Rollback(savedState);
    }

    public override void Uninstall(
        System.Collections.IDictionary savedState)
    {
        // Call the Uninstall() method of the base class
        base.Uninstall(savedState);
    }
```

5. Build the `GenerateNativeImage` project.

6. Select the `RandomNumberMergeModule` project in Solution Explorer. Open the File System Editor for this project. Move to the `RandNumCorp` folder in the Common Files Folder node. Add the Primary Output from GenerateNativeImage (Active) file to the folder by selecting Action, Add, Project Output.

7. Open the Custom Actions Editor for the merge module project. Select the Custom Actions node and select Add Custom Action from the context menu. The Select Item in Project dialog box appears. Select Primary Output from GenerateNativeImage (Active) by navigating to Common Files Folder, RandNumCorp. Click OK. The `Primary Output from GenerateNativeImage (Active)` file is added to all four nodes under Custom Actions.

8. Select the newly added custom action under the Install node. Open the Properties window and set the `CustomActionData` property to `/Args="[CommonFilesFolder]RandNumCorp\ RandomNumberGenerator.dll"`.

9. Build the `RandomNumberAppSetup` project. Install the project.

10. A precompiled native image of the `RandomNumberGenerator` assembly is added to the native image cache, as shown in Figure 13.40.

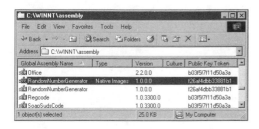

FIGURE 13.40
You can use Windows Explorer to view the contents of the native image cache.

In Step by Step 13.19, note the usage of the `CustomActionData` property in the Custom Actions Editor. This property is used to pass installation data from a setup program to the custom `Installer` class.

Another important thing to note from Step by Step 13.19 is the use of the term *native image cache*. The CLR stores all natively compiled assemblies in a central area called the native image cache, which is stored in a separate folder inside the assembly cache folder (usually `c:\WINNT\assembly` or `c:\Windows\assembly`), along with the GAC, as shown in Figure 13.40. You can identify whether an assembly is from the GAC or from the native image cache by looking at the Type field in the list. You can also list the contents of the native image cache by using the `/show` option with `ngen.exe`, as shown in Figure 13.41.

FIGURE 13.41
You can use `ngen.exe` to view the contents of the native image cache.

REVIEW BREAK

▶ The `System.Configuration.Install.Installer` class works as a base class for all the custom installers in the .NET Framework.

continues

continued

▶ The `Installer` class method `Install()` is called when an application is installed, and `Uninstall()` is called when an application is uninstalled. The `Commit()` method is executed if the `Install()` method executes successfully, and the `Rollback()` method is executed if the `Install()` method is not executed successfully.

▶ If you add predefined installation components (for example, a `PerformanceCounter` installation component) to the setup project, they are all added to the `ProjectInstaller` class. These are actually added to the `Installers` collection of the `ProjectInstaller` class.

▶ You can add your own custom `Installer` classes to a project to perform custom actions during installation—such as compiling code to native image format or creating a database on a target computer—through the Custom Actions Editor.

▶ You can compile MSIL code to native code by using the Native Image Generation tool (`ngen.exe`). The assemblies that are compiled into machine-specific native code are placed in the native image cache.

URL Remoting

Verify security policies for a deployed application.

• **Launch a remote application (URL remoting).**

The .NET Framework provides a *zero deployment* (or no-touch deployment) model for deploying Windows applications. The reason behind the name zero deployment is that users are not required to deploy the application before executing it. Users can instead just run the application, and the application installs itself. In this deployment model, you keep all the necessary code and configuration files on a Web server and the users execute the application by just pointing to the URL of the .exe file from Internet Explorer. Launching a remote application with a URL is known as *URL remoting*.

The Web-based deployment model does not require the .NET Framework to be installed on the server machine. (The server is not even required to be running Windows. You can even use a Solaris Web server!) All code and required configuration files are automatically downloaded from the Web server and are executed on the local machine. Of course, the local machine must have the .NET Framework installed on it.

This deployment model is very exciting because it gives you the ease of maintenance that is available from a Web application in addition to the rich user interface of Windows forms. This is certainly a big shift from how Windows applications have traditionally been deployed.

Launching a Remote Application

Step by Step 13.20 shows you how to deploy a simple Windows forms application on a Web server and launch it by referring to its URL (that is, by using URL remoting).

STEP BY STEP

13.20 Launching a Remote Application

1. In Solution Explorer, add a Visual C# Class Library project to the solution. Name the project SimpleUI.

2. Rename the Form1.cs file SimpleUI.cs in the project. Switch to the code view of the form and modify all references to Form1 so that they refer to SimpleUI instead.

3. Place a TextBox control (txtMessage), a Button control (btnDisplay), and a Label control (lblMessage) on the form. Set the TextAlign property of the Label control to MiddleCenter and set the font to a larger size.

4. Add the following code to the Click event handler of the Button control:

```
private void btnDisplay_Click(object sender,
    System.EventArgs e)
{
    lblMessage.Text = txtMessage.Text;
}
```

continues

continued

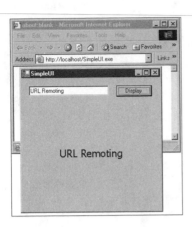

FIGURE 13.42
You can launch a remote Windows application from Internet Explorer via URL remoting.

> **NOTE**
>
> **ieexec.exe** When you launch a remote application by using a URL, no process is started by the name of the application. This is because a process with the name `ieexec.exe` launches the application. If you look at the current processes through Windows Task Manager, you should find one copy of `ieexec.exe` running for each application that has been launched through a URL.

5. Set the `SimpleUI` project as the startup project. Run the project. Enter some text in the text box and click the button. The text is displayed in the `Label` control.

6. Copy the `SimpleUI.exe` file to a Web server directory (such as `c:\inetpub\wwwroot`).

7. Launch Internet Explorer. Navigate to `http://localhost/SimpleUI.exe`. (This path may be different if you have a different server or path.)

8. If your Web server is local or within an intranet zone, the `SimpleUI` application is launched as shown in Figure 13.42. If instead you browse to a Web server over the Internet (by using an address such as `http://myserver.com/SimpleUI.exe`), you get a security exception. (I discuss how to deal with this security exception shortly.)

The Download Cache

The code downloaded from a URL is cached in a central location called the *download cache*. Unlike the GAC, the download cache always remember the original location from which its contents were downloaded. Therefore, the next time a request is made for the remote content, the download cache checks the timestamp of the requested assemblies on the server. If it finds requested assemblies with newer dates, it downloads them; otherwise, assemblies that have already been downloaded in the download cache are used.

This behavior makes the download cache useful for files that come from the Internet, where speed may be slow and caching of files may eliminate the additional time required to download an already downloaded file. The download cache also isolates the assemblies from other assemblies that are downloaded by other users or applications. The download cache is physically stored in a directory that is private to a user. For example, on my computer, the download cache is physically stored in the `C:\Documents and Settings\Administrator\Local Settings\Application Data\assembly\dl` folder.

The folder and subfolders in the download cache have cryptic names that do not easily convey information about the cache contents. To easily read the contents of the download cache, you can open Windows Explorer and navigate to the assembly cache folder (such as c:\winnt\assembly or c:\windows\assembly). The download cache is a subfolder attached to the assembly cache folder (see Figure 13.43). Although the download cache is not physically present in that location, shfusion.dll shows it there for easy access. If you want to see the contents of the download cache by using the command line, you can use gacutil.exe with the /ldl switch (see Figure 13.44).

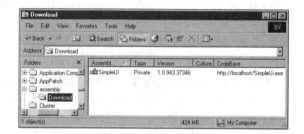

FIGURE 13.43
You can use Windows Explorer to view the contents of the download cache.

FIGURE 13.44
You can use the gacutil.exe with the /ldl switch to view the contents of the download cache.

Code Access Security Policy

Downloading code from remote sources may be a security risk. To help protect computers from malicious mobile code, the .NET Framework provides a security mechanism called code access security, which allows code to be trusted to varying degrees, depending on where the code originates, the publisher, the strong name, and the security zone.

To view the current code access security policy on your machine, follow the steps in Step by Step 13.21.

> **NOTE**
> **More on Code Access Security** You will learn more about Code Access Security in Chapter 15, "Configuring a Windows Application."

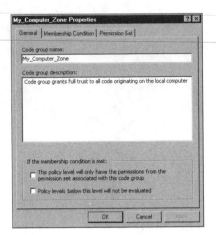

FIGURE 13.45
The My_Computer_Zone code group grants full trust to code originating from the local computer.

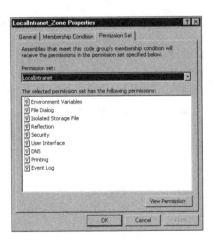

FIGURE 13.46
Code in the LocalIntranet_Zone group is partially trusted and is granted only selected permissions.

STEP BY STEP

13.21 Exploring the Code Access Security Policy for a Computer

1. Open the Administrative Tools section of Windows Control Panel. Open the tool named Microsoft .NET Framework Configuration.

2. Expand the Runtime Security Policy node, the Machine node, the Code Groups node, and the All_Code node. Select the My_Computer_Zone node. In the right pane, click the hyperlink Edit Code Group Properties. You should see the Properties window (see Figure 13.45). Select the Permission Set tab. Note that the default permission set for this code group is FullTrust.

3. In the left pane of the .NET Framework Configuration tool select LocalIntranet_Zone and in the right pane click the hyperlink Edit Code Group Properties. Select the Permission Set tab in the Properties window. Note that this code group is not fully trusted. It has only a partial set of permissions, as defined by the LocalIntranet permission set (see Figure 13.46).

4. Access the properties for Internet_Zone group. Note that the group's permission is set to Nothing.

When the CLR executes code, it can determine it's the code's origin by looking at the URL or path used to invoke it. This information is used to classify the code into one of the predefined zones listed in Table 13.3.

TABLE 13.3

CODE ACCESS SECURITY ZONES

Code Origin	Code Group
From a file path on a local computer, such as c:\inetpub\wwwroot\simpleUI.exe or c:\MyDir\SimpleUI.exe	My_Computer_Zone

Code Origin	*Code Group*
From a network share, such as \\server1\share1\ SimpleUI.exe, or from a Web server that is local within the network, such as http://server1/ SimpleUI.exe or http://192.168.1.1/ SimpleUI.exe	LocalIntranet_Zone
From an Internet address, such as www.myserver.com/ SimpleUI.exe or http://207.46.197.100/ SimpleUI.exe	Internet_Zone

As shown in Step By Step 13.21, the My_Computer_Zone code group has the FullTrust permission set associated with it. LocalIntranet_Zone is only partially trusted, as defined by the LocalIntranet permission set, whereas Internet_Zone has a permission set of Nothing. In Step by Step 13.20, when you use the URL http://localhost/SimpleUI.exe, the CLR determines from the URL that the code is coming from LocalIntranet_Zone. The assembly SimpleUI.exe is therefore only partially trusted. Still, SimpleUI.exe executes successfully because all its code is within the boundary of the permission set assigned to it. But if you upload SimpleUI.exe to a Web server that is addressable from the Internet and access the program by using a URL such as www.myserver.com/SimpleUI.exe, the runtime determines from the address that the code is downloaded from the Internet, and it applies the permission set for Internet_Zone to it, which is Nothing. As you can guess, the program execution fails and throws a security exception.

This behavior may look different from the behavior described in the product documentation installed with the final release of the .NET Framework SDK or Visual Studio .NET. Actually, following the Bill Gates initiative for Trustworthy Computing, the .NET Framework team decided to tighten the default security policy in the .NET Framework. Some of those changes were reflected in Version 1 of the .NET Framework, and others were made part of service packs of the Microsoft .NET Framework. At the time of this writing, the latest service pack available is Service Pack 2 (SP2), which includes updates from the previously released service packs. If you have not yet installed SP2 or later, I recommend you do it before proceeding with the rest of the chapter.

NOTE

Trustworthy Computing You can read about the Microsoft's initiative for trustworthy computing on the Wired Web site, at www.wired.com/ news/business/0,1367,49826, 00.html and on the Microsoft Web site, at www.microsoft.com/ PressPass/exec/craig/ 05-01trustworthywp.asp.

NOTE

The .NET Framework Service Packs The .NET Framework service packs are widely distributed as part of the Microsoft Windows Update service. Alternatively, you can download the service packs from the .NET Framework Web site, at msdn.microsoft.com/netframework/ downloads/updates/sp.

One of the significant changes in SP1 is the change of permission set for `Internet_Zone` from the `Internet` permission set to `Nothing`, thereby totally disabling the execution of mobile code originating from the Internet. This means that the mobile code unintentionally does not execute. If you are sure that an assembly coming from the Internet is safe, you can increase the level of trust and permissions associated with it by using the .NET Framework Configuration tool. (I cover how to do that a little later in this chapter.) If you do so, you can execute code coming from the Internet, too.

Calling Assemblies from the Partially Trusted Code (`AllowPartially TrustedCallersAttribute` Class)

Another important last-minute change to the Version 1 release of the .NET Framework that resulted from the Trustworthy Computing initiative was to ensure that by default, any strong named assembly can be called only from an assembly that is granted full trust by the security policy. This change protects strong-named assemblies from any possible misuse by partially trusted code.

The program `SimpleUI.exe` uses several assemblies from the .NET Framework: `System.dll`, `System.Data.dll`, `System.Drawing.dll`, `System.Windows.Forms`, and `System.Xml.dll`. All these assemblies are strongly named assemblies. When you execute `SimpleUI.exe` from a local Web server in Step By Step 13.20, it is partially trusted because the code originates from `LocalIntranet_Zone`. In Step by Step 13.20, `SimpleUI.exe` executes successfully. This means that a partially trusted assembly (such as `SimpleUI.exe`) is able to call strongly named assemblies (such as `System.Windows.Forms`). Doesn't this violate the statement "any strong named assembly can be called only from an assembly that is granted full trust by the security policy"?

The answer to this question can be explained with the help of the newly introduced `AllowPartiallyTrustedCallers` attribute, with which the .NET Framework has marked the following assemblies:

- ◆ `Accessibility.dll`

- ◆ `IEExecRemote.dll`

N O T E **Version 1 Security Changes** The .NET Framework team made some security-related changes just before shipping Version 1 of the .NET Framework. Some of these changes did not make it into the product document that is installed with the .NET Framework SDK. To get an overview of these changes, you can refer to the Version 1 Security Changes whitepaper, located at `http:// msdn.microsoft.com/library/ en-us/dnnetsec/html/ v1securitychanges.asp`.

- ◆ `mscorlib.dll`

- ◆ `Microsoft.VisualBasic.dll`

- ◆ `System.dll`

- ◆ `System.Data.dll`

- ◆ `System.Drawing.dll`

- ◆ `System.Web.Services.dll`

- ◆ `System.Windows.Forms.dll`

- ◆ `System.Xml.dll`

When a programmer applies the `AllowPartiallyTrustedCallers` attribute to a strong named assembly, the CLR allows a partially trusted assembly to call the given strong named assembly.

The advantage of this attribute is that the partially trusted assemblies can provide more functionality without making the user explicitly increase the trust level associated with the assemblies. But this has security considerations, too. As a programmer, before you mark an assembly with the `AllowPartiallyTrustedCallers` attribute, you must thoroughly test the assembly to make sure that it cannot potentially be misused by malicious callers to cause harm to users' computers. You can mark an assembly with the `AllowPartiallyTrustedCallers` attribute by using Visual Studio .NET by writing the following line of code in the `AssemblyInfo.cs` file of a project:

```
[assembly: AllowPartiallyTrustedCallers]
```

The `AllowPartiallyTrustedCallersAttribute` class belongs to the `System.Security` namespace. You also have to include the following using statement at the top of `AssemblyInfo.cs`:

```
using System.Security;
```

Now let's take a look at another assembly that is used earlier in this chapter, `NetSql.exe`. This assembly makes calls only to those assemblies from the .NET Framework that are marked with the `AllowPartiallyTrustedCallers` attribute. You can copy `Netsql.exe` to a local Web server on your network and execute it from Internet Explorer by using a URL similar to `http://localhost/NetSql.exe`.

FIGURE 13.47
Execution of the partially trusted assembly
`NetSql.exe` fails, with a security exception.

You should find that the execution fails with a security exception, as shown in Figure 13.47. What's the reason? What is `NetSql.exe` doing differently from `SimpleUI.exe`?

The answer is that some of the types in assemblies marked with the `AllowPartiallyTrustedCallers` attribute may require stronger permissions. One such type being used by the `NetSql.exe` assembly is `System.Data.SqlClient.SqlConnection`, and this is the reason `NetSql.exe`, which is a partially trusted assembly (as it is loaded from `LocalIntranet_Zone`), is not granted permission to execute. To get a complete list of types in assemblies marked with the `AllowPartiallyTrustedCallers` attribute that require stronger permissions to execute, see `http://msdn.microsoft.com/library/en-us/dnnetsec/html/Aptcatypes.asp`.

Setting the Runtime Security Policy for an Assembly

If you want to execute `NetSql.exe`, you have to configure the runtime security policy to increase the trust associated with `NetSql.exe`. Step by Step 13.22 shows you the process.

STEP BY STEP

13.22 Setting the Runtime Security Policy for an Assembly

1. Open the Administrative Tools section of Windows Control Panel. Open the tool named .NET Framework Configuration. Select the `Runtime Security Policy` folder in the left pane under the My Computer node, as shown in Figure 13.48.

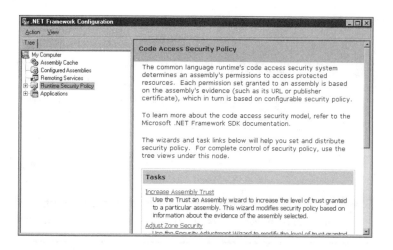

FIGURE 13.48◄

You can use the .NET Framework Configuration tool to configure the runtime security policy for an assembly.

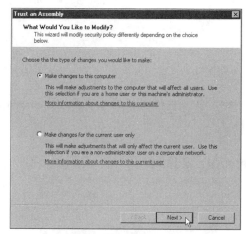

FIGURE 13.49▲

The Trust an Assembly Wizard allows you to trust an assembly for the logged-on user or for all users.

2. From the list of tasks in the right pane, click the hyperlink Increase Assembly Trust. The Trust an Assembly wizard appears, as shown in Figure 13.49. Choose the option Make Changes to This Computer and click the Next button.

3. In the next screen, type the URL for the NetSql.exe assembly, as shown in Figure 13.50. Click the Next button.

FIGURE 13.50◄

You can specify the path or URL of the assembly to be trusted.

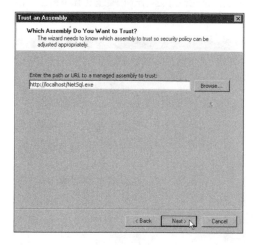

continues

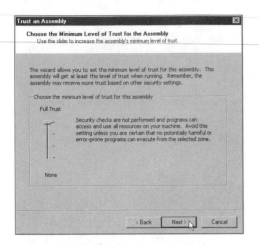

FIGURE 13.51
You can select one of four values to set the minimum level of trust for an assembly.

FIGURE 13.52
You can use Microsoft .NET Framework wizards to trust an assembly.

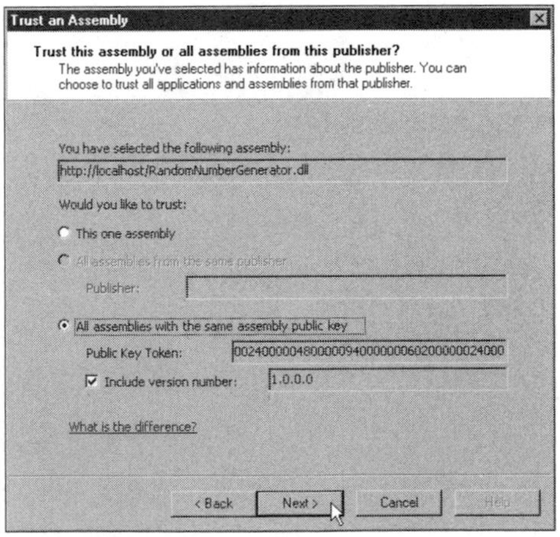

FIGURE 13.53
You can use the Trust an Assembly Wizard to trust all assemblies from the same publisher or all assemblies that have the same public key.

continued

4. The next screen asks you to select the minimum level of trust you want to associate with this assembly. A slider on the screen can take four positions: None, Internet, Local Intranet, and Full Trust. Change the default None level to Full Trust, as shown in Figure 13.51.

5. Click the Next button. The final screen of the wizard shows a summary of the operation. Click the Finish button to close the wizard.

6. Open Internet Explorer and navigate to the URL of `NetSql.exe`. `NetSql.exe` is invoked from the Web server.

In addition to using the method described in Step by Step 13.22, you can set the trust for an assembly by using a Microsoft .NET Framework Wizards shortcut, which you access from the Administrative Tools section of the Windows Control Panel (see Figure 13.52).

If you have a strong-named assembly, users see an additional screen in the Trust an Assembly Wizard, as shown in Figure 13.53. In this screen, you can choose to set a level of trust for all assemblies from the same publisher or for all assemblies that have the same public key.

Setting Runtime Security Policy for a Zone

In addition to the methods described in the preceding sections, there is another way to adjust security for code that is executing in the .NET Framework: You can use the Security Adjustment Wizard to modify the level of trust granted to all assemblies that come from a particular zone, such as Internet, Local Intranet, or My Computer. Step by Step 13.23 shows how to use this wizard to grant full trust to all assemblies coming from the Local Intranet zone.

STEP BY STEP

13.23 Setting the Runtime Security Policy for a Zone

1. Open the Microsoft .NET Configuration Wizards dialog box from the Administrative Tools section of the Windows Control Panel. Click the Adjust .NET Security icon. The Security Adjustment Wizard appears, as shown in Figure 13.54. (You can also invoke this wizard from the .NET Framework Configuration tool.) Choose Make Changes to This Computer and click the Next button.

2. In the next screen, select the Local Intranet zone and increase its level of trust to Full Trust, as shown in Figure 13.55. Click Next to continue.

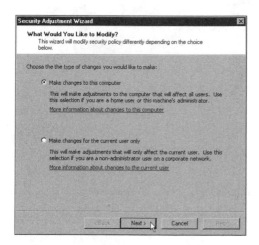

FIGURE 13.54
You can use the Security Adjustment Wizard to modify the level of trust granted to all assemblies coming from a particular zone, such as Internet, Local Intranet, or My Computer.

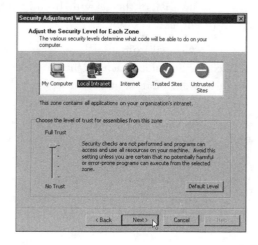

FIGURE 13.55
You can increase the level of trust for the Local Intranet zone.

continues

continued

3. The next screen of the wizard summarizes the changes made to the security policy for various zones. Click Finish to close the Wizard.

4. To confirm your changes, copy `RandomNumberGenerator.dll` and `RandomNumberApplication.exe` to the local Web server. Invoke them from a Web browser by using a URL such as `http://localhost/RandomNumberApplication.exe`. The application successfully executes.

WARNING

Increasing Trust for the `Internet` Zone Be aware that increasing the trust level for the Internet zone may increase the power of mobile code to do all kinds of operations on your machine. Normally increasing the trust level for the `Internet` is not recommended. If you want to trust code from selected Internet sites, a better option is to add those sites to the Trusted Sites zone (by selecting Tools, Internet Options, Security in Internet Explorer) and then set the trust level for the Trusted Sites zone.

When you set the runtime security policy for a zone, it has much wider implications than setting the runtime security policy for an assembly. Changes in the runtime security policy for a zone affect all the assemblies in that zone. Therefore, you need to be careful when you use this option.

Code access security and application configuration are discussed further in Chapter 15.

REVIEW BREAK

▶ URL remoting provides a zero deployment model for deploying a Windows application. The code and configuration files reside on a Web server, and you can execute the application by just pointing to the URL of the `.exe` file from Internet Explorer on the end user's computer.

▶ Code that is downloaded from a URL is cached in a central location called the download cache. When a subsequent request to the same content is made, the download cache checks the timestamp of the requested assemblies on the server and downloads the file from the server only if its timestamp has changed. Otherwise, it displays the cached copy to the user.

▶ Code Access Security allows code to be trusted to varying degrees, depending on where the code originates, the publisher, the strong name, and the security zone.

▶ If the `AllowPartiallyTrustedCallers` attribute is applied to a strong name assembly, it allows even partially trusted code to call this assembly.

▶ The .NET Framework Configuration tool can be used to configure the runtime security policy for an assembly or a zone.

METHODS OF DEPLOYMENT

Plan the deployment of a Windows-based application.

• **Plan a deployment that uses removable media.**

• **Plan a Web-based deployment.**

• **Plan a network-based deployment.**

After you have created a setup package, you can deploy your application from any location that's accessible to all of its potential users. You can use one of several deployment methods:

◆ Deployment via removable media

◆ Network-based deployment

◆ Web-based deployment

The following sections discuss each of these deployment options.

Deployment via Removable Media

Plan the deployment of a Windows-based application.

• **Plan a deployment that uses removable media.**

The most common examples of removable media are floppy disks, CD-ROMs, and DVDs. Deployment via removable media is suitable in three situations:

◆ When users are in many locations, without any common central connection.

◆ When not all users have access to the Internet.

◆ When application size is huge and not all users have access to high-speed Internet connections.

Deployment via removable media is becoming outdated with every new day. It involves costs for media, replication, and distribution that can easily be eliminated by using other deployment options. Still, deployment via removable media is the "lowest common denominator" solution and covers the maximum number of users.

Deployment projects in Visual Studio .NET can be used to create packages divided across multiple files, each with small size, as specified by the developer. These small-sized files can then be copied to floppy disks or CD-ROMs and distributed to users.

To create a setup project for removable media, you create a setup project as you would normally do, right-click the project in Solution Explorer, and select Properties from the shortcut menu. In the project's Property Pages dialog box, change Package Files to In Cabinet File(s). This enables the CAB size option. Set the CAB size to Custom and set the size depending on your media size, as shown in Figure 13.56.

FIGURE 13.56
You can set the setup project configuration properties to create an installation package in cabinet files of desired size.

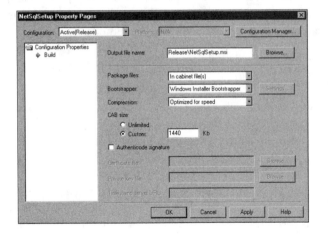

Next, you build the setup project to create a Windows Installer package (.msi file) and one or more CAB files, depending on the size of the application. If the Bootstrapper option is set to Windows Installer Bootstrapper, the setup project also creates a setup.exe file. When you copy all these files to the removable media, copy setup.exe and the .msi file to the first disk and then copy each CAB file to a separate disk.

Network-Based Deployment

Plan the deployment of a Windows-based application.

- **Plan a network-based deployment.**

Network-based installation is useful when users are sharing a common network. In such a case, applications can be installed via a shared network folder. This kind of deployment method is very common in corporate environments.

While creating a setup project for network-based deployment, you create a single setup package instead of creating multiple CAB files. After you have built the setup project, you copy all the setup files to a shared folder on the network and publish the address of the folder to the users. You might also want to make the network share a read-only share so that users cannot modify the setup files.

Administrative Installation

Administrative installation is a common method for deploying a customized version of an application to a large number of users. This is a very common method of installtion in corporate network environments. This method involves two steps:

1. The administrator creates an administrative installation point on a network by executing the Windows Installer package from the command line, using the `msiexec` command with the `/a` option, as in this example:

   ```
   msiexec /a netsql.msi
   ```

   This process needs to performed only once for the whole network. The administrative installation point is shared on the network for all the eligible users.

2. Users install the application by running `setup.exe` from the administrative installation point. The installation program picks up the required files and settings from the administrative installation point and does not ask installation-related questions of the user. The user installation needs to be performed for each user machine on the network.

Administrative installation offers several benefits in a corporate environment, including the following:

◆ Managing one set of application files from a central location

◆ Creating a standard application configuration for all users

◆ Controlling the installation options of an application

◆ Managing controlled upgrades of the application in the future

Web-Based Deployment

Plan the deployment of a Windows-based application.

- **Plan a Web-based deployment.**

Web-based deployment is the most popular form of deployment, especially for small applications. With the growth of high-speed Internet connections, this form of deployment is in much higher demand than deployment via removable media. Web-based deployment offers several advantages over other forms of application deployment:

◆ It reduces the costs of media, replication, and distribution.

◆ Management of software updates is simple. You can program an application to automatically check for updates on the Web, or you can instruct users to download an updater application from a Web page.

Creating a setup package for Web-based deployment is similar to doing so for network-based deployment. After the setup files are created, rather than copy them to a network share you copy them to a virtual directory on a Web server. You might also want to password-protect the deployment Web site so that only authorized users are able to download the application.

REVIEW BREAK

▶ You should select a deployment method that is convenient and accessible to all of the application's users.

▶ You can create installation packages in multiple cabinet files by choosing the In Cabinet File(s) option in the project's Property Pages dialog box.

▶ You can execute an administrative installation by using the `msiexec` command with the `/a` option. This installs a source image of the application onto the network that users in the workgroup can use to install the application on their machines.

▶ Web-based deployment reduces the costs of media, replication, and distribution. It also makes the management of software updates simple.

WINDOWS LOGO PROGRAM REQUIREMENTS

Plan the deployment of a Windows-based application.

- **Ensure that the application conforms to Windows Installer requirements and Windows Logo Program requirements.**

Microsoft provides logo programs to ensure the compatibility of applications with Microsoft operating systems. The logo programs provide guidelines to developers for writing applications that interoperate properly with Windows, providing greater stability, better maintenance, and improved management features. To earn a logo, an application must meet predefined specifications, and an independent lab must test it to confirm its compliance with the specifications.

Microsoft currently offers two different certification programs for applications designed for the Windows 2000 and Windows XP operating systems:

- ◆ The Certified for Microsoft Windows logo program
- ◆ The Designed for Microsoft Windows XP logo program

In addition to these operating system–based certification logo programs, Microsoft also recently launched a .NET Connected logo program. This program certifies applications that are built using the Microsoft .NET Framework and that expose and/or consume Extensible Markup Language (XML) Web services that comply with industry standards.

NOTE

Windows .NET Server With the release of Windows .NET Server, another certification program is being created to certify applications designed for the Windows .NET Server. Very likely, though, complying with the Windows 2000 and Windows XP requirements will prepare you well for this new program.

The Certified for Microsoft Windows Logo Program

The Certified for Windows logo program certifies an application for the Microsoft Windows 2000 operating system. To get this logo, applications must conform to the technical requirements defined in the application specifications for Windows 2000. After an independent testing lab successfully tests the application and the vendor signs the logo license agreement with Microsoft, the application may carry the Certified for Microsoft Windows logo.

The application specification for developing server-based applications differs from the one for desktop-based applications. You can get the complete specifications for both desktop-based and server-based applications by visiting the Certified for Windows Program home page, at `http://msdn.microsoft.com/certification`. For your quick reference, the following list summarizes the main points of the specification for developing logo-compliant desktop applications:

◆ **Windows Fundamentals**—Describes the requirements for consistent and stable functionality of a Windows application:

- Perform primary functionality and maintain stability

- Provide 32-bit components and document any 16-bit code

- Support long filenames and UNC paths

- Support printers with long filenames and UNC paths

- Do not read from or write to `Win.ini`, `System.ini`, `Autoexec.bat`, or `Config.sys` on any Windows operating system that is based on NT technology

- Ensure that nonhidden files outside the application's directory have file types associated with icons, descriptions, and actions

- Correctly perform Windows version checking

- Support AutoPlay of CD-ROM or DVD-ROM

- Ensure that any kernel mode drivers that your application installs pass verification testing on Windows 2000

- Ensure that any hardware drivers included with your application pass Windows Hardware Quality Labs (WHQL) testing

◆ **Windows Installer Service**—Describes the requirements for implementing the Windows Installer service, ensuring that the application can easily be deployed in a corporate environment:

  - Install by using a Windows Installer-based package that passes validation testing

  - Observe the rules for componentization

  - Identify shared components

  - Install to program files by default

  - Properly support Add/Remove Programs

  - Ensure that the application supports advertising

  - Ensure correct uninstall support

◆ **Component Sharing**—Describes the requirements for handling shared components so that applications can coexist with one another:

  - Do not attempt to replace files that are protected by Windows file protection

  - (For component producers) Build side-by-side components

  - (For application developers) Consume and install side-by-side components

  - Install any non–side-by-side shared files to the correct locations

◆ **Data and Settings Management**—Describes the requirements for ensuring that applications support roaming users, multiple users per machine, and simplified machine replacement. Applications that meet these requirements can also operate properly in secure Windows environments:

  - Default to My Documents for storage of user-created data

  - Correctly classify and store application data

  - Degrade gracefully on access denied

- Run in a secure Windows environment

- Adhere to system-level group policy settings

- Ensure that applications that create Administrative Template (.adm) files properly store their ADM file settings in the Registry

◆ **User Interface Fundamentals**—Describes the requirements for providing an accessible user interface:

- Support standard system size, color, font, and input settings

- Ensure compatibility with the high-contrast mode

- Provide documented keyboard access for all features

- Expose the location of the keyboard focus

- Do not rely exclusively on sound

- Do not place shortcuts to documents, help, or uninstallation in the Start menu

- Support multiple monitors

◆ **OnNow/ACPI Support**—Describes the requirements for ensuring that the application can participate in systemwide power management:

- For applications that are allowed to prevent sleep when busy, properly indicate busy application status

- In the nonconnected state, ensure that the application allows sleep and resumes normally

- In the connected state, handle sleep notifications properly

- Handle wake from normal sleep without losing data

- Properly handle wake from critical sleep

◆ **Application Migration**—Describes requirements for ensuring that an application continues to function correctly after the user upgrades to Windows 2000:

- Ensure that the application continues to function after upgrade to Windows 2000 Professional without reinstallation

The Designed for Microsoft Windows XP Logo Program

The Designed for Microsoft Windows XP logo program certifies an application for the Microsoft Windows XP operating system. To get the logo, an application must conform to the technical requirements defined in the Designed for Microsoft Windows XP application specifications. After an independent testing lab successfully tests the application and the vendor signs the logo license agreement with Microsoft, the application may carry the Designed for Microsoft Windows XP logo.

You can get the complete specifications for the Designed for Microsoft Windows XP logo program from the Windows Logo Program Web site, at `www.microsoft.com/winlogo`. For your quick reference, the following list summarizes the main points of this logo certification:

> **NOTE**
>
> **Designed for Windows XP—Optimized Status** If a product meets an extra set of requirements in addition to the core requirements mentioned in the Designed for Microsoft Windows XP application specifications, the product achieves Designed for Windows XP—Optimized status. The product still displays the Designed for Windows XP logo, but it enjoys additional marketing benefits, such as better placement in the Windows catalog.

◆ **Windows Fundamentals**—Describes the requirements for consistent and stable functionality of a Windows application:

- Perform primary functionality and maintain stability

- Ensure that any kernel-mode drivers that the application installs pass verification testing on Windows XP

- Ensure that any device or filter drivers included with the application pass Windows Hardware Compatibility Test (HCT)

- Correctly perform Windows version checking

- Support Fast User Switching and Remote Desktop

- Support new visual styles

- Support switching between tasks

◆ **Installation Requirements**—Describes the requirements for installing and uninstalling applications in Microsoft Windows XP to ensure that the application does not degrade the performance of the operating system or other applications:

- Do not attempt to replace files that are protected by Windows file protection

- Migrate from earlier versions of Windows

- Do not overwrite nonproprietary files with older versions

- Do not inappropriately require a reboot

- Install to `Program Files` by default

- Install any shared files that are not side-by-side to the correct locations

- Properly support Add/Remove Programs

- Support All Users installations

- Support AutoPlay for CDs and DVDs

◆ **Data and Settings Management**—Describes the requirements for ensuring that applications support the infrastructure provided by Windows XP for state separation of user data, user settings, and computer settings:

- Default to the correct location for storing user-created data

- Correctly classify and store application data

- Deal gracefully with access-denied scenarios

- Support running as a limited user

The Microsoft .NET Connected Logo Program

Microsoft recently launched another logo program that is based on Microsoft .NET technology. This logo program, announced in July 2002, is called the Microsoft .NET Connected logo program. This logo program certifies the applications that expose and/or consume XML Web services. There are two levels of compliance for participation in the Microsoft .NET Connected logo program:

◆ **The Base-Level Microsoft .NET Connected logo program**—This is the base level of the .NET Connected logo program. A certified application is identified by a silver Microsoft .NET Connected logo. This program certifies applications that are built using the Microsoft .NET Framework and that expose and/or consume XML Web services that comply with industry standards. Certified applications must be able to share information with other applications, across programming languages and platforms.

◆ **The Premium Level Microsoft .NET Connected logo program**—This is the premium level of the Microsoft .NET Connected logo program. A certified application is identified by a gold logo. This program certifies advanced-level applications that were built using the .NET Framework and that expose and/or consume XML Web services that comply with industry XML standards. Certified applications use the full capability of the .NET programming model for developing XML-based services that provide multilanguage support and added security, as well as enhanced flexibility, reliability, and performance.

> **NOTE**
>
> **The Optimized for Microsoft .NET Development Logo Program** Microsoft has introduced another logo program called the Optimized for Microsoft .NET Development logo program. This is a blue colored logo, which is used to identify the product and services specifically designed for developers who are programming for the Microsoft .NET platform.

You can learn more about the Microsoft .NET Connected logo program from the program's Web site, at www.microsoft.com/net/logo.

CHAPTER SUMMARY

This chapter focuses on how to deploy Windows-based applications. Some simple applications are as easy to deploy as just copying the files from one location to another, whereas some applications are complex and require reliance on the Microsoft Windows Installer service. This chapter discusses how to create setup projects to deploy Windows-based applications. It also discusses how to use various types of editors provided in the setup and deployment projects to perform specific tasks. Through these editors you can perform various tasks on the target machine, such as placing files in multiple folders (including the GAC), creating Registry keys and values in the Registry Editor, associating file types with the application, checking on dependencies, performing custom actions at different phases (such as during install, commit, rollback, and uninstall), and customizing the user interface of the installation process.

This chapter also discusses shared assemblies. You have learned how to use the Strong Name tool (sn.exe) to digitally sign an assembly. You can also use the Strong Name tool to perform delayed signing for an assembly. This chapter also discusses how you can add assemblies to the GAC through Windows Explorer, the Microsoft .NET Framework Configuration tool, the Global Assembly Cache tool (gacutil.exe), and the Microsoft Windows Installer (via setup and deployment projects).

> **KEY TERMS**
> - delay signing
> - deployment
> - merge module
> - native compilation
> - native image cache
> - URL remoting

continues

CHAPTER SUMMARY   *continued*

You have also learned how to precompile a Windows application during installation by creating an `Installer` class and adding the class to the custom actions.

The .NET Framework allows you to launch a remote application through a browser by just pointing to its URL. The Web Server need not have the .NET Framework installed. It just needs to have a copy of the executable file placed in a virtual directory. However, the clients should have the .NET Framework because the code is executed on their machines. This chapter shows how to set runtime security policies to include trust on the code that is executed over the network (an intranet or the Internet). It also summarizes the different ways in which Windows applications can be deployed.

Finally, this chapter discusses the Windows logo programs and Windows Installer requirements for Windows applications. You should make sure that your application conforms to these requirements in order to get the Certified for Windows 2000 logo or the Designed for Microsoft Windows XP logo. For the applications designed using the .NET Framework, Microsoft has also announced a new logo program, the .NET Connected logo program.

APPLY YOUR KNOWLEDGE

Exercises

13.1 Using Microsoft's Sample .NET Framework Bootstrapper

The setup projects created in this chapter assume that the .NET Framework is already installed on the target machine. You cannot use Visual Studio .NET setup and deployment projects to package the required .NET Framework along with a setup package. The .NET Framework has to be installed on the target machine by using a .NET Framework redistributable file (dotnetfx.exe) that is available through one of the following:

◆ The Windows Component Upgrade CD-ROM that comes with Visual Studio .NET

◆ The Microsoft MSDN Download Center (http://msdn.microsoft.com/downloads/sample.asp?url=/MSDN-FILES/027/001/829/msdncompositedoc.xml) or the Microsoft Windows Update Web site (http://windowsupdate.microsoft.com)

Ideally you would like a Windows application's installation program to perform a test for the availability of the .NET Framework on the target machine, and if the .NET Framework is not already installed, you need to install it by using the .NET Framework redistributable file (dotnetfx.exe).

In this exercise you will learn how to use Microsoft's sample .NET Framework bootstrapper Setup.exe file along with a setup package generated through Visual Studio .NET to check for the availability of the .NET Framework on the user's machine and install it by using the .NET Framework redistributable file if it is not already installed.

Estimated time: 20 minutes

1. Open the solution 316C13. In Solution Explorer, select the NetSqlSetup project.

2. Right-click the project and select Properties from the shortcut menu. In the NetSqlSetup Project project's Property Pages dialog box, change the Bootstrapper option to None. Click OK and build the project. Only the NetSqlSetup.msi file is created. It is created in the bin\Release folder of the NetSqlSetup project.

3. Download the Setup.exe bootstrapper sample from http://msdn.microsoft.com/downloads/sample.asp?url=/msdn-files/027/001/830/msdncompositedoc.xml.

4. Install the downloaded sample. It installs two files on your computer: setup.exe and settings.ini. Copy both files to the bin\Release folder of the NetSqlSetup project.

5. Open the settings.ini file in any text editor. Change its contents as follows:

```
[Bootstrap]
Msi=NetSqlSetup.msi
'LanguageDirectory=jpn
'ProductName=testproductname
'DialogText=
'CaptionText=
'ErrorCaptionText=
FxInstallerPath=d:\dotNetFramework
```

The value of FxInstallerPath is the path where you have stored the .NET Framework redistributable file, dotnetfx.exe. You can change the value to your actual path.

6. Open the setup.exe file. The installation is bootstrapped by the sample setup.exe file. It first tests for the availability of the .NET Framework. If the .NET Framework is not installed, it uses the path specified in FxInstallerPath to install the .NET Framework. Note that there are no bootstrap files for installing Microsoft Windows Installer.

APPLY YOUR KNOWLEDGE

This is because that check is a part of the .NET Framework installation and is automatically performed by dotnetfx.exe.

13.2 Creating a Database Script During Installation

In this chapter you have learned that the Custom Actions Editor allows you to perform custom actions during the installation process. In this exercise, you create a custom action to run the Northwind database installation script during installation of the NetSql project. You use osql, a command-line utility, to run the SQL script. This exercise assumes that you have Microsoft SQL Server installed on your machine.

Estimated time: 20 minutes

1. Open the solution 316C13. Add a Visual C# Class Library project to the solution. Name the project InstallNorthwind.

2. Add to the project the Northwind database installation script instnwnd.sql (which is usually available in the Microsoft SQL Server installation directory).

3. Right-click the project InstallNorthwind and choose Add, Add New Item from the context menu. The Add New Item dialog box appears. Add to the project an Installer class named InstallNorthwind.cs.

4. Open the InstallNorthwind.cs file in the code view. Add the following using directive:

   ```
   using System.Diagnostics;
   ```

5. Add the following code after the Component Designer generated code section in the class definition:

```csharp
public override void Install(
 System.Collections.IDictionary savedState)
{
    // call the Install() method
    // of the base class
    base.Install(savedState);
    string strSqlFilePath =
        this.Context.Parameters["Args"];

    // Run the osql process to
    // run the database script
    ProcessStartInfo psi =
        new ProcessStartInfo("osql.exe ",
        "-E -i " + "\"" +
        strSqlFilePath + "\"");
    psi.WindowStyle =
        ProcessWindowStyle.Hidden;
    try
    {
        Process p = Process.Start(psi);
        p.WaitForExit();
    }
    catch(Exception e)
    {
        // throw an InstallException with
        // the original exception message
        throw new
            InstallException(e.Message);
    }
}

public override void Commit(
 System.Collections.IDictionary savedState)
{
    // call the Commit() method
    // of the base class
    base.Commit(savedState);
}
public override void Rollback(
 System.Collections.IDictionary savedState)
{
    // call the Rollback() method
    // of the base class
    base.Rollback(savedState);
}

public override void Uninstall(
 System.Collections.IDictionary savedState)
{
    // call the Uninstall() method
    // of the base class
    base.Uninstall(savedState);
}
```

APPLY YOUR KNOWLEDGE

6. Build the `InstallNorthwind` project.

7. Select the `NetSqlSetup` project in Solution Explorer. Open the File System Editor. Select the Application Folder node and add the `Primary Output from InstallNorthwind (Active)` file to the folder by selecting Action, Add, Project Output.

8. Select the Application Folder node and add the `instnwnd.sql` file from the `InstallNorthwind` project to the folder by selecting Action, Add, File.

9. Open the Custom Actions Editor for the `NetSqlSetup` project. Select the Custom Actions node and select Add Custom Action from the context menu. The Select Item in the Project dialog box appears. Select Primary Output from InstallNorthwind (Active) by navigating to the Application Folder. Click OK. The Primary Output from InstallNorthwind (Active) file is added to all four nodes under Custom Actions.

10. Select the newly added custom action under the Install node. Move it before the Launch NetSql custom action. Open the Properties window and set the `CustomActionData` property to `/Args="[TARGETDIR]instnwnd.sql"`.

11. Build the `NetSqlSetup` project. Install the project. This time, during installation, the Northwind database installation script is also executed.

Review Questions

1. What are the advantages and disadvantages of `XCOPY` deployment?

2. What are the different parts of an assembly version?

3. What is the purpose of the File System Editor?

4. How can you customize the user interface of an installation process?

5. When can you call custom actions?

6. What are shared assemblies?

7. Where is the GAC located on a machine? How can you add items to the GAC?

8. What is meant by delay signing?

9. When should you use a merge module project?

10. How can you convert code into native code? Where are the precompiled assemblies placed?

11. What is the purpose of the `CustomActionData` property in the Custom Actions Editor?

12. What is meant by URL remoting?

13. What are some of the ways you can deploy a Windows application?

Exam Questions

1. You have created a database-driven Windows application. Using Microsoft SQL Server, you have also generated an installation script for your database. This script is stored in a file named `InstData.sql`. You want to deploy this application on your client's computer. When the application is deployed, the database should also be created on the client's computer. You are creating a setup project by using Visual Studio .NET. Which of the following actions should you take to create the database while deploying your application on the client's machine?

A. Create a component that derives from the `Installer` class. Override its `Install()` method to create the database. Add the component to the Install node of the Custom Actions Editor in the setup project.

B. Create a component that derives from the `Installer` class. Override its `Install()` method to create the database. Add the component to the Commit node of the Custom Actions Editor in the setup project.

C. Copy the `InstData.sql` file to the Application Folder on the File System on Target Machine by using the File System Editor. Add `InstData.sql` to the Install node of the Custom Actions Editor in the setup project.

D. Create a component that derives from the `Installer` class. Override its `Install()` method to create the database. Add the component to the Launch Conditions Editor in the setup project.

2. You are creating a setup project for a Windows application. In the Property Pages dialog box for the setup project, you have set the compression property to Optimized for speed. Which of the following options will be true as a result of this configuration option? (Select the two best answers.)

A. All assemblies in the application will be pre-compiled to native code so that they run faster.

B. The resulting assemblies will be larger.

C. The setup package will be larger.

D. The setup project will run faster.

3. You have developed a database-intensive Windows application. When the application is installed on the user's computer, the required database must also be installed. The execution of the program cannot continue without the database. Therefore, if the setup of the database fails, you would like to roll back the installation process. Which of the following editors would you use in the setup project to ensure that the database is properly installed on the target machine?

A. File System Editor

B. Custom Actions Editor

C. Launch Conditions Editor

D. Registry Editor

4. You have created a Windows application that uses some components that are not shared by other applications. Each of these components creates its own assemblies, and all these assemblies have strong names associated with them. The application that uses these components is not required to load a specific version of these components. You do not want to store the assemblies directly under the application's installation folder. Which of the following options is the best approach to store the assembly files for the application's components?

A. Store the components in the GAC.

B. Store the components anywhere you like and specify the path to them by using the `<codebase>` element in the application's configuration file.

C. Store the assemblies in one of the subdirectories under the application's installation directory and specify this subdirectory as part of the `<probing>` element in the application's configuration file.

APPLY YOUR KNOWLEDGE

D. Store the components in the `Windows system` directory.

5. When you install a Windows application on a target machine, you want to store the `ReadMe.txt` file in the installation directory selected by the user. You also want to create a shortcut for the `ReadMe.txt` file on the desktop of the target machine. While creating a setup project, which of the following actions would you take in the File System Editor to achieve this? (Select all that apply.)

A. Move the shortcut to the `ReadMe.txt` file from the Application Folder node to the User's Desktop in the File System on Target Machine node.

B. Add the `ReadMe.txt` file to the Application Folder node of the File System on Target Machine node.

C. Create a shortcut to the `ReadMe.txt` file that is available in the Application Folder node of the File System on Target Machine node.

D. Add the `ReadMe.txt` file to the User's Desktop node in the File System on Target Machine node.

E. Move the shortcut to the `ReadMe.txt` file from the User's Desktop node to the Application Folder in the File System on Target Machine node.

6. You have written a component that will be shared among multiple applications. You want to install the component to the GAC. Which of the following tools will you use to achieve this? (Select the two best answers.)

A. `sn.exe`

B. `gacutil.exe`

C. `ngen.exe`

D. `installutil.exe`

7. You are a developer in a large manufacturing company. You are developing a complex inventory control application with a team of 15 other developers. You have written two program modules, `inv1234.cs` and `inv5678.cs`, that are generic and will be used from several other applications within the company. You compiled both program modules by using a C# compiler to produce the `inv1234.netmodule` and `inv5678.netmodule` files. You now want to link both compiled modules into an assembly that you will install in the GAC to test some Windows forms that depend on this assembly. You have decided to keep the name of the assembly as `InvLib.dll`. You do not have access to the private key of the company, but you have access to the company's public key. The public key is stored in a file named `BigCoPublic.snk`. When the testing is completed, your project manager will use the private key (stored in the `BigCoPrivate.snk` file) to fully sign all the assemblies in the accounting software application. Which of the following commands would you choose to successfully sign your assembly?

A.
```
al.exe inv1234.netmodule,inv5678.netmodule
➥/delaysign /keyfile:BigCoPublic.snk
➥/out:InvLib.dll
```

B.
```
al.exe inv1234.netmodule,inv5678.netmodule
➥/delaysign+ /keyfile:BigCoPublic.snk
➥/out:InvLib.dll
```

C.
```
al.exe inv1234.netmodule,inv5678.netmodule
➥/delaysign- /keyfile:BigCoPublic.snk
➥/out:InvLib.dll
```

D.

```
csc.exe inv1234.cs,inv5678.cs
➥/delaysign /keyfile:BigCoPublic.snk
➥/out:InvLib.dll
```

8. You are using the Installer tool (`installutil.exe`) to install server resources by executing the installer components in three assemblies. You issued the following command:

```
installutil Assembly1.exe Assembly2.exe
Assembly3.exe
```

During the execution of this command, the installation of `Assembly3.exe` failed. Which of the following will happen?

A. Only `Assembly1.exe` will be installed.

B. Only `Assembly2.exe` will be installed.

C. Both `Assembly1.exe` and `Assembly2.exe` will be installed.

D. None of the assemblies will be installed.

9. You have written a Windows application for the time entry system at your company. All the employees in the company will use this application. For easy deployment, you are planning to copy the application to the Company's Web server and publish its URL on the company's intranet Web site. At a minimum, which of the following actions should you take in order to ensure that users can use this application?

A. Install the .NET Framework on all users' computers.

B. Install the .NET Framework on the Web server.

C. Install the .NET Framework on all users' computers as well as the Web server.

D. Install Visual Studio .NET on the Web server, and install the .NET Framework on users' computers.

10. You have designed a Windows application that will help users plan, manage, and file their income taxes. Because this market is competitive, you want to list the application in the Microsoft Windows catalog. Which of the following requirements must the application satisfy in order to get listed in the Windows catalog? (Select all that apply.)

A. Install to `Program Files` by default.

B. Properly support Add/Remove Programs.

C. Support AutoPlay for CDs and DVDs.

D. Fix all known bugs in the software.

11. You want to create a customized setup program for a Windows application. One of the screens shown during installation should be available only from the administrative installation of Microsoft Windows Installer. Other setup options should be available for both regular and administrative installations. Which of the following editors would allow you to create such an installation program?

A. File System Editor

B. User Interface Editor

C. Custom Actions Editor

D. Launch Conditions Editor

12. You have used the native compilation option for several assemblies in your Windows application.

APPLY YOUR KNOWLEDGE

During the testing of the application, you found that one of several parameters on the order entry forms is displayed incorrectly. You determined that classes involved in the problem are part of the native image cache. You want to analyze the contents of the native image cache on the user's computer to see if the correct versions of the assemblies are installed there. Which of the following methods could you use to view the contents of the native image cache? (Select all that apply.)

A. Use the Assembly Cache Viewer Shell Extension (`shfusion.dll`).

B. Use the Global Assembly Cache tool (`gacutil.exe`).

C. Use the Native Image Generator tool (`ngen.exe`).

D. Use the Assembly Binding Log Viewer (`fuslogvw.exe`).

13. You work as a software developer for a big pharmacy. You are writing some components that will be shared across several applications throughout the company. You want to place an assembly named `CommonComponents.dll` in the GAC for testing purpose. You do not have access to the company's private key, but you have stored the company's public key in the assembly manifest of `CommonComponents.dll`. Which of the following commands are you required to run to place your assembly in the GAC? (Select all that apply.)

A.

```
sn.exe -Vr CommonComponents.dll
```

B.

```
sn.exe -Vu CommonComponents.dll
```

C.

```
gacutil.exe /i CommonComponents.dll
```

D.

```
gacutil.exe /u CommonComponents.dll
```

14. You have created a Windows-based calendaring system that allows the salespeople in your company to synchronize their schedules with a central database on the company's Web site. Most of the time, salespersons are out of the office, participating in various sales events across the globe. Sales people would like to access the calendaring system from their laptops wherever they are. The company has standardized that all laptops will run Windows XP Professional with the .NET Framework installed; all laptops use Internet Explorer as the default browser.

To deploy the application, you have uploaded all the necessary files to the company's Web server, including the main application file, `Calendar.exe`, and several `.dll` files that implement other important functionality that is required in order for the application to run. To inform the sales people about the application, you are planning to send an email message to all of them, with the URL of the application, `www.BigSalesCompany.com/Cal/Calendar.exe`. You also want to give them instructions on how to configure their computers in order for the application to run properly. Which of the following instructions would ensure minimum security risk for all sales people while not affecting the functionality of the calendaring system? (Select all that apply.)

A. Using the .NET Framework Configuration Wizard, set the trust level for the `www.BigSalesCo.com/Cal/Calendar.exe` assembly to Full Trust.

B. Using the .NET Framework Configuration Wizard, increase the trust level for the My Computer zone to Full Trust.

C. Using Internet Explorer, add the company Web site to the Trusted Sites list.

D. Using the .NET Framework Configuration Wizard, increase the trust level for the Internet zone to Full Trust.

E. Using the .NET Framework Configuration Wizard, increase the trust level for the Trusted Sites zone to Full Trust.

15. You are designing a Windows application that will be downloaded to a user's computer from your company's Web server. After it is installed on the user's computer, the application might request and download more components from the Web site, as needed for the user's requirements. The application uses several components that need to be installed in the GAC on the user's machine. You want to sign your components with a cryptographic digital signature as well as with an Authenticode signature, so that the identity of your company is certified through an independent certifying authority. Which of the following options would you use for signing the components before they are packaged for deployment?

A. Use sn.exe to sign the assemblies.

B. Use signcode.exe to sign the assemblies.

C. Use sn.exe followed by signcode.exe to sign the assemblies.

D. Use signcode.exe followed by sn.exe to sign the assemblies.

Answers to Review Questions

1. XCOPY deployment is suitable for deploying small and simple applications that contain private assemblies. XCOPY deployment makes zero impact on the configuration of the target machine. However, XCOPY deployment lacks most of the amenities provided by Microsoft Windows Installer, such as copying files and shortcuts to different places on the target machine, associating file types with extensions, allowing custom actions to be performed during the installation process, providing the ability to roll back the installation process, uninstalling an application, repairing a component or an application, checking for dependencies and stopping the installation process when the dependencies do not exist, providing a user interface, and many more. Furthermore, XCOPY deployment is also not suitable when you want to place components or assemblies of an application in the GAC.

2. The different parts of an assembly version are <major>, <minor>, <build>, and <revision>.

3. The File System Editor provides mapping of the file system on the target machine. The folders are referred to by special names that are converted during the installation process to represent the folders as per the file system on the target machine.

4. The User Interface Editor allows you to create your own user interface for the installation process. There are three stages of installation: start, progress, and end. The editor allows you to add different types of dialog boxes to each of the different stages. It provides special properties whose values can be evaluated to perform the installation according to the end user's choice.

APPLY YOUR KNOWLEDGE

5. The custom actions can be performed in four phases: install, commit, rollback, and uninstall.

6. Shared assemblies are shared by multiple applications on a machine and are placed in the GAC. A shared assembly should have a strong name that consists of its text name (usually the name of the file, without the file extension), version number, culture information, and public key token.

7. The GAC is located in the assembly folder under the system folder on a machine. You can view shared assemblies in the GAC by navigating to the assembly folder in Windows Explorer. You can add shared assemblies to the GAC through Windows Explorer, the .NET Framework Configuration tool (mscorcfg.msc), the Global Assembly Cache tool (gacutil.exe), or the Windows Installer.

8. Delay signing is a process that allows you to place a shared assembly in the GAC by just signing the assembly with a public key. This allows the assembly to be signed with a private key at a later stage, when the development process is complete and the component or assembly is ready to be deployed.

9. Merge modules should be used to package shared components with their related resources, Registry entries, custom actions, and launch conditions. Merge modules cannot be installed directly; rather, they are merged into setup projects.

10. The compilation from MSIL to native code can be done by using the Native Image Generation tool (ngen.exe). The assemblies that are compiled into machine-specific native code are placed in the native image cache.

11. The CustomActionData property is used to pass custom data from a setup program to the custom installer class.

12. URL remoting provides a zero deployment model for deploying a Windows application. The code and configuration files reside on a Web server, and you can execute an application just by pointing to the URL of the .exe file from Internet Explorer on the end user's computer.

13. You can deploy applications in the following ways:

    • Deployment via removable media

    • Network-based deployment

    • Web-based deployment

Answers to Exam Questions

1. **A.** You can use the Custom Actions Editor to take custom actions such as database installations during application setup. If you have an Installer class or program that overrides the Install() method to create databases, it must be added to the Install node of the Custom Actions Editor. For more information, see the section "Creating Installation Components" in this chapter.

2. **C** and **D.** Changing a setup project's Compression property to Optimized for speed does not affect the size or the speed of the installed assemblies. Instead, the setup program compresses the assemblies by using a compression algorithm that is optimized for speed. As a result, you have a lower compression ratio, resulting in a large setup package that executes faster. For more information, see the section "Creating a Setup Project" in this chapter.

APPLY YOUR KNOWLEDGE

3. **B.** The Custom Actions Editor allows you to execute custom actions such as database installations while running the setup program. It also has provisions for performing an installation rollback if the installation operation fails. For more information, see the section "Using the Custom Actions Editor" in this chapter.

4. **C.** If the components are not shared between applications, it is not a good idea to store them in the GAC. You could use the <codebase> element in the application's configuration file, but in that case you must specify a version of the assembly. The applications in question are not specific about versions, so a good place to store the assemblies is in a folder inside the application's installation folder, with its location specified via the <probing> element in the application's configuration file. For more information, see the section "How the CLR Locates Assemblies" in this chapter.

5. **A, B,** and **C.** To copy the ReadMe.txt file to the installation directory selected by the user at install time, you would add it to the Application Folder node in the File System on Target Machine node. To create a shortcut, you first create a shortcut to the ReadMe.txt file stored in the Application Folder node in the File System on Target Machine node. Then you move this shortcut from the Application Folder node to the User's Desktop in the File System on Target Machine node. For more information, see the section "Using the File System Editor" in this chapter.

6. **A** and **B.** When you want to install a component to the GAC, you first assign it a strong name. You do this by using the Strong Name tool (sn.exe). You can place a strongly named assembly in the GAC by using the Global Assembly Cache tool (gacutil.exe).

For more information, see the section "Adding an Assembly to the Global Assembly Cache" in this chapter.

7. **B.** You can use the al.exe command to link already-compiled modules into an assembly. The process of including a public key in an assembly and signing it with a private key at a later stage is called delay signing. You can perform delay signing on an assembly by using al.exe with the /delay+ switch. For more information, see the section "Delay Signing Using the Assembly Linker Tool" in this chapter.

8. **D.** installutil.exe performs installation in a transactional manner. If one of the assemblies fails to install, installutil.exe rolls back the installations of all other assemblies. So if the installation of Assembly3.exe fails, none of the assemblies will be installed. For more information, see the section "Deploying an Installation Component by Using the Installer Tool (installutil.exe)" in this chapter.

9. **A.** You will have to install the .NET Framework only on all user computers. The .NET Framework and Visual Studio .NET do not have to be installed on the Web server. For more information, see the section "Launching a Remote Application" in this chapter.

10. **A, B,** and **C.** To be listed in the Windows catalog, an application must meet the requirements mentioned in the specifications of the Windows logo program. You are not required to fix all known bugs to be listed in the Windows catalog. For more information, see the section "Windows Logo Program Requirements" in this chapter.

APPLY YOUR KNOWLEDGE

11. **B.** You can customize the user interface of an installation program by using the User Interface Editor for both the regular installation and administrative installation. For more information, see the section "Using the User Interface Editor" in this chapter.

12. **A, B,** and **C.** The native image cache can be viewed with all the listed tools except for the Assembly Binding Log Viewer (`fuslogvw.exe`), which is used to display failed assembly binds. For more information, see the section "Performing Install-Time Compilation" in this chapter.

13. **A** and **C.** You have to first turn off the verification for partially signed assemblies. You can do this by using the `sn.exe` tool with the `-Vr` switch. Next, you can install the assembly to the GAC by using the `/i` switch with the `gacutil.exe` command. For more information, see the section "Delay Signing an Assembly" in this chapter.

14. **C** and **E.** In this scenario, although the salespeople connect to the calendaring system by using the Internet, all the content required for running the application is coming only from the company's Web site. The minimum-risk solution would be to add the company to the Trusted Sites list and then increase the trust level for trusted sites to Full Trust. Answer A is not the correct answer because the application consists of the `.exe` file and several other `.dll` files; if you just trust the `.exe` file, the code in `.dll` file is still not trusted. For more information, see the section "Setting the Runtime Security Policy for an Assembly" in this chapter.

15. **C.** `sn.exe` is used to sign an assembly with a cryptographic digital signature, whereas `signcode.exe` is used to sign an assembly with an Authenticode signature. When both are used together to sign an assembly, you should always use `sn.exe` before using `signcode.exe`. For more information, see the section "Delay Signing an Assembly" in this chapter.

APPLY YOUR KNOWLEDGE

Suggested Readings and Resources

1. The Visual Studio .NET Combined Help Collection:

   - "Deploying Applications and Components"

   - "Deployment Walkthroughs"

   - "Creating Installation Components"

2. Jeffrey Richter. *Applied Microsoft .NET Framework Programming*. Microsoft Press, 2002.

3. Information about .NET Framework version 1 security changes, msdn.microsoft.com/ library/en-us/dnnetsec/html/ v1securitychanges.asp.

4. The Certified for Microsoft Windows logo program Web site, msdn.microsoft.com/ certification.

5. The Designed for Microsoft Windows XP logo program Web site, www.microsoft.com/ winlogo.

6. The Microsoft .NET Connected logo Web site, www.microsoft.com/net/logo.

7. Deploying .NET Applications: Lifecycle Guide. www.microsoft.com/downloads/ release.asp?releaseid=40545

8. Microsoft Support WebCast: Microsoft .NET: Deploying Applications with .NET. support.microsoft.com/servicedesks/ webcasts/wc091902/wcblurb091902.asp.

MAINTAINING AND CONFIGURING A WINDOWS APPLICATION

This chapter covers the following Microsoft-specified objectives for the "Maintaining and Supporting a Windows-Based Application" section of Exam 70-316, "Developing and Implementing Windows-Based Applications with Microsoft Visual C# .NET and Microsoft Visual Studio .NET":

Optimize the performance of a Windows-based application.

▶ Performance is often defined as a part of the functional requirement of an application. If an application does not meet its performance requirement, it is considered broken. This exam objective tests your skills in developing a high-performance application for the .NET Framework. You should know some common performance patterns (do's) and anti-patterns (don'ts), and you should be able to use them in your programs to ensure that your applications meet their performance requirements.

Diagnose and resolve errors and issues.

▶ After an application has been deployed, you would ideally expect it to run smoothly. However, experience shows that even a well-tested application may misbehave for various reasons. You may be able to pinpoint problems if you log the behavior of your application. You might also want to design applications that can fine-tune themselves according to their environment. For example, you might want to create an application that can start or stop itself in response to performance measurements. The .NET Framework provides you with a variety of components and tools to publish, record, and analyze an application's performance. This exam objective requires you to know about the classes in the `System.Diagnostics` namespace that help you design an application that is easy to manage and maintain.

CHAPTER 14

Maintaining and Supporting a Windows Application

STUDY STRATEGIES

▶ Review the "Performance Tips and Tricks in .NET Applications" whitepaper from the Visual Studio .NET Combined Help Collection.

▶ Try out the walkthrough exercises related to `Process`, `EventLog`, and `PerformanceCounter` from the "Visual Basic and Visual C# Walkthroughs" section of the Visual Studio .NET Combined Help Collection.

▶ Review the "Design Goals—Performance" section of the "Designing Distributed Applications" topic from the Visual Studio .NET Combined Help Collection.

INTRODUCTION

The System.Diagnostics namespace provides various classes that help in managing and monitoring Windows applications. This chapter focuses on the following three important classes:

◆ **Process**—The Process class provides information about the processes that are running on a computer. You can also use this class to access process information for computers across the network. The Process class also facilitates starting and stopping a process on a local computer.

◆ **EventLog**—The EventLog class provides functionality to read and write information to the Windows event log. An application can monitor an event log to take actions when an entry is written to the log. An application may also publish its own events that may be of interest to other applications or to the system administrator.

◆ **PerformanceCounter**—The PerformanceCounter class can be used to get performance data for running processes. You can also use this class to publish performance data over a network.

In this chapter I show you how to use these classes, and I also describe how to use a number of supporting classes to monitor and manage processes, event logs, and performance counters. The System.Diagnostics namespace provides other classes, such as Trace and Debug, that help you test and debug applications. For more information on the Trace and Debug classes, see Chapter 12, "Testing and Debugging a Windows Application."

This chapter also discusses various techniques that may help you in improving the performance of applications.

MANAGING A WINDOWS PROCESS

Diagnose and resolve errors and issues.

A *process* is an application that is being executed. Each running process is uniquely identified on a computer with a process identifier.

When a process executes, it consumes resources such as processor time and primary memory. Managing a Windows process involves getting execution information about the running processes and, if required, starting or stopping a process.

The System.Diagnostics namespace provides several classes that help with process management. The key to working with processes is the Process class, which represents an instance of a process. You can either create instances of the Process class programmatically or you can use the Process component from the Windows Forms Designer's toolbox. Programmatic access is especially useful for dynamically representing multiple running processes.

Starting and Stopping Processes

To start a process, you use the Start() method of the Process class. This method is available in both static and nonstatic versions. To use the nonstatic version of the Start() method, you create an instance of the Process class, set its StartInfo property to specify the necessary startup information (such as the executable filename, arguments, environment variables, and working directory), and call the Start() method on it. The static version of the Start() method returns an instance of a created process when you pass the ProcessStartupInfo object or other arguments, such as the application's filename and environment.

Two methods can stop processes: CloseMainWindow() and Kill(). The CloseMainWindow() method requests a normal shutdown of a program that is equivalent to closing an application by clicking the close icon in its main window. CloseMainWindow() can stop only the processes that participate in the Windows message loop and have user interfaces. On the other hand, the Kill() method causes an abnormal program termination by forcibly killing an application. Using Kill() is the way to stop processes that do not have user interfaces or that do not participate in Windows message loops (such as MS-DOS–based programs).

Table 14.1 lists members of the Process class that are useful for starting and stopping processes.

NOTE

Starting and Stopping a Process The Process class allows you to start and stop only processes that are on the local machine. Although you can use Process to access process information for remote machines, you cannot start or stop processes on a remote machine by using this class.

WARNING

Use Kill() with Caution Using the Kill() method is the equivalent of killing a process by using Task Manager. It causes the program to terminate immediately, and all resources consumed by it are released. This may cause loss of data and should be used with caution.

TABLE 14.1

MEMBERS OF THE PROCESS CLASS THAT ARE USEFUL FOR STARTING AND STOPPING PROCESSES

Member	Type	Description
CloseMainWindow()	Method	Closes a process that has a user interface by sending a close message to the main window of the process.
EnableRaisingEvents	Property	Specifies whether the Exited event should be raised when the process terminates.
ExitCode	Property	Holds a value specified by the process when it exits.
Exited	Event	Occurs when a process exits.
ExitTime	Property	Specifies the time at which the process exited.
GetProcessById()	Method	Returns a Process object that represents an already running process with the given process identifier.
GetProcesses()	Method	Returns an array of Process objects in which each element represents an already existing process.
GetProcessesByName()	Method	Returns an array of Process objects in which each element represents an already running process with the specified process name.
HasExited	Property	Indicates whether the process has been terminated.
Id	Property	Specifies the unique identifier of the process.
Kill()	Method	Immediately stops the process.
StartInfo	Property	Specifies the properties to pass to the Start() method of the process. The only required StartInfo member is the FileName property. The specified filename does not have to be an executable file. Any file whose extension is associated with an installed application will work. For example, if the file has a .doc extension and if the .doc extension is associated with Microsoft Word in your operating system settings, the specified file is opened by using Microsoft Word.
WaitForExit()	Method	Sets the length of time to wait for the process to exit and blocks the current thread of execution until the time has elapsed or the process has exited.
WaitForInputIdle()	Method	Causes a Process object to wait for the process to enter an idle state.

Step by Step 14.1 shows how to start and stop a process.

STEP BY STEP

14.1 Starting and Stopping a Process

1. Launch Visual Studio .NET, select File, New, Blank Solution, and name it 316C14.

continues

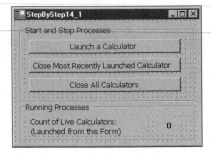

FIGURE 14.1
You can use the Process class to start and
stop a Windows process.

2. Add a Visual C# Windows Application project to the solution. Name the project StepByStep14_1.

3. Rename the Form1.cs file StepByStep14_1.cs in the project. Switch to the code view of the form and modify all references to Form1 so that they refer to StepByStep14_1 instead.

4. Place two GroupBox controls, three Button controls (btnLaunchCalculator, btnCloseRecentCaculator, and btnCloseAllCalculators), and two Label controls (one named lblLiveCaluclators) on the form and arrange them as shown in Figure 14.1.

5. Switch to the code view. Add the following using directive:

```
using System.Diagnostics;
```

6. Add the following code in the class definition:

```
// Declare an ArrayList to hold
// the process id of calculators
ArrayList arrCalculators = new ArrayList();
```

7. Add the following event handler to the class definition:

```
// Handles the Exited event of the Calculator process
private void Calculator_Exited(object sender,
                             System.EventArgs e)
{
  // Remove the process that has exited
  // from the ArrayList
  // Decrement the count of the live calculators
  Process p = (Process) sender;
  arrCalculators.RemoveAt(
     arrCalculators.IndexOf(p.Id));
  lblLiveCalculators.Text = (Int32.Parse(
     lblLiveCalculators.Text) - 1).ToString();
}
```

8. Attach default Click event handlers to the Button controls. Add the following code to the event handlers:

```
private void btnLaunchCalculator_Click(object sender,
                             System.EventArgs e)
{
   // Create a new process "calc.exe "
   // Add an event handler to the
   // Exited event of the process
   Process prcCalculator = new Process();
   prcCalculator.StartInfo.FileName = "calc.exe ";
   prcCalculator.EnableRaisingEvents = true;
   prcCalculator.Exited +=
          new EventHandler(Calculator_Exited);
```

```csharp
        // Start the process
        prcCalculator.Start();
        //Wait for process to enter idle state
        prcCalculator.WaitForInputIdle();
        // Add the Process Id of the calculator
        // to the ArrayList
        arrCalculators.Add(prcCalculator.Id);
        // Increment the count of the live calculators
        lblLiveCalculators.Text = (Int32.Parse(
            lblLiveCalculators.Text) + 1).ToString();
}

private void btnCloseRecentCalculator_Click(
        object sender, System.EventArgs e)
{

    if(arrCalculators.Count >0)
    {
        // Pick up the last process id
        // from the ArrayList
        int intId =
        (int) arrCalculators[arrCalculators.Count - 1];
        try
        {
            // Get access to the Process object
            // through the process id
            Process p = Process.GetProcessById(intId);
            // Close the process by closing
            // the calculator window
            p.CloseMainWindow();
        }
        catch(Exception ex)
        {
            Trace.WriteLine(ex.Message);
        }
    }
}

private void btnCloseAllCalculators_Click(
    object sender, System.EventArgs e)
{
    // Get all the processes by name "calc"
    Process[] arrCalculators =
        Process.GetProcessesByName("calc");

    // Close each process by closing
    // the calculator window
    foreach(Process prcCalculator
        in arrCalculators)
    {
        prcCalculator.CloseMainWindow();
    }
}
```

9. Set the project StepByStep14_1 as the startup project.

continues

continued

10. Run the project. Click the Launch a Calculator button multiple times. Multiple calculator windows open, and the Count of Live Calculators label keeps updating the count of the live calculators opened from this application. Click the Close Most Recently Launched Calculator button to close the last calculator process started.

11. Close a calculator by clicking its close button. The program receives a notification of its Exit event, and the Count of Live Calculators label is reduced by 1 by the Exited event handling code.

12. Start a Windows calculator from the Windows Start menu; position it separately onscreen to distinctly identify it from other calculators that are opened by the program. Click the Close Most Recently Launched Calculator button. The program closes only the last calculator started from this program, leaving the calculator that was externally started still active. Click the Close All Calculators button. The program closes all the open calculators, whether they were opened from this program or not.

Getting Process Information

You can create an instance of the Process class for any of the processes that are running on the local machine or on a remote machine. You can then use this process to get details about the running process. Some examples of execution details include the current processor usage, the memory usage, and whether the process is responding.

Access to this information in an application might help you decide whether you need to increase or decrease processing in the application based on the current system load. This information might also help you decide to terminate or restart misbehaving processes. Table 14.2 lists some important properties of the Process class for getting information about processes.

TABLE 14.2

SOME IMPORTANT PROPERTIES OF THE Process CLASS FOR GETTING INFORMATION ABOUT PROCESSES

Property	Description
MachineName	Specifies the name of the computer on which the process is running.
MainModule	Specifies the main module of the process.
MainWindowTitle	Specifies the caption of the main window of the process.
Modules	Specifies the modules that have been loaded by the associated process.
PriorityClass	Specifies the priority class for the process.
ProcessName	Specifies the name of the process.
ProcessorAffinity	Specifies the processors on which the threads in the process can be scheduled to run.
Responding	Indicates whether the user interface of the process is responding.
StandardError	Provides access to a StreamReader object through which you can read error output from the process.
StandardInput	Provides access to a StreamWriter object through which you can write input to the process.
StandardOutput	Provides access to a StreamReader object through which you can read output from the process.
StartTime	Specifies the time at which the process was started.
Threads	Gets the threads that are running in the associated process.
TotalProcessorTime	Specifies the total processor time spent on this process.
UserProcessorTime	Specifies the total user processor time spent on this process.
VirtualMemorySize	Specifies the size of the process's virtual memory.
WorkingSet	Specifies the process's physical memory usage.

Step by Step 14.2 uses some of these properties to display information about the processes that are running on the local machine and on remote machines.

STEP BY STEP

14.2 Getting Process Information

1. Add a Visual C# Windows application project to the solution. Name the project StepByStep14_2.

2. Rename the Form1.cs file StepByStep14_2.cs in the project. Switch to the code view of the form and modify all references to Form1 so that they refer to StepByStep14_2 instead.

3. Place five Label controls, one TextBox control (txtMachine), one Button control (btnLoad), and two ListView controls (lvwProcesses and lvwProcessInfo) on the form. Set the View property of the ListView controls to Details. Select the Columns property of the lvwProcesses control and click the ellipsis (...) button. The ColumnHeader Collection Editor window appears. Add two column headers, Process Name (chProcessName) and Process Id (chProcessId), as shown in Figure 14.2. Add to the lvwProcessInfo control two column headers, Property (chProperty) and Value (chValue). Arrange the controls as shown in Figure 14.3.

4. Switch to the code view. Add the following using directive:

```
using System.Diagnostics;
```

5. Add the following code in the class definition:

```
// Create a string member to hold the Machine Name
private string strMachineName;
```

6. Attach a Load event handler to the form, a Click event handler to the btnLoad control, and a SelectedIndexChanged event handler to the lvwProcesses control. Add the following code in the event handlers:

```
private void StepByStep14_2_Load(object sender,
                                System.EventArgs e)
{
    // Set the textbox with the System ComputerName
    strMachineName = txtMachine.Text =
                    SystemInformation.ComputerName;
}
```

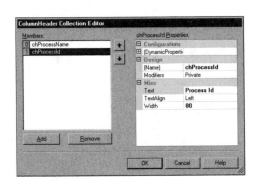

FIGURE 14.2
You can use the ColumnHeader Collection Editor to view and change the list of columns for a Windows Forms ListView control.

```
private void btnLoad_Click(object sender,
    System.EventArgs e)
{
    // Get the Machine name
    // Clear the list view controls
    strMachineName = txtMachine.Text;
    lvwProcesses.Items.Clear();
    lvwProcessInfo.Items.Clear();
    try
    {
        // Get all the processes
        Process[] arrProcesses;
        arrProcesses =
                Process.GetProcesses(strMachineName);
        foreach(Process p in arrProcesses)
        {
            // Add each process into the lvwProcesses
            ListViewItem lvwItem =
                new ListViewItem(new string[]
                    {p.ProcessName, p.Id.ToString()});
            lvwProcesses.Items.Add(lvwItem);
        }
    }
    catch(Exception ex)
    {
        MessageBox.Show(ex.Message);
    }
}

private void lvwProcesses_SelectedIndexChanged
    (object sender, System.EventArgs e)
{
    lvwProcessInfo.Items.Clear();
    // Get the Process Id of the selected process
    int intProcessId = Convert.ToInt32(
      this.lvwProcesses.FocusedItem.SubItems[1].Text);
    try
    {
        Process p = Process.GetProcessById(
            intProcessId, strMachineName);

        // Add Process information to the
        // lvwProcessInfo control
        ListViewItem lvwItem = new ListViewItem(new
            string[]{"StartTime",
            p.StartTime.ToString()});
        lvwProcessInfo.Items.Add(lvwItem);

        lvwItem = new ListViewItem(
            new string[]{"TotalProcessorTime",
            p.TotalProcessorTime.ToString()});
        lvwProcessInfo.Items.Add(lvwItem);
```

continues

continued

NOTE

Processes on a Remote Computer
You must have administrative
privileges on the remote computer in
order to get process information for
that computer.

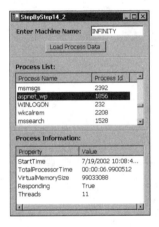

FIGURE 14.3
You can use the `Process` class to retrieve information about the running processes.

```
lvwItem = new ListViewItem(
    new string[]{"VirtualMemorySize",
    p.VirtualMemorySize.ToString()});
lvwProcessInfo.Items.Add(lvwItem);

if (strMachineName ==
    SystemInformation.ComputerName)
{
    lvwItem = new ListViewItem(new string[]{
        "Responding", p.Responding.ToString()});
    lvwProcessInfo.Items.Add(lvwItem);

    lvwItem = new ListViewItem(new string[]{
        "Threads", p.Threads.Count.ToString()});
    lvwProcessInfo.Items.Add(lvwItem);
}
}
catch(Exception ex)
{
    Debug.WriteLine(ex.Message);
}
}
```

7. Set the project `StepByStep14_2` as the startup project.

8. Run the project. Your computer name appears in the text box. Change the value and then click the Load Process Data button. A list of all the running processes appears in the Process List list view. Select a process from this list, and its information appears in the Process Information list view, as shown in Figure 14.3.

GUIDED PRACTICE EXERCISE 14.1

In this exercise, your objective is to create a form that allows you to start and stop a process. You should create a form with two `Button` controls. When you click the Launch Editor button, the program should launch MS-DOS Editor. When you click the Close MS-DOS Editor button, the program should close the editor. The program should allow you to launch only one instance of the editor at a time.

The `Process` component that is available in the Windows Forms toolbox is a convenient way to create processes in Windows Forms applications. How would you create the above-mentioned form that uses the `Process` component to create and kill the processes?

You should try working through this problem on your own first. If you get stuck or if you would like to see one possible solution, follow these steps:

1. Add a Visual C# Windows application project to the solution. Name the project `GuidedPracticeExercise14_1`.

2. Rename the `Form1.cs` file `GuidedPracticeExercise14_1.cs` in the project. Switch to the code view of the form and modify all references to `Form1` so that they refer to `GuidedPracticeExercise14_1` instead.

3. Place two `Button` controls (`btnLaunch` and `btnClose`) on the form. Select the Components tab in the toolbox and drag the `Process` component onto the form.

4. Access the Properties window for the `Process` component, change its `Name` property to `prcEditor`, and set `EnableRaisingEvents` to `true`. Expand the `StartInfo` property to access its subproperties. Change the `FileName` property to `Edit.com`.

5. Add the following event handling code to the `Exited` event of the `Process` component:

```
private void prcEditor_Exited(object sender,
                              System.EventArgs e)
{
    this.btnClose.Enabled = false;
    this.btnLaunch.Enabled = true;
}
```

6. Attach event handlers to the `Click` events of the `Button` controls and add the following code to them:

```
private void btnLaunch_Click(
    object sender, System.EventArgs e)
{
    // Start the process
    prcEditor.Start();
    this.btnClose.Enabled = true;
    this.btnLaunch.Enabled = false;
}
```

continues

continued

```
private void btnClose_Click(
    object sender, System.EventArgs e)
{
    // Kill the process
    prcEditor.Kill();
}
```

7. Set the project `GuidedPracticeExercise14_1` as the startup project.

8. Run the project. Click the Launch MS-DOS Editor button. The MS-DOS editor is launched, with the filename `Edit.com`, as shown in Figure 14.4. Click the Close MS-DOS Editor button to close the editor window.

FIGURE 14.4

GuidedPracticeExercise14_1 uses the Process component to start and kill the MS-DOS editor.

If you have difficulty following this exercise, review the section "Starting and Stopping Processes," earlier in this chapter. Also, spend some time looking at the various members of the `Process` class that are useful for starting and stopping a process (refer to Table 14.1), and then perform Step by Step 14.1. After doing that review, try this exercise again.

WORKING WITH EVENT LOGS

Event logging is the standard way in Windows for applications to log their events. You can easily monitor the behavior of an application by using the Event Viewer utility to analyze its messages in the event log.

In fact, you can also view events from the Visual Studio .NET environment, and you can access event logs through Server Explorer.

The Framework Class Libraries provide a set of classes that are designed to work with event logs. With the help of these classes, you can programmatically read or write to event logs. Programmatic access may even allow you to automate some of the administrative tasks associated with an application.

By default, three event logs are available: Application, Security, and System. Other applications or operating system components, such as Active Directory, include other event logs. Table 14.3 lists some important members of the EventLog class.

TABLE 14.3

SOME IMPORTANT MEMBERS OF THE EventLog CLASS

Member	Type	Description
CreateEventSource()	Method	Opens an event source so an application can write event information to an event log on the system.
Delete()	Method	Removes a log resource.
DeleteEventSource()	Method	Removes an application's event source from the event log.
EnableRaisingEvents	Property	Specifies whether the EventLog object receives notifications for the EntryWritten event.
Entries	Property	Gets the contents of an event log.
EntryWritten	Event	Occurs when an entry is written to an event log on the local computer.
Exists()	Method	Determines whether the specified log exists.
GetEventLogs()	Method	Creates an array of the event logs.
Log	Property	Specifies the name of the log to read from or write to.
LogDisplayName	Property	Specifies an event log's friendly name.
LogNameFromSourceName()	Method	Gets the name of the log to which the specified source is registered.
MachineName	Property	Specifies the name of the computer on which to read or write events.

continues

NOTE

The Log Property Only the first eight characters of a Log property name are significantly identified. Therefore, an event log with the name StepByStep14_2 would be treated as the same log as StepByStep14_3.

TABLE 14.3	*continued*

SOME IMPORTANT MEMBERS OF THE EventLog CLASS

Member	*Type*	*Description*
Source	Property	Specifies the source to register and use when writing to an event log.
SourceExists()	Method	Finds whether a given event source exists.
WriteEntry()	Method	Writes an entry in an event log.

Each application that is interested in interacting with an event log must register an event source with the log. When an event source is registered, its information is stored in the system registry and is available across application restarts.

The CreateEventSource() method allows you to register an application with an event log. If the event log does not already exist, this method creates it for you.

Writing to Event Logs

The WriteEntry() method of the EventLog object allows you to write messages to the event log specified by the event source. If the event source specified by the Source property of an EventLog object does not exist, the first call to WriteEntry() creates the event source before writing the entry to the event log.

You can write different types of messages (information, error, warning, success audit, and failure audit) to an event log. These types are specified by the values in the EventLogEntryType enumeration.

The sample application in Step by Step 14.3 demonstrates how to create an event log, register an application with the event log, unregister an application with an event log, write to an event log, and delete an event log.

STEP BY STEP

14.3 Creating and Writing to an Event Log

1. Add a Visual C# Windows application project to the solution. Name the project StepByStep14_3.

2. Rename the Form1.cs file StepByStep14_3.cs in the project. Switch to the code view of the form and modify all references to Form1 so that they refer to StepByStep14_3 instead.

3. Place two GroupBox controls, three Label controls, one TextBox control (txtMessage, with MultiLine set to true), four Button controls (btnCreate, btnRemoveSource, btnRemoveLog, and btnWrite), one ComboBox control (cbEventLogs), and five RadioButton controls (rbError, rbInformation, rbFailureAudit, rbSuccessAudit, and rbWarning) on the form. Arrange the controls as shown in Figure 14.5.

4. Switch to the code view. Add the following using directive:

```
using System.Diagnostics;
```

5. Add the following code in the class definition:

```
// Create a member to hold EventLogEntryType
private EventLogEntryType eletEntryType =
    EventLogEntryType.Error;
```

6. Add a new method named PopulateLogNames() to the class definition and call it from the form's Load event handler:

```
private void StepByStep14_3_Load(
    object sender, System.EventArgs e)
{
    PopulateLogNames();
}
private void PopulateLogNames()
{
    cbEventLogs.Items.Clear();
    // Add eventlogs in to the combo box.
    foreach(EventLog el in
        EventLog.GetEventLogs())
        cbEventLogs.Items.Add(el.Log);
}
```

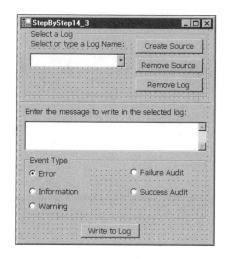

FIGURE 14.5

The StepByStep14_3 form uses the EventLog class to create an event log and write entries to it.

continues

continued

7. Attach a Click event handler to each Button control. Add the following code in the event handlers:

```csharp
private void btnCreate_Click(
    object sender, System.EventArgs e)
{
    if (cbEventLogs.Text != "")
    {
        string strSourceName = "StepByStep14_3_"
                            + cbEventLogs.Text;
        // Check whether the Source already exists
        if (!EventLog.SourceExists(strSourceName))
        {
            try
            {
                // Create event source and the
                // event log (if log doesn't exist)
                EventLog.CreateEventSource(
                    strSourceName,cbEventLogs.Text);
                PopulateLogNames();
                MessageBox.Show(
                    "Created EventSource " +
                    "for Selected EventLog");
            }
            catch(Exception ex)
            {
                MessageBox.Show(ex.Message);
            }
        }
        else
            MessageBox.Show("You already have an " +
            "EventSource attached to this EventLog",
            "Cannot Create EventSource");
    }
}

private void btnRemoveSource_Click(
    object sender, System.EventArgs e)
{
    if (cbEventLogs.Text != "")
    {
        string strSourceName = "StepByStep14_3" +
                            cbEventLogs.Text;
        if (EventLog.SourceExists(strSourceName))
        {
            // Delete the Event Source
            EventLog.DeleteEventSource(strSourceName);
            MessageBox.Show("Deleted the EventSource "
                + "for Selected EventLog");
        }
        else
            MessageBox.Show("There is currently no " +
                "EventSource for selected EventLog");
    }
}
```

```
private void btnRemoveLog_Click(
    object sender, System.EventArgs e)
{

    string strLogName = cbEventLogs.Text.ToUpper();
    // Do not delete system created logs
    if (strLogName == "APPLICATION" ||
        strLogName == "SECURITY" ||
        strLogName == "SYSTEM")
    {
        string strMessage = "This program does not " +
            "allow the deletion of system " +
            "created EventLogs as this may " +
            "cause undesirable effects on " +
            "the working of your computer.";
        MessageBox.Show(
            strMessage, "Dangerous Operation");
        return;
    }
    // If the log exists
    if (EventLog.Exists(cbEventLogs.Text))
    {
        // Confirm deletion from user
        string strMessage = "This operation will " +
         "delete the selected EventLog and " +
         "its associated EventSources, Are you Sure?";
        if(MessageBox.Show(
         strMessage, "Confirm Deletion",
         MessageBoxButtons.YesNo) == DialogResult.Yes)
            try
            {
                // Delete the Event Log
                EventLog.Delete(cbEventLogs.Text);
                PopulateLogNames();
            }
            catch(Exception ex)
            {
                MessageBox.Show(ex.Message,
                "Error Deleting EventLog");
            }
    }
    else
        MessageBox.Show("Selected EventLog does " +
          "not Exists", "Cannot Delete EventLog");
}

private void btnWrite_Click(object sender,
                   System.EventArgs e)
{
    if (cbEventLogs.Text != "")
    {
        string strSourceName = "StepByStep14_3_" +
            cbEventLogs.Text;
```

continues

continued

```
// If Source exists
if(EventLog.SourceExists(strSourceName))
    try
    {
        // Write an entry into event log
        EventLog.WriteEntry(strSourceName,
                      this.txtMessage.Text,
            this.eletEntryType);
        MessageBox.Show(
            "Entry Written to the " +
            "log Successfully");
    }
    catch(Exception ex)
    {
        MessageBox.Show(ex.Message,
          "Cannot Write to selected EventLog");
    }
    else
        MessageBox.Show(
            "There is no EventSource " +
            "for selected EventLog",
            "Event logging Failed");
    }
    else
        MessageBox.Show("Please Select an EventLog " +
                "to Write to.");
}
```

EXAM TIP

Deleting an Event Log   You should use the Delete() method to delete an event log cautiously. When an event log is deleted, all event sources registered with it are also deleted, so no application can continue writing to that log. Do not attempt to delete an event log that was created by Windows or any other application that is important to you; if you do, those applications might crash or behave in unexpected ways.

8. Add the following event handler in the class definition. Attach this event handler to all the RadioButton controls on the form:

```
private void rbEventType_CheckedChanged(
    object sender, System.EventArgs e)
{
    // Set the eletEntryType member
    if (sender == rbWarning)
        eletEntryType = EventLogEntryType.Warning;
    else if (sender == rbInformation)
        eletEntryType = EventLogEntryType.Information;
    else if (sender == rbSuccessAudit)
        eletEntryType =
            EventLogEntryType.SuccessAudit;
    else if (sender == rbFailureAudit)
        eletEntryType =
            EventLogEntryType.FailureAudit;
    else
        eletEntryType = EventLogEntryType.Error;
}
```

9. Set the project StepByStep14_3 as the startup project.

10. Run the project. Enter a name in the ComboBox control to create a source and log in to the System event log. Select from the combo box the log in which you want to write, enter the message in the message text box, select the type of the message from the radio button options, and click the Write button to write to the event log.

11. To view the logged messages, navigate to Server Explorer, expand the Servers node, and then select and expand the node that corresponds to your computer. Right-click the Events node and select Launch Event Viewer from the shortcut menu. This has the same effect as launching the Event Viewer from the Administrative Tools section of Windows Control Panel. Figure 14.6 shows the contents of a custom event log that is created by using the project StepByStep14_3.

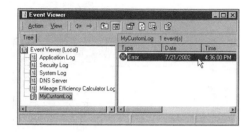

FIGURE 14.6
You can use the Windows Event Viewer to view the contents of the event logs.

> **NOTE**
>
> **The Security Log** The security log is read-only for all the users.

Reading and Listening to Event Logs

To read the contents of an event log, you can access the Entries property of the EventLog object. This property returns an EventLogEntryCollection object, and each of the elements in this collection object gives you access to an individual event log entry.

You can listen to an event log by registering an event handler for the EntryWritten event. However, before that, you have to set the EnableRaisingEvents property of the EventLog object to true.

> **NOTE**
>
> **Reading Entries from Remote Machines** Although the EventLog class allows you to access event log entries for the remote machines, it does not allow you to dynamically get notification for entries written to event logs on remote machines. You can only attach an event handler to the EntryWritten event for event logs on local machines.

GUIDED PRACTICE EXERCISE 14.2

In this exercise, you are required to create a Windows form like the one shown in Figure 14.7. Your objective is to select an event log and get its content. The application should be able to get dynamic notifications of any messages written to the event log after you first read it. You can test this application by using it along with the program written in Step by Step 14.3 to write to an event log.

How would you create such a form?

> **WARNING**
>
> **Listening to EventLog** The system responds to WriteEntry only if the last write event occurred at least five seconds previously. This means that if an application is writing to an event log too quickly, you might lose notifications for some of the recent entries written to the event log.

continues

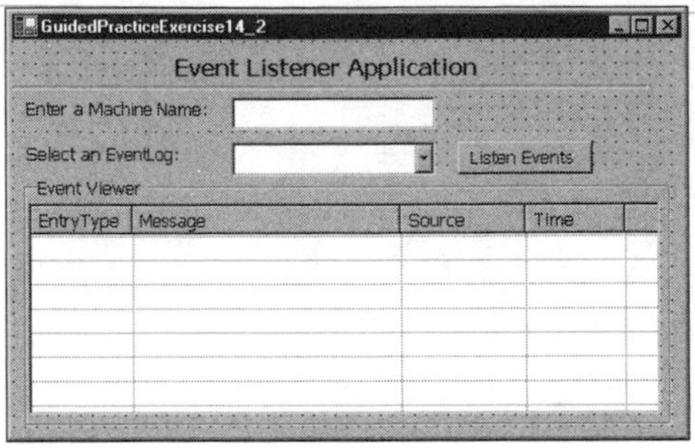

FIGURE 14.7

A possible design of a form that allows you to listen to a selected event log on a specified machine.

Referring to the Local Machine   You can easily refer to the local machine in all event log–related classes by specifying the local machine's name as a single dot (.).

continued

You should try working through this problem on your own first. If you get stuck, or if you'd like to see one possible solution, follow these steps:

1. Add a Visual C# Windows application project to the solution. Name the project GuidedPracticeExercise14_2.

2. Rename the Form1.cs file GuidedPracticeExercise14_2.cs in the project. Switch to the code view of the form and modify all references to Form1 so that they refer to GuidedPracticeExercise14_2 instead.

3. Place three Label controls, one TextBox control (txtMachineName), one Button control (btnListen), one ComboBox control (cbEventLogs), and one ListView control (lvwEvents) on the form. Add four column headers—Entry Type (chEntryType), Message (chMessage), Source (chSource), and Time (chTime)—to the ListView control. Arrange the controls as shown in Figure 14.7.

4. Add a new method named PopulateLogNames() and the form's Load event handler to the class definition:

```csharp
private void PopulateLogNames()
{
    cbEventLogs.Items.Clear();
    foreach(EventLog el in
      EventLog.GetEventLogs(txtMachineName.Text))
        cbEventLogs.Items.Add(el.Log);
}
private void GuidedPracticeExercise14_2_Load(
    object sender, System.EventArgs e)
{
    txtMachineName.Text =
        SystemInformation.ComputerName;
    // Add eventlogs in to the combo box.
    PopulateLogNames();
}
```

5. Attach an event handler to the Leave event of the txtMachineName control:

```csharp
private void txtMachineName_Leave(
  object sender, System.EventArgs e)
{
    try
    {
```

```
        // Add eventlogs in to the combo box.
        PopulateLogNames();
    }
    catch (Exception)
    {
        MessageBox.Show(
            "Please Enter a Different Computer Name",
       "Cannot Access EventLog for SpecifiedComputer");
        txtMachineName.Focus();
        txtMachineName.SelectAll();
    }
}
```

6. Add a `Click` event handler to the `Button` control and add the following the code to the class definition:

```
private void btnListen_Click(object sender,
System.EventArgs e)
{
    EventLog eventLog = new EventLog(cbEventLogs.Text,
        txtMachineName.Text);
    lvwEvents.Items.Clear();

    // Check if the machine to listen for events
    // is local machine
    if(this.txtMachineName.Text ==
      SystemInformation.ComputerName)
    {
        // Allow the Event log to raise events
        // Add an event handler for the EntryWritten
        // event
        eventLog.EnableRaisingEvents = true;
        eventLog.EntryWritten += new
          EntryWrittenEventHandler(
            eventLog_EntryWritten);
    }
    else
        MessageBox.Show(
            "EventLog class can't receive" +
            "notifications from remote computers." +
            " This program will just read the " +
            "current state of EventLog");

    foreach(EventLogEntry ele in eventLog.Entries)
    {
        // Add the entry in to the list view
        AddEntryToListView(ele);
    }
}

private void eventLog_EntryWritten(object source,
    EntryWrittenEventArgs e)
{
```

continues

continued

```
        // Add the entry in to the list view
        AddEntryToListView(e.Entry);
    }
    public void AddEntryToListView(EventLogEntry ele)
    {
        try
        {
            ListViewItem lviItem =
                new ListViewItem(new string[]
                    {
                        ele.EntryType.ToString(),
                        ele.Message.Trim(),
                        ele.Source,
                        ele.TimeGenerated.ToString()
                    });
            lvwEvents.Items.Add(lviItem);
        }
        catch(Exception ex)
        {
            Debug.WriteLine(ex.Message);
        }
    }
}
```

7. In Solution Explorer, right-click the solution and select Properties from the context menu. Select Startup Project from the left pane and choose the Multiple Startup Projects option. Select Start Action for StepByStep14_3 and GuidedPracticeExercise14_2 to set both projects as startup projects.

8. Run the application. In the form GuidedPracticeExercise14_2, select the desired log from the combo box and click the Listen Events button. A list of events that are maintained in the log appears. You can use the StepByStep14_3 form to add events to the log. Switch to the GuidedPracticeExercise14_2 form. The newly added event is added to the list view (see Figure 14.8).

If you have difficulty following this exercise, review the section "Reading and Listening to Event Logs," earlier in this chapter. After doing that review, try this exercise again.

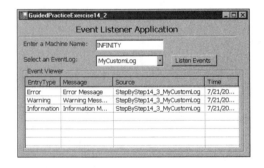

FIGURE 14.8
The Event Listener Application listens to events from the selected event log and dynamically updates the user interface.

WORKING WITH PERFORMANCE COUNTERS

Performance counters are the Windows way of collecting performance data from running processes. Microsoft Windows itself provides several hundred performance counters, each of which monitors a particular system parameter. In addition, various .NET server products, such as SQL Server, Exchange Server, and the various .NET Framework applications, also publish their own custom performance counters.

Windows organizes performance counters into categories. Each category defines a specific set of performance counters. For example, there are categories such as Memory, Processor, and PhysicalDisk. The Memory category has various counters such as Available Bytes, Cache Bytes, and Committed Bytes.

Some categories are further divided into instances. For example, the Process category is divided into several instances, each representing a running process on the computer. A new instance is added to the category whenever a new process is started, and the instance is removed when a process is killed. Each instance can have performance counters (such as I/O Read Bytes/sec) that specify the memory activity of a process. Usually all the instances in a category have the same list of performance counters. Of course each of the performance counters has unique performance data associated with it.

The PerformanceCounter class allows you to read performance samples for processes that are running on the local computer or on remote machines. By using this class, an application can even publish its own performance counter to inform the world about its performance level.

Table 14.4 lists some important members of the PerformanceCounter class.

	TABLE 14.4

SOME IMPORTANT MEMBERS OF THE PerformanceCounter CLASS

Member	Type	Description
CategoryName	Property	Specifies the performance counter category name.
Close()	Method	Closes the performance counter and frees all the resources.
CounterHelp	Property	Specifies the performance counter description.
CounterName	Property	Specifies the performance counter name.
CounterType	Property	Specifies the performance counter type.
Decrement()	Method	Decrements the performance counter value by one.
Increment()	Method	Increments the performance counter value by one.
IncrementBy()	Method	Increments or decrements the performance counter value by a specified amount.
InstanceName	Property	Specifies the instance name.
MachineName	Property	Specifies the computer name.
NextSample()	Method	Returns an object of type CounterSample that has properties such as RawValue, BaseValue, TimeStamp, and SystemFrequency. These properties provide detailed information on the performance data.
NextValue()	Method	Retrieves the current calculated value (a float type) for a performance counter.
RawValue	Property	Retrieves the raw, or uncalculated, value for a performance counter.
ReadOnly	Property	Indicates whether the PerformanceCounter object is in read-only mode.
RemoveInstance()	Method	Deletes an instance from the PerformanceCounter object.

NOTE

Performance Counters on Remote Machines   You can only read from (not modify) performance counters on remote machines. You can create custom performance counters only on the local computer.

Reading Performance Data of Running Processes

The process of reading a performance counter value is referred to as *sampling* the performance counter. When you sample a performance counter, you get a value that specifies the performance level of the process being monitored at that particular instant. The value of the performance counter may vary rapidly. A good way to analyze a performance counter is to graph sample values over time. Windows provides the Performance Monitoring tool (`perfmon.exe`) for this very purpose. You can quickly launch this tool by selecting Start, Run and typing `perfmon.exe` in the Run dialog box. You can also access it through the Performance option in the Administrative Tools section of Windows Control Panel.

Although tools such as `perfmon.exe` make it simple to monitor the performance of an application, it is sometimes also useful to read the values programmatically. This can be useful, for example, when you want a program to monitor the performance of another program and take actions depending on the performance data from that program. For example, you might want to run a processor-intensive `SalesAnalysis` application at a time when the critical `DownloadWebOrders` process is idle.

You can easily access the performance monitors installed on a computer through Server Explorer in Visual Studio .NET. You can drag and drop the performance counter of your choice to create an instance of a `PerformanceCounter` component. Step by Step 14.4 demonstrates how to use an instance of a `PerformanceCounter` component to monitor the currently available memory on a computer.

STEP BY STEP

14.4 Reading Performance Data

1. Add a Visual C# Windows application project to the solution. Name the project `StepByStep14_4`.

2. Rename the `Form1.cs` file `StepByStep14_4.cs` in the project. Switch to the code view of the form and modify all references to `Form1` so that they refer to `StepByStep14_4` instead.

continues

continued

3. Place a label control and a `ListView` control
(`lvwPerformance`) on the form. Add to the `ListView` control four column headers: CounterName
(`chChounterName`), Counter Type (`chCounterType`), Time
Stamp (`chTimeStamp`), and Raw Value (`chRawValue`).

4. Drag a `Timer` component onto the form. Set the Enabled
property to `true` and the `Interval` property to `1000`.

5. Open Server Explorer and select the server from the
Servers node. Select the Available Bytes performance
counter by navigating to Performance Counters, Memory,
Available Bytes from the server node (see Figure 14.9).
Drag the Available Bytes counter to the form, and name
the counter `pcMemory`.

6. Switch to the code view. Add the following using directive:

```
using System.Diagnostics;
```

7. Attach an event handler to the `Tick` event of the `Timer`
control and add the following code in the event handler:

```
private void timer1_Tick(
    object sender, System.EventArgs e)
{
    // Get the next performance data
    // Add the data to the ListView
    CounterSample csSample = pcMemory.NextSample();
    ListViewItem lviItem =
        new ListViewItem(new String[]
        {
            pcMemory.CounterName,
            csSample.CounterType.ToString(),
            csSample.TimeStamp.ToString(),
            csSample.RawValue.ToString()
        });
    this.lvwPerformance.Items.Add(lviItem);
}
```

8. Set project `StepByStep14_4` as the startup project.

9. Run the project. Every second, new performance counter
data is added as a new row to the list view in the Available
Bytes counter, as shown in Figure 14.10.

FIGURE 14.9
Server Explorer gives you access to a variety of
performance counters that are installed on your
computer.

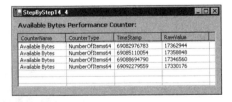

FIGURE 14.10
You can read the value of a performance
counter by using the `PerformanceCounter`
component.

Publishing Performance Data

The .NET Framework allows applications to create their own custom performance counters and publish their performance data. This performance data can then be monitored via the Performance Monitoring tool (perfmon.exe), or it can be monitored through any other application, such as the one you will create at the end of this chapter, in Exercise 14.2.

Visual Studio .NET makes it easy for you to create new performance categories and counters: It provides the Performance Counter Builder Wizard, which is available via Server Explorer. In Step by Step 14.5, you create a Windows application that publishes its performance and allows you to manually increase or decrease its performance.

STEP BY STEP

14.5 Publishing Performance Data

1. Add a Visual C# Windows application project to the solution. Name the project StepByStep14_5.

2. Rename the Form1.cs file StepByStep14_5.cs in the project. Switch to the code view of the form and modify all references to Form1 so that they refer to StepByStep14_5 instead.

3. Place five Label controls (one named lblCurrentLevel and two representing lines), one TextBox control (txtLevel), and three Button controls (btnInc, btnDec, and btnSet) on the form. Arrange the controls as shown in Figure 14.11.

4. Open Server Explorer and select from the Servers node the server in which you want to create a performance counter. Right-click the Performance Counters node and select the New Category option. The Performance Counter Builder dialog box appears. Enter the values in the dialog box, as shown in Figure 14.12, and then click OK.

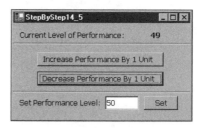

FIGURE 14.11
You can publish custom performance data for an application.

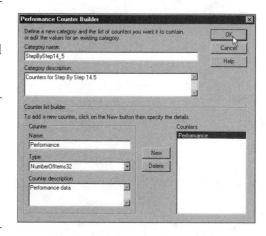

FIGURE 14.12
The Performance Counter Builder dialog box allows you to create a new performance counter category and specify one or more counters to be placed within it.

continues

continued

NOTE

Creating a Custom Performance Counter   When you create a new performance counter, you must specify a completely new category for your local computer. It is not possible to add a new performance counter to an existing category; however, you can add several performance counters to a new custom category.

It is also possible to create performance counter categories programmatically by using the PerformanceCounterCategory.Create() method.

5. Select the `StepByStep14_5` performance counter from the Performance Counters node in Server Explorer. Drag the performance counter that appears under the `StepByStep14_5` node to the form. Set the `Name` of the counter to `pc14_5` and the `ReadOnly` property to `false`.

6. Switch to the code view. Add the following using directive:

```
using System.Diagnostics;
```

7. Attach `Click` event handlers to the button controls and add the following code in the event handlers:

```
private void btnSet_Click(
    object sender, System.EventArgs e)
{
    // Set the performance counter value
    pc14_5.RawValue = Int32.Parse(txtLevel.Text);
    lblCurrentLevel.Text =
        pc14_5.NextValue().ToString();
}

private void btnInc_Click(object sender,
                            System.EventArgs e)
{
    pc14_5.Increment();
    lblCurrentLevel.Text =
        pc14_5.NextValue().ToString();
}

private void btnDec_Click(object sender,
                            System.EventArgs e)
{
    pc14_5.Decrement();
    lblCurrentLevel.Text =
        pc14_5.NextValue().ToString();
}
```

8. Attach `Load` and `Closed` event handlers to the form and add the following code in the event handlers:

```
private void StepByStep14_5_Load(
    object sender, System.EventArgs e)
{
    lblCurrentLevel.Text =
        pc14_5.NextValue().ToString();
}

private void StepByStep14_5_Closed(
    object sender, System.EventArgs e)
{
```

```
        pc14_5.RawValue = 0;
}
```

9. Set the project `StepByStep14_5` as the startup project.

10. Run the project. Enter a number in the text box and click the Set button. The label immediately reflects the current value of the performance counter. Click the increment and decrement buttons and notice the value changing in the label.

▶ A process is an application that is being executed. Each running process is uniquely identified on a computer with a process identifier.

▶ The `Process` class provides a large set of properties for getting information about running processes on a local or remote machine.

▶ The System event log provides a central repository for various issues that an application may encounter while it is executing. Using an event log to record such messages not only makes the job of system administrator easy, but it allows other applications to take appropriate action when an entry is written to a log.

▶ Multiple event sources can write into an event log. However, an event source can be used to write into only one event log.

▶ By default, events of the `Process` and `EventLog` classes are not enabled. You should set the `EnableRaisingEvents` property to `true` in order to instruct these classes to raise events.

▶ Performance counters are organized in categories, and each category defines a specific set of performance counters.

▶ The process of reading a performance counter value is called sampling the performance counter. The process of updating a performance counter value is called publishing a performance counter.

DESIGNING A WINDOWS APPLICATION FOR PERFORMANCE

Optimize the performance of a Windows-based application.

You should consider designing and developing an application for good performance early in its development cycle. Removing the performance glitches early in the development cycle is much less expensive than removing them later. The cost of rewriting modules, modifying code, or redistributing an application after the application has been fully developed or deployed goes up as an application moves beyond design and into implementation.

A common practice for ensuring the quality of code is to do frequent code reviews. You should also use the tests and techniques discussed previously in this chapter to see how two coding techniques compare in terms of performance and then adopt the best one.

The following are some of the commonly acknowledged best practices for writing high-performing applications by using the .NET Framework:

◆ **Avoid frequent boxing and unboxing**—When a value type (such as `struct`) is copied to a reference type (such as `class`), the compiler needs to create an object on the heap and copy the value of the value type from the stack to this newly created object on the heap. This process is called *boxing*, and it apparently requires more overhead than simply copying from value type to value type. When you copy a reference type to a value type, the value of the object from the heap is copied to the value type in the stack. This process is called *unboxing*. You should be aware of the overhead involved in boxing and unboxing and while designing the application, you should choose to represent data by using the types that minimize this overhead.

◆ **Use the `StringBuilder` class for complex string concatenations and manipulations**—The `String` type is immutable; this means that after a string is created, it can't be modified. When you modify a string, the Common Language Runtime (CLR) in fact creates a new string based on your modifications and returns it. The original string still hangs around in memory, waiting to be garbage collected. If an application is extensively modifying strings, you should consider using the `System.Text.StringBuilder` class. This class stores the string as an array of characters. The `StringBuilder` object is mutable and does in-place modification of strings. Using `StringBuilder` may help you achieve noticeable performance gains in an application that performs numerous string manipulations.

◆ **Use `AddRange()` with collections**—A large number of collection classes provide the `AddRange()` method, which you can use to add an array of items to the collection. Using `AddRange()` is much faster than adding elements by repeatedly calling the `Add()` method inside a loop.

◆ **Use native compilation to reduce startup time**—When you compile a program by using the C# compiler, the compiler generates Microsoft Intermediate Language (MSIL) code. When the program is loaded, this MSIL code is compiled into native code by the just-in-time (JIT) compiler as it executes. When a method is called for the first time, it is slower than usual because of the additional step of compilation, but successive calls to the method will be faster than the initial call because the code has already been converted to native code. Although this behavior should meet your requirements most of the time, in some cases, you might want to optimize an application's performance, even when the functions are loaded for the first time. In such a case, you might consider using the Native Image Generator tool (`ngen.exe`) to convert an application to native code before deploying it on the target machine. This way, you get maximum performance at all times. For example, Microsoft precompiles several libraries of the .NET Framework, such as `mscorlib.dll`, `System.Drawing.dll`, and `System.Windows.Forms.dll`, before deploying them on your machine because these classes are used by most applications.

◆ **Be careful about throwing exceptions**—Exceptions are cheap, until you throw one by using the `throw` statement. Throwing exceptions is a costly operation. You should be very careful when you throw exceptions from programs, and you should use exceptions only to signify exceptional error cases. You should not use exceptions just to manage normal program flow. You can use performance counters to keep track of the number of exceptions thrown by an application.

◆ **Avoid using unmanaged code**—Calls to unmanaged components involve costly marshaling operations, and therefore the performance of these programs may deteriorate. For maximum performance, you should rewrite the unmanaged components by using one of the languages supported by the CLR. If a rewrite is not possible, you should monitor the use of the unmanaged component to see if you can reduce the number of calls between the managed and unmanaged code, possibly by doing more work in each call rather than by making frequent calls to do small tasks.

◆ **Make fewer calls across processes**—Working with distributed applications involves the additional overhead negotiating network- and application-level protocols. Network speed may also be a bottleneck. The best approach is to get more done with fewer calls across the network. Reducing the number of calls is critical when you're creating high-performance distributed applications.

◆ **Compile the application by using** `Release` **configuration**— When you are ready to deploy an application, compile it in `Release` mode rather than in the default `Debug` mode. Applications compiled using `Debug` mode may run slowly because of the presence of extra debugging code.

◆ **Avoid automatic scaling of images**—One of the overloads of the `Graphics.DrawImage()` method allows you to specify an image and a point for the upper-left corner of the location where the image needs to be drawn. In such a case, because the height and width of the image are not specified, GDI+ attempts to auto-scale the image, and auto-scaling slows down the rendering of the image. To boost performance in this case, you should specify the height and width of the image, in addition to other parameters.

◆ **Use smart clipping and invalidation**—You can achieve better painting performance by redrawing only those areas of a form that have become invalidated. Using regions can help you exclude or paint only the specified areas of a form. Also, you should consolidate all your painting logic inside the `OnPaint()` and `OnPaintBackground()` methods, and you should avoid painting in the event handlers for `Resize`, `Load`, and `Show` events.

◆ **Avoid sophisticated painting**—When you use advanced painting features such as anti-aliasing or alpha-blending, more processing is required, and this leads to relatively slow performance of the application.

◆ **Use the optimized managed providers**—System.Data.OleDb is a generic provider that can access data exposed by any OleDb provider. Managed providers are specifically optimized for some databases. For example, when you use System.Data.OleDb to connect to a SQL Server database, System.Data.OleDb first passes your request to the OLE DB COM components, which in turn translate the requests to SQL Server Native Tabular Data Stream (TDS) format. However, when you use System.Data.SqlClient, it directly constructs the TDS packets and communicates with SQL Server. The removal of the extra translation step significantly increases the data access performance. So if you are connecting to a SQL Server database, you should use System.Data.SqlClient instead of the generic System.Data. OleDb. Similarly, you should use System.Data.OracleClient for connecting to Oracle databases.

> **NOTE**
>
> **The Managed Provider for Oracle**
> The Oracle managed provider is an add-on to the .NET Framework. You can download it from www.microsoft.com/downloads/ release.asp?releaseid=40032.

◆ **Use stored procedures instead of SQL statements**—When working with a relational database management system such as SQL Server, you should use stored procedures rather than a set of SQL statements given as a text command. This is because stored procedures are highly optimized for server-side data access, and their use usually improves data access performance significantly.

◆ **Tune the database**—Keeping up-to-date indexes greatly helps in improving performance for a database-intensive Windows application. You can run SQL Server's Profiler and Index Tuning Wizard to avoid any bottlenecks that are due to indexing. In addition, you can use SQL Server Query Analyzer to optimize a query's performance.

◆ **Prefer DataReader over DataSet for forward-only sequential access**—If you are reading a table sequentially, you should use DataReader rather than DataSet. DataReader creates a read-only, forward-only stream of data that increases application performance and reduces system overhead because only one row is in memory at a time.

EXAM TIP

User Identity and Connection Pooling   In order for connection pooling to work, multiple connections to the database must use exactly the same connection strings. If you are including user identity and password information in the connection string, the connection string for user Mahesh will not match with user Mary, for example, and you instead form two separate connection pools. To gain maximum performance gains, you must use a single identity and password in the connection string to a database.

◆ **Use connection pooling for the SQL Server .NET Data Provider**—The slowest database operation is establishing connection with the database. The SQL Server .NET Data Provider provides connection pooling to improve performance when connecting to a SQL Server database. In connection pooling, old connection information is stored in a connection pool so that it can be reused for the next connection. Saving on making new connections with each request provides significant performance gains. However, if you have dynamic connection strings (that is, you change parameters of the connection strings), you effectively disallow connection pooling because connections are only pooled on the exact connect string. To maximize the reuse of connections in a connection pool, you must use the same connection string for all the connections.

◆ **Avoid using auto-generated commands**—The `SqlCommandBuilder` and `OleDbCommandBuilder` classes enable you to automatically generate commands used to reconcile changes made to a data set. Although automatic generation of `INSERT`, `UPDATE`, and `DELETE` statements for changes to a data set makes database updates very convenient, it also requires extra trips to the server to get the schema information. Therefore, you should make convenience and performance trade-offs depending on the application's requirements.

◆ **Use transactions only when required**—Distributed transactions may have significant performance overhead. As a rule of thumb, you should use transactions only when required and keep the transactions as short-lived as possible.

◆ **Improve perceived performance**—This last technique has more to do with human behavior than with actual performance of an application. Studies have shown that showing an active splash screen during application startup may make your application appear as if it is loading faster. Similarly, showing a progress bar for long operation keeps users informed and in communication with the application. You can use these techniques to improve the perceived performance of your application.

CHAPTER SUMMARY

This chapter discusses the use of `Process`, `EventLog`, `PerformanceCounter`, and related classes that help in managing and monitoring Windows applications.

This chapter also discusses some well-known techniques for optimizing the performance of Windows applications. If you judiciously use these techniques while designing and developing applications, you might see a significant performance gain.

KEY TERMS

- boxing
- performance counter
- process
- unboxing

APPLY YOUR KNOWLEDGE

Exercises

14.1 Getting Module Information for a Process

When a process executes, it loads several other modules (generally .dll files) to help perform its functions. By using the Process class, you can determine what modules are loaded by an application. For each module, you can also determine various details, such as version number, entry point address, and memory size.

In this exercise, you learn how to work with the ProcessModule class and the ProcessModuleCollection class to get information about the modules loaded by a process that is executing.

Estimated time: 25 minutes

1. Launch Visual Studio .NET. Select File, New, Blank Solution, and name the new solution 316C14Exercises.

2. Add a new Windows application project to the solution. Name the project Exercise14_1.

3. Rename the Form1.cs file Exercise14_1.cs in the project. Switch to the code view of the form and modify all references to Form1 so that they refer to Exercise14_1 instead.

4. Place six Label controls (two representing lines), two TextBox controls (txtMachine and txtModuleInfo), one Button control (btnLoad), one ListBox control (lbModules), and a ListView control (lvwProcesses) on the form. Add two column headers, Process Name (chProcessName) and Process Id (chProcessId), to the ListView control. Set the MultiLine property of txtModuleInfo to true. Arrange the controls as shown in Figure 14.13.

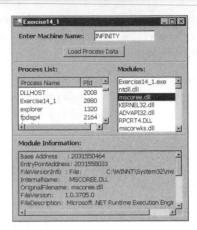

FIGURE 14.13
You can use the Modules property of the Process class to retrieve information about the modules that are loaded by the process.

5. Switch to the code view. Add the following using directive:

```
using System.Diagnostics;
using System.Text;
```

6. Add the following code in the class definition:

```
// Create a string member to
// hold the Machine Name
private string strMachineName;
```

7. Attach a Load event handler to the form, a Click event handler to the btnLoad control, and a SelectedIndexChanged event handler to the lvwProcesses and lbModules controls. Add the following code in the event handlers:

```
private void Exercise14_1_Load(
    object sender, System.EventArgs e)
{
    // Set the textbox with the
    // System ComputerName
    strMachineName = txtMachine.Text =
        SystemInformation.ComputerName;
}
```

APPLY YOUR KNOWLEDGE

```csharp
private void btnLoad_Click(
   object sender, System.EventArgs e)
{
    // Get the Machine name
    // Clear the listview, listbox
    // and textbox controls
    strMachineName = txtMachine.Text;
    lvwProcesses.Items.Clear();
    lbModules.Items.Clear();
    txtModuleInfo.Clear();
    try
    {
        // Get all the processes
        Process[] arrProcesses =
       Process.GetProcesses(strMachineName);
        foreach(Process p in arrProcesses)
        {
            // Add each process into the
            // lvwProcesses
            ListViewItem lvwItem =
              new ListViewItem(
                new string[]
                {p.ProcessName,
                 p.Id.ToString()});
            lvwProcesses.Items.Add(lvwItem);
        }
    }
    catch(Exception ex)
    {
        MessageBox.Show(ex.Message);
    }
}

private void
  lvwProcesses_SelectedIndexChanged(
  object sender, System.EventArgs e)
{
    lbModules.Items.Clear();
    txtModuleInfo.Clear();
    int intProcessId =
        Convert.ToInt32(
this.lvwProcesses.FocusedItem.SubItems[1].
    Text);
    try
    {
        Process p = Process.GetProcessById
           (intProcessId, strMachineName);
        foreach(ProcessModule pm
           in p.Modules)
        {
            lbModules.Items.Add(
                pm.ModuleName);
        }
```

```csharp
    }
    catch(Exception ex)
    {
        Debug.WriteLine(ex.Message);
    }
}

private void lbModules_SelectedIndexChanged
    (object sender, System.EventArgs e)
{
    txtModuleInfo.Clear();
    int intProcessId = Convert.ToInt32(
this.lvwProcesses.FocusedItem.SubItems[1].
    Text);
    try
    {
        // Get the Process Id of the
        // selected process
        Process p = Process.GetProcessById
           (intProcessId, strMachineName);
        // Get the Modules of the
        // selected process
        // Add module information to the
        // txtModuleInfo control
        foreach(ProcessModule pm
           in p.Modules)
        {
            if (pm.ModuleName ==
           lbModules.SelectedItem.ToString())
            {
                StringBuilder sb =
                    new StringBuilder();
                sb.Append(String.Format
                   ("Base Address     : {0}",
                   pm.BaseAddress.ToString()));
                sb.Append(String.Format
                ("\r\nEntryPointAddress: {0}",
                    pm.EntryPointAddress));
                sb.Append(String.Format
                  ("\r\nFileVersionInfo  : {0}",
                 pm.FileVersionInfo.ToString()));
                sb.Append(String.Format
                   ("\r\nModuleMemorySize : {0}",
                 pm.ModuleMemorySize.ToString()));
                txtModuleInfo.Text = sb.ToString();
                break;
            }
        }
    }
    catch(Exception ex)
    {
        Debug.WriteLine(ex.Message);
    }
}
```

8. Set the project Exercise14_1 as the startup project.

9. Run the project. Your computer name appears in the Enter Machine Name text box. Change the value if you want and then click the Load Process Data button. A list of all the running processes appears in the Process List list view. Select a process from the list. Its modules are listed in the list box. Select a module from the list box to obtain its information, as shown in Figure 14.13.

14.2 Getting Performance Information

Performance counters are categorized either by operating system or by the application that created them. Each performance counter category may also have zero or more instances. When a category has instances, you must specify the instance name along with the category when you want to read the value of a performance counter.

In this exercise, you create a performance monitor application that is similar to Windows perfmon.exe but does not draw graphs for performance. Instead, it just lists the raw value of the performance every second.

Estimated time: 35 minutes

1. Add a new Windows application project to the solution. Name the project Exercise14_2.

2. Rename the Form1.cs file Exercise14_2.cs in the project. Switch to the code view of the form and modify all references to Form1 so that they refer to Exercise14_2 instead.

3. Place two TextBox controls (txtMachineName and txtDescription), one ComboBox control (cbCategories), two ListBox controls (lbCounters and lbInstances), and a ListView control (lvwPerformance) on the form.

Add four column headers—Counter Name (chChounterName), Counter Type (chCounterType), Time Stamp (chTimeStamp), and Raw Value (chRawValue)—to the ListView control. Arrange the controls as shown in Figure 14.14.

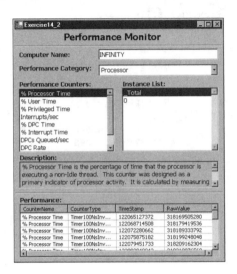

FIGURE 14.14
This performance monitor application is similar to Windows perfmon.exe.

4. Drag a Timer component (timer1) onto the form. Set its Enabled property to true and its Interval property to 1000.

5. Switch to the code view. Add the following using directive:

```
using System.Diagnostics;
```

6. Add the following code in the class definition. Attach the ListBox_SelectedIndexChanged event handler to the SelectedIndexChanged event of each ListBox control:

```
//currently selected performance counter
private PerformanceCounter pcCurrent;
private void PopulateCategoryList()
{
    this.cbCategories.Items.Clear();
    this.lvwPerformance.Items.Clear();
    this.lbCounters.Items.Clear();
    this.lbInstances.Items.Clear();

    // Get all the Performance Counter
    // category objects for the machine
    PerformanceCounterCategory [] pcc =
    PerformanceCounterCategory.GetCategories
    (this.txtMachineName.Text);
    // populate the category list
    // with category names
    foreach(PerformanceCounterCategory p
       in pcc)
        cbCategories.Items.Add(
            p.CategoryName);
}

// Event handler for SelectedIndexChaged
// event of both ListBoxes.
private void ListBox_SelectedIndexChanged
    (object sender, System.EventArgs e)
{
    timer1.Enabled = false;
    ListBox lb = sender as ListBox;
    // Select the appropriate item
    if(lb.Name == "lbCounters")
        if(lbInstances.Items.Count > 0 &&
            lbInstances.SelectedIndex == -1)
                lbInstances.SelectedIndex = 0;
    else
        if(lbCounters.Items.Count > 0 &&
            lbCounters.SelectedIndex == -1)
                lbCounters.SelectedIndex = 0;

    lvwPerformance.Items.Clear();
    PerformanceCounterCategory pcc =
        new PerformanceCounterCategory(
    (string)this.cbCategories.SelectedItem);
    PerformanceCounter pc;
    // get the PerformanceCounter object
    // based on current selection
    pc = new PerformanceCounter(
     pcc.CategoryName,
     (string)lbCounters.SelectedItem,
     (string)this.lbInstances.SelectedItem,
     this.txtMachineName.Text);
    pcCurrent = pc;
```

```
    //Display Description of
    //selected counter
    this.txtDescription.Text =
        pc.CounterHelp;
    // Enable the timer so that it can
    // update performance data for
    // the selected counter, every second
    timer1.Enabled = true;
}
```

7. Attach a Load event handler to the Form control, a Leave event handler to the TextBox control, a SelectedIndexChanged event handler to the ComboBox control, and a Tick event handler to the Timer control. Add the following code in the event handlers:

```
private void StepByStep14_4_Load(
    object sender, System.EventArgs e)
{
    // Get the name of local computer
    this.txtMachineName.Text =
        SystemInformation.ComputerName;
    // populate performance category list
    this.PopulateCategoryList();
}

private void txtMachineName_Leave(
    object sender, System.EventArgs e)
{
    // disable the timer so that no
    // performance data is updated
    timer1.Enabled = false;
    try
    {
        // Re-populate the category list if
        // a machine name is changed
        PopulateCategoryList();
    }
    catch (Exception)
    {
        // Alert user about
        // incorrect machine name
        MessageBox.Show(
        "Please Enter a Different " +
        "Computer Name",
        "Cannot Access PerformanceCounter"+
        " for Specified Computer");
        txtMachineName.Focus();
        txtMachineName.SelectAll();
    }
}
```

APPLY YOUR KNOWLEDGE

```
private void
   cbCategories_SelectedIndexChanged
   (object sender, System.EventArgs e)
{
   // disable the timer so that no
   // performance  data is updated
   timer1.Enabled = false;
   lbCounters.Items.Clear();
   lbInstances.Items.Clear();
   lvwPerformance.Items.Clear();

   // Get PerformanceCounter Categories
   // from the selected machine
   PerformanceCounterCategory pcc
       = new PerformanceCounterCategory
   (cbCategories.SelectedItem.ToString(),
      txtMachineName.Text);
   string [] arrInstanceNames =
      pcc.GetInstanceNames();
   lbInstances.Items.AddRange(
      arrInstanceNames);

   if(arrInstanceNames.Length == 0)
      foreach(PerformanceCounter pc
          in pcc.GetCounters())
            lbCounters.Items.Add(
               pc.CounterName);
   else
       foreach(PerformanceCounter pc in
      pcc.GetCounters(arrInstanceNames[0]))
         lbCounters.Items.Add(pc.CounterName);

}

private void timer1_Tick(
   object sender, System.EventArgs e)
{
   // Get the current performance data
   // for the selected counter
   CounterSample csSample =
       pcCurrent.NextSample();
   // Populate details in lvwPerformance
   ListViewItem lviItem =
     new ListViewItem(new String[]
       {
          pcCurrent.CounterName,
          csSample.CounterType.ToString(),
          csSample.TimeStamp.ToString(),
          csSample.RawValue.ToString()
       });
   this.lvwPerformance.Items.Add(lviItem);
}
```

8. Set project `Exercise14_2` as the startup project.

9. Run the project. Your system computer name appears in the Computer Name text box. Change the value if you want and then select a category from the Performance Category list box. A list of all the performance counters in the performance category selected appears, and a list of the instances listed in the Instances List list box appears. Select the desired performance counter and instance. The most recent data from the selected performance counter is added as a new row to the `ListView` control every second, as shown in Figure 14.14.

Review Questions

1. How do you stop a process that has a user interface? How do you stop a process that does not have a user interface?

2. What types of messages can you write into a message log?

3. Explain the terms *sampling a performance counter* and *publishing a performance counter*?

4. What is the purpose of the Native Image Generator tool (ngen.exe)?

5. When should you use `SqlDataReader` instead of `DataSet` for reading data?

Exam Questions

1. You have developed a database-intensive Windows forms application for a large pharmaceutical company. The database for the application is SQL Server 2000. Users of your application are complaining about the consistently slow nature of some reports.

APPLY YOUR KNOWLEDGE

Which of the following actions would you take to increase the performance of this application? (Select the two best answers.)

A. Compile the application to native code by using ngen.exe.

B. Run the SQL Server Index Tuning Wizard.

C. Convert all SQL statements to SQL Server stored procedures.

D. Add a PerformanceMonitor component to the code.

2. You have recently deployed an expense reporting system in your company. The application relies heavily on its SQL Server database. All employees in the company have similar access permissions to the database. You have created the application in such a way that it uses each employee's login name and password in the connection string to connect to SQL Server. Users of the application have reported significantly slow performance. Your task is to optimize the performance of this application. Which of the following steps would you take?

A. Compile the application to native code by using ngen.exe.

B. Run the SQL Server Index Tuning Wizard.

C. Increase the maximum size of the connection pool.

D. Use the same connection strings for each user.

3. You are designing a database-intensive Windows application for a large publishing house. You want to get maximum performance from the SQL queries that run to populate a combo box from a SQL Server database. Which of the following code segments would give you the fastest performance?

A.

```
SqlConnection conn =
    new SqlConnection(connStr);
conn.Open();
DataSet ds = new DataSet();
SqlDataAdapter ad = new SqlDataAdapter
    ("select * from authors", conn);
ad.Fill(ds);
```

B.

```
OleDbConnection conn =
    new OleDbConnection(connStr);
conn.Open();
DataSet ds = new DataSet();
OleDbDataAdapter ad = new OleDbDataAdapter
    ("select * from authors", conn);
ad.Fill(ds);
```

C.

```
SqlConnection conn =
    new SqlConnection(connStr);
SqlCommand cmd = new SqlCommand
    ("select * from authors", connStr);
conn.Open();
SqlDataReader reader;
reader = cmd.ExecuteReader();
```

D.

```
OleDbConnection conn =
    new OleDbConnection(connStr);
OleDbCommand cmd = new OleDbCommand
    ("select * from authors", connStr);
conn.Open();
OleDbDataReader reader;
reader = cmd.ExecuteReader();
```

4. You are working on a process management application that launches a Windows form, passes some keystrokes to the form, and then closes the application. Which of the following methods is the best method to use to close this application?

A. Close()

B. CloseMainWindow()

C. Dispose()

D. Kill()

APPLY YOUR KNOWLEDGE

5. You have developed a Windows application that calls large numbers of methods when the application is started. The application is database intensive and uses SQL Server as its database. Users are complaining about the slow startup time of the application. In order to improve the performance of the application, what would you do?

A. Use ngen.exe.

B. Use gacutil.exe.

C. Use the SQL Server Index Tuning Wizard.

D. Increase the size of the connection pool.

6. You are designing a Windows application that monitors the Application log for errors from a shipping and labeling application. You have written the following code in your application.

```
EventLog eventLog = new
    EventLog("Application", ".");
eventLog.EntryWritten +=
    new EntryWrittenEventHandler
    (eventLog_EntryWritten);
```

You are not receiving any notifications for the error. What should you do so this code will be notified of new event log entries?

A. Set eventLog.Enabled to true.

B. Set eventLog.EnableRaisingEvents to true.

C. Set eventLog.Enabled to false.

D. Set eventLog.EnableRaisingEvents to false.

7. Which of the following statements are true with respect to Windows performance counters? (Select the two best answers.)

A. Performance counters are categorized into performance counter categories.

B. Each performance counter category has zero or more instances associated with it

C. Each performance counter category has one or more instances associated with it.

D. Each instance has zero or more performance counter categories associated with it.

8. Which of the following statements is false with respect to the EventLog class?

A. You cannot write to any event log on a remote machine.

B. You can write to all event logs on a local machine.

C. You cannot get event-driven notifications when an entry is written to an event log on a remote machine.

D. You can get event-driven notifications when an entry is written to an event log on a local machine.

9. You have created an expense reporting system for a small manufacturing company. All computers in the company use Microsoft Excel as their default spreadsheet program. Which of following code segments would open the ExpenseReport.xls file by using Microsoft Excel on the user's computer?

A.
```
Process.Start(new ProcessStartInfo(
    "ExpenseReport.xls"));
```

B.
```
Process.Start(new ProcessStartInfo
        ("Excel ExpenseReport.xls"));
```

C.
```
Process.Start(new ProcessStartInfo(
    "Excel ExpenseReport"));
```

D.
```
Process.Start(new ProcessStartInfo
        ("Excel", "ExpenseReport.xls"));
```

APPLY YOUR KNOWLEDGE

10. You have created an expense reporting system for a small manufacturing company. The system allows users to launch expense files for editing in Microsoft Excel. Generally, the employees keep the editing session open for a long time; meanwhile, they need to select other options from the expense reporting system to verify what they are editing. You want to know when the user has finished editing the file so that you can archive it for later retrieval. Which of the following members of the Process class would be the best choice for achieving this? (Select the two best answers.)

    A. WaitForExit()

    B. HasExited

    C. Exited

    D. EnableRaisingEvents

11. You recently developed an expense reporting system. When you deployed the application, you found that some of the features of the application were not working as expected. You suspected that the application was using old versions of some of its components. You then created a small test application to get all the modules loaded by the application. Your program contains the following segment of code:

```
1:  Process p = Process.Start
       (new ProcessStartInfo(
          "ExpenseReport.exe "));
2:
3:  ProcessModuleCollection pmc =
       Process.GetProcessById(p.Id).Modules;
```

    When you analyzed the resulting collection of modules, you noted that not all the modules that were actually being used by the application were added to the ProcessModuleCollection object.

    To rectify this problem, which of the following statements would you add as line 2?

    A.
    ```
    p.Refresh();
    ```

    B.
    ```
    p.WaitForInputIdle();
    ```

    C.
    ```
    p.WaitForExit();
    ```

    D.
    ```
    p.CreateObjRef();
    ```

12. You have written an application that publishes its own custom performance counter. You want to decrease the value of the performance counter by 5. Which of the following methods is the best method to use to do this?

    A. Decrement()

    B. Increment()

    C. IncrementBy()

    D. NextValue()

13. You want to determine whether a given event log exists on a remote machine. Which of the following methods is the most efficient method to use to determine this?

    A. Exists()

    B. SourceExists()

    C. GetEventLogs()

    D. LogNameFromSourceName()

APPLY YOUR KNOWLEDGE

14. You want to create a high-performing graphics application. You have created several variations of a method that draws an image. Which of the following methods would have the best performance?

    A.

    ```
    public void DrawSampleImage(
        PaintEventArgs e)
    {
        Image newImage =
         Image.FromFile("SampImag.jpg");
        Point ulCorner = new Point(
          100, 100);
        e.Graphics.DrawImage(
          newImage, ulCorner);
    }
    ```

    B.

    ```
    public void DrawSampleImage(
        PaintEventArgs e)
    {
        Image newImage =
          Image.FromFile("SampImag.jpg");
        int x = 100;
        int y = 100;
        e.Graphics.DrawImage(
          newImage, x, y);
    }
    ```

    C.

    ```
    public void DrawSampleImage(
        PaintEventArgs e)
    {
        Image newImage =
          Image.FromFile("SampImag.jpg");
        Rectangle destRect =
            new Rectangle(
             100, 100, 450, 150);
        e.Graphics.DrawImage(
          newImage, destRect);
    }
    ```

    D.

    ```
    public void DrawSampleImage(
        PaintEventArgs e)
    {
        Image newImage =
           Image.FromFile("SampImag.jpg");
        float x = 100.0F;
        float y = 100.0F;
        e.Graphics.DrawImage(newImage, x, y);
    }
    ```

15. Which of the following coding constructs would have a negative impact on an application's performance and should be used cautiously?

    A. try

    B. catch

    C. finally

    D. throw

Answers to Review Questions

1. The `CloseMainWindow()` method of the `Process` class stops any process that participates in the Windows message loop and has a user interface. The `Kill()` method of the `Process` class stops any process that does not have a user interface or that does not participate in the Windows message loop. You can also use the `Kill()` method to kill applications that have interfaces.

2. The different types of messages that can be written into the event log are specified in the `EventLogEntryType` enumeration. The possible types are `Error`, `FailureAudit`, `Information`, `SuccessAudit`, and `Warning`.

3. The process of reading a performance counter value is known as sampling the performance counter. The process of updating a performance counter value is known as publishing a performance counter.

4. You use the Native Image Generator tool (ngen.exe) to convert an application to native code before deploying it on the target machine.

5. SqlDataReader provides high-performance data access for reading forward-only, read-only data. You should therefore use SqlDataReader instead of DataSet when you are reading data sequentially and updates are not required.

Answers to Exam Questions

1. **B** and **C.** The SQL Server's Index Tuning Wizard identifies any bottlenecks that are due to indexing. Using SQL Server stored procedure improves data access performance significantly. For more information, see the section "Designing a Windows Application for Performance" in this chapter.

2. **D.** Using different usernames and passwords when connecting to SQL Server creates a unique connection string for each database connection. This eliminates any gain that you might have because of connection pooling. To get the maximum benefit from connection pooling, you must use the same connection string every time you connect to the database. For more information, see the section "Designing a Windows Application for Performance" in this chapter.

3. **C.** When you are working with a SQL Server database, using the SQL Server managed provider gives you better performance than its OleDb counterpart. Also, when you are doing sequential read-only operations such as populating a combo box, the SqlDataReader object gives better performance than the SqlDataAdapter object. For more information, see the section "Designing a Windows Application for Performance" in this chapter.

4. **B.** The preferred way to close an application that has a user interface is to use the CloseMainWindow() method. For more information, see the section "Starting and Stopping a Process" in this chapter.

5. **A.** At application startup, JIT compilation involves additional overhead. Therefore, if a large number of methods are called at startup, compiling the application to native code using ngen.exe might improve the startup performance of the application. For more information, see the section "Designing a Windows Application for Performance" in this chapter.

6. **B.** The default value for EnableRaisingEvents is false. If this property is set to false, it does not raise the EntryWritten event for the event log. You should therefore set its value to true. For more information, see the section "Working with Event Logs" in this chapter.

7. **A** and **B.** Performance counters are categorized into various categories. Each performance counter category has zero or more instances associated with it. For more information, see the section "Working with Performance Counters" in this chapter.

8. **B.** Although it is possible to write to the event logs on the local machine, it is not possible to write to all of them. The security log that is created by the operating system itself is read-only; you cannot write to it, even on a local machine. For more information, see the section "Writing to Event Logs" in this chapter.

9. **A.** When you specify a filename, when the process is started, the operating system takes the default action based on the file extension. Because Excel is the default spreadsheet program used in the company, when the process starts, the file is automatically opened by Excel. For more information, see the section "Starting and Stopping Processes" in this chapter.

10. **C** and **D.** You can attach an event handler to the Exited event of the Process object to receive notification from a process when it exits. The default value of the EnableRaisingEvents property is false, so the Exited event is not raised. You should set this property to true so that you get event notification when the process is closed. For more information, see the section "Managing a Windows Process" in this chapter.

11. **B.** You should always retrieve the modules used by an application when it is completely loaded. You can ensure that an application is loaded and is ready to start by calling the WaitForInputIdle() method on its Process object. For more information, see the section "Managing a Windows Process" in this chapter.

12. **C.** Using the IncrementBy() method is the most efficient way to increase or decrease the value of a counter by the specified amount. For more information, see the section "Publishing Performance Data" in this chapter.

13. **A.** The easiest and the most efficient way to determine whether a log exists on a local or a remote machine is to use the static Exists() method of the EventLog class. For more information, see the section "Working with Event Logs" in this chapter.

14. **C.** Answer C gives the best performance because it specifies the destination size of the image, thereby avoiding any auto-scaling of the image. For more information, see the section "Designing a Windows Application for Performance" in this chapter.

15. **D.** The throw statement has the maximum performance penalty and should be used cautiously. For more information, see the section "Designing a Windows Application for Performance" in this chapter.

APPLY YOUR KNOWLEDGE

Suggested Readings and Resources

1. Visual Studio .NET Combined Help Collection:

   - "Managing Processes"

   - "Logging Application, Server, and Security Events"

   - "Monitoring Performance Thresholds"

   - "Performance Tips and Tricks in .NET Applications"

   - "Performance Considerations for Run-Time Technologies in the .NET Framework"

2. Kevin Burton. *.NET Common Language Runtime Unleashed*. Sams, 2002.

3. The .NET Show: Code Optimization. `msdn.microsoft.com/theshow/Episode027`.

4. The .NET Show: Inside the CLR. `msdn.microsoft.com/theshow/Episode020`.

5. Microsoft Support Web Cast: "Microsoft .NET Framework Performance: Tips, Tools, and Techniques." `support.microsoft.com/default.aspx?scid=/servicedesks/webcasts/wc050102/wcblurb050102.asp`.

6. Microsoft Support WebCast: Introduction to the Common Language Runtime Profiling API. `support.microsoft.com/servicedesks/webcasts/wc022802/wcblurb022802.asp`.

This chapter covers the following Microsoft-specified objectives for the "Creating User Services" and "Configuring and Securing a Windows-Based Application" sections of Exam 70-316, "Developing and Implementing Windows-Based Applications with Microsoft Visual C# .NET and Microsoft Visual Studio .NET":

Add controls to a Windows Form.

- **Configure control licensing.**

Configure a Windows-based application.

Configure security for a Windows-based application.

- **Select and configure authentication type. Authentication types include Windows Authentication, None, forms-based, Microsoft Passport, and custom authentication.**

- **Specify the security level for an application.**

- **Use custom attributes to configure security.**

Configure authorization.

- **Configure role-based authorization.**

- **Implement identity management.**

▶ If applications were used the same way by all users in all circumstances, there would be no need for configuration options. But in the real world, you often want to be able to change things about an application, even after it's installed on the user's computer. In this chapter, I explain some of the support that Visual C# .NET offers for runtime application configuration.

CHAPTER 15

Configuring a Windows Application

▶ After taking a brief look at control licensing, I talk about three main areas of configuration. The first area is runtime configuration using dynamic properties stored in configuration files. The .NET Framework offers good support for changing the behavior of applications at runtime by editing XML configuration files.

▶ The next area is code access security. By configuring security, you can control which applications are allowed to run on the computer and what privileges they have when running. The .NET Framework offers a comprehensive set of classes and attributes to manage code access security.

▶ The third area is authorization and role-based security. With role-based security, you can tie a program's privileges to the identity of the user who is running the program. This identity management lets you assign different levels of functionality to a program, depending on the identity of the user who is currently logged on.

▶ Use Visual Studio .NET to make the properties of some controls in your applications dynamic properties. View the resulting configuration files and investigate the effects of editing those files.

▶ Use the .NET Framework Configuration tool to adjust the configuration of your computer. Check the available options for the machine and application configurations.

▶ Use the .NET Framework Configuration tool to create a security policy for a test application. Experiment with the results of setting security policies at various levels, as well as with combinations of required, optional, refused, and demanded permissions.

INTRODUCTION

As a developer, your job does not end when you deliver an application to the end user. Users expect a well-designed Windows application to be configurable with a minimum of trouble and without needing to have code rewritten. As a simple example, if your application retrieves data from a database, you should provide some way for the end user to configure the name of the database server.

Administrators, too, want to configure applications. Administrative configuration often involves setting up security. In some cases, this involves computer security, designed to keep untrusted applications from harming the operating system or the user's critical data files. In others, this involves user security, designed to control who can use a particular application.

The .NET Framework offers you substantial control of these (and other) types of configuration. Dynamic properties and configuration files make most runtime configuration tasks a simple matter of editing Extensible Markup Language (XML) files. The .NET Framework also includes a complete security system that supports both code access and role-based security.

In this chapter, you'll learn how to design and code applications to take advantage of these configuration features and how to use these features to configure .NET applications at runtime.

CONFIGURING CONTROL LICENSING

Add controls to a Windows form.

- **Configure control licensing.**

Before we look at areas where .NET applications are designed to be configured, I should mention one area where configuration is almost never necessary: control licensing. The .NET Framework provides complete support for licensing of controls (and other classes), but this support is designed to be completely unobtrusive and transparent at runtime.

When you purchase a custom control for use in applications, it typically comes with a design-time license that's good for a limited number of computers. It also comes with a runtime license that allows end users to use applications that utilize the control without allowing them to embed the control in new applications. The .NET Framework handles this through use of a `LicenseProvider` object. The default `LicenseProvider` object checks at design time for the presence of a particular text file. If that text file is present, you can insert the control on a form; if it's not present, you cannot insert the control.

Assuming that you have a design-time license, everything else about control licensing is automatic. When you compile an application, the .NET Framework automatically converts the corresponding runtime license into a binary resource and embeds it into the executable file. This resource is available to the Common Language Runtime (CLR) at runtime. There's nothing to configure and nothing for the administrator to do. The control just works.

However, as with so many other things in the .NET Framework, this licensing structure is only the default. It's perfectly possible for a control author to implement his own custom `LicenseProvider` class to handle things in some fashion other than the default. A control might, for example, look for a particular registry key, a hardware dongle, a Web service, or even a configuration file before it runs. If you run across runtime licensing errors, they almost certainly come from such a custom licensing scheme. In such a case, your best course of action is to contact the control vendor directly for assistance.

CONFIGURING A WINDOWS-BASED APPLICATION

Configure a Windows-based application.

There are times when you want to leave some options in a program open until runtime. This might be something as central as the name of a database server or something as frivolous as the background color for a form. The .NET Framework lets you manage these options by using dynamic properties. *Dynamic properties* let you store some of an application's property values to an external file, from which they are retrieved at runtime. The .NET Framework provides all the infrastructure that you need to accomplish this, and Visual Studio .NET offers built-in support for dynamic properties.

With dynamic properties, you can make changes to an application's configuration without recompiling the application.

Using Dynamic Properties

Dynamic properties are managed by the `System.Configuration.AppSettingsReader` class at runtime, but you seldom need to work with this class directly. Instead, you can use the Visual Studio .NET Integrated Development Environment (IDE) to define dynamic properties for applications.

STEP BY STEP

15.1 Using Dynamic Properties

1. Create a new Visual C# .NET Windows application. Name the application 316C15. Add a form to the application.

2. Set the Text property of the form to StepByStep15_1. Set the ShowInTaskbar property of the form to false.

3. In the form's Properties window, click the + sign next to the Dynamic Properties entry. Click in the Advanced section and then click the ellipsis (…) button. The Dynamic Properties dialog box appears.

4. In the Properties list, select the check boxes for the ShowInTaskbar and Text properties. Accept the default key mapping for each of these properties. Figure 15.1 shows the Dynamic Properties dialog box. Click OK to close the dialog box.

5. Insert the Main() method to launch the form. Set the form as the startup object for the project.

6. Run the project. The form appears with the Text property that you set, and it is not displayed in the taskbar.

7. Stop the project. Double-click the app.config file in Solution Explorer. Edit the code in the file so it looks like this:

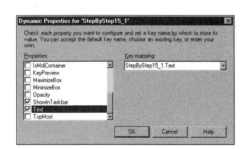

FIGURE 15.1
The Dynamic Properties dialog box allows you to configure dynamic properties by selecting the desired properties and their key names.

```
<?xml version="1.0" encoding="Windows-1252"?>
<configuration>
  <appSettings>
    <!--   User application and configured
        property settings go here.-->
    <!--   Example: <add key="settingName"
        value="settingValue"/> -->
    <add key="StepByStep15_1.ShowInTaskbar"
        value="True" />
    <add key="StepByStep15_1.Text"
        value="Set at Runtime"/>
  </appSettings>
</configuration>
```

8. Run the project again. The form has the Text property set to Set at Runtime, and it appears in the taskbar.

9. Stop the project.

10. Run the project by browsing to the bin directory of the project in Windows Explorer and double-clicking the project's executable file, 316C15.exe. The form opens with the Text property set to Set at Runtime, and it appears in the taskbar.

11. In a text editor, open the 316C15.exe.config file, which is in the project's bin\Debug or bin\Release directory. Edit the file so that it looks like this:

```
<?xml version="1.0" encoding="Windows-1252"?>
<configuration>
  <appSettings>
    <!--   User application and configured
       property settings go here.-->
    <!--   Example: <add key="settingName"
        value="settingValue"/> -->
    <add key="StepByStep15_1.ShowInTaskbar"
        value="False" />
    <add key="StepByStep15_1.Text"
        value="Compiled version" />
  </appSettings>
</configuration>
```

12. Run the project again. The form opens with the Text property set to Compiled version, and it does not appear in the taskbar.

Step by Step 15.1 demonstrates the key points of using dynamic properties for components on Windows forms:

◆ You can set any simple property (that is, any property whose value is not an instance of a class) to be a dynamic property by using the Dynamic Properties dialog box (via the Advanced section of the Dynamic Properties node in the Properties window).

◆ You can use the Properties window to edit dynamic properties, just as you can use it for other properties.

◆ When an application is running inside the IDE, the file `app.config` at the top level of the application holds the values for the dynamic properties.

◆ When you compile an application, a configuration file with the extension `.config` and the same name as the application's executable file holds the values for the dynamic properties.

Some components have default dynamic properties. For example, if you drag a SQL Server table from Server Explorer to a Windows form to create an `SqlConnection` component, an entry in the Dynamic Properties section of the Properties window for the connection string is automatically made, as shown in Figure 15.2.

All the forms, controls, and components in a project use a single configuration file. You can't change the default name of configuration file or use multiple configuration files in a single application.

If you remove a property from the Dynamic Properties list for a component, that property's key and last value remain in the configuration file. The configuration file does not retain any link to the application, so there's no way for it to determine that a particular key/value pair is no longer needed. This does not cause any problem for your applications, although you should keep it in mind. For example, if you use a dynamic property to store a password during development and then remove that property to ship the application, your last password remains in the configuration file. You can edit the configuration file by hand to remove this key and value.

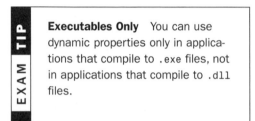

EXAM TIP

Executables Only   You can use dynamic properties only in applications that compile to `.exe` files, not in applications that compile to `.dll` files.

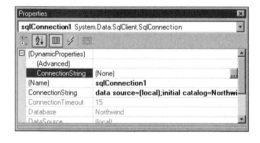

FIGURE 15.2
When some components, such as a `SqlConnection` component, are created, they automatically configure a few properties in the Dynamic Properties section of the Properties window.

Machine and Application Configuration Files

In addition to dynamic properties, the .NET Framework also supports runtime configuration through machine and application configuration files. For example, these files can direct the CLR to load a specific version of a particular assembly or enable just-in-time (JIT) debugging for Windows forms. These configuration files are XML files whose schemas are fully documented in the .NET Framework Developer's Guide. Most of the settings in these files are specific to ASP.NET applications, but some affect Windows applications as well.

Generally, application configuration files override the machine configuration file for those applications. However, the machine configuration file can include settings that direct it not to allow application settings. For example, an attempt to redefine the location of the CLR libraries on an application basis does not work because the `machine.config` file contains a section that prohibits this from being set at the application level. Of course, you could edit the `machine.config` file to remove that section (although that would be a very bad idea from a security point of view!).

The main use of machine and application configuration files for Windows applications is to specify the versions of assemblies that a particular application should use. By default, a .NET application loads only the exact version of an assembly that it was created with, but you can change that at the machine level or at the assembly level. Suppose, for example, that an application uses version 1.0.0.0 of an assembly whose name is CoolCode and whose strong name public key token is 6577fd6241e80701. You've tested the application, and you're satisfied that it works with this version of CoolCode. If the user installs version 1.1.0.0 of CoolCode on his or her computer, the application is unaffected; the application continues to use version 1.0.0.0.

However, you can use an application or a machine configuration file to override this default, by specifying a configured assembly. A *configured assembly* is a mapping from one version to another version. You could do this with the following section in the configuration file:

```
<runtime>
<assemblyBinding xmlns=
    "urn:schemas-microsoft-com:asm.v1">
```

```
<dependentAssembly>
  <assemblyIdentity name="CoolCode"
      publicKeyToken="6577fd6241e80701" />
  <bindingRedirect oldVersion="1.0.0.0"
      newVersion="1.1.0.0" />
</dependentAssembly>
</assemblyBinding>
</runtime>
```

If you add this section to the application configuration file, then the substitution can be made for the application. If you add this section to the machine configuration file (which is found, by default, in C:\WINNT\Microsoft.NET\Framework\v1.0.3705\CONFIG\machine. config), the specified version substitution can be made for any application that uses the CoolCode assembly.

Using the .NET Framework Configuration Tool

For the most part, you don't have to alter .NET configuration files by hand. That's because installing the .NET Framework gives you the .NET Framework Configuration tool (shown in Figure 15.3), which provides a Microsoft Management Console (MMC)-based way to edit these files. You can perform the following tasks with the .NET Framework Configuration tool:

FIGURE 15.3
The .NET Framework Configuration tool provides a graphical user interface (GUI) for editing configuration files.

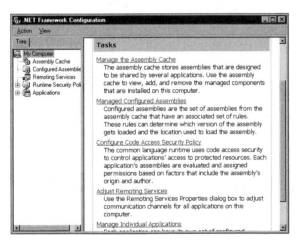

◆ Manage the contents of the global assembly cache (GAC), which provides assemblies to be used by all applications on the computer.

◆ Manage machinewide configured assemblies.

◆ Manage remoting channels, which allow communication with objects on remote computers.

◆ Manage security policy. (You'll learn more about .NET security later in this chapter.)

◆ Manage application settings. Applications can have their own rules for remoting and configured assemblies.

STEP BY STEP

15.2 Creating a Configured Assembly

1. Select Start, Programs, Administrative Tools, Microsoft .NET Framework Configuration.

2. Click the Applications node in the tree view.

3. Click the Add an Application to Configure link.

4. In the Configure an Application dialog box, scroll down the list until you find 316C15.exe. Select this application and click OK.

5. Expand the new node in the tree view and click the Configured Assemblies child node.

6. Click the Configure an Assembly link.

7. In the Configure an Assembly dialog box, select the option button to choose an assembly from the list of assemblies that this application uses. Click the Choose Assembly button. Select the System.Xml assembly and click Select, and then click Finish.

8. In the System.Xml Properties dialog box, select the Binding Policy tab. Enter 1.0.3300.0 as the requested version and 2.0.0.0 as the new version, as shown in Figure 15.4.

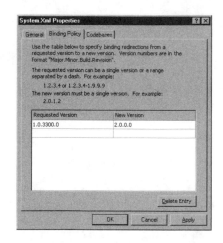

FIGURE 15.4
You can create a configured assembly and set its binding policy and other settings with the help of Microsoft .NET Framework Configuration tool.

continues

continued

> **WARNING**
>
> **No Validation**   As you can see in this example, the .NET Framework Configuration tool performs no validation to determine whether the specified new version of the assembly even exists.

FIGURE 15.5
You get a JIT debugging error if you attempt to load a nonexistent assembly.

9. Click OK to save the configured assembly information.

10. Double-click the `316C15.exe` file in Windows Explorer. You get a JIT debugging error, as shown in Figure 15.5, because the specified version of the `System.Xml` assembly doesn't actually exist.

11. Click No to dismiss the debugging dialog box. Open the `316C15.exe.config` file. It has the following contents if you've followed both Step by Step 15.1 and 15.2:

```xml
<?xml version="1.0" encoding="Windows-1252"?>
<configuration>
  <appSettings>
    <!--   User application and configured
           property settings go here.-->
    <!--   Example: <add key="settingName"
           value="settingValue"/> -->
    <add key="StepByStep15_1.ShowInTaskbar"
         value="False" />
    <add key="StepByStep15_1.Text"
         value="Compiled version" />
  </appSettings>
  <runtime>
    <assemblyBinding
        xmlns="urn:schemas-microsoft-com:asm.v1">
      <dependentAssembly>
        <assemblyIdentity name="System.Xml"
            publicKeyToken="b77a5c561934e089" />
        <bindingRedirect oldVersion="1.0.3300.0"
            newVersion="2.0.0.0" />
      </dependentAssembly>
    </assemblyBinding>
  </runtime>
</configuration>
```

12. Delete the entire `<runtime>` section of the configuration file. Save the file. Double-click the executable file again. Now that you have removed the configured assembly, the application once again launches.

REVIEW BREAK

▶ The .NET Framework stores runtime configuration information in XML files that you can edit without recompiling the application.

▶ Dynamic properties provide a built-in mechanism to let you store component properties in runtime configuration files.

▶ Machine and application configuration files hold administrative settings such as information about configured assemblies and remoting channels.

▶ The .NET Framework Configuration tool provides a GUI for editing runtime configuration files.

CONFIGURING SECURITY

Configure security for a Windows-based application.

- **Select and configure authentication type. Authentication types include Windows Authentication, None, forms-based, Microsoft Passport, and custom authentication.**

- **Specify the security level for an application.**

- **Use custom attributes to configure security.**

The .NET Framework offers a wide variety of security features. You can choose to run a machine in wide-open mode, with every user allowed to execute any .NET code, or you can lock things down selectively. You can control which programs have access to which resources or which users have the right to execute which programs.

Broadly speaking, .NET security can be broken down into two separate areas:

◆ **Code access security**—This type of security manages the security of .NET source code itself. You can tell the .NET Framework about the resources that your code needs in order to execute properly, and the .NET Framework checks for permission to access those resources on the machine at runtime. Code access security is very flexible; it includes the ability to define your own sets of necessary permissions. Administrators can also use code access security to make sure that undesirable code never gets a chance to run on a system.

◆ **Role-based security**—This type of security manages the user rather than the code. Using role-based security allows you to provide or deny access to resources based on which user account your code will execute under. In practical terms, this means that you can limit program execution to particular users or groups on the computer.

The following sections cover both of these types of security, beginning with code access security. The .NET Framework also includes other security features, notably public-key and private-key encryption, which are not a part of the exam 70-316, "Developing and Implementing Windows-Based Applications with Microsoft Visual C# .NET and Microsoft Visual Studio .NET," and are therefore not discussed in this chapter.

Understanding Code Access Security

Configure security for a Windows-based application.

• **Specify the security level for an application.**

Code access security controls what code can do on a computer. Code access security involves permissions to use resources. The .NET Framework has an entire object-oriented system for managing code access security and the associated permissions. In the following sections, you'll learn about some concepts that are involved in code access security, including permissions, code groups, and permission sets.

You'll also learn about the ways code access security can be managed. In particular, code can request permissions on a very fine-grained scale, and the administrator can choose to allow permissions on an equally fine-grained scale.

Understanding Permissions

Code access security is based on specific permissions that the CLR can grant or deny to code. For example, the ability to read or write information in the Windows Registry requires the `RegistryPermission` permission on the part of your code.

As you'll see later in this chapter, code can make four different types of permission request:

◆ It can request the minimum permissions that it requires to run.

◆ It can request optional permissions that it would like but does not require.

◆ It can refuse permissions, to ensure that it does not have access to particular resources.

◆ It can demand permissions on the part of the calling code.

The CLR decides, based on a variety of factors (including the origin of the code and information in the machine and application configuration files), whether a particular permission should be granted. If a piece of code is unable to obtain the minimum permissions that it requires, that piece of code does not execute. The security settings of the computer determine the maximum permissions that code can be granted, but code is allowed to request (and receive) fewer permissions than that maximum.

The .NET Framework groups permissions into three types:

◆ *Code access permissions* involve access to a protected resource or the ability to perform a protected operation.

◆ *Identity permissions* involve access based on credentials that are a part of the code itself.

◆ *Role-based permissions* involve access based on the user who is running the code.

Each permission in the .NET Framework is represented by a particular class that derives from `System.Security.CodeAccessPermission`. Table 15.1 lists these permissions.

TABLE 15.1

PERMISSIONS IN THE .NET FRAMEWORK

Permission	Explanation
Code Access Permissions	
DirectoryServicesPermission	Controls access to the System.DirectoryServices namespace
DnsPermission	Controls access to Domain Name System (DNS) services
EnvironmentPermission	Controls access to environment variables
EventLogPermission	Controls access to the Windows event log
FileDialogPermission	Controls access to files that are selected from the Open dialog box
FileIOPermission	Controls access to the reading and writing of files and directories
IsolatedStorageFilePermission	Controls access to private virtual file systems
IsolatedStoragePermission	Controls access to isolated storage
MessageQueuePermission	Controls access to message queuing via Microsoft Message Queue (MSMQ)
OleDbPermission	Controls access to data via the System.Data.OleDb namespace
PerformanceCounterPermission	Controls access to performance counters
PrintingPermission	Controls access to printers
ReflectionPermission	Controls access to the reflection features of .NET
RegistryPermission	Controls access to the Windows Registry
SecurityPermission	Controls access to unmanaged code
ServiceControllerPermission	Controls access to the starting and stopping of services
SocketPermission	Controls access to Windows sockets
SqlClientPermission	Controls access to data via the System.Data.SqlClient namespace
UIPermission	Controls access to the user interface
WebPermission	Controls access to making Web connections
Identity Permissions	
PublisherIdentityPermission	Represents the identity of the publisher, as determined by the code's digital signature
SiteIdentityPermission	Represents the Web site from which the code was downloaded
StrongNameIdentityPermission	Represents the strong name of the assembly
URLIdentityPermission	Represents the exact uniform resource locator (URL) where the code originated
ZoneIdentityPermission	Represents the security zone where the code originated; you can view security zones on the Security tab of the Internet Explorer Options dialog box
Role-Based Permissions	
PrincipalPermission	Represents the credentials of the user

Requesting Minimum Permissions

To start working in the .NET security framework, your code should request the minimum permissions that it needs to function correctly.

STEP BY STEP

15.3 Requesting Minimum Permissions

1. Add a new form to your Visual C# .NET application.

---

2. Place a Label control, a TextBox control (txtFileName), and a Button control (btnGetFile) on the form. Add an OpenFileDialog component (dlgOpen). Figure 15.6 shows the design for this form.

---

3. Switch to the code view and add the following code at the top:

```
using System.Security.Permissions;
[assembly:FileDialogPermissionAttribute(
    SecurityAction.RequestMinimum, Unrestricted=true)]
```

---

4. Double-click the Button control and add the following code to handle the Click event of the Button control:

```
private void btnGetName_Click(object sender,
    System.EventArgs e)
{
    try
    {
        if(dlgOpen.ShowDialog() == DialogResult.OK)
            txtFileName.Text = dlgOpen.FileName;
    }
    catch (Exception ex)
    {
        MessageBox.Show("Exception: " + ex.Message);
    }
}
```

---

5. Insert the Main() method to launch the form. Set the form as the startup object for the project.

---

6. Compile the project. Launch the executable file from Windows Explorer and verify that you can browse for a file.

NOTE

Custom Permissions   If none of the permissions in Table 15.1 are quite right for your application, you can also define custom permissions. Custom permissions are discussed later in this chapter, in the section "Using Custom Security Attributes."

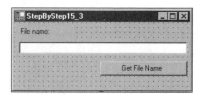

FIGURE 15.6
You can design a form to request minimum permissions required to run the form.

The code in Step by Step 15.3 requests permissions by applying an attribute to an assembly. The `FileDialogPermissionAttribute` allows the assembly to request the `FileDialogPermission` permission, which in turn allows access to the system's file dialog boxes. In this particular case, the code runs without any problem, which means that it was granted the requested permission. That's because by default you have full permissions to run any code that originates on your own computer. To see code access security in action, you need to learn how to manage the permissions granted to code on your computer. But first, you need to understand the concepts of code groups and permission sets.

Code Groups and Permission Sets

A *code group* is a set of assemblies that share a security context. You define a code group by specifying the membership condition for the group. Every assembly in a code group receives the same permissions from that group. However, because an assembly could be a member of multiple code groups, two assemblies in the same group might end up with different permissions.

The .NET Framework supports seven different membership conditions for code groups:

◆ **Application directory**—The application directory membership condition selects all the code in the installation directory of the running application.

◆ **Cryptographic hash**—The cryptographic hash membership condition selects all the code that matches a specified cryptographic hash. Practically speaking, this is a way to define a code group that consists of a single assembly.

◆ **Software publisher**—The software publisher membership condition selects all the code from a specified publisher, as verified by Authenticode signing.

◆ **Site**—The site membership condition selects all the code from a particular Internet domain.

◆ **Strong name**—The strong name membership condition selects all the code that has a specified strong name.

◆ **URL**—The URL membership condition selects all the code from a specified URL.

◆ **Zone**—The zone membership condition selects all the code from a specified security zone (Internet, local intranet, trusted sites, My Computer, or untrusted sites).

Permissions are granted in permission sets. A *permission set* is a set of one or more code access permissions that are granted as a unit. If you want to grant only a single permission, you must construct a permission set that contains only that single permission; you can't grant permissions directly. The .NET Framework supplies seven built-in permission sets:

◆ `Nothing`—The `Nothing` permission set grants no permissions.

◆ `Execution`—The `Execution` permission set grants permission to run but not to access protected resources.

◆ `Internet`—The `Internet` permission set grants limited permissions designed for code of unknown origin.

◆ `LocalIntranet`—The `LocalIntranet` permission set grants high permissions designed for code within an enterprise.

◆ `Everything`—The `Everything` permission set grants all permissions except for the permission to skip verification.

◆ `SkipVerification`—The `SkipVerification` permission set grants the permission to skip security checks.

◆ `FullTrust`—The `FullTrust` permission set grants full access to all resources. This permission set includes all permissions.

You can also create your own custom permission sets, as described in the section "Granting Permission," later in this chapter.

Granting Permission

The easiest way to grant or deny permissions in the .NET Framework is to use the Microsoft .NET Framework Configuration tool.

STEP BY STEP

15.4 Granting Permissions by Using the .NET Framework Configuration Tool

1. Select Start, Programs, Administrative Tools, Microsoft .NET Framework Configuration.

2. Expand the Runtime Security Policy node, then the User node, and then the Permission Sets node. You should see the built-in .NET permission sets.

3. Right-click the Everything permission set and select Duplicate. A new permission set named Copy of Everything is created.

4. Right-click the Copy of Everything permission set and select Rename. Rename the permission set No FileDialog.

5. With the No FileDialog permission set selected, click the Change Permissions link in the right panel of the configuration tool. In the Create Permission Set dialog box, select File Dialog and click Remove. Click Finish to save your changes.

6. Expand the Code Groups node and click the default All Code code group. Click the Add a Child Code Group link in the right panel of the configuration tool.

7. In the Create Code Group dialog box, name the new group Chapter15. Enter a description and click Next.

8. Choose the Hash condition. Click the Import button and browse to 316C15.exe. Click Open to calculate the hash for this file. Click Next.

9. Select the No FileDialog permission set and click Next. Click Finish to create the new code group.

10. Right-click the Chapter15 code group and select Properties. Check the box to make this code group exclusive, as shown in Figure 15.7. Click OK.

11. Run the 316C15.exe application by double-clicking it in Windows Explorer. A policy exception error box appears, indicating that the code cannot be run. Click No to dismiss the error box.

FIGURE 15.7
You can create a code group and grant or deny permissions in a GUI interface by using the Microsoft .NET Framework Configuration tool.

In Step by Step 15.4, you first create a permission set that includes every permission except for the permission to use the file dialog boxes. You then create a code group that contains the executable file for this chapter's examples, and then you assign the `No FileDialog` permission set to this code group. The result is that the code cannot run because it requires at a minimum the one permission that the new security policy cannot grant to it.

Imperative Security

Requesting permissions through the use of attributes is known as *declarative security*. There's a second method to request permissions, known as *imperative security*. With imperative security, you create objects to represent the permissions that your code requires.

STEP BY STEP

15.5 Imperative Security

1. Add a new form to your Visual C# .NET application.

2. Place a `Label` control, a `TextBox` control (`txtFileName`), and a `Button` control (`btnGetFile`) on the form. Add an `OpenFileDialog` component (`dlgOpen`). You can reuse the design from Figure 15.6 for this form.

3. Switch to the code view and add the following `using` directive:

```
using System.Security.Permissions;
```

4. Add this code to allow the user to browse for a filename when he or she clicks the button:

```
private void btnGetName_Click(object sender,
    System.EventArgs e)
{
    try
    {
        FileDialogPermission fdp = new
        FileDialogPermission(
            PermissionState.Unrestricted);
        // Check to see whether the code
        // has the specified permission
        fdp.Demand();
```

continues

continued

```
            if(dlgOpen.ShowDialog() == DialogResult.OK)
                txtFileName.Text = dlgOpen.FileName;
        }
        catch(Exception ex)
        {
            MessageBox.Show("Exception: " + ex.Message);
        }
    }
```

5. Comment out the `FileDialogPermissionAttribute` attribute in the code for `StepByStep15_3`. Otherwise, this attribute would apply to the entire assembly.

6. Insert the `Main()` method to launch the form. Set the form as the startup object for the project.

7. Compile the project. Launch the executable file from Windows Explorer and verify that you can browse for a file.

8. Run the Microsoft .NET Framework Configuration tool and locate the node for the `Chapter15` code group. Right-click the code group and select Properties. On the Membership Condition tab, select Import. Browse to the `316C15.exe` file and click Open. Click OK to close the dialog box.

9. Launch the `316C15.exe` file from Windows Explorer again. Click the Get File button. You should see the security exception message shown in Figure 15.8.

FIGURE 15.8
An exception is generated if the requested permission cannot be granted according to the current setting of the security policy.

> **EXAM TIP**
>
> **Imperative Versus Declarative Security**   The only time you absolutely have to use imperative security is when you need to make security decisions based on factors that are known only at runtime, such as the name of a particular file. In many other cases declarative security is easier to use.

In Step by Step 15.5 you construct a `FileDialogPermission` object that represents unrestricted access to the File dialog boxes. It then calls the `Demand()` method of that object to demand the permission from the operating system. When the security policy is such that the permission cannot be granted, the code throws an exception.

You might be confused about why the hash for the assembly has to be recalculated in order to have the proper code group apply. It is because the hash value is calculated when a mathematical formula is applied to all the code of the compiled program. When you make any change to an application, its hash code also changes.

Computing Permissions

Determining the actual permissions applied to any given piece of code is a complex process. To begin the process, you should think about permissions at the Enterprise level only. The CLR starts by examining the evidence that a particular piece of code presents, in order to determine its membership in code groups at that level. *Evidence* is just an overall term for the various identity permissions (publisher, strong name, hash, and so on) that can go into code group membership.

Code groups are organized into a hierarchy; in Step by Step 15.3 you create the Chapter15 code group as a child of the All Code code group. In general, the CLR examines all the code groups in the hierarchy to determine membership. However, any code group in the hierarchy may be marked as Exclusive (that's the effect of the check box that you select when creating the Chapter15 code group). The CLR stops checking for group membership if code is found to be a member of an Exclusive code group. Either way, code is determined to be a member of zero or more code groups as a first step.

Next, the CLR retrieves the permission set for each code group that contains the code. If the code is a member of an Exclusive code group, only the permission set of that code group is taken into account. If the code is a member of more than one code group and none of them is an Exclusive code group, all the permission sets of those code groups are taken into account. The permission set for the code is the *union* of the permission sets of all relevant code groups. That is, if code is a member of two code groups and one code group grants FileDialog permission but the other does not, the code has FileDialog permission from this step.

The process just described accounts for the permissions at one level (the Enterprise level). But there are actually four levels of permissions: Enterprise, Machine, User, and Application Domain. Only the first three of these levels can be managed within the .NET Framework Configuration tool. However, if you need specific security checking within an application domain (which, roughly speaking, is a session in which code runs), you can do this in code. An application domain can reduce the permissions granted to code within that application domain, but it cannot expand them.

The CLR determines which of the four levels are relevant by starting at the top (the Enterprise level) and working down. Any given code group can have the LevelFinal property, in which case the examination stops there. For example, if code is a member of a code group on the Machine level and that group has the LevelFinal property, only the Enterprise and Machine levels are considered when security is assigned. The CLR computes the permissions for each level separately and then assigns the code the intersection of the permissions of all relevant levels. That is, if code is granted FileDialog permission on the Enterprise and Machine levels but is not granted FileDialog permission on the User level, the code does not have FileDialog permission.

At this point, the CLR knows what permissions should be granted to the code in question, considered in isolation. But code does not run in isolation; it runs as part of an application. The final step of evaluating code access permissions is to perform a stack walk. In a *stack walk*, the CLR examines all code in the calling chain from the original application to the code being evaluated. The final permission set for the code is the intersection of the permission sets of all code in the calling chain. That is, if code is granted FileDialog permission but the code that called it was not granted FileDialog permission, the code is not granted FileDialog permission.

Requesting Other Types of Permissions

You might at times want to request a particular permission even though your application doesn't absolutely require that permission in order for a user to proceed. Optional permissions are used in such a case. If you refer to the code in Step by Step 15.3, you see that part of the permission attribute is the SecurityAction.RequestMinimum flag. To request optional permissions, you use the SecurityAction.RequestOptional flag.

To make use of optional permissions in Visual C# .NET, your code must have a Main() method with a try-catch block. If optional permissions for the assembly can't be granted, this block catches the exception. If minimum permissions can't be granted, the program is shut down, whether or not this block is present.

EXAM TIP

Determining Permissions   The Microsoft .NET Framework Configuration tool can help you determine the effective permissions for a piece of code. To determine the effective permissions, right-click the Runtime Security Policy node and select Evaluate Assembly. You can see the effective permissions for an assembly here, or you can get a list of all the code groups that contribute to the assembly's permissions.

You can also tell the CLR about permissions that you do not want your code to have. This can be useful if the code is potentially available to untrusted callers (for example, users who invoke the code over the Internet) and you want to limit the potential harm that they can do. The flag for this is `SecurityAction.RequestRefuse`.

Finally, you might want to ensure that all the code that calls your code has a particular permission. For example, you might want to raise an exception if any code in the calling stack doesn't have the `RegistryPermission` permission. You can do this by specifying `SecurityAction.Demand` in the declaration of the security attribute.

GUIDED PRACTICE
EXERCISE 15.1

One reason you might choose to use imperative security rather than declarative security is to be able to easily catch security violations and respond to them automatically.

In this exercise, you are required to extend the "browse for file" example in Step by Step 15.3 and use imperative security to selectively disable part of a user interface that the user isn't able to activate under the current security policy.

How would you use imperative security in this form?

You should try working through this problem on your own first. If you get stuck, or if you'd like to see one possible solution, follow these steps:

1. Add a new project to the solution. Name the new project `316C15GPE`.

2. Add a new form to the project. Name the form `GuidedPracticeExercise15_1`.

3. Place two `Label` controls, a `TextBox` control (`txtFileName`), and a `Button` control (`btnGetFile`) on the form. Name one of the `Label` controls `lblMessage` and clear its `Text` property. Add an `OpenFileDialog` component (`dlgOpen`).

4. Switch to the code view and add the following using directive:
   ```
   using System.Security.Permissions;
   ```

continues

continued

5. Attach default event handlers to the form and the Button control. Add the following code to the event handlers to check
   security at load time and to allow the user to browse for a filename when he or she clicks the button:

```
private void GuidedPracticeExercise15_1_Load(
    object sender, System.EventArgs e)
{
    try
    {
        FileDialogPermission fdp = new
        FileDialogPermission(
            PermissionState.Unrestricted);
        // Check to see whether the code
        // has the specified permission
        fdp.Demand();
    }
    catch(Exception ex)
    {
        btnGetFile.Enabled = false;
        lblMessage.Text =
            "You do not have permission " +
            "to browse for file names";
    }
}

private void btnGetFile_Click(object sender,
    System.EventArgs e)
{
    try
    {
        if(dlgOpen.ShowDialog() == DialogResult.OK)
            txtFilename.Text = dlgOpen.FileName;
    }
    catch (Exception ex)
    {
        MessageBox.Show("Exception: " + ex.Message);
    }
}
```

6. Insert the Main() method to launch the form. Set the form as
   the startup object for the project.

7. Compile the project. Run the compiled project from Windows
   Explorer. You should find it possible to browse for a file by
   clicking the Get File button.

8. Select Start, Programs, Administrative Tools, Microsoft .NET
   Framework Configuration.

9. Expand the Runtime Security Policy node, then the User node, then the Code Groups node, and finally the All_Code node. Click the Add a Child Code Group link in the right panel of the configuration tool.

10. In the Create Code Group dialog box, name the new group `Chapter15GPE`. Enter a description and click Next.

11. Choose the Hash condition. Click the Import button and browse to the executable file from this exercise. Click Open to calculate the hash for this file. Click Next.

12. Select the `No FileDialog` permission set (created in the Step by Step 15.5) and click Next. Click Finish to create the new code group.

13. Right-click the `Chapter15GPE` code group and select Properties. Check the box to make this code group exclusive. Click OK.

14. Run the program from Windows Explorer again. The `Button` control should be disabled, and the message shown in Figure 15.9 should appear.

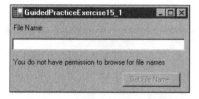

FIGURE 15.9
Choosing imperative security allows you to easily check for permissions and respond to them by taking custom actions such as customizing the user interface in the current instance.

In Guided Practice Exercise 15.1, the imperative security object is used to check the permissions that the application has as soon as the form is loaded. If the call to the `Demand()` method fails, you know that the user is not able to invoke the File dialog box. In that case, the code disables the button that would otherwise launch the File dialog box and shows a warning message instead.

If you had difficulty following this exercise, you should review the section "Imperative Security," earlier in this chapter. After this review you should try this exercise again.

Using Custom Security Attributes

Configure security for a Windows-based application.

- **Use custom attributes to configure security.**

In some cases, you might find that the built-in security permissions do not fit your needs. For example, say you have designed a custom class that retrieves confidential information from your company's database and you'd like to be able to restrict permission on it by a more specific means than limiting SQL permissions.

In such cases, you can create your own custom permissions and add them to the .NET security framework. This requires quite a bit of code, and most developers never need to perform this task. But just in case you do, I outline the process here. You'll find more in-depth information, including all the code for a simple custom permission, in the "Securing Applications" section of the .NET Framework Developer's Guide.

To implement a custom permission, you must create a class that inherits from the `CodeAccessPermission` class. Your new class must override five key methods to provide its own interfaces to the security system:

- ◆ `Copy()`—This method creates an exact copy of the current instance.

- ◆ `Intersect()`—This method returns the intersection of permissions between the current instance and a passed-in instance of the class.

- ◆ `IsSubsetOf()`—This method returns `true` if a passed-in instance includes everything allowed by the current instance.

- ◆ `FromXml()`—This method decodes an XML representation of the permission.

- ◆ `ToXml()`—This method encodes the current instance as XML.

Your class must support a constructor that accepts an instance of the `PermissionState` enumeration (which has a value of `Unrestricted` or `None`). You might also want to implement custom constructors related to your particular business needs. For example, a database-related permission might require a constructor that accepts a server name, if permissions should be handled differently on test and development servers.

Although it's not strictly required, your code should also implement a method named `IsUnrestricted()`, which returns `true` if the particular instance represents unrestricted access to the resource.

This makes your custom permission more compatible with the built-in permissions in the .NET Framework.

To support declarative security, you should also implement an attribute class for your permission. This attribute class should derive from CodeAccessSecurityAttribute (which in turn derives from SecurityAttribute). The class should override the CreatePermission member of the IPermission interface. Within this function, you should create an instance of your base custom permission class and set its properties according to the parameters from the declarative security invocation. Any attribute class must be marked with the Serializable attribute so that it can be serialized into metadata, along with the class to which it is applied.

For your custom permission to actually protect the intended resource, you need to make changes to both the resource and to the .NET Framework on the computers where the permission is to be used. The changes to the resource are simple: Whenever an operation that is protected by the custom permission is about to be performed, the code should demand an instance of the permission. If the calling code can't deliver the permission, your class should refuse to perform the operation.

The changes you need to make to the .NET Framework are somewhat more complex than resources. First, you need to create an XML representation of your custom permission in the format that is expected by the Code Access Security Policy tool (caspol.exe). You can create this XML representation by instantiating your permission and calling its ToXml() method. Given this XML representation, caspol.exe can add a permission set to the .NET Framework that contains your custom permission. It also adds the assembly that implements the custom permission to the list of trusted assemblies on the computer. You need to perform this step on every computer where your custom permission is to be used.

R E V I E W B R E A K

▶ Permissions control access to resources.

▶ Code can request the minimum permissions that it needs in order to run and optional permissions that it would like to have. It can also refuse permissions and demand permissions on behalf of calling code.

continues

continued

▶ Code access permissions represent access to resources, and identity permissions represent things that the .NET Framework knows about code.

▶ The .NET Framework supplies both attribute-based declarative security and class-based imperative security.

▶ A code group is a set of assemblies that share a security context.

▶ Permission sets are sets of permissions that can be granted as a unit.

▶ The CLR computes actual permissions at runtime based on code group membership and the calling chain of the code.

▶ Custom permissions allow you to create your own permissions to protect particular resources.

CONFIGURING AUTHORIZATION

Configure security for a Windows-based application.

- **Select and configure authentication types. Authentication types include Windows authentication, none, forms-based, Microsoft Passport, and custom authentication.**

Configure authorization.

- **Configure role-based authorization.**

- **Implement identity management.**

The final exam objective for this chapter involves the closely intertwined subjects of authentication and authorization. *Authentication* refers to the process of obtaining credentials from a user and verifying his or her identity. After an identity has been authenticated, it can be authorized to use various resources. *Authorization* refers to granting rights based on that identity.

In the Windows application world, authentication is simple: You're authenticated by Windows when you log on. That identity is available to .NET applications to use in making security decisions. Those decisions are handled by the role-based security scheme that is discussed in the remaining sections of this chapter.

Other authentication methods are available in the .NET Framework. These authentication methods apply only to ASP.NET applications, so you're unlikely to see them in conjunction with Windows applications. But you should know about the available choices becase it's possible for an ASP.NET application to invoke a Windows component (although it does so by using a Windows identity). These methods of authentication include the following:

◆ **None**—In many cases, there's no need for users of an ASP.NET application to be authenticated at all. Pages can simply be delivered to all comers.

◆ **Forms-based**—This form of authentication uses an HTML form to request credentials from the user. If the credentials are acceptable, the application sends back an identity key.

◆ **Windows**—ASP.NET applications can use the Windows authentication methods that are built into Internet Information Server to authenticate users in a Windows domain.

◆ **Passport**—Microsoft Passport is an Internet-based service from Microsoft that provides a centralized authentication and profile service for member sites.

◆ **Custom**—You can develop your own custom authentication scheme. You should be aware, though, that it is very difficult to design a secure authentication scheme; doing so is not recommended for anyone who doesn't have an advanced understanding of cryptography.

> **NOTE**
>
> **For More Authentication Information** For more details on ASP.NET authentication methods, refer to *MCAD/MCSD Training Guide (70-315): Designing and Implementing Web Applications with Visual C# .NET and Visual Studio .NET.*

Using the `WindowsIdentity` and `WindowsPrincipal` Objects

Within a Visual C# .NET Windows application, authorization is handled by the role-based security system. Role-based security revolves around two interfaces: `IIdentity` and `IPrincipal`.

NOTE

Custom Authorization   If for some reason you want to develop a custom authorization scheme, you can implement IIdentity and IPrincipal in your own classes. In use, these classes function very much like the Windows-based classes that are demonstrated in the remainder of this chapter.

For applications that use Windows accounts in role-based security, these interfaces are implemented by the WindowsIdentity and WindowsPrincipal objects, respectively.

The WindowsIdentity object represents the Windows user who is running the current code. The properties of this object allow you to retrieve information such as the username and his authentication method.

The WindowsPrincipal object adds functionality to the WindowsIdentity object. The WindowsPrincipal object represents the entire security context of the user who is running the current code, including any roles to which he belongs. When the CLR decides which role-based permissions to assign to your code, it inspects the WindowsPrincipal object.

STEP BY STEP

15.6 Using the WindowsIdentity and WindowsPrincipal Objects

1. Add a new form to your Visual C# .NET application.

2. Place a ListBox control (lbProperties) and a Button control (btnGetProperties) on the form.

3. Switch to the code view and add the following using directive:

```
using System.Security.Principal;
```

4. Double-click the Button control and add the following code to retrieve properties when the Button control is clicked:

```
private void btnGetProperties_Click(object sender,
    System.EventArgs e)
{
    // Tell the CLR which principal policy is in use
    AppDomain.CurrentDomain.SetPrincipalPolicy(
        PrincipalPolicy.WindowsPrincipal);
    lbProperties.Items.Clear();

    // Get the current identity
    WindowsIdentity wi = WindowsIdentity.GetCurrent();
```

```
        // Dump its properties to the listbox
        lbProperties.Items.Add("WindowsIdentity:");
        lbProperties.Items.Add("  Authentication type: " +
            wi.AuthenticationType);
        lbProperties.Items.Add("  Is Anonymous: " +
            wi.IsAnonymous);
        lbProperties.Items.Add("  Is Authenticated: " +
            wi.IsAuthenticated);
        lbProperties.Items.Add("  Is Guest: " +
            wi.IsGuest);
        lbProperties.Items.Add("  Is System: " +
            wi.IsSystem);
        lbProperties.Items.Add("  Name: " + wi.Name);
        lbProperties.Items.Add("  Token: " +
            wi.Token.ToString());

        // Get the current principal
        WindowsPrincipal prin = new WindowsPrincipal(wi);
        // Dump its properties to the listbox
        lbProperties.Items.Add("WindowsPrincipal:");
        lbProperties.Items.Add("  Authentication Type: " +
            prin.Identity.AuthenticationType);
        lbProperties.Items.Add("  Is Authenticated: "  +
            prin.Identity.IsAuthenticated);
        lbProperties.Items.Add("  Name: " +
            prin.Identity.Name);
        lbProperties.Items.Add("  Member of Users: " +
            prin.IsInRole(@"INFINITY\Users"));
    }
```

5. Insert the `Main()` method to launch the form. Set the form as the startup object for the project.

6. Run the project and click the Get Properties button. You should see output similar to that in Figure 15.10.

The code in Step by Step 15.6 first tells the CLR that you're using the standard Windows authentication method, by calling the `SetPrincipalPolicy()` method of the current application domain. It then retrieves the `WindowsIdentity` object of the current user by using the static `GetCurrent()` method of the `WindowsIdentity` object. After it displays some of the properties of the `WindowsIdentity` object, it gets the corresponding `WindowsPrincipal` object by passing the `WindowsIdentity` object to the constructor of the `WindowsPrincipal` class.

> **WARNING**
>
> **Modifying the Domain Name** This code contains a reference to a specific domain named INFINITY in its call to the `IsInRole()` method. You should change that to the name of your own domain in order to test this code.

FIGURE 15.10
The `WindowsIdentity` and `WindowsPrincipal` classes allow you to retreive current user information and also let you evaluate role membership for the current user.

Note that the properties of the `WindowsIdentity` object are somewhat richer than those of the `WindowsPrincipal` object but that the `WindowsPrincipal` object lets you evaluate role membership for the current user. If you only want to work with the `WindowsPrincipal` object, you can retrieve it from the `Thread.CurrentPrincipal()` static method.

Verifying Role Membership

One way to manage role-based security is to use the `IsInRole()` method of the `WindowsPrincipal` object to determine whether the current user is in a specific Windows group. The results of this method call can be used to modify your application's user interface or to perform other tasks.

STEP BY STEP

15.7 Verifying Role Membership

1. Add a new form to your Visual C# .NET application.

2. Place a `Label` control named `lblMembership` on the form.

3. Switch to the code view and add the following `using` directives:

```
using System.Security.Principal;
using System.Threading;
```

4. Double-click the form and add the following code to handle the `Load` event of the form:

```
private void StepByStep15_7_Load(object sender,
    System.EventArgs e)
{
    // Tell the CLR to use Windows security
    AppDomain.CurrentDomain.SetPrincipalPolicy(
        PrincipalPolicy.WindowsPrincipal);
    // Get the current principal object
    WindowsPrincipal prin =
        (WindowsPrincipal) Thread.CurrentPrincipal;
    // Determine whether the user is an admin
    Boolean fAdmin = prin.IsInRole(
        WindowsBuiltInRole.Administrator);
```

```
        // Display the results on the UI
        if(fAdmin)
            lblMembership.Text =
                "You are in the Administrators group";
        else
            lblMembership.Text =
                "You are not in the Administrators group";
}
```

5. Insert the `Main()` method to launch the form. Set the form as the startup object for the project.

6. Run the project. The form tells you whether you're in the Administrators group.

There are three available overloaded forms of the `IsInRole()` method:

◆ `IsInRole(WindowsBuiltInRole)`—This form uses one of the `WindowsBuiltInRole` constants to check for membership in the standard Windows groups.

◆ `IsInRole(String)`—This form checks for membership in a group with the specified name.

◆ `IsInRole(Integer)`—This form checks for membership in a group by using the specified role identifier (RID). RIDs are assigned by the operating system and provide a language-independent way to identify groups.

Using the `PrincipalPermission` Class

In the previous section I discussed the use of the `IsInRole()` method of the `WindowsPrincipal` object to manage role-based security. An alternative way to manage identities is to perform imperative or declarative security checking with role-based security by using the `PrincipalPermission` class or the `PrincipalPermissionAttribute` attribute.

STEP BY STEP

15.8 Using the `PrincipalPermission` Class

1. Add a new form to your Visual C# .NET application.

2. Switch to the code view and add the following using directives:

```
using System.Security.Permissions;
using System.Security.Principal;
```

3. Double-click the form and add the following code, which should run when the form is loaded:

```
private void StepByStep15_8_Load(object sender,
    System.EventArgs e)
{
    // Tell the CLR to use Windows security
    AppDomain.CurrentDomain.SetPrincipalPolicy(
      PrincipalPolicy.WindowsPrincipal);
    // Create a new PrincipalPermission object
    // This object matches any user
    // in a group named Developers
    PrincipalPermission pp = new PrincipalPermission(
        null, "Developers");
    // See if the user is in the group
    try
    {
        pp.Demand();
        MessageBox.Show(
            "You are in the Developers group");
    }
    catch (Exception ex)
    {
        MessageBox.Show("Exception: " + ex.Message);
    }
}
```

4. Insert the `Main()` method and set the form as the startup object for the project.

5. Run the project. If you're a member of a group named Developers, you see a message box that tells you so. If you are not a member of that group, you see a security exception message from the `PrincipalPermission` class.

Checking permissions by using role-based security is very similar to checking permissions by using code access security. The difference lies in what you are checking. The constructor for the `PrincipalPermission` class accepts both a name and a group name, so you can also use it to check whether a specific user is running the code.

▶ The .NET Framework supports both authentication and authorization. Authentication refers to verifying a user's identity. Authorization refers to granting rights based on that identity.

▶ The `WindowsPrincipal` and `WindowsIdentity` classes let you check the authentication status of the current user.

▶ You can use the `IsInRole()` method of the `WindowsPrincipal` object to check for membership in Windows groups.

▶ The `PrincipalPermission` class allows you to perform declarative and imperative role-based security operations.

CHAPTER SUMMARY

After you have finished writing an application, you might still need to configure it. In this chapter you have learned about several broad areas of configurability that are supported by the .NET Framework.

Dynamic properties allow you to set properties of forms, controls, and other components at runtime by editing XML files. Each assembly can have its own configuration file. You can also edit a master machine configuration file to make systemwide changes.

The .NET Framework also includes two complete security systems that administrators can configure. Code access security controls the access that the code has to sensitive resources. Code can determine exactly which resources it requires or would like, and administrators can determine exactly which resources to make available. The CLR checks whether the requested resources are available before it lets code run.

With role-based security, you can make decisions in your code based on the user who is currently logged on. You can check for a particular username or for membership in a built-in or custom Windows group and make decisions accordingly.

KEY TERMS

- authentication
- authorization
- code access security
- code group
- configured assembly
- declarative security
- imperative security
- permission
- permission set
- role-based security

APPLY YOUR KNOWLEDGE

Exercises

15.1 Sharing Dynamic Properties

When you are assigning dynamic properties to the components of a Windows application, you might want to use the same value for more than one property. You can do this by reusing the keys that are assigned to dynamic properties.

Estimated time: 15 minutes

1. Open a Visual C# .NET Windows application in the Visual Studio .NET IDE. Add a new form to the application.

2. Place three `Button` controls on the form.

3. Select the first `Button` control. In the `Button` control's Properties window, click the + sign next to the Dynamic Properties entry. Click in the Advanced section and then click the ellipsis button. The Dynamic Properties dialog box appears.

4. In the Dynamic Properties dialog box, select the Enabled property. Change its `Key mapping` value to `Button.Enabled`. Click OK.

5. Select the second `Button` control and repeat steps 3 and 4. Use the same name, `Button.Enabled`, for the `Key mapping` value.

6. Select the third `Button` control and repeat steps 3 and 4. Use the same name, `Button.Enabled`, for the `Key mapping` value.

7. Insert the `Main()` method and set the form as the startup object for the project.

8. Run the project. All three buttons are enabled.

9. Stop the project. Open the project's `app.config` file. Edit this file to change the stored value for `Button.Enabled` to `false`:

```xml
<?xml version="1.0"
    encoding="Windows-1252"?>
<configuration>
  <appSettings>
    <!--    User application and configured
        property settings go here.-->
    <!--    Example: <add key="settingName"
        value="settingValue"/> -->
    <add key="Button.Enabled"
        value="False" />
  </appSettings>
</configuration>
```

10. Run the project. All three buttons are disabled.

Any time you want two dynamic properties in the same project to stay synchronized, you just use the same key for all the properties. The original value of the property is the value from the first control to which you assigned the key mapping. It doesn't matter whether the components are on the same form or on different forms. For example, you might use a shared dynamic property to make sure that every form in your database-backed application gets the same connection string.

15.2 Using Declarative Role-Based Security

Just like code access security, role-based security can be declarative or imperative. This exercise shows how you can use declarative role-based security to cause an exception if the user is not in a specified group.

Estimated time: 15 minutes

1. Add a new form to your Visual C# .NET application.

2. Switch to the code view and add the following using directives:

```
using System.Security.Permissions;
using System.Security.Principal;
```

APPLY YOUR KNOWLEDGE

3. Modify the class declaration for the form to include a declarative security line with the `PrincipalPermissionAttribute` attribute:

```
[PrincipalPermissionAttribute(
    SecurityAction.Demand,
    Role="Administrators")]
public class Exercise15_2 :
    System.Windows.Forms.Form
```

4. Double-click the form to attach a `Load` event handler. Add the following code to the event handler:

```
private void Exercise15_2_Load(
    object sender, System.EventArgs e)
{
    MessageBox.Show(
        "You are a member of the " +
        "Administrators group");
}
```

5. Insert the `Main()` method to launch the form. Set the form as the startup object for the project.

6. Run the project. If you're not in the local Administrators group, you should see a security exception.

Review Questions

1. What types of projects can use dynamic properties?

2. What types of properties can you set to be dynamic properties?

3. What file contains the values that are assigned to dynamic properties?

4. How many configuration files can a single application contain?

5. What tasks can you perform with the .NET Framework Configuration tool?

6. What is the purpose of a configured assembly?

7. What types of permission requests can an application make?

8. What are the three types of permission objects?

9. What is the difference between declarative and imperative security?

10. What do the `WindowsIdentity` and `WindowsPrincipal` objects represent?

Exam Questions

1. You have developed a database application that stores a connection string as a dynamic property. You have finished testing the application and are now ready to switch to using the production server. You edit the connection string in the application's configuration file. What must you do to make the application use the new connection string?

   A. Nothing; the application automatically uses the new connection string.

   B. Restart the application.

   C. Recompile the application.

   D. Reboot Windows.

2. Users of your application have requested the ability to customize the main form of the application. Which of these form properties can you allow the users to set in a configuration file that has dynamic property support?

   A. `BackColor`

   B. `BackgroundImage`

   C. `Text`

   D. `Font`

3. You are using a .NET application from MegaSloth. This application uses a component from MiniControl to handle file browsing. MiniControl has released a new version of the component that has enhanced capabilities for browsing files over the Internet. You would like the MegaSloth application to use the new version of MiniControl. What should you do?

   A. Make a configured assembly entry in the MegaSloth application's configuration file to tell it to use the new version of the MiniControl component.

   B. Ask MegaSloth to compile a new version of its application that incorporates the new MiniControl component.

   C. Ask MiniControl to compile a new version of the MegaSloth application that incorporates the updated component.

   D. Just install the new version of the MiniControl component on your computer. All applications will automatically use the new version.

4. Your application requires the ability to read and write to the Windows Registry in order to function properly. Which .NET security feature should you use to ensure that your code has this ability?

   A. Code access security

   B. Role-based security

   C. Encryption

   D. Type safety

5. Your application requires the user to be in the Domain Admins group in order to activate certain functions. Which .NET security feature should you use to ensure that the user is in this group?

   A. Code access security

   B. Role-based security

   C. Encryption

   D. Type safety

6. You are using code access security to verify that your application has permission to perform file input/output (I/O) operations. As part of your testing procedure, you have created a permission set that denies file I/O permissions. You have also created a code group that uses a hash code membership condition to select your application's executable assembly, and you have assigned the permission set to this code group. You have set this code group to be an exclusive code group and verified that your program is unable to obtain file I/O permissions.

   To continue development, you change the code group to use the Everything permission set, and you continue to add new code to the application. When you're ready to test the security features, you change back to the permission set that does not have file I/O permissions. However, you find that your application is able to access files, even though you have not changed the declarative security within the application.

   Why is your code able to perform file I/O even though the code group denies file I/O permissions?

APPLY YOUR KNOWLEDGE

A. Changing code within the application changes its hash code, so it is no longer a member of the code group.

B. After you've assigned the Everything permission set to a code group, the code group ignores attempts to set more restrictive permissions.

C. The Exclusive property on a code group applies only when the code group is first created.

D. You must reboot your development computer to update the membership records of the code group.

7. Assembly A is a member of the following code groups (and only the following code groups in Table 1 below):

What permission does the CLR assign to Assembly A?

A. Everything

B. LocalIntranet

C. Internet

D. Nothing

8. Assembly B is a member of the following code groups (and only the following code groups in Table 2 below):

What permission does the CLR assign to Assembly B?

A. Everything

B. Nothing

C. Internet

D. LocalIntranet

TABLE 1

Level	Code Group	Permission Set	Exclusive	LevelFinal Property
Enterprise	All Code	Everything	No	No
Enterprise	Company Code	LocalIntranet	No	No
Enterprise	Restricted Code	Internet	No	No
Enterprise	Restricted Components	Nothing	No	No

TABLE 2

Level	Code Group	Permission Set	Exclusive	LevelFinal Property
Enterprise	All Code	Everything	No	No
Enterprise	Company Code	LocalIntranet	No	No
Machine	Restricted Code	Internet	No	No
User	Restricted Components	Nothing	No	No

APPLY YOUR KNOWLEDGE

9. Assembly C is a member of the following code groups (and only the following code groups in Table 3 below):

   What permission does the CLR assign to Assembly C?

   A. `Everything`

   B. `LocalIntranet`

   C. `Internet`

   D. `Nothing`

10. Assembly D is a member of the following code groups (and only the following code groups in Table 4 below):

    What permission does the CLR assign to Assembly D?

A. `Everything`

B. `LocalIntranet`

C. `Internet`

D. `Nothing`

11. Your code will be called from the Internet, and you want to minimize the chance that it can do unintentional damage to the local computer. As a result, you would like to ensure that your code is not granted file I/O permissions. Which `SecurityAction` flag should you use with the `FileIOPermissionAttribute` declaration?

   A. `SecurityAction.RequestMinimum`

   B. `SecurityAction.RequestOptional`

   C. `SecurityAction.Demand`

   D. `SecurityAction.RequestRefuse`

TABLE 3

Level	Code Group	Permission Set	Exclusive	LevelFinal Property
Enterprise	All Code	Everything	No	No
Enterprise	Company Code	LocalIntranet	Yes	No
Machine	Restricted Code	Internet	No	No
User	Restricted Components	Nothing	No	No

TABLE 4

Level	Code Group	Permission Set	Exclusive	LevelFinal Property
Enterprise	All Code	Everything	No	No
Enterprise	Company Code	LocalIntranet	No	No
Machine	Restricted Code	Internet	No	Yes
User	Restricted Components	Nothing	No	No

APPLY YOUR KNOWLEDGE

12. You want to be sure that all your code in the calling chain has file I/O permissions. Which `SecurityAction` flag should you use with the `FileIOPermission` object?

    A. `SecurityAction.RequestMinimum`

    B. `SecurityAction.RequestOptional`

    C. `SecurityAction.Demand`

    D. `SecurityAction.RequestRefuse`

13. Which of the following tasks requires you to use imperative security rather than declarative security?

    A. Ensuring that your application has access to a specific key in the Windows Registry

    B. Ensuring that your application can open a particular file whose name is specified by the user

    C. Ensuring that your application has access to a specific environment variable

    D. Ensuring that your application has access to SQL Server databases

14. Your application uses this code to check for membership in the Developers group:

```
private void frmSecure_Load(object sender,
    System.EventArgs e)
{
    // Get the current principal object
    Windows Principal prin =
        Thread.CurrentPricipal;
    // Determine whether the
    // user is a developer
    Boolean developer =
        prin.IsInRole("Developers");
    // Display the results on the UI
    if(developer)
        lblMembership.Text =
          "You are in the Developers group";
```

```
    else
        lblMembership.Text =
        "You are not in the Developers group";
}
```

Users report that the code claims that they are not in the Developers group even when they are. What must you do to fix this problem?

A. Use imperative security to make sure your code has access to the Windows environment variables.

B. Create a `WindowsIdentity` object by using `WindowsIdentity.GetCurrent`, and then use this object to construct the `WindowsPrincipal` object.

C. Use the `WindowsPrincipal.Name` property to retrieve the user's name, and then pass the user's name to the `IsInRole()` method.

D. Call `AppDomain.CurrentDomain.`
   `SetPrincipalPolicy(PrincipalPolicy.Window`
   `sPrincipal)` to specify the authentication mode.

15. Your application uses the same OLE DB connection string on the `OleDbConnection` objects on five different forms. You want to allow the user to set this connection string by editing the application's configuration file. What should you do to allow this with minimum effort?

A. Make the connection string a dynamic property of each `OleDbConnection` object. Use the same `Key` mapping value for all five connection strings.

B. Make the connection string a dynamic property of each `OleDbConnection` object. Use a different `Key` mapping value for each connection string.

C. Make the connection string a dynamic property of the OleDbConnection object on one form. Use code to copy this string to each of the other forms at runtime.

D. Make the connection string a dynamic property of the OleDbConnection object on one form. Open all connections from this same object.

Answers to Review Questions

1. You can use dynamic properties in any project that compiles to an .exe file. Dynamic properties cannot be used in .dll files.

2. You can set any simple property (that is, any property whose value is not an instance of a class or a structure) to be a dynamic property.

3. In the IDE, the app.config file contains the values assigned to dynamic properties. After your project is compiled, the configuration file has the same name as the project's executable file, with the added extension .config.

4. An application can have only a single configuration file, although it can also be affected by settings in the machine configuration file.

5. Manage the contents of the GAC, manage configured assemblies, manage remoting channels, manage security policy, and manage application settings.

6. The purpose of a configured assembly is to allow you to change the version of a library that is used by a particular .NET application.

7. An application can request minimum or optional permissions, refuse permissions, or demand permissions of its callers.

8. The .NET Framework groups permissions into three types of permission objects: code-based, identity, and role-based.

9. Declarative security works by assigning attributes to assemblies. Imperative security works by instantiating the various security classes and using them directly.

10. The WindowsIdentity object represents a logged-on user. The WindowsPrincipal object represents the entire security context of the logged-on user.

Answers to Exam Questions

1. **B.** Dynamic properties are applied only when a component is initialized. If your application is already running, you must restart the application (or somehow reload the applicable component) before it can see the changes in the configuration file. For more information, see the section "Using Dynamic Properties" in this chapter.

2. **C.** Only simple (that is, non-object) properties can be handled by automatic dynamic properties. For more information, see the section "Using Dynamic Properties" in this chapter.

3. **A.** By using a configured assembly, you can use the new component in an existing application without recompiling anything and without affecting other applications on the computer. .NET applications deliberately do not use new versions of components unless they are explicitly told to do so; automatically picking up new versions leads to DLL Hell in older versions of Windows. For more information, see the section "Machine and Application Configuration Files" in this chapter.

4. **A.** Checking whether code has a particular privilege is the function of code access security. For more information, see the section "Understanding Code Access Security" in this chapter.

5. **B.** Role-based security allows you to check whether a user is in a particular group. For more information, see the section "Using the WindowsIdentity and WindowsPrincipal Objects" in this chapter.

6. **A.** Hash codes are calculated from the Microsoft Intermediate Language code of an assembly, so changing the assembly's contents changes its hash code. For more information, see the sections "Imperative Security" and "Code Groups and Permission Sets" in this chapter.

7. **A.** Within a level, the permission set granted to an assembly is the union of all the permission sets of code groups on that level to which the assembly belongs. For more information, see the section "Computing Permissions" in this chapter.

8. **B.** Across levels, the permission set granted to an assembly is the intersection of all the permission sets of the levels. Because the user level grants no permissions to Assembly B, Assembly B gets no permissions from the CLR. For more information, see the section "Computing Permissions" in this chapter.

9. **B.** The Company Code code group is marked as an exclusive code group, so only its permission set is taken into account when determining the permission set for the assembly. For more information, see the section "Computing Permissions" in this chapter.

10. **C.** Because the code group on the Machine level is marked with the LevelFinal property, the code group on the user level is not taken into account when determining the permission set for this assembly. For more information, see the section "Computing Permissions" in this chapter.

11. **D.** SecurityAction.RequestRefuse tells the CLR that your assembly does not want to be granted the specified permission. For more information, see the section "Requesting Other Types of Permissions" in this chapter.

12. **C.** SecurityAction.Demand demands the specified permission of the calling code. For more information, see the section "Requesting Other Types of Permissions" in this chapter.

13. **B.** You must use imperative security to check access to resources whose names are not known until runtime. For more information, see the section "Imperative Security" in this chapter.

14. **D.** You must tell the CLR how users are authenticated, even when you're using a Windows application that automatically employs Windows authentication. For more information, see the section "Using the WindowsIdentity and WindowsPrincipal Objects" in this chapter.

15. **A.** By using the same Key mapping value for each of the five objects, you allow the user to change all five by changing a single entry in the configuration file. For more information, see the section "Using Dynamic Properties" and Guided Exercise 15.1 in this chapter.

APPLY YOUR KNOWLEDGE

Suggested Readings and Resources

1. Visual Studio .NET Combined Help Collection:

   - "Configuring Applications Using Dynamic Properties"

   - "Securing Applications"

   - "Configuring Applications"

2. Brian A. LaMacchia, et al. *.NET Framework Security*. Addison-Wesley, 2002.

3. Microsoft Support WebCast: .NET Code Access Security. support.microsoft.com/servicedesks/webcasts/wc041002/wcblurb041002.asp.

PART IV

FINAL REVIEW

Fast Facts

Practice Exam

Now that you've read this book, worked through the exercises, Guided Practice Exercises, and Step by Steps, and acquired as much hands-on experience using Visual C# .NET as you could, you are ready for the exam. This chapter is designed to be a "final cram in the parking lot" before you walk into the testing center. You can't reread the whole book in an hour, but you will be able to read this section in that time.

This chapter is organized by objective category, giving you not just a summary, but a review of the most important points from the book. Remember, this is just a review, not a replacement for the actual study material! It's meant to be a review of concepts and a trigger for you to remember useful bits of information you will need when taking the exam. If you know the information in here and the concepts that stand behind it, chances are good that the exam will be a snap.

Creating User Services

Create a Windows form by using the Windows Forms Designer.

Add and set properties on a Windows form.

◆ Properties let you customize the appearance and behavior of a Windows form.

◆ The Windows Forms Designer lets you define a form based on the properties that are available in its base class (which is usually the `System.Windows.Forms.Form` class).

Fast Facts

70-316

◆ You can add custom properties to a form.

◆ Properties let you encapsulate additional logic, in the form of the `get` and `set` accessors. These accessors let you preprocess data before you allow the programs to store them or read them from the field that originally stored the data.

◆ The `get` and `set` accessors allow read and write access, respectively, to a property. If you want to make a property read-only, you should not include a `set` accessor in its property definition. On the other hand, if you want a write-only property, you should not include a `get` accessor in the property definition.

◆ Attributes let you define the runtime behavior of a property.

Create a Windows form by using visual inheritance.

◆ With form inheritance, you can create a new form by inheriting it from a base form. This allows you to reuse and extend the code that you've already written.

◆ The Windows Forms Designer lets you inherit a form visually from an existing form through the Inheritance Picker dialog box. You can also visually manipulate inherited properties through the Properties window.

Build graphical interface elements by using the `System.Drawing` namespace.

◆ Windows forms follow a two-dimensional coordinate system. A point is an addressable location in this coordinate system.

◆ The `Graphics` object gives you access to a drawing surface that you can use to draw lines, text, curves, and a variety of shapes.

◆ The `ResizeRedraw` property, when set to `true`, instructs the form to redraw itself when it is resized. It's a good programming practice to design forms that resize their contents based on the form's size. The `Resize` event of a form can also be used to program the resizing logic.

◆ The `Graphics` class provides a set of `Draw` methods that are used to draw shapes such as rectangles, ellipses, and curves on a drawing surface. The `Graphics` class also provides a set of `Fill` methods that are used to create solid shapes.

◆ You can use an object of the `Bitmap` class to manipulate objects. The `System.Drawing` namespace classes can work with a variety of image formats.

Add controls to a Windows form.

Set properties on controls.

◆ You can add controls to a form in two ways: You can use the Windows Forms Designer or create them in code.

◆ The Windows Forms Designer in the Microsoft Visual Studio .NET IDE allows you to add controls to a form and manipulate them very easily.

◆ The Visual Studio .NET toolbox provides a variety of controls and components for creating common Windows GUI elements.

◆ You can set the properties of controls at design time by using the Properties window or at runtime by accessing them as *ControlName. PropertyName* in code.

◆ Some of the important properties of controls, such as `Anchor`, `Dock`, `Enabled`, `Font`, `Location`, `Name`, `Size`, `TabIndex`, `TabStop`, and `Visible`, are shared by most common Windows forms controls.

◆ A dialog box is used to prompt a user for input. A few built-in dialog boxes available, such as `ColorDialog`, `FontDialog`, `OpenFileDialog`, and `SaveFileDialog`. These function just like the Windows operating system's dialog boxes.

◆ You can build custom dialog boxes to meet custom requirements. You can create custom dialog boxes by first creating a form and setting a few properties of the form to enable the form to behave like a dialog box.

◆ Dialog boxes can be of two types: modal and modeless. You can call the `ShowDialog()` or `Show()` methods of the `Form` class to create modal and modeless dialog boxes, respectively.

◆ The `LinkLabel` control is derived from the `Label` control. The `LinkLabel` control allows you to add links to a control. The `Links` property of the `LinkLabel` control contains a collection of all the links referred to by the control.

◆ The `TextBox` control can be displayed as an ordinary text box, a password text box (where each character is masked by the character provided in the `PasswordChar` property), or a multiline textbox (if you set its `MultiLine` property to `true`). The `RichTextBox` control provides richer formatting capabilities than a `TextBox` control. It can also be drawn as a single-line or multiline text box. By default, the `RichTextBox` control has its `MultiLine` property set to `true`.

◆ `GroupBox` and `Panel` controls are container controls. They can be used to group other controls. The `Controls` property of these controls contains a collection of their child controls.

◆ In a group of `CheckBox` controls, you can check multiple check boxes. In a group of `RadioButton` controls, you can select only a single radio button at a time.

◆ The `CheckBox` control allows you to set three check states (`Checked`, `Unchecked`, and `Indeterminate`), if the `ThreeState` property is set to `true`.

◆ The `ComboBox` control allows you to select a value from a predefined list of values. You can also enter a value in the `ComboBox` control. The `ListBox` control only allows you to select a value from the list of values displayed.

◆ The `CheckedListBox` control derives from the `ListBox` control and inherits its functionality. However, a `CheckedListBox` control displays a `CheckBox` control along with each item in the list of items to be checked. The `CheckedListBox` control allows only two selection modes: `None` (no selection) and `One` (allows multiple selections).

◆ The `DomainUpDown` and `NumericUpDown` controls allow you to select from a list of defined values by pressing up and down buttons. You can also enter values in the controls unless their ReadOnly property is set to true.

◆ The `DateTimePicker` control allows you to select a date and time, and the `MonthCalendar` control allows you to select a date or range of dates. The `SelectionStart`, `SelectionEnd`, and `SelectionRange` properties return the start date, end date, and range of dates selected.

◆ The `TreeView` control is used to display data in a hierarchical collection of nodes. Each node is represented by a `TreeNode` object. The `AfterSelect` event of the `TreeView` control occurs when a node is selected and the `SelectedNode` property is set with the new selection.

◆ The `ListView` control is used to display items in different views—such as `List`, `Details`, `SmallIcon`, and `LargeIcon`—like the view options of Windows Explorer.

◆ Scrollbars can be associated with controls to provide scrolling functionality.

◆ The `TabControl` control provides a user interface that can be used to save space as well as to organize a large number of controls. You usually see a `TabControl` control used in wizards.

Load controls dynamically.

◆ Adding controls dynamically is a three-step process:

1. Create a private variable to represent each of the controls you want to place on the form.

2. In the form, place code to instantiate each control and to customize each control, using its properties, methods, or events.

3. Add each control to the form's control collection.

◆ While creating controls programmatically, be sure to add them to their parent container's `Controls` collection.

Write code to handle control events and add the code to a control.

◆ Control programming is event driven. Events are fired when the user interacts with a control. To take a specific action when an event occurs, you would write an event handler method and attach it to the event of a control via its delegate.

◆ Event handlers can be attached to controls either by using the Properties window or programmatically by adding delegate objects to `ControlName.EventName` by using the += operator.

Instantiate and invoke an ActiveX control.

◆ You can use the Windows Forms ActiveX Control Importer to create wrapper classes. These wrapper classes let you host an ActiveX control on a .NET Windows form.

◆ You can import an ActiveX control to a Visual Studio .NET project by adding it to the toolbox.

◆ After they're imported, ActiveX controls can be used just as native .NET controls are.

◆ ActiveX controls impose a performance penalty and have other drawbacks.

Configure control licensing.

◆ The default control licensing structure in the .NET Framework requires no configuration by either developer or administrator. If you encounter runtime licensing errors, they are almost certainly coming from a custom licensing scheme. In such a case, the best course of action is to contact the control vendor directly for assistance.

Create menus and menu items.

◆ There are two types of menus in Windows applications. The main menu is used to group all the available commands and options in a Windows application. A context menu is used to specify a relatively short list of options that apply to a control, depending on the application's current context.

◆ You can make keyboard navigation possible between menu items by including keyboard hotkeys in the `Text` properties of menu items. You can also associate shortcut keys with menus. Pressing a shortcut key directly invokes a command.

Implement navigation for the user interface (UI).

Configure the order of tabs.

◆ All controls with `TabStop` properties set to `true` appear in the tab order for a form. The order in which the Tab key moves the cursor to the controls is dictated by the `TabOrder` properties of the controls.

◆ The Tab Order Wizard provides a convenient way to set the `TabIndex` properties of controls to implement logical keyboard-based navigation in the form by using the Tab key.

Validate user input.

◆ It is generally a good practice to validate user input at the time of data entry. Thoroughly validated data results in consistent and correct data being stored by the application.

◆ When a user presses a key, three events are generated: `KeyDown`, `KeyPress`, and `KeyUp`, in that order.

◆ The `Validating` event is the ideal place for storing the field-level validation logic for a control.

◆ The `CausesValidation` property specifies whether validation should be performed. If it is set to `false`, the `Validating` and `Validated` events are suppressed.

◆ The `ErrorProvider` component in the Visual Studio .NET toolbox is used to show validation-related error messages to the user.

◆ A control cannot receive the focus and appears grayed out if its `Enabled` property is set to `false`.

Validate non-Latin user input.

◆ The `String.Compare()` method compares strings according to the rules of the `CultureInfo` object referenced by the `CurrentCulture` property.

◆ The `CultureInfo.CompareInfo` object searches for substrings according to the comparison rules of the current culture.

◆ The `Array.Sort()` method sorts the members of an array by the alphabetical order rules of the current culture.

◆ The `SortKey.Compare()` method compares strings according to the rules of the current culture.

Implement error handling in the UI.

Create and implement custom error messages.

◆ You can associate custom error messages with the exception classes defined by the CLR to provide more meaningful information to the caller code. The constructor of these classes that accepts the exception message as its parameter can be used to pass the custom error message.

◆ If the existing exception classes do not satisfy your exception handling requirements, you can create new exception classes that can be specific to your application. Custom exceptions should be derived from the `ApplicationException` class.

◆ Custom exceptions should have names that end with the word Exception and should implement three constructors (default, Message, Message and Exception) of their base classes.

◆ You can use the UnhandledException event of the AppDomain class to manage unhandled exceptions.

◆ You can use the EventLog class to log events to the Windows event log.

Create and implement custom error handlers.

◆ A try block consists of code that might raise an exception. A try block cannot exist on its own. It should be immediately followed by one or more catch blocks or a finally block.

◆ A catch block handles any exception raised by the code in the try block. The CLR looks for a matching catch block to handle the exception, which is the first catch block with either exactly the same exception type or any of the exception's base classes.

◆ If multiple catch blocks are associated with a try block, then the catch blocks should be arranged in top-to-bottom order of specific to general exception types.

◆ The finally block is used to enclose code that needs to be run, regardless of whether the exception is raised.

Raise and handle errors.

◆ An exception occurs when a program encounters any unexpected problem during normal execution.

◆ The Framework Class Library (FCL) provides two main types of exceptions: SystemException and ApplicationException. SystemException represents the exceptions thrown by the CLR, and ApplicationException represents the exceptions thrown by user programs.

◆ The System.Exception class represents the base class for all Common Language Specification (CLS)-compliant exceptions and provides the common functionality for exception handling.

◆ The throw statement is used to raise an exception.

Implement online user assistance.

◆ Visual Studio .NET includes the HTML Help SDK for the creation of HTML Help files.

◆ HTML Help files are composed of multiple HTML source files that are compiled into a single .chm file.

◆ You can create HTML Help topics with any HTML authoring tool. HTML Help Workshop provides a convenient way to organize help projects.

◆ An HTML Help file can include navigation aids such as a table of contents and an index.

◆ HTML Help 2 is Microsoft's latest standard for help files.

◆ The Visual Studio Help Integration Kit includes the tools necessary to build HTML Help 2 files, including Microsoft Help Workshop.

◆ The `HelpProvider` component is the bridge between a .NET Framework Windows application and an HTML Help file.

◆ You can use `HelpProvider` to display topics from a help file, Web pages, or pop-up help strings.

◆ Pop-up help is appropriate for dialog boxes, where you don't want the user to switch focus to another task.

◆ ToolTips let you provide quick help for individual controls.

Display and update data.

Transform and filter data.

◆ Server Explorer is a powerful tool for working with SQL Server data.

◆ You can edit and design SQL Server objects directly within Visual Studio .NET.

◆ The `DataView` object offers client-side sorting and filtering capabilities for data-bound objects.

◆ Using views on a server can be an efficient way to filter or transform data.

Bind data to the UI.

◆ Simple data binding refers to connecting a single entity in the data model to a single property of a control on the user interface.

◆ Any class that implements the `IBindingList`, `ITypedList`, or `IList` interface can deliver data via simple data binding.

◆ You can bind to almost any property of any control.

◆ Complex data binding binds a user interface control to an entire collection of data.

◆ To use complex data binding with a `ListBox` control or a `ComboBox` control, you set the control's `DataSource` and `DisplayMember` properties.

◆ A `ListBox` control or a `ComboBox` control can pull values from one data source and place them in another.

◆ You can cause a `ListBox` control or a `ComboBox` control to display one value while binding another by using the `DisplayMember` and `ValueMember` properties of the control.

◆ The `DataGrid` control displays an entire array of data in rows and columns. You specify the data to display by setting the `DataSource` property of the `DataGrid` control.

◆ The properties of the `DataGrid` control include many flexible formatting options.

◆ In one-way data binding, data from the data model is displayed on the form, but changes to the form do not affect the data model.

◆ In two-way data binding, data from the data model is displayed on the form, and changes to the form are written back to the database.

◆ The .NET Framework uses `BindingContext` and `CurrencyManager` objects to manage data binding.

◆ You can use events of the `CurrencyManager` object to help react to changes in bound data.

◆ The Data Form Wizard helps you create data-bound forms, both simple and complex, quickly. These forms draw their data from relational databases such as SQL Server databases.

Instantiate and invoke a Web service or component.

Instantiate and invoke a Web service.

◆ Web services provide you with the means to create objects and invoke their methods, even though your only connection to the server is via the Internet.

◆ Communication with Web services occurs via XML messages transported by HTTP.

◆ Because they communicate over HTTP, Web services are typically not blocked by firewalls.

◆ The Simple Object Access Protocol (SOAP) encapsulates object-oriented messages between Web service clients and servers.

◆ UDDI is a multivendor standard for discovering online resources, including Web services.

◆ Disco is Microsoft's standard format for discovery documents, which contain information about Web services.

◆ The Web Services Discovery tool, `disco.exe`, can retrieve discovery information from a server that exposes a Web Service.

◆ The Web Services Description Language (WSDL) lets you retrieve information on the classes and methods that are supported by a particular Web service.

◆ You can generate proxy classes for a Web service manually by using the Web Services Description Language tool (`wsdl.exe`).

◆ You can generate proxy classes for a Web service automatically by setting a Web reference to point to the Web service.

◆ You can test and debug a Web service without a client application by using one of several SOAP proxy tools.

Instantiate and invoke a COM or COM+ component.

◆ Using COM or COM+ components from .NET managed code requires the creation of an RCW.

◆ You can create an RCW for a COM component by using the Type Library Importer or by directly referencing the COM component from .NET code.

◆ To use COM components that you did not create, you should obtain a Primary Interop Assembly (PIA) from the creator of the component.

◆ RCWs impose a performance penalty on COM code.

Instantiate and invoke a .NET component.

◆ .NET components are classes that implement the `IComponent` interface.

◆ You can add .NET components to the Visual Studio .NET toolbox. They support the Visual Studio .NET interface with drag-and-drop functionality and the use of the Properties window.

◆ You can instantiate a .NET component by dragging it from the toolbox to a form or by declaring a new instance of the component's class in your code.

Call native functions by using platform invoke.

◆ You can use the .NET `PInvoke` facility to call functions from unmanaged libraries, including the Windows API.

Implement globalization.

Implement localizability for the UI.

◆ Localization is a three-step process that consists of globalization (identifying resources), localizability (verifying separation of resources from code), and localization (translating resources).

◆ Many resources may need to be localized, including user interface text, dates, times, currency amounts, and calendars.

◆ Cultures are identified by culture codes. A neutral culture code specifies only a location and cannot be used for localization. A specific culture code specifies both a location and a language, and it provides enough information for localization.

◆ The `CultureInfo` object represents a culture in the .NET Framework.

Convert existing encodings.

◆ Internally, .NET applications use 16-bit Unicode (UTF-16) as their preferred character encoding.

◆ The `System.Text.Encoding` class and its subclasses allow you to convert text from one encoding to another.

Implement right-to-left and left-to-right mirroring.

◆ In some languages, the user interface is read from right to left instead of from left to right. Converting a form for one of these languages is referred to as mirroring.

◆ The .NET Framework provides partial support for mirroring through the `RightToLeft` property on forms and controls.

Prepare culture-specific formatting.

◆ To iterate through the elements of a string in a world-ready application, you should use the `GetTextElementEnumerator()` method of the `StringInfo` class.

◆ Searching, sorting, and comparing strings in a world-ready application requires you to use standard objects and methods rather than clever programming tricks.

Create, implement, and handle events.

◆ Events allow a program to respond to changes in the code's environment.

◆ You can cause custom code to be executed when an event fires by registering the code with the event. These pieces of code that respond to an event are called event handlers.

◆ Event handlers are registered with events through delegate objects.

◆ A delegate object is a type of object that can store a reference to a method that has a specific signature. Events are objects whose type is delegate.

◆ To create and implement an event, you need to take care of the following steps:

1. Define the EventArgs class that will contain the event-related data. This is required only if you want to pass specific event-related information to the event handlers.

2. Create a delegate object that can store a reference to the event handler.

3. Define the event itself as an object of delegate type.

4. Define a method that notifies the registered objects of the event. Usually this method has a name such as OnChanged, where Changed is the event name.

5. Call the method defined in step 4 whenever the event occurs.

◆ You should always use += syntax when attaching an event handler to an event in order to add the delegate to a list of already existing delegates. Otherwise, all the previously existing delegates are canceled and receive no notification of the event.

Implement print capability.

◆ Printing in .NET is managed by the PrintDocument class. The PrintDocument class exposes a Graphics object that you can draw or write to with any of the System.Drawing methods.

◆ When you're ready to print, you call the Print() method of a PrintDocument object. This raises the PrintPage event, in which you can use the System.Drawing methods to construct the printout.

◆ If there is more to be printed when you are done constructing a page in the PrintPage() method, you should set e.HasMorePages to true to tell the CLR to trigger the event again for another page.

◆ The PrintDocument class supports the BeginPrint, EndPrint, and QueryPageSettings events.

◆ The PageSetupDialog component displays a dialog box that allows the user to set page-related printing properties.

◆ The PrintPreviewDialog component displays a preview of a document before it is printed.

◆ The PrintPreviewControl control lets you embed a print preview in a Windows form.

◆ The PrintDialog component allows the user to set printer-related printing properties.

Implement accessibility features.

◆ The .NET Framework supports the five basic principles of accessible design:

• **Flexibility**—The user interface should be flexible and customizable, so that users can adjust it to their own individual needs and preferences.

- **Choice of input methods**—Different users have different abilities and preferences when it comes to using the mouse or keyboard for performing tasks. All operations in an application should be accessible to the keyboard, and basic operations should be available via the mouse as well. In the future, voice and other types of input may also be considered as input methods.

- **Choice of output methods**—You should not depend on a single method of output (such as sound, color, or text) for important information.

- **Consistency**—Your application should be consistent with the Windows operating system and other applications in order to minimize difficulties related to learning and using new interfaces.

- **Compatibility with accessibility aids**—Windows includes a number of accessibility aids such as the Magnifier (which can blow up text or graphics to a larger size) and the Onscreen Keyboard (which enables keyboard input via the mouse). Your application should not circumvent these accessibility aids.

◆ Control properties that you should set to ensure accessibility include `AccessibleDescription`, `AccessibleName`, `AccessibleRole`, `BackColor`, `ForeColor`, `FontSize`, `BackgroundImage`, `TabIndex`, and `Text`.

◆ You can support high-contrast mode by setting the value of the Boolean `SystemInformation.HighContrast` property. The `SystemEvents.UserPreferenceChanged` event is raised whenever the HighContrast property changes.

CREATING AND MANAGING COMPONENTS AND .NET ASSEMBLIES

Create and modify a .NET assembly.

◆ Assemblies are the basic unit for reuse, versioning, security, and deployment of components that are created by using the .NET Framework. Each assembly includes an assembly manifest that stores the assembly's metadata.

◆ Depending on the number of files that make up an assembly, it is called a single-file or a multifile assembly.

◆ A private assembly is an assembly that is available only to clients in the same directory structure as the assembly. A shared assembly can be referenced by more than one application and is stored in the machinewide global assembly cache (GAC). A shared assembly must be assigned a cryptographically strong name.

Create and implement satellite assemblies.

◆ Satellite assemblies are assemblies that store culture-specific information for use in localizing an application.

Create resource-only assemblies.

◆ Resource-only assemblies are assemblies that contain just resources and no code. Resource-only assemblies may be satellite assemblies, or they may hold the default resources for all or part of an application.

Create a Windows control.

◆ The Microsoft .NET Framework allows programmers to create reusable code components. You can create a Windows component for use on forms by deriving from Component, Control, or UserControl or from any of their derived classes.

◆ If you want to create a control by assembling existing controls and you want to add custom-defined functionality to it, you should choose to inherit from the UserControl class. You should create a Windows Control Library template to create a user control.

◆ You can drag and drop a custom component from the toolbox to a form's surface and set its properties just as you can with any standard Windows component.

◆ When you create a control by extending it from the Control class, the control does not have any default user interface. You need to handle the control's Paint event to render its user interface.

◆ When you don't need any visual representation for components at runtime, you can extend them from the Component class. This class does not have any user interface to show on a form, but it does provide useful properties and events that can be used by its container to customize and control its behavior.

Create a Windows control by using visual inheritance.

◆ The technique of inheriting one visual object from another visual object is known as visual inheritance. When you inherit from a control by using visual inheritance, you inherit all the functionality and user interface of the base control. This allows you to reuse code.

Host a Windows control inside Microsoft Internet Explorer.

◆ When controls are hosted inside Internet Explorer, they are rendered as object elements that do not require any registration, unlike ActiveX objects. The class ID should be assigned the assembly (.dll) path and the control name to be hosted, separated with a # (pound sign).

◆ Controls can be hosted inside Internet Explorer if the assemblies exist in the same virtual directories where the Web page resides or in the GAC.

CONSUMING AND MANIPULATING DATA

Access and manipulate data from a Microsoft SQL Server database by creating and using ad hoc queries and stored procedures.

◆ Transact-SQL is the Microsoft SQL Server dialect of the ANSI SQL-92 standard query language.

◆ You can execute T-SQL statements from a variety of interfaces, including the Visual Studio .NET IDE, osql, SQL Query Analyzer, or custom applications.

◆ SELECT statements retrieve data from tables in a database.

◆ INSERT statements add new data to tables in a database.

◆ UPDATE statements modify existing data in tables in a database.

◆ DELETE statements remove data from tables in a database.

◆ You can create new stored procedures via Server Explorer and design them directly in Visual Studio .NET.

◆ To execute a query or stored procedure, you assign the text of the query or the name of the stored procedure to the CommandText property of a SqlCommand object. You use the Execute(), ExecuteReader(), ExecuteScalar(), or ExecuteNonQuery() method to execute the command. The Execute() method returns a DataSet object. The ExecuteReader() method returns a SqlDataReader object. The ExecuteScalar() method returns a single value. The ExecuteNonQuery() method does not return a result.

Access and manipulate data from a data store. Data stores include relational databases, XML documents, and flat files. Methods include XML techniques and ADO.NET.

◆ The ADO.NET object model includes both database-specific data provider classes and database-independent DataSet classes.

◆ Data providers contain implementations of the Connection, Command, Parameter, DataReader, and DataAdapter objects that are optimized for a particular database product. For example, OleDbConnection, OleDbCommand, OleDbParameter, OleDbDataReader, and OleDbDataAdapter are designed to work with any database that supports OLE DB, whereas the SqlConnection, SqlCommand, SqlParameter, SqlDataReader, and SqlDataAdapter classes are optimized for SQL Server. A separate implementation is optimized for Oracle database, too.

◆ The SqlConnection object represents a connection to a SQL Server database.

◆ The SqlCommand object represents a command that can be executed.

◆ The SqlParameter object represents a parameter of a stored procedure.

◆ The SqlDataReader object provides a fast way to retrieve a resultset from a command.

◆ The SqlDataAdapter object implements a two-way pipeline between the database and the data model.

◆ The DataSet object represents an entire relational database in memory. It's composed of DataTable, DataRelation, DataRow, and DataColumn objects.

◆ The DataView object provides a filtered row of the data from a DataTable object.

◆ You can change data in a DataSet object by treating the items in the DataSet object like any other variables.

◆ To persist changes from the data model to the underlying database, you must call the Update() method of the SqlDataAdapter object.

◆ The `UpdateCommand` property of the `SqlDataAdapter` object specifies a `SqlCommand` object to be executed for all changed rows.

◆ The `InsertCommand` property of the `SqlDataAdapter` object specifies a `SqlCommand` object to be executed for all new rows.

◆ The `DeleteCommand` property of the `SqlDataAdapter` object specifies a `SqlCommand` object to be executed for all deleted rows.

◆ The `DataGrid` control can provide a convenient way to handle data changes on the user interface.

◆ To retrieve data from disk files as raw bytes, you use the `FileStream` object.

◆ To retrieve data from disk files in a line-oriented fashion, you use the `StreamReader` object.

◆ To retrieve data from disk files that are formatted for binary storage, you use the `BinaryReader` object.

◆ To read data from XML files quickly, in a forward-only manner, where memory is a constraint, you use `XmlTextReader`.

◆ When memory is not a constraint and you want flexibility in retrieving, inserting, deleting, and updating data in any direction from XML files, you use `XmlDocument`. The `XmlDocument` class implements the W3C Document Object Model (DOM) Level 1 Core and the Core DOM Level 2 standards.

Handle data errors.

◆ Every real-world application should include error trapping. Data manipulation adds some special requirements to error trapping code.

◆ The `SqlException` and `SqlError` objects provide you with the means to retrieve SQL Server–specific error information.

◆ When you're designing update commands, you can choose between optimistic concurrency and "last one wins" concurrency.

TESTING AND DEBUGGING

Create a unit test plan.

◆ Testing is the process of executing a program with the intention of finding errors. You should design an effective test plan to ensure that your application is free from all detectable defects and errors.

◆ Unit testing ensures that each unit of an application functions as desired. It is the lowest level of testing.

◆ Integration testing ensures that different units of an application function as expected by the test plan after they are integrated.

Implement tracing.

Add trace listeners and trace switches to an application.

◆ Listeners are objects that receive trace and debug output. By default, there is one listener, `DefaultTraceListener`, attached to the `Trace` and `Debug` classes. This listener displays the messages in the output window.

◆ `Debug` and `Trace` objects share the same `Listeners` collection. Therefore, any `Listener` object that is added to the `Trace.Listeners` collection is also added to the `Debug.Listeners` collection.

◆ Trace switches provide a mechanism that allows you to change the type of messages traced by a program, depending on a value stored in the XML configuration file. You need not recompile the application for this change to take effect; you just restart it. You need to implement code to display the messages, depending on the value of the switch.

Display trace output.

◆ The `Trace` and `Debug` classes can be used to display informative messages in an application when the `DEBUG` and `TRACE` symbols are defined, respectively, at the time of compilation.

◆ By default, both the `TRACE` and `DEBUG` symbols are defined in the `Debug` configuration for compilation. Only the `TRACE` symbol is defined for the `Release` configuration of compilation.

◆ Visual C# .NET preprocessing directives allow you to define symbols in an application, mark regions of code, and conditionally skip code for compilation.

◆ The `Conditional` attribute allows you to conditionally add or skip a method for compilation, depending on the value of the symbol passed as a parameter to the attribute.

Debug, rework, and resolve defects in code.

Configure the debugging environment.

◆ Debugging is the process of finding the causes of errors in a program, locating the lines of code causing the errors, and then fixing the errors.

◆ The three options available during step-by-step execution are Step Into, Step Over, and Step Out.

◆ Breakpoints allow you to mark code that signals the debugger to pause execution. After you encounter a breakpoint, you can choose to continue step-by-step execution or resume normal execution by clicking F5 or the Resume button.

◆ The various tool windows, such as This, Locals, Autos, Watch, and Call Stack, can be of great help in tracking the execution path and the status of variables in the process of debugging an application in Visual Studio .NET.

Create and apply debugging code to components and applications.

◆ When an exception is thrown by an application, you can either choose to continue execution or break into the debugger (to start debugging operations such as step-by-step execution). You can customize this behavior for each exception object by using the Exceptions dialog box.

◆ You can attach a debugger to a running process (local or remote) with the help of the Processes dialog box.

Provide multicultural test data to components and applications.

◆ When an application is localized for multiple cultures, you should test the application's execution by using test data from each culture. You should use this test data both with the localized version of the application and with the default version of the application.

Execute tests.

◆ To test an application by using debugging features such as breakpoints, you should execute the application by using the default Debug configuration. Debugging features are disabled in the default Release configuration.

Resolve errors and rework code.

◆ Whenever the code is modified or a new feature is added in an application, you should run all the existing test cases, along with a new set of test cases, to check the new feature. This regression testing helps in developing robust applications.

DEPLOYING A WINDOWS-BASED APPLICATION

Plan the deployment of a Windows-based application.

◆ Although .NET supports XCOPY deployment, XCOPY is not sufficient for advanced deployment requirements. For advanced requirements, you should instead use the Microsoft Windows Installer to deploy applications.

◆ Microsoft Windows Installer 2.0 is the built-in installation and configuration service of the Windows operating system. In addition to providing several advanced installation features, it also provides the ability to roll back the installation process, uninstall an application, and repair a component or an application.

◆ Visual Studio .NET provides four types of deployment templates—Setup Project (for Windows-based applications), Web Setup Project (for Web-based applications), Merge Module Project (for shared components and assemblies), and Cab Project (for ActiveX components to be downloaded over the Internet). It also provides the Setup Wizard, which helps you create installation packages for any of these deployment projects.

Plan a deployment that uses removable media.

◆ Deployment via removable media is the "lowest common denominator" solution and covers the maximum number of users.

◆ To create a setup project for removable media, you create a setup project, right-click the project in Solution Explorer, and select Properties from the shortcut menu. In the Properties window, change Package Files to In Cabinet File(s). This enables the CAB size option. Set the CAB size to Custom, and set the size depending on your media size.

Plan a Web-based deployment.

◆ Web-based deployment reduces the costs of media, replication, and distribution. It also makes the management of software updates simple.

◆ Creating a setup package for Web-based deployment is similar to doing so for network-based deployment. After the setup files are created, rather than copy them to a network share, you copy them to a virtual directory on a Web server. You might also want to password-protect the deployment Web site so that only authorized users are able to download the application.

Plan a network-based deployment.

◆ Network-based installation is useful in a scenario in which multiple users are sharing a common network. In such a case, applications can be installed via a shared network folder. This kind of deployment method is very common in corporate environments.

◆ While creating a setup project for a network-based deployment, you create a single setup package instead of creating multiple CAB files. After you have built the setup project, you copy all the setup files to a shared folder on the network and publish the address of the network to the users.

Ensure that the application conforms to Windows Installer requirements and Windows Logo Program requirements.

◆ Microsoft provides logo programs to ensure the compatibility of applications with Microsoft operating systems. The logo programs provide guidelines to developers for writing applications that interoperate properly with Windows, providing greater stability, better maintenance, and improved management features.

◆ To earn a logo, an application must meet predefined specifications, and an independent lab must test it to confirm its compliance with the specification.

◆ The Certified for Windows logo program certifies compliance with Windows 2000.

◆ The Designed for Microsoft Windows XP logo program certifies compliance with Windows XP.

◆ The Windows Installer SDK contains requirements for the Windows Installer. If you build Windows Installer packages by using Visual Studio .NET, they will automatically meet these requirements.

Create a setup program that installs an application and allows for the application to be uninstalled.

Register components and assemblies.

◆ When you include a component in a Visual Studio .NET setup project, the Windows Installer automatically handles component and assembly registration.

◆ For shared components, you should create a merge module rather than a full installation package.

◆ The `System.Configuration.Install.Installer` class works as a base class for all the custom installers in the .NET Framework.

◆ The `Installer` class method `Install()` is called when an application is installed, and `Uninstall()` is called when an application is uninstalled. The `Commit()` method is executed if the `Install()` method executes successfully, and the `Rollback()` method is executed if the `Install()` method is not executed successfully.

◆ If you add predefined installation components (for example, a `PerformanceCounter` installation component) to a setup project, they are all added to the `ProjectInstaller` class. They are actually added to the `Installers` collection of this class.

◆ You can add your own custom `Installer` classes to a project to perform custom actions through the Custom Actions Editor during installation, such as compiling the code to its native image or creating a database on a target computer.

Perform an install-time compilation of a Windows-based application.

◆ MSIL can be compiled to native code via the Native Image Generator tool (ngen.exe). The assemblies that are compiled into machine-specific native code are placed in the Native Image Cache.

Deploy a Windows-based application.

Use setup and deployment projects.

◆ The File System Editor provides mapping of a file system on a target machine. The folders are referred to by special names that during the installation process are converted to represent the folder as it is named in the file system on the target machine.

◆ The Registry Editor allows you to specify Registry keys, subkeys, and values that are added to the Registry in the target machine during installation.

◆ The File Types Editor allows you to register a file extension with a Windows application.

◆ The User Interface Editor allows you to customize the user interface that is provided to the user during the installation process. Different types of user-interfaces are available for end user installation and administrative installation.

◆ The User Interface Editor and the Launch Conditions Editor for Search Elements provide special properties (such as Property and ButtonProperty) whose values can be evaluated to perform the installation according to the end user's choice.

◆ The Custom Actions Editor allows you to add custom actions to be performed during the installation process. It allows you to run .dll, .exe, and assembly files. There are four phases when custom actions can be performed: Install, Commit, Rollback, and Uninstall.

◆ The Launch Conditions Editor allows you to set conditions to be evaluated when the installation begins on the target machine. If the conditions are not met, the installation stops.

Add assemblies to the Global Assembly Cache.

◆ Shared assemblies are used by multiple applications on a machine. They are placed in the GAC and enjoy special priviliges, such as file security (because they are placed in the System folder), shared location, and side-by-side versioning.

◆ Public/private key pairs are generated by using the Strong Name tool (sn.exe). These pairs can be used to digitally sign an assembly.

◆ You can add a shared assembly to the GAC by using Windows Explorer, the .NET Framework Configuration tool, the Global Assembly Cache tool, or the Installer tool.

◆ The best way to add an assembly during deployment is to use using Microsoft Windows Installer. The Microsoft Windows Installer provides assembly reference-counting features and manages removal of the assembly at the time of uninstallation.

◆ When the Assembly Cache folder in the System folder is viewed in Windows Explorer, it displays assemblies from the GAC and Native Image Cache.

- The CLR first searches the GAC to locate assemblies before it looks into the files and folders where the assemblies are installed. Thus, shared assemblies placed in the GAC are more efficient because the CLR does not look into the `<codebase>` and `<probing>` elements of the applicable configuration files.

- Delay signing allows a shared assembly to be placed in the GAC by just having the assembly signed with the public key. This allows the assembly to be signed with private key at a later stage, when the development process is complete and the component or assembly is ready to be deployed. This process allows developers to work with shared assemblies as if they were strongly named and yet also secure the private key of the signature from being accessed at different stages of development.

- Merge modules allow you to create reusable components that help in deploying shared components. The merge modules cannot be directly installed. They need to be merged with installer programs of a Windows application.

Verify security policies for a deployed application.

- Code Access Security allows code to be trusted to varying degrees, depending on where the code originates, the publisher, the strong name, and the security zone.

- If `AllowPartiallyTrustedCallersAttribute` is associated with a strongly named assembly, even partially trusted assemblies are allowed to call it.

- The .NET Framework Configuration tool can be used to configure the runtime security policy for an assembly or a zone.

Launch a remote application (URL remoting).

- URL remoting provides a zero deployment model for deploying a Windows application. The code and configuration files reside on a Web server, and you can execute the application just by pointing to the URL of the `.exe` file from Internet Explorer.

- The code downloaded from a URL is cached in a central location called the download cache. When a second request is made to the same content, the download cache checks the timestamp of the requested assemblies on the server and downloads the file from the server only if its timestamp has changed. Otherwise, it displays the cached copy to the user.

MAINTAINING AND SUPPORTING A WINDOWS-BASED APPLICATION

Optimize the performance of a Windows-based application.

- You should use the `StringBuilder` class for strings that will be changed during the course of a program. The `StringBuilder` class can be changed in place, unlike the `String` class, which must be destroyed and re-created.

- You should use `AddRange` to add multiple objects to collections in a single operation.

- You should use native compilation to reduce startup time. Native images load faster than MSIL code the first time the code is used.

◆ You should throw exceptions only when necessary. Exceptions are time-consuming and should not be used for normal program flow.

◆ You should minimize calls to unmanaged code and use a chunky interface rather than a chatty one. The fewer calls to unmanaged code, the faster an application will run.

◆ You should minimize calls across processes. Cross-process calls are slower than in-process calls.

◆ You should compile an application by using the Release configuration. This removes unnecessary debugging code that can slow down an application.

◆ You should avoid scaling images and performing other advanced graphics operations.

◆ You should use data source–specific managed providers for data access. These providers (such as the SqlClient classes) are more efficient than the OleDb classes for their specific databases.

◆ You should use stored procedures instead of SQL statements. Stored procedures can be precompiled on the database server for speed of execution.

◆ You should use the DataReader classes for sequential table reading.

◆ You should use connection pooling for faster database connections. Connection pooling avoids the time-consuming process of creating a new connection for each database operation.

◆ You should avoid using auto-generated commands. Such commands are convenient but impose additional runtime overhead.

◆ You should avoid distributed transactions.

Diagnose and resolve errors and issues.

◆ A process is an application that is being executed. Each running process is uniquely identified on a computer via a process identifier (PID).

◆ The Process class provides a large set of properties for getting information about running processes on a local or remote machine.

◆ The event log is a central repository for various issues that an application may encounter while it is executing. Use of an event log to record such messages not only makes the job of the system administrator easier but also allows other applications to take appropriate action when an entry is written to a log.

◆ Multiple event sources can write into an event log. However, an event source can be used to write into only one event log.

◆ By default, events of the Process and EventLog classes are not enabled. You can set the EnableRaisingEvents property to true in order to instruct these classes to raise events.

◆ Performance counters are organized in categories that define specific sets of performance counters.

◆ The process of reading a performance counter value is called sampling the performance counter. The process of updating a performance counter value is called publishing a performance counter.

CONFIGURING AND SECURING A WINDOWS-BASED APPLICATION

Configure a Windows-based application.

◆ The .NET Framework stores runtime configuration information in XML files that can be edited without the application being recompiled.

◆ Dynamic properties enable you to store component properties in runtime configuration files.

◆ Machine and application configuration files hold administrative settings such as information about configured assemblies and remoting channels.

◆ The .NET Framework Configuration Editor is a GUI interface for editing runtime configuration files.

Configure security for a Windows-based application.

Select and configure authentication type. Authentication types include Windows Authentication, None, forms-based, Microsoft Passport, and custom authentication.

◆ Windows-based applications use Windows authentication to determine role membership.

You can also implement custom authentication schemes if the Windows user identity is not sufficient for your purposes.

Specify the security level for an application.

◆ Permissions control access to resources.

◆ Code can request the minimum permissions that it needs to run and the optional permissions that it would like to have. It can also refuse permissions and demand permissions on the part of calling code.

◆ Code access permissions represent access to resources, and identity permissions represent things that the .NET Framework knows about code.

◆ The .NET Framework supplies both attribute-based declarative security and class-based imperative security.

◆ A code group is a set of assemblies that shares a security context.

◆ A permission set is a set of permissions that can be granted as a unit.

◆ The CLR computes actual permissions at runtime based on code group membership and the calling chain of the code.

Use custom attributes to configure security.

◆ To implement a custom permission, you must create a class that inherits from the `CodeAccessPermission` class.

◆ Custom permissions allow you to create your own permissions to protect particular resources.

Configure authorization.

Configure role-based authorization.

◆ The .NET Framework supports both authentication and authorization. Authentication involves verifying a user's identity. Authorization involves granting rights based on that identity.

◆ Windows applications constructed with the .NET Framework automatically use Windows authentication.

◆ You can use the `IsInRole()` method of the `WindowsPrincipal` object to check for membership in Windows groups.

Implement identity management.

◆ The `WindowsPrincipal` and `WindowsIdentity` classes let you check the authentication status of the current user.

◆ The `PrincipalPermission` class allows you to perform declarative or imperative role-based security operations.

This practice exam contains 75 questions that are representative of what you should expect on the actual exam "Developing and Implementing Windows-Based Applications with Microsoft Visual C# .NET and Microsoft Visual Studio .NET" (Exam 70-316). The answers appear at the end of this practice exam. I strongly suggest that when you take this practice exam, you treat it just as you would the actual exam at the test center. Time yourself, read carefully, don't use any reference materials, and answer all the questions as best you can.

Some of the questions may be vague and require you to make deductions to come up with the best possible answer from the possibilities given. Others may be verbose, requiring you to read and process a lot of information before you reach the actual question. These are skills that you should acquire before attempting to take the actual exam. Take this practice exam, and if you miss more than 18 questions, try rereading the chapters that contain information on the subjects in which you were weak. You can use the index to find keywords to point you to the appropriate locations.

Practice Exam

EXAM QUESTIONS

1. You have used Visual C# .NET to develop a process manager application. Your application can identify any process on the system that has a user interface, and it allows you to collect information about the process. Now you want to add code that can shut down the identified process as well. Which method should you use to shut down these processes?

   A. `Process.Kill()`

   B. `Process.WaitForExit()`

   C. `Process.CloseMainWindow()`

   D. `Process.WaitForInputIdle()`

2. You would like to give the user the ability to customize your application so that it fits in better with his or her company's corporate look and feel. In particular, you want to let the user specify text to appear in the title bar of the main menu form. How should you add this ability to your application?

   A. Supply full source code with your application and tell users that they can edit the text and rebuild the application.

   B. Let the user edit the text in the Registry and use the `Microsoft.Win32.Registry` class to retrieve the value that the user saves.

   C. Make the `Text` property of the form a dynamic property and provide an XML file that the user can edit to set the value of the property.

   D. Run code in the form's `Load` event to retrieve the form's text from a text file by using a `FileStream` object.

3. You are distributing a .NET component to target computers. This component must be installed in the global assembly cache (GAC) so that it can be shared by every application on the target computer. In addition, you want to allow clients to check the identity of your company via a certificate from a third-party authority. How should you sign this component's code?

   A. Use `sn.exe` to sign the assembly.

   B. Use `signcode.exe` to sign the assembly.

   C. Use `signcode.exe` followed by `sn.exe` to sign the assembly.

   D. Use `sn.exe` followed by `signcode.exe` to sign the assembly.

4. Your application is failing when a particular variable equals 17. Unfortunately, you cannot predict when this will happen. Which debugging tool should you use to investigate the problem?

   A. Locals Window

   B. Output Window

   C. Immediate Window

   D. Conditional Breakpoint

5. Your graphics application creates and displays a `PrintPreviewControl` control at runtime. Users complain that the preview image is not of good quality. What should you do?

   A. Set the `UseAntiAlias` property to `true`.

   B. Set the `UseAntiAlias` property to `false`.

   C. Set the `AutoZoom` property to `true`.

   D. Set the `AutoZoom` property to `false`.

6. Your application is split into two parts: The server is implemented as a Web service, and the client is implemented as a Windows forms application. The server is still under active development, even though you are already shipping the client application. You anticipate that the data returned by the server will continue to change in the near future and that clients will need to adjust their means of working with the Web service to account for these changes. How should you provide user assistance for the client application?

   A. Ship an HTML Help file with the application and use a `HelpProvider` component to display the information. Ship periodic updates of the help file to the users.

   B. Include a readme file that contains instructions for running the application and email updates to the users.

   C. Place instructions in ToolTips and ship a new client application when the instructions change.

   D. Place the help file on an Internet server that is under your direct control and use a `HelpProvider` component to display the information.

7. Your project contains the following API declaration:

```
[DllImport("kernel32.dll")]
public static extern int GetComputerName(
    String buffer, ref uint size);
```

The project also contains the following code that uses the API to display the computer name:

```
public static void ShowName()
{
        String buf = "";
        UInt32 intLen=128;
        Int32 intRet;
```

```
        // Call the Win API method
        intRet = GetComputerName(
            buf, ref intLen);

        Console.WriteLine(
          "This computer is named " +
          buf.ToString());
}
```

Users report that no computer name is displayed. What should you do?

   A. Use `ref` with the variable `buf` in the call to the `GetComputerName()` function.

   B. Tell the users that their computers have no names set in their network properties.

   C. Replace the use of `String` with `StringBuilder` in the code.

   D. Use `out` with the variable `buf` in the call to the `GetComputerName()` function.

8. You are moving an existing COM-based application to .NET. Part of your existing application depends on a third-party COM-based library to which you do not have the source code. The library is implemented as a set of objects with no user interface. How should you proceed?

   A. Use the ActiveX Control Importer to import the library.

   B. Build a COM callable wrapper for the library.

   C. Build a runtime callable wrapper (RCW) for the library.

   D. Rewrite the library into managed code.

9. Your form allows the user to enter a telephone number into a `TextBox` control named `txtPhone`. You use the `Validating` event of this control to check whether the phone number is in the correct format. If the phone number is in an incorrect format, you do not allow the focus to leave the `txtPhone` control.

The form also includes a `Button` control, `btnCancel`, to cancel the data entry action. The user should be able to click this button any time, even when there is invalid data in the text box. What should you do to ensure that this is the case?

A. Set the `CausesValidation` property of the `TextBox` control to `true`.

B. Set the `CausesValidation` property of the `Button` control to `true`.

C. Set the `CausesValidation` property of the `TextBox` control to `false`.

D. Set the `CausesValidation` property of the `Button` control to `false`.

10. The main menu form of your application uses the `System.Drawing` objects to draw your company's logo on the background of the form. You want to redraw the logo whenever the form is resized, so that it always fills the entire form. What should you do?

A. Use a `Timer` control to call the `Invalidate()` method periodically.

B. Call the `Invalidate()` method within an event handler for the form's `Resize` event.

C. Call the `Invalidate()` method within an event handler for the form's `Paint` event.

D. Set the form's `ResizeRedraw` property to `true`.

11. You are designing a Windows application that has a variety of controls on its user interface. Some controls will be used infrequently. For these controls, you do not want the user to be able to tab to the control, but the user should still be able to activate the control by clicking it. Which of the following options should you use?

A. Set the control's `TabIndex` property to `0`.

B. Set the control's `TabIndex` property to `-1`.

C. Set the control's `TabStop` property to `false`.

D. Set the control's `Enabled` property to `false`.

12. How can you generate client-side proxy classes for a Web service? (Select the two best answers.)

A. Use a proxy tool such as the .NET WebService Studio tool.

B. Use the Web Services Description Language tool.

C. Use the Web Services Discovery tool.

D. Set a Web reference to point to the Web service.

13. You are designing a Windows service that will be used by computers in many countries. The service stores information related to computer uptime and page faults. For storing this information for future analysis, which culture should you use?

A. The invariant culture.

B. The `en-US` culture.

C. The culture specified by `Thread.CurrentThread.CurrentCulture`.

D. A culture selected by the user.

14. Your form uses `Label` controls to convey information. When the text in a `Label` control represents a higher-than-average value, you want to display it in bold type; when the text in the `Label` control represents a value that requires the user's attention, you want to display it in italic type. If both conditions are true, you want to display the text in bold italic type. How should you set the `Italic FontStyle` property for the control when the value requires attention so that it adds italic, whether the font is already bold or not?

A.

```
lblSampleText.Font.Style & FontStyle.Italic
```

B.

```
lblSampleText.Font.Style ^ FontStyle.Italic
```

C.

```
lblSampleText.Font.Style | FontStyle.Italic
```

D.

```
lblSampleText.Font.Style |
    (FontStyle.Underline And FontStyle.Bold)
```

15. Your application contains the following resource files that contain string resources:

```
AppStrings.resx
AppStrings.fr.resx
AppStrings.fr-FR.resx
AppStrings.en.resx
AppStrings.en-US.resx
```

The user executes the application on a computer that is running French (Canadian) software, so the CurrentUICulture property is set to fr-CA. What is the result?

A. The resources from AppStrings.fr.resx are used.

B. The resources from AppStrings.fr-FR.resx are used.

C. The resources from AppStrings.en-US.resx are used.

D. An exception is thrown.

16. You have created an array of Project objects named aProjects. Each Project object has a Name property and a DateDue property. You want to display all the Name property values in a ListBox control named lbProjects. Which code snippet should you use for this purpose?

A.

```
lbProjects.DataSource = aProjects;
lbProjects.ValueMember = Name;
```

B.

```
lbProjects.DataSource = aProjects;
lbProjects.DisplayMember = Name;
```

C.

```
lbProjects.DataSource = aProjects;
lbProjects.ValueMember = "Name";
```

D.

```
lbProjects.DataSource = aProjects;
lbProjects.DisplayMember = "Name";
```

17. You are creating a graphics application that will manipulate a variety of image formats. You have created an OpenFileDialog object in your program and have set its Filter property as follows:

```
ofdPicture.Filter=
    "Image Files (BMP, GIF, JPEG, etc.)|" +
    "*.bmp;*.gif;*.jpg;*.jpeg;" +
    "*.png;*.tif;*.tiff|" +
    "BMP Files (*.bmp)|*.bmp|" +
    "GIF Files (*.gif)|*.gif|" +
    "JPEG Files (*.jpg;*.jpeg)" +
    "|*.jpg;*.jpeg|" +
    "PNG Files (*.png)|*.png|" +
    "TIF Files (*.tif;*.tiff)" +
    "|*.tif;*.tiff|" +
    "All Files (*.*)|*.*";
```

You have created a Button control with its Text property set to Open Image.... When you click this button, you display the OpenFileDialog object to allow a selection. You want .bmp files to be the default choice in the dialog box. Which of the following values for the FilterIndex property must you choose to achieve this in the event handler of the Button control's Click event?

A. 0

B. 1

C. 2

D. 3

18. Your application uses a graphics library from a third-party developer. This library is implemented as a COM component. You are migrating your application to .NET. What should you do to continue to use the classes and methods within the graphics library?

  A. Use the Type Library Importer to create a signed RCW for the library. Install the RCW in the GAC.

  B. Use the Type Library Importer to create an unsigned RCW for the library. Install the RCW in the GAC.

  C. Create wrapper code that uses PInvoke to call functions from the library. Import this wrapper code into your application.

  D. Obtain a primary interop assembly (PIA) from the developer of the library. Install the PIA in the GAC.

19. You are using the PrintDocument class to print a graphical banner that should span multiple printed pages. However, only the first page of the banner prints. The variable e represents the PrintPageEventArgs object. What is the most likely cause of this problem?

  A. You have neglected to set e.HasMorePages to true when more than one page should be printed.

  B. You have neglected to set a sufficiently large value for e.MarginBounds.Height.

  C. You have neglected to set a sufficiently large value for e.PageBounds.Height.

  D. You have called the Print() method only once rather than once per page.

20. You have created an ASP.NET Web service project that includes a class named RefLibrary. The RefLibrary class contains this method:

```
public String Version()
{
    Version = "1.0.0.8";
}
```

You are able to instantiate the RefLibrary class from a Web service client project, but the Version() method is not available. What could be the problem?

  A. Only void methods can be part of the public interface of a Web service.

  B. You must mark the method with the WebService attribute.

  C. The methods of a Web service can return only Object data.

  D. You must mark the method with the WebMethod attribute.

21. You are planning to deploy an assembly into the GAC so that it can be used by any application on the target computer. What must you do?

  A. Sign the assembly with a strong name.

  B. Sign the assembly with an Authenticode certificate.

  C. Compile the assembly with the default Release configuration.

  D. Use regedit to add a key to the AssemblyFolders key in the Registry.

22. Your application contains the following code:

```
private void Form1_Load(
  System.Object sender, System.EventArgs e)
{
    EventLog eventLog = new EventLog(
        "Application", ".");
    // Add an event handler for
    // the EntryWritten event
    eventLog.EntryWritten += new
      EntryWrittenEventHandler(
      eventLog_EntryWritten);
}
```

```
private void eventLog_EntryWritten( _
  Object source , EntryWrittenEventArgs e)
{
    Debug.WriteLine(e.Entry.Message.Trim());
}
```

After you run this code, no event messages are written to the output window. You have verified that events are being posted to the Application event log. What could be the problem?

A. `EventLog` is not configured to receive `EntryWritten` event notifications.

B. You can monitor events from only the System event log.

C. The text of the event log entry is in the `EventLogEntry.Source` property.

D. You are not a member of the local `Administrators` group.

23. You wrote a COM component to accept data from an analog-to-digital converter card and made it available to your analysis program. Now you're moving that analysis program to .NET. The COM component is used nowhere else, and you have not shipped copies of it to anyone else. You want to call the objects in the COM server from your new .NET client. How should you proceed?

A. Use the Type Library Importer to create an unsigned RCW for the COM component.

B. Use the Type Library Importer to create a signed RCW for the COM component.

C. Set a direct reference from your .NET client to the COM server.

D. Use `PInvoke` to instantiate classes from the COM component.

24. Users of your application want to be able to set all properties of their printers, such as device settings and printer security, from within your application. Which component should you add to your form to easily enable this?

A. `PrintDocument`

B. `PrintDialog`

C. `PrintPreviewDialog`

D. `PageSetupDialog`

25. You are shipping a text-editing application to a variety of locales, including the United States, France, Israel, China, and Japan. One feature of the application is that the user can use it to search for text within long text passages. What should you use to perform this search?

A. `CultureInfo.CompareInfo`

B. `Array.Sort()`

C. `String.IndexOf()`

D. `String.IndexOfAny()`

26. You are invoking a Web service that returns a `StreamReader` object. Which project requires a reference to the `System.IO` namespace, where this object is defined?

A. The client project

B. Both the client project and the Web service project

C. The Web service project

D. Neither project

27. You have created a `DataSet` object that contains a single `DataTable` object named `Customers`. The `Customers` object has all the rows and columns from the Customers table in your database. Now you would like to bind only selected columns from the Customers table to a `DataGrid` control. How should you proceed?

A. Create a second `DataTable` object in the `DataSet` object. Copy the desired data to the second `DataTable` object. Bind the second `DataTable` object to the `DataGrid` control.

B. Create a `Command` object to retrieve the desired columns from the `DataTable` object. Bind the `Command` object to the `DataGrid` control.

C. Bind the `DataGrid` control to the entire `DataTable` object. Use the `Width` property of the columns in the `DataGrid` control to hide the columns that are not desired, by setting them to zero width.

D. Create a `DataView` object that retrieves only the desired tables from the `DataTable` object. Bind the `DataGrid` control to the `DataView` object.

28. You plan to use objects from the `System.Drawing` namespace to draw shapes on a form at runtime. You have already determined that you will draw these shapes during the form's `Paint` event. How should you create the `Graphics` object required by the `System.Drawing` classes?

    A. Call the `CreateGraphics()` method of the form.

    B. Retrieve the `Graphics` property of the `PaintEventArgs` object that is passed to the event.

    C. Pass the handle of the form to the `Graphics.FromHwnd()` method.

    D. Call the `CreateGraphics()` method of the control that has the focus.

29. Your application calls a Web service that retrieves and compares `traceroute` timing information from multiple servers around the world. Users complain that the user interface of the application is unresponsive while this information is being retrieved. What can you do to fix this problem?

    A. Move the application to a faster computer.

    B. Install a faster link to the Internet.

    C. Install more memory in the computer.

    D. Use asynchronous calls to invoke the Web service.

30. Your application includes a `SqlDataAdapter` object named `sqlDataAdapter1` that was created by dragging and dropping the Customers table from a database to your form. Your application also includes a `DataSet` object named `dsCustomers1`, that is based on this `SqlDataAdapter` object. What line of code should you use to load the data from the database into the `DataSet` object?

    A.
    ```
    dsCustomers1= sqlDataAdapter1.Fill(
        "Customers");
    ```

    B.
    ```
    sqlDataAdapter1.Fill(
        "dsCustomers1", "Customers");
    ```

    C.
    ```
    sqlDataAdapter1.Fill(
        dsCustomers1, "Customers");
    ```

    D.
    ```
    sqlDataAdapter1.Fill("dsCustomers1");
    ```

31. You are developing an accounting application that includes a class named `Transaction`. The `Transaction` class is inherited by subclasses such as `DepositTransaction` and `PaymentTransaction`. The `Transaction` class includes a method named `VerifyChecksum()`. The `VerifyChecksum()` method should be available to the `Transaction` class and to all classes derived from the `Transaction` class, but it should not be available to any other classes in the application. Which access modifier should you use in the declaration of the `VerifyChecksum()` method?

    A. `protected`

    B. `public`

C. `private`

D. `internal`

32. A `TextBox` control on your form should accept no more than three characters from the user. However, your code may need to place the value `Invalid` in the `TextBox` control. What value should you use for the `MaxLength` property of this control?

   A. `3`

   B. `4`

   C. `7`

   D. `8`

33. Your application contains a form, `Form1`, with its `BackColor` property set to `Red`. You add a new form, `Form2`, to the application by using visual inheritance to derive the new form from `Form1`. You set `Form2` to be the startup object for the application, and you set its `BackColor` property to `Blue`. Next, you change the `BackColor` property of `Form1` to `Yellow`. When you run the application, what is the `BackColor` of `Form2` set to?

   A. `Blue`

   B. `Red`

   C. `Yellow`

   D. `Control`

34. You have purchased a library of shared communications routines that is delivered as a .NET assembly. You want to make the classes in this assembly available to all your .NET applications. Where should you install the assembly?

   A. In the GAC

   B. In `C:\WINNT\System32`

   C. In each application's private directory

   D. In the directory specified by the `ASSEMBLY` environment variable

35. Your department is responsible for maintaining a variety of accounting applications. You've been assigned the task of creating a standard control to represent credit and debit accounts. The control will be made up of a collection of `TextBox` and `ComboBox` controls. On which class should you base this control?

   A. `Control`

   B. `UserControl`

   C. `Form`

   D. `Component`

36. Your application includes a `ListBox` control named `lbCourses` that displays a list of college courses. The `DisplayMember` property of the `ListBox` control is bound to the `CourseName` column of the `Courses` database table. The `ValueMember` property of the `ListBox` control is bound to the `CourseNumber` column of the `Courses` database table.

   Your form also contains a `TextBox` control named `txtCourseNumber`. This control uses simple data binding to display the `CourseNumber` column from the `StudentSchedules` table in your database.

   When the user selects a course name in the `ListBox` control, you want to display the corresponding `CourseNumber` value in the `txtCourseNumber` control. What should you do?

   A. Use simple data binding to bind the `SelectedValue` property of the `ListBox` control to the `CourseNumber` column of the `StudentSchedules` table.

   B. Use simple data binding to bind the `ValueMember` property of the `ListBox` control to the `Text` property of the `TextBox` control.

   C. Use the `SelectedIndexChanged` event of the `ListBox` control to copy the data from the `ListBox` control to the `TextBox` control.

D. Use simple data binding to bind the `SelectedValue` property of the `ListBox` control to the `CourseNumber` column of the `Courses` table.

37. You are planning to display invoices on a `DataGrid` control. The user will specify a customer, and then you'll retrieve from the database all the invoices for that customer. Which database object should you use to retrieve these invoices?

    A. A table

    B. A view

    C. An index

    D. A stored procedure

38. Your application's main form contains two `Button` controls, named `btnA` and `btnB`. When the user clicks either of these controls, or when the user moves the mouse over either of these controls, you want to run code to display a message on the form. The message is identical in all cases. How should you structure your code to fulfill this requirement?

    A. Write four separate event handlers, one each for the `Click` event of `btnA`, the `MouseMove` event of `btnA`, the `Click` event of `btnB`, and the `MouseMove` event of `btnB`.

    B. Write two event handlers, the first to handle both `Click` events and the second to handle both `MouseMove` events.

    C. Write two event handlers, the first to handle the `Click` and `MouseMove` events for `btnA` and the second to handle the `Click` and `MouseMove` events for `btnB`.

    D. Write a single event handler to handle the `Click` and `MouseMove` events of both controls.

39. Your application contains Unicode strings encoded in the UTF-16 format. You'd like to save a copy of those strings to disk in UTF-7 format. What should you do?

    A. Use the `Unicode.GetChars()` method to perform the conversion.

    B. Use the `Unicode.GetBytes()` method to perform the conversion.

    C. Use the `UTF7Encoding.GetChars()` method to perform the conversion.

    D. Use the `UTF7Encoding.GetBytes()` method to perform the conversion.

40. Your code uses the `Trace` class to produce debugging output. In which configuration(s) will this output be enabled?

    A. In the default `Release` configuration only.

    B. In the default `Debug` configuration only.

    C. In both the default `Release` configuration and the default `Debug` configuration.

    D. In neither the default `Release` configuration nor the default `Debug` configuration.

41. Your application executes the following code:

```
Trace.Listeners.Add(new
    TextWriterTraceListener("TraceLog.txt"));
```

When your application is running in the default `Release` configuration, where will messages from the `Trace` class appear?

    A. They will appear in the output window and in the `TraceLog.txt` file.

    B. They will appear in the output window only.

    C. They will appear in the `TraceLog.txt` file only.

    D. No trace messages will appear in this configuration.

42. You want your application to monitor for changes to the HighContrast setting at runtime, so that it can remove a background image from a form if necessary. Which event must you trap?

    A. SystemEvents.UserPreferenceChanged

    B. this.Paint

    C. SystemEvents.PaletteChanged

    D. this.Load

43. Your application allows the user to choose between two different sizes of text when printing reports. Users complain that when they choose the small font, there is excessive space between the lines of the report. What should you do to fix this problem?

    A. Call the Graphics.MeasureString() method to get the width of the text before it is printed.

    B. Call the Font.GetHeight() method to determine the vertical size of the font.

    C. Set the AutoZoom property of the associated PrintPreviewDialog component to true.

    D. Force the users to use the larger font.

44. You are supplying both an application and a help file for the application to your users. The help file is in HTML Help 1.3 format. There is a button on your form that you would like to use to display the table of contents of the help file. What should you use for this task?

    A. HelpProvider component

    B. HelpProvider class

    C. Help.ShowHelp() method

    D. ToolTip component

45. Your application displays the distance to various planets in a variety of units. You are beginning to sell this application in multiple countries. How should you ensure that the correct numeric formatting is used in all cases?

    A. Allow the user to select a culture from a list. Create a CultureInfo object based on the user's selection and assign it to the Thread.CurrentThread.CurrentCulture property. Use the ToString() method to format numeric amounts.

    B. Accept the Thread.CurrentThread.CurrentCulture property as it is set when you run the application. Use the ToString() method to format numeric amounts.

    C. Prompt the user for a numeric format and store it in the Registry.

    D. Allow the user to select a numeric format from a list of supported formats.

46. Your application uses a SqlDataReader object to retrieve patient information from a medical records database. When you find a patient who is currently hospitalized, you want to read the names of the patient's caregivers from the same database. You have created a second SqlDataReader object, based on a second SqlCommand object, to retrieve the caregiver information. Calling the ExecuteReader() method of the SqlCommand object is causing an error. What is the most likely cause of this error?

    A. You are using the same SqlConnection object for both of the SqlDataReader objects, and the first SqlDataReader object is still open when you try to execute the SqlCommand object.

    B. You must use a SqlDataAdapter object to retrieve the caregiver information.

C. You must use the `OleDbDataReader` object to retrieve information from the SQL Server database.

D. You are using the `ExecuteReader()` method of the `SqlCommand` object, but you should be using the `ExecuteScalar()` method instead.

47. You want to use a Web service that supplies travel weather information in your application. You know the URL of the `.asmx` file published by the Web service, but you do not know any details of the Web service's interface. What action should you take first?

    A. Run the Web Service Discovery tool.

    B. Open the `.asmx` file in a Web browser.

    C. Run the XML Schema Definition tool.

    D. Copy the `.asmx` file to your client project.

48. Your application retrieves data from the `Customers` and `Orders` tables in a database by using a view named `vwCustOrders`. This view is used to set the `CommandText` property for the `SelectCommand` property of a `DataAdapter` object. The application uses the `Fill()` method of this `DataAdapter` object to fill a `DataSet` object that is bound to a `DataGrid` control.

    Users report that changes they make to data displayed on the `DataGrid` control are not saved to the database. What could be the problem?

    A. The `DataGrid` control does not support editing data from a database.

    B. You cannot update a `DataSet` object that's based on a view.

    C. The `DataGrid` control does not support two-way data binding.

    D. Your application does not call the `Update()` method of the `DataAdapter` object.

49. Your application needs to store a large amount of data in a disk file between program runs. You'd like to store this information without wasting space. The disk file does not need to be easily readable by human beings. Which class should you use to accomplish this task?

    A. `StreamWriter`

    B. `FileStream`

    C. `BinaryWriter`

    D. `StringWriter`

50. You are designing a file-analysis application that will use heuristic methods to find information in arbitrary files. When the user specifies a disk file, you want to open that file and read it 1 byte at a time. Which .NET class can you use to accomplish this task?

    A. `BinaryReader`

    B. `StreamReader`

    C. `FileStream`

    D. `StringReader`

51. You have created a custom component for your application that monitors a bidirectional parallel port for error messages. This component raises an event named `PortError` whenever an error message is detected. At that point, you must make the error code available to the control container. How should you do this?

    A. Place the error code in a property of the component for the container to retrieve.

    B. Pass the error code as a parameter of the `PortError` cvcnt.

    C. Define a public variable in a separate class and place the value in that variable.

D. Define a custom `PortErrorEventArgs` class that inherits from the `EventArgs` class and pass an instance of the class as a parameter of the `PortError` event.

52. You are responsible for maintaining a COM component that is used by numerous applications throughout your company. You are not yet ready to migrate this COM component to .NET managed code, but you need to make it available to an increasing number of other projects that are being developed under the .NET Framework. What should you do?

   A. Set a direct reference to the existing COM component from each .NET project.

   B. Use the Type Library Importer to create and sign an assembly that will use the COM component. Place the COM component in the GAC.

   C. Obtain a PIA for the COM component.

   D. Set a direct reference from a single .NET project to the COM component. Include this project in each solution that must make use of the component.

53. Which of these applications cannot be deployed by the simple `XCOPY` method?

   A. An application that must deploy assemblies to the GAC.

   B. An application that makes use of private assemblies.

   C. An application that requires a configuration file.

   D. An application that is compiled in `Debug` mode.

54. You are using the Installer tool (`installutil.exe`) to install a set of components. You issue the following command to do so:

```
installutil Assembly1.exe Assembly2.exe
➡Assembly3.exe
```

`Assembly2` fails to install properly on the target computer. Which assemblies will be installed by the command?

   A. None of the assemblies will be installed.

   B. Only `Assembly1.exe` will be installed.

   C. Only `Assembly3.exe` will be installed.

   D. Both `Assembly1.exe` and `Assembly3.exe` will be installed.

55. You need to retrieve data from a SQL Server database. Which connection class should you use for maximum performance?

   A. `System.Data.SqlClient.SqlConnection`

   B. `System.Data.OleDb.OleDbConnection`

   C. `System.Data.ConnectionState`

   D. `System.Data.Odbc.OdbcConnection`

56. Your application depends on an assembly from another developer. This assembly isn't signed with an Authenticode key or a strong name, but you have determined that it can be trusted. You want to grant this code permissions by using the .NET Framework Configuration tool. Which type of membership condition should you use to create a code group that contains only this assembly?

   A. Software publisher

   B. Cryptographic hash

   C. Strong name

   D. URL

57. Your corporate counsel insists that the documents generated by your program be printed on legal-sized paper. Unfortunately, users sometimes use the Printer Setup dialog box to switch to letter-sized paper for their own convenience.

Which event of the `PrintDocument` class can you use to check and (if necessary) change the paper tray?

A. `BeginPrint`

B. `EndPrint`

C. `PrintPage`

D. `QueryPageSettings`

58. `Form1` contains a `TextBox` control named `TextBox1`. The `KeyPreview` property of `Form1` is set to true. The code for this form includes the following event handlers:

```
private void Form1_KeyPress(object sender,
  System.Windows.Forms.KeyPressEventArgs e)
{
    if(e.KeyChar == 'a')
    {
        Debug.WriteLine("Handled by form");
        e.Handled = true;
    }
}

private void TextBox1_KeyPress(
  object sender,
  System.Windows.Forms.KeyPressEventArgs e)
{
    if(e.KeyChar == 'a')
    {
        Debug.WriteLine(
            "Handled by textbox");
    }
}

private void textBox1_KeyDown(
   object sender,
   System.Windows.Forms.KeyEventArgs e)
{
    if(e.KeyCode == Keys.A)
    {
        Debug.WriteLine(
            "Handled by textbox");
    }
}
```

If the user presses the A key with the focus in `TextBox1`, what is the output?

A.

```
Handled by form
```

B.

```
Handled by textbox
Handled by form
Handled by textbox
```

C.

```
Handled by textbox
Handled by form
```

D.

```
Handled by textbox
```

59. You want to display a help button on the title bar of your Windows form. Which property settings should you make?

A. `HelpButton` = true, `MinimizeBox` = true, `MaximizeBox` = true

B. `HelpButton` = true, `MinimizeBox` = true, `MaximizeBox` = false

C. `HelpButton` = true, `MinimizeBox` = false, `MaximizeBox` = false

D. `HelpButton` = true, `MinimizeBox` = false, `MaximizeBox` = true

60. Your application allows you to select any event log on the local computer and monitor that event log for new entries. When a new entry is made to the event log, the application displays the text of the entry. You can then enter an explanatory note, if you like, which is posted back to the event log as another entry.

Now you are adding the capability to work with remote computers as well as the local computer. Which functionality must you disable for remote computers?

A. Retrieve a list of event logs on the remote computer.

B. Retrieve a list of entries in an event log.

C. Display the text of new entries.

D. Post notes back to the event log.

61. Your application will be used by people who depend on accessibility aids such as screen readers. Which properties should you explicitly set for every control? (Select the two best answers.)

    A. `ForeColor`

    B. `AccessibleName`

    C. `AccessibleRole`

    D. `AccessibleDescription`

62. You are creating a custom exception named `BusinessException` for your application. Which constructors should you implement for this class? (Select the three best answers.)

    A.
    ```
    public MyOwnCustomException ()
    ```

    B.
    ```
    public MyOwnCustomException (
      Exception inner) : base(inner)
    ```

    C.
    ```
    public MyOwnCustomException (
      string message) : base(message)
    ```

    D.
    ```
    public MyOwnCustomException(string message,
      Exception inner) : base(message, inner)
    ```

63. Your application requires the ability to access OLE DB data sources in order to function properly. Which .NET security feature should you use to ensure that your code has this ability?

    A. Role-based security

    B. Encryption

    C. Code access security

    D. Type safety

64. Your application connects to a SQL Server database by using the `System.Data.SqlClient.SqlConnection` object. It then runs a stored procedure by using a `System.Data.SqlClient.SqlCommand` object and retrieves the results into a `System.Data.SqlClient.SqlDataReader` object. The application reads two fields from each row of data and concatenates their values into a string variable. What can you do to optimize this application?

    A. Replace the `SqlConnection` object with an `OleDbConnection` object.

    B. Replace the stored procedure with a SQL statement.

    C. Replace the `SqlDataReader` object with a `DataSet` object.

    D. Replace the string variable with a `StringBuilder` object.

65. You are performing final acceptance testing on your application prior to shipping it. You have set a breakpoint inside the `SelectedIndexChanged` event handler for a combo box. However, when you select a new value in this combo box, the code does not stop at the breakpoint. What could be the problem?

    A. Selecting a value in a combo box does not fire the `SelectedIndexChanged` event.

    B. You are executing the project by using the default `Release` configuration.

    C. You have neglected to add the `[Conditional("DEBUG")]` attribute to the event handlers.

    D. You have neglected to add `const int DEBUGGING = 1` to the code.

66. Assembly A is a member of the following code groups (and only the following code groups):

Level	Code Group	Permission Set	Exclusive	LevelFinal
Enterprise	All Code	Everything	No	No
Enterprise	Special Code	LocalIntranet	No	No
Enterprise	Restricted Code	Nothing	No	No
Enterprise	Restricted Components	Nothing	No	No

What permission does the CLR assign to Assembly A?

A. Everything

B. LocalIntranet

C. Internet

D. Nothing

67. Your application includes a procedure that deletes many records from a database. When this procedure is invoked, you want the user to explicitly confirm his or her intention to delete the records. You have developed a form named frmConfirm to perform the confirmation. This form includes two Button controls, btnOK and btnCancel. The DialogResult property of btnOK is set to OK, and the DialogResult property of btnCancel is set to Cancel.

Which code snippet should you use to display frmConfirm and process the user's choice?

A.

```
frmConfirm frm = new frmConfirm();
frm.ShowDialog();
if(frm.DialogResult == DialogResult.OK)
{
    // Delete the records
}
```

B.

```
frmConfirm frm = new frmConfirm();
frm.Show();
if(frm.DialogResult == DialogResult.OK)
{
    // Delete the records
}
```

C.

```
frmConfirm frm = new frmConfirm();
frm.ShowDialog();
if(frm.btnOK.DialogResult ==
        DialogResult.OK)
{
    // Delete the records
}
```

D.

```
frmConfirm frm = new frmConfirm();
frm.Show();
if(frm.btnOK.DialogResult ==
        DialogResult.OK)
{
    // Delete the records
}
```

68. You have deployed your .NET application to several computers in the SALES domain that are not used for development. Your own computer is in the DEVELOPMENT domain. There is a two-way trust relationship established between the SALES domain and the DEVELOPMENT domain. Users report problems with the running application. You want to attach to the remote process for debugging, but you are unable to do so. What could be the problem?

A. The Machine Debug Manager (`mdm.exe`) is not installed on the computers in the SALES domain.

B. Visual Studio .NET does not support cross-domain debugging.

C. You cannot attach to a remote process that was compiled in the default `Release` configuration.

D. You must add a switch to the application's configuration file to enable remote debugging.

69. You are designing a custom control for use in industrial automation. This control will monitor a serial port and raise events based on data sent in through the serial port. This control will be hosted on forms, but it does not require any visual representation at runtime. From which class should you derive this control?

   A. `Control`

   B. `UserControl`

   C. `Form`

   D. `Component`

70. Your application includes a `CheckBox` control with its `ThreeState` property set to `true`. Your form displays this control in the indeterminate state. You want to take an action only if the user checks the `CheckBox` control. Which code snippet should you use?

   A.
```
if (chkTriState.CheckState ==
    CheckState.Checked)
{
    // Take action
}
```

B.
```
if (chkTriState.Checked)
{
    // Take action
}
```

C.
```
if (chkTriState.CheckState ==
    CheckState.Indeterminate)
{
    // Take action
}
```

D.
```
if (chkTriState.CheckState ==
    CheckState.Unchecked)
{
    // Take action
}
```

71. Your form requires a control that behaves exactly like a `TextBox` control, except that for certain values you want to display the text in red. From which class should you derive this control?

   A. `UserControl`

   B. `TextBox`

   C. `Control`

   D. `Component`

72. You have created a .NET component that will be used by multiple applications from your company. You want to be sure that this component is always installed in the same place and always has the same Registry settings. What type of installation should you create for the component?

   A. XCOPY installation

   B. Windows Installer merge module

   C. Windows Installer transform

   D. Windows Installer package

73. Your code would like file I/O permission, but it can run without this permission. You plan to request the permission and trap the error that occurs if the permission is not granted. Which `SecurityAction` flag should you use with the `FileIoPermission` object?

    A. `SecurityAction.RequestMinimum`

    B. `SecurityAction.RequestOptional`

    C. `SecurityAction.Demand`

    D. `SecurityAction.RequestRefuse`

74. The following code handles the `Click` event of `Button1`:

```csharp
private void Button1_Click(object sender, _
    System.EventArgs e)
{
        Int32 i, j;
        try
        {
            i = 0;
            j = 5 / i;
            Debug.WriteLine(
                "Result = " + j.ToString());
        }
        catch (ArithmeticException aex)
        {
            Debug.WriteLine(
                "Arithmetic Exception");
            goto EndIt;
        }
        catch (Exception ex)
        {
            Debug.WriteLine(
                "Unknown Exception");
            goto EndIt;
        }
        finally
        {
            Debug.WriteLine("Cleaning up");
            i = 0;
            j = 0;
        }
EndIt:
}
```

What is the output that appears when `Button1` is clicked?

A.
```
ArithmeticException
UnknownExcaption
```

B.
```
ArithmeticException
```

C.
```
Result =
ArithmeticException
Cleaning Up
```

D.
```
ArithmeticException
CleaningUp
```

75. Your application will use `SqlCommand` objects to directly manipulate the data in a SQL Server database. One of the tasks that you need to perform is to add a new row to a table in the database. Which SQL keyword should you use for this task?

    A. `SELECT`

    B. `UPDATE`

    C. `UNION`

    D. `INSERT`

ANSWERS TO EXAM QUESTIONS

1. **C.** You should use `Process.CloseMainWindow()` to shut down any application that has a user interface. This method gives the application a chance to clean up resources. `Process.Kill()` also shuts down the application, but it does not let normal cleanup processing proceed.

2. **C.** Dynamic properties provide a built-in mechanism to set properties at runtime without requiring you to write any code.

3. **D.** You need to sign the code with `sn.exe` to give it a strong name so that it can be stored in the GAC, and you need to sign it with `signcode.exe` to give it an Authenticode signature. The two tools should always be used in that order.

4. **D.** A conditional breakpoint lets you pause code only when a particular condition is true. In this case, you can use that capability to break into the code when the variable has the value 17.

5. **A.** Setting the `PrintPreviewControl.UseAntiAlias` property to `true` gives you a higher-quality print preview. The tradeoff is longer rendering times.

6. **D.** Because the application uses a Web service, you're assured that users have Internet access. Placing the help file on an Internet server allows you to display it on the form like any other help file but to change it quickly in one central location when it needs to be updated.

7. **C.** In the `PInvoke` calls, you should use `StringBuilder` instead of `String` to hold the return value.

8. **C.** RCWs let you call existing COM components from .NET code without requiring a code rewrite.

9. **D.** Setting the `CausesValidation` property of a control to `false` causes the `Validating` events of other controls to be ignored when the focus is shifted to the specified control.

10. **D.** The `Invalidate()` method triggers the `Paint` event, so calling it within the `Paint` event leads to an infinite regress. You could call the `Invalidate()` method periodically or in response to a `Resize` event, but using the `ResizeRedraw` property requires less code and is thus the preferable solution.

11. **C.** Setting the control's `TabStop` property to `false` removes the control from the tab order. If you set the control's `Enabled` property to `false`, the control cannot get the focus under any circumstances.

12. **B and D.** The .NET WebService Studio tool is used to invoke a Web service for testing. The Web Services Discovery tool can locate files that are related to a Web service, but it does not build any code. The other two methods can generate proxy classes for use in a client application.

13. **A.** For information that will not be directly displayed to an end user but that may need to be used from many different locales, the invariant culture provides a culture-neutral storage format.

14. **C.** Using the Or (|) operator sets the proper bit to represent the `Italic` `FontStyle` without altering any other bits that may already be set.

15. **A.** If resources from a specific culture are not found, the .NET Framework falls back to using resources from the appropriate neutral culture, in this case the `fr` culture.

16. **D.** To display values from an array in a `ListBox` control or a `ComboBox` control, you set the `DisplayMember` property of the control to a string that contains the name of the field.

17. **C.** The filters in the OpenFileDialog control are numbered, starting at 1. The first filter, `Image Files (BMP, GIF, JPEG, etc.)| "*.bmp;*.gif;*.jpg;*.jpeg;*.png;*.tif;*.tiff`, having `FilterIndex` set to 1, displays all the files; the second filter, `BMP Files (*.bmp)|*.bmp`, having `FilterIndex` set to 2, displays only the `.bmp` files.

18. **D.** Because the COM library comes from a third-party company, the only proper way to proceed is to obtain a PIA from that company. You should not import and sign code that you did not write yourself.

19. **A.** You need to set `PrintPageEventArgs.HasMorePages` to `true` in the `PrintPage` event when more than one page needs to be printed in the current print job.

20. **D.** The public, remotely accessible methods of a Web service are methods that are marked with the `WebMethod` attribute.

21. **A.** Only assemblies with strong names can be installed in the GAC. This allows the CLR to ensure that an assembly has not been tampered with and prevents naming collisions with assemblies from other developers.

22. **A.** You must set the `EventLog.EnableRaisingEvents` property to `true` to handle events from an event log in your code.

23. **C.** The COM component is used in only one project, so there's no penalty for using the easy direct reference method to use the objects in the COM component.

24. **B.** The `PrintDialog` component displays the standard Windows Print dialog box.

25. **A.** `Array.Sort` does not locate substrings. `String.IndexOf` and `String.IndexOfAny` can find substrings, but they are not culture-aware. Only the `CompareInfo` object can correctly handle the search in all character sets, including those that use 2 bytes per character.

26. **B.** Both the original object on the server and the proxy object on the client are instances of the same class, so both projects need a reference to the namespace that defines the class.

27. **D.** The `DataView` object provides a customized, bindable view of a `DataTable` object.

28. **B.** Because the `Graphics` object is so frequently needed during the `Paint` event, it is automatically passed to that event's handler.

29. **D.** Calls to a Web service will block other processing unless you use asynchronous calls to invoke the Web service.

30. **C.** To fill a `DataSet` object, you pass both the `DataSet` object and the name of the `DataTable` object to be created to the `Fill()` method of an appropriate `DataAdapter` object.

31. **A.** The `protected` modifier limits member access to the class that contains the member and to subclasses of that class. `public` allows any class to call the member. `private` limits access to the defining class only. `internal` limits access to classes within the same project, whether they are derived from the defining class or not.

32. **A.** The `MaxLength` property only has an effect on user input. It is not checked when you programmatically set the value of a control.

33. **A.** Assigning a value directly to the `BackColor` property of `Form2` overrides the inheritance from `Form1`. Further changes to the same property on `Form1` do not have any effect on `Form2`.

34. **A.** Assemblies installed in the GAC are available to all .NET code on the computer.

35. **B.** The `UserControl` class provides you with a design surface on which you can assemble constituent controls to create a custom control.

36. **A.** Using simple data binding is the easiest way to move values from one database table to another via controls on a Windows form.

37. **D.** A parameterized stored procedure allows you to pass in a parameter (in this case, the identifier for the customer) and use the parameter to limit the data returned.

38. **B.** You should avoid duplicating code if you don't have to. However, the `Click` and `MouseMove` event handlers of the `Button` control have different signatures. So you need to write two event handlers: one to handle both `Click` events and one to handle both `MouseMove` events.

39. **D.** The `GetBytes()` method of any encoding translates from Unicode characters to bytes that are appropriate for the `Encoding` object that's in use.

40. **C.** The `TRACE` symbol is defined in both the default `Debug` configuration and the default `Release` configuration. The `DEBUG` symbol is defined only in the default `Debug` configuration.

41. **A.** By default, Windows displays all `Trace` messages in the output window. If you add another `TraceListener` object to the `Listeners` collection of the `Trace` object, messages are sent to the new listener and to the output window.

42. **A.** The `UserPreferenceChanged` event is raised whenever the user changes display properties. You can check the `SystemInformation.HighContrast` property in this event to determine whether the user has entered high-contrast mode.

43. **B.** The `Font.GetHeight()` method allows you to determine the vertical size of the font so you can adjust the printing position of lines on the page.

44. **C.** The `Help.ShowHelp()` method displays the contents of a specified help file, without requiring a keyword or topic name.

45. **A.** Allowing the user to choose a culture is better than accepting the existing culture of the application because the user might be running a version of Windows that's not appropriate for his or her culture. There's no need to prompt for or store a numeric format because all necessary formats are stored in the .NET Framework.

46. **A.** You can have only a single `SqlDataReader` object open on a single `SqlConnection` object. If you need a second `SqlDataReader` object, you need to open a second `SqlConnection` object.

47. **A.** The Web Services Discovery tool uses the information in the `.asmx` file to locate the other important files for the Web service, including the WSDL file that specifies the Web service's interface.

48. **D.** Changes that are made to a `DataGrid` control that is bound to a `DataSet` control are automatically saved to the `DataSet` control. However, they are not persisted to the underlying data source until you call the `Update()` method of the `DataAdapter` object that was used to fill the `DataSet` control.

49. **C.** The `BinaryReader` class uses an efficient encoding method to write data to disk, but the results are not human readable.

50. **C.** The `FileStream` class is designed for byte-by-byte input and output. The other classes add additional functionality, but they require you to have prior knowledge of the structure of the file you're reading.

51. **D.** Using a class derived from `EventArgs` to pass event parameters is preferable to using individual arguments because it can more readily be extended in case you need to pass additional parameters in the future.

52. **B.** Using the Type Library Importer allows you to place the RCW assembly in the GAC so that it can be shared by all projects on the computer. A PIA is for code from other vendors, not for your own code.

53. **A.** An application that must deploy assemblies to the GAC should be deployed by using Windows Installer.

54. **A.** The `installutil.exe` tool treats each command line as a single transaction. If any of the assemblies listed in the command fails to install, the entire installation is rolled back.

55. **A.** `System.Data.SqlClient.SqlConnection` offers the best possible performance for SQL Server data sources because it talks directly to SQL Server by using the native TDS protocol.

56. **B.** A cryptographic hash uniquely identifies a particular version of a particular assembly. You can't use a software publisher membership condition because the code does not have an Authenticode signature.

57. **D.** The `QueryPageSettings` event fires before each page is printed and allows you to check and change page settings. Page settings cannot be changed in the `PrintPage` event.

58. **C.** The `KeyDown` event occurs before the `KeyPress` events. Setting the `Handled` property to `true` in the form's `KeyPress` event prevents the control's `KeyPress` event from firing.

59. **C.** The help button will be displayed on the title bar only if both the `MinimizeBox` and `MaximizeBox` properties are set to `false`.

60. **D.** You can enumerate and retrieve entries from the remote event logs, but you can only post new entries to an event log on the local computer.

61. **B** and **D.** The `AccessibleName` and `AccessbleDescription` properties provide information directly to screen reader programs.

62. **A, C,** and **D.** These are the three constructors that any `Exception` class should implement. Custom exception classes require the same three constructors that are defined in the base `System.Exception` class.

63. **C.** With code access security, you can use `OleDbPermission` to grant permission to use OLE DB data sources.

64. **D.** Strings in Visual C# .NET are immutable, so concatenating multiple values into a string requires you to delete and re-create the string many times. The `StringBuilder` object is optimized for changing textual data.

65. **B.** Breakpoints and other debugging features are not enabled in the default `Release` configuration.

66. **A.** Within a level, the permission set granted to an assembly is the union of all the permission sets of code groups on that level to which the assembly belongs.

67. **A.** To pause the rest of the application while the user makes a choice, you should use the `ShowDialog()` method rather than the `Show()` method to display the form. When the user clicks a button on the form, the value of the `DialogResult` property of that button is assigned to the `DialogResult` property of the form.

68. **A.** To enable remote debugging on a computer, the Machine Debug Manager must be installed. You can install this software by installing Visual Studio .NET on the remote machine or by installing Remote Components Setup on the remote machine.

69. **D.** When a custom control does not require a runtime user interface, the `Component` class provides the lowest overhead.

70. **A.** If a `CheckBox` control has its `ThreeState` property set to `true`, its `Checked` property returns `true` even if the check box is in the indeterminate state. You must evaluate the `CheckState` property to determine whether the check box is actually checked.

71. **B.** The easiest way to get a control to behave precisely like a `TextBox` control is to inherit from the `TextBox` class.

72. **B.** A Windows Installer merge module allows you to include the component in any installer package, and the merge module will have identical settings in every package. You cannot use `XCOPY` deployment to meet these requirements because the component requires Registry settings.

73. **B.** With a `SecurityAction.RequestOptional` request, you can trap the error if the permission is not granted.

74. **D.** An exception is handled by the most specific applicable `catch` block. A transfer-of-control statement (such as `goto`) does not skip a `finally` block.

75. **D.** The `INSERT` statement adds a new row to a SQL Server (or other ANSI SQL-compliant database) table.

Glossary

A-B

accessibility The process of making an application more readily available to users who have disabilities that interfere with their use of computer hardware or software.

accessor The code that is enclosed in a get and set block in a property definition. The get accessor is executed when the property value is read, and the set accessor is used when a value is assigned to the property. A property can contain a get accessor, a set accessor, or both.

ad hoc query A set of SQL statements that are executed immediately.

Application A class that provides a set of static methods and properties for managing an application.

assembly A logical unit of functionality that can contain one or more files. Every type that is loaded in the CLR belongs to an assembly.

assembly manifest A file that stores the assembly's metadata.

assembly metadata Information that provides the assembly's self-describing information, such as the name of the assembly, the version of the assembly, the files that are part of the assembly and their hash values, and the assemblies' dependencies on other assemblies. This subset of information in the manifest makes assemblies self-sufficient.

attribute A declarative tag that can be placed with certain code elements to provide additional information on the corresponding code element at runtime.

authentication The process of determining the identity of a user based on his or her credentials.

authorization The process of allowing a user to use specific resources based on his or her authenticated identity.

backing store A place where you can store a file.

boxing The process of converting a value type to a reference type in which the value in the stack is copied into the heap via the creation of a new instance of an object to hold its data.

C

CDATA section Raw data within an XML file.

class A reference type that encapsulates its data (constants and fields) and behaviors (methods, properties, indexers, events, operators, instance constructors, static constructors, and destructors).

Clipboard A mechanism by which you can transfer data between and within various Windows applications.

CLR (Common Language Runtime) A program that executes all managed code and provides code with various services at runtime, such as automatic memory management, cross-language integration, code access security, and debugging and profiling support.

code access security Security that is based on permission requests made by running code.

code group A group of zero or more modules that share a common security policy.

column All the values for one particular property in a table.

complex data binding   The process of connecting a user interface control to an entire collection of data rather than to a single data item.

component   A package of reusable code that implements the IComponent interface.

configured assembly   An assembly for which you have specified a runtime version substitution.

constructor   A method that allows control over initialization of a type. A constructor is executed when an instance of a type is created.

context menu   A menu that displays a small list of menu items that depend on the current working context. A context menu is associated with a control and is shown when the user right-clicks the control.

culture   A combination of language and location that is sufficient to dictate the formatting of resources.

culture code   An abbreviation that identifies a particular culture.

custom control   A control that is created by being derived directly or indirectly from the System.WindowsForms.Control class. A custom control renders its own user interface via its Paint event handler.

D

data binding   The process of connecting the controls on the user interface with the data stored in the data model.

data provider   The server-specific ADO.NET classes that supply data.

DataSet object   A server-independent store that can hold multiple tables and their relationships.

debugging   The process of locating logical or runtime errors in an application. Debugging involves finding the causes of the errors and fixing them.

declarative security   Security that is based on attributes that declare the desired permissions.

delay signing   A technique that allows you to place a shared assembly in the GAC just by signing the assembly with the public key. This allows the assembly to be signed with the private key at a later stage, when the development process is complete and the component or assembly is ready to be deployed. This process allows developers to work with shared assemblies as if they were strongly named and yet also secure the private key of the signature from being accessed at different stages of development.

delegate   A reference type that stores references to a method that has a specific signature. A delegate object can be used to dynamically invoke a method at runtime.

deployment   A process by which a Windows application or component is distributed in the form of installation package files to be installed on the other computers.

Disco   A Microsoft standard for Web service discovery.

DOM (Document Object Model)   The DOM class is an in-memory representation of an XML document that allows you to programmatically read, manipulate, and modify an XML document.

E

element   An XML tag and its contents.

encoding   A scheme for representing textual characters as numeric codes.

enumeration   A distinct type that has named constants. Enumeration types are defined by using the enum keyword. Enumeration types provide a type-safe way to work with constants.

event   A message that is sent by an object to signal an action. The action can be a result of user interaction, such as a mouse click, or it can be triggered by any other program.

event handling   The act of responding to an event handling can be accomplished by writing methods called event handlers that are invoked in response to events.

exception   A problem that occurs during the normal execution of a program.

exception handling The process of handling exceptions that are raised when a program executes.

F

FCL (Framework Class Library) A library of classes, interfaces, and value types that are included in the Microsoft .NET Framework. This library provides access to the system functionality and is designed to be the foundation on which the .NET Framework applications, components, and controls are built.

Field A variable that is associated with an object or a class.

foreign key An identifier in a database table that stores values from the primary key in another table. These values indicate to which row in the primary table each row in the other table is related.

G-H

GAC (global assembly cache) A code cache of assemblies that are supposed to be shared by many applications in a computer.

garbage collection A process of reclaiming all unused memory and returning it to the heap of available memory. The CLR garbage collector may be invoked when an application gets low on memory resources. The CLR also compacts the memory that is in use to reduce the working space needed for the heap.

GDI+ A modern implementation of the Windows Graphics Device Interface that allows you to create graphics, draw text, and manipulate graphical images.

globalization The process of identifying the resources to be localized in a particular application.

HTML Help Microsoft's online Help authoring system that creates help for software programs, multimedia titles, intranets, extranets, or the Internet.

I-J-K

identity A column whose value is automatically assigned by the server when a new row is entered.

IL (intermediate language) The language into which compilers that support the .NET Framework compile a program. IL has been ratified as an ECMA standard that calls IL common intermediate language (CIL). The Microsoft implementation of CIL is called Microsoft IL (MSIL).

imperative security Security that is based on instantiated classes.

inheritance A process through which you create a new type based on an existing type. In an inheritance relationship, the existing type is called the base type and the new type is called the derived type. When you use inheritance, the derived type automatically gets all the functionality of the base type—without any extra coding.

input validation A process by which an application examines user input to determine whether it is acceptable for the application.

JIT (just-in-time) compilation The process of converting IL code into machine code at runtime, just when it is required.

L-M

"last one wins" concurrency control A situation in which an update to a row always succeeds, whether another user has edited the row or not (as long as the row still exists).

localizability The process of verifying that all localizable resources have been separated from code.

localization The process of translating resources for another culture.

main menu　A menu that is used to group together various commands that are available in a Windows application. The main menu is displayed at the top of a form, just below the title bar, and it has several top-level menus. Each top-level menu can further have a hierarchy of menu items within itself. A Windows application can have just one main menu. In the case of an MDI application that consists of multiple forms, the menus of the child windows are merged together in the MDI container's main menu.

managed code　The code that runs under the services provided by the CLR. Managed code must expose necessary metadata information to the CLR in order to enjoy these services. *See* CLR.

MDI (multiple-document interface) application　An application that allows you to display and work with multiple documents at the same time. Each document is displayed in its own child window. You can recognize an MDI application by the inclusion of a Window menu that contains commands for switching among windows or documents. Common examples of MDI applications are Visual Studio .NET and Microsoft Excel.

merge module　A type of project that allows you to create reusable setup components that help in deploying shared components. Merge modules cannot be directly installed; instead, they must be merged with installers of applications that use the shared component packaged as a merge module.

metadata　Information about elements such as assemblies, types, and methods that helps the CLR manage garbage collection, object lifetime management, code access security, debugging, and so on for these elements.

N-O

namespace　A naming scheme that provides a way to logically group related types. Namespaces have two benefits: They are used to avoid naming conflicts and they make it easier to browse and locate classes.

native compilation　The process of precompiling assemblies in processor-specific machine code.

Native compilation can be done with the help of the Native Image Generation tool (`ngen.exe`).

native image cache　A cache that contains precompiled assemblies.

.NET Framework　A platform for building, deploying, and running XML Web services and applications. The .NET Framework consists of three main parts: the CLR, the FCLs, and a set of language compilers.

one-way data binding　A process in which the bound property of the control reflects changes to the data model, but changes to the control are not written back to the data model.

optimistic concurrency control　A situation in which an update to a row succeeds only if no one else has changed that row after it is loaded into the `DataSet` object.

osql　A SQL Server command-line tool for executing queries.

P-Q

parameter　A piece of information that is passed to a stored procedure at runtime.

performance counter　A Windows device that publishes performance-related data for applications and their components.

permission　A setting in .NET that controls access to a resource.

permission set　A set of one or more permissions that can be granted or denied as a unit.

PInvoke (platform invoke)　The feature of the .NET Framework that allows you to call the Windows API and other DLL procedures from managed code.

pop-up help　Help that is displayed in a pop-up window after the user has clicked the Help button on the form's caption followed by clicking on a control.

primary key　The unique identifier for a row in a database table.

PrintDocument A class that provides object-oriented access to all the features you need to print, either text or graphics.

private assembly An assembly that is available only to clients in the same directory structure as the assembly.

process An application that is being executed.

property A class member that is like a public field but that can also encapsulate additional logic within its get and set accessor methods.

R

RCW (runtime callable wrapper) A proxy that allows .NET code to make use of COM classes and members.

relational database A database that stores multiple tables and the relationships between them.

relationship A connection between two tables in a database.

resource file A file that contains string, bitmap, or other resources that can differ between cultures.

resource-only assembly An assembly that contains only resources and no executable code.

resultset A collection of data that is arranged in rows and columns.

role-based security Security that is based on the identity of the current user.

row All the values in a table that describe one instance of an entity.

S

satellite assembly A resource-only assembly that contains culture-specific information.

schema The structure of a database or an XML file.

SDI (single-document interface) application An application that allows you to work on a single document or form at a time. Common examples of SDI applications are the Windows Notepad and Wordpad applications.

shared assembly An assembly that can be referenced by more than one application. An assembly must be explicitly built to be shared; it must have a cryptographically strong name. Shared assemblies are stored in the machinewide GAC.

simple data binding The process of connecting a single value from the data model to a single property of a control.

SOAP (Simple Object Access Protocol) A standard for transmitting objects as XML over HTTP.

SQL-92 (Structured Query Language-92) The official ANSI specification for SQL.

SQL Query Analyzer A SQL Server graphical tool for executing queries.

stored procedure A set of SQL statements that are stored on the server for later execution.

stream A file that is viewed as a stream of bytes.

strong name A name that identifies an assembly globally. It consists of a simple text name, a version number, culture information (if provided), and a public key and is optionally signed using a digital signature. If the assembly contains more than one file, it is sufficient to generate a strong name just for the file that contains the assembly manifest.

structure User-defined value type. Like a class, a structure has constructors, fields, methods, properties, and so on. However, structures do not support inheritance.

T

T-SQL (Transact Structured Query Language) The SQL-92 dialect that is used in Microsoft SQL Server.

tab order The order in which controls receive focus when users navigate on a form by using the Tab key.

table   A collection of data about instances of a single entity.

testing   The process of executing programs and determining whether they worked as expected. Testing is the process of revealing errors by executing programs with various test cases and test data.

ToolTip   A small pop-up window that displays a brief description of a control's purpose when the mouse hovers over the control.

tracing   The process of displaying informative messages in an application at the time of execution. Tracing messages can be helpful for checking the health of a program or finding errors even though the program is already in production.

two-way data binding   A process in which changes to the control are written back to the data model.

U-V

UDDI (Universal Description, Discovery, and Integration)   A standard for discovering details of Web services and other business services that are available via the Internet.

unboxing   The process of converting a reference type to a value type in which the value from the heap is copied back into the stack.

Unicode   A universal character set that can represent more than 1 million characters. Unicode is the default internal language of the .NET Framework.

unmanaged code   Code written in a non-.NET environment that does not benefit from the services of the CLR.

URL remoting   The process of launching an application from a remote location.

user assistance   Any means of providing information about an application to the user.

user control   A control that is created by being derived directly or indirectly from the `System.WindowsForms.UserControl` class.

UTF-16   A 16-bit Unicode encoding format in which every character is encoded using 2 bytes.

visual inheritance   A process through which a visual element such as a form or a control is inherited based on an element that already exists. Visual inheritance helps reuse existing code and maintain consistency among visual elements.

W-X-Y-Z

Web method   A method of a Web service that can be invoked by client applications.

Web reference   Information in a Visual Studio .NET project that allows you to use objects that are supplied by a Web service.

Web service   A service that allows you to instantiate and invoke methods on objects over the Internet.

Windows Forms Designer   The rich visual environment provided by Visual Studio .NET that allows you to create Windows-based applications.

WSDL (Web Services Description Language)   An XML language that describes the interface of a Web service.

XML (Extensible Markup Language)   A text-based format that lets developers describe, deliver, and exchange structured data between a range of applications.

XML attribute   A property of an XML object.

XML declaration   The line in an XML file that identifies the file as an XML file.

XML namespace   A set of XML tags that is private to an application.

z-order   The order in which the controls are visually layered on a form along the form's z-axis, which specifies its depth. A control at the top of the z-order overlaps other controls, and other controls overlap a control that is at the bottom of the z-order.

Overview of the Certification Process

You must pass rigorous certification exams to become a Microsoft Certified Professional. These closed-book exams provide a valid and reliable measure of your technical proficiency and expertise. Developed in consultation with computer industry professionals who have experience with Microsoft products in the workplace, the exams are conducted by two independent organizations. Prometric offers the exams at more than 3,500 authorized Prometric testing centers around the world. Virtual University Enterprises (VUE) testing centers offer exams at more than 3,000 locations.

To schedule an exam, contact Prometric Testing Centers (800-755-EXAM or www.2test.com) or VUE (800-TEST-REG or www.vue.com/ms).

TYPES OF CERTIFICATION

Currently Microsoft offers seven types of certification, based on specific areas of expertise:

◆ **Microsoft Certified Professional (MCP)**—An MCP is qualified to implement a Microsoft product or technology as part of a business solution in an organization. Candidates can take elective exams to develop areas of specialization. MCP is the base level of expertise.

◆ **Microsoft Certified Systems Administrator (MCSA)**—An MCSA is qualified to implement, manage, and troubleshoot existing network and system environments based on the Microsoft Windows 2000 and Windows .NET Server platforms.

◆ **Microsoft Certified Systems Engineer (MCSE)**—An MCSE is qualified to analyze business requirements and design and implement the infrastructure for business solutions based on the Microsoft Windows 2000 platform and Microsoft server software. The MCSE credential is the next step up from the MCSA.

◆ **Microsoft Certified Application Developer (MCAD)**—An MCAD is qualified to use Microsoft technologies to develop and maintain department-level applications, components, Web or desktop clients, and back-end data services. This is the entry-level developer certification.

◆ **Microsoft Certified Solution Developer (MCSD)**—An MCSD is qualified to design and develop leading-edge business solutions by using Microsoft development tools, technologies, and platforms, including Microsoft Office and Microsoft BackOffice. MCSD is the highest level of expertise that has a focus on software development.

◆ **Microsoft Certified Database Administrator (MCDBA)**—An MCDBA is qualified to implement and administer Microsoft SQL Server databases.

◆ **Microsoft Certified Trainer (MCT)**—An MCT is instructionally and technically qualified by Microsoft to deliver Microsoft education courses at Microsoft-authorized sites. An MCT must be employed by a Microsoft Solution Provider Authorized Technical Education Center or a Microsoft Authorized Academic Training site.

> **NOTE**
>
> **Keeping Yourself Updated**
> Microsoft's certifications and the exams that lead to them are under constant revision. For up-to-date information about each type of certification, visit the Microsoft Training & Certification Web site, at www.microsoft.com/traincert. You also can contact the following sources:
>
> · Microsoft Regional Education Service Center for North America: 800-635-7544
>
> · MCPHelp@Microsoft.com

CERTIFICATION REQUIREMENTS

The following sections describe the certification requirements for the various types of Microsoft certification.

> **NOTE**
>
> **Discontinued Exams**   An asterisk following an exam in any of the lists below means that it is slated for retirement.

How to Become an MCP

Passing any Microsoft exam (with the exception of exam 70-058, "Networking Essentials") is all you need to do to become certified as an MCP.

How to Become an MCSA

You must pass three core exams and one elective exam to become an MCSA. The following sections show both the core requirements and the electives you can take to earn this certification.

MCSA Core Exams

You must pass three core exams from the following list to earn credit toward the MCSA certification:

◆ 70-210, "Installing, Configuring, and Administering Microsoft Windows 2000 Professional"

OR

70-270, "Installing, Configuring, and Administering Microsoft Windows XP Professional"

◆ 70-215, "Installing, Configuring, and Administering Microsoft Windows 2000 Server"

OR

70-275, "Installing, Configuring, and Administering Microsoft Windows .NET Server"

◆ 70-218, "Managing a Microsoft Windows 2000 Network Environment"

OR

70-278, "Managing a Microsoft Windows ,Net Server Network Environment"

MCSA Elective Exams

You must pass any one of the exams from the following list of electives exams to earn credit toward the MCSA certification:

◆ 70-028, "Administering Microsoft SQL Server 7.0"

◆ 70-081, "Implementing and Supporting Microsoft Exchange Server 5.5"*

◆ 70-086, "Implementing and Supporting Microsoft Systems Management Server 2.0"

◆ 70-088, "Implementing and Supporting Microsoft Proxy Server 2.0"*

◆ 70-214, "Implementing and Administering Security in a Microsoft Windows 2000 Network"

◆ 70-216, "Implementing and Administering a Microsoft Windows 2000 Network Infrastructure"

◆ 70-224, "Installing, Configuring, and Administering Microsoft Exchange 2000 Server"

◆ 70-227, "Installing, Configuring, and Administering Microsoft Internet Security and Acceleration (ISA) Server 2000 Enterprise Edition"

◆ 70-228, "Installing, Configuring, and Administering Microsoft SQL Server 2000 Enterprise Edition"

◆ 70-244, "Supporting and Maintaining a Microsoft Windows NT Server 4.0 Network"

◆ The CompTIA exam "A+" and "Network+"

◆ The CompTIA exams "A+" and "Server+"

The MCSA is the first Microsoft certification to recognize some third-party certification exams as electives. Two particular combinations of exams from CompTIA qualify as MCSA elective exams.

How to Become an MCSE

You must pass five core exams (four operating system exams and one design exam) and two elective exams to become an MCSE.

The following sections show the core requirements and the electives that you can take to earn MCSE certification.

MCSE Operating System Exams

You must pass these four core requirements to earn credit toward the MCSE certification:

◆ 70-210, "Installing, Configuring, and Administering Microsoft Windows 2000 Professional"

   OR

   70-270, "Installing, Configuring, and Administering Microsoft Windows XP Professional"

◆ 70-215, "Installing, Configuring, and Administering Microsoft Windows 2000 Server"

   OR

   70-275, "Installing, Configuring, and Administering Microsoft Windows .NET Server"

◆ 70-216, "Implementing and Administering a Microsoft Windows 2000 Network Infrastructure"

   OR

   70-276, "Implementing and Administering a Microsoft Windows .NET Server Network Infrastructure"

◆ 70-217, "Implementing and Administering a Microsoft Windows 2000 Directory Services Infrastructure"

OR

70-277, "Implementing and Administering a Microsoft Windows .NET Server Directory Services Infrastructure"

MCSE Design Exams

You must pass one of the design electives on this list to earn credit toward the MCSE certification:

◆ 70-219, "Designing a Microsoft Windows 2000 Directory Services Infrastructure"

◆ 70-220, "Designing Security for a Microsoft Windows 2000 Network"

◆ 70-221, "Designing a Microsoft Windows 2000 Network Infrastructure"

◆ 70-226, "Designing Highly Available Web Solutions with Microsoft Windows 2000 Server Technologies"

MCSE Elective Exams

You must pass two of the following elective exams to earn credit toward the MCSE certification:

◆ 70-019, "Designing and Implementing Data Warehouses with Microsoft SQL Server 7.0"

◆ 70-028, "Administering Microsoft SQL Server 7.0"

◆ 70-029, "Designing and Implementing Databases with Microsoft SQL Server 7.0"

◆ 70-056, "Implementing and Supporting Web Sites Using Microsoft Site Server 3.0"*

◆ 70-080, "Implementing and Supporting Microsoft Internet Explorer 5.0 by Using the Microsoft Internet Explorer Administration Kit"*

◆ 70-081, "Implementing and Supporting Microsoft Exchange Server 5.5"*

◆ 70-085, "Implementing and Supporting Microsoft SNA Server 4.0"*

◆ 70-086, "Implementing and Supporting Microsoft Systems Management Server 2.0"

◆ 70-088, "Implementing and Supporting Microsoft Proxy Server 2.0"*

◆ 70-214, "Implementing and Administering Security in a Microsoft Windows 2000 Network"

◆ 70-218, "Managing a Microsoft Windows 2000 Network Environment"

◆ 70-219, "Designing a Microsoft Windows 2000 Directory Services Infrastructure"

◆ 70-220, "Designing Security for a Microsoft Windows 2000 Network"

◆ 70-221, "Designing a Microsoft Windows 2000 Network Infrastructure"

◆ 70-222, "Migrating from Microsoft Windows NT 4.0 to Microsoft Windows 2000"

◆ 70-223, "Installing, Configuring, and Administering Microsoft Clustering Services by Using Microsoft Windows 2000 Advanced Server"

◆ 70-224, "Installing, Configuring, and Administering Microsoft Exchange 2000 Server"

◆ 70-225, "Designing and Deploying a Messaging Infrastructure with Microsoft Exchange 2000 Server"

◆ 70-226, "Designing Highly Available Web Solutions with Microsoft Windows 2000 Server Technologies"

◆ 70-227, "Installing, Configuring, and Administering Microsoft Internet Security and Acceleration (ISA) Server 2000 Enterprise Edition"

◆ 70-228, "Installing, Configuring, and Administering Microsoft SQL Server 2000 Enterprise Edition"

◆ 70-229, "Designing and Implementing Databases with Microsoft SQL Server 2000 Enterprise Edition"

◆ 70-230, "Designing and Implementing Solutions with Microsoft BizTalk Server 2000 Enterprise Edition"

◆ 70-232, "Implementing and Maintaining Highly Available Web Solutions with Microsoft Windows 2000 Server Technologies and Microsoft Application Center 2000"

◆ 70-234, "Designing and Implementing Solutions with Microsoft Commerce Server 2000"

◆ 70-244, "Supporting and Maintaining a Microsoft Windows NT Server 4.0 Network"

You cannot count the same exam as both a core exam and an elective exam to obtain MCSE certification.

How to Become an MCAD

You must pass two core exams and one elective exam to earn MCAD certification.

The following sections show the core requirements and the electives that you can take to earn MCAD certification.

MCAD Core Exams

You must pass two of the following core exams to earn credit toward the MCAD certification:

◆ 70-305, "Developing and Implementing Web Applications with Microsoft Visual Basic .NET and Microsoft Visual Studio .NET"

OR

70-306, "Developing and Implementing Windows-Based Applications with Microsoft Visual Basic .NET and Microsoft Visual Studio .NET"

OR

70-315, "Developing and Implementing Web Applications with Microsoft Visual C# .NET and Microsoft Visual Studio .NET"

OR

70-316, "Developing and Implementing Windows-based Applications with Microsoft Visual C# .NET and Microsoft Visual Studio .NET"

◆ 70-310, "Designing XML Web Services and Server Components with Microsoft Visual Basic .NET and the Microsoft .NET Framework"

OR

70-320, "Designing XML Web Services and Server Components with Microsoft Visual C# .NET and the Microsoft .NET Framework"

MCAD Elective Exams

You must pass one of the following elective exams to earn credit toward the MCAD certification:

◆ 70-229, "Designing and Implementing Databases with Microsoft SQL Server 2000 Enterprise Edition"

◆ 70-230, "Designing and Implementing Solutions with Microsoft BizTalk Server 2000 Enterprise Edition"

◆ 70-234, "Designing and Implementing Solutions with Microsoft Commerce Server 2000"

You may also count as an elective one of the four core exams 70-305, 70-306, 70-315, and 70-316. The one you can count as an elective is the exam from the opposite technology and language from the exam that you count as a core exam. For example, if you take the exam "Developing and Implementing Windows-Based Applications with Microsoft Visual Basic .NET and Microsoft Visual Studio .NET" (70-306) as a core exam, you can take the exam "Developing and Implementing Web Applications with Microsoft Visual C# .NET and Microsoft Visual Studio .NET" (70-315) as an elective.

How to Become an MCSD

There are two different tracks for the MCSD certification. The new track is for the MCSD for Microsoft .NET certification, and the old track covers the previous versions of Microsoft technologies. The requirements for both tracks are listed in the following sections.

The MCSD for Microsoft .NET Track

For the MCSD for Microsoft .NET certification, you must pass four core exams and one elective exam. Both the core and elective exams are listed in the following sections.

MCSD for Microsoft .NET Track Core Exams

You must pass four of the following core exams to earn credit toward the MCSD for Microsoft .NET certification:

◆ 70-305, "Developing and Implementing Web Applications with Microsoft Visual Basic .NET and Microsoft Visual Studio .NET"

OR

70-315, "Developing and Implementing Web Applications with Microsoft Visual C# .NET and Microsoft Visual Studio .NET"

◆ 70-306, "Developing and Implementing Windows-Based Applications with Microsoft Visual Basic .NET and Microsoft Visual Studio .NET"

OR

70-316, "Developing and Implementing Windows-Based Applications with Microsoft Visual C# .NET and Microsoft Visual Studio .NET"

◆ 70-310, "Designing XML Web Services and Server Components with Microsoft Visual Basic .NET and the Microsoft .NET Framework"

OR

70-320, "Designing XML Web Services and Server Components with Microsoft Visual C# .NET and the Microsoft .NET Framework"

◆ 70-300, "Analyzing Requirements and Defining .NET Solution Architectures"

MCSD for Microsoft .NET Track Elective Exams

You must pass one of the following elective exams to earn credit toward the MCSD for Microsoft .NET certification:

◆ 70-229, "Designing and Implementing Databases with Microsoft SQL Server 2000 Enterprise Edition"

◆ 70-230, "Designing and Implementing Solutions with Microsoft BizTalk Server 2000 Enterprise Edition"

◆ 70-234, "Designing and Implementing Solutions with Microsoft Commerce Server 2000"

The MCSD Old Track

For the old track for MCSD certification, you must pass three core exams and one elective exam. Both the core and elective exams are listed in the following sections.

MCSD Old Track Core Exams

You must pass three of the following core exams to earn credit toward the MCSD certification:

◆ 70-016, "Designing and Implementing Desktop Applications with Microsoft Visual C++ 6.0"

OR

70-156, "Designing and Implementing Desktop Applications with Microsoft Visual FoxPro 6.0"

OR

70-176, "Designing and Implementing Desktop Applications with Microsoft Visual Basic 6.0"

◆ 70-015, "Designing and Implementing Distributed Applications with Microsoft Visual C++ 6.0"

OR

70-155, "Designing and Implementing Distributed Applications with Microsoft Visual FoxPro 6.0"

OR

70-175, "Designing and Implementing Distributed Applications with Microsoft Visual Basic 6.0"

◆ 70-100, "Analyzing Requirements and Defining Solution Architectures"

MCSD Old Track Elective Exams

You must pass one of the following elective exams to earn credit toward the MCSD certification:

◆ 70-015, "Designing and Implementing Distributed Applications with Microsoft Visual C++ 6.0"

◆ 70-016, "Designing and Implementing Desktop Applications with Microsoft Visual C++ 6.0"

◆ 70-019, "Designing and Implementing Data Warehouses with Microsoft SQL Server 7.0"

◆ 70-029, "Implementing a Database Design on Microsoft SQL Server 7.0"

◆ 70-057, "Designing and Implementing Commerce Solutions with Microsoft Site Server 3.0, Commerce Edition"*

◆ 70-091, "Designing and Implementing Solutions with Microsoft Office 2000 and Microsoft Visual Basic for Applications"*

◆ 70-105, "Designing and Implementing Collaborative Solutions with Microsoft Outlook 2000 and Microsoft Exchange Server 5.5"

◆ 70-152, "Designing and Implementing Web Solutions with Microsoft Visual InterDev 6.0"

◆ 70-155, "Designing and Implementing Distributed Applications with Microsoft Visual FoxPro 6.0"

◆ 70-156, "Designing and Implementing Desktop Applications with Microsoft Visual FoxPro 6.0"

◆ 70-175, "Designing and Implementing Distributed Applications with Microsoft Visual Basic 6.0"

◆ 70-176, "Designing and Implementing Desktop Applications with Microsoft Visual Basic 6.0"

◆ 70-229, "Designing and Implementing Databases with Microsoft SQL Server 2000 Enterprise Edition"

◆ 70-230, "Designing and Implementing Solutions with Microsoft BizTalk Server 2000 Enterprise Edition"

◆ 70-234, "Designing and Implementing Solutions with Microsoft Commerce Server 2000"

To obtain MCSD certification, you cannot count the same exam as both a core exam and an elective exam.

How to Become an MCDBA

You must pass three core exams and one elective exam to earn MCDBA certification.

The following lists show the core requirements and the electives that you can take to earn MCDBA certification.

MCDBA Core Exams

You must pass the following three core exams to earn credit toward the MCDBA certification:

◆ 70-028, "Administering SQL Server 7.0"

OR

70-228, "Installing, Configuring, and Administering Microsoft SQL Server 2000 Enterprise Edition"

◆ 70-029, "Designing and Implementing Databases with Microsoft SQL Server 7.0"

OR

70-229, "Designing and Implementing Databases with Microsoft SQL Server 2000 Enterprise Edition"

◆ 70-215, "Installing, Configuring, and Administering Microsoft Windows 2000 Server"

OR

70-275, "Installing, Configuring, and Administering Microsoft Windows .NET Enterprise Server"

MCDBA Elective Exams

You must pass one of these elective exams to earn credit toward the MCDBA certification:

◆ 70-015, "Designing and Implementing Distributed Applications with Microsoft Visual C++ 6.0"

◆ 70-019, "Designing and Implementing Data Warehouses with Microsoft SQL Server 7.0"

◆ 70-155, "Designing and Implementing Distributed Applications with Microsoft Visual FoxPro 6.0"

◆ 70-175, "Designing and Implementing Distributed Applications with Microsoft Visual Basic 6.0"

◆ 70-216, "Implementing and Administering a Microsoft Windows 2000 Network Infrastructure"

◆ 70-276, "Implementing and Administering a Microsoft .NET Server Network Infrastructure"

◆ 70-305, "Developing and Implementing Web Applications with Microsoft Visual Basic .NET and Microsoft Visual Studio .NET"

◆ 70-306, "Developing and Implementing Windows-Based Applications with Microsoft Visual Basic .NET and Microsoft Visual Studio .NET"

- 70-310, "Designing XML Web Services and Server Components with Microsoft Visual Basic .NET and the Microsoft .NET Framework"

- 70-315, "Developing and Implementing Web Applications with Microsoft Visual C# .NET and Microsoft Visual Studio .NET"

- 70-316, "Developing and Implementing Windows-based Applications with Microsoft Visual C# .NET and Microsoft Visual Studio .NET"

- 70-320, "Designing XML Web Services and Server Components with Microsoft Visual C# .NET and the Microsoft .NET Framework"

How to Become an MCT

To understand the requirements and process for becoming an MCT, you need to obtain the MCT Program Guide document from the following Web site:

`www.microsoft.com/traincert/mcp/mct/guide`

The MCT Program Guide explains the four-step process of becoming an MCT. The general steps for the MCT certification are as follows:

1. Obtain one of the Microsoft premier certifications: MCSE, MCSD, or MCDBA.

2. Attend a classroom presentation of a Microsoft course taught by a Microsoft Certified Trainer at a Microsoft Certified Technical Education Center (CTEC).

3. Demonstrate instructional presentation skills by attending a Train-the-Trainer course or by providing proof of experience in technical training.

4. Complete the MCT application, which you can fill out on the above-mentioned Web site.

What's on the CD-ROM

This appendix provides a brief summary of what you'll find on the CD-ROM that accompanies this book. For a more detailed description of the *PrepLogic Practice Tests, Preview Edition*, exam simulation software, see Appendix D, "Using the *PrepLogic Practice Tests, Preview Edition* Software." In addition to the *PrepLogic Practice Tests, Preview Edition*, software, the CD-ROM includes an electronic version of the book, in Portable Document Format (PDF), and the source code used in the book.

THE *PREPLOGIC PRACTICE TESTS, PREVIEW EDITION*

PrepLogic is a leading provider of certification training tools. Trusted by certification students worldwide, we believe PrepLogic is the best practice exam software available. In addition to providing a means of evaluating your knowledge of the Training Guide material, *PrepLogic Practice Tests, Preview Edition*, features several innovations that help you to improve your mastery of the subject matter.

For example, the practice tests allow you to check your score by exam area or domain, to determine which topics you need to study more. Another feature allows you to obtain immediate feedback on your responses, in the form of explanations for the correct and incorrect answers.

PrepLogic Practice Tests, Preview Edition , exhibits most of the full functionality of the Premium Edition but offers only a fraction of the total questions. To get the complete set of practice questions and exam functionality, visit www.PrepLogic.com and order the Premium Edition for this and other challenging exam titles.

For a more detailed description of the features of the *PrepLogic Practice Tests, Preview Edition*, see Appendix D.

AN EXCLUSIVE ELECTRONIC VERSION OF THE TEXT

The CD-ROM also contains an electronic PDF version of this book. This electronic version comes complete with all figures as they appear in the book. You will find that the search capability of the reader is handy for study and review purposes.

COMPLETE CODE SAMPLES

You'll find the complete source code for every Step by Step, Guided Practice Exercise, and Exercise for the book on the CD. Just open any of the solution files in your copy of Visual Studio .NET, and you'll be ready to follow along with the text.

Using the *PrepLogic Practice Tests, Preview Edition Software*

This book includes a special version of the PrepLogic Practice Tests software, which is a revolutionary test engine designed to give you the best in certification exam preparation. PrepLogic offers sample and practice exams for many of today's most in-demand and challenging technical certifications. A special Preview Edition of the PrepLogic Practice Tests software is included with this book as a tool to use in assessing your knowledge of the training guide material while also providing you with the experience of taking an electronic exam.

This appendix describes in detail what *PrepLogic Practice Tests, Preview Edition*, is, how it works, and what it can do to help you prepare for the exam. Note that although the Preview Edition includes all the test simulation functions of the complete, retail version, it contains only a single practice test. The Premium Edition, available at www.preplogic.com, contains the complete set of challenging practice exams designed to optimize your learning experience.

THE EXAM SIMULATION

One of the main functions of *PrepLogic Practice Tests, Preview Edition*, is exam simulation. To prepare you to take the actual vendor certification exam, PrepLogic is designed to offer the most effective exam simulation available.

QUESTION QUALITY

The questions provided in the *PrepLogic Practice Tests, Preview Edition*, are written to the highest standards of technical accuracy. The questions tap the content of this book's chapters and help you review and assess your knowledge before you take the actual exam.

THE INTERFACE DESIGN

The *PrepLogic Practice Tests, Preview Edition*, exam simulation interface provides you with the experience of taking an electronic exam. This enables you to effectively prepare to take the actual exam by making the test experience familiar. Using this test simulation can help eliminate the sense of surprise or anxiety you might experience in the testing center because you will already be acquainted with computerized testing.

THE EFFECTIVE LEARNING ENVIRONMENT

The *PrepLogic Practice Tests, Preview Edition*, interface provides a learning environment that not only tests you through the computer but also teaches the material you need to know to pass the certification exam.

Each question includes a detailed explanation of the correct answer, and most of these explanations provide reasons the other answers are incorrect. This information helps to reinforce the knowledge you already have and also provides practical information you can use on the job.

SOFTWARE REQUIREMENTS

PrepLogic Practice Tests requires a computer with the following:

◆ Microsoft Windows 98, Windows Me, Windows NT 4.0, Windows 2000, or Windows XP

◆ A 166MHz or faster processor

◆ A minimum of 32MB of RAM

> **NOTE**   As with any Windows application, the more memory, the better the performance.

◆ 10MB of hard drive space

INSTALLING *PREPLOGIC PRACTICE TESTS, PREVIEW EDITION*

You can install *PrepLogic Practice Tests, Preview Edition*, by following these steps:

1. Insert the *PrepLogic Practice Tests, Preview Edition*, CD into your CD-ROM drive. The Autorun feature of Windows should launch the software. If you have Autorun disabled, select Start, Run. Go to the root directory of the CD and select setup.exe. Click Open, and then click OK.

2. The Installation Wizard copies the *PrepLogic Practice Tests, Preview Edition*, files to your hard drive. It then adds *PrepLogic Practice Tests, Preview Edition*, to your Desktop and the Program menu. Finally, it installs test engine components to the appropriate system folders.

REMOVING *PREPLOGIC PRACTICE TESTS, PREVIEW EDITION*, FROM YOUR COMPUTER

If you elect to remove the *PrepLogic Practice Tests, Preview Edition*, you can use the included uninstall process to ensure that it is removed from your system safely and completely. Follow these instructions to remove *PrepLogic Practice Tests, Preview Edition* from your computer:

1. Select Start, Settings, Control Panel.

2. Double-click the Add/Remove Programs icon. You are presented with a list of software installed on your computer.

3. Select the *PrepLogic Practice Tests, Preview Edition*, title you want to remove. Click the Add/Remove button. The software is removed from your computer.

USING *PREPLOGIC PRACTICE TESTS, PREVIEW EDITION*

PrepLogic is designed to be user friendly and intuitive. Because the software has a smooth learning curve, your time is maximized because you start practicing with it almost immediately. *PrepLogic Practice Tests, Preview Edition*, has two major modes of study: Practice Test and Flash Review.

Using Practice Test mode, you can develop your test-taking abilities as well as your knowledge through the use of the Show Answer option. While you are taking the test, you can expose the answers along with a detailed explanation of why the given answers are right or wrong. This gives you the ability to better understand the material presented.

Flash Review mode is designed to reinforce exam topics rather than quiz you. In this mode, you are shown a series of questions but no answer choices. Instead, you can click a button that reveals the correct answer to the question and a full explanation for that answer.

Starting a Practice Test Mode Session

Practice Test mode enables you to control the exam experience in ways that actual certification exams do not allow. To begin studying in Practice Test mode, click the Practice Test radio button from the main exam customization screen. This enables the following options:

◆ **The Enable Show Answer button**—Clicking this button activates the Show Answer button, which allows you to view the correct answer(s) and full explanation for each question during the exam. When this option is not enabled, you must wait until after your exam has been graded to view the correct answer(s) and explanation.

◆ **The Enable Item Review button**—Clicking this button activates the Item Review button, which allows you to view your answer choices. This option also facilitates navigation between questions.

◆ **The Randomize Choices option**—You can randomize answer choices from one exam session to the next. This makes memorizing question choices more difficult, thereby keeping questions fresh and challenging longer.

To your left, you are presented with the option of selecting the preconfigured practice test or creating your own custom test. The preconfigured test has a fixed time limit and number of questions. Custom tests allow you to configure the time limit and the number of questions in your exam.

The Preview Edition on this book's CD includes a single preconfigured practice test. You can get the compete set of challenging PrepLogic Practice Tests at www.preplogic.com to make certain you're ready for the big exam.

Click the Begin Exam button to begin your exam.

Starting a Flash Review Mode Session

Flash Review mode provides an easy way to reinforce topics covered in the practice questions. To begin studying in Flash Review mode, click the Flash Review radio button from the main exam customization screen. Select either the preconfigured practice test or create your own custom test.

Click the Best Exam button to begin your Flash Review mode session with the exam questions.

Standard *PrepLogic Practice Tests, Preview Edition*, Options

The following list describes the function of each of the buttons you see:

> **NOTE**
>
> Depending on the options, some of the buttons will be grayed out and inaccessible—or they might be missing completely. Buttons that are appropriate are active.

◆ **Exhibit**—This button is visible if an exhibit is provided to support the question. An *exhibit* is an image that provides supplemental information that is necessary to answer the question.

◆ **Item Review**—This button leaves the question window and opens the Item Review screen. From this screen you can see all questions, your answers, and your marked items. You can also see correct answers listed here, when appropriate.

◆ **Show Answer**—This option displays the correct answer, with an explanation about why it is correct. If you select this option, the current question is not scored.

◆ **Mark Item**—You can check this box to flag a question that you need to review further. You can view and navigate your marked items by clicking the Item Review button (if it is enabled). When grading your exam, you are notified if you have marked items remaining.

◆ **Previous Item**—You can use this option to view the previous question.

◆ **Next Item**—You can use this option to view the next question.

◆ **Grade Exam**—When you have completed your exam, you can click to end your exam and view your detailed score report. If you have unanswered or marked items remaining, you are asked if you would like to continue taking your exam or view your exam report.

Seeing Time Remaining

If the test is timed, the time remaining is displayed on the upper-right corner of the application screen. It counts down minutes and seconds remaining to complete the test. If you run out of time, you are asked if you want to continue taking the test or if you want to end your exam.

Getting Your Examination Score Report

The Examination Score Report screen appears when the Practice Test mode ends—as a result of time expiration, completion of all questions, or your decision to terminate early.

This screen provides a graphical display of your test score, with a breakdown of scores by topic domain. The graphical display at the top of the screen compares your overall score with the PrepLogic Exam Competency Score. The PrepLogic Exam Competency Score reflects the level of subject competency required to pass the particular vendor's exam. Although this score does not directly translate to a passing score, consistently matching or exceeding this score does suggest that you possess the knowledge needed to pass the actual vendor exam.

Reviewing Your Exam

From the Your Score Report screen, you can review the exam that you just completed by clicking on the View Items button. Navigate through the items, viewing the questions, your answers, the correct answers, and the explanations for those questions. You can return to your score report by clicking the View Items button.

GETTING MORE EXAMS

Each *PrepLogic Practice Tests, Preview Edition*, that accompanies your training guide contains a single PrepLogic practice test. Certification students worldwide trust PrepLogic practice tests to help them pass their IT certification exams the first time. You can purchase the Premium Edition of PrepLogic Practice Tests and get the entire set of all the new challenging Practice Tests for this exam. PrepLogic Practice Tests—because you want to pass the first time.

CONTACTING PREPLOGIC

If you would like to contact PrepLogic for any reason, including to get information about its extensive line of certification practice tests, please contact PrepLogic online at www.preplogic.com.

Customer Service

If you have a damaged product and need a replacement or refund, please call the following phone number:

800-858-7674

Product Suggestions and Comments

We value your input! Please email your suggestions and comments to the following address:

feedback@preplogic.com

LICENSE AGREEMENT

YOU MUST AGREE THE TERMS AND CONDITIONS OUTLINED IN THE END USER LICENSE AGREEMENT ("EULA") PRESENTED TO YOU DURING THE INSTALLATION PROCESS. IF YOU DO NOT AGREE TO THESE TERMS DO NOT INSTALL THE SOFTWARE.

Suggested Reading and Resources

.NET User Assistance

Your first source for help with any aspect of Visual Studio .NET should be the user assistance resources that Microsoft ships with its .NET products, which include the following:

- **.NET Framework Documentation**—All the classes, methods, properties, and other members of the .NET Framework Base Class Library are documented in this help file. This file is installed by the .NET Software Development Kit (SDK), and is also integrated into the Visual Studio .NET help file.

- **Visual Studio .NET Documentation**—This file includes help on all aspects of the Visual Studio interface, as well as a series of walkthroughs and samples that you can refer to for examples of using particular pieces of code.

- **Samples and QuickStart tutorials**—These tutorials are installed by the .NET Framework SDK. You can access them by selecting Start, Programs, Microsoft .NET Framework SDK, Samples, QuickStart Tutorials. This set of Hypertext Markup Language (HTML) pages shows examples of many aspects of the .NET Framework in both Visual Basic .NET and C#, and it includes links to both working copies and source code for each example.

Books

Ben Albahari, Peter Drayton, and Brad Merrill. *C# Essentials*. O'Reilly, 2002.

Bob Beauchemin. *Essential ADO.NET*. Addison-Wesley, 2002.

Don Box. *Essential .NET Vol.1: The Common Language Runtime*. Addison-Wesley, 2002.

Kevin Burton. *.NET Common Language Runtime Unleashed*. Sams, 2002.

Ethan Cerami. *Web Services Essentials*. O'Reilly, 2002.

David Chappell. *Understanding .NET*. Addison-Wesley, 2001.

Kalen Delaney. *Inside SQL Server 2000*. Microsoft Press, 2000.

Harvey M. Dietel. *C# How to Program*. Prentice Hall, 2001.

Richard Grimes. *Developing Applications with Visual Studio .NET*. Addison-Wesley, 2002.

Mike Gunderloy. *ADO and ADO.NET Programming*. Sybex, 2002.

Brian A. LaMacchia, et al. *.NET Framework Security*. Addison-Wesley, 2002.

Adam Nathan. *.NET AND COM: The Complete Interoperability Guide*. Sams, 2002.

Eric Newcomer. *Understanding Web Services: XML, WSDL, SOAP, and UDDI.* Addison-Wesley, 2002.

Charles Petzold. *Programming Microsoft Windows with C#.* Microsoft Press, 2001.

Jeffry Richter. *Applied Microsoft .NET Framework Programming.* Microsoft Press, 2001.

Kennard Scribner and Mark C. Stiver. *Applied SOAP: Implementing .NET Web Services.* Sams, 2001.

Scott Short. *Building XML Web Services for the Microsoft .NET Platform.* Microsoft Press, 2002.

Nick Symmonds. *Internationalization and Localization Using Microsoft .NET.* Apress, 2001.

Andrew Troelsen. *C# and the .NET Platform.* Apress, 2001.

Andrew Troelsen. *COM and .NET Interoperability.* Apress, 2002.

WEB SITES

msdn.microsoft.com/net—The Microsoft Developers Network (MSDN) Web site contains extensive technical documentation on all aspects of .NET development.

msdn.microsoft.com/vs/techinfo—The Visual Studio .NET Developer Center keeps you up-to-date on the latest headlines, code samples, and information related to developing applications by using Visual Studio .NET.

msdn.microsoft.com/architecture—The .NET Architecture Center contains a wealth of information on best practices for designing distributed .NET applications.

msdn.microsoft.com/theshow—The .NET Show keeps you up-to-date on cutting-edge technologies for Windows and Web applications.

www.gotdotnet.com—This is a Microsoft-sponsored community Web site that includes downloads and tools, samples, and user-contributed code.

www.windowsforms.net—This is a Microsoft-sponsored community Web site that includes downloads and tools, samples, and user-contributed code for developing Windows forms applications.

www.syncfusion.com/FAQ/winforms—The Windows forms FAQ site is an excellent compilation of frequently asked questions and answers from various Windows forms–related newsgroups and mailing lists.

Index

A

AbortRetryIgnore enumerator, 47
About dialog box, 196
AcceptChanges() method, DataSet class, 489
AcceptReturn member, TextBox class, 146
access modifiers, 31
accessibility, 680, 710
    control properties, 713-715
    design guidelines, 712-713
    implementing, 711-712, 715-716
    SQL-92, 432
    SQL Server, 431-439
    testing, 716-718
AccessibleDescription property, 713
AccessibleName property, 713
AccessibleRole property, 713
accessors, 59
Activation member, ListView control, 173
Active Accessibility SDK, 716
active study strategies, 10-11
ActiveLinkColor member, LinkLabel class, 144
ActiveMdiChild member, Form class, 211
ActiveX controls, 643-644, 650
    forms, 649-650
    importing with aximp.exe, 644-647
    importing with toolbox, 648-649
    properties, 648
    WebBrowser, 668
ad hoc queries, 431-432
    running, 432-433, 463-465
        custom forms, 437-440
        osql, 434-435
        SQL Query Analyzer, 436-437
        Visual Studio .NET IDE, 432-434
    statements. *See* statements
adaptive form exams, 12-16
Add Class command (Add menu), 327
Add Class Wizard, 327
Add Dialog dialog box, 861

Add Inherited Form command (Add menu), 61
Add menu commands
    Add Class, 327
    Add Inherited Form, 61
Add New Item dialog box, 316, 387, 898
Add Program dialog box, 326
Add Project Output Group dialog box, 856
Add Reference dialog box, 292, 877-878, 886
Add Web Reference dialog box, 572
Add() method, Binding class, 357
Added constant, 509
AddNew() member
    BindingManagerBase class, 380
    CurrencyManager class, 381
AddNew() method, DataView class, 494
AddRange() method, 973
administrative installation, network-based deployment, 917-918
ADO.NET object model, 480
    data providers, 480-481
        OLE DB, 481
        SQL Server, 481-489
    DataColumn object, 493
    DataRelation object, 491-492
    DataRow object, 492-493
    DataSet object, 489-490, 495
        finding data, 506-513
        moving in, 498-499
        multiple tables, 502-506, 551-553
        populating from databases, 496-497
        retrieving data, 498-499
        sorting data, 506-513
        strongly typed, 499-501
    DataTable object, 490-491
    DataView object, 494
        filtering data, 509-510
        sorting data, 509-510
    transactions, 553-554
AfterCheck member, TreeView control, 172
AfterCollapse member, TreeView control, 172

D

G

H

S

SelectedNode member, TreeView control, 172

SelectedRtf member, RichTextBox class, 148

SelectedTab member, TabControl control, 183

SelectedText member, ComboBox class, 160

SelectionBackColor property, DataGrid control, 373

SelectionColor member, RichTextBox class, 147

SelectionEnd member, MonthCalendar class, 169

SelectionFont member, RichTextBox class, 147

SelectionForeColor property, DataGrid control, 373

SelectionMode member
    CheckedListBox class, 156
    ListBox class, 156

SelectionRange member, MonthCalendar class, 169

SelectionStart member, MonthCalendar class, 169

SendToBack() method, ToolBar class, 207

Server Explorer, 393-394
    adding data connections, 394
    drag-and-drop operations, 396-399
    object design, 394-396
    performance counters, 968

server-side views, transforming data, 405-409

servers, Windows .NET Server, 919

service packs, 907

serviced components, 659

services (Web). See Web services

set accessors, 59

SetError() member, ErrorProvider class, 260

SetIconAlignment() member, ErrorProvider class, 260

SetIconPadding() member, ErrorProvider class, 260

SetLastError field (DllImportAttribute class), 664

SetPrincipalPolicy() method, 1023

setting
    culture properties, 611
    form properties
        programmatically, 51-56
        Visual Designer, 48-51

Setup Projects, 842-843
    creating, 846-850, 852
    customizing, 853
        Custom Actions Editor, 861-864
        File System Editor, 853-857
        File Types Editor, 858-860
        Launch Conditions Editor, 864-867
        Registry Editor, 857-858
        User Interface Editor, 860-861
    deploying installation components, 895-896

shapes, drawing, 85-94, 98-99

shared assemblies, 331, 868-869
    adding to GAC, 873
        Global Assembly Cache Tool, 876-877
        .NET Framework Configuration Tool, 874-876
        Windows Explorer, 873-874
        Windows Installer, 873
    CLR, 880-881
    compared to private assemblies, 331
    creating merge module projects, 884-889
    digital signing, 869
        creating public/private key pairs, 870
        delaying, 882-884
        verification, 870
    GAC, 331-332
    names, 869-873
    referencing from GAC, 877-878

Shift member, KeyEventArgs, 257

Shortcut member, MenuItem class, 189

Show Answer button, 1106

Show() method, 45, 55, 141

ShowCheckBox member, DateTimePicker control, 170

ShowDialog() method, 136, 141, 756

ShowInTaskbar property, Form class, 51

ShowToday member, MonthCalendar class, 169

ShowTodayCircle member, MonthCalendar class, 169

ShowToolTips member, ToolBar class, 207

ShowUpDown member, DateTimePicker control, 170

ShowWeekNumbers member, MonthCalendar class, 169

signatures, delegates, 295-296

signcode.exe, 332, 884

simple data binding, 356-358
    architecture, 363-364
    bindable entities, 358-361
    bindable properties, 361-362
    ComboBox control, 414
    DataGrid control, 374-378
    displaying array information, 411-412
    displaying database information, 412-414

Simple Object Access Protocol. See SOAP

SimpleUI.exe, 908

simulation questions, 14-17

single-document interface. See SDI

single-file assemblies, 324-325

single-table forms, creating with Data Form Wizard, 387-390

SANS PRESS

MASTER THE TOOLS OF THE NETWORK SECURITY TRADE WITH THE OFFICIAL BOOK FROM SANS PRESS!

SANS GIAC Certification:
Security Essentials Toolkit (GSEC)

Eric Cole, Mathew Newfield, John M. Millican

with foreword by Stephen Northcutt

0-7357-2774-9 • 384 pages • $49.99 US

You need more than a hammer to build a house, and you need more than one tool to secure your network. *Security Essentials Toolkit* covers the critical tools that you need to secure your site, showing you why, when, and how to use them. Based on the SANS Institute's renowned Global Information Assurance Certification (GIAC) program, this book takes a workbook-style approach that gives you hands-on experience and teaches you how to install, configure, and run the best security tools of the trade.

www.quepublishing.com

The Smartest Way To Get Certified™

EXAM CRAM™ 2

The test is in 2 weeks – are you ready?

You need a quick and efficient way to make sure you have what it takes to pass.

Where do you go?

Exam Cram 2!

Why?

Que Certification Exam Cram 2 titles have exactly what you need to pass your exam:

MCAD: Developing and Implementing Windows-based Applications with Visual C# .NET and Visual Studio .NET
Exam Cram 2 (Exam 70-316)
Kalani Kirk Hausman
0-7897-2902-4
$29.99 US/$46.99 CAN/£21.99 Net UK

- Key terms and concepts highlighted at the start of each chapter

- Notes, Exam Tips, and Alerts advise what to watch out for

- End-of-chapter sample Exam Questions with detailed discussions of all answers

- Complete text-based practice test with answer key at the end of each book

- The tear-out Cram Sheet condenses the most important items and information into a two-page reminder

- A CD that includes PrepLogic Practice Tests for complete evaluation of your knowledge

- Our authors are recognized experts in the field. In most cases, they are current or former instructors, trainers, or consultants—they know exactly what you need to know!

Que Certification: Your Complete Certification Resource!   www.examcram.com

CramSession

the difference between Pass ... or Fail

"On top of everything else, I find the best deals on training products and services for our CramSession members".

Jami Costin,
Product Specialist

CramSession.com is #1 for IT Certification on the 'Net.

There's no better way to prepare for success in the IT Industry. Find the best IT certification study materials and technical information at CramSession. Find a community of hundreds of thousands of IT Pros just like you who help each other pass exams, solve real-world problems, and discover friends and peers across the globe.

CramSession – #1 Rated Certification Site!

- *#1 by TechRepublic.com*
- *#1 by TechTarget.com*
- *#1 by CertMag's Guide to Web Resources.*

Visit Cramsession.com today!
...and take advantage of the best IT learning resources.

CramSession has IT all!

- **The #1 study guides on the 'Net.** With over 250 study guides for IT certification exams, we are the web site every techie visits before passing an IT certification exam.

- **Practice questions.** Get the answers and explanations with our CramChallenge practice questions delivered to you daily.

- **The most popular IT Forums.** Cramsession has over 400 discussion boards loaded with certification infomation where our subscribers study hard, work hard, and play harder.

- **e-Newsletters.** Our IT e-Newsletters are written by techs for techs: IT certification, technology, humor, career and more.

- **Technical Papers and Product Reviews.** Find thousands of technical articles and whitepapers written by industry leaders, trainers, and IT veterans.

- **Exam reviews.** Get the inside scoop before you take that expensive certification exam.

- **And so much more!**

CramSession
Prepare for Success!

www.cramsession.com